INTERNATIONAL COMMERCIAL DISPUTES

This is the fourth edition of this highly regarded work on the law of international commercial litigation as practised in the English courts. As such it is primarily concerned with how commercial disputes which have connections with more than one country are dealt with by the English courts. Much of the law which provides the framework for the resolution of such disputes is derived from international instruments, including recent Conventions and Regulations which have significantly re-shaped the law in the European Union. The scope and impact of these European instruments is fully explained and assessed in this new edition.

The work is organised in four parts. The first part considers the jurisdiction of the English courts and the recognition and enforcement in England of judgments granted by the courts of other countries. This part of the work, which involves analysis of both the Brussels I Regulation and the so-called traditional rules, includes chapters dealing with jurisdiction *in personam* and *in rem*, anti-suit injunctions and provisional measures. The work's second part focuses on the rules which determine whether English law or the law of another country is applicable to a given situation. The part includes a discussion of choice of law in contract and tort, with particular attention being devoted to the recent Rome I and Rome II Regulations. The third part of the work includes three new chapters on international aspects of insolvency (in particular, under the EC Insolvency Regulation) and the final part focuses on an analysis of legal aspects of international commercial arbitration. In particular, this part examines: the powers of the English courts to support or supervise an arbitration; the effect of an arbitration agreement on the jurisdiction of the English courts; the law which governs an arbitration agreement and the parties' dispute; and the recognition and enforcement of foreign arbitration awards.

International Commercial Disputes

Commercial Conflict of Laws in English Courts

Jonathan Hill
and
Adeline Chong

·H A R T·
PUBLISHING
OXFORD AND PORTLAND, OREGON
2010

Published in the United Kingdom by Hart Publishing Ltd
16C Worcester Place, Oxford, OX1 2JW
Telephone: +44 (0)1865 517530
Fax: +44 (0)1865 510710
E-mail: mail@hartpub.co.uk
Website: http://www.hartpub.co.uk

Published in North America (US and Canada) by
Hart Publishing
c/o International Specialized Book Services
920 NE 58th Avenue, Suite 300
Portland, OR 97213-3786
USA
Tel: +1 503 287 3093 or toll-free: (1) 800 944 6190
Fax: +1 503 280 8832
E-mail: orders@isbs.com
Website: http://www.isbs.com

British Library Cataloguing in Publication Data
Data Available

ISBN: 978-1-84113- 851-0

Typeset by Compuscript Ltd, Shannon
Printed and bound in Great Britain by
TJ International Ltd, Padstow, Cornwall

PREFACE

It is five years since the publication of the third edition of this work (the first by Hart Publishing). This fourth edition sees a variety of changes from the previous one—not least the addition of a co-author.

Although, since the last edition, there have been numerous minor changes throughout the topics considered in this work, there has also been a number of significant developments at the European level. First, two long-awaited instruments in the field of choice of law have finally been adopted: Regulation (EC) No 593/2008 on the law applicable to contractual obligations[1] (commonly known as the Rome I Regulation) and Regulation (EC) No 864/2007 on the law applicable to non-contractual obligations[2] (referred to as the Rome II Regulation). Secondly, the Lugano Convention of 1988 was revised in 2007—to bring it into line with the Brussels I Regulation. Although the revised Lugano Convention has not yet come fully into force, it is expected that it will do so in the not too distant future.[3] Accordingly, the text assumes that the revised Lugano Convention is in operation and readers who are interested in the position under 1988 Convention should refer to the third edition of this work.

Although the Brussels I Regulation and the revised Lugano Convention are, in substance, almost identical, in certain respects the terminology of the Convention differs from that of the Regulation. Whereas the Brussels I Regulation is divided into 'Chapters' and refers to 'Member States', the Lugano Conventions is divided into 'Titles' and refers to 'States bound by this Convention'. Throughout the book, the text takes the Brussels I Regulation as its starting point, only referring to the Lugano Convention (in footnotes) when it differs in some respect from the Regulation. If the text does not expressly refer to the Convention the reader should assume that it follows the Regulation (making appropriate allowances for differences in terminology). So, where the text states that 'the basic structure of Chapter II is to distinguish those bases of jurisdiction which apply regardless of the defendant's domicile from those which apply only to defendants who are domiciled in a Member State', the reader can also assume that the basic structure of Title II of the Lugano Convention is to distinguish those bases of jurisdiction which apply regardless of the defendant's domicile from those which apply only to defendants who are domiciled in a state bound by the Convention. Similarly, if there is nothing in the text or a footnote to indicate the contrary, where it is stated that 'Article 6(1) only applies if the proceedings are brought in the Member State in which one of the defendants is domiciled' the reader should conclude that Article 6(1) of the Convention only applies if the proceedings are

---

[1] [2008] OJ L177/6.
[2] [2007] OJ L199/40.
[3] The revised Lugano Convention entered into force between the EU and Norway on 1 January 2010. Switzerland has indicated that it will apply the Convention as from 1 January 2011.

brought in the state bound by the Lugano Convention in which one of the defendants is domiciled. And so on.

In structural terms, this edition largely follows the last one. However, we have re-structured the chapters which address choice of law issues and, prompted by the (positive) criticism of a reviewer of the previous edition, we have added three chapters dealing with international insolvency.

With a view to making the text easier to read and digest, we have taken a number of shortcuts in our use of terminology. In the context of the recognition and enforcement of foreign judgments and arbitral awards, the court which granted the judgment is referred to as the 'court of origin' or the 'original court'; the country (or state) in which the court of origin sits or in which the arbitral tribunal has its seat is referred to as the 'country of origin' (or 'state of origin'). The court in which recognition or enforcement of a foreign judgment or arbitral award is sought is referred to as the 'court addressed'; the country (or state) in which the court addressed sits is referred to as the 'country addressed' (or 'state addressed'). In addition, throughout the text, 'England' is used to signify 'England and Wales' and 'he', 'his' and 'him' to signify 'he or she', 'his or her' and 'him or her'.

We extend our thanks to Richard Hart and his team for the support and assistance they have provided. We are also grateful to the publishers and editors of the *International and Comparative Law Quarterly* for permission to reproduce material which appeared in that journal under the titles 'Some Private International Law Aspects of the Arbitration Act 1996' (1997) 46 *ICLQ* 274 and 'Choice of Law in Contract under the Rome Convention: the Approach of the UK Courts' (2004) 53 *ICLQ* 325. In addition, we would like to thank Prof Paul Torremans and Dr Sandra Frisby for helpful comments made. Adeline Chong would like to thank her family for their support, especially her father, Chong Poh. Jonathan Hill extends his usual thanks to Sheila.

As far as possible, we have tried to state the law as on 1 December 2009; we have, however, been able to incorporate some later material.

Bristol   JONATHAN HILL

Singapore   ADELINE CHONG

1 February 2010

CONTENTS

TABLE OF CASES

TABLE OF STATUTES

Decisions

Directives

Regulations

FRANCE

GERMANY

ITALY

NETHERLANDS

REPUBLIC OF SOUTH AFRICA

SWITZERLAND

UAE

UNITED STATES OF AMERICA

TABLE OF CONVENTIONS, ETC

TABLE OF STATUTORY
INSTRUMENTS AND RULES

1

INTRODUCTION

1.1 PRELIMINARY REMARKS

1.1.1　Where all the elements relevant to a situation are connected with England, a commercial dispute which cannot be settled amicably may normally be resolved in England by litigation; the claimant may apply for provisional measures from the court, the judge will apply English law and, if the claimant is awarded damages, the judgment will be enforceable against the assets of the defendant. If parties agree, such a dispute may be resolved by arbitration.[1]

　1.1.2　A variety of complications arise in international cases—that is, cases with a foreign element. In this context 'foreign' is not to be understood in a political sense. A state which has a unified legal system contains only one country or law district and legal relations operating exclusively within that state are domestic. So, a dispute arising out of a road accident in Limoges involving a Parisian motorist and a local cyclist is a domestic French dispute. However, in a state which comprises two or more legal systems, such as the United States of America or the United Kingdom, it is important to distinguish the state as a political unit from the separate countries or law districts within it. The United Kingdom contains three law districts—England, Scotland and Northern Ireland—and from the perspective of English private international law a dispute concerning a contract between an Englishwoman and a Scotsman is as much a case involving a foreign element as a dispute arising out of a contract between an Englishwoman and a Frenchman. Although disputes arising out of international commercial transactions take a myriad of different forms and involve a wide variety of different issues, the basic legal framework for their resolution is uniform. Broadly speaking, this framework can be broken down into three elements: (1) jurisdiction, (2) choice of law and (3) the recognition and enforcement of judgments and awards.

　1.1.3　The first issue is to identify the forum (or fora) in which the dispute may be resolved. In cases involving contractual disputes the parties may have agreed in advance to refer any dispute arising out of the transaction to the courts of a particular country or to arbitration. Where the dispute does not arise out of a contract, it is unusual for there to be an advance agreement between the parties and, even in cases involving international contracts, it is surprising how often the parties' agreement does not include a dispute-resolution clause. Whether or not the parties have agreed to litigation in a particular country or to arbitration, the first stage of an international commercial dispute involves questions of jurisdiction: which court or tribunal is competent in relation to the claim?

---

[1] If, however, the dispute is not capable of resolution by arbitration, the parties' arbitration agreement is unenforceable. See paras 21.2.10–21.2.12.

1.1.4   Where judgment is given by the court of a country in which the defendant has assets, a successful claimant may proceed to enforcement of the judgment immediately. However, the courts of the country where the defendant's assets are located may not be competent to determine the claim, or, even if those courts are competent, the claimant may seek procedural or other advantages by bringing proceedings against the defendant in another competent forum. Two problems arise in this situation. First, if the defendant does not have sufficient assets to satisfy the judgment in the country where the judgment is given, in what circumstances, if any, will the claimant be able to enforce the judgment in the country where sufficient assets are located? Secondly, can the courts of the country where the assets are located (or the courts of another country) grant provisional measures to ensure that the rights of the parties are not irreparably harmed pending the final judgment?

1.1.5   In the fields of jurisdiction and the recognition and enforcement of judgments, two very different types of regime have evolved. The traditional approach, which is reflected in the common law, is for the law to embrace the 'twin vices' of 'exorbitant national jurisdictional rules,[2] and extremely narrow judgment recognition practices resulting in a sort of "law of the jungle" in transnational enforcement'.[3] The narrowness of one country's rules for the recognition and enforcement of judgments given by the courts of other countries results—at least in part—from the breadth of other countries' jurisdiction rules. The alternative approach—which in practice can be achieved only by international agreement—is to limit the grounds on which jurisdiction can be assumed in international cases, as a result of which rules concerning the recognition and enforcement of foreign judgments can be less restrictive. This alternative approach is found in the Brussels I Regulation,[4] the Lugano Convention[5] and in the regime which operates within the United Kingdom.

1.1.6   The third important aspect of international commercial disputes involves choice of law. In an entirely domestic case it seems obvious that, as a general rule, the court should apply the law of the forum. However, in cases with a significant foreign element, there is a question whether the law governing the substance of the dispute should be the law of the forum or the law of another country.

1.1.7   Litigation is not the only method of resolving international disputes. On the international plane, arbitration is a dispute-resolution mechanism of increasing importance. Many of the questions which arise in the context of arbitration are similar to those which are central to international litigation. Can the claimant obtain provisional measures? Which law governs the merits of the dispute? Can a successful claimant enforce an award in a country other than that in which the award is given? There are, however, various problems which are particular to arbitration—notably, with regard to the relationship between the courts and the arbitral process.[6] Issues of

---

[2] Eg, Art 14 of the French civil code, which enables the French court to assume jurisdiction on the basis of the claimant's French nationality, or the rule according to which the English court may assume jurisdiction on the basis of the defendant's fleeting presence in England when the claim form is served (as in *Maharanee of Baroda v Wildenstein* [1972] 2 QB 283).

[3] PJ Borchers, 'Comparing Personal Jurisdiction in the United States and the European Community: Lessons for American Reform' (1992) 40 *Am J Comp L* 121, 128.

[4] Reg (EC) 44/2001, [2001] OJ L12/1.

[5] [2007] OJ L339/3.

[6] Chs 20–24.

jurisdiction, choice of law and the recognition of foreign judgments also arise in the context of insolvency proceedings—to which special rules apply.[7]

1.2 JURISDICTION AND THE RECOGNITION AND ENFORCEMENT OF FOREIGN JUDGMENTS

Basic Concepts

Jurisdiction[8]

1.2.1 The word 'jurisdiction' is employed in a number of different senses. For example, a rule which refers to a contract 'made within the jurisdiction' uses the term 'jurisdiction' to signify a geographical area. On the other hand, a rule which provides that, in certain circumstances, the courts of a particular country are to have 'exclusive jurisdiction', employs the term 'jurisdiction' to mean adjudicatory competence. An English court has jurisdiction, in the latter sense, if it can determine an issue which is brought before it by the claimant for its decision.

TWO ASPECTS TO JURISDICTION

1.2.2 The issue of jurisdiction is to be approached from two different angles. First, there are questions relating to the characteristics of the parties.[9] For example, there may be doubts whether a particular claimant or defendant is recognised by English law as having legal capacity to take part in proceedings in England. There may also be arguments over whether the defendant is entitled to immunity from suit. Secondly, there are general rules which circumscribe the jurisdiction of the courts in international cases (for example, where the defendant is resident in a foreign country or where the claim arises out of events which occurred abroad or where the parties agreed to submit their disputes to the courts of another country).[10] Although it is possible to imagine a legal system with no rules limiting the jurisdiction of the courts in international cases, in practice, the English courts are subject to a variety of limitations on their jurisdiction.

CLAIMS *IN PERSONAM* AND CLAIMS *IN REM*

1.2.3 When considering questions of jurisdiction it is important to draw a distinction between claims *in personam* and claims *in rem*. Proceedings *in personam*, which are directed against a named individual, are begun by service of the document instituting the proceedings on the defendant in accordance with the Civil Procedure Rules. The purpose of proceedings *in personam* is to make the defendant do something— such as perform a contract, or pay damages for breach—or to prevent the defendant

---

[7] Chs 17–19.
[8] Chs 2–11.
[9] Ch 2.
[10] Chs 4–9.

from doing something. If the claimant succeeds in his claim, the judgment is directed against the defendant who is bound by it. The judgment does not, however, directly affect the legal position of third parties. The bases on which the English courts may assume jurisdiction *in personam* are derived from three sources: first, international instruments, most notably the Brussels I Regulation and the Lugano Convention;[11] secondly, schedule 4 to the Civil Jurisdiction and Judgments Act 1982,[12] which in various circumstances confers jurisdiction on the courts of one or more of the countries which make up the United Kingdom;[13] and, thirdly, traditional rules, based primarily on the rules contained in Part 6 of the Civil Procedure Rules.[14]

1.2.4   Claims *in rem* arise in relation to a thing (*res*). Proceedings *in rem*, which in the commercial sphere are most commonly brought in respect of a ship, are commenced by serving the claim form on the *res* in connection with which the claim arises.[15] It is impossible to commence proceedings *in rem* unless the *res* is physically within the jurisdiction of the court. If proceedings *in rem* continue as such to judgment, the effect of the judgment *in rem* is to determine rights in the *res*, including the rights of third parties. In the commercial sphere, claims *in rem* fall within the jurisdiction of the Admiralty court.[16]

1.2.5   The fact that there is a basis on which the English court may assume jurisdiction—whether *in personam* or *in rem*—does not necessarily mean that litigation will be conducted in England. There are circumstances in which the English court is required to decline jurisdiction or may grant a stay of proceedings on the ground that the dispute between the parties should be determined by another forum.[17]

Recognition and Enforcement

1.2.6   Recognition of a foreign judgment is passive in the sense that it does not require any positive action by the court addressed. Enforcement, on the other hand, requires the court addressed to take the active step of authorising enforcement of the foreign judgment against the defendant's assets. Whereas there can be recognition without enforcement, there can be no enforcement without recognition. So, for

---

[11] Chs 4 and 5. The United Kingdom is also party to a large number of international conventions which seek to regulate the jurisdiction of the courts of the contracting states in specific areas, such as carriage by air, carriage by road and oil pollution. Legislation has been passed in order to discharge the United Kingdom's international obligations (eg, the Carriage by Air Act 1961 and the Carriage of Goods by Road Act 1965). For a list of the implementing legislation and a discussion of the relevant provisions see L Collins *et al*, *Dicey, Morris and Collins on The Conflict of Laws* (London, Sweet & Maxwell, 14th edn, 2006) ch 15. Generally speaking, under these legislative regimes, if the necessary jurisdictional requirements are met, the claimant is permitted to serve process on the defendant out of the jurisdiction without the court's permission.

[12] As amended by the Civil Jurisdiction and Judgments Order 2001, SI 2001/3929.

[13] Ch 6.

[14] Ch 7. There are additional bases of jurisdiction in particular circumstances. Eg, Pt 62 of the Civil Procedure Rules applies to cases concerning applications under the Arbitration Act 1996. See section 22.5.

[15] Where the claim arises in connection with a ship, there are various circumstances in which proceedings *in rem* may be commenced by service of the claim form on a ship other than that in relation to which the claim arose. See section 8.1.

[16] Ch 8. The admiralty court also has jurisdiction *in personam*.

[17] Ch 9 and section 21.2.

example, where A obtains a foreign judgment ordering B to pay damages for breach of contract, A may apply to enforce the judgment against B's assets in England. If the English court authorises enforcement, this necessarily entails recognition of the judgment. If, however, the foreign court dismisses A's claim on the basis that B had not breached the contract and A starts proceedings against B in England on the same claim B may seek to rely on the foreign judgment by way of defence. In this situation, the English court is asked to recognise the judgment as creating a bar to A's claim in England, but no question of enforcement is raised.

The Traditional Regime

1.2.7 In English law the traditional jurisdiction rules are relatively simple.[18] There are two key features: the rules are largely procedural in character in that the essence of the court's jurisdiction is the service of a claim form on the defendant and the limits of the court's jurisdiction are determined by reference to the exercise of a number of discretions. Broadly speaking, under the traditional rules, an English court has jurisdiction in proceedings *in personam* in three situations. First, a defendant may submit to the jurisdiction of the court. Secondly, an English court has jurisdiction over a defendant who is properly served with process within the jurisdiction. In such a case, however, the court has discretion to stay the proceedings on the basis that there is some more appropriate forum abroad (*forum non conveniens*). Thirdly, the court may assume jurisdiction over an absent defendant by giving the claimant permission to serve a claim form on the defendant out of the jurisdiction.[19] Permission, which is discretionary, depends on the claimant being able to satisfy certain conditions, one of which is that the court must be the most appropriate forum for the trial (*forum conveniens*). Although the traditional rules continue to apply in many cases, their scope has been significantly curtailed, most notably by the Brussels I Regulation, the Lugano Convention and the Civil Jurisdiction and Judgments Act 1982 (as amended). The traditional rules are residual in the sense that, if jurisdiction is determined by the Brussels regime, the claimant is unable to invoke any of the traditional bases of jurisdiction.

1.2.8 In theory, it is possible to imagine a situation where all foreign judgments are entitled to recognition and enforcement. Not surprisingly, however, there is no legal system which adopts this approach in practice. There are various reasons why, under the traditional regime, the automatic recognition and enforcement of foreign judgments is not a practical possibility.[20]

1.2.9 First, the original court may have assumed jurisdiction over the defendant on a basis which the court addressed does not regard as legitimate. In situations where the jurisdiction of the English court is based on the presence or submission of the defendant, a judgment given in the claimant's favour will normally be enforceable abroad. However, in cases where the claimant invokes the jurisdiction of the court

---

[18] Ch 7.
[19] CPR 6.36, PD 6B para 3.1.
[20] Ch 12.

under CPR 6.36 it is quite likely that, should the claimant have to seek enforcement abroad on account of the defendant having insufficient assets within the jurisdiction to satisfy the judgment, a foreign court will refuse enforcement on the ground that the judgment resulted from proceedings in which jurisdiction was assumed on an exorbitant basis. By the same token, at common law, a foreign judgment will not be recognised or enforced in England unless there was a sufficient connection between the defendant and the foreign court which, according to the standards imposed by English law, justified the assumption of jurisdiction.

1.2.10 Secondly, a foreign judgment is not entitled to recognition or enforcement in England if the foreign proceedings involved some substantial injustice. So, an English court will refuse to recognise or enforce a foreign judgment if the defendant was not given a proper opportunity to present his case in the foreign proceedings or if the defendant was given insufficient time to prepare a defence or if the claimant acted fraudulently (for example, by seeking to mislead the court with forged evidence) or if the foreign judgment offends against English public policy.

1.2.11 Thirdly, situations arise in which the courts of different countries reach incompatible decisions on the same or related issues. Where two foreign judgments conflict, the court addressed cannot respect both of them. Equally, the court addressed cannot be expected to recognise or enforce a foreign judgment which conflicts with one of its own judgments.

The Brussels I Regulation

1.2.12 The primary purpose of the Brussels I Regulation is to facilitate the recognition and enforcement of foreign judgments in civil and commercial matters within the Member States of the European Union. The almost identical Lugano Convention extends the same regime to Iceland, Norway and Switzerland. Although, at the level of detail, there are some minor differences between the Brussels I Regulation and the Lugano Convention, the structure of the two instruments is the same and the basic principles are common to both instruments. The core of the Brussels I Regulation is to be found in the first three groups of provisions: (1) Chapter I (scope);[21] (2) Chapter II (jurisdiction);[22] and (3) Chapter III (recognition and enforcement of judgments).[23] There are nine key principles.[24] First, the material scope of the Brussels I Regulation is limited to civil and commercial matters relating to property. Secondly, the Regulation contains rules of direct jurisdiction, which are applicable in the state in which the initial proceedings are brought and determine the court vested with jurisdiction. Thirdly, the defendant's domicile[25] is the point on which the rules on

---

[21] Section 3.3.
[22] Chs 4 and 5, sections 9.1 and 9.5.
[23] Ch 13.
[24] See Jenard-Möller Report [1990] OJ C189/6567, para 13.
[25] In English law 'domicile' for the purposes of the Brussels I Regulation is defined by the Civil Jurisdiction and Judgments Order 2001 (SI 2001/3929), sched 1, paras 9–12. See section 4.1. For the position under the Lugano Convention, see Civil Jurisdiction and Judgments Act 1982, ss 41–6.

jurisdiction hinge.[26] Fourthly, the Regulation contains precise and detailed rules of jurisdiction specifying the instances in which a person domiciled in a Member State may be sued in the courts of another Member State.[27] Fifthly, the defendant's rights must have been respected in the state of origin.[28] Sixthly, grounds for refusing recognition and enforcement are limited.[29] Seventhly, the enforcement procedure is unified and simplified.[30] Eighthly, the Regulation governs relations with other international conventions.[31] Ninthly, steps are taken to ensure that, as far as possible, interpretation of the Regulation and the Lugano Convention is uniform.[32]

Jurisdiction and the Recognition and Enforcement of Judgments within the United Kingdom

1.2.13   Whereas some of the jurisdiction rules contained in the Brussels I Regulation allocate jurisdiction to the courts of a 'place', others confer jurisdiction on the courts of a Member State. Since the United Kingdom is made up of three different law districts, some mechanism is required to allocate jurisdiction between the courts of England, Scotland and Northern Ireland. Moreover, the Brussels I Regulation does not allocate jurisdiction in cases which are entirely internal to the United Kingdom. Schedule 4 to the Civil Jurisdiction and Judgments Act 1982—which is largely based on Chapter II of the Brussels I Regulation—is the mechanism for allocating jurisdiction in civil and commercial matters within the United Kingdom.[33]

1.2.14   The Brussels I Regulation is also not concerned with the recognition and enforcement within the United Kingdom of judgments given by the courts of England, Scotland and Northern Ireland. A simplified system for the recognition and enforcement of judgments within the United Kingdom was introduced by the Civil Jurisdiction and Judgments Act 1982.[34]

Subsequent Developments

1.2.15   The success of the Brussels regime in facilitating the recognition and enforcement of judgments in Europe suggests a way forward for the creation of a worldwide regime. In the 1990s, the Hague Conference on Private International Law started work on a worldwide judgments convention and a Preliminary Draft Convention on Jurisdiction and Foreign Judgments in Civil and Commercial Matters was produced

---

[26] Although, as a general rule, the courts of the Member States may continue to apply traditional bases of jurisdiction as against defendants who are not domiciled in a Member State, the third principle must be read subject to a variety of provisions which apply regardless of domicile. See section 4.2.

[27] Ch 5.

[28] Section 4.4.

[29] Section 13.1.

[30] Section 13.1.

[31] Section 3.5.

[32] Section 3.2.

[33] Ch 6.

[34] Section 13.6.

in 1999. This draft, although differing in various respects from the Brussels regime, displayed several of the same characteristics. In particular, it was in the form of a double convention, which laid down rules of direct jurisdiction as well as making provision for the recognition and enforcement of judgments. A successful worldwide convention, adopted by a substantial number of significant commercial countries, would have had the effect of largely superseding the traditional rules (on both civil jurisdiction and the recognition and enforcement of judgments) of the participating states. However, negotiations at the Hague Conference stalled and the prospect of a worldwide convention along the lines originally intended has vanished for the foreseeable future.[35] In due course, negotiations were refocused on a more limited convention dealing with jurisdiction agreements and judgments resulting from proceedings based on such agreements (something along the lines of the 1958 New York Convention on the recognition and enforcement of foreign arbitral awards).[36] The Convention on Choice of Court Agreements[37] was concluded in 2005. By early 2010, although it had been signed both by the United States of America and the European Union, the Convention had not yet entered into force in any of the Member States of the Hague Conference because only one contracting state (Mexico) had ratified it.

1.3 CHOICE OF LAW

1.3.1 Every legal system must either expressly or impliedly contain choice of law rules for determining the substantive law to be applied to the merits of the dispute between the parties. At the most simple level a legal system may contain the rule that the law of the forum should be applied to all aspects of disputes coming before the courts, regardless of whether the dispute is domestic or international. While the application of the law of the forum can be justified in certain cases with a foreign element, the application of the law of the forum is often likely to defeat the legitimate expectations of foreign litigants. It is not difficult to envisage examples in which the application of the law of the forum seems inappropriate or unjust. Where, for example, parties enter a contract to be performed in France and agree that French law should govern their relations, the application of English law—if materially different from French law—may upset the economic balance of the contract. Similarly, where a claimant is injured in an accident abroad by a local resident, the natural expectation is that the defendant's liability should be governed by the law of the place where the accident occurred.

1.3.2 In view of the fact that there are significant differences between the systems of private law of different countries, a choice of law rule which requires the application of the law of the forum to international disputes leads to a situation where the outcome of a dispute may depend entirely upon where the litigation takes place. It is

---

[35] Details of the various stages of the negotiation process are available from the Hague Conference's website: http://hcch.e-vision.nl/index_en.php?act=progress.listing&cat=4. See also TC Hartley and M Dogauchi, *Explanatory Report* (2005) <http://www.hcch.net/upload/expl37e.pdf>.
[36] See sections 21.2 and 24.2.
[37] See <http://www.hcch.net/index_en.php?act=conventions.pdf&cid=98>.

to be expected that, if the courts of more than one country are competent to entertain proceedings, one of the factors which is relevant to the claimant's choice of forum is the likelihood of the substantive claim being successful.

1.3.3 Although it is almost impossible in practice to bring about a situation where the result of a dispute is the same irrespective of the forum in which it is litigated,[38] a step can be taken in that direction by the harmonisation of choice of law rules. The Rome Convention on the Law Applicable to Contractual Obligations, which was implemented in the United Kingdom by the Contracts (Applicable Law) Act 1990, introduced an (almost) uniform code for contractual choice of law questions throughout the Member States of the European Union; in 2008, this Convention was superseded by the Rome I Regulation,[39] which is closely modelled on the Convention which it replaced.[40] So, where a dispute arises out of an international contract, the courts of each of the Member States bound by the Regulation apply the same rules for determining the law to govern the substantive rights and obligations of the parties.[41] As regards non-contractual obligations, harmonisation of choice of law rules at the European level has also taken place. Subject to a number of exceptions to which pre-existing national choice of law rules continue to apply, choice of law with regard to non-contractual obligations is governed by the Rome II Regulation.[42]

1.3.4 It should not be thought that the application of the law of a foreign country is somehow incompatible with territorial sovereignty. Choice of law rules form part of the private international law of the forum. So, where an English choice of law rule directs the court to apply the law of a foreign country to the merits of the dispute, the foreign law is the applicable law by virtue of the application of English conflicts rules, not because English law is subordinate to the law of the foreign country in question. It follows that there are limits on the extent to which the forum will give effect to the laws of foreign countries, limits which are set by the forum itself.

1.3.5 Within any legal system, whereas some rules of law are optional, others are mandatory. Since mandatory rules are almost invariably designed to advance certain economic or social policies (such as restrictions on exchange control or consumer protection), each country has a legitimate interest in seeing that its mandatory rules are applied to situations which are intended to fall within their scope.[43] So, where the law which would normally apply to a particular situation is in conflict with a mandatory rule of the law of the forum, the mandatory rule will prevail.

1.3.6 Four further points should be made in the context of this introduction to choice of law. First, the distinction between substance and procedure is a crucial one. It is an almost universal principle that matters of procedure are governed by the

---

[38] Even if the substantive laws of different countries are harmonised by international conventions. See F Ferrari, '"Forum Shopping" Despite International Uniform Contract Law Conventions' (2002) 51 *ICLQ* 689.

[39] Reg (EC) 593/2008, [2008] OJ L177/6. The Regulation applies to contracts concluded on or after 17 December 2009.

[40] Ch 14.

[41] Certain issues and certain types of contract which are excluded from the Convention's scope continue to be governed by the common law.

[42] Reg (EC) 864/2007, [2007] OJ L199/40. See ch 15.

[43] See, eg, *Golden Acres Ltd v Queensland Estates Pty Ltd* [1969] Qd R 378 (Supreme Court, Queensland).

law of the forum. Where a dispute concerning an international contract is litigated in England, English rules of evidence and procedure are applied, irrespective of the law applicable to the merits of the dispute. So, English law governs questions such as whether a claimant in English proceedings is entitled to provisional measures (such as a freezing injunction)[44] or whether the court can grant an injunction restraining a litigant from proceeding abroad.[45] The dividing line between substance and procedure turns on the classification of the issue. It is provided, for example, that questions of limitation are to be determined by reference to the applicable law rather than the law of the forum.[46]

1.3.7   Secondly, even as regards substantive matters, it should not be assumed that the effect of choice of law rules is necessarily to refer all aspects of a particular legal relationship to the same law. For example, in a case relating to an international contract, issues such as formal validity, material validity and contractual capacity may be referred to the laws of different countries.

1.3.8   Thirdly, when a dispute is litigated in England the fact that, according to English choice of law rules, the law of a foreign country is the applicable law does not necessarily mean that the foreign law is applied to determine the rights and obligations of the parties. The general rule is that an English court does not have judicial notice of the laws of other countries. Accordingly, rules of foreign law have to be pleaded and proved by the party seeking to rely upon them. If the foreign law is not pleaded or cannot be proved, English law is applied by default.[47]

1.3.9   Finally, something should be said about the relationship between jurisdiction rules and choice of law rules. Historically, choice of law rules have formed the heartland of private international law. Until relatively recently English law permitted the exercise of jurisdiction in cases which had only a limited connection with England. The more distant the connection between the litigation and the forum, the more likely it is that the choice of law rules of the forum will direct that the law of a foreign country should be the applicable law. However, the trend in recent decades has been to use jurisdiction rules to steer legal proceedings towards a forum which is appropriate for the resolution of the dispute in question. In England this trend can be seen in the development of the doctrine of *forum non conveniens* by the courts and the introduction of the Brussels regime. Although there is no necessary connection between the allocation of jurisdiction and the determination of the applicable law, if the effect of jurisdiction rules is to direct litigation to an appropriate forum, there is an increased likelihood that the law of the forum will be the applicable law. The development of more sophisticated techniques for handling jurisdiction disputes has had the effect of reducing the importance of choice of law rules. Instead of private international law being concerned primarily with choice of law questions, the focus has shifted overwhelmingly to jurisdiction questions and, to a lesser extent, the recognition and enforcement of foreign judgments.

[44] Ch 10.
[45] Ch 11.
[46] As regards contractual obligations, see Rome I Reg, Art 12(1)(d); in relation to non-contractual obligations, see Rome II Reg, Art 15(h).
[47] Ch 16.

PART I

JURISDICTION AND THE RECOGNITION AND ENFORCEMENT OF FOREIGN JUDGMENTS

2

PERSONS WHO CAN AND CANNOT SUE OR BE SUED

2.0.1 In order to be able to take part in legal proceedings in England, whether as claimant or defendant, the party in question must have legal capacity in the eyes of English law (section 2.1). Although there are no general limitations on the types of person who can sue or be sued, at common law enemy aliens cannot in a time of war invoke the jurisdiction of the English courts; there are also certain types of claim which are not justiciable in the English courts (section 2.2). More importantly, there are certain categories of defendant who may have the benefit of immunity from suit in England—notably, foreign states, international organisations and their officers and employees (sections 2.3–2.6).

2.1 LEGAL CAPACITY TO SUE OR BE SUED

Foreign Corporations

2.1.1 The recognition of foreign corporations is normally relatively straightforward. It is a well-established principle of English private international law that the existence or dissolution of a foreign corporation duly created or dissolved under the law of a foreign country is recognised in England.[1] As a consequence of this principle, a foreign association which has legal personality under the law of the place where it is constituted can sue or be sued in England, even if a similar English association would not have legal personality under English law.

Other Foreign Juristic Entities

2.1.2 In English law there are essentially only two types of legal person: individuals and corporations or other personified groups of individuals. Other legal systems, however, may confer legal personality on entities which do not fall within these two categories. Can such foreign juristic entities take part in proceedings in England?

---

[1] L Collins *et al, Dicey, Morris and Collins on The Conflict of Laws* (London, Sweet & Maxwell, 14th edn, 2006) para 30R−009 (Rule 161). See, eg, *Lazard Brothers & Co v Midland Bank Ltd* [1933] AC 289. In certain situations, the courts of a Member State are required by EU law to recognise the legal personality of entities formed in accordance with the laws of another Member State: Case C−208/00 *Überseering BV v Nordic Construction Company Baumanagement GmbH* [2002] ECR I−9919. For consideration of some of the procedural problems which flow from takeovers and mergers involving foreign companies which are party to English proceedings, see *Toprak Enerji Sanayi AS v Sale Tinley Technology Plc* [1994] 1 WLR 840; *Industrie Chimiche Italia Centrale v Alexander G Tsavliris & Sons Maritime Co* [1996] 1 WLR 774.

2.1.3   In *Bumper Development Corporation v Commissioner of Police of the Metropolis*[2] the plaintiff purchased a bronze sculpture which was later seized by the police as part of a campaign of returning stolen religious artefacts to their owners. It was alleged that the sculpture had been stolen from a ruined temple in India. According to Indian law the temple was regarded as a legal person. When the plaintiff brought proceedings against the police for the return of the sculpture, the temple, acting through a representative, sought to assert its claim to the sculpture. The issue was 'whether a foreign legal person which would not be recognised as a legal person by our own law can sue in the English courts'.[3] Purchas LJ, who gave the judgment of the Court of Appeal, noted that English law's 'insistence on an essentially animate content in a legal person' gives rise to 'a formidable conceptual difficulty' in recognising as a party to English proceedings 'something which on one view is little more than a pile of stones'.[4] Nevertheless, the Court of Appeal held that the temple was capable of being recognised as a juristic entity with capacity to sue in England. Relying on the principle of comity, Purchas LJ thought that in the circumstances of the case there would not be 'any offence to English public policy in allowing a Hindu religious institution to sue in our courts'.[5] However, the limits of the court's approach should be noted: it was essential for the decision that the constitution of the temple empowered its representative to take all necessary steps in the proceedings on its behalf.[6]

Corporations Established under the Laws of Territories which are not States

2.1.4   Foreign corporations are entitled to recognition in England at common law because they are properly constituted and have legal personality according to the law of the country where they are constituted. A potential problem arises in relation to a business which is incorporated in a territory which is not recognised by HM Government as a state. Can such an organisation be recognised as having legal personality for the purposes of English law? The Foreign Corporations Act 1991 is designed to provide a simple answer to this question. The purpose of the 1991 Act is to ensure that a foreign corporation which operates under the law in force in a territory which is not recognised as a state by the United Kingdom is nevertheless treated in the same way as foreign corporations from recognised states. Section 1 of the Act provides:

(1) If at any time—

(a) any question arises whether a body which purports to have or, as the case may be, which appears to have lost corporate status under the laws of a territory which is not at that time a recognised State should or should not be regarded as having legal personality as a body corporate under the law of any part of the United Kingdom, and

---

[2] [1991] 1 WLR 1362. JG Collier, [1992] *CLJ* 39; PB Carter, (1991) 62 *BYIL* 452.
[3] Purchas LJ at [1991] 1 WLR 1362, 1371.
[4] [1991] 1 WLR 1362, 1371.
[5] [1991] 1 WLR 1362, 1372.
[6] [1991] 1 WLR 1362, 1373.

(b) it appears that the laws of that territory are at that time applied by a settled court system in that territory,

that question and any other material question relating to the body shall be determined (and account shall be taken of those laws) as if that territory were a recognised State.

(2) For the purposes of subsection (1) above—

(a) 'a recognised State' is a territory which is recognised by Her Majesty's Government in the United Kingdom as a State;
(b) the laws of a territory which is so recognised shall be taken to include the laws of any part of the territory which are acknowledged by the federal or other central government of the territory as a whole; and
(c) a material question is a question (whether as to capacity, constitution or otherwise) which, in the case of a body corporate, falls to be determined by reference to the laws of the territory under which the body is incorporated.

(3) Any registration or other thing done at a time before the coming into force of this section shall be regarded as valid if it would have been valid at that time, had subsections (1) and (2) above then been in force.

2.1.5 The essential condition for the recognition of a corporation which originates in a territory which is not recognised as a state is that 'it appears that the laws of that territory are at that time applied by a settled court system in that territory'. So, the 1991 Act allows an entity incorporated in the Turkish Republic of Northern Cyprus (which is recognised as a state only by Turkey) to take part in English proceedings.[7] However, the deceptively simple formula adopted by the legislation is surrounded by a penumbra of uncertainty. In the situation where a previously recognised state disintegrates into a number of breakaway territories, it may be difficult to determine the moment at which, for the purposes of section 1(1)(b), the court system becomes 'settled' in the new territories.

International Corporations[8]

Introduction

2.1.6 The term 'international corporation' is often used loosely to mean one of three different types of organisation. First, in the modern world there are numerous

---

[7] See, eg, *Re Polly Peck* The Times, 27 December 1996. In Case C–432/92 *R v Minister of Agriculture, Fisheries and Food, ex parte SP Anastassiou (Pissouri) Ltd* [1994] ECR I-3087 (Greenwood and Lowe, [1995] *CLJ* 4) the Court of Justice was called upon to rule on the implications of non-recognition of the Turkish Republic of Northern Cyprus for the Association Agreement between the European Community and the Republic of Cyprus. Following the accession of the Republic of Cyprus to the European Union, questions have arisen as to the implications of the fact that the operation of the *acquis communautaire* is suspended in the Turkish Republic of Northern Cyprus: see Case C–420/07 *Apostolides v Orams*, [2010] 1 All ER (Comm) 950 discussed at para 13.1.4.

[8] CW Jenks, 'The Legal Personality of International Organisations' (1945) 22 *BYIL* 267; FA Mann, 'International Corporations and National Law' (1967) 42 *BYIL* 145; JG Collier, 'The Status of an International Corporation' in P Feuerstein and C Parry (eds), *Multum Non Multa: Festschrift für Kurt Lipstein* (Heidelberg/Karlsruhe: CF Müller, 1980) 20–9; J Hill, 'International Corporations in the English Courts' (1992) 12 *OJLS* 135.

national corporations which have international business. International banks and other so-called multinational companies fall within this category. With regard to these corporations the international angle poses no special problems. Depending on their place of incorporation, English law treats such corporations quite simply as domestic or foreign legal persons. Multinational corporations of this type may take one of two forms. A national company may establish subsidiary companies in other countries. In such a case, the parent and the subsidiaries are separate legal persons and each subsidiary can own property, enter contracts on its own behalf and litigate. Because of the independent legal personality of each of the subsidiaries no special legal problems are posed by dealings between a subsidiary and the parent, between the subsidiaries *inter se* or between a subsidiary and third parties. The alternative organisational structure is where a multinational company merely establishes a presence in various countries. For example, a bank may set up branches in foreign countries, while remaining a single legal entity. Normally, a company which operates outside the frontiers of the country where it is incorporated is required by the laws of the territories where it carries on business to register its presence. For example, under English law an overseas company which establishes a branch or place of business in England is required to deliver various documents to the registrar of companies for registration.[9] However, an overseas company which is registered in England or which has a branch or a place of business in England is not a separate legal entity; English law simply recognises the company's legal personality under the law of the place where it is incorporated. Where this second form of organisation is adopted, the multinational company is one legal person operating in several countries. Secondly, there are corporations which are created under national law, but whose formation is contemplated in a treaty concluded between states. In such cases the conception of the company is international, but its birth is not. The corporation is national in character and is treated by English law in the same way as any other foreign corporation. For example, in the mid-20th century, an agreement between the United Kingdom, Australia and New Zealand provided for the creation of Tasman Empire Airways Ltd, a New Zealand company, to operate air services between Australia and New Zealand.[10] Thirdly, there are organisations which are established by treaties concluded between states and which owe their creation and existence to public international law. These are the only legal entities which are truly international corporations, rather than national corporations with an international dimension. It is this third category which has posed the greatest problems in English law.

Organisations under the International Organisations Act 1968

2.1.7 If the United Kingdom is a member of an international corporation (in the sense of a corporation formed by a treaty) and an Order in Council is made under the International Organisations Act 1968, the corporation is treated as having legal personality as an English corporation. The courts' approach to such international

9 Companies Act 2006, Pt 34. See paras 7.1.9–7.1.16.
10 See FA Mann, 'International Corporations and National Law' (1967) 42 *BYIL* 145, 146.

organisations is illustrated by *JH Rayner (Mincing Lane) Ltd v Department of Trade and Industry*.[11] The International Tin Council was established by a treaty after the Second World War for the purpose of regulating the market in relation to tin. The ITC, whose headquarters were in London, dealt on the London Metal Exchange, buying and selling tin with a view to supporting the world price. The Sixth International Tin Agreement, to which the United Kingdom was a party, was signed in New York in 1982. Article 16 of that agreement provided:

The Council shall have legal personality. It shall in particular have the capacity to contract, to acquire and dispose of movable and immovable property and to institute legal proceedings.

In order that the ITC could function properly in England, the International Tin Council (Immunities and Privileges) Order 1972[12] was made pursuant to section 1 of the International Organisations Act 1968. Article 5 of the Order stated that the 'Council shall have the legal capacities of a body corporate.' In 1985 the ITC announced that it could not meet the liabilities which it had incurred through its operations. At this time its debts stood at something in excess of £750 million. In the complex litigation which ensued—the main purpose of which was to seek to establish the liability of the parties to the Sixth International Tin Agreement for the debts of the ITC—one of the questions which the courts had to consider was the status of the ITC in English law.

2.1.8 The starting point for the decision was stated by Lord Oliver in the following terms:

as a matter of the constitutional law of the United Kingdom, the Royal Prerogative, whilst it embraces the making of treaties, does not extend to altering the law or conferring rights upon individuals or depriving individuals of rights which they enjoy in domestic law without the intervention of Parliament.[13]

Both Lord Templeman and Lord Oliver emphasised that the status of the ITC in English law depended on the International Tin Council (Immunities and Privileges) Order 1972 and not on the treaty:

Without the Order in Council the ITC had no existence in the law of the United Kingdom and no significance save in the name of an international body created by a treaty between sovereign states which was not justiciable by municipal courts.[14]

The ratio of the case is that, because of the doctrine of non-justiciability, an international corporation of which the United Kingdom is a member has no status to sue or be sued in England unless English law has conferred on it the characteristics of a body corporate.

International Corporations to which the United Kingdom is not a Party

2.1.9 What is the situation of international organisations which are not the subject of an Order under the 1968 Act? There are three possible ways of dealing with the

---

[11] [1990] 2 AC 418. C Greenwood, [1990] *CLJ* 8 and (1989) 60 *BYIL* 461.
[12] SI 1972/120.
[13] [1990] 2 AC 418, 500.
[14] Lord Oliver at [1990] 2 AC 418, 510.

question whether such organisations have legal capacity in England. First, it could be decided as a matter of English private international law that the existence of a legal person constituted under public international law can be recognised in the same way as legal persons constituted under foreign systems of domestic law. Secondly, the court could refuse recognition to an international corporation unless English law has conferred legal personality on it. Thirdly, an international corporation could be recognised if legal personality has been conferred upon it by the domestic law of the state in which its headquarters are situated (or by the domestic law of one or more of the states who were party to the treaty establishing it). While each of these possibilities gained some measure of support in *Arab Monetary Fund v Hashim (No 3)*,[15] the House of Lords ultimately decided—on the basis of its decision in *JH Rayner (Mincing Lane) Ltd v Department of Trade and Industry*[16]—that the third solution was the appropriate one.

ARAB MONETARY FUND V HASHIM (NO 3)[17]

2.1.10   The Arab Monetary Fund (AMF) was established by an agreement between 20 Arab states and Palestine in 1976. The purpose of the AMF, whose head office was located in Abu Dhabi (UAE), was to lay the monetary foundations of Arab economic integration and to accelerate the process of economic development throughout the Arab world. Article 2 of the agreement provided that the AMF was to have 'an independent juridical personality' and 'in particular, the right to own, contract and litigate'. The various signatories to the agreement subsequently took the steps necessary to bestow juridical personality on the AMF in their domestic systems. In the UAE, in accordance with the constitution, the treaty establishing the AMF was confirmed by the council of ministers and ratified by decree (Federal Decree No 35). The decree had the effect of conferring on the AMF independent legal personality and the capacity to sue and be sued under the law of the UAE. It was alleged that the defendant, the AMF's former director-general, had embezzled $50 million. When litigation was commenced in England to recover these sums, the defendant sought to have the claim struck out on the basis that the AMF did not have capacity to sue in England.

2.1.11   At first instance the judge inclined towards the recognition of the AMF in English law on the basis that it had legal personality under public international law.[18] The advantages of this solution (which had gained some acceptance in the Court of Appeal in *JH Rayner (Mincing Lane) Ltd v Department of Trade and Industry*[19]) were clearly set out in Hoffmann J's judgment:

Extending our conflict rule to international organisations seems to me sensible and practical. The rule as it applies to entities created by foreign domestic laws is based on the inconvenience of having legal entities which exist in one country but not in another. International organisations set up by foreign states do exist in fairly substantial numbers, trade with this country and bank in the City of London. They are invariably recognised as juridical entities by the domestic

---

[15] [1990] 3 WLR 139 (Hoffmann J and CA); [1991] 2 AC 114 (HL).
[16] [1990] 2 AC 418.
[17] [1991] 2 AC 114. PB Carter, (1991) 62 *BYIL* 447; FA Mann, 'International Organisations as National Corporations' (1991) 107 *LQR* 357; G Marston, [1991] *CLJ* 218.
[18] [1990] 3 WLR 139, 143.
[19] [1989] Ch 72. C Greenwood, [1989] *CLJ* 46.

systems of the parties to the treaty as well as by many other countries. ... It is difficult to see why an entity created by treaty between two or more foreign states should be less entitled to recognition than an entity created under the sovereign authority of a single foreign state within its domestic system.[20]

2.1.12   Following the House of Lords' decision in the *Tin Council* case, counsel for the AMF dropped the argument that the AMF should be recognised as an international organisation with personality under public international law.[21] Hoffmann J decided that the proper approach was to 'ignore the treaty and regard the AMF as constituted under Abu Dhabi law as a separate persona ficta'.[22] As such the AMF was entitled to recognition under English conflicts rules. This analysis was adopted by Lord Templeman in the House of Lords:

[W]hen sovereign states enter into an agreement by treaty to confer legal personality on an international organisation, the treaty does not create a corporate body. But when the AMF Agreement was registered in the UAE by means of Federal Decree No 35 that registration conferred on the international organisation legal personality and thus created a corporate body which English courts can and should recognise.[23]

2.1.13   This analysis achieves a practical result which is clearly more sensible than refusing recognition to the AMF altogether—the solution which had been reached by the majority of the Court of Appeal.[24] This does not mean, however, that the decision is devoid of difficulties. Although it is clear from the decision of the House of Lords that an international organisation on which legal personality has been conferred by one (or more) of the parties to the treaty establishing it is recognised as having legal personality in England, there is a question about what exactly is being recognised. If an organisation such as the AMF is recognised by virtue of the fact that it has been incorporated by the domestic laws of the parties to the treaty establishing it, does it follow that, although it has only one domicile and residence (in the headquarters state), it has multiple nationality and multiple personality because it is incorporated in numerous states?

WESTLAND HELICOPTERS LTD V ARAB ORGANISATION FOR INDUSTRIALISATION
2.1.14   The potential implications of the analysis adopted by the House of Lords which Hoffmann J had recognised as giving rise to 'questions of trinitarian subtlety'[25] were considered by Colman J in *Westland Helicopters Ltd v Arab Organisation for Industrialisation*.[26] The Arab Organisation for Industrialisation (AOI) was established in 1975 by a treaty between Egypt and a number of Gulf states. Its purpose was to create an Arab arms manufacturing industry. The treaty expressly provided that the AOI should have 'juridical personality' and that its headquarters were to be in Egypt. Subsequently, each of the states which was a party to the treaty passed domestic

---

[20] [1990] 3 WLR 139, 144.
[21] Strictly speaking, this was not necessary: the *Tin Council* case concerned an organisation of which the United Kingdom was a member; *Arab Monetary Fund v Hashim (No 3)* did not.
[22] [1990] 3 WLR 139, 147.
[23] [1991] 2 AC 114, 160.
[24] [1990] 3 WLR 139.
[25] [1990] 3 WLR 139, 148.
[26] [1995] 2 WLR 126. Anon, [1995] *CLJ* 230.

legislation giving legal personality to the AOI. After the signing of the peace treaty between Egypt and Israel in 1979, the other members of the AOI expressed an intention to liquidate the AOI. Egypt, however, refused to accept the termination of the AOI and passed legislation which purported to enable the AOI to continue as an Egyptian corporation.

2.1.15 Among the various questions which arose for decision was whether the AOI should be recognised as a national corporation (which was governed by Egyptian law) or as an international corporation (which, it was argued, should be governed by public international law). The essence of the argument on behalf of the Egyptian corporation was that, on the basis of the House of Lords' decision in *Arab Monetary Fund v Hashim (No 3)*, the AOI, although created by treaty, was to be recognised not as an international corporation but as a legal person created under the law of the headquarters state.

2.1.16 Colman J rejected this argument. Much turned on the proper interpretation of *Arab Monetary Fund v Hashim (No 3)*, in particular the passage in which Lord Templeman stated: 'I am unable to agree ... that Federal Decree No 35 only recognised an international organisation and did not create a corporate body.'[27] Taken out of context, this passage seems unequivocally to support the Egyptian corporation's argument. Colman J, however, took the view that:

Lord Templeman was ... clearly saying that the law of the UAE had created legal personality for the fund. He was not saying that the fund was a UAE corporation with all the legal attributes of such a body.[28]

According to Colman J, the analysis adopted by the House of Lords in *Arab Monetary Fund v Hashim (No 3)* does not give rise to problems of multiple personality:

English law will only recognise a foreign entity as having legal personality and therefore a capacity to sue or be sued if such a body has been accorded legal personality under the law of a foreign state recognised by this country.[29] In the case of a corporation one looks to see whether it has been incorporated under the law of a foreign state. In the case of an international organisation one looks to see whether it has been accorded the legal capacity of a corporation under the law of any of the member states or the state where it has its seat, if that state is not a member state. Where some or all of the member states have accorded to it the legal capacity of a corporation the English courts will also treat it as having the capacity of a corporation. The fact that several states have accorded to it that capacity under their law does not mean that there is more than one international organisation for the English court to recognise, but merely that there is more than one factual basis upon which recognition can be accorded to the same organisation.[30]

REMAINING PROBLEMS

2.1.17 Colman J's interpretation in the *Westland Helicopters* case of *Arab Monetary Fund v Hashim (No 3)* solves most of the potential problems that that decision was thought to have generated: an international organisation on which legal personality

---

[27] [1991] 2 AC 114, 160.
[28] [1995] 2 WLR 126, 139.
[29] This statement is qualified by the Foreign Corporations Act 1991. See para 2.1.4.
[30] [1995] 2 WLR 126, 141.

has been conferred by the law of one of the Member States (or by the law of the headquarters state) is not to be recognised as a national corporation, but as an international corporation. Nevertheless, the doctrine according to which an international organisation is recognised as having legal capacity by virtue of a foreign state having clothed it with legal personality (and thereby having 'created' a foreign corporation in the special sense of that word used by Lord Templeman) is not the ideal solution. If neither the United Kingdom nor any foreign country takes legislative steps to recognise or give effect to an international organisation established by treaty, it has no legal status in England; it is not able to sue or be sued, to enter into contracts or to hold property. The better approach is to recognise an international organisation on the basis that it has legal personality under public international law. This approach was, however, effectively blocked off by 'some ill-considered and unnecessary observations'[31] by members of the House of Lords in the *Tin Council* case. It has been suggested that, while the opinion of Lord Oliver in the *Tin Council* case was of sufficient weight to cause the abandonment of an alternative line of argument before Hoffmann J in *Arab Monetary Fund v Hashim (No 3)*, it may not be impregnable to a future attack at the level of the Supreme Court.[32] Should further problems concerning the legal capacity of international organisations arise, legislative intervention might be thought appropriate.[33]

Foreign States

2.1.18 A foreign state which is recognised by the United Kingdom has capacity to sue and—subject to various immunities[34]—be sued in England. It is equally well established that an unrecognised state cannot sue or be sued in an English court.[35] Although the two questions are not unrelated, from the perspective of English private international law, the crucial legal issue is not whether a territory is entitled to recognition as a state as a matter of public international law, but whether the state should be recognised by the English courts. It is possible for a territory to be recognised as a state by the general international community, but not by the United Kingdom. Such was the position of Southern Rhodesia following the unilateral declaration of independence in 1965. The current view is that the English courts regard Foreign Office certificates as conclusive. Accordingly, if the Foreign Office does not recognise a state, the English courts will not recognise it as an independent state with capacity to sue or be sued in England.

---

[31] JG Collier, [1992] *CLJ* 39, 41.

[32] G Marston, 'The Origin of the Personality of International Organisations in United Kingdom Law' (1991) 40 *ICLQ* 403, 424.

[33] See the correspondence between the Bank of England and the Lord Chancellor, cited by C Mercer, 'The Arab Monetary Fund and the Courts: The Status of Foreign Entitles Established by Treaty—Official Moves to Reassure the Markets' (1992) 13 *Bus LR* 159, 160.

[34] See section 2.3.

[35] For the development of the law in this area, see G Marston, 'The Personality of the Foreign State in English Law' [1997] *CLJ* 374.

2.1.19 In *GUR Corporation v Trust Bank of Africa Ltd*[36] the Court of Appeal introduced an exception to this general principle. The factual background to this case was the establishment of tribal homelands by the Republic of South Africa during the apartheid era. In 1981 the Republic of South Africa declared, by section 1 of the Status of Ciskei Act 1981, that the territory of Ciskei constituted a sovereign and independent state. The international community—including the United Kingdom—took no notice of this statutory provision and continued to regard the territory of Ciskei as subject to the sovereignty of South Africa. In 1983 the plaintiff contracted with the Republic of Ciskei's Department of Works to build a hospital and two schools in Ciskei. The plaintiff obtained from the defendant bank a guarantee in favour of Ciskei in return for a deposit of $300,000. In due course Ciskei demanded payment under the guarantee, but the defendant refused. When the plaintiff started proceedings to recover the security, the defendant sought to join Ciskei to the proceedings as third party.

2.1.20 At first instance the issue was raised whether Ciskei had *locus standi* to sue or be sued. Steyn J held that since Ciskei had not received official recognition as a state by the United Kingdom it could not be a party to litigation in England. The Court of Appeal took a different view. Although Ciskei could not be a party to litigation as an independent state this did not preclude the possibility of treating Ciskei's Department of Works as an emanation of the Republic of South Africa, which was regarded by the international community as still having sovereignty over the territory of Ciskei.

2.1.21 The approach adopted by the Court of Appeal was derived from *Carl Zeiss Stiftung v Rayner & Keeler Ltd (No 2)*,[37] in which the House of Lords was required to consider the validity of administrative acts of the German Democratic Republic (GDR). Although the USSR had purported to establish the GDR as an independent state it was not officially recognised as such by the United Kingdom. As far as the Foreign Office was concerned, the USSR was de jure entitled to exercise governing authority in respect of the territory which was known at the end of the Second World War as the Eastern Zone of Germany. Nevertheless, the House of Lords was prepared to recognise the administrative acts of the public authorities of the GDR as acts done by a subordinate body set up by the USSR to act on its behalf. In *GUR Corporation v Trust Bank of Africa Ltd* the Court of Appeal, applying the same reasoning, concluded that the government of the Republic of Ciskei was a subordinate body set up by the Republic of South Africa to act on its behalf and that it had *locus standi* as such in England.

2.1.22 The decision of the Court of Appeal was the subject of criticism. From the point of view of precedent it may be doubted whether the decision of the House of Lords in *Carl Zeiss Stiftung v Rayner & Keeler Ltd (No 2)* was decisive in *GUR Corporation v Trust Bank of Africa Ltd*. In the *Carl Zeiss* case the issue was whether the administrative acts of the GDR were effective; there was no question of the standing of the GDR to sue or be sued in England. In addition, *GUR Corporation v Trust Bank of Africa Ltd*, in which the named party was the Republic of Ciskei, appears to fly in the face of the

---

[36] [1987] QB 559. A Beck, 'A South African Homeland Appears in the English Courts: Legitimation of the Illegitimate?' (1987) 36 *ICLQ* 350; J Crawford, (1986) 57 *BYIL* 405; D Lloyd Jones, [1987] *CLJ* 7; FA Mann, 'The Judicial Recognition of an Unrecognised State' (1987) 36 *ICLQ* 348; C Warbrick, 'Unrecognised States and Domestic Law' (1987) 50 *MLR* 84.

[37] [1967] 1 AC 853. D Grieg, 'The Carl-Zeiss Case and the Position of Unrecognised Governments in English Law' (1967) 83 *LQR* 96.

doctrine that the source of a foreign state's *locus standi* in England is its recognition by the British Government.[38] The policy of the decision may also be questioned. The case raised competing policies: on the one hand, it is reasonable that the courts should seek to do their best to meet the needs and wishes of litigants; on the other, it is desirable that the courts should speak in terms which are not inconsistent with the foreign policy of HM Government. By effectively conferring status on the Republic of Ciskei the court undermined the stand taken by the international community against the policy of apartheid in South Africa, of which the creation of the tribal homelands was a part. The effect of the decision was that the party before the court was not the Republic of South Africa, but the unrecognised Republic of Ciskei, represented by its Department of Works. To have denied recognition to the Republic of Ciskei would undoubtedly have caused inconvenience to parties who contracted with the Republic of Ciskei, since they would have been unable to have their rights determined in England. However, such contracting parties would presumably have been able to bring proceedings against the Republic of Ciskei either in South Africa or in the territory of Ciskei itself.

Foreign Governments

2.1.23   The fact that a state is recognised does not in itself determine who is entitled to sue on behalf of that state. In cases of unconstitutional usurpation of power or the disintegration of constitutional authority there may be disagreement over who is entitled—as the government of a state—to litigate on behalf of that state and to enforce the rights which are vested in it. Before April 1980 the position of foreign governments was similar to that of foreign states; the right of a foreign government to litigate in England depended on its being recognised by the British Government. In April 1980 the Foreign Secretary announced that HM Government would no longer accord recognition to foreign governments.[39] It has therefore been left to the courts to formulate a test for determining whether or not an authority should be regarded as a government of a particular foreign state.

2.1.24   This important issue was considered in *Republic of Somalia v Woodhouse Drake and Carey (Suisse) SA*,[40] which concerned a cargo of rice which had been purchased by the Republic of Somalia. Following the refusal by the captain of the ship on which the cargo was loaded to enter the port of Mogadishu, the cargo was sold and the proceeds were paid into court. The issue facing the court was whether the so-called 'Interim Government' was entitled to the sum which had been paid into court. Hobhouse J thought that, in view of the state of relative chaos in Somalia, the claim of the 'Interim Government' should fail. The relevant test for deciding whether to recognise a government was formulated in the following terms:

[T]he factors to be taken into account in deciding whether a government exists as the government of a state are: (a) whether it is the constitutional government of the state; (b) the degree,

---

[38] G Marston, 'The Personality of the Foreign State in English Law' [1997] *CLJ* 374, 405.

[39] S Talmon, 'Recognition of Governments: An Analysis of the New British Policy and Practice' (1992) 63 *BYIL* 231.

[40] [1993] QB 54. B Kingsbury, 'Judicial Determination of Foreign "Government" Status' (1993) 109 *LQR* 377; C Warbrick, 'Recognition of Governments' (1993) 56 *MLR* 92.

nature and stability of administrative control, if any, that it of itself exercises over the territory of the state; (c) whether Her Majesty's Government has any dealings with it and if so what is the nature of those dealings; and (d) in marginal cases, the extent of international recognition that it has as the government of the state.[41]

Paragraphs (a) and (b) are alternative tests of being a government, although constitutionality and effectiveness normally coincide; paragraphs (c) and (d) are matters of evidence on which a court will rely to see if the test in paragraph (a) and/or paragraph (b) is satisfied.[42] Where the organisation claiming to be the government of a state is not the constitutional government (having attempted to seize power by a military coup) and does not have effective control over much of the country, the test is not satisfied.[43] The same is true if the usurper's control is only 'fragile and temporary'.[44]

2.1.25   The current policy of no longer according recognition to foreign governments has the practical advantage that it does not draw the British Government into an evaluation of competing claimants in circumstances of civil war or conflict and it avoids the possibility of misunderstanding or embarrassment. It does, however, have the potential disadvantage of uncertainty:

In doubtful cases a regime might be regarded as the constitutional government of a state by some courts but not by others. Further, 'degree' and 'stability' of administrative control are relative concepts which are often influenced by subjective, especially political, considerations of approval and disapproval of the regime in question. Thus, a regime while fulfilling the conditions of 'stability' and 'independence' in the eyes of some judges might not fulfil these conditions in the eyes of others. Another element of uncertainty would lie in the evaluation of the four criteria in case they led to conflicting results.[45]

Nevertheless, in cases where HM Government has dealings with a foreign body on a normal government-to-government basis, it is extremely unlikely that court will refuse to recognise that body as the government of the state in question; accordingly, that body will normally be regarded as entitled to litigate in England.[46]

2.2 PERSONS WHO CANNOT SUE AND NON-JUSTICIABLE CLAIMS

Enemy Aliens

2.2.1   As a general rule, a claimant is entitled to commence proceedings in England regardless of nationality, residence or domicile. However, at common law an alien enemy is not entitled to invoke the jurisdiction of the English courts. In order for someone to be an enemy alien there must be a state of war between the United Kingdom and the enemy country in question. Since the Second World War the traditional

---

[41] [1993] QB 54, 68.
[42] C Warbrick, 'Recognition of Governments' (1993) 56 *MLR* 92, 96.
[43] *Sierra Leone Telecommunications Co Ltd v Barclays Bank plc* [1998] 2 All ER 821.
[44] *Kuwait Airways Corporation v Iraqi Airways Co* [2001] 1 Lloyd's Rep 161, 221.
[45] S Talmon, 'Recognition of Governments: An Analysis of the New British Policy and Practice' (1992) 63 *BYIL* 231, 285.
[46] See *Kuwait Airways Corporation v Iraqi Airways Co* [1999] 1 LRC 223, 268 (Mance J) and [2001] 1 Lloyd's Rep 161, 218–21 (CA).

concept of war has virtually disappeared from state practice, although armed conflict continues to be used as an instrument of state policy; most situations involving armed conflict do not constitute a state of war from the legal point of view.[47]

2.2.2 The alien status of a person depends not on nationality, but on physical location. A British subject who voluntarily resides or carries on business in a foreign country which is at war with the United Kingdom is an enemy alien.[48] Similarly, a citizen of a country which is at war with the United Kingdom, but who resides in the United Kingdom with the permission of the Crown, is not an enemy alien for the purposes of English jurisdiction rules.[49] Furthermore, there is nothing to prevent a claimant from invoking the jurisdiction of the English courts against an enemy alien.[50]

Non-justiciable Claims

2.2.3 A related issue arises with regard to claims that are not justiciable in the English courts. In fact, there are two doctrines: the act of state doctrine and the broader (and somewhat ill-defined) principle of non-justiciability.[51] In both categories of case, although the claimant has capacity to sue in the English courts—because the claimant is recognised as having legal personality under English private international law—and the defendant is, in principle, subject to the personal jurisdiction of the court, the claim cannot be brought in England because the subject-matter of the litigation involves issues which the English court is not competent to adjudicate.

Act of State

2.2.4 Under English law, there is a relatively narrow doctrine of act of state, which covers, on the one hand, acts of the Crown performed in the course of its relations with a foreign state and executive acts which are authorised or ratified by the Crown in the exercise of sovereign power and, on the other, the executive and legislative acts of foreign states. Under this doctrine, the courts will not investigate the propriety of an act of state (whether of the United Kingdom or of a foreign state). Accordingly, a person who claims to have suffered injury or loss as a result of conduct which amounts to an act of state under English law is not able to obtain redress for such loss in English proceedings. In the 19th-century case of *Buron v Denman*,[52] for example, property belonging to the plaintiff, a Spaniard involved in the slave trade, was destroyed by the defendant, a British naval commander stationed on the coast of Africa with instructions to suppress the slave trade. When the plaintiff brought proceedings in England, the court refused to entertain the claim, notwithstanding the

---

[47] See, eg, *Amin v Brown* [2006] ILPr 67.

[48] *Porter v Freudenberg* [1915] 1 KB 857; *Sovfracht (V/O) v Van Udens Scheepvaart en Agentuur Maatschappij (NV Gebr)* [1943] AC 203.

[49] *Johnstone v Pedlar* [1921] 2 AC 262.

[50] *Robinson & Co v Continental Insurance Company of Mannheim* [1915] 1 KB 155; *Porter v Freudenberg* [1915] 1 KB 857.

[51] See *Kuwait Airways Corp v Iraqi Airways Co* [1999] 1 CLC 31.

[52] (1848) 2 Exch 167.

fact that the defendant's actions were tortious under the law of the place where they were committed, because the defendant's actions amounted to an act of state.

Non-justiciability

2.2.5   The decided cases in which the courts have held that an issue is non-justiciable tend to be rather complicated and it is not easy to reconcile them all. It has been said that an issue is justiciable 'if it is capable of being tried according to law'.[53] In the context of disputes with a foreign element, the issue of non-justiciability is most likely to arise in relation to issues that 'come within the exclusive province of the Executive and its prerogative'.[54] The application of the principle of non-justiciability (which, in effect, covers a number of sub-principles) can be illustrated by a few examples.

2.2.6   First, the English court will not investigate the legitimacy of action taken by a foreign sovereign state or adjudicate upon actions taken by the executive of a foreign state in the conduct of foreign affairs. This principle does not mean, however, that issues which are raised by allegations which might embarrass a foreign sovereign are *ipso facto* non-justiciable.[55] In *Buttes Gas & Oil Co v Hammer (No 3)*[56] a defamation claim incidentally raised the question whether a particular location in the Persian Gulf was within one emirate (Umm al Qawain) or another (Sharjah). The area of sea in question had been the subject of a long-running dispute between the two emirates and, in effect, the court was being asked 'to review transactions in which four sovereign states were involved, which they had brought to a precarious settlement, after diplomacy and the use of force, and to say that at least part of these were "unlawful" under international law'.[57] Lord Wilberforce said that this type of case was not suitable for adjudication because there were 'no judicial or manageable standards by which to judge these issues, ... the court would be in a judicial no-man's land'.[58]

2.2.7   Although there may be disagreement as to exactly what the *Buttes Gas* decision stands for, one plausible interpretation is that the decision supports a flexible principle according to which the court will decline to resolve issues concerning 'acts operating in the area of transactions between states' or 'transactions in the international field' if there are no 'judicial or manageable standards' by which to judge them.[59] This does not mean, however, that the courts will never adjudicate upon issues which involve the legality or legitimacy of the legislative or executive acts of a foreign state. For example, in *Kuwait Airways Corpn v Iraqi Airways Co (Nos 4 & 5)*[60] the House of Lords held that the defendant was liable for the loss of the plaintiff's aircraft, notwithstanding the fact that the aircraft had purportedly been vested in the defendant by a legislative decree of the Republic of Iraq. The House of Lords held

---

[53] FA Mann, *Foreign Affairs in English Courts* (Oxford, OUP, 1986) 63.
[54] *Ibid.*
[55] *Korea National Insurance Corp v Allianz Global Corporate & Specialty AG* [2008] 2 CLC 837.
[56] [1982] AC 888.
[57] Lord Wilberforce at [1982] AC 888, 938.
[58] [1982] AC 888, 938.
[59] See Mance J in *Kuwait Airways Corp v Iraqi Airways Co* [1999] 1 CLC 31, 61–2.
[60] [2002] 2 AC 883.

that, because the Iraqi decree involved a flagrant breach of established principles of public international law, the decree should not be recognised.

2.2.8   A second context in which the term 'non-justiciability' is used is where the dispute before the court involves, in some sense, relations between states on the plane of international law. For example, in the *International Tin* case[61] Lord Oliver said:

It is axiomatic that municipal courts have not and cannot have the competence to adjudicate upon or to enforce the rights arising out of transactions entered into by independent sovereign states between themselves on the plane of international law.[62]

This principle means that a treaty concluded by the Crown under the Royal prerogative does not create legal rights under English law and that the treaty itself cannot be the subject of litigation in England. It is only if the treaty has been given effect to by Act of Parliament that it can be the subject of litigation. Strictly speaking, the treaty is never enforced; the court enforces the statute which implements the convention.

2.2.9   By the same token, the English court is not competent to determine whether or not a foreign sovereign state has broken or effectively terminated a treaty.[63] In *Azov Shipping Co v Baltic Shipping Co*[64] it was argued that an arbitral award made in England should be set aside under section 67 of the Arbitration Act 1996 on the ground that the dispute which had been referred to arbitration was not justiciable (before either a court of civil jurisdiction or an arbitral tribunal) as it involved an intergovernmental agreement between Russia and Ukraine concerning the distribution of state-owned property following the collapse of the Soviet Union. In the words of Colman J:

The issue of non-justiciability ... depends in this case on whether the determination of the substantive issues in relation to [the claimant's claim] would involve determination of any matter as between Russia and Ukraine which either properly falls within the province of public international law or the resolution of which would affect the rights of either state as against the other.[65]

On the facts, however, the issues which arose for determination in the arbitration had nothing whatever to do with questions of public international law; resolution of the parties' dispute did not require a determination of whether the effect of the intergovernmental agreement in question was to vest title to any particular property in Russia or the Ukraine. As a result, the issues raised by the litigation could not be characterised as non-justiciable.

2.2.10   Thirdly, the English court 'will not exercise its own jurisdiction in aid of an excess of jurisdiction by [a] foreign State'.[66] In *Government of India v Taylor*,[67] Lord Keith explained that, where the claim of a foreign government involves 'an assertion of sovereign authority by one State within the territory of another, as distinct from a

---

[61] *JH Rayner (Mincing Lane) Ltd v Department of Trade and Industry* [1990] 2 AC 418.
[62] At 499.
[63] *British Airways Board v Laker Airways Ltd* [1985] AC 58. See also *Westland Helicopters Ltd v Arab Organisation for Industrialisation* [1995] QB 282.
[64] [1999] 2 Lloyd's Rep. 159.
[65] At 177.
[66] L Collins *et al, Dicey, Morris and Collins on The Conflict of Laws* (London, Sweet & Maxwell, 14th edn, 2006), para 5–021.
[67] [1955] AC 491, 511.

patrimonial claim by a foreign State', the claim will not be upheld in English proceedings. This principle is commonly expressed, perhaps slightly misleadingly, according to the terms of *Dicey, Morris and Collins'* Rule 3: 'English courts have no jurisdiction to entertain an action: (1) for the enforcement either directly or indirectly, of a penal, revenue or other public law of a foreign State; or (2) founded upon an act of state.' [68]

2.2.11   In *Mbasogo v Logo Ltd (No 1)* [69] the claimants, the Republic of Equatorial Guinea and its head of state, brought proceedings in England against the defendants, who were alleged to have been involved in an attempt to overthrow the government. The claim was for tortious damages—which included a claim for the costs incurred by the state in responding to the threat posed by the attempted coup and for the personal distress that the head of state claimed to have suffered. The defendants argued, *inter alia*, that the claims were not justiciable in the English courts. In terms of the justicia-bility of the claims, the fundamental distinction is between 'an exercise of sovereign power and an action brought by a sovereign state which might equally have been brought by an individual to recover losses for damage to property'. [70]

2.2.12   The Court of Appeal held that it would not determine or enforce a claim in a case where, in bringing the claim, the claimant was doing an act which was of a 'sovereign character' or which was done 'by virtue of sovereign authority' or which involved the exercise or assertion of a 'sovereign right'. [71] On the facts, the Court of Appeal dismissed the claims: the alleged losses arose as a result of decisions taken by the claimants to protect the state of Equatorial Guinea and its citizens; the claim was not justiciable because the claim for relief arose from the claimants' exercise of sovereign power in responding to the alleged attempted coup by the defendants. [72]

2.3 STATE IMMUNITY

Background

2.3.1   The purpose of the doctrine of sovereign immunity is to promote the functioning of all governments by protecting states from the burden of defending litigation abroad. In the 19th century foreign states were entitled to absolute immunity. The doctrine of absolute immunity was justified by the fact that state activities were limited to the public sphere. As regards both internal matters (such as law and order) and external matters (such as foreign policy and defence), it is reasonable that within the public sphere states should not be required to litigate in a foreign court against their will.

---

[68] L Collins *et al, Dicey, Morris and Collins on The Conflict of Laws* (London, Sweet & Maxwell, 14th edn, 2006), para 5R–019.

[69] [2007] QB 846.

[70] [2007] QB 846, 877 (at [67]).

[71] [2007] QB 846, 873 (at [50]).

[72] [2007] QB 846, 876 (at [63]). For application of the test formulated in *Mbasogo v Logo Ltd (No 1)*, see *Tasarruf Mevduati Sigorta Fonu v Demirel* [2007] 2 All ER 815. Although the case went on appeal ([2007] 1 WLR 2508), the Court of Appeal did not have to address the justiciability point. See also *Islamic Republic of Iran v Barakat Galleries Ltd* [2009] QB 22 in which the Court of Appeal held that Iran's claim to recover various antiquities was a patrimonial claim, rather than an attempt to exercise a sovereign right.

2.3.2 During the 20th century governments became involved in commercial activities which were scarcely any different in nature from the activities of private individuals and companies. When a foreign state enters the marketplace or when it acts as a private party would act, there is no justification for allowing the foreign state to avoid the economic costs of its actions. If, for example, an English company enters a contract to build a hospital in a foreign country, it is not obvious that, from a jurisdictional point of view, it should be regarded as legally relevant whether the other contracting party is a foreign company or a foreign government. The law should not permit the foreign state to shift the everyday burdens of the marketplace onto the shoulders of private parties. Accordingly, a distinction has to be drawn between those state activities which are public—and in relation to which a state may reasonably expect to be immune from legal proceedings in a foreign court—and those state activities which are private or commercial in nature—in relation to which a state cannot reasonably expect to be immune from litigation.[73] These different types of activity are given Latin labels: *acta jure imperii* and *acta jure gestionis* respectively.

2.3.3 Following the Second World War the English courts began to develop a doctrine of restrictive immunity at common law.[74] The rationale of the doctrine of restrictive immunity is that:

where the sovereign chooses to doff his robes and descend into the market place he must take the rough with the smooth, and having condescended to engage in mundane commercial activities he must also condescend to submit himself to an adjudication in a foreign court on whether he has in the course of those activities undertaken obligations which he has failed to fulfil.[75]

The law in this area was placed on a statutory footing by the State Immunity Act 1978[76] (which implements the European Convention on State Immunity of 1972).[77] The State Immunity Act 1978 is to a large extent based on the distinction between *acta jure imperii* and *acta jure gestionis*. The statutory rules do not apply to proceedings in respect of matters excluded from the scope of the Act or to events which occurred before the date on which the Act came into force.[78] Notwithstanding the fact that, for the purposes of English law, the doctrine of state immunity has been put on a statutory footing, it must be remembered that the doctrine derives from public international law. Legal instruments in the field of civil jurisdiction (whether domestic or international in nature) are impliedly subject to the international law of state immunity.[79] For example, the court of an EU Member State must decline jurisdiction if the

---

[73] See J Crawford, 'International Law and Foreign Sovereigns: Distinguishing Immune Transactions' (1983) 54 *BYIL* 75.

[74] See, in particular, *Trendtex Trading Corporation v Central Bank of Nigeria* [1977] QB 529 (B Markesinis, [1977] *CLJ* 211); *The I Congreso del Partido* [1983] 1 AC 244.

[75] Lord Mustill in *Kuwait Airways Corporation v Iraqi Airways Co* [1995] 1 WLR 1147, 1171.

[76] DW Bowett, [1978] *CLJ* 193; C Lewis, [1980] *LMCLQ* 1; FA Mann, (1979) 50 *BYIL* 43; G White, [1979] *JBL* 105; R White, (1979) 42 *MLR* 72.

[77] IM Sinclair, 'The European Convention on State Immunity' (1973) 22 *ICLQ* 254.

[78] State Immunity Act 1978, s 23(3). The Act came into force on 22 November 1978.

[79] Although it is not in force in the United Kingdom, the United Nations Convention on Jurisdictional Immunities of States and their Property (2004) provides guidance on the current extent of state immunity in public international law: see Aikens J in *AIG Capital Partners Inc v Republic of Kazakhstan* [2006] 1 WLR 1420, 1446–7 (at [80]); Sir Anthony Clarke in *Koo Golden East Mongolia v Bank of Nova Scotia* [2008] QB 717, 734–5 (at [47]).

defendant is entitled to claim immunity under the doctrine of state immunity, even if it has jurisdiction under the Brussels I Regulation.[80] However, it will normally be the case that a situation in which a defendant may be inclined to plead state immunity will not concern 'civil and commercial matters' and will, therefore, fall outside the material scope of the Brussels I Regulation.[81]

The Scope of Immunities

2.3.4 The 1978 Act seeks to distinguish government departments (which can claim immunity in the same way as a state) from state-owned and state-managed organisations (which are, as a general rule, to be treated in the same way as private corporations). A state's central bank is, however, subject to special rules.[82] The 1978 Act provides that immunity conferred by the legislation applies 'even though the state does not appear in the proceedings in question'.[83] This means that where, for example, a claim is brought against a defendant who is acting on behalf of a state bank in circumstances in which the state bank would be entitled to immunity under the 1978 Act, the claim fails.[84] Although the Act does not expressly deal with the situation where proceedings are brought against the servants or agents, officials or functionaries of a foreign state in respect of acts done by them as such, it is clear that, in such cases, the foreign state is entitled to claim immunity for its servants as it could if sued itself.[85] A foreign state's right to immunity cannot be circumvented simply by a claimant proceeding against a state's servants or agents, rather than against the state.

2.3.5 Section 14 of the 1978 Act deals differently with, on the one hand, governments and government departments and, on the other, so-called 'separate entities'; subsection (1) addresses the immunities of the former; subsection (2) is concerned with the latter. A state-owned company which has separate legal personality and which enjoys financial and administrative independence will normally be regarded as a separate entity for the purposes of the 1978 Act.[86]

2.3.6 Section 14 of the 1978 Act provides:

(1) The immunities and privileges conferred by this Part of this Act apply to any foreign or commonwealth State other than the United Kingdom; and references to a State include references to:

(a) the sovereign or other head of that State in his public capacity;
(b) the government of that State; and
(c) any department of that government,

---

[80] *Grovit v De Nederlandsche Bank* [2006] 1 WLR 3323.
[81] See Case C–292/05 *Lechouritou v Dimosio tis Omospondiakis Dimokratias tis Germanias* [2007] ECR I–1519; *Grovit v De Nederlandsche Bank* [2008] 1 WLR 51.
[82] See para 2.3.56.
[83] State Immunity Act 1978, s 1(2).
[84] *Koo Golden East Mongolia v Bank of Nova Scotia* [2008] QB 717.
[85] See Lord Bingham in *Jones v Ministry of the Interior of the Kingdom of Saudi Arabia* [2007] 1 AC 270, 281 (at [10]).
[86] See *The Altair* [2008] 2 Lloyd's Rep 90. See also *Wilhelm Finance Inc v Administrator del Astillero Rio Santiago* [2009] 1 CLC 867.

but not to any entity (hereafter referred to as a 'separate entity') which is distinct from the executive organs of the government of the State and is capable of suing or being sued.

(2) A separate entity is immune from the jurisdiction of the courts of the United Kingdom if, and only if—

(a) the proceedings relate to anything done by it in the exercise of sovereign authority; and
(b) the circumstances are such that a State ... would have been so immune.

The scope of the immunity of a separate entity under section 14(2) was considered by the House of Lords in *Kuwait Airways Corporation v Iraqi Airways Co.*[87] Fifteen aircraft belonging to the plaintiff had been seized by the Iraqi military forces on the invasion of Kuwait in 1991. Five were removed by the Iraqi airforce and the remaining 10 were handed over to the defendant, which integrated them into its domestic fleet. The plaintiff brought proceedings for the recovery of the aircraft which had not been destroyed and for damages. The question was whether or not the defendant could claim immunity under section 14(2).

2.3.7 Lord Goff (with whom Lord Jauncey and Lord Nicholls agreed) took as his starting point the proposition that the acts of the defendant were to be regarded as performed in the exercise of sovereign authority if such acts were *acta jure imperii*. Lord Goff decided that the defendant could not claim immunity:

[I]n the case of acts done by a separate entity, it is not enough that the entity should have acted on the directions of the state, because such an act need not possess the character of a governmental act. To attract immunity under section 14(2), therefore, what is done by the separate entity must be something that possesses that character. ... [I]n the absence of such character, the mere fact that the purpose or motive of the act was to serve the purposes of the state will not be sufficient to enable the separate entity to claim immunity under section 14(2) of the Act.[88]

Lord Goff decided that the events surrounding the seizure and detention of the plaintiff's aircraft had to be divided into two phases. First, the taking of the aircraft and their removal to Iraq constituted an exercise of governmental power by the Republic of Iraq. Secondly, after Iraq passed legislation vesting the aircraft in the defendant, the defendant could no longer claim immunity:

[A] separate entity of a state which receives nationalised property from the state cannot ipso facto claim sovereign immunity in respect of a claim by the former owner ... I for my part cannot see that the characterisation as an act jure imperii of the earlier involvement of the entity in the act of seizure can ... be determinative of the characterisation of the subsequent retention and use of the property by the state entity following the formal vesting of the property in the entity by a legislative act of the state.[89]

---

[87] [1995] 1 WLR 1147. MD Evans, 'When the State Taketh and the State Giveth' (1996) 45 *ICLQ* 401; H Fox, 'The Commerciality of the Spoils of War' (1996) 112 *LQR* 186. For consideration of the decisions of the High Court and the Court of Appeal, see: H Fox, 'A "Commercial Transaction" under the State Immunity Act 1978' (1994) 43 *ICLQ* 193; H Fox, 'States in the Market Place' (1994) 110 *LQR* 199; S Marks, [1994] *CLJ* 213; S Talmon, 'War Booty of "Separate Entity" Protected by Sovereign Immunity' (1995) 15 *OJLS* 295.
[88] [1995] 1 WLR 1147, 1160.
[89] [1995] 1 WLR 1147, 1163.

2.3.8   The minority (comprising Lord Mustill and Lord Slynn) took a different view. The minority's starting point was that the two conditions in section 14(2) are different, rather than overlapping requirements.[90] It was clear that section 14(2)(b) was satisfied: if the relevant defendant had been the Republic of Iraq, it would have been entitled to immunity under the State Immunity Act 1978 (since none of the exceptions to immunity would have applied).[91] Whether the retention of the aircraft was done by the defendant 'in the exercise of sovereign authority'—for the purposes of section 14(2)(a)—was the crux of the case. Lord Mustill took the view that:

Assuming ... that section 14(2)(b) is intended to create an additional requirement for immunity, one must ask again what is meant by the reference to things done by the entity in the exercise of a sovereign authority which the entity does not possess. ... [T]he entity is immune only if in some sense the act, although not done by the sovereign, is a manifestation of the sovereign's authority. ... In my opinion [the defendant] was not acting autonomously, but in harness with the Republic of Iraq, and under the shadow of the sovereign authority by which the latter itself was acting, so that its acts were a manifestation of that authority.[92]

Lord Slynn considered that the separation of the events following the seizure of the aircraft into two phases was unrealistic:

If ... this whole incident is to be regarded as one—ie the seizure, removal and use of the aircraft—then it is plain that it was being done under sovereign authority and not otherwise.[93]

2.3.9   The view of the minority is preferable to that of the majority, which effectively deprives section 14(2)(b) of all meaning (which Lord Goff recognised as something of a 'puzzle')[94] and which has been assessed as 'little short of disastrous for the law generally'.[95] If the doctrine of state immunity has a secure basis in policy terms, it seems not unreasonable that separate entities should be able to claim immunity 'when acting on the instruction of their sovereign in circumstances in which the sovereign, had it chosen to act directly rather than through an intermediary, would have itself been entitled to immunity'.[96] Lord Goff's concern that a separate entity might be able to claim immunity indefinitely was answered by Lord Slynn: 'The sale to another airline would break the chain of causation between Iraq's own acts and the exercise of sovereign authority pursuant to those acts.'[97]

2.3.10   It has to be conceded that the *Kuwait Airways Corporation* case is more problematical than most. In more typical cases, where a separate entity enters into a contract of a commercial nature (such as where a separate entity, owner of a cargo on board a vessel which has run aground, concludes a contract for salvage services with a salvage company), it is plain that the separate entity's act does not amount to a governmental act and that, in such circumstances, any attempt to claim immunity is bound to fail.[98]

---

[90] See Lord Mustill at [1995] 1 WLR 1147, 1171.
[91] See paras 2.3.14–2.3.38.
[92] [1995] 1 WLR 1147, 1172.
[93] [1995] 1 WLR 1147, 1175.
[94] [1995] 1 WLR 1147, 1159.
[95] H Fox, 'The Commerciality of the Spoils of War' (1996) 112 *LQR* 186, 187.
[96] MD Evans, 'When the State Taketh and the State Giveth' (1996) 45 *ICLQ* 401, 406.
[97] [1995] 1 WLR 1147, 1175.
[98] See, eg, *The Altair* [2008] 2 Lloyd's Rep 90.

The Scheme of the Act

The Principle of Immunity

2.3.11 The structure of the 1978 Act derives from the 19th-century position; the starting point is the principle of immunity. Section 1(1) provides:

A State is immune from the jurisdiction of the courts of the United Kingdom except as provided in the following provisions of this Part of this Act.

Exceptions to Immunity

2.3.12 The major part of the 1978 Act is concerned with the various exceptions to the principle of immunity. The legislation draws a distinction between adjudicative jurisdiction and enforcement jurisdiction: sections 2–11 deal with adjudicative jurisdiction; sections 13 and 14 regulate enforcement jurisdiction; section 12 is concerned with procedural issues. The boundaries of immunity from adjudicative jurisdiction and from enforcement jurisdiction are drawn differently, with the consequence that it is perfectly possible for an English court to hold a state liable for a debt but for there to be no means available to the judgment creditor to enforce the judgment in England.

The Burden of Proof

2.3.13 Is the court to presume that a state is entitled to immunity unless it is proved by the claimant to the contrary or should the burden of proof be on the party invoking immunity? It has been argued that, notwithstanding the way in which the Act is structured, the burden of proof should be on the defendant to establish that it is entitled to immunity.[99] Judicial opinion, however, is that the burden of proof falls on the claimant to show that the defendant is not entitled to immunity.[100] Furthermore, it is not enough that the claimant establishes a good arguable case. Even in those cases where the defendant does not seek to challenge the jurisdiction of the court, preferring to take no part at all in the proceedings, the question whether the defendant is entitled to immunity must be decided as a preliminary issue in favour of the claimant 'in whatever form and by whatever procedure the court may consider appropriate'.[101] If the claimant cannot establish on the balance of probabilities that the defendant is not entitled to immunity, the court will decline jurisdiction.[102]

Immunity from Adjudicative Jurisdiction

2.3.14 Sections 2–11 list the 10 areas in which states are not entitled to immunity from adjudicative jurisdiction. These 10 areas are not mutually exclusive; there are

---

[99] FA Mann, 'The State Immunity Act 1978' (1979) 50 *BYIL* 43, 62.
[100] *JH Rayner (Mincing Lane) Ltd v Department of Trade and Industry* [1987] BCLC 667, 678.
[101] Kerr LJ in *JH Rayner (Mincing Lane) Ltd v Department of Trade and Industry* [1989] Ch 72, 194.
[102] *Al-Adsani v Government of Kuwait (No 2)* [1996] 2 LRC 344.

certain points of overlap between them. Although it is thought that the exclusions from immunity are, for the most part, cumulative rather than alternative,[103] the Court of Appeal declined to express a concluded opinion on this point when it arose in *Intpro Properties (UK) Ltd v Sauvel*.[104]

Submission

2.3.15 Section 2(1) provides that a state is not immune 'as respects proceedings in respect of which it has submitted to the jurisdiction of the courts of the United Kingdom'. A state may submit after the dispute has arisen or by prior written agreement.[105] The simplest examples are situations in which a state enters into a contract which includes a jurisdiction clause in favour of the courts of a particular country. A choice of English law is not to be regarded as a submission to English jurisdiction.[106] As a general rule, a state is deemed to have submitted if it institutes proceedings or if it has intervened or taken any step in the proceedings.[107] A state which has taken a step in the proceedings will not be regarded as having submitted in a number of situations: first, where the state takes part in proceedings in order to claim immunity[108] (even if the state, in addition to claiming immunity, objects to the court's jurisdiction, for example by applying for a stay of execution, by contesting the validity of service, or by applying for a stay of proceedings on the basis of *forum non conveniens*);[109] secondly, where the state intervenes in proceedings to assert an interest in property in circumstances in which the state would have been entitled to immunity had the proceedings been brought against it[110]; thirdly, the state intervenes in proceedings in ignorance of facts entitling it to immunity if those facts could not reasonably have been ascertained and immunity is claimed as soon as reasonably practicable.[111]

2.3.16 A state can be regarded as submitting only by virtue of acts performed by its representatives. Submission may occur if a person has express authority to submit on the state's behalf. It is provided that the head of a state's diplomatic mission in the United Kingdom (or the person for the time being performing those functions) is deemed to have the authority to submit to the jurisdiction of the courts.[112] As a general rule, no other person is regarded as having deemed authority to submit.[113] However, where proceedings arise out of a contract, any person who has entered the contract on behalf of and with the authority of the state in question is deemed to have the necessary authority.[114] Once a state has submitted to proceedings, that

---

[103] See J Crawford, (1983) 54 *BYIL* 283, 284.
[104] [1983] QB 1019.
[105] State Immunity Act 1978, s 2(2). See *Ahmed v Government of the Kingdom of Saudi Arabia* [1996] 2 All ER 248.
[106] State Immunity Act 1978, s 2(2).
[107] State Immunity Act 1978, s 2(3).
[108] State Immunity Act 1978, s 2(4)(a).
[109] *Kuwait Airways Corporation v Iraqi Airways Co* [1995] 1 Lloyd's Rep 25.
[110] State Immunity Act 1978, s 2(4)(b).
[111] State Immunity Act 1978, s 2(5).
[112] State Immunity Act 1978, s 2(7).
[113] *Arab Republic of Egypt v Gamal-Eldin* [1996] 2 All ER 237.
[114] State Immunity Act 1978, s 2(7).

submission extends to any appeal or any counterclaim which arises out of the same legal relationship or facts as the claim.[115]

Arbitration

2.3.17   Section 9(1) provides:

Where a State has agreed in writing to submit a dispute which has arisen, or may arise, to arbitration, the State is not immune as respects proceedings in the courts of the United Kingdom which relate to the arbitration.

This provision does not apply where both the parties to the agreement are states or where the parties have agreed that immunity is to apply.[116] Although Article 12 of the European Convention on State Immunity of 1972, on which section 9 is based, is restricted to court proceedings relating to civil and commercial matters, there seems to be no such restriction in the law of the United Kingdom. What is meant by the word 'relate' in the context of section 9(1)? Of particular importance is the question whether the Act permits proceedings in England to enforce an arbitration award against a state. Both the wording of the European Convention on State Immunity and the structure of the 1978 Act—which draws a clear distinction between adjudicative jurisdiction and enforcement jurisdiction— indicate that the enforcement of awards is not within the scope of section 9, but falls to be determined by section 13.[117] Nevertheless, in *Svenska Petroleum Exploration AB v Government of the Republic of Lithuania (No 2)*[118] the Court of Appeal, having drawn attention to the fact that section 9 of the 1978 Act departs in certain respects from the European Convention on State Immunity, held that 'proceedings relating to arbitration' include proceedings relating to the enforcement of a foreign arbitral award. However, the Court of Appeal went on to add that: 'Enforcement by execution on property belonging to the state is another matter, as section 13 makes clear'. [119]

2.3.18   Does an agreement to arbitrate in country X amount to a waiver of immunity with regard to court proceedings relating to the arbitration in any forum or only to proceedings brought before the courts of country X? Academic opinion is divided. One view is that section 9 removes immunity only in respect of proceedings relating to arbitrations conducted in the United Kingdom[120]; the alternative view is that section 9 applies regardless of the seat of arbitration.[121] Given that in the *Svenska Petroleum* case the Court of Appeal held that section 9 extends to the enforcement of foreign arbitral awards, it follows that an agreement to arbitrate is effective to waive immunity not only in the country where the seat of arbitration is located, but also in other countries (such as countries where the claimant applies for provisional measures or countries in which a successful claimant seeks to enforce the arbitral award).

---

[115] State Immunity Act 1978, s 2(6).

[116] State Immunity Act 1978, s 9(2).

[117] H Fox, 'States and the Undertaking to Arbitrate' (1988) 37 *ICLQ* 1, 14–15.

[118] [2007] QB 886. A Kawharu, 'Enforcement of Arbitral Awards in Investment Disputes: Through the Smoke Screens' [2007] *LMCLQ* 136. For developments in the USA, see S Strong, 'Enforcement of Arbitral Awards Against States and State Agencies' (2006) 26 *Nw J Int'l L & Bus* 335.

[119] [2007] QB 886, 925 (at [117]). For discussion of s 13, see paras 2.3.40–2.3.54.

[120] H Fox, 'States and the Undertaking to Arbitrate' (1988) 37 *ICLQ* 1, 14.

[121] FA Mann, 'The State Immunity Act 1978' (1979) 50 *BYIL* 43, 58.

2.3.19   What is the effect of an arbitration agreement which is entered into by a state official who does not have authority to do so under the law of the state in question? It has been suggested that in this case the waiver is *ultra vires* and the court should not exercise jurisdiction.[122] The alternative (and preferable) view is that the waiver should be regarded as effective as long as the official who entered the agreement with the private party had the apparent authority to do so.[123]

Ships

2.3.20   Since some states own or operate fleets of merchant ships, one important area where the issue of immunity may be relevant is in the context of cases involving shipping. Section 10 applies to admiralty proceedings and proceedings on any claim which could be made the subject of admiralty proceedings.[124] Although the most usual way in which admiralty proceedings are commenced is by service of a claim form on a ship, a claim *in rem* is based on a claim *in personam* and the Supreme Court Act 1981—which defines the court's admiralty jurisdiction—provides that, subject to section 22 of that Act, 'an action *in personam* may be brought in the High Court in all cases within the Admiralty jurisdiction of that court'.[125] The exceptions to immunity contained in section 10 apply equally to proceedings *in rem* and *in personam*.[126]

2.3.21   Section 10(2) provides:

A State is not immune as respects:

(a) an action in rem against a ship belonging to that State; or
(b) an action in personam for enforcing a claim in connection with such a ship,

if, at the time when the cause of action arose, the ship was in use or intended for use for commercial purposes.

This subsection is qualified by subsection (3), which deals with the situation where the claimant starts proceedings *in rem* in respect of a sister ship (S2), rather than the ship in connection with which the claim arose (S1). The effect of subsection (3) is that both S1 and S2 must have been in use or intended for use for commercial purposes at the time when the claim arose in connection with S1.

2.3.22   Subsection (4) provides special rules for cargoes:

A State is not immune as respects:

(a) an action in rem against a cargo belonging to that State if both the cargo and the ship carrying it were, at the time when the cause of action arose, in use or intended for use for commercial purposes; or

---

[122] M Sornarajah, 'Problems of Applying the Restrictive Theory of Sovereign Immunity' (1982) 31 *ICLQ* 661, 685.
[123] RJ Oparil, 'Waiver of Sovereign Immunity in the United States and Great Britain by an Arbitration Agreement' (1986) 4(4) *J Int Arb* 61, 72; KI Vibhute, 'Waiver of State Immunity by an Agreement to Arbitrate and International Commercial Arbitration' [1998] *JBL* 550, 557–9.
[124] State Immunity Act 1978, s 10(1).
[125] Supreme Court Act 1981, s 21(1).
[126] For a discussion of jurisdiction in admiralty proceedings, see ch 8.

(b) an action in personam for enforcing a claim in connection with such a cargo if the ship carrying it was then in use or intended for use as aforesaid.

2.3.23 Although the exclusions from immunity in section 10 refer to ships and cargoes 'belonging to' a state, it is provided that 'references to a ship or cargo belonging to a state include references to a ship or cargo in its possession or control or in which it claims an interest'.[127] 'Commercial purposes' is defined by section 17(1) as 'purposes of such transactions or activities as are mentioned in section 3(3)'.[128]

2.3.24 Although the idea behind section 10 is relatively straightforward—states should not be able to claim immunity in respect of commercial shipping activity—the statutory provisions are rather complex. In particular, the distinction between ships and cargoes gives rise to some subtleties. The effect of subsections (2) and (4) can be illustrated by the following examples:

A warship which happens to be used for carrying motor cars for civilian use cannot be immune, but if a trading ship carries ammunition for military purposes both the ship and the cargo are immune, at least if there is no commercial cargo on board. Cement carried in a trading ship may be immune: the result depends on the purpose for which it will be used. If the consignee intends to sell the cement to the military administration, but is not contractually bound to do so, the non-commercial purpose does not in any legally relevant sense exist. If the consignee has sold an identifiable quantity being part of the cargo of cement for the building of military barracks, immunity extends to such quantity and it would probably be no counter-argument that one must not look beyond the consignee; what matter are the ultimate purposes in so far as they can be proven. Shoes for the army (to revert to an often-discussed example) are a cargo for a non-commercial purpose, but if they are consigned to a private merchant who only hopes to sell them to the army, the purpose remains commercial.[129]

2.3.25 Whereas normally the various exceptions to immunity can be applied cumulatively, where a situation falls within the scope of section 10(1) (ie, the claim is within the admiralty jurisdiction of the court) the exceptions from immunity contained in sections 3–5 (commercial transactions, contracts of employment and tort) do not apply if the following two requirements are met: first, the state is a party to the Brussels Convention of 1926 on Immunity of State-Owned Ships; secondly, the claim relates to the operation of a ship owned or operated by that state, or to the carriage of cargo or passengers on any such ship, or to the carriage of cargo owned by that state on any other ship.[130] Although the claimant cannot rely on sections 3–5 if both these requirements are satisfied, the other exceptions to immunity—notably section 2 (submission) and section 9 (arbitration)—are not excluded. Of course, if either of the requirements is not satisfied, the general provisions of sections 3, 4 and 5 may be relied upon by the claimant.

---

[127] State Immunity Act 1978, s 10(5).

[128] The definition of 'commercial transaction' for the purpose of s 3(3) includes: contracts for the supply of goods and services; loans and other transactions for the provision of finance; and other transactions and activities (of a commercial or analogous nature) into which a state enters or engages otherwise than in the exercise of sovereign authority. See para 2.3.27.

[129] FA Mann, 'The State Immunity Act 1978' (1979) 50 *BYIL* 43, 58–9.

[130] State Immunity Act 1978, s 10(6).

Commercial Activities

2.3.26 One of the most important exceptions to immunity is contained in section 3, which provides:

(1) A State is not immune as respects proceedings relating to—

(a) a commercial transaction entered into by the State; or
(b) an obligation of the State which by virtue of a contract (whether a commercial transaction or not) falls to be performed wholly or partly in the United Kingdom.

(2) This section does not apply if the parties to the dispute are States or have otherwise agreed in writing; and subsection (1)(b) above does not apply if the contract (not being a commercial transaction) was made in the territory of the State concerned and the obligation in question is governed by its administrative law.

Section 3(1)(b) has been given a broad interpretation by the English courts. Whereas section 3(1)(a) refers to a transaction 'entered into by the State', there is no similar reference in section 3(1)(b). The requirements of section 3(1)(b) are that the proceedings in question relate to obligations of the state, that those obligations are to be performed in the United Kingdom and that they have arisen by virtue of a contract; section 3(1)(b) does not require that the contract should have been entered into by the state.[131]

2.3.27 Section 3(3) defines what is meant by 'commercial transaction' in the following terms:

(a) any contract for the supply of goods or services;
(b) any loan or other transaction for the provision of finance or any guarantee or indemnity in respect of any such transaction or of any other financial obligation; and
(c) any other transaction or activity (whether of a commercial, industrial, financial, professional or other similar character) into which a State enters or in which it engages otherwise than in the exercise of sovereign authority;

but neither paragraph of subsection (1) above applies to a contract of employment between a State and an individual.

As regards paragraphs (a) and (b), it is the nature of the transaction, not its purpose, which is important. Accordingly, a contract for the sale of goods is a commercial transaction regardless of the purpose for which the goods are acquired and regardless of whether the state is engaged in the exercise of sovereign authority.[132] The sale of boots or the borrowing of money on which interest is payable are commercial transactions, notwithstanding the fact that the boots are for the army and the money is for munitions. As regards paragraph (c), the transaction or activity cannot be 'commercial' if the state enters into it in the exercise of sovereign authority. The dividing line between sovereign acts, on the one hand, and commercial acts, on the other, is notoriously difficult to draw. The 1978 Act essentially follows the distinction between *acta jure imperii* and *acta jure gestionis*. It is established that the distinction is based on the nature of

---

[131] *JH Rayner (Mincing Lane) Ltd v Department of Trade and Industry* [1989] Ch 72.
[132] See Burton J in *Orascom Telecom Holding SAE v Republic of Chad* [2008] 2 Lloyd's Rep 396, 400 (at [14]).

the transaction, rather than its purpose[133]; the test is objective, rather than subjective. The proper approach involves looking at all the circumstances in relation to the activities and their context and then considering all the factors together.[134] Applying this approach it has been held that *acta jure imperii* include the issue of banknotes[135] and the regulation and supervision of a nation's foreign exchange reserves.[136] Conversely, the issue of a letter of credit[137] or a promissory note[138] by a central bank is a commercial activity, as is the issue by a state of a series of bonds pursuant to a fiscal agency agreement[139] and the sale of shares in a subsidiary owned by a central bank to another state-owned bank following the central bank's reorganisation.[140]

Contracts of Employment[141]

2.3.28   Section 4, which contains special rules relating to contracts of employment, is drafted in a very complex manner. Subsection (1) provides that a state is not immune as regards 'proceedings relating to a contract of employment between the State and an individual where the contract was made in the United Kingdom or the work is to be wholly or partly performed there'. This exception to the principle of immunity is itself subject to exceptions in subsection (2), which in turn are subject to further exceptions in subsections (3) and (4):

(2) Subject to subsections (3) and (4) below, this section does not apply if—

(a) at the time when the proceedings are brought the individual is a national of the State concerned; or
(b) at the time when the contract was made the individual was neither a national of the United Kingdom nor habitually resident there; or
(c) the parties to the contract have otherwise agreed in writing.

(3) Where the work is for an office, agency or establishment maintained by the State in the United Kingdom for commercial purposes, subsection 2(a) and (b) above do not exclude the application of this section unless the individual was, at the time when the contract was made, habitually resident in that State.

(4) Subsection (2)(c) above does not exclude the application of this section where the law of the United Kingdom requires the proceedings to be brought before a court of the United Kingdom.

2.3.29   In *Sengupta v Republic of India*[142] the plaintiff, an Indian national, was employed by the Indian High Commission. When the plaintiff was dismissed he sued

---

[133] *The I Congreso del Partido* [1983] 1 AC 244.
[134] *Littrell v United States of America (No 2)* [1995] 1 WLR 82, 89 and 91.
[135] *Camdex International Ltd v Bank of Zambia (No 2)* [1997] 1 WLR 632.
[136] *Crescent Oil and Shipping Services Ltd v Banco Nacional de Angola* (1999, unreported).
[137] *Trendtex Trading Corpn v Central Bank of Nigeria* [1997] QB 529.
[138] *Cardinal Financial Investments Corporation v Central Bank of Yemen* [2001] Lloyd's Rep Banking 1.
[139] *NML Capital Ltd v Republic of Argentina* [2009] QB 579.
[140] *Re Banco Nacional de Cuba* [2001] 1 WLR 2039.
[141] For a comparative treatment, see H Fox, 'Employment Contracts as an Exception to State Immunity: Is All Public Service Immune?' (1995) 66 *BYIL* 97.
[142] [1983] ICR 221. J Crawford, (1983) 54 *BYIL* 279. Although the case was decided under the common law which was applicable before the entry into force of the 1978 Act, Browne-Wilkinson J considered the position under the legislation.

his employer in England. In these circumstances, the state was entitled to immunity since the employee was 'a national of the State concerned' for the purposes of section 4(2)(a) and the High Commission was not an 'establishment maintained by the State in the United Kingdom for commercial purposes' within the meaning of section 4(3). Similarly, the purposes of a medical office in London used by the Egyptian government to provide guidance, advice and expert care to patients referred for medical care in the United Kingdom are not 'commercial purposes'.[143]

2.3.30   It should also be noted that, by virtue of section 16(1)(a), section 4 does not apply to proceedings concerning the employment of the members of a diplomatic mission (as defined by the Diplomatic Privileges Act 1964) or to the members of a consular post (within the meaning of the Consular Relations Act 1968).[144] As Hutchison LJ noted in *Ahmed v Government of the Kingdom of Saudi Arabia*: 'It is a curious fact that ... s 16 appears almost completely to emasculate s 4.'[145]

Tort

2.3.31   Section 5 provides that a state is 'not immune as respects proceedings in respect of (a) death or personal injury, or (b) damage to or loss of tangible property, caused by an act or omission in the United Kingdom'. The wording of section 5 means that a state is immune in the United Kingdom in cases involving a wrongful act performed wholly outside the United Kingdom,[146] even if the damage to the claimant were to occur within the United Kingdom. The fact that the defendant is accused of breaches of peremptory norms of international law (*ius cogens*) does not prevent the defendant from relying on state immunity[147] and a decision by a national court to grant immunity in such circumstances does not amount to a breach of the claimant's right to a fair trial under Article 6 of the European Convention on Human Rights.[148] In cases where, as a result of a tort—whether committed in the United Kingdom or abroad—the claimant suffers pure economic loss, the general principle of immunity in section 1(1) applies.

2.3.32   It is provided by section 16(2) of the 1978 Act that section 5 does not apply to 'proceedings relating to anything done by or in relation to the armed forces of a State while present in the United Kingdom'. Whether a state has immunity in such proceedings is determined by the restrictive theory of immunity developed at common

---

[143] *Arab Republic of Egypt v Gamal-Eldin* [1996] 2 All ER 237.
[144] See, eg, *Arab Republic of Egypt v Gamal-Eldin* [1996] 2 All ER 237.
[145] [1996] 2 All ER 248, 256.
[146] *Al-Adsani v Government of Kuwait* [1996] 2 LRC 333; *Al-Adsani v Government of Kuwait (No 2)* [1996] 2 LRC 344. S Marks, [1997] *CLJ* 8.
[147] *Al-Adsani v Government of Kuwait* [1996] 2 LRC 333; *Al-Adsani v Government of Kuwait (No 2)* [1996] 2 LRC 344.
[148] *Al-Adsani v UK* (2002) 34 EHRR 273 (R Garnett, 'State Immunity Triumphs in the European Court of Human Rights' (2002) 118 *LQR* 367; D Lloyd Jones, 'Article 6 ECHR and Immunities Arising in Public International Law' (2003) 52 *ICLQ* 463; CJ Tams, [2003] *CLJ* 246; E Voyiakis, 'Access to Court v State Immunity' (2003) 52 *ICLQ* 297; X Yang, 'State Immunity in the European Court of Human Rights: Reaffirmations and Misconceptions' (2003) 74 *BYIL* 333); *Jones v Ministry of the Interior of the Kingdom of Saudi Arabia* [2007] 1 AC 270 (M Tomonori, 'Denying Foreign State Immunity on the Grounds of Alternative Means' (2008) 71 *MLR* 734).

law. For example, in *Littrell v United States of America (No 2)*[149] the plaintiff claimed that, while he was serving in the US air force in England, he suffered personal injury as a result of negligent medical treatment at a military hospital. The Court of Appeal held that the defendant was entitled to immunity at common law on the basis that the activities in question constituted *acta jure imperii*. Similarly, in *Holland v Lampen-Woolf*[150] the House of Lords held that the defendant enjoyed immunity under the common law doctrine of state immunity. The case concerned a defamation claim brought by an American university professor (who taught international relations at a US military base in England) against the education services officer at the base who had written a report questioning the plaintiff's professional competence.

Ownership, Possession and Use of Property

2.3.33 Section 6(1) provides that a state is not immune as respects proceedings relating to:

(a) any interest of that State in, or its possession or use of, immovable property in the United Kingdom; or
(b) any obligation of the State arising out of its interest in, or its possession or use of, any such property.

The basic principle in section 6(1) is subject to an exception in section 16 which provides that section 6(1) 'does not apply to proceedings concerning a State's title to or its possession of property used for the purposes of a diplomatic mission'.

2.3.34 The relationship between sections 6 and 16 was considered in *Intpro Properties (UK) Ltd v Sauvel*.[151] In 1979 the plaintiff let a house in London to the third defendant, the French government. The house was occupied by the first defendant, who was a financial counsellor at the French embassy in London. In 1983 dry rot was discovered in the house, but the plaintiff was unable to gain access to effect the necessary repairs. The plaintiff started proceedings with a view to recovering damages for the third defendant's refusal to allow the plaintiff entry to the premises. Counsel for the plaintiff relied on the exception to immunity contained in section 6(1)(b). Although it was accepted on the basis of section 13(2)(a) that it was not possible to obtain an injunction or an order for possession against the third defendant, the plaintiff argued that this did not bar the claim for damages for breach of covenant. Since the proceedings were plainly covered by section 6(1)(b) the question facing the court was whether the plaintiff's claim was excluded by section 16. The Court of Appeal's decision that section 16 did not apply was based on two reasons. First, the premises were not used for the purposes of a diplomatic mission. Although the first defendant used the premises for social functions associated with his employment, this was not enough to bring the case within the scope of the provision. Secondly, the proceedings in the present case did not concern the state's title to the premises or their possession

[149] [1995] 1 WLR 82. JG Collier, [1995] *CLJ* 7.
[150] [2000] 1 WLR 1573. M Tomonori, 'One Immunity Has Gone ... Another ...' (2001) 64 *MLR* 472; X Yang, [2001] *CLJ* 17.
[151] [1983] QB 1019. J Crawford, (1983) 54 *BYIL* 283.

of them within the meaning of section 16. Accordingly, the situation fell within the scope of section 6(1)(b) and the third defendant was not entitled to immunity.

2.3.35   Where proceedings are brought in relation to state-owned property which is in the possession of a third party, the state is being indirectly impleaded. In these circumstances section 6(4) allows the third party to raise immunity as a defence to the extent that the defence would have been available to the state in proceedings brought directly against it. As a result of section 6(4) a bank may be able to resist claims against funds belonging to a state which are deposited with it.

Intellectual Property Rights

2.3.36   Three points emerge from section 7. First, a state is not immune as respects proceedings relating to patents, trademarks and other intellectual property rights registered or protected in the United Kingdom. Secondly, there is no immunity in cases where a person alleges that a state has infringed his intellectual property rights in the United Kingdom.[152] Thirdly, there is no immunity in proceedings relating to the right to use a business name in the United Kingdom.

Membership of Organisations

2.3.37   Section 8 deals with proceedings relating to an organisation—whether 'a body corporate, an unincorporated body or a partnership'—of which a state is a member. The state does not enjoy immunity as regards proceedings arising between the state and the organisation or between the state and the other members of the organisation if two conditions are satisfied: first, the organisation has members which are not states; and, secondly, the organisation is incorporated under the law of the United Kingdom or is controlled from or has its principal place of business in the United Kingdom.

Taxes

2.3.38   A state is not immune as respects proceedings relating to its liability for value added tax, customs and excise duties and agricultural levies and business rates.[153]

Immunity from Enforcement Jurisdiction

Preliminary Remarks

2.3.39   As regards adjudicative jurisdiction, the exceptions to the general principle of immunity are extremely wide. In most cases of a commercial nature states and state entities (whether government departments or separate entities) are unable to invoke

---

[152] See the judgment of Millett LJ in *A Ltd v B Bank* [1997] FSR 165, 174.
[153] State Immunity Act 1978, s 11.

the doctrine of immunity in their favour. However, immunity from adjudicative jurisdiction is only part of the equation. It is not enough that a claimant is able to sue a state in England in respect of a commercial transaction; it is just as important that a successful claimant should be able to have recourse to the courts to enforce a judgment or award in his favour. It is in this regard that the 1978 Act might be thought to be lacking; the immunity from enforcement jurisdiction provided by sections 13 and 14 goes further than is necessary. The starting point is that a judgment against a foreign state cannot be enforced in England unless (i) it would have been enforceable if the judgment had been given against a person other than a state and (ii) the court of origin would have had jurisdiction on the basis of sections 2 to 11 of the State Immunity Act 1978.[154] From this starting point sections 13 and 14 of the 1978 Act makes provision for further immunities at the enforcement stage. The general point which emerges from sections 13 and 14 is that arbitration or litigation against a state is a far from secure process. A judgment or award against a state may prove to be no more than a Pyrrhic victory. It is not sufficient that the state submits to the adjudicative jurisdiction of national courts or to arbitration; to be sure of being able to enforce a judgment or award against a state, private parties need to bargain also for a waiver of immunity against enforcement jurisdiction.[155]

Immunity under Section 13(1) and (2)

2.3.40   Section 13(1) provides:

No penalty by way of committal or fine shall be imposed in respect of any failure or refusal by or on behalf of a State to disclose or produce any document or other information for the purposes of proceedings to which it is a party.

This subsection does not necessarily mean that a state can refuse to co-operate in disclosure of documents with impunity. The judge is entitled to draw the appropriate inference from a state's refusal to produce a relevant document.

2.3.41   The general principle of immunity from enforcement jurisdiction is extremely wide. Section 13(2) provides that:

(a) relief shall not be given against a State by way of injunction or order for specific performance or for the recovery of land or any other property; and
(b) the property of a State shall not be subject to any process for the enforcement of a judgment or arbitration award or, in an action in rem, for its arrest, detention or sale.

Although the Act does not define what is meant by 'injunction or order for specific performance', an order directed at a state to provide security for the other party's costs does not fall within the scope of section 13(1)(a): 'a simple order for the payment of money from no specified source' is not an injunction.[156] Conversely, an application

---

[154] Civil Jurisdiction and Judgments Act 1987, s 31. See *NML Capital Ltd v Republic of Argentina* [2009] QB 579.

[155] GR Delaume, 'Sovereign Immunity and Transnational Arbitration' (1987) 3 *Arb Int* 28, 44–5.

[156] Staughton LJ in *Soleh Boneh International Ltd v Government of the Republic of Uganda* [1993] 2 Lloyd's Rep 208, 213.

for a freezing injunction to prevent a state from dealing with any of its assets is clearly within the scope of section 13(2)(a).[157]

2.3.42 The enforcement immunity conferred by section 13(2) is subject to two exceptions. First, there is a general exception in cases where the defendant has waived immunity.[158] Secondly, there is a more specific exception to section 13(2)(b) in relation to property used for commercial purposes.[159]

Waiver of Immunity

2.3.43 Section 13(3) provides:

Subsection (2) above does not prevent the giving of any relief or the issue of any process with the written consent of the State concerned; and any such consent (which may be contained in a prior agreement) may be expressed so as to apply to a limited extent or generally; but a provision merely submitting to the jurisdiction of the courts is not to be regarded as a consent for the purposes of this subsection.

Subsection (5) goes on to provide that the head of a state's diplomatic mission in the United Kingdom (or the person for the time being performing his functions) is 'deemed to have authority to give on behalf of the State any such consent as is mentioned in subsection (3)'.

2.3.44 Section 13(3) was considered in *A Co Ltd v Republic of X*,[160] a case concerning the effect of the following terms contained in contracts for the sale of coffee and cocoa:

6. Sovereign Immunity

The Ministry of Finance hereby waives whatever defence it may have of sovereign immunity for itself or its property (present or subsequently acquired).

7. Governing Law & Arbitration

(a) This agreement shall be governed and construed in accordance with the laws of England without reference to conflict of the laws, and A Co and the Ministry of Finance hereby submit to the jurisdiction of the English courts.

As regards adjudicative jurisdiction, clause 7 of the contract was effective as a submission for the purposes of section 2 of the 1978 Act. In the course of proceedings the plaintiff applied for a freezing injunction to prevent the Republic from disposing of assets up to $12 million, which was the sum owed under the contracts. The question was whether clause 6 constituted 'written consent' for the purpose of section 13(3), thereby enabling the English court to grant the relief sought by the plaintiff. It was held that by expressly waiving 'whatever defence it may have of sovereign immunity for itself or its property' the defendant had waived its enforcement immunity. Where a contract includes a waiver of immunity clause, the courts will not strive to construe the clause restrictively. So, if a clause is phrased in terms of a general waiver covering

---

[157] *ETI Euro Telecom International NV v Republic of Bolivia* [2009] 1 WLR 665.
[158] State Immunity Act 1978, s 13(3).
[159] State Immunity Act 1978, s 13(4).
[160] [1990] 2 Lloyd's Rep 520. FA Mann, 'Waiver of Immunity' (1991) 107 *LQR* 362.

both adjudicative and enforcement jurisdiction, the state will not be able to claim immunity in proceedings in which the claimant applies for an anti-suit injunction to restrain the bringing of proceedings in another country.[161]

2.3.45   By contrast, in *Arab Banking Corporation v International Tin Council*[162] it was held that a submission by the defendant, the International Tin Council, in a banking facility to 'the non-exclusive jurisdiction of the English courts' did not involve a submission to the enforcement jurisdiction of the English courts. As a result, there was no power to grant a freezing injunction as the injunction sought by the plaintiff was ancillary to execution. Whether an agreement to arbitrate under the ICC Rules amounts to a waiver for the purposes of section 13(3) is uncertain.[163]

No Immunity in Respect of Property used for Commercial Purposes

2.3.46   Section 13(4) provides:

Subsection (2)(b) above does not prevent the issue of any process in respect of property which is for the time being in use or intended for use for commercial purposes; but, in a case not falling within section 10 above, this subsection applies to property of a State party to the European Convention on State Immunity only if—

(a) the process is for enforcing a judgment which is final within the meaning of section 18(1)(b) below and the State has made a declaration under Article 24 of the Convention; or
(b) the process is for enforcing an arbitration award.

The structure of subsection (4) is somewhat complex. The principle in subsection (2) is that a state's property cannot be the subject of an order for enforcement. Subsection (4) provides a general exception: an order for enforcement may be made against a state's commercial property—that is, property which is for the time being in use or intended for use for commercial purposes. There are, however, specific exceptions to the general exception.

2.3.47   The effect of these provisions is as follows. First, there can be no enforcement against a state's property which is not commercial property (unless there has been an express waiver of enforcement immunity). Secondly, an arbitration award can be enforced against the commercial property of a state.[164] Thirdly, in a situation which falls within the admiralty jurisdiction of the court, a judgment can be enforced against the commercial property of a state.[165] Fourthly, in a situation which does not fall within the admiralty jurisdiction of the court, a judgment can be enforced against the commercial property of a state which is not a party to the European Convention

---

[161] *Sabah Shipyard (Pakistan) Ltd v Islamic Republic of Pakistan* [2003] 2 Lloyd's Rep 571. G Wilkes, 'Enforcing Anti-Suit Injunctions against Sovereign States' (2004) 53 *ICLQ* 512.

[162] (1986) 77 Int LR 1.

[163] See the inconclusive discussion in *Orascom Telecom Holding SAE v Republic of Chad* [2008] 2 Lloyd's Rep 396, 404–8.

[164] See H Fox, 'State Immunity and Enforcement of Arbitral Awards: Do We Need an UNCITRAL Model Law Mark II for Execution Against State Property?' (1996) 12 *Arb Int* 89.

[165] For consideration of the special position of ships owned by the states which formerly comprised the USSR, see *The Guiseppe di Vittorio* [1998] 1 Lloyd's Rep 136; *The Guiseppe di Vittorio (No 2)* [1998] 1 Lloyd's Rep 661.

on State Immunity. Fifthly, in a situation which does not fall within the admiralty jurisdiction of the court, a judgment cannot be enforced against the commercial property of a state which is a party to the European Convention on State Immunity unless the judgment is final[166] and the state in question has made a declaration under Article 24 of the Convention.[167]

2.3.48 A preliminary question is what constitutes 'property' for the purposes of section 13 of the 1978 Act. In *Alcom Ltd v Republic of Colombia*[168] the House of Lords had no hesitation in concluding that a positive bank balance is 'property' of the account holder. A more comprehensive definition of 'property' within the context of section 13 was suggested in *AIG Capital Partners Inc v Republic of Kazakhstan*.[169] In the words of Aikens J:

'property' will include all real and personal property and will embrace any right or interest, legal, equitable, or contractual in assets that might be held by a state or any 'emanation of the state' ... or central bank or other monetary authority that comes within sections 13 and 14 of the Act.[170]

2.3.49 In determining whether or not property is intended for commercial purposes within the meaning of section 13(4), the legislation cross-refers to section 3 of the 1978 Act.[171] Section 13(5) provides that the certificate of the head of a state's diplomatic mission in the United Kingdom, or the person for the time being performing his functions, to the effect that any property is not in use or intended for use by or on behalf of the state for commercial purposes 'shall be accepted as sufficient evidence of that fact unless the contrary is proved'. The significance to be attached to an ambassadorial certificate which is very brief and plainly does not correspond to reality is very limited; indeed, in such cases, proving that the property in question is used for commercial purposes is not particularly onerous.[172]

2.3.50 Subsections (4) and (5) of section 13 were considered by the House of Lords in *Alcom Ltd v Republic of Colombia*.[173] The plaintiff, having obtained a default judgment against the Republic of Colombia, applied for an order to freeze the Republic's bank account to a specified amount which would be sufficient to satisfy the judgment. The account in question was the account used for the day-to-day running of the Republic's diplomatic mission in the United Kingdom. Since the Colombian ambassador had certified that the funds deposited at the bank were not used or intended for use for commercial purposes, section 13(5) placed the onus on the plaintiff to establish that the account was used for commercial purposes.

---

[166] A judgment is final if it 'is not or is no longer subject to appeal or, if given in default of appearance, liable to be set aside': State Immunity Act 1978, s 18(1)(b).

[167] The certificate of the Secretary of State as to whether a state is a party to the convention and has made a declaration under Art 24 is conclusive: State Immunity Act 1978, s 21(c).

[168] [1984] AC 580.

[169] [2006] 1 WLR 1420.

[170] [2006] 1 WLR 1420, 1438.

[171] See paras 2.3.26–2.3.27.

[172] See, eg, *Orascom Telecom Holding SAE v Republic of Chad* [2008] 2 Lloyd's Rep 396.

[173] [1984] AC 580. J Crawford, (1984) 55 *BYIL* 340; H Fox, 'Enforcement Jurisdiction, Foreign State Property and Diplomatic Immunity' (1985) 34 *ICLQ* 115; S Ghandi, 'Sovereign Immunity' (1984) 47 *MLR* 597; D Lloyd Jones, [1984] *CLJ* 222.

2.3.51 Once it was decided that the debt owed by the bank to the defendant, ie, the positive bank balance, was 'property' within the meaning of section 13(2)(b) and (4), the key question facing the House of Lords was whether this property was 'for the time being in use or intended for use for commercial purposes'. Lord Diplock said:

To speak of a debt as 'being used or intended for use' for any purposes by the creditor to whom the debt is owed involves employing ordinary English words in what is not their natural sense. ... What is clear beyond all question is that, if the expression 'commercial purposes' in section 13(4) bore what would be its ordinary and natural meaning in the context in which it there appears, a debt representing the balance standing to the credit of a diplomatic mission in a current bank account used for meeting the day-to-day expenses of running the mission would fall outside the subsection.[174]

2.3.52 The problem of interpretation flows from the definition of 'commercial purposes' in section 17(1). The expression 'commercial purposes' is defined by reference to 'commercial transaction' in section 3(3), which includes 'any contract for the supply of goods and services' irrespective of the purpose of the contract in question. This was the aspect of the case which had been regarded as crucial by Lord Donaldson MR in the Court of Appeal:

The purpose of money in a bank account can never be 'to run an embassy'. It can only be to pay for goods and services or to enter into other transactions which enable the embassy to be run.[175]

2.3.53 This interpretation did not find favour in the House of Lords. Notwithstanding the definition in section 17(1) Lord Diplock said:

Unless it can be shown by the judgment creditor who is seeking to attach the credit balance by garnishee proceedings that the bank account was earmarked by the foreign state solely (save for *de minimis* exceptions) for being drawn on to settle liabilities incurred in commercial transactions, as for example by issuing documentary credits in payment of the price of goods sold to the state, it cannot in my view, be sensibly brought within the crucial words of the exception for which section 13(4) provides.[176]

Lord Diplock's analysis was that, since the balance in an account cannot be dissected into the various uses to which the money drawn might be put in the future, it cannot be said that it is in use or intended for use for commercial purposes unless it is solely intended for use for commercial purposes. If it can be shown that an account is used solely for commercial purposes, the account is not immune from enforcement jurisdiction. In practice, however, embassy funds—which are invariably held in a general bank account either for mixed purposes or for general unallocated purposes—will always be exempt from execution. The result achieved in *Alcom Ltd v Republic of Colombia* is entirely justified on policy grounds. If it were possible to take enforcement measures against the bank account of a diplomatic mission in extreme cases the mission of a friendly foreign state might be required to close. Furthermore, the

---

[174] [1984] AC 580, 602–3.
[175] [1984] AC 580, 558–9.
[176] [1984] AC 580, 604.

decision of the House of Lords is consistent with public international law and the decision of the German Constitutional Court in a similar case.[177]

2.3.54   It has also been held that funds in an account which has been dormant for 18 months cannot be regarded as property which is used for commercial purposes.[178] Similarly, funds which formed part of a National Fund (created to assist in the management of the economy and government revenues of Kazakhstan) were held not to constitute property in use for commercial purposes even though the funds were traded; such dealings were all part of the overall exercise of sovereign authority by the Republic of Kazakhstan.[179] Conversely, funds in a 'borrower's account' set up to receive payments for the supply of goods and services and/or to be part of a system for repaying a loan granted by the World Bank are in use or intended for use for commercial purposes.[180]

Enforcement against Separate Entities

THE GENERAL RULE

2.3.55   For the purposes of the 1978 Act a separate entity within the meaning of section 14(1)[181] is, to the extent that it is entitled to immunity, to be treated in the same way as a state.[182] Section 14(3) provides:

If a separate entity (not being a State's central bank or other monetary authority) submits to the jurisdiction in respect of proceedings in the case of which it is entitled to immunity by virtue of subsection (2) above, subsections (1) to (4) of section 13 above shall apply to it in respect of those proceedings as if references to a State were references to that entity.

Where a separate entity has immunity, by virtue of the fact that the proceedings relate to something it has done in the exercise of sovereign authority, the mere fact of submission to the jurisdiction of the court does not entitle an English court to issue injunctions or allow enforcement against any of the separate entity's property. Conversely, where a separate entity is not entitled to immunity under section 14(2), it is treated in the same way as a private corporation; there are no special restrictions on enforcement procedures.

THE SPECIAL POSITION OF A STATE'S CENTRAL BANK

2.3.56   A judgment given against a state's central bank is of little comfort to the claimant if the judgment cannot be enforced against funds held by the bank. Nevertheless, section 14(4) places central banks in a privileged position:

Property of a State's central bank or other monetary authority shall not be regarded for the purposes of subsection (4) of section 13 above as in use or intended for use for commercial purposes; and where any such bank or authority is a separate entity subsections (1) to (3) of that section shall apply to it as if references to a State were references to the bank or authority.

---

[177]   *The Philippine Republic Case* (1977) 46 BVerfGE 342.
[178]   *AIC Ltd v Federal Government of Nigeria* (2003) 129 ILR 571.
[179]   *AIG Capital Partners Inc v Republic of Kazakhstan* [2006] 1 WLR 1420.
[180]   *Orascom Telecom Holding SAE v Republic of Chad* [2008] 2 Lloyd's Rep 396.
[181]   See para 2.3.6.
[182]   State Immunity Act 1978, s 14(2).

The effect of this subsection is to render the assets of a central bank inviolable; property of a state's central bank enjoys complete immunity from the enforcement process of the English courts, whether the property concerned is in use or intended for use for commercial purposes or not.[183] By making it effectively impossible to take enforcement measures in England, '[t]he legislator has ... rendered proceedings against a central bank almost wholly illusory, notwithstanding the fact that by virtue of section 14(2) a central bank which is a separate entity will be subject to jurisdiction as such in cases in which the proceedings relate to matters of a commercial character and the State itself would not be immune'.[184]

2.3.57 The position adopted by the State Immunity Act 1978 represents a triumph of economic expediency over commercial justice; it is supposed that the reason for making central banks immune from enforcement jurisdiction is to attract foreign funds to the City of London.[185] Notwithstanding the criticisms of section 14(4) on grounds of policy and the suggestion that a rule which grants absolute immunity to a central bank is inconsistent with Article 6(1) of the European Convention on Human Rights, it has been held that section 14(4) of the 1978 Act does not infringe the Convention.[186]

Service of Process in Proceedings against States

2.3.58 Section 12 lays down procedural requirements which must be followed in relation to proceedings brought against states. These requirements do not apply 'to proceedings against a State by way of counterclaim or to an action in rem'[187]; nor do they have to be followed in the context of proceedings brought against a separate entity.[188]

Instituting Proceedings

2.3.59 Once it has been established that a state is not substantively immune there are still questions concerning the exercise of jurisdiction and service of process. There are two valid methods whereby a claim form may be served on a foreign state. First, there is nothing to prevent service of process 'in any manner to which the State has agreed'.[189] Secondly, there is the method of service laid down by section 12(1), which provides that any document required to be served for instituting proceedings against a state:

shall be served by being transmitted through the Foreign and Commonwealth Office to the Ministry of Foreign Affairs of the State and service shall be deemed to have been effected when the writ or document is received at the Ministry.

---

[183] See Aikens J in *AIG Capital Partners Inc v Republic of Kazakhstan* [2006] 1 WLR 1420, 1441.
[184] FA Mann, 'The State Immunity Act 1978' (1979) 50 *BYIL* 43, 61−2.
[185] FA Mann, 'The State Immunity Act 1978' (1979) 50 *BYIL* 43, 62.
[186] See Aikens J in *AIG Capital Partners Inc v Republic of Kazakhstan* [2006] 1 WLR 1420, 1442–8.
[187] State Immunity Act 1978, s 12(7).
[188] See also *Wilhelm Finance Inc v Administrator del Astillero Rio Santiago* [2009] 1 CLC 867.
[189] State Immunity Act 1978, s 12(6); CPR 6.27. See *ABCI v Banque Franco-Tunisienne* [2003] 2 Lloyd's Rep 146.

2.3.60 Section 12(1) is drafted in mandatory terms; unless the foreign state has agreed to some other method of service, process 'shall be served' in the manner prescribed by the Act. Accordingly, service not in accordance with the terms of the Act will be set aside, as will any consequential default judgment.[190] Even where the parties have agreed on a method of service the claimant may choose to make use of the statutory procedure instead.[191] Although there is nothing in the Civil Procedure Rules to permit the court to dispense with service, a state 'which appears in proceedings cannot thereafter object that subsection (1) ... has not been complied with'.[192] As a result of the mandatory nature of section 12(1), where diplomatic relations between the United Kingdom and a foreign country have broken down, there may be no effective mechanism for service of process. In this situation the claimant is unable to proceed in England, notwithstanding the fact that the court has jurisdiction over the claim and the state party is not entitled to immunity under the 1978 Act.[193]

2.3.61 In *Kuwait Airways Corporation v Iraqi Airways Co*[194] the plaintiff sought to sue the Republic of Iraq (as well as the corporation to which the plaintiff's aircraft had been transferred by the Iraqi authorities). The writ was duly served on the corporation in England and on 11 January 1992 the plaintiff obtained permission to serve a concurrent writ on the second defendant, the Republic of Iraq. The British embassy in Baghdad was closed on 12 January 1992 and Iraq broke off diplomatic relations as from 6 February 1992. The documents instituting the proceedings against the second defendant were served at the Iraqi embassy in London and were received by an accredited diplomat. When the plaintiff obtained a default judgment the second defendant applied to have the judgment set aside on the basis of improper service. The House of Lords held that, as regards the second defendant, service had not been properly effected. Section 12(1) requires that service is to be effected by transmission 'to' the Ministry of Foreign Affairs and takes effect when the document is received 'at' the Ministry. Service of process at the embassy in London was ineffective.

2.3.62 It must be stressed that subsection (1) deals only with the method of service, it does not spell out the circumstances in which an English court may assume jurisdiction. In cases where the defendant does not have immunity but is not prepared to submit to the jurisdiction of the court, the claim form must be served out of the jurisdiction. Section 12(1) does not affect 'any rules of court whereby leave is required for the service of process outside the jurisdiction'.[195] In order to be able to serve a claim form out of the jurisdiction the claimant has to satisfy the requirements of Part 6 of the Civil Procedure Rules.[196]

---

[190] *Crescent Oil and Shipping Services Ltd v Importang UEE* [1998] 1 WLR 919.
[191] CPR 6.44(7).
[192] State Immunity Act 1978, s 12(3).
[193] See, eg, *Westminster City Council v Government of the Islamic Republic of Iran* [1986] 1 WLR 979. J Crawford, (1986) 57 *BYIL* 423.
[194] [1995] 1 WLR 1147.
[195] State Immunity Act 1978, s 12(7).
[196] See sections 4.3 and 7.3.

Judgments in Default

2.3.63   Section 12 contains special provisions dealing with judgments against states given in default of appearance:

(4) No judgment in default of appearance shall be given against a State except on proof that subsection (1) above has been complied with and that the time for entering an appearance as extended by subsection (2) above has expired.[197]

(5) A copy of any judgment given against a State in default of appearance shall be transmitted through the Foreign and Commonwealth Office to the Ministry of Foreign Affairs of that State and any time for applying to have the judgment set aside (whether prescribed by rules of court or otherwise) shall begin to run two months after the date on which the copy of the judgment is received at the Ministry.

Although process may validly be served on a state in any manner to which the state has agreed,[198] the same is not true with regard to service of a default judgment. It has been held that the 1978 Act requires service of a default judgment through the Foreign and Commonwealth Office and does not permit any derogation from that requirement.[199]

2.4 DIPLOMATIC IMMUNITY

Diplomatic Officers

2.4.1   It is a long-established principle that the representatives of foreign states should be immune from suit in England. Whereas diplomats used to enjoy absolute immunity, immunity under the Diplomatic Privileges Act 1964 is qualified. The 1964 Act implements certain provisions of the Vienna Convention on Diplomatic Relations of 1961,[200] the relevant parts of which are set out in schedule 1 to the Act. The Act divides persons who are entitled to immunity into three categories: diplomatic agents; members of the administrative and technical staff; and members of the service staff.

Diplomatic Agents

2.4.2   The Vienna Convention on Diplomatic Relations provides that diplomatic agents include the head of the mission and members of the diplomatic staff.[201] These diplomatic privileges also apply to a sovereign or other head of state as they apply to the head of a diplomatic mission.[202] Diplomatic agents are generally immune from suit, subject to three limitations, two of which are potentially important in the

---

[197] Sub-s (4) does not apply in cases where the parties have agreed on a method service different from that laid down in s 12(1): State Immunity Act 1978, s 12(6).

[198] See para 2.3.54.

[199] *Crescent Oil and Shipping Services Ltd v Importang UEE* [1998] 1 WLR 919.

[200] Diplomatic Privileges Act 1964, s 2(1).

[201] Art 1(d).

[202] State Immunity Act 1978, s 20(1). See *BCCI (in liquidation) v Price Waterhouse* [1997] 4 All ER 108 (J Hopkins, [1998] *CLJ* 4).

commercial context.[203] A diplomatic agent is immune neither in 'a real action relating to private immovable property ... unless he holds the property on behalf of the sending State for the purposes of the mission'[204] nor as regards 'an action relating to any professional or commercial activity exercised by the diplomatic agent in the receiving State outside his official functions'.[205]

2.4.3   These privileges and immunities are extended to members of the family of a diplomatic agent as long as they form part of the agent's household and they are not citizens of the United Kingdom.[206] Any diplomatic agent who is a citizen of or permanently resident in the United Kingdom has immunity from civil jurisdiction only 'in respect of official acts performed in the exercise of his functions'.[207]

Members of the Administrative and Technical Staff

2.4.4   Members of the administrative and technical staff are 'the members of the staff of the mission employed in the administrative and technical service of the mission'.[208] Clerical staff fall within this classification.[209] Broadly speaking, the immunity of members of the administrative and technical staff, together with members of their families forming part of their households who are not citizens of or permanently resident in the United Kingdom, enjoy the same immunities as diplomatic agents. There is, however, a significant restriction: the immunity of members of the administrative and technical staff does not extend to acts performed outside the course of their duties.[210]

Members of the Service Staff

2.4.5   Members of the service staff are staff 'in the domestic service of the mission',[211] such as cooks and cleaners. Members of the service staff who are not citizens of or permanently resident in the United Kingdom 'enjoy immunity in respect of acts performed in the course of their duties'.[212]

Waiver

2.4.6   Privileges conferred by the 1964 Act may be waived by the sending state.[213] Such a waiver must be express.[214] A waiver by the head of the diplomatic mission is

---

    [203] Art 31(1).
    [204] Art 31(1)(a). A diplomatic agent's private residence is not held for the purposes of the mission: *Intpro Properties (UK) Ltd v Sauvel* [1983] QB 1019.
    [205] Art 31(1)(c).
    [206] Art 37(1).
    [207] Art 38(1). This limited immunity may be extended by Order in Council under Diplomatic Privileges Act 1964, s 2(6).
    [208] Art 1(f).
    [209] *Sengupta v Republic of India* [1983] ICR 221.
    [210] Art 37(2). See *Re B (A Child)(Care Proceedings: Diplomatic Immunity)* [2003] 2 WLR 168.
    [211] Art 1(g).
    [212] Art 37(3).
    [213] Art 32(1).
    [214] Art 32(2).

deemed to be a waiver by the sending state.[215] A diplomatic officer who invokes the jurisdiction of the court by commencing proceedings in England cannot claim immunity in respect of any counterclaim directly connected with the principal claim.[216] However, a waiver of immunity from adjudicative jurisdiction is not sufficient to render any subsequent judgment enforceable against a diplomatic officer. There can be no enforcement unless there has been a separate waiver of immunity from enforcement jurisdiction.[217]

The Temporal Scope of Immunity

2.4.7 Those who are entitled to immunities and privileges enjoy them from the moment they enter the territory of the receiving state on proceeding to take up their post; if they are already in the receiving state, the immunities take effect from when the appointment is notified to the Foreign Office.[218] Once a diplomatic officer's functions have come to an end, the immunities conferred by the Act cease at the moment when he leaves the country or on expiry of a reasonable period in which to do so.[219] If a diplomatic officer dies, members of his family retain their immunities until the expiry of a reasonable period in which to leave the country.[220]

Consular Agents

2.4.8 The position of consular agents is governed by the Consular Relations Act 1968, which gives effect to certain provisions of the Vienna Convention on Consular Relations of 1963. Consular agents do not enjoy any immunity in relation to their private acts. Although immunity extends to the acts of consular agents performed in the exercise of their consular functions,[221] there is no immunity in relation to either civil proceedings relating to a contract, unless the agent expressly or impliedly contracted on behalf of the state in question, or civil proceedings brought by a third party for damage arising from an accident in the United Kingdom caused by a vessel, vehicle or aircraft.[222]

    2.4.9 The immunity conferred by the Consular Relations Act 1968 may be waived by the sending state.[223] Such waiver must be express and in writing. The institution of proceedings by a consular agent prevents the agent from claiming immunity in relation to a counterclaim directly connected with the claim. A waiver of immunity from adjudicative jurisdiction does not amount to a submission to execution, for which a separate waiver is required.

---

[215] Diplomatic Privileges Act 1964, s 2(3).
[216] Art 32(3).
[217] Art 32(4).
[218] Art 39(1).
[219] Art 39(2).
[220] Art 39(3).
[221] The words 'consular functions' are defined by Art 5 of the Vienna Convention on Consular Relations.
[222] Art 43.
[223] Art 45.

2.5 INTERNATIONAL ORGANISATIONS

2.5.1 By virtue of the International Organisations Act 1968, as amended by the International Organisations Act 1981, certain types of international organisation and their representatives may be granted immunities similar to those enjoyed by foreign states and their representatives.[224] The 1968 Act does not, however, grant blanket immunity in the same way as the State Immunity Act 1978 or the Diplomatic Privileges Act 1964. The organisations which are entitled to immunity and the particular immunities they enjoy are specified by Orders in Council made under the 1968 Act or under the legislation which it replaced.

2.5.2 In cases where the legislation does not apply a defendant may, nevertheless, be entitled to immunity under public international law. In *Zoersch v Waldock*[225] the Court of Appeal decided, *obiter*, that the former President of the European Commission on Human Rights was entitled to immunity in England as a matter of customary international law. Accordingly, in relation to acts performed in an official capacity immunity may continue to apply notwithstanding the fact that the defendant no longer holds office.

2.5.3 *Arab Monetary Fund v Hashim*[226] involved a claim to immunity in the context of proceedings brought by the AMF—an international organisation in relation to which no Order in Council has been made under the 1968 Act—against its former director-general. Evans J thought that 'the English courts should give effect to an immunity which is shown to exist under customary international law'.[227] However, to the extent that the immunity of officials of international organisations exists under international law it exists for the benefit of the organisation rather than the official. It follows that if the immunity is waived by the organisation there is no further bar to the proceedings against the official in England.[228]

---

[224] In addition, there is specific legislation dealing with specific bodies, such as the Specialized Agencies of the United Nations (Immunities and Privileges) Order 1974, SI 1974/1260.
[225] [1964] 1 WLR 675.
[226] [1993] 1 Lloyd's Rep 543.
[227] [1993] 1 Lloyd's Rep 543, 573.
[228] [1993] 1 Lloyd's Rep 543, 574.

3

THE BRUSSELS I REGULATION:
GENERAL CONSIDERATIONS

3.0.1 In the commercial sphere the most important international instrument which regulates jurisdiction and the recognition and enforcement of foreign judgments is the Brussels I Regulation[1] (section 3.1). This sets out a system for the allocation of jurisdiction in civil and commercial matters and for the reciprocal recognition and enforcement of judgments between the EU Member States. To ensure the uniform interpretation of the Brussels I Regulation references may be made by national courts to the Court of Justice (section 3.2). The material scope of the Regulation is limited to civil and commercial matters (section 3.3). The Regulation expressly regulates its relationship with other conventions in the areas of jurisdiction and the recognition and enforcement of judgments (section 3.4).

3.1 INTRODUCTION

3.1.1 Central to the operation of the European Union is the free movement of goods, services, workers and capital. Free movement on the scale envisaged by the Treaty establishing the European Community entails a vast network of international contracts for the sale of goods and the supply of services throughout the region. A massive increase in cross-border trade inevitably leads to an increase in international litigation. International trade depends in some measure on mutual trust and confidence derived from the availability of effective legal remedies in cases where disputes arise. Those who framed the original Treaty of Rome were aware that traditional approaches to conflict of laws problems would not achieve the co-operation which was required to bring about the level of economic integration which was envisaged. The nature of the problem can be illustrated by the following example. Suppose that the claimant, who is resident in country X, contracts to buy goods from the defendant, who is resident in country Y. A dispute follows and the claimant proceeds against the defendant in country X. The courts of country X exercise jurisdiction, notwithstanding the fact that the defendant has no connection with country X and takes no part in the proceedings. Having obtained a judgment

---

[1] Reg (EC) 44/2001, [2001] OJ L12/1. The predecessor to the Brussels I Regulation, the Brussels Convention, has been superseded in nearly all cases by the Regulation; the Convention applies only in relation to a limited number of territories of EU Member States which fall within the territorial scope of the Convention and which are excluded from the scope of the Regulation (namely, Aruba and the French overseas territories). See Brussels I Reg, Art 68. Other measures include Reg (EC) 861/2007 establishing a European Small Claims Procedure [2007] OJ L199/1; Reg (EC) 1896/2006 creating a European order for payment procedure [2006] OJ L399/1; Reg (EC) 805/2004 creating a European Enforcement order for uncontested claims [2004] OJ L143/15. For a discussion of these instruments, see JJ Fawcett and JM Carruthers, *Cheshire, North & Fawcett: Private International Law* (Oxford, OUP, 14th edn, 2008) 640–8.

in his favour in country X, the claimant seeks to enforce it against the defendant's assets in country Y. The courts of country Y refuse to enforce the judgment on the ground that the courts of country X exercised jurisdiction over the defendant on an exorbitant basis.

3.1.2   This example illustrates that the primary obstacles to the mutual recognition and enforcement of judgments are exorbitant jurisdiction rules. In order for a foreign judgment to be entitled to recognition and enforcement it must have been pronounced by a court having jurisdiction in the private international law sense. Once it is appreciated that international jurisdiction and the enforcement of foreign judgments 'should be recognised as branches of the same tree'[2] the obvious solution is to harmonise jurisdiction rules. If national courts are entitled to exercise jurisdiction over a foreign defendant on only a limited number of agreed bases, the recognition and enforcement of foreign judgments can be simplified. This is the approach adopted by the Brussels I Regulation.

3.1.3   The starting point for the development of a European regime for the allocation of jurisdiction and the recognition and enforcement of judgments is Article 220 of the original Treaty of Rome, which established the European Economic Community. Under this provision the Member States undertook to 'enter into negotiations with each other with a view to securing ... the simplification of formalities governing the reciprocal recognition and enforcement of judgments of courts or tribunals and of arbitration awards'. In due course, negotiations led to the adoption by the original six Member States[3] of the Convention on Jurisdiction and the Enforcement of Judgments in Civil and Commercial Matters (the Brussels Convention) in 1968. As the European Community expanded, the new Member States acceded to the Brussels Convention by means of a series of accession conventions in 1978,[4] 1982,[5] 1989[6] and 1996.[7] During this period, various amendments to the Brussels Convention were made by some of these accession conventions. In 1988 the EC Member States negotiated a parallel convention (the Lugano Convention), in almost identical terms to the Brussels Convention, with the six countries which were then members of EFTA.[8] The Lugano Convention was subsequently extended to Poland a few years prior to its accession to the European Community.

3.1.4   On the entry into force of the Treaty of Amsterdam, the European Community acquired legislative competence in relation to judicial co-operation in civil matters[9] and in the late 1990s work started on reforming the Brussels Convention and translating it into European legislation.[10] Council Regulation (EC) No 44/2001[11]

---

[2] FA Mann, 'The Doctrine of Jurisdiction in International Law' (1964) 111 *Hag Rec* 1, 75.

[3] Belgium, France, Germany, Italy, Luxembourg and the Netherlands.

[4] Denmark, Ireland and the United Kingdom.

[5] Greece.

[6] Portugal and Spain.

[7] Austria, Finland and Sweden.

[8] Austria, Finland, Iceland, Norway, Sweden and Switzerland. As regards Austria, Finland and Sweden, the Lugano Convention was partly superseded on their accession to the Brussels Convention.

[9] Arts 61 and 65 TEC, now Arts 67 and 81 TFEU. See O Remien, 'European Private International Law, the European Community and its Emerging Area of Freedom, Security and Justice' (2001) 38 *CML Rev* 53.

[10] See BJ Rodger, 'The Communitarisation of International Private Law: Reform of the Brussels Convention by Regulation' [2001] *Jur Rev* 59 and 69.

[11] [2001] OJ L12/1.

(the Brussels I Regulation), which diverges from the Brussels Convention in a number of ways, came into force on 1 March 2002.[12] Although both Ireland and the United Kingdom chose to opt into the Regulation, Denmark did not participate. However, on 19 October 2005, Denmark signed an agreement with the European Community[13] which provided for the application of the Brussels I Regulation[14] to Denmark from 1 July 2007.[15] The result is that the Brussels I Regulation applies in all EU Member States. Whereas the Brussels and Lugano Conventions had to be incorporated into domestic law by national legislation, the Brussels I Regulation is directly applicable throughout the Member States. Moreover, no further legislation is required—either at the European or domestic levels—when more countries accede to the European Union; the Brussels I Regulation applies in the new Member States as part of the *acquis communautaire*.[16]

3.1.5 When the Brussels Convention was transposed into a Regulation, the differences between the Brussels I Regulation and the Lugano Convention led to an impetus to revise the Convention to bring it into line with the Regulation. The two instruments are supposed to run in parallel and differences between them could be seen as an impediment to the circulation of judgments between the EU Member States and the Lugano states.[17] After negotiations, the revised Lugano Convention[18] was signed on 30 October 2007 between the European Community,[19] Denmark, Switzerland, Iceland and Norway.[20] The English court has to apply the Lugano Convention where the defendant is domiciled in Switzerland, Iceland or Norway, or where the exclusive jurisdiction rules set out in Article 22 or a choice of court agreement falling within Article 23 confer jurisdiction to the courts of those countries. The *lis pendens* provisions of Articles 27 and 28 are also applicable if there are concurrent proceedings in England and one of the Lugano states. Further, where the English court is asked to recognise or enforce a foreign judgment, the Lugano Convention applies where the

---

[12] Art 76.

[13] On the entering into force of the Treaty of Lisbon on 1 December 2009, the legal entity representing all Member States is the European Union, not the European Community.

[14] Subject to some minor amendments which are listed in the EC–Denmark Agreement, Art 2, [2005] OJ L299/64.

[15] Agreement between the European Community and the Kingdom of Denmark on jurisdiction and the recognition and enforcement of judgments in civil and commercial matters, [2005] OJ L299/62. For amendments in the United Kingdom to take the agreement into account, see the Civil Jurisdiction and Judgments Regs 2007, SI 2007/1655.

[16] Since the entry into force of the Brussels I Regulation, 12 Member States have acceded to the European Union: Bulgaria, the Czech Republic, Cyprus, Estonia, Hungary, Latvia, Lithuania, Malta, Poland, Romania, Slovakia and Slovenia.

[17] See Council Decision, [2008] OJ L339/1, para 4.

[18] [2007] OJ L339/3. References to the Lugano Convention is to be understood to be to the 2007 revised Convention unless otherwise indicated.

[19] The European Community had exclusive competence to conclude the revised Lugano Convention on behalf of all EU Member States with the exception of Denmark. See the opinion of the Court of Justice 1/03 [2006] ECR I–1145. N Lavranos, (2006) 43 *CML Rev* 1087.

[20] The European Community, Denmark and Norway have ratified the Convention. It entered into force between the EU and Norway on 1 January 2010. Iceland and Switzerland have yet to ratify it; Switzerland has announced that it will apply the Convention as from 1 January 2011. See also D Mavromati and R Rodriguez, 'The Revised Lugano Convention from a Swiss Perspective' [2009] *EBLR* 579, 589.

court of origin is from a Lugano state.[21] That said, for nearly all purposes, it does not matter whether the English court is applying the Brussels I Regulation or the Lugano Convention as the jurisdictional and recognition and enforcement rules in the revised Lugano Convention differ only in minor respects from the Brussels I Regulation. Therefore, the discussion below and in the subsequent chapters refers only to the Brussels I Regulation, although any significant differences between the two instruments are pointed out.

3.2 INTERPRETATION OF THE BRUSSELS I REGULATION

References to the Court of Justice

3.2.1 With the entry into force of the Treaty of Lisbon, any national court or tribunal is able to request preliminary rulings on the interpretation of the Brussels I Regulation from the Court of Justice.[22] This is in accordance with Article 267 of the Treaty on the Functioning of the European Union (TFEU), which establishes, first, that a court against whose decision there is no judicial remedy under national law 'shall' make a reference to the Court of Justice where it considers that a decision on a question of EU law is necessary for its decision and, secondly, that any other court or tribunal 'may' refer such matters.[23]

Methods of Interpretation[24]

3.2.2 The style of interpretation employed by the Court of Justice is teleological, rather than literal. Each of the different language versions of the Brussels I Regulation is equally authoritative; no single language version is to be regarded as self-sufficient. What appears to be an ambiguity in the English text may be resolved by having regard to other language versions. Since it may be impossible to interpret

---

[21] For amendments in the United Kingdom to take into account the Lugano Convention, see the Civil Jurisdiction and Judgments Regs 2009, SI 2009/3131 (in force on 1 January 2010).

[22] Art 68 TEC, which restricted the right to refer questions to the Court of Justice on the Brussels I Regulation to courts against whose decision there is no judicial remedy under national law, was repealed by the Treaty of Lisbon.

[23] The same also applies to a Danish court or tribunal in relation to the interpretation of the Brussels I Regulation; see EC–Denmark Agreement, Art 6, [2005] OJ L299/66.

[24] For a review of the case law of the Court of Justice under the Brussels Convention, see: A McClellan, 'The Convention of Brussels of September 27, 1968 on Jurisdiction and the Recognition and Enforcement of Judgments in Civil and Commercial Matters' (1978) 15 *CML Rev* 228; A McClellan, 'Jurisdiction and the Recognition and Enforcement of Judgments in Civil and Commercial Matters in the European Communities' (1979) 16 *CML Rev* 268; A McClellan and G Kremlis, 'The Convention of September 27, 1968 on Jurisdiction and Enforcement of Judgments in Civil and Commercial Matters' (1983) 20 *CML Rev* 529; S Pieri, 'The 1968 Brussels Convention on Jurisdiction and Enforcement of Judgments in Civil and Commercial Matters: Four Years' Case Law of the European Court of Justice' (1987) 24 *CML Rev* 635; S Pieri, 'The 1968 Brussels Convention on Jurisdiction and Enforcement of Judgments in Civil and Commercial Matters: the Evolution of the Case Law of the Court of Justice 1992–1996' (1997) 34 *CML Rev* 867.

the Regulation in a manner which is consistent with all the different language versions, the proper interpretation of a particular provision may fly in the face of the English text.

3.2.3 In private international law, the traditional approach is for questions of classification to be determined by the law of the forum. So, whether a particular issue raises a question of contractual or tortious liability, substance or procedure, formal or essential validity is to be decided by the classificatory scheme of the forum. If this traditional approach were applied to all aspects of the Brussels I Regulation its uniform application could be seriously compromised. It makes sense, therefore, to approach the interpretation of many of the concepts which are employed in the Regulation from a supranational or European perspective rather than from a purely national one. The Court of Justice is uniquely placed to formulate autonomous or independent interpretations which take account of the different legal traditions of the various Member States.

3.2.4 There is no simple answer to the question whether a particular rule or concept is to be given a national or autonomous interpretation.[25] Often the objectives of the Brussels I Regulation require that a particular concept should be given an independent interpretation; ultimately, however, the Court of Justice is faced by a question of policy. On the basis of the approach adopted to the Brussels Convention—an approach which is equally applicable in the context of the Regulation—the general principle is that concepts which may have a different content depending on the national law of the Member State, must be interpreted independently, by reference principally to the system and objectives of the Regulation.[26] Accordingly, the Court of Justice has favoured an autonomous interpretation in relation to the terms used in Chapter I, which defines the material scope of the Regulation, and the conceptual categories which determine the scope of the specific jurisdiction provisions (for example, 'matters relating to a contract' in Article 5(1) and 'rights *in rem* in immovable property' in Article 22(1)). The Court of Justice has also gone further and defined terms which might conceivably have been left to the law of the forum (such as 'the place where the harmful event occurred' for the purposes of Article 5(3)).[27] Nevertheless, the Regulation makes it clear that certain elements are to be defined by the internal law of the various Member States. For example, Article 59, which deals with the domicile of individuals, provides that it is for the law of the Member State in question to determine whether a person is domiciled in that state. Moreover, the Court of Justice has taken the view that matters which relate to procedural consequences or the detailed operation of legal concepts are to be interpreted by reference to national law. For example, in the context of Article 5(1), 'the place of

---

[25] For a discussion of this question, see C Kohler, 'The Case Law of the European Court on the Judgments Convention' (1982) 7 *EL Rev* 3, 7–13; A Layton, 'The Interpretation of the Brussels Convention by the European Court and English Courts' (1992) 11 *CJQ* 28, 32–5.

[26] See Case C–89/91 *Shearson Lehman Hutton v TVB Treuhandgesellschaft für Vermögensverwaltung und Beteiligungen mbH* [1993] ECR I–139, para 13; Case C–103/05 *Reisch Montage AG v Kiesel Baumaschinen Handels GmbH* [2006] ECR I–6827, para 29.

[27] Case 21/76 *Handelskwekerij GJ Bier BV v Mines de Potasse d'Alsace SA* [1976] ECR 1735.

performance' is referred to the applicable law as determined by the conflicts rules of the forum.[28]

Interpretation by National Courts[29]

3.2.5 In general terms, a national court should approach the interpretation of the Brussels I Regulation as would the Court of Justice.[30] The terse style in which the Regulation is drafted means that many important questions are left open. There are, for example, few provisions in the Regulation which seek to define the key concepts.[31] The courts may seek guidance from the reports of the working parties which negoti-ated the 1968 Convention and the subsequent accession conventions,[32] the report accompanying the Lugano Conventions[33] and the *travaux préparatoires* to the Brussels I Regulation.[34] These are useful starting points for fleshing out the provisions of the Regulation. Although the reports are helpful in providing answers to some of the ques-tions which are not answered by the wording of the Regulation itself, their importance must not be overstated. These materials are, however, far from comprehensive; they do not attempt to solve all the questions of interpretation that may arise. Furthermore, the reports are in no sense binding on the Court of Justice or national courts.

3.2.6 In commercial cases governed by the Brussels I Regulation, the Supreme Court (formerly the House of Lords) is normally the only court which has the obli-gation to refer questions of interpretation to the Court of Justice under Article 267 TFEU.[35] The procedure for making a reference is set out in CPR pt 68 and CPR PD 68. It is not mandatory for the courts below to make a reference to the Court of Justice.

---

[28] Case 12/76 *Industrie Tessili Italiana Como v Dunlop AG* [1976] ECR 1473.

[29] EU Member States may refer the interpretation of provisions of the Lugano Convention to the Court of Justice under Art 267 TFEU (see the Preamble to Protocol 2 of the Convention). With a view to ensuring uniformity of interpretation of the Lugano Convention by EU states and non-EU states, all states bound by the Convention shall 'pay due account' to the judgments by the national courts of states bound by the Convention and by the Court of Justice which relate to the Lugano Convention, the 1988 Lugano Convention and the instruments referred to in Art 64(1) of the Lugano Convention (of which the most important is the Brussels I Regulation): Protocol 2, Art 1. However, this applies only where the texts are the same and fully parallel; where the texts are different, the Lugano state courts will have to take account only of judgments that are delivered by national courts (F Pocar, Explanatory Report on the Lugano Convention, [2009] OJ C319/54, para 197). The principle of uniform interpretation is further facilitated by the setting up of a system of exchange of information concerning relevant judgments delivered pursuant to the Lugano Convention, the 1988 Lugano Convention and the instruments referred to in Art 64(1) of the revised Lugano Convention: Protocol 2, Art 3.

[30] See *Grupo Torras SA v Sheikh Fahad Mohammed al Sabah* [1995] ILPr 667; *Papanicolaou v Thielen* [1997] ILPr 37 (High Court, Ireland).

[31] See, however, Art 30, which defines what is meant by 'the court first seised' for the purposes of Arts 27–29: see paras 9.1.10–9.1.11.

[32] The most important are the Jenard Report ([1979] OJ C59/1) and the Schlosser Report ([1979] OJ C59/71). See also the Evrigenis-Kerameus Report ([1986] OJ C298/1) and the Almeida Cruz-Desantes Real-Jenard Report ([1990] OJ C189/35).

[33] Jenard-Möller Report, [1990] OJ C189/57 (1988 Lugano Convention); Pocar Report [2009] OJ C319/1 (2007 Lugano Convention).

[34] Principally, the European Commission's *Proposal for a Council Regulation (EC) on jurisdiction and the recognition and enforcement of judgments in civil and commercial matters*, COM (1999) 348 final.

[35] In certain cases involving the enforcement of judgments, the Court of Appeal acts as the final court of appeal: see para 13.4.14. It would then be obliged to refer a question of interpretation of the Regulation to the Court of Justice if it considers a decision on a question of EU law to be necessary for its decision.

However, the national court may have to consider whether a particular rule or concept should be given a national or independent interpretation. In these circumstances, it would be better for the national court to make a reference to the Court of Justice. Otherwise, if an autonomous interpretation is appropriate, it will be necessary for the court to refer, first, to the objectives and scheme of the Brussels I Regulation and, secondly, to the general principles which stem from the corpus of national legal systems.[36] The difficulty of such a task is not to be underestimated. Whereas the Court of Justice is a multilingual institution with the resources to undertake the necessary inquiries, a national court is in a less advantageous position. It is not clear how a national court, when working with the procedures and methods of its domestic legal system, could come to an independent interpretation which also fits in with the different context of other legal systems and could therefore persuade judges from all the other Member States.[37]

3.3 SCOPE OF THE BRUSSELS I REGULATION

Introductory Remarks

3.3.1   The scope of the Brussels I Regulation may be relevant to two stages of a dispute. First, when the claimant invokes the jurisdiction of the courts of a Member State in circumstances in which the court does not have jurisdiction under Chapter II, the defendant may seek to contest jurisdiction on the basis that the subject-matter of the dispute falls within the material scope of the Brussels I Regulation, as defined by Chapter I. Secondly, when a party seeks to have a judgment granted by the courts of one Member State recognised or enforced in another Member State under Chapter III the party against whom the judgment is invoked may seek to resist recognition or enforcement of the judgment on the basis that the subject-matter of the judgment does not fall within the Brussels I Regulation's scope. In these circumstances the court of the Member State in which recognition or enforcement is sought is not bound by a decision taken by the court of the state of origin as to the scope of Chapter I.

3.3.2   The Brussels I Regulation applies only where an international element is involved; therefore, it has no application in cases which are internal to a single Member State. However, the connection with another Member State does not have to be very strong to bring the Regulation into play. Where, for example, both parties to a contract have their place of business in one Member State, the fact that the contract contains a jurisdiction clause in favour of the courts of another Member State is to be regarded as an international element.[38]

3.3.3   A case which is entirely internal to the United Kingdom does not fall within the scope of the Brussels I Regulation, even if the forum would regard it as being of a non-domestic character; the Brussels I Regulation has no application to a dispute before the English courts which involves elements which are connected with Scotland or

---

[36] Case 29/76 *LTU Lufttransportunternehmen GmbH & Co KG v Eurocontrol* [1976] ECR 1541, para 3.
[37] H Jung, 'The Brussels and Lugano Conventions: The European Court's Jurisdiction; its Procedures and Methods' (1992) 11 *CJQ* 38, 49.
[38] *Anema BV v Broekman Motorships BV* [1991] ILPr 285 (District Court, Rotterdam).

Northern Ireland, but has no connection with any other country. Such a situation may, however, fall within the scope of schedule 4 to the Civil Jurisdiction and Judgments Act 1982 (which is a modified version of Chapter II of the Brussels I Regulation).[39]

3.3.4   The material scope of the Brussels I Regulation is determined by Article 1, the only provision in Chapter I, which refers to 'civil and commercial matters whatever the nature of the court or tribunal'. It is further provided that four matters are excluded from the regime's scope: (1) the status or legal capacity of natural persons, rights in property arising out of a matrimonial relationship, wills and succession; (2) bankruptcy, proceedings relating to the winding-up of insolvent companies or other legal persons, judicial arrangements, compositions and analogous proceedings; (3) social security; and (4) arbitration.

Civil and Commercial Matters

3.3.5   The first paragraph of Article 1 establishes that the Brussels I Regulation's material scope is determined by the subject-matter of the proceedings; the nature of the court in which those proceedings are brought is irrelevant. The Regulation covers civil claims brought before criminal courts[40] and applies to civil and commercial matters brought before administrative tribunals.[41]

3.3.6   The basic formula 'civil and commercial matters' is not defined, though Article 1 states that the expression 'civil and commercial matters' does not extend to 'revenue, customs or administrative matters'.[42] The Schlosser Report notes that:

The distinction between civil and commercial matters on the one hand and matters of public law on the other is well recognised in the legal systems of the original member states and is, in spite of some important differences, on the whole arrived at on the basis of similar criteria.[43]

The Court of Justice has added that the phrase 'civil and commercial matters' is to be given an autonomous meaning; it is not for national courts to determine the scope of Article 1 according to the conceptions of their own legal system.[44] From the perspective of a legal system which belongs to the common law tradition the Brussels regime's provisions are drafted in a foreign legal vocabulary. Although the public law/private law dichotomy has become a feature of the English legal system, the distinction does not permeate the thinking of common lawyers. Nevertheless, in practice, the phrase 'civil and commercial matters' presents few problems in the majority of cases. For example, it is obvious that litigation between private individuals or corporations (such as a dispute relating to a contract of employment)[45] falls within the scope of Article 1.

---

[39] See ch 6.

[40] Case C–172/91 *Sonntag v Waidmann* [1993] ECR I–1963, para 16.

[41] Jenard Report, [1979] OJ C59/9.

[42] Proceedings for the direct or indirect enforcement of a foreign state's revenue claim involve 'revenue matters' for the purposes of Art 1: *QRS 1 ApS v Frandsen* [1999] 1 WLR 2169. A Briggs, (1999) 70 *BYIL* 341; PStJ Smart, 'The Rule Against Foreign Revenue Laws' (2000) 116 *LQR* 360.

[43] [1979] OJ C59/82, para 23.

[44] Case 29/76 *LTU Lufttransportunternehmen GmbH & Co KG v Eurocontrol* [1976] ECR 1541, para 3.

[45] Case 25/79 *Sanicentral GmbH v Collin* [1979] ECR 3423.

3.3.7 Problems are most likely to arise in cases in which one of the parties to the litigation is a public authority.[46] The Court of Justice has taken the view that the dividing line between civil and commercial matters, on the one hand, and public law matters, on the other, is to be determined by a functional test, rather than an institutional one.[47] So, the fact that one of the parties is a public authority does not necessarily mean that the situation falls outside the scope of Article 1; by the same token the fact that a claim brought by a public authority is litigated in the ordinary courts and is not based on administrative law does not automatically entail the conclusion that the proceedings are to be regarded as involving civil and commercial matters.[48] The decisive factor is whether proceedings involve 'a public authority which acted in the exercise of its public authority powers'.[49] To assess whether this condition is satisfied the court must identify the legal relationship between the parties to the dispute and examine the basis and the detailed rules governing the bringing of the proceedings.[50] Where, for example, a public authority in the exercise of a right of recourse seeks to recover from the defendant sums paid to a third party by way of social assistance, the proceedings are to be regarded as 'civil' if the basis and the detailed rules relating to the bringing of such proceedings are governed by ordinary rules of law; if, however, the right of recourse is founded on 'provisions by which the legislature conferred on the public body a prerogative of its own', the proceedings cannot be regarded as 'civil' in nature.[51] Similarly, proceedings whereby a public body seeks to enforce a contract of guarantee are 'civil' in nature as long as the relationship between the public body and the guarantor does not entail the exercise by the former of powers going beyond those existing under the rules applicable to relations between private individuals.[52] This approach means that proceedings brought by a consumer protection organisation are covered by Article 1 if the subject-matter of the proceedings is not an exercise of public powers.[53]

3.3.8 In *Lechouritou v Dimosio*,[54] financial compensation was requested in respect of a massacre of Greek civilians by the German army during the Second World War. The Court of Justice observed that operations conducted by armed forces are one of

---

[46] Apart from this, the Report on the application of the Brussels I Regulation notes that the public/private law divide is also unclear when claims involve cross-border injunctions in environmental law matters and the enforcement of claims of private parties for damages and injunctions supported by public interests. See B Hess, T Pfeiffer and P Schlosser, *Report on the Application of Regulation Brussels I in the Member States*, Study JLS/C4/2005/03, Sept 2007, paras 73–9. See also, G Betlem and C Bernasconi, 'European Private Law, the Environment and Obstacles for Public Authorities' (2006) 122 *LQR* 124–37; A Scott, 'Exclusionary Principles and the Judgments Regulation' (2007) 3 *Journal of Private International Law* 309.

[47] Case 29/76 *LTU Lufttransportunternehmen GmbH & Co KG v Eurocontrol* [1976] ECR 1541, paras 3–4.

[48] Case 814/79 *Netherlands State v Rüffer* [1980] ECR 3807, para 13. TC Hartley, (1981) 6 *EL Rev* 215.

[49] Case C–172/91 *Sonntag v Waidmann* [1993] ECR I–1963, para 20. This means 'whether a public authority has exercised powers going beyond those existing, or which have no equivalent, in relationships between private individuals': Advocate General Ruiz-Jarabo Colomer in Case C–292/05 *Lechouritou v Dimosio* [2007] ECR I–1519, para 46.

[50] Case C–271/00 *Gemeente Steenbergen v Baten* [2002] ECR I–10527, para 31.

[51] Case C–271/00 *Gemeente Steenbergen v Baten* [2002] ECR I–10527, para 37. See also Case C–433/01 *Freistaat Bayern v Blijdenstein* [2004] ECR I–981, paras 20–1.

[52] Case C–266/01 *Préservatrice foncière TIARD SA v Netherlands State* [2003] ECR I–4867, para 36 (A Briggs, [2004] *LMCLQ* 313). See also Case C–265/02 *Frahuil SA v Assitalia SpA* [2004] ECR I–1543.

[53] Case C–167/00 *Verein für Konsumentinformation v Henkel* [2002] ECR I–8111.

[54] Case C–292/05 [2007] ECR I–1519.

the characteristic emanations of state sovereignty and are inextricably linked to the state's foreign and defence policy.[55] The fact that the proceedings brought in Greece were in the form of a civil action was irrelevant; the claim did not fall within the scope of Article 1.[56] Similarly, in *Netherlands State v Rüffer*,[57] the defendant, who was domiciled in Germany, owned a boat which sank in a public waterway for which the plaintiff, the Netherlands state, was responsible. The plaintiff removed the wreck and sold it. As the proceeds were insufficient to cover the full costs incurred, the plaintiff sued the defendant in the Dutch courts for the balance. Although the subject-matter of the proceedings was tortious according to Dutch law, the litigation fell outside the scope of Article 1 since, in recovering the wreck, the plaintiff had been acting in the exercise of its public powers pursuant to an international convention. The opposite conclusion was reached in *Sonntag v Waidmann*.[58] The plaintiffs' son was killed in an accident on a school excursion in Italy. The plaintiffs, having obtained an award of damages in proceedings in Italy against the teacher who had been in charge of the excursion, sought to enforce the judgment in Germany. The question arose whether the judgment fell within the scope of Article 1. The Court of Justice decided that 'the right to obtain compensation for injury suffered as a consequence of conduct regarded as culpable in criminal law is generally recognised as being a civil law right'.[59] In supervising pupils a teacher who works in the public sector acts on behalf of the state but does not exercise public authority powers. Accordingly, the Italian judgment was to be regarded as falling within the scope of Article 1.

3.3.9 It has also been held that a case involving a winding-up petition presented by the secretary of state under section 124A of the Insolvency Act 1986 did not involve civil and commercial matters: the plaintiff was a public authority acting pursuant to its public authority powers and was inviting the court 'to grant relief in the general public interest and not for the narrow purpose of enforcing private rights and obligations'.[60] The action of a bank in sending out a letter pursuant to governmental supervisory functions which had been delegated to it by the Dutch government was also of a public law nature, notwithstanding the fact that the letter contained allegedly libellous material.[61] Similarly, an action by a public body to recover money obtained by corrupt means is not 'civil and commercial' in nature.[62] Conversely, forfeiture proceedings in the magistrates' court, taken by a local authority under section 97 of the Trade Marks Act 1994, are to be regarded as civil proceedings; the local authority does not have a duty to bring such proceedings, which are predominantly concerned with the determination of the private interests of the individuals who stand to benefit if an order for the forfeiture of goods is made.[63]

---

[55] Case C–292/05 [2007] ECR I–1519, para 37.
[56] Case C–292/05 [2007] ECR I–1519, para 41.
[57] Case 814/79 [1980] ECR 3807.
[58] Case C–172/91 [1993] ECR I–1963. A Briggs, (1993) 13 *YBEL* 517.
[59] Case C–172/91 [1993] ECR I–1963, para 19.
[60] Sir Richard Scott V-C in *Re Senator Hanseatische Verwaltungsgesellschaft mbH* [1996] 2 BCLC 562, 580.
[61] *Grovit v De Nederlandsche Bank* [2008] 1 WLR 51.
[62] *Criminal Assets Bureau v JWPL* [2008] ILPr 298 (High Court, Ireland).
[63] *R v Harrow Crown Court, ex parte UNIC Centre SARL* [2000] 1 WLR 2112.

Exceptions

3.3.10 Matters falling outside the scope of Article 1 do so only if they constitute the principal subject-matter of the proceedings; they are thus not excluded when they come before the court as a subsidiary matter either in the main proceedings or in preliminary proceedings.[64]

First Exception: Family Law[65]

3.3.11 It emerges from the Jenard Report that the purpose of the first exception in Article 1 is to exclude all questions of family law other than matters relating to maintenance.[66] Two particular problems arise out of the wording of this exception. First, a distinction has to be drawn between 'rights in property arising out of a matrimonial relationship' which fall outside the scope of Article 1 and maintenance obligations which do not.[67] For example, a decision rendered in divorce proceedings ordering the payment of a lump sum and the transfer of certain property from one former spouse to the other concerns 'maintenance' and falls within the scope of Article 1.[68] Secondly, as far as the English legal system is concerned, there is a difficult dividing line to be drawn between property issues in general, which fall within the scope of Article 1, and 'rights in property arising out of a matrimonial relationship', which do not. Whereas legal systems derived from Roman law include matrimonial property regimes—particular rules which govern the property relations of spouses—in English law the general law (albeit with certain modifications) applies.[69]

3.3.12 The fact that matters relating to wills and succession[70] are excluded from its scope does not mean that the Brussels I Regulation has no application in a case which incidentally involves the transfer of property on death. *Re Hayward*[71] involved a villa in Spain which had been purchased jointly by the debtor and another Englishman (X)

---

[64] Jenard Report, [1979] OJ C59/10.
[65] Art 1(2)(a).
[66] [1979] OJ C59/10.
[67] Art 5(2) allocates special jurisdiction 'in matters relating to maintenance'. Since the entry into force of the Brussels I Regulation, there has been introduced a Regulation covering maintenance: Reg (EC) 4/2009 on jurisdiction, applicable law, recognition and enforcement of decisions and cooperation in matters relating to maintenance obligations [2009] OJ L7/1. Art 5(2) of the Lugano Convention has an additional jurisdictional base not found in Art 5(2) of the Brussels I Regulation to bring it into line with Art 3 of the Maintenance Obligations Regulation.
[68] Case C–220/95 *Van den Boogaard v Laumen* [1997] ECR I–1147. Cf *Lecombe v Bourotte* [2005] ILPr 106 (Court of Cassation, France) in which proceedings concerning the sale of shares under an agreement which defined the terms of a married couple's separation were held to fall within the exclusion in Art 1 relating to matrimonial property.
[69] Further consideration of these problems is beyond the scope of this work. For consideration of matrimonial jurisdiction, see CMV Clarkson and J Hill, *The Conflict of Laws* (Oxford, OUP, 3rd edn, 2006) ch 9.
[70] There are plans to harmonise the law in this area; see European Commission, *Proposal for a Regulation of the European Parliament and of the Council on jurisdiction, applicable law, recognition and enforcement of decisions and authentic instruments in matters of succession and the creation of a European Certificate of Succession*, COM (2009) 154 final. The UK government has decided not to opt into this proposed regulation.
[71] [1997] Ch 45.

in 1986. In 1987, shortly after he had been declared bankrupt, the debtor died intestate. A dispute arose in relation to the debtor's half-share in the villa between, on the one hand, the debtor's trustee in bankruptcy and, on the other, the debtor's widow, who claimed to be entitled under the debtor's intestacy, and X, who had become the sole registered proprietor of the villa. It was held that the case was not within the first exception. Rattee J did not think that the trustee's claim—that the debtor's half-share in the villa should be vested in the trustee—raised an issue of succession:

Succession was in no sense the principal subject-matter of the proceedings. The trustee's claim was simply on the basis that the bankrupt had been entitled to a half-share of the villa and that, on his appointment as trustee, the trustee had taken over the bankrupt's entitlement thereto. That in no sense ... raises any question of succession.[72]

Second Exception: Bankruptcy and Insolvency[73]

3.3.13 When the original Brussels Convention was being negotiated the Member States were also starting work on a Draft Convention on Bankruptcy, Winding up, Arrangements, Compositions and Similar Proceedings.[74] Accordingly, bankruptcy was excluded from Article 1. Work on the Draft Bankruptcy Convention proceeded very slowly.[75] Finally, after decades of negotiation and false starts, the Member States reached agreement on a text in 1995. However, the Convention never came in force as such. Instead, the approved text (with some minor amendments) was finally enacted into European law by means of a Council Regulation.[76]

3.3.14 It stands to reason that, if a claim falls within the scope of the Insolvency Regulation, it would necessarily fall within the scope of the second exception in Article 1 of the Brussels I Regulation. The inter-relationship between the two instruments was examined by the Court of Justice in *German Graphics Graphische Maschinen GmbH v van der Schee*.[77] The issue was whether a claim concerning the invocation of a reservation of title clause with respect to certain machines located on the premises of an insolvent company fell within the scope of the Insolvency Regulation or the Brussels I Regulation. The Court of Justice held that a broad definition should be given to the concept of 'civil and commercial matters' in the Brussels I Regulation; the corollary of this was that the scope of application of the Insolvency Regulation should not be broadly interpreted.[78] On the facts, it was held that the issue facing the court related to the ownership of the machines; this issue was independent of

---

[72] [1997] Ch 45, 53–4.
[73] Art 1(2)(b).
[74] Reaction to the Draft Bankruptcy Convention in the 1970s was mixed: JH Farrar, 'The EEC Draft Convention on Bankruptcy and Winding Up' [1977] *JBL* 320; I Fletcher, 'The Proposed Community Convention on Bankruptcy and Related Matters' (1977) 2 *EL Rev* 15; M Hunter, 'The Draft Bankruptcy Convention of the European Economic Communities' (1972) 21 *ICLQ* 682; M Hunter, 'The Draft EEC Bankruptcy Convention—A Further Examination' (1976) 25 *ICLQ* 310.
[75] For a review of the history of the Draft Bankruptcy Convention, see NA Aminoff, 'The EEC Draft Bankruptcy Convention—An Exercise in Harmonising Private International Law' [1990] 1 *LIEI* 121.
[76] Reg (EC) 1346/2000, [2001] OJ L160/1. For consideration of this Regulation, see ch 17. See also G Moss, I Fletcher and S Isaacs (eds), *The EC Regulation on Insolvency Proceedings* (Oxford, OUP, 2002).
[77] Case C–292/08 [2010] ILPr 15.
[78] Case C–292/08, [2010] ILPr 15, 21 (at [23]–[25]).

the law of insolvency. The action therefore fell outside the scope of the Insolvency Regulation. The Court of Justice went on to hold that the claim fell within the scope of the Brussels I Regulation.

3.3.15 In terms of the Insolvency Regulation's scope, the crucial question is whether a claim derives directly from, or is closely linked to, insolvency. For example, an action to set aside a transaction by virtue of a debtor's insolvency is closely related to insolvency proceedings and, therefore, falls within the scope of the Insolvency Regulation.[79] In *Gourdain v Nadler*[80] the French court had, on the application of a company's liquidator, ordered the *de facto* manager of a French company to pay a certain sum into the assets of the company. The liquidator then sought to enforce the French judgment in Germany. The Court of Justice decided that if the decision of the court of origin is given in the context of bankruptcy or analogous proceedings it falls within the scope of the second exception. As far as the Court of Justice was concerned, what was important was whether or not the decision of the French court was derived directly from the bankruptcy or winding-up.[81] The view according to which claims derived directly from or intimately linked to the bankruptcy or winding-up are within the second exception[82] and proceedings which are incidental to the bankruptcy or winding-up are not[83] is consistent with the general approach to the exceptions advocated by the Jenard Report.[84] Accordingly, where bankruptcy is not the principal subject-matter of the proceedings, a proprietary claim brought by a trustee in bankruptcy, whether in respect of assets held by a third party[85] or relating to a bankrupt's assets which, under English law, vested in the trustee on bankruptcy,[86] is not within the second exception.

3.3.16 Although the position with regard to the bankruptcy of individuals will normally be relatively straightforward, the position of companies is potentially more difficult. There are clearly many issues relating to companies which fall squarely within the Brussels I Regulation. For example, Article 22(2)[87] expressly allocates jurisdiction in respect of proceedings which have as their object the validity of the constitution, the nullity or the dissolution of companies or the decisions of their organs. Obviously, civil and commercial contracts entered into by companies also fall within Article 1. As regards the winding-up of companies, a number of distinctions need to be made. First, legal proceedings incidental to the voluntary winding-up of a company under the law of the United Kingdom are normal civil or commercial disputes within the scope of Article 1; this is also the position in cases involving winding-up subject to the supervision of the court. Secondly, in relation to winding-up by the court, if the company is insolvent, the proceedings are within the second exception; if the company is solvent the proceedings are not excluded. In cases where a company is wound up by

---

[79] Case C–399/07 *Seagon v Deko Marty Belgium NV* [2009] 1 WLR 2168.
[80] Case 133/78 [1979] ECR 733.
[81] Case 133/78 [1979] ECR 733, para 4.
[82] *Firswood Ltd v Petra Bank* [1996] CLC 608; Case C–111/08 *SCT Industri AB (in Liquidation) v Alpenblume AB* [2009] ILPr 743.
[83] *UBS AG v Omni Holding AG (in liquidation)* [2000] 1 WLR 916. See also *Re Société GPS* [2005] ILPr 697 (Court of Cassation, France).
[84] [1979] OJ C59/10.
[85] *Re Hayward* [1997] Ch 45.
[86] *Ashurst v Pollard* [2001] Ch 595.
[87] See paras 5.1.20–5.1.23.

the court what is important is not the legal ground on which the company is wound up, but whether the company is in fact solvent or insolvent.[88]

Third Exception: Social Security[89]

3.3.17   According to the Jenard Report, the purpose of the third exception is to exclude social security litigation which is concerned with 'disputes arising from relationships between the administrative authorities'.[90] However, the third exception does not apply to cases where:

the authority concerned relies on a direct right of recourse against a third party responsible for injury or damage, or is subrogated as against a third party to the rights of an injured party insured by it, since, in doing so, it is acting in accordance with ordinary legal rules.[91]

In *Gemeente Steebergen v Baten*,[92] the Court of Justice referred to this passage of the Jenard Report[93] and adopted the same basic approach. The claimant was a Dutch local authority which, having made social assistance payments to the defendant's former wife, took legal proceedings to recover the amount of these payments from the defendant. Having obtained a judgment in its favour from the Dutch courts, the plaintiff sought to enforce the judgment in Belgium and the question arose whether or not the enforcement proceedings concerned 'social security'. The Court of Justice ruled they did not:

[T]he concept of 'social security' does not encompass the action under a right of recourse by which a public body seeks from a person governed by private law recovery in accordance with the rules of the ordinary law of sums paid by it by way of social assistance.[94]

Fourth Exception: Arbitration[95]

3.3.18   The rationale behind the fourth exception is that arbitration is covered by the New York Convention of 1958, to which all EU Member States are parties.[96] However, the Report on the application of the Brussels I Regulation revealed difficulties in the context of the interface between the Regulation and arbitration[97] and the precise scope of the fourth exception has provoked considerable controversy.[98] A wide variety of disputes may arise out of arbitration and the question is whether all court proceedings which raise any issue relating to arbitration fall within the fourth exception. As things

---

[88] Schlosser Report, [1979] OJ C59/91, para 55.
[89] Art 1(2)(c).
[90] Jenard Report, [1979] OJ C59/13.
[91] *Ibid.*
[92] Case C–271/00 [2002] ECR I–10527.
[93] See also Advocate General Tizzano: Case C–271/00 [2002] ECR I–10527, para 41.
[94] Case C–271/00 [2002] ECR I–10527, para 49.
[95] Art 1(2)(d).
[96] Jenard Report, [1979] OJ C59/13.
[97] B Hess, T Pfeiffer and P Schlosser, *Report on the Application of Regulation Brussels I in the Member States*, Study JLS/C4/2005/03, Sept 2007, paras 106–14.
[98] See C Ambrose, 'Arbitration and the Free Movement of Judgments' (2003) 19 *Arb Int* 3.

currently stand, there may be parallel proceedings between courts and arbitral tribunals in different Member States with the result that an arbitration agreement may be held valid in one Member State and invalid in another.[99] The effectiveness of arbitration agreements is also undermined because procedural devices aimed at upholding such agreements are incompatible with the Regulation.[100] Furthermore, there is no uniform rule allocating jurisdiction with respect to ancillary proceedings in support of arbitration proceedings.[101] The Commission, in its Green Paper on the review of the Brussels I Regulation, has suggested a partial deletion of the exclusion of arbitration from the scope of the Regulation so that court proceedings in support of arbitration and the issue of provisional measures in support of arbitration might fall within the scope of the Regulation.[102] Although the majority of Member States are not in favour of the scope of Regulation being extended to arbitration,[103] the current state of affairs is unsatisfactory. There is no need for a European scheme to replace the New York Convention, which is acknowledged by many to be working well, but a partial reform of the Brussels I Regulation to support the New York Convention may be advisable.

3.3.19 Under the current situation, six different situations need to be considered: (1) legal proceedings relating to arbitration; (2) legal proceedings relating to arbitration in which the validity of the arbitration agreement arises as a preliminary question; (3) legal proceedings relating to the validity of an arbitration agreement; (4) legal proceedings in which the jurisdiction of the court is contested on the basis of an arbitration agreement; (5) legal proceedings to enforce an arbitration agreement by injunction; (6) legal proceedings for the recognition or enforcement of a foreign judgment given in defiance of an arbitration agreement.

LEGAL PROCEEDINGS RELATING TO ARBITRATION

3.3.20 Although there are some commentators who have suggested that the fourth exception applies only to arbitral proceedings themselves—with the consequence that no court proceedings relating to arbitration are within the fourth exception[104]—the orthodox view is that the Brussels regime does not apply 'for the purpose of determining the jurisdiction of courts and tribunals in respect of litigation relating to arbitration'.[105] In *Marc Rich & Co AG v Società Italiana Impianti PA* the Court of Justice held that the

[99] European Commission, 'Report from the Commission to the European Parliament, the Council and the European Economic and Social Committee on the application of Council Regulation (EC) No 44/2001 on jurisdiction and the recognition and enforcement of judgments in civil and commercial matters' (hereafter 'Commission Report'), COM (2008) 174 final, p 9.

[100] Case C–185/07 *Allianz SpA (formerly Riunione Adriatica Di Sicurta SpA) v West Tankers Inc* [2009] 1 AC 1138.

[101] Commission Report, COM (2009) 174 final, p 9.

[102] European Commission, Green Paper on the Review of Council Regulation (EC) No 44/2001 on jurisdiction and the recognition and enforcement of judgments in civil and commercial matters (hereafter 'Commission Green Paper'), COM (2009) 175 final, p 9.

[103] B Hess, T Pfeiffer and P Schlosser, *Report on the Application of Regulation Brussels I in the Member States*, Study JLS/C4/2005/03, Sept 2007, para 109. The House of Lords' European Union Committee supports the Commission's proposal to reform the arbitration exclusion: Green Paper on the Brussels I Regulation, HL Paper 148 (hereafter 'House of Lords' Green Paper'), July 2009, pp 26–7 (paras 95–7).

[104] See, eg, Schlosser, 'The 1968 Convention and Arbitration' (1991) 7 *Arb Int* 227.

[105] Jenard Report, [1979] OJ C59/13.

fourth exception is intended 'to exclude arbitration in its entirety, including proceedings brought before national courts'.[106] Accordingly, the fourth exception extends to:

court proceedings which are ancillary to arbitration proceedings, for example the appointment or dismissal of arbitrators, the fixing of the place for arbitration, the extension of the time limit for making awards or the obtaining of a preliminary ruling on questions of substance as provided by English law.[107]

However, it is important to note that a legal relationship does not fall outside the scope of the Regulation merely because the parties have entered into an arbitration agreement; the Regulation is still applicable if the substantive subject-matter of the dispute falls within the scope of the Regulation.[108]

3.3.21   The fourth exception also covers 'proceedings and decisions concerning applications for the revocation, amendment, recognition and enforcement of arbitration awards'.[109] So, a foreign judgment which makes an arbitral award enforceable as a judgment of the court concerns 'arbitration' and falls within the fourth exception.[110] However, in *Van Uden Maritime BV v Kommanditgesellschaft in Firma Deco-Line*[111] the Court of Justice ruled that, in a case where the parties have agreed to refer their substantive dispute to arbitration, court proceedings for provisional measures[112] do not thereby fall within the fourth exception. The Court thought that provisional measures are 'not ... ancillary to arbitration proceedings but are ordered in parallel to such proceedings and are intended as measures of support'.[113] This conclusion seems unsound in principle and is unlikely to promote legal certainty.[114] The view put forward by the English and German governments—that an application for interim relief in support of arbitration proceedings is ancillary to such arbitration proceedings and is within the fourth exception—is to be preferred.

3.3.22   The limits of the fourth exception were considered in *Lexmar Corporation and Steamship Mutual Underwriting Association (Bermuda) Ltd v Nordisk Skibsrederforening*.[115] The parties referred disputes arising out of a charter agreement to arbitration. In response to the arbitrator's order that the defendant should provide security for the plaintiff's costs in the arbitration, the defendant issued an appropriate letter of undertaking (which included an express choice of English law and jurisdiction). The arbitrator made an interim final award holding the defendant liable for the plaintiff's costs and the plaintiff sought to enforce the defendant's undertaking in legal proceedings. The question arose whether the substance of the proceedings

---

[106] Case C–190/89 [1991] ECR I–3855, para 18. See also Case C–391/95 *Van Uden Maritime BV v Kommanditgesellschaft in Firma Deco-Line* [1998] ECR I–7091, para 31.

[107] Schlosser Report, [1979] OJ C59/93, para 64(b).

[108] Advocate General Kokott in Case C–185/07 *Allianz SpA (formerly Riunione Adriatica Di Sicurta SpA) v West Tankers Inc* [2009] 1 AC 1138, 1151 (para 62).

[109] Schlosser Report, [1979] OJ C59/93, para 65(c).

[110] Advocate General Darmon in Case C–190/89 *Marc Rich & Co AG v Società Impianti Italiana PA* [1991] ECR I–3855, para 70; *Arab Business Consortium International Finance and Investment Co v Banque Franco-Tunisienne* [1996] 1 Lloyd's Rep 485.

[111] Case C–391/95 [1998] ECR I–7091.

[112] Under Brussels I Reg, Art 31.

[113] Case C–391/95 [1998] ECR I–7091, para 33.

[114] See G Petrochilos, 'Arbitration and interim measures: in the twilight of the Brussels Convention' [2000] *LMCLQ* 99.

[115] [1997] 1 Lloyd's Rep 289.

was 'arbitration' for the purposes of the fourth exception. The defendant argued that the plaintiff's claim to enforce the undertaking was effectively a claim to enforce the arbitrator's order. However, the court rejected the defendant's argument that, since the claim was ancillary to the arbitration, it should be regarded as falling within the fourth exception. Colman J concluded that only 'judicial proceedings which are directed to the regulation and support of arbitration proceedings and awards are covered by the [fourth] exception'.[116] Although the plaintiff's claim was to enforce a debt which arose out of events which were related to the arbitration, the proceedings did not fall within the fourth exception because the plaintiff's claim had 'nothing whatever to do with the exercise by the English courts of their curial law jurisdiction to regulate or support arbitration or their jurisdiction to enforce arbitral awards'.[117] In *Youell v La Réunion Aérienne*, the Court of Appeal held that 'it is the nature of the claim which is critical';[118] where a claimant is seeking a declaration of non-liability under an alleged contract containing a (disputed) French arbitration clause, the fact that the defendant is pursuing the mirror-image of those claims in French arbitration proceedings does not mean that the English claim falls within the fourth exception.

LEGAL PROCEEDINGS RELATING TO ARBITRATION IN WHICH THE VALIDITY
OF THE ARBITRATION AGREEMENT ARISES AS A PRELIMINARY QUESTION

3.3.23   The question which arose in *Marc Rich & Co AG v Società Italiana Impianti PA* was whether legal proceedings which are ancillary to arbitration proceedings are still within the fourth exception if the existence or validity of the arbitration agreement is challenged. In this case, the plaintiff, a Swiss company, offered by telex to buy a quantity of crude oil from the defendant, an Italian company. The defendant accepted the offer subject to certain further conditions. The plaintiff telexed again setting out the terms in greater detail; these terms included a clause providing for English law to govern the contract and for disputes to be referred to arbitration in London. The plaintiff alleged that the cargo of oil was contaminated and claimed damages. The defendant commenced legal proceedings in Italy with a view to obtaining a declaration of non-liability and the plaintiff started arbitration proceedings in England. When the defendant failed to appoint an arbitrator in accordance with the terms of the arbitration clause the plaintiff applied to the court for an arbitrator to be appointed on the defendant's behalf. The defendant contested the jurisdiction of the court, contending, first, that there was no arbitration agreement, secondly, that the case was not within the fourth exception, and thirdly, that, in view of the earlier proceedings in Italy, the English court was obliged to decline jurisdiction on the basis of the *lis pendens* rule.[119]

3.3.24   On a reference for a preliminary ruling from the Court of Appeal,[120] the Court of Justice accepted that the purpose of the fourth exception is to exclude all

---

[116] [1997] 1 Lloyd's Rep 289, 292.
[117] [1997] 1 Lloyd's Rep 289, 292. See also *The Xing Su Hai* [1995] 2 Lloyd's Rep 15, 21.
[118] [2009] 1 Lloyd's Rep 586, 591 (at [35]).
[119] For discussion of *lis pendens*, see section 9.1.
[120] [1989] 1 Lloyd's Rep 54. For a discussion of the case following the reference by the Court of Appeal but before the decision of the Court of Justice, see P Kaye, 'The Judgments Convention and Arbitration: Mutual Spheres of Influence' (1991) 7 *Arb Int* 289; DR Thomas, 'The Arbitration Exclusion in the Brussels Convention 1968: An English Perspective' (1990) 7(2) *J Int Arb* 43; F Davidson, 'Civil Jurisdiction and Arbitration' 1992 *SLT* 267.

court proceedings relating to arbitration. Accordingly, as the English proceedings for the appointment of an arbitrator by the court came within the sphere of arbitration, they were covered by the fourth exception.[121] Was this conclusion affected by the fact that the validity of the arbitration clause was challenged by the defendant? The defendant argued that a litigant should not be able to side-step the jurisdiction provisions of Title II of the Brussels Convention merely by alleging the existence of an arbitration agreement. The Court of Justice did not accept this argument:

> In order to determine whether a dispute falls within the scope of the Convention, reference must be made solely to the subject-matter of the dispute. If, by virtue of its subject-matter, such as the appointment of an arbitrator, a dispute falls outside the scope of the Convention, the existence of a preliminary issue which the court must resolve in order to determine the dispute cannot, whatever that issue may be, justify the application of the Convention. ... It follows that, in the case before the Court, the fact that a preliminary issue relates to the existence or validity of the arbitration agreement does not affect the exclusion from the scope of the Convention of a dispute concerning the appointment of an arbitrator.[122]

Litigation concerning the appointment of an arbitrator comes within the scope of the fourth exception 'even if the existence or validity of an arbitration agreement is a preliminary issue in that litigation'.[123] However, where the subject-matter of the dispute falls within the scope of the Regulation, a preliminary issue concerning the validity of an arbitration agreement also falls within the scope of the Regulation.[124]

LEGAL PROCEEDINGS RELATING TO THE VALIDITY OF AN ARBITRATION AGREEMENT

3.3.25   What is the position where the main issue in the legal proceedings is the existence of an arbitration agreement? This issue would arise where, for example, a party to a contract seeks a declaration from the court that an alleged arbitration clause is valid or invalid. In *Marc Rich & Co AG v Società Italiana Impianti PA* Advocate General Darmon considered that a dispute concerning the existence of an arbitration agreement falls within the fourth exception.[125] This conclusion is supported by the decision of the Court of Justice in *Effer SpA v Kantner*,[126] in which it was decided that a dispute concerning the existence of a contract is a matter 'relating to a contract' for the purposes of Article 5(1). By the same process of reasoning, a dispute over the existence of an arbitration agreement relates to arbitration for the purposes of the fourth exception. The English courts have accepted that proceedings in which the claimant seeks to establish that the defendant is bound by an arbitration agreement involve 'arbitration', notwithstanding the defendant's challenge to

---

[121] Case C–190/89 [1991] ECR I–3855, paras 18–19.
[122] Case C–190/89 [1991] ECR I–3855, paras 26 and 28.
[123] Case C–190/89 [1991] ECR I–3855, para 29.
[124] Case C–185/07 *Allianz SpA (formerly Riunione Adriatica Di Sicurta SpA) v West Tankers Inc* [2009] 1 AC 1138. See also *DHL GBS (UK) Ltd v Fallimento Finmatica SPA* [2009] 1 Lloyd's Rep 430, 434 (at [20]).
[125] Case C–190/89 [1991] ECR I–3855, para 35.
[126] Case 38/81 [1982] ECR 825.

the agreement's validity.[127] It has been suggested that, in order better to coordinate court proceedings and proceedings taking place before an arbitral tribunal, the courts of the Member State in which the seat of the arbitration is located should be given priority to determine the validity of the arbitration agreement.[128]

LEGAL PROCEEDINGS IN WHICH THE JURISDICTION OF THE COURT IS CONTESTED ON THE BASIS OF AN ARBITRATION AGREEMENT

3.3.26 In a case where the defendant contests the jurisdiction of the court of a Member State on the basis of an arbitration agreement, does the court have jurisdiction to determine the validity or existence of the arbitration agreement? It does not follow from the fact that Chapter II confers jurisdiction as regards the main issue, which falls within the scope of the Brussels I Regulation, that the court with jurisdiction over the main issue also has jurisdiction to deal with an incidental question falling within one of the exceptions; whether a court has jurisdiction to determine the existence or validity of an arbitration clause is a matter for the law of the court seised, not a matter to be determined by Chapter II.[129] Having said that, in the context of proceedings commenced in England, it seems that, once the claimant has invoked the jurisdiction of the court, the court would—on the basis of the claimant's submission— have jurisdiction to determine the validity or existence of an arbitration agreement invoked by the defendant in order to contest the court's jurisdiction. If the court rules that the arbitration clause is 'null and void'[130] the subject-matter of the dispute is not 'arbitration' and the proceedings fall outside the scope of the fourth exception. (A question may then arise in another Member State whether the decision declaring the alleged arbitration agreement to be invalid is a judgment which is entitled to recognition under Chapter III.)

LEGAL PROCEEDINGS TO ENFORCE AN ARBITRATION AGREEMENT BY INJUNCTION

3.3.27 Where proceedings are brought in another country in breach of the terms of an English arbitration clause, the defendant in the foreign proceedings may choose not only to contest the jurisdiction of the foreign court on the basis of the arbitration clause, but also to apply to the English court for an anti-suit injunction, that is, an injunction ordering the claimant in the foreign court to discontinue the proceedings.[131] The object of the English proceedings is to enforce the arbitration clause. Although the English courts have shown a willingness to grant an anti-suit injunction in such

---

[127] *The Lake Avery* [1997] 1 Lloyd's Rep 540; *The Ivan Zagubanski* [2002] 1 Lloyd's Rep 106; *A v B* [2007] 1 Lloyd's Rep 237; *Through Transport Mutual Insurance Association (Eurasia) Ltd v New India Assurance Co Ltd* [2005] 1 Lloyd's Rep 67 (The second part of the Court of Appeal's judgment, in which it was held that an injunction to restrain proceedings in another EU Member State court in breach of a valid arbitration agreement fell within Art 1(2)(d), is wrong in view of the Court of Justice's subsequent ruling in Case C–185/07 *Allianz SpA (formerly Riunione Adriatica Di Sicurta SpA) v West Tankers Inc* Case C–185/07 [2009] 1 AC 1138.)

[128] Commission Green Paper, COM (2009) 175 final, p 9; House of Lords' Green Paper, p 27 (para 96).

[129] Advocate General Darmon in Case C–190/89 *Marc Rich & Co AG v Società Impianti Italiana PA* [1991] ECR I–3855, para 44.

[130] Arbitration Act 1996, s 9(4).

[131] See ch 11.

circumstances,[132] the Court of Justice in *Allianz SpA (formerly Riunione Adriatica Di Sicurta SpA) v West Tankers Inc*[133] ruled that this English practice is inconsistent with the principle of mutual trust underpinning the Brussels I Regulation.[134]

THE RECOGNITION AND ENFORCEMENT OF JUDGMENTS GIVEN IN BREACH
OR DISREGARD OF AN ARBITRATION AGREEMENT

3.3.28 The final issues surrounding the fourth exception arise in the context of the recognition and enforcement of foreign judgments.[135] There are two separate, but related, questions to be considered. First, does the decision of a court of another state on the validity of an alleged arbitration agreement concern 'arbitration'? In *Marc Rich & Co AG v Società Italiana Impianti PA* Advocate General Darmon thought that this question should be given an affirmative answer.[136]

3.3.29 In *The Heidberg*[137] it was held that a French decision on the validity of an arbitration clause did not fall within the scope of the fourth exception. Following the decision of the Court of Justice in the *West Tankers*[138] case, it is clear that a judgment of a Member State court on the question whether an arbitration clause has been incorporated into a commercial contract between the parties is not to be characterised as involving 'arbitration' and, therefore, falls within the scope of the Regulation.[139] According to the terms of a key passage the Court of Justice's judgment:

[T]he court finds ... that if, because of the subject matter of the dispute, that is, the nature of the rights to be protected in proceedings, such as a claim for damages, those proceedings come within the scope of [the Brussels I Regulation], a preliminary issue concerning the applicability of an arbitration agreement, including in particular its validity, also comes within its scope of application.[140]

3.3.30 Secondly, what is the position where a national court adjudicates on the subject-matter of a dispute, because it overlooked an arbitration agreement or considered it inapplicable? Can recognition and enforcement of such a judgment be refused in another Member State on the ground that the arbitration agreement was valid and that the judgment falls within the scope of the fourth exception?[141] The Schlosser Report reveals that at the time of the negotiation of the 1978 Accession

---

[132] See, eg, *The Angelic Grace* [1995] 1 Lloyd's Rep 87.

[133] Case C–185/07 [2009] 1 AC 1138.

[134] See the discussion in paras 11.3.7–11.3.12.

[135] DT Hascher, 'Recognition and Enforcement of Judgments on the Existence and Validity of an Arbitration Clause under the Brussels Convention' (1997) 13 *Arb Int* 33; H van Houtte, 'May Court Judgments that Disregard Arbitration Clauses and Awards be Enforced under the Brussels and Lugano Conventions?' (1997) 13 *Arb Int* 85; J-P Beraudo, 'The Arbitration Exception of the Brussels and Lugano Conventions: Jurisdiction, Recognition and Enforcement of Judgments' (2001) 18(1) *J Int Arb* 13; JJ van Haersolte-van Hof, 'The Arbitration Exception: Further Comment' (2001) 18(1) *J Int Arb* 27.

[136] Case C–190/89 [1991] ECR I–3855, para 34; compare Evrigenis-Kerameus Report [1986] OJ C298/10, para 35.

[137] [1994] 2 Lloyd's Rep 287, 303. See also *The Xing Su Hai* [1995] 2 Lloyd's Rep 15, 21.

[138] Case C–185/07 *Allianz SpA (formerly Riunione Adriatica Di Sicurta SpA) v West Tankers Inc* [2009] 1 AC 1138.

[139] *DHL GBS (UK) Ltd v Fallimento Finmatica SPA* [2009] 1 Lloyd's Rep 430; *The Wadi Sudr* [2010] 1 Lloyd's Rep 193.

[140] Case C–185/07 [2009] 1 AC 1138, 1157 (at [26]).

[141] See Schlosser Report, [1979] OJ C59/92, para 62.

Convention there was disagreement on the precise scope of the arbitration exception in this area.[142]

3.3.31 The decision of the Court of Justice in *Marc Rich & Co AG v Società Italiana Impianti PA*[143] did not directly address the question, and opinion on its significance is divided.[144] On the one hand, it was suggested that the decision of the Court of Justice supported a wide interpretation of the arbitration exception and that, if the court of another Member State gave judgment in breach of an arbitration agreement, there was no obligation upon an English court to recognise that judgment.[145] On the other hand, it was argued that the decision of the Court of Justice in the *Marc Rich* case suggested that judgments in cases where there has been a breach of an agreement to go to arbitration were not within the scope of the fourth exception.[146]

3.3.32 The English cases also attested to the fact that, in the absence of clear guidance from the Court of Justice, the question was far from straightforward.[147] The recognition of a judgment which, having failed to give effect to an arbitration agreement, rules on the merits of the dispute is another issue which has effectively been resolved by the Court of Justice's decision in the *West Tankers* case.[148] The Court of Justice's analysis leads inexorably to the conclusion that, if the underlying dispute between the parties is civil and commercial in nature and within the scope of the Regulation, a judgment which resolves that dispute is also within the Regulation's scope; the fact that the parties had (in the eyes of the English court) agreed to refer the dispute to arbitration cannot lead to the conclusion that the judgment concerns 'arbitration'.[149]

3.4 THE RELATIONSHIP BETWEEN THE BRUSSELS I REGULATION AND OTHER INTERNATIONAL CONVENTIONS

3.4.1 Chapter VII concerns the relationship between the Brussels I Regulation and other international instruments. There is, for example, a list of certain conventions which are overridden by the Regulation.[150] It is provided, however, that those conventions continue to apply to matters to which the Brussels I Regulation does not apply.[151] The most important provision in Chapter VII is the one which preserves the effect of certain specialised

---

[142] [1979] OJ C59/92, para 61.

[143] Case C–190/89 [1991] ECR I–3855.

[144] The issue was mentioned but expressly left open by Advocate General Darmon: Case C–190/89 *Marc Rich & Co AG v Società Italiana Impianti PA* [1991] ECR I–3855, para 45.

[145] A Briggs, (1991) 11 *YBEL* 527, 529.

[146] JJ Fawcett and JM Carruthers, *Cheshire, North and Fawcett: Private International Law* (London, Butterworths, 14th edn, 2008) 630.

[147] A number of English cases took the view that a judgment on the merits given in breach of arbitration agreement is not within the fourth exception: *The Heidberg* [1994] 2 Lloyd's Rep 287; *Toepfer International GmbH v Molino Bosch Srl* [1996] 1 Lloyd's Rep 510; *Phillip Alexander Securities and Futures Ltd v Bamberger* [1997] ILPr 73; *Zellner v Phillip Alexander Securities and Futures Ltd* [1997] ILPr 730. The contrary position was taken in: *The Lake Avery* [1997] 1 Lloyd's Rep 540; *The Ivan Zagubanski* [2002] 1 Lloyd's Rep 106.

[148] Case C–185/07 *Allianz SpA (formerly Riunione Adriatica Di Sicurta SpA) v West Tankers Inc* [2009] 1 AC 1138.

[149] *The Wadi Sudr* [2010] 1 Lloyd's Rep 193.

[150] Art 69.

[151] Art 70.

conventions. Article 71[152] provides that the Brussels I Regulation shall not affect any conventions to which the Member States are parties and which, in relation to particular matters, govern jurisdiction or the recognition or enforcement of judgments.[153]

3.4.2 It is also provided that the Brussels I Regulation shall not prevent a court of a Member State which is a party to any such convention from assuming jurisdiction in accordance with that convention 'even where the defendant is domiciled in a Member State which is not a party to that convention'.[154] Furthermore, judgments given in a Member State by a court in the exercise of jurisdiction provided for in such a convention shall be recognised and enforced in other Member States in accordance with Chapter III.[155]

3.4.3 These provisions are of particular importance for the United Kingdom because of the significance of other conventions in the field of maritime law, in particular the International Convention for the Unification of Certain Rules relating to the Arrest of Seagoing Ships (the Arrest Convention) and the International Convention for the Unification of Certain Rules concerning Civil Jurisdiction in matters of Collision (the Collision Convention), both of which date from 1952. The jurisdiction provisions of these conventions are substantially implemented into English law by the Supreme Court Act 1981 and the effect of the Brussels I Regulation is to preserve the operation not only of special conventions, but also of the domestic legislation which translates the substance of the special conventions into English law.[156]

3.4.4 The European Union has signed up to the Hague Choice of Court Convention on behalf of all the Member States.[157] When the Convention comes into force, it will override the Regulation's rules where one or more of the parties reside in a state which is a contracting state to the Convention but which is not bound by the Regulation.[158] The Hartley and Dagouchi Report accompanying the Convention states that, in practice, conflicts of jurisdiction between the two instruments are likely to be rare.[159] The potential for inconsistency between the two instruments mainly arises in relation to the *lis pendens* rule which prevails over a choice of court agreement under the Regulation, but not under the Convention. Reform of Article 23 and/or Article 27 of the Brussels I Regulation to coordinate it with the Convention will be necessary later on.[160]

3.4.5 A number of points concerning the operation of the main provisions of Chapter VII of the Brussels I Regulation should be noted. First, the Regulation can be displaced only by special conventions which 'govern jurisdiction or the recognition or

---

[152] Lugano Convention, Art 67.

[153] See Case C–148/03 *Nürnberger Allgemeine Versicherungs AG v Portbridge Transport International BV* [2004] ECR I–10327.

[154] Art 71(2).

[155] Art 71(3).

[156] *The Po* [1991] 2 Lloyd's Rep 206; *The Anna H* [1995] 1 Lloyd's Rep 11.

[157] As of 1 December 2009, the Convention had also been signed by the United States of America and acceded to by Mexico. The Convention will only enter into force three months after two states have ratified or acceded to it: Article 31(1).

[158] Art 26(6)(a).

[159] T Hartley and M Dogauchi, Explanatory Report, 26 (the report is available on the Hague Convention website: http://www.hcch.net).

[160] B Hess, T Pfeiffer and P Schlosser, *Report on the Application of Regulation Brussels I in the Member States*, Study JLS/C4/2005/03, Sept 2007, paras 390–97, 884.

enforcement of judgments'.[161] A convention which governs substantive matters cannot override the Regulation. Secondly, if the convention in question concerns jurisdiction, the terms of the convention itself determine whether its jurisdiction rules override, or are additional (or alternative) to the rules in the Regulation. Thirdly, the court of a Member State may, relying on a special convention, assume jurisdiction over a defendant who is domiciled in a Member State which is not a party to the convention in question. In any event, the court hearing the claim must apply Article 26 of the Brussels I Regulation.[162] Fourthly, the operation of Chapter VII does not depend on it being shown that the Member State in which proceedings are brought has expressly implemented the special convention. Where jurisdiction is exercised under a special convention the crucial elements are: (1) that the Member State in which proceedings are brought is a party to the special convention in question; (2) that the forum has jurisdiction in accordance with its municipal law; and (3) that the exercise of jurisdiction is consistent with the terms of the special convention in question. If these three conditions are satisfied, a defendant who is domiciled in a Member State may be sued in another Member State, notwithstanding the fact that the courts in which the proceedings are brought do not have jurisdiction under Chapter II.[163]

---

[161] Art 71(1).
[162] For a discussion of Art 26, see section 4.4.
[163] See *The Nordglimt* [1988] QB 183; *The Deichland* [1990] 1 QB 361; *The Po* [1991] 2 Lloyd's Rep 206; *The Prinsengracht* [1993] 1 Lloyd's Rep 41. For further consideration of these cases, see section 8.2.

4

JURISDICTION *IN PERSONAM* UNDER THE BRUSSELS I REGULATION: INTRODUCTION

4.0.1 One of the key objectives of the Brussels I Regulation[1] is the harmonisation of jurisdictional bases in cases involving proceedings brought against defendants domiciled in the states concerned. Accordingly, although the application of the Brussels I Regulation is not restricted to proceedings in which the defendant is domiciled in one of the Member States, in many circumstances a defendant's domicile is 'the point on which the rules on jurisdiction hinge'[2] (section 4.1). The basic structure of Chapter II is to distinguish those bases of jurisdiction which apply regardless of the defendant's domicile from those which apply only to defendants who are domiciled in a Member State (section 4.2). As regards the service of documents abroad, the Brussels I Regulation is supplemented by the Civil Procedure Rules (section 4.3). Although the Regulation aims to simplify the recognition and enforcement of foreign judgments, this should not be at the cost of imposing procedural unfairness on the defendant (section 4.4).

4.1 DOMICILE UNDER THE BRUSSELS I REGULATION

The Domicile of Individuals

Introduction

4.1.1 Article 59 provides that, as regards natural persons, in order to determine whether a party is domiciled in a particular Member State, the court shall apply the law of that state.[3] So, whether someone is domiciled in the United Kingdom is a question of UK law. Under Article 2 a person domiciled in a Member State may be sued in the courts of the state in which he is domiciled. In the absence of a provision laying down a definition of domicile for the purposes of the Brussels I Regulation, the efficacy of this provision depends on the Member States sharing a broadly similar concept of domicile. Whereas in most of the Member States domicile means something akin to habitual residence, at common law domicile is a technical and artificial concept which approximates to a person's permanent home.

---

[1] Reg (EC) 44/2001, [2001] OJ L12/1.

[2] Jenard-Möller Report, [1990] OJ C189/65, para 13.

[3] The issue of whether 'domicile' should be given an autonomous meaning is raised by the European Commission in its 'Green Paper on the Review of Council Regulation (EC) No 44/2001 on jurisdiction and the recognition and enforcement of judgments in civil and commercial matters' (hereafter 'Commission Green Paper'), COM (2009) 175 final, p 10.

4.1.2 The application of the common law concept of domicile in the United Kingdom would seriously distort the operation of Chapter II; the English courts would be deprived of jurisdiction in cases where the defendant had made his home in England without establishing an intention to reside there permanently and jurisdiction would be conferred on the English courts in certain cases even though under the laws of nearly every other Member State the defendant would have been regarded as domiciled in a country other than England.[4] For this reason the implementing legislation in the United Kingdom includes a special definition of domicile for the purposes of the Brussels I Regulation. As regards natural persons, the definition of domicile is to be found in the Civil Jurisdiction and Judgments Order 2001.[5]

Domicile in the United Kingdom

4.1.3 The 2001 Order provides:

An individual is domiciled in the United Kingdom if and only if—

(a) he is resident in the United Kingdom; and
(b) the nature and circumstances of his residence indicate that he has a substantial connection with the United Kingdom.[6]

For the purposes of this rule, the word 'resident' must be given its ordinary meaning. In *Bank of Dubai Ltd v Abbas*[7] the Court of Appeal, drawing on earlier authorities decided in different contexts,[8] took the view that a person is to be regarded as resident in a part of the United Kingdom 'if that part is for him a settled or usual place of abode'.[9] As a settled or usual place of abode 'connotes some degree of permanence or continuity',[10] a person is not resident in England simply because he owns a home in England; there must be sufficient evidence that the person spends time in England. When domicile is being determined in this context, a 'numbers game' is inappropriate; what must be assessed is the nature and quality of the individual's visits to England.[11] Therefore, ownership of a £30 million property in England and an English football club did not indicate residence in England where the owner is not resident in the United Kingdom for tax purposes, enters the United Kingdom on a business visa and only spends intermittent and largely short-lived stays in England.[12]

4.1.4 The 2001 Order provides that where an individual has been resident in the United Kingdom for 'the last three months or more' it is to be presumed that that person has a substantial connection with the United Kingdom 'unless the contrary is proved'.[13] Of course, the 2001 Order does not stipulate that a person who has resided

---

[4] Schlosser Report, [1979] OJ C59/96, para 73(c).
[5] SI 2001/3929; as amended by SI 2005/617, SI 2007/1655 and SI 2009/871.
[6] Sched 1, para 9(2).
[7] [1997] ILPr 308. See also *High Tech International AG v Deripaska* [2007] EMLR 449; *Cherney v Deripaska* [2007] 2 All ER (Comm) 785; *OJSC Oil Company v Abramovich* [2008] EWHC 2613 (Comm).
[8] *Levene v Commissioners of Inland Revenue* [1928] AC 217.
[9] Saville LJ at [1997] ILPr 308, 311.
[10] Saville LJ in *Bank of Dubai Ltd v Abbas* [1997] ILPr 308, 311–12.
[11] *High Tech International AG v Deripaska* [2007] EMLR 449, 454 (at [24]).
[12] *OJSC Oil Company v Abramovich* [2008] EWHC 2613 (Comm). A Briggs, (2008) 79 *BYIL* 543.
[13] Sched 1, para 9(6).

in a particular country for less than three months is not to be regarded as having a substantial connection with that country. So, for example, an Italian student who travels to England intending to reside there for 12 months may be regarded as domiciled in England on his arrival.[14]

4.1.5   In certain circumstances it is not sufficient to know simply that a person is domiciled in the United Kingdom; some jurisdiction rules require the 'place' where a person is domiciled or the part of the United Kingdom in which a person is domiciled to be identified. As a general rule a person is domiciled in a particular part of the United Kingdom if and only if he is resident in that part and the nature and circumstances of his residence indicate that he has a substantial connection with that part.[15] A person who is resident in a part of the United Kingdom for the last three months or more is presumed to have a substantial connection with that part.[16] If an individual is domiciled in the United Kingdom but does not have a substantial connection with any part of the United Kingdom he is to be regarded as domiciled in the part of the United Kingdom where he is resident.[17] An individual is domiciled in a particular 'place' in the United Kingdom if he is domiciled in the part of the United Kingdom in which that place is situated and he is resident in that place.[18]

Domicile in Other States

4.1.6   If the application of the 2001 Order leads to the conclusion that a person is not domiciled in the United Kingdom, the method for ascertaining whether that person is domiciled in another Member State is to apply the law of that state. For instance, to determine whether a person is domiciled in Greece, Greek law must be applied.[19] If a person is not domiciled in the United Kingdom or in another Member State, it is not normally important to determine the particular non-Member State in which that person is domiciled.[20] Nevertheless, it is provided that a person is domiciled in a particular state (not being a Member State) if he is resident in that state and the nature and circumstances of his residence indicate that he has a substantial connection with that state.[21]

4.1.7   A person who is physically present within the Member States may be regarded as not domiciled in any of them. In such a case, the provisions of Chapter II are relevant only to the extent that they lay down rules which apply regardless of domicile.

The Domicile of Corporations[22]

4.1.8   The Brussels I Regulation lays down, in Article 60, a uniform rule which is independent from the laws of the Member States. Article 60(1) provides that for the

---

[14] See IK Mathers, 'The Brussels Convention of 1968: Its Implementation in the United Kingdom' (1983) 3 *YBEL* 49, 54.

[15] Civil Jurisdiction and Judgments Order 2001, sched 1, para 9(3).

[16] Civil Jurisdiction and Judgments Order 2001, sched 1, para 9(6).

[17] Civil Jurisdiction and Judgments Order 2001, sched 1, para 9(5).

[18] Civil Jurisdiction and Judgments Order 2001, sched 1, para 9(4).

[19] See *Haji-Ioannou v Frangos* [1999] 2 Lloyd's Rep 337.

[20] See, however, Brussels I Reg, Art 72.

[21] Civil Jurisdiction and Judgments Order 2001, sched 1, para 9(7).

[22] See, generally, MV Benedettelli, 'Conflicts of Jurisdiction and Conflicts of Law in Company Law Matters within the EU "Market for Corporate Models": Brussels I and Rome I after *Centros*' [2005] *EBLR* 55.

purposes of the Brussels I Regulation a company or other legal person or association of natural or legal persons[23] is domiciled at the place where it has (1) its statutory seat or (2) its central administration or (3) its principal place of business.[24] As the term 'statutory seat' has no legal significance in the United Kingdom, for the purposes of the law of the United Kingdom, 'statutory seat' means:

the registered office or, where there is no such office anywhere, the place of incorporation or, where there is no such place anywhere, the place under the law of which the formation took place.[25]

Although Article 60 envisages the possibility that a company's central administration and its principal place of business may be located at different places, it will often be the case that they overlap, especially in relation to small organisations.[26]

4.1.9 The effect of Article 60—which lays down alternative connecting factors— is that a corporation may be regarded as domiciled in England, notwithstanding the fact that it has effectively severed all meaningful links with England. In *Re Harrods (Buenos Aires) Ltd*,[27] for example, a company which had been incorporated in England in 1913 was regarded as domiciled in England even though its business was exclusively carried on in Argentina and its central management and control was exercised there.[28]

4.1.10 Whereas questions relating to the interpretation of the domicile provisions of the 2001 Order cannot be referred to the Court of Justice, the position is different with regard to Article 60. As Article 60 is a provision of EU law rather than domestic law, the Court of Justice has jurisdiction to interpret it and national courts should approach its interpretation from a European rather than a national perspective. Until the Court of Justice provides authoritative guidance on the meaning of the connecting factors employed by Article 60, the English courts will follow the approach adopted under the Brussels and Lugano Conventions.[29] When seeking to identify a company's administrative centre, the English courts have taken the view, first, that the most important factors are where the directors hold meetings and where major policy issues are decided[30] and, secondly, that it is doubtful whether a company can be regarded as having its central management and control in more than one place at the same time;[31] a company's principal place of business is its 'chief' or 'most important' place of

---

[23] Such as a limited liability partnership registered under the Limited Liability Partnerships Act 2000.

[24] There are special provisions in the Civil Jurisdiction and Judgments Order 2001 for determining the seat of companies for the purposes of (i) Art 22(2) of the Brussels I Regulation and (ii) the provisions relating to insurance, consumer and employment contracts: Civil Jurisdiction and Judgments Order 2001, sched 1, paras 10–11.

[25] Art 60(2). This rule also applies to Ireland.

[26] *King v Crown Energy Trading AG* [2003] ILPr 489.

[27] [1992] Ch 72.

[28] For discussion of some of the problems to which this case gave rise, see section 9.5.

[29] *King v Crown Energy Trading AG* [2003] ILPr 489.

[30] *The Rewia* [1991] 1 Lloyd's Rep 69, 74 (reversed on other grounds: [1991] 2 Lloyd's Rep 325); *Latchin (t/a Dinka Latchin Associates) v General Mediterranean Holdings SA* [2002] CLC 330. Cf *Alberta Inc v Katanga Mining Ltd* [2009] ILPr 175.

[31] See Andrew Smith J in *Latchin (t/a Dinka Latchin Associates) v General Mediterranean Holdings SA* [2002] CLC 330, 338 (at [34]). See, however, Lord Radcliffe in *Unit Construction Co Ltd v Bullock* [1940] AC 351, 366 (albeit in a somewhat different context).

business, rather than its 'main' place of business.[32] For example, the place where the day-to-day activities of the company are carried out may not be the principal place of business if those activities are subject to the control of senior management located elsewhere.[33] Domicile is also to be ascertained at the date on which proceedings were issued.[34] When the Court of Justice is required (under Article 267 of the Treaty on the Functioning of the European Union (TFEU)) to interpret Article 60, it seems likely that that decisions made in the context of the right of establishment of companies within the European Union will be significant as the three alternative connecting factors listed in Article 60(1) are also relevant in the context of Article 54 TFEU.[35]

Multiple Domiciles

4.1.11   It is implicit within the Brussels I Regulation that it is possible for a person to be domiciled in more than one Member State.[36] Although the question has not been considered by the Court of Justice, the United Kingdom courts have accepted that both an individual and a company may have more than one domicile. In *Daniel v Foster*[37] it was decided that the defendant was domiciled in Scotland for the purposes of the Civil Jurisdiction and Judgments Act 1982 even though his main home was in England. Similarly, in *Grupo Torras SA v Sheikh Fahad Mohammed al Sabah*[38] it was held that the defendant, who divided most of his time between the Bahamas and England, was resident in both countries and that, since the defendant had a substantial connection with England, he was domiciled in England for the purposes of Article 2. The approach adopted by the courts in these cases is equally applicable to cases involving two Member States. Given that a person may have more than one residence and that domicile for the purposes of the Brussels I Regulation is based on a residential test, it follows that a person may have more than one domicile for the purposes of the Regulation. The common law doctrine of domicile—under which a person can have only one domicile at any one time—is not relevant in this context.

4.1.12   It equally possible for a corporation to have more than one domicile. In *The Deichland*[39] the Court of Appeal held that a company which was incorporated in Panama, but whose central management and control was exercised in Germany, was domiciled in Germany. Although the courts have not expressly decided that a

[32] *The Rewia* [1991] 2 Lloyd's Rep 325.
[33] *Ministry of Defence and Support of the Armed Forces v Faz Aviation Ltd (Formerly FN Aviation Ltd)* [2007] ILPr 538, 546 (at [29]).
[34] *Canada Trust Co v Stolzenberg (No 2)* [2002] 1 AC 1; *Ministry of Defence and Support of the Armed Forces v Faz Aviation Ltd (Formerly FN Aviation Ltd)* [2007] ILPr 538.
[35] Previously Art 48 (ex Art 58) of the TEC. See European Commission, *Proposal for a Council Regulation (EC) on jurisdiction and the recognition and enforcement of judgments in civil and commercial matters* (hereafter "*Proposal*"), COM (1999) 348 final, p 24. Important decisions on companies and their right to freedom of establishment include: Case C–212/97 *Centros Ltd v Erhvervs-og Selskabsstyrelsen* [1999] ECR I–1459; Case C–208/00 *Überseering BV v Nordic Construction Company Baumanagement GmbH (NCC)* [2002] ECR I–9919; Case C–210/06 *Cartesio Oktató és Szolgáltató bt* [2009] Ch 354 (J Borg-Barthet, (2009) 58 *ICLQ* 1020).
[36] See Schlosser Report, [1979] OJ C59/96–7, para 75(e).
[37] 1989 SLT 90 (Sheriff Court, Dumbarton).
[38] [1995] 1 Lloyd's Rep 374.
[39] [1990] 1 QB 361. See also *Alberta Inc v Katanga Mining Ltd* [2009] ILPr 175, 188–9 (at [23]–[24]).

company can be domiciled in more than one Member State, it is perfectly possible for a corporation to satisfy the test laid down by Article 60 in relation to more than one Member State[40]—for example, where its central administration is in France and its statutory seat is in Germany. Moreover, there is no fundamental objection to two Member States having jurisdiction as a consequence of a corporation being domiciled in more than one Member State.[41]

4.2 THE BASIC STRUCTURE OF THE JURISDICTION RULES

Bases of Jurisdiction Applicable to Defendants Domiciled in a Member State: Articles 2 and 3

4.2.1   As regards proceedings which fall within the scope of Chapter I—by virtue of the fact that the proceedings concern civil and commercial matters and do not fall within the scope of any of the exceptions—a person who is domiciled in a Member State may generally be sued in the courts of a Member State only in accordance with the rules laid down in Chapter II. Under Article 2, persons domiciled in a Member State shall, whatever their nationality, be sued in the courts of that state. This provision, which enshrines the principle *actor forum sequitur rei* (the claimant must sue the defendant in the jurisdiction to which the defendant is subject), is in many respects the foundation of Chapter II as it applies to defendants domiciled in a Member State.

4.2.2   Notwithstanding its use of the word 'shall', Article 2 must be read in conjunction with Article 3 which provides that persons domiciled in a Member State may be sued in the courts of another Member State by virtue of the other jurisdiction rules set out in Chapter II. The effect of Article 3 is twofold: first, Article 2 is subordinate to the jurisdiction rules which override the domicile rule;[42] secondly, a claimant may have the option of proceeding against a person who is domiciled in a Member State either in the courts of the state in which the defendant is domiciled under Article 2 or in the courts of another Member State designated by, for example, Article 5 or Article 6.[43]

4.2.3   Various exorbitant bases of jurisdiction which cannot be applied against defendants who are domiciled in a Member State are listed.[44] This list includes the English rule which enables jurisdiction to be founded on the claim form instituting the proceedings having been served on the defendant during his temporary presence in England.[45] Strictly speaking, the specific outlawing of exorbitant bases of jurisdiction adds nothing as Article 3 makes the point that the courts of Member States may assume jurisdiction over defendants who are domiciled in a Member State only according to the rules set out in Chapter II.

---

[40] See Neill LJ at [1990] 1 QB 361, 375.
[41] See Stuart-Smith LJ at [1990] 1 QB 361, 379.
[42] In particular, Brussels I Reg, Arts 22–4.
[43] See ch 5.
[44] Brussels I Reg, Art 3(2) and Annex I.
[45] See, eg, *Maharanee of Baroda v Wildenstein* [1972] 2 QB 283.

4.2.4 It is important to note the operation of Article 71 of the Brussels I Regulation,[46] which provides that the Regulation shall not affect any conventions to which the Member States are or will be parties and which, in relation to particular matters, govern jurisdiction or the recognition or enforcement of judgments. The courts of a Member State which is a party to a convention on a particular matter may assume jurisdiction in accordance with that convention, even where the defendant is domiciled in another Member State which is not a party to that convention.[47]

Bases of Jurisdiction Applicable to Persons who are not Domiciled in a Member State: Article 4

4.2.5 The first paragraph of Article 4 involves two elements. First, it provides that, even in a case which falls within the scope of Article 1, if a defendant is not domiciled in a Member State, the jurisdiction of the courts of each Member State shall be determined by the law of that state. This basic rule presents few problems; if, for example, the defendant is a New York company, the English court is competent if it has jurisdiction under its traditional rules. Secondly, by way of exception, there are some provisions which apply to defendants regardless of their domicile.

4.2.6 The wording of the provision makes it clear that the basic rule in Article 4 is subject to the provisions of Article 22 concerning exclusive jurisdiction, which apply regardless of domicile. The text of Article 4 of the Brussels I Regulation also expressly states that the basic rule is subject to Article 23, the provision dealing with jurisdiction agreements.

4.2.7 Whether any other rules in Chapter II laying down jurisdictional bases should be applied in cases involving defendants who are not domiciled in a Member State is less certain. The main question relates to Article 24, the provision dealing with submission. Since the revised version of Article 4 of the Brussels I Regulation explicitly refers only to Article 22 (exclusive jurisdiction) and Article 23 (jurisdiction agreements), it may be questioned whether any other provision of Chapter II is applicable in cases where the defendant is not domiciled in a Member State.[48]

4.2.8 The second paragraph of Article 4 provides that, as regards a defendant who is not domiciled in a Member State, any person domiciled in a Member State may, whatever his nationality, avail himself in that state of the rules of jurisdiction there in force, and in particular those rules laying down exorbitant bases of jurisdiction (which are outlawed[49] in cases where the defendant is domiciled in a Member State), in the same way as the nationals of that state. So, a claimant who is domiciled in England may bring proceedings in France against a defendant who is not domiciled in a Member State under Article 14 of the French civil code, even though the jurisdiction provisions of the civil code were originally enacted solely for the benefit of French nationals. Article 4(2) makes no difference to practice in England, since under

---

[46] Lugano Convention, Art 67.

[47] Brussels I Reg, Art 71(2)(a). See sections 3.4 and 8.2.

[48] See *Big, Bättre Inköp I Grupp Aktiebolag I Likvidation v Isle of Man Assurance Limited* [2008] ILPr 221 (Supreme Court, Sweden). For further discussion, see section 5.2.

[49] By Brussels I Reg, Art 3(2) and Annex I.

English law the bases of jurisdiction set out in CPR PD 6B para 3.1[50] are available to claimants regardless of nationality.

Lis Pendens and Related Actions

4.2.9   The jurisdiction rules contained in Chapter II may be divided into two groups: first, the provisions which outline the circumstances in which the courts of a Member State may, in principle, assume jurisdiction in relation to proceedings brought against a particular defendant (whether or not domiciled in a Member State); secondly, the provisions which deprive the courts of a Member State of the jurisdiction which they would otherwise have had under the first group of provisions. This second category of rules seeks to deal with the problems posed by concurrent proceedings in the courts of two or more Member States.[51] These rules apply regardless of the domicile of the parties.[52]

The Standard of Proof

4.2.10   When a claimant invokes the jurisdiction of the courts of a Member State under Chapter II, what is the standard of proof which the claimant must satisfy? It is important to distinguish two different issues: first, the standard of proof which the claimant must establish as regards the merits of the dispute; secondly, the standard of proof as regards the jurisdiction of the court.

The Merits of the Dispute

4.2.11   One possibility is that the strength of the claim is totally irrelevant for the purposes of jurisdiction under the Brussels I Regulation.[53] Moreover, there is nothing in the reports which accompanied the Brussels and Lugano Conventions to suggest that for jurisdiction to be founded on Chapter II the claim on the merits must satisfy any particular standard of proof. In the context of CPR 6.36, one of the conditions for permission to serve a claim form out of the jurisdiction is that, as regards the merits, there is a serious question to be tried.[54] It would be surprising if a stricter test were applicable in cases in which service of process is to be effected under CPR 6.33 (which applies to cases covered by the Brussels I Regulation),[55] rather than under CPR 6.36. Accordingly, any suggestion that, in cases falling within the scope of the Brussels I Regulation, the claimant should have a good arguable case on the merits[56] is

---

[50] See section 7.3.
[51] Brussels I Reg, Arts 27–30.
[52] See section 9.1.
[53] C Kohler, 'Practical Experience of the Brussels Jurisdiction and Judgments Convention in the Six Original Contracting States' (1985) 34 *ICLQ* 563, 570–1. See also *Barclay v Sweeney* [1999] ILPr 288 (Court of Appeal, Paris).
[54] *Seaconsar Far East Ltd v Bank Markazi Jomhouri Islami Iran* [1994] 1 AC 438.
[55] See section 4.3.
[56] See, eg, *Mölnlycke AB v Procter & Gamble Ltd* [1992] 1 WLR 1112.

to be regarded as unsound in principle. The appropriate test should be no higher than that there is a serious issue to be tried.[57] This does not mean, however, that the court should ignore entirely the strength of the claim. It would, for example, be absurd if a court were unable to strike out proceedings which are vexatious or frivolous or otherwise an abuse of the process of the court.[58] A claim which is bound to fail does not raise 'a serious issue to be tried' and may be struck out as an abuse of process.[59]

Questions of Jurisdiction

4.2.12 The proper approach to cases involving questions of jurisdiction is outlined by the Schlosser Report, which states:

[A] court may assume jurisdiction only if it is completely satisfied of all the facts on which such jurisdiction is based; if it is not so satisfied it can and must request the parties to provide the necessary evidence, in default of which the action will be dismissed as inadmissible. In such circumstances the lack of jurisdiction would be declared by the court of its own motion, and not as a result of a challenge by one of the parties. Whether a court is itself obliged to investigate the facts relevant to jurisdiction, or whether it can, or must, place the burden of proof in this respect on the party interested in the jurisdiction of the court concerned, is determined solely by national law.[60]

4.2.13 In *Effer SpA v Kantner*[61] the plaintiff commenced proceedings for breach of contract in Germany on the basis that Germany was 'the place of performance of the obligation in question' for the purposes of Article 5(1). The defendant contested the jurisdiction of the court on the ground that no contract had been concluded between the parties. The nature of the problem facing the court in this type of case is obvious: a claimant should not be allowed to invoke the jurisdiction of the court simply by alleging the existence of a contract; by the same token, the defendant should not be allowed to circumvent the relevant jurisdictional provisions simply by denying a contract's existence. In the *Effer* case, the Court of Justice stated that, where the court's jurisdiction is invoked under Article 5(1):

the court called upon to decide a dispute arising out of a contract may examine, of its own motion even, the essential preconditions for its jurisdiction, having regard to conclusive and relevant evidence adduced by the party concerned, establishing the existence or the inexistence of the contract.[62]

Similarly, it has been held that a court which has jurisdiction in respect of proceedings involving tenancies of immovable property[63] is not deprived of jurisdiction where the dispute is concerned with the existence of the lease[64] and that, where a contract includes

---

[57] See *New England Reinsurance Corporation v Messoghios Insurance Co SA* [1992] 2 Lloyd's Rep 251.
[58] See *Lough Neagh Exploration Ltd v Morrice* [1999] NI 258 (Court of Appeal, Northern Ireland).
[59] *Newtherapeutics Ltd v Katz* [1991] Ch 226.
[60] [1979] OJ C59/82, para 22.
[61] Case 38/81 [1982] ECR 825.
[62] [1982] ECR 825, para 7. See *Karlung v Svensk Vägguide Comertex AB* [1999] ILPr 298 (Supreme Court, Norway).
[63] See Brussels I Reg, Art 22(1).
[64] Case 73/77 *Sanders v Van der Putte* [1977] ECR 2383.

a jurisdiction clause,[65] the chosen court has jurisdiction notwithstanding the fact that the proceedings seek to establish that the contract containing the clause is void.[66]

4.2.14   Any suggestion that the decision in *Effer SpA v Kantner* requires the claimant to satisfy the court at the interlocutory stage that the jurisdictional basis is satisfied on the balance of probabilities goes too far.[67] In *Seaconsar Far East Ltd v Bank Markazi Jomhouri Islami Iran*,[68] the House of Lords held that one of the conditions for permission to serve process out of the jurisdiction under what is now CPR 6.36 is that the claimant should have a good arguable case that the claim falls within the jurisdiction rule relied upon. It is clear from this decision that the requirement of a good arguable case imposes a stricter standard of proof than the requirement that there should be a serious question to be tried. Some of the issues under Chapter II are very similar to those which are relevant in the context of applications under CPR 6.36: for example, under Article 5(1) and CPR PD 6B para 3.1(6) the question may arise whether a contract was concluded between the parties; under Article 23 and CPR PD 6B para 3.1(6)(d) the existence of an agreement on jurisdiction may be disputed; under Article 5(3) and CPR PD 6B para 3.1(9) the parties may disagree on where the damage was sustained. There are good reasons of both principle and policy for the application of the same test, whether the claim is under the traditional rules (CPR 6.36) or the Brussels I Regulation (CPR 6.33).[69]

4.2.15   In *Canada Trust Co v Stolzenberg (No 2)*[70] the House of Lords confirmed that the English court may assume jurisdiction on the basis of a good arguable case.[71] So, in a situation where the claimant invokes the jurisdiction of the English court under Article 5(1) the court must be satisfied that the claimant has a good arguable case not only that the proceedings concern matters relating to a contract, but also that England is the place of performance of the obligation in question.[72] Similarly, if the court's jurisdiction is invoked under Article 2, the claimant must satisfy the court that there is a good arguable case that the defendant is domiciled in England.[73] If the

---

[65]   See Brussels I Reg, Art 23.

[66]   Case C–269/95 *Benincasa v Dentalkit Srl* [1997] ECR–I 3767.

[67]   Nicholls LJ in *Tesam Distribution Ltd v Schuh Mode Team GmbH* [1990] ILPr 149, 158.

[68]   [1994] 1 AC 438.

[69]   See Waller LJ in *Canada Trust Co v Stolzenberg (No 2)* [1998] 1 WLR 547, 553–9.

[70]   [2002] 1 AC 1. A Briggs, (2000) 71 *BYIL* 446; LC Ho, 'Pragmatism Rules' (2001) 50 *ICLQ* 632.

[71]   For earlier cases in which the High Court and Court of Appeal had applied this test see, eg: *Tesam Distribution Ltd v Schuh Mode Team GmbH* [1990] ILPr 149; *Medway Packaging Ltd v Meurer Maschinen GmbH* [1990] 2 Lloyd's Rep 112; *The Rewia* [1991] 2 Lloyd's Rep 325; *Mercury Publicity Ltd v Wolfgang Loerke GmbH* [1993] ILPr 142; *New England Reinsurance Corporation v Messoghios Insurance Co SA* [1992] 2 Lloyd's Rep 251; *Rank Film Distributors Ltd v Lanterna Editrice Srl* [1992] ILPr 58; *Mölnlycke AB v Procter & Gamble Ltd* [1992] 1 WLR 1112; *Agrafax Public Relations Ltd v United Scottish Society Incorporated* [1995] ILPr 753; *Boss Group Ltd v Boss France SA* [1997] 1 WLR 351; *Bank of Dubai Ltd v Abbas* [1997] ILPr 308; *Glencore International AG v Metro Trading International Inc* [1999] 2 Lloyd's Rep 632.

[72]   See *Deutsche Ruckversicherung AG v La Fondiara Assicurazioni SpA* [2001] 2 Lloyd's Rep 621.

[73]   Cases in which the courts have applied the test laid down in *Canada Trust Co v Stolzenberg (No 2)* include: *Deutsche Ruckversicherung AG v La Fondiara Assicurazioni SpA* [2001] 2 Lloyd's Rep 621; *Latchin (tla Dinka Latchin Associates) v General Mediterranean Holdings SA* [2002] CLC 330; *SSQ Europe SA v Johann & Backes OHG* [2002] 1 Lloyd's Rep 465; *Carnoustie Universal SA v International Transport Workers' Federation* [2002] 2 All ER (Comm) 657; *Evialis SA v SIAT* [2003] 2 Lloyd's Rep 377; *King v Crown Energy Trading AG* [2003] ILPr 489; *Provimi Ltd v Roche Products Ltd* [2003] 2 All ER (Comm) 683; *Ministry of Defence and Support of the Armed Forces for Iran v Faz Aviation Ltd (Formerly FN Aviation Ltd)* [2007] ILPr 538; *Alberta Inc v Katanga Mining Ltd* [2009] ILPr 175.

court's jurisdiction is challenged (for example, on the basis that parties agreed to the exclusive jurisdiction of another Member State[74] or that there are parallel proceedings in another Member State),[75] the burden remains on the claimant to satisfy the court that it is right for the English court to exercise jurisdiction. So, the claimant must have a good arguable case that the provisions which could have the effect of depriving the English court of jurisdiction are inapplicable[76] (for example, because the claim in question does not fall within the scope of the jurisdiction clause in the parties' contract).[77]

4.3 SERVICE ABROAD IN CASES FALLING WITHIN THE SCOPE OF THE BRUSSELS I REGULATION

4.3.1   The Civil Procedure Rules determine the circumstances in which a defendant who is not present within the jurisdiction may be served with a claim form out of the jurisdiction.[78] The general rule is that a defendant may be served abroad only with the court's permission.[79] However, CPR 6.33(2) creates a considerable exception in cases falling within the scope of Chapter II:

The claimant may serve the claim form on a defendant out of the United Kingdom where each claim made against the defendant to be served and included in the claim form is a claim which the court has power to determine under the Judgments Regulation[80] and—

(a) no proceedings between the parties concerning the same claim are pending in the courts of any other part of the United Kingdom or any other Member State; and

(b) (i) the defendant is domiciled in the United Kingdom or in any Member State;

　(ii) the proceedings are within article 22 of the Judgments Regulation; or

　(iii) the defendant is a party to an agreement conferring jurisdiction, within article 23 of the Judgments Regulation.

4.3.2   These rules are generally simple to apply. If the English court has jurisdiction under Chapter II the defendant may be served out of the jurisdiction without the court's permission.[81] However, the fact that the case falls within CPR 6.33 does not prevent the

---

[74]   Brussels I Reg, Art 23. See section 5.3.

[75]   Brussels I Reg, Art 27. See section 9.1.

[76]   *Carnoustie Universal SA v International Transport Workers' Federation* [2002] 2 All ER (Comm) 657, 673 (at [46]–[47]). Compare *Knauf UK GmbH v British Gypsum Ltd* [2001] 2 All ER (Comm) 332; *The Bank of Tokyo-Mitsubishi Ltd v Baskan Gida Sanayi Ve Pazarlama* [2004] ILPr 427.

[77]   *Provimi Ltd v Roche Products Ltd* [2003] 2 All ER (Comm) 683.

[78]   For methods of service in cases falling within the Brussels I Regulation where service is to be effected in another Member State, see Reg (EC) 1393/2007 (the 'Service Regulation'), [2007] OJ L324/79, which repeals Reg (EC) No 1348/2000, [2000] OJ L160/37. For discussion of the Convention on which the Service Regulation is based see W Kennett, 'Service of documents in Europe' (1998) 17 *CJQ* 284. See also the Hague Service Convention of 1965: http://www.hcch.net. The parties to this Convention include the United Kingdom, Denmark, Norway and Switzerland. For consideration of when the court will permit service by an alternative method in a case within the scope of the Brussels I Regulation, see *Knauf UK GmbH v British Gypsum Ltd* [2002] 1 WLR 907.

[79]   See section 7.3.

[80]   Ie, the Brussels I Regulation.

[81]   Although this principle is clear, the courts have not always applied it correctly. See, eg, *Newtherapeutics Ltd v Katz* [1991] Ch 226.

claimant from serving the relevant document on the defendant within the jurisdiction if that is possible (for example, because the defendant is physically present in England at the time of service).[82] In a case falling within CPR 6.33, the court is not allowed to give permission for service of process out of the jurisdiction.[83] However, if, in a case falling within the Brussels I Regulation, service is effected with permission under CPR 6.36, rather than under CPR 6.33, this is an irregularity that can be cured.[84] Where a claim form includes a number of claims against a defendant, some of which fall within the court's jurisdiction under the Brussels I Regulation and some of which do not, the claimant needs the court's permission to serve the claim form out of the jurisdiction. If, however, the claims which are not within the court's jurisdiction under Chapter II are struck out, there is no obstacle to service of the claim form out of the jurisdiction without permission.[85]

4.4 PROCEDURAL SAFEGUARDS

4.4.1   The first two paragraphs of Article 26 of the Brussels I Regulation provide:

1. Where a defendant domiciled in one Member State is sued in a court of another Member State and does not enter an appearance, the court shall declare of its own motion that it has no jurisdiction unless its jurisdiction is derived from the provisions of this Regulation.
2. The court shall stay the proceedings so long as it is not shown that the defendant has been able to receive the document instituting the proceedings or an equivalent document in sufficient time to enable him to arrange for his defence, or that all necessary steps have been taken to this end.

It is provided, however, that paragraph 2 is replaced by Article 19 of the Service Regulation[86] if the document instituting the proceedings was transmitted from one Member State to another pursuant to the Service Regulation.[87] Where, however, the Service Regulation is not applicable and the document instituting the proceedings was transmitted pursuant to the Hague Service Convention of 1965, Article 26(2) of the Brussels I Regulation is replaced by Article 15 of the Hague Service Convention.[88]

4.4.2   Article 26 is among the most important provisions of the Brussels I Regulation.[89] It applies where a defendant, who is domiciled in a Member State, does not enter an appearance. It does not, however, provide any protection for a defendant who is not domiciled in a Member State. Where a defendant, who is domiciled in a Member State,

---

[82] *Union Bank of Finland Ltd v Lelakis* [1997] 1 WLR 590.
[83] *Abdullah Ali Almunajem Sons Co v Recourse Shipping Co Ltd* [1995] ILPr 28; *The Bank of Tokyo-Mitsubishi Ltd v Baskan Gida Sanayi Ve Pazarlama AS* [2004] ILPr 427.
[84] *Waterford Wedgwood plc v David Nagli Ltd* [1999] ILPr 9.
[85] *Ocarina Marine Ltd v Marcard Stein & Co* [1994] 2 Lloyd's Rep 524.
[86] The reference in the Brussels I Regulation to Reg (EC) 1348/2000, [2000] OJ L160/37, must be understood to be a reference to Reg (EC) 1393/2007, [2007] OJ L324/79. Art 19(2) of both Regulations is in the same terms.
[87] Brussels I Reg, Art 26(3).
[88] Brussels I Reg, Art 26(4).
[89] Jenard Report, [1979] OJ C59/39.

does not enter an appearance, the court must of its own motion examine whether it has jurisdiction. If the court does not have jurisdiction under Chapter II (on the basis either of direct jurisdiction rules set out in Chapter II or of jurisdictional rules contained in a specialised convention, the effect of which is preserved by Article 71 of the Brussels I Regulation),[90] it must decline jurisdiction.[91] It is not sufficient for the court to accept the submissions of the claimant as regards jurisdiction; the court must itself ensure that the claimant proves that it has international jurisdiction.[92] These provisions introduced a fundamental change in England, since traditionally English courts are able to reach a decision only on the basis of submissions of fact or law made by the parties.[93] It does not, however, follow that the court must, of its own motion, investigate the facts relevant to deciding the question of jurisdiction. The only essential factor is that the uncontested assertions by the parties should not bind the court. As a result of Article 26 of the Brussels I Regulation, a court of a Member State may exercise jurisdiction only if it is completely satisfied of all the facts on which such jurisdiction is based; if it is not so satisfied it can and must request the parties to provide the necessary evidence, in default of which the claim will be dismissed as inadmissible.[94]

4.4.3 Article 26 is designed to ensure that a default judgment cannot be given against a defendant who is domiciled in a Member State unless appropriate steps to notify the defendant of the proceedings have been taken. Where Article 26(2) applies, it is not necessary that the defendant was actually notified of the proceedings in sufficient time:

The defendant must be responsible for any delay caused by his own negligence or by that of his relations or servants. The critical time is thus the time at which service was properly effected, and not the time at which the defendant received actual knowledge of the institution of proceedings.[95]

The court may give judgment in default:

even if no affidavit can be produced to confirm service on the defendant of the document instituting proceedings, provided it is shown that all the necessary approaches have been made to the competent authorities of the State in which the defendant is domiciled in order to reach him in sufficient time. Where necessary, it must also be shown that 'all investigations required by good conscience and good faith have been undertaken to discover the defendant'.[96]

4.4.4 In those cases where Article 26(3) of the Brussels I Regulation applies, because service has been effected pursuant to the Service Regulation, Article 19 of the Service Regulation provides considerable protection for the defendant. The effect of Article 19 of the Service Regulation is that where the defendant fails to enter an appearance, judgment shall not be given unless two conditions are satisfied. First, it must be estab-

---

[90] See section 3.4.
[91] Case C–148/03 *Nürnberger Allgemeine AG v Portbridge Transport International BV* [2004] ECR I–10327. See also *The Café Shop v Belbachir* [2006] ILPr 794 (Court of Cassation, France); *Jacob v Houssin* [2006] ILPr 730 (Court of Cassation, France).
[92] Jenard Report, [1979] OJ C59/39.
[93] Schlosser Report, [1979] OJ C59/81, para 22.
[94] Schlosser Report, [1979] OJ C59/82, para 22.
[95] Jenard Report, [1979] OJ C59/40.
[96] *Ibid.*

lished either that the originating process was served in accordance with the internal law of the country in question or that it was actually delivered to the defendant or his residence by a method provided for by the Service Regulation. Secondly, it must be established that the service or the delivery was effected in sufficient time to enable the defendant to defend. In a case falling within Article 26(4) of the Brussels I Regulation the procedural safeguard is provided by Article 15 of the Hague Service Convention. The effect of Article 15 of the Hague Service Convention is, in substance, the same as that produced by Article 19 of the Service Regulation, which is derived from it.

5

BASES OF JURISDICTION *IN PERSONAM* UNDER THE BRUSSELS I REGULATION

5.0.1 The direct jurisdiction rules of the Brussels I Regulation[1] are to be found in Chapter II. Chapter II contains a patchwork of rules whereby jurisdiction is conferred on the courts of the Member States. Within the bases of jurisdiction established by Chapter II, some are not dependent on where the defendant is domiciled; others apply only to defendants who are domiciled in a Member State. Subject to a small number of exceptions, nothing turns on whether or not the claimant is domiciled in a Member State.[2] There are four general bases of jurisdiction which apply both to defendants who are not domiciled in a Member State as well as to defendants who are so domiciled (sections 5.1 to 5.4). The remaining general bases of jurisdiction apply only in relation to defendants who are domiciled in a Member State: the general principle laid down in Article 2 is that a defendant who is domiciled in a Member State shall be sued in the courts of that state (section 5.5); Articles 5 and 6, however, define circumstances in which a defendant who is domiciled in a Member State may be sued in the courts of another Member State (sections 5.6 and 5.7); the Brussels I Regulation also includes provisions which allocate jurisdiction with regard to proceedings relating to insurance, consumer contracts and employment contracts (section 5.8). As regards a defendant who is not domiciled in a Member State, if the provisions of Chapter II do not allocate jurisdiction, Article 4 provides that the jurisdiction of the courts of each Member State shall be determined by the law of that state.[3]

5.0.2 It is important to note that the identification of a basis on which the English court may exercise jurisdiction is only the first stage of a two-stage process. The second stage involves consideration of provisions of the Brussels I Regulation (and, where appropriate, common law principles), the application of which may lead the English court to decline jurisdiction or to grant a stay of the proceedings.[4]

5.1 EXCLUSIVE JURISDICTION

5.1.1 The jurisdiction rules set out in Article 22 of the Brussels I Regulation are the predominant provisions of Chapter II. These jurisdiction rules are mandatory and exclusive; they may not be departed from either by an agreement purporting to confer jurisdiction on the courts of another Member State or by submission to the jurisdiction.[5]

---

[1] Reg (EC) 44/2001, [2001] OJ L12/1.
[2] Case C–412/98 *Group Josi Reinsurance Company SA v Universal General Insurance Company* [2000] ECR I–5925, paras 47 and 53.
[3] The traditional English bases of jurisdiction *in personam* are discussed in ch 7.
[4] The second stage is considered in ch 9.
[5] Jenard Report, [1979] OJ C59/34.

The matters referred to in these provisions are normally the subject of exclusive jurisdiction only if they constitute the principal subject-matter of the proceedings.[6] Where, however, litigation involves two related claims, if the principal claim falls within the scope of Article 22 of the Brussels I Regulation, it is reasonable to suppose that the court which has exclusive jurisdiction over the principal claim by virtue of Article 22 should also have jurisdiction over the other claim.[7] However, the Court of Justice has expressed the view that the exclusive jurisdiction provision 'must not be given a wider interpretation than is required by its objective'.[8]

5.1.2   The five bases of exclusive jurisdiction concern matters which are thought to be unsuited to adjudication by a foreign court: (1) certain proceedings relating to immovable property; (2) certain proceedings concerning the formation and dissolution of companies and the decisions of their organs; (3) certain proceedings concerning entries in public registers; (4) certain proceedings concerning intellectual property; (5) proceedings concerning the enforcement of judgments. Article 22 of the Brussels I Regulation applies in cases where it confers exclusive jurisdiction on the courts of the United Kingdom (or another Member State). Rather surprisingly, and almost certainly incorrectly, in *Choudhary v Bhattar*[9] the Court of Appeal decided that Article 22 does not apply to proceedings brought against persons who are not domiciled in a Member State—despite the clear wording that Article 22 applies 'regardless of domicile'.

Paragraph (1)

Preliminary Remarks

5.1.3   Article 22(1) of the Brussels I Regulation provides that the following courts shall have exclusive jurisdiction regardless of domicile:

in proceedings which have as their object rights *in rem* in immovable property or tenancies of immovable property, the courts of the Member State in which the property is situated.

This general principle is qualified by a second sentence which confers 'alternative' exclusive jurisdiction in certain cases involving short-term lettings:

However, in proceedings which have as their object tenancies of immovable property concluded for temporary private use for a maximum period of six consecutive months, the courts of the Member State in which the defendant is domiciled shall also have jurisdiction, provided that the tenant is a natural person and that the landlord and the tenant are domiciled in the same Member State.

5.1.4   In relation to disputes concerning immovable property, a number of reasons justify the allocation of exclusive jurisdiction to the courts of the country in which the

---

   [6]   Jenard Report, [1979] OJ C59/34.
   [7]   *Newtherapeutics Ltd v Katz* [1991] Ch 226. Some support for this analysis is to be found in the decision of the Court of Justice in Case 266/85 *Shenavai v Kreischer* [1987] ECR 239. See para 5.6.37 *ff*.
   [8]   Case C–115/88 *Reichert v Dresdner Bank* [1990] ECR I–27, para 9. See also Case 73/77 *Sanders v Van der Putte* [1977] ECR 2383, para 18.
   [9]   [2010] 2 All ER 1031. Cf Case C–281/02 *Owusu v Jackson* [2005] ECR I–1383, para 28.

property is situated.[10] First, proceedings concerning immovable property frequently entail a whole series of procedural acts which have to be carried out on the spot. There may be enquiries, verifications or surveys which, by definition, can only be carried out at the place where the property is situated. Secondly, local customs familiar only to the court of the particular place may be relevant. Thirdly, disputes relating to immovable property may concern entries in land registers at the place where the property is situated. In *Reichert v Dresdner Bank* the Court of Justice indicated that:

the essential reason for conferring exclusive jurisdiction on the courts of the … State in which the property is situated is that the courts of the *locus rei sitae* are the best placed, for reasons of proximity, to ascertain the facts satisfactorily and to apply the rules and practices which are generally those of the State in which the property is situated.[11]

Paragraph (1), First Sentence: Rights in Rem

GENERAL PRINCIPLES

5.1.5 A fundamental question concerning the operation of this ground of exclusive jurisdiction is whether the words 'rights *in rem*' are to be interpreted as an autonomous concept or by reference to the law of the *situs*. The Schlosser Report expressed a clear preference for the latter approach:

If an action relating to immovable property is brought in a particular State and the question whether the action is concerned with a right *in rem* …, the answer can hardly be derived from any law other than that of the *situs*.[12]

However, in *Reichert v Dresdner Bank*[13] the Court of Justice decided that the phrase 'proceedings which have as their object rights *in rem* in immovable property' must be given an independent definition in Community law[14] and ruled that paragraph (1) covers only proceedings which:

seek to determine the extent, content, ownership or possession of immovable property or the existence of other rights *in rem* therein and to provide the holders of those rights with the protection of the powers which attach to their interest.[15]

5.1.6 Following this approach it was held in *Re Hayward*[16] that an application in English proceedings by a trustee in bankruptcy for an order that he was entitled to a half-share of a villa in Minorca fell within the exclusive jurisdiction of the Spanish

---

[10] See the opinion of Advocate General Mischo in Case C–115/88 *Reichert v Dresdner Bank* [1990] ECR I–27, para 23.

[11] Case C–115/88 [1990] ECR I–27, para 10.

[12] [1979] OJ C59/121, para 168(c).

[13] Case C–115/88 [1990] ECR I–27. A Briggs, (1990) 10 *YBEL* 481; TC Hartley, (1991) 16 *EL Rev* 69.

[14] Case C–115/88 [1990] ECR I–27, para 8.

[15] Case C–115/88 [1990] ECR I–27, para 11. A Briggs (1990) 10 *YBEL* 481, 483—who criticised this ruling on the basis that it is too narrow—suggests that a claim should be regarded as concerning rights *in rem* in immovable property 'if it seeks to establish that a party has or does not have rights to immovable property, or that the rights he has are or are not subject to the rights of another in respect of that property'.

[16] [1997] Ch 45. J Harris, 'Rights *in Rem* and the Brussels Convention' (1997) 22 *EL Rev* 179; J Stevens, 'No Foot in Minorca? The Jurisdiction of the English Court in Clams to Title to Foreign Land' [1998] *Conv* 145.

courts. By contrast, in *Ashurst v Pollard*[17] the Court of Appeal held that the English court had jurisdiction to make an order for the sale of a villa situated in Portugal in a case where, following the bankruptcy of one of the owners, that person's trustee in bankruptcy applied for such an order.

5.1.7   A claim for compensation for use of immovable property is not within the scope of Article 22(1). *Lieber v Göbel*[18] concerned the transfer (in 1978) of a French apartment from the plaintiffs to the defendant. After the German court declared the transfer void (in 1987), the plaintiffs sought compensation for the nine years during which the defendant had used the apartment. In deciding that the plaintiffs' claim was not within the exclusive jurisdiction of the French courts the Court of Justice stated:

> It is evident that a claim for compensation for the use of immovable property can be raised only against the debtor and thus constitutes a right *in personam*, at any rate where the debtor does not dispute that the person bringing the claim is the owner of the immovable property in question.[19]

Similarly, an action which seeks to prevent a nuisance affecting land belonging to the claimant does not fall within the scope of Article 22(1) as while 'the basis of such an action is the interference with a right *in rem* in immovable property, ... the real and immovable nature of that right is ... of only marginal significance'.[20]

PROCEEDINGS RELATING TO CONTRACTS FOR THE SALE OF LAND
5.1.8   According to the Schlosser Report, claims based on contracts for the transfer of ownership or other rights *in rem* affecting immovable property do not have as their object rights *in rem* and do not fall within the exclusive jurisdiction rules.[21] In *Gaillard v Chekili*[22] the Court of Justice held that a claim for rescission of a contract for the sale of land and for consequential damages does not involve rights *in rem* for the purposes of paragraph (1). In a case where the vendor sues the purchaser for specific performance of the contract and the purchaser defends by questioning the vendor's title, it would seem that Article 22(1) does not apply to the proceedings as it is the defence rather than the claim which raises questions relating to rights *in rem* of immovable property.[23]

PROCEEDINGS RELATING TO TRUSTS OF LAND
5.1.9   A jurisdictional rule which turns on the distinction between rights *in rem* and rights *in personam* poses particular problems in England since it reflects the conceptual structure of the civil law systems of the states which negotiated the original Brussels Convention. In the context of the English legal system a key question is whether

---

[17] [2001] Ch 595. A Briggs (2000) 71 *BYIL* 443; J Harris, 'Ordering the sale of land situated overseas' [2001] *LMCLQ* 205.

[18] Case C–292/93 [1994] ECR I–2535. A Briggs, (1994) 14 *YBEL* 572.

[19] Case C–292/93 [1994] ECR I–2535, para 15.

[20] Case C–343/04 *Land Oberösterreich v CEZ AS* [2006] ECR I–4557, para 34.

[21] [1979] OJ C59/122, para 172. See *Sørensen v Pedersen* [2006] ILPr 606 (Eastern Court of Appeal, Denmark).

[22] Case C–518/99 [2001] ECR I–2771.

[23] See Case C–111/01 *Gantner Electronic GmbH v Basch Exploitatie Maatschappij BV* [2003] ECR I–4207.

the expression 'rights *in rem* in immovable property' includes only legal estates and interests in land or whether an interest under a trust of land comes within the scope of paragraph (1). The Schlosser Report suggests that since equitable interests can fulfil the same functions as rights *in rem* under continental legal systems they should be treated as such for jurisdictional purposes.[24]

5.1.10   In *Webb v Webb*[25] the Court of Justice took the contrary view. In this case the plaintiff acquired a flat in the south of France. The flat was put in the name of the defendant, the plaintiff's son. Subsequently, the plaintiff commenced proceedings in England for a declaration that the defendant held the property as trustee for the plaintiff and for an order requiring the son to execute such documents as were required to vest legal ownership in the plaintiff. The defendant contested the jurisdiction of the court on the basis that, since the plaintiff was bringing the claim in order to establish his rights of ownership of immovable property situated in France, the proceedings fell within the exclusive jurisdiction of the French courts. The Court of Justice ruled that, in order for the proceedings to be within the exclusive jurisdiction of the French courts, 'the action must be based on a right *in rem* and not on a right *in personam*'.[26] In the present case:

The aim of the proceedings before the national court is to obtain a declaration that the son holds the flat for the exclusive benefit of the father and that in that capacity he is under a duty to execute the documents necessary to convey ownership of the flat to the father. The father does not claim that he already enjoys rights directly relating to the property which are enforceable against the whole world, but seeks only to assert rights against the son. Consequently, his action is not an action *in rem* within the meaning of [paragraph (1)] but an action *in personam*.[27]

5.1.11   While there is no simple solution to the problem posed in *Webb v Webb*, the ruling of the Court of Justice has understandably been criticised. Since the concept 'rights *in rem*' is to be given an independent interpretation it is surprising that the Court of Justice seems to have attached so much significance to the principle that equity acts *in personam*. While an equitable property right may, in certain circumstances, be defeated by a sale to a bona fide purchaser—and therefore is not enforceable against the whole world—the Court of Justice's conclusion that the plaintiff's equitable interest in the flat was not a right *in rem* for the purposes of the exclusive jurisdiction provisions is somewhat artificial and flies in the face of the modern understanding of the place of equitable interests within the framework of English property law. For example, in *Tinsley v Milligan* Lord Browne-Wilkinson observed:

The reality of the matter is that ... English law has one single law of property made up of legal and equitable interests. Although for historical reasons legal estates and equitable estates have differing incidents, the person owning either type of estate has a right of property, a right in rem not merely a right in personam.[28]

---

[24] [1979] OJ C59/121, para 167.
[25] Case C–294/92 [1994] ECR I–1717. A Briggs, 'Trusts of Land and the Brussels Convention' (1994) 110 *LQR* 526; A Briggs, (1994) 14 *YBEL* 563; C MacMillan, [1996] *Conv* 125; P Rogerson, [1994] *CLJ* 462.
[26] Case C–294/92 [1994] ECR I–1717, para 14.
[27] Case C–294/92 [1994] ECR I–1717, para 15.
[28] [1994] 1 AC 340, 371.

Although a declaration by the court that the defendant holds the property on trust for the claimant does not effect a transfer of legal ownership, once such a declaration is made, the claimant is entitled to call for a conveyance. As the defendant argued, the father was 'ultimately seeking to secure ownership of the flat'.[29] In reality, the object of the proceedings was 'to determine ... ownership ... of immovable property';[30] accordingly, the object of the proceedings should have been regarded as being 'rights *in rem* of immovable property'. As one commentator has noted:

The father claimed that he was entitled to be, and should be made, legal owner of the flat. In all probability, he needed also to have the local register amended to perfect his entitlement ... As an entitlement to a right *in rem* sat at the very heart of claim and defence, it is difficult to see the decision of the Court ... as a very welcome addition to the jurisprudence.[31]

TENANCIES OF IMMOVABLE PROPERTY
5.1.12   In relation to disputes arising out of leases of immovable property the rationale for giving exclusive jurisdiction to the courts of the state in which the property is situated is:

the fact that tenancies are closely bound up with the law of immovable property and with the provisions, generally of a mandatory character, governing its use, such as legislation controlling the level of rents and protecting the rights of tenants, including tenant farmers.[32]

Tenancies of immovable property 'are generally governed by special rules and it is preferable, in the light of their complexity, that they be applied only by the courts of the states in which they are in force'.[33] Although proceedings involving tenancies will normally involve the landlord and the tenant, the application of paragraph (1) does not require this to be the case. Exclusive jurisdiction is conferred on the state where the immovable property is situated in a case where proceedings are brought against the tenant by a party who is subrogated to the rights of the owner of the property.[34]

LEASES FALLING WITHIN THE SCOPE OF THE FIRST SENTENCE OF PARAGRAPH (1)
5.1.13   In *Sanders v Van der Putte*[35] the Court of Justice decided that the words 'tenancies of immovable property' must be given an independent meaning, having regard to the purpose of the exclusive jurisdiction rules. This purpose does not justify extending the scope of the rules to a dispute arising out of agreement in relation to carrying on a business in a building rented from a third party.[36] However, a timeshare lease is a 'tenancy of immovable property' for the purposes of the first sentence of paragraph (1),[37]

---

[29]   Case C–294/92 [1994] ECR I–1717, para 12.
[30]   Case C–115/88 *Reichert v Dresdner Bank* [1990] ECR I–27, para 11.
[31]   A Briggs, (1994) 110 *LQR* 526, 530. See also J Stevens, 'No Foot in Minorca? The Jurisdiction of the English Court in Clams to Title to Foreign Land' [1998] *Conv* 145, 149–52.
[32]   Case 241/83 *Rösler v Rottwinkel* [1985] ECR 99, para 19.
[33]   Case 73/77 *Sanders v Van der Putte* [1977] ECR 2383, para 14.
[34]   Case C–8/98 *Dansommer v Götz* [2000] ECR I–393, para 36.
[35]   Case 73/77 [1977] ECR 2383. TC Hartley, (1978) 3 *EL Rev* 164.
[36]   Case 73/77 *Sanders v Van der Putte* [1977] ECR 2383, para 19.
[37]   *Jarrett v Barclays Bank Plc* [1999] QB 1.

even if the agreement between the parties requires the landlord to make available ancillary services (such as cleaning and security).[38]

5.1.14   Disputes arising out of short-term holiday lets also fall within the first sentence of paragraph (1). In *Rösler v Rottwinkel*[39] the plaintiff, who owned a villa in Italy, let it to the defendant for three weeks for a holiday. When disputes arose between the parties, both of whom were domiciled in Germany, the plaintiff started proceedings against the defendant in Germany. Notwithstanding the view expressed in the Schlosser Report that the underlying principle of paragraph (1) 'quite clearly does not require its application to short-term agreements for use and occupation such as, for example, holiday accommodation',[40] the Court of Justice decided that the exclusive jurisdiction rule applies to all lettings of immovable property, even for a short term and even where they relate to a holiday home.[41] By contrast, in *Hacker v Euro-Relais GmbH*[42] it was held that, even if the substance of the claim relates to the letting of accommodation, paragraph (1) does not apply to holiday contracts which include not only accommodation, but also other services, such as information and advice, the reservation of transport, reception on arrival and insurance against cancellation. The Court of Justice ruled that a complex contract of this type, which concerns a range of services in return for a lump sum paid by the customer, cannot constitute a 'tenancy agreement' within the meaning of paragraph (1).[43] However, the ruling in *Rösler v Rottwinkel* was confirmed in *Dansommer v Götz*[44]; the Court of Justice distinguished *Hacker v Euro-Relais GmbH* and ruled that paragraph (1) applies notwithstanding that the contract, in addition to making available a holiday home, automatically provides the tenant with travel and cancellation insurance.

PROCEEDINGS WHICH HAVE AS THEIR OBJECT ... TENANCIES
OF IMMOVABLE PROPERTY

5.1.15   Proceedings concerning the obligations of landlord and tenant are within the exclusive jurisdiction of the state in which the immovable property is situated on the basis that the tenancy is the object of such proceedings.[45] In *Rösler v Rottwinkel*[46] the Court of Justice held that:

any dispute concerning the existence of tenancies or the interpretation of the terms thereof, their duration, the giving up of possession to the landlord, the repair of damage caused by the tenant or the recovery of rent and of incidental charges payable by the tenant, such as

---

[38] *Re a Claim for Payment for a Timeshare* [1997] ILPr 524 (District Court, Darmstadt).
[39] Case 241/83 [1985] ECR 99.
[40] [1979] OJ C59/120, para 164.
[41] Case 241/83 [1985] ECR 99, para 25.
[42] Case C–280/90 [1992] ECR I–1111. A Briggs, (1992) 12 *YBEL* 657; TC Hartley, (1993) 17 *EL Rev* 550.
[43] Case C–280/90 [1992] ECR I–1111, para 15. See also Case C–73/04 *Klein v Rhodos Management Ltd* [2005] ECR I–8667 (in which the Court of Justice held that a complex timeshare contract, which included membership of a holiday club, was not within the scope of Art 22(1)); *Re Holiday Lettings* [1994] ILPr 276 (Federal Supreme Court, Germany).
[44] Case C–8/98 [2000] ECR I–393. E Peel, (2001) 20 *YBEL* 357.
[45] *Re the Sublease of a Shop* [1991] ILPr 292 (Court of Appeal, Düsseldorf).
[46] Case 241/83 [1985] ECR 99.

charges for the consumption of water, gas and electricity, falls within the exclusive jurisdiction conferred by [paragraph(1)].[47]

Even though the Jenard Report states that the exclusive jurisdiction rule 'was not intended by the committee to apply to proceedings concerned only with the recovery of rent',[48] the Court of Justice decided that a claim for the recovery of charges payable under the lease was within the scope of paragraph (1). Similarly, a claim for damages against a tenant for taking poor care of premises and causing damage to accommodation which had been rented for a few weeks' holiday falls within the first sentence of paragraph (1).[49]

5.1.16   By contrast, exclusive jurisdiction is not allocated in relation to 'disputes which are only indirectly related to the use of the property let, such as those concerning the loss of holiday enjoyment and travel expenses'.[50] So, jurisdiction in relation to a dispute arising out of a loan agreement is not conferred by paragraph (1)— notwithstanding the fact that the purpose of the loan is to finance the purchase of a lease of immovable property—if the claim is based on the finance agreement as opposed to the lease itself.[51]

Paragraph (1), Second Sentence: Short Leases

5.1.17   The conclusion reached by the Court of Justice in *Rösler v Rottwinkel* received little support from commentators[52] and its impact was curtailed by the amendment of paragraph (1). The second sentence of Article 22(1) applies where the tenant is a natural person and both parties are domiciled in the same Member State. If these conditions are satisfied—and the letting is 'for temporary private use for a maximum period of six consecutive months'—proceedings may be brought in the Member State in which the parties are domiciled.

5.1.18   The effect of the second sentence of paragraph (1) is not to deprive the courts of the Member State in which the immovable property is situated of jurisdiction in cases concerning short-term lettings; the courts of the *situs* have jurisdiction by virtue of the first sentence of Article 22(1). So, were the facts of *Rösler v Rottwinkel* to arise again, the claimant would be able to bring proceedings against the defendant in Italy. However, assuming that the conditions of the second sentence are satisfied, in cases involving short-term lettings, there are 'two exclusive jurisdictions, which might be described as alternative exclusive jurisdictions'.[53] Furthermore, the amendment does not reverse the decision of the Court of Justice in *Rösler v Rottwinkel* that claims solely for the recovery of rent fall within the scope of paragraph (1).

---

[47] Case 241/83 [1985] ECR 99, para 29.
[48] [1979] OJ C59/35. The working party for the 1978 Accession Convention had been unable to agree whether what is now Art 22(1) of the Brussels I Regulation applied to proceedings concerned only with the recovery of rent: Schlosser Report, [1979] OJ C59/120, para 164.
[49] Case C–8/98 *Dansommer v Götz* [2000] ECR I–393, para 38.
[50] Case 241/83 *Rösler v Rottwinkel* [1985] ECR 99, para 29.
[51] *Jarrett v Barclays Bank Plc* [1999] QB 1. A Briggs, (1996) 67 *BYIL* 577.
[52] See, eg, TC Hartley, (1985) 10 *EL Rev* 361; FA Mann, 'Exclusive Exotic Jurisdiction' (1985) 101 *LQR* 329.
[53] Jenard-Möller Report, [1990] OJ C189/75, para 52.

PROCEEDINGS CONCERNING IMMOVABLE PROPERTY IN MORE THAN
ONE MEMBER STATE

5.1.19 In *Scherrens v Maenhout*[54] the plaintiff claimed to be entitled under a single lease of a farm which consisted of 12 hectares in the Netherlands and five hectares in Belgium. The two plots were about seven kilometres apart. The Court of Justice held that the Dutch courts had exclusive jurisdiction in relation to the dispute over the Dutch land and the Belgian courts had exclusive jurisdiction to the extent that the dispute related to land situated in Belgium.[55] However, the result might be different where a dispute relates to a single plot of land which straddles a national boundary, especially if nearly all the plot is situated in one state only. In such a situation it might be appropriate for the courts of the state in which the greater part of the plot is situated to have exclusive jurisdiction in relation to the entirety of the dispute.[56]

Paragraph (2): Corporations

5.1.20 Article 22(2) of the Brussels I Regulation provides that 'in proceedings which have as their object the validity of the constitution, the nullity or the dissolution of companies or other legal persons or associations of natural or legal persons, or the decisions of their organs', the courts of the Member State in which the company, legal person or association has its seat has exclusive jurisdiction regardless of the defendant's domicile.[57] An English partnership qualifies as an 'association of ... natural persons' for the purposes of this paragraph (2).[58] The organs of a company include an administrator who is required to administer and manage a company's affairs.[59] 'Proceedings' has been held to be wide enough to encompass the claim and the likely defence.[60] In addition, Article 22(2) does not merely apply to 'internal' disputes but extends to disputes between a third party and a company.[61]

5.1.21 In *Grupo Torras SA v Sheikh Fahad Mohammed al Sabah* the Court of Appeal considered its purpose:

It is generally accepted as a matter of private international law that the law of the place of incorporation determines the capacity of the company, the composition and powers of the various organs of the company, the formalities and procedures laid down for them, the extent of an individual member's liability for the debts and liabilities of the company, and other matters of that kind. The objective of [paragraph (2)] is to confer exclusive jurisdiction to determine all such questions on the courts of the state where the company has its seat.[62]

---

[54] Case 158/87 [1988] ECR 3791. A Briggs, (1988) 8 *YBEL* 271.

[55] Case 158/87 [1988] ECR 3791, para 13.

[56] Case 158/87 *Scherrens v Maenhout* [1988] ECR 3791, para 14.

[57] For the meaning of 'seat' for the purposes of this rule, see Civil Jurisdiction and Judgments Order 2001, sched 1, para 10.

[58] Schlosser Report, [1979] OJ C59/120, para 162; *Phillips v Symes* [2002] 1 WLR 853.

[59] *Papanicolaou v Thielen* [1997] ILPr 37 (High Court, Ireland).

[60] *JP Morgan Chase Bank NA v Berliner Verkehrsbetriebe (BVG) Anstalt des Offentlichen Rechts* [2010] 2 WLR 29.

[61] *JP Morgan Chase Bank NA v Berliner Verkehrsbetriebe (BVG) Anstalt des Offentlichen Rechts* [2010] 2 WLR 690, 697–8.

[62] Stuart-Smith LJ at [1995] ILPr 667, 679.

The Jenard Report also mentions the need to avoid conflicting judgments being given in this area and that it is preferable to give exclusive jurisdiction to the courts of the state in which the company has its seat because it is in that state that information about the company will have been notified and made public.[63]

5.1.22 In *Hassett v South Eastern Health Board*,[64] two doctors challenged the decision of the Medical Defence Union (MDU) refusing to indemnify or make a contribution in respect of any sum which the doctors might have to pay pursuant to a professional negligence action maintained against them. MDU, which is a company incorporated under English law and which has its registered office in the United Kingdom, provides indemnity to its members in cases involving professional negligence. The doctors sued in Ireland but MDU argued that the English courts had exclusive jurisdiction under Article 22(2) as the claims against it concerned the validity of decisions adopted by its Board of Management. The Court of Justice held that Article 22(2):

must be interpreted as covering only disputes in which a party is challenging the validity of a decision of an organ of the company under the company law applicable or under the provisions governing the functioning of its organs, as laid down in its Articles of Association.[65]

In the instant case, the doctors were not challenging the fact that the MDU's Board of Management had the authority to reject their claim for indemnity under its Articles of Association, but rather they were challenging the manner in which that power was exercised. Consequently, the action did not fall under Article 22(2).

5.1.23 *Hassett v South Eastern Health Board* illustrates that Article 22(2) must be interpreted restrictively. The English courts have asked themselves 'what it is that the proceedings are in substance or principally concerned with'?[66] Whether particular proceedings fall within paragraph (2) has to be decided by reference to its purpose. The mere fact that the dispute arises between a company and its officers or between a shareholder and the company is, in itself, irrelevant. For example, a claim by an officer of a company for wrongful dismissal does not fall within paragraph (2). Similarly, Article 22(2) has no application to proceedings in which it is alleged that the officers of a company abused their authority and practised fraud on the company.[67] Conversely, a claim based on an allegation that the officers of a company acted without the authority of a properly convened and quorate board meeting is covered by paragraph (2).[68] Although in *Newtherapeutics Ltd v Katz*[69] Knox J held that paragraph (2) did not cover proceedings based on an allegation that a transaction to which the officers had committed a company was so detrimental to the interests of the company that no reasonable board of directors could properly have assented to

---

[63] [1997] OJ C59/35.

[64] Case C–372/07 [2008] ECR I–7403.

[65] Case C–372/07 [2008] ECR I–7403, para 26.

[66] Knox J in *Newtherapeutics Ltd v Katz* [1991] Ch 226, 245.

[67] *Grupo Torras SA v Sheikh Fahad Mohammed al Sabah* [1995] ILPr 667. See also *FKI Engineering Ltd v De Wind Holdings Ltd* [2007] ILPr 266, affirmed (without consideration of this point) [2009] 1 All ER (Comm) 118; *Calyon v Wytwornia Sprzetu Komunikacynego PZL Swidnik SA* [2009] 2 All ER (Comm) 603, 622–23 (at [87]–[97]); *Choudhary v Bhattar* [2010] 2 All ER 1031, 1047 (at [47]).

[68] *Newtherapeutics Ltd v Katz* [1991] Ch 226. See also *Speed Investments Ltd v Formula One Holdings Ltd (No 2)* [2005] 1 WLR 1936 (A Briggs, (2004) 75 *BYIL* 543).

[69] [1991] Ch 226.

it, this conclusion was doubted by the Court of Appeal in *Grupo Torras SA v Sheikh Fahad Mohammed al Sabah.*[70]

Paragraph (3): Public Registers

5.1.24 As regards 'proceedings which have as their object the validity of entries in public registers', Article 22(3) of the Brussels I Regulation allocates exclusive jurisdiction, regardless of domicile, on the courts of the state 'in which the register is kept'. Although the text indicates that paragraph (3) is limited to proceedings concerning the validity of entries in registers, the Jenard Report suggests that the rule covers 'proceedings relating to the validity *or effects* of entries' in public registers.[71]

5.1.25 The operation of paragraph (3) is relatively straightforward in relation to publicly owned registers. For example, proceedings brought with the purpose of having the Spanish property register rectified so that the claimant is registered as owner of immovable property situated in Spain falls within the exclusive jurisdiction of the Spanish courts.[72] There are, however, potential problems of interpretation because there is little guidance on what is to be understood by the words 'public register'. There would appear to be two possible interpretations. The narrow view is that a register should be regarded as public only if it is owned by a public authority; the broader view is that any register which is open to public inspection should be regarded as public, even if it is privately owned.

5.1.26 The broader view derives some support from the Jenard Report, which states that paragraph (3) applies not only to entries in land registers and land charges registers, but also to entries in commercial registers.[73] Although commercial registers are hardly known in England, they are very important in many continental systems. Their purpose is to provide a clear means of enabling anyone to find out who is a trader; they are usually maintained by the local chamber of commerce and they list the names and addresses of persons entitled to trade. The broader view has also been adopted by the English courts. In *Re Fagin's Bookshop Plc*[74] it was held that a public limited company's register of shareholders is a public register for the purposes of paragraph (3).

Paragraph (4): Intellectual Property[75]

5.1.27 Article 22(4) of the Brussels I Regulation provides that 'in proceedings concerned with the registration or validity of patents, trade marks, designs, or other similar

---

[70] [1995] ILPr 667.

[71] [1979] OJ C59/35. (Emphasis added.)

[72] *Re Hayward* [1997] Ch 45 (A Briggs, (1996) 67 *BYIL* 577). Compare, however, *Ashurst v Pollard* [2001] Ch 595 (and the trenchant criticism of A Briggs, (2000) 71 *BYIL* 443).

[73] [1979] OJ C59/35.

[74] [1992] BCLC 118.

[75] JJ Fawcett and P Torremans, *Intellectual Property and Private International Law* (Oxford, Clarendon Press, 1998) chs 1 and 2; E Jooris, 'Infringement of Foreign Copyright and the Jurisdiction of English Courts' [1996] 3 *EIPR* 127; C Wadlow, 'Intellectual Property and the Judgments Convention' (1985) 10 *EL Rev* 305.

rights required to be deposited or registered', the courts of the state 'in which the deposit or registration has been applied for, has taken place or is under the terms of an international convention deemed to have taken place' shall have exclusive jurisdiction, regardless of domicile.[76] The phrase 'proceedings concerned with the registration or validity of patents, trade marks, designs, or other similar rights' should be given a uniform interpretation, independent of national law.[77] Since the grant of a national patent is the exercise of national sovereignty, paragraph (4) provides for exclusive jurisdiction in proceedings concerned with the validity of patents.[78] Furthermore, it does not matter whether the issue of a patent's validity is raised by way of action or by a plea in objection.[79]

5.1.28   Since copyright is not a right which is 'required to be deposited or registered', Article 22(4) has no application to proceedings relating to copyright. Even as regards a registered right such as a patent, the exclusive jurisdiction rules do not cover any proceedings in which registration or validity is not in issue.[80] Accordingly, paragraph (4) does not provide for exclusive jurisdiction with regard to passing off proceedings or proceedings relating solely to the infringement of patents.[81] However, in *Coin Controls Ltd v Suzo International (UK) Ltd*,[82] which concerned the alleged infringement of a German patent, Laddie J held that, if the defendant challenges the validity of the patent in the context of the English infringement proceedings, the court is required to decline jurisdiction on the basis that the proceedings fall within the exclusive jurisdiction of the German courts: 'Once the defendant raises validity the court must hand the proceedings over to the court having exclusive jurisdiction over that issue.'[83] In this type of case, infringement and validity 'are so closely interrelated that they should be treated for jurisdiction purposes as one issue or claim'.[84] The Court of Appeal endorsed this approach in *Fort Dodge Animal Health Ltd v Akzo Nobel NV*[85] in the context of proceedings relating to the alleged infringement of a UK patent. According to Lord Wolff MR:

where there is a bona fide challenge to the validity of a United Kingdom patent, any proceedings for infringement must in English eyes be 'concerned with' the validity of the patent.

---

[76]   As regards Community trade marks jurisdiction is determined by the rules to be found in the Brussels I Regulation and in Reg (EC) 40/94 (the 'Trade Marks Regulation'), Arts 90–105. For the relationship between the Brussels I Regulation and the Trade Marks Regulation, see *Prudential Assurance Co Ltd v Prudential Insurance Co of America* [2003] 1 WLR 2295 (a case concerning the Brussels Convention).

[77]   Case 288/82 *Duijnstee v Goderbauer* [1983] ECR 3663, para 19.

[78]   Case 288/82 *Duijnstee v Goderbauer* [1983] ECR 3663, para 25.

[79]   Case C–4/03 *Gesellschaft für Antriebstechnik mbH & Co KG (GAT) v Lamellen und Kupplungsbau Beteiligungs KG (LuK)* [2006] ECR I–6509 (A Briggs, [2006] *LMCLQ* 447). Art 22(4) of the 2007 Lugano Convention expressly provides that exclusive jurisdiction is conferred 'irrespective of whether the issue is raised by way of an action or as a defence'.

[80]   Case 288/82 *Duijnstee v Goderbauer* [1983] ECR 3663, para 25.

[81]   Jenard Report, [1979] OJ C59/36. See, eg, *Mölnlycke AB v Procter & Gamble Ltd* [1992] 1 WLR 1112; *Chiron Corporation v Evans Medical Ltd* [1996] FSR 863.

[82]   [1999] Ch 33. See also *Knorr-Bremse Systems for Commercial Vehicles Ltd v Haldex Brake Products GmbH* [2008] ILPr 326.

[83]   [1999] Ch 33, 51. Compare *Expandable Grafts Partnership v Boston Scientific BV* [1999] FSR 352 (Court of Appeal, The Hague).

[84]   Laddie J in *Coin Controls Ltd v Suzo International (UK) Ltd* [1999] Ch 33, 51.

[85]   [1998] FSR 222. S Dutson, 'Intellectual property litigation' [1998] *LMCLQ* 505; I Karet, [1998] 2 *EIPR* 77.

Often, perhaps normally, the issue of validity will be the principal element of the dispute. No conclusion as to the chances of the claim of infringement succeeding can be made until a decision has been reached as to the strength of the allegations of validity.[86]

This analysis is also supported by the decision in *Gesellschaft für Antriebstechnik v Lamellen und Kupplungsbau*[87] in which the Court of Justice considered that Article 22(4) applies 'whatever the form of proceedings in which the issue of a patent's validity is raised'.[88]

Paragraph (5): Enforcement Proceedings

5.1.29 With regard to 'proceedings concerned with the enforcement of judgments', Article 22(5) of the Brussels I Regulation provides that the courts of the state in which 'the judgment has been or is to be enforced' shall have exclusive jurisdiction, regardless of the defendant's domicile. For the purpose of the Regulation, 'judgment' means 'any judgment given by a court or tribunal of a Member State'.[89] Accordingly, Article 22(5) does not apply to proceedings relating to judgments given by the courts of a non-Member State.[90] The reciprocal recognition and enforcement of the judgments of non-Member State A in Member States B and C depends wholly on the arrangements between state A and states B and C respectively.[91] In a case involving the enforcement of a judgment given by the court of a Member State, where enforcement proceedings are pending in two other Member States the effect of paragraph (5) is that each court in which enforcement proceedings are brought has exclusive jurisdiction over the proceedings within that state. So, if a claimant applies to enforce an English judgment both in England and France and seeks execution against money which the claimant believes the defendant holds in a French bank account, the English court has no jurisdiction to make a third party debt order[92] in relation to the debt situated in France.[93]

5.1.30 Paragraph (5) applies only in relation to proceedings which are directly concerned with the enforcement of judgments already delivered.[94] In *Reichert v Dresdner Bank (No 2)*[95] the Court of Justice confirmed that the rule applies to disputes which may arise from 'the use of force or constraint, or the dispossession of movables and immovables in order to obtain the physical implementation of judgments and measures' and that 'the difficulties to which these procedures give rise are within the exclusive jurisdiction of the court of the place where the judgment is to be enforced'.[96]

---

[86] [1998] FSR 222, 244. See also Chadwick LJ in *Prudential Assurance Co Ltd v Prudential Insurance Co of America* [2003] 1 WLR 2295, 2305 (at [21]).

[87] Case C–4/03 [2006] ECR I–6509.

[88] [2006] ECR I–6509, para 25.

[89] Art 32.

[90] Case C–129/92 *Owens Bank Ltd v Bracco* [1994] ECR I–117, para 24.

[91] See Parker LJ in *Owens Bank Ltd v Bracco* [1992] 2 AC 443, 452. A Briggs, 'Foreign Judgments, Fraud and the Brussels Convention' (1991) 107 *LQR* 531.

[92] Formerly, a garnishee order.

[93] *Kuwait Oil Tanker Co SAK v Qabazard* [2004] 1 AC 300. A Briggs, 'Owing, owning and the garnishing of foreign debts' [2003] *LMCLQ* 418; P Rogerson [2003] *CLJ* 576.

[94] See *Masri v Consolidated Contractors International (UK) Ltd (No 2)* [2009] QB 450.

[95] Case C–261/90 [1992] ECR I–2149. See also Jenard Report, [1979] OJ C59/36.

[96] Case C–261/90 [1992] ECR I–2149, para 28.

Examination of Jurisdiction

5.1.31   As a general rule it is for the defendant in proceedings to raise all the points which are relevant to his defence—whether these points are procedural or substantive. Chapter II produces an exception to this principle by requiring the court of a Member State whose jurisdiction is invoked to consider whether exclusive jurisdiction is conferred by Article 22 on the courts of another Member State—even if the defendant does not contest jurisdiction. Article 25 of the Brussels I Regulation, which is the corollary of the rule that submission by the defendant cannot override Article 22, provides:

Where a court of a Member State is seised of a claim which is principally concerned with a matter over which the courts of another Member State have exclusive jurisdiction by virtue of Article 22, it shall declare of its own motion that it has no jurisdiction.

5.1.32   The court's duty to declare that it has no jurisdiction whenever it finds that a court of another Member State has exclusive jurisdiction under Article 22 arises even where the procedural rules of the court limit the court's enquiry to the grounds raised by the parties.[97] Because a court has exclusive jurisdiction only if the principal subject-matter of the proceedings falls within one of the relevant provisions,[98] the operation of Article 25 of the Brussels I Regulation is not entirely straightforward. Where, for example, a court has jurisdiction under Article 2, but it appears that the courts of another Member State may have exclusive jurisdiction under Article 22 of the Brussels I Regulation, it may be far from simple to determine whether the principal subject-matter of the proceedings—rather than only a preliminary or incidental matter—falls within one of the paragraphs of Article 22. The dividing-line between the principal subject-matter and an incidental matter is not always a clear one.[99]

5.2 SUBMISSION

5.2.1   Nearly all systems of law accept that submission by the defendant is a basis on which a court is entitled to assume jurisdiction, even if the defendant has no other connection with the forum. If, once the dispute has arisen, the defendant agrees to make a voluntary appearance to defend the claim on the merits, there is no reason why the litigation should not go ahead in that forum. Article 24 of the Brussels I Regulation provides:

Apart from jurisdiction derived from other provisions of this Regulation, a court of a Member State before which a defendant enters an appearance shall have jurisdiction. This rule shall not apply where appearance was entered to contest the jurisdiction, or where another court has exclusive jurisdiction by virtue of Article 22.

Although submission by the defendant cannot override exclusive jurisdiction under Article 22, submission overrides all other jurisdictional rules contained in Chapter II.

---

[97]   Case 288/82 *Duijnstee v Goderbauer* [1983] ECR 3663.
[98]   Jenard Report, [1979] OJ C59/34.
[99]   See, eg, *Coin Controls Ltd v Suzo International (UK) Ltd* [1999] Ch 33.

For example, submission has the effect of superseding an earlier jurisdiction agreement between the parties.[100]

5.2.2 There is some doubt whether the submission rule applies regardless of the defendant's domicile. There is an argument for Article 24 being applicable only in cases where the defendant is domiciled in a Member State,[101] in which case each Member State's traditional rules on submission are applicable in situations involving defendants not domiciled in a Member State. The drafting of Article 4 of the Brussels I Regulation, which expressly singles out Articles 22 and 23 as being applicable regardless of the defendant's domicile, suggests that Article 24 applies only to defendants domiciled in a Member State. However, the text of Article 24 makes no reference to the domicile of the parties. Since the submission rule appears in the same section of Chapter II as Article 23,[102] the application of which is not restricted to defendants domiciled in a Member State, there is a case for treating the submission rule as applicable regardless of domicile. Furthermore, there is authority for the view that Article 24 applies even where the defendant is domiciled in a non-Member State.[103] As far as English law is concerned, it makes no practical difference whether the defendant's submission is determined by Article 24 of the Regulation or by the traditional rules.[104]

5.2.3 Under the procedural laws of some Member States a defendant is required to put forward certain defences in order to have a right of audience at all[105] or a defendant who restricts his argument to questions of jurisdiction is not permitted to defend on the merits at a later stage if the court assumes jurisdiction. In these circumstances, it is better, from a practical point of view, to allow a party not only to contend that the court has no jurisdiction, but also to argue that if the court rejects the jurisdiction defence it should decide in his favour on the merits. In *Elefanten Schuh GmbH v Jacqmain*[106] the Court of Justice held that the fact that the defendant puts forward a defence on the merits does not necessarily mean that he should be regarded as having submitted. The submission rule must be interpreted as meaning that a defendant should not be regarded as having submitted:

where the defendant not only contests the court's jurisdiction but also makes submissions on the substance of the action, provided that, if the challenge to jurisdiction is not preliminary to any defence as to the substance, it does not occur after the making of the submissions which under national procedural law are considered to be the first defence addressed to the court seised.[107]

5.2.4 A challenge to the jurisdiction of the court is effective to negative submission 'only if the plaintiff and the court seised of the matter are able to ascertain from the

---

[100] Case 150/80 *Elefanten Schuh GmbH v Jacqmain* [1981] ECR 1671, para 11. See also *SA CNV v S GmbH* [1991] ILPr 588 (Court of Appeal, Koblenz); *Servi Videoproduktions GmbH v Uniropa SA* [1995] ILPr 358 (Court of Appeal, Barcelona).

[101] See Jenard Report, [1979] OJ C59/38.

[102] Section 7 of Chapter II of the Brussels I Regulation.

[103] See Advocate General Darmon in Case C–318/93 *Brenner and Noller v Dean Witter Reynolds Inc* [1994] ECR I–4275, para 15. See also *Partenreederei ms Atlantic Duke v Frenave Agencia Maritima de Fretamentos e Consignçoes Sàrl* [1982] ECC 348 (District Court, Rotterdam); *SC Johnson & Son Inc v Mobilar Export Import GmbH* [1986] ECC 360 (District Court, Rotterdam).

[104] See section 7.2.

[105] See *Luis Marburg & Söhne GmbH v Società Ori Martin SpA* [1987] ECC 424 (Court of Cassation, Italy).

[106] Case 150/80 [1981] ECR 1671.

[107] Case 150/80 [1981] ECR 1671, para 17.

time of the defendant's first defence that it is intended to contest the jurisdiction of the court'.[108] So, a defendant does not submit to the jurisdiction if he states a defence on the merits provided he disputes the court's jurisdiction at the same time or earlier.[109] The defendant will not confer jurisdiction by submission when a substantive defence is presented as an alternative to be considered only if the jurisdictional defence fails.[110] However, a defendant who files a substantive defence before seeking to challenge the court's jurisdiction is to be regarded a having entered an appearance for the purposes of the submission rule.[111] Similarly, if the defendant submits to the court's jurisdiction at first instance but seeks to challenge jurisdiction on appeal, the court has jurisdiction.[112] Where a claimant applies for provisional or protective measures under Article 31, the defendant's participation in those proceedings should not be regarded as conferring jurisdiction by submission as regards the substantive claim.[113]

5.2.5   In the context of English procedural law, a defendant who wishes to defend proceedings, whether on the basis of jurisdiction or on the merits of the case, should acknowledge service of the claim form; failure to do so entitles the claimant to proceed to judgment in default.[114] The defendant's acknowledgment of service does not amount to submission as, by acknowledging service, the defendant does not thereby lose any right he may have to dispute the court's jurisdiction.[115] However, if the defendant fails to make an application challenging the court's jurisdiction within 14 days of the acknowledgment of service, he is treated as having submitted to the court's jurisdiction.[116] Procedural steps taken by the defendant before the expiry of the period for service of defence (such as an application for disclosure of documents or even for an extension of time for service of defence) do not amount to submission under Chapter II.[117]

5.3 JURISDICTION AGREEMENTS

Preliminary Considerations

The Text

5.3.1   It is not uncommon for an international commercial agreement to include a jurisdiction clause. A contractual jurisdiction clause is an agreement by the parties

---

[108] Case 150/80 [1981] ECR 1671, para 15.

[109] *Re a Shop Fitting Contract* [1993] ILPr 395 (Court of Appeal, Saarbrücken).

[110] *Machinale Glasfabriek de Maas BV v Emaillerie Alsacienne SA* [1984] ECC 123 (District Court, Arnhem); *SpA Officine Meccaniche Ventura v Prometal SA* [1990] ILPr 184 (District Court, Monza).

[111] *Re the Sublease of a Shop* [1991] ILPr 292 (Court of Appeal, Düsseldorf). See also *Re Submission to the Jurisdiction* [2002] ILPr 171 (Court of Appeal, Frankfurt).

[112] *Bernard Ghequières v Knuwer* [1990] ILPr 369 (Supreme Court, Netherlands); *Huwaert v Disclez* [1993] ILPr 286 (Court of Appeal, Luxembourg); *Proma di Fraco Gianotti v Société d'Exploitation des Etablissements Montuori SA* [1994] ILPr 744 (Court of Cassation, France).

[113] *Société Hanomag v Société Payant* [1996] ILPr 71 (Court of Appeal, Grenoble).

[114] CPR 10.2, 11(2).

[115] CPR 11(3).

[116] CPR 11(5).

[117] *Kurz v Stella Musical Veranstaltungs GmbH* [1992] Ch 196. R Thomas, 'Non-exclusive jurisdiction clauses and submission by appearance' [1992] *LMCLQ* 292.

to refer any dispute arising under the contract to the courts of a particular place or country. Article 23 of the Brussels I Regulation[118] provides:

1. If the parties, one or more of whom is domiciled in a Member State, have agreed that a court or the courts of a Member State are to have jurisdiction to settle any disputes which have arisen or which may arise in connection with a particular legal relationship, that court or those courts shall have exclusive jurisdiction. Such jurisdiction shall be exclusive unless the parties have agreed otherwise. Such an agreement conferring jurisdiction shall be either:

   (a) in writing or evidenced in writing, or
   (b) in a form which accords with practices which the parties have established between themselves, or
   (c) in international trade or commerce, in a form which accords with a usage of which the parties are or ought to have been aware and which in such trade or commerce is widely known to, and regularly observed by, parties to contracts of the type involved in the particular trade or commerce concerned.

2. Any communication by electronic means which provides a durable record of the agreement shall be equivalent to 'writing'.
3. Where such an agreement is concluded by parties, none of whom is domiciled in a Member State, the courts of other Member States shall have no jurisdiction over their disputes unless the court or courts chosen have declined jurisdiction. ...[119]
5. Agreements ... conferring jurisdiction shall have no legal force if they are contrary to Articles 13, 17 or 21, or if the courts whose jurisdiction they purport to exclude have exclusive jurisdiction by virtue of Article 22.

Basic Conditions

An Agreement on Jurisdiction

AN INDEPENDENT CONCEPT

5.3.2   Article 23 of the Brussels I Regulation deals with the situation where the parties 'have agreed' that the courts of a Member State are to have jurisdiction over disputes arising in connection with a legal relationship. The concept of 'an agreement conferring jurisdiction' should be regarded as an independent one.[120] Although a jurisdiction agreement normally takes the form of a contractual clause, the scope of the jurisdiction agreement provisions are not limited to simple contracts. In *Powell Duffryn Plc v Petereit*[121] the defendant, an English company, had purchased shares in a German company. Subsequently, the shareholders amended the company's Articles of association; under the amended Articles of association disputes between the shareholders and the

---

[118] See, generally, L Merrett, 'Article 23 of the Brussels I Regulation: A Comprehensive Code for Jurisdiction Agreements?' (2009) 58 *ICLQ* 545.

[119] Para (4) regulates jurisdiction agreements in relation to trusts.

[120] Case C–214/89 *Powell Duffryn Plc v Peteriet* [1992] ECR I–1745, para 14. See also *Nursaw v Dansk Jersey Eksport* [2009] ILPr 263; *Knorr-Bremse Systems for Commercial Vehicles Ltd v Haldex Brake Products GmbH* [2008] ILPr 326.

[121] Case C–214/89 [1992] ECR I–1745. A Briggs, (1992) 12 *YBEL* 664; TC Hartley, (1993) 18 *EL Rev* 225; MV Polak, (1993) 30 *CML Rev* 406; J Robinson, 'Articles of Association and Article 17 of the Brussels Convention' (1992) 13 *Bus LR* 260.

company were to be submitted to the court which normally had jurisdiction over the company. When, following the German company's bankruptcy, the liquidator brought proceedings in the German court designated by the Articles of association, the defendant contested the German court's jurisdiction. The Court of Justice ruled that, regardless of the applicable law, the company's Articles of association were to be regarded as 'a contract covering both the relations between the shareholders and also the relations between the shareholders and the company they set up'.[122] A jurisdiction clause which appears in the Articles of association of a limited company is binding on the shareholders and it is irrelevant whether the shareholder against whom the jurisdiction clause is invoked opposed the adoption of the clause or became a shareholder after the clause was adopted.[123]

THE LEGAL RELATIONSHIP
5.3.3   Where there are two or more different legal relationships between the same parties, a valid jurisdiction clause within the framework of one such contractual relationship is effective only with regard to the relationship of which it forms a part. Where, for example, parties to a distribution agreement (which does not include a jurisdiction clause) subsequently conclude—within the framework of that agreement—a number of individual contracts of sale (which do include a jurisdiction clause), the jurisdiction clauses in the contracts of sale do not extend to the distribution agreement.[124] The sales contracts and the distribution agreement are different legal relationships. Similarly, where parties enter a supply contract (which contains a jurisdiction clause) and, later, a repair contract (which contains no jurisdiction clause) under the terms of which the supplier undertakes to repair the goods supplied under the supply contract, the jurisdiction clause in the supply contract does not confer jurisdiction with regard to a dispute arising under the repair contract.[125]

Choice of the Courts of a Member State

5.3.4   If the parties choose a particular court in a Member State, the effect of Article 23 is to confer jurisdiction on that court, but not on other courts in the same country. So, if the parties agree that disputes are to be referred to the courts in Rome, this is not sufficient to confer jurisdiction on the courts of Milan. There is no requirement that there should be 'any objective connexion between the legal relationship in dispute and the court designated'.[126] Nor is it necessary for the chosen court to be directly specified from the wording of the agreement itself. It is very common for jurisdiction agreements in standard-form contracts to identify the agreed forum indirectly (for example, by referring contractual disputes arising under a bill of lading to the

---

[122] Case C–214/89 [1992] ECR I–1745, para 16.
[123] See also *Re Jurisdiction in Internal Company Matters* [1995] ILPr 424 (Federal Supreme Court, Germany).
[124] See *Bosma Huygen Meudelimpex BV v Häcker Küchen GmbH* [1992] ILPr 379 (Supreme Court, Netherlands).
[125] *WH Martin Ltd v Feldbinder Spezialfahrzeugwerke GmbH* [1998] ILPr 794.
[126] Case 56/79 *Zelger v Salinitri* [1980] ECR 89, para 4. See also Case C–159/97 *Trasporti Castelletti Spedizioni Internazionali SpA v Hugo Trumpy SpA* [1999] ECR I–1597, para 50.

courts for the place where the carrier has its principal place of business). In *Coreck Maritime GmbH v Handelsveem BV*[127] the Court of Justice held that:

It is sufficient that the clause states the objective factors on the basis of which the parties have agreed to choose a court or the courts to which they wish to submit disputes which have arisen or which may arise between them. Those factors, which must be sufficiently precise to enable the court seised to ascertain whether it has jurisdiction, may, where appropriate, be determined by the particular circumstances of the case.[128]

So, in a case involving the chartering of a Greek ship under a single-voyage charterparty containing a jurisdiction clause which refers disputes to the courts of the country of the flag of the vessel, the jurisdiction clause is no less effective than an agreement which expressly refers disputes to the Greek courts. However, an agreement which purports to confer jurisdiction by reference to subjective factors is not effective. For example, a clause purporting to refer disputes to the court 'most familiar with maritime law' would be invalid.[129]

5.3.5 In the situation where parties, none of whom is domiciled in a Member State, agree to refer their disputes to the courts of a Member State, the chosen court may, applying national law, decline jurisdiction.[130] If the chosen court declines jurisdiction the courts of other Member States may then exercise jurisdiction on the basis of national rules outside the Brussels I Regulation. However, it will be rare for the chosen court to decline jurisdiction; accordingly, the effect of the jurisdiction agreement provisions will normally be to prevent the courts of the other Member States from exercising jurisdiction.

5.3.6 Where parties, at least one of whom is domiciled in a Member State, agree to refer their disputes to the courts of a Member State, the effect of such an agreement is twofold. First, unless the jurisdiction agreement is, according to its terms, non-exclusive, it has the effect of preventing the courts of all the other Member States from exercising jurisdiction. Secondly, jurisdiction is conferred on the chosen courts,[131] although it should be remembered that Article 23 is subordinate to other provisions of Chapter II (notably, Article 22 and Article 24) which have the effect of depriving the chosen court of jurisdiction.[132] Before the decision of the Court of Justice in *Owusu v Jackson*[133] the English courts had taken the view that, notwithstanding the parties' choice of English jurisdiction, English proceedings may be stayed on the basis of *forum non conveniens* if the courts of a non-Member State provided a more appropriate forum.[134] This view was, to say the least, controversial—all the more so

---

[127] Case C–387/98 [2000] ECR I–9337. E Peel, (2001) 20 *YBEL* 344.

[128] Case C–387/98 [2000] ECR I–9337, para 15. Whether the clause in this case could be regarded as sufficiently certain is questionable: E Peel, (2001) 20 *YBEL* 344, 346.

[129] See Advocate General Alber in Case C–387/98 *Coreck Maritime GmbH v Handelsveem BV* [2000] ECR I–9337, para 33.

[130] Brussels I Reg, Art 23(3). See *Transocean Towage Co Ltd v Hyundai Construction Co Ltd* [1987] ECC 282 (Supreme Court, Netherlands).

[131] See Case C–387/98 *Coreck Maritime GmbH v Handelsveem BV* [2000] ECR I–9337, para 21.

[132] The disagreement over the relationship between the jurisdiction agreement provisions, on the one hand, and the provisions relating to concurrent proceedings, on the other, was determined by the Court of Justice in Case C–116/02 *Erich Gasser GmbH v MISAT Srl* [2003] ECR I–14693. See paras 9.1.41–9.1.43.

[133] Case C–281/02 [2005] ECR I–1383. See section 9.5.

[134] *Eli Lilly & Co v Novo Nordisk A/S* [2000] ILPr 73; *Sinochem International Oil (London) Co v Mobil Sales and Supply Corporation* [2000] 1 Lloyd's Rep 670; *UBS AG v Omni Holding AG* [2000] 1 WLR 916. In none of these cases, however, did the court grant a stay.

if the jurisdiction clause was exclusive, rather than non-exclusive; since the decision in the *Owusu* case, the view formerly taken by the English courts has become untenable.[135] Where the parties, one or more of whom is domiciled in a Member State, have referred their dispute to the courts of a Member State, the chosen courts cannot decline jurisdiction on a discretionary basis.

5.3.7   There are questions relating not only to whose domicile is relevant but also to the moment at which the domicile of the parties is relevant for the purposes of Article 23. As regards the former issue, the Court of Justice ruled in *Coreck Maritime GmbH v Handelsveem BV*[136] that it is the domicile of the original contracting parties—rather than the litigants—which is relevant. This ruling produces the perhaps surprising result that where a jurisdiction agreement in favour of the French courts is concluded between A (a Japanese company) and B (an English company), but the parties to the litigation are A and C (a New York company which succeeded to B's rights and obligations under the contract), the situation falls within Article 23(1) of the Brussels I Regulation, rather than Article 23(3). With regard to the question of timing, what is the position where, for example, one of the parties is domiciled in a Member State at the time when the agreement is concluded, but neither is domiciled in a Member State when proceedings are commenced? The Court of Justice has not been required to rule on this question, but the approach taken in *Coreck Maritime GmbH v Handelsveem BV* suggests that the relevant time is the time of contracting. Arguments based on principle point in the same direction; by entering an agreement on jurisdiction the parties assume reciprocal obligations, the nature and content of which should not be dependent on changes in circumstances following the conclusion of the agreement.

5.3.8   Article 23 applies in a situation where both parties are domiciled in the same Member State—for example, where two parties domiciled in Germany agree to refer disputes to the English courts.[137] Indeed, the courts have gone further and taken the view that Article 23 is not limited to disputes with an international element—so that a clause conferring exclusive jurisdiction on the courts of Forli in a contract with only Italian connecting factors must comply with the formal requirements of Article 23.[138]

Choice of the Courts of a Non-Member State

5.3.9   What is the situation where the parties agree to refer their disputes to the courts of a non-Member State? If the defendant is not domiciled in a Member State, Article 4 authorises the courts of each Member State to apply their own national jurisdiction rules. So, if A (an English company) and B (a New York company) enter an agreement which includes an English choice of law clause and a jurisdiction clause in favour of the courts of New York, A may apply for permission to serve process

---

[135]   *Equitas Ltd v Allstate Insurance Co* [2009] 1 All ER (Comm) 1137.

[136]   Case C–387/98 [2000] ECR I–9337, paras 20–1.

[137]   See *Re Leyland DAF Ltd* [1994] 1 BCLC 264; affirmed [1994] 2 BCLC 106 (a case concerning a Dutch jurisdiction clause in a contract regulating the relationship between two Dutch companies and the English subsidiary of one of them).

[138]   *British Sugar Plc v Fratelli Babbini di Lionello Babbini & Co SAS* [2005] 1 Lloyd's Rep 332. See also *Snookes v Jani-King (GB) Ltd* [2006] ILPr 433, 446–50 (at [39]–[45]).

on B out of the jurisdiction on the basis that the claim falls within CPR PD 6B para 3.1(6)(c).[139] In this situation Article 23 of the Brussels I Regulation is wholly irrelevant. While the court, applying traditional rules, will generally refuse permission to serve out in a case where the parties have agreed to the jurisdiction of a foreign court,[140] in exceptional circumstances permission may be given where the case is closely connected with England.[141]

5.3.10 More difficult is the situation where the defendant is domiciled in a Member State. The question arises whether an English court may stay proceedings brought against an English domiciliary on the basis that the parties agreed to refer their dispute to the courts of a non-Member State. In this type of case the court has jurisdiction by virtue of the defendant's domicile in England and there is nothing in Chapter II of the Brussels I Regulation to suggest that the court has any discretion. Nevertheless, the authorities—and common sense—suggest that the proceedings may be stayed in these circumstances.[142]

Formal Requirements

Introduction

5.3.11 The problem which Article 23 of the Brussels I Regulation is intended primarily to address is that posed by a jurisdiction clause in standardised general conditions of trade which may go unnoticed by one of the parties.[143] In a situation where contractual terms are not freely negotiated by the parties on the basis of equality there is 'the danger of [one of the parties] inadvertently finding himself bound by standard forms of agreement containing jurisdiction clauses without realising it'.[144]

5.3.12 The original version of Article 17 of the Brussels Convention took a very strict approach to jurisdiction clauses, which were valid only if they were 'in writing or evidenced in writing'. The Court of Justice took the view that this provision was premised on the consensus between the parties being 'clearly and precisely demonstrated'[145] and emphasised the importance of strict compliance with the formal requirements, so that there was 'certainty that the clause conferring jurisdiction was in fact part of the subject-matter of the contract properly so called'.[146] Experience showed, however, that the strictness of the formality requirements did not cater adequately for the customs and needs of international trade; on the occasion of

---

[139] See section 7.3.

[140] *Mackender v Feldia AG* [1967] 2 QB 590.

[141] *Evans Marshall & Co Ltd v Bertola SA* [1973] 1 WLR 349. For further discussion, see section 7.3.

[142] Schlosser Report, [1979] OJ C59/124, para 176. *Arkwright Mutual Insurance Co v Bryanston Insurance Co Ltd* [1990] 2 QB 649; *The Rewia* [1991] 1 Lloyd's Rep 69, 75, reversed on other grounds [1991] 2 Lloyd's Rep 325; *Re Harrods (Buenos Aires) Ltd* [1992] Ch 72. For further discussion, see section 9.5.

[143] Jenard Report, [1979] OJ C59/37.

[144] Schlosser Report, [1979] OJ C59/124, para 179.

[145] Case 24/76 *Estasis Salotti di Colzani Aimo v RÜWA Polstereimaschinen GmbH* [1976] ECR 1831, para 7; Case 25/76 *Galeries Segoura SPRL v Bonakdarian* [1976] ECR 1851, para 6.

[146] Case 24/76 *Estasis Salotti di Colzani Aimo v RÜWA Polstereimaschinen GmbH* [1976] ECR 1831, para 12.

subsequent accessions to the Brussels Convention in 1978 and 1989, the opportunity was taken to amend the formal requirements. The effect of the amended text is that actual consensus between the parties on the question of jurisdiction is no longer required:

actual consensus, which was initially essential and guaranteed only by writing or evidence in writing of an oral agreement, now yields in international trade to a presumption of actual consensus.[147]

5.3.13   The requirements set out in subparagraphs (a), (b) and (c) of paragraph (1) are alternative; the fact that an agreement on jurisdiction is not in writing or evidenced in writing does not necessarily mean that it is ineffective.[148] When an alleged jurisdiction agreement is challenged, the relevant standard of proof on the party seeking to rely on the agreement's existence is that of a 'good arguable case' and that party 'must show that they have a much better argument than the [other party] that, on the material available at present, the requirements of form in article 23(1) are met and that it can be established, clearly and precisely, that the clause conferring jurisdiction on the court was the subject of consensus between the parties'.[149]

5.3.14   Although the case law of the Court of Justice has been described as 'uncertain and sometimes contradictory',[150] in view of the relaxation of the formal requirements it should be relatively rare for a contractual agreement referring disputes to the courts of a Member State not to be effective to confer jurisdiction on the chosen court. Moreover, a jurisdiction clause is considered to be separable from the contract containing it so that even where a claim is advanced on the basis that the contract which includes the jurisdiction clause is void, the clause will still confer jurisdiction on the chosen court if the requirements of Article 23 are satisfied.[151] However, this is only true in so far as consensus can be said to have been reached on a contract; the fulfilment of the formal requirements set out in Article 23 is considered to establish consensus between the parties.[152] The fact that that consensus is alleged to be vitiated by factors such as mistake, misrepresentation, illegality, lack of authority or lack of capacity does not render the jurisdiction clause ineffective. There are two provisos to this: (i) the court will consider whether the jurisdiction clause can be relied upon if the jurisdiction clause itself, as opposed to the contract in which it is contained generally,

---

[147] Advocate General Tesauro in Case C–106/95 *Mainschiffahrts-Genossenschaft eG (MSG) v Les Gravières Rhénanes* [1997] ECR I–911, para 25.

[148] See, eg, *Graniti Fiandre v La Société Mothes* [2001] ILPr 164 (Court of Cassation, France).

[149] *Bols Distilleries BV (trading as Bols Royal Distilleries) v Superior Yacht Services Ltd* [2007] 1 WLR 12, 22 (at [28]). A Briggs, (2006) 77 *BYIL* 581. See also *Canada Trust v Stolzenberg (No 2)* [2002] 1 AC 1, 13; *Hewden Tower Cranes Ltd v Wolffkran GmbH* [2007] 2 Lloyd's Rep 138, 145 (at [46]); *WPP Holdings Italy Srl v Benatti* [2007] 1 WLR 2316, 2329–30 (at [42]–[44]).

[150] S Pieri, 'The 1968 Brussels Convention on Jurisdiction and Enforcement of Judgments in Civil and Commercial Matters: the Evolution of the Case Law of the Court of Justice 1992–1996' (1997) 34 *CML Rev* 867, 884.

[151] *Deutsche Bank AG v Asia Pacific Broadband Wireless Communications Inc* [2008] 2 Lloyd's Rep 619. A Briggs, (2008) 79 *BYIL* 557; A Sher, [2009] *LMCLQ* 275. Cf *The Mana* [2006] 2 Lloyd's Rep 319.

[152] Case C–24/76, *Estasis Salotti di Colzani Aimo v RÜWA Polstereimaschinen GmbH*, para 7. See also *Deutsche Bank AG v Asia Pacific Broadband Wireless Communications Inc* [2008] 2 Lloyd's Rep 619, 626 (at [30]); cf Flaux J at first instance: [2008] 2 Lloyd's Rep 177, 183–4 (at [34]).

is subject to specific attack[153]; and (ii) where the parties are still at the negotiating stage, no effect can be given to a jurisdiction clause even if it is in writing.[154]

In Writing or Evidenced in Writing[155]

IN WRITING

5.3.15 For a jurisdiction agreement to be 'in writing', it is not sufficient that the contractual clause in question is in a written or printed form; it is the consent of the contracting parties which must be in writing. Accordingly, the requirement of writing is fulfilled if the jurisdiction clause is contained in a document which is signed by both parties.[156] A jurisdiction agreement satisfies the requirement of writing if one party attaches its general terms and conditions (which include a jurisdiction clause) to an order form and the other party signs the order form and returns it.[157] The situation is more difficult in cases where the document signed by the parties does not set out the jurisdiction clause, but refers—either directly or indirectly—to standard terms and conditions which include a jurisdiction clause. There are various different situations to consider.

5.3.16 First, there are cases where the parties sign the front of a document which sets out, on the back, general conditions which include a jurisdiction clause. In *Estasis Salotti di Colzani Aimo v RÜWA Polstereimaschinen GmbH* the Court of Justice ruled that, in this situation, the requirement as to written form is satisfied 'only if the contract signed by both parties contains an express reference to those general conditions'.[158] In the absence of an express reference to printed terms on the back of the document signed by the parties, the jurisdiction clause does not satisfy paragraph (1)(a).[159]

5.3.17 Secondly, the document signed by the parties may refer to another document which refers to general conditions (which include a jurisdiction clause). This situation was also considered in *Estasis Salotti di Colzani Aimo v RÜWA Polstereimaschinen GmbH*.[160] The Court of Justice decided that—in the situation where a contract concluded by reference to earlier offers, which were themselves made with reference to the general conditions of one of the parties, including a jurisdiction clause—the requirement of writing is satisfied 'only if the reference is express

---

[153] *Deutsche Bank AG v Asia Pacific Broadband Wireless Communications Inc* [2008] 2 Lloyd's Rep 619, 624 (at [24]).

[154] *Bols Distilleries BV (trading as Bols Royal Distilleries) v Superior Yacht Services Ltd* [2007] 1 WLR 12.

[155] TC Hartley, (1977) 2 *EL Rev* 148.

[156] Case 71/83 *Partenreederei ms Tilly Russ v NV Haven- & Vervoerbedrijf Nova* [1984] ECR 2417, para 16. If, however, a jurisdiction clause is in illegible print, the requirements of Art 23(1)(a) are not met: *Richard SA v Pavan* [1998] ILPr 193 (Court of Cassation, France).

[157] See, eg, *Société Bretonne de Construction Navale v Société MB Marine* [1996] ILPr 133 (Court of Cassation, France). In the absence of confirmation by the other party, Art 23(1)(a) is not satisfied: *Mode Jeune Diffusion SA v Maglificio il Falco di Tizania Goti* [1998] ILPr 812 (Court of Cassation, France).

[158] Case 24/76 [1976] ECR 1831, para 10. See also *Jeumont-Schneider SA v Gruppo Industriale Ercole Marelli SpA* [1993] ILPr 12 (Court of Cassation, Italy).

[159] *Cotonfil Srl v Chemitex Sprl* [1983] ECC 8 (Court of Cassation, Italy); *Luz v Bertran* [1992] ILPr 537 (Court of Cassation, Italy); *Scan-Expo Wortmann GmbH v Ringkobling* [1994] ILPr 335 (Western Court of Appeal, Denmark).

[160] Case 24/76 [1976] ECR 1831.

and can therefore be checked by a party exercising reasonable care'[161] and 'only if it is established that the general conditions including the clause conferring jurisdiction have in fact been communicated to the other contracting party with the offer to which reference is made'.[162]

5.3.18   Thirdly, the contract signed by the parties may expressly refer to another document which contains general conditions (including a jurisdiction clause). While the judgment of the Court of Justice in *Estasis Salotti di Colzani Aimo v RÜWA Polstereimaschinen GmbH* does not expressly deal with this situation, it can be read as suggesting that the requirement of writing is satisfied in such a case.[163] In *Crédit Suisse Financial Products v Société Générale d'Entreprises*,[164] after the parties had concluded an agreement by telephone, the plaintiff sent a confirmation to the defendant, who signed and returned it. The confirmation expressly referred to a 'Master Agreement' which included an English jurisdiction clause. When the plaintiff started proceedings in England it was argued that the jurisdiction clause did not satisfy paragraph (1)(a) because the 'Master Agreement' had not been communicated to the defendant. The Court of Appeal interpreted *Estasis Salotti di Colzani Aimo v RÜWA Polstereimaschinen GmbH* as dealing only with the situation where there is a reference in the contract to another document (such as an offer), which in turn refers to conditions which include a jurisdiction clause. In the Court of Appeal's view the situation considered by the Court of Justice is distinguishable from the case where there is an express reference in the contract to general conditions which include a jurisdiction clause. The Court of Appeal, reversing the judge at first instance, decided that the requirement of writing is fulfilled if the general conditions (which include a jurisdiction clause) are incorporated by reference into a contract which is signed by both parties; it is irrelevant that the defendant does not have a readily available copy of the general conditions in his possession before signing the contract.[165]

5.3.19   Fourthly, a jurisdiction agreement contained in a company's Articles of association will satisfy paragraph (1)(a) 'if the statutes are lodged in a place to which the shareholder may have access, such as the seat of the company, or are contained in a public register'.[166] In these circumstances—even though the Articles of association are not directly communicated to the shareholders—'every shareholder is deemed to be aware of that clause and actually to have given consent to the assignment of jurisdiction for which it provides'.[167]

5.3.20   Where a contract containing or referring to a jurisdiction clause has not been signed by the party against whom it is invoked, the agreement is not 'in writing' for the purposes of paragraph (1)(a). What is the position, however, where A contracts with B on A's standard terms and B, who has not signed the contract, seeks to invoke the jurisdiction clause in the written contact against A? There is no obvious reason in this

---

[161] Case 24/76 [1976] ECR 1831, para 13.
[162] Case 24/76 [1976] ECR 1831, para 12.
[163] Case 24/76 [1976] ECR 1831, para 9.
[164] [1997] ILPr 165.
[165] See also *AIG Europe SA v QBE International Insurance Ltd* [2001] 2 Lloyd's Rep 268; *7E Communications Ltd v Vertex Antennentechnik GmbH* [2007] 1 WLR 2175; *Leo Laboratories Ltd v Crompton BV* [2005] 2 IR 225, 235 (Supreme Court, Ireland).
[166] Case C–214/89 *Powell Duffryn Plc v Petereit* [1992] ECR I–1745, para 28.
[167] Case C–214/89 *Powell Duffryn Plc v Petereit* [1992] ECR I–1745, para 28.

case why the jurisdiction clause should not be regarded as satisfying the requirements of paragraph (1)(a).[168]

5.3.21 *Iveco Fiat SpA v Van Hool NV*[169] concerned a jurisdiction clause in an agreement which had been concluded for a limited period. After the period had elapsed, the agreement was not formally renewed. Nevertheless, the parties continued dealing with each other for many years on the basis of the original agreement. The question was whether, in these circumstances, the parties could continue to rely on the jurisdiction clause. The Court of Justice held that, where the expired agreement continued to serve as the legal basis for the contractual relations between the parties, whether the jurisdiction clause was effective depended on the applicable law. If, for example, under the applicable law, the parties could validly renew the contract otherwise than in writing, the formal requirements would be met. If, however, under the applicable law, the parties could validly renew the contract only in writing, the requirement of writing would not be met unless either of the parties had confirmed in writing the jurisdiction clause or the group of clauses of which the jurisdiction clause formed a part without any objection from the other party to whom the written confirmation had been notified.[170]

EVIDENCED IN WRITING

5.3.22 The alternative requirement in subparagraph (a)—that a jurisdiction clause be evidenced in writing—has been interpreted by the Court of Justice as referring to the situation where a contract, which is concluded orally, is later confirmed in writing. A number of different situations should be distinguished.

5.3.23 The first situation arises where the oral agreement does not expressly include an agreement on jurisdiction. In *Galeries Segoura SPRL v Bonakdarian*[171] a contract of sale—which was concluded orally—was later confirmed by the seller in writing. The confirmation included the seller's standard terms and conditions, which incorporated a jurisdiction clause. The Court of Justice ruled:

Even if in an orally concluded contract the purchaser agrees to abide by the vendor's general conditions, he is not for that reason to be deemed to have agreed to any clause conferring jurisdiction which might appear in those general conditions. It follows that a confirmation in writing of the contract by the vendor, accompanied by the text of his general conditions, is without effect, as regards any clause conferring jurisdiction which it might contain, unless the purchaser agrees to it in writing.[172]

5.3.24 The second situation arises where there is an express oral agreement on jurisdiction which is subsequently confirmed in writing. In *F Berghöfer GmbH & Co*

---

[168] See Case 201/82 *Gerling Konzern Speziale Kreditversicherungs-AG v Amministrazione del Tesoro dello Stato* [1983] ECR 2503; *LAFI Office and International Business SL v Meriden Animal Health Ltd* [2000] 2 Lloyd's Rep 51.
[169] Case 313/85 [1986] ECR 3337.
[170] Case 313/85 [1986] ECR 3337, paras 7–8.
[171] Case 25/76 [1976] ECR 1851.
[172] Case 25/76 [1976] ECR 1851, para 8. See also *Polskie Ratownictwe Okretowe v Rallo Vito & C SNC* [2009] ILPr 922; *Re Yarn Sales* [1995] ILPr 180 (Federal Supreme Court, Germany). It is difficult to reconcile aspects of Henry LJ's judgment in *Agrafax Public Relations Ltd v United Scottish Society Incorporated* [1995] ILPr 753 with the decision of the Court of Justice.

KG v ASA SA[173] the Court of Justice decided that where jurisdiction is conferred by an express oral agreement the formal requirements are satisfied if one party sends written confirmation of that agreement to the other and the latter raises no objection. In this situation it does not matter which party sends the written confirmation.[174]

IN A FORM WHICH ACCORDS WITH PRACTICES WHICH THE PARTIES HAVE
ESTABLISHED BETWEEN THEMSELVES

5.3.25 Paragraph (1)(b) reflects the case law of the Court of Justice.[175] In *Partenreederei ms Tilly Russ v NV Haven- & Vervoerbedrijf Nova*[176] a contract of carriage had been concluded orally between the parties and then confirmed in writing when the carrier issued a bill of lading. The bill of lading, which included a jurisdiction clause, was signed by the carrier but not by the shipper. The Court of Justice held that the formal requirements were satisfied, notwithstanding the absence of express written agreement by the shipper, as long as the carrier and the shipper had a continuing business relationship which was governed as a whole by the carrier's general conditions which contained the jurisdiction clause.[177] If the conditions of paragraph (1)(b) are satisfied, it is immaterial whether the jurisdiction agreement was subject to prior oral agreement.[178]

5.3.26 Even in the context of a continuing trading relationship, paragraph (1)(b) will only come into play if the parties fail to conclude an agreement in writing which satisfies paragraph (1)(a). For example, if when a buyer orders goods the seller sends a written confirmation on the seller's general conditions (which include a jurisdiction clause) and the buyer signs and returns a tear-off slip agreeing to the seller's general conditions, the parties' agreement on jurisdiction satisfies the formal requirements of paragraph (1)(a). If, however, in relation to a particular contract the buyer fails to sign and return the tear-off slip and then a dispute arises out of that contract, the jurisdiction clause contained in the seller's general conditions is nevertheless valid because it satisfies the requirements of paragraph (1)(b).[179] Whether the dealings of parties to a continuing trading relationship are governed by the general conditions of one of them has to be determined on the facts of the case; paragraph (1)(b) will not be satisfied if, for example, a buyer regularly sends to the seller alternative sets of conditions of purchase and the seller habitually sends in return conflicting conditions of sale to the buyer.[180] Conversely, paragraph (1)(b) is satisfied where a buyer of goods repeatedly

---

[173] Case 221/84 [1985] ECR 2417, para 15.

[174] For criticism of this decision, see S Pieri, 'The 1968 Brussels Convention on Jurisdiction and Enforcement of Judgments in Civil and Commercial Matters: Four Years' Case Law of the European Court of Justice' (1987) 24 *CML Rev* 635, 644.

[175] See Case 25/76 *Galeries Segoura SPRL v Bonakdarian* [1976] ECR 1851; Case 71/83 *Partenreederei ms Tilly Russ v NV Haven- & Vervoerbedrijf Nova* [1984] ECR 2417.

[176] Case 71/83 [1984] ECR 2417.

[177] Case 71/83 [1984] ECR 2417, para 18. See also *Société Hanomag v Société Payant* [1996] ILPr 71 (Court of Appeal, Grenoble).

[178] *SSQ Europe SA v Johann & Backes OHG* [2002] 1 Lloyd's Rep 465. See also *Middle East Tankers & Freighters Bunker Services SA v Abu Dhabi Container Lines PJSC* [2002] 2 Lloyd's Rep 643.

[179] *Société Microstof Textiles v Société Laine Frères* [1990] ILPr 364 (Court of Appeal, Paris). See also *Re Missing Share Certificates* [1991] ILPr 298 (Court of Appeal, Munich); *Re a Purchase of Yarn* [1995] ILPr 479 (Federal Supreme Court, Germany).

[180] *Lafarge Plasterboard Ltd v Fritz Peters & Co KG* [2000] 2 Lloyd's Rep 689. See also *Oakley v Ultra Vehicle Design Ltd (In Liquidation)* [2005] ILPr 747, 762–64 (at [50]–[54]).

pays invoices which include a reference to the courts with jurisdiction without questioning the terms of the invoice.[181]

Trade Usages

5.3.27 The effect of paragraph (1)(c) is that:

Even in international trade or commerce, it is not sufficient that an agreement conferring jurisdiction be in a form which accords with practices (or a usage) in such trade or commerce of which the parties are or ought to have been aware. It is moreover required that the usage shall be, on the one hand, widely known in international trade or commerce and, on the other, regularly observed by parties to contracts of the type involved in the particular trade or commerce concerned.[182]

Although the Schlosser Report stressed that paragraph (c) does not obviate the need for an agreement on jurisdiction,[183] the reality is that, if the necessary conditions are satisfied, the agreement is presumed.[184] With regard to the interpretation of paragraph (1)(c), a number of points emerge from the decisions of the Court of Justice in *Mainschiffahrts-Genossenschaft eG (MSG) v Les Gravières Rhénanes*[185] and *Trasporti Castelletti Spedizioni Internazionali SpA v Hugo Trumpy SpA*.[186]

5.3.28 First, the court may presume that there is consensus between the parties to a jurisdiction clause if there are commercial practices in the relevant branch of international trade or commerce of which the parties are or ought to have been aware. Consensus will only be presumed, however, if the conduct of the parties is consistent with such a usage.[187]

5.3.29 Secondly, it is for the national court to determine whether the contract is one forming part of international trade or commerce and whether there is a usage in the branch of international trade or commerce in which the parties operate.[188] It is for the party seeking to rely on the alleged jurisdiction clause to establish that there is such a practice.[189]

---

[181] *Société Marcel Marie v Société Henco* [1998] ILPr 807 (Court of Appeal, Paris); *Clare Taverns v Gill* [2000] 2 ILRM 98 (High Court, Ireland). See also *Calyon v Wytwornia Sprzetu Komunikacynego PZL Swidnik SA* [2009] 2 All ER (Comm) 603.

[182] Jenard-Möller Report [1990] OJ C189/77, para 58.

[183] [1979] OJ C59/125, para 179.

[184] Case C–106/95 *Mainschiffahrts-Genossenschaft eG (MSG) v Les Gravières Rhénanes* [1997] ECR I–911; Case C–159/97 *Trasporti Castelletti Spedizioni Internazionali SpA v Hugo Trumpy SpA* [1999] ECR I–1597.

[185] Case C–106/95 *Mainschiffahrts-Genossenschaft eG (MSG) v Les Gravières Rhénanes* [1997] ECR I–911. TC Hartley, (1997) 22 *EL Rev* 360; E Peel, (1997) 17 *YBEL* 518; F Seatzu, 'Jurisdiction Agreements under Article 17(1)(c) of the Brussels Convention' (1998) 49 *NILQ* 327.

[186] Case C–159/97 [1999] ECR I–1597. TC Hartley, 'Jurisdiction agreements under the Brussels Jurisdiction and Judgments Convention' (2000) 25 *EL Rev* 178; E Peel, (2001) 20 *YBEL* 341.

[187] Case C–106/95 *Mainschiffahrts-Genossenschaft eG (MSG) v Les Gravières Rhénanes* [1997] ECR I–911, paras 19–20; Case C–159/97 *Trasporti Castelletti Spedizioni Internazionali SpA v Hugo Trumpy SpA* [1999] ECR I–1597, para 20.

[188] Case C–159/97 *Trasporti Castelletti Spedizioni Internazionali SpA v Hugo Trumpy SpA* [1999] ECR I–1597, para 23.

[189] See *Société Alusuisse France v Société Rodwer* [1990] ILPr 102 (Court of Appeal, Paris); *Société Aljoro v Société Iduga Filanova de Guebwiller* [1995] ILPr 616 (Court of Appeal, Paris).

5.3.30   Thirdly, whether a practice exists must be determined not by reference to international business or commerce in general, but by reference to the particular branch of international trade or commerce. It can be concluded that there is such a practice if:

a particular course of conduct is generally and regularly followed by operators in [the branch of international trade or commerce in question] when concluding contracts of a particular type.[190]

It is not necessary for such a course of conduct to be established in all the Member States. It will often be enough that there is a practice which is regularly followed by operators in the countries which play a prominent role in the branch of international trade or commerce in question.[191] Furthermore, although standard-form contracts will often follow guidelines issued by international organisations or by national associations (and the fact that this is the case may prove that a particular usage exists),[192] it is not necessary that publicity is given to the standard terms and conditions of certain types of contracts by such organisations or associations in order to prove that a usage exists.[193] It is also the case that a course of conduct satisfying the conditions indicative of a usage does not cease to be a usage just because it is challenged in the courts.[194]

5.3.31   Fourthly, parties will be presumed to be aware of a usage (regardless of any specific form of publicity[195]) either where they previously had commercial or trade relations between themselves or with other parties operating in the sector of international trade or commerce in question or where, in that sector, a particular course of conduct is sufficiently well known because it is generally and regularly followed when a particular type of contract is concluded, so that it may be regarded as being an established usage.[196] Since, in a case where rights and obligations under a contract are assigned to a third party, the validity of the jurisdiction agreement must be assessed by reference to the relationship between the original contracting parties,[197] it follows that it is the original parties whose awareness of the usage in question must be assessed.[198]

---

[190] Case C–106/95 *Mainschiffahrts-Genossenschaft eG (MSG) v Les Gravières Rhénanes* [1997] ECR I–911, para 23; Case C–159/97 *Trasporti Castelletti Spedizioni Internazionali SpA v Hugo Trumpy SpA* [1999] ECR I–1597, para 26.

[191] Case C–159/97 *Trasporti Castelletti Spedizioni Internazionali SpA v Hugo Trumpy SpA* [1999] ECR I–1597, para 27.

[192] See Advocate General Léger in Case C–159/97 *Trasporti Castelletti Spedizioni Internazionali SpA v Hugo Trumpy SpA* [1999] ECR I–1597, paras 153–4.

[193] Case C–159/97 *Trasporti Castelletti Spedizioni Internazionali SpA v Hugo Trumpy SpA* [1999] ECR I–1597, para 28.

[194] Case C–159/97 *Trasporti Castelletti Spedizioni Internazionali SpA v Hugo Trumpy SpA* [1999] ECR I–1597, para 29.

[195] Case C–159/97 *Trasporti Castelletti Spedizioni Internazionali SpA v Hugo Trumpy SpA* [1999] ECR I–1597, para 45.

[196] Case C–106/95 *Mainschiffahrts-Genossenschaft eG (MSG) v Les Gravières Rhénanes* [1997] ECR I–911, para 24; Case C–159/97 *Trasporti Castelletti Spedizioni Internazionali SpA v Hugo Trumpy SpA* [1999] ECR I–1597, para 43. See also *The Kribi* [2001] 1 Lloyd's Rep 76.

[197] Case 71/83 *Partenreederei ms Tilly Russ v NV Haven- & Vervoerbedrijf Nova* [1984] ECR 2417.

[198] Case C–159/97 *Trasporti Castelletti Spedizioni Internazionali SpA v Hugo Trumpy SpA* [1999] ECR I–1597, para 42.

Formal Requirements and Third Parties

5.3.32   In view of the way in which the formal requirements have been interpreted by the Court of Justice, potential problems arise in cases where the party to the litigation was not an original party to the agreement which incorporates the jurisdiction clause.[199] There are various issues to consider.

5.3.33   The first situation arises where a third party beneficiary wishes to rely on a contractual agreement on jurisdiction. In *Gerling Konzern Speziale Kreditversicherungs-AG v Amministrazione del Tesoro dello Stato*[200] the Court of Justice ruled that a third party beneficiary (in this case a beneficiary of a contract of insurance) can invoke a jurisdiction clause even if he has not signed it. The purpose of the jurisdiction agreement provisions are to ensure that the consent of the parties against whom the clause may be invoked is clearly and precisely expressed. From this point of view, there can be no reason for requiring a third party beneficiary to have signed the jurisdiction agreement.

5.3.34   The second situation arises where one of the parties to the original contract (which includes a jurisdiction clause) transfers his rights and obligations under the contract to a third party—whether voluntarily or by operation of law—and the other party to the original contract seeks to enforce the jurisdiction clause against the third party. In *Partenreederei ms Tilly Russ v NV Haven- & Vervoerbedrijf Nova*[201] the Court of Justice took the view that where a contract which includes a jurisdiction clause is concluded between A and B, the clause remains binding between A and C, a third party, if two conditions are met: (i) the jurisdiction clause is valid as between A and B; and (ii) under the applicable law C has succeeded to B's rights and obligations under the original contract.[202] So, in cases where a jurisdiction agreement is being invoked against a third party, to determine whether or not the formal requirements have been satisfied, the court first needs to focus on the contract between the original contracting parties.[203] However, it must not be forgotten that, even if the conditions laid down in *Partenreederei ms Tilly Russ v NV Haven- & Vervoerbedrijf Nova* are not satisfied (for example, because C does not succeed to the original party's rights and obligations under the relevant national law), this does not rule out the possibility of C being directly bound by the jurisdiction clause as a result of the relevant formal requirements being satisfied as against C[204] (for example, on the basis of a previous course of dealing between A and C).

---

[199] Where an agent who is authorised to act on behalf of his principal concludes a contract which is governed by English law and contains an English jurisdiction clause, the principal is bound: *Standard Steamship Owners Protection & Indemnity Association (Bermuda) Ltd v GIE Vision Bail* [2005] 1 All ER (Comm) 618.

[200] Case 201/82 [1983] ECR 2503.

[201] Case 71/83 [1984] ECR 2417. PM North, 'Jurisdiction clauses in bills of lading and the European Judgments Convention' [1985] *LMCLQ* 177; M Wilderspin, (1984) 9 *EL Rev* 456.

[202] Case 71/83 [1984] ECR 2417, para 26. See also Case C–387/98 *Coreck Maritime GmbH v Handelsveem BV* [2000] ECR I–9337; *Glencore International AG v Metro Trading International Inc* [1999] 2 Lloyd's Rep 632; *The Kribi* [2001] 1 Lloyd's Rep 76; *Knorr-Bremse Systems for Commercial Vehicles Ltd v Haldex Brake Products GmbH* [2008] ILPr 326.

[203] Case C–159/97 *Trasporti Castelletti Spedizioni Internazionali SpA v Hugo Trumpy SpA* [1999] ECR I–1597, paras 41–2.

[204] Case C–387/98 *Coreck Maritime GmbH v Handelsveem BV* [2000] ECR I–9337, para 27.

5.3.35 Thirdly, where a contract is assigned a question may arise whether the assignee can invoke the jurisdiction clause in the original contract. On the basis of the Court of Justice's ruling in *Partenreederei ms Tilly Russ v NV Haven- & Vervoerbedrijf Nova*, it has been decided (*obiter*) that where a contract of guarantee which includes a jurisdiction clause has been assigned, as long as the requirements are satisfied as between the original contracting parties, the assignee is entitled to take advantage of the jurisdiction clause against the guarantor.[205] In *Re Leyland DAF Ltd* [206] the question arose whether a jurisdiction clause in a contract between two companies was enforceable after one of the companies went into receivership. It was held that the jurisdiction clause remained binding regardless of whether proceedings were brought by the company receivers in the name of the company or were brought by an office-holder in his own name. The reality was that, despite the intervention of the receivers, the company—which was one of the original parties to the jurisdiction agreement—was the claimant in the litigation.

Formal Requirements and National Law

5.3.36 It is quite possible for there to be divergences between the formal requirements set out in Article 23 of the Brussels I Regulation and the requirements imposed by the applicable law (or the law of the forum). First, a jurisdiction clause, which is valid under the applicable law, may be formally invalid under Article 23. It should not be concluded, however, that in this situation the jurisdiction clause is entirely without effect. Of course, a jurisdiction clause which is invalid under the Brussels I Regulation cannot be invoked against a person who is domiciled in a Member State. However, the position may be different as regards a defendant who is not domiciled in a Member State. Article 4 provides that, as a general rule, a defendant who is not domiciled in a Member State may be sued in a Member State in accordance with traditional jurisdiction rules. If an English claimant issues proceedings in England against a New York company on the basis of an English jurisdiction clause, the invalidity of the clause under Article 23 of the Brussels I Regulation means simply that the claim form does not fall within CPR 6.33 and cannot be served on the defendant without the court's permission. However, under CPR 6.36 a claimant may apply for permission to serve the defendant out of the jurisdiction on the ground that the contract 'contains a term to the effect that the [English] court shall have jurisdiction to determine any claim in respect of the contract'.[207] As regards a defendant who is not domiciled in a Member State, if the jurisdiction clause is valid according to its proper law, the fact that the clause is formally invalid under Article 23 is no obstacle to permission to serve out being given under CPR 6.36.

5.3.37 Secondly, the applicable law may impose formal requirements which are more severe than those contained in the jurisdiction agreement provisions. In *Elefanten Schuh GmbH v Jacqmain*[208] the Court of Justice held that the formal requirements of the jurisdiction agreement provisions are both necessary and

---

[205] *Firswood Ltd v Petra Bank* [1996] CLC 608.
[206] [1994] 1 BCLC 264, affirmed [1994] 2 BCLC 106.
[207] CPR PD 6B para 3.1(6)(d). See para 7.3.28.
[208] Case 150/80 [1981] ECR 1671.

sufficient. Accordingly, a national law which lays down more stringent requirements cannot render formally invalid a jurisdiction agreement which satisfies the requirements of the Brussels I Regulation.[209] For example, it is irrelevant that national law would strike down a jurisdiction clause which is in a foreign language or which is printed in small type.[210] Similarly, in a case where a jurisdiction clause satisfies the requirements of paragraph (1)(c), the fact that statutory requirements of the law of the forum lay down additional requirements as to form is irrelevant.[211]

Material Validity and Interpretation

Material Validity[212]

5.3.38   A clause which is materially or essentially invalid is ineffective, regardless of whether the relevant formal requirements are satisfied. While it is clear that the Brussels regime determines the formal validity of a jurisdiction agreement, the extent to which it also regulates questions of material validity is more uncertain. For example, which law determines whether or not an alleged jurisdiction clause is void for mistake or whether such a clause may be set aside on the basis of duress? There are two possible views and the case law is not easy to reconcile.

5.3.39   One approach is that the requirements of Article 23 'are not strictly ones of formality'[213] and that Article 23 is a self-sufficient code which regulates both the formal and material validity of jurisdiction agreements under the Brussels I Regulation.[214] A clause is effective for the purposes of Article 23 only if the parties 'have agreed' that a court or the courts of a Member State are to have jurisdiction. It is arguable that whether or not the parties 'have agreed' is a question of European law. In the course of its judgment in *Benincasa v Dentalkit Srl* the Court of Justice seemed to advocate this approach:

A jurisdiction clause, which serves a procedural purpose, is governed by the provisions ... whose aim is to establish uniform rules of international jurisdiction. In contrast, the substantive provisions of the main contract in which that clause is incorporated, and likewise any dispute as to the validity of that contract, are governed by the *lex causae* determined by the private international law of the State of the court having jurisdiction.[215]

Similarly, in *Trasporti Castelletti Spedizioni Internazionali SpA v Hugo Trumpy SpA* the Court of Justice indicated that once the requirements of the jurisdiction agreement provision were satisfied, 'any further review of the validity of the clause and of the

---

[209] Case C–159/97 *Trasporti Castelletti Spedizioni Internazionali SpA v Hugo Trumpy SpA* [1999] ECR I–1597, para 37.
[210] *Fulgurit v La Compagnie d'Assurances FPA* [1996] ILPr 495 (Court of Cassation, France).
[211] Case C–159/97 *Trasporti Castelletti Spedizioni Internazionali SpA v Hugo Trumpy SpA* [1999] ECR I–1597, para 38.
[212] See AS Bell, 'Jurisdiction and Arbitration Agreements in Transnational Contracts, Part II' (1996) 10 *JCL* 97.
[213] David Steel J in *Knauf UK GmbH v British Gypsum Ltd* [2001] 2 All ER (Comm) 332, 341 (at [46]).
[214] See Aikens J in *Provimi Ltd v Roche Products Ltd* [2003] 2 All ER (Comm) 683, 713 (at [59]).
[215] Case C–269/95 [1997] ECR I–3767, para 25. See J Harris, 'Jurisdiction Clauses and Void Contracts' (1998) 23 *EL Rev* 279, 281–3.

intention of the party which inserted it must be excluded'.[216] Furthermore, in *Custom Made Commercial Ltd v Stawa Metallbau GmbH* Advocate General Lenz summarised the relationship between national law and Article 17 of the Brussels Convention (which has largely been superseded by Article 23 of the Brussels I Regulation) in the following terms:

Rules of the national law relating to the effective incorporation of contractual provisions and, in particular, of provisions set out in general business conditions and covering effective consensus and the form to be taken by such consensus are not applicable alongside Article 17 of the Brussels Convention. Accordingly, such rules of the national substantive law which is applicable in accordance with the conflicts rules of the court hearing the case cannot be used in order to determine whether a jurisdiction clause satisfying the conditions laid down by Article 17 has been validly incorporated into a contract.[217]

On the basis of these authorities, it would seem that once the conditions of Article 23 are satisfied, there no need to consider the question whether the clause is regarded as incorporated into the contract under the applicable law.[218] In addition, whether an alleged jurisdiction clause is, say, void for mistake or vitiated by duress raises the issue whether the parties 'have agreed' to the jurisdiction of particular courts and is to be determined by a European standard, rather than a national one.[219] The major problem with this approach is practical, rather than theoretical. Until appropriate European principles have been established by the Court of Justice a national court has little guidance as to what the European standard should be.

5.3.40 The alternative view is that the jurisdiction agreement provisions are concerned with formal validity and that the material validity of a jurisdiction clause is to be tested by reference to its governing law. According to this view, the governing law determines whether a jurisdiction clause is a term of the contract at all.[220] The Giuliano-Lagarde Report, which accompanies the Rome Convention on the Law Applicable to Contractual Obligations,[221] adopts this view—which also derives some support from the Court of Justice's ruling in *Powell Duffryn Plc v Petereit*.[222] On the

---

[216] Case C–159/97 [1999] ECR I–1597, para 51. It would seem that this ruling effectively reverses the effect of *The Hollandia* [1983] 1 AC 565 in which the House of Lords refused to give effect to a Dutch jurisdiction clause on the basis that this would be contrary to English mandatory rules (contained in the Carriage of Goods by Sea Act 1971): E Peel, (2001) 20 *YBEL* 342–3. Despite the Court of Justice's ruling in *Benincasa v Dentalkit Srl*, national courts will sometimes refer to national law, whether the *lex fori* or the *lex causae*, on a residual basis to determine the issue of consent to and validity of a jurisdiction clause: European Commission, 'Report from the Commission to the European Parliament, the Council and the European Economic and Social Committee on the application of Council Regulation (EC) No 44/2001 on jurisdiction and the recognition and enforcement of judgments in civil and commercial matters' (hereafter 'Commission Report'), COM (2008) 174 final, p 5.

[217] Case C–288/92 [1994] ECR I–2913, para 127.

[218] *AIG Europe SA v QBE International Insurance Ltd* [2001] 2 Lloyd's Rep 268 (A Briggs, (2001) 72 *BYIL* 452); *Siboti K/S v BP France SA* [2003] 2 Lloyd's Rep 364. Cf *Nestorway Ltd t/a Electrographic International v Ambaflex BV* [2007] ILPr 633, 638–9 (High Court, Ireland).

[219] See Judge Richard Siberry QC in *Carnoustie Universal SA v International Transport Workers' Federation* [2002] 2 All ER (Comm) 657, 690–1 (at [107]–[108]).

[220] See *AIG Europe (UK) v The Ethniki* [2000] 2 All ER 566; *LAFI Office and International Business SL v Meriden Animal Health Ltd* [2000] 2 Lloyd's Rep 51.

[221] [1980] OJ C282/11.

[222] Case C–214/89 [1992] ECR I–1745. See also *Re a Shop Fitting Contract* [1993] ILPr 395 (Court of Appeal, Saarbrücken).

assumption that questions of material validity are not governed by European law, the common law choice of law rules are relevant for determining the proper law as agreements on jurisdiction are excluded from the scope of the Rome I Regulation.[223] If a contract which contains a jurisdiction clause also contains an express choice of law, the chosen law is the proper law of the jurisdiction agreement. If there is no express choice, the law of the forum chosen by the parties is generally the proper law.[224] Potential problems may arise in cases where the existence of the jurisdiction clause (or the contract of which it forms a part) is contested. In such a case, the governing law is the putative proper law (ie, the law which would govern if the contract were valid).

Interpretation

5.3.41 At common law, the proper law governs the interpretation of a jurisdiction clause.[225] The Court of Justice, somewhat unhelpfully, has indicated only that 'it is for the national court to interpret the clause conferring jurisdiction invoked before it in order to determine which disputes fall within its scope'.[226] Whether textual ambiguities are to be resolved by reference to the canons of construction of the law of the forum or those of the proper law of the jurisdiction clause (as determined by the private international law of the forum) is not addressed.[227] From the point of view of principle, the proper law of the agreement should govern questions of substance (which include questions of interpretation).[228] Where, for example, the parties agree to refer disputes to 'British courts' the proper law should determine what is meant by 'British' in this context. Similarly, whether a jurisdiction agreement is exclusive or non-exclusive is an issue which should be referred to the proper law of the agreement. In an ordinary commercial contract which is governed by English law a clause which refers disputes to 'the jurisdiction of the English court' is normally interpreted as conferring exclusive jurisdiction, notwithstanding the fact that the word 'exclusive' is not used.[229] Even where the proper law of the jurisdiction clause is the law of a country other than England, the court will apply English law in the absence of any evidence of the relevant foreign law.[230]

5.3.42 A contractual jurisdiction agreement, if drafted in appropriate terms, may cover related tortious claims. Given the decision of the House of Lords in

---

[223] Art 1(2)(d). See para 14.1.14.

[224] *Hamlyn & Co v Talisker Distillery* [1894] AC 202; *Spurrier v La Cloche* [1902] AC 446.

[225] *Evans Marshall & Co Ltd v Bertola SA* [1973] 1 WLR 349. For an application of this rule, see *Provimi Ltd v Roche Products Ltd* [2003] 2 All ER (Comm) 683. See also O Kahn-Freund, 'Jurisdiction Agreements: Some Reflections' (1977) 26 *ICLQ* 825.

[226] Case C–214/89 *Powell Duffryn Plc v Petereit* [1992] ECR I–1745, para 37; Case C–269/95 *Benincasa v Dentalkit Srl* [1997] ECR I–3767, para 31.

[227] This point was not addressed by the Court of Appeal in *UBS AG v HSH Nordbank AG* [2009] 2 Lloyd's Rep 272, nor is it clear which approach was adopted.

[228] See Andrew Smith J in *Evialis SA v SIAT* [2003] 2 Lloyd's Rep 377, 389 (at [60]). See also Judge Richard Seymour QC in *British Sugar Plc v Fratelli Babbini di Lionello Babbini & Co SAS* [2005] 1 Lloyd's Rep 332, 343–4 (at [40]–[42]).

[229] *Sohio Supply Co v Gatoil (USA) Inc* [1989] 1 Lloyd's Rep 588; *British Aerospace Plc v Dee Howard Co* [1993] 1 Lloyd's Rep 368. Compare Waller J in *IP Metal Ltd v Ruote OZ SpA* [1993] 2 Lloyd's Rep 60, 67.

[230] See, eg, *Dresser UK Ltd v Falcongate Freight Management Ltd* [1992] 1 QB 502.

Fiona Trust & Holding v Privalov,[231] the preferable approach when construing the ambit of the jurisdiction clause is a generous one, taking a common sense view of what rational parties may have intended. In *Kitechnology BV v Unicor GmbH Rahn Plastmaschinen*[232] the parties had entered a confidentiality agreement which included an English jurisdiction clause. The plaintiff alleged that the defendant had misused confidential information and started proceedings in England claiming damages. It was held that a broadly drafted jurisdiction clause is not limited to contractual claims, but extends to other claims (such as claims in tort) which are so closely connected with the contractual claims that the parties can properly be taken to have intended that they should be decided by the same forum. Similarly, it has been held that, as regards a power of attorney which includes a jurisdiction clause in favour of Swiss courts and is governed by Swiss law, a claim arising out of an alleged breach of fiduciary duty in the exercise of the power of attorney falls within the scope of the jurisdiction agreement.[233] However, it seems that under the laws of Switzerland, Germany and France, even a widely drafted jurisdiction clause does not extend to claims for damages for infringement of Article 101 of the Treaty on the Functioning of the European Union.[234]

Situations where Jurisdiction is not Exclusive

Alternative Fora

5.3.43   Article 23 of the Brussels I Regulation refers to agreements conferring jurisdiction on a court or the courts of a single state. In *Meeth v Glacetal*[235] the Court of Justice decided that a clause conferring jurisdiction on alternative fora is valid. So, where a contract between A and B contains a jurisdiction clause which provides that if A sues B the courts of Germany are to have jurisdiction, but if B sues A the courts of France are to have jurisdiction, the jurisdiction clause falls within the scope of Article 23. Furthermore, if A sues B in Germany in accordance with the terms of the jurisdiction clause and B raises a set-off in the context of those proceedings, the German court has jurisdiction to consider 'a set-off connected with the legal relationship in dispute if such court considers that course to be compatible with the letter and spirit of the clause conferring jurisdiction'.[236]

---

[231] [2007] 4 All ER 951. A Briggs, [2008] *LMCLQ* 1.
[232] [1994] ILPr 568. See also *Maple Leaf Macro Volatility Master Fund v Rouvroy* [2009] 1 Lloyd's Rep 475, 507–8 (at [197]–[199]); *Skype Technologies SA v Joltid Ltd* [2009] EWHC 2783 (Ch); *Leo Laboratories Ltd v Crompton BV* [2005] 2 IR 225 (Supreme Court, Ireland). Cf *Hewden Tower Cranes Ltd v Wolffkran GmbH* [2007] 2 Lloyd's Rep 138.
[233] *Maimann v Maimann* [2001] ILPr 396.
[234] *Provimi Ltd v Roche Products Ltd* [2003] 2 All ER (Comm) 683. See also *Re the Termination of a Distribution Contract* [2003] ILPr 633 (Court of First Instance, Thessaloniki).
[235] Case 23/78 [1978] ECR 2133. TC Hartley, (1979) 4 *EL Rev* 125.
[236] Case 23/78 [1978] ECR 2133, para 8. The German Federal Supreme Court subsequently decided that, on its proper construction, the clause did not confer jurisdiction on the German courts as regards the defendant's counterclaim for set-off: *Glacetal Sàrl v Firma Meeth* [1979] ECC 455.

5.3.44 The liberal approach adopted by the Court of Justice suggests that, if a dispute-resolution clause purports to allow a claimant to refer disputes either to a particular court or to arbitration, the clause is effective to confer jurisdiction on the chosen court if the claimant elects to start proceedings in that court.[237] Similarly, a jurisdiction clause which provides that either party may bring proceedings against the other in the courts of two or more Member States would be effective. So, if a contract includes a term stating that 'all disputes arising under the contract shall be decided by the courts of England or France', either party would have a choice whether to bring proceedings in the English or French courts. If, in such a case, proceedings were commenced in more than one of the chosen fora on the same cause of action, any court other than the court first seised would be required to decline jurisdiction.[238]

Non-exclusive Jurisdiction Clauses[239]

5.3.45 Whether a jurisdiction clause is exclusive or non-exclusive is a matter of construction to be determined by reference to its proper law.[240] Article 23 of the Brussels I Regulation provides that, where the parties have agreed to the jurisdiction of a Member State, such jurisdiction is exclusive 'unless the parties have agreed otherwise'. Although, in a non-exclusive jurisdiction agreement, the non-exclusivity will normally be express, in appropriate circumstances, the non-exclusivity may be either implied or inferred from the wording of the agreement or the surrounding circumstances.[241] There are two aspects to a non-exclusive jurisdiction clause: first, it confers jurisdiction on the chosen court (or courts) and, secondly, it does not deprive the courts of other Member States of the jurisdiction which they enjoy under other relevant bases of jurisdiction.[242] So, if a German company and a French company agree to refer contractual disputes to the non-exclusive jurisdiction of the French courts, the French company has a choice of proceeding in the French courts (which have jurisdiction by virtue of Article 23) or the German courts (which have jurisdiction under Article 2).

Clauses for the Benefit of One Party Only

5.3.46 The Brussels I Regulation does not expressly deal with jurisdiction agreements which are concluded for the benefit of one of the parties to the agreement. The purpose of such an agreement is twofold: first, the party for whose benefit the agreement was made is permitted either to rely on the clause by proceeding in the courts of the country chosen by the parties or to bring proceedings in another country on the basis of other jurisdiction rules; secondly, the other party has no choice but to

---

[237] See *SA Ripi v Schumacher GmbH* [1989] ECC 50 (Commercial Court, Brussels).
[238] See section 9.1.
[239] See JJ Fawcett, 'Non-exclusive jurisdiction agreements in private international law' [2001] *LMCLQ* 234.
[240] See *McGowan v Summit at Lloyds*, 2002 SC 638 (Sheriff Court, Extra Division).
[241] *Evialis SA v SIAT* [2003] 2 Lloyd's Rep 377.
[242] *Insured Financial Structures Ltd v Elektrocieplownia Tychy SA* [2003] QB 1260.

proceed in the chosen forum.[243] For the purposes of the Brussels I Regulation, this is type of agreement is non-exclusive from the perspective of the party for whose benefit the agreement was concluded, but exclusive from the perspective of the other party. As Article 23 gives effect to both exclusive and non-exclusive jurisdiction agreements, there should be no doubts over the validity and effect of jurisdiction agreements concluded for the benefit of one party under the Brussels I Regulation.

5.4 PROVISIONAL MEASURES

5.4.1   Article 31 of the Brussels I Regulation provides:

Application may be made to the courts of a Member State for such provisional, including protective, measures as may be available under the law of that State, even if, under this Regulation, the courts of another Member State have jurisdiction as to the substance of the matter.

This provision applies to 'measures which … are intended to preserve a factual or legal situation so as to safeguard rights the recognition of which is sought elsewhere from the court having jurisdiction as to the substance of the matter'.[244] Although, according to this definition, freezing injunctions[245] and search orders[246] are provisional measures, the position of an interim anti-suit injunction is less clear.[247] To fall within Article 31, the measure in question must not have the effect of prejudging the substantive proceedings in another Member State.[248] If, for example, a court orders a defendant to make an interim payment to the claimant, such an order can constitute a provisional measure only if repayment to the defendant is guaranteed should the claimant be unsuccessful in the substantive claim and as long as the measure relates only to specific assets located within the jurisdiction of the court making the order.[249]

5.4.2   Article 31 does not in itself confer jurisdiction on an English court to grant freezing injunctions in support of foreign proceedings; it simply permits the courts of one Member State to grant protective measures in support of proceedings in another Member State; which measures can be granted and in what circumstances is a matter for the procedural law of the forum.[250] At common law, as a consequence of the decision of the House of Lords in *Siskina (Owners of cargo lately laden on board) v Distos*

---

[243] See, eg, *Ocarina Marine Ltd v Marcard Stein & Co* [1994] 2 Lloyd's Rep 524.

[244] Case C–261/90 *Reichert v Dresdner Bank (No 2)* [1992] ECR I–2149, para 34. A Briggs, (1992) 12 *YBEL* 660.

[245] Formerly known as *Mareva* injunctions.

[246] Formerly known as *Anton Piller* orders.

[247] See *Masri v Consolidated Contractors International (UK) Ltd (No 2)* [2009] QB 450.

[248] *Zinser Fleisch Import & Export Handelsgesellschaft v SA Salaisons du Jet Jean Laurent* [1994] ILPr 237 (Court of Appeal, Rennes).

[249] Case C–391/95 *Van Uden Maritime BV v Firma Deco-Line* [1998] ECR I–7091, para 47; Case C–99/96 *Mietz v Intership Yachting Sneek BV* [1999] ECR I–2277, para 43. See also *Bachy SA v Belbetoes Fundacoes e Betoes Especiais Lda* [1999] ILPr 743 (Court of Cassation, France); *Advanced Licensing GmbH v Studiocanal France* [2003] ILPr 550 (Court of Appeal, Paris).

[250] See *Re a Modelling Agency Agreement* [2003] ILPr 754 (Federal Supreme Court, Austria); *Frans Maas Rotterdam BV v Hans Ulrich Peterman Beratungs-und-Vertrub GmbH* [2005] ILPr 768 (Supreme Court, Netherlands).

Compania Naviera SA,[251] the court has no jurisdiction to grant interim relief unless it is 'properly seised of the substance of the claim'.[252] The Civil Jurisdiction and Judgments Act 1982, however, reverses the effect of the Siskina doctrine by providing that the High Court may grant interim relief in support of foreign proceedings. The court has power to grant interim relief under section 25(1) of the 1982 Act in support of proceedings being conducted in another country.[253] This power arises whether or not the defendant is otherwise amenable to the *in personam* jurisdiction of the court. Where, for example, proceedings have been commenced in France, even though the English court has no jurisdiction in relation to the substantive claim, the claimant may obtain in England an injunction freezing the defendant's assets—whether or not the defendant is domiciled in a Member State. Under the Civil Procedure Rules service of a claim form out of the jurisdiction claiming interim relief is permissible with the court's permission.[254]

5.5 THE DOMICILE RULE: ARTICLE 2

5.5.1   The effect of Article 2(1) is that, subject to other provisions of Chapter II, a person domiciled in a Member State shall, whatever their nationality, be sued in the courts of that state. Jurisdiction under Article 2 is general—in the sense that, as regards matters within the material scope of the Brussels I Regulation, there are no restrictions on the types of dispute which can be brought in the courts of the defendant's domicile. This means, for example, that it is possible for a defendant domiciled in England to be sued in England for infringement of a foreign intellectual property right.[255] The second paragraph of Article 2 makes it clear that national courts cannot discriminate against claimants on grounds of nationality. Traditionally, English jurisdiction rules have treated foreign claimants—with the exception of enemy aliens[256]— on exactly the same basis as English claimants.

5.5.2   Although Article 2 does not expressly address the question of when the defendant must be domiciled in a Member State, the only rational interpretation is that the relevant time is when the proceedings are started—otherwise the claimant 'may be shooting at a moving target'.[257] After some uncertainty in the lower courts,[258] the House of Lords held in *Canada Trust Co v Stolzenberg (No 2)*[259] that, in the

---

[251] [1979] AC 210.

[252] See Kerr LJ in *Babanaft International Co SA v Bassatne* [1990] Ch 13, 30.

[253] For further discussion, see ch 10.

[254] CPR 6.36, PD 6B para 3.1(5). See section 10.3.

[255] *Coin Controls Ltd v Suzo International (UK) Ltd* [1999] Ch 33 (S Dutson, 'Actions for Infringement of a Foreign Intellectual Property Right in an English Court' (1997) 46 *ICLQ* 918; R Fentiman, [1997] *CLJ* 503); *Pearce v Ove Arup Partnership Ltd* [2000] Ch 403 (A Briggs, (1999) 70 *BYIL* 337; R Fentiman, [1999] *CLJ* 286; J Harris, 'Justiciability, choice of law and the Brussels Convention' [1999] *LMCLQ* 360); *Fort Dodge Animal Health Ltd v Azko Nobel NV* [1998] FSR 222. But, see the country view in *Lucasfilm Ltd v Ainsworth* [2010] FSR 270.

[256] See paras 2.2.1–2.2.2.

[257] Mance J in *Grupo Torras SA v Sheikh Fahad Mohammed Al-Sabah* [1995] 1 Lloyd's Rep 374, 445.

[258] Mance J in *Grupo Torras SA v Sheikh Fahad Mohammed Al-Sabah* [1995] 1 Lloyd's Rep 374, 445 took the view that the crucial date was the issue of the writ (though, in any event, the writ was served on the following day). Rix J in *Trade Indemnity Plc v Försäkringsaktiebolaget Njord* [1995] 1 All ER 796, 822 left the question open.

[259] [2002] 1 AC 1.

context of Article 6 of the 1988 Lugano Convention,[260] the defendant's domicile is to be determined when process is issued, rather than when it is served. This approach is equally applicable in relation to Article 2.[261]

5.5.3   The first paragraph of Article 2 must be read in conjunction with Article 3, which provides that a person domiciled in a Member State may be sued in another Member State in accordance with the other provisions set out in Chapter II. In cases where jurisdiction is allocated by the jurisdiction provisions which override Article 2,[262] jurisdiction cannot be based on the defendant's domicile, notwithstanding the use of the word 'shall' in the first paragraph of Article 2. In cases where, on the basis of Article 2, the defendant may be sued in the courts of the Member State in which he is domiciled, the claimant often has the choice of invoking the jurisdiction of the courts of another Member State which has special jurisdiction.[263]

5.6 ALTERNATIVE FORA I: ARTICLE 5

Introduction

5.6.1   Article 5 provides a number of situations in which a person domiciled in a Member State may be sued in another Member State.[264] Article 5 contains seven paragraphs concerning the following matters: (1) 'matters relating to a contract'; (2) 'matters relating to maintenance'; (3) 'matters relating to tort, delict or quasi-delict'; (4) 'a civil claim for damages or restitution which is based on an act giving rise to criminal proceedings'; (5) 'a dispute arising out of the operations of a branch, agency or other establishment'; (6) certain proceedings relating to trusts; (7) 'a dispute concerning the payment of remuneration claimed in respect of the salvage of a cargo or freight'. Paragraph (2) does not concern commercial matters and is beyond the scope of this work; paragraph (4) is of very limited application as a basis of jurisdiction in England since under English law civil claims for damages in criminal proceedings are relatively unimportant in practice;[265] paragraph (7), which was added to the Brussels Convention by the 1978 Accession Convention, is discussed in a subsequent

---

[260]   The Lugano Convention was revised in 2007 and is nearly identical to the Brussels I Regulation. See para 3.1.5.

[261]   See Lord Steyn at [2002] 1 AC 1, 8.

[262]   See, eg, Arts 22 and 23.

[263]   Brussels I Reg, Arts 5–7.

[264]   One of the questions raised by the Commission Green Paper is whether the special jurisdiction rules of the Regulation should be applied to third state defendants: European Commission, Green Paper on the Review of Council Regulation (EC) No 44/2001 on jurisdiction and the recognition and enforcement of judgments in civil and commercial matters, COM (2009) 175 final, p 4. The House of Lords' European Union Committee, in its Green Paper on the Brussels I Regulation, issued a lukewarm response to this question; two particular concerns were that the creation of uniform rules in relation to third state defendants might increase the risk of parallel proceedings and that third states are not bound by the reciprocal system of jurisdictional rules set out in the Regulation. See HL Paper 148, pp 15–16 (paras 41–7).

[265]   Issues relating to the recognition or enforcement of judgments may arise where the courts of another Member State assumes jurisdiction under this provision. See Case C–7/98 *Krombach v Bamberski* [2000] ECR I–1935.

chapter.[266] In the present context, the most important elements of Article 5 are paragraphs (1), (3), (5) and (6).

5.6.2 Except with regard to cases falling within paragraph (6), the effect of Article 5 is to allocate jurisdiction to a 'place' rather than to a state. As far as the United Kingdom is concerned, the 'place' identified by Article 5 will be England, Scotland or Northern Ireland. The position in other Member States is somewhat different because of the operation of a system of regional courts. It cannot be assumed that, because the relevant 'place' is in the Netherlands, the claimant can sue the defendant anywhere in the Netherlands. Where the claimant relies on one of the paragraphs of Article 5, the claim must be brought in the district court where the 'place' in question is located; proceedings which are commenced in the wrong district court have to be transferred to (or terminated and restarted in) the proper court.[267]

5.6.3 In general, the connecting factors which justify jurisdiction under Article 5 are not ones which connect the defendant to the forum; the relevant factors are the factual connections between the claim and the forum. In this sense Article 5 is not unlike CPR PD 6B in inspiration.[268] Its operation is, however, very different. If the conditions of one of the provisions in Article 5 are satisfied, the claimant may sue the defendant either in the courts of the state which have jurisdiction under Article 2 (on the basis of the defendant's domicile) or in the courts of another state which have special jurisdiction under Article 5. The claimant has an entirely free choice. On the other hand, where a defendant is sued, in accordance with Article 2, in the country in which he is domiciled, he is not entitled to argue that he should have been sued in another country on the basis of Article 5.[269] If the claimant—in reliance on Article 5—sues in England the court has no discretion to stay the proceedings or decline jurisdiction in favour of the courts of another Member State (unless authorised to do so by Articles 27 to 29 of the Brussels I Regulation[270]).

5.6.4 Article 5 is a derogation from the general principle contained in Article 2; it gives the claimant the opportunity to proceed against the defendant in a Member State in which the defendant is not domiciled. The Court of Justice has taken the view that the derogations from the principle *actor forum sequitur rei* must be interpreted restrictively.[271] In *Somafer SA v Saar-Ferngas AG* the Court of Justice sought to justify the narrow interpretation of Article 5 on the ground that '[m]ultiplication of the bases of jurisdiction in one and the same case is not likely to encourage legal certainty and the effectiveness of legal protection throughout the territory of the Community' and is contrary to the objective of 'avoid[ing] a wide and multifarious interpretation of the exceptions to the general rule of jurisdiction contained in Article 2'.[272] In addition, the objective of strengthening legal protection of persons established in the Community requires that the jurisdictional rules which derogate from Article 2 should

---

[266] See paras 8.2.13–8.2.14.

[267] See, eg, *Allpac Holding BV v Maier am Tor* [1982] ECC 200 (Court of Appeal, Amsterdam).

[268] See section 7.3.

[269] *Codeviandes SA v Maillard* [2005] ILPr 600 (Court of Cassation, France).

[270] See section 9.1. On the question whether the English courts may stay proceedings on the basis that a non-Member State is a more appropriate forum, see section 9.5.

[271] Case 189/87 *Kalfelis v Bankhaus Schröder, Münchmeyer, Hengst & Co* [1988] ECR 5565, para 19.

[272] Case 33/78 [1978] ECR 2183, para 6.

be interpreted in a way which enables 'a normally well-informed defendant reasonably to predict before which courts, other than those of the State in which he is domiciled, he may be sued'.[273]

Jurisdiction in Matters Relating to Contract and Tort: Introduction

5.6.5 Article 5(1) confers jurisdiction as regards 'matters relating to a contract'; Article 5(3) deals with 'matters relating to tort, delict or quasi-delict'. A number of issues should be addressed by way of introduction. First, how should the interpretation of 'contract' and 'tort, delict or quasi-delict' be approached? Secondly, are paragraphs (1) and (3) mutually exclusive? Thirdly, are paragraphs (1) and (3) all-embracing or are there cases in which the claimant seeks to establish the liability of the defendant which fall within neither paragraph (1) nor paragraph (3)?

Methods of Interpretation

5.6.6 There is a potential problem surrounding the dividing line between 'contract', on the one hand, and 'tort, delict or quasi-delict', on the other. Different legal systems draw that dividing line in different places; what is a breach of contract in one legal system may be regarded as a tort in another. There are three possible ways of deciding whether proceedings are concerned with matters relating to a contract or matters relating to tort: (i) classify the issue according to the law of the forum; (ii) classify the issue according to the applicable law; (iii) formulate an independent or autonomous interpretation. It is not surprising that the Court of Justice has adopted the third of these approaches. According to the case law of the Court of Justice the phrase 'matters relating to a contract' is 'an independent concept' which 'must be interpreted by reference principally to the system and objectives of the [Brussels regime] in order to ensure that it is fully effective'.[274] The scope of Article 5(1) depends neither on the law of the forum nor the law governing the alleged contract.[275] For example, in *Jakob Handte & Co GmbH v Traitements Mécano-chimiques des Surfaces SA*[276] A (a German company) manufactured a component which was sold by B (a French company) to C (a Swiss company) who fitted it into a machine which was sold to D (another French company). When D brought proceedings in France against A, B and C one of the questions facing the court was whether jurisdiction could be exercised in relation to A. According to French law, as it then was,[277] D's claim against A was

---

[273] Case C–26/91 *Jakob Handte & Co GmbH v Traitements Mécano-chimiques des Surfaces SA* [1992] ECR I–3967, para 18.

[274] Case 9/87 *SPRL Acardo v SA Haviland* [1988] ECR 1539, para 11. A Briggs, (1988) 8 *YBEL* 269.

[275] Case 34/82 *Martin Peters Bauunternehmung GmbH v Zuid Nederlandse Aannemers Vereniging* [1983] ECR 987 (TC Hartley, (1983) 8 *EL Rev* 262); Case 9/87 *SPRL Acardo v SA Haviland* [1988] ECR 1539; Case C–26/91 *Jakob Handte & Co GmbH v Traitements Mécano-chimiques des Surfaces SA* [1992] ECR I–3967.

[276] Case C–26/91 [1992] ECR I–3967. M Decker, 'Contract or Tort: A Conflict of Classification' (1993) 42 *ICLQ* 366.

[277] The French courts have since decided that the claim of the sub-buyer is not contractual in nature: A Briggs, *The Conflict of Laws* (Oxford, OUP, 2nd edn, 2008) 76, n 145.

contractual in nature and France was the place of performance of the obligation in question. In most European states a manufacturer's liability towards a subsequent purchaser for defects in the product sold is considered to be non-contractual. The Court of Justice explained that 'how the legal relationship in question before the national court is classified by the relevant national law' is immaterial.[278] Similarly, in *Kalfelis v Bankhaus Schröder, Münchmeyer, Hengst & Co* the Court of Justice decided that the term 'tort, delict or quasi-delict' in Article 5(3) must be regarded as an autonomous concept.[279]

5.6.7 It follows from the approach adopted by the Court of Justice that, in certain circumstances, a claim—which, for jurisdictional purposes, has to be classified as contractual—is, from the point of view of the substantive law to be applied by the forum, to be regarded as tortious. The classification for jurisdictional purposes has no bearing on the substance of the case:

A court that acquires jurisdiction under Article 5(1) is not prevented ... from proceeding with the action on the basis that it is delictual and a court that acquires jurisdiction under Article 5(3) is not prevented ... from proceeding with the action on the basis that it is contractual.[280]

Are Paragraphs (1) and (3) Mutually Exclusive?

5.6.8 From the decision of the Court of Justice in *Kalfelis v Bankhaus Schröder, Münchmeyer, Hengst & Co* it is clear that paragraphs (1) and (3) are to be regarded as mutually exclusive.[281] This is in marked contrast to the traditional English approach which regards tort and contract as overlapping categories.[282] From the point of view of jurisdiction, Article 5 does not give the claimant a choice whether to frame the claim in contract or in tort. In *Burke v Uvex Sports GmbH*,[283] the plaintiff had purchased a motorcycle helmet from the defendant. The helmet caused the plaintiff to suffer severe injuries when he was involved in an accident in Ireland. He sued in Ireland on the basis of Article 5(3). The High Court of Ireland decided that it could not 'overlook the existence of the contractual relationship, however basic, between the plaintiff and the ... defendant' and that the plaintiff could not 'avoid the consequences of the existence of that contract by seeking his remedy solely in tort'.[284] This case illustrates that if the proceedings concern 'matters relating to a contract' jurisdiction cannot be derived from Article 5(3), even if the claim is regarded as being in tort by the law of the forum. Where, for example, the claimant has, on the same facts, both a claim for breach of contract and a claim for damages in tort for negligent misstatement,

---

[278] Case C–26/91 [1992] ECR I–3967, para 10.
[279] Case 189/87 [1988] ECR 5565, para 16. A Briggs, (1988) 8 *YBEL* 272. See also Case C–261/90 *Reichert v Dresdner Bank (No 2)* [1992] ECR I–2149.
[280] Advocate General Jacobs in Case C–26/91 *Jakob Handte & Co GmbH v Traitements Mécano-chimiques des Surfaces SA* [1992] ECR I–3967, para 24.
[281] Case 189/87 [1988] ECR 5565, para 19. See also *Agnew v Länsförsäkringsbolagens AB* [2001] 1 AC 223.
[282] *Matthews v Kuwait Bechtel Corporation* [1959] 2 QB 57; *Coupland v Arabian Gulf Oil Co* [1983] 1 WLR 1136; *Base Metal Trading Ltd v Shamurin* [2002] CLC 322; *Base Metal Trading Ltd v Shamurin* [2005] 1 WLR 1157.
[283] [2005] ILPr 348 (High Court, Ireland).
[284] [2005] ILPr 348, 354 (at [31]).

both claims are to be regarded as involving 'matters relating to a contract' for the purposes of Article 5(1).[285] Similarly, if the proceedings concern 'matters relating to tort, delict or quasi-delict' the court may not exercise jurisdiction under Article 5(1) on the basis that the claim is regarded by the law of the forum as contractual.[286] Furthermore, where a claimant has a claim against a defendant part of which is based in contract and another part of which is based in tort 'a court which has jurisdiction under Article 5(3) over an action in so far as it is based on tort or delict does not have jurisdiction over that action in so far as it is not so based'.[287] However, if the court assumes jurisdiction on the basis of either Article 5(1) or (3), whether concurrent claims which are regarded as being contractual and tortious under domestic law are allowed will be up to the procedural law of the forum.[288] The next issue if concurrent claims are permitted is whether the Rome I Regulation will apply to the contract claim and the Rome II Regulation will apply to the tortious claim or if the concurrent claims will be decided under one regime. Given that the Brussels I Regulation, the Rome I Regulation and the Rome II Regulation are supposed to work in tandem with each other, the autonomous meaning ascribed to 'matters relating to a contract' (Article 5(1)) and 'matters relating to tort' (Article 5(3)) must largely correspond with matters falling within the scope of the Rome I and Rome II Regulations respectively. This means that if the court assumes jurisdiction on the basis of Article 5(1), the Rome I Regulation will normally be applicable notwithstanding that the claimant may be advancing a claim that would be characterised as tortious under domestic law. Similarly, if the court exercises jurisdiction on the basis of Article 5(3), the Rome II Regulation will usually be applicable irrespective of any domestic contractual classification of the claim. That said, this will not be true for all cases because the ambit of 'matters relating to a contract' and 'matters relating to a tort' is not identical to the ambit of the Regulations. For example, an unjust enrichment claim arising out of a valid contract[289] has been suggested to be a 'matter relating to a contract' for jurisdictional purposes[290] but such a claim clearly falls within the Rome II Regulation. So the court may assume jurisdiction on the basis of Article 5(1), but for choice of law purposes, it would have to apply the Rome II Regulation.

---

[285] *Source Ltd v TUV Rheinland Holding AG* [1998] QB 54; *Mazur Media Ltd v Mazur Media GmbH* [2004] 1 WLR 2966, 2974 (at [30]). See also *Re Missing Share Certificates* [1991] ILPr 298 (Court of Appeal, Munich); *Re an Italian Cargo of Adulterated Wine* [1991] ILPr 473 (Court of Appeal, Koblenz).

[286] Case C–26/91 *Jakob Handte & Co GmbH v Traitements Mécano-chimiques des Surfaces SA* [1992] ECR I–3967.

[287] Case 189/87 *Kalfelis v Bankhaus Schröder, Münchmeyer, Hengst & Co* [1988] ECR 5565, para 19. See also *Rudolph Roock Transeuropa Haus-Haus Speditions KG v Boulanger Belgique* [2005] ILPr 251 (Court of Cassation, France); *NV Euro Boat v Sarl Team Boat* [2006] ILPr 336 (Commercial Court, Veurne).

[288] *Base Metal Trading Ltd v Shamurin* [2005] 1 WLR 1157; *Coupland v Arabian Gulf Oil Co* [1983] 1 WLR 1136.

[289] According to the House of Lords in *Kleinwort Benson v Glasgow City Council* [1999] 1 AC 153, a restitutionary claim arising out of a void contract does not fall within Art 5(1) (majority), nor Art 5(3) (unanimous). See paras 5.6.15 and 5.6.17.

[290] Lord Goff accepted this possibility in *Kleinwort Benson Ltd v Glasgow City Council* [1999] 1 AC 153, 170–1.

Are Paragraphs (1) and (3) All-embracing?

5.6.9 A consideration of this question must take as its starting point the decision in *Kalfelis v Bankhaus Schröder, Münchmeyer, Hengst & Co.*[291] In the course of its judgment the Court of Justice stated that Article 5(3) must be regarded as covering 'all actions which seek to establish the liability of a defendant and which are not related to a "contract" within the meaning of Article 5(1)'.[292] This formula has been repeated in subsequent cases.[293] On the face of it, this passage would appear to endorse the view that Article 5(1) and Article 5(3), taken together, cover all situations in which the claimant seeks to establish the civil liability of the defendant. In *Jakob Handte & Co GmbH v Traitements Mécano-chimiques des Surfaces SA* Advocate General Jacobs expressed the view that '[d]elictual liability is ... a residual category encompassing liability that is not contractual'.[294] According to this view, Article 5(3) covers claims based on unjust enrichment (to the extent that they do not concern matters relating to a contract).

5.6.10 The expansive interpretation of Article 5(3) may, however, be questioned. First, it has been argued that, looking at the decision in *Kalfelis v Bankhaus Schröder, Münchmeyer, Hengst & Co* as a whole, the Court of Justice accepted the possibility that there may be situations in which an obligation is excluded from the scope of Article 5(3) if it is not tortious, but is not covered by Article 5(1) either, if its contractual nature cannot be established.[295] Secondly, this argument is supported by the original judgment (in German). The relevant German word (*Schadenshaftung*) which is translated in the English report as 'liability' is the equivalent of the French term *responsabilité* and means 'liability for damage'. It follows that a claim based on unjust enrichment does not fall within the words 'matters relating to tort, delict and quasi-delict'.[296] Thirdly, in *Reichert v Dresdner Bank (No 2)* Advocate General Gulmann noted:

[T]here may be difficulties in distinguishing actions which may be regarded as actions for compensation covered by either Article 5(1) or Article 5(3) from those which cannot be regarded as actions for compensation in matters either of contract or of tort, delict or quasi-delict. In such cases the result of the demarcation may be that there is no special jurisdiction for the action in question, which can therefore be brought only before the court of the State in which the defendant is domiciled.[297]

Fourthly, in *Kleinwort Benson Ltd v Glasgow City Council*[298]—a case involving schedule 4 to the 1982 Act—the House of Lords rejected the argument that claims which

---

[291] Case 189/87 [1988] ECR 5565. A Briggs, (1988) 8 *YBEL* 272.

[292] Case 189/87 [1988] ECR 5565, para 17.

[293] See, eg, Case C–51/97 *Réunion Européenne SA v Spliethoff's Bevrachtingskantoor BV* [1998] ECR I–6511, para 22; Case C–167/00 *Verein für Konsumentinformation v Henkel* [2002] ECR I–8111, para 36.

[294] Case C–26/91 [1992] ECR–I 3967, para 11.

[295] F Pocar, 'Jurisdiction in Matters Relating to Tort or Delict' in HD Tebbens, T Kennedy and C Kohler (eds), *Civil Jurisdiction and Judgments in Europe* (London, Butterworths, 1992) 111.

[296] See Staughton LJ in *Source Ltd v TUV Rheinland Holding AG* [1998] QB 54, 63. See also R Stevens, 'Restitution and the Brussels Convention' (1996) 112 *LQR* 391, 396; Lord Clyde in *Kleinwort Benson Ltd v Glasgow City Council* [1999] 1 AC 153, 185.

[297] Case C–261/90 [1992] ECR I–2149, 2169.

[298] [1999] 1 AC 153. See also *Davenport v Corinthian Motor Policies at Lloyd's* [1991] SLT 774 (a case involving a claim for recovery of a statutory indemnity) in which the Court of Session held – also in the context of sched 4 to the 1982 Act – that proceedings which raise questions of the defendant's liability may involve neither matters relating to a contract nor matters relating to tort.

fall outside Article 5(1) necessarily fall within the scope of Article 5(3). Lord Goff considered that restitutionary claims could not fall within Article 5(3) 'if only because a claim based on unjust enrichment does not, apart from exceptional circumstances, presuppose either a harmful event or a threatened wrong'.[299]

5.6.11   Indeed, the proposition that paragraphs (1) and (3) of Article 5 are not all-embracing is more consistent with the Court of Justice's view:

> the provisions on 'special jurisdiction' in Articles 5 and 6 … constitute derogations from the principle that jurisdiction is vested in the courts of the State of the defendant's domicile, laid down in the general provisions of Article 2 and 3 and, therefore, those provisions on special jurisdiction must be interpreted restrictively.[300]

It must always be remembered that the conclusion that, in specific circumstances, the proceedings fall neither within Article 5(1) nor Article 5(3) does not entail the consequence that there is no forum in which the claim can be brought: 'If a claim cannot be brought within Article 5, it can always be pursued in the courts of the defendant's domicile'.[301]

Jurisdiction in Matters Relating to a Contract

5.6.12   The general rule is that a person domiciled in a Member State may be sued in another Member State 'in matters relating to a contract, in the courts for the place of performance of the obligation in question'.[302] This general rule does not apply to insurance, consumer and employment contracts.[303] Furthermore, there are specific rules under the Brussels I Regulation for allocating jurisdiction with regard to contracts for the sale of goods and contracts for the provision of services in cases where the place of performance of the characteristic obligation (ie, the obligation to deliver the goods or to provide the services) is in a Member State.[304]

Matters Relating to a Contract

5.6.13   In most instances there will be few problems in determining whether or not the proceedings relate to a contract. Article 5(1) 'is not to be understood as covering a situation where there is no obligation freely assumed by one party towards another'.[305] So, where A, on behalf of D, enters a contract with C, C's claim against

---

[299] [1999] 1 AC 153, 172.

[300] Case 32/88 *Six Constructions Ltd v Humbert* [1989] ECR 341, para 18.

[301] Millett LJ in *Kleinwort Benson Ltd v Glasgow City Council* [1996] QB 678, 698.

[302] Brussels I Reg, Art 5(1)(a).

[303] See section 5.8.

[304] See paras 5.6.21–5.6.29. For a comparison between Art 5(1) of the Brussels I Regulation and the equivalent provision of the Brussels Convention, see K Takahashi, 'Jurisdiction in matters relating to contract: Article 5(1) of the Brussels Convention and Regulation' (2002) 27 *EL Rev* 530.

[305] Case C–26/91 *Jakob Handte & Co GmbH v Traitements Mécano-chimiques des Surfaces SA* [1992] ECR I–3967, para 15; Case C–51/97 *Réunion Européenne SA v Spliethoff's Bevrachtingskantoor BV* [1998] ECR I–6511, para 17. See also Case C–96/00 *Gabriel* [2002] ECR I–6367; *Re a Mail Order Promise of Win in a Draw* [2003] ILPr 737 (Federal Supreme Court, Germany); *Koogar v AMS Neve* [2006] ILPr 796 (Court of Cassation, France).

D does not fall within Article 5(1) if D was not a party to the contract and did not authorise its conclusion.[306] However, where A and D enter into a contract which provides for C to have directly enforceable rights against D under that contract, C's action against D falls within Art 5(1).[307] Although different legal systems adopt different approaches to what exactly constitutes a contract, 'at its irreducible minimum a contract is a consensual arrangement intended to create legal relations and to be legally enforceable'.[308] Because, for the purposes of Article 5(1) 'contract' must be given an autonomous interpretation, particular aspects of domestic law—such as the English doctrines of consideration and privity—cannot be used to determine the boundaries of Article 5(1). For example, a dispute relating to a promise to make a gift falls within the scope of Article 5(1).[309] In *Atlas Shipping Agency (UK) Ltd v Suisse Atlantique Société d'Armement Maritime SA*[310] it was held that proceedings to enforce a promise given by the first defendant to the second defendant to pay a sum of money to the plaintiff involved 'matters relating to a contract' for the purposes of Article 5(1). Conversely, the potential liability of a manufacturer of goods to a sub-buyer is not to be regarded as contractual, regardless of the characterisation of the law of the forum, because the manufacturer does not voluntarily assume any obligations towards the sub-buyer.[311] In *Réunion Européenne SA v Spliethoff's Bevrachtingskantoor BV*[312] the Court of Justice was faced by a situation in which A purchased a cargo of pears which were shipped under a bill of lading issued by B, but the actual carrier was D. The goods arrived in a damaged condition and A made an insurance claim against C. C, who was subrogated to the rights of A, brought proceedings against D. The Court of Justice ruled that, as there was no contractual nexus between C and D, the situation did not fall within Article 5(1).[313] Similarly, where C, a consumer organisation, brings proceedings against D, a trader, with a view to preventing D from including certain types of terms in its contracts with consumers, the absence of any contractual nexus between C and D means that the case does not fall within Article 5(1).[314] Although, in *Kleinwort Benson Ltd v Glasgow City Council*,[315] the majority of the House of Lords held that, in a case involving a contract which was void *ab initio*, claims for restitution are not within Article 5(1), this does not mean that all restitutionary claims necessarily fall outside the scope of this

---

[306] Case C–265/02 *Frahuil SA v Assitalia SpA* [2004] ECR I–1543, para 26.

[307] *WPP Holdings Italy Srl v Benatti* [2007] 1 WLR 2316, 2332–3 (at [53]–[55]).

[308] Millett LJ in *Kleinwort Benson Ltd v Glasgow City Council* [1996] QB 678, 698 (a case decided under sched 4 to the 1982 Act).

[309] See Case C–27/02 *Engler v Janus Versand GmbH* [2005] ECR I–481 (promise to award a prize which was independent of any order for goods by the prize-winner was a 'matter relating to a contract').

[310] [1995] 2 Lloyd's Rep 188.

[311] Case C–26/91 *Jakob Handte & Co GmbH v Traitements Mécano-chimiques des Surfaces SA* [1992] ECR I–3967. For criticism of this decision, see A Briggs, (1992) 12 *YBEL* 667; TC Hartley, 'Unnecessary Europeanisation under the Brussels Jurisdiction and Judgments Convention: the Case of the Dissatisfied Sub-Purchaser' (1993) 18 *EL Rev* 506.

[312] Case C–51/97 [1998] ECR I–6511. A Briggs, 'Claims against sea carriers and the Brussels Convention' [1999] *LMCLQ* 333; TC Hartley, 'Carriage of goods and the Brussels Jurisdiction and Judgments Convention' (2000) 25 *EL Rev* 89; E Peel, (1998) 18 *YBEL* 700.

[313] For criticism of this decision, see, eg, K Takahashi, 'Jurisdiction over direct action against sub-carrier under the Brussels Convention' [2001] *LMCLQ* 107.

[314] Case C–167/00 *Verein für Konsumentinformation v Henkel* [2002] ECR I–8111, paras 39–40.

[315] [1999] 1 AC 153.

provision. Lord Goff accepted the possibility that Article 5(1) may be broad enough to encompass a claim for the recovery of money paid under a valid contract where the basis of the claim is a failure of consideration comprising the non-performance of a valid contractual obligation.[316] It would also seem that a restitutionary claim which arises from a voidable or unenforceable contract is covered by Article 5(1)[317] and there is an argument that a restitutionary claim which arises from a frustrated contract should be regarded as sufficiently closely connected with a contract to fall within the scope of Article 5(1).[318]

DENIAL OF AN ALLEGED CONTRACT'S EXISTENCE

5.6.14   The Court of Justice held that a denial of the existence of an alleged contract by the defendant does not, in itself, deprive the court of jurisdiction under Article 5(1).[319] The ruling was applied by the Court of Appeal in a case where it was the plaintiff—rather than the defendant—who denied the alleged contract's existence. In *Boss Group Ltd v Boss France SA*[320] the defendant, a French company, asserted that the conduct of the plaintiff, an English company, amounted to a breach of an alleged exclusive distribution agreement between the parties. The plaintiff denied that any such agreement existed and applied for a declaration from the English court to that effect. The defendant also started proceedings in France for breach of the alleged agreement. The jurisdictional question raised by the English proceedings was whether an application for a declaration that an alleged contract did not exist concerned 'a matter relating to a contract' for the purposes of Article 5(1) and, if so, whether England was the place of performance of the obligation in question. The Court of Appeal held that the proceedings fell within the scope of Article 5(1):

[Article 5(1)] allows a party to be sued in matters relating to a contract in the courts for the place of performance of the obligation in question. That party in the present case is the defendant company. It seems to me to that it is entirely illogical and wrong for that party to assert that there is a contract and that the plaintiff has broken it (which is what the defendant has done in France, where it has relied upon Article 5(1)), whilst simultaneously contending the contrary here to avoid the application of Article 5(1). ... Once one has removed the self-contradictory stance taken up by the defendant, it seems to me self-evident that there are matters relating to a contract between the parties.[321]

While this aspect of the Court of Appeal's decision may be supportable, it is unclear if the same can be said in relation to the court's analysis of the 'obligation in question'.[322]

---

[316] [1999] 1 AC 153, 170–71.
[317] Lord Hutton in *Kleinwort Benson Ltd v Glasgow City Council* [1999] 1 AC 153, 195.
[318] See G Virgo, 'Jurisdiction over Unjust Enrichment Claims' (1998) 114 *LQR* 386, 389.
[319] Case 38/81 *Effer SpA v Kantner* [1982] ECR 825. TC Hartley, (1982) 7 *EL Rev* 235.
[320] [1997] 1 WLR 351. C Forsyth, 'Brussels Convention jurisdiction "in matters relating to a contract" when the plaintiff denies the existence of a contract' [1996] *LMCLQ* 329; E Peel, 'Jurisdiction over Non-Existent Contracts' (1996) 112 *LQR* 541; I Turkki, (1996) 21 *EL Rev* 419. See also *Youell v La Réunion Aérienne* [2009] 1 All ER (Comm) 301, affirmed [2009] 1 Lloyd's Rep 586 (CA) (without consideration of this point).
[321] Saville LJ at [1997] 1 WLR 351, 356–7.
[322] See paras 5.6.32 and 5.6.33.

OBLIGATIONS IN CASES INVOLVING VOID CONTRACTS

5.6.15 In *Kleinwort Benson Ltd v Glasgow City Council*,[323] a case decided under schedule 4 to the 1982 Act, the House of Lords reversed the decision of the Court of Appeal[324] and held that Article 5(1) does not extend to restitutionary obligations in cases where an intended contract is a nullity. In this case the plaintiff, an English bank, brought proceedings for the restitution of money paid under a contract which was a nullity because the defendant, a Scottish local authority, had acted *ultra vires*. According to English law, the plaintiff's claim was for restitution rather than for breach of contract. The House of Lords held, by a bare majority, that the proceedings did not fall within Article 5(1). According to the majority, the words 'in the courts for the place of the obligation in question' help to define what is meant by the phrase 'matters relating to a contract'.[325] Because the connecting factor which determines jurisdiction is the place of performance of a particular obligation and there is 'no other obligation which could ... be intended than an obligation based on contract',[326] the scope of Article 5(1) does not cover a case where the disputed obligation is based on the principle of unjust enrichment:

Where ... the claim is for money paid under a supposed contract which in law never existed, it seems impossible to say that the claim for the recovery of the money is based upon a particular contractual obligation.[327]

Accordingly, a claim based on a restitutionary obligation arising out of a void contract cannot be within Article 5(1). One of the arguments in favour of this interpretation is that, where there is no contractual obligation and no place for the performance of a contractual obligation, there is no close connecting factor and no justification for the invocation of Article 5(1). This argument should not be pushed too far, however, since, even in simple contractual situations, Article 5(1) may confer jurisdiction on a forum which has a very limited connection with the dispute between the parties.[328]

5.6.16 Lord Nicholls, with whom Lord Mustill agreed, adopted the same basic approach as the majority of the Court of Appeal. According to this view, Article 5(1) should be interpreted as covering matters relating to a 'void contract'—that is to say, a situation where negotiations between the parties led to an agreement in fact, but there is no contract in law because of some defect (such as one of the parties' lack of capacity, public policy or failure to comply with the applicable formal requirements); 'without undue straining of language',[329] the 'obligation in question' may be regarded as referring to a restitutionary obligation rather than a contractual one. Of course, it

---

[323] [1999] 1 AC 153. A Briggs, (1996) 67 *BYIL* 580; PA McGrath, '*Kleinwort Benson v Glasgow City Council*: A simple point of jurisdiction' (1999) 18 *CJQ* 41; G Maher, [1998] *Jur Rev* 131; SGA Pitel, [1998] *CLJ* 19; E Peel, 'Jurisdiction over restitutionary claims' [1998] *LMCLQ* 22; G Virgo, 'Jurisdiction over Unjust Enrichment Claims' (1998) 114 *LQR* 386.

[324] [1996] QB 678. A Briggs, (1997) 68 *BYIL* 331; A Reed, 'Article 5(1) of the Brussels Convention, Restitutionary Claims and the Need for a New Approach' (1997) 48 *NILQ* 243; J Riley, 'Void contracts, restitution and jurisdiction' [1996] *LMCLQ* 183; R Stevens, 'Restitution and the Brussels Convention' (1996) 112 *LQR* 391.

[325] Lord Hutton at [1999] 1 AC 153, 189.

[326] Lord Clyde at [1999] 1 AC 153, 181.

[327] Lord Goff at [1999] 1 AC 153, 167.

[328] See Case C–288/92 *Custom Made Commercial Ltd v Stawa Metallbau GmbH* [1994] ECR I–2913.

[329] Lord Nicholls at [1999] 1 AC 153, 176.

should be noted that this view would not entail the consequence that all claims for restitution based on unjust enrichment would fall within the scope of Article 5(1); there could be no application of Article 5(1) in a case where the basis of the claim was other than obligations resulting from a contract which, for one reason or another, failed.[330]

5.6.17   The strongest argument in favour of the majority view is that the extension of Article 5(1) to restitutionary claims arising out of void contracts is not consistent with the principle that the derogations from Article 2 set out in Article 5 should be interpreted restrictively[331]; the interpretation favoured by the minority would tend to confer jurisdiction on the courts of the claimant's domicile (because that is where the defendant's restitutionary obligation would normally have to be performed), whereas the principle in Article 2 is that litigation should generally be conducted in the courts of the defendant's domicile. Conversely, a number of arguments support the approach of the minority. First, the approach of the majority requires a distinction to be drawn between, on the one hand, claims which result from contracts which are void (which fall outside the ambit of Article 5(1)) and, on the other, those which arise out of contracts which are voidable or unenforceable (which fall within the provision's scope). Since different legal systems may draw that dividing line differently, it is hard to see how the analysis advocated by the majority—if it were shared by the Court of Justice—would promote uniformity throughout the Member States. Secondly, the minority view has significant practical advantages. In particular, if Article 5(1) were interpreted to cover claims arising out of a void contract, the court with jurisdiction to rule on the validity or invalidity of an alleged contract would, if it decided that the alleged contract was void, also have jurisdiction to determine the consequences of nullity:

It would be surprising and unfortunate if, having decided that the contract is null and void, the same court cannot proceed to decide on the restitutionary consequences following directly from this.[332]

Thirdly, because the Rome I Regulation applies without any reservations in England, the consequences of the nullity of a contract should be characterised as contractual in nature, rather than restitutionary.[333] It is to be hoped that, in a case falling within the scope of the Brussels I Regulation, the place of restitutionary obligations within Article 5 will in due course be considered by the Court of Justice.[334]

PRE-CONTRACTUAL OBLIGATIONS

5.6.18   Whether Article 5(1) also covers pre-contractual obligations has troubled the English courts. In *Trade Indemnity Plc v Försäkringsaktiebolaget Njord*,[335] a case

---

[330] See Roch LJ at [1996] QB 678, 696.
[331] Case 189/87 *Kalfelis v Bankhaus Schröder, Münchmeyer, Hengst & Co* [1988] ECR 5565, para 19.
[332] Lord Nicholls at [1999] 1 AC 153, 175.
[333] See Rome I Reg, Art 12(1)(e). The United Kingdom had entered into a reservation against its predecessor, Art 10(1)(e) of the Rome Convention: Contracts (Applicable Law) Act 1990, s 2(2).
[334] The difference in views on this point has not been resolved by the advent of the Rome I and Rome II Regulations. There is a degree of overlap between the two Regulations; namely, unjust enrichment claims arising out of a void contract could fall under both Regulations. This is not particularly problematic as the choice of law rules on this issue for both Regulations lead to the same law; but it is not helpful for the purpose of resolving the jurisdictional uncertainty.
[335] [1995] 1 All ER 796.

involving the 1988 Lugano Convention, Rix J considered that Article 5(1) applies only to cases involving contractual obligations and does not extend to a claim based on the defendant's alleged failure to comply with a pre-contractual duty of disclosure. Although in *Kleinwort Benson Ltd v Glasgow City Council* the question whether, for the purposes of Article 5(1), the word 'contract' is capable of including 'anticipated contract' was left open, in *Agnew v Länsförsäkringsbolagens AB*,[336] another case under the 1988 Lugano Convention, a bare majority of the House of Lords decided that a case concerning a pre-contractual obligation could fall within Article 5(1). In the *Agnew* case the plaintiff sought to avoid a contract of reinsurance on the ground that the defendant had failed to comply with the duty to make fair presentation of the risk. Although, as a matter of English law, the defendant's obligation arose under the general law, rather than under an express term of the contract, the House of Lords held that the proceedings involved 'matters relating to a contract' for the purposes of Article 5(1).

5.6.19   It should be stressed that in *Agnew v Länsförsäkringsbolagens AB*, although the dispute related to a pre-contractual obligation, that obligation was closely linked to a contract which was subsequently concluded by the parties.[337] The position is different when one of the parties is in breach of a pre-contractual obligation and the parties fail to enter a contractual relationship at all.[338] In *Fonderie Officine Meccaniche Tacconi SpA v Heinrich Wagner Sinto Maschinenfabrik GmbH*[339] the question facing the Court of Justice was whether a claim based on the defendant's breach of duty to act in good faith, in the context of the negotiation and formation of a contract, fell within the scope of Article 5(1) or Article 5(3) (or neither). The claimant sought damages to make good the loss it had suffered as a result of the defendant having unjustifiably broken off negotiations. The Court of Justice repeated the view that Article 5(1) does not cover a situation in which there is no obligation freely assumed by one party to another.[340] As no contract had been concluded and the obligation on which the claim was based was imposed by a source external to the parties,[341] there was no obligation freely assumed by the defendant to the claimant. As the Court of Justice pointed out: 'In those circumstances, it is clear that any liability which may follow from the failure to conclude [a] contract … cannot be contractual'.[342]

5.6.20   Whether the House of Lords' decision in *Agnew v Länsförsäkringsbolagens AB* can stand with the Court of Justice's ruling is debatable. On the one hand, the cases are distinguishable on their facts: whereas, in the *Agnew case*, the parties had entered a contractual relationship, in *Fonderie Officine Meccaniche Tacconi SpA v*

---

[336] [2001] 1 AC 223. A Briggs, (2000) 71 *BYIL* 451; I Pester, 'Reinsurance, good faith and art 5(1) of the Brussels Convention' [2000] *LMCLQ* 289.

[337] See, however, *Alfred Dunhill Ltd v Diffusion Internationale de Maroquinerie de Prestige SARL* [2001] CLC 949 (in which it was it was held that Art 5(3), rather than Art 5(1), covered a claim for damages for a misrepresentation which had induced the representee to enter a contract with the representator). See also *Crucial Music Corp v Klondyke Management AG* [2007] ILPr 733.

[338] See the opinion of Advocate General Darmon in Case C–89/91 *Shearson Lehman Hutton v TVB Treuhandgesellschaft für Vermögensverwaltung und Beteiligungen mbH* [1993] ECR I–139, paras 95–97.

[339] Case C–344/00 [2002] ECR I–7377.

[340] Case C–344/00 [2002] ECR I–7377, para 23.

[341] The duty of good faith arose under Art 1337 of the Italian civil code.

[342] Case C–334/00 [2002] ECR I–7377, para 26. See also *Wiehag GmbH v Coverall srl* [2009] ILPr 237 (Court of Cassation, Italy).

Heinrich Wagner Sinto Maschinenfabrik GmbH they had not. On the other hand, the whole thrust of the Court of Justice's ruling is that a pre-contractual obligation which is imposed by the general law is not contractual for the purposes of Article 5.

Contracts Governed by Article 5(1)(b)

5.6.21   One of the problems of the original version of Article 5(1), as interpreted by the Court of Justice, was that it could allocate jurisdiction to a court with little connection with the dispute, particularly in cases where the claim was based on the defendant's breach of a payment obligation. In response to these criticisms, Article 5(1) of the Brussels I Regulation was re-drafted. Article 5(1)(b) provides that, for the purposes of the rule that jurisdiction in matters relating to a contract is allocated to the courts for the place of performance of the obligation in question, that place is:

— in the case of the sale of goods, the place in a Member State where, under the contract, the goods were delivered or should have been delivered,
— in the case of the provision of services, the place in a Member State where, under the contract, the services were provided or should have been provided.

The objective of the redrafting is to set up rules of jurisdiction which are highly predictable so that the claimant can identify easily the court in which he may sue and the defendant can reasonably foresee before which court he may be sued.[343] Underlying the two indents of Article 5(1)(b) is the idea that the court for the place where the characteristic obligation of the contract is to be performed has a close link to the contract.[344] In *Color Drack GmbH v Lexx International Vertriebs GmbH*,[345] the Court of Justice held that the rule of special jurisdiction contained in Article 5(1)(b) 'establishes the place of delivery as the autonomous linking factor to apply to all claims founded on one and the same contract for the sale of goods rather than merely to the claims founded on the obligation of delivery itself'.[346] Therefore, the problem of the courts of the place of characteristic performance being allocated jurisdiction even though the performance (or non-performance) which is the subject-matter of the claim is not the characteristic performance also arises under the redrafted provision. For example, in a contract of sale of goods which provides for delivery in France, the French courts will have jurisdiction under the first indent of Article 5(1)(b) even though the dispute relates to non-payment rather than the delivery of the goods.[347] However, since Article 5(1)(b) is prefaced with the phrase 'unless otherwise agreed', in the example given, if the parties have agreed on Italy being the place of payment, it can be argued that Article 5(1) allocates jurisdiction to the courts of Italy.[348]

---

[343] Case C–386/05 *Color Drack GmbH v Lexx International Vertriebs GmbH* [2007] ECR I–3699, paras 19–20.
[344] Case C–386/05 *Color Drack GmbH v Lexx International Vertriebs GmbH* [2007] ECR I–3699, para 23.
[345] Case C–386/05 [2007] ECR I–3699.
[346] Case C–386/05 [2007] ECR I–3699, para 26.
[347] See *DPT (Duroplast Technik) GmbH v Chemiplastica SpA* [2009] ILPr 229 (Court of Cassation, Italy).
[348] JJ Fawcett and JM Carruthers, *Cheshire, North & Fawcett: Private International Law* (Oxford, OUP, 14th edn, 2008) 242–3.

5.6.22 There are two ways in which the places of performance identified in the two indents of Article 5(1)(b) might be determined. Under the first approach, focus is on the place of performance as a question of law. This means that the place of delivery (in relation to a contract for the sale of goods) or the place of performance of the services (in relation to a contract for the provision of services) will be identified by the applicable law, as determined by the choice of law rules of the forum.[349] For example, in *Scottish & Newcastle International Ltd v Othon Ghalanos Ltd*,[350] the contract of sale, governed by English law, concerned the sale of cider which was to be shipped from Liverpool to Limassol. The buyer argued that since Limassol was entered as the 'Place of delivery' on the invoices, the courts of England did not have jurisdiction under Article 5(1)(b). However, the bills of lading were made out to the buyers as consignees, were stipulated as non-negotiable and were forwarded to the buyers immediately after shipment; property and risk passed to the buyers upon delivery of the goods to the carrier in Liverpool. In short, the seller had no continuing interest in the cider after shipment. The House of Lords applied section 32(1) of the Sale of Goods Act 1979 and held that the seller had delivered the goods to the buyer when the goods were delivered to the carrier in Liverpool. Accordingly, the English court had jurisdiction under Article 5(1)(b).

5.6.23 The facts of *Scottish & Newcastle International Ltd v Othon Ghalanos Ltd* were quite clear-cut; more difficult situations may arise—such as where the shipping documents and property in the goods may be transferred to the buyer at another point in time. In such situations, it may not be easy to identify or reasonably foresee the place where these events may occur[351] (for example, the seller may retain property in the goods and the shipping documents until payment, but the goods may be on the high seas when that occurs). This leads to the second approach—according to which the relevant connecting factor under Article 5(1)(b) is the physical place of performance.[352] This was the preference of Lord Mance in *Scottish & Newcastle International Ltd v Othon Ghalanos Ltd* in an *obiter dictum*;[353] Lords Bingham and Rodger reserved their opinion on this point.[354]

5.6.24 The foregoing discussion is subject to the qualification that, whether Article 5(1)(b) is to be interpreted as referring to the legal place of performance or the

---

[349] Case 12/76 *Industrie Tessili Italiana Como v Dunlop AG* [1976] ECR 1473; Case C–288/92 *Custom Made Commercial Ltd v Stawa Metallbau GmbH* [1994] ECR I–2913. See *Bourjois SAS v Gommatex Poliuretani SpA* [2008] ILPr 373 (Court of Cassation, Italy); *DPT (Duroplast Technik) GmbH v Chemiplastica SpA* [2009] ILPr 229 (Court of Cassation, Italy); *Franke GmbH v Fallimento Rubinetterie Rapetti SPA* [2009] ILPr 165 (Court of Cassation, France).

[350] [2008] 2 All ER 768. A Briggs, (2008) 79 *BYIL* 508; L Merrett, [2008] *CLJ* 244; C Hare and P Hinks, [2008] *LMCLQ* 353.

[351] Lord Mance at [2008] 2 All ER 768, 784 (at [52]).

[352] See Case C–381/08 *Car Trim GmbH v Key Safety Systems Srl*, Advocate General Mazák, 24 September 2009.

[353] At least for all fob contracts. Although the contract in the *Scottish & Newcastle* case was expressed as a cfr (cost and freight) contract, it had the characteristics of a fob (free on board) contract; Lord Mance thought that it was, to all intents and purposes, an fob contract: [2008] 2 All ER 768, 778 (at [33]). In international trade, the two of the most common forms of contract are cif (cost insurance and freight) and fob, though there is considerable flexibility within each type of contract. This means that, for the purposes of Art 5(1)(b), the content of the particular contract needs to be scrutinised (as illustrated by *Scottish & Newcastle International Ltd v Othon Ghalanos Ltd*).

[354] Lord Bingham at [2008] 2 All ER 768, 772 (at [7]); Lord Rodger at 775 (at [19]–[20]).

physical place of performance, the parties can effectively select the connecting factor under Article 5(1)(b) by an agreement on the place of performance; as already noted, Article 5(1)(b) starts with the words 'unless otherwise agreed'. In *Zelger v Salinitri*[355] the Court of Justice held that, if the place of performance of a contractual obligation has been specified by the parties in a clause which is valid according to the law applicable to the contract, the court for that place has jurisdiction in relation to disputes relating to that obligation under Article 5(1). Furthermore, the Court of Justice ruled that, although a jurisdiction agreement must satisfy the relevant formal requirements,[356] an agreement on the place of performance will confer jurisdiction under Article 5(1) irrespective of whether the formal conditions of Article 23 have been observed. So, where an Italian defendant expressly agrees to perform contractual services in England, the English court has jurisdiction in relation to disputes arising out of the contract as long as the parties' agreement is valid according to the applicable law. Similarly, where disputes arise in relation to machines sold by a German seller to an English buyer, the English court does not have jurisdiction under Article 5(1) if the contract provides that delivery of the machines was to be 'ex works' in Germany.[357] Accordingly, it is perfectly possible for Article 5(1) to confer jurisdiction when one party tacitly accepts the other party's general conditions (which stipulate the place of performance).[358] Whether the parties have agreed on the place of delivery or on the place for the performance of services is a question of construction of the contract. In appropriate circumstances, such an agreement may be implied from the terms of the contract and the surrounding circumstances.[359] In *Mainschiffahrts-Genossenschaft eG (MSG) v Les Gravières Rhénanes*,[360] the Court of Justice ruled that the general principle—that an agreed place of performance determines jurisdiction under Article 5(1) as long as the agreement is valid according to the applicable law—does not apply if the agreed place of performance has 'no real connection with the reality of the contract'.[361] The Court of Justice held that an agreement on the place of performance 'which is designed not to determine the place where the person liable is actually to perform the obligations incumbent upon him, but solely to establish that the courts for a particular place have jurisdiction'[362] will not determine jurisdiction under Article 5(1).[363] A 'fictitious'[364] agreement of this type will be effective to confer jurisdiction on the courts for the agreed place of performance only if the agreement satisfies the requirements of Article 23 of the Brussels I Regulation.[365]

5.6.25   While it is not difficult to understand why the Court of Justice sought to outlaw the circumvention of rules relating to formal requirements of jurisdiction

---

[355] Case 56/79 [1980] ECR 89. TC Hartley, (1981) 6 *EL Rev* 61. For an application of this decision, see *Re the M/S Hoop* [1982] ECC 533 (Federal Supreme Court, Germany).
[356] See para 5.3.11 *ff*.
[357] See *Viskase Ltd v Paul Kiefel GmbH* [1999] 1 WLR 1305. A Briggs, (1999) 70 *BYIL* 336. 'Ex works' means that the seller makes the goods available for collection by the buyer at the seller's place of business.
[358] *Re the Recovery of Unpaid Customs Duty* [1985] ECC 311 (Federal Supreme Court, Germany).
[359] *Re the Sale of Shares in a German Company* [2002] ILPr 240 (Court of Appeal, Stuttgart).
[360] Case C–106/95 [1997] ECR I–911.
[361] Case C–106/95 [1997] ECR I–911, para 31.
[362] Case C–106/95 [1997] ECR I–911, para 35.
[363] See *Re the Supply of Wooden Panels* [1998] ILPr 100 (District Court, Stuttgart).
[364] Case C–106/95 [1997] ECR I–911, para 33.
[365] See section 5.2.

agreements, the judgment presents certain difficulties. In particular, in the course of its judgment the Court of Justice vacillated between an objective test ('a place of performance which has no actual connection with the real subject-matter of the contract'[366]) and a subjective one (a 'place of performance which is designed ... solely to establish that the courts for a particular place have jurisdiction'[367]). It is not difficult to apply the decision of the Court of Justice in a case where the agreed place of performance is wholly inappropriate to the subject-matter of the contract (for example, where a contract for the carriage of goods by sea stipulates Prague as the place of delivery). However, the application of the decision will not always be so simple. What is the proper solution in a case where, in a contract between an Irish seller and a Greek buyer, it is provided that the seller will deliver the goods in London? If the seller fails to deliver the goods, can the buyer invoke the English court's jurisdiction under Article 5(1)? How is the court to decide whether or not the parties' agreement on the place of delivery was designed 'solely to establish' the jurisdiction of the English courts? To what extent does the answer to this question depend on a consideration of subjective intentions as opposed to objective criteria?

5.6.26 The smooth operation of Article 5(1)(b) depends upon national courts being able to distinguish contracts for the sale of goods and for the provision of services from other contracts. In most cases, it may be imagined that this task will not be too onerous. It is normally simple enough to determine whether the subject-matter of a contract is goods or not. A contract for the sale of land or company shares or a contract for the assignment of an intellectual property right is clearly not a contract for the sale of goods. A contract of exchange is not a sale of goods; nor is a contract for the hire of goods.[368] By the same token, contracts for services—such as contracts for services provided by architects, lawyers, accountants and other professionals—are normally reasonably easy to identify. However, a contract whereby the owner of an intellectual property right permits another party to use that right is not a contract for the provision of services as the owner undertakes merely to permit the licensee to exploit the right freely.[369] There are, nevertheless, difficult borderlines: is a single contract which is partly barter and partly sale a contract for the sale of goods for the purposes of Article 5(1)(b)? Similarly, how is a contract for both the sale of goods and the supply of services[370] to be characterised within the scheme of Article 5(1)? It might be anticipated that, over the course of time, the Court of Justice will be required to draw some difficult dividing lines.

5.6.27 Another significant problem which Article 5(1)(b) does not expressly address is that posed by the situation where, as regards a contract for the sale of goods, there is more than one place of delivery or, in relation to a contract of services, there is more than one place of performance. In *Color Drack GmbH v Lexx International*

---

[366] Case C–106/95 [1997] ECR I–911, para 33.

[367] Case C–106/95 [1997] ECR I–911, para 35.

[368] But see the contrary view of A Briggs, *The Conflict of Laws* (Oxford, OUP, 2nd edn, 2008) 78.

[369] Case C–533/07 *Falco Privatstiftung, Thomas Rabitsch v Gisela Weller-Lindhorst* [2009] ECR I–3327.

[370] Such as the contract in *Société Nouvelle des Papeteries de l'Aa SA v BV Machinefabriek BOA* (1992 Nederlands Jurisprudentie 750); noted and discussed by THD Struycken, 'Some Dutch reflections on the Rome Convention, Art 4(5)' [1996] *LMCLQ* 18.

Vertriebs GmbH,[371] the Court of Justice answered in the affirmative when it was asked whether Article 5(1)(b) applies in the case of a sale of goods involving deliveries in several places within one single Member State.[372] The Court of Justice further held that Article 5(1)(b) should be used to identify only one court in that single Member State (in this case, Austria) notwithstanding that the goods should have been delivered to several places within that state. 'Place of performance' was to be understood to be the 'place of the principal delivery, which must be determined on the basis of economic criteria'.[373] If a principal place of delivery cannot be ascertained, the plaintiff may sue the defendant in the court for the place of delivery of its choice.[374] Although the Court of Justice in *Color Drack* was careful to state that its observations in that case applied solely to the situation where there are several places of delivery within one Member State and were without prejudice to the situation where there are several places of delivery in a number of Member States, the principles laid down are equally applicable in the latter situation and, needless to say, in cases concerning the provision of services. This was confirmed in *Rehder v Air Baltic Corporation*[375] where the issue was where an airline performed its obligations towards its passengers. The Court of Justice held that, where there are several places at which services are provided within different Member States, the place where the main provision of services is carried out is the place most closely connected with the contract.[376] The Court agreed with the referring court that the place of the registered office or the principal place of establishment of the airline (where merely logistical and preparatory services, such as the provision of aircraft and crew, are carried out), the place where the contract is concluded and the place where the ticket is issued do not have the necessary close link to the contract. Instead, the main provision of services with respect to a contract for air transport is carried out at the places of departure and arrival of the aircraft.[377] As these services are indivisible, neither the place of departure nor the place of arrival can be identified as the 'principal' place of performance—in terms of the economic value of the services provided.[378] Accordingly, on the basis of Article 5(1)(b), a claimant can choose to sue either in the court for the place of departure or the court for the place of arrival, or the claimant can sue in the court of the defendant's domicile under Article 2.

5.6.28   These two judgments clear up some, but not all, of the questions surrounding Article 5(1)(b). It is of particular note that the obligation at issue in *Rehder* was

---

[371] Case C–386/05 [2007] ECR I–3699. J Harris, (2007) 123 *LQR* 522; A Gardella, (2007) 9 *Yearbook of Private International Law* 439.

[372] Case C–386/05 [2007] ECR I–3699, para 38.

[373] Case C–386/05 [2007] ECR I–3699, para 40.

[374] Case C–386/05 [2007] ECR I–3699, para 42.

[375] Case C–204/08 [2009] ILPr 752.

[376] Case C–204/08 [2009] ILPr 752, 762 (para 38). See also Case 266/85 *Shenavai v Kreischer* [1987] ECR 239.

[377] The essential services being the checking-in and boarding of passengers, the on-board reception of those passengers at the agreed place of take-off, the departure of the aircraft at the scheduled time, the transport of the passengers and their luggage from the place of departure to the place of arrival, the care of passengers during the flight and the disembarkation of the passengers safely at the place of landing and at the time scheduled in the contract. The place where the aircraft may stop over does not have a close link to the essential services: Case C–204/08 [2009] ILPr 752, 762 (para 40).

[378] Case C–204/08 [2009] ILPr 752, 762 (para 42).

genuinely non-divisible. However, what if under the contract the seller undertook divisible obligations (for example, to sell and deliver goods of the same economic value to country X and country Y), but only carried out his obligations in country X? It cannot be that, as no principal place of delivery can be identified, the claimant will have a free choice whether to sue in country X or country Y; Article 5(1)(b) must allow the claimant to sue only in country Y. Conversely, if the seller contracted to sell and deliver goods of the same economic value to countries X, Y and Z but failed to deliver in the last two countries, the claimant will have a free choice whether to sue in country Y or country Z for the non-performance in both countries. Nevertheless, the Court of Justice decided under the Brussels Convention that where the claim is based on the breach by the defendant of more than one obligation in circumstances where the obligations are of equal rank, Article 5(1) allocates jurisdiction to the courts for each place of performance with regard to the dispute arising out of the obligation which should have been performed at that place.[379] It is unclear whether this principle also applies under Article 5(1)(b) of the Regulation: with reference to the example given above, does the claimant have the options of: (i) a choice between suing in country Y or country Z for the non-performance in both countries, and, (ii) suing in country Y for the non-performance in country Y and suing in country Z for the non-performance in country Z? In practical terms though, if both options were open to a claimant, it would be highly likely that he would want to concentrate his resources and pursue proceedings in only one country.

5.6.29   The Court of Justice's recent jurisprudence also does not address the situation where there is a multiplicity of obligations, such as breach of an undertaking not to do something where that undertaking applies without any geographical limit. Giving a free choice to the claimant in these circumstances would clearly not fulfil the criterion that the defendant should be able to foresee where he may be sued. In a case decided under the Brussels Convention, the Court of Justice held that where the relevant obligation has been, or is to be, performed in a number of places, no court has jurisdiction under Article 5(1) as, for the purposes of that provision, a single place of performance for the obligation in question must be identified.[380] Bearing in mind that Article 5(1) is a derogation from the rule in Article 2 and must thus be restrictively construed, it is suggested that the same rule should apply under the Regulation[381] and the claimant has no choice but to rely upon Article 2.

Other Contracts

5.6.30   Article 5(1)(b) of the Brussels I Regulation does not allocate jurisdiction in all situations involving contractual obligations. Even as regards contracts for the sale

---

[379] Case C–420/97 *Leathertex Divisione Sintetici SpA v Bodetex BVBA* [1999] ECR I–6747.

[380] Case C–256/00 *Besix SA v Wasserreinigungsbau Alfred Kretzschmar GmbH & Co KG (Wabag)* [2002] ECR I–1699. Further, where there is a choice as to where the relevant obligation is to be performed, no single jurisdiction can be established under Art 5(1): *Mora Shipping Inc v Axa Corporate Solutions Assurance SA* [2005] 2 Lloyd's Rep 769.

[381] The Court of Justice has confirmed that its case law on provisions of the Brussels Convention which correspond to provisions of the Brussels I Regulation remain authoritative for the purposes of interpreting the latter in the absence of any reason for interpreting the two provisions differently: Case C–533/07 *Falco Privatstiftung, Thomas Rabitsch v Gisela Weller-Lindhorst*, 23 April 2009, para 51.

of goods or for the provision of services falling within the scope of the Brussels I Regulation, if paragraph (b) fails to allocate jurisdiction to the courts of a Member State (because the place of performance of the characteristic obligation is not in a Member State), the general rule (according to which the courts for the place of performance of the obligation on which the claim is based have jurisdiction) applies.[382] So, where an English seller of goods sues a German buyer for the unpaid purchase price, the place of performance of the buyer's payment obligation will determine jurisdiction under the general rule (found in Article 5(1)(a) of the Brussels I Regulation) if the place of delivery of the goods is not in a Member State.[383] Similarly, Article 5(1)(a) applies if the dispute relates to a contract which is neither a contract for the sale of goods nor a contract for the provision of services.

5.6.31   The connecting factor which determines jurisdiction for the purposes of the general rule is 'the place of performance of the obligation in question'. The interpretation of this phrase is the issue under the Brussels Convention which has been considered by the Court of Justice more frequently than any other. Although many of the situations in which a reference has been made would now be governed by Article 5(1)(b) of the Brussels I Regulation rather than the general rule, the body of case law developed by the Court of Justice remains relevant for those cases in which jurisdiction is still determined by the general rule.

THE OBLIGATION IN QUESTION

5.6.32   As regards the determination of 'the obligation in question' the rule first laid down by the Court of Justice in *Ets A de Bloos SPRL v Société en commandite par actions Bouyer* is that, for the purposes of jurisdiction in matters relating to a contract, 'the obligation to be taken into account is that which corresponds to the contractual right on which the plaintiff's action is based'.[384] This is the obligation which the contract imposes on the defendant, the non-performance of which is relied upon by the claimant in support of his claim. For example, where the claimant sues the defendant for having failed to pay royalties due under a recording contract, the obligation in question is the obligation to pay the royalties.[385] In an action for a declaration of non-liability by a carrier when goods in its care are stolen in France while en route to England, France is the place of performance of the 'obligation in question' as the central issue is whether the carrier is liable for the loss of the goods in France.[386] For the purposes of Article 5(1)(a), it is immaterial where other obligations under the contract—which are not relevant to the legal proceedings—were to be performed.[387]

---

[382] Art 5(1)(c).

[383] For a different interpretation of the interrelationship of subparas (a), (b) and (c) of Art 5(1) of the Brussels I Regulation, see K Takahashi, 'Jurisdiction in matters relating to contract: Article 5(1) of the Brussels Convention and Regulation' (2002) 27 *EL Rev* 530, 540.

[384] Case 14/76 [1976] ECR 1497, para 13. This ruling was confirmed in a series of later cases, including: Case 266/85 *Shenavai v Kreischer* [1987] ECR 239, para 20; Case C–288/92 *Custom Made Commercial Ltd v Stawa Metallbau GmbH* [1994] ECR I–2913, paras 23–25. See also *Royal & Sun Alliance Insurance Plc v MK Digital FZE (Cyprus) Ltd* [2006] 2 Lloyd's Rep 110, 125 (at [90]).

[385] *Barbier v Music for Pleasure Ltd* [1990] ILPr 172 (Court of First Instance, Brussels).

[386] *Royal & Sun Alliance Insurance Plc v MK Digital FZE (Cyprus) Ltd* [2006] 2 Lloyd's Rep 110.

[387] Advocate General Alber in Case C–256/00 *Besix SA v Wasserreinigungsbau Alfred Kretzschmar GmbH & Co KG (Wabag)* [2002] ECR I–1699, para 16. See also *Fisher v Unione Italiana de Riassicurazione SPA*

By the same token, unless the claim is based on the defendant's breach of the obligation which characterises the contract, it is not the characteristic obligation which determines jurisdiction under the general rule.[388]

5.6.33   In *Effer v Kantner,*[389] an agent had been promised payment by a company which later became insolvent. The issue was whether this company's promise was made in its own name or in the name of its principal. The principal company denied the existence of any contract between it and the agent. The Court of Justice held that the claim fell within Article 5(1). In *Effer v Kantner* the existence of a contractual obligation was not denied; the issue was who owed that obligation which raised the preliminary question whether there was a contract between the company and the agent. The Court of Appeal went further in *Boss Group Ltd v Boss France SA*[390] in which it assumed jurisdiction under Article 5(1) with regard to the plaintiff's application for a declaration that it had not entered a contract with the defendant. On the one hand, it is doubtful whether *Boss Group Ltd v Boss France SA* was correctly decided[391] as the Court of Justice's case law insists on there being a contractual obligation in the first place. Since, where proceedings are brought for a declaration that no contract was ever concluded between the parties, the claimant is unable to identify any obligation (breached by the defendant) as a basis for the claim and Article 5(1) cannot allocate jurisdiction.[392] On the other hand, the Court of Justice's observation in *Effer v Kantner*—that Article 5(1) 'would be deprived of its legal effect' if it is accepted that 'in order to defeat the rule contained in that provision it is sufficient for one of the parties to claim that the contract does not exist'[393]—holds true *a fortiori* for the situation where the existence of the contract is the only issue at stake.

5.6.34   For the purposes of Article 5(1)(a), 'the obligation in question' is the original obligation, not any subsidiary obligation which may arise on breach of the original obligation.[394] So, if B sues A for failure to make available a suitable vehicle in accordance with the terms of a contract of hire, jurisdiction is determined by the place

---

[1998] CLC 682; *MBM Fabri-Clad Ltd v Eisen- und Hüttenwerke Thale AG* [2000] ILPr 505; *Handelsagentur Dieter Nienaber GmbH & Co KG v Impex-Euro Srl* [1988] ECC 150 (Court of Cassation, Italy); *Vauth & Söhn KG v Lindig* [1989] ECC 212 (Court of Appeal, Versailles).

[388] See *Royal & Sun Alliance Insurance Plc v MK Digital FZE (Cyprus) Ltd* [2006] 2 Lloyd's Rep 110, 125 (at [90]); *Société Européenne d'Expansion (SEDEX) v Société Vetex* [1990] ILPr 254 (Court of Cassation, France);

[389] Case 38/81 [1982] ECR 825.

[390] [1997] 1 WLR 351. C Forsyth, 'Brussels Convention jurisdiction "in matters relating to a contract" when the plaintiff denies the existence of a contract' [1996] *LMCLQ* 329; E Peel, 'Jurisdiction over Non-Existent Contracts' (1996) 112 *LQR* 541; I Turkki, (1996) 21 *EL Rev* 419.

[391] K Hertz, *Jurisdiction in Contract and Tort under the Brussels Convention* (Copenhagen, DJØF Publishing, 1998) 153–4. The same goes for *USF Ltd (t/a USF Memcor) v Aqua Technology Hanson NV/ SA* [2001] 1 All ER (Comm) 856 (which followed the decision in the *Boss Group* case). Compare A Briggs, (1996) 67 *BYIL* 583 (supporting the decision).

[392] However, the decision in the *Boss Group* case was approved by Lord Clyde in *Kleinwort Benson Ltd v Glasgow City Council* [1999] 1 AC 153, 182 and by Lord Hope in *Agnew v Länsförsäkringsbolagens AB* [2001] 1 AC 223, 258, although, in the later case, Lord Millett doubted the decision's correctness: [2001] 1 AC 223, 264.

[393] Case 38/81 [1982] ECR 825, para 7.

[394] See, eg, *Medway Packaging Ltd v Meurer Maschinen GmbH* [1990] 2 Lloyd's Rep 112. In addition, the existence of the particular obligation must be established according to the terms of the contract where there is insufficient evidence that custom implies that the obligation exists in a particular trade: *Gard Marine & Energy Ltd v Tunicliffe* [2010] Lloyd's Rep IR 62.

of performance of A's obligation to provide the vehicle, not the place of performance of A's obligation to pay compensation for having failed to do so.[395] Similarly, where a distributor sues a manufacturer for wrongful termination of a distributorship, the obligation in question is not the manufacturer's obligation to pay compensation; depending on the circumstances, it is either the manufacturer's obligation to give reasonable notice of the termination[396] or the obligation to continue supplying the distributor with products.[397]

5.6.35   According to the analysis of the Court of Justice the identification of the obligation in question depends, in many situations, on which party is claimant and which party is defendant. Consider, for example, the situation where, under a charter agreement, A (a French company) makes available a particular vessel to B (an English company) and B repudiates the contract on the basis that the vessel in question is unseaworthy and refuses to pay the hire. If B sues A for damages for breach of contract, the obligation which forms the basis of the proceedings is A's obligation to make available a seaworthy vessel; but if A sues B for non-payment of the hire, the obligation on which the proceedings are based is B's obligation to pay.[398] Although in each situation, 'the obligation in question' is different, it is likely that the same fundamental issues are involved.

MULTIPLE OBLIGATIONS

5.6.36   In many cases proceedings arising out of a contractual dispute involve breaches of different obligations under the contract. What is the correct approach to the situation where, for example, the defendant is in breach of two obligations, one to be performed in England and the other to be performed in Belgium? One possible solution is for Article 5(1) to be interpreted simply as allocating jurisdiction to the English courts for the first claim and to the Belgian courts for the second claim. According to this view, the only way in which the claimant could have both claims resolved in the same forum would be to bring proceedings in the state in which the defendant is domiciled. Alternatively, Article 5(1) could be interpreted as allocating jurisdiction in relation to both claims to the courts for the place where the principal obligation in dispute is to be performed.

5.6.37   In *Shenavai v Kreischer*[399] the Court of Justice took the opportunity to confirm the general rule that the obligation in question is the contractual obligation which forms the actual basis of the legal proceedings. However, in a passage which was not strictly necessary for the decision, the Court of Justice considered the problem

---

[395] See *SAE SpA v Maas und See* [1992] ILPr 194 (Court of Appeal, Genoa); *Gracechurch Container Line Ltd v SpA Assicurazioni Generali* [1994] ILPr 206 (Court of Cassation, Italy).

[396] *Audi-NSU Auto Union AG v Adelin Petit et Cie SA* [1980] ECC 235 (Court of Cassation, Belgium).

[397] *Meyer v La Société Charles Wednesbury Ltd* [1996] ILPr 299 (Court of Appeal, Paris).

[398] See cases involving contracts for the sale of goods and for the provision of services decided under Art 5(1) of the Brussels Convention: *WH Martin Ltd v Feldbinder Spezialfahrzeugwerke GmbH* [1998] ILPr 794; *Machinale Glasfabriek de Maas BV v Emaillerie Alsacienne SA* [1984] ECC 123 (District Court, Arnhem); *Société Alusuisse France v Société Rodwer* [1990] ILPr 102 (Court of Appeal, Paris); *SIPAL Rexons Società Italiana Prodotti Auto e Locomozione SpA v Sprl Gold's Products* [1990] ILPr 386 (Court of Appeal, Mons); *Promac Sprl v SA Sogeservice* [1993] ILPr 309 (Court of Appeal, Paris).

[399] Case 266/85 [1987] ECR 239. WA Allwood, (1988) 13 *EL Rev* 60.

posed by a dispute concerned with a number of obligations arising under the same contract and forming the basis of the claim:

[I]n such a case the court before which the matter is brought will, when determining whether it has jurisdiction, be guided by the maxim *accessorium sequitur principale*; in the other words, where various obligations are at issue, it will be the principal obligation which will determine its jurisdiction.[400]

5.6.38 One must be careful not to read too much into this passage; the mere fact that one obligation is more important than another does not necessarily mean that the less important obligation is ancillary to the more important one. It is important to draw a distinction between, on the one hand, a contract which contains a number of independent obligations and, on the other, a contract which contains a principal obligation and one or more ancillary obligations. In the first case, Article 5(1) allocates jurisdiction in respect of each obligation to the courts for the place where the particular obligation is to be performed. *Leathertex Divisione Sintetici SpA v Bodetex BVBA*[401] involved disputes arising out of the termination of an agency contract. For a number of years C, a Belgian company, had acted in Belgium and the Netherlands as commercial agent for D, an Italian company; C received 5% commission by way of remuneration. After it had failed to receive payment of commission which it claimed was owing, C regarded the agreement as having been terminated and brought proceedings in Belgium claiming the unpaid commission and compensation in lieu of notice. According to the law governing the contract the obligation to pay commission was to be performed in Italy (the debtor's place of business) but the place of performance of the obligation to give notice of termination was Belgium (the agent's place of business). The Belgian courts, which regarded the two obligations as separate and of equal rank, made a reference to the Court of Justice on the interpretation of Article 5(1) in these circumstances. The Court of Justice ruled that where two obligations of equal rank are to be performed in different states, Article 5(1) does not allocate jurisdiction to the court for the place where only one of them is to be performed.[402]

5.6.39 This ruling has no direct bearing on how the principal obligation proviso should be applied, given that the Belgian court had not concluded that either obligation was the principal one. However, the Court of Justice, in response to an argument presented on behalf of the United Kingdom government, did clarify one important point. It was argued that the question posed by the Belgian court should be reformulated because, rather than the two obligations being of equal rank, the obligation to pay the commission was the principal one. The Court of Justice rejected this argument and indicated that 'it is for the national court to assess the relative importance of the contractual obligations at issue'.[403] In a case involving two or more obligations to be performed in different states, Article 5(1) does not require the national

[400] Case 266/85 [1987] ECR 239, para 19.
[401] Case C–420/97 [1999] ECR I–6747. G Panagopoulos, 'Jurisdiction in relation to a contract split between two states' [2000] *LMCLQ* 150.
[402] Case C–420/97 [1999] ECR I–6747, para 42. This ruling was foreshadowed by an *obiter dictum* in the judgment of Lloyd LJ in *Union Transport Plc v Continental Lines SA* [1991] 2 Lloyd's Rep 48, 51–2.
[403] Case C–420/97 [1999] ECR I–6747, para 21.

court to classify one of the obligations as the principal one, so that jurisdiction under Article 5(1) is necessarily allocated to a single forum.[404]

5.6.40   Where one of the obligations allegedly breached by the defendant can be categorised as the principal obligation, Article 5(1) allocates jurisdiction—in relation to claims concerning both the principal obligation and the ancillary obligation or obligations—to the courts for the place where the principal obligation is to be performed.[405] In *Union Transport Plc v Continental Lines SA*[406] it was alleged that as a result of an exchange of telexes the parties had concluded a contract for the charter of a vessel to be nominated by the defendant to load a cargo of telegraph poles in Florida for carriage to Bangladesh. The defendant, a Belgian company, argued that there was no contract. When the defendant failed to nominate a vessel the plaintiff started proceedings in England. On the assumption that the parties had concluded a contract the defendant was in breach of two obligations—to nominate and to provide a vessel. Since the second obligation was to be performed in Florida, the only basis on which the English court might have jurisdiction was that the obligation to nominate was to be performed in England. The defendant argued that, even though the obligation to nominate was to be performed in England, the court did not have jurisdiction under Article 5(1) since the obligation to provide a vessel was the primary obligation to which the obligation to nominate was ancillary. Both the Court of Appeal and the House of Lords concluded, in the plaintiff's favour, that the obligation to nominate was the principal obligation.

5.6.41   In deciding which obligation is principal and which one is ancillary a number of points should be considered. First, the precise terms of the contract are crucial. Had the vessel been named in the charter the failure to tender the vessel would have been the principal obligation.[407] Having said that, there is no reason why the principal obligation cannot be an implied, rather than express, term of the contract.[408] Secondly, the time sequence does not determine which obligation is principal and which obligation is ancillary; the first obligation breached by the defendant is not necessarily the principal obligation. In *AIG Europe UK Ltd v The Ethniki*[409] the Court of Appeal accepted the argument that it would be wrong to equate 'principal' with 'first in time'.[410] Thirdly, if the breach of the particular obligation does not, in itself, give rise to a complete cause of action that obligation is unlikely to be the principal obligation. In *Union Transport Plc v Continental Lines SA* Lloyd LJ noted that:

The very fact that a complete cause of action could have been based on the failure to nominate a vessel without referring to the provision of a vessel goes a long way to show that the failure to nominate was the principal obligation.[411]

---

[404]   See, eg, *Figot v Leithauser GmbH and Co* [2001] ILPr 28 (Court of Cassation, France).
[405]   See, eg, *William Grant & Sons International Ltd v Société Marie Brizard et Roger International* [2000] ILPr 774 (Court of Cassation, France).
[406]   [1991] 2 Lloyd's Rep 48 (CA); [1992] 1 WLR 15 (HL). A Briggs, 'The Brussels Convention Reaches the House of Lords' (1992) 108 *LQR* 186.
[407]   See Lord Goff at [1992] 1 WLR 15, 22.
[408]   *Raiffeisen Zentralbank Österreich Aktiengesellschaft v National Bank of Greece SA* [1999] 1 Lloyd's Rep 408.
[409]   [2000] 2 All ER 566.
[410]   See Evans LJ at [2000] 2 All ER 566, 573.
[411]   [1991] 2 Lloyd's Rep 48, 51.

5.6.42 Following the House of Lords' decision in the *Union Transport* case, the English courts have sought to identify the principal obligation by reference to the fundamental obligation or real cause of complaint.[412] In a case involving a claim to payment under a letter of credit, the principal obligation is the obligation of the bank to pay the beneficiary, not the bank's obligation to take up and examine the documents presented by the beneficiary.[413] In the context of a bill of lading which incorporates the Hague-Visby Rules, it has been held that the 'fundamental obligation' is not 'the obligation to keep and return (subject to proof that any loss or damage has occurred without fault), but the obligation to exercise due diligence'.[414] Depending on the precise nature of the claim and the defendant's default, the place of performance may be the port of loading, the high seas or the port of discharge.[415] In *AIG Europe UK Ltd v The Ethniki*[416] the question was whether the principal obligation in a contract of reinsurance was the claims control clause, under which the defendant's obligation was to notify the claim under the policy within a stipulated time limit (which was to be performed in England), or the ascertainment of loss obligation, according to which the defendant was required to investigate the claim fully and timeously (which was to be performed in Greece). The Court of Appeal, dismissing the defendant's appeal, held that the obligation under the claims control clause was the principal one. In the words of Evans LJ, the plaintiff's claim was 'based essentially on [the defendant's] failure to inform it promptly of the claim received in Athens'.[417] In *Source Ltd v TUV Rheinland Holding AG*[418] the plaintiffs, an English company, sought to sue the defendants, two German companies, in England for breach of contract. The plaintiffs alleged that the defendants were in breach of a contractual obligation to exercise reasonable skill and care in presenting reports to the plaintiffs concerning the quality of certain goods. The defendants were under a number of obligations under the contract: an obligation to inspect the goods, an obligation to refer defects to the factories, an obligation to make out a report and to send it to the plaintiffs in England. The Court of Appeal decided that the obligation to inspect the goods (which was not to be performed in England) was the principal obligation—inspection of the goods was the 'principal task for which the plaintiffs engaged the German companies'[419]—and that the court did not have jurisdiction under Article 5(1).[420] In *Barry v Bradshaw*[421] the defendant, an Irish accountant, was retained by the claimants, who had moved from England to Ireland, to represent, conduct and settle their tax affairs in the United Kingdom. When the claimants alleged that the defendant had acted negligently and started proceedings in England, the defendant contested the court's jurisdiction on the

---

[412] Compare *Société Filtertechniek Nederland BV v Hoff* [1998] ILPr 196 (Court of Appeal, Paris) in which the principal obligation was regarded as the one which gave rise to the largest amount of compensation.

[413] *Crédit Agricole Indosuez v Chailease Finance Corporation* [2000] ILPr 776.

[414] Rix J in *RPS Prodotti Siderurgici SRL v The Sea Maas* [2000] 1 All ER 536, 541.

[415] See, however, *Gracechurch Container Line Ltd v Assicurazioni Generali* [1994] ILPr 206 (Court of Cassation, Italy).

[416] [2000] 2 All ER 566.

[417] [2000] 2 All ER 566, 573.

[418] [1998] QB 54.

[419] Staughton LJ at [1998] QB 54, 61.

[420] See also *Ferndale Films Ltd v Granada Television Ltd* [1994] ILPr 180 (Supreme Court, Ireland).

[421] [2000] CLC 455.

basis that he was domiciled in Ireland and that Ireland, rather than England, was the place of performance of his obligations under the contract. However, the Court of Appeal accepted the claimants' argument that England, as the place where the Inland Revenue is situated, was the place of performance of the defendant's obligations. Although Ireland was the place where the defendant's obligations to communicate with the Inland Revenue (by correspondence written in Ireland) were performed, the principal obligation was the defendant's obligation to represent the claimants at a hearing before the General Commissioners, which necessarily could be performed only in England.

5.6.43   The fact that there is a principal/accessory relationship between various of the defendant's contractual obligations does not mean that litigation concerning any of those obligations, if not brought in the Member State of the defendant's domicile (under Article 2), must be brought in the place of performance of the principal obligation. Where the defendant fails to perform not only the primary obligation in England but also secondary obligations in France, there is nothing to stop the claimant choosing to litigate disputes concerning the secondary obligations (but not the primary obligation) in the place of performance of the secondary obligations (ie, France).[422]

Place of Performance

5.6.44   Should the place of performance be determined by reference to the law of the forum, the applicable law or an independent interpretation? In *Industrie Tessili Italiana Como v Dunlop AG*[423] the Court of Justice held that the place of performance of the obligation in question is to be determined by the law which governs that obligation according to the conflicts rules of the court before which the matter is brought.[424] If English jurisdiction is invoked in a case where jurisdiction is not allocated by Article 5(1)(b) of the Brussels I Regulation and the place of performance is disputed, the court must, first, decide by reference to English choice of law rules which law is applicable to the contractual obligation in question and, then, determine the place of performance by reference to the applicable law (which may or may not be English law). If, however, the place of performance cannot be ascertained, Article 5(1) 'does not provide for any jurisdiction alternative to that of the domicile of the defendant'.[425]

5.6.45   It has already been noted, in the context of the discussion of Article 5(1)(b) of the Brussels I Regulation, that the parties may, subject to certain limitations, expressly designate the place of performance.[426] Whether the parties have made such an agreement is a question of construction. It has been held, for example, that

---

[422] *Hoff v Filtertechniek Nederland BV* [2001] ILPr 82 (Court of Cassation, France).

[423] Case 12/76 [1976] ECR 1473, para 15.

[424] This ruling was confirmed in Case C–288/92 *Custom Made Commercial Ltd v Stawa Metallbau GmbH* [1994] ECR I–2913 and Case C–440/97 *GIE Group Concorde v Master of the vessel Suhadiwarno Panjan* [1999] ECR I–6309. See also *Commercial Marine Piling Ltd v Pierse Contracting Ltd* [2009] ILPr 909.

[425] Morritt LJ in *Viskase Ltd v Paul Kiefel GmbH* [1999] 1 WLR 1305, 1316–17.

[426] See paras 5.6.21, 5.6.24 and 5.6.25. An architect who draws up plans in Denmark in relation to the renovation of property in England and manages the renovation project performs his obligation in England: *Heifer International Inc v Christiansen* [2008] 2 All ER (Comm) 831.

where the parties to a charterparty agreed that 'general average ... shall be adjusted in London', this did not constitute a binding agreement as to the place of payment for the purposes of Article 5(1).[427] Similarly, where a claimant brings proceedings to recover commission due under an agency contract, if previously commission has been paid in London and Paris, it cannot be assumed that the parties reached agreement on the place of performance.[428]

5.6.46   In the absence of agreement on the place of performance or where the parties' agreement, without satisfying the formal requirements of Article 23, designates a fictitious place of performance (for example, where a charter agreement between an owner of an ocean-going liner and a demise charterer stipulates Vienna as the place of performance of the owner's obligations), the English court will have jurisdiction only if the claimant can establish a good arguable case that, according to the applicable law, the obligation must have been performed in England; it is not enough that the obligation in question might have been performed in England.[429] If the parties have not agreed on the place of performance (or if the parties' agreement is fictitious) the significance of the applicable law to questions of jurisdiction may be considerable. Where the claim is based on the defendant's failure to perform adequately the obligation to deliver goods, depending on the type of contract in question and the applicable law, the place of performance may be, for example, the place where the goods are located at the moment of sale[430] or the place where the seller is established.[431]

5.6.47   The applicable law is of particular importance in cases where the proceedings involve a contractual obligation to pay.[432] For example, in a situation where an English shipowner charters a vessel to a German charterer, who refuses to pay the hire, which court has jurisdiction in relation to the shipowner's claim for the unpaid hire may turn on the law governing the contract. Whereas under English law the debtor must, as a general rule, seek out the creditor at his place of business and pay him there,[433] under German law the general rule is that an obligation to pay is to be discharged at the debtor's domicile or seat.[434] Accordingly, in this type of case, Article 5(1) makes provision for English jurisdiction only if English law is the applicable law.[435]

---

[427]   *The World Hitachi Zosen* The Times, 8 April 1996.

[428]   See, eg, *Khawam v Huppmann Handel GmbH* [1990] ILPr 115 (Court of Appeal, Paris).

[429]   *Hanbridge Services Ltd v Aerospace Communications Ltd* [1993] ILPr 778 (Supreme Court, Ireland).

[430]   *SpA Officine Meccaniche Ventura v Prometal SA* [1990] ILPr 184 (District Court, Monza), applying Art 1609 of the French civil code.

[431]   *SIPAL Rexons Società Italiana Prodotti Auto e Locomozione SpA v Sprl Gold's Products* [1990] ILPr 386 (Court of Appeal, Mons), applying the International Sale of Goods Convention 1964.

[432]   See C Forsyth and P Moser, 'The Impact of the Applicable Law of Contract on the Law of Jurisdiction under the European Conventions' (1996) 45 *ICLQ* 190.

[433]   *Robey & Co v Snaefell Mining Co Ltd* (1887) 20 QBD 152; *Rein v Stein* [1892] QB 753; *The Eider* [1893] P 119. The position is the same under Danish and Swedish law: *PC Express AB v Columbus IT Partner A/S* [2001] ILPr 314 (Eastern Court of Appeal, Denmark).

[434]   BGB, para 269. The same basic rule is to be found in Art 1247 of the French civil code (see *Société Lorraine des Produits Métallurgiques v SA Banque Paribas Belgique* [1995] ILPr 175 (Court of Appeal, Paris); *Société Eureco v Société Confezioni Liviam di Crespi Luigi* [1990] ILPr 50 (Court of Appeal, Paris); *Swissport International Ltd v Holco* [2005] ILPr 596 (Court of Cassation, France)) and in the International Sale of Goods Convention 1964 (see *Società Kretschner v Muratori* [1991] ILPr 361 (Court of Cassation, Italy)).

[435]   See, eg, *Gamlestaden Plc v Casa de Suecia SA* [1994] 1 Lloyd's Rep 433.

5.6.48   Determining the place of performance of an obligation to make payment is not always simple.[436] There is, for example, the problem of ascertaining where an obligation to pay money to an international bank or other corporation with branches worldwide is to be performed. As a general proposition, it is reasonable to suppose that if the place of payment is not stipulated, the creditor's principal place of business should be regarded as the place of performance. However, where an obligation to pay a sum of money to a bank (for example, under a guarantee) is intimately connected with a bank account which is held at a particular branch, the place of performance should be the location of the branch where the account is held.[437] Similarly, a bank's obligation to make payment out of an account is to be regarded as an obligation to make payment at the branch where the account is kept.[438] It should also be noted that there are exceptions to the general rules which determine the place of payment. For example, under German law, although as a general rule the debtor's residence is the place of payment, where a lawyer seeks to recover fees from a client for advocacy work the place of payment is where the lawyer's office is situated.[439] Equally, it is not an immutable rule of English law that, in the absence of any express provision in the contract, a debtor's obligation to pay is to be performed at the creditor's place of business.[440] Specific types of contract contain special rules. For example, in a contract of reinsurance, premiums are payable in cash at the insurer's principal place of business and claims are payable at the address of the reinsured, unless the contract provides expressly or by implication to the contrary[441]; in *Royal Bank of Scotland v Cassa di Risparmio delle Provincie Lombard,*[442] in the context of a dispute relating to letters of credit governed by the Uniform Customs and Practice for Documentary Credits, it was held that the place of performance of the defendant's obligation to reimburse the plaintiff was where claims for reimbursement by the plaintiff were to be made, rather than where the plaintiff's principal place of business was located.

5.6.49   The determination of the place of performance of certain other obligations also may present problems.[443] In English law it seems that, in the absence of an agreement to the contrary, an obligation to give notice—such as notice of termination of an agreement[444]—is to be performed at the place of business of the party who is to be notified.[445] There are also problems in trying to identify the place of performance of

---

[436] See *Domicrest Ltd v Swiss Bank Corporation* [1999] QB 548 (in which the court had to consider evidence on Swiss law, which governed the contract).

[437] *Bank of Scotland v Seitz* [1990] SLT 584 (Court of Session, Scotland).

[438] *Richardson v Richardson* [1927] P 228.

[439] See *Re a German Lawyer's Fee Agreement* [1992] ILPr 395 (Federal Supreme Court, Germany). For the position in France, see *Swissport International Ltd v Holco* [2005] ILPr 596 (Court of Cassation, France).

[440] See, eg, *Masri v Consolidated Contractors International (UK) Ltd* [2005] 1 CLC 1125, 1146 (at [82]); affirmed without consideration of this point [2006] 1 WLR 830 (CA).

[441] R Hunter, 'Reinsurance Litigation and the Civil Jurisdiction and Judgments Act 1982' [1987] *JBL* 344, 347.

[442] The Financial Times, 21 January 1992.

[443] See, eg, *Crucial Music Corp v Klondyke Management AG* [2007] ILPr 733 (warranty of intellectual property rights being transferred by assignment is performed at the time when and the place where the transfer is effected).

[444] See, eg, Case 14/76 *Ets A de Bloos SPRL v Société en commandite par actions Bouyer* [1976] ECR 1497.

[445] *Medway Packaging Ltd v Meurer Maschinen GmbH* [1990] 2 Lloyd's Rep 112. See also *Carl Freudenberg KG v Bureau RC Van Oppens Sarl* [1986] ECC 366 (Court of Cassation, Belgium).

a negative obligation—such as the obligation under a worldwide exclusive distribution agreement not to supply anyone other than the party entitled under the agreement— as such an obligation is 'probably performable everywhere'.[446] In *Besix SA v Wasserreinigungsbau Alfred Kretzschmar GmbH & Co KG (Wabag)*[447] the Belgian claimant and the German defendants had submitted a joint tender for a water supply project in Cameroon. After the project was awarded to another consortium, in which the German defendants were involved, the claimant sought to sue the defendants in Belgium for breach of their contractual undertaking to 'act exclusively and not ... commit themselves to other partners'. The question was whether Belgium could be regarded as the place of performance of this obligation, given that the obligation was to be honoured throughout the world—as a result of which there were numerous potential places of performance. The Court of Justice took the view that Article 5(1) does not confer jurisdiction on the courts of any state if, in the circumstances of the case, the relevant obligation has been, or is to be, performed in a number of places[448]; for the purposes of Article 5(1), 'a single place of performance for the obligation in question must be identified'.[449] Given that the defendants were contractually obliged to honour the non-competition agreement throughout the world, the performance of the obligation in question was not capable of being identified with a specific place and was not linked with one forum rather than another. In these circumstances, Article 5(1) did not confer jurisdiction on the Belgian courts (or any other forum) and the claimant had no choice but to sue the defendants in Germany in reliance on Article 2.

5.6.50 It is worth emphasising that the reason why, in the *Besix* case, the negative obligation in question could not be localised was because it was 'not subject to any geographical limit'.[450] Where, in a case involving a claim based on the breach of a negative obligation, there is clearly a single location for the effects to be avoided, this place should serve to identify the place of performance of the obligation in question.[451] So, in a case involving an exclusive distribution agreement which relates to one Member State, if the claim is based on breach by the supplier of its obligation not to supply anyone other than the claimant, it is not unreasonable to regard the contract area as the place of performance.[452]

The Jurisprudence of the Court of Justice in the Light of the Purpose of Article 5(1)

5.6.51 Although it is said that Article 5 'is justified by the fact that there must be a close connecting factor between the dispute and the court with jurisdiction to resolve it',[453] the jurisprudence of the Court of Justice often led to Article 5(1) of the Brussels

---

[446] Saville LJ in *Boss Group Ltd v Boss France SA* [1997] 1 WLR 351, 357. Cf *Nestorway Ltd t/a Electrographic International v Ambaflex BV* [2007] ILPr 633 (High Court, Ireland); *SARL Noge v Gotz GmbH* [1998] ILPr 189 (Court of Cassation, France).

[447] Case C–256/00 [2002] ECR I–1699.

[448] Case C–256/00 [2002] ECR I–1699, para 28.

[449] Case C–256/00 [2002] ECR I–1699, para 29.

[450] Case C–256/00 [2002] ECR I–1699, para 55.

[451] K Hertz, *Jurisdiction in Contract and Tort under the Brussels Convention* (Copenhagen, DJØF Publishing, 1998) 150.

[452] See *Carl Stuart Ltd v Biotrace* [1994] ILPr 554 (Supreme Court, Ireland).

[453] Jenard Report, [1979] OJ C59/22.

Convention conferring jurisdiction on a forum with little connection with the dispute. This is why, as regards disputes arising out of contracts for the sale of goods and for the provision of services, Article 5(1)(b) of the Brussels I Regulation allocates jurisdiction to the courts for the place of performance of the characteristic obligation. Although the amended version of Article 5(1) of the Brussels I Regulation is a definite improvement, for a variety of reasons it still falls a long way short of finding an ideal solution to the problem of the allocation of jurisdiction over contractual disputes.

5.6.52   First, and most fundamentally, Article 5(1) attempts to allocate jurisdiction by reference to a single connecting factor. Such a one-dimensional rule is unlikely to allocate jurisdiction to a closely connected forum on a consistent basis.[454] Secondly, if jurisdiction is not allocated by Article 5(1)(b), the general rule—which focuses on the specific obligation allegedly breached by the defendant—applies. In these cases, all the problems associated with the original version of Article 5(1) remain. The exercise of jurisdiction by an inappropriate forum is most likely in cases where the 'obligation in question' is the defendant's obligation to pay (whose place of performance may have little connection with the real substance of the dispute) and/or the claim is based on the defendant's failure to perform (in which case the dispute may well have little connection with the place where the defendant should have performed).[455] Although the Court of Justice has repeatedly been encouraged to reconsider its earlier jurisprudence,[456] on each occasion it has confirmed the rulings in *Ets A de Bloos SPRL v Société en commandite par actions Bouyer*[457] and *Industrie Tessili Italiana Como v Dunlop AG*.[458] The claimant is entitled to sue the defendant in the place of performance of the obligation 'even where the court thus designated is not that which has the closest connection with the dispute'.[459]

Jurisdiction in Matters Relating to Tort

5.6.53   Article 5(3) of the Brussels I Regulation provides that 'in matters relating to tort, delict or quasi-delict' a person domiciled in a Member State may be sued in another Member State 'in the courts for the place where the harmful event occurred or may occur'.[460] This wording makes it clear that Article 5(3) covers cases where the

---

[454] See J Hill, 'Jurisdiction in Civil and Commercial Matters: Is there a Third Way?' (2001) 54 *CLP* 439, 471–4.

[455] See, eg, *Promac Sprl v SA Sogeservice* [1993] ILPr 309 (Court of Appeal, Paris).

[456] See, eg, the opinion of Advocate General Lenz in Case C–288/92 *Custom Made Commercial Ltd v Stawa Metallbau GmbH* [1994] ECR I–2913, 2915–2948; the opinion of Advocate General Léger in Case C–420/97 *Leathertex Divisione Sintetici SpA v Bodetex BVBA* [1999] ECR I–6747, paras 118–136 and the opinion of Advocate General Ruiz-Jarabo Colomer in Case C–440/97 *GIE Group Concorde v Master of the vessel Suhadiwarno Panjan* [1999] ECR I–6309, paras 95–108.

[457] Case 14/76 [1976] ECR 1497.

[458] Case 12/76 [1976] ECR 1473.

[459] Case C–288/92 *Custom Made Commercial Ltd v Stawa Metallbau GmbH* [1994] ECR I–2913, para 21.

[460] On jurisdiction and internet torts, see JJ Fawcett, J Harris and M Bridge, *International Sale of Goods in the Conflict of Laws* (Oxford, OUP, 2005) 549–82; O Bigos, 'Jurisdiction over Cross-Border Wrongs on the Internet' (2005) 54 *ICLQ* 585; BP Werley, 'Aussies Rules: Universal Jurisdiction over Internet Defamation' (2004) 18 *Temple Int'l & Comp LJ* 199; HP Hestermeyer, 'Personal Jurisdiction for Internet Torts: Towards an International Solution?' (2005–06) 26 *Nw J Int'l L & Bus* 267.

claimant is seeking to prevent the defendant from committing an anticipated wrong as well as cases where a wrong is alleged to have already been committed.

Matters Relating to Tort, Delict or Quasi-delict

5.6.54 The Court of Justice has not been required to provide a positive definition of what constitutes matters relating to 'tort, delict or quasi-delict'. What emerges from the cases is that, in the standard case, for proceedings to fall within the scope of Article 5(3) there must be a claim seeking to establish the liability of a defendant[461] and the claim must not relate to an obligation which has been freely entered into by one party to another.[462] It is important to note, however, that Article 5(3) uses the phrase 'matters relating to tort', rather than 'tortious claims'. In *Danmarks Rederiforening v LO Landsorganisation i Sverige*[463] the question was whether proceedings in a particular Danish court, which had exclusive jurisdiction to rule on the legality of industrial action, fell within the scope of Article 5(3) notwithstanding the fact that any claim for compensation (which might be brought if the industrial action was declared to be illegal) would be heard by the regular Danish courts. The Court of Justice ruled that, even though the proceedings were not directly concerned with the liability of the defendant, they were covered by Article 5(3). The English court has decided that a claim for contribution under the Civil Liability (Contribution) Act 1978 also falls within Article 5(3).[464] The nature of the relief sought by the claimant is not generally relevant to the applicability of Article 5(3). An application either for a declaration that the defendant has committed a tort or for an injunction to restrain possible future torts[465] falls within Article 5(3), whether or not the claimant also claims compensation. Moreover, and more controversially, it has been held that an application for a declaration that the claimant is not liable for a tort is within Article 5(3).[466]

5.6.55 Although the question is not entirely free from doubt,[467] it seems unlikely that Article 5(3) is to be regarded as a residual category which includes all claims seeking to establish liability which do not fall within Article 5(1). At the very least Article 5(3) is premised on the existence of two elements: 'One is that there must have been "wrongful" conduct, and the other that that conduct must have caused a "harmful event"'.[468] The use of the words 'harmful event' in Article 5(3), while entirely appropriate for claims in tort or equitable wrongs, 'seems most inappropriate for restitutionary claims'.[469] Accordingly, a claim based on constructive trust for wrongdoing (such

---

[461] Case C–261/90 *Reichert v Dresdner Bank (No 2)* [1992] ECR I–2149, para 20.

[462] Case 189/87 *Kalfelis v Bankhaus Schröder, Münchmeyer, Hengst & Co* [1988] ECR 5565; Case C–26/91 *Jakob Handte & Co GmbH v Traitements Mécano-chimiques des Surfaces SA* [1992] ECR I–3967.

[463] Case C–18/02 [2004] ECR I–1417.

[464] *Hewden Tower Cranes Ltd v Wolffkran GmbH* [2007] 2 Lloyd's Rep 138.

[465] See *Re Action for a Prohibitory Injunction* [2006] ILPr 790 (Federal Supreme Court, Germany).

[466] *Equitas Ltd v Wave City Shipping Co Ltd* [2005] 2 All ER (Comm) 301. Cf *BL Macchine Automatiche SpA v Windmoller & Holscher KG* [2004] ILPr 350 (Court of Cassation, Italy).

[467] See paras 5.6.9–5.6.11.

[468] Advocate General Gulmann in Case C–261/90 *Reichert v Dresdner Bank (No 2)* [1992] ECR I–2149, 2169.

[469] Hirst J in *Barclays Bank Plc v Glasgow City Council* [1993] QB 429, 443.

as dishonest assistance) is within the scope of Article 5(3),[470] as is a claim for breach of fiduciary duty.[471] There is, however, a good argument for saying that a claim based on knowing receipt which is not based on wrongdoing by the defendant should fall outside the scope of Article 5(3) as it is restitutionary in nature.[472]

A Harmful Event

5.6.56 The concept of 'harmful event' is broad in scope. For example, it has been held that, in the context of consumer protection, it is wide enough to cover not only the situation where an individual has sustained injury, but also the undermining of legal stability by the use of unfair terms in consumer contracts.[473] When seeking to determine the act which constitutes the 'harmful event' for the purposes of Article 5(3) the court must identify the causative event underlying the infliction of harm. For example, where the defendant lawfully photographs the claimant in Germany, but wrongfully publishes those photographs in the Netherlands, the relevant event is the publication, rather than the taking of the photographs.[474] Similarly, where an English domiciliary, who is injured in a road accident in France and receives damages for his injuries, later seeks further compensation for deterioration of his condition, the deterioration (which takes place in England) is not a 'harmful event' for the purposes of Article 5(3); the harmful event is the defendant's negligence in causing the accident.[475] Further, where sound recordings should have been delivered to England but were wrongfully retained and used in Germany, Germany was the place where the event giving rise to damage occurred.[476]

5.6.57 Which law determines whether or not an event is to be regarded as 'harmful'? In *Shevill v Presse Alliance SA*[477] the plaintiff started proceedings in England alleging that she had been defamed by a newspaper article published by the defendant, a French company. The defendant argued that the plaintiff could not rely on Article 5(3) in a libel case where the plaintiff, rather than proving that there had been a harmful event, sought to rely solely on the presumption of harm. Among the questions which the House of Lords referred to the Court of Justice was the following:

Does the phrase 'harmful event' include an event actionable under national law without proof of damage, where there is no evidence of actual damage or harm?[478]

---

[470] *Casio Computer Co Ltd v Sayo* [2001] ILPr 694; *Dexter Ltd v Harley* The Times, 2 April 2001; *Cronos Containers NV v Palatin* [2003] 2 Lloyd's Rep 489.

[471] *WPP Holdings Italy Srl v Benatti* [2007] 1 WLR 2316. For an alternative viewpoint, see paras 15.1.86–15.1.91.

[472] A Briggs, (2001) 72 *BYIL* 470, 473; TM Yeo, 'Constructive Trustees and the Brussels Convention' (2001) 117 *LQR* 560, 564.

[473] Case C–167/00 *Verein für Konsumentinformation v Henkel* [2002] ECR I–8111, para 42.

[474] *Re the Unauthorised Publication of Approved Photographs* [1991] ILPr 468 (District Court, Hamburg).

[475] *Henderson v Jaouen* [2002] 1 WLR 2971. A Briggs, (2002) 73 *BYIL* 458. See also *Athanasakos v Hatramo Haven en Transportbedrijf Moerdijk BV* [2005] ILPr 699 (Supreme Court, Greece).

[476] *Mazur Media Ltd v Mazur Media GmbH* [2004] 1 WLR 2966 (however, Lawrence Collins J went on to hold that the damage which occurred was merely indirect damage).

[477] Case C–68/93 [1995] ECR I–415.

[478] The questions referred by the House of Lords are reproduced in the Court of Justice's judgment: Case C–68/93 [1995] ECR I–415, para 16.

5.6.58 The Court of Justice decided that, as long as the effectiveness of the Brussels regime is not impaired, the criteria for assessing whether or not the defendant's conduct constitutes a 'harmful event' for the purposes of Article 5(3) 'must ... be settled solely by the national court seised, applying the substantive law determined by its national conflict of laws rules'.[479] Not surprisingly, when it came to applying the Court of Justice's ruling, the House of Lords held that:

where English law presumes the publication of a defamatory statement is harmful to the person defamed without specific proof thereof that is sufficient for the application of Article 5(3).[480]

The Place

5.6.59 In a road accident case there can be little doubt over where the harmful event occurs. If, as a result of the negligence of an English motorist, a person is injured in France, the victim may bring proceedings against the driver either in England (Article 2) or in France (Article 5(3)). The road accident case is simple, first, because the defendant's act and the claimant's damage occur in the same place and, secondly, because the claimant's damage consists of personal injury or property damage. More difficult are the cases where the defendant acts in one place and the claimant suffers injury in another and/or the harm suffered by the claimant is in the nature of pure economic loss.

MULTIPLE LOCALITY CASES

5.6.60 If the defendant, in France, shoots with a gun and injures the claimant, who is standing on the other side of the border with Germany, where does the harmful event occur for the purposes of Article 5(3)? The answer given by the Court of Justice to this question is that, notwithstanding the fact that Article 5(3) refers to the 'place' in the singular, the harmful event occurs 'either at the place where the damage occurred or the place of the event giving rise to it'.[481] In *Handelskwekerij GJ Bier BV v Mines de Potasse d'Alsace SA*[482] the plaintiff alleged that the defendant, a French company, discharged effluent into the Rhine in France; the pollution flowed down-river and the plaintiff, a Dutch horticulturist, suffered loss as a result of the pollution of the water supply. The plaintiff invoked the jurisdiction of the Dutch courts, relying on Article 5(3). The defendant contested jurisdiction on the basis that the harmful event occurred in France rather than in the Netherlands. The Court of Justice decided that 'the place of the event giving rise to the damage no less than the place where damage occurred can, depending on the case, constitute a significant connecting factor from the point of view of jurisdiction'.[483] Accordingly, the plaintiff was entitled to sue the defendant in the Netherlands (where the damage occurred) and was not required

---

[479] C–68/93 [1995] ECR I–415, para 39.
[480] Lord Jauncey at [1996] AC 959, 983.
[481] Case 21/76 *Handelskwekerij GJ Bier BV v Mines de Potasse d'Alsace SA* [1976] ECR 1735, para 19. See also *Haftpflichtverband der Deutsche Industrie Versicherungsverein auf Gegenseitigkeit (HDI) v Société Axa France IARD* [2007] ILPr 373 (Court of Cassation, France).
[482] Case 21/76 [1976] ECR 1735. TC Hartley, (1977) 2 *EL Rev* 143.
[483] Case 21/76 [1976] ECR 1735, para 15.

to proceed in France (where the defendant was domiciled). In *Zuid-Chemie BV v Philippo's Mineralenfabriek NV/SA*,[484] micromix was manufactured by the defendant, delivered in Belgium and subsequently used by the claimant in the Netherlands in the production of fertiliser. Because the micromix had contained the wrong proportion of cadmium, the fertiliser was rendered unusable. The issue was which 'damage' was relevant for the purposes of Article 5(3)—the delivery of the defective product in Belgium or the normal use of the product for the purpose for which it was intended in the Netherlands. The Court of Justice decided that the 'place where the harmful event occurred' was not Belgium, where the defendant had manufactured and delivered the contaminated micromix,[485] but in the Netherlands, where the claimant had used it to produce contaminated fertiliser. The Court of Justice cautioned that:

The place where the damage occurred must not, however, be confused with the place where the event which damaged the product itself occurred, the latter being the place of the event giving rise to the damage. By contrast, the 'place where the damage occurred'... is the place where the event which gave rise to the damage produces its harmful effects, that is to say, the place where the damage caused by the defective product actually manifests itself.[486]

It should be stressed that, where a claimant has a choice under Article 5(3), that choice is not subject to any constraints. The claimant does not have to justify why he selected one competent forum rather than another and the defendant is not entitled to contest jurisdiction on the basis that the claimant opted for a forum which was less competent or appropriate than another.[487] Where, however, it is impossible to determine the place where the event giving rise to the damage occurred, the claimant who wishes to rely on Article 5(3) has no choice but to bring proceedings at the place where the damage occurred.[488]

5.6.61   The interpretation of Article 5(3) in the context of proceedings for libel, invasion of privacy or breach of copyright raises potential problems since a single publication might be disseminated in a number of places. In *Shevill v Presse Alliance SA*[489] the plaintiff alleged that she had been defamed in an article published by the defendant, a French company, in a newspaper which had a circulation of many thousands in France and only a handful in England. When the plaintiff started proceedings in England, the defendant contested the court's jurisdiction on the basis that England was not the place where the harmful event occurred.

5.6.62   As regards the place of the event giving rise to the damage, the Court of Justice ruled that, in the context of a libel, the relevant place is 'the place where the publisher of the newspaper in question is established, since that is the place where the harmful event originated and from which the libel was issued and put into circulation'.[490]

---

[484] Case C–189/08 [2009] ECR I–6917.

[485] Although Belgium was acknowledged by both parties to be the place of the event giving rise to the damage.

[486] Case C–189/08 [2009] ECR I–6917, para 27.

[487] *Schimmel Pianofortefabrik GmbH v Bion* [1992] ILPr 199 (Court of Cassation, France).

[488] Case C–51/97 *Réunion Européenne SA v Spliethoff's Bevrachtingskantoor BV* [1998] ECR I–6511, para 33.

[489] Case C–68/93 [1995] ECR I–415. A Briggs, (1995) 15 *YBEL* 487; C Forsyth, [1995] *CLJ* 515; A Reed and TP Kennedy, 'International torts and *Shevill*: the ghost of forum shopping yet to come' [1996] *LMCLQ* 108.

[490] Case C–68/93 [1995] ECR I–415, para 24.

As regards the place where the damage occurred, the Court of Justice decided that the place is 'where the event giving rise to the damage, entailing tortious, delictual or quasi-delictual liability, produced its harmful effects upon the victim'.[491] The basis of this decision was that:

In the case of an international libel through the press, the injury caused by a defamatory publication to the honour, reputation and good name of a natural or legal person occurs in the places where the publication is distributed, when the victim is known in those places.[492]

5.6.63   The effect of this ruling was that the plaintiff was entitled to sue the defendant in France (the place of the event giving rise to the damage) or in England (the place where some of the damage occurred). However, the Court of Justice added an important proviso. If a claimant sues in the place of the event giving rise to the damage the court has jurisdiction to hear the claim for damages 'for all the harm caused by the unlawful act'.[493] If, however, a claimant sues in another Member State—on the basis that some of the damage occurred there—the courts of that state have jurisdiction to rule only on the injury caused to the victim's reputation in that state.[494] So, on the facts of *Shevill v Presse Alliance SA*, if the plaintiff had sued the defendant in France she could have recovered damages for all injury to her reputation, wherever suffered, but by suing in England she was limited to recovering for any loss of reputation which she had suffered in the United Kingdom.[495]

5.6.64   In a case where the claimant alleges that he has suffered loss to his reputation as a result of the publication of defamatory material in a number of different places, the Court of Justice's ruling runs the risk that the same (or very similar) issues may be litigated in two or more states. It must be remembered, however, that the claimant can avoid such multiplicity of proceedings by 'bringing his entire claim before the courts either of the defendant's domicile or of the place where the publisher of the defamatory publication is established'.[496]

5.6.65   Problems may also arise in cases involving property damage. In *Réunion Européenne SA v Spliethoff's Bevrachtingskantoor BV*[497] a cargo of pears was damaged at some point between the place where they were shipped (in Australia) and their ultimate destination, a town in France. The cargo had been carried (in sealed containers) by the defendant to Rotterdam, from where the containers were carried (by a third party) to the final destination. It was only when the sealed containers were opened in France that it was discovered that the cargo had perished. In the context of the claim brought by the cargo-owners' insurers against the defendant, the Court of

---

[491] Case C–68/93 [1995] ECR I–415, para 28.

[492] Case C–68/93 [1995] ECR I–415, para 29.

[493] Case C–68/93 [1995] ECR I–415, para 25.

[494] Case C–68/93 [1995] ECR I–415, para 30. See *Barclay v Sweeney* [1998] ILPr 288 (Court of Appeal, Paris); *Sola v Le Tribune de Genève* [2000] ILPr 795 (Court of Appeal, Paris).

[495] For application of the *Shevill* ruling in a case governed by sched 4 to the Civil Jurisdiction and Judgments Act 1982, see *McCarten, Turkington and Breen v Lord St Oswald* [1996] NI 65 (High Court, Northern Ireland). For an application of the *Shevill* ruling in context of breach of copyright, see *Wegmann v Elsevier Science Ltd* [1999] ILPr 379 (Court of Cassation, France).

[496] Case C–68/93 *Shevill v Presse Alliance SA* [1995] ECR I–415, para 32.

[497] Case C–51/97 [1998] ECR I–6511.

Justice ruled that, in the circumstances of the case, the place where the damage arose was 'the place where the actual maritime carrier was to deliver the goods'.[498]

CASES INVOLVING ECONOMIC LOSS

5.6.66 The application of the ruling in *Handelskwekerij GJ Bier BV v Mines de Potasse d'Alsace SA* is less straightforward in cases involving economic loss than in cases which give rise to personal injury and/or property damage. The localisation of the defendant's wrongful act and the claimant's damage is inherently difficult because both the wrongful act and the damage are intangible.

5.6.67 Although the Court of Justice seems to have taken a relatively liberal view of Article 5(3), it is important to remember that Article 5(3) is a derogation from Article 2 which must be interpreted restrictively. In *Dumez France SA v Hessische Landesbank*[499] the plaintiff was a French company which owned two German subsidiaries. The plaintiff alleged that as a result of tortious acts by the defendant, a German bank, the German subsidiaries had become insolvent. The plaintiff claimed damages for the loss suffered as a consequence and started proceedings in France. The defendant contested the jurisdiction of the French courts on the basis that France was not 'the place where the harmful event occurred'. Although Germany was obviously the place of the event giving rise to the damage, the plaintiff's argument was that France was the place of the damage, since it was in France that the plaintiff suffered the loss. The Court of Justice thought that the fallacy of the plaintiff's argument was to equate the place where the damage occurred with the place where the injury was suffered. Although the plaintiff suffered loss in France—it was in France that the plaintiff suffered a depletion of its assets—the injury suffered by the plaintiff was only an indirect consequence of harm inflicted on the German subsidiaries. The damage occurred in Germany, where the defendant's action caused injury to the immediate victim. For the purposes of Article 5(3) the place where the damage occurs is:

the place where the event giving rise to the damage, and entailing tortious, delictual or quasi-delictual liability, directly produced its harmful effects upon the person who is the immediate victim of the event.[500]

So, where A (a French domiciliary) negligently kills B (the husband of C, a German domiciliary) in England, C may bring proceedings against A in France (on the basis of Article 2) or in England (on the basis of Article 5(3)), but not in Germany. Despite the superficial attraction of the plaintiff's argument in *Dumez France SA v Hessische Landesbank*, the Court of Justice could hardly have reached any other conclusion. Acceptance of the plaintiff's argument would have significantly undermined Article 2 in the context of claims relating to economic loss:

[A] plaintiff usually suffers financial loss where he ... is domiciled so that to allow him ... to sue there is tantamount to conferring jurisdiction on the courts of the plaintiff's domicile rather than those of the defendant's.[501]

---

[498] Case C–51/97 [1998] ECR I–6511, para 35.
[499] Case 220/88 [1990] ECR I–49. A Briggs, (1990) 10 *YBEL* 484; TC Hartley, (1991) 16 *EL Rev* 71.
[500] Case 220/88 [1990] ECR I–49, para 20.
[501] JG Collier, [1996] *CLJ* 216, 218.

So, where A (an Austrian domiciliary) enters an investment contract with B (a German domiciliary) and transfers funds into a German investment account, if A loses part of the sum invested and receives back only part of the capital invested, Germany is the place where the harmful event occurs; Article 5(3) does not confer jurisdiction on the place where A is domiciled or where A's assets are concentrated.[502]

5.6.68   The same basic analysis was adopted in *Marinari v Lloyds Bank plc*.[503] The plaintiff lodged with the defendant's Manchester branch promissory notes with an exchange value of more than $750 million. The defendant's staff refused to return the promissory notes and advised the police of the allegedly dubious origin of the notes. This led to the arrest of the plaintiff and the sequestration of the notes. After his release the plaintiff started proceedings in Italy against the defendant for compensation for the damage he claimed to have suffered as a result of the conduct of the defendant's employees. The defendant challenged the Italian court's jurisdiction on the basis that Italy was not the place where the harmful event occurred. The Court of Justice decided that Article 5(3) does not 'encompass any place where the adverse consequences of an event that has already caused actual damage elsewhere can be felt'.[504] The Court concluded that Article 5(3) 'cannot be construed as including the place where, as in the present case, the victim claims to have suffered financial damage consequential on initial damage arising and suffered by him in another … state'.[505] Accordingly, the Italian courts did not have jurisdiction.

5.6.69   Although both *Dumez France SA v Hessische Landesbank* and *Marinari v Lloyds Bank Plc* were, according to the Court of Justice's interpretation, single locality cases—that is to say, the place of the damage was also the place of the event giving rise to the damage—it is quite possible for a case involving pure economic loss to be a multiple locality case. As the decision in *Shevill v Presse Alliance SA*[506] shows, the approach adopted in *Handelskwekerij GJ Bier BV v Mines de Potasse d'Alsace SA*[507] is applicable to such cases. In a case where D, in France, gives negligent advice to C, in England, the place of the event giving rise to the damage is France, where the statement originates (not England where the statement is received); this is so whether the advice is given by post or by some instantaneous mode of communication.[508] In cases involving loss resulting from reliance on negligent advice, the place of the damage is quite likely to be the claimant's economic centre—where the advice is received and acted upon.[509] Similarly, where damages in tort are claimed for the breaking-off of contractual negotiations, the place where the harmful event occurs is where the claimant receives notification of the termination of negotiations.[510] However, the fact

---

[502]   Case C–168/02 *Kronhofer v Maier* [2004] ECR I–6009, para 21.
[503]   Case C–364/93 [1995] ECR I–2719. A Briggs, 'The uncertainty of special jurisdiction' [1996] *LMCLQ* 27; A Briggs, (1995) 15 *YBEL* 511; JG Collier, [1996] *CLJ* 216; TC Hartley, (1996) 21 *EL Rev* 164.
[504]   Case C–364/93 [1995] ECR I–2719, para 14.
[505]   Case C–364/93 [1995] ECR I–2719, para 15.
[506]   Case C–68/93 [1995] ECR I–415.
[507]   Case 21/76 [1976] ECR 284.
[508]   *Domicrest Ltd v Swiss Bank Corporation* [1999] QB 548; *Alfred Dunhill Ltd v Diffusion Internationale de Maroquinerie de Prestige SARL* [2001] CLC 949.
[509]   See, eg, *London Helicopters Ltd v Heliportugal LDA-INAC* [2006] ILPr 614.
[510]   *Bus Berzelius Umwelt-Service AG v Chemconserve BV* [2004] ILPr 183 (Supreme Court, Netherlands).

that the place of the damage cannot be equated with the claimant's home forum is illustrated by *Domicrest Ltd v Swiss Banking Corporation*.[511] The plaintiff, an English company, relied upon a negligent misstatement given by the defendant, a Swiss bank. The misstatement was made in the context of a telephone conversation between the parties in which the defendant guaranteed the creditworthiness of a third party to whom the plaintiff had supplied goods. The plaintiff's reliance took the form of releasing to the third party goods which were then stored in Switzerland and Italy. Rix J thought that, in these circumstances, the damage occurred in Switzerland and Italy, where the goods were released without prior payment.[512] *Domicrest Ltd v Swiss Banking Corporation* involved a situation where the claimant has lost his money or his goods.[513] This situation has been distinguished in *Dolphin Maritime and Aviation Services Ltd v Sveriges Angfartygs Assurans Forening*[514] from that where the claimant has not received money which he ought to have received. Christopher Clarke J held that the place where the harm occurs in this scenario is the place where the money ought to have been received,[515] which, on the facts of the case, pointed towards the claimant's domicile.

5.6.70 In *Kitechnology BV v Unicor GmbH Rahn Plastmaschinen*[516] the Court of Appeal decided that, in a case involving an allegation of breach of confidence, the English court cannot assume jurisdiction under Article 5(3) unless the alleged activities of the defendants occurred in England or those activities had direct repercussions in England. It was suggested, however, that a harmful event would have occurred in England if the plaintiff's commercial interests in England had suffered in England through the defendant's activities. In *Modus Vivendi Ltd v British Products Canmex Co Ltd*[517] the question was whether the English court had jurisdiction in relation to the tort of passing off. The plaintiff, an English company, alleged that the defendant, a Scottish company, had committed passing off by selling goods similar to the plaintiff's goods in China. The plaintiff sought to invoke the court's jurisdiction on the basis that the harmful event occurred in England. Applying the jurisprudence of the Court of Justice, Knox J concluded that the English court did not have jurisdiction. The place of the damage was where the goods in question were sold and where the alleged deception took place, namely China; the place of the event giving rise to the damage was Scotland, where the defendant's operations were centred. It was not sufficient that the plaintiff felt the loss in England and the fact that some subsidiary aspects of the production of the goods occurred in England was not sufficient to

---

[511] [1999] QB 548. A Read, 'Special Jurisdiction and the Convention: The Case of *Domicrest Ltd v Swiss Bank Corporation*' (1999) 18 *CJQ* 218. See also *Alfred Dunhill Ltd v Diffusion Internationale de Maroquinerie de Prestige SARL* [2001] CLC 949; *Newsat Holdings Ltd v Zani* [2006] 1 Lloyd's Rep 707.

[512] [1999] QB 548, 568. The approach taken by Rix J (who did not follow the decision of Steyn J in *Minister Investments Ltd v Hyundai Precision and Industry Co Ltd* [1988] 2 Lloyd's Rep 621) was approved by the Court of Appeal in *ABCI v Banque Franco-Tunisienne* [2003] 2 Lloyd's Rep 146.

[513] See also *The Seaward Quest* [2007] 2 Lloyd's Rep 308 (a case decided under the Civil Jurisdiction and Judgments Act 1982, sched 4).

[514] [2009] 2 Lloyd's Rep 123.

[515] See also Case C–51/97 *Réunion Européenne SA v Spliethoff's Bevrachtingskantoor BV* [1998] ECR I–6511; cf *Mazur Media Ltd v Mazur Media GmbH* [2004] 1 WLR 2966, 2978–9 (at [51]).

[516] [1994] ILPr 56.

[517] [1996] FSR 790.

justify the view that the event giving rise to the damage had occurred in England.[518] Where, however, it is alleged that, as a result of passing off, the claimant suffers loss of goodwill and damage to reputation in England—because England is where the alleged deception takes place—the English court may exercise jurisdiction under Article 5(3) on the basis that England is the place where the damage occurs (even if the event giving rise to the damage occurs abroad).[519] Of course, if infringement of a UK intellectual property right takes place in England, the English court has jurisdiction—as in these circumstances England is both the place of the event giving rise to the damage and the place where the damage occurred.[520] Even if a UK trade mark is infringed by an internet website, the trade mark owner can bring proceedings for infringement in England; the fact that the website can be accessed in England means that England is where the damage occurs.[521] Although there are potential problems with the identification of the place where the harmful event occurs in respect of tortious claims based on the defendant's anti-competitive behaviour,[522] the most obvious solution is to treat the place where the defendant's conduct produces a decline in the claimant's sales as the relevant place for the purposes of Article 5(3).[523]

Branch, Agency or Other Establishment[524]

5.6.71 Article 5(5) provides that 'as regards a dispute arising out of the operations of a branch, agency or other establishment' a person domiciled in a Member State may be sued in another Member State 'in the courts for the place in which the branch, agency or other establishment is situated'. So, where a French company sets up a branch in England, those who deal with the company through the branch can sue the French company in England in relation to any dispute which arises out of the operations of the branch. Where a claimant has been dealing with more than one branch, jurisdiction under Article 5(5) should be determined by the location of the branch with which the claimant had the most significant dealings, having regard to the

---

[518] See also *Waterford Wedgwood plc v David Nagli Ltd* [1999] ILPr 9.

[519] *Mecklermedia Corporation v DC Congress GmbH* [1998] Ch 40. See also *GEP Industries v HSM Schuhmarketing* [2008] ILPr 866 (Court of Cassation, France), a case involving the analogous tort of unfair competition; *Re Jurisdiction in Relation to Domain Name Grabbing* [2009] ILPr 16 (Supreme Court, Austria).

[520] *Fort Dodge Animal Health Ltd v Azko Nobel NV* [1998] FSR 222. See also *Aredal Foam Systems HB v Msr Dosiertechnik GmbH* [2008] ILPr 103 (Supreme Court, Sweden).

[521] See *Re the Maritim Trademark* [2003] ILPr 297 (District Court, Hamburg). See also *Saint-Tropez A/S v Reuven's II (Société)* [2009] ILPr 836 (Court of Cassation, France), a case concerning the alleged breach of copyright, an unregistered intellectual property right.

[522] See C Withers, 'Jurisdiction and Applicable Law in Antitrust Tort Claims' [2002] *JBL* 250. See also BJ Rodger, 'Competition Law in a Scottish Forum' [2003] *Jur Rev* 247. See *SanDisk Corp v Koninklijke Philips Electronics NV* [2007] ILPr 325.

[523] See *Soba Mølnlycke AS v Procter & Gamble Scandinavia Inc* [1997] ILPr 704 (Court of Appeal, Tønsberg); *Re Vitamin Cell Complex* [2006] ILPr 125 (Federal Supreme Court, Germany); *Re Jurisdiction in Claim for Damages Caused by Vitamin Cartel* [2007] ILPr 754 (Regional Court, Dortmund).

[524] JJ Fawcett, 'Methods of Carrying on Business and Article 5(5) of the Brussels Convention' (1984) 9 *EL Rev* 326; N March Hunnings, 'Agency and Jurisdiction in the EEC Conflict of Laws' [1982] *JBL* 244; M Bogdan, 'Web-Sites, Establishment and Private International Law' (2006) 17 *KCLJ* 97.

purpose of the contract (or other transaction) between the parties.[525] Not surprisingly the Court of Justice has held that the concepts 'operations' and 'a branch, agency or other establishment' must be given autonomous interpretations.[526] In many situations Article 5(5) overlaps with Article 5(1).

Branch, agency or other establishment

5.6.72   As regards the words 'other establishment', the Court of Justice has decided that 'the concept of "establishment" ... shall be based on the same essential characteristics as a branch or agency'.[527] A number of general criteria are relevant when considering the characteristics which a branch, agency or other establishment must display in order to fall within Article 5(5).

5.6.73   First, the Court of Justice has said that 'one of the essential characteristics of the concepts of branch or agency is the fact of being subject to the direction and control of the parent body'.[528] In *Blanckaert and Willems PVBA v Trost*[529] it was held that the requirement of 'direction and control' is not satisfied where the agent is an independent commercial agent who is free to arrange his own work, may represent several firms at the same time, and merely passes orders to the parent body, being involved neither in the terms of orders nor with their execution.

5.6.74   The subsequent case law of the Court of Justice establishes that the requirement of direction and control is not of universal application. In *SAR Schotte GmbH v Parfums Rothschild SARL*[530] C, a German company, sold goods to D, the French subsidiary of P, a German company. C had corresponded and negotiated with P, the German parent. When a dispute arose as to the quality of the products, C started proceedings in Germany. The question facing the court was whether P could be regarded as a 'branch, agency or other establishment' of D, the French subsidiary. The Court of Justice laid particular emphasis on the impression given by the arrangement between the parent and the subsidiary:

[T]hird parties doing business with the establishment which acts as an extension of another company must be able to rely on the appearance thus created and regard that establishment as an establishment of the other company even if, from the point of view of company law, the two companies are independent of each other.[531]

Although the test of direction and control is a useful one, it yields to 'the way in which these two undertakings behave in their business relations and present themselves vis-à-vis third parties in their commercial dealings'.[532] This decision has been criticised

---

[525]   *Société Comebo v Société Strafor Development* [1996] ILPr 552 (Court of Appeal, Paris).
[526]   Case 33/78 *Somafer SA v Saar-Ferngas AG* [1978] ECR 2183.
[527]   Case 14/76 *Ets A de Bloos SPRL v Société en commandite par actions Bouyer* [1976] ECR 1497, para 21.
[528]   Case 14/76 *Ets A de Bloos SPRL v Société en commandite par actions Bouyer* [1976] ECR 1497, para 20.
[529]   Case 139/80 [1981] ECR 819, para 13. TC Hartley, (1981) 6 *EL Rev* 481.
[530]   Case 218/86 [1987] ECR 4905. WA Allwood, (1988) 13 *EL Rev* 213.
[531]   Case 218/86 [1987] ECR 4905, para 15. See also *Zellner v Phillip Alexander Securities and Futures Ltd* [1997] ILPr 716 (District Court, Krefeld).
[532]   Case 218/86 [1987] ECR 4905, para 16.

on the ground that the doctrine of 'appearance' is inherently vague.[533] For example, is the simple fact that one company appears to be acting on behalf of another sufficient or is it important that the companies have the same name—as was the case in *SAR Schotte GmbH v Parfums Rothschild SARL* itself?

5.6.75 Secondly, a branch, agency or other establishment must have 'a place of business which has the appearance of permanency'.[534] Thirdly, a branch, agency or other establishment has 'a management and is materially equipped to negotiate business with third parties'; although third parties know that there may be a legal link with the parent which is located abroad, they do not have to deal directly with the parent but may transact business at the place of business of the branch or agency.[535]

Operations

5.6.76 In *Somafer SA v Saar-Ferngas AG*[536] the defendant, a French demolition company, was engaged to blow up a bunker in Germany. In Germany the defendant dealt with its customers through a representative. The plaintiff, a German enterprise, undertook safety measures to protect the gas supply in the vicinity of the demolition work and alleged that the defendant's German representative had agreed to reimburse the plaintiff for the cost of the safety precautions. The plaintiff brought proceedings against the defendant in Germany with a view to recovering its expenses. One of the questions was whether, for the purposes of Article 5(5), the dispute arose out of the 'operations' of the representative.

5.6.77 The Court of Justice decided that operations include three things: (i) actions relating to rights and obligations concerning the management of the agency, branch or establishment itself such as those concerning the building of the branch or the engagement of staff to work there; (ii) actions relating to obligations which have been undertaken at the place of business of the branch in the name of the parent and which must be performed in the state where the branch is established; and (iii) actions concerning non-contractual obligations arising from the activities which the branch has undertaken at the place in which it is established on behalf of the parent.[537]

5.6.78 It has been suggested that this narrow definition excludes from the scope of Article 5(5) the situation where a manufacturer, domiciled in one Member State, uses a branch office to sell in another Member State goods which are defective, if the branch does no more than enter into the contract of sale on behalf of the parent; if, however, the branch office gives undertakings as to delivery of the goods and the action concerns delivery, the dispute clearly arises out of the operations of the branch.[538]

---

[533] JC Schultz, 'Jurisdiction in Matters Relating to Tort and Delict' in HD Tebbens, T Kennedy and C Kohler (eds), *Civil Jurisdiction and Judgments in Europe* (London, Butterworths, 1992) 106–8.
[534] Case 33/78 *Somafer SA v Saar-Ferngas AG* [1978] ECR 2183, para 12.
[535] Case 33/78 *Somafer SA v Saar-Ferngas AG* [1978] ECR 2183, para 12.
[536] Case 33/78 [1978] ECR 2183. TC Hartley, (1979) 4 *EL Rev* 127.
[537] Case 33/78 [1978] ECR 2183, para 13.
[538] JJ Fawcett, 'Methods of Carrying on Business and Article 5(5) of the Brussels Convention' (1984) 9 *EL Rev* 326, 334.

5.6.79   Although the place where the operations are carried out will normally also be the place where the branch or agency is established, the application of Article 5(5) does not depend on this being so. In *Lloyd's Register of Shipping v Société Campenon Bernard*[539] the plaintiff, a French company, purchased a quantity of steel to fulfil a contract in Kuwait. The defendant, a United Kingdom corporation, contracted with the plaintiff to check that the steel complied with a particular standard. Although the contract was concluded in France through the defendant's French branch, the contract provided that the checks were to be carried out by the defendant's Spanish branch. Although the Spanish branch certified that the steel complied with the relevant standard, the contractor in Kuwait rejected the steel. When the plaintiff started proceedings against the defendant in France, the question was whether Article 5(5) confers jurisdiction in a case where, although the branch is located in one country (France), the operations out of which the dispute arises take place in another (Spain).

5.6.80   In contesting the French courts' jurisdiction the defendant sought to rely on a passage from the Court of Justice's judgment in *Somafer SA v Saar-Ferngas AG* in which it is stated that 'operations' include 'actions ... relating to undertakings which have been entered into at the place of business [of the branch] in the name of the parent body and *which must be performed ... where the place of business is established*'.[540] Advocate General Elmer took the view that the passage from *Somafer SA v Saar Ferngas AG* relied upon by the defendant was in the nature of an *obiter dictum*[541] and the Court of Justice ruled that Article 5(5) 'does not presuppose that the undertakings in question entered into by the branch in the name of the parent body are to be performed in the ... state in which the branch is established'.[542] If the defendant's argument had been accepted, Article 5(5) would have been rendered largely redundant, as the courts for the place of performance of the contractual obligation giving rise to the dispute normally have jurisdiction under Article 5(1).[543]

5.6.81   In *Anton Durbeck GmbH v Den Norske Bank ASA*[544] the English courts followed the approach adopted by the Court of Justice in *Lloyd's Register of Shipping v Société Campenon Bernard* in the context of a claim in tort. The Court of Appeal held that, where there is such a nexus between the activities of the branch and the claim in tort that it is natural to describe the dispute as one arising out of the operations of the branch, the claimant is entitled to rely upon Article 5(5), 'regardless of where those activities take effect'.[545] Since, in matters relating to tort, the court where the harmful event occurs already has jurisdiction by virtue of Article 5(3), if Article 5(5) were interpreted as requiring the activities of the branch to bring about the harmful event giving rise to the dispute within the jurisdiction of the court, this would effectively deprive Article 5(5) of an independent role with regard to claims in tort.[546]

---

[539] Case C–439/93 [1995] ECR I–961. TC Hartley, (1996) 21 *EL Rev* 162.
[540] Case 33/78 [1978] ECR 2183, para 13 (emphasis added).
[541] Case C–439/93 [1995] ECR I–961, para 12.
[542] Case C–439/93 [1995] ECR I–961, para 22.
[543] Advocate General Elmer in Case C–439/93 *Lloyd's Register of Shipping v Société Campenon Bernard* [1995] ECR I–961, para 16.
[544] [2003] QB 1160.
[545] Lord Phillips at [2003] QB 1160, 1173 (at [43]).
[546] See Lord Phillips at [2003] QB 1160, 1173 (at [44]).

5.6.82 In *Lloyd's Register of Shipping v Société Campenon Bernard* the Court of Justice repeated the view that the justification for Article 5 is the existence of 'a specially close connecting factor between the dispute and the court with jurisdiction to resolve it'.[547] There are two problems with this aspect of the judgment. First, it is far from obvious that the dispute in *Lloyd's Register of Shipping v Société Campenon Bernard* had a particularly close connection with France. It seems clear that Spain was the factual centre of gravity of the dispute and, unless the contract between the parties contained an express choice of French law (which seems very unlikely), French law would not have been the applicable law.[548] Secondly, it has been questioned whether Article 5(5) really is founded on the notion of closest connection: 'The rationale of Article 5(5) lies in the analogy with Article 2, not with Article 5(1) or 5(3).'[549] In *Anton Durbeck GmbH v Den Norske Bank ASA*[550] the Court of Appeal recognised that Article 5(5) 'provides a quasi defendant's domicile basis of jurisdiction'.[551]

Relations Between a Branch and the Parent Body

5.6.83 One of the issues surrounding Article 5(5) is whether, in a case where a dispute arises between an agent and the parent body, the agent may rely on Article 5(5) to bring proceedings against the parent body in the courts for the place where the agent is situated. Although this question has not been directly addressed by the Court of Justice, Advocate General Reischl expressed the view that:

Article 5(5) ... has the sole purpose of facilitating legal proceedings for *third parties* who are involved with a subsidiary establishment in that they are not obliged to lodge their application where the parent company is situate. Thus it was solely for their benefit that jurisdiction was established in a place nearer to that in which the cause of action arose.[552]

This analysis is clearly correct.[553] One of the fundamental objectives of the Brussels regime is to eliminate the categories of exorbitant jurisdiction based in particular on the claimant's domicile. Since there is no reason why there should be a general basis of jurisdiction which enables an agent to sue the parent body in the agent's home forum, the scope of Article 5(5) should be limited to disputes in which third parties are involved.[554]

Trusts

5.6.84 Article 5(6) provides that a person domiciled in a Member State may be sued in another Member State 'as settlor, trustee or beneficiary of a trust created by the

---

[547] Case C–439/93 [1995] ECR I–961, para 21.

[548] J Hill, 'Jurisdiction under Article 5(5) of the Brussels Convention' (1996) 15 *CJQ* 94, 95–6.

[549] A Briggs, (1995) 15 *YBEL* 496, 497. See also Advocate General Elmer in Case C–439/93 *Lloyd's Register of Shipping v Société Campenon Bernard* [1995] ECR I–961, para 18; compare Jenard, [1979] OJ C59/22.

[550] [2003] QB 1160.

[551] Lord Phillips at [2003] QB 1160, 1173 (at [43]).

[552] Case 14/76 *Ets A de Bloos SPRL v Société en commandite par actions Bouyer* [1976] ECR 1497, 1519 (emphasis in original). See also Case 139/80 *Blanckaert and Willems PVBA v Trost* [1981] ECR 819, 838.

[553] TC Hartley, (1977) 2 *EL Rev* 57, 61.

[554] A McClellan, 'The Convention of Brussels of September 27, 1968 on Jurisdiction and the Recognition and Enforcement of Judgments in Civil and Commercial Matters' (1978) 15 *CML Rev* 228, 237.

operation of a statute, or by a written instrument, or created orally and evidenced in writing, in the courts of the Member State in which the trust is domiciled'.

5.6.85 The rule in paragraph (6) is based on the argument that trusts, even though they have no legal personality, may be said to have a geographical centre of operation.[555] The domicile of a trust is determined by the forum's rules of private international law.[556] For the purposes of English law, a trust 'is domiciled in a part of the United Kingdom only if the system of law of that part is the system of law with which the trust has its closest and most real connection'.[557] Note must also be taken of the Recognition of Trusts Act 1987, which enacts the Hague Convention on the Law Applicable to Trusts and their Recognition into English law. The Convention provides that a trust shall be governed by the law chosen by the settlor[558]; in the absence of choice, the trust is governed by the law with which it is most closely connected.[559] In *Gomez v Gomez-Monche Vives*,[560] the Court of Appeal had to decide whether it had jurisdiction over a defendant domiciled in Spain who was alleged to be an overpaid beneficiary of a trust stipulated to be governed by English law. The claim had no other connections with England. The court held that the system of law with which the trust had its closest and most real connection was not to be determined by weighing up the connecting factors (which would arguably have pointed towards Liechtenstein, as most of the trustees were based there and the administration of the trust was carried out there). A choice of the law governing the trust was not conclusive, but, apart from a choice that is made to evade the imposition of mandatory rules, the court thought it was difficult to see what other circumstances would be sufficient to outweigh that choice as an indication of the system of law with which the trust had its real and closest connection. Lawrence Collins LJ observed that:

A trust is not like a commercial contract where it is only necessary to consider the content of the applicable law in exceptional circumstances. Trustees in particular have to be intimately aware of their responsibilities under the general law applicable to the trust. They may have to know whether they can lawfully accumulate income. Resort to the law governing the trust is central to their responsibilities.[561]

Consequently, the trust had its closest and most real connection with England and was domiciled in England. The Court of Appeal assumed jurisdiction under Article 5(6) although there was no connection between the trust and England apart from the governing law.[562]

5.6.86 It must be remembered that Article 5(6) provides an alternative forum to that directed by Article 2; a trustee of an English trust who has gone to Corsica can

---

[555] Schlosser Report, [1979] OJ C59/106–07, para 114(a).
[556] Art 60(3).
[557] Civil Jurisdiction and Judgments Order 2001, sched 1, para 12.
[558] Hague Trusts Convention, Art 6.
[559] Hague Trusts Convention, Art 7.
[560] [2009] Ch 245. A Briggs, (2008) 79 *BYIL* 533.
[561] [2009] Ch 245, 287 (at [64]).
[562] The second part of the claim involved an allegation that the defendant had abused her position as the donee of a fiduciary power by exercising it in favour of herself. The court held that it did not have jurisdiction over this part of the claim as, although the power exercised may be fiduciary, there was no basis to extend Art 5(6) to persons with fiduciary powers who do not come within the normal meaning of a 'trustee'.

also be sued in the courts there.[563] Furthermore, jurisdiction under Articles 2 and 5(6) can be ousted by the stipulation of an exclusive jurisdiction by the settlor.[564]

5.6.87   Unlike the other paragraphs of Article 5, paragraph (6) allocates jurisdiction to the courts of a state rather than the courts for a 'place'. Where the courts of the United Kingdom have jurisdiction by virtue of Article 5(6), schedule 4 to the 1982 Act allocates jurisdiction between the various parts of the United Kingdom.[565]

5.7 ALTERNATIVE FORA II: ARTICLE 6

Introduction

5.7.1   The primary objective of the Brussels regime is not the harmonisation of jurisdiction rules for its own sake, but the free movement of judgments between the various states involved. A simplified system for the recognition and enforcement of judgments depends, at least in part, on the avoidance of conflicting judgments. However, the direct jurisdiction rules contained in Chapter II often give the claimant a choice of fora in relation to a particular claim. Moreover, Article 5, as interpreted by the Court of Justice, creates situations in which courts of more than one state have jurisdiction over different claims arising out of one set of facts. Article 6 counteracts other jurisdiction rules which might generate a multiplicity of proceedings in different states by enabling related claims to be heard together.[566] Article 6 achieves this—rather paradoxically—by providing alternatives to the courts stipulated by Articles 2 and 5.[567]

5.7.2   Although in many respects Article 6 is similar in its purpose to CPR PD 6B para 3.1(3) and (4),[568] its operation is very different. Whereas the exercise of jurisdiction under CPR 6.36 depends on the court being satisfied that England is the most appropriate forum, there is no element of discretion under Article 6, which gives the claimant 'an unfettered right of choice'.[569]

Multiple Defendants

5.7.3   The effect of Article 6(1) is that a person domiciled in a Member State may be sued 'where he is one of a number of defendants in the courts for the place where any one of them is domiciled'.[570] For the purposes of this rule, whether a defendant is to be regarded as domiciled in a Member State is to be determined when the proceedings

---

[563] Schlosser Report, [1979] OJ C59/107, para 118.

[564] Brussels I Reg, Art 23(4).

[565] See para 6.2.9.

[566] See JJ Fawcett, 'Multi-Party Litigation in Private International Law' (1995) 44 *ICLQ* 744, 749–54; ZS Tang, 'Multiple Defendants in the European Jurisdiction Regulation' (2009) 34 *EL Rev* 80.

[567] Brussels I Reg, Art 7 is considered at para 8.2.16.

[568] See paras 7.3.13–7.3.16.

[569] Hirst J in *Aiglon Ltd v Gau Shan Co Ltd* [1993] 1 Lloyd's Rep 164, 174.

[570] Art 6(1) cannot be invoked against a defendant who is not domiciled in a Member State: *Société Kenya Airways v Airbus SAS* [2009] ILPr 26 (Court of Appeal, Orleans).

are issued.[571] It is important to emphasise the limits of this provision. First, Article 6(1) applies only if the proceedings are brought in the Member State in which one of the defendants is domiciled.[572] So, if C sues D1 (domiciled in France) in England on the basis of Article 5(1), C cannot rely on Article 6(1) to sue D2 (domiciled in Germany) in England. Similarly, where C brings proceedings against D1, who is domiciled in a non-Member State, Article 6(1) does not provide for D2, who is domiciled in a Member State, to be joined to those proceedings.[573] Secondly, for Article 6(1) to apply, there must be an appropriate connection between the claims against the various defendants. Article 6(1) of the Brussels I Regulation applies only if the claims between the defendants 'are so closely connected that it is expedient to hear and determine them together to avoid the risk of irreconcilable judgments resulting from separate proceedings'.[574] It is unclear, though, whether 'irreconcilable' should be given a broad interpretation (meaning 'contradictory') as has been adopted for the purposes of the rules on *lis pendens*.[575] The Court of Justice in *Roche Nederland BV v Primus*[576] refused to be drawn into this question, but indicated that if the broader interpretation is to be preferred, it agreed with Advocate General Léger[577] that the divergence must arise in the context of the same situation of law and fact.[578]

5.7.4   Article 6(1) may lead to litigation being conducted in a relatively inappropriate forum—for example, where the domicile of one of the defendants is completely irrelevant to the substance of the dispute. Where a Spanish claimant is injured in England as a result of the negligence of the first defendant, a Spanish driver, and/or the second defendant, an English driver, the claimant may sue both defendants in Spain, even though—in terms of the factual centre of gravity of the dispute—England obviously provides a more appropriate forum.[579]

5.7.5   On the one hand, it does not follow from the fact that claims against two defendants arise out of the same set of facts that the claims should necessarily be heard together; on the other, although there has to be a close relationship between the claims, the operation of Article 6(1) does not depend on there being a single claim brought against several defendants on the basis of a single legal relationship.[580]

---

[571] *Petrotrade Inc v Smith* [1999] 1 WLR 457; *Canada Trust Co v Stolzenberg (No 2)* [2002] 1 AC 1.

[572] Case C–51/97 *Réunion Européenne SA v Spliethoff's Bevrachtingskantoor BV* [1998] ECR I–6511, para 44.

[573] Case C–51/97 *Réunion Européenne SA v Spliethoff's Bevrachtingskantoor BV* [1998] ECR I–6511, para 46.

[574] Although this proviso is not part of the text of Art 6(1) of the Brussels Convention, there is no substantive difference between the different versions of Art 6(1) as the proviso in Art 6(1) of the Regulation is derived from the Court of Justice's interpretation of Art 6(1) of the Brussels Convention in Case 189/87 *Kalfelis v Bankhaus Schröder, Münchmeyer, Hengst & Co* [1988] ECR 5565, para 13 (A Briggs, (1988) 8 *YBEL* 272; TC Hartley, (1989) 14 *EL Rev* 172). The inspiration for the Court of Justice's ruling was Art 22(3) of the Brussels Convention (the equivalent of Art 28(3) of the Brussels I Regulation), which defines what is meant by 'related actions'. See para 9.1.47 *ff*.

[575] See section 9.1.

[576] Case C–539/03 [2006] ECR I–6535.

[577] See the lengthy analysis in Advocate General Léger's opinion in Case C–539/03 [2006] ECR I–6535, paras 58–105.

[578] Case C–539/03 [2006] ECR I–6535, paras 25–6.

[579] See *Garcia v England* [1995] ILPr 433 (Court of Appeal, Vittoria).

[580] *Ruffini v Fornato* [1981] ECC 541 (Court of Appeal, Milan). See also *Hodder-Dargaud Ltd v Egmont International Holdings A/S* [2003] ILPr 665 (Court of Cassation, France).

The crucial question is whether there is a danger of irreconcilable judgments: 'It is for the national court to verify in each individual case whether that condition is satisfied.'[581] So, a claimant who sues D1 in England for infringement of a UK patent is not able to rely on Article 6(1) to join D2 to the proceedings where the claim against D2 relates to infringement of the equivalent Dutch patent; because the claims against D1 and D2 relate to different national rights, there is no risk of irreconcilable judgments—even though the issues raised by the two claims will be very similar.[582] The position is the same in relation to a European patent falling under the European Patent Convention. In *Roche Nederland BV v Primus*,[583] a number of companies established in various contracting states to the Convention, but belonging to the same group of companies, allegedly infringed a European patent. The Court of Justice held that: 'in order that decisions may be regarded as contradictory it is not sufficient that there be a divergence in the outcome of the dispute, but that divergence must also arise in the context of the same situation of law and fact.'[584] Although the companies may have acted in an identical or similar manner in accordance with a common policy, the Convention provides for the patent to be governed by the national law of each of the contracting states for which it has been granted. This means that, although the factual situation may be the same with respect to each infringement, the legal situation is not. Therefore, there would be no risk of contradictory decisions if a composite claim is not allowed. The connection required for Article 6(1) was not established. However, in a case where disputes arise out of identical contracts concluded between the claimant and more than one defendant (such as where an insurer reinsures the risk with several reinsurers), there is a sufficient connection between the claims against the defendants to justify the application of Article 6(1).[585] Similarly, Article 6(1) is applicable where a claimant pursues two actions for damages for breach of contract against different defendants where the only difference between the claims is the identity of the parties to the contract.[586]

5.7.6 The concern to prevent irreconcilable judgments, however, took a back seat to a literal interpretation of the Regulation in *Glaxosmithkline and Laboratoires Glaxosmithkline v Rouard*.[587] In this case, the Court of Justice rather surprisingly held that Article 6(1) could not be used by an employee in the context of proceedings brought against joint employers who were domiciled in different Member States. The Court observed that Section 5 of Chapter II of the Regulation, which covers jurisdiction in relation to individual contracts of employment, expressly preserves the application of other provisions of Chapter II to employment contracts but does not refer to Article 6(1) at all. A literal interpretation of the Regulation led to the conclusion that Section 5 precludes any recourse to Article 6(1). However, as Advocate General

---

[581] Case 189/87 *Kalfelis v Bankhaus Schröder, Münchmeyer, Hengst & Co* [1988] ECR 5565, para 13.
[582] *Fort Dodge Animal Health Ltd v Azko Nobel NV* [1998] FSR 222.
[583] Case C–539/03 [2006] ECR I–6535. A Briggs, [2006] *LMCLQ* 447.
[584] Case C–539/03 [2006] ECR I–6535, para 26.
[585] See, however, *International Credit Insurance Corporation v Pohjola Insurance Company Ltd* [2003] ILPr 50 (Supreme Court, Sweden) in which a majority of 3:2 decided that the condition was not satisfied in this type of case.
[586] *Masri v Consolidated Contractors Group SAL* [2006] 1 WLR 830. See also *FKI Engineering Ltd v De Wind Holdings Ltd* [2009] 1 All ER (Comm) 118; *Et Plus SA v Welter* [2006] 1 Lloyd's Rep 251, 265–6.
[587] Case C–462/06 [2008] ECR I–3965.

Poiares Maduro pointed out in his opinion, this literal interpretation disregards the contextual scope of the Regulation. Under the Brussels Convention, Article 6(1) was applicable to contracts of employment and there was no reason to believe that the authors of the Regulation intended to amend this principle: 'It would be surprising if, in adopting [the Brussels I Regulation], the legislature had intended to deprive employees of the benefit of the more favourable rules which applied under the Brussels Convention prior to the entry into force of that regulation.'[588] Furthermore, the Court of Justice's literal interpretation fails to protect the employee, the weaker contracting party, as he would be required to sue each defendant individually in the courts having jurisdiction in each Member State.[589] The result of the Court of Justice's judgment is that a claimant who is not an employee would be able to invoke Article 6(1) whereas a claimant who is an employee and in need of more favourable rules of jurisdiction would not be able to.[590] It is suggested that the Advocate General's opinion makes more sense than the Court's ruling, not least because there is a risk that the courts hearing the claims, based on the same factual and legal context, against the different employers, could come to divergent decisions.

5.7.7   A literal interpretation of Article 6(1) was also favoured by the Court of Justice in *Reisch Montage AG v Kiesel Baumaschinen Handels GmbH*,[591] this time with the effect of widening the scope of Article 6(1). The claimant, a company established in Liechtenstein, brought an action for payment in Austria against a debtor, who was domiciled in Austria, and the guarantor, who was based in Germany. However, the action against the debtor was barred by Austrian procedural rules because of ongoing bankruptcy proceedings. The issue was whether Article 6(1) could still be relied upon to sue the German guarantor in Austria when the action was inadmissible against the Austrian debtor. The Court of Justice held that Article 6(1) was not one of the provisions which provide expressly for the application of domestic rules and hence it cannot be interpreted in such a way as to make its application dependent on the effects of domestic rules.[592] Thus, it was held that, apart from the situation where Article 6(1) is abused by a claimant for the sole purpose of removing a defendant from the jurisdiction of the courts of the Member State in which that defendant is domiciled,[593] it could be relied upon in the context of an action brought in a Member State against a defendant domiciled in that state and a co-defendant domiciled in another Member State even where, by the time it is brought, the action is inadmissible in relation to the first defendant.[594]

---

[588] Advocate General Poiares Maduro at Case C–462/06 [2008] ECR I–3965, para 21.

[589] Advocate General Poiares Maduro at Case C–462/06 [2008] ECR I–3965, para 21.

[590] J Harris, (2008) 124 *LQR* 523. See also Recital 13. The Court of Justice took a different view on this point: it held that allowing an employee to rely on Art 6(1) to sue his employers would mean that an employer would likewise be permitted to rely on Art 6(1) to sue its employees. The latter result would be contrary to the objective of protecting the position of employees in contracts of employment: Case C–462/06 [2008] ECR I–3965, paras 29–30.

[591] Case C–103/05 [2006] ECR I–6827. A Briggs, [2006] *LMCLQ* 447.

[592] Case C–103/05 [2006] ECR I–6827, para 30.

[593] See para 5.7.10.

[594] Case C–103/05 [2006] ECR I–6827, paras 32–3. Cf the contrary view of Advocate General Ruiz-Jarabo Colomer in his opinion.

5.7.8   In *Gascoine v Pyrah*[595] the Court of Appeal permitted the plaintiff to join the second defendant, who was domiciled in Germany, to proceedings commenced in England against the first defendant, who was domiciled in England, even though the claims against the two defendants were, in legal terms, entirely separate. Whereas the claim against the first defendant was for breach of contract, the claim against the second defendant was based on negligence, there being no contractual relationship between the plaintiff and the second defendant. Nevertheless, in factual terms, the plaintiff's claims against the two defendants were closely interwoven. The Court of Appeal decided that Article 6(1) applies to a case involving a risk of inconsistent findings of fact if separate proceedings were brought in different states, just as it applies to a case which involves a risk of conflicting findings of law.

5.7.9   However, in *Réunion Européenne SA v Spliethoff's Bevrachtingskantoor BV*[596] the Court of Justice appeared to adopt a much more restrictive approach than that taken by the Court of Appeal. In the course of its ruling, the Court of Justice indicated that:

Two claims in one action for compensation against different defendants and based in one instance on contractual liability and in the other on liability in tort … cannot be regarded as connected.[597]

At first, the exact scope of this ruling was unclear,[598] with some commentators arguing (with good reason) that, if the Court of Justice in the *Réunion Européenne* case had intended to lay down a general rule that the conditions of Article 6(1) can never be satisfied in a case where C has a claim against A in contract and a claim against B in tort, the Court was wrong.[599] In *Freeport plc v Arnoldsson*,[600] the Court of Justice took the opportunity to clarify what it had appeared to say in *Réunion Européenne*. Arnoldsson had entered into an agreement with Freeport plc (a company incorporated under English law) under which the claimant would receive £500,000 as a success fee when a factory shop was opened in Sweden. Under the terms of the agreement, Arnoldsson was to be paid by the company which was to become the owner of the factory site. When the factory was opened, a company incorporated under Swedish law, Freeport AB, became its owner. Neither Freeport plc nor Freeport AB paid the fee. Arnoldsson then brought an action before the Swedish courts against both companies, basing his action in relation to Freeport plc on Article 6(1). Freeport plc argued that Article 6(1) was inapplicable because the action against it was based in contract whereas the action against Freeport AB, with whom Arnoldsson did not have a contractual relationship, was based in tort, delict or quasi-delict. In its judgment, the Court of Justice pointed out that *Réunion Européenne* had concerned an action brought before the court of a Member State in which none of the defendants had been domiciled and that, consequently, there was no question of Article 6(1)

---

[595] [1994] ILPr 82.
[596] Case C–51/97 [1998] ECR I–6511.
[597] Case C–51/97 [1998] ECR I–6511, para 50.
[598] See *Watson v First Choice Holidays and Flights Ltd* [2001] 2 Lloyd's Rep 339 and *Daly v Irish Travel Group Ltd, t/a 'Crystal Holidays'* [2003] ILPr 623 (High Court, Ireland).
[599] A Briggs and P Rees, *Civil Jurisdiction and Judgments* (London, LLP, 5th edn, 2009) para 2.203. See also Cooke J in *Andrew Weir Shipping Ltd v Wartsila UK Ltd* [2004] 2 Lloyd's Rep 377, 393.
[600] Case C–98/06 [2007] ECR I–8319. A Scott, [2008] *LMCLQ* 113.

being applicable in that case. So, in terms of the issue which arose in the *Freeport* case, the judgment in *Réunion Européenne* (whatever it may or may not have said) was largely irrelevant. As for the question raised in the *Freeport* case, the Court of Justice's interpretation of Article 6(1) was clear: where an action is brought before the court for the place where one of the defendants has its head office, Article 6(1) applies notwithstanding the fact that the claims brought against different defendants have different legal bases. Because, on the facts of the case, the claims against the two defendants were related, Arnoldsson was entitled to bring proceedings in Sweden against Freeport AB on the basis of Article 2 (in tort) and Freeport plc on the basis of Article 6(1) (for breach of contract).

5.7.10   The courts should be vigilant in ensuring that a claimant is not permitted to abuse Article 6(1). It would be wrong if a claimant could invoke Article 6(1) against D2, who is domiciled in another Member State, simply by bringing a speculative claim against D1 in England under Article 2. However, there have been mixed messages from the Court of Justice on this point.[601] In *Freeport plc v Arnoldsson*,[602] the Court of Justice replied in the affirmative when asked whether Article 6(1) remained available where claims are brought with the sole object of ousting the jurisdiction of the courts of the Member State where one of the defendants is domiciled.[603] A literal approach to the text of the Regulation was (again) adopted to justify this ruling; the Court noted that Article 6(1), unlike Article 6(2), does not expressly make provision prohibiting such a course of action.[604] This part of the judgment is hard to reconcile with *Reisch Montage AG v Kiesel Baumaschinen Handels GmbH*,[605] in which the Court was careful to exclude from the scope of its judgment the situation where claims are brought under Article 6(1) for the sole purpose of removing a defendant from the jurisdiction of the courts of the Member State in which that defendant is domiciled.[606]

5.7.11   In cases concerning multiple defendants, some of whom are domiciled in Member States and some of whom are not, the combined effect of Article 6(1) and the Civil Procedure Rules[607] will often be to allow the claimant to proceed against all the defendants in England. Where, for example, D1 is domiciled in England, D2 is domiciled in New York and D3 is domiciled in Germany the claimant may obtain permission to serve D2 out of the jurisdiction under CPR 6.36 on the basis of the rule in CPR PD 6B para 3.1(3) and D3 can be joined as a party to English proceedings

---

[601] For English and Irish cases on this point, see *The Rewia* [1991] 2 Lloyd's Rep 325; *Zair v Eastern Health and Social Services Board* [1999] ILPr 823; *Andrew Weir Shipping Ltd v Wartsila UK Ltd* [2004] 2 Lloyd's Rep 377; *Kelly v McCarthy* [1994] ILPr 29 (High Court, Ireland); *Gannon v B & I Steam Packet Co Ltd* [1994] ILPr 405 (Supreme Court, Ireland); *The Xing Su Hai* [1995] 2 Lloyd's Rep 15; *Chiron Corporation v Evans Medical Ltd* [1996] FSR 863.

[602] Case C–98/06 [2007] ECR I–8319.

[603] Case C–98/06 [2007] ECR I–8319, para 54. Freeport plc had argued that the action brought against Freeport AB was devoid of legal merit and was brought solely for the purpose of suing Freeport plc in Sweden.

[604] Case C–98/06 [2007] ECR I–8319, para 51. Cf the opinion of Advocate General Mengozzi, paras 47–68.

[605] Case C–103/05 [2006] ECR I–6827.

[606] Case C–103/05 [2006] ECR I–6827, para 32. See also Case 189/87 *Kalfelis v Bankhaus Schröder Munchmeyer Hengst & Co* [1988] ECR 5565, paras 8–9.

[607] CPR 6.36, PD 6B para 3.1(3).

under Article 6(1). However, in a situation where D1 is domiciled in New York and D2 is domiciled in Germany, in order to proceed in England the claimant must have an independent basis of jurisdiction against D2. The fact that the English court is prepared to give permission to serve out as against D1 does not mean that D2 can be sued in England under Article 6(1).[608]

Third Party Proceedings

5.7.12   Whereas Article 6(1) concerns the situation where the claimant wishes to proceed against two or more defendants, Article 6(2) deals with the situation where a defendant wishes, in the event of being found liable, to pass liability on to a third party. Third party proceedings (now known as Part 20 claims) provide an important procedural device for related proceedings to be resolved together, thereby preventing separate proceedings being conducted in different countries. Article 6(2) provides that a person domiciled in a Member State may be sued:

as a third party in an action on a warranty or guarantee or in any other third party proceedings, in the court seised of the original proceedings, unless these were instituted solely with the object of removing him from the jurisdiction of the court which would be competent in his case.

The Jenard Report provides an example of the importance of this provision:

A German exporter delivers goods to Belgium and the Belgian importer resells them. The purchaser sues the importer for damages in the court for the place of his domicile, for example in Brussels. The Belgian importer has a right of recourse against the German exporter and consequently brings an action for breach of warranty against that exporter in the court in Brussels, since it has jurisdiction over the original action.[609]

5.7.13   As Article 6(2) does not define what is meant by 'other third party proceedings', whether proceedings are to be regarded as third party proceedings for the purposes of Article 6(2) is, as a general rule, a question to be answered by reference to the procedural rules of the law of the forum.[610] Where, for the purposes of Part 20 of the Civil Procedure Rules, there is a connection between C's claim against D1 and D1's claim against D2, the court is entitled to exercise jurisdiction over D2 on the basis of Article 6(2).[611] However, if the court would, in the circumstances, refuse to allow the bringing of a Part 20 claim were the case a domestic one, it may normally exercise discretion against allowing D1 to rely upon Article 6(2).[612] According to the terms of Article 6(2), reliance upon Article 6(2) is not allowed where the proceedings are instituted solely with the object of removing D2 from the jurisdiction of the court

---

[608] Case C–51/97 *Réunion Européenne SA v Spliethoff's Bevrachtingskantoor BV* [1998] ECR I–6511, para 46.

[609] [1979] OJ C59/27.

[610] See Schlosser Report, [1979] OJ C59/111, para 135; *National Justice Compania Naviera SA v Prudential Assurance Co Ltd (No 2)* [2000] 1 WLR 603.

[611] *Kinnear v Falconfilms NV* [1996] 1 WLR 920; cf *Barton v Golden Sun Holidays Ltd (In Liquidation)* [2007] ILPr 804.

[612] *Waterford Wedgwood plc v David Naldi Ltd* [1999] ILPr 9.

which would be competent otherwise; it is for the national court to determine whether an abuse of process has occurred.[613]

5.7.14   There is an important qualification to the general principle that what constitutes third party proceedings for the purposes of Article 6(2) is to be determined by the procedural law of the forum. In *Kongress Agentur Hagen GmbH v Zeehaghe BV*[614] the plaintiff, relying on Article 5(1), started proceedings in the Netherlands against the first defendant, a German company, claiming damages for breach of contract. The first defendant applied for permission to join the second defendant, another German company, under Article 6(2). One of the questions which arose was whether the Dutch court was entitled to assess the admissibility of the application for permission in the light of the procedural rules of its national law (and to refuse to allow the second defendant to be joined, for example, on the ground that this would delay and complicate the proceedings). The Court of Justice drew a distinction between jurisdiction and procedure:

With regard to an action on a warranty or guarantee, Article 6(2) ... merely determines which court has jurisdiction and is not concerned with conditions for admissibility properly so called.[615]

Although national courts will apply national procedural rules to the question of admissibility:

an application for leave to bring an action on a warranty or guarantee may not be refused expressly or by implication on the ground that the third parties sought to be joined reside or are domiciled in a ... state other than that of the court seised of the original proceedings.[616]

Accordingly, Article 6(2) does not require the national court to accede to the request for permission to bring third party proceedings; the court may apply the procedural rules of its national law in order to determine whether that action is admissible, provided that the effectiveness of the Brussels regime is not impaired.

5.7.15   Whereas Article 6(1) applies only if one of the defendants is sued in the courts of his domicile there is no such limitation in Article 6(2). The purpose of Article 6(2) is to enable the entire dispute to be heard by a single court; it is not important, for example, whether jurisdiction over the first defendant is based on Article 2 or Article 5.[617] The wording of Article 6(2) does not appear to rule out the possibility of a third party who is domiciled in a Member State being joined to proceedings even where the first defendant is not domiciled in a Member State and the basis of jurisdiction in the original proceedings is an exorbitant one. However, this interpretation of Article 6(2) conflicts with the general framework of Chapter II; a more plausible

---

[613] Case C–77/04 *Groupement d'Intérêt Économique (GIE) Réunion Européenne v Zurich España* [2005] ECR I–4509. For further proceedings, see *GIE Réunion Européenne v Zurich Seguros* [2007] ILPr 301 (Court of Cassation, France). See also *Siplast SA v Delbouw Roermond BV* [2005] ILPr 66 (Supreme Court, Netherlands).

[614] Case C–365/88 [1990] ECR I–1845. A Briggs, (1990) 10 *YBEL* 487; TC Hartley, (1991) 16 *EL Rev* 73.

[615] Case C–365/88 [1990] ECR I–1845, para 18.

[616] Case C–365/88 [1990] ECR I–1845, para 21.

[617] Case C–365/88 *Kongress Agentur Hagen GmbH v Zeehaghe BV* [1990] ECR I–1845. See also *Rutschi Pumpen AG v SA Pompes Rutschi Mulhouse* [2002] ILPr 59 (Court of Appeal, Grenoble).

interpretation is that Article 6(2) is limited to cases where jurisdiction in the original proceedings is derived from the direct jurisdiction rules set out in Chapter II.

Counterclaims

5.7.16   As a general principle, a claimant who invokes the jurisdiction of a court cannot legitimately complain if the same court exercises jurisdiction over a counterclaim which arises out of the same facts. Article 6(3) provides that a person domiciled in a Member State may be sued 'on a counterclaim arising from the same contract or facts on which the original claim was based, in the court in which the original claim is pending'.

5.7.17   The scope of Article 6(3) was considered by the Court of Justice in *Danvaern Production A/S v Schuhfabriken Otterbeck GmbH & Co.*[618] The plaintiff, a German company, and the defendant, a Danish company, concluded an agreement under the terms of which the defendant was given the exclusive right to sell certain of the plaintiff's products in Denmark. Having purported to terminate the agreement, the plaintiff started proceedings in Denmark for outstanding payments. The defendant argued that the plaintiff's claim should be dismissed and counterclaimed for damages for wrongful termination of the agreement. In the Danish proceedings the question arose whether Article 6(3) applies to counterclaims and/or to set-offs. (In Danish the same word is used to cover both concepts.) The Court of Justice analysed the essential differences between these concepts: a case involves set-off 'where the defendant pleads, as a defence, the existence of a claim which he allegedly has against the plaintiff, which would have the effect of wholly or partially extinguishing the plaintiff's claim'; by contrast, a counterclaim, which arises 'where the defendant, by a separate claim made in the context of the same proceedings, seeks a judgment or decree ordering the plaintiff to pay him a debt, ... can be made for an amount exceeding that claimed by the plaintiff and ... can be proceeded with even if the plaintiff's claim is dismissed'.[619]

5.7.18   Within this analytical framework, Article 6(3) is concerned only with counterclaims—that is, claims by a defendant for a separate judgment against the claimant. Article 6(3) establishes that the court which has jurisdiction over the claimant's claim also has jurisdiction over the defendant's counterclaim; the only condition being that the counterclaim should arise from the contract or from the facts on which the claim was based.[620] It is not enough, however, that D's counterclaim is in some sense related to C's claim.[621] Furthermore, it has been held that Article 6(3) can be relied upon only by the original defendant. Where, for example, C sues D1 in England (on the basis of Article 2) and D1 joins D2 to those proceedings (under Article 6(2)),

---

[618]   Case C–341/93 [1995] ECR I–2053. A Briggs, (1995) 15 *YBEL* 498; TC Hartley, (1996) 21 *EL Rev* 166.
[619]   Case C–341/93 [1995] ECR I–2053, para 12.
[620]   See *Re a Counterclaim under Italian Law* [1995] ILPr 133 (Federal Supreme Court, Germany); *Cha Cha Denmark A/S v Commercial Textiles Lda* [2002] ILPr 53 (Supreme Court, Denmark); *Re the Assertion of a Set-Off and Counterclaim* [2003] ILPr 543 (Federal Supreme Court, Germany).
[621]   *Dollfus Mieg & Cie v CDW International Ltd* [2004] ILPr 232.

D2 cannot rely on Article 6(3) to bring a counterclaim against C in the context of the proceedings under Article 6(2).[622]

5.7.19   Article 6(3) does not apply to set-off as a defence. Whether the defendant may raise set-off as a defence is a procedural question to be determined by the national court according to the procedural law of the forum: 'The defences which may be raised and the conditions under which they may be raised are determined by national law'.[623]

Contractual Claims Involving Matters Relating to Rights *in Rem* in Immovable Property

5.7.20   As regards proceedings which have as their object rights *in rem* in immovable property, exclusive jurisdiction is allocated to the courts of the Member State in which the property is situated.[624] Jurisdiction in matters relating to a contract is normally governed by Articles 2 and 5(1). In the absence of Article 6(4), this division of jurisdiction could lead to proceedings arising out of the same set of facts being heard in different courts:

When a person has a mortgage on immovable property the owner of that property is quite often also personally liable for the secured debt. Therefore it has been made possible in some States to combine an action concerning the personal liability of the owner with an action for the enforced sale of the immovable property. This presupposes of course that the court for the place where the immovable property is situated also has jurisdiction as to actions concerning the personal liability of the owner.[625]

5.7.21   Article 6(4) provides that a person domiciled in a Member State may be sued:

in matters relating to a contract, if the action may be combined with an action against the same defendant in matters relating to rights *in rem* in immovable property, in the court of the Member State in which the property is situated.

The effect of this provision is that an action concerning the personal liability of the owner of immovable property can be combined with an action for the enforced sale of the property in those states where such a combination of actions is possible.[626]

Article 6 and Jurisdiction Agreements

5.7.22   Although there are good practical arguments for allowing a court to assume jurisdiction over related claims brought against different defendants, the extended jurisdiction provided for by Article 6 is, nevertheless, subordinate to the jurisdiction which is conferred by an exclusive jurisdiction agreement. Consider the following

---

[622] *Dollfus Mieg & Cie v CDW International Ltd* [2004] ILPr 232.
[623] Case C–341/93 *Danvaern Production A/S v Schuhfabriken Otterbeck GmbH & Co* [1995] ECR I–2053, para 13.
[624] Brussels I Reg, Art 22(1). See section 5.1.
[625] Jenard-Möller Report, [1990] OJ C189/74, para 46.
[626] Jenard-Möller Report, [1990] OJ C189/74, para 46.

situation: A (an Italian manufacturer) sells goods to B (an English wholesaler); this contract contains an agreement referring disputes to the exclusive jurisdiction of the Italian courts; B sells the goods to C (a French retailer), who claims that the goods are defective and starts proceedings in England against B. Of course, it would be in B's interests to join A to these proceedings under Article 6(2) of the Brussels I Regulation; if the English court finds that the goods are defective and orders B to pay damages, B will want to recover its loss from A. Furthermore, in terms of the efficient administration of justice, there is an argument for the consolidation of C's claim against B and B's claim against A as the same issues will arise in the context of both claims. From A's perspective, however, there is no obvious reason why the exclusive jurisdiction clause in its contract with B should not be enforced under Article 23(1) of the Brussels I Regulation. So, which rule takes priority: Article 6(2) or Article 23(1)? Although the matter is not explicitly addressed either by Article 23 or by Article 6, the whole structure of the Brussels I Regulation accords priority to the enforcement of jurisdiction agreements in these circumstances.[627] The analysis is the same in cases where there is a conflict between Article 6(1) and Article 23; the latter takes priority.[628]

5.8 INSURANCE, CONSUMER CONTRACTS AND EMPLOYMENT CONTRACTS

5.8.1   Chapter II contains provisions dealing with jurisdiction in matters relating to insurance,[629] consumer contracts[630] and employment contracts.[631] Two general points should be made by way of introduction. First, the basic aim of these provisions is to protect the party who from the socio-economic point of view is weaker. In the context of insurance the weaker party may be the policy-holder, the insured or the beneficiary; in a consumer contract, the consumer is in a weaker position than the supplier; in an employment contract, the employee is the weaker party. The effect of the relevant provisions is that, regardless of whether he is the defendant or the claimant, the weaker party generally has the option of requiring the litigation to take place in his home forum. Secondly, the requirements for jurisdiction agreements in such contracts are stricter than in the context of other contracts with the consequence that only in limited circumstances may such agreements be enforced against the weaker party.

Insurance

5.8.2   In matters relating to insurance, jurisdiction is determined by Section 3 of Chapter II;[632] there is no attempt to define what is meant by 'insurance' for these

---

[627] See *Hough v P&O Containers Ltd* [1999] QB 834. A Briggs, (1998) 69 *BYIL* 342. Compare *Ammerlaan Agro Projecten BV v Les Serres de Cosquerou* [1999] ILPr 627 (Court of Cassation, France).
[628] *Deforche (Société) v Tomacrau (Société)* [2007] ILPr 367 (Court of Cassation, France).
[629] Arts 8–14.
[630] Arts 15–17.
[631] Arts 18–21.
[632] Art 8.

purposes. The Schlosser Report takes the view that, since reinsurance contracts cannot be equated with insurance contracts, the provisions concerning matters relating to insurance do not apply to reinsurance contracts.[633] Although the Court of Justice left the question open in *Overseas Union Insurance Ltd v New Hampshire Insurance Co*,[634] in *Agnew v Länsförsäkringsbolagens AB*[635] the House of Lords held that Section 3 does not apply to reinsurance and, in *Group Josi Reinsurance Company SA v Universal General Insurance Company*,[636] the Court of Justice confirmed that the insurance provisions do not cover disputes between a reinsurer and a reinsured in connection with a reinsurance contract. It also does not cover third party proceedings between insurers based on alleged multiple insurance or co-insurance as none of the parties come under the underlying aim of Section 3 to protect the weaker party.[637]

5.8.3   Generally speaking, Section 3 applies independently of the rest of Chapter II. However, it is provided that the operation of Section 3 shall not prejudice Article 4 or Article 5(5)[638] and the jurisdiction rules contained in Section 3 are superseded if the defendant voluntarily puts in an appearance to contest the claim on the merits.[639] Although Section 3 was intended to protect the small policy-holder against the more powerful insurer, the scope of Section 3 is not limited to cases in which it can be shown that the policy-holder is weak and in need of protection.[640]

Proceedings Brought against Insurers

5.8.4   Section 3 contains detailed rules for determining jurisdiction over insurers who are domiciled in a Member State.[641] For the purposes of these rules an insurer who is not domiciled in a Member State but has a branch, agency or other establishment in one of the Member States shall, in disputes arising out of the operations of the branch, agency or other establishment, be deemed to be domiciled in that state.[642] The effect of the provisions of Section 3 is to give the policy-holder a wide choice of fora in which to bring proceedings against the insurer.

5.8.5   Article 9(1) provides that an insurer domiciled in a Member State may be sued: (i) in the courts of the state where he is domiciled or (ii) in another Member State, in the courts for the place where the policy-holder, the insured or a beneficiary is domiciled, or (iii) if he is a co-insurer, in the courts of a Member State in which proceedings are brought against the leading insurer. The domicile of the policy-holder which is relevant for the purposes of the second option is the domicile existing at the

---

[633]   [1979] OJ C59/117, para 151.
[634]   Case C–351/89 [1991] ECR I–3317.
[635]   [2001] 1 AC 223.
[636]   Case C–412/98 [2000] ECR I–5925, para 76. E Peel, (2001) 20 *YBEL* 353.
[637]   Case C–77/04 *Groupement d'Intérêt Économique (GIE) Réunion Européenne v Zurich España* [2005] ECR I–4509. See also *Youell v La Réunion Aerienne* [2009] 1 All ER (Comm) 301, affirmed [2009] 1 Lloyd's Rep 586 (CA) (without consideration of this point).
[638]   Art 8.
[639]   Art 24.
[640]   *New Hampshire Insurance Co v Strabag Bau AG* [1992] 1 Lloyd's Rep 361.
[641]   Arts 9–11.
[642]   Art 9(2). These provisions are implemented in the United Kingdom by Civil Jurisdiction and Judgments Act 1982, s 44 and Civil Jurisdiction and Judgments Order 2001, sched 1, para 11.

time when the proceedings are instituted.[643] If the policy-holder is not domiciled in a Member State, the second option is not available.[644] The third option reflects the same policy considerations as those underlying Article 6(1).[645] In addition, Article 11(2) has the effect of widening the scope of Article 9(1)(b) in allowing an injured party who is not the policy holder, the insured or the beneficiary of the insurance contract to sue the insurer in the injured party's domicile.[646] Whether this principle extends to allowing persons stepping into the shoes of the injured party to sue in their domiciliary forum depends on the identity of the claimant. It has been held that the principle does not cover a social security institution who is the statutory assignee of the rights of the injured party, although it would cover a statutory assignee such as the heirs of the person injured in an accident; the former cannot be considered to be a weaker party requiring the protection of the special rules in Section 3.[647]

5.8.6 As regards liability insurance or insurance of immovable property, Article 10[648] makes it possible to sue the insurer in the courts for the place where the harmful event occurred. The same rule applies 'if movable and immovable property are covered by the same insurance policy and both are adversely affected by the same contingency'. The effect of this rule is that if a cottage in the Lake District and its contents are insured on the same policy, the insurer can be sued in England in relation to a claim arising out of a fire which causes damage to both the cottage and the contents. The rule also applies if 'the movables are covered by an endorsement to the policy covering the immovable property'.[649]

5.8.7 Article 11(1) provides that, in respect of liability insurance, 'the insurer may also, if the law of the court permits it, be joined in proceedings which the injured party has brought against the insured'. From a practical perspective, this rule is likely to be of greatest significance in road accident cases. So, where the victim of a road accident sues the driver in the courts of a Member State which would not have jurisdiction over the driver's insurer under other bases of jurisdiction, the driver is able to join the insurer as third party, but only 'if the court seised of the matter has jurisdiction in such a case under its own law'.[650]

5.8.8 According to Article 11(2), the other provisions which allocate jurisdiction with regard to claims brought against insurers[651] 'shall apply to actions brought by the injured party directly against the insurer, where such direct actions are permitted'. The Jenard Report states that the phrase 'where such direct actions are permitted' has

---

[643] Jenard Report, [1979] OJ C59/31.

[644] *Lassin v Payne* [1995] ILPr 17 (Court of Appeal, Paris).

[645] See paras 5.7.3–5.7.11.

[646] Case C–463/06 *FBTO Schadeverzekeringen NV v Odenbreit* [2007] ECR I–11321. The Court of Justice also held that it did not matter if an action pursued under Art 9(1)(b) is classified as a tort under national law as national classifications were irrelevant for the application of the provisions of the Regulation. See also *Maher v Groupama Grand Est* [2009] 1 WLR 1752, 1755–6 (at [4]–[8]).

[647] Case C–347/08 *Vorarlberger Gebietskrankenkasse v WGV-Schwäbische Allgemeine Versicherungs AG* [2010] ILPr 25.

[648] The phrase 'the place where the harmful event occurred' should be given the interpretation as that attributed by the Court of Justice to the same phrase in Art 5(3): *Rutschi Pumpen AG v SA Pompes Rutschi Mulhouse* [2002] ILPr 59 (Court of Cassation, France).

[649] Jenard Report, [1979] OJ C59/32.

[650] Jenard Report, [1979] OJ C59/32.

[651] Arts 8–10.

been used 'specifically to include the conflict of laws rules of the court seised of the matter',[652] and suggests that choice of law rules must be used to decide whether the law to be applied is 'the law of the place where the harmful event occurred, the law governing the contract of insurance or the *lex fori*'.[653]

5.8.9   How is this rule to be applied in a situation where a claimant is injured in a road accident in Belgium as a result of the negligence of a driver who is insured with an English insurance company? Which law determines whether the claimant may bring a direct action against the insurer in England? It is submitted that the traditional English approach would be to regard this question as procedural rather than substantive, with the consequence that English law, as the law of the forum, would determine the question. Under English law direct actions against insurers are allowed in limited circumstances.[654]

5.8.10   It should be noted that, because the provisions concerned with matters relating to insurance are without prejudice to Article 5(5),[655] an insurer who is domiciled in a Member State may be sued in the courts of another Member State 'as regards a dispute arising out of a branch, agency or other establishment, in the courts for the place in which the branch, agency or other establishment is situated'.[656]

5.8.11   The jurisdiction rules set out in the foregoing paragraphs must be read in conjunction with the provisions relating to jurisdiction agreements. In various circumstances a jurisdiction agreement may authorise the bringing of proceedings against an insurer in a Member State which does not normally have jurisdiction over claims brought against insurers and prevent proceedings being brought in a Member State which does normally have jurisdiction under the foregoing provisions.[657]

Proceedings Brought against the Policy-holder, the Insured or a Beneficiary

5.8.12   Where the defendant in proceedings concerning matters relating to insurance is not the insurer, the general principle is that the courts of the defendant's domicile have jurisdiction. Article 12(1) provides that:

an insurer may bring proceedings only in the courts of the Member State in which the defendant is domiciled, irrespective of whether he is the policy-holder, the insured or a beneficiary.

This general principle, which applies whether or not the insurer is domiciled in a Member State,[658] is subject to exceptions.

5.8.13   First, Article 11(3) provides that in certain circumstances the policy-holder or insured can be joined to actions brought, under Article 10(2), by an injured party directly against the insurer:

If the law governing such direct actions provides that the policy-holder or the insured may be joined as a party to the action, the same court shall have jurisdiction over them.

---

[652] [1979] OJ C59/32.
[653] [1979] OJ C59/32, n 4.
[654] See Third Parties (Rights Against Insurers) Act 1930 and Road Traffic Act 1988, s 151.
[655] Art 8.
[656] See para 5.6.71 *ff*.
[657] See paras 5.8.14–5.8.23.
[658] *Jordan Grand Prix Ltd v Baltic Insurance Group* [1999] 2 AC 127. A Briggs, (1998) 69 *BYIL* 345.

The Jenard Report justifies this exception to the general rule in the following terms:

In the interests of the proper administration of justice, it must be possible for the actions to be brought in the same court to prevent different courts from giving judgments which are irreconcilable. The procedure will in addition protect the insurer against fraud.[659]

Secondly, Article 12(2) provides that the provisions of Section 3 'shall not affect the right to bring a counterclaim in the court in which, in accordance with this Section, the original claim is pending'. If, for example, the policy-holder starts proceedings against the insurer in the courts of a Member State in which the policy-holder is not domiciled, the insurer may bring a counterclaim in those courts. However, such a counterclaim may be brought only against the original claimant; it is not possible for the insurer to join third parties to the counterclaim.[660] Thirdly, in limited circumstances, a jurisdiction agreement between the parties will enable proceedings to be brought against the policy-holder in a Member State in which the defendant is not domiciled.

Jurisdiction Agreements

5.8.14 The general jurisdiction rules contained in Articles 8 to 12 must be read in conjunction with the provisions which deal with the validity of jurisdiction agreements in matters relating to insurance.[661] It is provided that the provisions of Section 3 may be departed from only by a jurisdiction agreement which satisfies one of five alternative conditions set out in Article 13. Before the conditions are considered, a few general points should be noted. First, the purpose of the rules relating to jurisdiction agreements in insurance contracts is to prevent parties from limiting the choice offered to the policy-holder and to prevent the insurer from avoiding the restrictions imposed by the domicile rule.[662] Secondly, the Schlosser Report indicates[663] that jurisdiction agreements in consumer contracts must, in so far as they are permitted at all, comply with the formal requirements which apply to jurisdiction agreements in general.[664] There is no reason why, on this point, a distinction should be made between consumer contracts and insurance contracts. Thirdly, the provisions relating to jurisdiction agreements in insurance contracts are intended to uphold the validity of exclusive jurisdiction clauses in certain types of insurance policy (such as policies of marine insurance) in which the policy-holder is unlikely to require the protection given by the provisions in Section 3. Fourthly, whether a particular jurisdiction agreement is permitted depends on a number of factors, including whether it was concluded before or after the dispute arose, whether the jurisdiction clause is exclusive or non-exclusive, the domicile of the policy-holder and the nature of the risk involved.

---

[659] [1979] OJ C59/32.
[660] *Jordan Grand Prix Ltd v Baltic Insurance Group* [1999] 2 AC 127.
[661] Arts 13 and 14.
[662] Jenard Report, [1979] OJ C59/33.
[663] [1979] OJ C59/120, para 161a.
[664] Art 23.

THE FIVE ALTERNATIVE CONDITIONS

5.8.15   Article 13(1) provides that a jurisdiction clause 'which is entered into after the dispute has arisen' is permissible:

After a dispute has arisen, that is to say as soon as the parties disagree on a specific point and legal proceedings are imminent or contemplated, the parties completely regain their freedom.[665]

If the condition in paragraph 1 is satisfied, the clause will be upheld whether it is exclusive or non-exclusive.

5.8.16   The second condition, in Article 13(2), refers to a jurisdiction agreement 'which allows the policy-holder, the insured or a beneficiary to bring proceedings in courts other than those indicated in this Section'. A jurisdiction clause in a contract of insurance which purports to confer exclusive jurisdiction on the courts of a single Member State does not satisfy this condition (although it may satisfy one of the other conditions). The main purpose of Section 3 is to give the policy-holder a choice of fora in which to sue the insurer. A jurisdiction clause which gives the policy-holder more choice is perfectly valid; a clause which limits that choice is not compatible with the general aims of Chapter II.

5.8.17   It has been seen that, in proceedings brought by the injured party against the insured, the insured may be permitted to join the insurer as a third party.[666] The Jenard Report alludes to the problem which may arise where the insured and the insurer are domiciled in the same state:

For example, where an accident is caused in France by a German domiciled in Germany who is insured with a German company, should third party proceedings, which are recognised under French law, be possible even though the litigation concerns a contract of insurance between a German insured person and a German insurer? As it is subject to German law, should this contract not be litigated in a German court?[667]

5.8.18   The third condition, which was inserted to deal with this situation, provides that the rules in Section 3 may be departed from by an agreement:

which is concluded between a policy-holder and an insurer, both of whom are at the time of conclusion of the contract domiciled or habitually resident in the same Member State, and which has the effect of conferring jurisdiction on the courts of that State even if the harmful event were to occur abroad, provided that such agreement is not contrary to the law of that State.[668]

Accordingly, in the example given by the Jenard Report, if the contract of insurance between the insurer and the insured contains an exclusive jurisdiction clause in favour of the German courts, the French courts have no jurisdiction over the insurer, notwithstanding the terms of Article 11(1) of the Brussels I Regulation. However, a beneficiary under the insurance contract who has not expressly subscribed to the jurisdiction clause and is domiciled in a Member State other than that of the policy-holder

---

[665] Jenard Report, [1979] OJ C59/33.
[666] Art 11(1).
[667] [1979] OJ C59/32.
[668] Art 13(3).

and the insurer is not bound by the clause.[669] This is to preserve the underlying aim of protecting the economically weaker party by upholding his right to defend himself before the courts of his own domicile.

5.8.19 One of the general purposes of Chapter II is to provide jurisdictional safeguards for defendants who are domiciled in a Member State. The Brussels I Regulation takes a less protective attitude towards parties who are not domiciled in a Member State. The fourth condition allows effect to be given to a jurisdiction agreement which is concluded with a policy-holder who is not domiciled in a Member State, except in so far as the insurance is compulsory or relates to immovable property in a Member State.[670]

5.8.20 The fifth condition was added to the Brussels Convention by the 1978 Accession Convention in response to the United Kingdom's request for special rules for the insurance of large risks. Section 3 (as originally drafted) was focused on the problems posed by domestic insurance contracts in which there is a disparity in economic power between the policy-holder and the insurer. The concept of social protection underlying a restriction on the admissibility of provisions conferring jurisdiction in insurance matters was not thought to be justified in situations where the policy-holder is a powerful undertaking.[671] The fifth condition is intended to give special treatment to jurisdiction agreements in contracts of marine insurance and some sectors of aviation insurance. (There are, however, no special provisions in the case of risks relating to transport by land.) Nevertheless, in certain circumstances the effect of Section 3 is to give protection to a policy-holder whose position is no weaker than that of the insurer.

5.8.21 The fifth condition permits jurisdiction agreements in contracts of insurance 'in so far as' they cover specified risks.[672] In *Charman v WOC Offshore BV* Hirst J decided that the phrase 'in so far as' should be given a literal interpretation, so that a jurisdiction agreement is valid only to the extent that it relates to the specified risks.[673] As a result of this interpretation litigation arising out of a contract which covers some specified risks and other non-specified risks might be split between two jurisdictions. It is, however, open to the parties in this type of situation to enter a second jurisdiction agreement after the dispute has arisen. Such an agreement is valid, regardless of the nature of the risk.[674]

5.8.22 Article 14 contains a list of the specified risks:

1. any loss or damage to—

   (a) sea-going ships, installations situated offshore or on the high seas, or aircraft, arising from perils which relate to their use for commercial purposes;
   (b) goods in transit other than passengers' baggage where the transit consists of or includes carriage by such ships or aircraft;

---

[669] Case C–112/03 *Société Financière et Industrielle du Peloux v Axa Belgium* [2005] ECR I–3707.

[670] Art 13(4).

[671] Schlosser Report, [1979] OJ C59/114, para 140.

[672] Arts 13(5) and 14.

[673] [1993] 1 Lloyd's Rep 378, 384. This issue was expressly left open by the Court of Appeal: [1993] 2 Lloyd's Rep 551. See also *Ministry for Agriculture, Food and Forestry v Alte Leipziger Versicherung Aktiengesellshaft* [2001] 2 IR 82 (Supreme Court, Ireland).

[674] Art 13(1).

2. any liability, other than for bodily injury to passengers or loss of or damage to their baggage—

   (a) arising out of the use or operation of ships, installations or aircraft as referred to in point 1(a) in so far as, in respect of the latter, the law of the Member State in which such aircraft are registered does not prohibit agreements on jurisdiction regarding insurance of such risks;

   (b) for loss or damage caused by goods in transit as described in point 1(b);

3. any financial loss connected with the use or operation of ships, installations or aircraft as referred to in point (1)(a), in particular loss of freight or charter-hire;

4. any risk or interest connected with any of those referred to in points 1 to 3 above;

5. notwithstanding points 1 to 4, all 'large risks' as defined in Council Directive 73/239/EEC, as amended by Council Directives 88/357/EEC and 90/618/EEC, as they may be amended.

5.8.23   The Schlosser Report gives some guidance as to the scope of these specified risks. First, point 1(a) applies only to hull insurance and not to liability insurance, and the term 'sea-going ships' means all vessels intended to travel on the sea.[675] Secondly, point 1(b) covers the value of goods destroyed or lost in transit, but not liability insurance for any loss or damage caused by those goods[676]; it is irrelevant during which section of the transport the circumstances causing liability occurred.[677] Thirdly, an example of insurance against ancillary risks within point 4 would be shipowner's disbursements consisting of exceptional operation costs, such as harbour dues accruing while the ship remains disabled.[678] For the purposes of point 4 the words 'connected with' are to be given a narrow construction. Where a contract of insurance covers marine risks (within points 1 to 3) and non-marine risks, the non-marine risks do not qualify as specified risks simply by virtue of the fact that they are covered by the same policy as the marine risks; to fall within point 4 the risks in question must be 'ancillary to' or 'accessory to' the risks set out in points 1 to 3.[679] Fourthly, there is uncertainty as to the scope of point 2(a):

Whether these provisions also cover all liability arising in connection with the construction, modification and repair of a ship; whether therefore the provision includes all liability which the shipyard incurs towards third parties and which was caused by the ship; or whether the expression 'use or operation' has to be construed more narrowly as applying only to liability arising in the course of a trial voyage—all these are questions of interpretation which still await an answer.[680]

Consumer Contracts[681]

5.8.24   Section 4 of Chapter II contains the jurisdiction provisions which apply to certain consumer contracts. Like Section 3, Section 4 is independent from the rest of Chapter II; the jurisdiction rules which apply to contracts generally do not apply to consumer

---

[675] [1979] OJ C59/115, para 141.

[676] [1979] OJ C59/115, para 142.

[677] [1979] OJ C59/115, para 145.

[678] [1979] OJ C59/115–116, para 147.

[679] *Charman v WOC Offshore BV* [1993] 2 Lloyd's Rep 551; *Tradigrain SA v SIAT SpA* [2002] 2 Lloyd's Rep 553.

[680] [1979] OJ C59/115, para 144.

[681] J Hill, *Cross-Border Consumer Contracts* (Oxford, OUP, 2008) chs 3 and 4.

contracts within the scope of Section 4. However, Section 4 operates without prejudice to Articles 4 and 5(5) and it must be assumed that Section 4 can be overridden by the defendant's submission.[682] In its basic aim, Section 4 is no different from Section 3; its purpose is to protect the weaker party, which—in the context of Section 4—is the consumer.

The Scope of Section 4[683]

5.8.25 Not all proceedings involving consumers fall within the scope of Section 4. For the consumer provisions to apply, various conditions must be satisfied.[684] First, the proceedings must concern a concluded contract.[685] Secondly, the contract must have been concluded by 'a person for a purpose which can be regarded as being outside his trade or profession'.[686] The concept 'consumer' must be given an independent interpretation.[687] In the context of unfair terms in consumer contracts, the Court of Justice has ruled that only natural persons (and not legal persons) can qualify as consumers.[688] There is every reason to think that the same approach should be followed with regard to the Brussels I Regulation. The Court of Justice has indicated an unwillingness to extend the consumer provisions to persons for whom the protection provided by Section 4 is not required. In *Benincasa v Dentalkit Srl*[689] the plaintiff, having entered into a franchise agreement with an Italian company, sought to rely on the consumer provisions. The essence of the argument was that, since at the time of the conclusion of the contract the plaintiff had not yet set up the franchised shop which was envisaged by the agreement, he was a consumer. The Court of Justice rejected this argument and ruled that a plaintiff who enters a contract with a view to pursuing a trade or profession in the future is not to be regarded as a consumer.[690] In the course of its judgment the Court of Justice indicated that:

only contracts concluded for the purpose of satisfying an individual's needs in terms of private consumption come under the provisions designed to protect the consumer as the weaker party economically.[691]

---

[682] Art 24. See Advocate General Lenz in Case C–99/96 *Mietz v Intership Yachting Sneek BV* [1999] ECR I–2277, para 31. See also *Re Jurisdiction in a Consumer Contract* [2002] ILPr 157 (Court of Appeal, Koblenz).

[683] P Cachia, 'Consumer Contracts in European Private International Law: The Sphere of Operation of the Consumer Contract Rules in the Brussels I and Rome I Regulations' (2009) 34 *EL Rev* 476.

[684] A number of the concepts which are used to fix the boundaries of Section 4 are derived from the provisions of the draft treaty which ultimately became Art 5 of the Rome Convention on the Law Applicable to Contractual Obligations; Art 5 of the Convention was replaced (with some amendments) by Art 6 of the Rome I Regulation. See section 14.5.

[685] See Case C–96/00 *Gabriel* [2002] ECR I–6367; Case C–27/02 *Engler v Janus Versand GmbH* [2005] ECR I–481, paras 32–43; Case C–180/06 *Ilsinger v Dreschers* [2009] ECR I–3961.

[686] Art 15(1).

[687] Case C–89/91 *Shearson Lehman Hutton v TVB Treuhandgesellschaft für Vermögensverwaltung und Beteiligungen mbH* [1993] ECR I–139, para 13; Case C–269/95 *Benincasa v Dentalkit Srl* [1997] ECR I–3767, para 12. See *Ghandour v Arab Bank (Switzerland)* [2008] ILPr 527 (Court of Appeal, Athens).

[688] Cases C–541/99 and C–542/99 *Cape Snc v Idealservices Srl; Ideal Service MN RE Sas v OMAI Srl* [2001] ECR I–9049.

[689] Case C–269/95 [1997] ECR I–3767. J Harris, 'Jurisdiction Clauses and Void Contracts' (1998) 23 *EL Rev* 279; E Peel, (1997) 17 *YBEL* 530.

[690] Case C–269/95 [1997] ECR I–3767, para 19.

[691] Case C–269/95 *Benincasa v Dentalkit Srl* [1997] ECR I–3767, para 17.

5.8.26   A similarly strict interpretation of a consumer contract was taken in *Gruber v Bay Wa AG*,[692] which concerned a farmer buying roof tiles for his farm building and ancillary buildings used principally for the farm. The Court of Justice held that the farmer should not benefit from the rules of Section 4. Where a contract has a dual purpose, ie it is concluded partly for trade purposes and partly for non-trade purposes, Section 4 is inapplicable, notwithstanding the fact that the private use is predominant, as long as the proportion of the professional usage is not negligible.[693] In addition, the Court stated that the person who claims to be a consumer must not have behaved in such a way as to give the other party to the contract the impression that he was acting for business purposes; otherwise, he would lose the protection afforded by Section 4.[694] However, the value of the contract is irrelevant to whether it falls within Section 4. It is, for example, perfectly possible for a contract for the purchase of a yacht to qualify as a consumer contract if the relevant conditions of Section 4 are satisfied.[695] It is less clear whether certain types of contracts in the area of financial services can be said to satisfy a person's 'needs in terms of private consumption'. Although it has been held in England that an agreement between a bank and a wealthy married couple (a civil engineer and his wife) relating to foreign exchange margin trading was covered by the consumer contract provisions contained in Section 4,[696] the Greek courts took the opposite view.[697]

5.8.27   The Court of Justice has ruled that the consumer contract provisions apply only to the extent that a consumer is a party to the dispute. In *Shearson Lehman Hutton v TVB Treuhandgesellschaft für Vermögensverwaltung und Beteiligungen mbH*[698] a German national had instructed the defendant to carry out currency futures transactions on a commission basis. The original contracting party assigned his rights under the contract to the plaintiff, a German company, which brought proceedings against the defendant. The plaintiff was not a consumer, but sought to rely on the consumer provisions on the basis that the original contracting party had dealt with the defendant as a consumer. The Court of Justice held that Section 4 protects the consumer only in so far as he personally is the plaintiff or defendant in proceedings.[699] A plaintiff who acts in the exercise of his trade or profession rather than in his private capacity is not a consumer for the purposes of Section 4 and cannot invoke the special rules on jurisdiction laid down as regards consumer contracts.[700] Similarly, a consumer protection organisation which brings proceedings as an association on behalf of consumers cannot rely on the consumer contract provisions.[701]

---

[692]   Case C–464/01 [2005] ECR I–439.
[693]   Case C–464/01 [2005] ECR I–439, para 41.
[694]   Case C–464/01 [2005] ECR I–439, paras 51–3.
[695]   Case C–99/96 *Mietz v Intership Yachting Sneek BV* [1999] ECR I–2277. E Peel, (2001) 20 *YBEL* 359.
[696]   *Standard Bank London Ltd v Apostolakis* [2000] ILPr 766. See also *Re Jurisdiction in a Consumer Contract* [2002] ILPr 157 (Court of Appeal, Koblenz).
[697]   *Standard Bank of London v Apostolakis* [2003] ILPr 499 (Court of First Instance, Athens).
[698]   Case C–89/91 [1993] ECR I–139. A Briggs, (1993) 13 *YBEL* 511.
[699]   Case C–89/91 [1993] ECR I–139, para 23.
[700]   Case C–89/91 [1993] ECR I–139, para 22. A management agreement between a professional footballer and a company providing management services is not a consumer contract: *Prostar Management Ltd v Twaddle* 2003 SLT 181 (Sheriff Court, Glasgow). See also *Maple Leaf Macro Volatility Master Fund v Rouvroy* [2009] 1 Lloyd's Rep 475, 509.
[701]   Case C–167/00 *Verein für Konsumentinformation v Henkel* [2002] ECR I–8111.

5.8.28 Thirdly, the contract must fall within one of three categories: (i) contracts for the sale of goods on instalment credit terms[702]; (ii) contracts for a loan repayable by instalments, or for any other form of credit, made to finance the sale of goods[703]; (iii) situations where:

the contract has been concluded with a person who pursues commercial or professional activities in the Member State of the consumer's domicile or, by any means, directs such activities to that Member State or to several States including that Member State, and the contract falls within the scope of such activities.[704]

The purpose of this formulation is to include 'consumer contracts concluded via an interactive website accessible in the state of the consumer's domicile'[705] within the protective ambit of the consumer contract provisions.[706] However, it is not intended that Section 4 should extend to situations where, prior to entering the contract, the consumer acquires knowledge of a service or of the possibility of buying goods via a passive website.[707] In a Joint Declaration concerning Article 15 of the Brussels I Regulation, the Council and Commission stress that:

the mere fact that an Internet site is accessible is not sufficient for Article 15 to be applicable, although a factor will be that this Internet site solicits the conclusion of distance contracts and that the contract has actually been concluded at a distance, by whatever means. In this respect, the language or currency which a website uses does not constitute a relevant factor.[708]

5.8.29 Fourthly, although contracts of transport are excluded, contracts which for an inclusive price provide for a combination of travel and accommodation (such as package holidays) are not.[709]

Proceedings Brought against the Consumer

5.8.30 Proceedings may be brought against a consumer by the other party to the contract only in the courts of the Member State in which the consumer is domiciled.[710] The relevant time for determining the consumer's domicile is when the proceedings are instituted, rather than when the contract was concluded.[711] It should also be noted that the other party has 'the right to bring a counterclaim in the court in which ... the

---

[702] This also covers hire purchase: Schlosser Report, [1979] OJ C59/118, para 157. For the limits of this category, see Case C–99/96 *Mietz v Intership Yachting Sneek BV* [1999] ECR I–2277.

[703] The Commission has observed that Art 15(1)(a) and (b) does not cover the new types of credit products that have been developed, such as reflected in Dir 2008/48/EC on credit agreements for consumers and repealing Dir 87/102/EEC [2008] OJ L133/66: Commission Report, COM (2009) 174 final, p 10.

[704] Art 15(1).

[705] European Commission, *Proposal*, COM (1999) 348 final, p 16.

[706] See Y Farah, 'Allocation of Jurisdiction and the Internet in EU Law' (2008) 33 *EL Rev* 257.

[707] European Commission, *Proposal*, COM (1999) 348 final, p 16. See K Vasiljeva, '1968 Brussels Convention and EU Council Reg No 44/2001: Jurisdiction in Consumer Contracts Concluded Online' (2004) 10 *Euro LJ* 123.

[708] The *Europa* website indicates that the Joint Declaration can be found at the following web address: http://europa.eu.int/justice_home/unit/civil/justciv_conseil/justciv_en.pdf.

[709] Art 15(3).

[710] Art 16(2).

[711] Jenard Report, [1979] OJ C59/33.

original claim is pending'.[712] So, if the consumer sues the other party in the courts of that party's domicile, the latter may bring a counterclaim against the consumer, even though the consumer is not domiciled in that state.

Proceedings Brought against the Other Party

5.8.31   The consumer is given a choice of fora in which to proceed against the other party. A consumer may bring proceedings against the other party to a contract either in the courts of the Member State in which that party is domiciled or in the courts of the state in which he is himself domiciled.[713] The other party may be deemed, for certain purposes, to be domiciled in a Member State, even though for the purposes of Articles 2 to 4 he is not domiciled in a Member State. It is provided that where a consumer enters into a contract with a party who is not domiciled in a Member State but has a branch, agency or other establishment in one of the Member States, that party shall, in disputes arising out of the operations of the branch, agency or establishment, be deemed to be domiciled in that state.[714]

5.8.32   It is provided that the consumer contract provisions are without prejudice to Article 4.[715] Accordingly, if the other party is not domiciled in a Member State, and is not deemed to be so domiciled, Section 4 does not apply and jurisdiction must be determined by reference to traditional rules.[716] The consumer contract provisions are also expressed to be without prejudice to Article 5(5).[717] This means that a defendant who is domiciled in a Member State may be sued in the courts of another Member State 'as regards a dispute arising out of a branch, agency or other establishment, in the courts for the place in which the branch, agency or other establishment is situated'.[718]

Jurisdiction Agreements

5.8.33   The Brussels I Regulation restricts the extent to which the parties to a consumer contract can depart from the jurisdiction rules set out in Section 4 by means of a jurisdiction agreement. The basic approach to jurisdiction agreements in consumer contracts mirrors that adopted in the context of insurance contracts. According to the Schlosser Report,[719] jurisdiction agreements in consumer contracts, in so far as they are permitted at all, must comply with the formal requirements which apply to jurisdiction agreements in commercial contracts.[720]

---

[712] Art 16(3).
[713] Art 16(1).
[714] Art 15(2).
[715] Art 15(1).
[716] Case C–318/93 *Brenner and Noller v Dean Witter Reynolds Inc* [1994] ECR I–4275. A Briggs, (1994) 14 *YBEL* 578.
[717] Art 15(1).
[718] For a discussion of Art 5(5), see para 5.6.71 *ff*.
[719] Schlosser Report, [1979] OJ C59/120, para 161a. See also *Weber v SA Eurocard Belgium-Luxembourg* [1993] ILPr 55 (Court of Appeal, Luxembourg).
[720] Art 23.

5.8.34 Article 17[721] provides that jurisdiction agreements in consumer contracts are to be given effect in three situations. First, there is no objection to a jurisdiction agreement which is entered into after the dispute has arisen.[722] Such agreements are not likely to be very common in practice. Secondly, the courts will give effect to a jurisdiction agreement which allows the consumer to bring proceedings in courts other than those indicated by the other consumer contract provisions.[723] Again, such agreements are likely to be rare. Thirdly, effect will be given to a jurisdiction agreement which is entered into by the consumer and the other party to the contract, both of whom are at the time of conclusion of the contract domiciled or habitually resident in the same state, and which confers jurisdiction on the courts of that state, provided that such an agreement is not contrary to the law of that state.[724] This third possibility is designed to protect the other party to a consumer contract who finds that, after the contract has been concluded, the consumer moves to another country. Although, under Article 16(2), the consumer ought to be sued in the country of his new domicile, fairness requires that the other party should be able to rely on a jurisdiction agreement in favour of the courts of the country of their common domicile at the time of the conclusion of the contract.[725] The use of domicile and habitual residence as alternative connecting factors means that:

a seller or a lender need not sue the defendant abroad in the courts of the State in which the defendant is domiciled, if, when the proceedings are instituted, the defendant is still resident in the State in which the contract was concluded.[726]

5.8.35 It should also be noted that a jurisdiction clause in a consumer contract may be rendered unenforceable by virtue of the operation of the Unfair Terms in Consumer Contracts Regulations 1999[727] (which implement the relevant Council Directive[728]).[729] It is doubtful, however, whether the 1999 Regulations can have much of an impact on jurisdiction clauses in cases governed by Section 4 of Chapter II.[730] (The position is different where the case is internal to a single Member State[731] or where the contract, although involving a consumer, falls outside the scope of Section 4—such as a contract of transport.) Where a jurisdiction clause in a consumer contract falls within one of the three permitted categories, it is difficult to see how the basic requirements of the Regulations can be satisfied. If the agreement is concluded after the

---

[721] Art 17.
[722] Art 17(1).
[723] Art 17(2).
[724] Art 17(3).
[725] Jenard Report, [1979] OJ C59/33.
[726] Jenard Report, [1979] OJ C59/34.
[727] SI 2083/1999.
[728] Dir (EEC) 13/93, [1993] OJ L95/29.
[729] See Joined Cases C–240/98 and C–244/98 *Océano Grupo Editorial SA v Rocío Murciano Qunitero; Salvat Editores SA v Prades* [2000] ECR I–4941 (S Whittaker, 'Judicial Intervention and Consumer Contracts' (2001) 117 *LQR* 215); *Standard Bank London Ltd v Apostolakis (No 2)* [2001] Lloyd's Rep Banking 240 (C Withers, 'Jurisdiction clauses and the Unfair Terms in Consumer Contract Regulations' [2002] *LMCLQ* 56).
[730] The discussion of the 1999 Regs in *Standard Bank London Ltd v Apostolakis (No 2)* [2001] Lloyd's Rep Banking 240 was *obiter*.
[731] As was the case in Joined Cases C–240/98 and C–244/98 *Océano Grupo Editorial SA v Rocío Murciano Qunitero; Salvat Editores SA v Prades* [2000] ECR I–4941.

dispute has arisen (the first category), the clause will almost certainly be 'individually negotiated'[732] and therefore is not governed by the Regulations. If the clause gives the consumer a wider choice of fora than that provided by the provisions of Section 4 (the second category), it does not cause 'a significant imbalance in the parties' rights and obligations to the detriment of the consumer'[733] as required by the Regulations. If the clause allocates jurisdiction to the courts of the parties' common domicile (the third category), to the extent there is any detriment to the consumer, it is caused by the fact that the consumer moves to a new country after the conclusion of the contract, rather than by the clause itself. Indeed, as this third category was included expressly in order to avoid unfairness to the other party to the contract,[734] it would be perverse to characterise clauses in the third category as unfair to the consumer.

Jurisdiction in Relation to Employment Contracts

Introduction

5.8.36   As originally drafted, the Brussels Convention of 1968 did not include any provisions dealing expressly with contracts of employment, notwithstanding the fact that from the point of view of inequality of bargaining power individual contracts of employment raise similar problems to consumer contracts and insurance contracts. The preliminary draft of the 1968 Convention had included specific provisions concerned with employment contracts, but after prolonged consideration by the committee they were not inserted into the final text.[735] However, as the Brussels regime evolved, specific rules relating to individual contracts of employment were developed[736] and individual employment contracts were finally put on a par with consumer contracts. Chapter II contains a block of provisions—Section 5, which comprises Articles 18 to 21—devoted to jurisdiction in relation to employment contracts.

Individual Contracts of Employment

5.8.37   Although it is reasonable to assume that the words 'individual contracts of employment' are to be given an autonomous interpretation, until the matter is referred to the Court of Justice the precise scope of the employment contract rules will remain a matter for speculation. Nevertheless, a number of points are relevant in this context. First, collective agreements between employers and workers' representatives

---

[732] Unfair Terms in Consumer Contracts Regs 1999, reg 5.

[733] Unfair Terms in Consumer Contracts Regs 1999, reg 5.

[734] Jenard Report, [1979] OJ C59/33.

[735] The reasons for their exclusion are to be found in the Jenard Report, [1979] OJ C59/24.

[736] Through its interpretation of Art 5(1) of the Brussels Convention, the Court of Justice created a new rule of 'special jurisdiction' for employment contracts (see Case 133/81 *Ivenel v Schwab* [1982] ECR 1891; Case C–125/92 *Mulox IBC Ltd v Geels* [1993] ECR I–4075; Case 32/88 *Six Constructions Ltd v Humbert* [1989] ECR 341; see also WA Allwood, 'Characteristic Performance and Labour Disputes under the Brussels Convention: Pandora's Box' (1987) 7 *YBEL* 131). This case law was, to a certain extent, incorporated into Art 5(1) of the Brussels Convention and forms part of the background to the employment contract provisions of the Brussels I Regulation.

cannot be regarded as individual contracts of employment.[737] Secondly, a contract of employment 'presupposes a relationship of subordination of the employee to the employer'.[738] So, a contract for work on a self-employed basis should not fall within the scope of the employment contract rules. Thirdly, in *Shenavai v Kreischer*,[739] a case decided under the original text of Article 5(1) of the Brussels Convention, the Court of Justice stated that the significant characteristics of contracts of employment are that:

they create a lasting bond which brings the worker to some extent within the organisational framework of the business of the undertaking or employer, and they are linked to the place where the activities are pursued, which determines the application of mandatory rules and collective agreements.[740]

Fourthly, the special rules which apply to individual contracts of employment should not be applied by analogy to other types of contract which share some of the same characteristics. In *Mercury Publicity Ltd v Wolfgang Loerke GmbH*[741] the Court of Appeal refused to apply the employment contract rules to a contract under the terms of which the plaintiff employed the defendant company as a commercial agent. The Court of Appeal rejected the idea that the special jurisdiction rules could be extended to a contract between two independent corporations. Fifthly, the special rules which apply to individual employment contracts do not apply to all proceedings involving an employer and employee. Where an employer brings a claim against a defendant who is (or was) his employee, in circumstances where the defendant's status as employee is legally irrelevant or where it can truly be said that the subject-matter of the dispute does not involve 'matters relating to individual contracts of employment' (for example, where the claim is based on the tort of conspiracy), the employer is able to rely on the jurisdictional bases which apply to defendants in general.[742]

Proceedings Brought against the Employer

5.8.38   An employer domiciled in a Member State can be sued in that Member State.[743] In addition, the Brussels I Regulation provides that an employer which is not domiciled in a Member State—but which has a branch, agency or other establishment in a Member State—is deemed to be domiciled in that Member State as regards disputes arising out of the operations of the branch, agency or establishment. To the extent that an employer can be sued in a Member State other than that in which it is domiciled (or deemed to be domiciled), much turns on whether or not the employee habitually carries on work in a single country. If the employee carries out all his work in non-Member States, the employer cannot be sued other than in the courts of its domicile.[744]

---

[737]   Jenard-Möller Report, [1990] OJ C189/73, para 42.
[738]   Jenard-Möller Report, [1990] OJ C189/73, para 41.
[739]   Case 266/85 [1987] ECR 239.
[740]   Case 266/85 [1987] ECR 239, para 16.
[741]   [1993] ILPr 142.
[742]   *Swithenbank Foods Ltd v Bowers* [2002] 2 All ER (Comm) 974.
[743]   Art 19(1).
[744]   Case 32/88 *Six Constructions Ltd v Humbert* [1989] ECR 341, para 22. See also *Shell International Limited v Liem* [2004] ILPr 347 (Court of Cassation, France).

5.8.39   Where the employee habitually carries out his work in a single country (and that country is a Member State), the employee may sue the employer in the courts for the place where the employee habitually carries out his work.[745] If the employee no longer habitually works for the employer in a Member State, proceedings can be brought at the place where the employee last did so.[746] If the employee does not habitually carry out his work in any one country, the employee can sue the employer in the courts for the place where the business which engaged the employee is or was situated (as long as that place is in a Member State).[747] This rule was suggested by Article 6 of the Rome Convention on the Law Applicable to Contractual Obligations, which provides that, in relation to a contract of employment, if the parties have not chosen the applicable law and the employee does not habitually work in one particular country, the applicable law is normally the law of the country in which the place of business through which he was engaged is situated.[748] According to the Jenard-Möller Report, the term 'place of business' is to be understood in a broad sense; in particular, it covers any entity such as a branch or an agency with no legal personality.[749] It has also been established that work carried out by an employee on oil or gas installations positioned on or above the part of the continental shelf adjacent to a state is to be regarded as work carried out in the territory of that state.[750]

THE PLACE WHERE AN EMPLOYEE HABITUALLY WORKS
5.8.40   To determine where an employee habitually works, national law is irrelevant; the court must apply uniform criteria as laid down by the Court of Justice.[751] In *Rutten v Cross Medical Ltd*[752] the Court of Justice ruled that 'the place where the employee habitually carries out his work' is the place where the employee 'has established the effective centre of his working activities'.[753] If, for example, an employee spends two-thirds of his working time in one state, in which he has an office from which he organises his activities for his employer and to which he returns after business trips abroad, the place where the employee habitually works is the place where the office is located. However, the ruling in the *Rutten* case has no application in a case where, although the employee works in more than one state, he does not have an office from which he organises his working life. In this type of case the employee is normally to be regarded as habitually working in the place where he spends most of his working time engaged in his employer's business.[754] Of course, where an employee performs similar work for the employer in more than one place, it may be impossible to say that the employee works habitually in any particular place. In this situation, the

---

[745]   Art 19(2)(a).
[746]   This is expressly provided by Brussels I Reg, Art 19(2)(a). See *Four Winds Charter (Société) v Latoja* [2009] ILPr 839 (Court of Cassation, France). .
[747]   Art 19(2)(b).
[748]   The Rome I Regulation does not make substantive changes in this area. See para 14.5.29 *ff*.
[749]   [1990] OJ C189/73, para 43.
[750]   Case C–37/00 *Weber v Universal Ogden Services Ltd* [2002] ECR I–2013, para 36.
[751]   Case C–37/00 *Weber v Universal Ogden Services Ltd* [2002] ECR I–2013, para 62.
[752]   Case C–383/95 [1997] ECR I–57. E Peel, (1997) 17 *YBEL* 515.
[753]   Case C–383/95 [1997] ECR I–57, para 27. See *Re Employment in More than One State* [2003] ILPr 540 (Federal Labour Court, Germany).
[754]   Case C–37/00 *Weber v Universal Ogden Services Ltd* [2002] ECR I–2013, para 50.

relevant connecting factor for jurisdictional purposes is the place of business through which the employee was engaged.[755]

5.8.41 The determination of where an employee habitually works is made more difficult in a case where a person employed by employer A is either seconded to employer B or suspends employment with employer A and works for employer B. In *Pugliese v Finmeccanica SpA*[756] the claimant was engaged in 1990 to work for the Italian defendant in Turin. However, the claimant never worked in Turin; by agreement, her employment with the defendant was suspended for at least three years and she started work with a German company in Munich. The suspension of the claimant's contract of employment was extended by the defendant until 1998. When the claimant failed to report for work in Turin in July 1998 the defendant imposed disciplinary measures against her and then terminated her employment. The claimant brought proceedings in Germany for reimbursement of various expenses during her period of employment with the German company and to challenge her dismissal. Questions concerning the jurisdiction of the German court were referred to the Court of Justice. A central issue was whether, during the suspension of her employment with the defendant, the place where the claimant worked for the German employer could be regarded as the place where she habitually carried out her work under her contract of employment with the defendant.

5.8.42 The Court of Justice decided that:

when an employee is connected to two different employers, the first employer can be sued before the courts of the place where the employee carries out his work for the second employer only when, at the time of the conclusion of the second contract of employment, the first employer itself has an interest in the employee's performance of the service for the second employer in a place decided upon by the latter.[757]

The Court of Justice also laid down a series of factors which help to determine whether the first employer has such an interest; these include matters such as: whether the second contract of employment was envisaged when the first contract was concluded; whether there are organisational or economic links between the two employers; and whether the first employer can determine the length of the employee's work for the second employer.[758]

Proceedings Brought against the Employee

5.8.43 An employer may bring proceedings in the courts of the Member State in which the employee is domiciled.[759] It is reasonable to suppose that the domicile of the employee is to be determined when the proceedings are issued—as this is the rule that applies in relation to consumer contracts. However, if the employee sues the employer

---

[755] Case C–37/00 *Weber v Universal Ogden Services Ltd* [2002] ECR I–2013, para 58.
[756] Case C–437/00 [2003] ECR I–3573.
[757] Case C–437/00 [2003] ECR I–3573, para 23.
[758] Case C–437/00 [2003] ECR I–3573, para 24.
[759] Art 20(1). See *Swithenbank Ltd v Bowers* [2002] 2 All ER (Comm) 974.

in a forum other than that in which the employee is domiciled, the employer is entitled to bring a counterclaim in the court in which the original claim is pending.[760]

JURISDICTION AGREEMENTS

5.8.44 In view of the fact that an employee is, from the socio-economic point of view, the weaker party in the contractual relationship, it is to be expected that the effectiveness of jurisdiction clauses in individual contracts of employment should be regulated. Article 21 of the Brussels I Regulation provides:

The provisions of this Section may be departed from only by an agreement on jurisdiction:

1. which is entered into after the dispute has arisen; or
2. which allows the employee to bring proceedings in courts other than those indicated in this Section.

The result of this provision is that, where an individual contract of employment contains a jurisdiction clause, the employee has, in his capacity as claimant, a free choice between the courts of the state of the defendant's domicile or the courts for the place where the employee habitually works or the courts to which prorogation has been made.[761] The employer, however, cannot rely on the clause.

---

[760] Art 20(2).
[761] Almeida Cruz-Desantes Real-Jenard Report, [1990] OJ C189/48, para 27(f). See *Re Jurisdiction Agreement in Employment Contract* [2002] ILPr 233 (Court of First Instance, Piraeus).

BASES OF JURISDICTION *IN PERSONAM* UNDER SCHEDULE 4 TO THE CIVIL JURISDICTION AND JUDGMENTS ACT 1982

6.0.1 The regime for the allocation jurisdiction within the United Kingdom mirrors the system which exists on the international plane. In civil and commercial matters jurisdiction is determined by schedule 4 to the Civil Jurisdiction and Judgments Act 1982 ('schedule 4') which, to a significant extent, reflects Chapter II of the Brussels I Regulation.[1] So far as the English court is concerned, the effect of schedule 4 is that Scotland and Northern Ireland are (subject to modifications) treated as if they were Member States.[2] If the defendant is domiciled in another part of the United Kingdom the English court will have jurisdiction only if it would have had jurisdiction if the defendant had been domiciled in another Member State. Accordingly, as regards disputes which fall within the scope of Article 1 of the Brussels I Regulation, the English court cannot assume jurisdiction on the basis of the traditional rules if the defendant is domiciled in another part of the United Kingdom. However, if the proceedings are not within the material scope of the Brussels I Regulation, schedule 4 does not apply and jurisdiction is determined by the traditional rules.[3]

6.1 JURISDICTION IN CIVIL AND COMMERCIAL MATTERS: SCHEDULE 4 TO THE 1982 ACT

The Scope of Schedule 4

6.1.1 Questions surrounding the allocation of jurisdiction within the United Kingdom in civil and commercial matters can arise in two different contexts. First, although there are certain jurisdiction rules within the Brussels I Regulation which allocate jurisdiction to 'the courts for a place' within one of the Member States, the Brussels I Regulation also contains provisions which confer jurisdiction on the courts of the United Kingdom but do not determine whether the courts of England, Scotland or Northern Ireland are competent. Whereas, for example, Article 5(3) provides that

---

[1] Reg (EC) 44/2001, [2001] OJ L12/1. On the entry into force of the Brussels I Regulation, sched 4 to the 1982 Act (which had been based on the Brussels Convention and was known as the 'Modified Convention') was completely replaced by provisions set out in sched 2 to the Civil Jurisdiction and Judgments Order 2001 (SI 2001/3929). In the current version of sched 4 to the 1982 Act, no attempt is made to follow the numbering of provisions to be found in the Brussels I Regulation.

[2] See generally, KJ Hood, *Conflict of Laws within the UK* (Oxford, OUP, 2007) 188–200.

[3] See ch 7.

in matters relating to tort the 'courts for the place where the harmful event occurred' have jurisdiction, Article 2 of the Brussels I Regulation simply states that a person domiciled in a Member State 'shall ... be sued in the courts of that Member State'.

6.1.2   Secondly, cases arise which, from the perspective of other Member States, do not involve questions of international jurisdiction—since they are entirely internal to the United Kingdom—but which, from the perspective of the English court, are cases with a foreign element since not all the relevant elements are connected with England. Where, for example, an English motorist injures a Scottish pedestrian in Northern Ireland, the Brussels I Regulation—which is concerned only with international jurisdiction—does not provide an answer to the question of which court has jurisdiction.

6.1.3   The mechanism for allocating jurisdiction in these two types of case is schedule 4 to the Civil Jurisdiction and Judgments Act 1982. Section 16(1) of the 1982 Act provides:

The provisions set out in Schedule 4 (which contains a modified version of Chapter II of the Regulation) shall have effect for determining, for each part of the United Kingdom, whether the courts of law of that part, or any particular court of law in that part, have or has jurisdiction in proceedings where—

(a) the subject-matter of the proceedings is within the scope of the Regulation as determined by Article 1 of the Regulation (whether or not the Regulation has effect in relation to the proceedings); and
(b) the defendant ... is domiciled in the United Kingdom or the proceedings are of a kind mentioned in Article 22 of the Regulation (exclusive jurisdiction regardless of domicile).

6.1.4   The scope of section 16 is limited in the sense that the rules in schedule 4 do not apply to all situations where the effect of the Brussels I Regulation is to allocate jurisdiction to the courts of the United Kingdom, rather than to the courts for a place within the United Kingdom. There are two points to note. First, some matters which fall within the material scope of Article 1 of the Brussels I Regulation are excluded from schedule 4.[4] Secondly, with the exception of rule 11[5] (which applies regardless of domicile), schedule 4 applies only where the defendant is domiciled in the United Kingdom.[6] This creates potential problems as regards Article 23 of the Brussels I Regulation.

6.1.5   Where, for example, a dispute between a Scotsman and a Brazilian arises under a contract which contains an English jurisdiction clause, if the Brazilian sues the Scotsman for breach of contract in the United Kingdom, jurisdiction is determined by the combined effect of the Brussels I Regulation and schedule 4, whereas if the Scotsman sues the Brazilian, only the Brussels I Regulation applies. What, therefore, is the effect of a jurisdiction clause in favour of the English courts in a case falling within the Brussels I Regulation but not within schedule 4? In the usual case, where the parties have identified the courts of a part of the United Kingdom, Article 23 should be interpreted as allocating jurisdiction to the courts of that part. There is no obvious solution, however, to the situation where the parties expressly agree to the jurisdiction of 'the courts of the United Kingdom' or to the jurisdiction of the

---

[4] Civil Jurisdiction and Judgments Act 1982, s 17 and sched 5.
[5] Rule 11 is the equivalent of Art 22 of the Brussels I Reg.
[6] Civil Jurisdiction and Judgments Act 1982, s 16(1)(b).

'British courts'. The indications are that such clauses will be interpreted—at least in England—as agreements in favour of the English courts.[7]

The Text of Schedule 4

6.1.6   Many of the provisions of schedule 4 reproduce the text of Chapter II of the Brussels I Regulation, substituting the words 'part of the United Kingdom' or 'part' for 'Member State'. There are, however, various provisions of schedule 4 which differ from the equivalent provisions of the Brussels I Regulation; there are also some additions and some omissions.

6.1.7   As regards the provisions which set out the bases on which a court may exercise jurisdiction, the major omission is that schedule 4 contains no special jurisdiction rules dealing with matters relating to insurance. Where Section 3 of Chapter II confers jurisdiction on the courts of the United Kingdom (rather than on the courts for a place within the United Kingdom) or where a dispute relating to insurance is internal to the United Kingdom, the general jurisdiction rules of schedule 4 have to be applied. Schedule 4 also contains no provisions which are equivalent to Articles 27 to 30.[8]

Interpretation

6.1.8   To the extent that the provisions of the Brussels I Regulation and schedule 4 are the same they should be interpreted in the same way. Section 16(3) of the 1982 Act provides:

In determining any question as to the meaning or effect of any provision contained in Schedule 4—

(a) regard shall be had to any relevant principles laid down by the European Court in connection with Title II of the 1968 Convention or Chapter II of the Regulation and to any relevant decision of that court as to the meaning or effect of any provision of that Title or that Chapter; and

(b) without prejudice to the generality of paragraph (a), the reports mentioned in section 3(3)[9] may be considered and shall, so far as relevant, be given such weight as is appropriate in the circumstances.

6.1.9   Even though many of the provisions of schedule 4 are identical (or nearly identical) to the equivalent provisions of the Brussels I Regulation (and the Brussels Convention), the Court of Justice has no jurisdiction under Article 267 of the Treaty on the Functioning of the European Union to rule on the interpretation of schedule 4. In *Kleinwort Benson Ltd v City of Glasgow District Council*[10] the Court of Appeal referred

---

[7] *The Komninos S* [1990] 1 Lloyd's Rep 541. See para 14.2.17.
[8] See ch 9.
[9] See para 3.2.5.
[10] Case C–346/93 [1995] ECR I–615. G Betlem, (1996) 33 *CML Rev* 137; EM Bishop, 'Kleinwort Benson: A Good Example of Judicial Self-Restraint' (1995) 20 *EL Rev* 495; A Briggs, (1995) 15 *YBEL* 492; L Collins, 'The Brussels Convention within the United Kingdom' (1995) 111 *LQR* 541; E Peel, 'Non-admissibility and restitution in the European Court of Justice' [1996] *LMCLQ* 8.

various questions concerning the interpretation of the provision of schedule 4 which corresponded to Article 5 of the Brussels Convention. The Court of Justice's conclusion that it did not have jurisdiction was largely based on the fact that under section 16(3) of the Civil Jurisdiction and Judgments Act 1982 the courts of the United Kingdom are required only to have regard to the jurisprudence of the Court of Justice with the consequence that any ruling would not be binding on the court making the reference.[11]

6.2 BASES OF JURISDICTION UNDER SCHEDULE 4

6.2.1   Schedule 4 takes as its starting point the principle that a person 'domiciled in a part of the United Kingdom shall be sued in the courts of that part'.[12] The only circumstances in which a person domiciled in a part of the United Kingdom may be sued in the courts of another part of the United Kingdom are those set out in the other provisions of schedule 4 itself.

Exclusive Jurisdiction

6.2.2   Article 22 of the Brussels I Regulation confers exclusive jurisdiction on a Member State. Where that state is the United Kingdom, rule 11 of schedule 4 allocates jurisdiction to the courts of part of the United Kingdom. Rule 11 also allocates jurisdiction in cases which are internal to the United Kingdom.[13] Where the courts of one part of the United Kingdom have exclusive jurisdiction under rule 11, a court in another part of the United Kingdom must declare of its own motion that it has no jurisdiction.[14]

6.2.3   In the main rule 11 of schedule 4 is in the same form as Article 22 of the Brussels I Regulation. There are, however, two differences. First, rule 11 does not reproduce Article 22(4), which deals with certain proceedings relating to intellectual property rights. Indeed, proceedings concerned with the registration or validity of patents, trade marks, designs or other similar rights are excluded from the scope of schedule 4 altogether.[15] Since all the United Kingdom registers concerned with patents, trade marks and designs are located in England, the practical effect of Article 22(4) of the Brussels I Regulation is to allocate exclusive jurisdiction to the English courts.

6.2.4   Secondly, Article 22(2) of the Brussels I Regulation allocates exclusive jurisdiction with regard to various proceedings involving companies, including proceedings concerning the decisions taken by the organs of companies. Rule 11(b) adopts the approach of the Brussels I Regulation as regards proceedings concerning the constitution, the nullity or the dissolution of companies. However, as regards

---

[11]   Case C–346/93 [1995] ECR I–615, paras 23–4.
[12]   Sched 4, r 1.
[13]   Civil Jurisdiction and Judgments Act 1982, s 16(1)(b).
[14]   Sched 4, r 14.
[15]   Civil Jurisdiction and Judgments Act 1982, s 17 and sched 5, para 2.

proceedings concerned with the decisions of the organs of companies, rule 4 (which has no counterpart in the Brussels I Regulation) provides:

Proceedings which have as their object a decision of an organ of a company or other legal person or of an association of natural or legal persons may, without prejudice to the other provisions of this Schedule, be brought in the courts of the part of the United Kingdom in which that company, legal person or association has its seat.[16]

Prorogation of Jurisdiction

Submission

6.2.5 Rule 13 of schedule 4, which is in terms similar to Article 24 of the Brussels I Regulation, applies only where the defendant is domiciled in the United Kingdom.[17] So, where a person domiciled in Scotland enters an appearance in England the effect of rule 13 is to confer jurisdiction on the English court. This rule does not apply where the defendant appears to contest jurisdiction or where another court has exclusive jurisdiction under rule 11.[18]

Jurisdiction Agreements

6.2.6 Rule 12 of schedule 4 provides a mechanism for allocating jurisdiction to the courts of England, Scotland or Northern Ireland not only in cases where the dispute is internal to the United Kingdom[19] (for example, where a contractual dispute between a Scotsman and a company domiciled in Northern Ireland arises out of an agreement which contains an English jurisdiction clause), but also where Article 23 of the Brussels I Regulation confers jurisdiction on the courts of the United Kingdom and the defendant is domiciled in a part of the United Kingdom.[20] Rule 12(1) provides:

If the parties have agreed that a court or the courts of a part of the United Kingdom are to have jurisdiction to settle any disputes which have arisen or which may arise in connection with a particular legal relationship, and, apart from this Schedule, the agreement would be effective to confer jurisdiction under the law of that part, that court or those courts shall have jurisdiction.

6.2.7 It is also provided that agreements on jurisdiction shall have no legal force if they are contrary to the provisions of rule 9 (which limits the effectiveness of jurisdiction clauses in consumer contracts) or if the courts whose jurisdiction they purport to exclude have exclusive jurisdiction by virtue of rule 11.[21] Furthermore, in relation to

---

[16] For the purposes of Art 22(2) of the Brussels I Reg, 'seat' is to be determined by Civil Jurisdiction and Judgments Order 2001, sched 1, para 10.
[17] Civil Jurisdiction and Judgments Act 1982, s 16(1)(a).
[18] Sched 4, r 13(2).
[19] See, eg, *Snookes v Jani-King* [2006] ILPr 433, 451–3 (at [56]–[62]).
[20] Civil Jurisdiction and Judgments Act 1982, s 16(1)(a).
[21] Sched 4, r 12(3).

individual contracts of employment, a jurisdiction agreement is effective only if it is entered into after the dispute has arisen or if it allows the employee to bring proceedings in courts other than those indicated by rule 10.[22]

6.2.8   The first paragraph of rule 12 is drafted differently from Article 23(1) of the Brussels I Regulation in two respects. First, whereas Article 23 of the Brussels I Regulation provides that jurisdiction is exclusive 'unless the parties have agreed otherwise', rule 12(1) states merely that the courts of the part of the United Kingdom chosen by the parties 'shall have jurisdiction'. So, if a contractual dispute arises between a Scotsman and a German in circumstances in which the English courts have jurisdiction under Article 5(1) of the Brussels I Regulation (because England is the place of performance of the obligation in question) and the Scots courts have jurisdiction by virtue of the parties' agreement, if the German starts proceedings in England for breach of contract, neither Article 23 of the Brussels I Regulation nor rule 12 of schedule 4 requires the court to stay the proceedings in favour of the courts of Scotland.[23] Similarly, where a contract between one party domiciled in Scotland and the other domiciled in England includes an English jurisdiction clause, the courts of Scotland and England have concurrent jurisdiction in respect of proceedings brought against the party domiciled in Scotland—under rules 1 and 12 respectively.[24] Secondly, rule 12 does not impose any requirements as to form. Instead it is provided that to confer jurisdiction on the courts of a part of the United Kingdom the agreement must be effective under the law of that part.

Special Jurisdiction

6.2.9   In most cases falling within its scope, Article 5 of the Brussels I Regulation allocates jurisdiction to the courts for a place in a Member State. In general, therefore, rule 3 of schedule 4, which is based on Article 5 of the Regulation, is relevant only in cases which are internal to the United Kingdom. However, as regards proceedings concerning trusts which are domiciled in the United Kingdom,[25] because Article 5(6) of the Brussels I Regulation allocates jurisdiction to a Member State rather than a place, rule 3(f), the equivalent provision of schedule 4, applies to cases involving international jurisdiction as well as to internal cases. Rule 3(f) does not apply, however, in cases where the trust is domiciled in the United Kingdom but the defendant is not.[26] Where Article 5(6) of the Brussels I Regulation confers jurisdiction on the courts of the United Kingdom (because the trust is domiciled in the United Kingdom) and rule 3(f) of schedule 4 does not apply (because the defendant is not domiciled in the

---

[22]   Sched 4, r 10(5).

[23]   If, however, the parties' agreement purported to confer exclusive jurisdiction, one would normally expect the English court to stay any proceedings brought in breach of the terms of the jurisdiction clause. See section 9.5.

[24]   *British Steel Corporation v Allivane International Ltd* [1988] ECC 405 (Sheriff Court, Airdrie); *McGowan v Summit at Lloyds* 2003 SC 638 (Court of Session, Scotland).

[25]   For the purposes of the Brussels I Reg, the domicile of a trust is determined by the Civil Jurisdiction and Judgments Order 2001, sched 1, para 12.

[26]   Civil Jurisdiction and Judgments Act 1982, s 16(1)(b).

United Kingdom) it is provided that the proceedings 'shall be brought in the courts of the part of the United Kingdom in which the trust is domiciled'.[27]

6.2.10   Rule 3 is in most respects in the same form as Article 5 of the Brussels I Regulation: a person domiciled in a part of the United Kingdom may, in certain circumstances, be sued in the courts for a place identified by various paragraphs of rule 3. Two points should, however, be noted. First, rule 3(a) follows Article 5(1) of the Brussels Convention, rather than Article 5(1) of the Brussels I Regulation. Accordingly, in cases internal to the United Kingdom, jurisdiction in matters relating to a contract is determined by the place of performance of the obligation on which the claim is based;[28] there are no special rules for determining that place in cases involving contracts for the sale of goods or for the provision of services. Secondly, rule 3 of schedule 4 includes an eighth paragraph, which provides that a person domiciled in a part of the United Kingdom may also be sued:

in proceedings—

(a) concerning a debt secured on immovable property; or
(b) which are brought to assert, declare or determine proprietary or possessory rights, or rights of security, in or over movable property, or to obtain authority to dispose of movable property,

in the courts of the part of the United Kingdom in which the property is situated.

6.2.11   Rules 5 and 6 of schedule 4 reproduce, as between the different parts of the United Kingdom, Articles 6 and 7 of the Brussels I Regulation which apply as between the Member States. Rule 6 and the first three paragraphs of rule 5 apply only to internal cases as the provisions of the Brussels I Regulation from which they are derived allocate jurisdiction to the courts for a place rather than to the courts of a Member State in general. Like rule 3(f), rule 5(d) of schedule 4 plays a dual role in the sense that it not only applies to internal cases, but supplements Article 6(4) of the Brussels I Regulation where the effect of that provision is to allocate jurisdiction to the courts of the United Kingdom.

Consumer Contracts and Individual Contracts of Employment

6.2.12   Rules 7–9 of schedule 4 are, in general terms, in the same form as Articles 15–17 of the Brussels I Regulation. They do not apply to contracts of insurance.[29] Furthermore, schedule 4 does not apply in cases where a consumer who is domiciled in the United Kingdom brings proceedings against a defendant who is domiciled elsewhere.[30] Where a claimant, in reliance on Article 16(1) of the Brussels I Regulation, brings proceedings in the United Kingdom on the ground that he is a consumer domiciled in the United Kingdom such proceedings should be brought 'in the courts

---

[27] Civil Jurisdiction and Judgments Act Order 2001, sched 1, para 7(2).
[28] See paras 5.6.30–5.6.50.
[29] Sched 4, r 7(2).
[30] Civil Jurisdiction and Judgments Act 1982, s 16(1)(b).

of the part of the United Kingdom in which he is domiciled'.[31] Rule 10 of schedule 4 covers jurisdiction in relation to individual contracts of employment and closely follows Articles 18–21 of the Brussels I Regulation.

Procedural Matters and Provisional Measures

6.2.13   Where the High Court has jurisdiction under schedule 4 the claimant may serve the claim form out of the jurisdiction on the defendant without the court's permission.[32] However, if the defendant does not enter an appearance, the English court must declare of its own motion that it has no jurisdiction unless jurisdiction is derived from schedule 4 itself.[33] Furthermore, the court shall stay the proceedings unless it has been shown that the defendant has been able to receive the originating process in sufficient time to enable him to arrange for his defence.[34] Finally, rule 16, which corresponds to Article 31 of the Brussels I Regulation, provides that the courts of part of the United Kingdom may grant provisional measures in support of proceedings in another part of the United Kingdom. For example, where proceedings within the scope of Article 1 of the Brussels I Regulation are brought in Scotland, the English court may grant a freezing injunction in aid of those substantive proceedings.[35]

---

[31]   Civil Jurisdiction and Judgments Act Order 2001, sched 1, para 8(1).
[32]   CPR 6.32.
[33]   Sched 4, r 15(1).
[34]   Sched 4, r 15(2).
[35]   Civil Jurisdiction and Judgments Act 1982, s 25(1). See sections 5.4 and 10.3.

7

BASES OF JURISDICTION *IN PERSONAM* UNDER TRADITIONAL RULES

7.0.1 Under traditional English jurisdiction rules there are three general situations in which the court may assume jurisdiction: where the defendant is present within the jurisdiction (section 7.1); where the defendant submits to the jurisdiction of the court (section 7.2); and where the case is a proper one for the court to give permission for service of process on the defendant out of the jurisdiction (section 7.3).[1]

7.0.2 These bases of jurisdiction are, however, subject to three qualifications. First, the traditional rules must be read subject to the provisions of the Brussels I Regulation[2] and the Lugano Convention which allocate jurisdiction to the courts of the various states concerned.[3] Secondly, the court may be deprived of the jurisdiction which it otherwise would have by the existence of concurrent proceedings in the courts of another Member State.[4] Thirdly, in cases where jurisdiction is based on the defendant's presence in England when the claim form was served, the court may grant a stay of the proceedings or decline jurisdiction (indeed, the court may be under a duty to do so) on one of a number of grounds: that there is a more appropriate forum abroad;[5] that the parties agreed to refer their dispute to the courts of another country;[6] that the dispute relates to foreign land or a foreign intellectual property right;[7] or that the parties agreed to refer their dispute to arbitration.[8]

7.1 PRESENCE

Individuals

Personal Service

7.1.1 The most straightforward method of invoking the jurisdiction of the court is to serve the claim form personally on the defendant in England. Except in those situations where the court has discretion to allow service abroad, service must be effected within the jurisdiction.[9] The Civil Procedure Rules provide that proceedings against

---

[1] It should also be noted that the English court may have jurisdiction in relation to certain types of claim under specific legislation (such as the Carriage by Air Acts (Application of Provisions) Order 1967).
[2] Reg (EC) 44/2001, [2001] OJ L12/1.
[3] See ch 5.
[4] Section 9.1.
[5] Section 9.2.
[6] Section 9.3.
[7] Section 9.4.
[8] Section 21.2.
[9] CPR 6.6(1).

an individual may be started by personal service;[10] a claim form is served personally on an individual 'by leaving it with that individual'.[11] If the defendant is physically within the jurisdiction, personal service presents no problems; the claimant or his agent simply hands a copy of the relevant document to the defendant. The rationale behind jurisdiction based on presence is said to be allegiance. In *Carrick v Hancock* Lord Russell of Killowen CJ said that 'the jurisdiction of a court was based upon the principle of territorial dominion, and that all persons within territorial dominion owe their allegiance to its sovereign power and obedience to all its laws and to the lawful jurisdiction of its courts'.[12] When jurisdiction is founded on the defendant's presence in England it is wholly irrelevant that the cause of action arose abroad and that the claim form was served while the defendant was present within the jurisdiction only for a short period.[13] However, if the claimant, through fraud, induces the defendant to enter the jurisdiction, the claim may be struck out as an abuse of process.[14]

7.1.2 A classic illustration of the assumption of jurisdiction on the basis of the defendant's presence is *Maharanee of Baroda v Wildenstein*.[15] In this case a contractual dispute arose between two French residents who happened to share an interest in horseracing. The plaintiff issued a writ against the defendant and the writ was served on him at the Ascot racecourse during his temporary presence in England. The validity of the service was upheld:

[U]nless the plaintiff knows full well that she has no cause of action (and that is not suggested), she did no wrong in taking out a High Court writ in the first place (foreigner though she is) and serving it here at the first available opportunity upon the defendant (foreigner though *he* also is). Both in taking it out and serving it (albeit when the defendant was fleetingly on British soil) she was doing no more than our law permits, even though it may have ruined his day at the races. Some might regard her action as bad form; none can legitimately condemn it as an abuse of legal process.[16]

7.1.3 There are numerous situations where personal service is not possible. For example, many defendants in commercial disputes are limited companies or partnerships for which different rules apply.[17] There are also special rules for service in Admiralty claims *in rem*[18] and in cases where the defendant is a foreign state.[19] In addition, it is provided that personal service is not possible where a solicitor is authorised to accept service on behalf of a party; in this situation, service must be effected on the solicitor—unless personal service is required by some other rule.[20] Finally, it should be emphasised that, in civil and commercial matters falling within the scope of the Brussels I Regulation, jurisdiction based merely on the defendant's

---

[10] CPR 6.3(1)(a).
[11] CPR 6.5(3)(a).
[12] (1895) 12 TLR 59, 60.
[13] *Colt Industries Inc v Sarlie (No 1)* [1966] 1 WLR 440. PB Carter, (1965–66) 41 *BYIL* 447.
[14] *Watkins v North American Land and Timber Co Ltd* (1904) 20 TLR 534.
[15] [1972] 2 QB 283.
[16] Edmund-Davies LJ at [1972] 2 QB 283, 294.
[17] See paras 7.1.6–7.1.18.
[18] See ch 8.
[19] See paras 2.3.58–2.3.62.
[20] CPR 6.7.

presence in England when process is served cannot be invoked against a defendant domiciled in a Member State.[21]

7.1.4 In terms of the place of service, the Civil Procedure Rules provide that, where no solicitor is acting for the party to be served and that party has not given an address for service, process may be served at the individual's 'usual or last known residence';[22] alternatively, if the person to be served is a proprietor of a business, service may be effected at the 'principal or last known place of business'.[23] As regards the mode of service, process may be served by first class post,[24] by leaving the claim form at the relevant address, by document exchange or by fax or other means of electronic communication.[25] It used to be thought that, where service is effected by post at the defendant's last known residence in England, the defendant must be present in England at the time of service for service to be valid.[26] This view was not followed, however, in *City & Country Properties Ltd v Kamali*.[27] The Court of Appeal held that postal service on the defendant's English address was valid even though, as the claimant was well aware, the defendant was not present at that address when service was effected and was out of the country at the relevant time. This decision is contrary to principle and can only be regarded as having been wrongly decided; the Court of Appeal appeared to lose sight of the fact that, unless the claimant obtains permission to serve a defendant out of the jurisdiction, the court's jurisdiction is based on the defendant's presence in England, whatever method of service is employed.

7.1.5 If the claimant serves the claim form in England in accordance with the terms of a contract between the parties and the claim form contains only a claim relating to that contract, the claim form is deemed to be served on the defendant if it is served by a method specified in the contract.[28] In appropriate circumstances, the court may authorise service by a method not permitted by the Civil Procedure Rules[29] or may even dispense with service.[30]

Companies[31]

7.1.6 Process may be served on companies in England either in accordance with the relevant provisions of the Companies Act 2006 (and regulations made under it) or under CPR 6.9.[32]

---

[21] See para 4.2.3.
[22] CPR 6.9(2). See *Cranfield v Bridgegrove Ltd* [2003] 1 WLR 2441; *Burns-Anderson Independent Network plc v Wheeler* [2005] ILPr 528.
[23] CPR 6.9(2). See *Phillips v Symes* [2002] 1 WLR 853.
[24] See *Crescent Oil and Shipping Services Ltd v Importang UEE* [1998] 1 WLR 919.
[25] CPR 6.3.
[26] *Chellaram v Chellaram (No 2)* [2002] 3 All ER 17.
[27] [2007] 1 WLR 1219. A Briggs, (2007) 78 *BYIL* 600.
[28] CPR 6.11.
[29] CPR 6.15.
[30] CPR 6.16. See, eg, *Olafsson v Gissurarson (No 2)* [2007] 1 Lloyd's Rep 188.
[31] For a critical assessment of the territorial approach of English law, see JJ Fawcett, 'A New Approach to Jurisdiction over Companies in Private International Law' (1988) 37 *ICLQ* 645.
[32] See P Rogerson, 'English Court's Jurisdiction over Companies: How Important is Service of the Claim Form in England?' (2000) 3 *CFILR* 272.

Companies Act 2006

UK COMPANIES

7.1.7   In cases where proceedings are brought against companies which are incorporated in the United Kingdom, the overwhelming majority concern civil and commercial matters falling within the scope of the Brussels I Regulation. In these cases, jurisdiction has to be determined by reference to Chapter II of the Brussels I Regulation and the rules laid down in the Civil Jurisdiction and Judgments Order 2001.[33] When jurisdiction is not determined by the Brussels I Regulation, the Companies Act 2006 is applicable.

   7.1.8   In relation to a company registered under the Companies Act 2006, a document may be served on the company by leaving it at, or sending it by post to, the company's registered office (which may be in England, Wales, Scotland or Northern Ireland[34]).[35] This is true even if the company carries on business abroad and conducts no business in England.[36] For the purposes of this rule, a foreign company which has a branch in England and registers under Part 34 of the Companies Act 2006 is not to be regarded as a company registered in England.[37] A company which is registered in Scotland or Northern Ireland, but which carries on business in England, may be served by leaving the claim form at, or by sending it to, the company's principal place of business in England; in such a case a copy must be sent by post to the company's registered office.[38] A company which is registered in Scotland or Northern Ireland, but which does not carry on business in England, may be served in Scotland or Northern Ireland only in accordance with the rules which apply to extraterritorial jurisdiction.[39]

OVERSEAS COMPANIES

7.1.9   A company is a legal person, but it has no physical existence. Accordingly, the rule which states that jurisdiction may be exercised on the basis of the defendant's physical presence in England could apply to companies only by analogy. The common law evolved various tests to determine whether a foreign company was 'here'—so that it could be served within the jurisdiction. These rules have, however, been superseded by legislation. Subject to the provisions of the Brussels I Regulation and the Lugano Convention, Part 34 of the Companies Act 2006 lays down various requirements relating to 'overseas companies' which are defined as companies 'incorporated outside the United Kingdom'.[40]

---

[33] See ch 5.
[34] Companies Act 2006, s 9(2).
[35] Companies Act 2006, s 1139(1). The Civil Procedure Rules provide that a company registered in England and Wales may be served at the 'principal office of the company' or at 'any place of business of the company within the jurisdiction which has a real connection with the claim': CPR 6.5(6).
[36] *International Credit and Investment Co (Overseas) Ltd v Adham* [1994] 1 BCLC 66.
[37] See the analysis of Longmore J in *Sea Assets Ltd v PT Garuda Indonesia* [2000] 4 All ER 371 (in the context of the Companies Act 1985).
[38] Companies Act 2006, s 1139(4).
[39] See section 7.3.
[40] Companies Act 2006, s 1044.

7.1.10   The rules for the service of process on overseas companies are to be found in the Companies Act 2006 (and the regulations made under it[41]) and the Civil Procedure Rules; the claimant may rely on either set of rules.[42] Under the 2006 Act and the 2009 Regulations an overseas company which 'opens a UK establishment' is required to deliver to the registrar of companies specified particulars of the establishment,[43] including the establishment's address[44] and the 'name and service address of every person resident in the United Kingdom authorised to accept service of documents on behalf of the company in respect of the establishment, or a statement that there is no such person'.[45] For the purposes of this rule, an 'establishment' means either a branch within the meaning of the Eleventh Company Law Directive (89/666/EEC) or 'a place of business that is not such a branch'.[46]

7.1.11   The Eleventh Company Law Directive does not attempt to define the word 'branch' and there is no case law of the Court of Justice specifically on the point. However, it may be supposed that the Court of Justice's jurisprudence developed in the context of Article 5(5) of the Brussels Convention is relevant.[47] According to the decision in *Somafer SA v Saar-Ferngas AG* a branch is:

a place of business which has the appearance of permanency, such as the extension of a parent body, has a management and is materially equipped to negotiate business with third parties so that the latter, although knowing that there will if necessary be a legal link with the parent body, the head office of which is abroad, do not have to deal directly with such parent body but may transact business at the place of business constituting the extension.[48]

7.1.12   Under the Companies Act 1985 the courts took a flexible approach to the phrase 'place of business' and there is every reason to think that the same approach is appropriate under the 2006 Act and Overseas Companies Regulations 2009. In *South India Shipping Corporation Ltd v Export-Import Bank of Korea*[49] the question was whether the office (in London) rented by a Korean bank amounted to a place of business within the meaning of the companies legislation. No business transactions were conducted from the London office, which was used solely for the purpose of gathering information and maintaining public relations with other banking and financial institutions in the United Kingdom and Europe. The Court of Appeal rejected the contention that, for premises in England to constitute a place of business, the company must be carrying on a substantial part of its business within the jurisdiction and held that the London office was a place of business for the purposes of the legislation. There is no rule of law that a company cannot establish a presence within the jurisdiction by means of activities which might be described as incidental to the company's main business.[50] It has also been held that a one-ship company with no freehold or

---

[41] Overseas Companies Regulations 2009, SI 2009/1801.
[42] CPR PD 6B 3.1(2).
[43] Companies Act 2006, s 1046; Overseas Companies Regs 2009, reg 4.
[44] Companies Act 2006, s 1046; Overseas Companies Regs 2009, reg 7(1)(a).
[45] Companies Act 2006, s 1046; Overseas Companies Regs 2009, reg 7(1)(e).
[46] Companies Act 2006, s 1046; Overseas Companies Regs 2009, reg 2.
[47] See paras 5.6.72–5.6.75.
[48] Case 33/78 [1978] ECR 2183, para 12.
[49] [1985] 1 WLR 585.
[50] See Ackner LJ at [1985] 1 WLR 585, 592.

leasehold premises in England may nevertheless be regarded as having a place of business in England if it appears that the company is run from England and the only address given by the company for correspondence is an English address.[51]

7.1.13 The rule requiring information to be provided to the companies registrar imposes an obligation to deliver a return containing the specified particulars 'within one month of having opened a UK establishment'.[52] There is, however, no requirement (as there was under the Companies Act 1985) that the overseas company's place of business should be 'established'. Accordingly, the case law on this question[53] has no obvious role to play in the 2006 Act's scheme.

7.1.14 Under section 1139(2)(a), a document may be served on an overseas company registered under the Companies Act 2006 by leaving it at, or sending it by post to, the registered address of any person resident in the United Kingdom who is authorised to accept service of documents on the company's behalf. Where an overseas company is registered under the 2006 Act, service may be effected by complying with this rule even if the company has ceased to have a place of business in England when the proceedings are commenced.[54] If there is no person authorised to accept service or if an authorised person refuses service or, for some other reason, service cannot be effected, the overseas company can be served by leaving the claim form at, or sending it by post to, any place of business of the company in the United Kingdom.[55]

7.1.15 The claimant may rely on section 1139(2) notwithstanding the fact that the dispute has no connection with the English forum; there is no requirement under section 1139 that the proceedings should relate to the business conducted in England. If any injustice results from the assumption of jurisdiction under the Companies Act 2006—for example, where the jurisdiction of the court is invoked under section 1139(2) in relation to a claim which arises after the company has ceased to have a place of business within the jurisdiction—this may, in certain circumstances, be remedied by the exercise of the court's discretion to stay the proceedings on the basis of *forum non conveniens*.[56]

Civil Procedure Rules

7.1.16 Part 6 of the Civil Procedure Rules also provides a simple mechanism for invoking the court's jurisdiction over a company which has a presence in England. Under CPR 6.9(2), in a case where a foreign company has not given an address for service and is not represented by a solicitor on whom service can be effected, service of process may be made by sending the claim form to 'any place of business of the company within the jurisdiction'.[57] For the purposes of CPR 6.9(2), a company

---

[51] *Domansa v Derin Shipping and Trading Co Inc* [2001] 1 Lloyd's Rep 362.

[52] Overseas Companies Regs 2009, reg 4(1).

[53] See, in particular, *Re Oriel* [1986] 1 WLR 180; *Cleveland Museum of Art v Capricorn Art International SA* [1990] 2 Lloyd's Rep 166.

[54] *Rome v Punjab National Bank (No 2)* [1989] 1 WLR 1211.

[55] Companies Act 2006, s 1139(2)(b).

[56] See section 9.2.

[57] A limited liability partnership can be served in England either at the principal office of the partnership or at any place of business of the partnership within the jurisdiction which has a real connection with the claim: CPR 6.9(2).

can have a place of business without it having a very substantial connection with England.[58] Some of the older common law cases—such as *Dunlop Pneumatic Tyre Co Ltd v Actien-Gesellschaft für Motor und Motorfahrzeugbau Vorm Cudell & Co*,[59] in which it was held that a German company which occupied a stand at a trade fair in England for nine days was present within the jurisdiction—would satisfy the test laid down in CPR 6.9(2). Like section 1139 of the Companies Act 2006, CPR 6.9(2) has no requirement that the claim should have any connection with the defendant's business in England.[60] Nevertheless, it is not unreasonable to suppose that, where the claimant relies upon CPR 6.9(2), the defendant will apply for (and normally obtain) a stay of proceedings on the basis of *forum non conveniens* if the claim is wholly unconnected with the defendant's activities in England.

Partnerships

7.1.17   A partnership is not a corporate body and therefore does not fall within the scope of the rules contained in the Companies Act 2006. The Civil Procedure Rules provide that a document is served personally on a partnership where the partners are being sued in the name of their firm by leaving it with a partner or with a person who has management of the partnership business (as long as the document is left at the principal place of business).[61] To constitute good service, the claimant may either serve the claim form on the partners personally or rely on another valid method of service. Where, for example, the claimant chooses to effect service by post, unless the partner has provided an address for service, the claim form must be sent either to the partner's 'usual or last known residence' or the 'principal or last known place of business of the partnership'.[62] In a situation where the partnership has no place of business in England, the partnership cannot be sued by service of process on a person who has management of the partnership business. However, the claimant can choose to sue the partnership by reference to the individual partners as partners; in such a case, if the partners can be served in England, the claimant can invoke the English court's jurisdiction.[63] Where the claimant chooses to make individual partners parties to proceedings brought against the partnership, as regards any partner who cannot be served within the jurisdiction, the claimant needs to obtain the court's permission to serve out of the jurisdiction under CPR 6.36.[64] In these circumstances, the claimant will normally be able to rely on CPR PD 6B para 3.1(3) on the basis that the partner in question is 'a necessary or proper party' to the claim brought against the partnership.[65]

---

[58] *Domansa v Derin Shipping and Trading Co Inc* [2001] 1 Lloyd's Rep 362.
[59] [1902] 1 KB 342.
[60] *Sea Assets Ltd v PT Garuda Indonesia* [2000] 4 All ER 371.
[61] CPR 6.5(3).
[62] CPR 6.9(2).
[63] *Oxnard Financing SA v Rahn* [1998] 1 WLR 1465.
[64] See section 7.3.
[65] *West of England Steamship Owners' Protection and Indemnity Association Ltd v John Holman & Sons* [1957] 1 WLR 1164.

7.1.18   Where partners are sued in the name of the firm, service of process on one of the partners is effective as regards all the partners, including those who are abroad, whether service takes place in England[66] or abroad.[67] If process is served on the person having control or management of the partnership business at the principal place of business, this is effective service on all the partners—even those whose who are not within the jurisdiction.[68]

Staying Proceedings Founded on the Defendant's Presence

7.1.19   In cases where the defendant may be served with a claim form on the basis of presence in England, the court may nevertheless be required to decline jurisdiction under Article 27 of the Brussels I Regulation because of parallel proceedings in another Member State, or it may stay the proceedings under Article 28 because of related proceedings in another Member State or under the court's inherent jurisdiction (for example, because there is a more appropriate forum for the trial of the claim abroad).[69]

7.2 SUBMISSION

7.2.1   Whereas jurisdiction based on presence is ultimately derived from the state's authority or territorial dominion, jurisdiction based on submission derives from the consent of the defendant. It is important in this context to distinguish three different situations.

Jurisdiction Agreements

7.2.2   Prior to the issue of the claim form the parties may enter an agreement to refer an existing dispute or potential disputes arising from a particular legal relationship to the English courts. Jurisdiction clauses take many different forms. For example, the parties to a bill of lading may agree to refer any dispute arising under the contract to the courts of the country where the carrier has its principal place of business.

   7.2.3   In cases where the parties to a dispute have agreed to English jurisdiction the court is not seised of proceedings simply by virtue of the issue of a claim form in England; process must be served on the defendant. Where the effect of Article 23 of the Brussels I Regulation[70] is to confer jurisdiction on the English court, the court's permission to serve the defendant out of the jurisdiction is not required; the claim form may be served on the defendant as of right.[71] Article 23 is not effective to confer

---

[66] *Lysaght Ltd v Clark & Co* [1891] 1 QB 552.
[67] *Hobbs v Australian Press Association* [1933] 1 KB 1.
[68] *Worcester City and County Banking Co v Firbank, Powling & Co* [1894] 1 QB 784.
[69] See ch 9.
[70] See section 5.3 and paras 6.2.6–6.2.8.
[71] CPR 6.33.

jurisdiction in cases where either the subject-matter of the proceedings does not fall within the scope of Article 1 of the Brussels I Regulation or neither party is domiciled in a Member State.[72] In these situations, if the defendant—whether an individual or a corporation—cannot be served within the jurisdiction and declines to put in a voluntary appearance, the claimant needs to obtain the court's permission to serve the claim form out of the jurisdiction;[73] the jurisdiction agreement, on its own, does not constitute 'submission'.

Agreements to Submit

7.2.4 An agreement to submit involves an agreement between the parties on the method whereby process is to be served. Where parties have agreed to English jurisdiction and the contract specifies the method of service, service of the claim form in accordance with the terms of the contract constitutes good service.[74] In cases governed by Article 23 of the Brussels I Regulation, there is no need for the court's permission, whether service is to be effected in England or abroad.[75] In cases where the agreement between the parties does not provide for service of process in England, the claimant must obtain the court's permission to serve the defendant out of the jurisdiction if the subject-matter of the proceedings does not fall within the scope of the Brussels I Regulation or if neither party is domiciled in a Member State.[76]

Voluntary Appearance

7.2.5 In cases where the subject-matter of the proceedings falls within the scope of the Brussels I Regulation and the defendant is domiciled in a Member State, whether the defendant has submitted to the jurisdiction of the court by voluntary appearance falls to be determined by Article 24 of the Brussels I Regulation.[77] In cases not falling within the Regulation's scope, regard should be had exclusively to the traditional rules. It is not wholly clear whether Article 24 of the Brussels I Regulation applies to defendants who are not domiciled in a Member State. In practice, however, it makes no difference whether the issue of submission is judged according to Article 24 or under the traditional rules.

7.2.6 A defendant who neither is present in England nor has agreed to submit to English jurisdiction may nevertheless confer jurisdiction on the court by appearing to

---

[72] Under the Hague Choice of Court Convention (not yet in force), the effect of a jurisdiction clause in favour of the English court will be determined by Art 5 of the Convention (rather than Art 23 of the Brussels I Regulation) if one or more of the parties to the litigation is resident in a contracting state to the Convention which is not an EU Member State: Art 26(6). Under Art 5, the forum designated by an exclusive jurisdiction clause has jurisdiction over disputes within the scope of the agreement and may not decline jurisdiction on the ground that the dispute should be decided in a court of another state.

[73] CPR 6.36, PD 6B para 3.1(6)(d). For the text of the relevant jurisdictional basis, see para 7.3.17.

[74] CPR 6.11.

[75] CPR 6.33.

[76] CPR 6.11(2).

[77] See section 5.2.

defend the case on the merits. Submission arises where, independently of any prior agreement between the parties, the defendant accepts the jurisdiction of the court by acknowledging service of the claim form without challenging the court's jurisdiction.[78] For a submission to be voluntary it must be directed to the determination of the claim which is the subject-matter of the proceedings. A challenge to jurisdiction is not a submission:

> [A] person voluntarily submits to the jurisdiction of the court if he voluntarily recognises, or has recognised, that the court has jurisdiction to hear and determine the claim which is the subject-matter of the relevant proceedings. In particular, he makes a voluntary submission to the jurisdiction if he takes a step in proceedings which in all the circumstances amounts to a recognition of the court's jurisdiction in respect of the claim which is the subject-matter of those proceedings.[79]

For example, an application for an extension of time in which to lodge a substantive defence is a sufficient step to amount to submission.[80] The same is true of an application to strike out the claim on the ground that it discloses no cause of action.[81] Whereas a request for disclosure of documents referred to in the particulars of claim does not amount to submission,[82] the position is different if the application is for disclosure of all the documents relevant to the substantive issue with a view to arguing that the claimant has no cause of action.[83] A useful test for deciding whether the steps taken by the defendant constitute submission is to ask whether a disinterested bystander with knowledge of the case would regard the acts of the defendant or his solicitor as inconsistent with the making and maintaining of his challenge to the court's jurisdiction.[84]

7.2.7   The procedure set out in the Civil Procedure Rules is to allow a defendant who is not otherwise subject to the jurisdiction of the court to agree to litigation in England. Whether or not the defendant intends to challenge the court's jurisdiction, he must acknowledge service under Part 10 of the Civil Procedure Rules; failure to do so within the specified time period entitles the claimant to obtain a default judgment.[85] A defendant submits to the jurisdiction if he chooses to acknowledge service of process and to defend on the merits. However, by acknowledging service, the defendant is not deprived of the right to challenge the court's jurisdiction.[86] Although a defendant cannot take a step in the proceedings and then challenge the court's jurisdiction, he will not be regarded as having submitted if he makes his challenge to the court's jurisdiction at the outset, even if, at the same time, he raises other objections to the claim.[87]

---

[78] *Williams & Glyn's Bank Plc v Astro Dinamico Compania Naviera SA* [1984] 1 WLR 438. See, eg, *Global Multimedia International Ltd v ARA Media Services* [2007] 1 All ER (Comm) 1160.

[79] Goff LJ in *The Messiniaki Tolmi* [1984] 1 Lloyd's Rep 266, 270.

[80] *Sage v Double A Hydraulics Ltd; Chambers v Starkings* The Times, 2 April 1992.

[81] *The Messiniaki Tolmi* [1984] 1 Lloyd's Rep 266.

[82] *Kurz v Stella Musical Veransstaltungs GmbH* [1992] Ch 196.

[83] *Caltex Trading Pte Ltd v Metro Trading International Inc* [1999] 2 Lloyd's Rep 724.

[84] See Farquharson LJ in *Sage v Double A Hydraulics Ltd; Chambers v Starkings* The Times, 2 April 1992.

[85] CPR 10.2.

[86] CPR 11(3).

[87] *Prudential Assurance Co Ltd v Prudential Insurance Co of America* [2003] 1 WLR 2295.

7.3 SERVICE OUT OF THE JURISDICTION UNDER CPR 6.36

Introduction

7.3.1 There are situations where it is appropriate for proceedings against a foreign defendant to be brought in England notwithstanding the fact that the court cannot assume jurisdiction on the basis of the defendant's presence or submission. For example, England would appear to be an appropriate forum for dealing with disputes relating to contracts which have a close connection with England or with claims arising out of accidents which occur in England. The purpose of CPR 6.36 is to enable the court to assume jurisdiction over foreign defendants in circumstances where the subject-matter of the dispute has a sufficient connection with England. Nevertheless, CPR 6.36 incorporates bases of jurisdiction which are exorbitant—in the sense that they are not founded on a close connection between the defendant and the forum. In cases falling within the material scope of the Brussels I Regulation, the bases of jurisdiction in CPR PD 6B para 3.1 cannot be invoked against a defendant who is domiciled in a Member State.[88] Furthermore, even as regards a defendant who is not domiciled in a Member State, the English court may be precluded from exercising jurisdiction under CPR 6.36 because of concurrent proceedings in another Member State.[89]

Three Issues

7.3.2 CPR 6.37(3) provides that permission to serve a defendant out of the jurisdiction shall not be granted unless the court is satisfied that England is 'the proper place in which to bring the claim'. In deciding whether or not to exercise its discretion to allow service on a defendant out of the jurisdiction the court will have regard to three issues. First, as regards the merits of the claim, there must be a 'serious issue to be tried'.[90] Secondly, the claimant must establish a good arguable case that the claim falls within one of the grounds set out in CPR PD 6B para 3.1.[91] Thirdly, the court must be satisfied that England is the *forum conveniens*—that is, the forum in which the case can most suitably be tried in the interests of the parties and the ends of justice.[92]

7.3.3 Following a number of conflicting decisions of the Court of Appeal,[93] in *Seaconsar Far East Ltd v Bank Markazi Jomhouri Islami Iran*[94] the House of Lords determined the relationship between the three elements of the enquiry. Lord Goff, with whom the other members of the House of Lords agreed, indicated that the

---

[88] Art 3.
[89] See section 9.1.
[90] *Seaconsar Far East Ltd v Bank Markazi Jomhouri Islami Iran* [1994] 1 AC 438.
[91] *Ibid.*
[92] *Spiliada Maritime Corporation v Cansulex Ltd* [1987] AC 460.
[93] See *Attock Cement Co Ltd v Romanian Bank for Foreign Trade* [1989] 1 WLR 1147; *Metall und Rohstoff AG v Donaldson Lufkin & Jenrette Inc* [1990] 1 QB 391; *Overseas Union Insurance Ltd v Incorporated General Insurance Ltd* [1992] 1 Lloyd's Rep 439; *Société Commerciale de Réassurance v ERAS (International) Ltd* [1992] 1 Lloyd's Rep 570; *Banque Paribas v Cargill International SA* [1992] 2 Lloyd's Rep 19; *Seaconsar Far East Ltd v Bank Markazi Jomhouri Islami Iran* [1993] 1 Lloyd's Rep 236.
[94] [1994] 1 AC 438. A Briggs, 'Service out of the jurisdiction gets easier: defendant, beware!' [1994] *LMCLQ* 1; PB Carter, (1993) 64 *BYIL* 464; J Perkins, [1994] *CLJ* 244.

proper approach to an application for permission to serve out of the jurisdiction is to look at each of the three aspects separately:

[A] judge faced with a question of leave to serve proceedings out of the jurisdiction ... will in practice have to consider both (1) whether jurisdiction has been sufficiently established ... under one of the paragraphs of [CPR PD 6B para 3.1], and (2) whether there is a serious issue to be tried, so as to enable him to exercise his discretion to grant leave, before he goes on to consider the exercise of that discretion, with particular reference to the issue of *forum conveniens*.[95]

The strength or weakness of the claim does not affect the way in which the court's discretion should be exercised. In the course of his speech, Lord Goff said:

Suppose that, for example, the plaintiff's case is very strong on the merits. If so, I cannot see that a case particularly strong on the merits can compensate for a weak case on *forum conveniens*. Likewise, in my opinion, a very strong connection with the English forum cannot justify a weak case on the merits, if a stronger case on the merits would otherwise be required. In truth, as I see it, the two elements are separate and distinct.[96]

Procedure

7.3.4 An application for permission to serve a defendant out of the jurisdiction must be supported by evidence stating the ground (or grounds) in CPR PD 6B para 3.1 relied upon; the applicant must also state that he believes that the claim has a reasonable prospect of success and indicate in what place or country the defendant is likely to be found.[97] The claimant must make full and frank disclosure of the material circumstances of the claim, but not of the possible defences to the claim.[98] Furthermore, if relevant facts come to light after the making of the order (such as the prior commencement of parallel proceedings abroad), the claimant is obliged to go back to the court to obtain clarification on whether, in light of the new facts, the order giving permission for service out of the jurisdiction should be set aside.[99] Although the omission of any material fact is sufficient to justify the discharge of the order giving permission,[100] the decision whether or not to discharge the order turns on the court's overriding objective of dealing with the case justly. The court may, for example, decide that, notwithstanding non-disclosure by the claimant, the order giving permission to serve out of the jurisdiction should stand and that the proper response to the non-disclosure is that a sanction in terms of costs should be imposed on the claimant.[101] If permission to serve out is given, the defendant may challenge the court's jurisdiction under Part 11 of the Civil Procedure Rules. Where the exercise of the court's discretion is contested, the defendant's application to have service set aside should not be confused with an application for a stay on the basis of *forum non conveniens* in cases where the defendant is served within the jurisdiction as of right.

95 [1994] 1 AC 438, 456–7.
96 [1994] 1 AC 438, 456.
97 CPR 6.37(1).
98 See, eg, *MRG (Japan) Ltd v Engelhard Metals Japan Ltd* [2004] 1 Lloyd's Rep 731.
99 See *Network Telecom (Europe) Ltd v Telephone Systems International Inc* [2004] 1 All ER (Comm) 418.
100 *The Hagen* [1908] P 189.
101 *Albon v Naza Motor Trading Sdn Bhd* [2007] 2 All ER 719.

Where the defendant who has been served abroad seeks to have service set aside on the ground that England is not the *forum conveniens*, the burden of proof rests on the claimant to show that—on the date on which the order giving permission was made—England was the *forum conveniens*.[102] There is a right of appeal to a judge of the High Court against decisions of the master;[103] appeals to the Court of Appeal from the High Court may be brought with permission.[104]

7.3.5   Where the claimant obtains permission to serve process out of the jurisdiction the claim form may be served in one of a variety of different ways, including by any method permitted by the law of the country in which process is to be served.[105] There is, however, an overriding condition that the Civil Procedure Rules do not require or permit the claimant to do anything which is contrary to the law of the country in which service is effected.[106] To be good service, the method of service does not have to be expressly permitted by the foreign law; it is enough that the method of service does not contravene the law of the country of service.[107] In the event of service being defective, the court has discretion to cure the defect and to regard service as valid.[108] Whether or not the court will exercise its discretion depends on the circumstances of the case. For example, the court will not normally exercise its discretion in the claimant's favour in a case where service of the claim form on the defendant is contrary to the local law.[109] Where, however, the defect relates only to administrative procedures—rather than fundamentals—and there is no doubt that the claim form expressly came to the defendant's notice, the court may decide to exercise its discretion in favour of curing the defect.[110]

A Serious Question to be Tried

7.3.6   A full investigation of the merits of the case at the jurisdictional stage of proceedings would involve an enormous waste of effort and resources. It would, however, be unfair on the defendant if the claimant could obtain permission to serve out of the jurisdiction without having to establish that he has a plausible claim. The requirement that the evidence should disclose that there is a serious issue to be tried is an attempt to balance these competing tensions. Some of the confusion in the earlier case law resulted from the fact that arguments relating to the merits may arise in two superficially similar, but crucially different, contexts. It is important to distinguish, on the one hand, the situation where jurisdiction and the merits are inextricably bound up together and, on the other, the situation where the issues which go to jurisdiction and the issues which go to the merits of the case are quite distinct.

---

[102]   *ISC Technologies Ltd v Guerin* [1992] 2 Lloyd's Rep 430; *Limit (No 3) Ltd v PDV Insurance Co* [2005] 1 CLC 515.
[103]   CPR Pt 52 and CPR PD 52.
[104]   Supreme Court Act 1981, s 18(1).
[105]   See CPR 6.24 and 6.25.
[106]   CPR 6.24(2). See *Arros Invest Ltd v Nishanov* [2004] ILPr 366.
[107]   *Habib Bank Ltd v Central Bank of Sudan* [2007] 1 WLR 470.
[108]   CPR 3.10.
[109]   *The Sky One* [1988] 1 Lloyd's Rep 238. See also *Leal v Dunlop Bio-Processes International Ltd* [1984] 1 WLR 874; *Camera Care Ltd v Victor Hasselblad* [1986] ECC 373.
[110]   *The Goldean Mariner* [1990] 2 Lloyd's Rep 215; *National Commercial Bank v Haque* [1994] CLC 230.

7.3.7 An example of a situation within the first category is where a claimant applies for permission to serve out under CPR PD 6B para 3.1(6)(a)—on the basis that the claim relates to a contract which was made in England—and the defendant challenges the court's jurisdiction by denying that there was a binding contract between the parties. In this type of case the existence of the contract is relevant both to jurisdiction and to the merits and the same standard of proof must be applied to both issues.[111] Obviously, the proper standard to be applied in this situation is the test which is applicable to questions of jurisdiction.[112] An example of the second type of case is where the claimant invokes the court's jurisdiction under CPR PD 6B para 3.1(1) on the basis that the defendant is domiciled in England and the defendant resists jurisdiction on the ground that there is no basis for the claim. In this situation the question of jurisdiction (is the defendant domiciled in England?) is distinct from the question of the merits (is the claim well-founded?). Although it used to be thought that, as regards the second question, the relevant test is that the claimant should establish a good arguable case on the merits,[113] in *Seaconsar Far East Ltd v Bank Markazi Jomhouri Islami Iran*[114] the House of Lords indicated that the courts had been proceeding on the basis of a misunderstanding—largely as a result of a misinterpretation of the decision of the House of Lords in *Vitovice Horni a Hutni Tezirstvo v Korner*.[115] There is no requirement that the claimant should establish a good arguable case on the merits: the standard of proof in respect of the cause of action is whether, on the written evidence before the court, 'there is a serious question to be tried'.[116]

7.3.8 Such a serious question arises if there is a substantial question of fact or law (or both) which the claimant bona fide desires the court to try.[117] Where, however, the alleged facts, if proved, would not support the claim, there is no 'serious issue to be tried' and permission to serve out of the jurisdiction must be refused. A case cannot be a proper one for service out of the jurisdiction if the court is satisfied that the claim must fail.[118] Under the Civil Procedure Rules the claimant's application for permission to serve out must be supported by a statement that the claimant believes that his claim has a reasonable prospect of success.[119] This test, which is 'not a high one' and requires no more than the claimant's 'chances of success are not fanciful',[120] has been held to be substantially the same as the test laid down in the *Seaconsar* case.[121]

---

[111] *Seaconsar Far East Ltd v Bank Markazi Jomhouri Islami Iran* [1994] 1 AC 438.

[112] See paras 7.3.35–7.3.37.

[113] See, eg, Parker LJ in *Banque Paribas v Cargill International SA* [1992] 2 Lloyd's Rep 19, 25; Stuart-Smith LJ in *Seaconsar Far East Ltd v Bank Markazi Jomhouri Islami Iran* [1993] 1 Lloyd's Rep 236, 248; Slade LJ in *Metall und Rohstoff AG v Donaldson Lufkin & Jenrette Inc* [1990] 1 QB 391, 434.

[114] [1994] 1 AC 438.

[115] [1951] AC 869.

[116] Lord Goff at [1994] 1 AC 438, 452.

[117] *Ibid.*

[118] See *Barings Plc v Coopers & Lybrand* [1997] ILPr 12; *Re Banco Nacional de Cuba* [2001] 1 WLR 2039; *The Prestrioka* [2003] 2 Lloyd's Rep 327.

[119] CPR 6.37(1)(b).

[120] Clarke LJ in *Carvill America Incorporated v Camperdown UK Ltd* [2005] 2 Lloyd's Rep 457, 465 (at [24]). Notwithstanding the low threshold in terms of the merits of the claim, some claims fall below the required level: see, eg, *Ophthalmic Innovations International (UK) Ltd v Ophthalmic Innovations International Inc* [2005] ILPr 109.

[121] *De Molestina v Ponton* [2002] 1 Lloyd's Rep 271; *Swiss Reinsurance Company Limited v United India Insurance Company* [2004] ILPr 53; *BAS Capital Funding Corporation v Medfinco Ltd* [2004] ILPr 305;

The Heads of CPR PD 6B para 3.1

7.3.9 CPR PD 6B para 3.1 lists the circumstances in which 'the claimant may serve a claim form out of the jurisdiction with the permission of the court under rule 6.36'. The various jurisdictional grounds are to be found in paragraphs (1)–(20). Apart from other statutory bases for the exercise of extraterritorial jurisdiction, the code set out in Part 6 of the Civil Procedure Rules is comprehensive; the court has no inherent power to allow service of process out of the jurisdiction in a case not falling within the scope of the rules.[122]

Jurisdiction Based on Domicile

7.3.10 (1) A claim is made for a remedy against a person domiciled[123] within the jurisdiction.

Where the proceedings concern civil and commercial matters within the meaning of Article 1 of the Brussels I Regulation the claimant may serve a defendant who is domiciled—but not physically present—in England as of right.[124] However, certain matters, such as arbitration, are excluded from the scope of the Regulation. In such a case, a defendant who is domiciled in England but not physically present may be served out of the jurisdiction with the court's permission.

Injunctions

7.3.11 (2) A claim is made for an injunction ordering the defendant to do or refrain from doing an act within the jurisdiction.

On the basis of the authority of the House of Lords' decision in *Siskina (Owners of cargo lately laden on board) v Distos Compania Naviera SA*,[125] where a claimant applies to the court for an injunction against a foreign defendant the application for an injunction cannot stand alone as a basis of jurisdiction. So, to be able to rely on CPR PD 6B para 3.1(2) the claimant must be able to bring the substantive claim within one of the other heads of CPR PD 6B para 3.1.

7.3.12 Obviously, an application for an anti-suit injunction—restraining a litigant from commencing or continuing proceedings abroad—cannot fall within the scope of paragraph (2).[126] Similarly, an application for a freezing injunction is not a claim which falls within the scope of what is now CPR PD 6B para 3.1(2).[127] However, given the desirability of the courts of one country being able to grant provisional

Ophthalmic Innovations International (UK) Ltd v Ophthalmic Innovations International Inc [2005] ILPr 109; *NABB Brothers Ltd v Lloyd's Bank International (Guernsey) Ltd* [2005] ILPr 506.

[122] *Re Busfield* (1886) 32 ChD 123; *Re Anglo African Steamship Co* (1886) 32 ChD 348. In cases covered by the Brussels I Regulation service may be effected out of the jurisdiction under CPR 6.33 without permission. See section 4.3.

[123] For the purposes of this provision 'domicile' is to be determined by reference to the relevant provisions of the Civil Jurisdiction and Judgments Order 2001 (SI 2001/3929): CPR 6.31(1)(i). See section 4.1.

[124] CPR 6.33(2).

[125] [1979] AC 210. K Lipstein, [1978] *CLJ* 241.

[126] *Amoco (UK) Exploration Co v British American Offshore Ltd* [1999] 2 Lloyd's Rep 772.

[127] See *Mercedes Benz AG v Leiduck* [1996] 1 AC 284.

measures in support of foreign proceedings (whether ongoing or imminent), CPR PD 6B para 3.1(5) allows permission for service out to be given where the claim is made for 'an interim remedy' under section 25(1) of the Civil Jurisdiction and Judgments Act 1982.[128] The court's power under section 25 of the 1982 Act applies whether or not the proceedings fall within the scope of the Brussels I Regulation and regardless of where the substantive proceedings are being (or will be) pursued.[129]

Multiple Defendants

7.3.13   (3) A claim is made against a person ("the defendant") on whom the claim form has been or will be served (otherwise than in reliance on this paragraph) and—

(a) there is between the claimant and the defendant a real issue which it is reasonable for the court to try; and

(b) the claimant wishes to serve the claim form on another person who is a necessary or proper party to that claim.

Paragraph (3) is a head of jurisdiction which is extremely important in practice. In a situation where there are two or more potential defendants, it may be very inconvenient if the claimant cannot proceed against them all in the same forum.[130] Paragraph (3) provides a mechanism whereby defendants who are not otherwise amenable to the jurisdiction of the court may be served out of the jurisdiction.[131]

7.3.14   There are various situations where paragraph (3) may be invoked. First, where the first defendant is sued in England as of right, other defendants may be served out of the jurisdiction under paragraph (3). Secondly, where the first defendant is served out of the jurisdiction under another of the heads of CPR PD 6B para 3.1, other defendants may be served out of the jurisdiction under paragraph (3). Paragraph (3) does not apply in cases where the substantive proceedings are abroad and the court's jurisdiction over the first defendant is based on section 25 of the Civil Jurisdiction and Judgments Act 1982.[132] Nor does paragraph (3) apply to third party proceedings (which the Civil Procedure Rules refer to as Part 20 claims). However, CPR PD 6B para 3.1 enables service out in cases where:

(4) A claim is an additional claim under Part 20 and the person to be served is a necessary or proper party to the claim or additional claim.[133]

Consider the situation where C, a manufacturer, sells goods to B, a wholesaler, who sells them to A, a retailer. Where A sues B in England (on the basis that the goods are defective) B may, if C is not otherwise amenable to the English court's jurisdiction, apply to join C to those proceedings under CPR PD 6B para 3.1(4).

---

[128]   For further discussion, see section 10.3.

[129]   Civil Jurisdiction and Judgments Act 1982 (Interim Relief) Order 1997, SI 1997/302.

[130]   See, eg, *The Goldean Mariner* [1990] 2 Lloyd's Rep 215; *Credit Agricole Indosuez v Unicof Ltd* [2004] 1 Lloyd's Rep 196.

[131]   See JJ Fawcett, 'Multi-Party Litigation in Private International Law' (1995) 44 *ICLQ* 744, 746–9.

[132]   *Belletti v Morici* [2009] ILPr 960.

[133]   See *Société Commerciale de Réassurance v ERAS (International) Ltd* [1992] 1 Lloyd's Rep 570; *The Berge Sisar* [1997] 1 Lloyd's Rep 635.

7.3.15 While paragraphs (3) and (4) provide advantages for claimants (including Part 20 claimants) they present certain risks for defendants. First, paragraph (3) is potentially open to abuse. It would be entirely wrong if a claimant were able to start proceedings in England against a 'dummy' defendant simply as a means of bringing a foreign defendant before the court. It is for this reason that the courts approach paragraphs (3) and (4) with a certain degree of caution.[134] Furthermore, the Civil Procedure Rules provide a measure of protection for defendants in these circumstances. Where the application is made under paragraph (3) the written evidence supporting the application must state 'the grounds on which the claimant believes that there is between the claimant and the defendant a real issue which it is reasonable for the court to try'.[135] This requirement is intended to ensure that the claim was brought bona fide against the first defendant and not merely to bring in the foreign defendant as a necessary or proper party.[136] If the claimant does not have a cause of action against the first defendant or if the claim is not a genuine one, the court will refuse to allow other defendants to be served out of the jurisdiction under paragraph (3).[137] Secondly, in cases falling within paragraphs (3) and (4), there is a danger that the court will exercise jurisdiction over defendants who have little or no connection with England in relation to causes of action which similarly have little or no connection with England—simply on the basis that they have a relationship with the proceedings between the claimant and the first defendant.[138]

7.3.16 To satisfy paragraph (3) or (4) all the claimant has to show is that the defendant in question is a necessary or proper party; if the defendant is a proper party the fact that he is not also a necessary party is not relevant. In deciding whether a defendant is a proper party for the purposes of paragraph (3) or (4) the court should ask itself the following question:

[S]upposing both parties had been within the jurisdiction would they both have been proper parties to the action? If they would, and only one of them is in this country, then the rule says that the other may be served, just as if he had been within the jurisdiction.[139]

A second defendant will normally be regarded as a necessary or proper party if the claim against the second defendant arises out of the same transactions as the claim against the first defendant or where the two claims give rise to common questions of fact.[140] A claimant may be able to join a second defendant to proceedings in England

---

[134] See *Multinational Gas and Petrochemical Co v Multinational Gas and Petrochemical Services Ltd* [1983] Ch 258. JJ Fawcett, 'Jurisdiction over Foreign Companies' (1984) 100 *LQR* 17.

[135] CPR 6.37(2). The substance of this phrase can be traced back to a passage in the judgment of Morton J in *Ellinger v Guinness, Mahon & Co* [1939] 4 All ER 16, 22 which was cited with approval by members of the House of Lords in *The Brabo* [1949] AC 326. The statement required by CPR 6.37(2) is in addition to the information required by CPR 6.37(1). See paras 7.3.4 and 7.3.8.

[136] See Lawrence Collins J in *Konamaneni v Rolls-Royce Industrial Power (India) Ltd* [2002] 1 All ER 979, 992 (at [44]).

[137] *New Hampshire Insurance Co v Aerospace Finance Ltd* [1998] 2 Lloyd's Rep 539; *Chase v Ram Technical Services Ltd* [2000] 2 Lloyd's Rep 418.

[138] See, eg, *The Kapetan Georgis* [1988] 1 Lloyd's Rep 352; J Hill, 'Jurisdiction in Civil and Commercial Matters: Is There a Third Way?' (2001) 54 *CLP* 439, 467–8.

[139] Lord Esher MR in *Massey v Heynes & Co* (1888) 21 QBD 330, 338. See *Carvill America Incorporated v Camperdown UK Ltd* [2005] 2 Lloyd's Rep 457, 468.

[140] See, eg, *United Film Distribution v Chhabria* [2001] 2 All ER (Comm) 865; *Alberta Inc v Katanga Mining Ltd* [2009] ILPr 175.

under paragraph (3), notwithstanding the fact that jurisdiction under CPR PD 6B para 3.1 could not have been exercised in relation to that defendant if he had been the primary defendant.[141]

Contract

7.3.17   (6) A claim made in respect of a contract where the contract—

        (a) was made within the jurisdiction;
        (b) was made by or through an agent trading or residing within the jurisdiction;
        (c) is governed by English law; or
        (d) contains a term to the effect that the court shall have jurisdiction to determine any claim in respect of the contract.

Another ground under CPR PD 6B para 3.1 is where:

(8) A claim is made for a declaration that no contract exists where, if the contract was found to exist, it would comply with the conditions set out in paragraph (6).

GENERAL SCOPE

7.3.18   As a general rule, for the purposes of paragraph (6), the contract which is the subject-matter of the litigation is a contract between the claimant and the defendant.[142] A claim by X for a declaration that a contract between Y and Z has come to an end does not fall within paragraph (6).[143] However, the claim of an assignee to enforce rights arising under a contract does fall within the scope of paragraph (6), as does a claim that liabilities under a contract have been transferred to the defendant.[144] Similarly, where C incurs a loss on behalf of B and that loss is covered by a contract of insurance between B and A (the insurer), C's claim for contribution (under the Civil Liability (Contribution) Act 1978) against A may be 'in respect of a contract' for the purposes of paragraph (6).[145] Furthermore, in a case where C has a claim for breach of contract against either D1 or D2, the fact that, when the proceedings are commenced, it is not clear which of the two defendants should properly be regarded as having assumed the obligations which have been breached is not an obstacle to the claims against each defendant being regarded as falling within paragraph (6).[146] It has been held that the word 'contract' must be interpreted strictly; paragraph (6) does not extend to the relationship created by the appointment of a company director, even though such a relationship is analogous to a contractual relationship.[147]

---

[141]   *ISC Technologies Ltd v Guerin* [1992] 2 Lloyd's Rep 430.
[142]   *Finnish Marine Insurance Co Ltd v Protective National Insurance Co* [1990] 1 QB 1078 (PB Carter, (1990) 61 *BYIL* 395); *Bastone & Firminger Ltd v Nasima Enterprises (Nigeria) Ltd* [1996] CLC 1902; *Amoco (UK) Exploration Co v British American Offshore Ltd* [1999] 2 Lloyd's Rep 772; *United Film Distribution v Chhabria* [2001] 2 All ER (Comm) 865.
[143]   *HIB Ltd v Guardian Insurance Co Inc* [1997] 1 Lloyd's Rep 412.
[144]   *DR Insurance Co v Central National Insurance Co* [1996] 1 Lloyd's Rep 74.
[145]   *Greene Wood & McLean v Templeton Insurance Ltd* [2009] 1 WLR 2013.
[146]   *The Ines* [1993] 2 Lloyd's Rep 492.
[147]   *Newtherapeutics Ltd v Katz* [1991] Ch 226.

7.3.19   Paragraph (6) encompasses a claim for a declaration that a contract has been rescinded for misrepresentation or a claim that a contract has been discharged by frustration,[148] as well as a claim for a declaration that a contractual term remains enforceable between the parties.[149] Because of uncertainties under the old Rules of the Supreme Court,[150] paragraph (8) makes it clear that permission to serve out may be given in cases where the claimant asserts that no contract with the defendant was ever concluded.

7.3.20   Although the words 'in respect of' are very wide,[151] in order to fall within paragraph (6), the claim must be designed to ascertain the substantive rights of the claimant.[152] Where a claimant seeks a declaration that, even if the terms of a contract have been broken, the defendant suffered no loss, the claim falls within paragraph (6).[153] As a general rule, it is not sufficient that a contract provides part of the factual background to the claim; paragraph (6) requires 'some direct effect upon the relevant contract'.[154] However, there has been a suggestion that, in certain circumstances, where there is a direct link between two contracts, a claim arising out of a contract which, viewed in isolation, cannot be the subject of permission to serve out of the jurisdiction, may nevertheless be regarded as falling within the scope of paragraph (6) if that claim affects another contract which is covered by one or more of subparagraphs (a)–(d).[155] But, even this approach has limits:

[S]uppose that an English company has two contracts with a contractor. The first is a foreign contract for some prefabrication which is entirely outside [CPR PD 6B para 3.1]. The second is a construction contract to be performed in this country by means of the materials to be prefabricated abroad under the foreign contract. Suppose that there is then a breach of the foreign contract. … [I]t could not possibly be right that the company could obtain leave to serve abroad a claim under the foreign prefabrication contract merely on the ground that its breach has had some consequences for, or repercussions upon, the due performance of the English contract.[156]

7.3.21   There is some uncertainty over the extent to which restitutionary claims fall within the scope of paragraph (6). Some of the older authorities suggest that any restitutionary claim may be brought within paragraph (6) on the basis that a claim which is founded on quasi-contract relates to a contract.[157] Such an approach is difficult to reconcile with more recent developments in the law of restitution. The older cases were decided at a time when the implied contract theory of restitution, a theory which has

---

[148]   *BP Exploration Co (Libya) Ltd v Hunt* [1976] 1 WLR 788.

[149]   *Gulf Bank KSC v Mitsubishi Heavy Industries Ltd* [1994] 1 Lloyd's Rep 323.

[150]   See *The Olib* [1991] 2 Lloyd's Rep 108; *DR Insurance Co v Central National Insurance Co* [1996] 1 Lloyd's Rep 74.

[151]   The courts took an expansive interpretation to the equivalent paragraph of RSC Order 11, r 1(1): see Kerr J in *BP Exploration Co (Libya) Ltd v Hunt* [1976] 1 WLR 788, 795.

[152]   *Cool Carriers AB v HSBC Bank USA* [2001] 2 All ER (Comm) 177 (a claim for interpleader relief is not a claim made in respect of a contract).

[153]   *HIB Ltd v Guardian Insurance Co Inc* [1997] 1 Lloyd's Rep 412.

[154]   Knox J in *Re Baltic Real Estate (No 2)* [1993] BCLC 503, 505. See also *ABCI v Banque-Franco-Tunisienne* [2003] 2 Lloyd's Rep 146.

[155]   *EF Hutton & Co (London) Ltd v Monfarrij* [1989] 1 WLR 488.

[156]   Kerr LJ in *EF Hutton & Co (London) Ltd v Monfarrij* [1989] 1 WLR 488, 494.

[157]   *Bowling v Cox* [1926] AC 751; *Re Jogia* [1988] 1 WLR 484.

been definitively rejected by modern commentators, held sway.[158] On the one hand, as a matter of principle, a restitutionary claim which is wholly unconnected with a contract should not fall within paragraph (6) and it seems that modern authorities accept that not every claim which can be described as restitutionary or quasi-contractual necessarily falls within paragraph (6).[159] On the other hand, a claim does not have to be contractual to fall within the scope of CPR PD 6B para 3.1(6); the claim has only to be 'in respect of a contract', a phrase which is wider than 'under a contract'.[160] It can be argued, on the basis of the House of Lords' decision in *Kleinwort Benson Ltd v Glasgow City Council*[161]—a case concerning the meaning of the phrase 'matters relating to a contract' for the purposes of schedule 4 to the Civil Jurisdiction and Judgments Act 1982—that, whereas a claim involving a restitutionary claim which arises out of a contract which is voidable or unenforceable falls within the scope of paragraph (6), a restitutionary claim arising out of a contract which is void *ab initio* does not. However, as the House of Lords drew attention to the fact that the wording of paragraph (6) differs from the wording of Article 5(1),[162] it has been doubted whether *Kleinwort Benson Ltd v Glasgow City Council* provides much assistance in cases not governed by the Brussels I Regulation.[163] A further argument against restitutionary claims being within paragraph (6) is that the Civil Procedure Rules (unlike the Rules of the Supreme Court which they replaced) contain, in paragraph (16), a separate head of jurisdiction covering claims for restitution.[164] Nevertheless, it has been held that a claim for restitution of overpayments made under a mistake of fact by the claimant to the defendant in the course of performance of a contract between the parties falls within the scope of CPR PD 6B para 3.1(6).[165]

CONTRACTS MADE WITHIN THE JURISDICTION

7.3.22 It is for English law as the law of the forum to determine whether or not a contract is made within the jurisdiction. The traditional view is that, whereas a contract concluded by exchange of letters is made where the acceptance of the offer is posted,[166] a contract concluded by telephone or telex is made where the offeror receives notification of acceptance.[167] By analogy, a contract concluded by fax is concluded where the acceptance is received. The position in relation to a contract concluded by an exchange of emails or via an interactive website has yet to be addressed by the courts. There is a good argument that such a contract should be treated in the same way as contracts concluded by telex or fax.[168] In certain situations, analysis in

---

[158] See A Briggs, 'Jurisdiction under Traditional Rules' in FD Rose (ed), *Restitution and the Conflict of Laws* (Oxford, Mansfield Press, 1995) 49–63.

[159] See, eg, Clarke J in *The Kurnia Dewi* [1997] 1 Lloyd's Rep 552, 561.

[160] See Lightman J in *Albon v Naza Motor Trading Sdn Bhd* [2007] 2 All ER 719, 729 (at [26]).

[161] [1997] 1 AC 153.

[162] Lord Hutton at [1997] 3 WLR 973, 955.

[163] *Albon v Naza Motor Trading Sdn Bhd* [2007] 2 All ER 719.

[164] See para 7.3.32.

[165] *Albon v Naza Motor Trading Sdn Bhd* [2007] 2 All ER 719.

[166] *Benaim & Co v Debono* [1924] AC 514.

[167] *Entores Ltd v Miles Far East Corporation* [1955] 2 QB 327; *Brinkibon Ltd v Stahag Stahl und Stahlwarenhandelsgesellschaft mbH* [1983] 2 AC 34.

[168] See J Hill, *Cross-Border Consumer Contracts* (Oxford, OUP, 2008) 23–8.

terms of offer and acceptance is extremely forced and the designation of a single juris-diction as the place where the contract was made seems both arbitrary and artificial. For example, where, during the course of a telephone conversation, two contracting parties in different countries finally indicate their consent to a contract which they have previously negotiated, the contract should be regarded as having been made in both countries; as long as England is one of the countries, the requirements of CPR PD 6B para 3.1(6)(a) are satisfied.[169]

7.3.23 Potential problems arise in cases where a contract is negotiated in one country but formally signed in another or where a contract is concluded in one country and then confirmed or amended in another. It has been held that a contract may be regarded as made within the jurisdiction, notwithstanding the fact that it was preceded by a less formal agreement which was made abroad. In *Gibbon v Commerz und Creditbank AG*[170] the parties reached an agreement in Hamburg, but letters were subsequently exchanged in London. The Court of Appeal decided that the agreement was made in London on the basis that the written agreement superseded what was agreed in Hamburg.[171] However, it would follow that, in a situation where a written agreement signed in England merely evidences a concluded oral contract which was made abroad, the claimant should not be able to rely on CPR PD 6B para 3.1(6)(a).

7.3.24 In *BP Exploration Co (Libya) Ltd v Hunt*[172] the parties had entered an agreement in London in 1960. In 1967 this agreement was partly amended in Texas. The 1967 amendment could not, however, stand alone; it merely amended certain provisions of the 1960 agreement. It was argued on behalf of the defendant that, since the contract had been made partly in England and partly in Texas, the court was unable to allow service out of the jurisdiction. Two propositions emerge (albeit *obiter*) from Kerr J's judgment. First, if the effect of the amendment is to discharge completely the original agreement, the contract is to be regarded for jurisdictional purposes as having been made at the place where it is amended. Conversely, a contract concluded in England, but amended abroad, is 'made within the jurisdiction' for the purposes of CPR PD 6B, para 3.1(6)(a).[173] Secondly, where a contract is made partly within the jurisdiction and partly abroad, 'it is sufficient for the purposes of the rule if the contract which is the subject-matter of the action was substantially made within the jurisdiction'.[174]

CONTRACTS CONCLUDED THROUGH AN AGENT IN ENGLAND
7.3.25 Subparagraph (b) applies to cases where the contract is negotiated by an agent in England, but is concluded by the principal abroad. (If the agent concludes the contract in England on the principal's behalf, the case falls within subparagraph (a).) The existence of this head of jurisdiction is justified on the basis that if for-eigners choose to carry on business in England by means of agents it is only right and proper that claimants should be able to serve them even though they are out of

---

[169] See *Apple Corps Limited v Apple Computer Inc* [2004] ILPr 597.
[170] [1958] 2 Lloyd's Rep 113.
[171] See Morris LJ at [1958] 2 Lloyd's Rep 113, 120.
[172] [1976] 1 WLR 788. PB Carter, (1976–7) 48 *BYIL* 371.
[173] *Sharab v Al-Saud* [2009] 2 Lloyd's Rep 160.
[174] [1976] 1 WLR 788, 798.

the jurisdiction.[175] Where it is the claimant rather than the defendant who conducts business in England through an agent, there is no justification for the exercise of jurisdiction over the foreign defendant. Accordingly, subparagraph (b) is relevant only where the agent through whom the contract was made was acting on behalf of the defendant; a claimant cannot obtain permission to serve a claim form on a defendant outside the jurisdiction on the basis that the contract was made through the former's English agent.[176]

CONTRACTS GOVERNED BY ENGLISH LAW

7.3.26 Applications for permission to serve out of the jurisdiction on the ground that the dispute relates to a contract governed by English law have provided numerous opportunities for the development and interpretation of contractual choice of law rules by the English courts.[177] As a general rule, the law governing a contract is determined by one of three choice of law regimes: (i) for contracts either concluded before 1 April 1991 or concerning matters falling outside the material scope of the Rome Convention or the Rome I Regulation, the common law choice of law rules apply; (ii) as regards contracts concluded between 1 April 1991 (the date on which the Rome Convention on the Law Applicable to Contractual Obligations was implemented into English law by the Contracts (Applicable Law) Act 1990) and 17 December 2009 (the day before the entry into force of the Rome I Regulation[178]), the choice of law rules set out in the Rome Convention apply; (iii) with regard to contracts concluded on or after 17 December 2009, the Rome I Regulation applies.[179]

7.3.27 As one of the matters excluded from the scope of the Rome Convention and the Rome I Regulation is 'procedure',[180] it might be argued that the common law rules should determine whether a contract is governed by English law for the purposes of subparagraph (c). Although the Civil Procedure Rules are procedural, they incorporate issues of substantive law. The law governing a contract for the purposes of subparagraph (c) is a substantive question, which—as regards any contract falling within the Rome I Regulation's scope—is to be determined by reference to the rules contained in the Regulation.[181]

JURISDICTION CLAUSES IN FAVOUR OF THE ENGLISH COURTS

7.3.28 Many contracts contain a jurisdiction clause, that is, an agreement to refer disputes arising out of a legal relationship to the courts of a particular country. If

---

[175] Atkin LJ in *National Mortgage and Agency Co of New Zealand Ltd v Gosselin* (1922) 38 TLR 832, 833.

[176] *Union International Insurance Co Ltd v Jubilee Insurance Co Ltd* [1991] 1 WLR 415.

[177] Eg, *Amin Rasheed Shipping Corporation v Kuwait Insurance Co* [1984] AC 50. See JJ Fawcett, 'The Interrelationships of Jurisdiction and Choice of Law in Private International Law' (1991) 44 *CLP* 38.

[178] Reg (EC) 593/2008, [2008] OJ L177/6.

[179] Art 28. For a discussion of choice of law in contract, see ch 14.

[180] Rome Convention, Art 1(2)(h); Rome I Reg, Art 1(3).

[181] See, in the context of the Rome Convention, *Bank of Baroda v Vysya Bank* [1994] 2 Lloyd's Rep 87, *Egon Oldendorff v Libera Corporation* [1996] 1 Lloyd's Rep 380; *HIB Ltd v Guardian Insurance Co* [1997] 1 Lloyd's Rep 412; *Marubeni Hong Kong and South China Ltd v Mongolian Government* [2002] 2 All ER (Comm) 873; *Tiernan v The Magen Insurance Co Ltd* [2000] ILPr 517; *Marconi Communications International Inc v PT Pan Indonesia Bank Ltd Tbk* [2007] 2 Lloyd's Rep 72.

the agreement provides a contractual method for the service of process within the jurisdiction the claimant may employ that agreed method.[182] In most situations CPR PD 6B para 3.1(6)(d) is displaced by Article 23 of the Brussels I Regulation,[183] under which the claimant may serve a foreign defendant out of the jurisdiction without the court's permission.[184] In cases where jurisdiction is not allocated by the Regulation, the claimant requires the court's permission for service out of the jurisdiction.[185] There seems to be no reported case in which the court has refused to give permission in a situation where the claim falls within CPR PD 6B para 3.1(6)(d) (or its predecessors). It should be noted, however, that there is no jurisdiction under paragraph (6)(d) where the parties have agreed to refer a claim in tort to English jurisdiction.[186]

Breach of Contract within the Jurisdiction

7.3.29 (7) A claim is made in respect of a breach of contract committed within the jurisdiction.

For paragraph (7) to apply there must have been a contract between the parties, the defendant must be guilty of breach and the breach must have occurred in England. In principle, where the contract is breached by non-performance, the place where the breach has been committed should be determined by the law which governs the contract. In the context of cases involving a claim based on breach of a payment obligation, there are some English authorities which support this proposition.[187] However, such instances are the exception; in the majority of cases the parties do not plead the relevant foreign law and the courts apply English law to determine the place of breach.

Tort

7.3.30 (9) A claim is made in tort where—

> (a) damage was sustained within the jurisdiction; or
> (b) the damage sustained resulted from an act committed within the jurisdiction.

Until 1987 service out in tort cases was possible only if the claim was 'founded on a tort committed within the jurisdiction'. The current verbal formulation, which was inspired by the Court of Justice's interpretation of Article 5(3) of the Brussels Convention,[188] avoids the problems associated with having to determine the place of the tort in cases where the wrongful act is committed in one country and the damage

---

[182] CPR 6.11.
[183] See section 5.3.
[184] CPR 6.33.
[185] It can be assumed that, after the entry into force of the Hague Choice of Court Convention (see paras 7.3.47–7.3.50), when the English court has jurisdiction under that Convention, service out of the jurisdiction will not require the court's permission.
[186] *The Anna L* [1994] 2 Lloyd's Rep 379.
[187] See, eg, *Malik v Narodni Banka Ceskoslovenska* [1946] 2 All ER 663.
[188] Case 21/76 *Handelskwekerij GJ Bier BV v Mines de Potasse d'Alsace SA* [1976] ECR 1735.

is sustained in another. In order for the claimant to be able to rely on paragraph (9) the court must be satisfied, first, that the claim is founded on a tort and, secondly, that either the damage was sustained within the jurisdiction or the damage resulted from an act committed within the jurisdiction. When the court is considering the second of these issues, it seems that the case law of the Court of Justice (and the English courts) with regard to Article 5(3)[189] may be regarded as being of, at least, persuasive authority.[190]

7.3.31   First, to decide whether or not the claim is 'founded on a tort' within the meaning of paragraph (9) 'the courts will apply exclusively English law'.[191] So, where the claimant alleges that he was libelled by an article in a magazine with a worldwide circulation, the claimant may invoke paragraph (9) even if only a very small number of the magazines were distributed in England as, under English law, each publication constitutes a separate tort.[192] Claims to equitable restitutionary remedies for breach of trust or breach of fiduciary duty are not 'founded on a tort' and therefore must be brought within some other paragraph of CPR PD 6B para 3.1.[193] Secondly, for the purposes of paragraph (9), it is enough that 'some significant damage has been sustained in England'.[194] It has generally been held that the damage caused must be direct rather than indirect and the fact that the defendant's conduct has had an effect on the claimant's financial position in England is not sufficient to bring the case within the scope of paragraph (9).[195] So, an English company is not able to rely on paragraph (9) simply on the basis that its financial interests have suffered because it is the parent of a foreign company which has been damaged by a tort abroad. Rather surprisingly, in *Booth v Phillips*[196] a widow claiming under the Fatal Accident Acts following the death of her husband working abroad was able to rely on paragraph (9) on the basis that her loss of financial dependency was damage sustained in England (where she lived). Equally surprisingly, the case was followed in *Cooley v Ramsay*,[197] a case in which the victim of a traffic accident in Australia successfully applied for service out under CPR PD 6B para 3.1(9) on the basis that economic loss consequent upon the accident occurred in England. If it is alleged that defamatory material posted on an internet website has damaged the claimant's reputation in England, the claim falls within CPR PD 6B para 3.1(9) if the website can be accessed and the material downloaded in England; it is irrelevant that the website is accessible all over the world.[198] Thirdly, in the context of CPR PD 6B para 3.1(9) the 'central question

---

[189] See paras 5.6.53–5.6.70.

[190] *ABCI v Banque Franco-Tunisienne* [2003] 2 Lloyd's 146.

[191] Slade LJ in *Metall und Rohstoff AG v Donaldson Lufkin & Jenrette Inc* [1990] 1 QB 391, 443. PB Carter, (1989) 60 *BYIL* 485; R Fentiman, [1989] *CLJ* 191.

[192] *Berezovsky v Michaels* [2000] 1 WLR 1004. A Briggs, (2000) 71 *BYIL* 440; C Hare, [2000] *CLJ* 461; J Harris, 'Forum Shopping in International Libel' (2000) 116 *LQR* 562.

[193] *ISC Technologies Ltd v Guerin* [1992] 2 Lloyd's Rep 430.

[194] Slade LJ in *Metall und Rohstoff AG v Donaldson Lufkin & Jenrette Inc* [1990] 1 QB 391, 437. See also *Newsat Holdings Ltd v Zani* [2006] 1 Lloyd's Rep 707.

[195] *Beecham Group Plc v Norton Healthcare Ltd* [1997] FSR 81; *Bastone & Firminger Ltd v Nasima Enterprises (Nigeria) Ltd* [1996] CLC 1902.

[196] [2004] 2 Lloyd's Rep 457.

[197] [2008] ILPr 345.

[198] *King v Lewis* [2004] ILPr 546. In this type of case the claimant is restricted to damages for loss of reputation in England; he cannot claim damages for worldwide loss of reputation.

is whether there is a link between the putative defendant and the English forum'[199] to justify the assumption of jurisdiction. Accordingly, when considering whether the damage resulted from acts committed within the jurisdiction, the court will regard as relevant only the acts of the putative defendant.[200] Paragraph (9) does not require all the acts to have been committed within the jurisdiction; it is not sufficient, however, that the claimant can point to some relatively minor or insignificant act committed, perhaps fortuitously, within the jurisdiction.[201] The court is required:

to look at the tort alleged in a common sense way and ask whether damage has resulted from substantial and efficacious acts committed within the jurisdiction (whether or not other substantial and efficacious acts have been committed elsewhere): if the answer is yes, permission may (but of course need not) be given.[202]

Constructive Trusts and Restitution

7.3.32   (15) A claim is made for a remedy against the defendant as constructive trustee where the defendant's alleged liability arises out of acts committed within the jurisdiction.

(16) A claim is made for restitution where the defendant's alleged liability arises out of acts committed within the jurisdiction.

In cases involving a claim for restitution against a defendant who is alleged to be holding the claimant's property as constructive trustee,[203] there is a considerable overlap between paragraphs (15) and (16). Although, on the one hand, paragraph (16) is, in certain respects, broader in scope, as it extends to cases such as those in which it is alleged that the claimant paid money to a defendant under a mistake of fact or law, on the other hand, paragraph (16) depends on the claim being 'for restitution', thereby potentially raising difficult doctrinal questions relating to the boundaries of restitution.[204] Whereas paragraph (16) is limited to claims for restitution, paragraph (15) covers remedies other than restitution which might be claimed against a constructive trustee—such as remedies based on the constructive trustee's duty to account.

7.3.33   One of the purposes of paragraph (15), which is a revised version of a rule introduced in 1990, is to enable proceedings to be brought in fraud cases against a foreign entity which has not participated in the fraud, but which has been used by the persons who control it as a receptacle for the proceeds of the fraud. The scope of paragraph (15) also extends to other cases involving breach of fiduciary duty. The basic factual connection which justifies the assumption of jurisdiction under paragraphs (15) and (16) is that acts which give rise to the defendant's liability took place within the

---

[199] Neill LJ in *Arab Business Consortium International Finance and Investment Co v Banque Franco-Tunisienne* [1997] 1 Lloyd's Rep 531, 536.

[200] *Arab Business Consortium International Finance and Investment Co v Banque Franco-Tunisienne* [1996] 1 Lloyd's Rep 485; affirmed [1997] 1 Lloyd's Rep 531.

[201] *Arab Business Consortium International Finance and Investment Co v Banque Franco-Tunisienne* [1996] 1 Lloyd's Rep 485.

[202] Slade LJ in *Metall und Rohstoff AG v Donaldson Lufkin & Jenrette Inc* [1990] 1 QB 391, 437. See also *Ashton Investments Ltd v OJSC Rusal Aluminium* [2007] 1 Lloyd's Rep 311.

[203] For consideration of the circumstances in which a defendant may be regarded as a constructive trustee, see *NABB Brothers Ltd v Lloyd's Bank International (Guernsey) Ltd* [2005] ILPr 506.

[204] See, eg, *NABB Brothers Ltd v Lloyd's Bank International (Guernsey) Ltd* [2005] ILPr 506.

jurisdiction.[205] In this sense, paragraphs (15) and (16) are narrower than paragraph (9), which covers claims in tort and permits service on the basis of damage sustained in England or on the basis of damage (wherever sustained) resulting from an act committed in England. It has been held that paragraph (15) does not require the claimant to show that all the acts giving rise to the alleged liability were committed within the jurisdiction; it is sufficient that some of them were[206]—at least if the acts committed within the jurisdiction are a substantial part of the acts on which the defendant's alleged liability is based.[207] There is no reason why the same approach should not be adopted with regard to paragraph (16). So, for example, for jurisdiction to be established under paragraph (15), it is not essential that the defendant acquired the knowledge upon which a claim to enforce an alleged constructive trust is based within the jurisdiction.[208]

Other Heads of Jurisdiction

7.3.34   (10) A claim is made to enforce any judgment or arbitral award.[209]

   (11) The whole subject matter of a claim relates to property located within the jurisdiction.[210]

   (12) A claim is made for any remedy which might be obtained in proceedings to execute the trusts of a written instrument where—

   (a) the trusts ought to be executed according to English law; and
   (b) the person on whom the claim form is to be served is a trustee of the trusts.[211]

   (13) A claim is made for any remedy which might be obtained in proceedings for the administration of the estate of a person who died domiciled within the jurisdiction.

   (14) A probate claim or a claim for the rectification of a will.

   (17) A claim is made by the Commissioners for HM Revenue and Customs relating to duties or taxes against a defendant not domiciled in Scotland or Northern Ireland.

   (18) A claim is made by a party to proceedings for an order that the court exercise its power under section 51 of the Supreme Court Act 1981 to make a costs order in favour of or against a person who is not a party to those proceedings.[212]

   (19) A claim is—

   (a) in the nature of salvage and any part of the services took place within the jurisdiction; or
   (b) to enforce a claim under section 153, 154, 175 or 176A of the Merchant Shipping Act 1995.

---

[205] *Nycal (UK) Ltd v Lacey* [1994] CLC 12.

[206] *ISC Technologies Ltd v Guerin* [1992] 2 Lloyd's Rep 430.

[207] *Pakistan v Zardari* [2006] 2 CLC 667.

[208] *Polly Peck International Plc v Nadir* The Independent, 2 September 1992.

[209] The presence of assets within the jurisdiction is not a pre-condition for the assumption of jurisdiction under this rule: *Tasarruf Mevduarti Sigorta Fonu v Demirel* [2007] 1 WLR 2508. For a discussion of jurisdiction in cases relating to the enforcement of arbitral awards, see paras 24.2.13–24.2.15.

[210] See *Re Banco Nacional de Cuba* [2001] 1 WLR 2039; *Pakistan v Zardari* [2006] 2 CLC 667. It has been held that confidential information amounts to 'property' for the purposes of what is now CPR PD 6B para 3.1(11): *Ashton Investments Ltd v OJSC Russian Aluminium* [2007] 1 Lloyd's Rep 311.

[211] See *Chellaram v Chellaram (No 2)* [2002] 3 All ER 17.

[212] This head of jurisdiction was added following the observations of the Court of Appeal in *National Justice Compania Naviera SA v Prudential Assurance Co Ltd (No 2)* [2000] 1 WLR 603.

(20) A claim made—

    (a) under an enactment which allows proceedings to be brought and those proceedings are not covered by any of the other grounds referred to in this paragraph;[213] or

    (b) under the Directive of the Council of the European Communities dated 15 March 1976 No 76/308/EEC, where service is to be effected in a Member State of the European Union.

Interpretation and Standard of Proof

7.3.35 As regards the merits of the claim, the requirement is that there is a serious question to be tried.[214] What, however, is the relevant test when there is a dispute as to whether the claim falls within the scope of one of the heads of CPR PD 6B para 3.1? In *Seaconsar Far East Ltd v Bank Markazi Jomhouri Islami Iran*[215] the House of Lords decided that there must be 'a good arguable case' that the claim falls within the paragraph being relied upon. It is important to note that this test applies not only where the question of jurisdiction is separate from questions as to the merits, but also where these two issues are interrelated. Where, for example, the claimant invokes the jurisdiction of the court under CPR PD 6B para 3.1(6)(a), the claimant must establish a good arguable case not only that there was a contract, but that the alleged contract was made within the jurisdiction;[216] it is not enough merely to show that if the contract existed it was made within the jurisdiction.[217] If the court's jurisdiction is invoked under CPR PD 6B para 3.1(6)(c) the claimant must establish a good arguable case not only that there was a contract between the claimant and the defendant, but also that the alleged contract was governed by English law.[218] Similarly, where the claimant seeks to rely on CPR PD 6B para 3.1(7), there must be a good arguable case, first, that there was a contract, secondly, that the contract was broken and, thirdly, that the breach was committed within the jurisdiction; it is not enough for the claimant to show that if there was a contract and it had been broken such breach was committed within the jurisdiction.[219]

7.3.36 The formula 'a good arguable case' is inherently vague. Nevertheless, it is certainly the case that the adjective 'good' is meant to add something to the simple word 'arguable'; so, the fact that there may be plenty to argue about does not in itself assist the claimant in establishing a good arguable case.[220] Some cases which

---

[213] See, eg, Nuclear Installations Act 1965; Social Security Contributions and Benefits Act 1992; Drug Trafficking Offences Act 1994; Part VI of the Criminal Justice Act 1988; Inheritance (Provision for Family and Dependants) Act 1975; Part II of the Immigration and Asylum Act 1999; sched 2 to the Immigration Act 1971; Financial Services and Markets Act 2000; Pensions Act 1995; Pensions Act 2004.

[214] See paras 7.3.6–7.3.8.

[215] [1994] 1 AC 438.

[216] See *Apple Corps Limited v Apple Computer Inc* [2004] ILPr 597.

[217] Lord Goff at [1994] 1 AC 438, 454–5.

[218] *The Kurnia Dewi* [1997] 1 Lloyd's Rep 552; *Maritrop Trading Corp v Guangzhou Ocean Shipping Co* [1998] CLC 224; *Marconi Communications Ltd v PT Pan Indonesia Bank Ltd TBK* [2004] 1 Lloyd's 594. Compare *Chellaram v Chellaram (No 2)* [2002] 3 All ER 17, 44 (at [136]).

[219] Lord Goff in *Seaconsar Far East Ltd v Bank Markazi Jomhouri Islami Iran* [1994] 1 AC 438, 453–54. See *Hewitson v Hewitson* [1999] 2 FLR 74.

[220] See Mance LJ in *ABCI v Banque Franco-Tunisienne* [2003] 2 Lloyd's Rep 146, 167.

suggest that the claimant must show that he is 'probably right'[221] or that there is 'a strong probability that the claim falls within the letter and the spirit of the [rule] relied upon'[222] go too far. The requirement that the claimant should establish a good arguable case is less stringent than a balance of probabilities;[223] the claimant does not have to satisfy the judge that at the end of the day it is more probable than not that he will win. The threshold which the claimant must surmount has been articulated in different ways: according to one approach, a good arguable case may be equated with 'a strong argument' or 'a strong case for argument';[224] another suggestion is that all that is required is a good arguable case 'with a fair prospect of success';[225] yet another formulation, which seems to have gained general acceptance in more recent cases, requires the claimant to have 'a much better argument on the material available'.[226]

7.3.37 It is important to note the limits of the decision in *Seaconsar Far East Ltd v Bank Markazi Jomhouri Islami Iran*. The House of Lords' attention was directed to a situation where the dispute between the parties on the question of jurisdiction turned on disputed questions of fact or on disputes as to the legal conclusions which may be drawn from the facts (such as whether the defendant's conduct amounts to a breach of contract). The application of the test of 'a good arguable case' in this context is designed to ensure that, as far as possible, applications for service out under CPR 6.36 are not turned into trials on written evidence—an obviously unsatisfactory procedure. The House of Lords did not, however, address the situation in which there is no dispute on the salient facts of the case, but the parties disagree on the construction of the words of the paragraph of the rules being relied upon by the claimant. In this type of case—in which the court is faced with a pure question of law which must be determined one way or the other—it is reasonable to expect the claimant to establish that the case comes clearly within one of the heads of CPR PD 6B para 3.1 and that 'it comes not merely within the letter but also within the spirit of the rule'.[227] When confronted with a problem concerning the correct construction and application of provisions of CPR PD 6B para 3.1 to a particular situation, the court must decide whether the claimant is right or wrong; this type of situation does not involve or require any further investigation and therefore it is not enough for the claimant to say that, even if he cannot bring himself within both the letter and the spirit of CPR PD 6B para 3.1, he nevertheless has a good arguable case.[228] If there is any ambiguity in the construction of the rules, such ambiguity must be resolved in the defendant's favour.[229]

---

[221] Staughton LJ in *Attock Cement Co Ltd v Romanian Bank for Foreign Trade* [1989] 1 WLR 1147, 1155.

[222] Slade LJ in *Metall und Rohstoff AG v Donaldson Lufkin & Jenrette Inc* [1990] 1 QB 391, 434.

[223] *Carvill America Incorporated v Camperdown UK Ltd* [2005] 2 Lloyd's Rep 457, 468; *Konkola Copper Mines plc v Coromin* [2006] 1 Lloyd's Rep 410, 424.

[224] Lord Goff in *Seaconsar Far East Ltd v Bank Markazi Jomhouri Islami Iran* [1994] 1 AC 438, 453.

[225] Henry LJ in *Agrafax Public Relations Ltd v United Scottish Society Incorporated* [1995] ILPr 753, 763.

[226] Waller LJ in *Canada Trust Co v Stolzenberg (No 2)* [1998] 1 WLR 547, 555. See also *Cherney v Deripaska (No 2)* [2009] 1 All ER (Comm) 333.

[227] Lloyd J in *Atlantic Underwriting Agencies Ltd v Compagnia di Assicurazione di Milano SpA* [1979] 2 Lloyd's Rep 240, 245.

[228] *EF Hutton & Co (London) Ltd v Monfarrij* [1989] 1 WLR 488.

[229] *The Hagen* [1908] P 189; *Siskina (Owners of cargo lately laden on board) v Distos Compania Naviera SA* [1979] AC 210.

Forum Conveniens

7.3.38   The third requirement is that the claimant must establish that England is the most appropriate forum. In essence, this raises the same critical question posed by an application by a defendant for a stay of proceedings on the basis of *forum non conveniens*.[230]

The Test

7.3.39   According to the test laid down by the House of Lords in *Spiliada Maritime Corporation v Cansulex Ltd*,[231] the court's task is to identify the forum 'in which the case can be tried more suitably for the interests of the parties and for the ends of justice'.[232] In an application for service out under CPR 6.36 the burden of persuasion rests on the claimant to show that England is the *forum conveniens*. According to Lord Templeman, the claimant who seeks permission to serve out of the jurisdiction must satisfy the court that England is 'the most appropriate forum to try the action'.[233] Lord Goff thought that the burden of proof on the claimant is not simply to persuade the court that England is the appropriate forum for the trial of the action, but 'to show that this is clearly so'.[234] It is doubtful whether there is a difference of substance between these alternative verbal formulations.

When is Appropriateness to be Assessed?

7.3.40   A question arises whether the test of appropriateness should be applied by reference to the circumstances as they existed at the date on which the order granting (or refusing) permission was made or whether, in cases where the decision to grant or refuse permission to serve out is subsequently challenged, the court should have regard to events which occurred after the original decision was made. In *ISC Technologies Ltd v Guerin*[235] Hoffmann J considered that events which take place after the decision to give (or refuse) permission to serve out are relevant only to the extent that they throw light on those factors which were relevant considerations when the decision was made. However, in *BMG Trading Ltd v AS McKay*[236] Phillips LJ expressed reservations about this aspect of Hoffmann J's judgment. Phillips LJ thought that it would not be proper for the court to continue to assert jurisdiction over a second defendant under what is now CPR PD 6B para 3.1(3) (on the basis that the second defendant is a necessary party to the claim against the first defendant) if, by the time the court comes

---

[230]   For further discussion of the doctrine of *forum non conveniens*, see section 9.2.
[231]   [1987] AC 460. A Briggs, 'Forum non conveniens—the last word?' [1987] *LMCLQ* 1; PB Carter, (1986) 57 *BYIL* 429; JG Collier, [1987] *CLJ* 33; J Jacob, (1987) 6 *CJQ* 89. For a policy-based evaluation, see JJ Fawcett, 'Trial in England or Abroad: The Underlying Policy Considerations' (1989) 9 *OJLS* 205.
[232]   Lord Goff at [1987] AC 460, 474 (citing Lord Kinnear in *Sim v Robinow* (1892) 19 R 665, 668).
[233]   [1987] AC 460, 465.
[234]   [1987] AC 460, 481.
[235]   [1992] 2 Lloyd's Rep 430, 434.
[236]   [1998] ILPr 691.

to consider the second defendant's application to set aside service, the claim against the first defendant has, for whatever reason, become a dead letter.[237]

The First Stage of the Test

7.3.41   The test laid down in *Spiliada Maritime Corporation v Cansulex Ltd* is applied in two stages. At the first stage, the court must, in deciding whether the case is a proper one for permission to be given, take into account 'the nature of the dispute, the legal and practical issues involved, such questions as local knowledge, availability of witnesses and their evidence and expense'.[238] Furthermore, it is necessary to take into account both the residence or place of business of the defendant and the ground (or grounds) of CPR PD 6B para 3.1 invoked by the claimant. The significance of the different grounds under CPR PD 6B para 3.1 varies greatly from case to case. For example, in some cases the fact that the applicable law is English is of considerable importance; in others it is almost wholly irrelevant.[239] If, having regard to all the relevant factors, the court concludes that England is the appropriate forum, permission to serve out will be given. Although there are cases which suggest that the court should not generally look favourably on claims for negative declaratory relief,[240] more recent authority adopts a much less hostile approach to such claims.[241] If England is clearly the appropriate forum, the court will not refuse permission to serve out simply because of the nature of the relief sought by the claimant.[242]

7.3.42   It is quite possible for the various factors relevant to the exercise of discretion to point in different directions. For example, in a case where English law is the applicable law and England is the factual centre of gravity of the dispute the court may, nevertheless, refuse to give permission to serve out of the jurisdiction on the ground that concurrent proceedings on the same issues have already been commenced in another forum.[243]

The Second Stage of the Test

7.3.43   The second stage of the test requires the court to assess not only the practicalities of the case, but also whether justice will be done abroad. If England is not the most closely connected forum the court should not be deterred from exercising its discretion against giving permission simply because the claimant will be deprived of a legitimate personal or juridical advantage by having to litigate in a foreign forum rather than in England. However, permission to serve out of the jurisdiction may be

---

[237] [1998] ILPr 691, 694.

[238] Lord Wilberforce in *Amin Rasheed Shipping Corporation v Kuwait Insurance Co* [1984] AC 50, 72.

[239] Lord Goff in *Spiliada Maritime Corporation v Cansulex Ltd* [1987] AC 460, 481.

[240] *Insurance Corporation of Ireland v Strobus International Insurance* [1985] 2 Lloyd's Rep 138; *The Volvox Hollandia* [1988] 2 Lloyd's Rep 361; *DR Insurance Co v Central National Insurance Co* [1996] 1 Lloyd's Rep 74.

[241] *Messier-Dowty Ltd v Sabena SA* [2000] 1 WLR 2040; *Ark Therapeutics plc v True North Capital Ltd* [2006] 1 All ER (Comm) 138.

[242] *HIB Ltd v Guardian Insurance Co Inc* [1997] 1 Lloyd's Rep 412.

[243] *DR Insurance Co v Central National Insurance Co* [1996] 1 Lloyd's Rep 74.

granted, notwithstanding the fact that there is an alternative forum abroad which is more closely connected, if the court is not satisfied that 'substantial justice will be done in the available appropriate forum'.[244] The court may conclude, for example, that substantial justice will not be done abroad if the delays in the foreign forum are excessive or if a successful claimant is not able to recover his costs in the foreign forum.[245]

The Impact of a Jurisdiction Clause

7.3.44   In cases involving an agreement in favour of English jurisdiction, if one or more of the parties is domiciled in a Member State, the English court has jurisdiction by virtue of Article 23 of the Brussels I Regulation;[246] in such cases CPR 6.36 is irrelevant. Where, however, none of the parties is domiciled in a Member State or a state bound by the Lugano Convention, the situation falls within CPR PD 6B para 3.1(6)(d) if the claim is made 'in respect of a contract ... [which] contains a term to the effect that the court shall have jurisdiction to determine any claim in respect of the contract'.

7.3.45   When the claim falls within CPR PD 6B para 3.1(6)(d), the question arises whether the jurisdiction clause is to be weighed in the balance as one of the factors within the *Spiliada* test, or whether some other principle is to be applied. Since in *Spiliada Maritime Corporation v Cansulex Ltd*[247] the House of Lords did not consider the effect of jurisdiction clauses, the principle adopted in *The Chaparral*[248]—a case which pre-dates the *Spiliada* case by more than 20 years—should be applied. In *The Chaparral* a dispute arose in relation to a contract which provided that any dispute arising 'must be treated before the London Court of Justice'. When the plaintiff obtained leave to serve the writ out of the jurisdiction, the defendant applied to have leave set aside on the ground that England was not the appropriate forum and that proceedings had already been started in Florida. The Court of Appeal refused to set aside service. Although the court retains a discretion, 'it is a discretion which, in the ordinary way and in the absence of strong reason to the contrary, will be exercised in favour of holding parties to their bargain'.[249]

7.3.46   Where the parties have agreed to litigate in a foreign country, it does not automatically follow that the court will refuse permission to serve out of the jurisdiction; all depends on whether or not the court is satisfied that England is the proper place in which to bring the claim. Although, as a general rule, the court will refuse permission, thereby preventing the claimant from going back on his word,[250] there may be circumstances in which the court considers it appropriate to give permission

---

[244]   Lord Goff in *Spiliada Maritime Corporation v Cansulex Ltd* [1987] AC 460, 482.

[245]   *Roneleigh Ltd v MII Exports Inc* [1989] 1 WLR 619.

[246]   See section 5.3. When the Hague Choice of Court Convention of 2005 enters into force, the provisions of the Convention will prevail over Art 23 in cases where one or more of the parties is resident in a contracting state to the Convention which is not an EU Member State: Art 26(6). See paras 7.3.47–7.3.50.

[247]   [1987] AC 460.

[248]   [1968] 2 Lloyd's Rep 158.

[249]   Willmer LJ at [1968] 2 Lloyd's Rep 158, 163. See also *BAS Capital Funding Corporation v Medfinco Limited* [2004] ILPr 305.

[250]   *Mackender v Feldia AG* [1967] 2 QB 590.

notwithstanding the parties' prior agreement to refer their disputes to another forum. Where proceedings are brought in England in breach of an exclusive jurisdiction clause the court should apply the same basic principles whether the case involves an application for a stay of English proceedings brought as of right or an application for permission to serve a claim form out of the jurisdiction on an absent defendant.[251] If the parties have agreed to the exclusive jurisdiction of a foreign forum, the court should refuse to give permission to serve out unless 'strong cause for not doing so is shown'.[252] It seems that the court is most likely to conclude that a case is 'one of those exceptional cases'[253] in which it is proper to give permission notwithstanding an agreement to refer any dispute to the courts of another country, if it involves multiple defendants. In a case where the claimant has related claims against two defendants, the court may disregard the fact that, as regards one of the defendants, the claimant agreed to the exclusive jurisdiction of a foreign court, if England provides a convenient forum in which the claims against both defendants can be tried together.[254]

The Hague Choice of Court Convention

7.3.47 In the 1990s the Hague Conference on Private International Law started work on what, it was hoped, would result in a world-wide convention along the lines of the Brussels Convention. During the course of negotiations, it became clear that it was going to be impossible to reach agreement on certain key questions. As a result, the scope of the project was narrowed; the aim was to produce a convention which would guarantee the enforcement of exclusive jurisdiction agreements and the enforcement of judgments which result from litigation in which the court of origin assumes jurisdiction on the basis of such an agreement. Although the Brussels Convention was the archetype for the project as originally conceived, the model for the Hague Choice of Court Convention which was finally agreed in 2005 was the New York Convention of 1958 (which makes provision for the enforcement of arbitration agreements and for the recognition and enforcement of arbitral awards).[255]

7.3.48 When the Hague Convention enters into force,[256] it will determine the jurisdictional impact of exclusive jurisdiction agreements which refer the parties' dispute (or disputes) to the courts of a contracting state. Subject to various exceptions (such as family law matters, consumer contracts and employments contracts[257]), the Hague Convention applies to 'exclusive choice of court agreements concluded in civil or commercial matters'.[258] Where a choice of court agreement designates an EU Member State as the contractual forum, it is important to be aware of the dividing line between

---

[251] *Citi-March Ltd v Neptune Orient Lines Ltd* [1996] 1 WLR 1367. See section 9.3.

[252] Brandon J in *The Eleftheria* [1970] P 94, 99.

[253] Cairns LJ in *Evans Marshall & Co Ltd v Bertola SA* [1973] 1 WLR 349, 385.

[254] See *Evans Marshall & Co Ltd v Bertola SA* [1973] 1 WLR 349; *Citi-March Ltd v Neptune Orient Lines Ltd* [1996] 1 WLR 1367.

[255] See sections 21.2 and 24.2.

[256] As of 1 January 2010, the Convention had been signed by the United States of America and the European Union (on behalf of all the Member States) and had been acceded to by Mexico. The Convention will only enter into force three months after two states have ratified or acceded to it: Art 31(1).

[257] See Art 2.

[258] Art 1(1).

the Brussels I Regulation and the Hague Convention. Notwithstanding the terms of Article 23(1) of the Brussels I Regulation (which purports to cover cases where either the claimant or the defendant is domiciled in a Member State), following the entry into force of the Hague Convention, the Convention will apply where one of the parties is resident in a contracting state to the Convention which is not an EU Member State.[259] So, when the Convention is in force in the United States and the European Union, the effect of a choice of court agreement in favour of the English courts will be determined by the Hague Convention if one of the parties is resident in the United States; if, however, none of the parties is resident in a contracting state which is not an EU Member State, Article 23 of the Brussels I Regulation will continue to apply.

7.3.49   To fall within the scope of the Convention, the jurisdiction agreement must (i) satisfy the relevant formal requirements and (ii) designate the courts of a contracting state as the contractual forum.[260] The basic jurisdiction rules in Article 5 are that the contractual forum 'shall have jurisdiction to decide a dispute to which the agreement applies, unless the agreement is null and void under the law of that State' and that the contractual forum 'shall not decline to exercise jurisdiction on the ground that the dispute should be decided in a court of another State'. As far as the assumption of jurisdiction by the English court in cases where the English court is the contractual forum, the implementation of the Convention into English law will not bring about a significant change; under the traditional rules, there appears to be no reported case in which the English court has failed to assume jurisdiction in a situation where the parties have concluded an exclusive jurisdiction agreement designating England as the contractual forum.

7.3.50   As regards cases where the contractual forum is a contracting state to the Convention which is not an EU Member State, the English court will not be entitled to assume jurisdiction under the traditional rules (whether on the basis of the defendant's presence in England or by service out of the jurisdiction under CPR 6.36) unless the case comes within one of the five situations set out in Article 6:

(a) the agreement is null and void under the law of the State of the chosen court;
(b) a party lacked the capacity to conclude the agreement under the law of the State of the court seised;
(c) giving effect to the agreement would lead to a manifest injustice or would be manifestly contrary to the public policy of the State of the court seised;
(d) for exceptional reasons beyond the control of the parties, the agreement cannot reasonably be performed; or
(e) the chosen court has decided not to hear the case.

The effect of Article 6 is that, although some of the cases involving foreign jurisdiction clauses under the traditional rules would be decided in the same way under the Hague Convention (for example, because giving effect to the agreement would lead to a manifest injustice), the English court will very rarely be able to assume jurisdiction in a case where the parties have agreed to refer their dispute to the jurisdiction of the courts of a contracting state to the Convention.

---

[259] Art 26(6).
[260] Art 3. The agreement must be 'in writing' or be concluded 'by any other means of communication which renders information accessible so as to be usable for subsequent reference'.

8

BASES OF JURISDICTION IN ADMIRALTY PROCEEDINGS

8.0.1 The jurisdiction of the admiralty court is largely based on the scheme established by the Supreme Court Act 1981 (section 8.1). Some of the bases of jurisdiction set out in the 1981 Act are derived from international conventions, notably the International Convention for the Unification of Certain Rules Relating to the Arrest of Sea-Going Ships (the Arrest Convention) and the International Convention for the Unification of Certain Rules concerning Civil Jurisdiction in matters of Collision (the Collision Convention), both of which date from 1952. While the framework is established by domestic legislation, the Brussels I Regulation[1] and the Lugano Convention have a significant impact on the operation of jurisdiction rules in relation to proceedings falling within their scope (section 8.2).

8.0.2 It must be remembered that there are circumstances in which proceedings in admiralty matters may be stayed or in which jurisdiction must be declined. Where admiralty proceedings are started in England—whether *in rem* or *in personam*—the court must, in appropriate cases, apply the relevant provisions of the Brussels regime.[2] If jurisdiction is not declined (or the proceedings stayed) under the Brussels I Regulation or the Lugano Convention, there are circumstances in which the court may stay the proceedings under its inherent jurisdiction.[3] As regards the staying of proceedings under the traditional rules, there are no special principles which apply to proceedings *in rem*; indeed, many of the cases in which the courts have worked out the general principles upon which a stay should be granted under the court's inherent jurisdiction have involved admiralty proceedings. Where the parties have agreed to arbitration the court is obliged to grant a stay of proceedings under the Arbitration Act 1996.[4]

8.0.3 Admiralty proceedings may be brought *in personam* against a named defendant (for example, by service of a claim form on an English registered company in England[5]) or *in rem* by service of process on a *res*. In a claim *in rem*, the *res* is usually a ship, but may be cargo, freight or, in certain circumstances, other property.[6] A claimant may commence proceedings both *in rem* and *in personam* in relation to the same claim. In such a case it is necessary for two claim forms to be issued. Proceedings *in rem* enable the claimant to arrest the ship, so that the ship can be sold and the claim satisfied out of the proceeds. Although proceedings *in rem* are commenced by service

---

[1] Reg (EC) 44/2001, [2001] OJ L12/1.
[2] See section 9.1.
[3] See sections 9.2–9.5.
[4] See section 21.2.
[5] See, eg, *The Western Regent* [2005] 2 Lloyd's Rep 359.
[6] Proceedings *in rem* may be brought in relation to an aircraft (Supreme Court Act 1981, s 21(5)) or a hovercraft (Hovercraft Act 1968, s 2(1)). Proceedings *in rem* involving aircraft are very unusual.

of process on the *res* and they are sometimes regarded as brought against the *res*, the owner (or charterer) of the *res*, rather than the *res* itself, is the defendant.[7] Where proceedings are brought *in rem*, it is common for the owner or charterer of the ship to submit to the jurisdiction and put up security for the claim, thereby preventing the ship's arrest or obtaining its release if it has already been arrested. If a shipowner or charterer acknowledges service of process in England, the proceedings in England take on a hybrid character; the proceedings become *in personam* but do not lose their *in rem* character.[8] Whereas a judgment *in rem* is restricted to the value of the *res*, there is no such restriction as regards a judgment *in personam*. However, a judgment *in rem*, unlike a judgment *in personam*, determines the status of the *res* and may affect third parties.

8.1 JURISDICTION UNDER THE SUPREME COURT ACT 1981[9]

The Admiralty Jurisdiction of the High Court: Section 20

8.1.1   The admiralty jurisdiction of the High Court is defined by sections 20–24 of the Supreme Court Act 1981.[10] Jurisdiction does not depend on the nationality of the ship, the residence or domicile of the owners or the place where the event giving rise to the claim occurred.[11] As regards those heads of jurisdiction which are based on the Arrest Convention 'a broad and liberal construction should be given to them'.[12] Furthermore, the court will have regard to the Convention[13] and, where appropriate, the *travaux préparatoires*[14] to assist in the construction of the Act. The provisions of the 1981 Act are complex and involve a wide range of overlapping bases of jurisdiction.

Section 20(1)(a) and (b)

8.1.2   Paragraphs (a) and (b) of section 20(1) refer to various statutory heads of jurisdiction which are listed in subsections (2) and (3) respectively.[15] Since a number of the bases of jurisdiction overlap, it is quite common for a claim to fall within more than one head of the court's admiralty jurisdiction. Subsection (3) sets out three bases of jurisdiction:

---

[7] See *Republic of India v India Steamship Co (No 2)* [1998] AC 878.

[8] *The Gemma* [1899] P 285; *The August 8* [1983] 2 AC 450; *The Maciej Rataj* [1992] 2 Lloyd's Rep 552.

[9] DC Jackson, 'Admiralty jurisdiction—the Supreme Court Act 1981' [1982] *LMCLQ* 236.

[10] The court does not have jurisdiction over any claim certified by the secretary of state to be one which falls to be determined in accordance with the provisions of the Rhine Navigation Convention: Supreme Court Act 1981, s 23.

[11] Supreme Court Act 1981, s 20(7). See, however, section 8.2.

[12] Lord Brandon in *The Antonis P Lemos* [1985] AC 711, 725.

[13] *The Evpo Agnic* [1988] 1 WLR 1090.

[14] *Gatoil International Inc v Arkwright-Boston Manufacturers Mutual Insurance Co* [1985] AC 255.

[15] These provisions are largely derived from s 1(1) of the Administration of Justice Act 1956.

(a)   any application to the High Court under the Merchant Shipping Act 1995;
(b)   any action to enforce a claim for damage, loss of life or personal injury arising out of—

    (i)   a collision between ships; or
    (ii) the carrying out of or omission to carry out a manoeuvre in the case of one or more
          of two or more ships; or
    (iii) non-compliance, on the part of one or more of two or more ships, with the collision
          regulations;

(c)   any action by shipowners or other persons under the Merchant Shipping Act 1995 for the
      limitation of the amount of their liability in connection with a ship or other property.[16]

Subsection (2) provides that the admiralty jurisdiction of the High Court includes
the matters set out in paragraphs (a)–(s), the most important of which are considered
below.

DISPUTES BETWEEN CO-OWNERS
8.1.3   (b) any question arising between the co-owners of a ship as to possession, employment
          or earnings of that ship;[17]

Paragraph (b) includes 'power to settle any account outstanding and unsettled between
the parties in relation to the ship, and to direct that the ship, or any share thereof, shall
be sold, and to make such other order as the court thinks fit'.[18]

MORTGAGES AND CHARGES
8.1.4   (c) any claim in respect of a mortgage of or charge on a ship or any share therein;

In this context 'charge' means a charge in the nature of a mortgage and does not
include a maritime lien.[19]

DAMAGE TO A SHIP
8.1.5   (d) any claim for damage received by a ship;[20]

Although many cases which fall within paragraph (d) also fall within paragraph (e),
since the damage results from a collision between two ships, paragraph (d) extends to
cases where damage is done by something other than a ship, for example, by a pier[21]
or a buoy.[22] The 1981 Act makes no provision for the enforcement of a claim within
paragraph (d) other than by means of proceedings *in personam*.[23]

---

[16] See *The Western Regent* [2005] 2 Lloyd's Rep 359.
[17] See, eg, *The Vanessa Ann* [1985] 1 Lloyd's Rep 549.
[18] Supreme Court Act, s 20(4).
[19] *The St Merriel* [1963] P 247; *The Acrux* [1965] P 391.
[20] *The Father Thames* [1979] 2 Lloyd's Rep 364.
[21] *The Zeta* [1893] AC 469.
[22] *The Upcerne* [1912] P 160.
[23] Supreme Court Act 1981, s 21. See, however, DC Jackson, *Enforcement of Maritime Claims* (London,
LLP, 4th edn, 2005) 56–7.

DAMAGE DONE BY A SHIP

8.1.6   (e) any claim for damage done by a ship;

Damage is a prerequisite for jurisdiction under paragraph (e); where there is a collision between two ships but no damage is inflicted, no cause of action arises.[24] However, there is no requirement that there should be physical contact between the ship by which the damage is done and the property which is damaged.[25] So, this basis of jurisdiction is satisfied in a case where the negligent navigation of a vessel causes two other ships to collide.[26] For the purposes of paragraph (e) what is important is that the damage is the direct result or natural consequence of something done by those engaged in the navigation of the ship and that the ship itself is the actual instrument by which the damage was done;[27] it is not sufficient for the ship to have been used in some way in the chain of events which led to the infliction of damage.[28] Where a ship is deliberately driven off fishing grounds by another vessel the ensuing economic or financial damage is, in principle, within the scope of paragraph (e).[29] By contrast, the fact that the claimant has suffered economic loss by virtue of a failure by the shipowners or charterers to complete the contractual voyage is not enough to bring the claim within paragraph (e); such loss is not caused by 'the physical act of the whole or part of the ship or by those engaged in the navigation or management of the ship in a physical sense'.[30]

8.1.7   Paragraph (e) includes not only damage done to a ship, but also damage done to other property such as a breakwater,[31] oyster beds,[32] a pier[33] or an underwater cable.[34] Paragraph (e) extends to any claim in respect of liability for oil pollution under Chapter III of Part VI of the Merchant Shipping Act 1995 and to any claim in respect of a liability falling on the International Oil Pollution Compensation Fund 1984 under Chapter IV of Part VI of the Merchant Shipping Act 1995.[35]

CARRIAGE AND HIRE

8.1.8   (h) any claim arising out of any agreement relating to the carriage of goods in a ship or to the use or hire of a ship;

In general, the courts have construed paragraph (h) broadly, giving the words 'their ordinary wide meaning'.[36] So, a claim arising out of a charterparty is an agreement 'relating … to the use or hire of a ship'.[37] There are four aspects to paragraph (h) which have been the subject of judicial consideration.

---

[24] *The Margaret* (1881) 6 PD 76.
[25] *The Industrie* (1871) LR 3 A&E 303.
[26] *Ibid.*
[27] *The Eschersheim* [1976] 1 WLR 430.
[28] *The Rama* [1996] 2 Lloyd's Rep 281.
[29] *The Dagmara* [1988] 1 Lloyd's Rep 431.
[30] Clarke J in *The Rama* [1996] 2 Lloyd's Rep 281, 298.
[31] *The Uhla* (1867) 19 LT 89.
[32] *The Swift* [1901] P 168.
[33] *The Merle* (1874) 31 LT 447.
[34] *The Clara Killam* (1870) LR 3 A&E 161.
[35] Supreme Court Act 1981, s 20(5).
[36] Lord Diplock in *The Eschersheim* [1976] 1 WLR 430, 438.
[37] *The Tjaskemolen* [1997] 2 Lloyd's Rep 465.

8.1.9 First, the phrase 'agreement relating to the carriage of goods in a ship' suggests that 'the carriage of goods by sea is the central matter to which the agreement relates'.[38] On this basis, a claim arising out of a cif contract for the sale of goods is not within the scope of paragraph (h).[39] Where a contract includes some elements which relate to the use of a ship and others which do not, if severance of the contract is possible, a claimant may invoke the jurisdiction of the admiralty court in relation to claims arising out of that part of the contract involving the use of a vessel; the part of a cif contract concerning demurrage is not within paragraph (h).[40]

8.1.10 Secondly, paragraph (h) cannot be relied upon if the claim relates to the carriage of goods on an unidentified ship.[41] Furthermore, where the claimant in reliance on paragraph (h) brings proceedings *in rem* under section 21(4),[42] the ship in connection with which the claim arises must be the same ship as that to which the agreement for the carriage of goods or for the use or hire relates.[43] So, a claimant must establish not only that the agreement relates to the use or hire of ship X or to the carriage of goods in ship X, but that the claim arises in connection with ship X.

8.1.11 Thirdly, the words 'arising out of' should be construed as meaning 'connected with', rather than 'arising under'.[44] Accordingly, paragraph (h) is wide enough to cover claims based in contract or tort[45] and to claims for contribution and indemnity under the Civil Liability (Contribution) Act 1978.[46] There is no requirement that the agreement out of which the claim arises should be an agreement between the parties to the litigation;[47] paragraph (h) may extend, for example, to a claim in tort by a subcharterer against a shipowner.[48]

8.1.12 Fourthly, the breadth of paragraph (h) results from the use of the words 'any agreement relating to', rather than the narrower expression 'any agreement for'.[49] It has been held that paragraph (h) includes within its scope an agreement for mooring and unmooring and other services of a ship[50] and an agreement for salvage services (as involving the use of a salvage vessel).[51] Nevertheless, there are limits to the scope of paragraph (h) since:

It would ... be unreasonable to infer from the expression actually used ... that it is intended to be sufficient that the agreement in issue should be in some way connected, however remotely, with the carriage of goods in a ship or with the use or hire of a ship.[52]

---

[38] Phillips J in *Petrofina SA v AOT Ltd* [1992] QB 571, 576.
[39] *Petrofina SA v AOT Ltd* [1992] QB 571.
[40] *Ibid.*
[41] *The Lloyd Pacifico* [1995] 1 Lloyd's Rep 54.
[42] See paras 8.1.26–8.1.38.
[43] *The Lloyd Pacifico* [1995] 1 Lloyd's Rep 54.
[44] *The Antonis P Lemos* [1985] AC 711.
[45] *The St Elefterio* [1957] P 179.
[46] *The Hamburg Star* [1994] 1 Lloyd's Rep 399.
[47] *The St Elefterio* [1957] P 179.
[48] *The Antonis P Lemos* [1985] AC 711.
[49] *Gatoil International Inc v Arkwright-Boston Manufacturers Mutual Insurance Co* [1985] AC 255.
[50] *The Queen of the South* [1968] P 449.
[51] *The Eschersheim* [1976] 1 WLR 430. Compare *The Tesaba* [1982] 1 Lloyd's Rep 397.
[52] Lord Keith in *Gatoil International Inc v Arkwright-Boston Manufacturers Mutual Insurance Co* [1985] AC 255, 270–1.

To fall within paragraph (h) there must be 'some reasonably direct connection' with the stipulated activities.[53] So, the following are not connected with the carriage of goods in a ship or the use or hire of a ship in a sufficiently direct sense to be capable of coming within paragraph (h): a claim in connection with an agreement for the hire by shipowners of containers to be carried on a ship;[54] a claim for the payment of premiums under a contract of insurance in relation to a cargo of oil;[55] a claim arising out of a contract of marine insurance.[56] Whether paragraph (h) confers jurisdiction on the admiralty court in the situation where a dispute arising out of a charterparty has been referred to arbitration and the successful claimant seeks to enforce the award by means of a claim *in rem* has given rise to conflicting decisions. According to one strand in the case law, where the court has jurisdiction to enforce a charterparty, it also has jurisdiction to enforce an arbitral award based on it.[57] The opposing—and preferable—view is that, since paragraph (h) requires the claim to have a reasonably direct connection with the use or hire of a ship, this condition is not satisfied where the contemplated proceedings in England are for the enforcement of an arbitral award.[58]

SALVAGE
8.1.13 (j) any claim—

> (i) under the Salvage Convention 1989;
> (ii) under any contract for or in relation to salvage services; or
> (iii) in the nature of salvage not falling within (i) or (ii) above;

or any corresponding claim in connection with an aircraft;

For the purposes of this basis of jurisdiction salvage services include services rendered in saving life from a ship.[59] Paragraph (j) is concerned with claims for salvage services and does not include a claim against the salvor (for example, for negligent salvage).[60]

GOODS SUPPLIED TO A SHIP
8.1.14 (m) any claim in respect of goods or materials supplied to a ship for her operation or maintenance;

Paragraph (m) covers a contract of supply, whether by way of sale or hire, between the claimant and a shipowner. It is important to note, however, that the expression

---

[53] Lord Keith in *Gatoil International Inc v Arkwright-Boston Manufacturers Mutual Insurance Co* [1985] AC 255, 271.

[54] This proposition follows from the fact that the House of Lords overruled *The Sonia S* [1983] 2 Lloyd's Rep 63 in *Gatoil International Inc v Arkwright-Boston Manufacturers Mutual Insurance Co* [1985] AC 255.

[55] *Gatoil International Inc v Arkwright-Boston Manufacturers Mutual Insurance Co* [1985] AC 255.

[56] *The Aifanourios* 1980 SC 346.

[57] *The Saint Anna* [1983] 1 WLR 895 in which Sheen J sought to derive support from *Bremer Oeltransport GmbH v Drewry* [1933] 1 KB 753.

[58] *The Beldis* [1936] P 51; *The Bumbesti* [2000] QB 559.

[59] Supreme Court Act 1981, s 20(6). There is no claim for salvage in respect of services rendered to a ship in danger in navigable non-tidal inland waters: *The Goring* [1988] AC 831.

[60] *The Tesaba* [1982] 1 Lloyd's Rep 397.

used in paragraph (m) is 'supplied to a ship' and not 'supplied to a shipowner'.[61] Furthermore, it has been held that the expression 'goods or materials' should not be construed too narrowly and extends to all necessaries, including the provision of crew services.[62] In *The River Rima* Lord Brandon took the view that, while paragraph (m) includes within its scope a contract which 'expressly provides that the goods or materials are required for the use of a particular ship, the identity of which is specified in the contract or will be specified by the time when the contract comes to be performed', it does not extend to a contract which 'contains no reference to a particular ship for the use of which the goods or materials are required, leaving the shipowner to make his own decision about that later'.[63]

8.1.15 In *The Kommunar*[64] it was held that paragraph (m) was applicable to a claim for the reimbursement of sums which the plaintiffs had paid to subagents who had actually supplied goods to the defendant shipowners. Clarke J concluded on the facts that:

the plaintiffs were not simply acting as bankers, they were not advancing moneys to the shipowner for the shipowner to purchase supplies. By the terms of the contract it was their responsibility to pay for necessaries supplied by the supplier of the necessaries.[65]

WAGES

8.1.16 (o) any claim by a master or member of the crew of a ship for wages (including any sum allotted out of wages or adjudged by a superintendent to be due by way of wages);

Paragraph (o), which applies whether or not the wages are earned on board the ship,[66] is satisfied where the claimants have a valid claim in debt against a defendant who is contractually obliged to pay remuneration, regardless of whether the claimants are also employed by another person.[67] The extent of the claim to wages is always quantified in accordance with the terms of the contract under which the services to the ship were provided.[68] Paragraph (o) also covers a claim for unpaid employers' contributions to a pension fund, since the contributions are, in principle, part of the employee's total earnings.[69] However, claims for severance payments[70] or unpaid statutory social insurance benefits[71] are not within the scope of paragraph (o).

---

[61] Lord Brandon in *The River Rima* [1988] 1 WLR 758, 763.
[62] *The Edinburgh Castle* [1999] 2 Lloyd's Rep 362; *Lavington International Ltd v The Nore Challenger and The Nore Commander (Bareboat Charterers)* [2001] 2 All ER (Comm) 667.
[63] [1988] 1 WLR 758, 763.
[64] [1997] 1 Lloyd's Rep 1.
[65] [1997] 1 Lloyd's Rep 1, 7.
[66] *The Tacoma City* [1991] 1 Lloyd's Rep 330.
[67] *The Turiddu* [1999] 2 Lloyd's Rep 401.
[68] *The Ever Success* [1999] 1 Lloyd's Rep 824.
[69] *The Halcyon Skies* [1977] QB 14.
[70] *The Tacoma City* [1991] 1 Lloyd's Rep 330.
[71] *The Acrux* [1965] P 391.

DISBURSEMENTS

8.1.17   (p) any claim by a master, shipper, charterer or agent in respect of disbursements
             made on account of a ship;

Paragraph (p) does not cover the situation where an insurer seeks to recover from the
owner sums paid out by the insurer under a policy of marine insurance.[72]

OTHER BASES OF JURISDICTION

8.1.18   (a) any claim to the possession or ownership of a ship or to the ownership of any
             share therein;
           (f) any claim for loss of life or personal injury sustained in consequence of any defect
             in a ship or in her apparel or equipment, or in consequence of the wrongful act,
             neglect or default of—

              (i) the owners, charterers or persons in possession or control of a ship; or
              (ii) the master or crew of a ship, or any other person for whose wrongful acts,
                 neglects or defaults the owners, charterers or persons in possession or control
                 of a ship are responsible,

             being an act, neglect or default in the navigation or management of the ship,
             in the loading, carriage or discharge of goods on, in or from the ship, or in the
             embarkation, carriage or disembarkation of persons on, in or from the ship;
           (g) any claim for loss of or damage to goods carried in a ship;[73]
           (k) any claim in the nature of towage in respect of a ship or an aircraft;[74]
           (l) any claim in the nature of pilotage in respect of a ship or an aircraft;
           (n) any claim in respect of the construction, repair or equipment of a ship or in
             respect of dock charges or dues;
           (q) any claim arising out of an act which is or is claimed to be a general average act;
           (r) any claim arising out of bottomry;
           (s) any claim for the forfeiture or condemnation of a ship or of goods which are
             being or have been carried, or have been attempted to be carried, in a ship, or
             for the restoration of a ship or any such goods after seizure, or for droits of
             Admiralty.[75]

Section 20(1)(c)

8.1.19   Section 20(1)(c) provides that the High Court has 'any other Admiralty jurisdiction which it had immediately before the commencement of [the 1981] Act'. This
takes one back to section 1 of the Administration of Justice Act 1956, which states
that the admiralty jurisdiction of the High Court extends to:

any other jurisdiction which either was vested in the High Court of Admiralty immediately
before the date of commencement of the Supreme Court of Judicature Act 1873 ... or is

---

[72] *Bain Clarkson Ltd v Owners of 'Sea Friends'* [1991] 2 Lloyd's Rep 322.
[73] See, eg, *The Pia Vestra* [1984] 1 Lloyd's Rep 169.
[74] See, eg, *The Leoborg* [1962] 2 Lloyd's Rep 146.
[75] See, eg, *The Skylark* [1965] P 474.

conferred by or under an Act which came into operation on or after that date on the High Court as being a court with Admiralty jurisdiction.

The effect of these provisions is that the admiralty court is competent in relation to matters within the Admiralty Act 1840 and the Admiralty Court Act 1861 and in relation to matters within the court's inherent jurisdiction.

8.1.20 For nearly all practical purposes the jurisdiction conferred by the 1840 and 1861 Acts is fully reflected in the statutory heads of jurisdiction under the 1981 Act. Although it is relatively rare for the court's inherent jurisdiction to be invoked, it may still occasionally be relevant in relation to 'injurious acts on the high seas'[76] or in relation to the enforcement of a foreign judgment *in rem*. In *The Despina GK*[77] the plaintiff sought to enforce a Swedish judgment *in rem* by means of proceedings *in rem* in England, reliance being placed on the decision of Sir Robert Phillimore in *The City of Mecca*.[78] It was held that the admiralty court's inherent jurisdiction covers proceedings *in rem* for the enforcement of a foreign judgment *in rem* provided that the *res* is still the property of the judgment debtor at the time when it is arrested.

Section 20(1)(d)

8.1.21 Whereas section 20(1)(c) looks to the past, section 20(1)(d) looks to the future and provides that the jurisdiction of the admiralty court shall include:

any jurisdiction connected with ships or aircraft which is vested in the High Court apart from this section and is for the time being by rules of court made or coming into force after the commencement of this Act assigned to the Queen's Bench Division and directed by the rules to be exercised by the Admiralty Court.

Jurisdiction *in Rem*: Section 21(2)–(8)

8.1.22 Subsections (2)–(4) of section 21 define the three categories of case in which the various bases of admiralty jurisdiction may be invoked by way of proceedings *in rem* in respect of a ship.[79] Where the ship or other property which is the subject-matter of the proceedings *in rem* is sold in the exercise of the court's admiralty jurisdiction,[80] the court has the necessary jurisdiction to determine any question concerning title to the proceeds of sale.[81]

---

[76] *The Tubantia* [1924] P 78.

[77] [1983] QB 214.

[78] (1879) 5 PD 28; reversed on appeal on the ground that the foreign judgment was in fact a judgment *in personam*: (1881) 6 PD 106.

[79] Proceedings *in rem* may be brought in respect of an aircraft only in the case of claims in the nature of towage or pilotage: Supreme Court Act 1981, s 21(5). See *Re Glider Standard Austria SH 1964* [1965] P 463.

[80] For the circumstances in which the court will order sale, see *The Myrto* [1977] 2 Lloyd's Rep 243, 259–60.

[81] Supreme Court Act 1981, s 21(6).

Section 21(2): Cases Falling Within Section 20(2)(a)–(c) and (s)

8.1.23   Section 21(2) provides that:

In the case of any such claim as is mentioned in section 20(2)(a), (c) or (s) or any such question as is mentioned in section 20(2)(b), an action *in rem* may be brought in the High Court against the ship or property in connection with which the claim or question arises.

Claims falling within this provision are truly *in rem* in the sense that they may be brought only by service of process on the *res* in connection with which they arose.

Section 21(3): Maritime Liens

8.1.24   Subsection (3) provides that:

In any case in which there is a maritime lien or other charge on any ship, aircraft or other property for the amount claimed, an action *in rem* may be brought in the High Court against that ship, aircraft or property.

The 1981 Act does not define what is meant by a maritime lien nor the circumstances in which such a lien comes into existence.

MARITIME LIENS[82]

8.1.25   A maritime lien is a privileged claim upon a ship, which attaches to the ship as soon as the claim arises. Of particular significance is that a maritime lien gives the claimant priority over other creditors and may be enforced against the ship even if the ship is sold to a third party after the claim arises. A maritime lien arises in respect of claims for damage caused by a ship and for certain services rendered to a ship (namely, salvage, wages, master's disbursements and bottomry).[83] These claims fall within paragraphs (e), (j), (o), (p) and (r) of section 20(2).

'OR OTHER CHARGE'

8.1.26   Section 21(3) does not apply to mortgages of ships, which are specifically dealt with by section 21(2).[84] In *The St Merriel*[85] Hewson J decided that the word 'charges' includes statutory charges, which are equated to maritime liens, but not a repairer's possessory lien.

Section 21(4): Cases Falling within Section 20(2)(e)–(r)

8.1.27   Subsection (4) is rather different from subsections (2) and (3) in that it provides that proceedings *in rem* may be brought in respect of one of a number of ships, but only if the ship in relation to which the claim is brought is owned (or, in

---

[82]   DR Thomas, *Maritime Liens* (London, Stevens, 1980).
[83]   DC Jackson, *Enforcement of Maritime Claims* (London: LLP, 4th edn, 2005) 29–50.
[84]   Referring to s 20(2)(c) of the Supreme Court Act 1981. See Hewson J in *The St Merriel* [1963] P 247, 251–2.
[85]   [1963] P 247, 254.

certain circumstances, chartered) by the person who would be the defendant were the proceedings brought *in personam*. Section 21(4), which unlike subsections (2) and (3) does not provide for proceedings *in rem* to be brought in respect of any property other than a ship, states:

In the case of any such claim as is mentioned in section 20(2)(e) to (r), where—

(a) the claim arises in connection with a ship; and
(b) the person who would be liable on the claim in an action in personam ('the relevant person') was, when the cause of action arose, the owner or charterer of, or in possession or in control of, the ship,

an action in rem may (whether or not the claim gives rise to a maritime lien on that ship) be brought in the High Court against—

(i) that ship, if at the time when the action is brought the relevant person is either the beneficial owner of that ship as respects all the shares in it or the charterer of it under a charter by demise; or
(ii) any other ship which at the time when the action is brought, the relevant person is the beneficial owner as respects all the shares in it.

Section 21(4) introduces a much greater degree of flexibility than subsections (2) and (3) since it provides for proceedings *in rem* to be brought in respect of either the ship which was directly involved in the events which gave rise to the claim in question or, in certain circumstances, another ship. The operation of section 21(4) is based on four notions: 'the relevant person'; 'the particular ship';[86] 'other ship'; and 'beneficial owner'.

THE RELEVANT PERSON (WHEN THE CAUSE OF ACTION AROSE)

8.1.28   A person is the relevant person only if a double requirement is satisfied: the relevant person not only must be the person who would be liable on the claim *in personam*, but also must have been the owner or charterer of the ship (or must have been in possession or control of it) when the cause of action arose. As regards the first requirement, the burden of proof is on the claimant. However, the claimant does not have to establish the relevant person's liability as a preliminary issue: 'So long as a [claimant's] case is not bound to fail so that he has an arguable case he is entitled … to proceed with it.'[87] The imposition of the second requirement means that section 21(4) cannot be invoked if:

the person who owns the vessel to be proceeded against is a different legal person from the person who was the owner or charterer of the vessel at the time when its claim arose or who was in possession or control of it at that time.[88]

In *The Kommunar (No 2)* Colman J gave the following example:

[I]f corporation A was the owner of the vessel at the time when the cause of action arose and, at that time, the person who would have been liable for the claim if pursued in personam, and if, subsequently, the debts of corporation A are transferred by law to corporation B, so that

---

[86] This is the expression used in Art 3 of the 1952 Arrest Convention.
[87] Clarke J in *The Yuta Bondarovskaya* [1998] 2 Lloyd's Rep 357, 361.
[88] Colman J in *The Kommunar (No 2)* [1997] 1 Lloyd's Rep 8, 11.

it alone can now be sued in personam for the claim in question, an action in rem cannot be brought against a vessel owned by corporation B unless it is possible to identify corporation B as the same legal person as corporation A.[89]

Where a claim arises in connection with a ship which, at that time, was owned by a Russian state enterprise, the claimant cannot proceed *in rem* in relation to that ship if, before the commencement of proceedings, the vessel becomes vested—through the process of privatisation—in a new Russian private joint stock company. Even if the private company succeeds to the assets and liabilities of the state enterprise, section 21(4) cannot apply because, in the absence of any provision of Russian law providing for the continuity of the legal personality of the state enterprise, it is not possible to identify the private company as the same legal person as the state enterprise.

8.1.29 In the context of section 21(4)(b) 'owner' means registered owner.[90] As regards the expression 'charterer', the position is less clear. There is no doubt that 'charterer' includes a demise charterer;[91] the question is whether it also covers other types of charterer. Although the majority of the Court of Appeal in *The Span Terza*[92] indicated that a time charterer was within the scope of the equivalent provision of the Administration of Justice Act 1956, in *The Evpo Agnic* Lord Donaldson MR, who had dissented in *The Span Terza*, reiterated his view that 'charterer' must mean demise charterer.[93] More recently, however, the Court of Appeal in *The Tychy*[94] reviewed the earlier cases and decided that, for the purposes of section 21(4)(b), 'charterer' includes a time charterer, a voyage charterer and a slot charterer.[95] The expression 'in possession or control' refers to a person—such as a salvor—who is in the position of a demise charterer, albeit not under a demise charter.[96]

8.1.30 In determining, for the purpose of subsection (4), whether a person would be liable on a claim *in personam* it should be assumed that he has his habitual residence or a place of business in England.[97] It should be stressed, however, that this provision is relevant only for determining the jurisdiction *in rem* of the court; it does not give the court jurisdiction *in personam* over the relevant person.

THE PARTICULAR SHIP: SECTION 21(4)(B)(I)

8.1.31 The particular ship is the ship in connection with which the claim arises. The claimant may bring proceedings *in rem* in relation to the particular ship if, at the time when the proceedings are brought, the relevant person is either the beneficial owner[98] of all the shares in the ship or a demise charterer. Normally, to establish that the relevant person is a demise charterer of the particular ship for the purposes of

---

[89] [1997] 1 Lloyd's Rep 8, 11.

[90] Lord Donaldson MR in *The Evpo Agnic* [1988] 1 WLR 1090, 1096.

[91] Lord Donaldson MR in *The Evpo Agnic* [1988] 1 WLR 1090, 1095. For the meaning of 'demise charter', see para 8.1.31.

[92] [1982] 1 Lloyd's Rep 225.

[93] [1988] 1 WLR 1090, 1095.

[94] [1999] 2 Lloyd's Rep 11. For conflicting views on the merits of this decision, see S Baughen, 'Slot charters and "sister-ship" arrests' [2000] *LMCLQ* 129; B Davenport, 'Slot Charters' (2000) 116 *LQR* 36.

[95] A slot charter is a voyage charter of part of a ship.

[96] Lord Donaldson MR in *The Evpo Agnic* [1988] 1 WLR 1090, 1095–6.

[97] Supreme Court Act 1981, s 21(7).

[98] See paras 8.1.32–8.1.36.

section 21(4)(b)(i), the claimant will have to point to a contract between the owner of the vessel and the person alleged to be the demise charterer; the contract will be regarded as a demise charter only if the owner has relinquished to the charterer his rights of possession and control, including the right to employ the master, officer and crew.[99] However, a contractual arrangement between the owner and charterer is not always required. In *The Guiseppe di Vittorio*[100] it was held that, where a government-owned ship was managed and operated by a state-owned corporation, the corporation could be regarded as the demise charterer for the purposes of section 20(4)(b)(i) if the rights enjoyed by the corporation under the legislation which determined its relationship with the owner were equivalent to those of a demise charterer under a contractual arrangement with the owner.

OTHER SHIP: SECTION 21(4)(B)(II)

8.1.32   In order for the claimant to be able to bring proceedings *in rem* in respect of any ship other than the particular ship, the relevant person must be the beneficial owner[101] of it; that the relevant person is a demise charterer is not sufficient. Generally speaking, where the court has jurisdiction *in rem* in respect of a ship by virtue of section 21(4)(b)(ii) that ship is a sister ship of the particular ship. However, section 21(4) is not limited to cases where the other ship and the particular ship are both owned by the relevant person. Where, for example, the relevant person is the charterer of one ship and the owner of another, if the claim arises in connection with the chartered vessel, the claimant may bring proceedings in respect of the ship owned by the relevant person in respect of liabilities incurred by the relevant person as charterer.[102]

BENEFICIAL OWNER

8.1.33   Although there has been judicial disagreement over the meaning of the words 'beneficial owner',[103] the accepted view is that beneficial ownership means equitable ownership, whether or not accompanied by legal ownership; it does not include possession and control (for example, under a charter by demise) falling short of legal or equitable ownership.[104] As a general rule, the registered owner is also the beneficial owner. However, section 21(4)(b) enables the claimant to arrest a ship which has been transferred into different legal ownership, the relevant person retaining beneficial ownership of the ship.[105] It has been said that 'where there is a suggestion of a trusteeship or a nominee holding, there is no doubt that the court can investigate it'.[106]

8.1.34   Various problems may arise in the determination of the beneficial ownership of a foreign ship. First, as the division between legal and equitable ownership has

---

[99] See Evans LJ in *The Guiseppe di Vittorio* [1998] 1 Lloyd's Rep 136, 156–8.
[100] [1998] 1 Lloyd's Rep 136. S Baughen, 'The *de facto* demise charterer' [1998] *LMCLQ* 161.
[101] See paras 8.1.33–8.1.38.
[102] *The Span Terza* [1982] 1 Lloyd's Rep 225.
[103] *The Andrea Ursula* [1973] QB 265; *The I Congreso del Partido* [1978] QB 500.
[104] The view of Robert Goff J in *The I Congreso del Partido* [1978] QB 500 was preferred in *The Father Thames* [1979] 2 Lloyd's Rep 364 and was endorsed by the Court of Appeal in *The Nazym Khikmet* [1996] 2 Lloyd's Rep 362.
[105] See *The Saudi Prince* [1982] 2 Lloyd's Rep 255.
[106] Slynn J in *The Aventicum* [1978] 1 Lloyd's Rep 184, 187.

no counterpart in many legal systems, it may be difficult to decide whether or not the rights of a foreign corporation under the relevant foreign law should be characterised as 'beneficial ownership' for the purposes of section 21(4). *The Nazym Khikmet*[107] concerned a vessel which was legally owned by the state of Ukraine, but which was managed and operated by a Ukrainian trading corporation. The plaintiff sought to establish that, in view of the range of rights enjoyed by the company under the law of Ukraine, the company should be regarded as the 'beneficial owner' of the ship. The Court of Appeal decided that, even though the company had a wide measure of commercial discretion in the operation of the ship, it did not enjoy what English law recognises as the rights of an equitable owner.[108]

8.1.35   Secondly, the proliferation of one-ship companies and complex corporate structures may make the determination of the beneficial ownership of a ship less than straightforward. Although 'the court in all cases can and in some cases should look behind the registered owner to determine the true beneficial ownership',[109] the court is not inclined to pierce the corporate veil unless there is a clear indication that the apparent arrangements are a sham or façade. So, in the absence of special circumstances, section 21(4) does not allow the claimant to bring proceedings *in rem* in relation to a ship owned by a subsidiary company of the relevant person or by a sister company.

8.1.36   In *The Maritime Trader*[110] the plaintiff issued a writ *in rem* in relation to a claim arising out of a charter concluded between the plaintiff and a German company. The writ was served on a ship owned by a subsidiary of the German company. The court had no jurisdiction in these circumstances since, although the German company owned all the shares in the subsidiary, it had no legal or equitable property in the assets of the subsidiary and it could not be said that the ship was beneficially owned by the relevant person. Similarly, in *The Evpo Agnic*[111] the plaintiffs owned a cargo being carried by a ship belonging to a one-ship Panamanian company. The ship sank and the plaintiffs brought proceedings *in rem* in relation to a ship owned by a second one-ship Panamanian company. Both companies had the same president, vice-president and shareholders. The Court of Appeal held that the court did not have jurisdiction *in rem* under section 21(4) and ordered the unconditional release of the vessel which had been arrested. The two ships were not in the same beneficial ownership, notwithstanding the fact that a number of vessels, including those owned by the two companies, were run as a fleet under the management of a third company.

8.1.37   By contrast, in *The Tjaskemolen*[112] the plaintiff sought to bring a claim arising out of a charterparty with a company known as Bayland. Proceedings were issued *in rem* and a vessel was arrested. The defendant applied for the vessel's release on the basis that it was the owner, having purchased the vessel from Bayland before the issue of the writ and the arrest of the vessel. The plaintiff argued that the sale from

---

[107] [1996] 2 Lloyd's Rep 362. E Haslam, 'The Odessa File: Post Socialist Property Rights in English Courts' (1997) 60 *MLR* 710. See also E Halsam, 'Post Soviet property rights in English courts' [1999] *LMCLQ* 491.
[108] See also *The Guiseppe di Vittorio* [1998] 1 Lloyd's Rep 136.
[109] Slynn J in *The Aventicum* [1978] 1 Lloyd's Rep 184, 187.
[110] [1981] 2 Lloyd's Rep 153.
[111] [1988] 1 WLR 1090.
[112] [1997] 2 Lloyd's Rep 465.

Bayland to the defendant was a sham and that therefore Bayland remained the vessel's beneficial owner for the purposes of section 21(4)(b)(ii). Clarke J held that the court did have jurisdiction under section 21(4): the sale to the defendant was a sham—in the sense that, rather than being a genuine commercial transaction, it was designed simply as a means of trying to prevent the arrest of Bayland's vessel—and did not have the effect of depriving Bayland of beneficial ownership of the ship.

8.1.38   For proceedings *in rem* to be maintained under section 21(4) the relevant person must have been the owner or charterer of the particular ship at the time when the cause of action arose and that person must also be the beneficial owner (or, in the case of proceedings concerning the particular ship, the demise charterer) of the ship in relation to which the proceedings are brought at the time when the proceedings are brought. Accordingly, where a ship has changed hands before proceedings are commenced the court has no jurisdiction *in rem* in relation to that ship.[113]

The Relationship between Section 21(3) and (4)

8.1.39   Subsections (3) and (4) overlap in certain respects. For example, in a salvage case in which the salvor has a maritime lien over the salved ship, the salvor's claim falls within section 21(4)—on the basis that the court has jurisdiction under section 20(2)(j)—as well as under section 21(3). A similar overlap exists in cases giving rise to a maritime lien which fall within one of paragraphs (e), (o), (p) and (r) of section 20(2). In these cases the claimant may proceed under either subsection. If the claimant relies on section 21(3), proceedings *in rem* may be brought only against the ship or other property in connection with which the claim arises. If the appropriate conditions are satisfied, the claimant may proceed under section 21(4) against either the particular ship or another ship, but not against other property.

Jurisdiction in Actions *In Personam*: Section 21(1) and Section 22

8.1.40   Proceedings *in personam* may be brought in relation to all cases coming within the admiralty jurisdiction of the High Court.[114] Indeed, as regards claims falling within section 20(2)(d) and section 20(3), the 1981 Act makes no provision for the claimant to enforce the claim otherwise than by proceedings *in personam*. Whereas a claim form *in rem* may not be served out of the jurisdiction, the Civil Procedure Rules make provision in certain circumstances for service out of the jurisdiction of a claim form *in personam*.[115] Special rules apply to collision claims and limitation claims. Section 22(2) of the 1981 Act provides:

The High Court shall not entertain any action in personam to enforce a claim to which this section applies unless—

---

[113] *The Mawan* [1988] 2 Lloyd's Rep 459.
[114] Supreme Court Act 1981, s 21(1).
[115] CPR 6.33, 6.36.

(a) the defendant has his habitual residence or a place of business within England or Wales; or

(b) the cause of action arose within inland waters of England or Wales or within the limits of a port of England or Wales; or

(c) an action arising out of the same incident or series of incidents is proceeding in the court or has been heard and determined in the court.[116]

So, a claim form in a collision claim cannot be served out of the jurisdiction unless the case falls within section 22(2)(a), (b) or (c) of the 1981 Act or the defendant has submitted to or agreed to submit to the jurisdiction and the court gives permission for service out of the jurisdiction in accordance with Part 6 of the Civil Procedure Rules.[117] Similarly, as regards limitation claims, service out of the jurisdiction is permissible only if (i) the case falls within section 22(2)(a), (b) or (c) of the 1981 Act or (ii) the defendant has submitted to or agreed to submit to the jurisdiction or (iii) the admiralty court has jurisdiction over the claim under any applicable convention and the court gives permission for service out of the jurisdiction in accordance with Part 6 of the Civil Procedure Rules.[118]

8.1.41   It should be noted that the restrictions imposed as regards collision claims apply only in cases where the claimant seeks permission to serve out of the jurisdiction and do not apply to claims *in rem*. Paragraphs (e) and (f) of section 20(2) confer jurisdiction on the admiralty court in relation to 'any claim for damage done by a ship' and certain claims 'for loss of life or personal injury'. Claims falling within these paragraphs may be enforced by means of proceedings *in rem*.[119]

Commencing Admiralty Proceedings

8.1.42   The relevant rules for the commencement of admiralty proceedings are to be found in Part 61 of the Civil Procedure Rules. Admiralty proceedings *in rem* are commenced by service of a claim form on the *res*. In addition, the claimant may obtain the arrest of the ship. Admiralty proceedings *in personam* are commenced by service of a claim form on the defendant. The tendency is for claimants to prefer to commence proceedings *in rem* where possible, since this is the most effective way of obtaining security for the claim.

Proceedings in Rem

8.1.43   The High Court's jurisdiction in admiralty proceedings *in rem* is strictly territorial. A claim form *in rem* must be served on the *res* within the jurisdiction of the court—which means in English territorial waters. There is no provision for a claim form *in rem* to be served out of the jurisdiction.[120] The basic rule is that a claim form *in rem* may be served by fixing it to the outside of the property in respect of which the

---

[116] See also CPR 61.4 (collision claims) and CPR 61.11 (limitation claims).
[117] CPR 61.4(7).
[118] CPR 61.11(5). See *ICL Shipping Ltd v Chin Tai Steel Enterprise Co Ltd* [2004] 1 WLR 2254.
[119] Supreme Court Act 1981, s 21(4).
[120] *Castrique v Imrie* (1870) LR 4 HL 414.

proceedings are brought.[121] It is not enough for the claimant to serve the claim form on the master on board the ship.[122]

8.1.44 In a typical case involving proceedings *in rem* involving a ship, the claim form may be served by fixing a copy of it on the outside of the ship in a position which may reasonably be expected to be seen.[123] However, in practice, the claim form is often served on a solicitor authorised to accept service[124] or in accordance with an agreement of the parties providing for service of proceedings.[125] A warrant for arrest is served in the same manner as an *in rem* claim form.[126]

8.1.45 A claim form and a warrant for arrest may be issued at the same time, whether or not the vessel is physically within the jurisdiction of the English court; either the claim form or the warrant for arrest may be served first. Only the Admiralty Marshal (or his substitute) may serve a warrant for arrest.[127] If the owner of the ship puts up security, the claimant will generally refrain from arresting the ship. Nevertheless, a claimant who satisfies the relevant statutory criteria and the provisions of the Civil Procedure Rules has a right of arrest.[128] Once an arrest has been effected, the owner of the ship may put up security in order to obtain the ship's release. Security may take the form of bail, which is an undertaking given to the court, or a guarantee or undertaking given out of court, usually by a bank or insurance company. Bail may be given only after acknowledgment of the claim form and in these cases the owner of the *res* is taken to have submitted personally to the court's jurisdiction.[129] Contractual security—for example, in the form of a letter of guarantee given out of court by the shipowner's P&I Club—may be given without the owner of the *res* submitting or agreeing to submit to the jurisdiction.[130] However, where—in return for not arresting the vessel—the P&I Club undertakes to appoint solicitors for the service of process, the court can order specific enforcement of this undertaking, thereby effectively forcing the defendant's submission.[131]

8.1.46 In cases falling within the scope of section 21(2) and (3) the claimant may bring proceedings only against the property in relation to which the claim arises. Under subsection (4), however, the claimant may have a choice as to the ship against which to proceed *in rem*. Where the court has jurisdiction *in rem* under section 21(4), by virtue of the fact that the claim falls within section 20(2)(e)–(r), the claimant may issue a claim form *in rem* against a number of ships (for example, the particular ship and one or more sister ships). Indeed, where possible, it is sensible to name in the claim

---

[121] CPR PD 61 para 3.6(1)(a). Where the claim concerns freight, service is to be effected on the cargo or the ship in which the cargo is carried: CPR PD 61 para 3.6(1)(b). See also *Owners of the Ship or Vessel Mt Rowan v Owners of the Ship or Vessel or Property Singapura Timur* [2004] 1 LRC 538 (High Court, Malaysia) in which, following a collision which led to the defendant's vessel sinking in the Straits of Malacca, a writ *in rem* was served on the defendant's vessel by a court-appointed diver.

[122] *The Prins Bernhardt* [1964] P 117.

[123] CPR PD 61 para 3.6(1)(a). If the property is freight, see CPR PD 61 para 3.6(1)(b).

[124] CPR PD 61 para 3.6(5).

[125] CPR PD 61 para 3.6(6).

[126] CPR PD 61 para 5.5(1).

[127] CPR 61.5(8).

[128] *The Varna* [1993] 2 Lloyd's Rep 253. M Dockray, 'Disclosure and Arrest of Ships' (1994) 110 *LQR* 382.

[129] *The Prinsengracht* [1993] 1 Lloyd's Rep 41.

[130] *The Deichland* [1990] 1 QB 361. For consideration of the importance of the form of security, see paras 8.2.9–8.2.10.

[131] *The Juntha Rajprueck* [2003] 2 Lloyd's Rep 107.

form as many of the ships against which proceedings *in rem* may be brought as can be identified, since it may not be possible to add further names to the claim form at a later stage.[132] Section 21(8) of the 1981 Act provides that once a ship has been served with process or arrested in proceedings *in rem* brought to enforce a claim under section 20(2)(e)–(r), no other ship may be served with process or arrested in that or any other proceedings *in rem* to enforce that claim. In such a case the claim form should be amended by deleting all the other names upon it.[133] The position is, therefore, that the claimant can keep his options open when the claim form is issued, but may proceed *in rem* against only one of the named ships.[134] Where a ship is arrested abroad and later released, section 21(8) does not prevent the subsequent arrest of the same vessel in England in the context of English proceedings *in rem*.[135] The court may, however, order the release of the vessel if it is satisfied that in the circumstances the arrest of the vessel is vexatious or oppressive or otherwise an abuse of the process of the court.[136]

Proceedings in Personam

8.1.47   Whereas a claim form *in rem* may be served only in England, a claim form commencing admiralty proceedings *in personam* may, in certain circumstances, be served out of the jurisdiction. In cases where the defendant is domiciled in a Member State, jurisdiction may be exercised only under Chapter II or under one of the special conventions whose effect is preserved by Article 71 of the Brussels I Regulation.[137] If jurisdiction is not regulated by the Brussels I Regulation (or the Lugano Convention), service out of the jurisdiction depends on the permission of the court. The conditions for the giving of permission in cases within the jurisdiction of the admiralty court are governed by the principles formulated under Part 6 of the Civil Procedure Rules; permission will not be given unless England is the 'proper place in which to bring the claim'.[138] Accordingly, in addition to the claim falling within the jurisdiction of the court, the evidence must reveal a serious question to be tried and the English court must be the *forum conveniens*.[139]

8.2 THE IMPACT OF THE BRUSSELS I REGULATION[140]

Introduction

The Basic Scheme

8.2.1   The Brussels I Regulation is intended to provide a comprehensive framework for the allocation of jurisdiction between the courts of the Member States in matters

---

[132] See, eg, *The Prevese* [1973] 1 Lloyd's Rep 202.
[133] *The Al Battani* [1993] 2 Lloyd's Rep 219.
[134] *The Berny* [1979] QB 80; *The Helene Roth* [1980] QB 273; *The Freccia del Nord* [1989] 1 Lloyd's Rep 388.
[135] *The Kommunar (No 2)* [1997] 1 Lloyd's Rep 8; *The Tjaskemolen (No 2)* [1997] 2 Lloyd's Rep 477.
[136] *The Tjaskemolen (No 2)* [1997] 2 Lloyd's Rep 477.
[137] See section 8.2 (Lugano Convention, Art 67).
[138] CPR 6.37(3).
[139] See section 7.3.
[140] TC Hartley, 'The Effect of the 1988 Brussels Judgments Convention on Admiralty Actions in Rem' (1989) 105 *LQR* 640.

falling within the Regulation's material scope. Since the Regulation applies to civil and commercial matters, proceedings within the jurisdiction of the admiralty court are almost invariably covered by Article 1.

8.2.2 According to the basic scheme of the jurisdiction rules contained in Chapter II, a defendant domiciled in a Member State may be sued either in the courts of the Member State in which he is domiciled or in the courts of another Member State in accordance with the provisions of Chapter II but not otherwise. Although, as a general rule, Chapter II does not allocate jurisdiction with regard to proceedings brought against a defendant who is not domiciled in a Member State, a number of the provisions of Chapter II apply regardless of the defendant's domicile.

Does the Brussels I Regulation Apply to Proceedings in Rem?

8.2.3 The jurisdiction rules in Chapter II are drafted with proceedings *in personam* in mind. For example, Article 2 provides that a person domiciled in a Member State may be sued in the courts of his domicile. As regards admiralty proceedings it is very common for proceedings to be brought *in rem*. What is the impact of Chapter II in these circumstances? Since in proceedings *in rem* service is effected on the *res*, there is potentially an argument that the Brussels I Regulation has no application because the defendant is not a person domiciled in a Member State. Although this argument was accepted by Sheen J in *The Deichland*,[141] it was rejected by the Court of Appeal.[142] The essential facts were very simple: the plaintiff commenced an action *in rem* in England by serving a writ on a vessel chartered by the defendant, a German company; security for the plaintiff's claim was put up on the defendant's behalf in consideration of the plaintiff refraining from arresting the vessel. The defendant sought a declaration that the English court had no jurisdiction and that, as a result of Article 2, the plaintiff should have brought the proceedings in Germany. The Court of Appeal decided that, even where proceedings are solely *in rem*, the person who is interested in contesting liability and against whom the plaintiff would wish to proceed *in personam* if an appearance were entered is being 'sued' for the purposes of Articles 2 and 3. So, proceedings *in rem* are governed by Chapter II in the same way as proceedings *in personam* even before the person who is interested in contesting liability has submitted to the jurisdiction. In *Republic of India v India Steamship Co (No 2)*[143] the House of Lords largely rejected the personification theory of proceedings *in rem* and confirmed the Court of Appeal's analysis in *The Deichland*. In the words of Lord Steyn:

The idea that a ship can be a defendant in legal proceedings was always a fiction. ... [A]n action in rem is an action against the owners from the moment that the Admiralty Court is seized with jurisdiction. ... From that moment the owners are parties to the proceedings in rem.[144]

---

[141] [1988] 2 Lloyd's Rep 454.
[142] [1990] 1 QB 361. G Hogan, (1990) 15 *EL Rev* 81, 82–4.
[143] [1998] AC 878. B Davenport, 'End of an Old Admiralty Belief' (1998) 114 *LQR* 169; FD Rose, 'The nature of Admiralty proceedings' [1998] *LMCLQ* 27. For a more critical view of the decision, see N Teare, 'The Admiralty action *in rem* and the House of Lords' [1998] *LMCLQ* 33.
[144] [1998] AC 876, 913.

The Preservation of Special Conventions

8.2.4   Chapter II does not contain the only bases of jurisdiction authorised by the Brussels I Regulation. As a general principle, the Regulation preserves the effect of special conventions concerning civil jurisdiction; Article 71 provides that it 'does not affect any conventions to which the Member States are parties and which, in relation to particular matters, govern jurisdiction'. Moreover, the courts of a Member State which is party to a special convention may assume jurisdiction in accordance with that convention even against a defendant who is domiciled in a Member State which is not a party to that convention[145]—although in such a situation the court must apply the procedural safeguards which Article 26 of the Brussels I Regulation[146] requires. The most important conventions in admiralty matters are the Arrest and Collision Conventions of 1952. Although attempts have been made to bring English law into line with the treaty obligations assumed by the United Kingdom under these conventions, the Supreme Court Act 1981 does not implement these conventions into English law as such.[147]

The Practical Effect of the Brussels I Regulation

8.2.5   Where the person who is interested in contesting the claim in proceedings *in rem* is not domiciled in a Member State, the rule is that the admiralty jurisdiction of the English court is based exclusively on the relevant provisions of the 1981 Act. Where, however, the defendant is domiciled in a Member State, it is not always sufficient that the claimant brings his claim within one of the heads of jurisdiction under the 1981 Act. On the basis of the Court of Appeal's decision in *The Deichland*,[148] the combined effect of Chapter II and Article 71 is that, if the person who is interested in contesting the claim in proceedings *in rem* is domiciled in a Member State, the court has jurisdiction under sections 20–24 of the 1981 Act only if the exercise of jurisdiction under these sections is consistent either with the terms of the Arrest Convention or the Collision Convention or with one of the heads of jurisdiction set out in Chapter II.[149] This proposition can be illustrated by a number of examples.

8.2.6   Suppose that a collision occurs in Rio de Janeiro harbour between the claimant's vessel and a vessel owned by the defendant, an Italian corporation; as a result of the collision the claimant's vessel is a constructive total loss; the claimant commences proceedings *in rem* by serving a claim form on the defendant's vessel in English

---

[145]   Brussels I Reg, Art 71(2). (Lugano Convention, Art 67(2).)

[146]   See section 4.4.

[147]   The precise relationship between the Brussels I Regulation and the jurisdictional provisions of the special conventions is uncertain. One possibility is that the provisions on jurisdiction contained in special conventions are to be treated as if they were provisions of the Brussels I Regulation itself: Schlosser Report, [1979] OJ C59/140, para 240(b); another is that the effect of Art 71 is to achieve 'an indirect incorporation' of the special conventions into English municipal law: Hobhouse J in *The Nordglimt* [1988] QB 183, 197. The idea that Art 71 could achieve indirect incorporation is controversial: see Lloyd LJ in *The Po* [1991] 2 Lloyd's Rep 206, 211.

[148]   [1990] 1 QB 361.

[149]   See Jenard Report, [1979] OJ C59/59.

waters; to prevent arrest security is put up by the defendant's P&I Club. It could be argued that, since the case concerns civil and commercial matters and the defendant is domiciled in Italy, the English court has no jurisdiction and the proceedings should be brought in Italy under Article 2. However, even though the Collision Convention as such does not form part of English law, the English court has jurisdiction not only under the 1981 Act, but under Article 1(1)(b) of the Collision Convention, which provides that proceedings in relation to a claim for collision occurring between seagoing vessels may be introduced 'before the court of the place ... where arrest could have been effected and bail or other security has been furnished'. In these circumstances, the claimant is able to rely on the terms of the Collision Convention.[150] The preservation of special conventions by Article 71 of the Brussels I Regulation does not depend on it being shown that the Member State has implemented the special convention; it is enough that the United Kingdom is a party to the special convention in question and that the English court has jurisdiction both under English domestic law and under the special convention. If these conditions are satisfied, it does not matter whether the special convention is part of English municipal law.[151]

8.2.7 Although the United Kingdom is a party to the Arrest Convention, it has never been given the force of law in English municipal law; Parliament has simply given effect to certain of the provisions of the Arrest Convention in sections 21 and 22 of the 1981 Act. Suppose that the plaintiff starts proceedings *in rem* in England in respect of a vessel owned by a defendant domiciled in a Member State; the vessel is arrested and security is put up for her release. Can the claimant rely on the 1981 Act notwithstanding the fact that proceedings fall within the scope of Article 1 of the Brussels I Regulation and the defendant is domiciled in a Member State? Although, in this situation, the court's jurisdiction is based on the 1981 Act, the assumption of jurisdiction is consistent with the terms of the Arrest Convention. As long as the assumption of jurisdiction is consistent with a special convention to which the United Kingdom is a party (and which is preserved by Article 71 of the Brussels I Regulation), the court is entitled to assume jurisdiction.[152]

8.2.8 The position is different, however, if the claimant seeks to rely on the 1981 Act but, in the circumstances of the case, the claimant does not proceed to arrest the defendant's vessel. Suppose that the claimant brings proceedings *in rem* in respect of a vessel chartered by the defendant, a German company, but the ship is not arrested, because security is put up in consideration of the claimant refraining from arresting the vessel. If the defendant were not domiciled in a Member State, the only relevant rules would be those contained in the 1981 Act—according to which the court has jurisdiction over the proceedings. However, if the defendant is domiciled in a Member State, the court is not competent unless it has jurisdiction either under Chapter II of the Brussels I Regulation or under a special convention preserved by Article 71. In a case where proceedings *in rem* are brought in England against a German defendant and the court does not have jurisdiction under Chapter II, the crucial question is

---

[150] *The Po* [1991] 2 Lloyd's Rep 206. TC Hartley, 'Coming to terms with the Brussels Jurisdiction and Judgments Convention' [1991] *LMCLQ* 446.
[151] Lloyd LJ in *The Po* at [1991] 2 Lloyd's Rep 206, 211.
[152] *The Nordglimt* [1988] QB 183.

whether the court has jurisdiction under the Arrest Convention. Although the 1981 Act incorporates the substance of the Arrest Convention, it is wider than the Arrest Convention itself; the 1981 Act is framed in such a way that the jurisdiction of the court is based on the service of process on the ship within the jurisdiction whether or not the ship is arrested. Article 7 of the Arrest Convention, however, is premised on the vessel in question having been arrested and confers jurisdiction on 'courts of the country in which the arrest was made'. By virtue of Article 71 of the Brussels I Regulation, where the defendant is domiciled in a Member State, the provisions of the 1981 Act are to be given effect only so far as they implement the Arrest Convention and not otherwise.[153]

8.2.9 Accordingly—except in those situations falling within the Collision Convention, under which jurisdiction does not depend on the ship having been arrested—a claimant who wishes to proceed in the admiralty court *in rem* in respect of a ship owned or chartered by a defendant who is domiciled in a Member State must ensure either that the ship is arrested or that the defendant submits or agrees to submit to the jurisdiction. In a case where contractual security is given without the defendant submitting to the jurisdiction, the claimant should proceed to arrest the vessel in order to found the jurisdiction of the court. Where the defendant puts up security in the form of a bail bond the court has jurisdiction over the defendant on the basis of submission and there is no need either to obtain an agreement to submit or to arrest the vessel.[154] This is because it is impossible for bail to be given unless the defendant has entered an appearance by voluntarily acknowledging service of process.

8.2.10 The effect of Article 71 is that, to the extent that the Arrest and Collision Conventions lay down positive jurisdiction rules, these rules prevail over the provisions of the Brussels I Regulation.[155] In collision proceedings, for example, the question whether it is possible to join further defendants to the proceedings has to be answered by reference to the terms of Article 3(3) of the Collision Convention (as implemented by domestic legislation), rather than according to Article 6 of the Brussels I Regulation.[156] What is the position, however, with regard to jurisdictional issues which are not directly addressed by the special conventions? If, for example, the Arrest Collision is silent on a particular point, to what extent is the gap filled by the Brussels I Regulation in cases where the person being sued is domiciled in a Member State? There is an argument for saying that, because the Brussels I Regulation preserves the effect of, *inter alia*, the Arrest Convention, the provisions of Chapter II cannot have the effect of restricting the English court's jurisdiction under the Arrest Convention (as implemented by the Supreme Court Act 1981). On the basis of the decision of Clarke J in *The Bergen*,[157] where a claimant starts proceedings *in rem* in England with a view to enforcing a claim under a bill of lading which contains a jurisdiction agreement in favour of the courts of another Member State, the court should

---

[153] *The Deichland* [1990] 1 QB 361. PB Carter, (1989) 60 *BYIL* 489.

[154] *The Prinsengracht* [1993] 1 Lloyd's Rep 41.

[155] *The Anna H* [1995] 1 Lloyd's Rep 11. TC Hartley, 'Jurisdiction under competing conventions' [1995] *LMCLQ* 31.

[156] *Doran v Power* [1997] ILPr 52 (Supreme Court, Ireland).

[157] [1997] 1 Lloyd's Rep 380. See also *Srl Siamar v Srl Spedimex* [1990] ILPr 266 (Court of Cassation, Italy).

not apply Article 23 of the Brussels I Regulation (which would require the court to decline jurisdiction). The argument in favour of this approach is that the application of Article 23 would have the effect of depriving the English court of the jurisdiction which it enjoys under the Supreme Court Act 1981 (to the extent that it implements the Arrest Convention). It might be questioned whether Clarke J's analysis is consistent with the decision of the Court of Justice in *Owners of the cargo lately laden on board the ship Tatry v Owners of the ship Maciej Rataj*.[158] In this case the Court of Justice ruled that, because the Arrest Convention contains no provisions dealing with concurrent proceedings, the provisions of the Brussels Convention relating to concurrent proceedings were applicable, notwithstanding the fact that the English court's jurisdiction was based on the Arrest Convention. It would seem that the application of this reasoning to a case like *The Bergen* should lead to the conclusion that, because the Arrest Convention is silent as to the effect of a jurisdiction clause, the court should apply Article 23 of the Brussels I Regulation and decline jurisdiction in favour of the courts of the Member State chosen by the parties.[159]

8.2.11   It should be noted that, in practical terms, the outcome in the majority of cases should be the same whether or not Article 23 of the Brussels I Regulation is held to be applicable.[160] Even if Article 23 is not applicable—and, as a result, the court is not required by the Regulation to decline jurisdiction—the court, in the exercise of its discretion, will normally hold the parties to their bargain and grant a stay of proceedings in favour of the chosen court.[161]

Limitation and Salvage

8.2.12   There are two provisions in the Brussels I Regulation which apply specifically to proceedings within the admiralty jurisdiction of the High Court.

Salvage of Cargo or Freight

8.2.13   Many matters relating to admiralty jurisdiction are governed by special conventions which are preserved by Article 71 of the Brussels I Regulation. Although the Arrest Convention allows a claimant to invoke the jurisdiction of a state in which a ship has been arrested on account of a salvage claim,[162] there is no equivalent jurisdiction in relation to salvaged cargo and freight. Under English law, however, the admiralty court has jurisdiction in respect of claims connected with salvaged cargo and freight.[163] In the absence of Article 5(7), the English court would no longer be able to exercise admiralty jurisdiction over defendants domiciled in a Member State in relation to such claims.

---

[158] Case C–406/92 [1994] ECR I–5439. See para 9.1.7.
[159] See KM Siig, 'Maritime jurisdiction agreements in the EU' [1997] *LMCLQ* 362.
[160] Following a subsequent application, the English proceedings were stayed under the court's inherent jurisdiction: *The Bergen (No 2)* [1997] 2 Lloyd's Rep 710.
[161] *The El Amria* [1981] 2 Lloyd's Rep 119. See section 9.4.
[162] Art 7(1)(b) of the 1952 Arrest Convention.
[163] Supreme Court Act 1981, s 20(2)(j).

8.2.14 Article 5(7) provides that a person domiciled in a Member State may be sued:

as regards a dispute concerning the payment of remuneration claimed in respect of the salvage of a cargo or freight, in the court under the authority of which the cargo or freight in question:

(a) has been arrested to secure such payment, or
(b) could have been so arrested, but bail or other security has been given;

provided that this provision shall apply only if it is claimed that the defendant has an interest in the cargo or freight or had such an interest at the time of salvage.

The limitations of this provision should be noted. It applies only where the defendant had an interest in the cargo or freight at the time of salvage and if the cargo or freight was arrested (or could have been arrested). The purpose of Article 5(7) is:

to confer jurisdiction only with regard to those claims which are secured by a maritime lien. If the owner of a ship in difficulties has concluded a contract for its salvage, as his contract with the cargo owner frequently obliges him to do, any disputes arising from the former contract will not be governed by this provision.[164]

Limitation of Liability

8.2.15 In English law the limitation of the liability of the owner of a seagoing ship may arise in one of two ways. First, where a claimant starts proceedings against the shipowner, limitation of liability may be raised by the shipowner by way of counterclaim. Secondly, if a shipowner anticipates a liability claim, it may be in his interest to take the initiative, in which case the proceedings take the form of originating proceedings against one or more of the potential claimants.

8.2.16 Article 7 of the Brussels I Regulation provides:

Where by virtue of this Regulation a court of a Member State has jurisdiction in actions relating to liability arising from the use or operation of a ship, that court, or any other court substituted for this purpose by the internal law of that Member State, shall also have jurisdiction over claims for limitation of such liability.

This provision is relevant where the shipowner brings an independent action against an actual or potential claimant with a view to limiting his liability.[165] In the situation where the shipowner takes the initiative he may, of course, rely on Articles 2–6. However, Articles 2–6 do not allow the shipowner to bring limitation proceedings in the courts of his domicile. Since the shipowner could be sued in the courts of his domicile, it is desirable also to allow the shipowner to have recourse to this jurisdiction. It is the purpose of Article 7 of the Brussels I Regulation to provide for this. The value of this provision to the shipowner is that it enables all proceedings concerning limitation to be concentrated in his home forum.[166]

---

[164] Schlosser Report, [1979] OJ C59/109, para 123(b).
[165] Schlosser Report, [1979] OJ C59/110, para 127.
[166] Schlosser Report, [1979] OJ C59/110, para 128(a).

9

DECLINING JURISDICTION
AND STAYING PROCEEDINGS

9.0.1 Since the main purpose of the Brussels I Regulation[1] is to facilitate the free flow of judgments it is important that the risks of irreconcilable judgments should be minimised. Accordingly, there are circumstances in which, although the courts of a Member State have *prima facie* jurisdiction under one of the bases set out in Chapter II (or under the court's traditional rules), it is provided that proceedings must be stayed or that jurisdiction must be declined; in some cases the courts of a Member State have a discretion as to whether to allow proceedings to continue (section 9.1).

9.0.2 Where proceedings are not stayed on the basis of the Brussels I Regulation, there are circumstances in which proceedings may nevertheless be stayed under the court's inherent jurisdiction. The exercise of the court's discretion is of fundamental importance when considering the boundaries of jurisdiction under traditional English rules. The most common basis for the grant of a stay is the doctrine of *forum non conveniens*.[2] In a case where the claim form is served in England as of right the defendant may obtain a stay of the proceedings by satisfying the court that the courts of another country provide a more appropriate forum. The general principles governing the circumstances in which a stay will be granted apply equally to proceedings *in personam* and proceedings *in rem* (section 9.2).[3] Where the parties have agreed to the jurisdiction of the courts of a particular country, special considerations apply (section 9.3). According to traditional rules, the English court will also decline jurisdiction in certain cases involving foreign land or foreign intellectual property rights (section 9.4). A further question is whether, in a case where the English court has jurisdiction by virtue of the provisions of the Brussels I Regulation, the court may nevertheless grant a stay in the exercise of its inherent jurisdiction or on some other basis (section 9.5).

---

[1] Reg (EC) 44/2001, [2001] OJ L12/1.

[2] In addition, CPR r 3.1 confers on the court, as part of its case management powers, the power to stay the whole or part of any proceedings either generally or until a specified date or event; this power is one of the ordinary and general powers of the court conferring a wide discretion to manage the proceedings as it thinks fit. The line of cases which has considered the staying of proceedings on the 'case management' basis includes: *Reichhold Norway ASA v Goldman Sachs International* [2000] 1 WLR 173; *National Westminster Bank v Utrecht-America Finance Company* [2001] 3 All ER 733; *Affymetrix Inc v Multilyte Ltd* [2005] ILPr 470; *CNA Insurance Co Ltd v Office Depot International (UK) Ltd* [2007] Lloyd's Rep IR 89; *Deutsche Bank AG v Sebastian Holdings Inc* [2010] 1 All ER (Comm) 808.

[3] The doctrine of *forum non conveniens* may be excluded, either expressly or impliedly, by statute in relation to certain types of claim. Eg, in *Milor SRL v British Airways Plc* [1996] QB 702 the Court of Appeal held, in a case where the English court had jurisdiction under the Warsaw Convention (as implemented by the Carriage by Air Acts (Application of Provisions) Order 1967), that there was no scope for the application of the doctrine of *forum non conveniens*. See also the similar decisions in *Royal & Sun Alliance Insurance plc v MK Digital Fze (Cyprus) Ltd* [2005] 2 Lloyd's Rep 679 and *Hatzl v XL Insurance Co Ltd* [2009] 1 Lloyd's Rep 555 in the context of the CMR Convention (on the carriage of goods by road).

9.1 DECLINING JURISDICTION AND STAYING
PROCEEDINGS UNDER THE BRUSSELS I REGULATION

9.1.1   The primary aim of the Brussels I Regulation is to achieve the simplification of the recognition and enforcement of judgments. The attainment of this goal depends, to a certain extent, on reducing the number of situations in which the courts of different states may render conflicting judgments.[4] The jurisdiction rules contained in Article 6 are designed to facilitate the consolidation of related actions in a single forum. Of more significance are the provisions which are 'intended, in the interests of the proper administration of justice ..., to prevent parallel proceedings before the courts of different [Member States] and to avoid conflicts between decisions which might result therefrom'.[5] In a situation where there are concurrent proceedings in two or more Member States, Articles 27–29 of the Brussels I Regulation give priority to the court first seised.[6] Article 27 is concerned with parallel proceedings or *lis pendens*—that is, proceedings in two or more Member States between the same parties and involving the same cause of action. If the conditions of this rule are satisfied any court other than the court first seised must stay its proceedings or decline jurisdiction. The effect of Article 28, which deals with situations where related actions are pending in the courts of different Member States, is that any court other than the court first seised may, as a matter of discretion, stay its proceedings or, in certain circumstances, decline jurisdiction. Article 29 applies where a dispute falls within the exclusive jurisdiction of more than one Member State; it provides that any court other than the court first seised must decline jurisdiction.

9.1.2   These provisions appear to have been devised to deal primarily with relatively simple situations involving a single claim (such as a breach of contract or a tort). Experience has shown that Articles 27 and 28 give rise to various problems and work less well in complex situations involving parallel claims involving similar, but not identical, subject-matters—particularly in the context of intellectual property disputes involving a range of similar (but distinct) national rights.[7]

General Considerations

The Significance of the Brussels I Regulation

9.1.3   The provisions concerning concurrent proceedings are limited to cases where 'proceedings'[8] in two or more Member States fall within the scope of Article 1.

---

[4] Case 144/86 *Gubisch Maschinenfabrik KG v Palumbo* [1987] ECR 4861, para 8.

[5] Case 144/86 *Gubisch Maschinenfabrik KG v Palumbo* [1987] ECR 4861, para 8.

[6] See PE Herzog, 'Brussels or Lugano, Should You Race to the Courthouse or Race for a Judgment?' (1995) 43 *Am J Comp L* 379, 381–4.

[7] See *Research in Motion UK Ltd v Visto Corp* [2008] FSR 499; CJS Knight, 'Complicating Simplicity: The "Court First Seised" and "Related Actions" in Article 28' (2008) 27 *CJQ* 454. With regard to Art 6, see also Case C–539/03 *Roche Nederland BV v Primus* [2006] ECR I–6535.

[8] The term 'proceedings' includes an application for the establishment of a liability fund under the Convention relating to the Limitation of Liability of Owners of Sea-Going Ships of 1957: Case C–39/02 *Maersk Olie & Gas A/S v Firma M de Haan en W de Boer* [2004] ECR I–9657.

Where, for example, A starts proceedings in Finland in breach of an arbitration clause against B and B applies to the English court for a declaration that A is bound by the agreement, Articles 27 and 28 of the Brussels I Regulation are inapplicable because the English proceedings are covered by the fourth exception to Article 1.[9] In *The Lake Avery*[10] the plaintiff alleged that the parties had concluded a contract which included an arbitration clause. The defendant started proceedings against the plaintiff in the Netherlands, the Dutch court exercising jurisdiction under Article 5(1). When the plaintiff subsequently sought a declaration from the English court to the effect that the alleged contract (including the arbitration clause) was binding on the defendant, the defendant applied for a stay. Clarke J held that, because the subject-matter of the English proceedings was 'arbitration' within the fourth exception in Article 1, the provisions relating to concurrent proceedings were not applicable.

Parties not Domiciled in a Member State

9.1.4   In *Overseas Union Insurance Ltd v New Hampshire Insurance Co*[11] there arose between the plaintiff, a company incorporated in Singapore, and the defendant, a company incorporated in New Hampshire but with business in France, a dispute on whether the plaintiff was bound by a reinsurance contract. The defendant started proceedings against the plaintiff in France to enforce the contract. When the plaintiff, having disputed the jurisdiction of the French court, started proceedings against the defendant in England with a view to obtaining a declaration that it was no longer bound by the contract, the defendant sought a stay of the English proceedings. One of the questions facing the court was whether the *lis pendens* rule applied in a situation where neither party was domiciled in a Member State.

9.1.5   The Court of Justice noted that the *lis pendens* rule 'makes no reference to the domicile of the parties to the proceedings'[12] and ruled that it must be applied regardless of the domicile of the parties. The purpose of the *lis pendens* rule is best served if it is interpreted 'as broadly as possible'[13]—so that it can be applied in all cases of proceedings pending before the courts of different Member States which are capable of leading to irreconcilable decisions. It is reasonable to suppose that the approach taken by the Court of Justice in *Overseas Union Insurance Ltd v New Hampshire Insurance Co* applies equally to all the provisions which seek to regulate concurrent proceedings.

---

[9] *Through Transport Mutual Insurance Association (Eurasia) Ltd v New India Assurance Co Ltd* [2005] 1 Lloyd's Rep 67. The applicability of the *lis pendens* rule in cases involving arbitration was referred by the Court of Appeal in Case C–190/89 *Marc Rich & Co AG v Società Italiana Impianti PA* [1991] ECR I–3855, but the issue was not directly addressed by the Court of Justice. See also B Audit, 'Arbitration and the Brussels Convention' (1993) 9 *Arb Int* 1, 23.

[10] [1997] 1 Lloyd's Rep 540.

[11] Case C–351/89 [1991] ECR I–3317. A Briggs, (1991) 11 *YBEL* 521; TC Hartley, (1992) 17 *EL Rev* 75.

[12] [1991] ECR I–3317, para 13.

[13] Advocate General Van Gerven in Case C–351/89 *Overseas Union Insurance Ltd v New Hampshire Insurance Co* [1991] ECR I–3317, para 9.

The Bases of Jurisdiction on which the Concurrent Proceedings are Founded

9.1.6   The scope of the provisions dealing with concurrent proceedings is not limited to cases where the courts have assumed jurisdiction under the direct juris-diction provisions contained in Chapter II. The Court of Justice's interpretation in *Overseas Union Insurance Ltd v New Hampshire Insurance Co* means that Article 27 applies in cases where, in accordance with the provisions of Article 4, a court of a Member State assumes jurisdiction by virtue of the law of that state over a defendant who is not domiciled in a Member State.[14] For example, in a case involving a dispute between A, a French national domiciled in New York, and B, a Mexican corpora-tion, if the French court assumes jurisdiction on the basis of A's French nationality and B starts parallel proceedings in England by serving a claim form on A during A's temporary presence in England, the English court is required to apply Article 27 of the Brussels I Regulation, even though neither party is domiciled in a Member State and none of the direct jurisdiction provisions of Chapter II of the Regulation is relevant.

    9.1.7   The notion that the provisions dealing with concurrent proceedings should be regarded as having a broad scope was confirmed in *Owners of the cargo lately laden on board the ship Tatry v Owners of the ship Maciej Rataj*.[15] One of the ques-tions raised by this case is whether the concurrent proceedings provisions are appli-cable in a situation where the English court exercises jurisdiction under the Arrest Convention of 1952, one of the special conventions preserved by the Brussels I Regulation.[16] The Court of Justice adopted the approach of the Schlosser Report, according to which the provisions of the Brussels regime apply to the extent that a special convention does not contain rules covering a particular matter.[17] The effect of the Court of Justice's ruling is that, when a specialised convention (such as the Arrest Convention) contains certain rules of jurisdiction but no provisions on *lis pendens* or related actions, Articles 27 and 28 of the Brussels I Regulation determine the priority of concurrent proceedings brought in two or more Member States.[18] However, if a specialised convention does expressly deal with the problem of con-current proceedings, the relevant provisions of the specialised convention apply and displace Articles 27 and 28.[19] The Court of Justice's ruling in the *Tatry* case is not uncontroversial and its reasoning has been the subject of criticism[20] on the

---

[14]   [1991] ECR I–3317, para 13.
[15]   Case C–406/92 [1994] ECR I–5439.
[16]   Brussels I Reg, Art 71. See section 8.2.
[17]   [1979] OJ C59/140, para 240(b).
[18]   Case C–406/92 [1994] ECR I–5439, paras 25–7. It is difficult to reconcile the decision of Judge Brice QC in *Deaville v Aeroflot Russian International Airlines* [1997] 2 Lloyd's Rep 67 (a case involving the Warsaw Convention) with this ruling.
[19]   In the context of claims within the scope of the CMR Convention, see *Andrea Merzario Ltd v Internationale Spedition Leitner Gesellschaft GmbH* [2001] 1 Lloyd's Rep 490; *Royal & Sun Alliance Insurance plc v MK Digital Fze (Cyprus) Ltd* [2005] 2 Lloyd's Rep 679 (reversed on appeal, but without the Court of Appeal having to address the concurrent proceedings issue: [2006] 2 Lloyd's Rep 110); *Sony Computer Entertainment Ltd v RH Freight Services Ltd* [2007] ILPr 314; *Hatzl v XL Insurance Co Ltd* [2009] 1 Lloyd's Rep 555. See also the view of the German courts in *Re Parallel Proceedings relating to an International Contract of Carriage of Goods by Road* [2004] ILPr 356 (Federal Supreme Court, Germany).
[20]   See A Briggs, (1994) 14 *YBEL* 579, 581.

basis that the effect of the ruling is to allow jurisdiction exercised under the Arrest Convention to be defeated by the concurrent proceedings provisions, even though it is provided that such provisions 'shall not affect' the specialised conventions to which the Member States are parties.[21] Nevertheless, the decision can be supported on policy grounds. There is no convincing reason why the general principles concerning *lis pendens* which are applicable to claims *in personam* should not also apply to claims *in rem*.[22]

Enforcement Proceedings

9.1.8 A question arises whether the provisions relating to concurrent proceedings apply only to original proceedings—that is, proceedings which might lead to a judgment—or whether enforcement proceedings also fall within their scope. On the basis of the Court of Justice's ruling in *Owens Bank Ltd v Bracco*,[23] it is clear that Articles 27 and 28 of the Brussels I Regulation do not apply to proceedings, or issues arising in proceedings, concerning the recognition and enforcement of judgments given in civil and commercial matters in non-Member States.[24] So, where a claimant seeks to enforce a New York judgment, first in Italy and secondly in England, the English court is not required to decline jurisdiction or grant a stay of proceedings, even if the defendant resists enforcement in both Member States by raising the defence of fraud. The fact that proceedings in Italy and England to enforce a judgment granted by the New York courts may raise the same factual issues does not bring Articles 27 and 28 into play.

9.1.9 There is some doubt whether all enforcement proceedings fall outside the scope of the provisions dealing with concurrent proceedings or whether only proceedings concerning the enforcement of judgments granted by the courts of non-Member States are excluded. In *Owens Bank Ltd v Bracco* Advocate General Lenz favoured the view that the concurrent proceedings provisions should apply only to original proceedings,[25] but the Court of Justice's judgment does not expressly decide the issue.[26] Accordingly, it should not be assumed that concurrent proceedings involving the enforcement of a judgment given by the courts of a Member State fall outside the scope of Articles 27 and 28. Having said that, it should be stressed that the only provision which might potentially be relevant is Article 28; there is no basis on which Article 27 or Article 29 might apply in a case involving the enforcement of the same judgment in more than one Member State.[27]

---

[21] Brussels I Reg, Art 71.

[22] See TC Hartley, (1995) 20 *EL Rev* 409, 413–14.

[23] Case C–129/92 [1994] ECR I–117. A Briggs, (1994) 14 *YBEL* 557; R Fentiman, [1994] *CLJ* 239; E Peel, 'Recognition and Enforcement under the Brussels Convention' (1994) 110 *LQR* 386.

[24] Case C–129/92 *Owens Bank Ltd v Bracco* [1994] ECR I–117, para 37. See also *Dubai Bank Ltd v Abbas* [1998] ILPr 391.

[25] Case C–129/92 [1994] ECR I–117, para 62.

[26] Case C–129/92 [1994] ECR I–117, paras 17–25.

[27] See Advocate General Lenz in Case C–129/92 *Owens Bank Ltd v Bracco* [1994] ECR I–117, paras 63–7.

The Court First Seised

9.1.10 A concept which is central to the operation of the provisions dealing with concurrent proceedings is 'the court first seised'. Under the Brussels Convention, the question of when a court becomes 'seised' was governed by the national law of the court concerned.[28] There are two main problems with this approach. First, the court has to determine and apply foreign law, which makes the proceedings longer and more complex than might otherwise be the case.[29] Secondly, because of different procedural systems in different Member States, C may, by starting proceedings against D in one Member State, have an (arguably) arbitrary advantage over D, who starts proceedings against C in another Member State.

9.1.11 During the negotiations which led to the enactment of the Brussels I Regulation, it was decided that the new provisions would lay down a uniform rule for defining the date on which proceedings are 'pending'. Article 30 of the Brussels I Regulation provides that, for the purposes of Articles 27–29, a court becomes seised:

1. at the time when the document instituting the proceedings or an equivalent document is lodged with the court, provided that the plaintiff has not subsequently failed to take the steps he was required to take to have service effected on the defendant, or
2. if the document has to be served before being lodged with the court, at the time when it is received by the authority responsible for service, provided that the plaintiff has not subsequently taken the steps he was required to take to have the document lodged with the court.

The aim of this provision is to provide a level playing field, notwithstanding the fact that different procedural models operate in different Member States.[30] The effect of Article 30 is that the court becomes seised as soon as the claimant takes the first substantial step required by the procedural law of the forum in question to institute proceedings (either lodging the document instituting the proceedings with the court or setting in motion the procedure for service of process of the defendant). However, in order for the first step in the procedure to be treated as the time when the court is seised, the claimant must subsequently take the further steps necessary for the proceedings to become definitively pending. As far as English proceedings are concerned, the court becomes seised for the purposes of Article 30 when the claim form

---

[28] Under the Brussels Convention (and the original Lugano Convention), a court was seised when 'the requirements for proceedings to become definitively pending are ... fulfilled' and the relevant requirements are 'to be determined in accordance with the national law of each of the courts concerned': Case 129/83 *Zelger v Salinitri (No 2)* [1984] ECR 2397, para 16 (TC Hartley, (1985) 10 *EL Rev* 56). Under the Brussels Convention, if proceedings were commenced in England and Greece, it was for English law to determine when the English court was seised and for Greek law to determine when the Greek court was seised: *Tavoulareas v Tsavliris* [2004] 1 Lloyd's Rep 445. On the question of when the English court became seised for the purposes of the Brussels Convention and the original Lugano Convention, see *The Freccia del Nord* [1989] 1 Lloyd's Rep 388; *Dresser UK Ltd v Falcongate Freight Management Ltd* [1992] 1 QB 502; *The Sargasso* [1994] 3 All ER 180; *Phillips v Symes (No 3)* [2008] 1 WLR 180.

[29] See, eg, *Grupo Torras SA v Sheikh Fahad Mohammed al Sabah* [1995] ILPr 667; *Molins Plc v GD SpA* [2000] 2 Lloyd's Rep 234; *Carnoustie Universal SA v International Transport Workers' Federation* [2002] 2 All ER (Comm) 657.

[30] See European Commission, *Proposal for a Council Regulation (EC) on jurisdiction and the recognition and enforcement of judgments in civil and commercial matters* (hereafter '*Proposal*'), COM (1999) 348 final, p 20.

is issued—so long as the claimant does not subsequently fail to effect service of the claim form on the defendant. If difficulties relating to the interpretation of Article 30 arise, the provision should be given its ordinary and natural meaning.[31]

Concurrent Proceedings Commenced on the Same Day

9.1.12 The provisions relating to concurrent proceedings are premised on one court being seised of proceedings before another (or others). It is not easy to see how these provisions can be applied in cases where the courts of two or more Member States are seised of proceedings on the same day. It is almost impossible for the court to determine accurately the precise moment in the day on which the originating documents were either issued or served. One possible solution is that Articles 27 and 28 do not apply if the competing courts were seised on the same day—with the consequence that each set of proceedings may proceed to judgment.[32] In the event that the concurrent proceedings produce irreconcilable judgments, the solution has to be found in Chapter III.[33]

Concurrent Proceedings

9.1.13 The rules concerning concurrent proceedings apply only to the extent that proceedings are continuing in two or more Member States. Accordingly, if proceedings commenced in the court first seised are 'definitively terminated'—so that the court first seised is no longer seised of the proceedings—Articles 27 and 28 are not applicable to the proceedings in the court second seised.[34] As Morison J noted in *Internationale Nederlanden Aviation Lease BV v Civil Aviation Authority*, if the provisions relating to concurrent proceedings 'are directed at the problems caused by *lis alibi pendens*, once the *lis* has ceased, so that the court is no longer seised of the matter, the Articles have no application'.[35] The proceedings in the two (or more) Member States 'must both be current so that they can be said to be concurrent'.[36]

9.1.14 Equally, where the proceedings in the court first seised have been concluded by virtue of judgment having been given, the provisions designed to deal with concurrent proceedings can have no application.[37] If the courts of a Member State (state A) have already given judgment and one of the parties seeks to litigate the same or related matters before the courts of another Member State (state B), to determine whether or not the proceedings in state B are barred by the proceedings in state A,

---

[31] See, eg, *WPP Holdings Italy Srl v Benatti* [2007] 1 WLR 2316.

[32] See *SA CNV v S GmbH* [1991] ILPr 588 (Court of Appeal, Koblenz).

[33] Brussels I Reg, Art 34(3) and (4). See paras 13.3.35–13.3.39.

[34] Case C–39/02 *Maersk Olie & Gas A/S v Firma M de Haan en W de Boer* [2004] ECR I–9657, para 41.

[35] [1997] 1 Lloyd's Rep 80, 93.

[36] Morison J in *Internationale Nederlanden Aviation Lease BV v Civil Aviation Authority* [1997] 1 Lloyd's Rep 80, 93. See also *Tavoulareas v Alexander G Tsavliris and Sons Maritime Co (No 2)* [2006] 1 All ER (Comm) 130.

[37] See Dillon LJ in *Berkeley Administration Inc v McClelland* [1995] ILPr 201, 209. See also *Tavoulareas v Alexander G Tsavliris and Sons Maritime Co (No 2)* [2006] 1 All ER (Comm) 130.

regard must be had to the rules relating to the recognition of judgments to be found in Chapter III, rather than those dealing with concurrent proceedings.[38] A judgment which is entitled to recognition gives rise to an estoppel *per rem judicatam* which prevents the parties reopening matters which were decided by the court first seised.

Lis Pendens

The Operation of Article 27

9.1.15   Article 27 of the Brussels I Regulation provides:

1. Where proceedings involving the same cause of action and between the same parties are brought in the courts of different Member States, any court other than the court first seised shall of its own motion stay its proceedings until such time as the jurisdiction of the court first seised is established.
2. Where the jurisdiction of the court first seised is established, any court other than the court first seised shall decline jurisdiction in favour of that court.

The effect of Article 27 is that, if the relevant conditions are satisfied, any court other than the court first seised must, depending on the circumstances, either stay its proceedings or decline jurisdiction. If the claimant starts proceedings in Italy and the defendant contests the jurisdiction of the Italian court and starts proceedings against the claimant in England, Article 27(1) requires the English court to stay the proceedings. If the defendant's challenge to the Italian court's jurisdiction is upheld, the English court may lift the stay and allow the English proceedings to continue. If, however, the defendant's challenge to the Italian court's jurisdiction is rejected, the jurisdiction of the court first seised 'is established' and the English court must decline jurisdiction under Article 27(2).[39] Similarly, if the jurisdiction of the court first seised is not contested, jurisdiction must be declined.[40]

The Same Cause of Action

9.1.16   Although the English and German versions of the text refer to the 'same cause of action', the duty to stay or dismiss proceedings on the basis of Article 27 does not arise unless the proceedings involve 'the same cause of action' and 'the same object' (or 'subject-matter'). This interpretation results from the fact that other language versions draw a distinction between the cause of action and the object of the proceedings.[41] To determine whether proceedings between the same parties in different Member States involve the same cause of action, the court should only take into account the claims of the two claimants, to the exclusion of the defence

---

[38] Chadwick LJ in *Prudential Assurance Co Ltd v Prudential Insurance Co of America* [2003] 1 WLR 2295, 2307 (at [26]). For consideration of Chapter III of the Regulation, see ch 13.
[39] See *Société Belt Buckle v Guenoun* [2006] ILPr 801 (Court of Cassation, France).
[40] *Protis Sàrl v Cidue SpA* [1991] ILPr 312 (Court of Cassation, France).
[41] Case 144/86 *Gubisch Maschinenfabrik KG v Palumbo* [1987] ECR 4861, para 14.

submissions raised by the defendants.[42] The concepts employed in Article 27 should be given an autonomous EU interpretation and should not be understood by reference to national law.[43]

9.1.17   *Gubisch Maschinenfabrik KG v Palumbo*[44] concerned a dispute relating to the validity of a contract for the sale of goods. The German 'seller' started proceedings in Germany against an Italian 'buyer' to enforce the terms of the disputed contract. When the 'buyer' started proceedings in Rome with a view to obtaining a declaration that the alleged contract was not binding on him, the 'seller' contested the jurisdiction of the Italian courts. The main question facing the court was whether the German and Italian proceedings could be said to have the same cause of action and the same object 'when the first seeks to enforce the contract and the second seeks its rescission or discharge'[45] or whether the two sets of proceedings merely involved related actions.

9.1.18   Advocate General Mancini thought that two sets of proceedings did not involve either the same object or the same cause of action since the Italian action was 'for a *declaration* that a contract of sale is *inoperative* because the offer was revoked', whereas the claim in German proceedings assumed that the contract was valid and sought 'to *obtain judgment* for the amount of the price'.[46] According to the Advocate General, the *lis pendens* rule should be interpreted strictly on the basis that a broad interpretation confuses matters which are meant to be kept apart, namely related actions and *lis pendens*.[47] The Court of Justice did not agree with the Advocate General's analysis and decided, first, that the German and Italian proceedings involved the same cause of action, because the proceedings arose out of the same contractual relationship, and secondly, that they involved the same object, since the question whether the contract was binding between the parties lay at the heart of the two actions.[48]

9.1.19   The scope of Article 27 is not limited to claims which are entirely identical.[49] It follows that parallel proceedings *in personam* and *in rem* in different Member States may be regarded as involving the same cause of action and the same object.[50] Although there are differences in character between a claim *in rem* and a claim *in personam* there are no differences between the essential elements of the cause of action in the two types of proceedings. Whether a claim is brought *in personam* or *in rem* the underlying complaint is the same and the essential facts which the claimant must

---

[42] Case C-111/01 *Gantner Electronic GmbH v Basch Exploitatie Maatschappij BV* [2003] ECR I-4207, para 26; Case C-39/02 *Maersk Olie & Gas A/S v Firma M de Haan en W de Boer* [2004] ECR I-9657, para 36. See also *Re Termination of an Agency Contract* [1998] ILPr 815 (Court of Appeal, Munich).

[43] See *Société Normane de Transit et de Consignation v Sarl Jarry Plastique* [2006] ILPr 732 (Court of Cassation, France).

[44] Case 144/86 [1987] ECR 4861. TC Hartley, (1988) 13 *EL Rev* 216.

[45] Case 144/86 [1987] ECR 4861, para 15.

[46] Case 144/86 [1987] ECR 4861, para 4. (Emphasis in original.)

[47] Case 144/86 [1987] ECR 4861, para 3.

[48] Case 144/86 [1987] ECR 4861, para 16. See also *Re an Application for a Stay of Proceedings* [2003] ILPr 640 (Federal Supreme Court, Germany).

[49] Case 144/86 [1987] ECR 4861, para 17.

[50] Case C-406/92 *Owners of the cargo lately laden on board the ship Tatry v Owners of the ship Maciej Rataj* [1994] ECR I-5439, para 48.

establish to support his right to the judgment of the court are the same.[51] (This still leaves the question whether the parties to the two sets of proceedings are the same.[52]) In a case where, following a collision between vessel X and vessel Y, foreign liability proceedings are commenced by parties interested in vessel Y and English limitation proceedings are brought by the owners of vessel X, there is a good argument for saying that the concurrent proceedings involve the same object or subject-matter.[53] The position is more difficult where there is only a partial overlap between the substance of two claims—for example, where the second cause of action is broader than the first. One solution is to apply Article 28—rather than Article 27—on the basis that the two actions are 'related'. In view of the overriding consideration of reducing the incidence of conflicting judgments, the preferable solution is for the court second seised to be regarded as under a duty to grant a stay or to decline jurisdiction (as the case may be).[54]

9.1.20 The logic of the decision in *Gubisch Maschinenfabrik KG v Palumbo* is perhaps rather surprising; if proceedings for a negative declaration are started first, this will have the effect of paralysing any subsequent proceedings in another forum. This was the conclusion reached by the Court of Justice in *Owners of the cargo lately laden on board the ship Tatry v Owners of the ship Maciej Rataj*.[55] The shipowners started proceedings in the Netherlands with a view to obtaining a declaration that the cargo owners were not entitled to the remedy of damages against them. Subsequently, the cargo owners claimed damages in proceedings brought against the shipowners in England. One of the bases on which the shipowners contested the jurisdiction of the English court was the *lis pendens* rule.

9.1.21 The Court of Justice decided that the Dutch proceedings for a declaration of non-liability and the English claim for damages involved the same cause of action—which the Court of Justice defined as 'the facts and the rule of law relied on as the basis of the action'.[56] Furthermore, the object of each action—that is, 'the end the action has in view'[57]—was the same even though the first was seeking a declaration that the plaintiff was not liable for damage as claimed by the defendants, while the second was seeking to have the plaintiff in the Dutch proceedings held liable for causing loss and ordered to pay damages:

As to liability, the second action has the same object as the first, since the issue of liability is central to both actions. The fact that the plaintiff's pleadings are couched in negative terms

---

[51] *The Deichland* [1990] 1 QB 391; *The Kherson* [1992] 2 Lloyd's Rep 261.

[52] See paras 9.1.24–9.1.34.

[53] See Saville LJ in *The Happy Fellow* [1998] 1 Lloyd's Rep 13, 18 (doubting the contrary view of the judge at first instance: [1997] 1 Lloyd's Rep 130).

[54] *William Grant & Sons International Ltd v Marie Brizzard et Roger International SA* [1997] ILPr 391 (Court of Session, Scotland).

[55] Case C–406/92 [1994] ECR I–5439. A Briggs, (1994) 14 *YBEL* 579; A Briggs, 'The Brussels Convention tames the Arrest Convention' [1995] *LMCLQ* 161; B Davenport, 'Forum Shopping in the Market' (1995) 111 *LQR* 366; R Fentiman, [1995] *CLJ* 261; TC Hartley, (1995) 20 *EL Rev* 409. The decision was applied in *Re a Clothing Sale Contract* [1995] ILPr 172 (Court of Appeal, Munich); *Re a Sale of Shares* [1996] ILPr 292 (Federal Supreme Court, Germany).

[56] Case C–406/92 [1994] ECR I–5439, para 39. See also Case C–39/02 *Maersk Olie & Gas A/S v Firma M de Haan en W de Boer* [2004] ECR I–9657, para 38; *Glencore International AG v Metro Trading International Inc* [1999] 2 Lloyd's Rep 632.

[57] Case C–406/92 [1994] ECR I–5439, para 41.

in the first action, whereas in the second action they are couched in positive terms by the defendant, who has become plaintiff, does not make the object of the dispute different.

As to damages, the pleas in the second action are the natural consequence of those relating to the finding of liability and thus do not alter the principal object of the action. Furthermore, the fact that a party seeks a declaration that he is not liable for loss implies that he disputes any obligation to pay damages.[58]

In a case involving both a contractual claim (under a contract between C and D) and a tortious claim (based on allegations of fraud on the part of D), the tortious claim does not involve the same cause of action as the contractual claim even though both claims arise out of the same overall factual situation.[59] Claims arising out of a single contract will normally involve the same cause of action, though it does not follow that all such claims involve the same object. Where, for example, a distribution contract between C (the distributor) and D (the manufacturer) is terminated by D, the claim by C for commission earned prior to the termination does not have the same object as proceedings brought by D for a declaration that the contract was validly terminated.[60] Similarly, an application for damages (which seeks to have the defendant declared liable) does not have the same subject-matter as an application to limit liability under the 1957 Convention relating to the Limitation of Liability of Owners of Sea-Going Ships (which is designed to ensure that any liability will be limited to an amount calculated in accordance with the 1957 Convention).[61]

9.1.22 A simple rule which requires all courts other than the court first seised to decline jurisdiction might be thought not to be a very satisfactory way of dealing with the problems posed by proceedings for a negative declaration, since in a case such as *Owners of the cargo lately laden on board the ship Tatry v Owners of the ship Maciej Rataj* it may lead to the more appropriate forum for the trial of the proceedings being displaced in favour of the forum in which the negative declaration is sought. However, the relative appropriateness of the competing fora is not a significant factor in the resolution of jurisdictional issues under the Brussels I Regulation and there is no reason why, as far as the operation of jurisdiction rules is concerned, claims for a negative declaration should be singled out for different treatment.[62] Furthermore, it has been convincingly argued that it is far too simplistic to equate an application for negative declaratory relief with forum shopping.[63]

9.1.23 Notwithstanding the broad approach to the phrase 'cause of action' adopted by the Court of Justice, the English courts have been keen to police the boundary between Article 27 and Article 28 carefully.[64] English proceedings to enforce the terms of a loan agreement do not involve the same cause of action as preliminary proceedings in Spain which do not lead to a determination of the merits, their object

---

[58] Case C–406/92 [1994] ECR–5439, paras 39–44. See also *JP Morgan v Primacom* [2005] 2 Lloyd's Rep 665.

[59] *Bank of Tokyo-Mitsubishi v Baskan Gida Sanayi Ve Pazarlama* [2004] 2 Lloyd's Rep 395.

[60] *Re Termination of an Agency Contract* [1998] ILPr 815 (Court of Appeal, Munich).

[61] Case C–39/02 *Maersk Olie & Gas A/S v Firma M de Haan en W de Boer* [2004] ECR I–9657, para 35.

[62] See *Messier-Dowty Ltd v Sabena SA* [2000] 1 WLR 2040; *Bristow Helicopters Ltd v Sikorsky Aircraft Corporation* [2004] 2 Lloyd's Rep 150. Compare *The Volvox Hollandia* [1988] 2 Lloyd's Rep 361.

[63] A Bell, 'The Negative Declaration in Transnational Litigation' (1995) 111 *LQR* 674.

[64] See also *Re a Claim by a German Lottery Company* [2005] ILPr 492 (Court of Appeal, Cologne).

being simply to convert the loan agreement into a 'public document' which can be relied upon in subsequent proceedings.[65] German proceedings concerning the alleged infringement of a German registered trade mark do not involve the same cause of action as English passing off proceedings.[66] Greek proceedings for the recovery of money do not have the same cause of action as English proceedings for the tracing of the money into assets acquired with it and the establishment of beneficial ownership of such assets.[67] Spanish proceedings in which the claimant seeks damages on the basis that the defendant's misrepresentation induced the claimant to enter a contract with one of the defendant's subsidiary companies do not involve the same cause of action as English proceedings in which the claimant seeks damages from the defendant for non-performance of the contract with the subsidiary on the basis that the defendant is liable for the subsidiary's default.[68] English proceedings involving claims founded on breaches of contract do not involve the same cause of action as Greek proceedings which concern claims arising outside the contract and founded on tort or statute.[69]

The Same Parties

9.1.24   The requirement that the parallel proceedings should involve the same parties is satisfied in a case where C sues D in one state and D sues C in another state. The question whether the parties are the same cannot depend on the procedural position of each of them in the two sets of proceedings; the claimant in the first proceedings may be the defendant in the second.[70] In addition, the court should not adopt too formalistic an approach in cases where different persons have identical legal interests. In *Drouot Assurances SA v Consolidated Metallurgical Industries (CMI Industrial Sites)*[71] the Court of Justice had to decide when (if ever) an insurer is to be regarded as the same party as the insured. The litigation arose out of problems encountered by a barge which was carrying a cargo from the Netherlands to France. Proceedings were brought in the Netherlands by C (the charterer of the barge and owner of the cargo) and P (the South African insurer of the cargo) against V (the master and owner of the barge).[72] Proceedings were then brought in France by D (the insurer of the vessel) against C, P and G (P's European representative). In the French proceedings, C and P

---

[65]   *Gamlestaden Plc v Casa de Suecia SA* [1994] 1 Lloyd's Rep 433.

[66]   *Mecklermedia Corporation v DC Congress GmbH* [1998] Ch 40.

[67]   *Haji-Ioannou v Frangos* [1999] 2 Lloyd's Rep 337.

[68]   *Sarrio SA v Kuwait Investment Authority* [1997] 1 Lloyd's Rep 113. See also *Glencore International AG v Shell International Trading and Shipping Co Ltd* [1999] 2 Lloyd's Rep 692; *The Winter* [2000] 2 Lloyd's Rep 298; *Re Cover Europe Ltd* [2002] 2 BCLC 61.

[69]   *Underwriting Members of Lloyd's Syndicate 980 v Sinco SA* [2009] 1 All ER (Comm) 272.

[70]   Case C–406/92 *Owners of the cargo lately laden on board the ship Tatry v Owners of the ship Maciej Rataj* [1994] ECR I–5439, para 31. See also *Re a Sale of Shares* [1996] ILPr 292 (Federal Supreme Court, Germany).

[71]   Case C–351/96 [1998] ECR I–3075. KR Handley, '*Res Judicata* in the European Court' (2000) 116 *LQR* 191; Peel (1998) 18 *YBEL* 689; F Seatzu, 'The meaning of "same parties" in Article 21 of the Brussels Jurisdiction and Judgments Convention' (1999) 24 *EL Rev* 540.

[72]   At the time of the events giving rise to the dispute, the barge was owned by W and the French proceedings were brought against W as well as V. However, by the time the reference to the Court of Justice was heard, W had died and V had become the owner of the barge.

challenged the court's jurisdiction. The central question was whether, for the purposes of the *lis pendens* rule, D and V should be regarded as the same party.

9.1.25 The Court of Justice accepted that there are circumstances in which an insurer and the insured must be considered to be one and the same party. If a judgment delivered against the insurer has the force of *res judicata* as against the insured, such as where the insurer, by virtue of its right of subrogation, brings or defends proceedings in the name of the insured, the insurer and insured are the same party for the purposes of the *lis pendens* rule.[73] However, the conditions of the rule are not satisfied in cases where the interests of the insurer and the insured diverge.[74] On the facts of the *Drouot Assurances* case, the requirement that the interests of D, the insurer, and those of V, the insured, be 'identical ... and indissociable' was not satisfied.[75]

9.1.26 It is clear that the ruling in the *Drouot Assurances* case is not limited to insurance cases; the principle which emerges from the judgment is of more general application. For example, for the purposes of Article 27, a company liquidator acting on behalf of X & Co and X & Co itself ought to be treated as the same party.[76] Similarly, in a case where X Ltd makes a valid legal assignment of its cause of action to Y Ltd, the two companies are 'the same party'; their interests are identical and indissociable and a judgment granted in an action involving Y Ltd would be binding on X Ltd.[77]

MULTIPLE PARTIES

9.1.27 On the basis of the Court of Justice's ruling in *Owners of the cargo lately laden on board the ship Tatry v Owners of the ship Maciej Rataj*,[78] where some of the parties are the same as the parties to proceedings which have already been started, Article 27 requires the second court seised to decline jurisdiction only to the extent to which the parties to the proceedings pending before it are also parties to the proceedings previously started before the court of another Member State; it does not, however, prevent the proceedings from continuing between the other parties.[79] While the Court of Justice recognised that this interpretation involves fragmenting proceedings, this problem is to some extent mitigated by the rule according to which the court second seised may stay related proceedings.[80]

9.1.28 So, in a situation where disputes arise out of a joint venture agreement involving four parties (A, B, C, and D), if A and B start proceedings against D in France, and D starts proceedings against A and C in Germany, the German courts are required to apply Article 27 as regards A, but so far as the German courts are concerned the proceedings brought by D against C are related proceedings falling within the scope of Article 28.

---

[73] Case C–351/96 [1998] ECR I–3075, para 19. See *Sony Computer Entertainment Ltd v RH Freight Services Ltd* [2007] 2 Lloyd's Rep 463.

[74] Case C–351/96 [1998] ECR I–3075, para 20.

[75] Case C–351/96 [1998] ECR I–3075, para 23.

[76] See *Re Cover Europe Ltd* [2002] 2 BCLC 61.

[77] *Kolden Holdings Ltd v Rodette Commerce Ltd* [2008] 1 Lloyd's Rep 435.

[78] Case C–406/92 [1994] ECR I–5439, para 34.

[79] For application of this ruling, see *Glencore International AG v Metro Trading International Inc* [1999] 2 Lloyd's Rep 632.

[80] Brussels I Reg, Art 28.

PARALLEL PROCEEDINGS *IN PERSONAM* AND *IN REM*

9.1.29   Article 27 applies to proceedings *in rem* as well as to proceedings *in personam*.[81]
So, if the claimant starts proceedings *in rem* in one Member State in relation to a specific vessel and then, after the vessel's release, commences proceedings *in rem* in relation
to the same vessel in another Member State, the two sets of proceedings involve the
same parties for the purposes of the *lis pendens* rule. More problematical are cases
involving parallel proceedings *in personam* and *in rem* in different states. Where, for
example, the claimant commences proceedings *in personam* against the defendant in one
Member State and then starts proceedings *in rem* by arresting a ship which is owned
by the defendant (or in which the defendant has an interest) in another Member State,
are the parties to the two sets of proceedings the same? There are two situations to
consider.

   9.1.30   First, it is not unusual in cases where proceedings are commenced *in rem*
for the person who would be the defendant were the proceedings to be brought *in
personam* (typically, the shipowner or the charterer) to acknowledge service of the
claim form in England. In this situation the proceedings in England take on a hybrid
character; the action becomes *in personam* but does not lose its character of being an
action *in rem*.[82] Where A sues B *in personam* in another Member State and then B
starts proceedings *in rem* in England against a vessel owned by A, who acknowledges
service of the claim form, the English proceedings do not cease to be between the
same parties on account of the fact that the English proceedings continue both *in rem*
and *in personam*.[83]

   9.1.31   Secondly, it is possible for a claim which is commenced *in rem* to continue
solely *in rem*. One possible view, which was adopted in *The Nordglimt*,[84] is that, as the
parties to a claim *in rem* are the claimant and the vessel, where a claim *in personam* is
brought abroad and a claim *in rem* is brought in England, the *lis pendens* rule does not
apply while the English litigation proceeds solely *in rem*. This approach is, however,
inconsistent with the analysis of the Court of Appeal in *The Deichland*[85] and was
definitively rejected by the House of Lords in *Republic of India v India Steamship Co
Ltd (No 2)*.[86]

   9.1.32   In *The Deichland* the plaintiff commenced an action *in rem* in England by
serving a writ on a vessel chartered by the defendant, who was domiciled in Germany.
The question arose whether the English court had jurisdiction or whether Article 2
obliged the plaintiff to bring proceedings in Germany. The Court of Appeal rejected
the argument that, while the action was solely *in rem*, Article 2 did not apply because
the defendant was not being sued. Looking at the reality of the matter, it was the
defendant who was interested in contesting liability and it was against the defendant
that the plaintiff would have wanted to proceed *in personam* if that were possible.[87]

---

   [81]   Case C−406/92 *Owners of the cargo lately laden on board the ship Tatry v Owners of the ship Maciej
Rataj* [1994] ECR I−5439, para 47.
   [82]   *The Gemma* [1899] P 285; *The August 8* [1983] 2 AC 450; *The Maciej Rataj* [1992] 2 Lloyd's Rep 552.
   [83]   Case C−406/92 *Owners of the cargo lately laden on board the ship Tatry v Owners of the ship Maciej
Rataj* [1994] ECR I−5439, para 48.
   [84]   [1988] QB 183.
   [85]   [1990] 1 QB 361.
   [86]   [1998] AC 878.
   [87]   See Neill LJ at [1990] 1 QB 361, 374.

Accordingly, it was held that the defendant was being 'sued' for the purposes of Article 2—even when the proceedings were solely *in rem*. It is implicit in this decision that if a defendant is sued *in personam* in one Member State and is 'sued' *in rem* in another Member State the two sets of proceedings involve the same parties for the purposes of Article 27.

9.1.33   The analysis suggested in *The Deichland* was favoured by the House of Lords in *Republic of India v India Steamship Co Ltd (No 2)*,[88] a case involving the meaning of the words 'the same parties' in the context of section 34 of the Civil Jurisdiction and Judgments Act 1982.[89] The House of Lords held that 'an action *in rem* is an action against the owners from the moment that the Admiralty court is seized with jurisdiction'.[90] Even though the decision of the House of Lords concerned the interpretation of section 34 of the 1982 Act, it would be strange if the meaning of 'the same parties' in respect of section 34 was different from the meaning of the same words in the context of the *lis pendens* rule.[91] Accordingly, Article 27 applies to cases involving parallel proceedings *in rem* and *in personam* on the same cause of action and to cases where a claimant starts proceedings *in rem* in respect of a ship owned by the defendant in one Member State and subsequently brings proceedings *in rem* in connection with a sister ship in another Member State. This interpretation is consistent with the objective of preventing parallel proceedings in different Member States and avoiding conflicting judgments. The Court of Justice has stressed that the purpose of the *lis pendens* rule is best served if it is interpreted broadly, since this reduces the risks of conflicting judgments.[92] Conflicting judgments could result if, following the bringing of a claim *in personam* against a shipowner in one state, a claim *in rem* on the same cause of action were allowed to be brought in another Member State.[93]

9.1.34   It does not necessarily follow that all parallel proceedings *in personam* and *in rem* involve the same parties. Different considerations may apply in a case where the vessel is in new ownership or for any other reason the person who acknowledges service of the claim form *in rem* is not the person who would be liable in an action *in personam*.[94]

The Relationship between the Court First Seised and the Court Second Seised

THE GENERAL RULE

9.1.35   In a case where Article 27 applies, is the court second seised restricted either to staying its proceedings or declining jurisdiction, or may the court second seised examine whether the court first seised has jurisdiction? In *Overseas Union Insurance Ltd v New Hampshire Insurance Co*,[95] in which various questions relating to the *lis*

---

[88] [1998] AC 878.
[89] See para 12.3.4.
[90] Lord Steyn at [1998] AC 878, 913.
[91] See Lord Steyn at [1998] AC 878, 910.
[92] Case C–351/89 *Overseas Union Insurance Ltd v New Hampshire Insurance Co* [1991] ECR I–3317, para 16.
[93] TC Hartley, 'The Effect of the 1968 Brussels Judgments Convention on Admiralty Actions in Rem' (1989) 105 *LQR* 640, 656.
[94] Staughton LJ in *Republic of India v India Steamship Co Ltd (No 2)* [1997] 2 WLR 538, 554.
[95] Case C–351/89 [1991] ECR I–3317.

pendens rule were referred to the Court of Justice, it was decided that the court second seised may not, as a general rule, investigate whether the foreign court assumed jurisdiction on a proper basis:

[I]n no case is the court second seised in a better position than the court first seised to determine whether the latter has jurisdiction. Either the jurisdiction of the court first seised is determined directly by the rules of the [Brussels I Regulation], which are common to both courts and may be interpreted and applied with the same authority by each of them, or it is derived, by virtue of Article 4 ..., from the law of the State of the court first seised, in which case that court is undeniably better placed to rule on the question of its own jurisdiction.[96]

Where, for example, C brings proceedings in Greece against D1, a Greek domiciliary, and, relying on Article 6(1), against D2, who is domiciled in England, and then D2 sues C in England on the same cause of action, the English court must stay the proceedings between D2 and C (or, if the jurisdiction of the Greek court is established, decline jurisdiction). The court is not entitled to permit the English proceedings to continue on the basis that the claim against D1 was contrived in order to enable C to bring proceedings against D2 in Greece.[97] Such a result follows from the Court of Justice's insistence that it is for the court first seised to decide whether it has jurisdiction and that the court second seised must respect that decision. Furthermore, the court second seised cannot decide to refuse a stay under Article 27(1) on the basis that proceedings in the court first seised may last an excessively long time;[98] nor can a stay granted Article 27(1) be lifted on the ground that the proceedings before the court first seised are not progressing.[99]

LIMITS TO THE DUTY TO STAY PROCEEDINGS OR DECLINE JURISDICTION

9.1.36   Where more than one Member State has exclusive jurisdiction (under Article 22 of the Brussels I Regulation), any court other than the court first seised must decline jurisdiction.[100] This rule requires the court second seised to consider the basis on which the court first seised exercised jurisdiction. What is the situation, however, where the English court has exclusive jurisdiction under Article 22 of the Brussels I Regulation, but before the English claim form is issued, proceedings are commenced in another Member State which does not have exclusive jurisdiction?

9.1.37   The framework of the Brussels I Regulation, if not the wording of Article 27 itself, supports the view that, where the court second seised has exclusive jurisdiction and the court first seised does not, the *lis pendens* rule should not apply so as to require the court with exclusive jurisdiction to stay its proceedings or decline jurisdiction. Although, as a general rule, where the recognition of a judgment given in one Member State is sought in another Member State the jurisdiction of the court of origin may not be reviewed,[101] Article 35(1) of the Brussels I Regulation provides that a judgment given by the courts of a Member State shall be refused recognition

---

[96] Case C–351/89 [1991] ECR I–3317, para 23.
[97] See *Phillips v Symes* [2002] 1 WLR 853.
[98] Case C–116/02 *Erich Gasser GmbH v MISAT Srl* [2003] ECR I–14693, para 73. See also *Re an Application for a Stay of Proceedings* [2003] ILPr 640 (Federal Supreme Court, Germany).
[99] *Re Lifting a Stay of Proceedings* [1999] ILPr 291 (Court of Appeal, Munich).
[100] Brussels I Reg, Art 29.
[101] Brussels I Reg, Art 35(3).

if it conflicts with Article 22 or the jurisdiction rules relating to insurance matters or consumer contracts.[102] Where, for example, the court which is second seised has exclusive jurisdiction under Article 22 of the Brussels I Regulation and the court first seised does not, it makes no sense for the court second seised to decline jurisdiction, since the judgment of the court first seised is not, in any event, entitled to recognition under Chapter III. Indeed, the possibility that there is an exception to the *lis pendens* rule in cases where the court second seised has exclusive jurisdiction was admitted by the Court of Justice in *Overseas Union Insurance Ltd v New Hampshire Insurance Co*[103] and in *Erich Gasser GmbH v MISAT Srl.*[104] Not surprisingly, the English courts have accepted that Article 22 constitutes an implied derogation from the mandatory requirements of Article 27.[105] Since Article 35(1) also provides that recognition of a judgment may be refused on the basis that the court of the state of origin misapplied the jurisdiction provisions relating to insurance matters or consumer contracts, the foregoing arguments could be applied, *mutatis mutandis*, to cases concerning these provisions. However, it seems that the Court of Justice does not envisage that any provisions other than those relating to exclusive jurisdiction take priority over the *lis pendens* rule.[106]

ARTICLE 27 AND JURISDICTION AGREEMENTS

9.1.38   Although the English courts used to think that jurisdiction agreements prevail over the *lis pendens* rule, the Court of Justice has made it clear that this view is incorrect. In *Continental Bank NA v Aeakos Compania Naviera SA*[107] the defendant brought proceedings in Greece against the plaintiff bank in breach of a jurisdiction agreement which, in the eyes of the English court, was effective to confer exclusive jurisdiction on the English courts. When the plaintiff subsequently brought proceedings in England, the defendant applied for a stay of the English proceedings on the basis of the parallel proceedings in Greece. The Court of Appeal refused to grant a stay, accepting the argument that the English jurisdiction clause took precedence over the *lis pendens* rule.[108] Steyn LJ, who gave the judgment of the Court of Appeal, thought that the structure and logic of the Brussels regime convincingly pointed to this conclusion.[109] In Steyn LJ's view, if priority were not given to the jurisdiction clause, a party would be able to override an exclusive jurisdiction agreement by pre-emptively suing in the court of another country, which would be the court first seised, as a consequence of which the court chosen by the parties would then be obliged to decline jurisdiction, or, if the jurisdiction of the other court is contested, to stay its proceedings.[110] The decision of the Court of Appeal on this point, which was binding

---

[102] Brussels I Reg, Arts 8–17. For further discussion see paras 13.3.3–13.3.8.
[103] Case C–351/89 [1991] ECR I–3317, para 20.
[104] Case C–116/02 [2003] ECR I–14693.
[105] *Speed Investments Ltd v Formula One Holdings Ltd (No 2)* [2005] 1 WLR 1936.
[106] Case C–116/02 *Erich Gasser GmbH v MISAT Srl* [2003] ECR I–14693, paras 44–5.
[107] [1994] 1 WLR 588.
[108] See also the earlier decisions in *Klöckner & Co AG v Gatoil Overseas Inc* [1990] 1 Lloyd's Rep 177; *Rank Film Distributors Ltd v Laterna Editrice Srl* [1992] ILPr 58; *Denby v Hellenic Mediterranean Lines Co Ltd* [1994] 1 Lloyd's Rep 320.
[109] [1994] 1 WLR 588, 596.
[110] [1994] 1 WLR 588, 596–7.

on the courts in England[111] and was followed in Scotland,[112] provoked considerable criticism from commentators.

9.1.39 The unacceptable consequences which the Court of Appeal thought would flow from the view that the *lis pendens* rule takes precedence, thereby requiring the English court to stay the proceedings in spite of an English jurisdiction clause, is premised on the court first seised failing to apply the relevant jurisdiction rules correctly. In a case such as *Continental Bank NA v Aeakos Compania Naviera SA* the court first seised will assume jurisdiction only if it is satisfied that for some reason the jurisdiction agreement does not confer exclusive jurisdiction on the English court— for example, because the dispute falls outside the scope of the agreement or because the formal requirements of Article 23 of the Brussels I Regulation are not satisfied or because the defendant submitted to the jurisdiction of the court first seised, thereby superseding the prior agreement.[113] The Court of Appeal's refusal to grant a stay (pending the Greek court's decision on whether its jurisdiction was established) was inconsistent with the Court of Justice's statement of principle in the *Overseas Union Insurance* case that 'in no case is the court second seised in a better position than the court first seised to determine whether the latter has jurisdiction'.[114] Although the *Overseas Union Insurance* case was cited in *Continental Bank NA v Aeakos Compania Naviera SA* it seems that the Court of Appeal simply ignored it. As one commentator observed:

Overseas Union should have been seen as an absolute answer to the pretensions of the English court to hear the case. The refusal of the court in *Continental Bank* even to mention that decision in its judgment is astonishing.[115]

9.1.40 Although the conclusion of the Court of Appeal in *Continental Bank NA v Aeakos Compania Naviera SA* is hard to defend considering that one of the fundamental objectives of the Brussels regime is to avoid as far as possible the incidence of conflicting judgments, some attempted to support the decision on policy grounds.[116] Moreover, some of the practical implications of requiring the court second seised to stay proceedings—simply for the purpose of allowing the court first seised to decline jurisdiction—might be thought to be unattractive. It was, for example, suggested that 'it really would indeed be strange'[117] if the English court were required to grant a stay of proceedings in a case where the defendant, although not denying the existence of an exclusive jurisdiction clause in favour of the English courts, applies for a stay on the basis of earlier proceedings in another Member State.

9.1.41 Nevertheless, it came as no surprise that, when the Court of Justice was given the opportunity to consider the relationship between jurisdiction agreements and the *lis pendens* rule, it decided that the approach adopted by the Court of Appeal in the *Continental Bank* case is heretical and ruled that the *lis pendens* rule takes priority.

---

[111] *IP Metal Ltd v Ruote OZ Spa (No 2)* [1994] 2 Lloyd's Rep 560; *Glencore International AG v Metro Trading International Inc* [1999] 2 Lloyd's Rep 632.
[112] *Bank of Scotland v SA Banque Nationale de Paris* [1996] ILPr 668 (Court of Session, Scotland).
[113] See A Bell, 'Anti-Suit Injunctions and the Brussels Convention' (1994) 110 *LQR* 204, 208.
[114] Case C–351/89 [1991] ECR I–3317, para 23.
[115] A Briggs, 'Anti-European teeth for choice of court clauses' [1994] *LMCLQ* 158, 161.
[116] See TC Hartley, (1994) 19 *EL Rev* 548; P Rogerson, [1994] *CLJ* 241.
[117] Waller J in *IP Metal Ltd v Ruote OZ SpA (No 2)* [1994] 2 Lloyd's Rep 560, 564.

In *Erich Gasser GmbH v MISAT Srl*,[118] a reference from the Austrian courts, D brought proceedings in Italy against C, *inter alia*, for a declaration that the contract between them had been terminated and that C had not failed to perform the contract. Several months later, C started proceedings against D in Austria to obtain payment of outstanding invoices. All the invoices had contained a jurisdiction clause in favour of the Austrian courts. The United Kingdom government made representations in support of the approach which the Court of Appeal had adopted in the *Continental Bank* case[119] and this was supported by Advocate General Léger, who proposed that the *lis pendens* rule should be interpreted as meaning that:

the court second seised and having exclusive jurisdiction by virtue of an agreement conferring jurisdiction may, by way of exception …, rule on the dispute without waiting for the court first seised to decline jurisdiction when there is no doubt as to the jurisdiction of the court second seised.[120]

However, the Court of Justice brushed aside the UK government's concerns and reiterated the line that it had taken in the *Overseas Union Insurance* case; other than in cases where the court second seised has exclusive jurisdiction *stricto sensu*,[121] 'the court second seised is never in a better position than the court first seised to determine whether the latter has jurisdiction'.[122] Accordingly, the Court of Justice ruled that:

a court second seised whose jurisdiction has been claimed under an agreement conferring jurisdiction must nevertheless stay proceedings until the court first seised has declared that it has no jurisdiction. [123]

9.1.42 Perhaps not surprisingly, this decision has been greeted with dismay—especially in England.[124] By giving Article 27 priority over Article 23 and effectively sanctioning the litigation manoeuvre known as the 'Italian torpedo',[125] the Court of Justice has allowed a situation to arise in which litigants can engage in delaying tactics and effectively paralyse proceedings in the contractual forum. By taking the initiative and starting proceedings in a Member State whose courts are very slow—even in the resolution of apparently simple jurisdictional issues—a potential defendant can seriously disrupt the claimant's legitimate attempt to bring a claim to court in the contractually agreed forum. Even if it is perfectly clear that the court first seised does not have jurisdiction, the contractual forum cannot rule on the substance of the dispute until the court first seised has ruled that it does not have jurisdiction.[126] Furthermore, the fact that the delay in the non-contractual forum is expected to be excessively long does not justify

---

[118] Case C−116/02 [2003] ECR I–14693. Y Baatz, 'Who decides on jurisdiction clauses?' [2004] *LMCLQ* 25; R Fentiman, [2004] *CLJ* 312; R Fentiman, (2005) 42 *CML Rev* 241; J Mance, 'Exclusive Jurisdiction Agreements and European Ideals' (2004) 120 *LQR* 357. See also P de Vareilles-Sommières (ed), *Forum Shopping in the European Judicial Area* (Oxford, Hart Publishing, 2007).
[119] See Case C−116/02 [2003] ECR I–14693, paras 29−33.
[120] Case C−116/02 [2003] ECR I–14693, para 83.
[121] That is, jurisdiction under Brussels I Reg, Art 22.
[122] Case C−116/02 [2003] ECR I–14693, para 48.
[123] Case C−116/02 [2003] ECR I–14693, para 54. See also *JP Morgan v Primacom* [2005] 2 Lloyd's Rep 665.
[124] In addition to the discussions noted above (at nn 115 and 118), see TC Hartley, 'The European Union and the Systematic Dismantling of the Common Law of Conflict of Laws' (2005) 54 *ICLQ* 813.
[125] See M Franzoni, 'Worldwide Patent Litigation and the Italian Torpedo' [1997] 7 *EIP Rev* 392.
[126] See, eg, *JP Morgan v Primacom* [2005] 2 Lloyd's Rep 665.

the contractual forum (the court second seised) in seeking to pre-empt the decision of the court first seised on the jurisdictional issue.[127]

9.1.43 The practical problems resulting from the Court of Justice's ruling in the *Gasser* case have led commentators to advocate an amendment to the text of the Brussels I Regulation and the possibility of legislative change has been put firmly on the agenda.[128] One suggestion is that, in a case involving a choice of court agreement, the priority rule in Article 27 should be reversed so that 'the court designated by the agreement would have priority to determine its jurisdiction and any other court seized would stay proceedings until the jurisdiction of the chosen court is established'.[129]

THE RELATIONSHIP BETWEEN CONCURRENT PROCEEDINGS AND PROVISIONAL MEASURES

9.1.44 Article 31 of the Brussels I Regulation[130] provides that the courts of a Member State may grant provisional, including protective measures, even though the courts of another Member State have jurisdiction over the substance of the matter. Normally, proceedings involving provisional measures in one Member State will not prevent the courts of another Member State exercising jurisdiction over the substantive dispute. So, if the French court sets in motion the judicial expertise process (which, under French law, is seen as interim proceedings and classed as a provisional or protective measure), this does not prevent the English court from exercising jurisdiction as regards the substantive dispute between the parties.[131] Similarly, substantive proceedings in one Member State do not restrict the jurisdiction of the courts of other Member States to grant provisional measures[132]; the substantive proceedings and the application for provisional measures do not involve the same cause of action.[133] If, for example, the claimant commences French proceedings against a defendant domiciled in France, the English court may, in support of those proceedings, grant a freezing injunction in respect of the defendant's assets and Article 27 of the Brussels I Regulation is not applicable.[134] However, if there arises, in the course of proceedings concerned with provisional measures, a substantive matter in respect of which the decision will be decisive of the litigation, there is no reason in principle why Articles 27 and 28 should not be applied.[135] It has also been argued, on the basis of the Court of Justice's ruling

---

[127] Case C–116/02 *Erich Gasser GmbH v Misat Srl* [2003] ECR I–14693. On the question of whether the Court of Justice's approach to Art 27 raises potential problems under Art 6(1) of the ECHR, see JJ Fawcett, 'The Impact of Article 6(1) of the ECHR on Private International Law' (2007) 56 *ICLQ* 1, 13–16; see also TC Hartley, 'The European Union and the Systematic Dismantling of the Common Law of Conflict of Laws' (2005) 54 *ICLQ* 813, 821 n 35. There is also the difficult question whether the claimant in the contractual forum would be able to recover damages for the defendant's breach by starting proceedings in a non-contractual forum; see L Merrett, 'The Enforcement of Jurisdiction Agreements within the Brussels Regime' (2006) 55 *ICLQ* 315.

[128] See the European Commission's Green Paper on the review of the Brussels I Regulation: COM (2009) 175 final, pp 5–6.

[129] European Commission, COM (2009) 175 final, p 5.

[130] See sections 5.4 and 10.3.

[131] *Miles Platts Ltd v Townroe Ltd* [2003] 1 All ER (Comm) 561.

[132] Case C–391/95 *Van Uden Maritime BV v Kommanditgesellschaft in Firma Deco-Line* [1998] ECR I–7091.

[133] See, eg, *JP Morgan v Primacom* [2005] 2 Lloyd's Rep 665.

[134] *Republic of Haiti v Duvalier* [1990] 1 QB 202.

[135] See Thomas J in *The Winter* [2000] 2 Lloyd's Rep 298, 302.

in *Italian Leather SpA v WECO Polstermöbil GmbH & Co*,[136] that Article 27 should be applied in circumstances where proceedings for provisional measures are brought in more than one Member State and there is a risk that, if the court second seised does not stay its proceedings or decline jurisdiction, irreconcilable judgments may result.[137]

THE RELATIONSHIP BETWEEN PARALLEL PROCEEDINGS AND RELATED ACTIONS
9.1.45   In the context of the Brussels I Regulation, multiparty litigation may generate problems surrounding the relationship between Article 27 and Article 28. The following example illustrates the nature of the problem. Disputes arise between A, B, C, and D out of a joint venture in which all four parties are involved: first, A and B commence proceedings against C in England; secondly, C commences proceedings against D in Italy; finally, D commences proceedings in England against C and B. If the Italian court stays the proceedings between C and D (or declines jurisdiction) under Article 28, the English court may exercise jurisdiction over the proceedings brought by D against B and C. If, however, the Italian court does not stay the proceedings or decline jurisdiction, the main question, as regards Article 27, is this: in relation to D's claim against C in England, must the English court stay or dismiss the proceedings under Article 27 in favour of the Italian courts on the basis that the proceedings are between the same parties and involve the same cause of action as the Italian proceedings?
9.1.46   The case law of the Court of Justice is of some assistance. In *Overseas Union Insurance Ltd v New Hampshire Insurance Co* the Court of Justice laid down the general rule that 'in no case is the court second seised in a better position than the court first seised to determine whether the latter has jurisdiction'.[138] The decision to stay proceedings or decline jurisdiction under Article 28 is a discretionary one; it is not for the courts of one Member State to review the exercise of discretion by the courts of another Member State.[139] Accordingly, as regards the proceedings commenced by D against C in England, the English court must stay the proceedings or decline jurisdiction under Article 27. The fact that there is not complete identity between the parties to the litigation as a whole in England and Italy is not relevant;[140] all that is required is that the particular proceedings in the two jurisdictions are between the same parties and involve the same cause of action and the same object.

Related Actions

9.1.47   Article 28 of the Brussels I Regulation provides:

1. Where related actions are pending in the courts of different Member States, any court other than the court first seised may stay its proceedings.

---

[136] Case C−80/00 [2002] ECR I−4995. See para 13.3.37.
[137] XE Kramer, (2003) 40 *CML Rev* 953, 960−1.
[138] Case C−351/89 [1991] ECR I−3317, para 23.
[139] *Assurances Générales de France v Chiyoda Fire and Marine Co (UK) Ltd* [1992] 1 Lloyd's Rep 325.
[140] Case C−406/92 *Owners of the cargo lately laden on board the ship Tatry v Owners of the ship Maciej Rataj* [1994] ECR I−5439.

2. Where these actions are pending at first instance, any court other than the court first seised may also, on the application of one of the parties, decline jurisdiction if the court first seised has jurisdiction over the actions in question and its law permits the consolidation thereof.

3. For the purposes of this Article, actions are deemed to be related where they are so closely connected that it is expedient to hear and determine them together to avoid the risk of irreconcilable judgments resulting from separate proceedings.

This provision deals with the problem where related actions are brought in the courts of different Member States. Its purpose is to confer discretion on a court other than the court first seised to stay its proceedings or to decline jurisdiction.[141]

THE PROVISION DOES NOT CONFER JURISDICTION

9.1.48   Where the courts of a Member State have jurisdiction under Chapter II in relation to a particular claim, the effect of Article 28 is not to confer jurisdiction over related claims. The specific provision which determines jurisdiction in relation to multiple defendants is Article 6.[142] The Court of Justice's ruling in *Elefanten Schuh GmbH v Jacqmain*[143] makes it clear that the related actions rule is intended to establish how related actions which have been brought before courts of different Member States are to be dealt with; the provision does not allocate jurisdiction to a court of a Member State in respect of a claim related to another claim over which that court does have jurisdiction under Chapter II.[144]

WHAT ARE 'RELATED ACTIONS'?

9.1.49   The third paragraph of Article 28 indicates the criterion which determines whether actions are related ('they are so closely connected that it is expedient to hear and determine them together to avoid the risk of irreconcilable judgments resulting from separate proceedings'). In *Owners of the cargo lately laden on board the ship Tatry v Owners of the ship Maciej Rataj* the Court of Justice decided that the concept of related actions 'must be given an independent interpretation'[145] and that such interpretation 'must be broad and cover all cases where there is a risk of conflicting decisions, even if the judgments can be separately enforced and their legal consequences are not mutually exclusive'.[146] However, the notion of 'related proceedings' should not be pushed too far. For example, proceedings are not related simply

---

[141] It seems to be accepted that, even in a case which falls within the scope of the Brussels I Regulation and which involves related proceedings in another Member State, a defendant may apply for a temporary stay on case management grounds, rather than on the basis of Art 28: *Curtis v Lockheed Martin UK Holdings Ltd* [2008] 1 CLC 219.

[142] See section 5.7.

[143] Case 150/80 [1981] ECR 1671.

[144] Case 150/80 [1981] ECR 1671, para 19. See also *Société Lorraine des Produits Metallurgiques v SA Banque Paribas Belgique* [1995] ILPr 175 (Court of Appeal, Paris); *Société Bretonne de Construction Navale v Société MB Marine* [1996] ILPr 133 (Court of Cassation, France); *Société des Etablissements J Verdier v Da Silva* [2001] ILPr 34 (Court of Cassation, France).

[145] Case C−406/92 [1994] ECR I−5439, para 51.

[146] Case C−406/92 [1994] ECR I−5439, para 52. For consideration of the defence of 'irreconcilability' in the context of the recognition and enforcement of judgments under the Brussels I Regulation, see paras 13.3.35–13.3.39.

because they arise from the same general factual situation; furthermore, proceedings are not related—even if there is a very small risk of irreconcilable judgments—if it is not expedient for the actions to be determined together.[147] In *Sarrio SA v Kuwait Investment Authority*[148] the House of Lords took the view that, when considering whether two actions are related, the court should not embark upon too technical an analysis of the extent to which they overlap:

there should be a broad commonsense approach to the question whether the actions are related, bearing in mind the objective of the Article, applying the simple wide test set out in [the rule] and refraining from an over sophisticated analysis of the matter.[149]

This approach is considerably more flexible than that suggested by the case law of the Court of Justice in the context of Article 6(1)[150] and further clarification from the Court of Justice of the words 'related actions' is likely to be needed. Despite such uncertainties, it goes without saying that for proceedings to be regarded as related 'it is not necessary there should be the same parties and the same cause of action'.[151]

STAYING PROCEEDINGS UNDER PARAGRAPH (1)

9.1.50   Under Article 28(1) of the Brussels I Regulation, in order for the court to be able to exercise its discretion in favour of granting a stay, there must be related actions pending in the courts of two or more Member States, but there is no requirement that the related proceedings should be pending at first instance.[152] If the proceedings are not related—because there is no risk of irreconcilable judgments—no question of a stay under Article 28 can arise.[153] When there arises the possibility of proceedings being stayed under Article 28(1) the court need not at that time be satisfied that both actions can be brought together in the court first seised.[154] If a stay is granted under Article 28(1) the court may subsequently revoke the stay (for example, on the ground that the two actions cannot in fact be brought together in the court first seised).[155]

---

[147]   *Research in Motion UK Ltd v Visto Corp* [2008] FSR 499. See also *Prifti v Musini Sociedad Anonima de Seguros y Reaseguros* [2004] 1 CLC 517.

[148]   [1999] 1 AC 32. A Briggs, (1997) 68 *BYIL* 339; J Harris, 'Related actions and the Brussels Convention' [1998] *LMCLQ* 145.

[149]   Lord Saville at [1999] 1 AC 32, 41.

[150]   See paras 5.7.3–5.7.11.

[151]   Judge Buxton QC in *De Pina v MS 'Birka' Buetler Schiffahrts KG* [1994] ILPr 695, 701.

[152]   The equivalent provision of the Brussels Convention (Art 22(1)) did not apply unless the concurrent proceedings were pending at first instance. This requirement appears to have been 'an anomaly originating in the negotiations for the 1968 Brussels Convention': European Commission, *Proposal*, COM (1999) 348 final, p 19.

[153]   See, eg, *Mecklermedia Corporation v DC Congress GmbH* [1998] Ch 40; *JP Morgan v Primacom* [2005] 2 Lloyd's Rep 665.

[154]   The contrary view of Judge Buxton QC in *De Pina v MS 'Birka' Beutler Schiffahrts KG* [1994] ILPr 695 confuses the first two paragraphs of the related actions rule and is inconsistent with the later decision of the Court of Justice in Case C–406/92 *Owners of the cargo lately laden on board the ship Tatry v Owners of the ship Maciej Rataj* [1994] ECR I–5439. Not surprisingly, it was not followed in *Centro Internationale Handelsbank AG v Morgan Grenfell Trade Finance Ltd* [1997] CLC 870.

[155]   See Rix J in *Centro Internationale Handelsbank AG v Morgan Grenfell Trade Finance Ltd* [1997] CLC 870, 889.

9.1.51 There is no indication of the basis on which the discretion conferred by Article 28(1) should be exercised. The authorities are not consistent and there are various strands in the case law. First, on the basis of the Jenard Report—which states that where actions are related 'the first duty of the court is to stay its proceedings'[156]—it has been said that, where an application for a stay under the related actions rule is made, a strong presumption lies in favour of the applicant.[157] This view was questioned, however, in *Centro Internationale Handelsbank AG v Morgan Grenfell Trade Finance Ltd* by Rix J, who considered that the burden of proof or persuasion should be on the party making the application for a stay.[158] The text of the provision itself does not suggest that the court should approach the matter with any presumption other than that it should support the Brussels I Regulation's obvious concern about the undesirability of irreconcilable judgments.[159] If the circumstances surrounding the foreign proceedings make it inappropriate for a stay to be granted, the court will exercise its discretion in the claimant's favour.[160]

9.1.52 Secondly, the English courts have been troubled by the relationship between the related actions rule and the doctrine of *forum non conveniens*.[161] One question—on which the High Court is divided[162]—is whether all the factors which an English court takes into account when applying the doctrine of *forum non conveniens* are relevant to an application for a stay on the basis of Article 28. In his opinion in *Owens Bank v Bracco* Advocate General Lenz highlighted three factors which may be relevant to the exercise of discretion under paragraph (1): 'the extent of the relatedness and the risk of mutually irreconcilable decisions; the stage reached in each set of proceedings; and the proximity of the courts to the subject-matter of the case'.[163] While there is some overlap between these three factors and the factors which are considered under the doctrine of *forum non conveniens*, it would be wrong to conclude that the traditional English approach to the staying of proceedings on the basis of *forum non conveniens* can be imported wholesale into Article 28.[164] It must be remembered that the primary concern of the Brussels I Regulation is to reduce the incidence of irreconcilable judgments. Where the risk of irreconcilable judgments is small, the court second seised may legitimately choose not to stay the proceedings.[165] Similarly, when the possibility of irreconcilable judgments cannot be avoided—whether or not the court second seised grants a stay—the argument in favour of a stay on the basis of Article 28(1) is far from overwhelming.[166]

---

[156] [1979] OJ C59/41.

[157] Ognall J in *Virgin Aviation Services Ltd v CAD Aviation Services* [1991] ILPr 79, 88.

[158] [1997] CLC 870, 891–92. See also *Mecklermedia Corporation v DC Congress GmbH* [1998] Ch 40.

[159] See Rix J in *Centro Internationale Handelsbank AG v Morgan Grenfell Trade Finance Ltd* [1997] CLC 870, 892.

[160] See *Haji-Ioannou v Frangos* [1999] 2 Lloyd's Rep 337.

[161] For a discussion of *forum non conveniens*, see section 9.2.

[162] Compare *Virgin Aviation Services Ltd v CAD Aviation Services* [1991] ILPr 79 and *The Maciej Rataj* [1991] 2 Lloyd's Rep 458.

[163] Case C–129/92 [1994] ECR I–117, para 76.

[164] Schlosser Report, [1979] OJ C59/125, para 181.

[165] *The Maciej Rataj* [1991] 2 Lloyd's Rep 458, reversed on other grounds [1992] 2 Lloyd's Rep 552.

[166] *Centro Internationale Handelsbank AG v Morgan Grenfell Trade Finance Ltd* [1997] CLC 870.

9.1.53 The proper approach to cases where the proceedings in the court first seised were seemingly brought in breach of an exclusive jurisdiction agreement in favour of the English courts is not easy. If the policy of upholding jurisdiction agreements is to be supported, there is an argument for saying that, even in a case where there is a serious risk of irreconcilable judgments, the English court should not stay its proceedings under Article 28 if the parties agreed to the exclusive juris- diction of the English courts and one of the parties has started proceedings in another Member State in breach of the terms of the agreement.[167] However, since the doctrine advanced by the Court of Appeal in *Continental Bank NA v Aeakos Compania Naviera SA*[168] was overturned by the Court of Justice in *Erich Gasser GmbH v MISAT Srl*,[169] the validity of this argument is questionable. The case law of the Court of Justice indicates that the policy of avoiding conflicting judgments takes priority over the upholding of jurisdiction clauses (by the allegedly chosen court). Where the jurisdiction of the other Member State has been challenged, but not yet established, the English court may legitimately assume that the court first seised will reach the same conclusion on the question of the validity of the jurisdic- tion agreement. If, however, the court first seised, having decided that the jurisdiction agreement does not satisfy the requirements of Article 23, assumes jurisdiction, the English court ought to be prepared to grant a stay if, without the stay, there is a real risk of irreconcilable judgments.

DECLINING JURISDICTION UNDER PARAGRAPH (2)

9.1.54 Under Article 28(2) of the Brussels I Regulation, where related actions are pending at first instance in the courts of two Member States, the court second seised may decline jurisdiction in a situation where the court first seised has jurisdiction over both actions and its law allows the actions to be consolidated.[170] For the pur- poses of this rule, it is important that the court first seised should have jurisdiction over both actions; it is not enough that the two actions may be brought in different courts of the Member State in which the court first seised is situated; the discretion to decline jurisdiction arises only if 'the actual court first seised has jurisdiction over both actions'.[171]

Rival Exclusive Jurisdictions

9.1.55 Article 29 of the Brussels I Regulation provides:

Where actions come within the exclusive jurisdiction of several courts, any court other than the court first seised shall decline jurisdiction in favour of that court.

---

[167] *IP Metal Ltd v Ruote OZ SpA* [1993] 2 Lloyd's Rep 60; *Bankers Trust International Plc v RCS Editori SpA* [1996] CLC 899; *Lexmar Corporation and Steamship Mutual Underwriting Association (Bermuda) Ltd v Nordisk Skibsrederforening* [1997] 1 Lloyd's Rep 289.

[168] [1994] 1 WLR 588. See para 9.1.38.

[169] Case C–116/02 [2003] ECR I–14693.

[170] The revised wording of Art 28(2) of the Regulation corrects an error contained in Art 22(2) of the Brussels Convention.

[171] Judge Buxton QC in *De Pina v MS 'Birka' Beutler Schiffahrts KG* [1994] ILPr 695, 698.

This provision, which is needed to prevent an impasse which would otherwise be created by the rule that any court must of its own motion decline jurisdiction if the subject-matter is within the exclusive jurisdiction of the courts of another Member State,[172] follows the same approach as Article 27: first come, first served. Although it is not likely that this provision will be frequently invoked, it is possible for the courts of more than one Member State to have exclusive jurisdiction. For example, the courts of two Member States may have exclusive jurisdiction under Article 22(1) of the Brussels I Regulation (where a dispute between two parties who are domiciled in Belgium arises in relation to a short-term letting of immovable property situated in Italy) or under Article 22(2) (where a company's seat is in France under French law but is in Germany under German law).

9.1.56   Under the Brussels I Regulation, Article 29 is applicable only where the rival courts have exclusive jurisdiction under Article 22. If, by virtue of a jurisdiction agreement between the parties, the court first seised assumes jurisdiction under Article 23, but the second court has exclusive jurisdiction under Article 22, the court second seised should not be required to decline jurisdiction. It would make no sense for the court second seised to decline jurisdiction, since by virtue of Article 35(1) the judgment of the court first seised is not entitled to recognition under Chapter III in these circumstances.[173]

Concurrent Proceedings within the United Kingdom

9.1.57   Although there is no provision in schedule 4 to the Civil Jurisdiction and Judgments Act 1982 equivalent to Articles 27–29 of the Brussels I Regulation, the Civil Procedure Rules provide that, in cases where the English court has jurisdiction in civil and commercial matters, service of a claim form out of the jurisdiction is permissible without the court's permission only as long as 'no proceedings between the parties concerning the same claim are pending in the courts of any other part of the United Kingdom'.[174]

9.1.58   As a general rule, this provision ensures that the same claim will not be litigated in more than one part of the United Kingdom. There are, however, various gaps in the solution provided by the Civil Procedure Rules. First, the Civil Procedure Rules prevent concurrent proceedings involving the same claim only where the claim form is to be served out of the jurisdiction. Where, for example, A (domiciled in England) brings proceedings in Northern Ireland against B (domiciled in Northern Ireland) and B subsequently issues proceedings in England against A concerning the same claim, there is nothing in the Civil Procedure Rules to prevent the claim form being served on A in England and there is nothing in schedule 4 of the 1982 Act to require the English court to stay its proceedings. Secondly, neither schedule 4 nor the Civil Procedure Rules have anything to say about related actions. In cases which fall within these gaps the question arises whether the English court has discretion to stay the proceedings in the exercise of its inherent jurisdiction.[175]

---

[172] Brussels I Reg, Art 25.
[173] See para 13.3.5.
[174] CPR 6.32(1)(a).
[175] See paras 9.5.24–9.5.28.

9.2 STAYING PROCEEDINGS ON THE BASIS OF THE DOCTRINE OF *FORUM NON CONVENIENS*

Forum Shopping

9.2.1   The fact that many systems of procedural law include exorbitant jurisdiction rules means that, in the context of an international dispute, the claimant often has a choice between two or more countries in which to proceed against the defendant. The existence of alternative fora may give rise to forum shopping[176]—a practice which has been defined as a claimant 'by-passing his natural forum and bringing his action in some alien forum which would give him relief or benefits which would not be available to him in his natural forum'.[177] Of course, this definition raises more questions than it answers: 'What is the natural forum? Is it the forum with which the dispute is most closely connected or the forum in which it can be resolved most conveniently?'[178] Indeed, the value of the concept of the 'natural forum' may be questioned. Although there are some cases where the situation has a strong connection with only one country (which might, accordingly, be termed the 'natural forum'), there are many others which either have a strong connection with more than one country or a relatively insubstantial connection with several countries. In these cases, it hardly seems helpful either to describe or to seek to identify any of the potential fora as the 'natural' one.[179]

9.2.2   Nevertheless, the commencement of proceedings in countries which have no more than a limited connection with the dispute is commonplace. Of course, forum shopping is not confined to foreign claimants trying to obtain the perceived benefits of English justice. There is also a history of claimants trying their luck in the United States in the hope of obtaining higher damages awards: 'As a moth is drawn to the light, so is a litigant drawn to the United States.'[180] A striking example is the litigation following the crash near Paris of a DC-10 owned by a Turkish airline in 1974. Eleven hundred plaintiffs from all over the world brought proceedings in California against a number of defendants, including the manufacturers of the aircraft. Having failed to persuade the Californian court to decline jurisdiction on the basis of *forum non conveniens* the defendants agreed not to contest liability. Following proceedings in which the quantum of damages was contested, damages were awarded to two plaintiffs and the remaining claims were settled.[181]

9.2.3   There is no consensus on whether forum shopping (in the sense of a claimant bringing proceedings in a forum which does not have a substantial connection with the dispute) is an evil which ought to be discouraged or prevented. According to one school

---

[176] See JJ Fawcett, 'Forum Shopping—Some Questions Answered' (1984) 35 *NILQ* 141.

[177] Lord Pearson in *Boys v Chaplin* [1971] AC 356, 401.

[178] AG Slater, 'Forum Non Conveniens: A View from the Shop Floor' (1988) 104 *LQR* 554, 560.

[179] See J Hill, 'Jurisdiction in Civil and Commercial Matters: Is There a Third Way?' (2001) 54 *CLP* 439, 459–60.

[180] Lord Denning MR in *Smith, Kline and French Laboratories Ltd v Bloch* [1983] 1 WLR 730, 733. See also *Castanho v Brown & Root (UK) Ltd* [1981] AC 557.

[181] *In re Paris Air Crash of March 3, 1974* 399 F Supp 732 (1975). See FK Juenger, 'Forum Shopping Domestic and International' (1989) 63 *Tulane LR* 553, 560–2.

of thought, forum shopping is not something which merits condemnation. Forum shopping 'is only a pejorative way of saying that, if you offer a plaintiff a choice of jurisdictions, he will naturally choose the one in which he thinks his case can be most favourably presented: this should be a matter neither for surprise nor for indignation'.[182] The question may be asked: 'Is it necessarily objectionable to bring proceedings in an alien forum if that forum is one of the established centres for the resolution of disputes and offers specialised services or facilities not available in the natural forum?'[183] There is also an economic angle to forum shopping, since international dispute resolution can be a valuable source of invisible exports.

9.2.4   On the other hand, there are strong arguments against allowing claimants to proceed in a forum which does not have a substantial connection with the dispute. First, while it would be wrong to deprive prospective claimants of all choice—since there may well be more than one forum which would be suitable for the trial of the claim—forum shopping may lead to injustice to the defendant. For example, forum shopping may be used by a claimant to put pressure on a defendant to settle a claim on terms which are more favourable to the claimant than would have been the case had proceedings been brought in a more suitable forum. Secondly, it is said that forum shopping is contrary to the public interest in the sense that it is wasteful of the time of witnesses and of others. Thirdly, forum shopping may be thought to be incompatible with the principle of comity in that to allow foreigners to litigate in England when there is a more suitable forum elsewhere is in some way derogatory of foreign courts or foreigners generally.[184] Thinking along these lines has given birth to the contrasting expressions 'judicial chauvinism' (which is evidenced by a liberal attitude towards forum shopping) and 'judicial comity' (which is typified by a commitment to directing litigation to its most appropriate forum). In *The Abidin Daver* Lord Diplock expressed the view that the evolution of English law during the 1970s and 1980s was proof of the fact that in England 'judicial chauvinism has been replaced by judicial comity'.[185]

The Development of English Law

9.2.5   From a doctrinal point of view there are two different strands in the case law. On the one hand, because of the potentially exorbitant nature of jurisdiction under what is now CPR 6.36, it has long been established that the court will not give permission for service of process on a defendant out of the jurisdiction unless the claimant shows that England is the appropriate forum. Although the phrase *'forum conveniens'* does not seem to have been used regularly until after the decision of the Court of Appeal in *Rosler v Hilbery*[186] in 1925, in English law the concept can be traced back to the late 19th century.[187]

---

[182] Lord Simon in *The Atlantic Star* [1974] AC 436, 471.
[183] AG Slater, 'Forum Non Conveniens: A View from the Shop Floor' (1988) 104 *LQR* 554, 560–1.
[184] AG Slater, 'Forum Non Conveniens: A View from the Shop Floor' (1988) 104 *LQR* 554, 562.
[185] [1984] AC 398, 411.
[186] [1925] Ch 250.
[187] *Société Générale de Paris v Dreyfus Brothers* (1885) 29 ChD 239.

9.2.6 By contrast, in cases where jurisdiction is invoked as of right—on the basis of the defendant's presence in England at the time of service—the traditional approach of the courts was to decline jurisdiction only in exceptional cases. This approach was exemplified by the decision of the Court of Appeal in *St Pierre v South American Stores (Gath and Chaves) Ltd.*[188] The underlying premise was that '[t]he right of access to the King's court must not be lightly refused'.[189] According to Scott LJ, if a defendant who had been served within the jurisdiction requested the court to exercise its inherent jurisdiction to stay the proceedings, a stay would generally be refused unless the defendant could show that the proceedings would either be 'oppressive or vexatious' to the defendant or would be 'an abuse of the process of the court in some other way' and that the grant of a stay would 'not cause an injustice' to the plaintiff.[190] Since a mere balance of convenience was not a sufficient ground for depriving a plaintiff of the advantages of pursuing his action in England, a stay of proceedings would normally be refused even in a case where neither party was resident in or otherwise closely connected with England and the cause of action related to events which had taken place abroad.[191] This endorsement of forum shopping was a reflection of the view that 'if the forum is England, it is a good place to shop in, both for the quality of the goods and the speed of service'.[192]

9.2.7 There was, however, a tension between the approach adopted to applications for permission to serve out under what is now CPR 6.36 and applications for a stay of proceedings under the court's inherent jurisdiction. The exercise of extraterritorial jurisdiction undermines the idea that jurisdiction is based on territorial sovereignty. If process can be served anywhere in the world on the basis that the litigation has a sufficient connection with the forum, the automatic exercise of jurisdiction on the basis of the defendant's fleeting presence becomes open to question. Jurisdiction based on service of process abroad shows that the theoretical foundation of jurisdiction is not territorial sovereignty and suggests an approach to jurisdiction based on contacts between the case and the forum, whether or not the defendant is served within the jurisdiction.[193]

9.2.8 In the 1970s and early 1980s the first steps were taken towards integrating the divergent common law rules. In a trio of cases—*The Atlantic Star*,[194] *MacShannon v Rockware Glass Ltd*[195] and *The Abidin Daver*[196]—the House of Lords dismissed the traditional approach as recalling 'the good old days, the passing of which many may regret,

---

[188] [1936] 1 KB 382.

[189] Scott LJ at [1936] 1 KB 382, 398.

[190] [1936] 1 KB 382, 398.

[191] See, eg, *Maharanee of Baroda v Wildenstein* [1972] 2 QB 283.

[192] Lord Denning MR in *The Atlantic Star* [1973] QB 364, 382.

[193] See M Pryles, 'The Basis of Adjudicatory Competence in Private International Law' (1973) 21 *ICLQ* 61.

[194] [1974] AC 436. A Bridge, 'Changing Attitudes to Jurisdiction' (1973) 36 *MLR* 649; PB Carter, (1972–3) 46 *BYIL* 428; JG Collier, [1973] *CLJ* 240; JD McClean, 'Foreign Collisions and *Forum Conveniens*' (1973) 22 *ICLQ* 748.

[195] [1978] AC 795. PB Carter, (1978) 49 *BYIL* 291; J Weiler, 'Forum Non Conveniens—An English Doctrine?' (1978) 41 *MLR* 739. For developments immediately after *MacShannon v Rockware Glass Ltd*, see PB Carter, (1979) 50 *BYIL* 245.

[196] [1984] AC 398. A Barma and D Elvin, 'Forum Non Conveniens; Where Do We Go from Here?' (1985) 101 *LQR* 48; PB Carter, (1984) *BYIL* 351; JJ Fawcett, '*Lis Alibi Pendens* and the Discretion to Stay' (1984) 47 *MLR* 481.

when the inhabitants of this island felt an innate superiority over those unfortunate enough to belong to other races'[197] and indicated a far greater willingness to stay English proceedings in cases where England was not the appropriate forum. In *The Atlantic Star* the House of Lords suggested that the words 'vexatious and oppressive' in the *St Pierre* formula should be given a 'liberal'[198] or 'wide'[199] interpretation. In *MacShannon v Rockware Glass Ltd* the House of Lords went further and reformulated the *St Pierre* test. According to the test laid down by Lord Diplock:

In order to justify a stay ... (a) the defendant must satisfy the court that there is another forum to whose jurisdiction he is amenable in which justice can be done between the parties at substantially less inconvenience or expense, and (b) the stay must not deprive the plaintiff of a legitimate personal or juridical advantage which would be available to him if he invoked the jurisdiction of the English court.[200]

In *The Abidin Daver* the more flexible approach which had been advocated in *MacShannon v Rockware Glass Ltd* was extended to the situation where proceedings between the same parties and concerning the same cause of action were brought in England and abroad.

9.2.9 Towards the middle of the 1980s it became increasingly clear that similar considerations were relevant both in cases where the defendant applied for a stay of proceedings commenced in England and in cases where the plaintiff applied for permission to serve process on the defendant out of the jurisdiction.[201] The decision of the House of Lords in *Spiliada Maritime Corporation v Cansulex Ltd*,[202] in which English law fully embraced the doctrine of *forum non conveniens*,[203] was the logical conclusion of this realisation.

The Test of Appropriateness

General Considerations

9.2.10 The key features of the test of appropriateness emerge from Lord Goff's speech in *Spiliada Maritime Corporation v Cansulex Ltd*,[204] which has been considered and applied in dozens of subsequent cases. The same fundamental principles apply to

---

[197] Lord Reid in *The Atlantic Star* [1974] AC 436, 453.

[198] See Lord Reid at [1974] AC 436, 454.

[199] See Lord Wilberforce at [1974] AC 436, 466.

[200] [1978] AC 795, 812.

[201] A Briggs, 'Forum Non Conveniens—Now We Are Ten?' (1983) 3 *LS* 74; A Briggs, 'The staying of actions on the ground of "forum non conveniens" today' [1984] *LMCLQ* 227; R Schuz, 'Controlling Forum-Shopping: The Impact of MacShannon v Rockware Glass Ltd' (1986) 35 *ICLQ* 374.

[202] [1987] AC 460. A Briggs, 'Forum non conveniens—the last word?' [1987] *LMCLQ* 1; PB Carter, (1986) 57 *BYIL* 429; JG Collier, [1987] *CLJ* 33; J Jacob, (1987) 6 *CJQ* 89. For a policy-based evaluation, see JJ Fawcett, 'Trial in England or Abroad: The Underlying Policy Considerations' (1989) 9 *OJLS* 205.

[203] This doctrine had long been established in other jurisdictions. For a discussion of the development of the law in the United States see DW Robertson, 'Forum Non Conveniens in America and England: "A Rather Fantastic Fiction"' (1987) 103 *LQR* 398, 400–9. The leading Scots cases are *Sim v Robinow* (1892) 14 R 665 and *Société du Gaz de Paris v Société Anonyme de Navigation 'Les Armateurs Français'* 1926 SC (HL) 13.

[204] Lord Templeman gave a short concurring speech. The other members of the House of Lords agreed with both speeches.

cases where the defendant seeks a stay of proceedings which have been started as of right in England (*forum non conveniens*) and where the claimant applies for permission to serve a claim form on the defendant out of the jurisdiction under CPR 6.36 (*forum conveniens*).[205] In adopting this approach the House of Lords rejected the view expressed by Lord Wilberforce in *Amin Rasheed Shipping Corporation v Kuwait Insurance Co*[206] that the principles which had been formulated as regards the staying of proceedings were of little assistance in deciding applications for permission to serve out of the jurisdiction.

9.2.11 The word '*conveniens*' is not to be equated with convenience. Notwithstanding the Latin label 'it is most important not to allow it to mislead us into thinking that the question at issue is one of "mere practical convenience"'.[207] In Lord Goff's view, 'the question is not one of convenience, but of suitability or appropriateness of the jurisdiction'.[208] Whether the case involves an application for a stay or an application for permission to serve out of the jurisdiction the court's task is to identify the forum 'in which the case can be tried more suitably for the interests of the parties and for the ends of justice'.[209]

9.2.12 As regards the time at which the relative appropriateness of the alternative fora should be determined, there are three possibilities: when process is served; when the application for a stay is made; or when the application for a stay is heard. It has been held that the court should take into account the circumstances as they exist at the date on which the defendant's application for a stay is heard.[210] By assessing the situation as it is at that date—rather than as it was at some earlier date—the court should 'avoid the absurdity of ordering a stay which is patently unjust through a change in circumstances'.[211] It should also be noted that, even in circumstances in which the defendant might expect the application to be successful, the court may refuse to grant a stay if the defendant is guilty of delay: 'application for a stay on the ground that there is another more suitable forum should be made promptly'.[212] Furthermore, a defendant may maintain an application for a stay so long as he has not taken any step in the proceedings which amounts to submission to the court's jurisdiction. If, for example, a defendant, after having obtained permission to appeal against the judge's decision to refuse a stay, serves a defence to the claim on the merits, he is thereby barred from pursuing the appeal. Service of a defence on the merits is inconsistent with the continuation of an application for a stay on the basis of *forum non conveniens*.[213]

---

[205] Where a claimant starts litigation both in England and abroad on the same claim, exceptionally the claimant may apply for a stay of the English proceedings. For the approach of the courts in such cases, see *Attorney-General v Arthur Anderson & Co* [1989] ECC 224; *Advanced Portfolio Technologies Inc v Ainsworth* [1996] FSR 217 (J Harris, 'The Ambivalent Plaintiff and the Scope of Forum Non Conveniens' (1996) 15 *CJQ* 279).

[206] [1984] AC 50, 72.

[207] Lord Goff in *Spiliada Maritime Corporation v Cansulex Ltd* [1987] AC 460, 474.

[208] [1987] AC 460, 474.

[209] [1987] AC 460, 474 (citing Lord Kinnear in *Sim v Robinow* (1892) 14 R 665, 668).

[210] *ISC Technologies Ltd v Guerin* [1992] 2 Lloyd's Rep 430, 434; *Lubbe v Cape plc* [2000] 1 WLR 1545, 1565–6.

[211] Evans LJ in *Mohammed v Bank of Kuwait and the Middle East KSC* [1996] 1 WLR 1483, 1493.

[212] Staughton LJ in *Lee v Mindel* [1994] ILPr 217, 223.

[213] *Ngcobo v Thor Chemicals Holdings Ltd* The Times, 10 November 1995.

9.2.13   When applying the test of appropriateness the court should not be drawn into a consideration of the advantages and disadvantages of the systems of administering justice in foreign countries as compared with the system of administering justice in England:

For an English court to investigate such a matter and to pronounce a judgment on it is not consistent with the mutual respect which the courts of friendly states, each of which has a well developed system for the administration of justice, owe, or should owe to each other.[214]

However, given that the second stage of the *Spiliada* test requires the court to ask whether substantial justice will be done in the alternative foreign forum, it is almost inevitable that, on occasions, the court will implicitly or explicitly pronounce judgment on the perceived weaknesses of foreign judicial systems.[215]

A Two-Stage Test

9.2.14   As regards the staying of proceedings under the court's inherent jurisdiction, the basic principle is that a stay will be granted on the ground of *forum non conveniens* only where the court is satisfied that there is some other available forum, having competent jurisdiction, which is the appropriate forum for the trial of the action.[216] This basic test is applied in two stages.

THE FIRST STAGE

9.2.15   At the first stage of the test, the burden of proof is on the defendant to satisfy the court that there is some other forum which *prima facie* is the appropriate forum for the trial of the action. The burden on the defendant is not simply to show that England is not the natural or appropriate forum for the trial, but to establish that there is another available forum having competent jurisdiction which is clearly or distinctly more appropriate than the English forum. (On this point, proper regard must be paid to the fact that jurisdiction has been founded in England as of right.[217]) If the arguments for and against the English court and the alternative forum are evenly balanced, a stay will be refused.[218]

9.2.16   The first stage involves a consideration of the factors which point in the direction of another forum as that with which the dispute has the most real and substantial connection. Such factors may not only affect convenience and expense (such as the availability of witnesses), but may relate to the applicable law and the places where the parties reside or carry on business.[219] There are certain situations

---

[214] Brandon LJ in *The El Amria* [1981] 2 Lloyd's Rep 119, 126. See also Lord Diplock and Lord Wilberforce in *Amin Rasheed Corporation v Kuwait Insurance Co* [1984] AC 50, 67–8 and 72 and the speech of Lord Brandon in *The Abidin Daver* [1984] AC 398, 425.

[215] See, eg, *Lubbe v Cape plc* [2000] 1 WLR 1545.

[216] Lord Goff in *Spiliada Maritime Corporation v Cansulex Ltd* [1987] AC 460, 476.

[217] Lord Goff in *Spiliada Maritime Corporation v Cansulex Ltd* [1987] AC 460, 477. See also *Bank of Credit and Commerce Hong Kong Ltd v Sonali Bank* [1995] 1 Lloyd's Rep 227.

[218] *Domansa v Derin Shipping and Trading Co Inc* [2001] 1 Lloyd's Rep 362; *XN Corporation Ltd v Point of Sale Ltd* [2001] ILPr 35.

[219] Lord Goff in *Spiliada Maritime Corporation v Cansulex Ltd* [1987] AC 460, 477–8.

in which the court is likely to assume that a particular country is the natural forum. For example, the courts of the place of incorporation will almost invariably be the most appropriate forum for the determination of issues which relate to the right of shareholders to sue on behalf of the company.[220] Similarly, in a case involving a claim to title to real property situated in England 'it is almost impossible to imagine circumstances in which England would not be the appropriate forum'.[221] The English court will often be the natural and appropriate forum for the trial of an action concerning misrepresentation or non-disclosure in the negotiation and placement of a reinsurance with London underwriters[222] and where a claim is based on a tort allegedly committed within a certain jurisdiction, 'it is not easy to imagine what other facts could displace the conclusion that the courts of that jurisdiction are the natural forum'.[223] Nevertheless, in a libel case, the court may grant a stay even though allegedly defamatory material has been published in England, if the claimant does not have connections with England which give rise to a sufficient reputation to protect in England;[224] furthermore, in certain circumstances where the connection with England is slight and the damage in England is, at most, minimal, the English court may consider it appropriate to strike out the claim or grant a stay on the basis that the proceedings are an abuse of the process of the court.[225]

9.2.17 If the court concludes that prima facie there is no other forum which is clearly more appropriate for the trial of the action, it will ordinarily refuse a stay.[226] Furthermore, if there is no natural forum for the trial of the action, the court is entitled to refuse to grant a stay.[227] Such cases are likely to occur in commercial disputes, where connecting factors may point to a number of different jurisdictions[228] and in Admiralty cases involving collisions on the high seas.[229]

9.2.18 At the first stage of the *Spiliada* case, the question is whether there is a more appropriate alternative forum which is 'available' to the claimant.[230] One view was that a court is 'available' only if it is 'available to the [claimant] in a practical sense as an alternative forum for the resolution of [the] dispute'.[231] According to

---

[220] See Lawrence Collins J in *Konamaneni v Rolls-Royce Industrial Power (India) Ltd* [2002] 1 All ER 979, 1010 (at [128]).

[221] Lawrence Collins J in *Pakistan v Zardari* [2006] 2 CLC 667, 706 (at [172]).

[222] *Markel International Insurance Co Ltd v La Republica Compania Argentina de Seguros Generales SA* [2005] Lloyd's Rep IR 90. See also *Münchener Rückversicherungs-Gesellschaft AG (t/a Munich Reinsurance Co) v Commonwealth Insurance Co* [2004] 2 CLC 665.

[223] Robert Goff LJ in *The Albaforth* [1984] 2 Lloyd's Rep 91, 96. See also *Metall und Rohstoff AG v Donaldson Lufkin & Jenrette Inc* [1990] 1 QB 391; *ISC Technologies Ltd v Guerin* [1992] Lloyd's Rep 430; *Caltex Singapore Pte Ltd v BP Shipping Co* [1996] 1 Lloyd's Rep 286; *Schapira v Ahronson* [1998] ILPr 587; *Berezovsky v Michaels* [2000] 1 WLR 1004; *King v Lewis* [2004] ILPr 546. But see, *Booth v Phillips* [2004] 1 WLR 3292 (in which jurisdiction was assumed in relation to a widow's claim following the death of her husband in an accident in Egypt); *Cooley v Ramsay* [2008] ILPr 345 (in which the English court assumed jurisdiction in a case concerning a tort which had a occurred in New South Wales).

[224] *Chadha & Osicom Technologies Inc v Dow Jones & Co Inc* [1999] ILPr 829.

[225] *Jameel v Dow Jones & Co Ltd* [2005] QB 946. A Briggs, (2005) 76 *BYIL* 668.

[226] Lord Goff in *Spiliada Maritime Corporation v Cansulex Ltd* [1987] AC 460, 478. See, eg, *The Hamburg Star* [1994] 1 Lloyd's Rep 399; *Meridien Baio Bank GmbH v Bank of New York* [1997] 1 Lloyd's Rep 437.

[227] Lord Goff in *Spiliada Maritime Corporation v Cansulex Ltd* [1987] AC 460, 477.

[228] See, eg, *European Asian Bank AG v Punjab and Sind Bank* [1982] 2 Lloyd's Rep 356.

[229] *The Vishva Abha* [1990] 2 Lloyd's Rep 312.

[230] Lord Goff at [1987] AC 460, 476.

[231] Evans LJ in *Mohammed v Bank of Kuwait and the Middle East KSC* [1996] 1 WLR 1483, 1496.

this approach, a forum would not be available if the claimant could not afford to travel to the alternative forum and would be unable to instruct local lawyers to act on his behalf there. However, this view of whether or not a forum is 'available' confuses the first and second stages of the *Spiliada* test. At the first stage the court's task is to evaluate the connecting factors with the competing courts with a view to identifying which of these courts has the most real and substantial connection with the dispute. Whether the claimant will obtain substantial justice in the court with which the dispute is most closely connected is something to be considered at the second stage of the *Spiliada* test, rather than as a facet of the availability of that forum at the first stage of the test.

9.2.19 The correct view is that a court is 'available' if it is a 'tribunal having competent jurisdiction'.[232] For the purposes of the first stage of the *Spiliada* test, the basis on which the alternative forum may assume jurisdiction over the claim is irrelevant. Of course, a foreign court is available—as a court of competent jurisdiction—if it can exercise jurisdiction as of right over the defendant. However, the claimant cannot argue that the foreign court is not available simply because, to the extent that the alternative court may exercise jurisdiction, the defendant is prepared to submit to it. In *Lubbe v Cape plc*[233] the defendant was an English company, but the situation was more closely connected with South Africa. In response to the defendant's application for a stay of the English proceedings the plaintiffs argued that South Africa was not an available forum as the South African courts did not have jurisdiction over the defendant. The House of Lords rejected this argument as the defendant had agreed to submit to South African jurisdiction:

The ground on which the jurisdiction of the courts in the other forum is available to be exercised is of no importance either one way or the other in the application to the case of the *Spiliada* principles.[234]

THE SECOND STAGE

9.2.20 If the court concludes that there is some available forum which *prima facie* is clearly more appropriate, it will ordinarily grant a stay unless justice requires that a stay should not be granted. At the second stage, the burden of proof is on the claimant to establish that there are special circumstances by reason of which justice requires that the trial should proceed in England.[235] At the second stage the court will

---

[232] See Lord Kinnear in *Sim v Robinow* (1892) 14 R 665, 668, cited by Lord Goff in *Spiliada Maritime Corporation v Cansulex Ltd* [1987] AC 460, 474. See also the analysis in *Connelly v RTZ Corporation Plc* [1998] AC 854 and the discussion by A Briggs, (1996) 67 *BYIL* 587. Notwithstanding the clarification in the *Connelly* case, the analytical error in *Mohammed v Bank of Kuwait and the Middle East KSC* [1996] 1 WLR 1483 was repeated by Tomlinson J in *Alberta Inc v Katanga Mining Ltd* [2009] ILPr 175 (a case in which the alternative forum was the Democratic Republic of Congo); it was held that, because of the lack of a developed infrastructure within which the rule of law could be confidently and consistently upheld, the alternative forum was not 'available' for the purposes of the *Spiliada* test.

[233] [2000] 1 WLR 1545. A Briggs, (2000) 71 *BYIL* 435.

[234] Lord Hope at [2000] 1 WLR 1545, 1566 (a stay was, however, refused for other reasons: see para 9.2.44). See also *Konamaneni v Rolls-Royce Industrial Power (India) Ltd* [2002] 1 All ER 979, 999 [at [72]]; *Hindocha v Gheewala* [2004] 1 CLC 502 (L Merrett, [2004] *CLJ* 309). See also the discussion of L Merrett, 'Uncertainties in the First Limb of the *Spiliada* Test' (2005) 54 *ICLQ* 211.

[235] Lord Goff in *Spiliada Maritime Corporation v Cansulex Ltd* [1987] AC 460, 476.

consider all the circumstances of the case, including circumstances which go beyond the connecting factors with other jurisdictions which were taken into account at the first stage; of prime significance is the question whether the claimant would obtain justice in the foreign jurisdiction.[236]

9.2.21 In *MacShannon v Rockware Glass Ltd* Lord Diplock had thought that the court should not grant a stay if it would 'deprive the plaintiff of a legitimate personal or juridical advantage which would be available to him if he invoked the jurisdiction of the English court'.[237] In the *Spiliada* case Lord Goff was eager to play down the importance of such advantages; the mere fact that the claimant has a legitimate personal or juridical advantage in proceeding in England should not be decisive.[238] The court should not be deterred from granting a stay of proceedings simply because the claimant will be deprived of such an advantage 'provided that the court is satisfied that substantial justice will be done in the available appropriate forum'.[239]

The Application of the Test: Factors to be Taken into Account

9.2.22 When applying the test of appropriateness there is almost no limit to the range of factors which the court may, in the specific circumstances, consider to be relevant. The decided cases show that regard may be had to procedural factors (such as delay and costs) as well as to substantive factors (such as the applicable law). Of course, not all the factors are relevant in any particular case. The decided cases illustrate that certain types of factor are considered at the first stage; others at the second stage.

Factors Considered at the First Stage

CONVENIENCE AND EXPENSE

9.2.23 Although the doctrine of *forum non conveniens* is concerned with appropriateness rather than simply practical convenience, it is important not to lose sight of the fact that considerations of convenience and expense are relevant. So, the court should have regard to matters such as the residence and place of business of the parties as well as the availability of witnesses and other evidence.[240] Not infrequently, it is the place where the relevant events took place which provides the most appropriate forum.[241]

LIS ALIBI PENDENS

9.2.24 It is generally undesirable that the same dispute should be litigated in more than one forum. The additional inconvenience and expense which results from allowing two sets of legal proceedings to be pursued concurrently in two different countries

---

[236] Lord Goff in *Spiliada Maritime Corporation v Cansulex Ltd* [1987] AC 460, 478.
[237] [1978] AC 795, 812.
[238] [1987] AC 460, 482–4.
[239] Lord Goff in *Spiliada Maritime Corporation v Cansulex Ltd* [1987] AC 460, 482.
[240] See, eg, *The Lakhta* [1992] 2 Lloyd's Rep 269; *The Polessk* [1996] 2 Lloyd's Rep 40.
[241] See, eg, *International Marine Services Inc v National Bank of Fujairah* [1997] ILPr 468.

where the same facts are in issue and the testimony of the same witnesses required is considerable. Furthermore, if both sets of proceedings continue to judgment there is a risk of inconsistent decisions being handed down, which in turn may lead to problems of enforcement. Accordingly, the court should strive to avoid the risk of inconsistent decisions and should favour the litigation of issues only once, in the most appropriate forum.[242] Where parallel proceedings between the same parties concerning the same cause of action are brought in the courts of two or more Member States any court other than the court first seised *must* stay its proceedings or decline jurisdiction.[243] However, in cases not regulated by the Brussels I Regulation, the *Spiliada* doctrine confers a discretion on the court.[244] The court's discretion to grant a stay under its inherent jurisdiction extends to cases where the other proceedings are arbitration proceedings not involving identical parties. The court may, for example, stay proceedings between B and C pending the outcome of an arbitration (whether in England or abroad) between A and B.[245] The grant of a stay in such a case is exceptional and only temporary.

9.2.25   Prior to *Spiliada Maritime Corporation v Cansulex Ltd* the leading authority on the staying of proceedings in cases where litigation on the same issue was pending in a foreign country (*lis alibi pendens*) was the House of Lords' decision in *The Abidin Daver*.[246] In *de Dampierre v de Dampierre*, however, Lord Goff indicated that the general principle laid down in *Spiliada Maritime Corporation v Cansulex Ltd* is applicable 'whether or not there are other relevant proceedings already pending in the alternative forum'.[247] Although there appear to be slight differences between the approach advocated by Lord Diplock in *The Abidin Daver* and the *Spiliada* test, it has come to be accepted that there is in fact no conflict between the cases.[248]

9.2.26   To obtain a stay the defendant must show that the existence of parallel proceedings abroad, along with all the other relevant factors, has the effect of making the foreign court the more appropriate forum. The existence of parallel proceedings abroad does not raise a presumption in favour of a stay so as to reverse the burden of proof.[249] The undesirability of there being concurrent proceedings in two countries is merely one of the considerations to be weighed as part of the overall assessment; it cannot necessarily lead to a stay.[250] The weight to be attached to the existence of *lis alibi pendens* depends on the circumstances of the case, including the stage reached in the proceedings

---

[242]   Bingham LJ in *EI du Pont de Nemours & Co v Agnew* [1987] 2 Lloyd's Rep 585, 589.

[243]   Brussels I Reg, Art 27.

[244]   A claimant who sues the defendant in more than one country will normally be required to elect which proceedings to pursue: *Australian Commercial Research and Development v ANZ McCaughan Merchant Bank Ltd* [1989] 3 All ER 65. However, if it is not vexatious for the claimant to pursue the litigation in both countries (eg, where he is not able to bring the whole of his claim in one forum) he will not be put to election: see *Merrill Lynch, Pierce Fenner & Smith Inc v Raffa* [2001] ILPr 437.

[245]   *Reichhold Norway ASA v Goldman Sachs International* [2000] 1 WLR 173.

[246]   [1984] AC 398.

[247]   [1988] AC 92, 108.

[248]   See, eg, *Cleveland Museum of Art v Capricorn Art International SA* [1990] 2 Lloyd's Rep 166. It seems, however, that the practice adopted in cases involving parallel proceedings in the European Patent Office (EPO) may be slightly different from the more usual commercial cases; this is explicable by the specific context in which litigation at the EPO takes place: *Glaxo Group Ltd v Genentech Inc* [2007] FSR 840 (Lewison J), [2008] FSR 459 (CA).

[249]   Hirst J in *Meadows Indemnity Co Ltd v Insurance Corporation of Ireland Plc* [1989] 1 Lloyd's Rep 181, 189.

[250]   Bingham LJ in *EI du Pont de Nemours & Co v Agnew* [1987] 2 Lloyd's Rep 585, 589.

abroad,[251] the connections with the foreign court,[252] the basis on which the foreign court assumed jurisdiction[253] and the likely outcome of any jurisdictional challenge in the foreign forum.[254] For example, the court is more likely to grant a stay if the foreign proceedings are already well advanced when the English proceedings are commenced. Conversely, the court will refuse to stay English proceedings if the foreign court has assumed jurisdiction on an exorbitant basis, the proceedings are still at a preliminary stage and it is likely that they will not survive a jurisdictional challenge. Similarly, in a case where elements of the parties' dispute are almost bound to be litigated in more than one forum—whether or not the English proceedings are stayed—the court is likely not to attach as much weight to the parallel proceedings as in cases where the proceedings in the alternative forum will deal with all the issues between the parties.[255]

9.2.27 In modern practice, when one party who asserts a positive claim has brought (or intends to bring) proceedings in one jurisdiction, the other party may bring proceedings for a negative declaration in another jurisdiction. Although claims for a negative declaration are still less common than claims for positive relief (in the form of damages or a specific remedy, such as an injunction or an order for specific performance), the court should not be reluctant to grant a negative declaration if to do so would assist in achieving justice.[256] Accordingly, from the point of view of the question of appropriateness, there is no reason why the court should treat a claim for a negative declaration any differently from a claim for some form of positive relief,[257] so long as the claim for a negative declaration serves a useful purpose.[258] In a case where the claim is for a negative declaration, the court may consider it appropriate to exercise jurisdiction, even if this will involve there being parallel proceedings in England and abroad.[259]

MULTIPLE DEFENDANTS

9.2.28 It is clearly inconvenient in a case where there is more than one defendant if the claimant is required to pursue litigation against each defendant in a different jurisdiction. Furthermore, unless multiparty disputes are heard by the same court there is a risk of inconsistent decisions.[260] A claimant therefore has a legitimate interest in trying to consolidate the claims into one set of proceedings. CPR PD 6B para 3.1(3)

---

[251] *Cleveland Museum of Art v Capricorn Art SA* [1990] 2 Lloyd's Rep 166.

[252] *The Olympic Galaxy* [2006] 2 Lloyd's Rep 27.

[253] *The Volvox Hollandia* [1988] 2 Lloyd's Rep 361; *Chase v Ran Technical Services Ltd* [2000] 2 Lloyd's Rep 418.

[254] *Meridien Biao Bank GmbH v Bank of New York* [1997] 1 Lloyd's Rep 437.

[255] See, eg, *Smyth v Behbehani* [1999] ILPr 584.

[256] Lord Woolf MR in *Messier-Dowty Ltd v Sabena SA* [2000] 1 WLR 2040, 2050. For discussion of this case, see A Briggs, (2000) 71 *BYIL* 455.

[257] See L Collins, 'Negative Declarations and the Brussels Convention' (1992) 108 *LQR* 545, 547.

[258] See, eg, *EI du Pont de Nemours & Co v Agnew* [1987] 2 Lloyd's Rep 585; *New Hampshire Insurance Co v Phillips Electronics North America Corporation* [1998] ILPr 256; *Tiernan v The Magen Insurance Co* [2000] ILPr 517; *Bristow Helicopters Ltd v Sikorsky Aircraft Corporation* [2004] 2 Lloyd's Rep 150; *Bhatia Shipping and Agencies Pvt Ltd v Alcobex Metals Ltd* [2005] 2 Lloyd's Rep 336; *Ark Therapeutics plc v True North Capital Ltd* [2006] 1 All ER (Comm) 138.

[259] *CGU International Insurance plc v Szabo* [2002] 1 All ER (Comm) 83.

[260] See, eg, *Bouygues Offshore SA v Caspian Shipping Co (Nos 1, 3, 4 and 5)* [1998] 2 Lloyd's Rep 461. A Briggs, (1998) 69 *BYIL* 342.

enables a claimant to serve a claim form out of the jurisdiction on a defendant who is a necessary or proper party to litigation being brought against another defendant in England; CPR PD 6B para 3.1(4) allows service of additional claims under Part 20 (formerly known as third party proceedings) on a defendant abroad.[261]

9.2.29 If a foreign court has jurisdiction to determine all the claims in multiparty proceedings this is a factor which points against the assumption of jurisdiction by the English court.[262] Conversely, where all the potential defendants can be sued in England—by virtue of their being served within the jurisdiction as of right or out of the jurisdiction with the court's permission—this is a factor which points towards England as the appropriate forum.[263] Indeed, this factor may be decisive. There are circumstances in which, simply by virtue of the fact that CPR PD 6B para 3.1 enables there to be a single trial with all effective parties present and bound by the result, the English court is the most appropriate forum even if factual connections with another forum are stronger.[264] Furthermore, in cases involving multiple parties, some of whom are domiciled in a Member State and some of whom are not, there will be a tendency for the English court to refuse to grant a stay on the basis of *forum non conveniens*. As regards the defendants who are domiciled in a Member State, if the English court's jurisdiction is derived from the Brussels I Regulation, the Court of Justice's ruling in *Owusu v Jackson*[265] means that the court cannot stay the proceedings on the basis that another country is a more appropriate forum. Accordingly, if the claims against all the defendants are to be resolved in a single set of proceedings, the English court will also have to assume jurisdiction under the traditional rules with regard to the defendants who are not domiciled in a Member State.[266]

9.2.30 In cases where reliance is placed on CPR PD 6B para 3.1(3) or (4) there appears to be a degree of circularity in the reasoning if the existence of exorbitant jurisdiction is relied upon to justify the assumption of that jurisdiction.[267] Accordingly, the court must exercise caution in cases where the claimant attempts 'to persuade the courts of one country to arrogate for themselves a jurisdiction which belongs more properly to the courts of another country'.[268] The fact that an English court may—by virtue of CPR 6.36—exercise a wider and more flexible jurisdiction than the courts of many other countries does not mean that England is always the appropriate forum in cases where the litigation involves a number of foreign defendants.[269] Although the court is entitled to make liberal use of English procedural rules whenever it is appropriate in the interests of doing justice between all the parties concerned, these rules

---

[261] See paras 7.3.13–7.3.16.

[262] *The Oinoussin Pride* [1991] 1 Lloyd's Rep 126.

[263] See *Booth v Phillips* [2004] 2 Lloyd's Rep 457.

[264] *The Kapetan Georgis* [1988] 1 Lloyd's Rep 352; *Meadows Indemnity Co Ltd v Insurance Corporation of Ireland Plc* [1989] 2 Lloyd's Rep 298; *The Goldean Mariner* [1990] 2 Lloyd's Rep 215; *Barings Plc v Coopers & Lybrand* [1997] ILPr 12, affirmed [1997] ILPr 576; *Credit Agricole Indosuez v Unicof Ltd* [2004] 1 Lloyd's Rep 196.

[265] Case C–281/02 [2005] ECR I–1383.

[266] See *Attorney General of Zambia v Meer Care & Desai* [2006] 1 CLC 436. See also *Global Multimedia International Ltd v Ara Media Services* [2007] 1 All ER (Comm) 1160.

[267] *The Goldean Mariner* [1990] 2 Lloyd's Rep 215.

[268] Sir Michael Kerr in *First National Bank of Boston v Union Bank of Switzerland* [1990] 1 Lloyd's Rep 32, 38. See also *Cleveland Museum of Art v Capricorn International SA* [1990] 2 Lloyd's Rep 166.

[269] See, eg, *Haji-Ioannou v Frangos* [1999] 2 Lloyd's Rep 337.

'must not be abused by exorbitant uses in international contexts'.[270] It must never become the practice to bring foreign defendants to England as a matter of course on the ground that the only alternative requires more than one suit in different jurisdictions.[271] Nevertheless, in cases where a Part 20 claimant seeks contribution under the Civil Liability (Contribution) Act 1978, the absence of similar legislation in the alternative forum is a significant factor in favour of allowing the claimant to rely on CPR PD 6B para 3.1(4) and giving permission for service out under CPR 6.36.[272]

THE '*CAMBRIDGESHIRE* FACTOR'

9.2.31   In *Spiliada Maritime Corporation v Cansulex Ltd*[273] very few of the factual connections were with England; neither party was English and all the events which gave rise to the claim occurred abroad. Nevertheless, the House of Lords concluded that England was the *forum conveniens*. The dispute between the parties concerned a cargo of sulphur which had been loaded by the defendant, a company incorporated in British Columbia, on a ship owned by the plaintiff. The plaintiff alleged that the sulphur was wet when loaded, thereby causing corrosion to the hold of the ship. A similar cargo had been loaded at the same time on another ship, the *Cambridgeshire*, which was owned by an English company. When the plaintiff applied for permission to serve out under what is now CPR 6.36, many of the key elements of the dispute were already the subject of litigation in England in respect of the *Cambridgeshire*.[274]

9.2.32   The House of Lords decided that it was right to take into account the fact that there would be benefits in terms of efficiency, expedition and economy by having available experienced teams of lawyers and experts who were familiar with the legal and factual issues raised by the case by virtue of their involvement in the *Cambridgeshire* litigation. As Lord Goff noted:

[A]nyone who has been involved, as counsel, in very heavy litigation of this kind, with a number of experts on both sides and difficult scientific questions involved, knows only too well what the learning curve is like, how much information and knowledge has to be, and is, absorbed, not only by the lawyers but really by the whole team, including both lawyers and experts, as they learn about the interrelation of law, fact and scientific knowledge, having regard to the contentions advanced by both sides in the case, and identify in their minds the crucial matters on which attention has to be focused, why these are the crucial matters, and how they are to be assessed.[275]

In subsequent cases the so-called '*Cambridgeshire* factor' has been advanced, albeit with very little success, as a relevant consideration in the context of both applications for a stay of proceedings[276] and applications for permission to serve out of the jurisdiction.[277]

---

[270] Sir Michael Kerr in *First National Bank of Boston v Union Bank of Switzerland* [1990] 1 Lloyd's Rep 32, 38.

[271] Lloyd LJ in *The Goldean Mariner* [1990] 2 Lloyd's Rep 215, 222.

[272] *Petroleo Brasiliero SA v Mellitus Shipping Inc* [2001] 1 All ER (Comm) 993.

[273] [1987] AC 460.

[274] *Bibby Bulk Carriers Ltd v Cobelfret NV* [1989] QB 155.

[275] [1987] AC 460, 485.

[276] *Owens Bank Ltd v Bracco* [1992] 2 AC 443; *British Aerospace Plc v Dee Howard Co* [1993] 1 Lloyd's Rep 368.

[277] *Metall und Rohstoff AG v Donaldson Lufkin & Jenrette Inc* [1990] 1 QB 391; *The Kapetan Georgis* [1988] 1 Lloyd's Rep 352; *The Goldean Mariner* [1989] 2 Lloyd's Rep 390, affirmed [1990] 2 Lloyd's Rep 215.

THE APPLICABLE LAW

9.2.33 Where a dispute arises out of a contract which is governed by English law, the basis of jurisdiction which enables the claimant to apply for permission to serve the defendant out of the jurisdiction is to be found in CPR PD 6B para 3.1(6)(c). Since in certain sectors of the economy (such as shipping and insurance) it is common for English choice of law clauses to be included in contracts which, from a purely factual point of view, have no meaningful connection with England, the courts traditionally took the view that where reliance is placed on the contract being governed by English law, the burden on the claimant to show that England is the *forum conveniens* is a particularly heavy one.[278] However, more recently it has come to be acknowledged that the importance to be attached to the fact that English law is the applicable law depends on the circumstances of the case.[279] Although there are cases in which the applicable law is treated as a significant factor,[280] the fact that English law is the governing law is not a weighty factor in favour of English jurisdiction when there is no reason to suppose that the law applicable in the alternative forum is any different[281] or when the issues between the parties are primarily questions of fact.[282]

9.2.34 In some cases where English law is the applicable law the court is prepared to place very considerable emphasis on the fact that English judges are better placed than others to rule on questions of English law.[283] (This line of reasoning suggests that it is also preferable that questions of foreign law should be decided by the relevant foreign court.[284]) The English courts are also best equipped to apply English canons of construction in cases where the dispute between the parties requires the court to construe the terms of a contract governed by English law,[285] particularly if the contract was concluded on a standard form with which the English court is more familiar than the alternative forum.[286] If the task is undertaken by a foreign court, expense and inconvenience result from the court having to rely on the expert evidence of English lawyers.[287] However, it should be stressed that a choice of law is only one factor in the equation; the court should not fall into the error of thinking that by choosing the law of country X to govern their contractual relationship the parties thereby choose to confer jurisdiction of the courts of country X.[288] In a case where the parties' contract

---

[278] See, eg, Lord Diplock's speech in *Amin Rasheed Shipping Corporation v Kuwait Insurance Co* [1984] AC 50, 68.

[279] See Lord Goff in *Spiliada Maritime Corporation v Cansulex Ltd* [1987] AC 470, 481. See *Novus Aviation Ltd v Onur Air Tasimacilik AS* [2009] 1 Lloyd's Rep 576.

[280] See, eg, *Ark Therapeutics plc v True North Capital Ltd* [2006] 1 All ER (Comm) 138; *Novus Aviation Ltd v Onur Air Tasimacilik AS* [2009] 1 Lloyd's Rep 576.

[281] See Lawrence Collins J in *Chellaram v Chellaram (No 2)* [2002] 3 All ER 17, 50 (at [150]).

[282] *Navigators Insurance Co v Atlantic Methanol Production Co LLC* [2004] Lloyd's Rep IR 418; *Limit (No 3) Ltd v PDV Insurance Co* [2005] 1 CLC 515.

[283] *Coast Lines Ltd v Hudig & Veder Chartering NV* [1972] 2 QB 34; *Zivlin v Baal Taxa* [1998] ILPr 106; *Tryg Baltica International (UK) Ltd v Boston Compania de Seguros SA* [2005] Lloyd's Rep IR 40.

[284] See Robert Goff J in *Trendtex Trading Corporation v Crédit Suisse* [1980] 3 All ER 721, 735; *The Nile Rhapsody* [1992] 2 Lloyd's Rep 399.

[285] *CGU International Insurance plc v Szabo* [2002] 1 All ER (Comm) 83; *New Hampshire Insurance Co v Phillips Electronics North America Corporation* [1998] ILPr 256; *Apple Corps Limited v Apple Computer Inc* [2004] ILPr 597; *Sawyer v Atari Interactive Inc* [2006] ILPr 129.

[286] *Latchin (t/a Dinkha Latchin Associates) v General Mediterranean Holdings SA* [2002] CLC 330.

[287] *Standard Steamship Owners' Protection and Indemnity Association (Bermuda) Ltd v Gann* [1992] 2 Lloyd's Rep 528.

[288] *Macsteel Commercial Holdings (Pty) Ltd v Thermasteel V (Canada) Inc* [1996] CLC 1404.

is governed by English law, if the most closely connected forum is another common law jurisdiction whose law is similar to English law, the court may well conclude that the foreign court will have no difficulty in applying English law and that the English proceedings should be stayed.[289]

9.2.35 The importance of the applicable law is increased in cases involving questions of public policy. Where an issue of English public policy arises in the context of a dispute concerning a contract governed by English law it is highly desirable that that issue should be decided by an English court.[290] A question of English public policy is not 'a question capable of fair resolution in any foreign court, however distinguished and well instructed'.[291] By the same token, an English court would normally be unwilling to adjudicate upon the public policy of another country.[292]

LANGUAGE

9.2.36 In certain circumstances the fact that the dispute between the parties raises questions of construction of documentary material is a factor which strengthens the case for regarding a particular court as the appropriate forum. Where a decision depends upon the construction of a document in one language and the rival courts are, on the one hand, courts whose native language is that of the document and, on the other, courts whose native language is not that of the document, the matter may be more suitably tried in the former courts.[293] So, in a dispute relating to the interpretation of a document in the English language, if the alternative forum is Egypt, there is a natural inclination to regard England as the *forum conveniens*.[294] However, in cases where the language of the alternative forum is not English, it does not automatically follow from the fact that the dispute relates to documents in English that England is the appropriate forum; the courts of a foreign country may be the *forum conveniens* if the applicable law is the law of that country and it is by reference to that law that the documents have to be interpreted.[295] Furthermore, it has been stated that, 'it would not normally be right to treat the use of the English language in negotiations as a matter of great weight. In international business the use of the English (or, in reality, the American) language has become ubiquitous'.[296]

Factors Considered at the Second Stage

TIME BARS

9.2.37 What significance should the court attach to the fact that the claim is time barred in the alternative forum? This was another of the issues considered by the

---

[289] *Chase v Ran Technical Services Ltd* [2000] 2 Lloyd's Rep 418.

[290] *Mitsubishi Corporation v Alafouzos* [1988] 1 Lloyd's Rep 191.

[291] Bingham LJ in *EI du Pont de Nemours & Co v Agnew* [1987] 2 Lloyd's Rep 585, 594.

[292] Toulson J in *CGU International Insurance plc v Szabo* [2002] 1 All ER (Comm) 83, 90 (at [24]–[25]).

[293] Parker LJ in *The Magnum* [1989] 1 Lloyd's Rep 47, 51. See also *Haji-Ioannou v Frangos* [1998] CLC 61, 80, affirmed [1999] 2 Lloyd's Rep 337; *Dellar v Zivy* [2007] ILPr 868.

[294] *The Al Battani* [1993] 2 Lloyd's Rep 219; *The Magnum* [1989] 1 Lloyd's Rep 47 (PB Carter, (1989) 60 *BYIL* 482).

[295] *The Nile Rhapsody* [1992] 2 Lloyd's Rep 399.

[296] Lawrence Collins LJ in *Novus Aviation Ltd v Onur Air Tasimacilik AS* [2009] 1 Lloyd's Rep 576, 585 (at [80]).

House of Lords in *Spiliada Maritime Corporation v Cansulex Ltd.*[297] It does not automatically follow that the court will assume jurisdiction whenever the claim is time barred in the alternative forum. Lord Goff gave the following examples:

[S]uppose that the plaintiff allowed the limitation period to elapse in the appropriate jurisdiction, and came here simply because he wanted to take advantage of a more generous time bar applicable in this country; or suppose that it was obvious that the plaintiff should have commenced proceedings in the appropriate jurisdiction, and yet he did not trouble to issue a protective writ there; in cases such as these, I cannot see that the court should hesitate to stay the proceedings in this country, even though the effect would be that the plaintiff's claim would inevitably be defeated by a plea of the time-bar in the appropriate jurisdiction.[298]

There may, however, be cases where the claimant has acted reasonably, but finds that he is time barred in the appropriate jurisdiction; in this type of case, it would be unjust for the court to deprive the claimant of the opportunity of having his claim judicially determined. The court either may refuse to grant a stay or may grant a stay on condition that the defendant undertakes to waive the time bar when the claimant commences proceedings in the alternative forum.[299]

DELAY

9.2.38   Delay in the foreign forum is a factor which the court will take into account when considering the question of justice.[300] Although the court may regard the anticipated delay in the alternative forum as decisive if it is excessive,[301] such cases are relatively rare.[302]

COSTS

9.2.39   In principle, the court should not assume jurisdiction simply on the basis that there is a costs advantage to the claimant if the litigation takes place in England rather than abroad; the issue of costs is but one factor which must be weighed in the balance.[303] Although an advantage to the claimant in litigating in England is not normally decisive, the *Spiliada* test entitles the court to assume jurisdiction if substantial justice will not be done in the foreign forum. In *Roneleigh Ltd v MII Exports Inc*[304] the Court of Appeal upheld the judge's decision to allow service out of the jurisdiction, even though all the relevant connecting factors pointed towards New Jersey as the appropriate forum. The basis of the decision was that, since the law of New Jersey does not allow a successful claimant to recover costs, substantial justice would not be done in the foreign forum.[305]

---

[297] [1987] AC 460.
[298] [1987] AC 460, 483.
[299] *Baghlaf Al Safer Factory Co BR for Industry Ltd v Pakistan National Shipping Co* [1998] 2 Lloyd's Rep 229; *The Prestrioka* [2003] 2 Lloyd's Rep 327.
[300] *The Al Battani* [1993] 2 Lloyd's Rep 219.
[301] *The Vishva Ajay* [1989] 2 Lloyd's Rep 558.
[302] For examples where delay in the alternative forum was not decisive, see *Radhakrishna Hospitality Service Private Ltd v EIH Ltd* [1999] 2 Lloyd's Rep 249; *Konamaneni v Rolls-Royce Industrial Power (India) Ltd* [2002] 1 All ER 979.
[303] *The Oinoussin Pride* [1991] 1 Lloyd's Rep 126.
[304] [1989] 1 WLR 619.
[305] See also *The Vishva Ajay* [1989] 2 Lloyd's Rep 558.

DAMAGES

9.2.40 As a general rule, the fact that the claimant, if successful, will recover higher damages in England than abroad does not mean that the English court is more appropriate than the forum with which the dispute is more closely connected. There are, however, certain circumstances in which the difference between the damages which could be recovered in England and abroad is so great that the court may take the view that it would amount to an injustice if the defendant were required to pursue his claim abroad.[306] In *Caltex Singapore Pte Ltd v BP Shipping Ltd*[307] Clarke J decided that, notwithstanding the fact that Singapore was a more closely connected forum, proceedings should not be stayed. Whereas, in English proceedings, damages would be calculated by reference to the Convention on Limitation of Liability for Maritime Claims 1976, the courts of Singapore would apply the 1957 version of the convention, which provides for a lower level of recovery. This decision was, however, disapproved by the Court of Appeal in *Herceg Novi (owners) v Ming Galaxy (owners)*,[308] another case in which Singapore was the more closely connected forum. The fact that the more closely connected foreign court would apply the 1957 version of the convention rather than the 1976 version was not sufficient to justify refusal of a stay. According to Sir Christopher Staughton:

[I]n terms of abstract justice, neither convention is objectively more just than the other. [The court's] task is not to decide whether our law is better than the law of Singapore. It is to decide whether substantial justice will be done in Singapore.[309]

As the Court of Appeal considered that substantial justice would be done in Singapore, the appeal against the judge's refusal to grant a stay was allowed.

RESOURCES

9.2.41 If the claimant cannot afford to pursue his claim in the alternative forum, but does have the funds to litigate in England, this may, depending on the precise circumstances of the case, encourage the court to decide that England is the appropriate forum, notwithstanding the fact that the dispute is more closely connected with the foreign forum. In *Connelly v RTZ Corporation Plc*[310] proceedings were commenced in England against the defendant, an English company, in respect of injuries which the plaintiff had allegedly suffered while working in Namibia for one of the defendant's subsidiaries. The defendant applied for a stay. On the basis of the first stage of the *Spiliada* test, Namibia was the country with which the dispute had its most real and substantial connection. However, the plaintiff sought to resist the grant of a stay on the basis that, because of financial factors, substantial justice would not be done in Namibia. Although the plaintiff had the resources to pursue the litigation in England—either by virtue of legal aid or a conditional fee arrangement with his legal advisers—he was unable to fund litigation in Namibia and was not entitled to financial assistance for such litigation.

---

[306] *The Vishva Abha* [1990] 2 Lloyd's Rep 312.
[307] [1996] 1 Lloyd's Rep 286.
[308] [1998] 4 All ER 238. A Briggs, (1998) 69 *BYIL* 340.
[309] [1998] 4 All ER 238, 247.
[310] [1998] AC 854. A Briggs, (1997) 68 *BYIL* 357. See also *Carlson v Rio Tinto plc* [1999] CLC 559.

9.2.42   Lord Goff, with whom the majority of the House of Lords agreed, concluded that a stay should not be granted. The starting point was that:

at least as a general rule, the court will not refuse to grant a stay simply because the plaintiff has shown that no financial assistance, for example in the form of legal aid, will be available to him in the appropriate forum, whereas such financial assistance will be available to him in England.[311]

Even though the absence of legal aid in the most closely connected jurisdiction does not of itself justify the refusal of a stay on the basis of *forum non conveniens*, 'the availability of financial assistance in this country, coupled with its non-availability in the appropriate forum, may exceptionally be a relevant factor'.[312] For the majority of the House of Lords the crucial factor was that, given the complexity of the issues raised by the case, there was no realistic prospect of the plaintiff being able to bring the claim without the benefit of professional assistance. Since, in practical terms, the case could not be tried in Namibia, a stay should be refused. However, Lord Goff added an important qualification:

If the position had been, for example, that the plaintiff was seeking to take advantage of financial assistance available here to obtain a Rolls Royce presentation of his case, as opposed to a more rudimentary presentation in the appropriate forum, it might well have been necessary to take a different view.[313]

9.2.43   It is worth noting the dissenting speech of Lord Hoffmann, who took the view that there was no defensible principle which could justify a refusal to grant a stay. The consequences of the majority decision were spelt out in the following terms:

It means that the action of a rich plaintiff will be stayed while the action of a poor plaintiff in respect of precisely the same transaction will not. It means that the more speculative and difficult the action, the more likely it is to be allowed to proceed in this country with the support of public funds. Such distinctions will do the law no credit.[314]

9.2.44   A related issue was raised in *Lubbe v Cape plc*[315] which involved claims for personal injury or death by over 3,000 plaintiffs (nearly all of whom were South African citizens). The defendant was an English company which owned a number of subsidiary companies involved in the mining and processing of asbestos in South Africa. The plaintiffs were either employees of the defendant's subsidiaries or people who lived in close proximity to the subsidiaries' industrial operations in South Africa; they claimed that their injuries resulted from the defendant's failure to ensure the adoption of proper working practices by its subsidiaries. In the context of the defendant's application for a stay it was clear that, under the first stage of the *Spiliada* test, South Africa was the most closely connected forum. However, the plaintiffs argued

---

[311] [1998] AC 854, 873. See *Hewitson v Hewitson* [1999] 2 FLR 74.
[312] [1998] AC 854, 873.
[313] [1998] AC 854, 874.
[314] [1998] AC 854, 876.
[315] [2000] 1 WLR 1545. P Muchlinski, 'Corporations in International Litigation: Problems of Jurisdiction and the United Kingdom Asbestos Cases' (2001) 50 *ICLQ* 1; E Peel, '*Forum Non Conveniens* Revisited' (2001) 117 *LQR* 187; AC Sinclair, 'Funding decisive: asbestos group action to proceed in England' [2001] *LMCLQ* 197. For discussion of the two Court of Appeal decisions—reported at [1999] ILPr 471 and [2000] 1 Lloyd's Rep 139—see A Briggs, (1998) 69 *BYIL* 336 and (1999) 70 *BYIL* 319.

that a stay should be refused because substantial justice could not be done in South Africa. The plaintiffs' argument contained two elements. The first was essentially the issue that had been raised in the *Connelly* case: if the English proceedings were stayed, the plaintiffs would have no means of obtaining the professional representation and expert evidence which would be essential for their claims to be justly determined. The second element was the absence in South Africa of developed procedures for handling group actions involving large numbers of plaintiffs. The House of Lords considered that in these circumstances substantial justice could not be done in South Africa and the English proceedings should not be stayed.

COMPETING CHOICE OF LAW RULES

9.2.45   Each legal system has choice of law rules for deciding which substantive rules to apply to disputes which come before its courts. While in certain areas there has been some measure of harmonisation, there are considerable divergences between the choice of law rules applied in different countries. As a result, a claimant may have a claim which will fail if brought in one forum, but will succeed if brought in another.

9.2.46   The nature of the problem which arises from such divergences may be illustrated by *The Magnum*,[316] a case which concerned a dispute arising out of a contract of insurance which contained an express choice of English law. When the plaintiff made a claim under the policy the defendant, a Spanish insurance company, denied liability. The plaintiff's claim would fail if it were pursued in Spain because the Spanish court would disregard the choice of law clause and, applying domestic Spanish law, would disallow the plaintiff's claim on the basis of public policy. Since under English conflicts rules the applicable law was English law according to which the plaintiff had a valid claim under the contract, the plaintiff applied for permission to serve the defendant out of the jurisdiction. In this type of case, how should the court balance the factual connections in favour of the foreign country against the fact that the choice of law rules applied by the foreign court lead to a result which is the opposite of that reached by the application of English conflicts rules?

9.2.47   The cases show that, in situations where the English choice of law rules and the choice of law rules of a foreign country conflict in this way, the court will regard the conflict as a factor which points towards England as the *forum conveniens*, particularly in a case where parties to a contractual dispute have expressly chosen English law to govern their contract and there is a possibility that the alternative forum will not apply the chosen law.[317] In *Irish Shipping Ltd v Commercial Union Co Plc*, in which the issue was whether England or Belgium was the appropriate forum,[318] Staughton LJ said:

In an ideal world there would be no difference between the conflict rules applied by all nations. ... But unfortunately uniformity is far from achieved. It is by no means improbable

---

[316] [1989] 1 Lloyd's Rep 47.
[317] See *Coast Lines Ltd v Hudig and Veder Chartering NV* [1971] 2 Lloyd's Rep 390, affirmed [1972] 1 Lloyd's Rep 53.
[318] Although the case did not concern an application for service out under what is now CPR PD 6B para 3.1, the situation was considered by Staughton LJ as being 'somewhat akin' to such an application ([1991] 2 QB 206, 229) and the *Spiliada* test was regarded by the Court of Appeal to be relevant.

that the Belgian and English conflict rules differ in their application to this case. In those circumstances, it seems to me fairly arguable that a plaintiff is entitled to claim the benefit of the conflict rules prevailing here. So far as concerns domestic law, it would be wrong to suppose that our system is better than any other. But in the case of conflict rules, which ought to be but are not the same internationally, there is a case for saying that we should regard our rules as the most appropriate.[319]

9.2.48   The significance of the exercise of jurisdiction by the English court—so that English conflicts rules are applied in preference to those of another country—is illustrated by *Banco Atlantico SA v British Bank of the Middle East*.[320] The plaintiff, a Spanish bank, was the holder of bills of exchange, which were drawn on a third party, but in relation to which the defendant, an English bank, acted as guarantor. When the bills were not paid on presentment, the plaintiff started proceedings in England. The defendant applied for a stay of proceedings on the basis that the courts of Sharjah (UAE) were clearly a more appropriate forum. Although there could be no doubt that the underlying factual matrix of the case was most closely connected with the UAE, a stay was refused. Of particular importance was the fact that the choice of law rules applied by the courts of Sharjah were fundamentally different from the English rules. If the litigation took place in England, the court would—on the basis of English conflicts rules[321]—conclude that the applicable law was Spanish law, under which the plaintiff had an arguable claim. However, the evidence before the Court of Appeal indicated that the Sharjah court would apply its own domestic law, under which the plaintiff's claim was bound to fail. The Court of Appeal decided that to grant a stay of proceedings—thereby forcing the plaintiff to pursue the defendant in a jurisdiction in which it would be bound to face summary rejection of its claims—would not be 'conducive to justice'.[322]

9.2.49   It has been questioned whether this approach—which is routinely followed[323]—is the correct one to take. If it is not appropriate for the English court to embark upon a comparison of the procedures or methods or reputation or standing of the courts of one country as compared with those of another, it is not obvious why it should be thought appropriate for the court to embark on such a comparison in substantive matters.[324]

PROCEDURAL ADVANTAGES/FAIRNESS

9.2.50   There are cases in which the court regards the ease of enforceability of a judgment in the claimant's favour to be a significant factor. If, for example, the alternative fora are England and Libya and it is clear that it would be significantly easier for the claimant to enforce an English judgment in England, than a Libyan judgment, the court may conclude that England is the appropriate forum.[325]

---

[319]   [1991] 2 QB 206, 229–30.
[320]   [1990] 2 Lloyd's Rep 504.
[321]   Bills of Exchange Act 1882, s 72.
[322]   Bingham LJ at [1990] 2 Lloyd's Rep 504, 509.
[323]   See, eg, *Akai Pty Ltd v People's Insurance Co Ltd* [1998] 1 Lloyd's Rep 90; *Tiernan v The Magen Insurance Co Ltd* [2000] ILPr 517.
[324]   PB Carter, (1989) 60 *BYIL* 482, 484–5.
[325]   *Sharab v Al-saud* [2009] 2 Lloyd's Rep 160.

9.2.51 If the defendant asserts that he will not receive a fair hearing in the alternative forum, does this factor tilt the balance in favour of England as the *forum conveniens*? In considering the answer to this question, the starting point is the principle that the English court is not permitted to embark on a comparison of the respective merits and failings of the English legal system and the legal systems of foreign countries. Accordingly, the party which seeks to invoke the jurisdiction of the English court will not be permitted to bring into the equation perceived defects of the legal system of the alternative forum (such as the competence of the judiciary or the system of civil procedure). It would, for example, be:

wholly wrong for an English court, with quite inadequate experience of how it works in practice in a particular country, to condemn as inferior to that of our own country a system of procedure for the trial of issues of fact that has long been adopted by a large number of both developed and developing countries in the modern world.[326]

A litigant's fears as to the quality of justice in the alternative forum are not relevant.[327] Similarly, the court will not take into account the fact that a foreign court is, in comparison with the English court, relatively inexperienced 'unless it can be shown that the [foreign] court will not apply the relevant law to the facts or that it will not properly find the facts'.[328]

9.2.52 However, if the litigant can show that he would not receive a fair trial in the alternative forum—for example, for political, racial or religious reasons—this is a factor which the court ought to take into account when considering the question of appropriateness.[329] It has also been argued that, if proceedings in the alternative forum would not satisfy the requirements of the right to a fair trial under Article 6 of the ECHR, the English court, in order to comply with its obligations under the Human Rights Act 1998, should refuse to grant to stay.[330]

9.2.53 A claimant who wishes to argue for English jurisdiction on the basis that he will not be treated fairly in the most closely connected forum 'must assert this candidly and support his allegations with positive and cogent evidence'.[331] It is rare that the claimant in English proceedings is able to satisfy the court that there are legitimate reasons for thinking that he will not receive even-handed justice in the alternative forum. For example, in *Askin v ABSA Bank Ltd*[332] the plaintiff sought to resist a stay in favour of the courts of South Africa on the ground that, although the dispute was most closely connected with South Africa, he faced criminal charges in South Africa and feared for his safety there. The Court of Appeal agreed with the judge that the plaintiff could not rely on his unwillingness to return to South Africa to face criminal charges as a basis for arguing that justice required his claim to be

---

[326] Lord Diplock in *Amin Rasheed Shipping Corporation v Kuwait Insurance Co* [1984] AC 50, 67. See *The Bergen (No 2)* [1997] 2 Lloyd's Rep 710.

[327] *Jeyaretnam v Mahmood* The Times, 21 May 1992.

[328] Clarke J in *The Varna (No 2)* [1994] 2 Lloyd's Rep 41, 48. See also *Ceskoslovenska Obchodni Banka AS v Nomura International plc* [2002] ILPr 321.

[329] *Carvalho v Hull, Blyth (Angola) Ltd* [1979] 1 WLR 1228. See also *Al-Bassam v Al-Bassam* [2004] EWCA Civ 857.

[330] See JJ Fawcett, 'The Impact of Article 6(1) of the ECHR on Private International Law' (2007) 56 *ICLQ* 1, 37–42.

[331] Lord Diplock in *The Abidin Daver* [1984] AC 398, 411.

[332] [1999] ILPr 471. A Briggs, (1999) 70 *BYIL* 319.

tried in England. As for the plaintiff's personal safety, the court did not think that there was an objective basis to the plaintiff's fear of being assassinated or suffering serious harm if he returned to South Africa. Accordingly, the plaintiff's appeal against the stay of the English proceedings was dismissed.

The Weighing of Factors

9.2.54 Following the House of Lords' decision in *Spiliada Maritime Corporation v Cansulex Ltd* it was suggested that the legal community could 'look forward to some peace and quiet on this front and fewer reported cases'.[333] However, the flow of reported cases concerned with *forum (non) conveniens* has continued unabated. The decided cases show that there is a vast array of potentially relevant factors, many of which point in different directions, and that it is not always easy to predict the weight which the court, in the exercise of its discretion, will attach to any particular factor.[334] For example, in some cases a costs advantage to the claimant is crucial; in others it is of marginal significance. In *Spiliada Maritime Corporation v Cansulex Ltd* Lord Templeman observed:

The factors which the court is entitled to take into account in considering whether one forum is more appropriate are legion. The authorities do not, perhaps cannot, give any guidance as to how these factors are to be weighed in any particular case.[335]

9.2.55 It seems that uncertainty is an inevitable feature of the traditional English system of jurisdiction. Perhaps not surprisingly, some remain to be convinced of the virtues of the doctrine of *forum (non) conveniens*.[336] From a practical point of view it is not essential that jurisdiction rules should be simple, but it is highly desirable that they be certain.[337] A system of jurisdiction rules based on the test of appropriateness can lead to certainty only if the natural forum is self-evident in most cases and trial judges apply the test in a consistent and impartial manner. The cases do not suggest that these conditions can be satisfied. In cases where a defendant who is served within the jurisdiction applies for a stay, what is the court to do if the defendant shows that there is another more closely connected forum and the claimant shows that a stay would deprive him of a legitimate personal or juridical advantage? In these circumstances the court must apply 'the underlying fundamental principle'.[338] This, however, requires the court to strike a balance between largely unbalanceable considerations.[339]

---

[333] JG Collier, [1987] *CLJ* 33, 35.

[334] See J Hill, 'Jurisdiction in Civil and Commercial Matters: Is There a Third Way?' (2001) 54 *CLP* 439, 450–2.

[335] [1987] AC 460, 465.

[336] DW Robertson, '*Forum Non Conveniens* in America and England: "A Rather Fantastic Fiction"' (1987) 103 *LQR* 398; AG Slater, '*Forum Non Conveniens*: A View from the Shop Floor' (1988) 104 *LQR* 554; PA Stone, 'The Civil Jurisdiction and Judgments Act 1982: Some Comments' (1983) 32 *ICLQ* 477.

[337] PB Carter, (1972–3) 46 *BYIL* 428, 430.

[338] Lord Goff in *Spiliada Maritime Corporation v Cansulex Ltd* [1987] AC 460, 482.

[339] PB Carter, (1986) 57 *BYIL* 429, 433.

9.2.56   From a theoretical point of view a system of jurisdiction rules which seeks to locate each international commercial dispute in the most appropriate forum for its resolution has an obvious appeal. However, such a system depends for its realisation on the exercise of discretion, rather than the application of predictable rules. Accordingly, the theoretical attractions of the doctrine of *forum (non) conveniens* are bought at a price—namely, uncertainty, delay and expense—which has to be paid by litigants. It is arguable that the doctrine costs more than its worth.[340]

Appeals Against the Exercise of Discretion

9.2.57   In the *Spiliada* case Lord Templeman considered that in cases where the parties are litigating about where to litigate the decision of the trial judge should normally be final: 'An appeal should be rare and the appellate court should be slow to interfere'.[341] The fact that the Court of Appeal disagrees with the weight that the trial judge has given to the various relevant factors is not sufficient to justify intervention:

It can only interfere in three cases: (1) where the judge has misdirected himself with regard to the principles in accordance with which his discretion is to be exercised; (2) where the judge in exercising his discretion has taken into account matters which he ought not to have done, or failed to take into account matters which he ought to have done; or (3) where his decision is plainly wrong.[342]

9.2.58   Whether the Court of Appeal always adheres to the principle that the appellate courts should be 'slow to interfere' may be doubted. If the Court of Appeal does not agree with the exercise of discretion it is not difficult to pay lip-service to the principle of non-interference, but to decide that the judge in the lower court erred in principle, or misdirected himself in some significant manner, or failed to consider a relevant factor, or considered a factor which he should have ignored.[343]

9.3 THE IMPACT OF A JURISDICTION CLAUSE

9.3.1   In cases falling within the scope of the Brussels I Regulation a jurisdiction clause in favour of the courts of a Member State is effective to confer jurisdiction on the courts of that state—so long as the agreement on jurisdiction satisfies the formal and other requirements of Article 23.[344] Where the English courts have jurisdiction

---

[340] DW Robertson, 'Forum Non Conveniens in America and England: "A Rather Fantastic Fiction"' (1987) 103 *LQR* 398, 426.

[341] [1987] AC 460, 465. See *New Hampshire Insurance Co v Phillips Electronics North America Corporation* [1998] ILPr 256; *Smyth v Behbehani* [1999] ILPr 584; *International Credit and Investment Co (Overseas) Ltd v Shaikh Kamal Adham* [1999] ILPr 302; *Dornoch Ltd v Mauritius Union Assurance Co Ltd* [2006] 2 Lloyd's Rep 475; *Glaxo Group Ltd v Genentech Inc* [2008] FSR 459.

[342] Lord Brandon in *The Abidin Daver* [1984] AC 398, 420.

[343] See *Berezovsky v Michaels* [2000] 1 WLR 1004 in which the House of Lords was divided on whether the Court of Appeal had been justified in interfering. For consideration of some of the problems posed by the potential for appeals under the traditional rules, see J Hill, 'Jurisdiction in Civil and Commercial Matters: Is There a Third Way?' (2001) 54 *CLP* 439, 447–50.

[344] See section 5.3.

under Article 23 of the Brussels I Regulation the claimant does not require the court's permission to serve the defendant out of the jurisdiction.[345] If the defendant is domiciled in a Member State the effect of Article 23 is normally mandatory.[346] As a general rule, the chosen courts may not decline jurisdiction and the courts of other Member States may not assume jurisdiction. However, if neither party is domiciled in a Member State, the courts chosen by the parties may decline jurisdiction.[347]

The Traditional Rules

9.3.2   The traditional rules have a residual character; they apply only where the provisions of the Brussels regime do not determine jurisdiction. It is reasonable to expect that, in cases governed by the traditional rules, if parties agree to refer their disputes to the courts of a particular country, the English court will, as a general rule, enforce that agreement.[348] This is certainly the case where the parties have agreed to English jurisdiction. There seems to be no reported case in which English proceedings have been stayed at the behest of a defendant seeking to escape an English jurisdiction agreement, nor a reported case where jurisdiction is invoked under CPR PD 6B para 3.1(6)(d) (or its predecessors) in which the court has refused permission to serve out of the jurisdiction. The fact that a refusal to grant a stay (or a decision to allow service out) means that the parties will be involved in parallel proceedings in England and abroad is accorded less weight than the desirability of upholding the parties' contractual agreement on jurisdiction.[349] Where the parties have agreed to English jurisdiction, whether the jurisdiction clause is exclusive or non-exclusive makes little or no difference to the way in which the court's discretion is exercised.[350]

9.3.3   At common law a jurisdiction clause in favour of a foreign court does not oust the English court's jurisdiction. Accordingly, it cannot be assumed that such jurisdiction clauses will be enforced as a matter of course. Whether a claimant is able to proceed in England depends on the exercise of the court's discretion.[351] The special considerations to which situations involving jurisdiction clauses give rise suggest that the general test laid down in *Spiliada Maritime Corporation v Cansulex Ltd*[352] should not apply. The case law supports the view that, where parties to a contract have

---

[345]   CPR 6.33.

[346]   See the approach of the Court of Justice in Case C–281/02 *Owusu v Jackson* [2005] ECR I–1383.

[347]   Brussels I Reg, Art 23(3).

[348]   *The Chaparral* [1968] 2 Lloyd's Rep 158; *OT Africa Line Ltd v Magic Sportswear Corp* [2005] 2 Lloyd's Rep 170.

[349]   See Thomas J in *Akai Pty Ltd v People's Insurance Co Ltd* [1998] 1 Lloyd's Rep 90, 107.

[350]   *Commercial Bank of the Near East Plc v A* [1989] 2 Lloyd's Rep 319; *Standard Steamship Owners' Protection and Indemnity Association (Bermuda) Ltd v Gann* [1992] 2 Lloyd's Rep 528; *British Aerospace Plc v Dee Howard Co* [1993] 1 Lloyd's Rep 368; *Mercury Communications Ltd v Communications Telesystems International* [1999] 2 All ER 33; *JP Morgan Securities Asia Private Ltd v Malaysian Newsprint Industries Sdn Bhd* [2001] 2 Lloyd's Rep 41; *Import Export Metro Ltd v Compania Sud Americana de Vapores SA* [2003] 1 Lloyd's Rep 405. See also JJ Fawcett, 'Non-exclusive jurisdiction agreements in private international law' [2001] *LMCLQ* 234.

[351]   See E Peel, 'Exclusive jurisdiction agreements: purity and pragmatism in the conflict of law' [1998] *LMCLQ* 182.

[352]   [1987] AC 460.

entered a jurisdiction agreement, special rules govern the way in which the court's discretion is exercised.[353]

9.3.4   Where the parties have agreed to the jurisdiction of a foreign court, one of the parties should not generally be able to bring proceedings in England in breach of the terms of the agreement. Where the claimant serves a claim form on the defendant as of right the court should normally stay the English proceedings on the defendant's application; if the claimant applies for permission to serve out under CPR 6.36 permission should generally be refused. The relevant principles applicable in cases where the defendant applies for a stay of proceedings brought in breach of a jurisdiction clause in favour of a foreign forum were summarised in *The Eleftheria* by Brandon J:

(1) Where plaintiffs sue in England in breach of an agreement to refer disputes to a foreign court, and the defendants apply for a stay, the English court, assuming the claim to be otherwise within its jurisdiction, is not bound to grant a stay but has a discretion whether to do so or not. (2) The discretion should be exercised by granting a stay unless strong cause for not doing so is shown. (3) The burden of proving such strong cause is on the plaintiffs. (4) In exercising its discretion the court should take into account all the circumstances of the particular case. (5) In particular, but without prejudice to (4), the following matters, where they arise, may properly be regarded: (a) In what country the evidence on the issues of fact is situated, or more readily available, and the effect of that on the relative convenience and expense of trial as between the English and foreign courts. (b) Whether the law of the foreign court applies and, if so, whether it differs from English law in any material respects. (c) With what country either party is connected, and how closely. (d) Whether the defendants genuinely desire trial in the foreign country, or are only seeking procedural advantages. (e) Whether the plaintiffs would be prejudiced by having to sue in the foreign court because they would: (i) be deprived of security for their claim; (ii) be unable to enforce any judgment obtained; (iii) be faced by a time bar not applicable in England; or (iv) for political, racial, religious or other reasons be unlikely to get a fair trial.[354]

These principles are applicable not only in cases where English proceedings are brought in breach of the terms of an exclusive jurisdiction clause. The same principles are applicable in a case where proceedings are brought in England notwithstanding the fact that the parties agreed to the non-exclusive jurisdiction of the courts of another country and proceedings are already pending in that country.[355] By contrast, in cases where the parties have agreed to the non-exclusive jurisdiction of another country, but there are no proceedings pending in the contractual forum, if the claimant seeks to bring proceedings in England (whether as of right or by obtaining permission to serve out of the jurisdiction), the English court will determine its jurisdiction by reference to the *Spiliada* test; if, notwithstanding a non-exclusive jurisdiction clause in favour of another forum, there is as between the parties a clear balance in terms of justice and fairness in favour of England, the court will exercise jurisdiction (either by refusing to grant a stay or by giving permission to serve out).[356]

---

[353] See, eg, *Sinochem International Oil (London) Co Ltd v Mobil Sales and Supply Corporation* [2000] 1 Lloyd's Rep 670.
[354] [1970] P 94, 99–100.
[355] *The Rothnie* [1996] 2 Lloyd's Rep 206.
[356] *BP plc v Aon Ltd* [2006] 1 Lloyd's Rep 549.

9.3.5 Although the test laid down in *The Eleftheria* appears not to be entirely consistent with earlier decisions of the Court of Appeal,[357] there is no doubt that Brandon J's judgment in *The Eleftheria* correctly states the law.[358] Furthermore, since there was no jurisdiction clause involved in the *Spiliada* case, any suggestion that cases involving jurisdiction clauses should be decided by reference to the *Spiliada* test and that the only effect of a foreign jurisdiction clause is to reverse the burden of proof under that test[359] is unsound in principle.[360] As Lord Hobhouse noted in *Turner v Grovit*, a litigant 'does not have to show that the contractual forum is more appropriate than any other; the parties' contractual agreement does that for him'.[361]

9.3.6 Although the application of the *Eleftheria* test should normally lead to English proceedings being stayed in cases where the parties have entered a jurisdiction agreement in favour of the courts of another country,[362] the court may refuse to grant a stay whenever 'strong cause for not doing so is shown'.[363] If there is clear and cogent evidence that there would not be a fair trial in the contractual forum, the English court will not grant a stay.[364] More controversial are cases where, notwithstanding the jurisdiction agreement, there are arguments of convenience in favour of the English proceedings continuing. Where, for example, the claimant has claims in contract (which fall within the foreign jurisdiction clause) and claims in tort (which are not covered by the clause), the court may allow the contractual claims to proceed in England if the court has jurisdiction over the tort claims and the contractual claims form only a small part of the litigation.[365] More importantly, the court will often be prepared to exercise its discretion against the grant of a stay if there are related proceedings in England involving the same issues and it is thought 'essential, in order to avoid the risk of different decisions on the same issues by courts in two different countries, that the two actions should be tried together'.[366] Indeed, the paradigm case in which the court is most likely to refuse a stay—notwithstanding the existence of a foreign jurisdiction clause—is one involving two or more defendants. The fact that the claimant can proceed against all the defendants in England, but cannot do so in the contractual forum, is frequently regarded as justifying English

---

[357] See, in particular, *The Fehmarn* [1958] 1 WLR 159. This decision was widely criticised and is now explained on the basis of its unusual facts.

[358] *The El Amria* [1981] 2 Lloyd's Rep 119. See also *The Pioneer Container* [1994] 2 AC 324 (Toh Kian Sing, 'Jurisdiction clauses in bills of lading—the cargo claimant's perspective' [1995] *LMCLQ* 183) and *Donohue v Armco Inc* [2002] 1 All ER 749.

[359] See *The Nile Rhapsody* [1992] 2 Lloyd's Rep 399, affirmed [1994] 1 Lloyd's Rep 382. A Briggs, 'Jurisdiction Clauses and Judicial Attitudes' (1993) 109 *LQR* 382.

[360] See Rix J in *The MC Pearl* [1997] 1 Lloyd's Rep 566, 576. There are, however, some reported cases involving a jurisdiction agreement in which the court decides whether or not to grant a stay of proceedings by reference to the *Spiliada* test (with the jurisdiction agreement being given particular weight): see, eg, *Catlin Syndicate Ltd v Adams Land & Cattle Co* [2006] 2 CLC 425.

[361] [2002] 1 WLR 107, 118 (at [25]).

[362] See, eg, *Burrows v Jamaica Private Power Company Ltd* [2002] 1 All ER (Comm) 374; *ACP Capital Ltd v IFR Capital plc* [2008] ILPr 719; *Middle Eastern Oil LLC v National Bank of Abu Dhabi* [2009] 1 Lloyd's Rep 251.

[363] Brandon J in *The Eleftheria* [1970] P 94, 99.

[364] *Carvalho v Hull, Blyth (Angola) Ltd* [1979] 1 WLR 1228. See also *Middle Eastern Oil LLC v National Bank of Abu Dhabi* [2009] 1 Lloyd's Rep 251 (in which a stay was refused).

[365] *Domansa v Derin Shipping and Trading Co Inc* [2001] 1 Lloyd's Rep 362.

[366] Brandon LJ in *The El Amria* [1981] 2 Lloyd's Rep 119, 129.

jurisdiction.[367] The Privy Council has indicated that the fact that the claimant has allowed the limitation period to expire in the contractual forum is not in itself a sufficient 'strong cause'.[368] It seems generally to be accepted that if the claimant has acted unreasonably in failing to protect its position in the agreed forum by issuing protective proceedings within the limitation period, the court should nevertheless stay the English proceedings.[369] However, where the claimant has acted reasonably in starting litigation in England and not commencing proceedings in the contractual forum (for example, where the jurisdiction clause is void under English law), the court may decide either to allow the proceedings to take place in England or to make the grant of a stay conditional on the defendant waiving any limitation defence it may have in the contractual forum.[370] If it later transpires that the defendant is unable to waive the time bar in the foreign proceedings, the court will permit the proceedings to continue in England.[371]

9.3.7 There is a strand in the case law which suggests that the party seeking to escape the effect of a jurisdiction agreement needs to be able to point to some factor which could not have been foreseen in order to displace the bargain which has been agreed.[372] Where a claimant concludes similar contracts but with inconsistent dispute-resolution clauses (for example, some contracts making express provision for English law and jurisdiction and others including a choice of the law and jurisdiction of another country), the court may refuse to allow related disputes arising from all the contracts to be consolidated in English proceedings; although it might be more convenient if the claimant were able to override the foreign jurisdiction clause, it should not be open to a party seeking to justify the bringing of English proceedings in contravention of a foreign jurisdiction clause to rely on the risk of inconsistent decisions of different courts as grounds for strong cause when he ought to have appreciated the existence of that risk at the time when he entered into the contract containing the exclusive jurisdiction clause.[373] As a general rule, claimants should not be permitted 'to avoid the foreseeable consequences of the contractual structure which they have created'.[374]

9.3.8 The court should give full weight to the *prima facie* desirability of holding claimants to their agreement, and 'must be careful not just to pay lip-service to the principle involved, and then fail to give effect to it because of a mere balance of

---

[367] See *The Rewia* [1991] 1 Lloyd's Rep 69 (reversed on other grounds [1991] 2 Lloyd's Rep 325); *The Vishva Prabha* [1989] 2 Lloyd's Rep 286; *Standard Chartered Bank v Pakistan National Shipping Corporation* [1995] 2 Lloyd's Rep 365; *Citi-March Ltd v Neptune Orient Lines Ltd* [1996] 1 WLR 1367; *The MC Pearl* [1997] 1 Lloyd's Rep 566; *Sinochem International Oil (London) Co Ltd v Mobil Sales and Supply Corporation* [2000] 1 Lloyd's Rep 670.

[368] See *The Pioneer Container* [1994] 2 AC 324.

[369] *Citi-March Ltd v Neptune Orient Lines Ltd* [1996] 1 WLR 1367; *The MC Pearl* [1997] 1 Lloyd's Rep 566; *The Bergen (No 2)* [1997] 2 Lloyd's Rep 710.

[370] *Baghlaf Al Safer Factory Co BR for Industry Ltd v Pakistan National Shipping Co* [1998] 2 Lloyd's Rep 229; *Insurance Company "Ingosstrakh" Ltd v Latvian Shipping Co* [2000] ILPr 164. See also *BMG Trading Ltd v AS McKay* [1998] ILPr 690.

[371] *Baghlaf Al Safer Factory Co BR for Industry Ltd v Pakistan National Shipping Co (No 2)* [2000] 1 Lloyd's Rep 1.

[372] See, eg, *British Aerospace plc v Dee Howard Co* [1993] 1 Lloyd's Rep 368; *Mercury Communications Ltd v Communication Telesystems International* [1999] 2 All ER (Comm) 33; *Ace Insurance SA-NV v Zurich Insurance Co* [2001] 1 Lloyd's Rep 618.

[373] See Colman J in *Konkola Copper Mines plc v Coromin (No 2)* [2006] 2 Lloyd's Rep 446, 452 (at [32]).

[374] Colman J in *Konkola Copper Mines plc v Coromin (No 2)* [2006] 2 (at [42]).

convenience'.[375] Notwithstanding the presumption in favour of a stay, it has been suggested that, since the rules give discretion to the court and virtually every case has factors pointing in opposite directions, in practice, 'an English court is about as likely to retain the case as to give effect to the choice of forum clause'.[376] There is no doubt that the approach adopted by the English courts is open to criticism from the point of view of principle. It has been plausibly suggested that:

except in circumstances where there has been an unforeseeable change in the procedure of the courts submitted to or the general socio-political situation of the [foreign] forum, the exploitation of fairly bargained for procedural advantages through the enforcement of exclusive jurisdiction ... clauses should be permitted, even where those advantages relate to the type of remedies available in the foreign jurisdiction, timebars, time delays, exchange control restrictions, and other aspects of the procedure of the foreign court such as interest on damages and cost of proceedings.[377]

9.3.9 While the procedural effect of a jurisdiction clause is a matter of English law as the law of the forum, its existence, validity and interpretation are normally determined by reference to its (putative) proper law. Whether an exclusive jurisdiction agreement is to be regarded as precluding the parties from seeking provisional measures in a court other than the chosen court is also a question of interpretation to be referred to the proper law of the agreement.[378] The proper law may, in certain circumstances, be overridden by mandatory rules of the forum.[379]

The Hague Choice of Court Convention

9.3.10 When the Hague Choice of Court Convention comes into force, the traditional rules will be largely displaced in cases where the contractual forum is a state which is a party to the Convention.[380] Article 6 of the Convention provides that, as a general rule, a non-contractual forum must 'suspend or dismiss proceedings to which an exclusive choice of court agreement applies'. There are, however, five exceptions. The obligation to decline jurisdiction does not arise if: (a) the agreement is null and void under the law of the contractual forum; (b) a party to the jurisdiction agreement lacked capacity to conclude the agreement; (c) giving effect to the agreement would lead to a manifest injustice or would be manifestly contrary to the public policy of the forum state; (d) for exceptional reasons beyond the control of the parties, the agreement cannot reasonably be performed; or (e) the chosen court has decided not to hear the case.

---

[375] Brandon J in *The Eleftheria* [1970] P 94, 103.

[376] MF Sturley, 'Bill of lading choice of forum clauses: comparisons between United States and English law' [1992] *LMCLQ* 248, 251.

[377] A Bell, 'Jurisdiction and Arbitration Agreements in Transnational Contracts, Part I' (1996) 10 *JCL* 53, 65 (footnotes omitted).

[378] *The Lisboa* [1980] 2 Lloyd's Rep 546. Of course, a jurisdiction agreement may not only allocate exclusive jurisdiction to the courts of a particular country as regards the merits but also expressly provide that the parties are free to bring proceedings in other countries for the purpose of obtaining provisional measures.

[379] *The Hollandia* [1983] 1 AC 565; *Baghlaf Al Safer Factory Co BR for Industry Ltd v Pakistan National Shipping Co* [1998] 2 Lloyd's Rep 229.

[380] At 1 January 2010, only Mexico had ratified the Convention; the European Union and the United States of America had signed it.

9.3.11 The effect of Article 6 of the Hague Convention will be that the range of circumstances in which the English court may assume jurisdiction in defiance of a foreign jurisdiction clause will be progressively narrowed as more states accede to the Convention. For example, it is not obvious that the Hague Convention would justify the English court in refusing to grant a stay of proceedings in a case such as *The El Amria*.[381] By contrast, it is reasonable to suppose that were a case such as *Carvalho v Hull, Blyth (Angola) Ltd*[382] to arise under the Hague Convention, it would be legitimate for the English court to assume jurisdiction, notwithstanding the jurisdiction clause in favour of a foreign court, on the basis that, on the particular facts of the case, giving effect to the agreement would lead to a manifest injustice.

9.4 JURISDICTION IN CASES INVOLVING FOREIGN LAND AND FOREIGN INTELLECTUAL PROPERTY RIGHTS

Cases Involving Foreign Land

9.4.1 Under Article 22(1) of the Brussels I Regulation, in proceedings which have as their object rights *in rem* in, or tenancies of immovable property, the courts of the Member State in which the property is situated have exclusive jurisdiction—regardless of the defendant's domicile.[383] So, where the proceedings are within the scope of Article 1 and the principal subject-matter of the dispute concerns rights *in rem* of immovable property located in another Member State, there can be no question of proceedings being brought in England.

9.4.2 The common law rules are applicable in cases where the situation does not fall within the scope of Article 1 or if the immovable property is located in a non-Member State. At least, this is the position if the defendant is not domiciled in a Member State. More difficult is the situation where the defendant is domiciled in a Member State. Consider the situation where the immovable property is situated in New York and the defendant is domiciled in England. Article 22 of the Brussels I Regulation does not apply and there is nothing in Chapter II to suggest that the courts of a Member State cannot exercise jurisdiction under the Regulation. However, where an English defendant is sued in England in relation to a dispute concerning immovable property located in New York, the Brussels I Regulation should not be regarded as preventing the court from declining jurisdiction. There would be little to recommend a system of jurisdiction rules which obliges the English court to hear and determine a dispute concerning title to land in New York between a French claimant and an English defendant. In these circumstances the court should be able to stay the proceedings.[384]

---

[381] [1981] 2 Lloyd's Rep 119.
[382] [1979] 1 WLR 1228.
[383] See section 5.1.
[384] *Re Polly Peck International plc (in administration) (No 2)* [1998] 3 All ER 812. For further discussion, see section 9.5.

9.4.3   At common law, the general principle is that the court has no jurisdiction to entertain an action for the determination of the title to, or the right to possession of, any immovable property situated outside England.[385] There are three well-established exceptions to this general principle. First, if the court has jurisdiction *in personam* over a defendant, the court may exercise jurisdiction in respect of a contract or an equity affecting foreign land.[386] However, where jurisdiction is founded on presence, the defendant may apply for a stay on the basis of the doctrine of *forum non conveniens*;[387] where the claimant seeks to invoke the jurisdiction of the court under CPR 6.36 permission to serve out will be given only if the England is the most appropriate forum.[388] Secondly, in certain cases involving the administration of estates, the court may determine questions of title to foreign land.[389] Thirdly, the court may exercise jurisdiction *in rem* against a ship to enforce a claim for damage done to foreign land.[390]

9.4.4   It used to be the case that the court could not exercise jurisdiction in an action for the recovery of damages for trespass or for other torts to immovable property outside England.[391] This rule was, however, reversed by section 30 of the Civil Jurisdiction and Judgments Act 1982, which provides:

(1) The jurisdiction of any court in England and Wales or Northern Ireland to entertain proceedings for trespass to, or any other tort affecting, immovable property shall extend to cases in which the property in question is situated outside that part of the United Kingdom unless the proceedings are principally concerned with a question of the title to, or the right to possession of, that property.
(2) Subsection (1) has effect subject to the 1968 Convention and the Lugano Convention and the [Brussels I] Regulation and to the provisions set out in Schedule 4.

In *Re Polly Peck International plc (in administration) (No 2)*[392] the question was whether the English court had jurisdiction in a case where the plaintiffs alleged that the defendant company's subsidiaries had trespassed on the plaintiffs' land in northern Cyprus during the Turkish invasion of 1974. On the facts of the case, it was held that, although the claim was concerned with a question of the title to, or the right to possession of, foreign immovable property, it was not 'principally' (which was interpreted as meaning 'chiefly')[393] concerned with this question. Furthermore, the Court of Appeal considered that it did not have to be established on the balance of probabilities that the English court had jurisdiction under section 30 of the 1982 Act; it was sufficient for the plaintiff to be able to demonstrate a good arguable case that it did.[394]

---

[385] *British South Africa Co v Companhia de Moçambique* [1893] AC 602. See S Lee, 'Jurisdiction over Foreign Land: A Reappraisal' (1997) 26 *Anglo-Am LR* 273.
[386] *Penn v Lord Baltimore* (1750) 1 Ves Sen 444.
[387] See section 9.3.
[388] See section 7.3.
[389] This topic is beyond the scope of the present work.
[390] *The Tolten* [1946] P 135. See para 8.1.5.
[391] *Hesperides Hotels Ltd v Aegean Turkish Holidays Ltd* [1979] AC 508.
[392] [1998] 3 All ER 812. A Briggs, (1998) 69 *BYIL* 356; A Dickinson, 'Jurisdictional trespass' [1998] *LMCLQ* 519.
[393] See Mummery LJ at [1998] 3 All ER 812, 828.
[394] [1998] 3 All ER 812, 827. Compare Rattee J, at first instance, who had taken the contrary view: [1997] 2 BCLC 630, 641–2.

Cases Involving Foreign Intellectual Property Rights

9.4.5   Intellectual property rights share certain characteristics with rights relating to land. For the most part, intellectual property rights are territorially limited and may be regarded as analogous to other forms of immovable property. In civil and commercial matters falling within the scope of the Article 1, the relevant provisions of the Brussels I Regulation must be applied. Article 22(4)—like Article 22(1) in relation to proceedings concerning immovable property situated in a Member State—confers exclusive jurisdiction in relation to proceedings concerning the validity of patents, trade marks, designs and analogous rights on the courts of the Member State in which the interest in question is registered. As regards other types of dispute concerning intellectual property rights—for example, a simple claim for damages for passing off or for breach of copyright—the general jurisdictional bases set out in Chapter II are relevant and, if the defendant is domiciled in a Member State, there is no scope for the application of the common law rules.[395]

9.4.6   Where, for example, the intellectual property right in question is registered in a non-Member State and the defendant is not domiciled in a Member State, the Brussels I Regulation does not apply. It used to be thought that, for the purposes of the rule in *British South Africa Ltd v Companhia de Moçambique*[396] (in which the House of Lords denied jurisdiction in respect of a dispute over foreign land), intellectual property rights should be regarded as analogous to immovable property.[397] For example, in *Coin Controls Ltd v Suzo International (UK) Ltd*, Laddie J said:

The principles which applied to land in the *Moçambique* case apply equally well to attempts to litigate foreign intellectual property rights in English courts. Those rights give rise to monopolies or quasi-monopolies which are strictly territorial in nature. In the case of patents, historically their purpose was to encourage and protect local industry. So courts following the common law tradition have declined to entertain actions concerned with the enforcement of foreign intellectual property rights.[398]

According to this approach, a claim for breach of American copyright is not justiciable in England.[399]

9.4.7   However, in *Pearce v Ove Arup Partnership Ltd*,[400] the Court of Appeal (in the context of a case governed by the Brussels Convention) questioned the applicability of the *Moçambique* rule to cases involving foreign intellectual property rights—especially in situations involving infringement, rather than validity. As the reasoning of the decision is not dependent on issues specific to the Brussels Convention, the *Moçambique* rule would no longer appear to have any role to play in cases involving

---

[395]   *Coin Controls Ltd v Suzo International (UK) Ltd* [1999] Ch 33; *Pearce v Ove Arup Partnership Ltd* [2000] Ch 403. A Briggs, 'Two Undesirable Side-Effects of the Brussels Convention' (1997) 113 *LQR* 364; LJ Cohen, 'Intellectual Property and the Brussels Convention' [1997] 7 *EIP Rev* 379; M Tugendhat, 'Media Law and the Brussels Convention' (1997) 113 *LQR* 360. See, however, *Lucasfilm Ltd v Ainsworth* [2010] FSR 270.

[396]   [1893] AC 602.

[397]   GW Austin, 'The Infringement of Foreign Intellectual Property Rights' (1997) 113 *LQR* 321.

[398]   [1999] Ch 33, 43.

[399]   *Tyburn v Conan Doyle* [1990] 1 All ER 910. See also *LA Gear v Whelan* [1991] FSR 670; *Plastus Kreativ AB v Minnesota Mining and Manufacturing Co* [1995] RPC 438.

[400]   [2000] Ch 403. A Briggs, (1999) 70 *BYIL* 337; R Fentiman, 'The Justiciability of Foreign Copyright Claims' [1999] *CLJ* 286; J Harris, 'Justiciability, choice of law and the Brussels Convention' [1999] *LMCLQ* 360.

foreign intellectual property rights—even if the court's jurisdiction is based entirely on the traditional rules.[401] Whether the application of the decision in *Pearce v Ove Arup Partnership Ltd* in cases where jurisdiction is based on the traditional rules will produce a significant change in the practice of the English courts is, however, doubtful.[402] In cases which concern the validity of a foreign intellectual property right, it is difficult to see how the English court could be regarded as an appropriate forum; in practice, it does not much matter whether the English court declares that the claim is not justiciable in England (on the basis of the *Moçambique* rule) or grants a stay of the English proceedings (on the basis of the doctrine of *forum non conveniens*). In infringement cases, the place where the acts of infringement took place will normally be the natural forum—even if the facts do not raise any question over the validity of the intellectual property right in question. Accordingly, where English proceedings involve the infringement abroad of a foreign intellectual property right, the defendant should normally be able to obtain a stay of the English proceedings on the ground that another forum is more appropriate.

9.5 STAYING PROCEEDINGS UNDER THE COURT'S INHERENT JURISDICTION IN CASES INVOLVING THE BRUSSELS I REGULATION

Introduction

9.5.1 The philosophy of the jurisdictional code contained in Chapter II is fundamentally different from that which lies behind the traditional English jurisdiction rules. The provisions of the Brussels I Regulation are, in the main, mechanical and formalistic. In cases where there are already proceedings in another Member State, the court must stay proceedings (or decline jurisdiction) if the foreign proceedings involve the same cause of action and the same parties;[403] the court may grant a stay if the foreign proceedings are related.[404] By contrast, the boundaries of English jurisdiction in international cases have traditionally been fixed by open-textured principles which confer on judges considerable discretion.

9.5.2 If the English court has jurisdiction under the Brussels I Regulation (for example, because the defendant is domiciled in England or because, in the context of a claim in tort, the defendant is domiciled in a Member State and England is the place where the harmful event occurred), the question arises whether the court can grant a stay of proceedings under its inherent jurisdiction—whether on the basis that the dispute concerns foreign land or that the parties have agreed to the jurisdiction of the courts of a non-Member State or that, for some other reason, there is a more appropriate forum abroad. The question of when, if ever, it is consistent with the

---

[401] W Kennett, (1999) 48 *ICLQ* 966, 968. See also *Griggs Group Ltd v Evans (No 2)* [2005] Ch 153.

[402] In addition to the *forum non conveniens* point considered in this paragraph, it has been argued that the courts cannot apply foreign intellectual property laws which are, by their nature, territorially limited: K Lipstein, 'Intellectual Property: Jurisdiction or Choice of Law' [2002] *CLJ* 295.

[403] Brussels I Reg, Art 27.

[404] Brussels I Reg, Art 28.

Brussels I Regulation to stay proceedings on a discretionary basis has been one of the most controversial issues in the field of civil jurisdiction.

9.5.3 Part of the problem is that the Brussels I Regulation contains no provisions which expressly address this question.[405] In England a body of case law emerged on the relationship between the Brussels Convention and the doctrine of *forum non conveniens*. In *Re Harrods (Buenos Aires) Ltd*[406] various questions were referred to the Court of Justice by the House of Lords, but the reference[407] was withdrawn when the case was settled; in *Lubbe v Cape plc*[408] the House of Lords would have made a reference to the Court of Justice on the compatibility of the doctrine of *forum non conveniens* with the Brussels Convention if it had been necessary for its decision.[409] It was not until the reference by the Court of Appeal in *Owusu v Jackson*[410] that the Court of Justice was presented with an opportunity to rule on the issue. Although the Court of Justice's decision in this case[411] answers some of the questions raised by the English case law, it leaves several issues unresolved.

Cases where Jurisdiction is Founded on the Traditional Rules

9.5.4 Generally speaking, the effect of Article 4 is that, if the defendant is not domiciled in a Member State, the jurisdiction of the English court is founded on the traditional rules.[412] In such cases the court should be able to grant a stay on the basis of *forum non conveniens* at least where the alternative forum is a non-Member State.[413] Whether the position is the same where the alternative forum is another Member State is more controversial.[414] Nevertheless, in *The Xin Yang*[415] Clarke J decided that he was not precluded from granting a stay in favour of the Dutch courts in a case where

---

[405] According to s 49 of the Civil Jurisdiction and Judgments Act 1982, the English courts may grant a stay of proceedings where to do so is not inconsistent with the Lugano Convention. This provision is largely devoid of substance, since it says nothing about what is or is not inconsistent with the Convention. It would seem that if s 49 had not been enacted the law would have been exactly the same and there is no equivalent provision relating to the Brussels I Regulation.

[406] [1992] Ch 72. A Briggs, 'Forum Non Conveniens and the Brussels Convention Again' (1991) 107 *LQR* 180; TC Hartley, (1992) 17 *EL Rev* 553; P Kaye, 'The EEC Judgments Convention and the Outer World: Goodbye to Forum Non Conveniens?' [1992] *JBL* 47.

[407] Case C–314/92 *Ladenimor SA v Intercomfinanz SA*.

[408] [2000] 1 WLR 1545.

[409] See Lord Bingham at [2000] 1 WLR 1545, 1562.

[410] [2002] ILPr 45. A Briggs, (2002) 73 *BYIL* 453; A Briggs, '*Forum non conveniens* and ideal Europeans' [2005] *LMCLQ* 378; A Briggs, 'The Death of Harrods: *Forum non Conveniens* and the European Court' (2005) 121 *LQR* 535; G Cuniberti, 'Forum non conveniens and the Brussels Convention' (2005) 54 *ICLQ* 973; R Fentiman, 'English Domicile and the Staying of Actions' [2005] *CLJ* 303; R Fentiman, 'Civil Jurisdiction and Third States: *Owusu* and After' (2006) 43 *CML Rev* 705; C Hare, 'Forum non conveniens in Europe: Game Over or Time for "Reflexion"?' [2006] *JBL* 157; J Harris, 'Stays of Proceedings and the Brussels Convention' (2005) 54 *ICLQ* 933; E Peel, 'Forum non conveniens and European ideals' [2005] *LMCLQ* 363; B Rodger, '*Forum Non Conveniens* Post-*Owusu*' (2006) 2 *Journal of Private International Law* 71. See also *American Motorists Insurance Co v Cellstar Corporation* [2003] ILPr 370 in which the Court of Appeal proposed referring similar questions.

[411] Case C–281/02 [2005] ECR I–1465.

[412] See paras 4.2.5–4.2.8.

[413] See Advocate General Léger in Case C-281/02 *Owusu v Jackson* [2005] ECR I–1383, para 235.

[414] See A Briggs, 'Some Points of Friction between English and Brussels Convention Jurisdiction' in M Andenas and F Jacobs, *European Community Law in the English Courts* (OUP, Oxford, 1998) 281–4.

[415] [1996] 2 Lloyd's Rep 217. JJ Newton, '*Forum non conveniens* in Europe (again)' [1997] *LMCLQ* 337.

English proceedings *in rem* had been brought in connection with a vessel owned by a Chinese corporation.[416] The Court of Appeal's analysis in *Haji-Ioannou v Frangos*[417] confirmed that, where the defendant is not domiciled in a Member State and the court is authorised by Article 4 to exercise jurisdiction under its traditional rules, the court which would otherwise be first seised is entitled to decline to exercise jurisdiction on the ground of *forum non conveniens* even if the alternative forum is a Member State.[418] It should be emphasised, however, that these cases pre-date the Court of Justice's decision in *Owusu v Jackson*.[419]

9.5.5   The doctrine of *forum non conveniens* is potentially relevant only if the proceedings are not stayed (or jurisdiction declined) on the basis of Article 27 or Article 28. If, for example, parallel proceedings involving the same parties and the same cause of action have already been commenced in another Member State the English court must stay the proceedings or decline jurisdiction in accordance with Article 27 of the Brussels I Regulation—even if neither party is domiciled in a Member State and the court's jurisdiction is derived from the traditional rules rather than the jurisdictional bases set out in Chapter II.[420] In this situation, there can be no room for the application of the doctrine of *forum non conveniens*.

Cases where Jurisdiction is Founded on Chapter II and the Alternative Forum is a Member State

9.5.6   If jurisdiction is founded on Chapter II the English court is not entitled to stay the proceedings on the basis that another Member State is more appropriate. Where, for example, English proceedings are brought against a defendant domiciled in England, the court cannot stay the proceedings on the ground that France, being the place of performance of the obligation in question for the purposes of Article 5(1) or the place where the harmful event occurred for the purposes of Article 5(3), is a more appropriate forum.[421] Similarly, the court cannot stay the proceedings on the ground that the courts of another Member State are more appropriate if the claimant sues the defendant in England on the basis of Article 5[422] or if proceedings are brought in England against the first defendant (under Article 2) and the second defendant (under Article 6(1)).[423] Such cases are governed exclusively by the rules contained in the Brussels I Regulation.

---

[416] [1996] 2 Lloyd's Rep 217, 222.

[417] [1999] 2 Lloyd's Rep 337. A Briggs, (1999) 70 *BYIL* 326.

[418] See also *Sarrio SA v Kuwait Investment Authority* [1997] 1 Lloyd's Rep 113, 124. For discussion of this aspect of the decision, see J Harris, 'Staying Proceedings for a Contracting State to the Brussels Convention' (1997) 113 *LQR* 557. Although the House of Lords allowed the appeal ([1999] 1 AC 32), this aspect of the Court of Appeal's decision was not considered.

[419] Case C–281/02 [2005] ECR I–1383.

[420] Case C–351/89 *Overseas Union Insurance Ltd v New Hampshire Insurance Co* [1991] ECR I–3317.

[421] See Advocate General Léger in Case C–281/02 *Owusu v Jackson* [2005] ECR I–1383, para 242. See also *Aiglon Ltd v Gau Shan Co Ltd* [1993] 1 Lloyd's Rep 164; *Mahme Trust Reg v Lloyds TSB Bank plc* [2004] 2 Lloyd's Rep 637; *DC v WOC* [2001] 2 IR 1 (High Court, Ireland).

[422] *Gomez v Gomez-Moche Vives* [2008] 3 WLR 309. The decision was affirmed by the Court of Appeal, though the argument that the English proceedings could be stayed was not pursued on appeal: [2009] Ch 245.

[423] *Viking Line ABP v International Transport Workers' Federation* [2005] ILPr 50.

Cases where Jurisdiction is Founded on Chapter II and the Alternative Forum is a Non-Member State

Forum non Conveniens

9.5.7 One of the questions which has generated most controversy is whether the English court may apply the doctrine of *forum non conveniens* and stay proceedings in favour of the courts of a non-Member State in a case where the court has jurisdiction under Article 2 (because the defendant is domiciled in England) or under the special jurisdiction provisions (Articles 5 and 6). One view is that, in these circumstances, the doctrine of *forum non conveniens* is generally incompatible with the Brussels I Regulation. This was the view taken by the High Court in *S & W Berisford plc v New Hampshire Insurance Co*[424] and *Arkwright Mutual Insurance Co v Bryanston Insurance Co Ltd.*[425] In the former case, where the English court had jurisdiction over the defendant under Article 2 of the Brussels Convention, Hobhouse J succinctly stated the rationale for the exclusion of the doctrine of *forum non conveniens*:

It is clear that the [Brussels] Convention is designed (subject to Article 4) to achieve uniformity and to 'harmonise' the relevant procedural and jurisdictional rules of the courts of the contracting states. The Convention leaves no room for the application of any discretionary jurisdiction by the courts of this country; the availability of such a discretion would destroy the framework of the Convention and create lack of uniformity in the interpretation and implementation of the Convention.[426]

9.5.8 However, the view that the doctrine of *forum non conveniens* is not necessarily incompatible with the Brussels regime[427] was accepted by the Court of Appeal in *Re Harrods (Buenos Aires) Ltd;*[428] a stay was granted on the ground that Argentina was a more appropriate forum, notwithstanding the fact that the English court had jurisdiction under Article 2 of the Brussels Convention. The Court of Appeal held that, if the conflict is between the English court and the courts of a non-contracting state, the English court retains its inherent jurisdiction to stay the proceedings. In subsequent years, the *Harrods* doctrine was consistently followed by the English courts—even in cases where the situation concerned not only connections with England and a non-Member State but also connections with another Member State.[429]

9.5.9 As some predicted,[430] the Court of Justice ruled that this whole line of cases is not consistent with the Brussels regime. In *Owusu v Jackson*[431] the claimant, who

---

[424] [1990] 2 QB 631.

[425] [1990] 2 QB 649. A Briggs, '*Spiliada* and the Brussels Convention' [1991] *LMCLQ* 10; L Collins, '*Forum Non Conveniens* and the Brussels Convention' (1990) 106 *LQR* 535.

[426] [1990] 2 QB 631, 645.

[427] See, eg, L Collins, '*Forum Non Conveniens* and the Brussels Convention' (1990) 106 *LQR* 535; P Kaye, *Civil Jurisdiction and Enforcement of Foreign Judgments* (Abingdon, Professional Books, 1987) 1244–5.

[428] [1992] Ch 72. A Briggs, '*Forum Non Conveniens* and the Brussels Convention Again' (1991) 107 *LQR* 180; TC Hartley, (1992) 17 *EL Rev* 553; P Kaye, 'The EEC Judgments Convention and the Outer World: Goodbye to *Forum Non Conveniens*?' [1992] *JBL* 47.

[429] See, eg, *The Po* [1991] 2 Lloyd's Rep 206; *Ace Insurance SA-NV v Zurich Insurance Co* [2001] 1 Lloyd's Rep 618; *Anton Durbeck GmbH v Den Norske Bank ASA* [2003] QB 1160; *Travellers Casualty and Surety Company of Europe Ltd v Sun Life Assurance Company of Canada (UK) Ltd* [2004] ILPr 793.

[430] See, eg, W Kennett, '*Forum Non Conveniens* in Europe' [1995] *CLJ* 552.

[431] Case C–281/02 [2005] ECR I–1383.

was domiciled in England, was severely injured during a holiday in Jamaica when he dived into the sea and struck his head on a submerged sandbank. He commenced proceedings for breach of contract against the first defendant (also domiciled in England), who had let a holiday villa to the claimant. The claimant also brought a tort claim against a number of Jamaican companies, alleging that they had negligently failed to warn swimmers of the danger posed by submerged sandbanks at the beach where the claimant was injured. The question referred to the Court of Justice was whether the English court could stay the proceedings between the claimant and the first defendant on the basis that Jamaica was a more appropriate forum.

9.5.10   The Court of Justice ruled that a court on which jurisdiction is conferred by Article 2 of the Brussels Convention is precluded from declining that jurisdiction on the ground that a court of a non-contracting state would be a more appropriate forum even if the jurisdiction of no other contracting state is in issue or the proceedings involve no factors connecting the situation with another contracting state.[432] Although the *Owusu* case was a reference under the Brussels Convention, there can be no doubt that the position under the Brussels I Regulation is the same.[433] Furthermore, the Court of Justice's rejection of the doctrine of *forum non conveniens* necessarily covers not only situations where the English court's jurisdiction is based on Article 2 but also cases where the court's jurisdiction is founded on other bases set out in Chapter II. So, a stay in favour of the courts of a non-Member State cannot be granted either in a case where the English court has jurisdiction under Article 5(1),[434] Article 22,[435] or Article 23 of the Brussels I Regulation.[436]

9.5.11   What emerges from the Court of Justice's ruling is that the Court of Appeal had been wrong in the *Harrods* case to place so much emphasis on the reciprocal recognition and enforcement of judgments at the expense of other aspects of the Brussels regime. For example, the Court of Justice identified 'respect for the principle of legal certainty' as one of the objectives of the Brussels regime.[437] This echoes an important passage from the Schlosser Report:

A plaintiff must be sure which court has jurisdiction. He should not have to waste his time and money risking that the court concerned may consider itself less competent than another.[438]

Given that the operation of the doctrine of *forum non conveniens* depends on the exercise of discretion (and is inherently uncertain), application of the doctrine 'is liable to undermine the predictability of the rules of jurisdiction laid down by the Brussels Convention, in particular that of Article 2, and consequently to undermine the principle of legal certainty'.[439]

---

[432] Case C–281/02 [2005] ECR I–1383, para 46.

[433] See Advocate General Léger in Case C–281/02 *Owusu v Jackson* [2005] ECR I–1383, para 194.

[434] The suggestion to the contrary by the Court of Appeal in *Ace Insurance SA-NV v Zurich Insurance Co* [2001] 1 Lloyd's Rep 618 cannot be accepted.

[435] *Choudhary v Bhattar* [2009] ILPr 842, reversed on other grounds [2010] 2 All ER 1031.

[436] *Equitas Ltd v Allstate Insurance Co* [2009] 1 All ER (Comm) 1137. The contrary view of the Court of Appeal in cases decided before the decision in *Owusu* (*Eli Lilly & Co v Novo Nordisk A/S* [2000] ILPr 73, *Sinochem International Oil (London) Co v Mobil Sales and Supply Corporation* [2000] 1 Lloyd's Rep 670 and *UBS AG v Omni Holding AG* [2000] 1 WLR 916) cannot be accepted.

[437] Case C–281/02 *Owusu v Jackson* [2005] ECR I–1383, para 38.

[438] [1979] OJ C59/97, para 78. See also Recital 11 to the Brussels I Regulation which states that '[t]he rules of jurisdiction must be highly predictable'.

[439] Case C–281/02 *Owusu v Jackson* [2005] ECR I–1383, para 41.

9.5.12 In addition, the Court of Justice implicitly supported the view expressed by Hobhouse J in *S & W Berisford plc v New Hampshire Insurance Co*[440] (before the Court of Appeal formulated the *Harrods* doctrine). As one of the objectives of the Brussels regime is to establish a uniform system for the allocation of jurisdiction, the doctrine of *forum non conveniens* has no role to play in that regime:

allowing *forum non conveniens* in the context of the Brussels Convention would be likely to affect the uniform application of the rules of jurisdiction contained therein in so far as that doctrine is recognised in only a limited number of Contracting States, whereas the objective of the Brussels Convention is precisely to lay down common rules to the exclusion of derogating national rules.[441]

Unresolved Questions

9.5.13 The decision in the *Owusu* case deals with a relatively narrow issue and leaves many questions unanswered. In particular, there is nothing in the judgment of the Court of Justice or the opinion of Advocate General Léger which expressly indicates whether it would be incompatible with the Brussels I Regulation for a national court to decline jurisdiction in a case where (i) there is a connection with a non-Member State of a type which, were the connection with a Member State, would confer exclusive jurisdiction on that other state under Article 22, (ii) there is a jurisdiction agreement in favour of a non-Member State or (iii) there are concurrent proceedings in a non-Member State.[442] Indeed, Advocate General Léger was at pains to emphasise that the proceedings in the *Owusu* case concerned a situation where the court of a non-contracting state 'has not been designated by any jurisdiction clause, has not previously had brought before it any claim liable to give rise to *lis alibi pendens* or related actions and the factors connecting the dispute with that non-Contracting State are of a kind other than those referred to in Article 16 of the Brussels Convention'.[443] The fact that both the Court of Justice and the Advocate General delimited the question in *Owusu* so narrowly appears to leave open the possibility of national courts declining jurisdiction in the three categories of case outlined above. Indeed, as Lawrence Collins LJ stated in *Masri v Consolidated Contractors International (UK) Ltd (No 2)*: '[i]n such cases it would be odd if the Brussels I Regulation did not permit the English court to stay its proceedings'.[444]

9.5.14 On the other hand, the Court of Justice's observation 'that Article 2 ... is mandatory in nature and that, according to its terms, there can be no derogation from the principle it lays down except in the cases expressly provided for'[445] appears to point in the opposite direction. Notwithstanding these uncertainties, it is unlikely that the Court of Justice was seeking to lay down a hard-and-fast rule requiring the English courts (or the courts of other Member States) to exercise jurisdiction under Article 2 regardless of the degree of connection between the claim and a non-Member State.

---

[440] [1990] 2 QB 631, 645.
[441] Case C–281/02 *Owusu v Jackson* [2005] ECR I–1383, para 43.
[442] Case C–281/02 [2005] ECR I–1383, paras 69–70, 277, 280 (AG Léger); [2005] ECR I–1383, para 48 (ECJ).
[443] Case C–281/02 [2005] ECR I–1383, para 277.
[444] [2009] QB 450, 485 (at [125]).
[445] Case C–281/02 [2005] ECR I–1383, para 37.

9.5.15 It does not follow, however, that the Court of Justice is prepared to permit the application of the doctrine of *forum non conveniens* by the English courts in the three situations identified as giving rise to issues which did not have to be addressed in the *Owusu* case.[446] Throughout its judgment, the Court of Justice displayed a pronounced hostility to the notion that jurisdictional questions under the Brussels regime should be determined by reference to discretionary criteria.[447] This hostility towards the doctrine of *forum non conveniens* is not based solely on the fact that, because of its discretionary nature, it undermines the predictability of jurisdiction rules. Other black marks against the doctrine include the fact that, being found only in two Member States (the United Kingdom and Ireland), it is alien to the Member States of the civil law tradition which originally drafted the Brussels Convention[448] and the suggestion that, because the grant of a stay involves delay, the operation of the doctrine of *forum non conveniens* might be incompatible with the requirements of Article 6 of the European Convention on Human Rights.[449] Accordingly, it is possible that, if exceptions to the mandatory operation of the jurisdiction rules in Chapter II are permissible, it has to be through the operation of hard-edged rules, rather than through the application of discretionary doctrines.

9.5.16 The practical argument for allowing some exceptions to the rigid application of the jurisdiction rules contained in Chapter II is overwhelming. If no exceptions are permitted, it would be possible to sue a defendant domiciled in England in relation to a dispute concerning a right *in rem* in immovable property situated in a non-Member State, even though not only is it an almost universal principle that proprietary claims relating to immovable property should be determined by the courts of the country in which the property is situated but also the English court would have to decline jurisdiction over the same type of dispute were the property situated in a Member State.[450] Similarly, in a case where two contracting parties (one of them domiciled in England) agree to the exclusive jurisdiction of the courts of New York, the court would have to exercise jurisdiction under Article 2 if proceedings were brought in England against the party domiciled in England, notwithstanding the fact that, by virtue of Article 23, the court would have no jurisdiction if the parties had agreed to refer their disputes to the courts of another Member State.[451] The English court would also have to exercise jurisdiction over claims brought against a defendant

---

[446] See, eg, B Rodger, '*Forum Non Conveniens* Post-*Owusu*' (2006) 2 *Journal of Private International Law* 71, 97.

[447] See, eg, Case C–281/02 [2005] ECR I–1383, para 41.

[448] See Advocate General Léger at Case C–281/02 [2005] ECR I–1383, para 220.

[449] See Advocate General Léger at Case C–281/02 [2005] ECR I–1383, para 270. For consideration of the significance (if any) of the ECHR in the context of jurisdictional disputes, see JJ Fawcett, 'The Impact of Article 6(1) of the ECHR on Private International Law' (2007) 56 *ICLQ* 1.

[450] Art 25.

[451] Such a conclusion could be said to be in conflict with Case C–387/98 *Coreck Maritime GmbH v Handelsveem BV* [2000] ECR I–9337 in which the Court of Justice stated that the validity of a jurisdiction clause in favour of the courts of a non-Member State is governed by its applicable law (as determined by the forum's choice of law rules). It is reasonable to interpret this passage as an implicit acceptance by the Court of Justice that, in a case where a jurisdiction clause in favour of a non-Member State is valid, the court of a Member State is entitled to give effect to the jurisdiction clause under its national law (for example, by staying its proceedings or declining jurisdiction) notwithstanding the fact that its jurisdiction is derived from the Brussels I Regulation.

domiciled in England even though the same (or similar) claims were being litigated in a non-Member State.

9.5.17 One way of providing for exceptions to the strict application of the jurisdiction rules set out in Chapter II is to give 'reflex effect'[452] to the provisions of Chapter II relating to exclusive jurisdiction, jurisdiction agreements, *lis pendens* and related actions—thereby allowing Member State courts to stay proceedings or decline jurisdiction in cases which display a relevant connection with a non-Member State. But, even assuming that the Court of Justice is willing to accept the theory of 'reflex effect', which version of the theory would they endorse? There are, at least, three variations of the theory and each of them potentially presents problems.

9.5.18 According to the strictest version of the reflex effect theory (version 1), the courts of Member States would apply the rules in Articles 22, 23, 27 and 28 by analogy to cases involving the relevant connections with non-Member States. For example, in a case involving a jurisdiction agreement in favour of the courts of a non-Member State, the English court would decline jurisdiction if the circumstances were such that, had the agreement referred the dispute to the courts of a Member State, the effect of Article 23 would have been to confer exclusive jurisdiction on those courts. In the same way, jurisdiction would have to be declined in a case involving concurrent proceedings in a non-Member State if, had the concurrent proceedings been brought in a Member State, Article 27 would have required the English court to decline jurisdiction. However, this version presents certain difficulties. In particular, it seems inappropriate to apply by analogy hard-edged rules—such as Articles 23 and 27—in cases involving connections with a non-Member State; the provisions of the Regulation requiring effect to be given without any qualification to foreign choice of court agreements or giving unqualified priority to the court first seised 'seem[..] ... to be intimately linked to the principle of mutual trust between the courts of the Member States'.[453] It is also obvious that this approach is unlikely to appeal to the English courts (or to English commentators[454])—especially in the context of *lis pendens* and related actions. Whereas the imposition of a duty to decline jurisdiction in cases involving rights *in rem* in immovable property situated in a non-Member State and in cases where the parties to a dispute have agreed to the exclusive jurisdiction of the courts of a non-Member State would not usually produce results very different from those reached by the application of traditional common law doctrines,[455] the same cannot be said in relation to cases involving concurrent proceedings. The primacy accorded to the court first seised under Articles 27 and 28 has no counterpart in

---

[452] See Advocate General Léger in Case C–281/02 *Owusu v Jackson* [2005] ECR I–1383, para 70.

[453] A Nuyts, *Study on Residual Jurisdiction: General Report* (2007) p 143 (para 183). This report (which is available at http://ec.europa.eu/justice_home/doc_centre/civil/studies/doc/study_residual_jurisdiction_en.pdf) was commissioned as part of the background to the European Commission's 2009 project relating to the possible reform of the Brussels I Regulation.

[454] See, eg, A Briggs, '*Forum non conveniens* and ideal Europeans' [2005] *LMCLQ* 378.

[455] At common law the court generally has no jurisdiction to entertain a claim for the determination of title to, or the right to possession of, any immovable property situated outside England: *British South Africa Co v Companhia de Moçambique* [1893] AC 602. Similarly, unless the claimant can show 'strong cause', the court will, under its inherent jurisdiction, stay English proceedings brought in breach of a foreign jurisdiction clause: *The Eleftheria* [1970] P 94; *The El Amria* [1981] 2 Lloyd's Rep 119; *Donohue v Armco Inc* [2002] 1 All ER 749.

the doctrine of *forum non conveniens* which treats concurrent proceedings as only one factor (of variable weight) to be taken into account by the court.[456]

9.5.19   The obvious alternative to the application of Articles 22, 23 and 27 by analogy is to adopt a more flexible approach to the 'reflex effect' theory by allowing a Member State court to stay its proceedings or decline jurisdiction under the Regulation in accordance with national law. The most flexible version of the reflex effect theory (version 2) looks more to the underlying policies behind Articles 22, 23 and 27, rather than to their precise wording. According to this approach, in a case which involves a connection with a non-Member State which, were the connection with a Member State, would bring one of the 'reflex effect' provisions of the Regulation into play, the national court is entitled to stay its proceedings (or not) in accordance with its national law. Under version 2, in a case where the English court has jurisdiction under Article 2 of the Regulation, but there is a jurisdiction agreement in favour of a non-Member State, whether the English court grants a stay or not depends on the application of the doctrine laid down in *The Eleftheria*.[457] Under version 2, it would be sufficient for the jurisdiction agreement to be valid under the (private international) law of the forum; the party seeking a stay of the proceedings would not have to demonstrate that, had the jurisdiction agreement been in favour of a Member State, the agreement would have satisfied all the requirements of Article 23 of the Regulation. The problem with this approach, however, is that it runs the risk of introducing the kind of discretion, uncertainty and lack of uniformity which the Court of Justice considered to be so objectionable in the *Owusu* case. Accordingly, it seems unlikely that the Court of Justice would find version 2 of the 'reflex effect' theory an acceptable answer to the problems posed by jurisdictional conflicts between Member States and non-Member States.

9.5.20   A third version of the 'reflex effect' theory lies somewhere between the previous two. According to version 3, a Member State court is able to apply its national law to stay its proceedings notwithstanding the fact that its jurisdiction is derived from the Regulation, but only in a situation where, had the connection with the non-Member State been a connection with a Member State, the court would have been obliged to stay its proceedings or decline jurisdiction under the Regulation. The idea behind version 3 is to allow Member State courts a degree of flexibility (under national law) in staying its proceedings or declining jurisdiction in cases involving a relevant connection with a non-Member State, but to identify with a high degree of precision the circumstances in which staying proceedings under national law is permitted. The operation of version 3 of the reflex effect theory can be illustrated by a couple of simple examples. Suppose that disputes arise between two parties (A, a New York resident, and B, who is domiciled in England); A initiates proceedings against B in England and, a few days later, B starts proceedings against A in New York and applies for a stay of the English proceedings. Under version 3 of the 'reflex effect' theory, the English court would not be able to grant a stay its proceedings on the basis of *forum non conveniens* in these circumstances; because the English court is the court first seised (and, therefore, would not have been obliged to decline jurisdiction under Article 27 had the foreign proceedings been brought in a Member State rather than a non-Member State); on the other

---

[456] See paras 9.2.24–9.2.27.
[457] [1970] P 94, 99–100.

hand, if the priority of the English and New York proceedings were reversed, version 3 of the 'reflex effect' theory would allow the English court, as the court second seised, to stay its proceedings on the basis of the *Spiliada* doctrine (or to decline to do so); unlike version 1, version 3 would not require the English court to decline jurisdiction through the application of Article 27 by analogy.

9.5.21 There can be little doubt that an approach to cases involving appropriate connections with non-Member States based on the 'reflex effect' of Article 22, 23, 27 and 28 is preferable to the strict application of Articles 2, 5, and 6 without any exceptions. There is, however, no obviously right answer to the question of how broadly or narrowly the 'reflex effect' theory should be circumscribed. As the implications of the decision in *Owusu v Jackson* can only be regarded as uncertain, further guidance from the Court of Justice is required in order for national courts to know exactly how they should deal with cases involving a range of connections with non-Member States (ie, connections of the kind found in Article 22, jurisdiction agreements and concurrent proceedings).[458] It is not easy to predict whether or not the Court of Justice will favour the 'reflex effect' of Articles 22, 23, 27 and 28 and, if so, which version of the theory will gain the Court's approval. Until further guidance emanates from the Court of Justice (or the Brussels I Regulation is amended[459]), it seems that the English courts will treat the ruling in *Owusu v Jackson*[460] as limited to its facts and may continue to be tempted to apply traditional doctrines in cases involving disputes relating to immovable property situated in non-Member States, concurrent proceedings in such states and jurisdiction agreements in favour of such states.[461] In *Konkola Copper Mines plc v Coromin*, for example, Colman J took the view (*obiter*) that the decision in *Owusu v Jackson* 'has not disturbed the approach to the applicability of foreign jurisdiction clauses explained in *The El Amria*'.[462]

Cases Involving Schedule 4 to the 1982 Act

9.5.22 When considering the inherent jurisdiction of the English court to stay its proceedings in cases regulated by schedule 4 to the 1982 Act, a distinction needs to

---

[458] In January 2009, the Irish Supreme Court decided to refer to the Court of Justice the question whether the existence of earlier parallel proceedings in the United States meant that proceedings brought against a company domiciled in Ireland could be stayed and, if so, on what basis: *Goshawk Dedicated Ltd v Life Receivables Ireland Ltd* [2009] ILPr 435. It appears, however, that the matter was resolved before the reference was made: see *Catalyst Investment Group Ltd v Lewisohn* [2010] 2 WLR 839, 861 at [85]. The Irish High Court had thought that, on the basis of the *Owusu* decision, there was no basis upon which the Irish proceedings could be stayed in these circumstances: [2008] ILPr 816. A similar question could have been addressed in *Karafarin Bank v Mansoury-dara* [2009] 2 Lloyd's Rep 289, but Teare J side-stepped the issue.

[459] See the European Commission's Report on the application of the Brussels I Regulation (COM (2009) 174 final) and the Green Paper on the review of the Regulation (COM (2009) 175 final), which is the first step in the possible amendment of the Regulation.

[460] Case C–281/02 [2005] ECR I–1383.

[461] As in *The Nile Rhapsody* [1994] 1 Lloyd's Rep 382; *Ace Insurance SA-NV v Zurich Insurance Co* [2001] 1 Lloyd's Rep 618.

[462] [2005] 2 Lloyd's Rep 555, 574 (at [101]). Although the case went on appeal, the decision of the Court of Appeal casts no light on this issue: [2006] 1 Lloyd's Rep 410. See C Knight, '*Owusu* and *Turner*: The Shark in the Water?' [2007] *CLJ* 288. Compare, however, *Catalyst Investment Group Ltd v Lewisohn* [2010] 2 WLR 839 in which Barling J did not accede to arguments based on the 'reflex effect' of Art 27.

be drawn between, on the one hand, cases which are internal to the United Kingdom and, on the other, situations where schedule 4 supplements a provision of the Brussels I Regulation which allocates jurisdiction to the courts of the United Kingdom (rather than to the courts for a place).

Internal Disputes

9.5.23   In cases which are internal to the United Kingdom—where schedule 4 applies alone—the Brussels I Regulation does not prevent the English court from granting a stay of proceedings. It is not in any way inconsistent with the Brussels I Regulation for the English court to stay proceedings in an internal case—for example, on the ground that Scotland or Northern Ireland is a more appropriate forum than England. In *Foxon v Scotsman Publications Ltd*[463] it was held by Drake J that English proceedings could not be stayed in favour of the Scots courts on the basis of *forum non conveniens*. However, the same judge subsequently reached the opposite conclusion in *Cummings v Scottish Daily Record and Sunday Mail Ltd*[464] and it is the approach adopted in this later decision which is the correct one and which has been followed in subsequent cases.[465] *A fortiori*, if the parties have agreed to the exclusive jurisdiction of the courts of part of the United Kingdom, the courts of other parts may (and normally will) stay proceedings which are brought in breach of the terms of the agreement.[466]

Cases Governed by the Brussels I Regulation and Schedule 4

9.5.24   The position is more complex in cases where schedule 4 operates in tandem with the Brussels I Regulation. A variety of different situations should be considered.

THE ALTERNATIVE FORUM IS THE COURT OF ANOTHER MEMBER STATE
9.5.25   Where proceedings are started in England and the alternative forum is the court of another Member State the position is straightforward. If there are parallel proceedings in England and another Member State, any court other than the court first seised must stay its proceedings or decline jurisdiction if proceedings involve the same parties and the same cause of action; the court may grant a stay if the proceedings are related.[467] In circumstances not covered expressly by Articles 27 and 28, there is no room for the exercise of the court's inherent jurisdiction to stay proceedings, whether on the basis of *forum non conveniens* or on some other basis.

---

[463] The Times, 17 February 1994. L Collins and B Davenport, 'Forum Conveniens within the United Kingdom' (1994) 110 *LQR* 325.

[464] The Times, 9 June 1995. L Collins, 'The Brussels Convention within the United Kingdom' (1995) 111 *LQR* 541.

[465] *Lennon v Scottish Daily Record* [2004] EMLR 332; *The Seaward Quest* [2007] 2 Lloyd's Rep 308. See also *McCarten, Turkington and Breen v Lord St Oswald* [1996] NI 65 (High Court, Northern Ireland) in which the court exercised its discretion against staying defamation proceedings in favour of the English courts.

[466] *Buchanen, t/a Warnocks v Brook Walker and Company* [1988] NI 116 (High Court, Northern Ireland).

[467] Brussels I Reg, Arts 27–29.

THE ALTERNATIVE FORUM IS THE COURT OF A NON-MEMBER STATE

9.5.26 As regards a conflict of jurisdiction between the English court and the court of a non-Member State, the decision in *Owusu v Jackson*[468] establishes that the exercise of the court's inherent jurisdiction is incompatible with the Brussels I Regulation. Where the parties have agreed to the exclusive jurisdiction of a non-Member State or where proceedings have already been commenced in a non-Member State or where there is a close connection (of the type listed in Article 22) with a non-Member State, there is a good case for saying that the court should refuse to exercise jurisdiction. Whether Articles 22, 23, 27 and 28 should be given 'reflex effect', thereby depriving the court of jurisdiction, is uncertain. It seems unlikely, however, that the court retains its inherent jurisdiction in such cases.[469]

THE ALTERNATIVE FORUM IS THE COURT OF ANOTHER PART
OF THE UNITED KINGDOM

9.5.27 A difficult question arises where the combined effect of schedule 4 and the Brussels I Regulation is to allocate non-exclusive jurisdiction to more than one part of the United Kingdom. So, for example, where a foreign claimant is injured in an accident in Scotland as a result of the negligence of an English defendant, Article 5(3) of the Brussels I Regulation confers jurisdiction on the courts of Scotland and the combined effect of Article 2 of the Brussels I Regulation and Rule 1 of schedule 4 is to confer jurisdiction on the English courts. The logic of the decision in *Owusu v Jackson*[470] prevents the English court from granting a stay under its inherent jurisdiction in this type of case where the alternative forum is another part of the United Kingdom. Nevertheless, the English courts have taken the view that they retain their discretion to stay proceedings on the basis of *forum non convneiens* in such circumstances.[471]

9.5.28 Because the Civil Procedure Rules may not be entirely effective in preventing parallel proceedings involving the same cause of action from being brought in different parts of the United Kingdom and schedule 4 does not contain provisions dealing with concurrent proceedings,[472] it is important that the English court should be able to stay proceedings in circumstances where, if a stay were refused, there would be risk of irreconcilable judgments being given by the courts of different parts of the United Kingdom. Furthermore, in cases where the parties have entered a jurisdiction agreement in favour of the courts of a part of the United Kingdom the court should seek to uphold the parties' agreement. Accordingly, a stay might be appropriate in a case where proceedings are commenced in England—for example, under Article 5(1) of the Brussels I Regulation—on the basis that the parties agreed to refer disputes to the exclusive jurisdiction of the courts of another part of the United Kingdom.

---

[468] Case C–281/02 [2005] ECR I–1383.
[469] See paras 9.5.13–9.5.21.
[470] Case C–281/02 [2005] ECR I–1383.
[471] *Ivax Pharmaceutical UK Ltd v Akzo Nobel BV* [2007] FSR 888. The authority of this decision is not, however, strong: not only was *Owusu v Jackson* not cited, but also the only case on which the judge relied involved a situation which was internal to the United Kingdom.
[472] See paras 9.1.57–9.1.58.

10

PROVISIONAL MEASURES

10.0.1 In any legal system it is inevitable that there will be delays between the commencement of proceedings by the claimant and the final resolution of the claim. Delays in litigation may lead to the claimant's efforts to vindicate his rights being frustrated if the defendant is allowed either to thwart the legal process (for example, by destroying evidence) or to deprive the successful claimant of the fruits of success (for example, by dissipating his assets and making himself judgment-proof). The same dangers exist in the context of disputes which the parties have agreed to refer to arbitration. Accordingly, the courts have developed a range of provisional measures, the purpose of which is to ensure that, as far as possible, the rights of the parties are not irreparably harmed pending the final judgment or award (section 10.1). The jurisdiction of the courts to grant provisional measures has been clarified and extended (sections 10.2 and 10.3). Provisional measures may be granted in relation to acts or things within the jurisdiction or abroad. Although the courts must exercise caution when considering the grant of provisional measures with extraterritorial effect, the courts have become increasingly aware of the importance (as well as the dangers) of granting such measures (section 10.4). Notwithstanding developments on the international plane, the cross-border enforcement of provisional measures remains fraught with difficulty (section 10.5).

10.1 DIFFERENT TYPES OF PROVISIONAL MEASURE

Introduction

10.1.1 Broadly speaking, provisional measures can be divided into three categories. First, some measures are designed to maintain the status quo pending the final decision on the merits. In English law the court may grant interlocutory injunctions (which, in appropriate circumstances, may be obtained without the defendant having been given notice of the application)[1] with a view to ensuring that justice can be done when the dispute is ultimately determined. So, for example, a claimant employer may apply for an injunction to prevent the defendant contractor from ceasing work on a construction project.[2] Similarly, the court may make an order 'for the detention, custody or preservation of relevant property'.[3]

10.1.2 Secondly, the court may take measures which are designed to secure the ultimate judgment or award by preventing the defendant from disposing of assets pending the final determination of the proceedings. Perhaps the most simple

---

[1] That is, what used to be known as an *ex parte* application.
[2] *Channel Tunnel Group Ltd v Balfour Beatty Construction Ltd* [1993] AC 334.
[3] CPR 25.1(1)(c)(i).

and effective provisional measure in this context is a court order which allows the claimant to attach property within the court's jurisdiction. In matters falling within the jurisdiction of the admiralty court the claimant may, in certain circumstances, bring proceedings *in rem* by serving a claim form on the *res* (normally a ship) within the jurisdiction.[4] Where proceedings are commenced *in rem* the claimant is also entitled to arrest the *res*. In practice, either the *res* is sold and the judgment or award is enforced out of the proceeds of sale or the owner puts up security for the claim to obtain the release of the *res* or, if it has not yet been arrested, to prevent the claimant from arresting it. In any event the claimant obtains security for his claim.

10.1.3   In cases not falling within the jurisdiction of the admiralty court, there is no equivalent to a claim *in rem*. Indeed, the presence of the defendant's assets in England does not, in itself, entitle the court to assume jurisdiction over the claim.[5] Modern technological conditions—particularly the development of systems for the electronic transfer of funds—make it increasingly difficult for a party who obtains a judgment or an award in his favour to execute the judgment or award against the assets of the losing party. Legal and practical problems surrounding enforcement have led to the development in England of new provisional measures. The courts developed the *Mareva*[6] injunction (referred to by the Civil Procedure Rules as a 'freezing injunction'),[7] which enables a claimant to obtain an order freezing the defendant's assets.

10.1.4   Thirdly, provisional measures include procedural orders of an investigative nature. For example, the English courts have the power to make orders for the inspection of property or for the taking of samples.[8] In *CFEM Façades SA v Bovis Construction Ltd*[9] the court was faced with an application to enforce a French order appointing experts to inspect a building in London and to take evidence from potential witnesses. The most significant development in this area in English law was the birth of the *Anton Piller*[10] order (referred to by the Civil Procedure Rules as a 'search order'),[11] which requires the defendant to permit the claimant to enter the defendant's premises with a view to collecting evidence.

10.1.5   While there are statutory provisions and procedural rules concerned with specific measures, section 37(1) of the Supreme Court Act 1981 provides the foundation of the court's broad discretionary jurisdiction to grant provisional measures:

The High Court may by order (whether interlocutory or final) grant an injunction or appoint a receiver in all cases in which it appears to the court to be just and convenient to do so.

---

[4] See section 8.1.
[5] *Siskina (Owners of cargo lately laden on board) v Distos Compania Naviera SA* [1979] AC 210.
[6] *Mareva Compania Naviera SA v International Bulk Carriers SA* [1975] 2 Lloyd's Rep 509. *Nippon Yusen Kaisha v Karageorgis* [1975] 1 WLR 1093 was, however, the first English case in which a freezing injunction was granted.
[7] CPR 25.1(1)(f).
[8] CPR 25.1(1)(c)(ii) and (iii).
[9] [1992] ILPr 561.
[10] *Anton Piller KG v Manufacturing Processes Ltd* [1976] Ch 55.
[11] See Civil Procedure Act 1997, s 7; CPR 25.1(1)(h).

The extreme generality of section 37(1) means that the principles according to which provisional measures are granted are mainly to be gleaned from the cases.

Interlocutory Injunctions

10.1.6 Any consideration of the law relating to interlocutory injunctions must take as its starting point the decision of the House of Lords in *American Cyanamid Co v Ethicon Ltd*.[12] It should be stressed, however, that this decision should be regarded as no more than a set of useful guidelines.[13] The decision contains no principle of universal application and it must always be remembered that an injunction should be granted only if it is just and convenient to do so. The guidelines in *American Cyanamid Co v Ethicon Ltd* indicate that, in deciding whether or not to grant an interlocutory injunction, the court should have regard to a number of questions. First, as a general rule, the court should be satisfied that there is a serious question to be tried. Secondly, the court should consider the balance of convenience. This means, for example, that an injunction should normally be refused in a case where the claimant, if successful, will be adequately compensated by an award of damages. However, as Lord Diplock noted: 'Where other factors appear to be evenly balanced it is a counsel of prudence to take such measures as are calculated to preserve the status quo.'[14] Thirdly, unless the court exercises restraint, an application for provisional measures may draw the court into a mini-trial on the merits at the interlocutory stage. So, as a general rule, the court should not be concerned with the relative strength of the parties' arguments (subject, of course, to the court being satisfied that there is a serious question to be tried). However, where it is clear that the claim is unanswerable on the facts or that the case involves a simple point of law (for example, concerning the interpretation of a statutory or contractual provision) which will obviously be resolved in the claimant's favour, the court will generally grant the relief sought. Where the case will be effectively determined by the decision to grant (or to refuse) the measure sought by the claimant the court has no choice but to look at the merits of the claim.

10.1.7 It is important to draw attention to the limits of the guidelines in *American Cyanamid Co v Ethicon Ltd*. For example, the guidelines are inappropriate in cases where there is no prospect of a trial. Similarly, it would seem that the guidelines do not apply to mandatory interlocutory injunctions;[15] the court will seldom grant a mandatory injunction at the interlocutory stage. Finally, special principles have been worked out by the courts in relation to freezing injunctions and search orders.

---

[12] [1975] AC 396.
[13] *Cambridge Nutrition Ltd v British Broadcasting Corporation* [1990] 3 All ER 523.
[14] *American Cyanamid Co v Ethicon Ltd* [1975] AC 396, 408.
[15] *Leisure Data v Bell* [1988] FSR 367.

Freezing Injunctions

Background

10.1.8 Perhaps the most important function of provisional measures in the context of international litigation is to secure the ultimate judgment by preventing the defendant from disposing of his assets before the final determination of the proceedings. From the point of view of the claimant, what is needed is a mechanism whereby the defendant is, first, required to disclose the extent and location of his assets and, then, prevented from dealing with his assets to the extent which is necessary to ensure that, as far as possible, any judgment obtained by the claimant can be satisfied. From the point of view of the defendant, however, it is important that remedies which are made available to the claimant are not so extensive that they may be used as an instrument of oppression.

10.1.9 Many civil law countries have a mechanism—which in France is known as the *saisie conservatoire*—whereby at the very outset of proceedings the assets of a defendant may be seized so that there will be property against which the claimant, if successful, will be able to levy execution. Often, in practice, the defendant provides security for the claim to obtain the release of his assets. Although, until relatively recently, there was no equivalent institution in English law, in the 1970s the freezing injunction was born. The purpose of a freezing injunction should not be to put unfair pressure on the defendant or to hold the defendant to ransom; it is:

to prevent parties to actions frustrating [the court's] orders by moving assets out of the jurisdiction, or dissipating assets in one way or another, with a view to making themselves proof against a future judgment.[16]

This is achieved by the court making an order which freezes the defendant's assets (often a credit balance in a bank account) so that, if the claim is upheld by the court, there will be property of the defendant out of which the judgment can be satisfied.[17] A freezing injunction may be granted by the court either before or after the granting of the judgment on the merits of the dispute.

10.1.10 In view of the basic purpose of a freezing injunction, assets of the defendant which, although of value to the defendant, have no value in the open market should not be made subject to such an injunction. In *Camdex International Ltd v Bank of Zambia (No 2)*[18] the plaintiff, having secured a judgment against the defendant, the central bank of Zambia, obtained an injunction freezing the defendant's assets in England. The Court of Appeal acceded to the defendant's application to have some newly printed Zambian bank notes exempted from the injunction. Even though the defendant might have been prepared to pay a considerable sum of money to gain possession of the bank notes—in order to fulfil its obligations as a central bank—the notes had no value in the open market. In its original form the injunction was being

---

[16] Lord Donaldson MR in *Jet West Ltd v Haddican* [1992] 1 WLR 487, 489.
[17] Brandon J in *The Rena K* [1979] QB 377, 407.
[18] [1997] 1 WLR 632.

used 'in an attempt to pressurise the defendant into discharging part of its liability under the judgment'.[19]

Obtaining a Freezing Injunction

10.1.11   An application for a freezing injunction may be made at the interlocutory stage. Because speed and the element of surprise are important, the claimant's application is usually made without notice.[20] Notwithstanding the generality of section 37(1) of the 1981 Act, where the relief sought is the freezing of assets within the jurisdiction, a freezing injunction will not be granted unless the claimant shows that there is at least a good arguable case that he will succeed at the trial and the court considers that, on the whole of the evidence then before it, the refusal of a freezing injunction would involve a real risk that a judgment or award in favour of the claimant would remain unsatisfied.[21] Although many cases in which the claimant makes an application for a freezing injunction involve allegations of fraud or similar types of wrongdoing on the part of the defendant, the mere fact that the claimant alleges fraud is not sufficient; something more is required—such as plausible evidence that the defendants are 'the sort of people who will stop at nothing to frustrate the [claimant] from making any substantial recovery by dissipating their assets, unless restrained by the freezing order'.[22]

10.1.12   When making an application for a freezing injunction, the claimant 'should identify the prospective judgment whose enforcement the defendant is not to be permitted, by dissipating his assets, to frustrate'.[23] In the context of a without notice application, it is not appropriate for the court to grant a freezing injunction 'in the absence of any formulation of the case for substantive relief that the applicant for the order intend[s] to institute';[24] the claimant 'must at least point to proceedings already brought, or proceedings about to be brought, so as to show where and on what basis he expects to recover judgment against the defendant'.[25] Furthermore, where the claimant is seeking an order freezing assets within the jurisdiction, it must be shown that the defendant has assets within the jurisdiction. Originally, freezing injunctions were subject to three limitations: (1) they were granted only against persons resident outside the jurisdiction; (2) they were granted only against persons who had property within the jurisdiction; and (3) they were granted only to restrain the removal of property from the jurisdiction.[26] None of these limitations applies today.

10.1.13   The factual context which gave birth to the freezing injunction was litigation in England involving a foreign defendant who had assets in England.[27] On the

---

[19]   Phillips LJ at [1997] 1 WLR 632, 640.

[20]   See CPR PD 25 para 4.

[21]   *Nimemia Maritime Corporation v Trave Schiffahrtsgesellschaft mbH und Co KG* [1983] 1 WLR 1412; *Refco Inc v Eastern Trading Co* [1999] 1 Lloyd's Rep 159; *Laemthong International Lines Co Ltd v Artis* [2005] 1 Lloyd's Rep 100.

[22]   Flaux J in *The Nicholas M* [2009] 1 All ER (Comm) 479, 500 (at [53]).

[23]   Lord Bingham in *Fourie v Le Roux* [2007] 1 WLR 320, 322 (at [3]).

[24]   Lord Scott in *Fourie v Le Roux* [2007] 1 WLR 320, 334 (at [35]).

[25]   Lord Bingham in *Fourie v Le Roux* [2007] 1 WLR 320, 323 (at [3]).

[26]   See Neill LJ in *Derby & Co Ltd v Weldon (Nos 3 & 4)* [1990] Ch 65, 89.

[27]   *Nippon Yusen Kaisha v Karageorgis* [1975] 1 WLR 1093; *Mareva Compania Naviera SA v International Bulk Carriers* [1975] 2 Lloyd's Rep 509.

basis of the early cases, it was uncertain whether it was a requirement for the exercise of the *Mareva* jurisdiction that the defendant should be either a foreign company or a foreign resident. Cases decided in 1980 indicated that a freezing injunction could also be granted against an English resident.[28] The approach adopted by the courts was endorsed by section 37(3) of the Supreme Court Act 1981, which provides:

The power of the High Court under subsection (1) to grant an interlocutory injunction restraining a party to any proceedings from removing from the jurisdiction of the High Court, or otherwise dealing with, assets located within that jurisdiction shall be exercisable in cases where that party is, as well as in cases where he is not, domiciled, resident or present within that jurisdiction.

10.1.14 Until the 1990s it was generally assumed that the scope of the *Mareva* jurisdiction was limited to assets within the jurisdiction.[29] The practice of the courts has changed in this regard. In appropriate circumstances a freezing injunction affecting assets abroad may be granted.[30]

10.1.15 In the early cases, freezing injunctions took the form of orders restraining the defendant from removing assets from the jurisdiction of the court. Subsequently, in *Rahman (Prince Abdul) bin Turki al Sudairy v Abu-Taha*[31] Lord Denning MR expressed the opinion that a freezing injunction could be obtained if there was a danger that the defendant would dispose of his assets within the jurisdiction. Although this *dictum* was for a time doubted, section 37(3) refers to 'removing from the jurisdiction of the High Court, or otherwise dealing with, assets'. If any doubt persisted after the entry into force of the 1981 Act, *Nimemia Maritime Corporation v Trave Schiffahrtsgesellschaft mbH und Co KG*[32] established that a freezing injunction could be granted where there is a risk that the defendant will either dissipate his assets within the jurisdiction or remove them from the jurisdiction.

10.1.16 Freezing injunctions confer on the claimant 'draconian powers'[33] to interfere with the defendant's life and privacy without the defendant being able to put his side of the argument. Because the defendant is unable to take part at this initial stage, the courts impose two requirements on the claimant. First, a claimant making an application without notice must disclose to the court all matters relevant to the exercise of the court's discretion whether to grant relief before giving the defendant the opportunity to be heard.[34] In a case where an injunction is granted without notice, but the claimant failed to make proper disclosure, the injunction will usually be discharged on the defendant's application.[35] Secondly, the claimant will normally be required to give an undertaking in damages in the event of the claim

---

[28] *Chartered Bank v Daklouche* [1980] 1 WLR 107; *Barclay-Johnson v Yuill* [1980] 1 WLR 1259; *Rahman (Prince Abdul) bin Turki al Sudairy v Abu-Taha* [1980] 1 WLR 1268.

[29] *Ashtiani v Kashi* [1987] QB 888.

[30] See section 10.4.

[31] [1980] 1 WLR 1268, 1273.

[32] [1983] 1 WLR 1412.

[33] Browne-Wilkinson V-C in *Tate Access Floors Inc v Boswell* [1991] Ch 512, 533.

[34] See, eg, Mummery LJ in *Memory Corpn v Sidhu (No 2)* [2000] 1 WLR 1443, 1460. For a summary of the relevant principles, see *Brinks-Mat Ltd v Elcombe* [1988] 1 WLR 1350 and *Yukong Line Ltd v Rendsburg Investments Corporation* [2001] 2 Lloyd's Rep 113.

[35] The court, however, has a discretion not to discharge a freezing injunction, notwithstanding non-disclosure by the claimant: see, eg, *Dadourian Group International Inc v Simms* [2009] 1 Lloyd's Rep 601.

being unsuccessful[36] or in the event of any third party suffering injury by reason of the injunction.[37] In an appropriate case a claimant may be required to support his undertaking by a payment into court or by provision of a bond from an insurance company.

The Effect of a Freezing Injunction

INJUNCTIONS OPERATE *IN PERSONAM*

10.1.17   A freezing injunction may be granted against the totality of the defendant's assets or a defendant may be restrained from dealing with assets in such a way that their unencumbered value remains above a specified value. Normally, the maximum to which a claimant is entitled is an injunction for the highest amount in respect of which he has a good arguable case (including a sum for interest and costs).[38] A freezing injunction is not, however, a proprietary remedy; it is not intended to give security for the claim in advance of judgment, but merely to prevent the defendant from defeating the claimant's chances of recovery.[39] A freezing injunction operates *in personam*[40] and does not attach to the defendant's property as such. Accordingly, a claimant who obtains a freezing injunction does not thereby obtain priority over other creditors.[41] The effect of a freezing injunction is that the person to whom it is addressed is in contempt of court if he fails to comply with the terms of the injunction. Depending on the seriousness of the contempt, penalties may range from an immediate prison sentence,[42] a fine or sequestration of the defendant's assets[43] to an order simply requiring the party who is in breach of the terms of the injunction to restore to the frozen assets any sums which have been unlawfully dissipated.[44]

10.1.18   The courts must strike a balance between the interests of the parties and should not allow a freezing injunction to act oppressively against the defendant. If a freezing injunction is granted before notice is given to the defendant, the defendant

---

[36] *Hoffmann-La Roche & Co AG v Secretary of State for Trade and Industry* [1975] AC 295. In appropriate circumstances (for example, in a case where the claimant is a public body acting in the performance of a public duty), the court may dispense with an undertaking: *Securities and Investment Board v Lloyd-Wright* [1993] 4 All ER 210; *United States Securities and Exchange Commission v Manterfield* [2010] 1 WLR 172.

[37] See *Tharros Shipping Co Ltd v Bias Shipping Ltd* [1994] 1 Lloyd's Rep 577. For consideration of some of the problems surrounding the court's jurisdiction to determine damages, see *Balkanbank v Taher* [1995] 1 WLR 1056; *Balkanbank v Taher (No 2)* [1995] 1 WLR 1067. See also *Al-Rawas v Pegasus Energy Ltd* [2009] 1 All ER 346.

[38] The cases show that it is not always easy to determine how the appropriate figure should be calculated; see, eg, *Pacific Maritime (Asia) Ltd v Holystone Overseas Ltd* [2008] 1 Lloyd's Rep 371.

[39] *Hitachi Shipbuilding and Engineering Co Ltd v Viafiel Compania Naviera SA* [1981] 2 Lloyd's Rep 498; *Polly Peck International Plc v Nadir* [1992] 2 Lloyd's Rep 238. See also Lord Bingham in *Fourie v Le Roux* [2007] 1 WLR 320, 322 (at [3]).

[40] Lord Denning MR expressed the view that *Mareva* injunctions operated *in rem*: *Z Ltd v A-Z and AA-LL* [1982] QB 558, 573. It has since been decided that this observation was made *per incuriam*: see Lord Ackner in *Attorney General v Times Newspapers Ltd* [1992] 1 AC 191, 215.

[41] *Cretanor Maritime Co Ltd v Irish Marine Management Ltd* [1978] 1 WLR 966; *Iraqi Ministry of Defence v Arcepey Shipping Co* [1981] QB 65; *K/S A/S Admiral Shipping v Portlink Ferries Ltd* [1984] 2 Lloyd's Rep 166; *Flightline Ltd v Edwards* [2003] 1 WLR 1200; *Kastner v Jason* [2005] 1 Lloyd's Rep 397.

[42] *Pospischal v Phillips* The Times, 20 January 1988; *Guildford Borough Council v Valler* The Times, 15 October 1993.

[43] *Fakih Brothers v A P Moller (Copenhagen) Ltd* [1994] 1 Lloyd's Rep 103.

[44] *TDK Tape Distributor UK Ltd v Videochoice Ltd* [1986] 1 WLR 141.

may at any time apply for the variation or discharge of the injunction either on the basis that the original terms of the injunction are oppressive or on the basis of a material change of circumstances. When deciding the extent to which the defendant should be prevented from dealing with his assets the courts must bear in mind that '[i]t is not the purpose of a *Mareva* injunction to prevent a defendant acting as he would have acted in the absence of a claim against him'.[45] This means that, before judgment, the defendant must be given access to sufficient funds for usual living expenses (which may amount to a considerable total)[46] and for the payment of legal fees incurred in defending the claim.[47] So:

While a defendant who is a natural person can and should be enjoined from indulging in a spending spree undertaken with the intention of dissipating or reducing his assets before the day of judgment, he cannot be required to reduce his ordinary standard of living with a view to putting by sums to satisfy a judgment which may or may not be given in the future.[48]

Similarly, before judgment, a freezing injunction ought not to interfere with the defendant's ordinary course of business. No defendant, whether a natural or legal person, should be prevented from carrying on his business in the ordinary way or from meeting his debts or other obligations as they come due prior to judgment being given.[49] This principle makes the grant of a freezing injunction against a bank—or, at any rate, a bank carrying on a normal banking business—very difficult, since a bank must be able to repay its depositors in accordance with the terms on which the deposits are held. However, it seems to have become accepted that, once the claimant has obtained a judgment (or arbitral award) in his favour, a judgment debtor is not free to dispose of his assets in the ordinary course of business.[50] Furthermore, there may be exceptional circumstances (such as where, to avoid an attachment of assets pursuant to foreign court proceedings, parties collaborate with a view to ensuring that no debts or other financial benefits accrue to one of the parties) in which the court considers it appropriate to make an order restraining a person from making payments due under transactions between that person and the judgment debtor.[51]

THIRD PARTIES

10.1.19 A freezing injunction may affect third parties. It is usual to serve notice of a freezing injunction on third parties, who hold the defendant's assets. A person who has notice of the injunction and who knowingly aids and abets the defendant to deal with his assets in breach of the terms of the injunction, is guilty of a contempt of court.[52]

---

[45] Lord Donaldson MR in *Polly Peck International Plc v Nadir* [1992] 2 Lloyd's Rep 238, 249.
[46] *Babanaft International Co SA v Bassatne* [1990] Ch 13.
[47] *Cala Cristal SA v Emran Al-Borno* The Times, 6 May 1994. For consideration of the position of solicitors who are paid fees in cases where the claim against the defendant is proprietary in nature, see *United Mizrahi Bank Ltd v Doherty* [1998] 1 WLR 435.
[48] Lord Donaldson MR in *Polly Peck International Plc v Nadir* [1992] 2 Lloyd's Rep 238, 249.
[49] *Iraqi Ministry of Defence v Arcepey Shipping Co* [1981] QB 65; *Avant Petroleum Inc v Gatoil Overseas Inc* [1986] 2 Lloyd's Rep 236; *Polly Peck International Plc v Nadir* [1992] 2 Lloyd's Rep 238.
[50] See Sir Thomas Bingham MR in *Camdex International Ltd v Bank of Zambia (No 2)* [1997] 1 WLR 632, 634.
[51] See *Kensington International Ltd v Republic of Congo* [2008] 1 Lloyd's Rep 161.
[52] *Seaward v Paterson* [1897] 1 Ch 545; *Z Ltd v A-Z and AA-LL* [1982] QB 558.

FREEZING INJUNCTIONS AND THE PROVISION OF SECURITY

10.1.20   Whereas in proceedings *in rem* the arrest (or threat of arrest) of the *res* ensures that the claimant obtains security for the claim, a freezing injunction, which operates *in personam*, is not a form of attachment of assets. Nevertheless, it has been argued that, notwithstanding the courts' attempt to balance the interests of the parties, the *Mareva* jurisdiction involves the unequal treatment of defendants in the sense that it denies the defendant the right to be heard at the initial stage, thereby giving the claimant a powerful leverage against the defendant.[53] Although a freezing injunction does not in itself provide security for the claim, it may lead to this result. Once a freezing injunction has been granted (particularly one which prevents the defendant from disposing of any of his assets within the jurisdiction), the defendant may put up security (for example, by way of a third party guarantee or bond) in order to obtain the discharge of the injunction.

Ancillary and Related Orders

DISCLOSURE ORDERS

10.1.21   If the defendant's assets are to be frozen, the claimant must first locate them. In international disputes the availability of a disclosure order,[54] ancillary to a freezing injunction, is an extremely valuable weapon in the claimant's armoury. Furthermore, disclosure of the extent and whereabouts of the defendant's assets is essential for the smooth operation of the *Mareva* jurisdiction:

The defendant may have more than one asset within the jurisdiction—for example, he may have a number of bank accounts. The plaintiff does not know how much, if anything, is in any of them; nor does each of the defendant's bankers know what is in the other accounts. Without information about the state of each account it is difficult, if not impossible, to operate the *Mareva* jurisdiction properly: for example, if each banker prevents the drawing from his account to the limit of the sum claimed, the defendant will be treated oppressively, and the plaintiff may be held liable on his undertaking in damages. … Furthermore, the very generality of the order creates difficulty for the defendant's bankers, who may for example be unaware of the existence of other assets of the defendant within the jurisdiction; indeed, if a more specific order is possible, it may give much needed protection for the defendant's bankers, who are after all simply the innocent holders of one form of the defendant's assets.[55]

10.1.22   The court has 'the power to make such ancillary orders as appear to the court to be just and convenient, to ensure that the exercise of the *Mareva* jurisdiction is effective to achieve its purpose'.[56] Such orders include disclosure orders requiring the defendant to provide information relating to the extent and whereabouts of his assets. Indeed, the court may insist that the defendant orders his bank to disclose

---

[53] AAS Zuckerman, 'Interlocutory Remedies in Quest of Procedural Fairness' (1993) 56 *MLR* 325, 335. See also J Grunert, 'Interlocutory Remedies in England and Germany: A Comparative Perspective' (1996) 15 *CJQ* 18.

[54] CPR 25.1(1)(g). See C McLachlan, 'The Jurisdictional Limits of Disclosure Orders in Transnational Fraud Litigation' (1998) 47 *ICLQ* 3.

[55] Robert Goff J in *A v C* [1981] QB 956, 959–60. See also *Motorola Credit Corp v Uzan* [2002] 2 All ER (Comm) 945.

[56] Ackner LJ in *AJ Bekhor & Co Ltd v Bilton* [1981] QB 923, 940. See also *Allied Arab Bank Ltd v Hajjar* [1988] QB 787.

information about his account and the fact that a foreign bank will not (or may not) comply with a request for disclosure of documents relating to the account of one of its clients is not, by itself, a ground for refusing to make the order.[57] It is also established that where the court has granted a post-judgment freezing injunction against the defendant the court has jurisdiction to make a disclosure order against a third party who has 'become mixed up' in the defendant's arrangements to defeat execution of the judgment—even though the claimant has no independent cause of action against the third party.[58]

10.1.23   As a general rule, where the court makes a disclosure order ancillary to a freezing injunction the disclosure order should not go beyond the ambit of the injunction.[59] However, in *Derby & Co Ltd v Weldon (Nos 3 & 4)* Neill LJ left open the possibility that 'in certain circumstances a discovery order can be made with a wider ambit than the injunction to which it is ancillary'.[60] Subsequently, it has been held that, in a case where the claimant has already obtained a judgment or arbitral award in his favour, the court has jurisdiction to make an order which includes both a freezing injunction confined to assets within the jurisdiction and a disclosure order in respect of worldwide assets.[61]

10.1.24   Although the court may make an order affecting both assets within and outside the jurisdiction,[62] in practice, where a disclosure order reveals the existence of assets abroad, there are many circumstances in which it is more effective for the claimant to bring attachment proceedings in the country or countries where the assets are located, rather than to seek the grant of a worldwide freezing injunction in England.[63] Often it is only by taking action in the country where the assets are located that the claimant can obtain an order which is binding on parties other than the defendant.[64]

10.1.25   After judgment has been given in the claimant's favour, the court also has the power to make a disclosure order against the judgment debtor under Part 71 of the Civil Procedure Rules. This type of order is quite distinct from a disclosure order which is ancillary to a freezing injunction. A disclosure order may be made under Part 71 without the claimant having to establish the preconditions required for the grant of a freezing injunction. So, a post-judgment disclosure order under Part 71 of the Civil Procedure Rules can be made without the claimant having to show that there is a risk of removal or dissipation of the defendant's assets.

RECEIVERSHIP ORDERS

10.1.26   The court's jurisdiction to appoint a receiver is derived from the same statutory source as its jurisdiction to grant an interlocutory injunction.[65] The parties to the

---

[57] *Bank of Crete SA v Koskotas* [1991] 2 Lloyd's Rep 587.

[58] *Mercantile Group (Europe) AG v Aiyela* [1994] QB 366; *C Inc Plc v L* [2001] 2 Lloyd's Rep 459. See also P Devonshire, 'Mareva Injunctions and Third Parties: Exposing the Subtext' (1999) 62 *MLR* 539.

[59] Neill LJ in *Derby & Co Ltd v Weldon (Nos 3 & 4)* [1990] Ch 65, 94. See also *AJ Bekhor & Co Ltd v Bilton* [1981] QB 923.

[60] [1990] Ch 65, 94.

[61] *Gidrxslme Shipping Co v Tantomar-Transportes Maritimos Lda* [1995] 1 WLR 299.

[62] See section 10.4.

[63] L Collins, 'Fraudulent Conduct in International Law' (1989) 42 *CLP* 255, 274.

[64] See section 10.5.

[65] Supreme Court Act 1981, s. 37(1). For the text of this provision, see para 10.1.5.

proceedings are required to relinquish control of the assets specified in the order to the receiver, who is an officer of the court. Any person who, with knowledge of the appointment of the receiver, attempts to deal with the assets which are the subject-matter of the receivership order may be liable for contempt of court. The appointment of a receiver and the grant of a freezing injunction are separate remedies. Depending on the circumstances, the court may decide to grant one remedy or the other—or to grant both.[66]

Search Orders

10.1.27 There are certain circumstances in which there is a serious danger that the defendant may dispose of or destroy property which is relevant to a claim against him. For example, where the defendant has made copies of a recording in breach of the claimant's intellectual property rights, the illegal copies are important evidence which is liable to be destroyed by the defendant once legal proceedings are started. A remedy in the context of an *inter partes* application is not likely to be effective, since the element of surprise is lost.

10.1.28 Although search orders are an established feature of English commercial litigation, the basis of the court's jurisdiction was uncertain until the matter was put on a statutory footing by section 7 of the Civil Procedure Act 1997.[67] Section 7(1) provides:

The court[68] may make an order under this section for the purpose of securing, in the case of any existing or proposed proceedings in the court—

(a) the preservation of evidence which is or may be relevant, or
(b) the preservation of property which is or may be the subject-matter of the proceedings or as to which any question arises or may arise in the proceedings.

A search order may direct any person to permit whomever is designated by the order to enter premises[69] in England and Wales and while on the premises, to take various steps in accordance with the terms of the order.[70] The 'steps' which may be taken include: carrying out searches and making inspections; making or obtaining copies, photographs and samples.[71] Although the 1997 Act is the primary source of the courts' power to grant search orders, the court may still make an order under section 37 of the Supreme Court Act 1981 or under its inherent jurisdiction.

10.1.29 A search order, which may be the subject of an application without notice,[72] requires the defendant to permit the claimant (or his representatives) to enter the defendant's premises in order to search for and remove items such as documents, other evidence or specified property. Normally, a search order should be carried out by or

---

[66] *Derby & Co Ltd v Weldon (Nos 3 & 4)* [1990] Ch 65.
[67] See M Dockray and KR Thomas, 'Anton Piller orders: the new statutory scheme' (1998) 17 *CJQ* 272.
[68] This means the High Court: Civil Procedure Act 1997, s 7(8).
[69] 'Premises' includes any vehicle: Civil Procedure Act 1997, s 7(8).
[70] Civil Procedure Act 1997, s 7(3).
[71] Civil Procedure Act 1997, s 7(4).
[72] See CPR PD 25 para 4.

under the supervision of a supervising solicitor—that is, an experienced solicitor who has some familiarity with the operation of search orders and who is not a member of the firm acting for the claimant.[73]

10.1.30   A search order will not be made unless the claimant has an extremely strong *prima facie* case, the potential or actual damage to the claimant's interests is very serious, there is clear evidence that the defendant has in his possession property which is incriminating and there is a serious possibility that the property in question will be disposed of or destroyed before an *inter partes* application can be made.[74] As in cases involving applications for a freezing injunction, the claimant is required to give an undertaking in damages. While the usefulness of search orders to the claimant can hardly be doubted, there are some indications that search orders have on occasion been granted too readily and operated oppressively.[75]

10.2 JURISDICTION TO GRANT PROVISIONAL MEASURES: PROCEEDINGS *IN REM*

10.2.1   In cases involving admiralty proceedings *in rem*, the claimant is entitled to have the *res* arrested.[76] The claimant issues both a claim form *in rem*, which the claimant may serve, and a warrant for arrest, which must be served by the Admiralty Marshal.[77] The claim form and warrant are often served at approximately the same time, but either may be served first. The owner of the *res* may obtain the consent of the claimant to release the *res*—or to refrain from arresting it—by giving bail (which is given to the court) to the claimant's satisfaction. Normally, however, the claimant will not require bail, but will be satisfied with a guarantee or undertaking given out of court, typically by a bank or insurance company.

10.2.2   The original purpose of the system for the provision of security for the claim in proceedings *in rem* was to ensure that a successful claimant could enforce the judgment against assets in England. What, however, is the position where the dispute is to be resolved by the courts of another country or by arbitrators? Is the claimant entitled to obtain security in England for his claim in a situation where the English court is not the proper forum for the determination of the substantive dispute? Before the entry into force of section 26 of the Civil Jurisdiction and Judgments Act 1982 the view adopted by the courts was that the purpose of the jurisdiction *in rem* was to provide security in respect of the claim *in rem*, not to provide security in some other proceedings—for example, arbitration proceedings.[78] The position was radically altered by section 26 of the 1982 Act (which has since been amended and partially replaced by section 11 of the Arbitration Act 1996).

---

[73] See CPR PD 25 paras 7 and 8.
[74] *Anton Piller KG v Manufacturing Processes Ltd* [1976] Ch 55.
[75] *Columbia Picture Industries v Robinson* [1987] Ch 38; *Universal Thermosensors Ltd v Hibben* [1992] 1 WLR 840.
[76] For a discussion of the circumstances in which proceedings may be brought *in rem*, see ch 8.
[77] CPR 61.5(8).
[78] See Robert Goff LJ in *The Andria now renamed Vasso* [1984] QB 477, 490.

10.2.3 Section 26 of the 1982 Act (as amended) provides:

(1) Where in England and Wales ... a court stays or dismisses Admiralty proceedings on the ground that the dispute in question should be submitted to the determination of the courts of another part of the United Kingdom or of an overseas country, the court may, if in those proceedings property has been arrested or bail or other security has been given to prevent or to obtain release from arrest—

(a) order that the property arrested be retained as security for the satisfaction of an award or judgment which—
   (i) is given in respect of the dispute in the legal proceedings in favour of which those proceedings are stayed or dismissed; and
   (ii) is enforceable in England and Wales ... ; or
(b) order that the stay or dismissal of those proceedings be conditional on the provision of equivalent security for the satisfaction of any such award or judgment.

(2) Where a court makes an order under subsection (1), it may attach such conditions to the order as it thinks fit, in particular conditions with respect to the institution or prosecution of the relevant legal proceedings.

(3) Subject to any provision made by rules of court and to any necessary modifications, the same law and practice shall apply in relation to property retained in pursuance of an order made by a court under subsection (1) as would apply if it were held for the purposes of proceedings in that court.

10.2.4 Section 11 of the Arbitration Act 1996 makes similar provision for cases where a *res* is arrested to provide security for arbitration proceedings:

(1) Where Admiralty proceedings are stayed on the ground that the dispute in question should be submitted to arbitration, the court granting the stay may, if in those proceedings property has been arrested or bail or other security has been given to prevent or to obtain release from arrest—

(a) order that the property arrested be retained as security for the satisfaction of any award given in the arbitration in respect of that dispute, or
(b) order that the stay of those proceedings be conditional on the provision of equivalent security for the satisfaction of any such award.

(2) Subject to any provision made by rules of court and to any necessary modifications, the same law and practice shall apply in relation to property retained in pursuance of an order as would apply if it were held for the purposes of proceedings in the court making the order.

10.2.5 The effect of these sections is both to clarify the law and sweep away the unnecessarily complex rules formulated by the courts.[79] The position under section 26 of the 1982 Act and section 11 of the 1996 Act is that a court which stays or dismisses a claim *in rem* may order the retention of the *res* which has been arrested or may order that the stay or dismissal of proceedings be conditional on the provision of security for the award or judgment. It is important to note, however, that the statutory jurisdiction under section 26 and section 11 is linked to the court's jurisdiction over the *res*. The statutory provisions should not apply in cases where the court is incompetent from the outset (for example, where the proceedings commenced *in rem* is not within

---

[79] See *The Andria now renamed Vasso* [1984] QB 477; *The Tuyuti* [1984] QB 838.

the jurisdiction of the admiralty court as defined by the Supreme Court Act 1981).[80] Where the court does not have jurisdiction over the claim, the proper course is for the court to dismiss the claim and order the unconditional release of any security obtained by reason of the arrest.

10.2.6   The power to order the retention of arrested property or other security may be exercised, first, when the stay of proceedings is granted in favour of the courts of another Member State on the basis of the provisions of the Brussels I Regulation[81] or, secondly, under the court's inherent jurisdiction (for example, where a stay is granted on the basis of the doctrine of *forum non conveniens*[82] or on the basis of a jurisdiction agreement in favour of the courts of another country)[83] or, thirdly, on the ground that the matter should be referred to arbitration whether in England or abroad.[84] However, in cases within the third category—where the court grants a mandatory stay on the basis of an arbitration agreement under section 9 of the Arbitration Act 1996 (which implements Article II of the New York Convention of 1958)—the court cannot attach conditions to the grant of the stay.[85] Under section 11 of the 1996 Act the court may either maintain the arrest or discharge the vessel. Similarly, where a mandatory stay is granted under the Brussels I Regulation, the court may not impose any conditions—for the simple reason that, where the grant of a stay is mandatory, it is not open to the court to lift the stay in the event of a condition not being complied with.[86] Nevertheless, if the defendant wants to obtain the release of the *res*, he has little choice but to put up security.

10.2.7   Under a previous version of the rules of court, the claimant was required to make full and frank disclosure of material facts at the time of the application for arrest;[87] failure to do so could lead to the court making an unconditional order for the release of the *res* and the discharge of any security obtained by reason of the arrest.[88] However, the rules of court were amended and, under the current version of the Civil Procedure Rules, it is normally the case that a warrant of arrest is issued as of right on the claimant making the necessary declaration.[89]

10.2.8   The statutory provisions apply whether or not foreign proceedings (or arbitration proceedings) on the substance of the dispute have already been commenced.[90] It follows that if arbitration has been commenced a claimant who has not obtained security in the arbitration proceedings may quite properly issue a claim form *in rem* for the sole purpose of obtaining security.[91] Where a stay has been granted without the ship having been arrested, the court may lift the stay temporarily in order that

---

[80] Hobhouse J in *The Nordglimt* [1988] QB 183, 204.
[81] Hobhouse J in *The Nordglimt* [1988] QB 183, 204.
[82] *The Emre II* [1989] 2 Lloyd's Rep 182.
[83] *The Havhelt* [1993] 1 Lloyd's Rep 523.
[84] See, eg, *The Jalamatsya* [1987] 2 Lloyd's Rep 164.
[85] *The World Star* [1986] 2 Lloyd's Rep 274.
[86] L Collins *et al, Dicey, Morris and Collins on The Conflict of Laws* (London, Sweet & Maxwell, 14th edn, 2006) para 8–039.
[87] *The Andria now named Vasso* [1984] QB 477.
[88] *The Kherson* [1992] 2 Lloyd's Rep 261. This case was mistakenly decided under the old rules, notwithstanding the fact that new rules had entered into force.
[89] CPR 61.5(4).
[90] *The Nordglimt* [1988] 1 QB 183.
[91] Sheen J in *The Jalamatsya* [1987] 2 Lloyd's Rep 164, 165.

arrest may be effected and an order made under section 26 or section 11, as the case may be.[92]

10.2.9 The final point concerns the question of discretion. The effect of the statutory provisions is that the court may, first, order the retention of the property which has been arrested or, secondly, order the unconditional release of the property or, thirdly, in cases where a stay is not mandatory (under either the Arbitration Act 1996 or the Brussels I Regulation), order the release of the property on condition that the defendant provide equivalent security for the claim.[93] How should the court exercise its discretion? In cases where the third option is available, the court will, as a general rule, only exercise its discretion to release the *res* on the provision of sufficient security to cover the amount of the claim with interest and costs on the basis of the claimant's 'reasonably arguable best case'.[94] Where, for example, the court is of the view that the claim is 'certain or nearly certain'[95] to fail or the claim is 'likely to fail'[96] or will 'probably'[97] fail, the proper course of action is to release the *res* free from conditions. Where, however, the claimant has 'an arguable claim on fact or law'[98] security should not be released.[99] The fact that, because the *res* is heavily mortgaged, it seems unlikely that the claimant will recover anything from its value is not a basis on which the court should exercise its discretion to order the unconditional release of the *res*.[100] Where the court has little evidence on the likelihood of the claim being successful in legal proceedings abroad, the court may, by virtue of the powers conferred by section 26(2), order that, as a condition of the *res* being retained, the claimant must provide security for the losses which the owner of the *res* is likely to sustain as a result of the *res* not being released.[101]

10.3 JURISDICTION TO GRANT PROVISIONAL MEASURES: PROCEEDINGS *IN PERSONAM*

Background: The Position at Common Law

10.3.1 Where England is the forum for the trial of the claim, the court has jurisdiction to grant the full range of provisional measures available under English law in relation to those proceedings.[102] So, where the English court has substantive jurisdiction over a defendant (whether under the Brussels I Regulation or the traditional rules),

---

[92] *The Silver Athens (No 2)* [1986] 2 Lloyd's Rep 583.
[93] *The Bazias 3, The Bazias 4* [1993] QB 673.
[94] *The Moschanthy* [1971] 1 Lloyd's Rep 37; *The Bazias 3, The Bazias 4* [1993] QB 673.
[95] Brandon J in *The Moschanthy* [1971] 1 Lloyd's Rep 37, 43.
[96] Saville J in *The Havhelt* [1993] 1 Lloyd's Rep 523, 525.
[97] Saville J in *The Havhelt* [1993] 1 Lloyd's Rep 523, 526.
[98] Brandon J in *The Moschanthy* [1971] 1 Lloyd's Rep 37, 43.
[99] See also *The Yuta Bondarovskaya* [1998] 2 Lloyd's Rep 357.
[100] *The Havhelt* [1993] 1 Lloyd's Rep 523.
[101] *The Havhelt* [1993] 1 Lloyd's Rep 523.
[102] Case C–391/95 *Van Uden Maritime BV v Firma Deco-Line* [1998] ECR I–7091; Case C–99/96 *Mietz v Intership Yachting Sneek BV* [1999] ECR I–2277. See also *Spray Network NV v Telenor AS* [2004] ILPr 586 (Supreme Court, Netherlands).

the court may, where appropriate, grant interim relief; in such cases, because the court has jurisdiction over the substance of the case, it also derives its jurisdiction to grant interim relief (on both pre-judgment and post-judgment bases) from the jurisdictional rule conferring substantive jurisdiction.[103] In such cases, the restrictions which apply where jurisdiction is derived from Article 31 of the Brussels I Regulation are not relevant.[104] More problems have been caused by cases where the court has no jurisdiction over the claim or where, although the defendant is amenable to the court's jurisdiction, either no proceedings have been brought in England or English proceedings have been stayed.

10.3.2   As one leading commentator has observed:

Common sense would suggest that if proceedings are pending in one country, and the defendant's assets are situate in another country, the plaintiff ought to be able to obtain protective or interim relief by way of attachment in the latter country. That is indeed the law in most countries.[105]

The process whereby English law ultimately attained the common sense position—that is, the court may grant an injunction if it has *in personam* jurisdiction over the person against whom the injunction is sought[106]—is somewhat tortuous. As the common law singularly failed to respond to the requirements of international litigation, the answer had to be provided by legislation.

10.3.3   In *Siskina (Owners of cargo lately laden on board) v Distos Compania Naviera SA*[107] the House of Lords, relying on the principle that an injunction may be granted only in support of the invasion of a legal or equitable right which is enforceable in England,[108] held that, if the court had no jurisdiction over the substantive claim, there was no jurisdiction to grant a freezing injunction (under what is now CPR PD 6B para 3.1(2)) in relation to assets located in England. Although the *Siskina* doctrine was the subject of widespread criticism, it was subsequently applied in a number of cases[109] and confirmed by the Privy Council.[110]

10.3.4   The effect of the *Siskina* doctrine was that provisional measures could be granted only in support of a claim over which the court had jurisdiction by virtue of the defendant's presence or submission or on the basis of one of the grounds of long-arm jurisdiction (other than what is now CPR PD 6B para 3.1(2)). For example, in *Channel Tunnel Group Ltd v Balfour Beatty Construction Ltd*[111] the House of Lords held that the court had jurisdiction to grant an interlocutory injunction under section 37(1) of the

---

[103]   *Masri v Consolidated Contractors International (UK) Ltd (No 2)* [2009] QB 450. See also *Masri v Consolidated Contractors International (UK) Ltd (No 4)* [2009] 2 WLR 699.

[104]   *Ibid.* See also *Re Grant of an Extraterritorial Injunction* [2009] ILPr 22 (Supreme Court, Austria).

[105]   L Collins, 'The Siskina Again: an Opportunity Missed' (1996) 112 *LQR* 8.

[106]   Lord Scott in *Fourie v Le Roux* [2007] 1 WLR 320, 332 (at [30]).

[107]   [1979] AC 210. K Lipstein, [1978] *CLJ* 241.

[108]   *North London Railway Co v Great Northern Railway Co* (1883) 11 QBD 30.

[109]   *The Veracruz I* [1992] 1 Lloyd's Rep 353 (P Marshall, 'The conditional or anticipatory *Mareva* injunction' [1992] *LMCLQ* 161; L Collins, 'The Legacy of *The Siskina*' (1992) 108 *LQR* 175); *Zucker v Tyndalls Holdings Plc* [1992] 1 WLR 1127 (DC Wilde, 'Jurisdiction to grant interlocutory (*Mareva*) injunctions' [1993] *LMCLQ* 309).

[110]   *Mercedes Benz AG v Leiduck* [1996] 1 AC 284. N Andrews, [1996] *CLJ* 12; L Collins, 'The Siskina Again: an Opportunity Missed' (1996) 112 *LQR* 8; IR Scott, 'Extra-territorial Jurisdiction and *Mareva* Relief' (1996) 15 *CJQ* 6.

[111]   [1993] AC 334.

Supreme Court Act 1981 in support of an arbitration being conducted in Belgium.[112] Since the defendant was duly served with the originating process in England, the court's jurisdiction was not excluded by the *Siskina* doctrine. Whether or not the defendant was entitled to a stay—for example, on the basis that another court was clearly a more appropriate forum or on the basis of a jurisdiction clause or arbitration agreement— was an irrelevant consideration.[113] However, the court would have had no jurisdiction to grant provisional measures in support of the Belgian arbitration if the plaintiff had not been able to effect service on the defendant in England.

10.3.5 From a policy point of view the common law position was not easy to defend and it is widely thought that '[t]he law took a wrong turning in *The Siskina*'.[114] The effects of the *Siskina* doctrine—at least in relation to the court's jurisdiction to grant provisional measures in support of proceedings abroad—were finally reversed by legislation. The relevant statutory provisions empower the court to grant provisional measures in support of any legal or arbitral proceedings which have been (or will be) commenced abroad.

Jurisdiction to Grant Provisional Measures in Support of Foreign Proceedings

Section 25 of the Civil Jurisdiction and Judgments Act 1982

10.3.6 Article 31 of the Brussels I Regulation[115] provides:

Application may be made to the courts of a Member State for such provisional, including protective, measures as may be available under the law of that State, even if, under this Regulation, the courts of another Member State have jurisdiction as to the substance of the matter.

In *Reichert v Dresdner Bank (No 2)*, the Court of Justice indicated that provisional measures falling within the scope of Article 31 are measures which, in matters within the scope of Article 1, 'are intended to preserve a factual or legal situation so as to safeguard rights'.[116] This approach means that 'a measure ordering the hearing of a witness for the purpose of enabling the applicant to decide whether or not to bring a case, determine whether it would be well founded and assess the relevance of evidence which might be adduced in that regard' is not a provisional measure for the purposes of Article 31.[117] Within the context of Article 31, courts making orders in support of substantive proceedings in another Member State 'must take into consideration the need to impose conditions or stipulations such as to guarantee their provisional or protective character'.[118] So, if a court orders a defendant to make an interim payment

---

[112] In the exercise of its discretion, however, the House of Lords declined to grant the relief sought by the plaintiff.

[113] Lord Browne-Wilkinson at [1993] AC 334, 343. See also *Phonogram Ltd v Def American Ltd* The Times, 7 October 1994.

[114] Lord Nicholls in *Mercedes Benz AG v Leiduck* [1996] 1 AC 284, 307. See L Collins, 'The End of The Siskina?' (1993) 109 *LQR* 342.

[115] See G Maher and BJ Rodger, 'Provisional and Protective Remedies: The British Experience of the Brussels Convention' (1999) 48 *ICLQ* 302.

[116] Case C–261/90 [1992] ECR I–2149, para 34.

[117] Case C–104/03 *St Paul Dairy Industries NV v Unibel Exser BVBA* [2005] ECR I–3481, para 25.

[118] Case C–391/95 *Van Uden Maritime BV v Firma Deco-Line* [1998] ECR I–7091, para 41.

to the claimant, the order will not qualify as a provisional or protective measure for the purposes of the Brussels I Regulation unless, in the event of the claimant being unsuccessful, repayment to the defendant of the sum awarded is guaranteed.[119] Furthermore, such a measure must relate only to specific assets located within the jurisdiction of the court making the order.[120] According to the Court of Justice in *Van Uden Maritime BV v Firma Deco-Line,* jurisdiction to grant provisional measures under Article 31 of the Brussels I Regulation is 'conditional on ... the existence of a real connecting link between the subject-matter of the measures sought and the territorial jurisdiction of the ... State of the court before which those measures are sought'.[121]

10.3.7 Because of the decision of the House of Lords in the *Siskina* case, Article 31 of the Brussels I Regulation does not give the English court jurisdiction to grant provisional measures unless the court also has jurisdiction over the claim.[122] Section 25 of the Civil Jurisdiction and Judgments Act 1982, however, reverses the effect of the *Siskina* doctrine, whether the substantive proceedings are being conducted in another Member State or in any other country.[123] Although the original impetus for the enactment of section 25 of the 1982 Act was the need to give effect to the Brussels Convention, the current position is that the English courts have 'power to grant interim relief in aid of substantive proceedings elsewhere of whatever kind and wherever taking place'.[124] There can be no doubt that the foreign proceedings to which section 25 is referring are proceedings on the substance of the matter and that the term 'proceedings' in section 25 means judicial proceedings and does not extend to arbitration proceedings.[125]

10.3.8 Service may be effected out of the jurisdiction with the permission of the court if '[a] claim is made for an interim remedy under section 25(1) of the Civil Jurisdiction and Judgments Act 1982'.[126] For the purposes of the court's jurisdiction to grant provisional measures in support of foreign proceedings, the domicile of the defendant and the basis on which the foreign court assumed jurisdiction are irrelevant. The English court may grant interim relief in support of French proceedings whether the French court assumed jurisdiction over a defendant domiciled in a Member State under Chapter II of the Brussels I Regulation[127] or over a defendant not domiciled in a Member State under its traditional rules.[128] The court may also

---

[119] Case C–391/95 *Van Uden Maritime BV v Firma Deco-Line* [1998] ECR I–7091, para 47; Case C–99/96 *Mietz v Intership Yachting Sneek BV* [1999] ECR I–2277, para 43.

[120] Case C–391/95 *Van Uden Maritime BV v Firma Deco-Line* [1998] ECR I–7091, para 47; Case C–99/96 *Mietz v Intership Yachting Sneek BV* [1999] ECR I–2277, para 43. See also *Wermuth v Wermuth* [2003] 1 WLR 942; *Comet Group Plc v Unika Computer SA* [2004] ILPr 10.

[121] Case C–391/95 [1998] ECR I–7091, para 40.

[122] Kerr LJ in *Babanaft International Co SA v Bassatne* [1990] Ch 13, 30.

[123] Originally, s 25 of the 1982 Act was limited to cases falling within the scope of the Brussels regime. However, it was extended to all foreign proceedings by the Civil Jurisdiction and Judgments Act 1982 (Interim Relief) Order 1997, SI 1997/302. See D Capper, 'Further Trans-Jurisdictional Effects of Mareva Injunctions' (1998) 17 *CJQ* 35.

[124] Millett LJ in *Crédit Suisse Fides Trust SA v Cuoghi* [1998] QB 818, 825.

[125] Lawrence Collins LJ in *ETI Euro Telecom International NV v Republic of Bolivia* [2009] 1 WLR 665, 682–86 (at [70]–[98]).

[126] CPR PD 6B para 3.1(5).

[127] *Republic of Haiti v Duvalier* [1990] 1 QB 202.

[128] *X v Y* [1990] 1 QB 220.

grant interim relief in support of proceedings abroad where the foreign proceedings are entirely domestic.[129] In a suitable case, the court may grant a worldwide freezing injunction in support of foreign proceedings.[130]

The Exercise of the Power

DISCRETION

10.3.9   Section 25(2) of the 1982 Act provides:

On an application for any interim relief under subsection (1) the court may refuse to grant that relief if, in the opinion of the court, the fact that the court has no jurisdiction apart from this section in relation to the subject-matter of the proceedings in question makes it inexpedient for the court to grant it.

There is an argument for saying that each Member State is required to make available, in aid of court proceedings in other Member States, such provisional and protective measures as its own domestic law would afford if its courts were trying the substantive action.[131] However, the better view is that the courts have discretion over the granting of provisional measures in support of foreign proceedings whether or not the foreign proceedings are taking place in a Member State.[132] The most significant questions in the context of section 25 concern the way in which the court should exercise its discretion.

10.3.10   The significance to be attached to section 25(2) was considered by the Court of Appeal in *Crédit Suisse Fides Trust SA v Cuoghi*.[133] The plaintiff, having started proceedings against the defendant in Switzerland, obtained from the English court a freezing injunction to restrain the defendant, who was resident and domiciled in England, from dealing with his assets worldwide. The defendant applied for the injunction to be limited to his assets in England. The Court of Appeal took the view that the injunction should not be varied. Although section 25(2) is not particularly well drafted its purpose is clear enough:

On an application for interim relief under subsection (1), the court is not bound to grant relief but may decline to do so if in its opinion the fact that it is exercising an ancillary jurisdiction in support of substantive proceedings elsewhere make it inexpedient to grant it. It is the ancillary or subordinate nature of the jurisdiction rather than its source which is material, and the test is one of expediency.[134]

10.3.11   There is one situation where it would appear that the court is required by the Brussels I Regulation to order protective measures in favour of a judgment creditor. Where the claimant obtains permission to enforce a foreign judgment in a Member State under Chapter III, the defendant may appeal against the enforcement order.[135]

---

[129] *Alltrans Inc v Interdom Holdings Ltd* [1991] 4 All ER 458.
[130] *Crédit Suisse Fides Trust SA v Cuoghi* [1998] QB 818. See para 10.4.15.
[131] Staughton LJ in *Republic of Haiti v Duvalier* [1990] 1 QB 202, 212.
[132] L Collins, 'Provisional and Protective Measures in International Litigation' in *Essays in International Litigation and the Conflict of Laws* (Oxford, Clarendon Press, 1994) 37.
[133] [1998] QB 818.
[134] Millett LJ at [1998] QB 818, 825–6.
[135] Brussels I Reg, Art 43.

In this situation, it is provided that 'no measures of enforcement may be taken other than protective measures taken against the property of the party against whom enforcement has been sought'.[136] A claimant who obtains an enforcement order, the effect of which is suspended pending the defendant's appeal, is entitled to protective measures from the courts of the Member State where enforcement is sought.[137]

THE IMPACT OF AN EXCLUSIVE JURISDICTION CLAUSE

10.3.12   In a situation where the court may, in principle, grant a freezing injunction in the claimant's favour, what significance, if any, should the court attach to an agreement by the parties to refer the dispute to the court of another country? In cases covered by the Brussels I Regulation the existence of a jurisdiction clause in favour of another Member State does not affect the jurisdiction of the English court to grant provisional or protective measures. Where, for example, the French courts have exclusive jurisdiction by virtue of Article 23, the English court may, by virtue of Article 31 and section 25 of the 1982 Act, grant provisional measures.[138] Similarly, in cases governed by schedule 4 to the Civil Jurisdiction and Judgments Act 1982, a jurisdiction clause in favour of the courts of one part of the United Kingdom is no obstacle to provisional measures being granted by the courts of another part.[139] Any other solution would be wholly inconsistent with the framework established by the Brussels I Regulation and the 1982 Act.

10.3.13   In cases where the parties have entered a jurisdiction agreement which is not regulated by Article 23, the court should be equally prepared to grant provisional measures notwithstanding the fact that the parties have agreed to the exclusive jurisdiction of a foreign court. If the originating process cannot be served on the defendant in England it may be served out of the jurisdiction with the court's permission.[140] Where the parties have agreed to refer their disputes to the exclusive jurisdiction of the courts of a particular country, the English court should, as a general rule, hold the parties to their bargain as regards the substantive dispute between them. However, unless there are very clear words to the contrary in the agreement itself, an application for provisional or protective measures should not be regarded as falling within the scope of the jurisdiction agreement.[141] So, in a case where an Englishman and a New Yorker enter a contract which contains an exclusive jurisdiction clause in favour of the courts of New York, if the New Yorker starts proceedings in England and applies for an injunction freezing the Englishman's assets, the court should not be deterred from granting interim relief by the fact that the defendant may apply for (and will normally be entitled to) a stay of the substantive proceedings.[142] The same approach should be adopted in cases where the claimant starts proceedings *in rem* in England

---

[136]   Brussels I Reg, Art 49.

[137]   Case 119/84 *Capelloni v Pelkmans* [1985] ECR 3147. See G Hogan, 'The Judgments Convention and *Mareva* Injunctions in the United Kingdom and Ireland' (1989) 14 *EL Rev* 191, 200–4.

[138]   L Collins, 'Provisional Measures, the Conflict of Laws and the Brussels Convention' (1981) 1 *YBEL* 249, 258.

[139]   *Coca-Cola Bottlers (Ulster) Ltd v The Concentrate Manufacturing Co of Ireland, t/a Seven-Up International* [1990] NI 77 (High Court, Northern Ireland).

[140]   CPR 6.36, PD 6B para 3.1(5).

[141]   See the judgment of Lord Denning MR in *The Lisboa* [1980] 2 Lloyd's Rep 546, 548–9.

[142]   See *Channel Tunnel Group Ltd v Balfour Beatty Construction Ltd* [1993] AC 334.

notwithstanding the existence of a jurisdiction clause in favour of the courts of another country. Although the English proceedings *in rem* will normally be stayed on account of the jurisdiction clause, the court may order the retention of the *res* which has been arrested or order that the stay or dismissal of proceedings be conditional on the provision of security.[143]

THE SIGNIFICANCE OF PARALLEL PROCEEDINGS IN ANOTHER MEMBER STATE

10.3.14   In the context of the Brussels I Regulation, where there are parallel proceedings between the same parties involving the same cause of action before the courts of two or more Member States, any court other than the court first seised must decline jurisdiction or stay its proceedings.[144] In *Republic of Haiti v Duvalier*[145] it was argued that, because the substantive proceedings had been brought in France, the effect of the *lis pendens* rule was to deprive the English court of jurisdiction to grant provisional measures under section 25(1) of the 1982 Act in support of those proceedings. The Court of Appeal had no hesitation in rejecting this argument:

> Either a claim for interim relief does not involve or concern any cause of action, or it is based on a new and distinct cause of action created by section 25.[146]

According to this approach, the English court's jurisdiction over a substantive claim is not removed by earlier French proceedings involving only provisional measures.[147] Indeed, it would make nonsense of the framework of the Brussels I Regulation if, for the purposes of Article 27, the main proceedings in one Member State and the application for a freezing injunction in aid of those proceedings in another Member State were regarded as 'involving the same cause of action'.

POST-JUDGMENT PROVISIONAL MEASURES

10.3.15   In those cases falling within the scope of Article 1 a potential jurisdictional problem arises as regards post-judgment measures. Article 22(5) of the Brussels I Regulation provides that, in proceedings concerned with the enforcement of judgments, the courts of the Member State in which the judgment is to be enforced shall have exclusive jurisdiction.[148] It has been argued that the effect of Article 22(5) is that, where a claimant intends to enforce a judgment in another Member State, the English court is precluded from granting a post-judgment freezing injunction in respect of the judgment debtor's assets.[149] This argument is in part based on the framework of the Brussels I Regulation as a whole, which treats post-judgment protective measures as part of the enforcement process.[150]

---

[143] Civil Jurisdiction and Judgments Act 1982, s 26(1). See section 10.2.
[144] Brussels I Reg, Art 27. See section 9.1.
[145] [1990] 1 QB 202.
[146] Staughton LJ at [1990] 1 QB 202, 211.
[147] *Miles Platt Ltd v Townroe Ltd* [2003] 1 All ER (Comm) 561.
[148] See paras 5.1.29–5.1.30.
[149] See G Hogan, 'The Judgments Convention and *Mareva* Injunctions in the United Kingdom and Ireland' (1989) 14 *EL Rev* 191, 197–200.
[150] See, in particular, Brussels I Reg, Art 47.

10.3.16 The English cases, however, reject this interpretation. According to the analysis of Kerr LJ in *Babanaft International Co SA v Bassatne*,[151] although proceedings concerning the enforcement of judgments are within the exclusive jurisdiction of the state where the assets are situated, there is no reason why the courts of other states should not have jurisdiction to grant provisional measures (such as a freezing injunction over foreign assets), pending enforcement of the judgment. According to the case law of the Court of Justice, measures of enforcement are measures involving 'the use of force or constraint, or the dispossession of movables and immovables in order to obtain the physical implementation of judgments'.[152] As a freezing injunction involves no such element of force, constraint, or the dispossession of property, an application for a post-judgment freezing injunction is not to be viewed as 'proceedings concerned with the enforcement of judgments' for the purposes of Article 22(5); such an injunction is correctly characterised as an interim measure: post-judgment freezing injunctions 'may pave the way for execution, but they are not proceedings concerned with enforcement of judgments'.[153] The same analysis may be applied to the grant of an independent post-judgment disclosure order under Part 71 of the Civil Procedure Rules[154] in support of foreign enforcement proceedings.[155] It has been argued, however, that a disclosure order which is not ancillary to a freezing injunction cannot properly be regarded as a provisional measure.[156]

10.3.17 The effect of Article 47(1) of the Brussels I Regulation is that, where a judgment granted by the court of another Member State has been registered in England, the English court has jurisdiction to grant provisional, including protective, measures in accordance with English law. Nevertheless, such protective measures are regulated by Article 31 and are subject to the limitations imposed by that provision. In *Banco Nacional de Commercio Exterior SNC v Empresa de Telecommunicaciones de Cuba SA*[157] an application was made to the English court for a worldwide freezing injunction in support of proceedings to enforce an Italian judgment in England. The Court of Appeal held that, while there is no doubt that the English court may grant a domestic freezing order in this context, the court is not entitled to grant a worldwide freezing order in support of English enforcement; as regards assets not located in England, the requirement laid down by the Court of Justice in the *Van Uden* case[158] that there be a 'real connecting link' between the subject-matter of the measures sought and the territorial jurisdiction of the English court is not satisfied.

---

[151] [1990] Ch 13, 35.

[152] Case C–261/90 *Reichert v Dresdner Bank (No 2)* [1992] ECR I–2149, para 28.

[153] Lawrence Collins LJ in *Masri v Consolidated Contractors International (UK) Ltd (No 2)* [2009] QB 450, 484–5 (at [124]).

[154] Formerly RSC, Ord 48.

[155] L Collins *et al, Dicey, Morris and Collins on The Conflict of Laws* (London, Sweet & Maxwell, 14th edn, 2006) para 11–418.

[156] P Kaye, 'Property Restraint and Disclosure Orders in the English Courts: Extraterritorial Developments' (1989) 10 *Company Lawyer* 227, 230.

[157] [2007] 2 Lloyd's Rep 484. L Merrett, 'Worldwide Freezing Injunctions in Europe' [2007] *CLJ* 495.

[158] Case C–391/95 *Van Uden Maritime BV v Firma Deco-Line* [1998] ECR I–709. See para 10.4.12.

Jurisdiction to Grant Provisional Measures in Support of Arbitration Proceedings

10.3.18 The Arbitration Act 1996 determines the circumstances in which the English court may intervene in arbitration proceedings.[159] Section 44(1) provides that, in the absence of a contrary agreement by the parties,[160] the court has, in relation to arbitration proceedings, the same power of making orders about various matters as it has in relation to legal proceedings. One of the matters listed in section 44(2) is 'the making of an interim injunction or the appointment of a receiver'.[161] Where an application is made under section 44, the originating process may be served out of the jurisdiction with the court's permission.[162] In a suitable case, the court will make an order under section 44 'to help the arbitral process to operate effectively'.[163]

10.3.19 The court's power to grant interim relief under section 44 of the 1996 Act applies regardless of the seat of arbitration and whether or not the seat of arbitration has been designated.[164] This does not mean, however, that the English courts will readily grant freezing injunctions or other interim relief in support of foreign arbitrations. Section 2(3) of the Act emphasises that the court may refuse to exercise the powers conferred by section 44 if:

in the opinion of the court, the fact that the seat of arbitration is outside England and Wales ..., or that when designated or determined the seat is likely to be outside England and Wales ..., makes it inappropriate to do so.

In a situation where an application is made for a worldwide freezing injunction, the court will not consider making such an order under section 44 of the 1996 Act unless the case has a sufficiently strong connection with England (for example, because there are substantial assets of the defendant situated within the jurisdiction).[165]

10.3.20 It must always be remembered that where the seat of arbitration is located in a foreign country the court of that country is 'the natural court for the source of interim relief'.[166] If, in a case involving an arbitration being conducted abroad, an application for interim relief is made in England, it is for the claimant to show why the English court, rather than the relevant foreign forum, should grant relief. If, for example, a particular form of relief is not available under the law of the seat, this is

---

[159] Arbitration Act 1996, s 1(c). For the position prior to the 1996 Act, see *Channel Tunnel Group Ltd v Balfour Beatty Construction Ltd* [1993] AC 334.

[160] Where parties have agreed to ICSID arbitration (see paras 24.5.8–24.5.10), they have agreed not to seek interim measures from national courts (see *ETI Euro Telecom International NV v Republic of Bolivia* [2009] 1 WLR 665) and neither party may invoke the court's powers under s 44(1) of the 1996 Act.

[161] The correctness of the apparent suggestion of the Court of Justice in Case C–391/95 *Van Uden Maritime BV v Firma Deco-Line* [1998] ECR I–709, paras 24–5 that, in cases where the defendant is domiciled in a Member State, the court's power to grant provisional measures in support of arbitration proceedings is derived solely from Art 24 of the Brussels Convention (now Art 31 of the Regulation) has been doubted: L Collins *et al, Dicey, Morris and Collins on The Conflict of Laws* (London, Sweet & Maxwell, 14th edn, 2006) para 8–034 n 93.

[162] CPR 62.5.

[163] See Teare J in *Emmott v Michael Wilson & Partners Ltd (No 2)* [2009] 1 Lloyd's Rep 233, 245 (at [90]), citing an extract from Departmental Advisory Committee, *Report on the Arbitration Bill* (1996), para 214.

[164] Arbitration Act 1996, s 2(3).

[165] *Mobil Cerro Negro Ltd v Petroleos de Venezuela SA* [2008] 1 Lloyd's Rep 684.

[166] Lord Mustill in *Channel Tunnel Group Ltd v Balfour Beatty Construction Ltd* [1993] AC 334, 368.

a factor which the English court has to weigh in the balance. It does not follow, however, that the absence of a remedy in the foreign forum would, without more, justify the intervention of the English court. The court should be wary about intervening in a foreign arbitration if there is a danger that it will come into conflict with the courts of the seat.[167]

10.3.21   The relationship between the courts' powers under section 44 of the 1996 Act and the Brussels I Regulation is unclear. The most straightforward view is that the Regulation has no bearing on the operation of section 44; if the grant of provisional measures in support of arbitration concerns 'arbitration', such measures fall within the fourth exception to Article 1. However, in *Van Uden Maritime BV v Firma Deco-Line*, the Court of Justice ruled that, even in cases where the parties have agreed to refer their substantive dispute to arbitration, provisional measures do not 'concern ... arbitration as such but the protection of a wide variety of rights'.[168] Furthermore, the approach of the Court of Justice seems to suggest[169] that, in a case where the defendant is domiciled in a Member State, the court's power to grant provisional measures in support of arbitration proceedings is derived solely from Article 31 of the Brussels I Regulation. The implications of this approach would appear to be, first, that in cases where the defendant is domiciled in a Member State, the English courts' powers under section 44 of the 1996 Act are limited to granting measures which can be regarded as 'provisional' as that term is understood by the Court of Justice[170] and, secondly, the grant of provisional measures under section 44 is conditional on the existence of a real connecting link between the subject-matter of the measures sought and the territorial jurisdiction of the English court.[171]

10.4 EXTRATERRITORIAL PROVISIONAL MEASURES[172]

Introduction

10.4.1   Since equitable remedies operate *in personam*, there is no theoretical reason why, as long as the defendant is amenable to the court's jurisdiction, provisional measures granted by the court should be limited to acts performed or assets situated within the jurisdiction.[173] In principle, an act committed by the defendant anywhere in the world in breach of the terms of an injunction or other equitable remedy is a contempt which may be punished by the court. So, the court has power under section 37(1) to appoint a receiver over assets not within the court's jurisdiction[174] even though the appointment may not prove effective without assistance from the

---

[167] See also ch 22.
[168] Case C-391/95 [1998] ECR I-7091, para 33.
[169] Case C-391/95 [1998] ECR I-7091, para 25.
[170] See para 10.3.6.
[171] See para 10.4.12.
[172] D Capper, 'Worldwide *Mareva* Injunctions' (1991) 54 *MLR* 329; L Collins, 'The Territorial Reach of *Mareva* Injunctions' (1989) 105 *LQR* 262; A Rogers, 'The extraterritorial reach of the *Mareva* injunction' [1991] *LMCLQ* 231.
[173] See *BAS Capital Funding Corporation v Medfinco Limited* [2004] ILPr 305, 321.
[174] *Duder v Amsterdamsch Trustees Kantoor* [1902] 2 Ch 132.

appropriate foreign court.[175] Similarly, even though the power to make search orders under section 7 of the Civil Procedure Act 1997 is limited to premises located in England, the court may, under its inherent jurisdiction, make a search order in respect of foreign premises.[176] In *Cook Industries Inc v Galliher*[177] the court ordered a foreign defendant to disclose the contents of a flat in his name situated in France and to permit the flat to be inspected by a French *avocat*. However, the decision in *Protector Alarms Ltd v Maxim Alarms Ltd*[178]—in which the court declined to make a search order in respect of Scottish premises on the basis that it would be better for the plaintiff to seek an equivalent order from the local courts—suggested that search orders ought not to be made against foreign defendants in respect of foreign premises.

10.4.2 In *Altertext Inc v Advanced Data Communications Ltd* Scott J indicated that '*Anton Piller* orders to be executed in respect of foreign premises ought not to be granted … except against defendants over whom the court has unquestionable jurisdiction'.[179] So, in a case where the claimant seeks a search order and the only basis on which the court may exercise jurisdiction over the defendant is one of the heads of CPR PD 6B para 3.1, the search order ought not to be executed until the foreign defendant has been given the opportunity to apply to set aside permission to serve out of the jurisdiction:

It would be wrong … for the court to assume jurisdiction over a foreign defendant on an *ex parte* application, and then to require a mandatory order of an *Anton Piller* character to be executed by the foreign defendant before he has had an opportunity to challenge the court's assumption of jurisdiction over him.[180]

10.4.3 For a number of years the English courts granted freezing injunctions (and ancillary orders) only in relation to assets located within the jurisdiction. In *Ashtiani v Kashi*[181] the Court of Appeal, in refusing to grant an injunction restraining the defendant from dealing with his foreign assets, attached some weight to section 37(3) of the 1981 Act which refers to the power to grant injunctions restraining a party from dealing with assets located 'within the jurisdiction of the High Court'. However, following this decision the pressure on the courts to change their practice became considerable. As Lord Donaldson MR noted in *Derby & Co Ltd v Weldon (Nos 3 & 4)*:

We live in a time of rapidly growing commercial and financial sophistication and it behoves the courts to adapt their practices to meet the current wiles of those defendants who are prepared to devote as much energy to making themselves immune from the courts' orders as to resisting the making of such orders on the merits of their case.[182]

Furthermore, following the decision in *Ashtiani v Kashi* there was an evolution of the practice of the courts in related areas. In *Interpool Ltd v Galani*[183] it was held that

---

[175] *In Re Maudslay, Sons & Field* [1900] 1 Ch 602.
[176] C McLachlan, 'Transnational Applications of *Mareva* Injunctions and *Anton Piller* Orders' (1987) 36 *ICLQ* 669, 678–9.
[177] [1979] Ch 439.
[178] [1978] FSR 442.
[179] [1985] 1 WLR 457, 463.
[180] Scott J at [1985] 1 WLR 457, 462–3.
[181] [1987] QB 888.
[182] [1990] Ch 65, 77.
[183] [1988] QB 738.

an order for the disclosure of assets after judgment under RSC Order 48[184] could extend to assets located outside the jurisdiction and in *Maclaine Watson & Co Ltd v International Tin Council (No 2)*[185] the defendants were ordered to make full disclosure of the location of their assets both within and outside the jurisdiction.

10.4.4   In *Babanaft International Co SA v Bassatne*[186] the Court of Appeal decided that the earlier decision in *Ashtiani v Kashi* was to be regarded as merely a reflection of the way in which the jurisdiction to grant freezing injunctions had been developed in England up to that point.[187] There is nothing to preclude the court from granting a freezing injunction which extends to assets outside the jurisdiction; the purpose of section 37(3) is not to limit the geographical scope of the court's power but to prevent discrimination against defendants who are not domiciled, resident or present within the jurisdiction.

10.4.5   The possibility of granting an extraterritorial or worldwide freezing injunction was confirmed in a number of cases decided towards the end of the 1980s,[188] notably *Republic of Haiti v Duvalier*,[189] *Derby & Co Ltd v Weldon*,[190] *Derby & Co Ltd v Weldon (Nos 3 & 4)*[191] and *Derby & Co Ltd v Weldon (No 6)*.[192] As a result of these cases it can be definitively stated that:

> The jurisdiction of the court to grant a *Mareva* injunction against a person depends not on territorial jurisdiction of the English court over assets within its jurisdiction, but on the unlimited jurisdiction of the English court in personam against any person, whether an individual or a corporation, who is, under English procedure, properly made a party to proceedings pending before the English court.[193]

Although the problems surrounding extraterritorial provisional measures are not limited to freezing injunctions, it is in this area that issues concerning the exercise of discretion to grant extraterritorial measures have arisen most frequently.

10.4.6   In relation to provisional measures with extraterritorial effect, it is easy to fall into the trap of thinking that the limits of the English court's jurisdiction are determined by the *in personam* jurisdiction of the court over the defendant. However, this would be to take too narrow a view of the jurisdictional issue: a key concern is (or ought to be) 'what is permissible … as a matter of international law'.[194] One of the important features of the Court of Appeal's decision in *Masri v Consolidated Contractors International (UK) Ltd (No 2)*[195] is Lawrence Collins LJ's analysis of the jurisdictional limits imposed by international law and it is against the background of this analysis that the practice of the English courts should be understood.

---

[184] Now CPR Pt 71.
[185] [1989] Ch 286.
[186] [1990] Ch 13.
[187] See the judgment of Neill LJ (who was a member of the Court of Appeal in both *Ashtiani v Kashi* [1987] QB 888 and *Babanaft International Co SA v Bassatne* [1990] Ch 13).
[188] For a brief discussion, see N Andrews, [1989] *CLJ* 199.
[189] [1990] 1 QB 202.
[190] [1990] Ch 48.
[191] [1990] Ch 65.
[192] [1990] 1 WLR 1139. D Capper, 'The worldwide *Mareva* marches on' [1991] *LMCLQ* 26.
[193] Dillon LJ in *Derby & Co Ltd v Weldon (No 6)* [1990] 1 WLR 1139, 1149.
[194] A Johnson, 'Interim Injunctions and International Jurisdiction' (2008) 27 *CJQ* 433, 444.
[195] [2009] QB 450.

As Lawrence Collins LJ makes clear: 'the mere fact that an order is *in personam* and is directed towards someone who is subject to the personal jurisdiction of the English court does not exclude the possibility that the making of the order would be contrary to international law or comity, and outside the subject matter jurisdiction of the English court.'[196] To avoid falling foul of the principles of public international law, the court needs to consider '(a) the connection of the person who is the subject of the order with the English jurisdiction; (b) whether what they are ordered to do is exorbitant in terms of jurisdiction; and (c) whether the order has impermissible effects on foreign parties'.[197] It is apparent that 'it is not permissible as a matter of international law for one state to trespass upon the authority of another, by attempting to seize assets situated within the jurisdiction of the foreign state or compelling its citizens to do acts within the foreign state's boundaries'.[198]

Extraterritorial Freezing Injunctions

Conditions and Discretion

10.4.7 The most fundamental conditions for the grant of an extraterritorial freezing injunction are the same as those which apply to any freezing injunction: the claimant must have a good arguable case on the merits and the court must consider that the refusal of an injunction would involve a real risk that a judgment (or award) in favour of the claimant would remain unsatisfied.[199] There is, however, no requirement that the defendant should have any assets within the jurisdiction. In *Derby & Co Ltd v Weldon (Nos 3 & 4)* Lord Donaldson MR stated:

The existence of sufficient assets within the jurisdiction is an excellent reason for confining the *Mareva* jurisdiction to such assets, but other considerations apart, the fewer the assets within the jurisdiction the greater the necessity for taking protective measures in relation to those outside it.[200]

10.4.8 However, the mere fact that the claimant shows a good arguable case and a real risk of English assets being dissipated or hidden—the requisites for a domestic freezing injunction—cannot by itself be sufficient to justify an extraterritorial freezing injunction.[201] Before the court will grant an extraterritorial freezing injunction it must be satisfied that the defendant has insufficient English assets to satisfy the claim (if successful) and that there is a high risk that the defendant will dispose of his foreign assets. Furthermore, since equity does not act in vain, the court will not grant an extraterritorial freezing injunction if 'there is doubt about whether the order will be obeyed and if, should that occur, no real sanction would exist'.[202]

---

[196] [2009] QB 450, 465 (at [35]).
[197] [2009] QB 450, 472 (at [59]).
[198] [2009] QB 450, 469 (at [47]).
[199] *Nimemia Maritime Corporation v Trave Schiffahrtsgesellschaft mbH und Co KG* [1983] 1 WLR 1412.
[200] [1990] Ch 65, 79.
[201] See Parker LJ in *Derby & Co Ltd v Weldon* [1990] Ch 48, 56.
[202] Lord Donaldson MR in *Derby & Co Ltd v Weldon (Nos 3 & 4)* [1990] Ch 65, 81. For the application of this principle, see *Derby & Co Ltd v Weldon (No 6)* [1990] 1 WLR 1139.

10.4.9   When considering what constitutes a 'real sanction' for the purposes of this principle it is important to bear in mind the distinction between cases where a world-wide freezing injunction is sought in the context of substantive proceedings in England, on the one hand, and cases where the application is for worldwide relief in support of foreign proceedings, on the other. In *Derby & Co Ltd v Weldon (Nos 3 & 4)*, a case in which the substantive proceedings were being conducted in England, the Court of Appeal decided that the fact that, in the case of disobedience, the court could bar the defendant's right to defend was a sufficient sanction since, if the court barred the right to defend, the defendant 'would become a fugitive from a final judgment given against it without its explanations having been heard and which might well be enforced against it by other courts'.[203] However, where the application is for a worldwide freezing order in support of foreign proceedings, the court has no effective sanction for disobedience if the defendant is neither resident in England nor has any assets in England.[204] The requirement that there should be a sanction for disobedience does not mean, however, that the court should be satisfied that an extraterritorial freezing injunction will be recognised abroad or otherwise be made binding.[205]

10.4.10   In the context of domestic freezing injunctions, the effect of the injunction is to prevent the removal of the assets from the jurisdiction or their dissipation within the jurisdiction. In cases concerning an application for a freezing injunction in respect of foreign assets, the question arises whether the court may go further and order the transfer of assets from one country to another. In *Derby & Co Ltd v Weldon (No 6)*[206] the Court of Appeal decided that, having regard to the fact that the object of a freezing injunction (and any ancillary orders) is to ensure as far as possible that any judgment obtained by the claimant will be satisfied, a freezing injunction in respect of foreign assets is not necessarily limited to ordering that the assets should be frozen; there is no reason why, in principle, a freezing injunction should not be extended to ordering the transfer of assets from a jurisdiction in which that judgment will not be recognised to a jurisdiction in which the court's judgment will be recognised.[207]

10.4.11   The English courts have recognised that, in the context of an application for a provisional measure which is designed to have extraterritorial effect, the mere fact that the defendant is amenable to the *in personam* jurisdiction of the English court does not of itself justify the grant of such measures. As Lawrence Collins LJ noted in *Masri v Consolidated Contractors International (UK) Ltd (No 2)*[208] (a case involving an application for a receivership order by way of equitable execution), 'an *in personam* order against a person subject to the English jurisdiction may be contrary to international comity'.[209]

10.4.12   Special care is needed in cases governed by the Brussels I Regulation, where an application is made for a freezing injunction in support of substantive

[203] Lord Donaldson MR at [1990] Ch 65, 81.
[204] *Motorola Credit Corpn v Uzan (No 2)* [2004] 1 WLR 113. See also *Belletti v Morici* [2009] ILPr 960.
[205] *Derby & Co Ltd v Weldon (Nos 3 & 4)* [1990] Ch 65; *Derby & Co Ltd v Weldon (No 6)* [1990] 1 WLR 1139. P Kaye, 'Extraterritorial *Mareva* Orders and the Relevance of Enforceability' (1990) 9 *CJQ* 12.
[206] [1990] 1 WLR 1139.
[207] Dillon LJ at [1990] 1 WLR 1139, 1151.
[208] [2009] QB 450.
[209] [2009] QB 450, 469 (at [47]).

proceedings in another Member State. The Court of Justice's decision in *Van Uden Maritime BV v Firma Deco-Line*[210] states that jurisdiction to grant provisional measures under Article 31 of the Brussels I Regulation is 'conditional on … the existence of a real connecting link between the subject-matter of the measures sought and the territorial jurisdiction of the … State of the court before which those measures are sought'.[211] Although the concept of a 'real connecting link' is rather imprecise, there is a strong argument for saying that, as regards freezing injunctions, the English court's jurisdiction to make orders in support of proceedings in another Member State is limited to cases where the assets to be frozen are located in England and/or the defendant is personally subject to the court's jurisdiction (typically, by virtue of being domiciled in England).[212] For example, in *Banco Nacional de Commercio Exterior SNC v Empresa de Telecommunicaciones de Cuba SA*,[213] in the context of proceedings to enforce an Italian judgment against a Cuban company in England, the Court of Appeal granted a domestic freezing order, but refused to grant a worldwide freezing injunction. In the words of Tuckey LJ: 'Any assets here are protected by the domestic order. The worldwide order is only directed at assets outside the jurisdiction. There is therefore no connecting link at all between the subject matter of the measure sought and the territorial jurisdiction of this court.'[214]

10.4.13 From this perspective, the decision of the Court of Appeal in *Republic of Haiti v Duvalier*,[215] in which a worldwide freezing injunction was granted in support of French proceedings, even though the defendant was not domiciled in England and the defendant had no assets in England must be regarded as of questionable authority.[216] Although the fact that the defendant's English solicitors held assets for the defendant abroad hardly qualifies as a 'real connecting link',[217] in *Masri v Consolidated Contractors International (UK) Ltd (No 2)*[218] Lawrence Collins LJ repeated his view that there is nothing in the *Van Uden* ruling which casts any doubt on the correctness of the decision of *Republic of Haiti v Duvalier*. Another borderline case, perhaps, is *Motorola Credit Corpn v Uzan (No 2)*.[219] In this case, the claimant sought worldwide freezing injunctions in support of substantive proceedings in New York. Accordingly, although the Court of Appeal referred to the *Van Uden* case, the provision which is now Article 31 of the Brussels I Regulation was not directly relevant. Nevertheless, the Court of Appeal seems to have proceeded on

---

[210] Case C–391/95 [1998] ECR I–7091.

[211] Case C–391/95[1998] ECR I–7091, para 40.

[212] Although the Court of Justice ruled in Case C–391/95 *Van Uden Maritime BV v Firma Deco-Line* [1998] ECR I–7091, para 47 and Case C–99/96 *Mietz v Intership Yachting Sneek BV* [1999] ECR I–2277, para 43 that an order for interim payment is a provisional measure for the purposes of what is now Art 31 of the Brussels I Reg only if it is limited to specific assets located within the jurisdiction of the court making the order, it is doubtful that this limitation is intended to apply to provisional measures in general.

[213] [2007] 2 Lloyd's Rep 484.

[214] [2007] 2 Lloyd's Rep 484, 489 (at [29]). See also the discussion of Pumfrey J in *SanDisk Corporation v Koninlijke Philips Electronics NV* [2007] ILPr 325, 344–7 (at [49]–[58]).

[215] [1990] 1 QB 202.

[216] E Peel, (1998) 18 *YBEL* 693, 698. See also A Johnson, 'Interim Injunctions and International Jurisdiction' (2008) 27 *CJQ* 433, 440.

[217] For a different view, see L Collins *et al*, *Dicey, Morris and Collins on The Conflict of Laws* (London, Sweet & Maxwell, 13th edn, 2006) para 8–031.

[218] [2009] QB 450, 481 (at [106]).

[219] [2004] 1 WLR 113.

the assumption that the test to be applied is the same whether or not the substantive proceedings are being conducted in a Member State and that the 'real connecting link' requirement has to be satisfied in any case where the court's jurisdiction derives from section 25 of the 1982 Act. The defendants were four members of a Turkish family. As regards the second and third defendants, who neither lived in England, nor had any assets in England, there was no basis for a worldwide order.[220] Conversely, the grant of a worldwide injunction against the fourth defendant, who resided in England and had assets both in England and abroad, was entirely justified. The first defendant's position fell between these two extremes: he did not reside in England and the bulk of his assets were outside the jurisdiction, but he did own a valuable house in London. The Court of Appeal upheld the grant of a worldwide injunction in this situation. Given that the first defendant was not resident or domiciled in England, it may be questioned whether the fact that he owned a house in London should be regarded as sufficient to establish a real connecting link between the jurisdiction of the English court and the assets located outside the jurisdiction.[221]

10.4.14   In *Babanaft International Co SA v Bassatne* Kerr LJ noted that:

some situations, which are nowadays by no means uncommon, cry out—as a matter of justice to [claimants]—for disclosure orders and *Mareva* type injunctions covering foreign assets of defendants even before judgment.[222]

With regard to extraterritorial orders, the courts are conscious that they are operating in a sensitive area and that orders affecting foreign assets should be considered with care. Although the courts have the power to grant an injunction affecting assets which are not located within the jurisdiction, judges frequently state that they are prepared to exercise that power only in exceptional circumstances.[223] Nevertheless, worldwide freezing injunctions 'are nowadays routinely made in cases of international fraud'.[224] As regards injunctions ordering the transfer of foreign assets from one country to another, special care is required in view of the questions of comity which arise. In *Derby & Co Ltd v Weldon (No 6)* Staughton LJ sounded the following note of caution:

If it ever became common practice for English courts not merely to assume jurisdiction over defendants abroad under [CPR 6.36], but also to order them to transfer assets here so that any eventual judgment could be more readily enforced, that would in my view justifiably be regarded as unacceptable chauvinism by the international community.[225]

---

[220] See also *Belletti v Morici* [2009] ILPr 960 (in which the defendants had no connection with England).

[221] Support for this view may be derived from *Banco Nacional de Commercio Exterior SNC v Empresa de Telecommunicaciones de Cuba SA* [2007] 2 Lloyd's Rep 484. See the discussion of L Merrett, 'Worldwide freezing injunctions in Europe' [2008] *LMCLQ* 71.

[222] [1990] Ch 13, 33.

[223] Members of the Court of Appeal have used various phrases to describe the exceptional nature of a freezing injunction covering a defendant's assets outside the jurisdiction. Such injunctions will be granted 'in extreme situations' (Kerr LJ in *Babanaft International Co SA v Bassatne* [1990] Ch 13, 37); 'it will only be in an exceptional case that the court will make such an order' (May LJ in *Derby & Co Ltd v Weldon* [1990] Ch 48, 55); 'cases where it will be appropriate to grant such an injunction will be rare—if not very rare indeed' (Staughton LJ in *Republic of Haiti v Duvalier* [1990] 1 QB 202, 215; a worldwide pre-judgment freezing injunction will be granted 'only in an unusual case' (Butler-Sloss LJ in *Derby & Co Ltd v Weldon (Nos 3 & 4)* [1990] Ch 65, 96).

[224] Millett LJ in *Crédit Suisse Fides Trust SA v Cuoghi* [1998] QB 818, 824.

[225] [1990] 1 WLR 1139, 1153.

10.4.15 Various factors have been thought relevant to the exercise of discretion. First, the court is more inclined to grant *Mareva* relief in cases where the claim is proprietary rather than personal.[226] Secondly, although the court's powers to grant an extraterritorial freezing injunction are, in principle, the same whether the claimant's application is made before or after judgment 'as a matter of discretion, such orders will in practice no doubt be made more readily after judgment'.[227] Where an injunction is granted after judgment it should normally be limited in duration. The claimant should be encouraged to proceed swiftly with proper methods of execution since 'perpetual injunctions restraining a defendant from dealing with his assets until the crack of doom are undesirable'.[228] Thirdly, where the claimant seeks an injunction in support of foreign proceedings, it used to be thought that 'apart from the very exceptional case, the proper attitude of the English courts ... is to confine themselves to their own territorial area'.[229] According to this view, where the court has jurisdiction to grant provisional measures in support of substantive proceedings abroad, the court should normally restrict its orders to assets within the jurisdiction. More recently, however, in *Crédit Suisse Fides Trust SA v Cuoghi*[230] the Court of Appeal indicated that, if it is expedient to do so, the English court should grant worldwide interim relief in support of foreign proceedings:

Where a defendant and his assets are located outside the jurisdiction of the court seised of the substantive proceedings, it is ... most appropriate that protective measures should be granted by those courts best able to make their orders effective. In relation to orders taking direct effect against the assets, this means the courts of the state where the assets are located; and in relation to orders in personam, including orders for disclosure, this means the courts of the state where the person enjoined resides.[231]

Accordingly, in cases where the substantive proceedings are not being pursued in England, it should be very exceptional for the English court to grant an injunction with extraterritorial effect if the defendant is neither domiciled in England nor has any English assets.[232] Furthermore, for reasons already considered,[233] in cases within the scope of the Brussels I Regulation, it is questionable whether the English court is empowered to grant a worldwide freezing injunction in support of proceedings in another Member State unless the defendant is domiciled in England.

10.4.16 In those cases involving a defendant who is domiciled in England, where there is no obstacle to the English court granting a worldwide freezing injunction in support of foreign proceedings,[234] it must always be remembered that the English court 'must recognise that its role is subordinate to and must be supportive of that of the primary court'.[235] It follows that the English court should take into account a

---

[226] *Republic of Haiti v Duvalier* [1990] 1 QB 202.
[227] Kerr LJ in *Babanaft International Co SA v Bassatne* [1990] Ch 13, 37. See also *Masri v Consolidated Contractors International SA Sal* [2008] ILPr 146.
[228] Staughton LJ in *Republic of Haiti v Duvalier* [1990] 1 QB 202, 213–14.
[229] Lord Donaldson MR in *Rosseel NV v Oriental Commercial Shipping (UK) Ltd* [1990] 1 WLR 1387, 1389. See also *The Xing Su Hai* [1995] 2 Lloyd's Rep 15; *S&T Bautrading v Nordling* [1997] 3 All ER 718.
[230] [1998] QB 818.
[231] Millett LJ at [1997] 3 All ER 724, 730.
[232] See, eg, *Motorola Credit Corpn v Uzan (No 2)* [2004] 1 WLR 113.
[233] See para 10.4.12.
[234] *Crédit Suisse Fides Trust SA v Cuoghi* [1998] QB 818.
[235] Lord Bingham CJ at [1998] QB 818, 832.

number of factors when deciding whether it would be inexpedient to make the order: first, whether making the order would interfere with the management of the case by the foreign court with jurisdiction over the substantive dispute; secondly, whether it is the policy of that court not to make worldwide freezing orders; thirdly, whether there is a danger of there being conflicting or overlapping orders if the English court grants the relief sought; fourthly, whether at the time the order is sought there is likely to be a potential conflict as to jurisdiction; fifthly, whether the court will be able to enforce the order if it is disobeyed.[236] The question whether the English court should normally refrain from granting worldwide freezing orders in cases where the court with jurisdiction over the substantive dispute either has no jurisdiction to grant such measures or would, in the circumstances of the case, refuse to exercise their jurisdiction to grant worldwide relief on the merits has divided the Court of Appeal.[237]

10.4.17 Finally, in *Rosseel NV v Oriental Commercial Shipping (UK) Ltd*[238] it was held that the court should not, as a general rule, grant an extraterritorial freezing injunction in a case where the claimant is seeking to enforce a foreign judgment or award in England. However, this decision has subsequently been described by the Court of Appeal as 'surprising'.[239]

The Protection of the Defendant and Third Parties

10.4.18 In *Derby & Co Ltd v Weldon* Parker LJ said that:

there is every justification for a worldwide *Mareva*, so long as, by undertaking or proviso or a combination of both, (a) oppression of the defendants by way of exposure to a multiplicity of proceedings is avoided, (b) the defendants are protected against the misuse of information gained from the ordinary order for disclosure in aid of the *Mareva*, and (c) the position of third parties is protected.[240]

PROTECTING THE DEFENDANT AGAINST A MULTIPLICITY OF PROCEEDINGS
AND THE MISUSE OF INFORMATION

10.4.19 In *Babanaft International Co SA v Bassatne*[241] Neill and Nicholls LJJ thought that a plaintiff should be required to undertake that information disclosed under an extraterritorial disclosure order would not be used abroad (for example, as the basis for legal proceedings in a foreign country) without the consent of the defendant or the court's permission.[242] That such undertakings should normally be required was subsequently confirmed by the Court of Appeal[243] and by a practice

---

[236] See Potter LJ in *Motorola Credit Corpn v Uzan (No 2)* [2004] 1 WLR 113, 147.
[237] See *Crédit Suisse Fides Trust SA v Cuoghi* [1998] QB 818; *Refco Ltd v Eastern Trading Co* [1999] 1 Lloyd's Rep 159; *Motorola Credit Corpn v Uzan (No 2)* [2004] 1 WLR 113.
[238] [1990] 1 WLR 1387.
[239] Millett LJ in *Crédit Suisse Fides Trust SA v Cuoghi* [1998] QB 818, 828.
[240] [1990] Ch 48, 57.
[241] [1990] Ch 13.
[242] For consideration of when the court may give permission for the claimant to make use of evidence obtained in injunction proceedings in the context of other proceedings, see *Dadourian Group International Inc v Simms (No 2)* [2007] 1 All ER 329.
[243] *Republic of Haiti v Duvalier* [1990] 1 QB 202; *Derby & Co Ltd v Weldon* [1990] Ch 48; *Derby & Co Ltd v Weldon (Nos 3 & 4)* [1990] Ch 65.

direction issued jointly by the Lord Chief Justice, the President of the Family Division and the Vice-Chancellor in 1994.[244] In view of the fact that an order restraining the defendant from dealing with any of his assets overseas and requiring him to disclose details of all his assets wherever located is a draconian order, a worldwide freezing injunction normally includes an undertaking by the claimant not to bring any proceedings to enforce the injunction in another jurisdiction without the court's permission.[245] It is not sufficient merely that the claimant makes the relevant undertaking. Before the court makes a disclosure order in respect of foreign assets, it will normally need to be satisfied that the court has a sufficient degree of control over the claimant (for example, by virtue of the claimant's continuing connection with England) to ensure compliance with any orders it may make regarding the use of information.[246]

10.4.20 Whether or not the claimant is required to make undertakings and, if so, what form they should take depends on the particular circumstances of the case. As Nolan LJ noted in *Re Bank of Credit and Commerce International SA*: 'Each case must be considered as to its facts.'[247] For example, the Court of Appeal decided in *Republic of Haiti v Duvalier* that it was not appropriate to require undertakings from a foreign state which 'has complied scrupulously with its undertaking in the past'.[248] Equally, in *Re Bank of Credit and Commerce International SA*[249] it was decided that the English liquidators of a foreign company should not be required to give an undertaking to obtain permission from the English court before taking any steps which might lead to the commencement of criminal proceedings against the defendants abroad. Nevertheless, as a general rule, the claimant will be required to make undertakings.

10.4.21 In *Dadourain Group International Inc v Simms*,[250] following an arbitration in the United States, the claimants had obtained a worldwide freezing injunction from the English courts. The claimants had made an undertaking not to seek to enforce the injunction in any country other than England or France. Subsequently, when the claimants applied to vary the injunction so that they could seek to enforce it in Switzerland, the court was faced with the question of how its discretion to permit enforcement of a worldwide freezing injunction abroad should be exercised. The Court of Appeal laid down a series of guidelines of which the most important are: the overriding objective is to ensure the effectiveness of the injunction in a way that is not oppressive to the defendant or to third parties; the relief granted should be proportionate and should not result in the claimant obtaining abroad relief which is superior to that granted by the injunction itself; the claimant must show that there is a real prospect that there are assets located in the foreign country in question and that there is evidence of a risk that those assets will be dissipated.[251]

---

[244] *Practice Direction (Mareva Injunctions and Anton Piller Orders)* [1994] 1 WLR 1233. For the current position, see CPR PD 25.

[245] See Arden LJ in *Dadourian Group International Inc v Simms* [2006] 1 WLR 2499, 2500–01 (at [1]).

[246] See Nicholls LJ in *Babanaft International Co SA v Bassatne* [1990] Ch 13, 47.

[247] [1994] 1 WLR 708, 717.

[248] Staughton LJ at [1990] 1 QB 202, 217.

[249] [1994] 1 WLR 708.

[250] [2006] 1 WLR 2499.

[251] [2006] 1 WLR 2499, 2502 (at [25]).

THE PROTECTION OF THIRD PARTIES: THE BABANAFT PROVISO

10.4.22   Although an injunction operates *in personam*—against the person to whom it is addressed—it may have an indirect effect on third parties.[252] It is well established that a person who is not a party to the injunction may nevertheless be in contempt of court if, having been notified of the terms of the injunction, he does acts which assist the defendant in breaking them. When a third party has knowledge of a freezing injunction he must do what he reasonably can to preserve the assets affected; if he knowingly assists in any way in their disposal or in prohibited dealing with them, he will be in contempt of court.[253] In *Z Ltd v A-Z and AA-LL*,[254] for example, the plaintiff had obtained freezing injunctions against a number of defendants. A bank, which held assets of one of the defendants against whom the injunction had been granted, had been served with a copy of the injunction (and therefore had notice of it) even though the defendant had not been served. It was held that the bank would be in contempt by disposing of the defendant's assets after having received notice of the injunction, even though the defendant could not at that time be in contempt for failing to comply with the court's order. It is, however, important that the potential liability of third parties is subject to reasonable limits. Under public international law, 'it would be an exorbitant exercise of jurisdiction to put a third party abroad in the position of having to choose between being in contempt of an English court and having to dishonour its obligations under a law which does not regard the English order as a valid excuse'. [255]

10.4.23   In *Babanaft International Co SA v Bassatne*,[256] when the Court of Appeal first decided that the court could restrain by injunction a defendant from dealing with foreign assets, it was clear that an extraterritorial freezing injunction posed novel problems for third parties. Although a whole range of individuals and corporations might be affected by a freezing injunction, banks are in the most vulnerable position. Freezing injunctions are often directed to all the defendant's assets, many of which will be held in accounts in various banks in numerous countries. If these banks have branches in London, they are *prima facie* within the contempt jurisdiction of the English courts.

10.4.24   In *Babanaft International Co SA v Bassatne* the members of the Court of Appeal agreed that a worldwide freezing injunction should not expose third parties to unreasonable risks of liability for contempt of court and subsequent cases confirmed the principle that a worldwide freezing injunction should contain appropriate provisos for the protection of third parties.[257] The crucial question, however, concerns the

---

[252]   See P Devonshire, 'The implications of third parties holding assets subject to a *Mareva* injunction' [1996] *LMCLQ* 268; A Malek and C Lewis, 'Worldwide *Mareva* injunctions: the position of international banks' [1990] *LMCLQ* 88.

[253]   Failure to comply with a freezing injunction in such circumstances does not, however, expose the third party to liability to the claimant in negligence: *Customs and Excise Commissioners v Barclays Bank plc* [2007] 1 AC 181.

[254]   [1982] QB 558.

[255]   Lawrence Collins LJ in *Masri v Consolidated Contractors International (UK) Ltd (No 2)* [2009] QB 450, 469 (at [47]).

[256]   [1990] Ch 13.

[257]   See, eg, *Ghoth v Ghoth* [1992] 2 All ER 920.

form which such protective provisions should take. In *Babanaft International Co SA v Bassatne*, whereas Neill and Nicholls LJJ took the view that the injunction should be binding only on the defendant, Kerr LJ would have preferred a proviso which would not affect third parties 'unless and to the extent that [the injunction] is enforced by the courts of the states in which any of the defendants' assets are located'.[258] This aspect of Kerr LJ's judgment is the seed from which the so-called *Babanaft* proviso has grown.

10.4.25   The appropriate level of protection for third parties was the subject of further consideration by the Court of Appeal. In *Derby & Co Ltd v Weldon (Nos 3 & 4)* Lord Donaldson MR suggested a reformulation of the *Babanaft* proviso so that a worldwide freezing injunction would have extraterritorial effect on a third party only if either it was declared enforceable by a foreign court or the third party was subject to English jurisdiction and was able to prevent the acts abroad which constitute a breach of the terms of the injunction.[259] This reformulation was substantially adopted by a practice direction jointly issued in 1994 by the Lord Chief Justice, the President of the Family Division and the Vice-Chancellor[260] and repeated in the model freezing injunction set out in the Civil Procedure Rules.[261] Although it is to be expected that the model freezing injunction will be followed in most cases, the court may modify it as appropriate in any particular case.[262] As regards worldwide freezing injunctions, the model includes the following proviso:

(1) Except as provided in paragraph (2) below, the terms of this order do not affect or concern anyone outside the jurisdiction of this court.

(2) The terms of this order will affect the following persons in a country or state outside the jurisdiction of this court—

    (a) the Respondent or his officer or agent appointed by power of attorney;

    (b) any person who—

       (i) is subject to the jurisdiction of this court;

       (ii) has been given written notice of this order at his residence or place of business within the jurisdiction of this court, and

       (iii) is able to prevent acts or omissions outside the jurisdiction of this court which constitute or assist in a breach of the terms of this order.

    (c) any other person, only to the extent that this order has been declared enforceable by or is enforced by a court in that country or state.

10.4.26   As a general rule a third party will not be affected by a freezing injunction in respect of acts performed abroad unless and until the courts of the country where the assets are located have recognised and enforced the injunction. Even in such a case the third party is affected only to the extent decided by the foreign court. In practice, in only very limited circumstances will an English freezing injunction be entitled to recognition and enforcement abroad.[263]

---

[258] [1990] Ch 13, 37.
[259] [1990] Ch 65, 84.
[260] *Practice Direction (Mareva Injunctions and Anton Piller Orders)* [1994] 1 WLR 1233.
[261] CPR PD 25.
[262] CPR PD 25 para 6.2.
[263] See section 10.5.

10.4.27 As an exception to the general rule, a third party may be affected by a freezing injunction in respect of actions undertaken abroad, notwithstanding the fact that the injunction is not entitled to recognition in the country where the assets are located. In order for the exception to apply, three conditions must be satisfied. First, the third party in question must be subject to English jurisdiction. Secondly, the third party must have been given written notice in England of the injunction; there can be no question of a third party being exposed to the risk of contempt until he has received notice of the injunction. Thirdly, an extraterritorial freezing injunction affects a third party only if the individual or establishment in England is able to prevent acts or omissions outside the jurisdiction of the court. This third condition raises very difficult questions, particularly with regard to banks. In what circumstances, for example, can a bank in England be regarded as having the necessary control over branches in other countries? As regards an English bank with branches abroad, the effect of the *Babanaft* proviso is that the English bank will be liable for contempt if, in breach of the terms of the injunction, foreign branches allow the defendant to make withdrawals from accounts held at the foreign branches.[264] As regards foreign banks with branches in England, the effect of the *Babanaft* proviso should be that, as a general rule, activities conducted abroad will not incur liability for contempt in England even though, by virtue of its presence in England, the bank is subject to English jurisdiction. A leading commentator has suggested:

[I]t will only be in exceptional cases (eg, where the account abroad is under its control) in which [the English branch] will be 'able to prevent acts or omissions outside the jurisdiction'. The mere fact that a foreign bank with a branch in London is part of one juridical entity should not mean, for this purpose, that the foreign bank is in contempt because of the acts of one of its branches outside England.[265]

10.4.28 Nevertheless, in *Baltic Shipping Co v Translink Shipping Ltd*[266] it was assumed that a French bank with a branch in England might be liable for contempt in relation to acts committed abroad by a subsidiary company. Clarke J thought, however, that the bank should not be placed in a situation where it runs the risk both of being in breach of the terms of a worldwide freezing injunction if its foreign subsidiary meets a customer's demand and of being liable for breach of contract if it does not. Accordingly, a proviso was added to the injunction to enable the French bank's subsidiary to comply with what it reasonably believed to be its obligations, contractual or otherwise, under the law of the country where the subsidiary was established.[267]

10.4.29 In 1993 it had been suggested by Saville J in his end of year statement as judge in charge of the commercial court that, in appropriate circumstances, a worldwide freezing injunction should include a proviso along the lines of that subsequently added in *Baltic Shipping Co v Translink Shipping Ltd* (the *Baltic* proviso). Although the *Baltic* proviso is essential to protect third parties in cases where there is a conflict between the worldwide injunction and the law of the country where the defendant's

---

[264] *Securities and Investments Board v Pantell SA* [1990] Ch 426.
[265] L Collins, 'Provisional and Protective Measures in International Litigation' in *Essays in International Litigation and the Conflict of Laws* (Oxford, Clarendon Press, 1994) 92.
[266] [1995] 1 Lloyd's Rep 673.
[267] See Clarke J in *Baltic Shipping Co v Translink Shipping Ltd* [1995] 1 Lloyd's Rep 673, 675.

assets are located, no such proviso was added to the standard-form freezing injunction set out in the 1994 practice direction.[268] However, in *Bank of China v NBM LLC*[269] the Court of Appeal approved *Baltic Shipping Co v Translink Shipping Ltd* and held that third parties who might be adversely affected by worldwide freezing injunctions should be given reasonable protection. According to Tuckey LJ, the *Baltic* proviso should be added to a worldwide freezing injunction 'unless the court considers on the particular facts of the case that this is inappropriate'[270] and reiterated the view that this proviso should be included in the standard form. The model worldwide freezing injunction appended to the Civil Procedure Rules includes a paragraph which closely follows the *Baltic* proviso:

Nothing in this order shall, in respect of assets located outside England and Wales, prevent any third party from complying with—

(1) what it reasonably believes to be its obligations, contractual or otherwise, under the laws and obligations of the country or state in which those assets are situated or under the proper law of any contract between itself and the Respondent;

(2) any orders of the courts of that country or state, provided that reasonable notice of any application for such an order is given to the Applicant's solicitors.[271]

The Dangers of Extraterritorial Freezing Injunctions

10.4.30 Although the worldwide freezing injunction has taken root in England, it would be foolish to think that the practice of the courts is entirely free from dangers and problems. Attention may be drawn to three issues.[272] First, even though the elaborate structure of the *Babanaft* proviso is designed to lessen the invasive impact of a worldwide freezing injunction, the grant of an extraterritorial order may come very close to an unwarranted interference with the jurisdiction of the courts of the country where the assets are situated. Secondly, the theoretical justification for the grant of extraterritorial orders—namely, that the order acts only *in personam*—is not entirely convincing, especially in cases where the court appoints a receiver who is entitled to take possession of the assets. The worldwide freezing injunction 'smacks too much of the arrogance of a former imperial power sending a gun-boat where there is trouble abroad'.[273] Thirdly, an extraterritorial freezing injunction is not effective against defendants who are not resident in England. The sanction for disobedience is normally simply that the defendant is barred from defending the substantive proceedings. The sanction may prove to be illusory, since if the defendant is not allowed to defend the proceedings it is possible that the courts of foreign countries where the defendant's assets are located will refuse to recognise or enforce the final judgment of the English court on public policy grounds.[274] Although the answers to these concerns would

---

[268] *Practice Direction (Mareva Injunctions and Anton Piller Orders)* [1994] 1 WLR 1233.

[269] [2002] 1 WLR 844.

[270] [2002] 1 WLR 844, 852 (at [22]).

[271] CPR PD 25.

[272] See N Browne-Wilkinson, 'Territorial Jurisdiction and the New Technologies' (1991) 25 *Israel LR* 145, 152–3.

[273] *Ibid*, 153.

[274] See Case C–394/07 *Gambazzi v DaimlerChrysler Canada Inc* [2009] ILPr 637.

seem to lie in closer international co-operation, it is not easy to see how significant advances can be made. The Brussels I Regulation shows how difficult it is to achieve an effective system for the reciprocal enforcement of provisional measures.

10.5 ENFORCEMENT OF FOREIGN PROVISIONAL MEASURES

10.5.1 The swift and easy transfer of assets across frontiers means that a claimant may seek protective measures in a country where the defendant's assets are no longer located. If the court makes an order—notwithstanding the fact that the assets are elsewhere—the question arises whether the order should be entitled to enforcement in countries where the assets are to be found. The question of the enforcement of foreign provisional measures has not yet loomed large in English practice. For reasons of practical convenience, a claimant will often apply for provisional measures in the country where those measures are intended to take effect. Moreover, until recently there could be no question of seeking enforcement of foreign provisional measures in England; the only foreign judgments which are entitled to enforcement at common law or under the statutory regimes which are based on the common law[275] are judgments for a fixed sum of money.

10.5.2 In theory, the position under the Brussels I Regulation is different from that which exists at common law. The enforcement provisions in Chapter III do not distinguish between judgments on interlocutory matters and final judgments or between money judgments and judgments *in specie*.[276] Although there is, in principle, no problem surrounding the enforcement under the Brussels I Regulation of a freezing injunction which has issued from an *inter partes* procedure,[277] where one Member State grants a provisional measure without the defendant being given notice of the claimant's application, the court's order is not entitled to enforcement in other Member States under Chapter III.[278] In addition, protective measures (other than orders for the making of an interim payment) granted by the courts of Scotland and Northern Ireland are not enforceable in England under Part II of the 1982 Act.[279]

---

[275] Administration of Justice Act 1920; Foreign Judgments (Reciprocal Enforcement) Act 1933.
[276] Case 143/78 *de Cavel v de Cavel* [1979] ECR 1055, paras 8–9.
[277] See *Stolzenberg v DaimlerChrysler Canada Inc* [2005] ILPr 266 (Court of Cassation, France); *Re Grant of an Extraterritorial Injunction* [2009] ILPr 22 (Supreme Court, Austria).
[278] Case 125/79 *Denilauler v Snc Couchet Frères* [1980] ECR 1553, para 18. See para 13.1.6.
[279] Civil Jurisdiction and Judgments Act 1982, s 18(5)(d).

11

ANTI-SUIT INJUNCTIONS

11.0.1 There are many situations in which the courts of more than one country have jurisdiction over a particular dispute. Under traditional English jurisdiction rules where, for example, A sues B in a foreign country and B sues A on the same cause of action in England, A may apply for a stay of the English proceedings on the basis that the foreign court is the more appropriate forum.[1] If England is the more appropriate forum, may the claimant in the English proceedings obtain an anti-suit injunction—that is, an injunction requiring the other party not to commence or to discontinue proceedings in a foreign court? Because anti-suit injunctions raise delicate questions of comity, the court will not restrain a litigant from proceeding abroad simply on the basis that England is the *forum conveniens* (section 11.1). An anti-suit injunction will not normally be granted unless either the proceedings in the foreign forum are 'vexatious or oppressive' or the bringing of the proceedings infringes a legal or equitable right of the defendant in the foreign proceedings (for example, where proceedings are brought in breach of a dispute resolution agreement concluded between the parties) (section 11.2). Special factors should be considered in cases where the foreign proceedings concern civil and commercial matters and the foreign court's jurisdiction derives from the Brussels I Regulation[2] (section 11.3).

11.1 PRELIMINARY REMARKS

11.1.1 An English court cannot directly limit the jurisdiction of foreign courts. This does not mean, however, that an English court may not indirectly affect foreign proceedings by issuing an injunction ordering a defendant to do (or not to do) something. In theory, an anti-suit injunction does not interfere with the foreign court because it operates *in personam*: 'it is directed against the [defendant] and not the courts of the other jurisdiction.'[3] Failure by the defendant to comply with the order amounts to contempt for which the defendant may be punished, but it does not have an impact on the foreign proceedings as such. Of course, proceedings continue only as long as the parties take the necessary procedural steps. In reality, therefore, the grant of an anti-suit injunction interferes indirectly with the foreign court's jurisdiction and runs counter to the idea of comity.[4] So, although anti-suit injunctions can play an important role in international litigation, it is rare for the grant of an anti-suit injunction to be appropriate:

Injunctive relief with extraterritorial effect … must be an exceptional remedy. It ought only to be granted in exceptional circumstances. It is, after all, inconsistent with normal relations

---

[1] See section 9.2.
[2] Reg (EC) 44/2001, [2001] OJ L12/1.
[3] Lord Woolf MR in *Fort Dodge Animal Health Ltd v Akzo Nobel NV* [1998] FSR 222, 246.
[4] TC Hartley, 'Comity and the Use of Anti-suit Injunctions in International Litigation' (1987) 35 *Am J Comp L* 487, 506.

between friendly sovereign states, and it is subversive of the best interests of the international trade system.[5]

Furthermore, the effectiveness of an anti-suit injunction will normally depend entirely on the effectiveness of any sanctions imposed by the English court for contempt of court in the event of the defendant refusing to comply with the terms of the injunction. This is because a foreign court is likely to regard an English anti-suit injunction as an attempt to infringe its own jurisdiction and, accordingly, will not recognise or enforce it.[6]

11.1.2   As a general proposition, an application for an anti-suit injunction is not a separate cause of action; it is ancillary to a substantive cause of action. Where, as is usual, the English court has substantive jurisdiction over the defendant (whether under the Brussels I Regulation or the traditional rules), there is no jurisdictional obstacle to the grant of an anti-suit injunction: 'As a matter of English law, once the court has jurisdiction over the substance of the case, it has jurisdiction to make ancillary orders, including anti-suit injunctions to protect the integrity of its process.'[7] Such an injunction may be granted on either a pre-judgment or post-judgment basis and there is no requirement that the claimant should establish an independent basis of jurisdiction with regard to the anti-suit injunction itself: 'Where a party is properly before a court, an anti-suit injunction is not a separate claim requiring its own basis of jurisdiction. In alternative forum cases, it is not necessary for the applicant to rely on a cause of action establishing a separate right not to be sued.'[8]

11.1.3   The position would appear to be different, however, in so-called 'single forum' cases (assuming that an anti-suit injunction may be granted in such cases[9]). In a case in which there is no question of the claimant seeking a substantive remedy in English proceedings, an anti-suit injunction could not be granted unless the claimant is able to establish a basis of jurisdiction against the defendant (under the Brussels I Regulation or under the traditional rules, as the case may be). In a case governed by the traditional rules, if the defendant cannot be served with process in England or does not submit to the jurisdiction of the court, the claimant may apply for permission to serve process abroad. For example, in an appropriate case, permission to serve out of the jurisdiction may be given under CPR 6.36 on the basis that, if the claim is in respect of a contract governed by English law, it falls within the scope of CPR PD 6B, para 3.1(6)(c).[10]

---

[5] Steyn J in *ED & F Man (Sugar) Ltd v Haryanto (No 2)* [1991] 1 Lloyd's Rep 161, 168.

[6] See, eg, *Re the Enforcement of an English Anti-suit Injunction* [1997] ILPr 320 (Court of Appeal, Düsseldorf). J Harris, 'Restraint of Foreign Proceedings—the View from the Other Side of the Fence' (1997) 16 *CJQ* 283.

[7] Lawrence Collins LJ in *Masri v Consolidated Contractors International (UK) Ltd (No 3)* [2009] QB 503, 525 (at [59]).

[8] Lawrence Collins LJ in *Masri v Consolidated Contractors International (UK) Ltd (No 3)* [2009] QB 503, 535 (at [99]).

[9] See paras 11.2.3–11.2.4, 11.2.17–11.2.18.

[10] *Schiffahrtsgesellschaft Detlev von Appen GmbH v Voest Alpine Intertrading GmbH* [1997] 2 Lloyd's Rep 279; *Shell International Petroleum Co Ltd v Coral Oil Co Ltd* [1999] 1 Lloyd's Rep 72; *Youell v Kara Mara Shipping Co Ltd* [2000] 2 Lloyd's Rep 102; *The Ivan Zagubanski* [2002] 1 Lloyd's Rep 106; *Albon v*

11.1.4   In the early 1980s there emerged the idea that the same basic test should be applied to applications for a stay of English proceedings and applications for an anti-suit injunction.[11] However, as the test for the grant of a stay of English proceedings became more liberal, it became clear that, if the English courts were to avoid interfering excessively (albeit indirectly) in foreign proceedings, a stricter test would have to be formulated in the context of applications for an injunction to restrain the defendant from litigating abroad. If the rules for the grant of an anti-suit injunction were the mirror image of the test laid down in *Spiliada Maritime Corporation v Cansulex Ltd*[12] the position would be as follows:

To justify the grant of an injunction, the defendant [in the foreign proceedings] must show: (a) that the English court is the natural forum for the trial of the action, to whose jurisdiction the parties are amenable; *and* (b) that justice does not require that the action should nevertheless be allowed to proceed in the foreign court.[13]

11.1.5   For a litigant to be prevented from pursuing proceedings abroad simply on the basis that the English court regards itself as the natural forum would be inconsistent with the principle of comity. Although an injunction granted to one party to restrain the other from beginning or continuing proceedings in a foreign court is one of the forms of injunction which the court has power to grant, the court should exercise this jurisdiction with caution 'because it involves indirect interference with the process of the foreign court concerned'.[14] Accordingly, the test to be applied to an application for an anti-suit injunction is not the same as the test which applies to an application for a stay of English proceedings. It is well established that the mere fact that England is the *forum conveniens* does not, without more, entitle a claimant to an injunction restraining the defendant from litigating abroad.[15] As Glidewell LJ stated in *Barclays Bank plc v Homan*:

If the only issue is whether an English or foreign court is the more appropriate forum for the trial of an action, that question should normally be decided by the foreign court on the principle of *forum non conveniens*, and the English court should not seek to interfere with that decision.[16]

It follows that, in a case where there are concurrent proceedings in England and a foreign country, the English court may conclude, first, that the English proceedings should not be stayed (because the foreign forum is not clearly more appropriate) and, secondly, that the situation is not one in which an anti-suit injunction should be granted. In this type of case, unless the foreign court stays its proceedings, a party may have little choice but to litigate simultaneously in two jurisdictions.

Naza Motor Trading Sdn Bhd (No 4) [2007] 2 Lloyd's Rep 420; *Steamship Mutual Underwriting Association (Bermuda) Ltd v Sulpicio Inc* [2008] 2 Lloyd's Rep 269.

[11]   *Castanho v Brown & Root (UK) Ltd* [1981] AC 557. A Briggs, 'No Interference with Foreign Court' (1982) 31 *ICLQ* 189; DG Morgan, 'Discretion to Stay Jurisdiction' (1982) 31 *ICLQ* 582.

[12]   [1987] AC 460.

[13]   Lord Goff in *Société Nationale Industrielle Aérospatiale v Lee Kui Jak* [1987] AC 871, 895.

[14]   Lord Brandon in *South Carolina Insurance Co v Assurantie Maatschappij 'De Zeven Provincien' NV* [1987] AC 24, 40. PB Carter, (1986) 57 *BYIL* 434; C Forsyth, [1988] *CLJ* 177.

[15]   *Société Nationale Industrielle Aérospatiale v Lee Kui Jak* [1987] AC 871, 895.

[16]   [1993] BCLC 680, 701.

11.2 THE BASES ON WHICH AN ANTI-SUIT
INJUNCTION MAY BE GRANTED

11.2.1   Although the modern view is that the court's discretion to grant injunctive relief should not be regarded as limited to a fixed number of categories,[17] in the context of anti-suit injunctions the circumstances in which the court will consider granting relief generally fall into one of two situations: first, 'where one party to an action has behaved, or threatens to behave, in a manner which is unconscionable' and secondly, 'where one party to an action can show that the other party has either invaded, or threatens to invade, a legal or equitable right of the former for the enforcement of which the latter is amenable to the jurisdiction of the court'.[18]

Unconscionable Conduct

11.2.2   In *South Carolina Insurance Co v Assurantie Maatschappij 'De Zeven Provincien' NV* Lord Brandon said that, although it was probably not wise to attempt to provide an exhaustive definition of 'unconscionable conduct', that term includes 'conduct which is oppressive or vexatious'.[19] This formula was applied in *Société Nationale Industrielle Aérospatiale v Lee Kui Jak*.[20] Lord Goff said:

> [W]here a remedy for a particular wrong is available both in the English ... court and in a foreign court, the English ... court will, generally speaking, only restrain the plaintiff from pursuing proceedings in the foreign court if such pursuit would be vexatious or oppressive. This presupposes that, as a general rule, the English ... court must conclude that it provides the natural forum for the trial of the action; and further, since the court is concerned with the ends of justice, that account must be taken not only of injustice to the defendant if the plaintiff is allowed to pursue the foreign proceedings, but also of injustice to the plaintiff if he is not allowed to do so. So the court will not grant an injunction if, by doing so, it will deprive him of advantages in the foreign forum of which it would be unjust to deprive him.[21]

What emerges from this passage is that to obtain an anti-suit injunction on the basis of unconscionable conduct the claimant must, as a general rule, satisfy two criteria: first, England must be the natural forum and, secondly, it must be shown that to allow the foreign proceedings to continue would cause positive injustice (which, in most cases, is established by showing that the foreign proceedings are vexatious or oppressive).

---

[17] See the speeches of Lord Goff and Lord Mackay in *South Carolina Insurance Co v Assurantie Maatschappij 'De Zeven Provincien' NV* [1987] AC 24; *Société Nationale Industrielle Aérospatiale v Lee Kui Jak* [1987] AC 871.

[18] Lord Brandon in *South Carolina Insurance Co v Assurantie Maatschappij 'De Zeven Provincien' NV* [1987] AC 24, 40. For some of the procedural problems surrounding anti-suit injunctions in multiparty cases, see *Société Commerciale de Réassurance v Eras International Ltd (No 2)* [1995] 2 All ER 278.

[19] [1987] AC 24, 41.

[20] [1987] AC 871. A Briggs, 'Restraint of foreign proceedings' [1987] *LMCLQ* 391; PB Carter, (1988) 59 *BYIL* 342; C Forsyth, [1988] *CLJ* 177; PF Kunzlik, [1987] *CLJ* 406.

[21] [1987] AC 871, 896.

England is the Natural Forum

11.2.3 Whereas under the doctrine of *forum non conveniens* the defendant merely has to establish that another forum is more appropriate, where an anti-suit injunction is sought from the English court the general rule is that it must be shown not only that the foreign forum is not the natural forum, but that England is. Whether there are any exceptions to this general principle is uncertain. There have been instances in which the court has granted an anti-suit injunction notwithstanding the fact that the foreign court is the only forum in which the claim can be pursued (so-called 'single forum' cases)[22] and, in *Airbus Industrie GIE v Patel*,[23] the House of Lords left open the possibility of the English court granting injunctive relief in cases where it is not the natural forum. Lord Goff considered that the court could grant an anti-suit injunction, even in a case where it did not have jurisdiction over the parties' dispute, 'in extreme cases, for example where the conduct of the foreign state exercising jurisdiction is such as to deprive it of the respect normally required by comity'.[24]

11.2.4 However, considerable doubt has been cast in these cases by the speech of Lord Hobhouse in *Turner v Grovit*.[25] In his summary of the law, Lord Hobhouse considered that 'an important restriction' upon the willingness of the English courts to grant an anti-suit injunction is that the party seeking the anti-suit injunction 'is a party to litigation in this country'.[26] Furthermore, Lord Hobhouse stated that 'English law requires the applicant to show a clear need to protect existing English proceedings'.[27] If the need to satisfy both of these conditions is to be regarded as a hard-and-fast rule (rather than a general rule to which there may be exceptions), it is no longer the case that the English court has the power to grant an anti-suit injunction either in single forum cases or in other cases where proceedings relating to the substantive dispute between the parties have not already been commenced in England.[28] Even if it is still possible for the English court to grant an anti-suit injunction in single forum cases, 'it would be a highly unusual case in which the English court would grant an anti-suit injunction in a single forum case against a non-English party, and (I would add) an even rarer case in which it would have jurisdiction to do so'.[29]

---

[22] See, eg, *Midland Bank plc v Laker Airways Ltd* [1986] QB 689. See also *British Airways Board v Laker Airways Ltd* [1985] AC 58.

[23] [1999] 1 AC 119. A Briggs, (1998) 69 *BYIL* 332; R Fentiman, [1998] *CLJ* 467; S Males, 'Comity and anti-suit injunctions' [1998] *LMCLQ* 543; E Peel, 'Anti-Suit Injunctions—the House of Lords Declines to Act as International Policeman' (1998) 114 *LQR* 543.

[24] [1999] 1 AC 119, 140.

[25] [2002] 1 WLR 107.

[26] [2002] 1 WLR 107, 119 (at [27]).

[27] [2002] 1 WLR 107, 120 (at [28]). See also *Glencore International v Exter Shipping Ltd* [2002] 2 All ER (Comm) 1.

[28] See the inconclusive observations of Lawrence Collins LJ in *Masri v Consolidated Contractors International (UK) Ltd (No 3)* [2009] QB 503, 524–5 (at [56]–[57]). Lawrence Collins LJ discussed *Turner v Grovit* and the fact that the rationale for the grant of an anti-suit injunction is the need to protect existing English proceedings, but also referred to the 'single forum' cases without addressing the relationship between such cases and this rationale.

[29] Lawrence Collins LJ in *Masri v Consolidated Contractors International (UK) Ltd (No 3)* [2009] QB 503, 524 (at [56]).

Vexatious or Oppressive

11.2.5   There are problems with any test which is formulated in a very open-textured way. The requirement that the grant of an anti-suit injunction depends on it being established that the foreign proceedings are vexatious or oppressive is such a test as there is no satisfactory definition of conduct which amounts to vexation or oppression. Nevertheless, factors which indicate vexation or oppression include 'the institution of proceedings which are bound to fail, or bringing proceedings which interfere with or undermine the control of the English court of its own process, or proceedings which could and should have formed part of an English action brought earlier'.[30]

11.2.6   In *Société Nationale Industrielle Aérospatiale v Lee Kui Jak* Lord Goff indicated that the court should not grant an anti-suit injunction 'if, by doing so, it will deprive [the claimant] of advantages in the foreign forum of which it would be unjust to deprive him'.[31] By contrast, an anti-suit injunction will be granted if the foreign proceedings are vexatious or oppressive. This raises the question how to draw the dividing line between the claimant seeking a legitimate advantage, on the one hand, and acting in a vexatious or oppressive manner, on the other.

11.2.7   It is not enough that acts should be 'vexatious or oppressive' in the ordinary domestic sense in which claims might be summarily struck out under the Civil Procedure Rules; something more is required.[32] The mere fact that the law applied by the foreign forum is different from English law does not mean that the foreign proceedings are inherently oppressive.[33] Where the question is simply one of justice between litigants the court should be slow to intervene unless it is satisfied that justice can be achieved only by granting an injunction. The power to restrain a litigant in foreign proceedings by injunction is 'to be exercised with great caution so as to avoid even the appearance of interference with another court'.[34]

11.2.8   It is not easy to extract clear principles from the decided cases, each of which turns on its own particular facts. In deciding whether to grant an anti-suit injunction 'the court must seek to strike a balance'[35] between the possible injustice to the defendant in the foreign proceedings if the injunction is not granted and the possible injustice to the foreign claimant if it is. The likelihood of the court granting an anti-suit injunction seems to be related to the strength of the connection between the dispute and the foreign forum. Where the foreign forum is either an appropriate forum—or at least not an inappropriate one—the court will normally be unwilling to interfere by granting an anti-suit injunction.[36] In the words of Leggatt LJ:

The very fact that the foreign court constitutes a natural forum usually means that the institution of proceedings in it is not unconscionable.[37]

---

[30] Lawrence Collins LJ in *Elektrim SA v Vivendi Holdings 1 Corporation* [2009] 1 Lloyd's Rep 59, 71 (at [83]).

[31] [1987] AC 871, 896.

[32] *Arab Monetary Fund v Hashim (No 6)* The Financial Times, 24 July 1992.

[33] *Barclays Bank Plc v Homan* [1993] BCLC 680.

[34] Lord Denning MR in The Lisboa [1980] 2 Lloyd's Rep 546, 549.

[35] Glidewell LJ in *Barclays Bank plc v Homan* [1993] BCLC 680, 701.

[36] Eg, *Société Commerciale de Réassurance v Eras International Ltd (No 2)* [1995] 2 All ER 278; *Satyam Computer Services Ltd v Upaid Systems Ltd* [2008] 2 All ER (Comm) 465.

[37] *Barclays Bank plc v Homan* [1993] BCLC 680, 705.

The court is more likely to regard foreign proceedings as vexatious or oppressive if the foreign forum is regarded as an inappropriate (or clearly inappropriate) forum.[38] Where, for example, a claimant starts proceedings on the same cause of action both in England and abroad, the defendant may legitimately apply to the English court for an anti-suit injunction so that he does not have to fight the same claim on two fronts. In this type of case, the court is likely to grant an anti-suit injunction if satisfied that England is the more appropriate forum.[39] Similarly, in a case where the defendant 'is seeking to re-litigate in a foreign jurisdiction matters which are already *res judicata* between himself and the [claimant] by reason of an English judgment', an anti-suit injunction restraining the defendant from continuing with the foreign proceedings may be granted.[40] Conversely, where the claimant, having commenced proceedings as of right in the foreign forum, will benefit from an obvious advantage abroad (such as security for its claim), it would be inappropriate for the English court to grant an anti-suit injunction.[41]

11.2.9 Where foreign proceedings have not yet been commenced and are not contemplated the court will be extremely unwilling to grant an anti-suit injunction. In *ED & F Man (Sugar) Ltd v Haryanto (No 2)*[42] the parties had entered two contracts for the sale of sugar, both of which were governed by English law. After protracted arbitration and legal proceedings the parties made a settlement agreement. Subsequently, the defendant obtained a judgment from the Indonesian courts to the effect that the original contracts and the settlement agreement were illegal and of no effect. In the context of proceedings in England to enforce the settlement agreement, the plaintiff also sought a general worldwide ban to prevent the defendant from relying on the Indonesian judgment, whether by way of offence or defence. The injunction sought by the plaintiff was not, however, aimed at specific foreign proceedings; indeed, it was not even known whether the defendant was contemplating further proceedings abroad. The Court of Appeal upheld Steyn J's refusal to grant the injunction on the basis that the grant of an injunction would be 'an illegitimate interference (albeit indirectly) with the processes of the courts worldwide'.[43]

11.2.10 The majority of cases in which the English court has been faced with an application for an anti-suit injunction on the basis of vexation or oppression can be divided into a number of groups. The first comprises choice of forum cases in which the claimant seeks to establish that the foreign proceedings are vexatious or oppressive because the substantive or procedural law applied by the foreign court is different from that which would be applied in the natural forum. The second group involve cases where it is alleged that the bringing of the foreign proceedings is not in good faith. The third category of cases involves situations where the claimant

---

[38] See Lord Hobhouse in *Turner v Grovit* [2002] 1 WLR 107, 118 (at [25]). See, eg, *General Star International Indemnity Ltd v Sterling Cooke Brown Reinsurance Brokers Ltd* [2003] ILPr 314.
[39] *Advanced Portfolio Technologies Inc v Ainsworth* [1996] FSR 217.
[40] Lawrence Collins LJ in *Masri v Consolidated Contractors International (UK) Ltd (No 3)* [2009] QB 503, 530 (at [82]). See A Briggs, 'Enforcing and reinforcing an English judgment' [2008] *LMCLQ* 421.
[41] See, eg, *The Irini A* [1999] 1 Lloyd's Rep 196.
[42] [1991] 1 Lloyd's Rep 429.
[43] [1991] 1 Lloyd's Rep 161, 168.

seeks an injunction to restrain arbitration proceedings, rather than foreign court proceedings. In a fourth group are cases in which a party to English litigation brings proceedings abroad with the purpose of collecting evidence which will subsequently be used in English proceedings. The fifth group, the so-called 'single forum' cases, includes situations where the claimant alleges that the foreign proceedings involve the extraterritorial application by the foreign court of the law of that country. However, not all cases where the application for an anti-suit injunction is based on unconscionability obviously fall within one of these five categories. In these miscellaneous situations, the court will not normally seek to interfere in the foreign proceedings.[44]

SUBSTANTIVE AND PROCEDURAL DIFFERENCES

11.2.11   Several of the cases have involved applications to restrain a litigant from pursuing proceedings in the United States. The advantages which may be sought in American proceedings include the contingency fee system, broad rules on pre-trial disclosure and generous damages awards. The pursuit of such advantages is not in itself vexatious or oppressive, though it may be regarded as such if the foreign forum is thought to be inappropriate.[45]

11.2.12   *Société Nationale Industrielle Aérospatiale v Lee Kui Jak*[46] concerned proceedings brought following a helicopter crash in Brunei in which the plaintiff's husband was killed. The helicopter had been manufactured by a French company and operated by a Malaysian company. The plaintiff started proceedings against both companies in Brunei and against the French company in Texas. The French company applied to the Brunei courts for an injunction restraining the plaintiff from continuing with the proceedings in Texas. The basis of the application was that, whereas in the context of the Brunei proceedings the French company—if found liable—could claim indemnity from the Malaysian company, there was no such possibility in Texas. Furthermore, there was no advantage to the plaintiff in pursuing the Texas proceedings, since the French company had given undertakings which ensured that any potential advantages to the plaintiff in the Texan proceedings would also be available in Brunei. The Privy Council decided that, in these circumstances, the proceedings in Texas were oppressive and that the grant of an injunction was appropriate.

ABSENCE OF GOOD FAITH

11.2.13   Where foreign proceedings are not brought bona fide, the court may regard the action of the claimant in the foreign proceedings to be vexatious. So, the court will consider the defendant's conduct to be vexatious and may seek to restrain the defendant from continuing with the foreign proceedings in a case where the defendant in English proceedings commences proceedings in bad faith in another jurisdiction[47]—for example, with the express purpose of frustrating or disrupting parallel

---

[44] See, eg, *The Western Regent* [2005] 2 Lloyd's Rep 359.
[45] See, eg, *Simon Engineering Plc v Butte Mining Plc (No 2)* [1996] 1 Lloyd's Rep 91.
[46] [1987] AC 871.
[47] See *Turner v Grovit* [2000] 1 QB 345 (CA) and the speech of Lord Hobhouse at [2002] 1 WLR 107, 120 (at [29]). See also *Cadre SA v Astra Asigurari SA* [2006] 1 Lloyd's Rep 560.

proceedings in England[48] or of making a collateral attack on an English judgment[49] or an English arbitration.[50] It should be emphasised, however, that the purpose of an anti-suit injunction 'is not to ensure that an English judgment is recognised by a friendly foreign state, but to prevent unconscionable conduct'.[51] The continuation of foreign proceedings in relation to matters on which the English court has rendered judgment is not, without more, vexatious and oppressive; in the absence of exceptional circumstances, the English court should not interfere, albeit indirectly, with the process of the foreign court and the right of the foreign court to decide in accordance with its own laws whether or not to recognise or enforce the English judgment.[52] Where the defendant in English proceedings is unable to show any legitimate interest in bringing proceedings abroad—for example, where the issues raised abroad either have been or could have been raised in ongoing English proceedings—the court will conclude that it is appropriate to grant an anti-suit injunction on the basis that the bringing of the foreign proceedings is vexatious.[53]

ANTI-ARBITRATION INJUNCTIONS

11.2.14 The English court also has jurisdiction to grant an anti-suit injunction to restrain the defendant from pursuing arbitration proceedings whether in England or in another country.[54] However, it is not normally possible for the claimant to satisfy the conditions for the grant of an anti-suit injunction in such cases.[55] Indeed, where court proceedings are brought in breach of the terms of a binding arbitration agreement between the parties, the duty of the court is to grant a stay of those proceedings.[56] There are, however, exceptional cases in which the courts are prepared to grant an anti-arbitration injunction on the basis that, in the circumstances, the pursuit of arbitration proceedings is vexatious or oppressive. For example, in *Albon v Naza Motor Trading Sdn Bhd (No 4)*[57] the claimant argued that the alleged arbitration agreement was a forgery and the court granted a temporary anti-arbitration injunction to enable the allegation of forgery to be decided by the English court. Similarly, if there has already been a judgment (whether in England or abroad) declaring the alleged arbitration agreement to be invalid, it may be appropriate for the English court to grant an injunction to restrain one of the parties from commencing or

---

[48] See, eg, *Albon v Naza Motor Trading Sdn Bhd (No 4)* [2007] 2 Lloyd's Rep 420, affirmed [2008] 1 Lloyd's Rep 1. See also *Tonicstar Ltd v American Home Assurance Co* [2005] Lloyd's Rep IR 32.

[49] *Trafigura Beheer BV v Kookmin Bank Co (No 2)* [2007] 1 Lloyd's Rep 669. A Briggs, 'A further consequence of choice of law?' (2007) 123 *LQR* 18.

[50] *Noble Assurance Co v Gerling-Konzern General Insurance Co* [2007] 1 CLC 87 (on the facts of the case, the court in its discretion granted relief in declaratory rather than injunctive form).

[51] Clarke LJ in *The Western Regent* [2005] 2 Lloyd's Rep 359, 369 (at [48]).

[52] See Clarke LJ in *The Western Regent* [2005] 2 Lloyd's Rep 359, 369–70 (at [50]). See also *Akai Pty Ltd v People's Insurance Co Ltd* [1998] 1 Lloyd's Rep 90, 108.

[53] *Glencore International AG v Exter Shipping Ltd* [2002] 2 All ER (Comm) 1. A Briggs, (2002) 73 *BYIL* 463. See also *Shell International Petroleum Co Ltd v Coral Oil Co Ltd* [1999] 1 Lloyd's Rep 606.

[54] There appears to be some doubt as to whether this jurisdiction is derived from s 44 of the Arbitration Act 1996 or s 37(1) of the Supreme Court Act 1981 (or both): *Republic of Kazakhstan v Istil Group (No 2)* [2008] 1 Lloyd's Rep 382; *Sheffield United FC Ltd v West Ham United FC plc* [2009] 1 Lloyd's Rep 167.

[55] See, eg, *Elektrim SA v Vivendi Universal SA (No 2)* [2007] 2 Lloyd's Rep 8. Compare, however, *Albon v Naza Motor Trading Sdn Bhd (No 4)* [2008] 1 All ER (Comm) 351.

[56] Arbitration Act 1996, s 9. See section 21.2.

[57] [2008] 1 Lloyd's Rep 1.

pursuing arbitration proceedings, rather than leaving the question of the arbitrator's jurisdiction to be decided by the arbitrator.[58]

COLLECTING EVIDENCE ABROAD

11.2.15 In principle, a party to English proceedings may seek to obtain evidence from abroad. Such evidence can be sought in the context of the English proceedings themselves.[59] Alternatively, a litigant may bring separate proceedings abroad in accordance with the procedural law of the foreign country in question with a view to obtaining evidence for use in the English proceedings. If a litigant chooses to follow the latter course, the English court will not, as a general rule, grant an anti-suit injunction preventing the litigant from pursuing the foreign proceedings. So long as the foreign proceedings do not interfere with the English court's control over its own process there is no reason for the court to interfere.[60]

11.2.16 However, the court may conclude on the facts of a particular case that foreign proceedings, the purpose of which is to collect evidence to support English proceedings, are vexatious or oppressive. For example, in *Bankers Trust International Plc v PT Dharmala Sakti Sejahtera*[61] the court granted an injunction to prevent the defendant from pursuing proceedings in New York, purportedly to obtain evidence for use in English proceedings. There were various reasons why the New York proceedings were regarded as oppressive. Of particular significance was the fact that the English proceedings had already been completed (though judgment had not yet been given). Accordingly, the obtaining of any new evidence in New York would have necessitated re-opening the English proceedings, thereby causing delay. Furthermore, the New York proceedings were highly speculative in nature.[62]

SINGLE FORUM CASES

11.2.17 There is some support in the cases for the view that, if the foreign court is the only available forum for the trial of the claim, an anti-suit injunction may be granted in exceptional circumstances notwithstanding the fact that the effect of an anti-suit injunction in such a case is to deprive the claimant in the foreign proceedings of any remedy. What emerges from the decisions of the House of Lords in *British Airways Board v Laker Airways Ltd*[63] and of the Court of Appeal in *Midland Bank Plc v Laker Airways Ltd*[64] is that an anti-suit injunction may be granted in a single forum case if two conditions are satisfied. First, the foreign proceedings must be, in their nature, oppressive or unconscionable. The English courts have tended to regard US anti-trust suits under the Sherman and Clayton Acts as oppressive. Secondly, the foreign proceedings must involve the extraterritorial application of the law of the foreign forum, which turns on the extent to which the dispute has a meaningful connection with the

---

[58] See *Republic of Kazakhstan v Istil (No 2)* [2008] 1 Lloyd's Rep 382.
[59] CPR Pt 34.
[60] *South Carolina Insurance Co v Assurantie Maatschappij 'De Zeven Provincien' NV* [1987] AC 24.
[61] [1996] CLC 252.
[62] See also *Omega Group Holdings Ltd v Kozeny* [2002] CLC 132.
[63] [1985] AC 58.
[64] [1986] QB 689. J Crawford, (1986) 57 *BYIL* 414.

foreign forum. Both conditions were fulfilled in the *Midland Bank* case,[65] in which an injunction was granted to restrain the defendant from pursuing an anti-trust suit in the United States against the plaintiff, an English bank. According to the defendant, the plaintiff had conspired with British Airways and British Caledonian to drive the defendant out of the market. In view of the oppressive nature of the United States procedures, it was unconscionable and unjust for the plaintiff to invoke the United States jurisdiction under the Sherman and Clayton Acts against an English company, whose dealings with the defendant had taken place entirely in England and who had not submitted to the jurisdiction of the United States courts.[66] By contrast, an anti-suit injunction was not granted in *British Airways Board v Laker Airways Ltd*.[67] The defendant had brought anti-trust proceedings in the United States against two UK airlines, British Airways and British Caledonian. The airlines applied for an anti-suit injunction, relying on the allegedly oppressive nature of the US proceedings. The House of Lords discharged the anti-suit injunction which had been granted at first instance and upheld by the Court of Appeal. Lord Diplock placed particular emphasis on the fact that the airlines, by conducting business operations in the United States, could be regarded as having 'voluntarily submitted' to US law as a consequence of which the anti-trust proceedings were not 'unconscionable'.[68] In these circumstances, it could not be said that the defendant was seeking the extraterritorial application of US anti-trust law. Accordingly, there was no legitimate reason for the English court to interfere.

11.2.18 It is questionable whether the decision in *Midland Bank Plc v Laker Airways Ltd*[69] is still good law. Lord Hobhouse's speech in *Turner v Grovit*[70] emphasised that the justification for anti-suit injunctions is the need to protect existing legal proceedings in England—a condition which cannot be satisfied in cases where there can be no question of the parties' dispute being litigated in England. Nevertheless, there is no discussion in *Turner v Grovit* of the single forum cases; nor did the House of Lords expressly consider the possibility of exceptions to the general rule as suggested by Lord Goff in *Airbus Industrie GIE v Patel*.[71]

Infringement of a Legal or Equitable Right

11.2.19 If A invades or threatens to invade a legal or equitable right of B for the enforcement of which A is amenable to the jurisdiction of the English court, the court may grant an injunction restraining A.[72] Accordingly, the court may grant an anti-suit injunction when a litigant has a legal or equitable right not to be sued in a foreign court on the cause of action in question. A right not to be sued abroad may

---

[65] [1986] QB 689.
[66] See Dillon LJ at [1986] QB 689, 704.
[67] [1985] AC 58.
[68] [1985] AC 58, 84.
[69] [1986] QB 689.
[70] [2002] 1 WLR 107.
[71] [1999] 1 AC 119.
[72] Lord Brandon in *South Carolina Insurance Co v Assurantie Maatschappij 'De Zeven Provincien' NV* [1987] AC 24, 40.

be contractual (for example, where there is an arbitration clause or a clause conferring exclusive jurisdiction on the English courts) or arise by virtue of an equitable defence to the claim (such as estoppel, election, waiver, or laches).[73]

11.2.20 In practice, the possibility of a litigant obtaining an anti-suit injunction to protect a legal or equitable right arises most frequently where foreign proceedings have been brought in breach of an arbitration clause or an exclusive jurisdiction clause.[74] How should the courts exercise their discretion in these circumstances? Although, where the parties have agreed to litigate in a particular forum, whether in England or abroad, the court seeks to hold the parties to their bargain, it does not necessarily follow that the court should restrain a litigant from pursuing foreign proceedings brought in breach of a dispute-resolution clause as readily as it would stay English proceedings which are brought in breach of a foreign jurisdiction clause. In the context of an application for an anti-suit injunction the question of comity is more prominent.

11.2.21 Notwithstanding considerations of comity, the trend in recent cases has been for the courts to grant anti-suit injunctions in cases involving foreign proceedings brought in breach of a dispute-resolution agreement almost as a matter of course. The start of this trend was the decision of the Court of Appeal in *Continental Bank NA v Aeakos Compania Naviera SA*.[75] The Court of Appeal decided that, in the absence of special countervailing factors, a case where proceedings are brought abroad in breach of an exclusive jurisdiction clause in favour of the English courts is 'the paradigm case' for the grant of an anti-suit injunction.[76] In this type of situation an anti-suit injunction is 'the only effective remedy' for the defendant's breach of contract.[77] A similar approach was taken in *The Angelic Grace*,[78] a case in which the defendant commenced Italian proceedings in breach of an English arbitration clause. The Court of Appeal had little hesitation in acceding to the plaintiff's application for an anti-suit injunction. According to Millett LJ:

[W]here an injunction is sought to restrain a party from proceeding in a foreign court in breach of an arbitration agreement governed by English law, the English court need feel no diffidence in granting the injunction, provided that it is sought promptly and before the foreign proceedings are too far advanced. I see no difference in principle between an injunction to restrain proceedings in breach of an arbitration clause and one to restrain proceedings in breach of an exclusive jurisdiction clause. ... The justification for the grant of the injunction in either case is that without it the plaintiff will be deprived of its contractual rights in a situation in which damages are manifestly an inadequate remedy. The jurisdiction is, of course, discretionary and is not exercised as a matter of course, but good reason needs to be shown why it should not be exercised in any given case.[79]

---

[73] *British Airways Board v Laker Airways Ltd* [1985] AC 58. JG Collier, [1984] *CLJ* 253; B Davenport, 'Restraining foreign proceedings' [1984] *LMCLQ* 563.

[74] Where the parties have agreed to the non-exclusive jurisdiction of the English court, the commencement of foreign proceedings by one of the parties is not a breach of contract; in such a case the court will only grant an anti-suit injunction if the pursuit of the foreign proceedings is vexatious or oppressive: *Sabah Shipyard (Pakistan) Ltd v Islamic Republic of Pakistan* [2003] 2 Lloyd's Rep 571; *Royal Bank of Canada v Coöperatieve Centrale Raiffeisen-Boerenleenbank BA* [2004] 1 Lloyd's Rep 471; *Deutsche Bank AG v Highland Crusader Offshore Partners LP* [2009] 2 Lloyd's Rep 617.

[75] [1994] 1 WLR 588. For further consideration of this case, see section 11.3.

[76] Steyn LJ at [1994] 1 WLR 588, 598.

[77] *Ibid*.

[78] [1995] 1 Lloyd's Rep 87. N Pengelley, 'Judicial comity and angelic grace' [1998] *ADRLJ* 196.

[79] [1995] 1 Lloyd's Rep 87, 96. See also the similar comments of Neill LJ at [1995] 1 Lloyd's Rep 87, 97.

11.2.22 The effect of these decisions is to raise a presumption that an anti-suit injunction will be granted to restrain proceedings brought in breach of an English jurisdiction clause or arbitration agreement. No longer is it necessary for judges at first instance to pay lip-service to the principle that an anti-suit injunction should be available only in exceptional circumstances. Where the parties have agreed to English jurisdiction:

the Court should not be reluctant to grant an injunction on the ground that to do so might be thought to be an interference with the exercise of a jurisdiction by a Court of competent jurisdiction elsewhere. It would not be such an interference but merely the enforcement of a contractual promise.[80]

11.2.23 The general principle that 'the parties should be kept to their bargain unless there is a good reason to the contrary'[81] was endorsed by the House of Lords in *Donohue v Armco Inc.*[82] Lord Bingham summarised the position in the following terms:

If contracting parties agree to give a particular court exclusive jurisdiction to rule on claims between those parties, and a claim falling within the scope of the agreement is made in proceedings in a forum other than that which the parties have agreed, the English court will ordinarily exercise its discretion (whether ... by restraining the prosecution of proceedings in the non-contractual forum abroad, or by such other procedural order as is appropriate in the circumstances) to secure compliance with the contractual bargain, unless the party suing in the non-contractual forum (the burden being on him) can show strong reasons for suing in that forum.[83]

Accordingly, in the absence of special circumstances, anti-suit injunctions are routinely granted in cases where foreign proceedings are brought in breach of a dispute-resolution agreement.[84] However, the burden on the applicant is to show a high degree of probability that its case is right (in particular, that the parties are bound by the alleged dispute-resolution clause).[85] The court will not grant an

---

[80] Clarke J in *A/S D/S Svendborg v Wansa* [1996] 2 Lloyd's Rep 559, 569.

[81] Clarke J in *A/S D/S Svendborg v Wansa* [1996] 2 Lloyd's Rep 559, 570.

[82] [2002] 1 All ER 749.

[83] [2002] 1 All ER 749, 759 (at [24]). See also the speech of Lord Hobhouse in *Turner v Grovit* [2002] 1 WLR 107.

[84] See *Akai Pty Ltd v People's Insurance Co Ltd* [1998] 1 Lloyd's Rep 90 (FMB Reynolds, 'Overriding policy of the forum: the other side of the coin' [1998] *LMCLQ* 1); *Toepfer International GmbH v Société Cargill France* [1998] 1 Lloyd's Rep 379; *Credit Suisse First Boston (Europe) Ltd v MLC (Bermuda) Ltd* [1999] 1 Lloyd's Rep 767; *Bankers Trust Co v PT Jakarta International Hotels and Development* [1999] 1 Lloyd's Rep 910; *Shell International Petroleum Co Ltd v Coral Oil Co Ltd* [1999] 1 Lloyd's Rep 72; *XL Insurance Ltd v Owens Corning* [2000] 2 Lloyd's Rep 500; *The Kribi* [2001] 1 Lloyd's Rep 76; *The Ivan Zagubanski* [2002] 1 Lloyd's Rep 106; *Society of Lloyd's v White (No 1)* [2002] ILPr 85; *Society of Lloyd's v White (No 2)* [2002] ILPr 104; *The Epsilon Rosa* [2003] 2 Lloyd's Rep 509; *Beazley v Horizon Offshore Contractors Inc* [2005] ILPr 123; *OT Africa Line Ltd v Magic Sportswear Corp* [2005] 2 Lloyd's Rep 170; *The Hornbay* [2006] 2 Lloyd's Rep 44; *General Motors Corp v Royal & Sun Alliance Insurance plc* [2007] 2 CLC 507; *C v D* [2008] 1 Lloyd's Rep 239; *Starlight Shipping Co v Tai Ping Insurance Co Ltd* [2008] 1 Lloyd's Rep 230; *Standard Bank plc v Agrinvest International Inc* [2008] 1 Lloyd's Rep 532; *Steamship Mutual Underwriting Association (Bermuda) Ltd v Sulpicio Lines Inc* [2008] 2 Lloyd's Rep 269; *The Duden* [2009] 1 Lloyd's Rep 145; *Sheffield United FC Ltd v West Ham United FC plc* [2009] 1 Lloyd's Rep 167; *Vitol SA v Arcturus Merchant Trust Ltd* [2009] EWHC 800 (Comm); *Rimpacific Navigation Inc v Daehan Shipbuilding Co Ltd* [2009] EWHC 2941 (Comm). See also cases in which, although there was no dispute-resolution agreement as such, the claimant in the foreign proceedings had contractually agreed not to bring those proceedings: *National Westminster Bank v Utrecht-America Finance Company* [2001] 3 All ER 733; *CNA Insurance Co Ltd v Office Depot International (UK) Ltd* [2007] Lloyd's Rep IR 89. For a similar approach in a case involving a 'no action clause' in a bond issue, see *Elektrim SA v Vivendi Holdings 1 Corporation* [2009] 1 Lloyd's Rep 59.

[85] *Bankers Trust Co v PT Jakarta International Hotels and Development* [1999] 1 Lloyd's Rep 910. If the foreign proceedings fall outside the scope of a dispute-resolution clause between the parties, the case in

anti-suit injunction if it is no more than arguable that the foreign proceedings in question were brought in breach of contract.[86] *A fortiori*, in a case where part of the factual background is a contract which includes an English jurisdiction clause, the court will not grant an anti-suit injunction if the foreign proceedings do not fall within the scope of the clause.[87] Conversely, an anti-suit injunction may be obtained in a case where the effect of the foreign proceedings—even if not strictly in breach of the dispute-resolution clause—would be to frustrate the claimant's contractual entitlement to have the substantive dispute resolved by the contractual forum.[88]

11.2.24   This approach has been erroneously extended to cases where the exclusive jurisdiction of the English court is imposed by statute. In *Samengo-Turner v Marsh & McLennan (Services) Ltd*[89] a dispute arose under a contract of employment which included a jurisdiction clause in favour of the New York courts. When the employer[90] started proceedings in New York against three of its employees, the employees (who were domiciled in England) applied to the English court for an anti-suit injunction to restrain the continuation of those proceedings. The employees' argument was that, as the New York jurisdiction clause, which had been entered into before the dispute arose, was not enforceable against them,[91] they had a legal right under Article 20 of the Brussels I Regulation not to be sued other than in the courts of the Member State in which they were domiciled. Although Tuckey LJ did not consider that the argument in favour of the grant of an injunction was as strong as in cases where foreign proceedings are brought in breach of a dispute-resolution agreement,[92] the Court of Appeal granted an anti-suit injunction to protect the employees' right under the Regulation to be sued only in the English courts. The decision has justifiably been described as 'quite extraordinary' and 'calamitous'[93] and it has been convincingly argued that the case was decided *per incuriam*; the Court of Appeal was led into error by regarding the Brussels I Regulation as the source of a 'right' to be sued in the English courts.[94] The correct analysis is that the Brussels I Regulation merely directs the courts of Member States either to assume or decline jurisdiction in certain circumstances and does not confer rights (or impose obligations) on natural and legal persons. As a result, the grant of an anti-suit injunction in this type of case is wholly inappropriate and unsupportable in terms of principle or policy.

---

favour of an anti-suit injunction being granted falls away: *Brave Bulk Transport Ltd v Spot on Shipping Ltd* [2009] 2 Lloyd's Rep 115.

[86] *American International Specialty Lines Insurance Co v Abbott Laboratories* [2003] 1 Lloyd's Rep 267.
[87] *AWB (Geneva) SA v North America Steamships Ltd* [2007] 2 Lloyd's Rep 315.
[88] *The Kallang* [2007] 1 Lloyd's Rep 160.
[89] [2007] 2 All ER (Comm) 813.
[90] Technically, the claimant in the New York proceedings was an entity which was part of the same economic group as the employer and which the Court of Appeal treated as being in the same position as the employer.
[91] See Brussels I Reg, Art 21.
[92] [2007] 2 All ER (Comm) 813, 823 (at [41]).
[93] A Briggs, (2007) 78 *BYIL* 615, 620.
[94] A Briggs, 'Who Is Bound by the Brussels Regulation?' [2007] *LMCLQ* 433. See also the more muted criticisms of A Dickinson, 'Resurgence of the Anti-Suit Injunction: The Brussels I Regulation as a Source of Civil Obligations?' (2008) 57 *ICLQ* 465.

Reasons for not Granting an Anti-suit Injunction

11.2.25   The English authorities have produced a situation where, in a case involving foreign proceedings which are brought in breach of a contractual dispute-resolution clause, the focus of the inquiry has shifted away from a consideration of the reasons for granting an anti-suit injunction to an examination of the possible grounds on which the grant of such an injunction may be refused. It must always be remembered that the fundamental question is whether, in all the circumstances, it is just and convenient for the court to grant the relief sought by the claimant. The court may, for example, refuse to grant an anti-suit injunction in a case where allegations made in the context of the foreign proceedings involve an impeachment of the contract containing the jurisdiction clause.[95] The court will not grant an anti-suit injunction if it will serve no purpose. Where, for example, it is clear that the English proceedings will be concluded before the foreign proceedings are scheduled to commence, an anti-suit injunction should not be granted, even though the foreign proceedings are brought in breach of the terms of an English jurisdiction clause.[96]

FOREIGN PROCEEDINGS FOR PROVISIONAL MEASURES OR SECURITY

11.2.26   In a case where, notwithstanding the fact that the parties agreed to English jurisdiction or to arbitration, legal proceedings are brought in a foreign court, a distinction should be drawn between proceedings concerning the substantive issues and proceedings relating to provisional or protective measures. Where the litigation abroad concerns the merits of the dispute there are good reasons why the defendant should seek an anti-suit injunction from the English court. The position is different, however, where the foreign proceedings are concerned only with provisional measures or security. Where, for example, a cargo owner who has agreed to the exclusive jurisdiction of the English courts, has a claim against a one-ship company, if the exclusive jurisdiction agreement entitles the ship owner to an injunction preventing the cargo owner from taking protective measures in a foreign forum where the ship is located, this is tantamount to depriving the cargo owner of any effective remedy.[97]

11.2.27   It is perfectly possible for the express terms of the parties' dispute-resolution clause to confer exclusive jurisdiction as regards substantive disputes to the English courts, but to permit either party to seek provisional measures in other courts.[98] In this type of case, there can be no question of the claimant being entitled to an anti-suit injunction from the English court to restrain the defendant from applying for provisional measures abroad. What is the position, however, if the dispute-resolution clause does not expressly address the issue of provisional measures? There are two possible solutions. First, depending on the precise wording of the dispute-resolution clause, the court may interpret the clause as relating only to substantive proceedings and not to proceedings concerned with provisional measures, security or enforcement.[99] Secondly, in a case where the foreign proceedings do not involve the substance

---

[95] *Credit Suisse First Boston (Europe) Ltd v Seagate Trading Co Ltd* [1999] 1 Lloyd's Rep 784.
[96] *Banque Cantonale Vaudoise v Waterlily Maritime Inc* [1997] 2 Lloyd's Rep 347.
[97] Lord Denning MR in *The Lisboa* [1980] 2 Lloyd's Rep 546, 548–9.
[98] See, eg, *Ultisol Transport Contractors Ltd v Bouygues Offshore SA* [1996] 2 Lloyd's Rep 140.
[99] See, eg, Lord Denning MR in *The Lisboa* [1980] 2 Lloyd's Rep 546, 548.

of the dispute (for example, where proceedings *in rem* are commenced abroad for the purpose of obtaining security), the court may refuse to grant an anti-suit injunction unless the party seeking the injunction tenders alternative security for the claim.[100]

DELAY

11.2.28   It must always be remembered that the court has discretion whether to grant an anti-suit injunction—even in cases where proceedings abroad are brought in breach of a dispute-resolution agreement. One of the factors which will have an impact on the way in which the court exercises its discretion is delay. As a general rule, the claimant who wishes to restrain the other party from litigating abroad should seek injunctive relief 'promptly and before the foreign proceedings are too far advanced'.[101]

11.2.29   In *Schiffahrtsgesellschaft Detlev von Appen GmbH v Voest Alpine Intertrading GmbH*[102] Brazilian proceedings were commenced in February 1993 in breach of an English arbitration clause. Although the plaintiff did not apply for an anti-suit injunction until December 1994 Morison J granted the relief sought by the plaintiff[103] and this decision was upheld by the Court of Appeal.[104] While the delay was not serious enough for the grant of an anti-suit injunction to be refused, the plaintiff was required to indemnify the defendant for the extra costs occasioned by the delay. There was a different outcome in *Toepfer International GmbH v Molino Bosch Srl.*[105] Notwithstanding the fact that the contract between the parties contained an English arbitration clause, the defendant started proceedings against the plaintiff in Italy. Although the Italian proceedings were commenced in 1988 the plaintiff did not start proceedings in England with a view to obtaining an anti-suit injunction until 1995. Even though an injunction would almost certainly have been granted had the application been made promptly, Mance J decided that, in view of the delay between the commencement of the Italian proceedings and the plaintiff's application, the discretion should be exercised against granting the relief sought.[106] *A fortiori*, where a litigant has obtained a foreign judgment in proceedings brought in breach of a dispute-resolution clause, the court will not grant an injunction to restrain proceedings to enforce the judgment in England.[107] It should be noted, however, that foreign judgments, the enforcement of which is governed by the common law or one of the statutory regimes based on the common law,[108] are not normally entitled to recognition and enforcement if the bringing of the proceedings abroad was contrary to an arbitration clause or jurisdiction agreement.[109]

---

[100] *Petromin SA v Secnev Marine Ltd* [1995] 1 Lloyd's Rep 603.

[101] Millett LJ in *The Angelic Grace* [1995] 1 Lloyd's Rep 87, 96.

[102] [1997] 2 Lloyd's Rep 279.

[103] [1997] 1 Lloyd's Rep 179.

[104] See also *Advent Capital plc v GN Ellinas Importers-Exporters* Ltd [2004] ILPr 377; *Markel International Co Ltd v Craft, The Norseman* [2007] Lloyd's Rep IR 403.

[105] [1996] 1 Lloyd's Rep 510.

[106] See also *The Golden Anne* [1984] 2 Lloyd's Rep 489; *The Skier Star* [2008] 1 Lloyd's Rep 652.

[107] *The Eastern Trader* [1996] 2 Lloyd's Rep 585.

[108] Administration of Justice Act 1920; Foreign Judgments (Reciprocal Enforcement) Act 1933.

[109] Civil Jurisdiction and Judgments Act 1982, s 32(1). This ground for denying effect to a foreign judgment does not apply to judgments granted by the courts of Member States in cases falling within the scope of Art 1 of the Brussels I Regulation. For further discussion, see paras 12.4.19–12.4.22.

CHALLENGE TO THE FOREIGN COURT'S JURISDICTION

11.2.30 As a general rule, if the claimant in the English proceedings submits to the jurisdiction of the foreign court, it is reasonable for the court to assume that the claimant has waived the jurisdiction clause and to refuse to grant an anti-suit injunction—though exceptional circumstances may nevertheless justify relief being granted.[110] However, it will normally be the case that, where proceedings are commenced abroad in breach of a dispute-resolution clause, the jurisdiction of the foreign court will be challenged by the defendant in the foreign proceedings. If an application for an anti-suit injunction is made before the foreign court has ruled on its own jurisdiction, the grant of an anti-suit injunction by the English court would appear premature. At such an early stage, foreign courts should be 'left in control over their own proceedings'.[111] In principle, it is more appropriate for the foreign court to determine its own jurisdiction than for the English court to make an order restraining a litigant from participating in foreign proceedings.[112] Accordingly, as a general rule, the grant of an anti-suit injunction should be made (if at all) only after the foreign court has ruled on its own jurisdiction.

11.2.31 It would seem, however, that in cases involving foreign proceedings brought in breach of the parties' dispute-resolution agreement, the courts are not willing to await the decision of the foreign court and are prepared to grant an anti-suit injunction before the foreign court has ruled on its own jurisdiction.[113] In *The Angelic Grace* Millett LJ rejected the notion that for the English court to seek to pre-empt the decision of the foreign court in this way involves a breach of comity:

I cannot accept the proposition that any court would be offended by the grant of an injunction to restrain a party from invoking a jurisdiction which he had promised not to invoke and which it was its own duty to decline.[114]

This approach is premised, however, on the dubious assumption that foreign courts will necessarily share the English court's view on issues such as the validity of the dispute-resolution clause.

CASES INVOLVING MULTIPLE PARTIES

11.2.32 It is well established that the court may refuse to stay English proceedings between A and B, notwithstanding the fact that A and B agreed to the exclusive jurisdiction of a foreign court, on the ground that A has a related claim against C and England provides the most appropriate forum where A's claims against B and C can be heard together.[115] In such a case, the court may take the view that there is 'strong cause' why A should not be held to the jurisdiction agreement.[116] It has been suggested that the same principles apply whether the contractual forum is England or another country[117] and that the test which is applied in cases involving foreign jurisdiction clauses (where the defendant applies for a stay) should also be applied in cases involving an English jurisdiction

---

[110] *A/S D/S Svendborg v Wansa* [1997] 2 Lloyd's Rep 183.

[111] Colman J in *Sokana Industries Inc v Freyre Co Inc* [1994] 2 Lloyd's Rep 57, 66.

[112] See Judge Brice QC in *Deaville v Aeroflot Russian International Airlines* [1997] 2 Lloyd's Rep 67, 75.

[113] *Continental Bank NA v Aeakos Compania Naviera SA* [1994] 1 WLR 588.

[114] [1995] 1 Lloyd's Rep 87, 96.

[115] *The El Amria* [1981] 2 Lloyd's Rep 119.

[116] See section 9.3.

[117] See Thomas J in *Akai Pty Ltd v People's Insurance Co Ltd* [1998] 1 Lloyd's Rep 90, 104.

clause (where the claimant applies for an anti-suit injunction).[118] Accordingly, where A brings proceedings abroad against B, notwithstanding the fact that A and B have agreed to the exclusive jurisdiction of the English court, the English court should refuse to grant an anti-suit injunction if A has a related claim against C and the foreign court provides the most appropriate forum for the determination of A's claims against B and C.

11.2.33 *Bouygues Offshore SA v Caspian Shipping Co (Nos 1, 3, 4 and 5)*[119] concerned complex litigation involving a number of parties. The factual background was the loss of a barge belonging to B during a voyage between the Congo and South Africa. At the relevant time, the barge was under tow by a tug, owned by C, but managed by U, which was the towage contractor. The towage contract between B and U contained an English jurisdiction clause. The tow line parted in stormy conditions as the vessels were approaching Cape Town and the barge was driven ashore onto rocks. It was alleged that P, the Cape Town harbour authority, was partly responsible for the accident. B started proceedings against C and U in South Africa by arresting the tug and P was made a party to those proceedings. On the basis of the English jurisdiction clause in the towage contract, U applied for an anti-suit injunction to restrain B from continuing with the South African proceedings against it.

11.2.34 At first instance, Clarke J granted the relief sought by U.[120] Although it was recognised that it was desirable that B's claims against U and the other parties to the South African litigation 'should be tried at the same time and by the same tribunal',[121] the judge took the view that this was not 'sufficient to lead to the conclusion that [B] should not be held to its contract'.[122] The Court of Appeal, however, allowed B's appeal. '[N]otwithstanding the near-conclusive effect of the exclusive jurisdiction clause between [B] and [U]',[123] as South Africa was the most appropriate forum in which all the related claims could be pursued together, this was an exceptional situation in which it was not appropriate for the court to seek to enforce the jurisdiction clause by granting an anti-suit injunction against B. Allowing B to proceed with its claim against U (and the other defendants) in South Africa was 'the only way to minimize, if not avoid altogether, the risk of inconsistent decisions in different jurisdictions'.[124]

11.2.35 This approach was confirmed by the House of Lords in *Donohue v Armco Inc*.[125] While acknowledging that, where the interests of other parties are involved, the court will ordinarily seek to enforce a jurisdiction clause by granting an injunction to restrain the pursuit of proceedings in a non-contractual forum, the House of Lords accepted that the position is different in cases involving multiple parties. Notwithstanding the claimant's contractual right to have disputes resolved by the agreed forum, there are strong reasons against enforcing a jurisdiction clause in a case where the grant of an anti-suit injunction would have the effect of increasing the chances of different courts

---

[118] See Clarke J in *Ultisol Transport Contractors Ltd v Bouygues Offshore SA* [1996] 2 Lloyd's Rep 140, 149 and in *A/S D/S Svendborg v Wansa* [1996] 2 Lloyd's Rep 559, 569.
[119] [1998] 2 Lloyd's Rep 461.
[120] *Ultisol Transport Contractors Ltd v Bouygues Offshore SA* [1996] 2 Lloyd's Rep 140.
[121] [1996] 2 Lloyd's Rep 140, 150.
[122] [1996] 2 Lloyd's Rep 140, 152.
[123] Evans LJ at [1998] 2 Lloyd's Rep 461, 467.
[124] Sir John Knox at [1998] 2 Lloyd's Rep 461, 470.
[125] [2002] 1 All ER 749.

handing down conflicting judgments. In a case involving more than two parties, some of whom are not contractually bound by a jurisdiction clause:

the interests of justice are best served by the submission of the whole dispute to a single tribunal which is best fitted to make a reliable, comprehensive judgment on all the matters in issue. A procedure which permitted the possibility of different conclusions by different tribunals, perhaps made on different evidence, would ... run directly counter to the interests of justice.[126]

11.2.36 Where the court declines to grant an anti-suit injunction, notwithstanding the fact that the foreign proceedings are brought in breach of a contractual dispute-resolution agreement, the defendant in the foreign proceedings is, in principle, entitled to damages.[127]

11.3 THE BRUSSELS I REGULATION

11.3.1 Although the Brussels I Regulation does not seek to harmonise the procedural laws of the Member States[128]—and therefore does not directly forbid the English courts from exercising their inherent jurisdiction to grant anti-suit injunctions in the interests of justice—it is important to remember that national procedural law cannot be allowed to impair the effectiveness of the Regulation. Accordingly, to the extent that the grant of an anti-suit injunction impedes the proper functioning of the Regulation, it is incompatible with it. Looking at the matter from a European perspective, it is difficult to see how it could be appropriate for the English court to seek to interfere, even indirectly, with the jurisdiction of the courts of another Member State, given that the Brussels I Regulation is designed to provide a uniform code for the allocation of jurisdiction in civil and commercial matters between the Member States. Furthermore, the Brussels I Regulation, through the provisions dealing with concurrent proceedings,[129] contains a mechanism for dealing with the jurisdictional conflicts which may arise from proceedings involving the same or related issues being pursued in different Member States (by requiring any courts other than the court first seised to stay its proceedings or decline jurisdiction).[130] Where concurrent proceedings are brought first in England and then in France, the English court should not seek to pre-empt the decision of the French court by granting

---

[126] Lord Bingham at [2002] 1 All ER 749, 764 (at [34]). See also *Verity Shipping SA v NV Norexa* [2008] 1 Lloyd's Rep 652.

[127] See Lord Bingham in *Donohue v Armco Inc* [2002] 1 All ER 749, 765 (at [36]). See also *Union Discount Co Ltd v Union Discount Cal Ltd* [2002] 1 WLR 1517. A Briggs, (2001) 72 *BYIL* 446. The courts have taken the view that where damages are awarded for the costs of defending proceedings brought in breach of a dispute-resolution clause, costs should be assessed on an indemnity basis (rather than the standard basis): *A v B (No 2)* [2007] 1 All ER (Comm) 633; *National Westminster Bank plc v Rabobank Nederland (No 3)* [2008] 1 Lloyd's Rep 16. See, generally, D Tan and N Yeo, 'Breaking promises to litigate in a particular forum: are damages an appropriate remedy?' [2003] *LMCLQ* 435; N Yeo and D Tan, 'Damages for Breach of Exclusive Jurisdiction Clauses' in S Worthington (ed), *Commercial Law and Commercial Practice* (Oxford, Hart Publishing, 2003) 403–31). For a different view, see CH Tham, 'Damages for breach of English jurisdiction clauses: more than meets the eye' [2004] *LMCLQ* 46.

[128] Case C–365/88 *Kongress Agentur Hagen GmbH v Zeehaghe BV* [1990] ECR I–1845, para 17.

[129] Brussels I Reg, Arts 27–9.

[130] See section 9.1.

an anti-suit injunction against the claimant in the French proceedings;[131] it is for the French court to decide if the conditions of Article 27 or 28 of the Brussels I Regulation are satisfied and whether to stay its proceedings or decline jurisdiction. Similarly, for example, where the claimant sues a defendant for breach of contract in the courts for the place of performance of the obligation in question there can be no question of the English court restraining the claimant from proceeding in the courts which have jurisdiction under Article 5(1) rather than in the courts with jurisdiction under Article 2.

11.3.2   Nevertheless, the English courts took the view that there are certain circumstances where it is not inappropriate to grant an anti-suit injunction to restrain a litigant from commencing or continuing with proceedings in another Member State. First, the doctrine espoused by the Court of Appeal in *Continental Bank NA v Aeakos Compania Naviera SA*[132] means that in a situation where proceedings are brought in the courts of another Member State, notwithstanding an exclusive jurisdiction agreement in favour of the English courts, the English court is not required to stay its proceedings under the *lis pendens* rule and is entitled to grant an anti-suit injunction on the basis that the continuance of the foreign proceedings amounts to conduct which is vexatious and oppressive.

11.3.3   This decision is not compatible with the framework and spirit of the Brussels I Regulation and was widely criticised.[133] The fallacy on which the Court of Appeal's decision was based is the proposition that a jurisdiction clause takes precedence over the *lis pendens* rule. There is nothing in the jurisdiction provisions to suggest that this is the case. In a case such as *Continental Bank NA v Aeakos Compania Naviera SA* if the court first seised exercises jurisdiction it can only be on the basis that the jurisdiction clause does not confer exclusive jurisdiction on the English courts (for example, because the agreement does not satisfy the formal requirements or because the dispute does not fall within the scope of the clause). In these circumstances it is inappropriate for the English court to review (or to seek to pre-empt) the decision of the court first seised on the effect of the jurisdiction clause. If the defendant in proceedings brought in another Member State wishes to challenge the assumption of jurisdiction, the appropriate forum is the Member State in question rather than England. As the *Continental Bank* case was binding on both the High Court and the Court of Appeal it was routinely followed,[134] although some judges expressed reservations.[135] However, the decision of the Court of Justice in *Erich Gasser GmbH v MISAT Srl*[136] indicated that the approach of the Court of Appeal in the *Continental Bank* case was fundamentally mistaken. According to the Court of Justice, the court second seised, even if it is the court allegedly chosen by the

---

[131] *First National Bank Association v Compagnie Nationale Air Gabon* [1999] ILPr 617.

[132] [1994] 1 WLR 588. See paras 9.1.36–9.1.38.

[133] See, eg, R Asariotis, 'Antisuit Injunctions for Breach of a Choice of Forum Agreement: A Critical Review of the English Approach' (1999/2000) 19 *YBEL* 447; A Briggs, 'Anti-European teeth for choice of court clauses' [1994] *LMCLQ* 158.

[134] See, eg: *Bankers Trust International Plc v RCS Editori SpA* [1996] CLC 899; *Charterers Mutual Assurance Association Ltd v British and Foreign* [1998] ILPr 838; *Gilkes v Venizelos ANESA* [2000] ILPr 487; *The Kribi* [2001] 1 Lloyd's Rep 76; *Comet Group Plc v Unika Computer SA* [2004] ILPr 10.

[135] See, in particular, the observations of Leggatt LJ in *Phillip Alexander Securities & Futures Ltd v Bamberger* [1997] ILPr 73, 117 and those of Phillips LJ in *Toepfer International GmbH v Société Cargill France* [1998] 1 Lloyd's Rep 379, 386.

[136] Case C–116/02 [2003] ECR I–14693.

parties, must stay its proceedings pending the decision of the court first seised on the effect of the alleged jurisdiction clause.[137] Although the decision in the *Gasser* case does not address the issue of anti-suit injunctions as such, its implications are clear. If the court second seised is not entitled to determine whether there is an effective jurisdiction agreement, there can be no question of it granting a remedy for breach of that agreement.[138]

11.3.4 Notwithstanding the problems with the *Continental Bank* decision, it was extended in *Turner v Grovit*.[139] The plaintiff in the English proceedings had been employed by the second defendant; although he ordinarily worked in Britain, the plaintiff had temporarily worked in Spain. After resigning his employment, he started proceedings in England against the second defendant, claiming constructive dismissal. Proceedings for breach of contract were then commenced in Spain against the plaintiff by the third defendant, which was part of a group of companies which included the second defendant. The plaintiff then applied for an anti-suit injunction against the second and third defendants and their alleged owner and controller, the first defendant. At first instance, the judge refused to grant the relief sought by the claimant on the basis that the Spanish court should be allowed to decide for itself whether to assume jurisdiction or to stay its proceedings or decline jurisdiction under the concurrent proceedings provisions.[140] The Court of Appeal, however, held that, even in a case where jurisdiction is determined exclusively by the Brussels Convention, the situations in which the court may grant an anti-suit injunction are not limited to those where the parties have conferred exclusive jurisdiction on the English court.[141] Laws LJ had 'no doubt' that where proceedings are brought in another Member State 'for no purpose other than to harass and oppress a party who is already a litigant [in England]', the court 'possesses the power to prohibit by injunction the plaintiff in the other jurisdiction from continuing with the foreign process'.[142] As might have been expected, this decision received an even more hostile reaction than that which had greeted the *Continental Bank* case[143] and the defendants appealed to the House of Lords. Although the House of Lords indicated that it considered the case suitable for the grant of an anti-suit injunction, it sought a ruling from the Court of Justice.[144]

11.3.5 In its ruling,[145] the Court of Justice was not at all sympathetic to the approach of the English courts. Advocate General Ruiz-Jarabo Colomber had no hesitation in declaring the English practice inconsistent with the Brussels Convention:

---

[137] See para 9.1.39.

[138] See Y Baatz, 'Who decides on jurisdiction clauses?' [2004] *LMCLQ* 25, 28–9.

[139] [2000] 1 QB 345 (CA); [2002] 1 WLR 107 (HL).

[140] [1999] 1 All ER (Comm) 445.

[141] See Laws LJ at [2000] 1 QB 345, 358.

[142] [2000] 1 QB 345, 357.

[143] See, eg, A Briggs, (1999) 70 *BYIL* 332; J Harris, 'Use and Abuse of the Brussels Convention' (1999) 115 *LQR* 576. For a more sympathetic view, see C Ambrose, 'Can Anti-Suit Injunctions Survive European Community Law?' (2003) 52 *ICLQ* 401; TC Hartley, 'Anti-suit Injunctions and the Brussels Jurisdiction and Judgments Convention' (2000) 49 *ICLQ* 166.

[144] [2002] 1 WLR 107. A Briggs, (2001) 72 *BYIL* 437.

[145] Case C–159/02 [2004] ECR I–3565. A Briggs, 'Anti-Suit Injunctions and Utopian Ideals' (2004) 120 *LQR* 529; A Dickinson, 'A charter for tactical litigation in Europe?' [2004] *LMCLQ* 273; C Hare, 'A Lack of Restraint in Europe' [2004] *CLJ* 570; T Kruger, 'The Anti-Suit Injunction in the European Judicial Space: *Turner v Grovit*' (2004) 53 *ICLQ* 1030. See also A Clarke, 'The Differing Approaches to Commercial Litigation in the European Court of Justice and the Courts of England and Wales' [2007] *EBLR* 101.

European judicial cooperation ... is imbued with the concept of mutual trust, which presupposes that each State recognises the capacity of the other legal systems to contribute independently, but harmoniously, to attainment of the stated objectives of integration. No superior authorities have been created to exercise control, beyond the interpretative role accorded to the Court of Justice; still less has authority been given to the authorities of a particular State to arrogate to themselves the power to resolve the difficulties which the European initiative itself seeks to deal with. It would be contrary to that spirit for a judicial authority in Member States to be able, even if only indirectly, to have an impact on the jurisdiction of the Court of another Contracting State to hear a given case.[146]

Not surprisingly, the Court of Justice, adopting the same approach as the Advocate General, ruled that national courts are precluded from granting an injunction which 'prohibits a party to proceedings pending before it from commencing or continuing legal proceedings before a court of another Contracting State, even where that party is acting in bad faith with a view to frustrating the existing proceedings'.[147]

11.3.6   The Court of Justice's ruling deals directly with much of the English case law: the approach to anti-suit injunctions adopted by the English courts in both the *Continental Bank* case and *Turner v Grovit* is incompatible with the Brussels I Regulation. This leaves, however, two other situations to consider. The first is where, in civil and commercial matters, a Member State court exercises jurisdiction in relation to, say, a New York domiciliary under its traditional jurisdiction rules (as authorised by Article 4). It could be argued that in this type of case, where the jurisdiction of the foreign court is not directly determined by Chapter II, the Brussels I Regulation does not constrain the English courts' inherent jurisdiction to grant an anti-suit injunction in the interests of justice. However, it does not follow from Article 4 that the court should be willing to grant an anti-suit injunction in cases where the court of a Member State assumes jurisdiction on a basis of jurisdiction outside the Brussels I Regulation. Because the Regulation provides for the free movement of judgments in civil and commercial matters regardless of the basis on which the court of origin assumed jurisdiction, it is only if the provisions dealing with concurrent proceedings are given a broad interpretation that the goal of reducing the possibility of irreconcilable judgments being rendered by the courts of different Member States can be achieved. In *Overseas Union Insurance Ltd v New Hampshire Insurance Co*[148] the Court of Justice decided that the *lis pendens* rule was applicable regardless of the parties' domicile and regardless of the basis on which the court first seised assumed jurisdiction. In the course of its judgment the Court of Justice stressed that 'in no case is the court second seised in a better position than the court first seised to determine whether the latter has jurisdiction'.[149] Furthermore, the Court of Justice's ruling in *Turner v Grovit* displays marked hostility towards attempts by the courts of one state to pre-empt the decisions of the courts of other states on questions of jurisdiction. Accordingly, in cases within the material scope of Article 1, the English court may not grant an anti-suit injunction even where the jurisdiction of the courts of another Member State is not derived from the direct jurisdiction provisions of Chapter II.

---

[146] Case C–159/02 [2004] ECR I–3565, paras 31–2.
[147] Case C–159/02 [2004] ECR I–3565, para 31.
[148] Case C–351/89 [1991] ECR I–3317.
[149] Case C–351/89 *Overseas Union Insurance Ltd v New Hampshire Insurance Co* [1991] ECR I–3317, para 23.

11.3.7 The second situation is where proceedings are commenced in the courts of another Member State in circumstances where, from the perspective of the English court, the foreign proceedings are brought in breach of an arbitration agreement between the parties. The argument for treating the grant of an anti-suit injunction in such a case as not incompatible with the Brussels I Regulation is based on the idea that, because the proceedings involve arbitration, they are outside the scope of Article 1.[150] Of course, if the foreign court regards the arbitration clause as binding on the parties, it will refer the parties to arbitration,[151] in which case the claimant in the foreign proceedings will have no choice but to arbitrate the dispute, whether or not the English court grants an injunction. More problematical is the situation where the foreign court considers that the arbitration agreement is not binding (in which case its view is that the situation falls within the scope of Article 1), but the English court regards the arbitration agreement to be binding (as a result of which it considers the English proceedings to be covered by Article 1(2)(d)). There was conflicting first instance authority on the question whether proceedings involving an application for an injunction to enforce an arbitration clause (by restraining a litigant from continuing with foreign proceedings) concern 'arbitration'[152] and the implications of the Court of Justice's ruling in *Van Uden Maritime BV v Firma Deco-Line*[153] were unclear. In *West Tankers Inc v RAS Riunione Adriatica di Sicurta*[154] the House of Lords considered the issue to be sufficiently problematical to justify the reference of the following question to the Court of Justice:

Is it consistent with EC Regulation 44/2001 for a court of a Member State to make an order to restrain a person from commencing or continuing proceedings in another Member State on the ground that such proceedings are in breach of an arbitration agreement?[155]

11.3.8 The prevailing view in England was that proceedings involving an application for an anti-suit injunction to restrain proceedings commenced in breach of an arbitration clause concern 'arbitration' and the English courts' practice of enforcing arbitration agreements by anti-suit injunctions—as exemplified by *The Angelic Grace*[156]—was not called into question by the Court of Justice's ruling in *Turner v Grovit*.[157] As Lord

---

[150] See the discussion of P Gross, 'Anti-suit injunctions and arbitration' [2005] *LMCLQ* 10.

[151] New York Convention, Art II. See section 21.2.

[152] The majority view was that such proceedings are within the fourth exception: *Toepfer International GmbH v Société Cargill France* [1997] 2 Lloyd's Rep 98; *The Ivan Zagubanski* [2002] 1 Lloyd's Rep 106; *The Hari Bhum* [2004] 1 Lloyd's Rep 206; *West Tankers Inc v RAS Riunione Adriatica di Sicurta* [2005] 2 Lloyd's Rep 257; the contrary position had, however, been advocated: *Charterers Mutual Assurance Association Ltd v British and Foreign* [1998] ILPr 838. See, generally, L Flannery, 'Anti-suit Injunctions in Support of Arbitration' [2003] *EBLR* 143; H Seriki, 'Anti-Suit Injunctions and Arbitration: A Final Nail in the Coffin?' (2006) 23(1) *J Int Arb* 25.

[153] Case C–391/95 [1998] ECR I–7091. See paras 3.3.19 and 10.3.19.

[154] [2007] 1 Lloyd's Rep 391. R Fentiman, 'Arbitration and the Brussels Regulation' [2007] *CLJ* 493. For consideration of the decision at first instance ([2005] 2 Lloyd's Rep 257), see J Hill, 'Anti-suit injunctions and arbitration' [2006] *LMCLQ* 166. See also M Ilmer and I Naumann, 'Yet another blow: anti-suit injunctions in support of arbitration agreements within the European Union' [2007] *Int Arb LR* 147.

[155] [2007] 1 Lloyd's Rep 391, 395 at [25].

[156] [1995] 1 Lloyd's Rep 87.

[157] See *Through Transport Mutual Insurance Association (Eurasia) Ltd v New India Assurance Co Ltd* [2005] 1 Lloyd's Rep 67. A Briggs, (2004) 75 *BYIL* 549; L Merrett, 'To What Extent Does an Agreement to Arbitrate Exclude the Brussels Regulation?' [2005] *CLJ* 308; N Pengelley, 'The European Court of Justice, English Courts and the Continued Use of the Anti-suit Injunction in Support of Agreements to Arbitrate:

Hoffmann noted in the *West Tankers* case, proceedings for an injunction to restrain proceedings brought in breach of an arbitration clause 'are entirely to protect the contractual right to have the dispute determined by arbitration'.[158]

11.3.9   However, in *Allianz SpA (formerly Riunione Adriatica Di Sicurta SpA) v West Tankers Inc*[159] the Court of Justice was no more sympathetic to the English practice of granting anti-suit injunctions than it had been in *Turner v Grovit*. As the Advocate General pointed out, the central flaw in the position taken by the English courts was to focus on the substance of the English proceedings without having regard to the subject-matter of the proceedings in another Member State which the anti-suit injunction is designed (indirectly) to restrain. In the *West Tankers* case, there was no case for saying that the foreign proceedings (in this case, in Italy) concerned arbitration; the Italian proceedings involved civil and commercial matters (namely, a claim in tort, possibly also in contract, for damages) and fell squarely within the scope of Article 1 and outside the scope of the arbitration exception. This conclusion was not invalidated by the fact that, in the context of the Italian proceedings, a preliminary issue arose as to the jurisdictional effect of an arbitration clause. In the words of the Advocate General:

a legal relationship does not fall outside the scope of [the Brussels I Regulation] simply because the parties have entered into an arbitration agreement. Rather the Regulation becomes applicable if the substantive subject-matter is covered by it. The preliminary issue to be addressed by the court seised as to whether it lacks jurisdiction because of an arbitration clause and must refer the dispute to arbitration in application of the New York Convention is a separate issue. An anti-suit injunction which restrains a party in that situation from commencing or continuing proceedings before the national court of a Member State interferes with proceedings which fall within the scope of the Regulation.[160]

This analysis leads to the conclusion that the approach adopted by the Court of Justice in *Turner v Grovit* is equally applicable in the situation where an application is made for an anti-suit injunction to restrain a litigant from commencing or pursuing proceedings in breach of an arbitration clause.

11.3.10   The Court of Justice followed the Advocate General's opinion: the grant of an anti-suit injunction in a case such as *West Tankers* is objectionable because 'the use of an anti-suit injunction to prevent a court of a Member State, which normally has jurisdiction to resolve a dispute under [the Brussels I Regulation], from ruling in accordance with Article 1(2)(d) …, on the very applicability of the regulation to the dispute brought before it necessarily amounts to stripping that court of the power to rule on its own

---

Through Transport v New India' (2006) 2 *Journal of Private International Law* 397. See also G Blanke, 'The ECJ's Recent Jurisprudence on Anti-Suit Injunctions under the Brussels Convention: A Promising *Début* for a more Prominent Role for Arbitration in European Commercial Dispute Resolution at the Dawn of the 21st Century?' [2005] *EBLR* 591.

[158]   [2007] 1 Lloyd's Rep 391, 394 (at [16]).
[159]   Case C–185/07 [2009] 1 AC 1138. A Briggs, 'Fear and Loathing in Syracuse and Luxembourg' [2009] *LMCLQ* 161; R Fentiman, 'Arbitration and Anti-Suit Injunctions in Europe' [2009] *CLJ* 278; H Meidanis and A Giannakoulias, (2009) 46 *CML Rev* 1709; E Peel, 'Arbitration and Anti-Suit Injunctions in the European Union' (2009) 125 *LQR* 365. See also K Noussia, 'Antisuit Injunctions and Arbitration Proceedings: What Does the Future Hold?' (2009) 26(3) *J Int Arb* 311.
[160]   Case C–185/07 [2009] 1 AC 1138, 1151 (at [62]).

jurisdiction under [the Brussels I Regulation]'.[161] Accordingly, an anti-suit injunction which aims to enforce an arbitration clause 'is contrary to the general principle … that every court seised itself determines, under the rules applicable to it, whether it has jurisdiction to resolve the dispute before it'[162] and 'runs counter to the trust which Member States accord to one another's legal systems and judicial institutions and on which the system of jurisdiction under [the Brussels I Regulation] is based'. [163]

11.3.11 In policy terms, the problems with the *West Tankers* case mirror many of those engendered by the decision in *Erich Gasser GmbH v MISAT Srl*.[164] A disputant who wants to disrupt the agreed method of dispute resolution and harass the other party can start proceedings in any Member State which, but for the arbitration agreement, would have had jurisdiction over the substantive dispute and drag those proceedings out by contesting the validity of the arbitration agreement. Even if such a tactic will have the effect of neither preventing the other party referring the substantive dispute to arbitration nor requiring the arbitration proceedings to be stayed pending the determination of the litigation, it will generate aggravation and the wasting of costs.[165]

11.3.12 These concerns inevitably lead to thoughts about how the Brussels I Regulation might be amended. There is a good case for seeking to make better provision for the protection of arbitration agreements (as well as jurisdiction agreements). Instead of the situation resulting from the *Erich Gasser* and *West Tanker* cases—under which all Member State courts are regarded as equally competent to determine the question whether a dispute-resolution agreement is valid and binding—it would make sense for this question to be within the exclusive jurisdiction of a single court. Obviously, the court with exclusive jurisdiction would be the contractual forum (for jurisdiction agreements) or the court of the seat of arbitration (for arbitration agreements). To accommodate such a rule, court proceedings (or, at least, some court proceedings) relating to arbitration would have to be brought within the scope of the Regulation. In some ways, this would be unfortunate: the idea that arbitration should, in its entirety, be excluded from the Brussels I Regulation is an attractive one. However, given the way the Court of Justice has largely emasculated the arbitration exception in the *West Tankers* case, the most plausible way forward appears to require an amendment to the scope of the Regulation and the formulation of a jurisdictional regime better designed to uphold the integrity of (and give primacy to) dispute-resolution clauses.

---

[161] Case C–185/07 [2009] 1 AC 1138, 1157 (at [28]).
[162] Case C–185/07 [2009] 1 AC 1138, 1157 (at [29]).
[163] Case C–185/07 [2009] 1 AC 1138, 1158 (at [30]).
[164] Case C–116/02 [2003] ECR I–14693.
[165] For a more sanguine view of the potential implications of the *West Tankers* case, see C Kessler and J Hope, 'The ECJ Reference in The Front Comor: Much Ado About Nothing?' (2008) 25 *Arb Int* 331.

12

RECOGNITION AND ENFORCEMENT OF FOREIGN JUDGMENTS UNDER THE COMMON LAW AND UNDER RELATED STATUTORY REGIMES

12.0.1 The basic principles underlying the law relating to the recognition and enforcement of foreign judgments at common law are reasonably clear (section 12.1). Notwithstanding Lord Bridge's view that the enforcement of foreign judgments is primarily governed by statutory codes,[1] the common law is still of very considerable significance in that it applies to judgments given by the courts of most countries in the Middle East and some countries in Eastern Europe as well as to most non-commonwealth countries in the Americas (including the United States of America), Africa and Asia (sections 12.2–12.5). There are, however, statutory regimes which either supplement or supersede the common law: Part II of the Administration of Justice Act 1920 provides a scheme for the enforcement (but not the recognition) of judgments given by various commonwealth jurisdictions; the Foreign Judgments (Reciprocal Enforcement) Act 1933, which is a virtual codification of the common law rules, introduced a framework for the implementation of bilateral treaties between the United Kingdom and various foreign countries as well as for the recognition and enforcement of judgments given in proceedings where the original court exercised jurisdiction under the provisions of various international conventions (section 12.6).

12.1 INTRODUCTION

Why Recognise Foreign Judgments?

12.1.1 In the modern world, where so much commerce is international in nature, the international community has a general interest in ensuring that judgments operate as a form of international currency. If judgments were only valid and enforceable in the country of origin, international trade would be an even more hazardous enterprise. In *Adams v Cape Industries Plc* Slade LJ suggested that underlying the system for the recognition and enforcement of foreign judgments is:

an acknowledgement that the society of nations will work better if some foreign judgments are taken to create rights which supersede the underlying cause of action, and which may be directly enforced in countries where the defendant or his assets are to be found.[2]

---

[1] *Owens Bank Ltd v Bracco* [1992] 2 AC 443, 489.
[2] [1990] Ch 433, 552. Note that the absence of assets in England is not a bar to enforcement if there is a reasonable possibility that the judgment debtor will have assets in England in the future. See *Tasarruf Mevduati Sigorta Fonu v Demirel* [2007] 1 WLR 2508, 2519 (at [40]).

Although this idea may explain why some foreign judgments should be entitled to recognition or enforcement, it does not provide an answer to the question of which judgments should—and should not—be recognised or enforced.

Which Foreign Judgments Should Be Entitled to Recognition and Enforcement?

12.1.2 Broadly speaking, there are two possible theories for the recognition and enforcement of foreign judgments: the doctrine of reciprocity and the doctrine of obligation. Although the English courts have from time to time flirted with the doctrine of reciprocity, it is the doctrine of obligation which underpins the common law and the statutory regimes which are based on it. The theory of obligation flows from a jurisdiction-based approach to the recognition and enforcement of foreign judgments. If, on the one hand, there exists between the country of origin and the person against whom the judgment was given a connection which is sufficient to justify the exercise of jurisdiction by the original court, the judgment creates an obligation which the courts of other countries ought to recognise and, where appropriate, enforce; if, on the other hand, the connection is not sufficient, the judgment does not create any obligation outside the country of origin. The doctrine of obligation was accepted as part of English common law in *Schibsby v Westenholz*[3] and the statutory schemes which are based on the common law—Part II of the Administration of Justice Act 1920 and the Foreign Judgments (Reciprocal Enforcement) Act 1933—adopt the same underlying approach.

12.2 CONDITIONS FOR ENFORCEMENT AT COMMON LAW

12.2.1 A foreign judgment is entitled to enforcement in England only if the person seeking to rely on the judgment (the judgment creditor) is able to establish that certain basic requirements are met: (1) the original court must have been a court of competent jurisdiction; (2) the judgment must be final and conclusive; (3) the judgment must be for a fixed sum of money, not being a tax or penalty. If these three conditions are satisfied, the judgment is *prima facie* entitled to enforcement. However, the fact that the basic conditions for the enforcement of a foreign judgment have been satisfied does not guarantee that the judgment will be enforced. The party against whom the judgment is invoked (the judgment debtor) may resist enforcement by establishing one of a number of defences. Some defences have been formulated by the courts, others are the creation of Parliament.[4]

The Jurisdiction of the Original Court

Introductory Remarks

12.2.2 As a general proposition, an English court which is called upon to recognise or enforce a foreign judgment is not concerned with the internal law of the country

---

[3] (1870) LR 6 QB 155.
[4] See section 12.4.

of origin. Even if, as a result of a defect, the judgment may be set aside on appeal, the judgment is nevertheless *prima facie* enforceable in England unless and until it is set aside by the courts of the country of origin. As a general rule, whether the original court had jurisdiction over the person against whom the judgment is invoked according to its own rules is irrelevant; the question is whether—as a matter of English law—the original court is to be regarded as a court of competent jurisdiction in the private international law sense.[5] In other words, was the connection between the country of origin and the person against whom the judgment is invoked sufficient to create an obligation which the English court should recognise or enforce? The traditional starting point for a discussion of this question is a passage taken from the judgment of Buckley LJ in *Emanuel v Symon*:

In actions in personam there are five cases in which the courts of this country will enforce a foreign judgment: (1) where the defendant is a subject of the foreign country in which the judgment has been obtained; (2) where he was resident in the foreign country when the action began; (3) where the defendant in the character of plaintiff has selected the forum in which he is afterwards sued; (4) where he has voluntarily appeared; and (5) where he has contracted to submit himself to the forum in which the judgment was obtained.[6]

It is doubtful whether case (1) would be held to give rise to jurisdiction.[7] The remaining categories effectively boil down to two types of case: first, where the party against whom the judgment is invoked submitted to the jurisdiction of the original court (cases (3), (4) and (5)); secondly, where there is a sufficient territorial connection between the party against whom the judgment is invoked and the country of origin (case (2)). In the second type of case there are three questions to consider. What is the appropriate territorial connection in the case of individuals? The traditional view—based on *Emanuel v Symon*—is that residence within the jurisdiction of the original court is necessary. The law was, however, re-examined by the Court of Appeal in *Adams v Cape Industries Plc*.[8] What is the relevant test in cases involving corporations? When considering the connection between the country of origin and the person against whom the judgment is invoked, what is the relevant territorial unit in the case of a political state, such as the United States of America, comprising different law districts which have different rules of law and different legal procedures?

Submission

12.2.3   The original court is regarded as a court of competent jurisdiction if the person against whom the judgment is invoked submitted to the jurisdiction of the court.[9] Where a person is regarded as having submitted in respect of a claim brought against him in foreign proceedings, the submission extends not only to the original

---

[5] *Buchanan v Rucker* (1808) 9 East 192.
[6] [1908] 1 KB 302, 309.
[7] See para 12.2.23.
[8] [1990] Ch 433. PB Carter, (1990) 61 *BYIL* 402; JG Collier, [1990] *CLJ* 416.
[9] See, eg, *Pattni v Ali* [2007] 2 AC 85; A Briggs, (2006) 77 *BYIL* 575; CH Tham, [2007] *LMCLQ* 129. Where the judgment debtor submitted to the jurisdiction of the original court, that court is a court of competent jurisdiction as regards the determination of contractual rights to movables or intangible property situated in another country: Lord Mance in *Pattni v Ali* [2007] 2 AC 85, 100 (at [27]).

claim, but to claims concerning the same subject matter as the original claim and to related claims.[10] However, such an extension of submission beyond the original claim depends upon, first, the further claims being properly brought under the rules of procedure of the foreign court and, secondly, the further claims being brought either by the original claimant or by others who were parties to the foreign litigation at the time of the submission.[11]

12.2.4   Section 33(1) of the Civil Jurisdiction and Judgments Act 1982 provides:

For the purposes of determining whether a judgment given by a court of an overseas country should be recognised or enforced in England and Wales ..., the person against whom the judgment was given shall not be regarded as having submitted to the jurisdiction of the court by reason only of the fact that he appeared (conditionally or otherwise) in the proceedings for all or any one or more of the following purposes, namely—

(a) to contest the jurisdiction of the court;
(b) to ask the court to dismiss or stay the proceedings on the ground that the dispute in question should be submitted to arbitration or to the determination of the courts of another country;
(c) to protect, or obtain the release of, property seized or threatened with seizure in the proceedings.

This provision, which has the effect of reversing the position at common law,[12] does not provide a positive definition of acts which amount to submission; rather it identifies a range of procedural acts which are not to be regarded as amounting to submission. The effect of section 33 is that a litigant who contests the jurisdiction of the original court, requests the original court to decline jurisdiction (for example, on the basis of *forum non conveniens* or because the parties had agreed to arbitration)[13] or appears to protect his property, is not regarded as having submitted. In situations where the procedure of the original court is similar to the procedure under CPR 6.36, a litigant is not to be regarded as having submitted by applying to have service out of the jurisdiction set aside,[14] although this situation does not obviously fall within the express wording of paragraph (b).

12.2.5   A defendant is to be regarded as having submitted to the jurisdiction of the original court if he voluntarily appears in the proceedings to defend the claim on the merits, if he counterclaims in those proceedings or if he agrees to submit to the jurisdiction of the court (for example, in a contractual jurisdiction clause). Contesting the jurisdiction and the merits of the case in the alternative also amounts to submission.[15] In a situation where the original court rejects the defendant's challenge to its jurisdiction and the defendant proceeds to fight the case on the merits (without reserving the position on jurisdiction), the defendant must be regarded as having

---

[10]   *Murthy v Sivajothi* [1999] 1 **WLR** 467. A Briggs, (1998) 69 *BYIL* 349.
[11]   Evans LJ in *Murthy v Sivajothi* [1999] 1 **WLR** 467, 476.
[12]   *Harris v Taylor* [1915] 2 KB 580; *Henry v Geoprosco International Ltd* [1976] QB 726 (PB Carter, (1974–75) 47 *BYIL* 379; JG Collier, [1975] *CLJ* 219; G Solomons, 'Enforcement of Foreign Judgments: Jurisdiction of Foreign Court' (1976) 25 *ICLQ* 665).
[13]   *Tracomin SA v Sudan Oil Seeds Ltd (No 1)* [1983] 1 WLR 662, affirmed [1983] 1 WLR 1026 (although the only point raised on appeal was the temporal scope of s 33).
[14]   *Akande v Balfour Beatty Construction Ltd* [1998] ILPr 110.
[15]   *Boissière & Co v Brockner & Co* (1889) 6 TLR 85.

submitted.[16] However, the defendant will not be regarded as having submitted to the jurisdiction of the original court if he 'makes it clear in his first defence rather than in some subsequent defence that he is contesting the jurisdiction'; for the purposes of this rule it does not matter if the jurisdictional defence includes 'additional material which constitutes a plea to the merits of the case'.[17]

12.2.6 There may be a difficult dividing line to be drawn between, on the one hand, contesting jurisdiction and the merits in the alternative and, on the other, contesting jurisdiction while reserving the possibility of fighting on the merits should the plea as to jurisdiction fail. Accordingly, the court should not be too quick to conclude that the defendant has submitted. Where the foreign procedure requires a defendant to contest the jurisdiction and plead to the merits at the same time, there is no submission, unless the defendant takes 'some step which is only necessary or only useful if the objection [to jurisdiction] has been actually waived, or if the objection has never been entertained at all'.[18] If the defendant's participation in the foreign proceedings does not amount to submission according to the law of the original court, such acts should not be regarded as submission for the purposes of English private international law—even if, had such steps been taken in English proceedings, they would have been regarded as submission to the jurisdiction of the English court.[19] However, the converse is not necessarily the case; as the important question is whether the defendant is to be regarded as having submitted for the purposes of English private international law, the fact that, under the law of the original court, the defendant submitted to the foreign court's jurisdiction is not decisive.[20]

12.2.7 In complex, multiparty litigation there is a question whether submission in one set of proceedings can be regarded as submission (or an agreement to submit) to related proceedings involving the same issues. In *Adams v Cape Industries Plc*[21] an English company, which was involved (through subsidiary companies) in the mining and sale of asbestos, was the defendant in two sets of proceedings (the Tyler 1 actions and the Tyler 2 actions) brought by more than 600 asbestos workers in Texas. Although the defendant took part in the Tyler 1 actions, which were settled, as regards the Tyler 2 actions, the defendant contested the jurisdiction of the court and took no further part in the proceedings. In enforcement proceedings in England the plaintiffs in the Tyler 2 actions argued that the defendant, by taking part in the Tyler 1 actions, had effectively submitted to the jurisdiction of the court in relation to the Tyler 2 actions. Scott J rejected the argument that the two sets of proceedings in reality constituted 'one unit of litigation' and held that the steps taken by the defendant in the Tyler 1 actions could not be regarded as constituting consent to the Tyler 2 actions.[22]

---

[16] *Marc Rich & Co AG v Società Italiana Impianti PA (No 2)* [1992] 1 Lloyd's Rep 624. P Kaye, 'Forensic Submission as a Bar to Arbitration' (1993) 12 *CJQ* 359.

[17] Neill LJ in *Marc Rich & Co AG v Società Italiana Impianti PA (No 2)* [1992] 1 Lloyd's Rep 624, 633.

[18] See Cave J in *Rein v Stein* (1892) 66 LT 469, 471; approved by Lord Fraser in *Williams & Glyn's Bank plc v Astro Dinamico Compania Naviera SA* [1984] 1 WLR 438, 444. See also *Starlight International Inc v Bruce* [2002] ILPr 617.

[19] *Adams v Cape Industries Plc* [1990] Ch 433; *The Eastern Trader* [1996] 2 Lloyd's Rep 585.

[20] *Akai Pty Ltd v People's Insurance Co Ltd* [1998] 1 Lloyd's Rep 90.

[21] [1990] Ch 433.

[22] [1990] Ch 433, 462–3.

12.2.8   A defendant who expressly agrees to the jurisdiction of the original court[23] is regarded as having submitted, even if the judgment is given in default. So, if parties agree to refer a dispute to the exclusive jurisdiction of the courts of country X, a judgment given in the claimant's favour by the courts of country X in a matter falling within the scope of the jurisdiction agreement is *prima facie* entitled to enforcement in England. However, a jurisdiction agreement in favour of a particular court in a particular country is not to be regarded as amounting to a general submission to all the courts in that country. For example, an agreement to submit to the courts of St Petersburg is not an agreement to submit to any court in Russia and in such circumstances the courts of Moscow are not to be regarded as having jurisdiction in the private international law sense.[24]

12.2.9   More problematical are cases where it is alleged that the person against whom the judgment is invoked impliedly agreed to submit to the jurisdiction of the original court. The generally accepted view is that an agreement to submit must be express.[25] For example, a contractual choice of the law of country X is not an implied agreement to submit to the jurisdiction of the courts of country X.[26] Whether an agreement to submit is express is a question of interpretation which, as a matter of principle, should be determined by the law governing the agreement. *Blohn v Desser*[27] is often cited for the proposition that an agreement to submit may be implied. The defendant in that case had been a sleeping partner in a firm which carried on business in Austria. The plaintiff, having obtained a judgment against the firm in Vienna, sought to enforce the judgment in England against the defendant. The defendant, whose name was on the commercial register in Vienna, had taken no part in the Austrian proceedings. Diplock J thought that it was 'clear law that [a contract] to submit to the forum in which the judgment was obtained, may be express or implied'.[28] This observation was, however, *obiter*. In *Vogel v R & A Kohnstamm Ltd*[29] Ashworth J rejected the notion that an implied agreement to submit could be a sufficient basis of jurisdiction. Further doubt was cast on *Blohn v Desser* in *Adams v Cape Industries Plc*, Scott J taking the view that the minimum that is required is 'a clear indication of consent to the exercise by the foreign court of jurisdiction'.[30]

12.2.10   In principle, consent to the jurisdiction of the original court—even if it does not form part of a contractually enforceable agreement—should be sufficient to confer jurisdiction in the private international law sense if it gives rise to an estoppel. However, if it is alleged that the defendant consented to the jurisdiction of the

---

[23] See A Briggs, *Agreements on Jurisdiction and Choice of Law* (Oxford, OUP, 2008) ch 9.

[24] See Shaw and Goff LJJ in *SA Consortium General Textiles v Sun and Sand Agencies Ltd* [1978] QB 279.

[25] L Collins *et al*, *Dicey, Morris and Collins on The Conflict of Laws* (London, Sweet & Maxwell, 14th edn, 2006) para 14–072.

[26] This principle is supported by commonwealth authorities: *Mattar and Saba v Public Trustee* [1952] 3 DLR 399 (Appellate Division, Alberta); *Dunbee Ltd v Gilman & Co (Australia) Pty Ltd* [1968] 2 Lloyd's Rep 394 (Court of Appeal, New South Wales).

[27] [1962] 2 QB 116. PB Carter, (1962) 38 *BYIL* 493; J Jacob, [1961] *CLJ* 184; PRH Webb, 'Enforcement of Foreign Judgments: Implied Submission' (1962) 25 *MLR* 96.

[28] [1962] 2 QB 116, 123.

[29] [1973] QB 133. PB Carter, (1971) 45 *BYIL* 415; EJ Cohn, 'Submission to Foreign Jurisdiction' (1972) 21 *ICLQ* 157.

[30] [1990] Ch 433, 466.

original court otherwise than by a contractual agreement such consent is 'of no legal effect if not acted upon or if withdrawn before being acted on'.[31] Similarly, if proceedings in the original court are instituted and brought to judgment against an absent defendant without reliance on the defendant's representation of willingness to submit to the jurisdiction, or in ignorance of it, the representation cannot subsequently be relied on by the claimant as a consensual basis for establishing the court's jurisdiction. Furthermore, if a non-contractual representation is to be relied upon as establishing the original court's jurisdiction, it must be a representation intended to be relied upon or, at least, be a representation that the claimant believed and had reasonable ground for believing was intended to be acted upon.

A Sufficient Territorial Connection

INDIVIDUALS

12.2.11   Although *Adams v Cape Industries Plc*[32] was concerned with the question whether the original court had jurisdiction in the private international law sense over a company, the decision of the Court of Appeal includes a comprehensive review of cases involving foreign judgments given against individuals. In *Carrick v Hancock*,[33] for example, proceedings had been started in Sweden, the defendant having been served with the document instituting the proceedings during a short visit to Sweden. Although the defendant took part in the proceedings—and therefore the decision of the English court to enforce the judgment can be justified on the basis of the defendant's submission—Lord Russell of Killowen CJ is reported as saying that:

the jurisdiction of a Court was based upon the principle of territorial dominion, and that all persons within any territorial dominion owe their allegiance to its sovereign power and obedience to all its laws and to the lawful jurisdiction of its Courts.[34]

12.2.12   The Court of Appeal decided in *Adams v Cape Industries Plc* that, in the absence of any form of submission, the jurisdiction of the original court depends upon the physical presence of the person against whom the judgment is invoked in the country concerned at the date of service of the originating process. The requirement of physical presence will not normally be satisfied in a case involving cross-border e-commerce; where, for example, a seller based in England advertises goods on a website which is accessible in the United States and sells and delivers goods to customers there, the seller is not present in the United States.[35] To found jurisdiction in the private international law sense, presence in the country of origin must have been voluntary. The temporary presence of a litigant in the country of origin will not found jurisdiction if it was induced by compulsion, fraud or duress.[36]

---

[31] Scott J in *Adams v Cape Industries Plc* [1990] Ch 433, 466.
[32] [1990] Ch 433.
[33] (1895) 12 TLR 59.
[34] (1895) 12 TLR 59, 60. See also *Sirdar Gurdyal Singh v Rajah of Faridkote* [1894] AC 670; *Employers' Liability Assurance Corporation Ltd v Sedgwick, Collins & Co Ltd* [1927] AC 95.
[35] *Lucasfilm Ltd v Ainsworth* [2010] FSR 270, 321–23 (at [187]–[195]). It makes no difference whether the seller is an individual or a company.
[36] Slade LJ in *Adams v Cape Industries Plc* [1990] Ch 433, 518. See also *Colt Industries Inc v Sarlie (No 1)* [1966] 1 WLR 440. PB Carter, (1965–66) 41 *BYIL* 447.

12.2.13   The acceptance of temporary presence in the foreign country as a basis of jurisdiction in the private international law sense may appear reasonable in view of the fact that, under the Civil Procedure Rules, the temporary presence of a foreigner in England at the time of service of process is regarded as justifying the exercise of jurisdiction by the English court.[37] However, the apparent symmetry between the rules which govern English jurisdiction, on the one hand, and those which determine whether a foreign court is a court of competent jurisdiction, on the other, is false. Where the jurisdiction of the English court is invoked on the basis of the defendant's temporary presence in England, the court normally has a discretion to stay its proceedings on the ground of *forum non conveniens* and 'the exercise of the discretion is likely to be an issue when jurisdiction is founded on mere presence'.[38] Furthermore, the cases relied upon by the Court of Appeal in *Adams v Cape Industries Plc* pre-date the adoption of the doctrine of *forum non conveniens* in England. It has been suggested that, in view of the development of the doctrine of *forum non conveniens*, it would be rational to determine the competence of a foreign court in the private international law sense by the application of a test based on the appropriateness of the foreign forum, rather than on relatively inflexible factors such as presence or residence.[39]

12.2.14   If temporary presence is an acceptable basis of jurisdiction in the private international law sense the defendant's residence within the jurisdiction of the original court must also be acceptable—at least where residence is accompanied by presence. What, however, is the position where the person against whom the judgment is invoked is resident within the jurisdiction of the original court but was not physically present when process was served? This question was expressly left open by the Court of Appeal in *Adams v Cape Industries Plc*.[40] There is, however, no obvious reason why residence—which is a more substantial connection than mere presence—should not be sufficient, whether or not accompanied by presence at the moment when the foreign proceedings are commenced.

COMPANIES

12.2.15   Whereas, in the context of individuals, presence and residence are relatively straightforward concepts to apply, the presence of a company is more metaphysical. In considering the presence of a company the courts have distinguished two types of situation: first, cases where it is alleged that a company has direct presence in the foreign country; secondly, cases of indirect presence in which it is alleged that the company is present in the foreign country through a representative.

12.2.16   In order for direct presence to be established the company must be carrying on business in the foreign country at a definite and, to some extent, permanent

---

[37] *Maharanee of Baroda v Wildenstein* [1972] 2 QB 283. See paras 7.1.1–7.1.2. In cases within the material scope of Art 1 of the Brussels I Regulation, this basis of jurisdiction cannot be invoked against a defendant who is domiciled in a Member State: see paras 4.2.1–4.2.3.

[38] JJ Fawcett and JM Carruthers, *Cheshire, North and Fawcett: Private International Law* (Oxford, OUP, 14th edn, 2008) 518.

[39] A Briggs, 'Which Foreign Judgments Should We Recognise Today?' (1987) 36 *ICLQ* 240. Compare J Harris, 'Recognition of Foreign Judgments at Common Law—The Anti-Suit Injunction Link' (1997) 17 *OJLS* 477.

[40] Slade LJ at [1990] Ch 433, 518.

place at the time when proceedings are commenced.[41] Indirect presence poses greater difficulty. In deciding whether a company is present in a foreign country through a representative, the court has regard to all the circumstances of the case. Of particular significance, however, is whether the representative is empowered to conclude contracts on the company's behalf. If the representative is no more than a channel of communication between the company and third parties, the company cannot realistically be regarded as present in the foreign country.[42]

12.2.17 The question of corporate presence was subjected to an exhaustive review by the Court of Appeal in *Adams v Cape Industries Plc*.[43] After a lengthy examination of the authorities, the Court of Appeal concluded:

(1) The English courts will be likely to treat a trading corporation incorporated under the law of one country ('an overseas corporation') as present within the jurisdiction of the courts of another country only if either (i) it has established and maintained at its own expense (whether as owner or lessee) a fixed place of business of its own in the other country and for more than a minimal period of time has carried on its own business at or from such premises by its servants or agents (a 'branch office' case), or (ii) a representative of the overseas corporation has for more than a minimal period of time been carrying on *the overseas corporation's* business in the other country at or from some fixed place of business.

(2) In either of these two cases presence can only be established if it can fairly be said that *the overseas corporation's* business (whether or not together with the representative's own business) has been transacted at or from the fixed place of business. In the first case, this condition is likely to present few problems. In the second, the question whether the representative has been carrying on the overseas corporation's business or has been doing no more than carry on his own business will necessitate an investigation of the functions which he has been performing and all aspects of the relationship between him and the overseas corporation.

(3) In particular, but without prejudice to the generality of the foregoing, the following questions are likely to be relevant on such investigation: (a) whether or not the fixed place of business from which the representative operates was originally acquired for the purpose of enabling him to act on behalf of the overseas corporation; (b) whether the overseas corporation has directly reimbursed him for (i) the cost of his accommodation at the fixed place of business; (ii) the cost of his staff; (c) what other contributions, if any, the overseas corporation makes to the financing of the business carried on by the representative; (d) whether the representative is remunerated by reference to transactions, eg by commission, or by fixed regular payments or in some other way; (e) what degree of control the overseas corporation exercises over the running of the business conducted by the representative; (f) whether the representative reserves (i) part of his accommodation, (ii) part of his staff for conducting business related to the overseas corporation; (g) whether the representative displays the overseas corporation's name at his premises or on his stationery, and if so, whether he does so in such a way as to indicate that he is a representative of the overseas corporation; (h) what business, if any, the representative transacts as principal exclusively on his own behalf; (i) whether the representative makes contracts with customers or other third parties in the name of the overseas corporation, or otherwise in such manner as to bind it; (j) if so, whether the

---

[41] *Littauer Glove Corporation v FW Millington (1920) Ltd* (1928) 44 TLR 746.
[42] *Vogel v R & A Kohnstamm Ltd* [1973] QB 133. PB Carter, (1971) 45 *BYIL* 415; EJ Cohn, 'Submission to Foreign Jurisdiction' (1972) 21 *ICLQ* 157.
[43] [1990] Ch 433.

representative requires specific authority in advance before binding the overseas corporation to contractual obligations.[44]

12.2.18 In *Adams v Cape Industries Plc* the plaintiffs argued that the defendant, an English company, was carrying on business within the jurisdiction of the original court through subsidiary marketing companies, which were incorporated in Illinois. The Court of Appeal rejected the plaintiffs' argument based on direct presence. Although the economic reality of the situation was that the defendant controlled the activities of the group of subsidiary companies involved in the mining and marketing of asbestos, the defendant and the subsidiary companies were separate legal persons. The fact that the defendant organised its affairs so that its potential liability would be limited was not in itself sufficient to justify lifting the corporate veil. The Court of Appeal also rejected the plaintiffs' argument based on indirect presence. Although the activities of the subsidiary companies were of assistance to the defendant, the subsidiary companies were not empowered to bind the defendant and were primarily carrying on business on their own account.

THE PROBLEM OF FEDERAL STATES

12.2.19 What is the relevant territorial unit for the purposes of the rule that the original court is to be regarded as a court of competent jurisdiction if the defendant was present when process was served? This question was considered, albeit *obiter*, by the Court of Appeal in *Adams v Cape Industries Plc*.[45]

12.2.20 Where the judgment is granted by the courts of a unitary state, there can be no dispute over the relevant territorial jurisdiction. If a judgment creditor seeks to enforce an Egyptian judgment in England, the question is whether the judgment debtor was present in Egypt at the commencement of proceedings. The solution is not so obvious, however, where the judgment is granted by the courts of a political state which is made up of a number of different law districts. In the context of the facts of *Adams v Cape Industries Plc*, the question was this: did the plaintiffs have to establish that the defendant was present within Texas (the state or law district in which the proceedings took place) or was presence somewhere within the United States of America (the federal state) sufficient? The Court of Appeal tentatively concluded that presence somewhere in the United States would have been enough. This conclusion was based, first, on a distinction between state and federal matters and, secondly, on the view that there is a national jurisdiction in federal matters under the law of the United States.

12.2.21 The distinction between state and federal matters seems logical. In proceedings concerning the enforcement of a state judgment, the important question, in the absence of submission by the defendant, is whether the person against whom the judgment is invoked was present in the state in question. For example, a judgment by a Texas court against an English resident who carries on business in France is not entitled to recognition or enforcement in England. The same is true if the English resident establishes himself in Illinois: 'The fact that Chicago is in the United States does not make Texas any the less a foreign court for a resident in Illinois than if Chicago were in France.'[46]

---

[44] Slade LJ at [1990] Ch 433, 530–1.
[45] [1990] Ch 433.
[46] Slade LJ at [1990] Ch 433, 555.

12.2.22   As regards federal judgments it would seem reasonable that presence within the federal state should be sufficient—but only if there is a national jurisdiction in federal matters. But, is there a national jurisdiction in federal matters in the United States? Although the three members of the Court of Appeal thought, 'albeit with varying degrees of doubt',[47] that there is, the better view is that there is not. Statutory provisions exist for the registration of federal court judgments in other states of the Union and, under the law of the United States, a judgment of a federal court is no different from a judgment of a state court—in the sense that it is regarded as a foreign judgment for enforcement purposes.[48] The view suggested by the Court of Appeal could lead to the unfortunate situation where the judgment of a federal court sitting in Texas would be enforceable in England, even though it would not be enforceable in other parts of the United States.[49]

No Other Bases of Jurisdiction

12.2.23   Although there are *dicta* to the contrary,[50] it is generally thought that the fact that the person against whom the judgment is invoked is a national of the country where the foreign judgment is obtained is not sufficient to justify the recognition or enforcement of the judgment.[51] Logically, it would follow that the fact that the person against whom the judgment is invoked is domiciled within the jurisdiction of the original court is insufficient. It is also clear that a foreign court is not to be regarded as competent in the private international law sense simply because the party against whom the judgment is invoked owns assets within the jurisdiction of the original court.[52] Similarly, the fact that the claim arose out of events which occurred within the jurisdiction of the original court is, in itself, irrelevant.[53] Finally, it should be noted that, although the English courts are prepared to exercise jurisdiction over a foreign defendant under CPR 6.36 in cases where England is thought to be the *forum conveniens*,[54] a foreign judgment is not entitled to recognition or enforcement in England on the ground that the original court exercised jurisdiction over the defendant on a similar basis.[55]

Judgments Concerning Foreign Immovable Property

12.2.24   At common law the English court will not normally adjudicate on questions relating to title to, or the right to the possession of, immovable property outside England.[56] By the same token, a foreign court will not be regarded as a court of

---

[47]   Slade LJ at [1990] Ch 433, 557.
[48]   JG Collier, [1990] *CLJ* 416, 418.
[49]   PB Carter, (1990) 61 *BYIL* 402, 404.
[50]   In particular, in *Emanuel v Symon* [1908] 1 KB 302.
[51]   L Collins *et al*, *Dicey, Morris and Collins on The Conflict of Laws* (London, Sweet & Maxwell, 14th edn, 2006) para 14–078.
[52]   *Emanuel v Symon* [1908] 1 KB 302.
[53]   *Sirdar Gurdyal Singh v Rajah of Faridkote* [1894] AC 670.
[54]   See section 7.3.
[55]   This follows from *Schibsby v Westenholz* (1870) LR 6 QB 155.
[56]   See section 9.4.

competent jurisdiction on questions relating to title to, or the right to the possession of, immovable property outside its country.[57] Even if the defendant was present or resident in the country of origin at the commencement of the proceedings or submitted to the jurisdiction of the original court, the judgment will not be recognised or enforced in England.

Final and Conclusive

12.2.25 In order for a judgment to be regarded as final and conclusive it must definitively determine the dispute between the parties.[58] Interlocutory decisions which only provisionally determine the parties' rights cannot be enforced. A judgment is not final and conclusive if issues determined by the judgment can be re-opened before the original court[59] or if the original court may alter its terms.[60] It seems, however, that a judgment is to be regarded as final and conclusive even though it remains possible for there to be an adjustment to the damages on the application of either the claimant or the defendant.[61]

12.2.26 Not all judgments which may be described as interlocutory are provisional. A distinction has to be drawn between decisions which are provisional or subject to revision (such as a decision to grant an interlocutory injunction) and procedural decisions which are interlocutory in the sense that permission to appeal to the Court of Appeal is required.[62] The first category of decisions, which are made pending the final determination of the case, are not final and conclusive. By contrast, it is perfectly possible that a decision in the second category finally determines the issue which is raised.

12.2.27 The existence of the possibility of an appeal to a higher court in the country of origin does not deprive a judgment of its finality.[63] Furthermore, the fact that an appeal is pending in the country of origin at the time when the judgment creditor brings proceedings in England is not a bar to enforcement. However, where an appeal against the judgment is pending abroad, the court will normally stay enforcement proceedings until the appeal has been heard.[64]

For a Fixed Sum

12.2.28 At common law foreign injunctions or orders for specific performance are not enforceable in England; only judgments for a fixed sum of money are entitled to

---

[57] L Collins *et al, Dicey, Morris and Collins on The Conflict of Laws* (London, Sweet & Maxwell, 14th edn, 2006) para 14R–099 (Rule 40).

[58] See, eg, *Buehler AG v Chronos Richardson Ltd* [1998] 2 All ER 960.

[59] *Kirin-Amgen Inc v Boehringer Mannheim GmbH* [1997] FSR 289.

[60] *Nouvion v Freeman* (1889) 15 App Cas 1; *Carl Zeiss Stiftung v Rayner & Keeler Ltd (No 2)* [1967] 1 AC 853.

[61] *Lewis v Eliades* [2004] 1 WLR 692, 705 (at [54]). Although the first instance decision was confirmed by the Court of Appeal, leave to appeal was not given on the question whether the foreign judgment was final and conclusive: see Potter LJ at [2004] 1 WLR 692, 699–700 (at [28]).

[62] See Stuart-Smith LJ in *Desert Sun Loan Corporation v Hill* [1996] 2 All ER 847, 863.

[63] *Nouvion v Freeman* (1889) 15 App Cas 1; *The Irini A (No 2)* [1999] 1 Lloyd's Rep 189. See also *Deighan v Sunday Newspapers Ltd* [1997] NI 105 (High Court, Northern Ireland).

[64] *Colt Industries Inc v Sarlie (No 2)* [1966] 1 WLR 1287.

enforcement.[65] In some common law jurisdictions, however, it is now accepted that the court has the discretion to enforce foreign non-money judgments. In *Pro-Swing v Elta*,[66] the Supreme Court of Canada held that the 'time is ripe' for a revision of the traditional common law rule that limits the enforcement of foreign judgment, to final money judgments.[67] Such a development must take place incrementally and in a principled way,[68] and with a view to the principle of comity—albeit '[c]omity does not require receiving courts to extend greater judicial assistance to foreign litigants than it does to its own litigants ...'[69] This development has been followed in Jersey and the Cayman Islands.[70] Whether English courts will follow suit is unclear.[71] The costs and potential difficulties to which attempting to enforce non-money foreign judgments may give rise (for example, where the form of the foreign order is vague) will be issues militating against overturning the traditional rule. Further, although English courts are themselves prepared to hand down non-money judgments that may require enforcement in other courts,[72] reciprocity[73] is not a feature of the English common law rules on recognition and enforcement.[74] That said, there may be good reasons to follow in the Canadian footsteps; under the Brussels I Regulation, in civil and commercial matters, English courts are already required to enforce non-money judgments emanating from the courts of other EU Member States. There is also a good argument for saying that, although there are valid historical reasons for the common law's traditional refusal to enforce foreign non-money judgments,[75] those reasons do not justify the retention of the traditional approach in the 21st century.

---

[65] *Sadler v Robins* (1808) 1 Camp 253; *Beatty v Beatty* [1924] 1 KB 807. However, it has been argued that this is a misplaced reading of the scope of the court's powers and that there exists an equitable jurisdiction to enforce foreign non-money judgments: RW White, 'Enforcement of Foreign Judgments in Equity' (1980–82) 9 *Sydney LR* 630. See also D Buzard, 'US Recognition and Enforcement of Foreign Country Injunctive and Specific Performance Decrees' (1989–90) 20 *Cal W Int LJ* 91.

[66] [2006] 2 SCR 612, (2006) 273 DLR (4th) 663. RF Oppong, (2007) 70 *MLR* 654; SGA Pitel, (2007) 3 *Journal of Private International Law* 241.

[67] Deschamps J at [2006] 2 SCR 612, para 15.

[68] McLachlin CJC at [2006] 2 SCR 612, para 79.

[69] Deschamps J at [2006] 2 SCR 612, para 31. On the facts of the case however, a majority of the court did not think that the foreign judgment should be enforced.

[70] *Brunei and Bandone v Fidelis* [2008] JRC 152 (Royal Court, Jersey) (E Mackereth, (2009) 15 *Trust & Trustees* 25); *Miller v Gianne and Redwood Hotel Investment Corporation* [2007] CILR 18 (Grand Court, Cayman Islands).

[71] Smellie CJ in *Miller v Gianne and Redwood Hotel Investment Corporation* [2007] CILR 18, 39–40 relied on the Privy Council decision of *Pattni v Ali* [2007] 2 AC 85, 100 (at [27]); but it is suggested that this was reading too much into the decision. The Privy Council did not evince any intention to overrule the long-established rule that enforcement depends on the foreign judgment being for a fixed sum of money. Furthermore, the case concerned the recognition of a foreign non-money judgment as a defence and not the enforcement of that judgment. For academic discussion of the enforcement of non-money judgments, see RF Oppong, 'Enforcing Foreign Non-Money Judgments: An Examination of Some Recent Developments in Canada and Beyond' (2006) 39 *UBC Law Review* 257; V Black, 'Enforcement of Foreign Non-Money Judgments: *Pro Swing v ELTA*' (2005) 42 *Can Bus LJ* 81.

[72] Eg, a worldwide freezing injunction. See section 10.4.

[73] The other sense in which reciprocity can be used in the context of recognition and enforcement is that a judgment of a foreign court would be enforced in England if that foreign court would also enforce an English judgment. This has never been a doctrine adopted in England. See L Collins *et al, Dicey, Morris and Collins on The Conflict of Laws* (London, Sweet & Maxwell, 14th edn, 2006) para 14–080.

[74] *Schibsby v Westenholz* (1870) LR 6 QB 155. Cf *Travers v Holley* [1953] P 246.

[75] The rule can be traced back to the position prior to the Judicature Act 1873, where a foreign judgment could be enforced only by way of an action in debt or *assumpsit*, which required that a sum certain in

12.2.29   Where the foreign judgment is in the nature of a fine or other penalty, it will not be enforced.[76] Similarly, since an English court will not enforce, either directly or indirectly, foreign revenue laws, a foreign judgment which orders the payment of taxes is not enforceable in England.[77] A third category, that of judgments involving 'other public laws',[78] although an amorphous category,[79] is generally also unenforceable. The common justification for the exclusion of such judgments is that the enforcement of public laws will be 'an assertion of sovereign authority by one State within the territory of another ... contrary to all concepts of independent sovereignties'.[80] In all instances, however:

The critical question is whether in bringing a claim, a Claimant is doing an act which is of a sovereign character or which is done by virtue of sovereign authority; and whether the claim involves the exercise or assertion of a sovereign right. If so, then the court will not determine or enforce the claim. On the other hand, if in bringing the claim the Claimant is not doing an act which is of a sovereign character or by virtue of sovereign authority and the claim does not involve the exercise or assertion of a sovereign right and the claim does not seek to vindicate a sovereign act or acts, then the court will both determine and enforce it.[81]

12.2.30   In *United States of America v Inkley*[82] the Court of Appeal confirmed the common law rule that the English courts will not enforce the penal laws of a foreign state. In the course of his judgment Purchas LJ set out the following principles:

(1) the consideration of whether the claim sought to be enforced in the English courts is one which involves the assertion of foreign sovereignty, whether it be penal, revenue or other public law, is to be determined according to the criteria of English law; (2) that regard will be had to the attitude adopted by the courts in the foreign jurisdiction which will always receive serious attention and may on occasions be decisive; (3) that the category of the right of action, ie whether public or private, will depend on the party in whose favour it is created, on the purpose of the law or enactment in the foreign state on which it is based and on the general context of the case as a whole; (4) that the fact that the right, statutory or otherwise, is penal in nature will not deprive a person, who asserts a personal claim depending thereon, from having recourse

---

money was owed to the plaintiff. See RW White, 'Enforcement of Foreign Judgments in Equity' (1980–82) 9 *Sydney LR* 630, 631.

[76] *Huntington v Attrill* [1893] AC 150.

[77] *Government of India v Taylor* [1955] AC 491. See A Briggs, 'The Revenue Rule in the Conflict of Laws: Time for a Makeover' [2001] *Sing JLS* 280.

[78] *A-G of New Zealand v Ortiz* [1984] AC 1, 20–1; *United States of America v Inkley* [1989] QB 255, 265; *Government of the Islamic Republic of Iran v Barakat Galleries Ltd* [2009] QB 22 (P Rogerson, [2008] *CLJ* 246; A Rushworth, [2008] *LMCLQ* 123). See generally, L Collins, 'Revolution and Restitution: Foreign States in National Courts' (2007) *Hag Rec* 13, especially 58–64.

[79] Lord Denning in *AG of New Zealand v Ortiz* [1984] AC 1, 20 thought that 'other public laws' are 'laws which are eiusdem generis with "penal" or "revenue" laws'. L Collins *et al*, *Dicey, Morris and Collins on The Conflict of Laws* (London, Sweet & Maxwell, 14th edn, 2006) para 5–034 admits that: 'There is, it is true, very little authority which deals directly with the general principle that foreign public laws will not be enforced in the English court.'

[80] Lord Keith in *Government of India v Taylor* [1955] AC 491, 511. Lord Keith was referring specifically to the application of a foreign tax law, but the *dictum* also explains the exclusion of foreign penal and other public laws.

[81] Sir Anthony Clarke MR in *Mbasogo v Logo Ltd (No 1)* [2007] QB 846, 873 (at [50]). For discussion of this case, which involved claims by the President of Equatorial Guinea and the Republic of Equatorial Guinea for damages arising out of an attempted coup d'état, see A Briggs, (2007) 123 *LQR* 182; A Mills, [2007] *CLJ* 3; A Scott, [2007] *LMCLQ* 296. See also the decision of the Privy Council in related litigation: *Equatorial Guinea v Royal Bank of Scotland International* [2006] UKPC 7 (A Dickinson, (2006) 122 *LQR* 569).

[82] [1989] QB 255. PB Carter, (1988) 59 *BYIL* 347.

to the courts of this country; on the other hand, by whatever description it may be known if the purpose of the action is the enforcement of a sanction, power or right at the instance of the state in its sovereign capacity, it will not be entertained; (5) that the fact that in the foreign jurisdiction recourse may be had in a civil forum to enforce the right will not necessarily affect the true nature of the right being enforced in this country.[83]

The context of the dispute in *United States of America v Inkley* was an action by the government of the United States to enforce a judgment for the amount of an appearance bond given by the defendant in civil proceedings in Florida. Applying the relevant principles the Court of Appeal concluded that 'the general context and background against which the appearance bond was executed was criminal or penal', particularly since 'the whole purpose of the bond was to ensure, so far as it was possible, the presence of the executor of the bond to meet justice at the hands of the state in a criminal prosecution'.[84] While the case is consistent with established authority, it is arguable that the approach of the English courts is too restrictive:

What public interest of this country could conceivably be said to have been advanced by *United States of America v Inkley*? How the interests of justice are advanced by a blanket refusal to enforce foreign penal or revenue laws is unclear.[85]

12.2.31 By contrast, in *SA Consortium General Textiles v Sun and Sand Agencies Ltd*[86] the defendants had been ordered by a French judgment to pay in addition to compensatory damages a sum by way of further damages for *résistance abusive*—a head of damage awarded where a defendant has unreasonably refused to satisfy an obviously good claim. The Court of Appeal rejected the defendant's argument that the extra head of damage was a penalty. According to Lord Denning MR a penalty is 'a sum payable to the state by way of punishment and not a sum payable to a private individual, even though it is payable by way of exemplary damages'.[87]

12.2.32 In *United States Securities and Exchange Commission v Manterfield*,[88] it was claimed that the award of an interim freezing order in support of proceedings in Massachusetts would fall foul of the principle of non-enforcement of foreign penal laws. In the Massachusetts proceedings, the claimant, the United States Securities and Exchange Commission (SEC), sought not only the disgorgement of gains fraudulently acquired by the defendant, but also a civil monetary penalty. The claimant gave an undertaking that any assets recovered pursuant to the freezing order, if granted, would be offset against the sum to be disgorged and distributed to investors. The evidence showed that the amount to be disgorged was greater than the value of the assets in England; this meant that none of the English assets would go towards enforcement of the civil penalty. The Court of Appeal held that it is the substance of what is being sought to be enforced which is important for the purposes of the rule; in the instant case, the substance was the disgorgement of the alleged proceeds of fraud.[89] Nor did

---

[83] [1989] QB 255, 265.
[84] Purchas LJ at [1989] QB 255, 265.
[85] JG Collier, [1988] All ER Ann Rep 46, 48.
[86] [1978] QB 279.
[87] [1978] QB 279, 299–300.
[88] [2009] 2 All ER 1009. D Capper, (2009) 28 *CJQ* 454.
[89] [2009] 2 All ER 1009, 1016 (at [24]). In so holding, the Court of Appeal appeared to be influenced by the decision of the Court of Appeal of New South Wales in *Robb Evans of Robb Evans & Associates v*

the court place any importance on the fact that the SEC was a foreign regulatory body rather than a private individual.[90] The rule against enforcement of foreign penal laws was therefore not breached. The case affirms that if a foreign judgment can be severed into non-penal and penal components, the former can be enforced.[91]

12.3 CONDITIONS FOR RECOGNITION AT COMMON LAW

Introduction

12.3.1 Although the majority of cases concerning foreign judgments involve proceedings commenced by a judgment creditor for the enforcement of a money judgment in England, there are various situations in which a party seeks recognition of a foreign judgment rather than its enforcement. Whether a foreign judgment should be regarded as an effective bar to the subsequent proceedings in England depends on the doctrine of estoppel *per rem judicatam*.[92] In order for a foreign judgment to be an effective bar to subsequent proceedings in England it must create either a cause of action estoppel or an issue estoppel. Cause of action estoppel:

prevents a party to an action from asserting or denying, as against the other party, the existence of a particular cause of action, the non-existence or existence of which has been determined by a court of competent jurisdiction in previous litigation between the same parties.[93]

Issue estoppel is narrower. Indeed, a cause of action estoppel may involve two or more issue estoppels:

[W]ithin one cause of action, there may be several issues raised which are necessary for the determination of the whole case. The rule then is that, once an issue has been raised and distinctly determined between the parties, then, as a general rule, neither party can be allowed to fight that issue all over again.[94]

The doctrine of estoppel *per rem judicatam* has been developed on two grounds: first, it is in the public interest that there should be an end to litigation and, secondly, justice to the individual requires that a litigant should not be vexed twice for the same cause.[95] Accordingly, as a general rule, where a judgment creates an estoppel, the estoppel will extend not only 'to points upon which the court was actually required

---

European Bank Ltd [2004] 61 NSWLR 75 (DFC Thomas, (2005) 121 *LQR* 380; A Briggs, [2004] *LMCLQ* 313; M Burston, (2004) 26 *Sydney LR* 439).

[90] [2010] 1 WLR 172, 179 (at [23]). Cf *Schemmer v Property Resources Ltd* [1975] Ch 273, 288, where Goulding J had characterised the SEC as the 'financial police of the American Union'. The case involved the enforcement of a US statute which was held to be a penal law. Although a judgment concerning a private individual may possibly be enforceable in England, proceedings commenced by a receiver (a public officer) appointed by the US District Court pursuant an application by the SEC did not qualify for enforcement in England.

[91] *Raulin v Fischer* [1911] 2 KB 93.

[92] See PR Barnett, *Res Judicata, Estoppel and Foreign Judgments* (Oxford, OUP, 2001).

[93] Diplock LJ in *Thoday v Thoday* [1964] P 181, 197.

[94] Lord Denning MR in *Fidelitas Shipping Co Ltd v V/O Exportchleb* [1966] 1 QB 630, 640.

[95] Slade LJ in *Charm Maritime Inc v Kyriakou* [1987] 1 Lloyd's Rep 433, 440. For the more limited effect of foreign default judgments, see *New Brunswick Railway Co Ltd v British and French Trust Corporation Ltd* [1939] AC 1; *Masters v Leaver* [2000] ILPr 387.

by the parties to form an opinion and pronounce a judgment', but 'to every point which properly belonged to the subject of litigation, and which the parties, exercising reasonable diligence, might have brought forward at the time'.[96]

12.3.2 A judgment does not create an estoppel unless a number of conditions (the first two of which overlap with the conditions for enforcement) are satisfied. First, the judgment must have been given by a court of competent jurisdiction. In cases where estoppel *per rem judicatam* is raised as a defence by a defendant in English proceedings the claimant will normally have been the claimant in the foreign proceedings. In this type of case the original court is obviously to be regarded as a court of competent jurisdiction.[97] Where, however, the claimant in English proceedings invokes cause of action estoppel against a defendant, the foreign judgment will be entitled to recognition only if the original court had jurisdiction by virtue of the defendant's presence in the country of origin or the defendant's submission to the jurisdiction of its courts.[98] Secondly, the judgment in the earlier proceedings relied on as creating an estoppel must be final and conclusive.[99] The foreign court itself must consider that the judgment is final and conclusive and the English court should not give a foreign judgment greater preclusive effect in England than it would have in that foreign jurisdiction.[100] Thirdly, the judgment must be 'on the merits'. Fourthly, the parties (or their privies) in the earlier proceedings relied on as creating the estoppel must be the same as those in the later proceedings in which that estoppel is raised as a bar. Finally, the cause of action (or issue) in the later proceedings in which the estoppel is raised must be the same cause of action (or issue) as that decided by the court in the earlier proceedings. If these conditions are satisfied, the person seeking to resist recognition of the foreign judgment may, nevertheless, seek to rely on any of a number of defences.[101]

12.3.3 In general terms, a litigant may seek the recognition of a foreign judgment, rather than its enforcement, in one of three types of situation. First, the paradigm case involving the recognition of a foreign judgment arises when the defendant seeks to rely on a foreign judgment as a defence to proceedings in England. Recognition by way of defence is raised where A sues B for breach of contract in a foreign country, the court dismisses A's claim, A starts proceedings on the same cause of action in England and B relies on the foreign judgment as a bar to the proceedings in England.

12.3.4 Secondly, where a claimant who has been successful in foreign proceedings—but less successful than he might have hoped—wishes to re-litigate the same cause of action in England, the defendant may wish to rely on the foreign judgment as a bar to the English proceedings. It used to be the case that in English law a foreign judgment in the claimant's favour did not operate to extinguish the cause of action. Accordingly, a judgment creditor who had obtained an award of damages in foreign proceedings might choose between applying to enforce the judgment and suing the judgment debtor in England on the original cause of action in the hope of obtaining a

---

[96] Wigram V-C in *Henderson v Henderson* (1843) 3 Hare 100, 115. See also *ED & F Man (Sugar) Ltd v Haryanto (No 2)* [1991] 1 Lloyd's Rep 429.
[97] *Emanuel v Symon* [1908] 1 KB 302.
[98] See paras 12.2.3–12.2.22.
[99] See paras 12.2.25–12.2.27.
[100] *Barrett v Universal-Island Records Ltd* [2006] EMLR 567, 624 (at [189]).
[101] See section 12.4.

higher award. This rule, which gave a litigant two bites at the cherry, was indefensible. The doctrine of non-merger was abolished by the Civil Jurisdiction and Judgments Act 1982, section 34 of which provides:

No proceedings may be brought by a person in England or Wales ... on a cause of action in respect of which a judgment has been given in his favour in proceedings between the same parties, or their privies, in a court in another part of the United Kingdom or in a court of an overseas country, unless that judgment is not enforceable or entitled to recognition in England or Wales ... .

12.3.5   A question concerning the operation of section 34 is whether it is a mandatory provision limiting the jurisdiction of the court or whether it merely makes available a defence to a party to the proceedings in which the foreign judgment was given. In *Republic of India v India Steamship Co Ltd*[102] the Court of Appeal decided that the effect of section 34 is mandatory and cannot be overridden by the agreement of the parties. This decision was strongly criticised[103] and reversed on appeal by the House of Lords.[104] Having examined the common law prior to the entry into force of section 34 and the purpose behind the legislation, the House of Lords concluded that section 34 does no more than establish a defence which is capable of being defeated by estoppel, waiver or contrary agreement.[105] Whether the conduct of the defendant constitutes a waiver or gives rise to an estoppel (by convention or by acquiescence) depends on the particular facts of the case.[106]

12.3.6   Thirdly, a judgment creditor may seek to rely on a foreign judgment in order to prevent the judgment debtor from resisting enforcement of the judgment on certain grounds in England. For example, if the original court, having decided that the defendant authorised a local lawyer to accept service of the originating process on his behalf, exercises jurisdiction on the basis of the defendant's submission, the claimant may wish to rely on this aspect of the foreign judgment. If the defendant is barred from re-opening the factual issues which were definitively determined by the original court, the foreign judgment may be regarded as establishing that the defendant submitted to the jurisdiction of the original court for the purposes of English private international law (as well as under the local law), thereby preventing the defendant from challenging the foreign judgment on the ground that the original court was not a court of competent jurisdiction.[107]

On the Merits

12.3.7   In order to be entitled to recognition in England, a foreign judgment must be 'on the merits'. This condition raises potentially difficult questions. For example, is a judgment a decision on the merits if the original court dismissed the claim on the

---

[102] [1992] 1 Lloyd's Rep 124.
[103] L Collins, 'Illogical Survivals and Astonishing Results' (1992) 108 *LQR* 393.
[104] [1993] AC 410. PB Carter, (1993) 64 *BYIL* 470.
[105] Lord Goff at [1993] AC 410, 473.
[106] See *Republic of India v India Steamship Co Ltd (No 2)* [1998] AC 878.
[107] See *Desert Sun Loan Corporation v Hill* [1996] 2 All ER 847.

basis that the court had no jurisdiction or on the basis that the claim was time-barred? Is a decision by the original court that the defendant submitted to the court's jurisdiction a judgment on the merits?

12.3.8 The Foreign Limitation Periods Act 1984 introduced the rule that a foreign judgment based on limitation is to be regarded as a decision on the merits. Section 3 of the 1984 Act provides:

Where a court in any country outside England and Wales has determined any matter wholly or partly by reference to the law of that or any other country (including England and Wales) relating to limitation, then, for the purposes of the law relating to the effect to be given in England and Wales to that determination, that court shall, to the extent that it has so determined the matter, be deemed to have determined it on its merits.[108]

12.3.9 The question whether a decision of the original court on a procedural or jurisdictional matter is a judgment on the merits has been considered in two important cases. In *The Sennar (No 2)*[109] the plaintiff, a German company, started proceedings *in rem* in relation to a vessel owned by the defendant, a Sudanese company, in Rotterdam. The plaintiff's claim, which arose out of a bill of lading relating to a cargo of groundnuts, was that the master of the ship had committed a tort against the plaintiff by incorrectly dating the bill of lading. The defendant contested the jurisdiction of the Dutch court on the basis that the bill of lading conferred exclusive jurisdiction on the courts of Sudan. The Dutch court dismissed the claim on the ground that, as a party to the bill of lading, the plaintiff was entitled to found the claim only in contract and was bound by the jurisdiction clause. When the plaintiff subsequently started proceedings against the defendant in England with a view to obtaining damages in tort, the defendant sought to rely on the Dutch judgment in support of its application for a stay of the English proceedings. The central question facing the House of Lords was whether the plaintiff's claim was barred by the Dutch judgment. The plaintiff's main argument was that the judgment, being on a procedural question (namely, the jurisdiction of the Dutch courts), was not a judgment on the merits. It was the defendant's contention that the Dutch judgment created an issue estoppel on the question whether the plaintiff's claim fell within the scope of the jurisdiction clause contained in the bill of lading.

12.3.10 On the question whether the Dutch judgment was a decision on the merits Lord Brandon said:

Looking at the matter negatively a decision on procedure alone is not a decision on the merits. Looking at the matter positively a decision on the merits is a decision which establishes certain facts proved or not in dispute; states what are the relevant principles of law applicable to such facts; and expresses a conclusion with regard to the effect of applying those principles to the factual situation concerned.[110]

The Dutch judgment was a decision on the merits in this positive sense as regards two issues: first, that the plaintiff's only claim against the defendant was for breach of the contract of carriage and, secondly, that the effect of the jurisdiction clause was to

---

[108] The effect of this section is to reverse *Black-Clawson International Ltd v Papierwerke Waldhof-Aschaffenburg AG* [1975] AC 591. PB Carter, (1974–5) 47 *BYIL* 381; AJE Jaffey, 'Recognition of a Defendant's Foreign Judgment' (1975) 38 *MLR* 585.

[109] [1985] 1 WLR 490.

[110] [1985] 1 WLR 490, 499.

make any remedy for breach of that contract enforceable only in the Sudanese courts (unless the defendant elected otherwise).[111] Accordingly, the defendant could rely on the Dutch judgment to support its application for a stay of the English proceedings.

12.3.11   In *Desert Sun Loan Corporation v Hill*[112] the plaintiff issued proceedings in Arizona against, *inter alios*, a partnership (of which the defendant had been a member) and the defendant (as one of a number of guarantors of the partnership's liabilities). One of the defendant's former partners authorised a US attorney to accept service on behalf of the partners (including the defendant). The Arizona court decided that the defendant had submitted to the court's jurisdiction and held that he was liable as guarantor for a proportion of the partnership's debts. The plaintiff sought to enforce the judgment in England and claimed that the decision of the Arizona court on the jurisdictional point was a decision on the merits which barred the defendant's argument that, because he had not in fact authorised his former partner to instruct the US attorney to act on his behalf, the Arizona court was not a court of competent jurisdiction.

12.3.12   On the facts of the case the Court of Appeal concluded that the Arizona court, in considering whether the defendant had submitted to its jurisdiction under the law of Arizona, had not decided that the defendant had expressly authorised his former partner to instruct the US attorney to act on his behalf. However, it was accepted that if, in the context of its decision on the jurisdictional issue, the Arizona court had decided, as a question of fact, that the defendant had authorised his former partner to instruct a US attorney to act on his behalf, the defendant would not have been able to re-open that factual question in the English enforcement proceedings.

12.3.13   What emerges from these cases is that, even though the decision of the original court does not determine the substantive dispute between the parties, this does not necessarily mean that it is not a decision on the merits; a foreign judgment which, in general terms, decides a procedural or jurisdictional question may be regarded as determining an issue (or a number of issues) on the merits. In order for the decision of the original court on such an issue to be regarded as a decision on the merits two conditions must be satisfied: first, there must have been an express submission of the procedural or jurisdictional issue in question to the original court and, secondly, the specific issue of fact must have been raised before, and decided by, that court.[113]

Identity of the Parties

12.3.14   Whether the plea is based on cause of action estoppel or issue estoppel, it is essential that there is identity between the parties in the earlier action (which is relied on as creating the estoppel) and the parties in the later action (in which the judgment is relied upon). The requirement of identity is obviously satisfied if the parties are exactly the same. In *Black v Yates*[114] the plaintiff's husband had been killed in Spain in a motor accident which had been caused by the defendant's negligence. The defendant

---

[111]   Lord Diplock at [1985] 1 WLR 490, 494–5.
[112]   [1996] 2 All ER 847. A Briggs, (1996) 67 *BYIL* 596; P Rogerson, 'Issue Estoppel and Abuse of Process in Foreign Judgments' (1998) 17 *CJQ* 91.
[113]   See the judgment of Evans LJ in *Desert Sun Loan Corporation v Hill* [1996] 2 All ER 847, 858.
[114]   [1992] QB 526. PB Carter, (1991) 62 *BYIL* 458.

was prosecuted and convicted in Spanish criminal proceedings to which the plaintiff joined a civil claim for damages, as permitted by Spanish procedural law. The court, applying the same principles as those which would have been applied by a civil court, awarded the plaintiff the equivalent of £18,000 by way of compensation. When the plaintiff commenced proceedings against the defendant in England—claiming damages under the Fatal Accidents Acts—the defendant sought to rely on the Spanish judgment (under section 34 of the Civil Jurisdiction and Judgments Act 1982).[115] It was held that the plaintiff's claim was barred:

[Section 34] contemplates proceedings of whatever character in the court of an overseas country in which the plaintiff and defendant in English proceedings have previously participated as opposing parties for the purposes of adjudicating a cause of action between them, in respect of which the English plaintiff has obtained a judgment in his favour enforceable or entitled to recognition in England and Wales.[116]

There is no requirement that the English claimant should have been the original party in the overseas proceedings or that the foreign proceedings were exclusively civil in character.[117]

12.3.15 More problematical is the situation where the proceedings leading to the foreign judgment concern a claim *in personam* against a named defendant and the subsequent proceedings in England involve an Admiralty claim *in rem* (or vice versa). Since it is not desirable that the same issues should be tried in two or more courts of competent jurisdiction, a judgment *in personam* may operate as a bar to subsequent proceedings *in rem* in England on the same cause of action. Whether or not there is identity of the parties should be looked at from a realistic perspective—rather than from a technical one. In *Republic of India v India Steamship Co Ltd (No 2)*[118] the House of Lords held that, for the purposes of section 34 of the Civil Jurisdiction and Judgments Act 1982, the parties to foreign proceedings *in personam* are the same as the parties to English proceedings brought by the same claimant in relation to a ship owned by the defendant in the foreign proceedings. The rationale of this decision is that the owner of the vessel served in the Admiralty proceedings *in rem* is the person who would be liable in a claim *in personam*.

12.3.16 It does not follow that a foreign judgment *in personam* will necessarily bar subsequent proceedings *in rem* on the same cause of action in England.[119] In *Republic of India v India Steamship Co Ltd (No 2)* the Court of Appeal decided not to consider the situation where, in a case involving a maritime lien, a claim *in rem* is brought in respect of a ship in new ownership or where, for some other reason, the person who acknowledges service in the proceedings *in rem* did not take part (whether as claimant or defendant) in the earlier foreign proceedings[120] and the House of Lords also chose not to express a final view on the matter.[121]

---

[115] For the text of the provision, see para 12.3.4.
[116] Phillips J at [1992] QB 526, 546.
[117] *Ibid.*
[118] [1998] AC 878. A Briggs, (1997) 68 *BYIL* 355.
[119] See M West, 'Arbitrations, Admiralty actions *in rem* and the arrest of ships in the Hong Kong SAR: in the twilight of *The Indian Grace (No 2)*' [2002] *LMCLQ* 259.
[120] Staughton LJ at [1997] 2 WLR 538, 554.
[121] Lord Steyn at [1998] AC 878, 912.

12.3.17 In *Carl Zeiss Stiftung v Rayner & Keeler Ltd (No 2)*[122] the House of Lords took a more technical approach to a not dissimilar question. Carl Zeiss Stiftung, a foundation which had been established in the Grand Duchy of Saxe-Weimar in 1891, was located at Jena, which at the time of the litigation—prior to German reunification— was in the German Democratic Republic. The English proceedings were started in 1955 by solicitors instructed by the Council of Gera, which, it was alleged, was the legal representative of Carl Zeiss Stiftung (Jena). One of the purposes of the proceedings was to prevent the defendant, a West German corporation known as Carl Zeiss Stiftung (Heidenheim, Brenz), from passing off optical and glass instruments with the name 'Carl Zeiss' or 'Zeiss'. In 1953 the Council of Gera had brought proceedings in West Germany with a view to preventing the defendant from using the name 'Carl Zeiss', but in 1960 the Federal Supreme Court dismissed the claim. Although the plaintiffs in the English proceedings were the English solicitors, rather than the Council of Gera, the defendant argued that the parties in both proceedings were effectively the same.

12.3.18 Although the majority of the House of Lords rejected the plaintiff's contentions, Lord Wilberforce dissented on this point. According to Lord Wilberforce the correct approach is to look to see who in reality is behind the proceedings. In the present case the reality was that the Council of Gera was behind the proceedings both in West Germany and England and in each case on behalf of Carl Zeiss Stiftung (Jena). It is hard to resist Lord Wilberforce's conclusion that to treat the solicitors as the parties to the English proceedings was both lacking in reality and unduly technical.[123]

12.3.19 The parties to litigation are also to be regarded as the same for the purposes of cause of action estoppel or issue estoppel if there is privity between a party to the earlier litigation and the later proceedings. In this context, privity signifies privity of blood, title or interest.[124] The common feature of these three categories of privity is that privies all have an interest in the subject-matter of the proceedings. So, in a case involving property which is held on trust, a judgment given against the trustees would bar a subsequent claim by the beneficiaries, because there is sufficient privity between the trustees and the beneficiaries.[125] On the facts of a particular case, shareholders and their company may be regarded as privies.[126] Such would be the case where a company is effectively the alter ego of a sole shareholder.[127]

12.3.20 The fact that a third party has a commercial interest in the outcome of litigation between the claimant and the defendant does not justify the conclusion that the judgment should be regarded as binding on the third party. For privity of interest to exist between two parties involved in separate proceedings:

> there must be a sufficient degree of identification between the two parties to make it just to hold that the decision to which one was a party should be binding in proceedings to which the other is a party.[128]

---

[122] [1967] 1 AC 853.
[123] [1967] 1 AC 853, 968–9.
[124] Lord Reid in *Carl Zeiss Stiftung v Rayner & Keeler Ltd (No 2)* [1967] 1 AC 853, 910.
[125] *Gleeson v J Whipple & Co Ltd* [1977] 1 WLR 510.
[126] *Matai Industries Ltd v Jensen* [1989] 1 NZLR 525 (High Court, New Zealand).
[127] *Barakot Ltd v Epiette Ltd* [1997] 6 Bank LR 28.
[128] Megarry V-C in *Gleeson v J Whipple & Co Ltd* [1977] 1 WLR 510, 515.

The courts have not attempted to formulate a definition of privity in this context, being content to observe that '[e]ach case has to be decided in light of its particular facts'.[129]

Identity of the Cause of Action or Issue

Cause of Action Estoppel

12.3.21   Where there is any dispute about whether the causes of action in the two sets of proceedings are the same, this question must be determined by English law; whether the causes of action would be regarded as identical by the domestic law of the country of origin is irrelevant.[130] The English authorities are not entirely satisfactory. The general principle is that a cause of action consists of the minimum facts which a claimant is required in law to plead and (if necessary) prove in order to obtain the relief which he claims.[131] The doctrine of *res judicata* requires that 'damages resulting from one and the same cause of action must be assessed and recovered once [and] for all'.[132] It follows that cause of action estoppel extends not only to the issues actually decided by the original court, but 'to every point which properly belonged to the subject of the litigation, and which the parties, exercising reasonable diligence, might have brought forward at that time'.[133]

12.3.22   Potential problems are posed by situations where a single event gives rise to a variety of injuries or losses. In cases involving the tort of negligence the cases show that some judges have sought to draw a distinction between, on the one hand, different losses falling within a particular head of damage and, on the other, different heads of damage arising out of a single set of facts. Different losses within a particular head of damage clearly result from the same cause of action. A claimant cannot justify proceedings for the loss of an eye by the defendant's negligence when he has already recovered for the loss of a foot by the same negligence by saying that in the first action he only gave particulars of the loss of his foot.[134] However, in *Brunsden v Humphrey*[135] the majority of the Court of Appeal thought that it is possible to segregate different causes of action by reference to different heads of damage. According to this view, if as a result of an accident a claimant suffers both personal injury and property damage he has two distinct causes of action, one for his personal injuries and the other for damage to his property. The decision in *Brunsden v Humphrey*, the logic of which has been questioned,[136] was not followed by the Court of Appeal in *Talbot v Berkshire County Council*[137] and the better view is that a cause of action should be

---

[129]   Aldous LJ in *Kirin-Amgen Inc v Boehringer Mannheim GmbH* [1997] FSR 289, 307.
[130]   *Republic of India v India Steamship Co Ltd* [1992] 1 Lloyd's Rep 124, reversed by the House of Lords on other grounds: [1993] AC 410; *Barrett v Universal-Island Records Ltd* [2006] EMLR 567, 624 (at [188]).
[131]   *Letang v Cooper* [1965] 1 QB 232.
[132]   Bowen LJ in *Brunsden v Humphrey* (1884) 14 QBD 141, 147.
[133]   Lord Denning MR in *Fidelitas Shipping Co Ltd v V/O Exportchleb* [1966] 1 QB 630, 643.
[134]   Talbot J in *Conquer v Boot* [1928] 2 KB 336, 345.
[135]   (1884) 14 QBD 141.
[136]   *Buckland v Palmer* [1984] 1 WLR 1109.
[137]   [1994] QB 290.

regarded as encompassing different heads of damage arising out of a single set of facts.

12.3.23   With regard to cases involving a breach of contract which gives rise to different losses the position is made clear by the decision of the House of Lords in *Republic of India v India Steamship Co Ltd.*[138] Litigation arose out of bills of lading under which the plaintiff's cargo had been carried from Sweden to India in a ship owned by the defendant. During the course of the voyage there was a fire on board the ship as a result of which some of the plaintiff's cargo was jettisoned and the rest was damaged. In proceedings commenced by the plaintiff in India the court awarded damages for short delivery. When the plaintiff started proceedings in England with a view to recovering compensation for the damage to the cargo—by far the larger part of the plaintiff's losses—the defendant applied to strike out the English proceedings. The plaintiff alleged that the cause of action in the English proceedings related to damages for delivery of the cargo in a damaged condition, whereas the Indian judgment concerned only damages for short delivery. The question facing the court was whether the Indian and English proceedings involved two different causes of action or one cause of action involving two kinds of damage.

12.3.24   The House of Lords decided that, since proof of damage is not necessary to establish the cause of action, the cause of action in the Indian and English proceedings was the same:

> [I]t is necessary to identify the relevant breach of contract; and if it transpires that the cause of action in the first action is a breach of contract which is the same breach of contract which constitutes the cause of action in the second, then the principle of res judicata applies, and the plaintiff cannot escape from the conclusion by pleading in the second action particulars of damage which were not pleaded in the first.[139]

Issue Estoppel

12.3.25   Although the basic framework of issue estoppel and cause of action estoppel is the same, issue estoppel gives rise to greater problems. Whatever may be the difficulties in determining whether proceedings in two different countries involve the same cause of action, those difficulties are more extreme where the question is whether proceedings in two countries involve the same issue. Because of such difficulties, it is well established that an issue estoppel can arise only in respect of findings of a foreign court which were essential for its decision.[140]

12.3.26   In *Carl Zeiss Stiftung v Rayner & Keeler Ltd (No 2)*[141] it had been held in the earlier German proceedings that the constitution of Carl Zeiss Stiftung (Jena)

---

[138] [1993] AC 410. S Beckwith, 'Res Judicata and Foreign Judgments: The *Indian Grace*' (1994) 43 *ICLQ* 185.

[139] Lord Goff at [1993] AC 410, 420. For consideration of cause of action estoppel in the context of transfer of title to movables, see *Air Foyle Ltd v Center Capital Ltd* [2003] 2 Lloyd's Rep 753.

[140] *The Good Challenger* [2004] 1 Lloyd's Rep 67. See also, eg, *Kirin-Amgen Inc v Boehringer Mannheim GmbH* [1997] FSR 289.

[141] [1967] 1 AC 853. The relevant background facts are set out in para 12.3.17.

had been rendered ineffective—as a result of which the Council of Gera did not have authority to act as the foundation's legal representative. One of the questions facing the House of Lords was whether the decision of the Federal Supreme Court created an issue estoppel which determined that the plaintiffs were acting without the authority of Carl Zeiss Stiftung (Jena). On this question it was argued by the plaintiffs that, whereas in the German proceedings the issue was whether the Council of Gera representing Carl Zeiss Stiftung (Jena) could sue in respect of certain matters in Germany, in the English proceedings the issue was whether this could be done in England. This somewhat artificial distinction was rejected by the majority of the House of Lords. As Lord Wilberforce noted, the issue which arose in both the English and the German proceedings was whether Carl Zeiss Stiftung (Jena) had become paralysed or its organs rendered ineffective so that the Council of Gera was not authorised to act on the foundation's behalf.[142]

12.3.27 Issue estoppel raises practical problems which do not arise in relation to cause of action estoppel:

Suppose the first case is one of trifling importance but it involves for one party proof of facts which would be expensive and troublesome; and that party can see the possibility that the same point may arise if his opponent later raises a much more important claim. What is he to do? The second case may never be brought. Must he go to great trouble and expense to forestall a possible plea of issue estoppel if the second case is brought? This does not arise in cause of action estoppel: if the cause of action is important, he will incur the expense; if it is not, he will take the chance of winning on some other point.[143]

Not surprisingly the English courts have counselled caution in the application of the doctrine of estoppel *per rem judicatam* in cases of issue estoppel. In *Carl Zeiss Stiftung v Rayner & Keeler Ltd (No 2)* Lord Reid, echoing the observations of Lord Brougham in *Houlditch v Donegal*,[144] provided two reasons for caution: first, the English courts, not being familiar with modes of procedure in many foreign countries, may not be sure that a particular issue has been decided by the original court and may be unsure whether that issue was a basis of the foreign judgment; secondly, where the foreign proceedings were of a trivial character as a result of which the defendant chose not to participate in them, it might be unjust to prevent the defendant from raising issues which were decided against him in his absence by the original court.[145] If the court has doubts whether the foreign court decided the specific issue raised in the English proceedings, the foreign judgment will not be recognised as creating an estoppel.[146]

12.3.28 The impact of issue estoppel is further limited by two factors. First, on the basis of the decision in *Carl Zeiss Stiftung v Rayner & Keeler Ltd (No 2)*, the court has a general discretion not to recognise a foreign judgment if it would be unjust to do so, even if the conditions for the creation of an issue estoppel are

---

[142] [1967] 1 AC 853, 967–8.
[143] Lord Reid in *Carl Zeiss Stiftung v Rayner & Keeler Ltd (No 2)* [1967] 1 AC 853, 917. See also Toulson J in *Baker v Ian McCall International Ltd* [2000] CLC 189, 198.
[144] (1834) 8 Bligh NS 301, 338.
[145] [1967] 1 AC 853, 918. See *Baker v Ian McCall International Ltd* [2000] CLC 189.
[146] *Desert Sun Loan Corporation v Hill* [1996] 2 All ER 847.

satisfied. Secondly, the principle of issue estoppel may be held not to operate in a case where, after the foreign judgment has been pronounced, further material, which could not by reasonable diligence have been adduced in the foreign proceedings, becomes available.[147]

12.4 DEFENCES TO RECOGNITION AND ENFORCEMENT AT COMMON LAW

12.4.1   The existence of a system of legal rules for the recognition and enforcement of foreign judgments is premised on the idea that, having obtained a judgment on the merits in an appropriate jurisdiction, a litigant should be able to rely on that judgment in another country. Although in English law the basis of the common law rules on recognition and enforcement of foreign judgments is not reciprocity in a strict sense, the foundation of private international law in this area is the collective interest of the world's legal systems in the free movement of judgments. Accordingly, practical common sense points towards defences to the recognition and enforcement of foreign judgments being kept to a minimum. As a general rule, the person against whom a foreign judgment is invoked is not allowed to raise defences in the English proceedings which were raised, or could have been raised, in the foreign proceedings.[148] Where, however, new evidence comes to light after judgment in the foreign proceedings has been given, the person against whom the judgment is invoked should be able to rely on such evidence in the context of proceedings in England. An English judgment may be set aside on the basis of fresh evidence and there is no good reason why a foreign judgment should be treated more favourably.

12.4.2   Notwithstanding the fact that the number of defences to recognition and enforcement of foreign judgments should be limited, an English court should not be obliged to give effect to a foreign judgment which either offends English standards of justice (whether substantive or procedural) or conflicts with an earlier judgment whether granted by an English court or entitled to recognition in England. This does not mean, however, that the court addressed is entitled to act as though it were a court of appeal in respect of the original court. Under English law it is not generally open for the person against whom the judgment was given to attack a foreign judgment on the merits. So, the fact that the original court made an error of fact or an error of law (even of English law) is not a ground for refusing recognition or enforcement.[149] Similarly, lack of internal competence under the domestic law of the country of origin is not a defence,[150] although in the unlikely event of a foreign judgment being a complete nullity under the law of the country of origin—rather than simply irregular—it should not be recognised or enforced in England.[151]

---

[147]   *C (A Minor) v Hackney LBC* [1996] 1 WLR 789 (a case involving a domestic judgment).
[148]   *Ellis v McHenry* (1871) LR 6 CP 228; *Israel Discount Bank of New York v Hadjipateras* [1984] 1 WLR 137. The defences of fraud and natural justice are exceptions to this general rule. See paras 12.4.3–12.4.13.
[149]   *Godard v Gray* (1870) LR 6 QB 139.
[150]   Lindley LJ in *Pemberton v Hughes* [1899] 1 Ch 781, 791.
[151]   JD McClean and K Beevers, *Morris: The Conflict of Laws* (London, Sweet & Maxwell, 7th edn, 2009) para 7–037. See, however, *Merker v Merker* [1963] P 283.

Natural Justice

Traditional Categories

12.4.3 It used to be assumed, on the authority of *Jacobson v Frachon*,[152] that a foreign judgment could be refused recognition or enforcement in England on the ground that the foreign proceedings involved a breach of the principles of natural justice in only two situations: first, where the defendant was not given notice of the proceedings in the original court; secondly, where the person against whom the judgment was given was not presented with a proper opportunity to present his case. Whether there has been a breach of natural justice in either of these senses is to be assessed by English standards; the fact that a foreign court might take a different view on whether the principles of natural justice have been observed is irrelevant. Indeed, the person against whom the judgment is invoked should be able to raise the question of natural justice in the context of proceedings in England even if the original court ruled on the question in the other party's favour in the original proceedings.[153] The English courts have been loath to refuse to recognise or enforce foreign judgments on these traditional grounds.

Substantial Justice

12.4.4 Prior to the decision of the Court of Appeal in *Adams v Cape Industries Plc*[154] it was reasonable to suppose that if a foreign judgment was challenged on the basis of a procedural defect which fell within neither of the traditional categories the party seeking to resist recognition or enforcement would have to show that, by virtue of the defect, the foreign judgment was contrary to English public policy. However, in *Adams v Cape Industries Plc* the Court of Appeal decided, albeit *obiter*, that the natural justice defence extends to situations involving procedural defects which lead to 'breach of an English court's views of substantial justice'.[155]

12.4.5 In *Adams v Cape Industries Plc*—a case involving proceedings for the enforcement of a foreign judgment which had awarded damages to more than 200 plaintiffs for personal injuries—the foreign proceedings had not involved a judicial investigation of the injuries of any of the individual plaintiffs. The judge directed that the average award for each of the plaintiffs should be $75,000 and counsel placed the plaintiffs into four groups—according to the seriousness of their injuries. In the view of the Court of Appeal, substantive justice requires that the amount of compensation should not be fixed subjectively by or on behalf of the plaintiff: 'the extent of the defendant's obligation is to be assessed objectively by the independent judge upon proof by the plaintiff of the relevant facts.'[156] Even had the original court been regarded as a court of competent jurisdiction,[157] enforcement of the judgment would

---

[152] (1928) 138 LT 386.
[153] *Jet Holdings Inc v Patel* [1990] 1 QB 335.
[154] [1990] Ch 433.
[155] Slade LJ at [1990] Ch 433, 564.
[156] Slade LJ at [1990] Ch 433, 567. See also *Masters v Leaver* [2000] ILPr 387.
[157] On this question, see section 12.2.

have been refused on the basis that the procedure adopted was contrary to English notions of substantial justice.

12.4.6   The defence based on contravention of English notions of substantial justice is different from and more general than the defence of natural justice: 'It could almost be seen as an ultimate discretion to withhold recognition simply because in the eyes of the English forum justice was palpably not done.'[158] The substantial justice defence formulated by the Court of Appeal in *Adams v Cape Industries Plc* is more analogous to the defence of public policy than the defence of natural justice as traditionally understood.

12.4.7   In considering whether a foreign judgment should be refused enforcement on the basis that it contravenes English notions of substantial justice, the court must take account not only of the injustice caused by the procedure adopted by the original court, but any possibilities for the party against whom the judgment is invoked to correct procedural irregularities under the law of the country of origin. The relevance of the existence of a remedy in the country of origin and the weight to be attached to it depend upon factors which include the nature of the procedural defect and the reasonableness in the circumstances of requiring or expecting the party resisting recognition or enforcement to make use of the remedy.[159]

12.4.8   If the person against whom the judgment is invoked had notice of an irregularity in the procedure adopted by the original court and the procedural law of the country of origin offers him a fair opportunity of correcting that error, it would not be appropriate for recognition or enforcement of the foreign judgment to be refused in England in a case where that opportunity was not taken. However, if the party against whom the judgment is invoked is not aware of the procedural defect, or if there are no means whereby the original court is able to remedy the defect, or if it is not reasonable to expect the party in question to avail himself of the remedies available in the original court, the English court may legitimately refuse to recognise or enforce the foreign judgment on the basis that it contravenes English notions of substantial justice.[160]

Fraud

General Principles

12.4.9   The defence of fraud is anomalous in a number of respects. First, although an English court cannot normally review the decision of the original court on the merits, an exception is made in cases involving allegations of fraud. Secondly, whereas it is not, as a general rule, possible to raise in English proceedings defences which were raised or could have been raised in the foreign proceedings, the 19th-century authorities[161] show that a foreign judgment will not be recognised or enforced in England if

---

[158] PB Carter, (1988) 59 *BYIL* 360, 363.
[159] Slade LJ at [1990] Ch 433, 570.
[160] See *Masters v Leaver* [2000] ILPr 387.
[161] *Abouloff v Oppenheimer & Co* (1882) 10 QBD 295; *Vadala v Lawes* (1890) 25 QBD 310.

it was obtained by fraud—even if the allegation of fraud was investigated and rejected by the original court. Thirdly, there is clear authority for the proposition that an English court may investigate the question of fraud even if the person against whom the judgment was given chose not to raise the matter in the course of the foreign proceedings.[162] Finally, although as regards the setting aside of an English judgment on the ground of fraud the rule is that the person challenging the judgment must produce fresh evidence which 'entirely changes the aspect of the case'[163] or which 'would probably have an important influence on the result of the case',[164] no such requirement applies to cases involving foreign judgments. Although the 19th-century cases were extensively criticised, they were upheld by decisions of the Court of Appeal[165] and the House of Lords[166] in the late 20th century.

12.4.10   There are, however, two qualifications to these rules. First, a defence based on fraud will be struck out as an abuse of process unless there is 'plausible evidence disclosing at least a *prima facie* case of fraud'.[167] Secondly, a litigant is not permitted to raise the question of fraud if there has been a separate foreign judgment which creates an issue estoppel on that question. In *House of Spring Gardens Ltd v Waite*[168] the plaintiff obtained a judgment in Ireland against the defendant for nearly £3.5 million (the first judgment).[169] After the appeal to the Irish Supreme Court had been dismissed, the defendant started proceedings in the Irish High Court with a view to having the first judgment set aside on the basis of fraud. The defendant's allegation of fraud was rejected (the second judgment). When the plaintiff sought to enforce the first judgment in England the question arose whether the defendant could raise the defence of fraud again. The Court of Appeal decided that the facts were distinguishable from the earlier cases and that the scope of the defence of fraud should not be extended. In the present case the allegation of fraud had been raised in separate proceedings, the purpose of which had been to investigate the question of fraud in the original proceedings. The Court of Appeal took the view that, unless the second judgment itself was impeachable for fraud, the second judgment should be regarded as creating an issue estoppel on the question whether the first judgment had been obtained by fraud. The result should be the same if the question of fraud is determined in separate proceedings in a country other than that in which the original judgment was given.[170]

---

[162] *Syal v Heyward* [1948] 2 KB 443.

[163] Earl Cairns LC in *Phosphate Sewage Co Ltd v Molleson* (1879) 4 App Cas 801, 814.

[164] Denning LJ in *Ladd v Marshall* [1954] 1 WLR 1489, 1491. See also Lord Diplock in *Hunter v Chief Constable of the West Midlands Police* [1982] AC 529, 545.

[165] *Jet Holdings Inc v Patel* [1990] 1 QB 335.

[166] *Owens Bank Ltd v Bracco* [1992] 2 AC 443. A Briggs, 'Foreign Judgments: More Surprises' (1992) 109 *LQR* 549; JG Collier, [1992] *CLJ* 441.

[167] Lord Templeman in *Owens Bank Ltd v Etoile Commerciale SA* [1995] 1 WLR 44, 51. See also *Clarke v Fennoscandia Ltd (No 3)* 2008 SLT 33, where the House of Lords refused to entertain an allegation of fraud where the real reason for raising the issue of fraud was not to oppose the recognition or enforcement of the foreign judgment but to undermine a foreign judgment which was the product of a fair hearing.

[168] [1991] 1 QB 241. PB Carter, (1990) 61 *BYIL* 405.

[169] The Irish judgment was granted before 1 June 1988, the date on which the Brussels Convention came into force between the Republic of Ireland and the United Kingdom.

[170] Parker LJ in *Owens Bank Ltd v Bracco* [1992] 2 AC 443, 471.

The Application of the Principles to Different Types of Fraud

12.4.11   At the most general level, fraud may take two forms.[171] On the one hand, a party to litigation may raise an allegation of fraud affecting the cause of action upon which the claimant based his claim in the foreign proceedings (for example, an allegation that a contract was procured by fraud). In these cases, the general rule applicable to the setting aside of an English judgment is the relevant one.[172] The party seeking to resist the judgment must produce fresh evidence in support of the allegation that there was fraud relating to the underlying transaction.

12.4.12   On the other hand, one of the parties may raise an allegation of fraud affecting the conduct of the proceedings of the original court itself. In relation to these cases the English courts have been rather unsophisticated and the principle laid down in *Abouloff v Oppenheimer & Co* and *Vadala v Lawes* has been applied indiscriminately. A better approach would be to look more closely at different types of fraud affecting the conduct of the proceedings. Three different factual situations emerge from the cases. First, the most common cases of fraud involve allegations that the original court was misled by one of the litigants. For example, it may be alleged that the document which was used to prove the existence of a disputed transaction was forged.[173] Secondly, the party against whom the judgment is invoked may allege fraud in cases where he was deprived of an opportunity to take part in the foreign proceedings, whether as a result of a trick by the other party or as a result of threats. For example, in *Ochsenbein v Papelier*[174] the plaintiff, having started proceedings in France, tricked the defendant into thinking that the action would be discontinued by burning the originating process in the defendant's presence. The plaintiff, in fact, continued with the French proceedings behind the defendant's back and obtained a default judgment in his favour. More recently, in *Jet Holdings Inc v Patel*,[175] it was argued that a Californian judgment should be refused enforcement in England because the defendant, having previously been threatened and attacked by employees of the plaintiff company, had been afraid to visit the United States and take part in the Californian proceedings. Thirdly, allegations of fraud may concern the conduct of the original court itself.[176] A rare, and extreme example of this category of fraud occurred in *Korea National Insurance Corporation v Allianz Global Corporate & Specialty AG*[177] in which aspersions were cast against not only the foreign judiciary, but also the foreign state. It was alleged that a North Korean judgment concerning a reinsurance claim by a North Korean insurance company against foreign reinsurers had been procured by fraud which was instigated or at least approved by the North Korean state and its senior officials. On the basis of these allegations it was argued that the North Korean judgment should not be enforced as the North Korean

---

[171] See the judgment of the Court of Appeal in *Owens Bank Ltd v Bracco* [1992] 2 AC 443, 459.

[172] Parker LJ in *Owens Bank Ltd v Bracco* [1992] 2 AC 443, 459. This aspect of the Court of Appeal's decision was not considered by the House of Lords.

[173] See *Owens Bank Ltd v Bracco* [1992] 2 AC 443.

[174] (1873) LR 8 Ch App 695.

[175] [1990] 1 QB 335.

[176] *Price v Dewhurst* (1837) 8 Sim 279.

[177] [2008] 2 CLC 837.

judiciary was not independent from the state. At first instance, Field J thought that the issues raised had the potential for straining diplomatic relations between the governments of the United Kingdom and North Korea and were thus non-justiciable.[178] On appeal, however, the Court of Appeal held that: 'There is no general rule that if an allegation might embarrass a foreign sovereign it follows that that will also embarrass diplomatic relations with the United Kingdom and that thus such embarrassing issues are non-justiciable.'[179] Where in a commercial context allegations were made against the state, not in relation to a sovereign act carried out in its own jurisdiction, but in relation to acts which affect the rights of a party under a commercial contract, the English court would normally look into those allegations unless the UK government has indicated that such a move will embarrass diplomatic relations between the United Kingdom and that state.[180]

12.4.13   The law should draw a distinction between these three categories of fraud affecting the conduct of the proceedings of the original court. In relation to the first category the person against whom the judgment was given will *prima facie* have been given the opportunity to raise the question of fraud before the original court. Since the English court is in no better a position than the original court to assess whether or not one of the parties was attempting to practise deception, a litigant should not be allowed to raise this type of fraud in proceedings in England—except in cases where fresh evidence has come to light after the conclusion of the foreign proceedings. This type of case should be treated in the same way as cases involving allegations of fraud affecting the cause of action. As regards the second category it is legitimate to allow the question of fraud to be raised at the stage of recognition or enforcement if the conduct of the party seeking to rely on the judgment has effectively prevented the other party from taking a full part in the proceedings. The rule in *Abouloff v Oppenheimer & Co* is also justified in those rare cases falling within the third category. Where the alleged fraud involves matters such as judicial bias, the opportunity to raise the matter before the original court is effectively meaningless. The party against whom the judgment was given should therefore be free in such circumstances to raise the question of fraud in the English proceedings.

Public Policy

12.4.14   Public policy plays a role in many areas of private international law, including the recognition and enforcement of foreign judgments. It would be unreasonable to expect an English court to enforce a foreign judgment which conflicts with English public policy.[181] Even though the content of public policy is notoriously open-textured, in the civil and commercial sphere it will be only in very exceptional circumstances that

---

[178] [2008] 2 CLC 825.

[179] Waller LJ at [2008] 2 CLC 837, 848 (at [30]).

[180] [2008] 2 CLC 837, 848 (at [32]).

[181] Foreign courts refuse to enforce English judgments on similar grounds; eg, the courts of the United States will not enforce an English judgment which is incompatible with the protection of free speech guaranteed by the First Amendment. See KH Youm, 'The Interaction between American and Foreign Libel Law: US Courts Refuse to Enforce English Libel Judgments' (2000) 49 *ICLQ* 131.

a judgment will be refused recognition or enforcement on this basis.[182] Most of the cases cited in the text-books in which public policy has been successfully invoked concern family law matters and the courts seem to have taken an uncharacteristically relaxed view of foreign judgments outside that limited area. For example, there is nothing contrary to English public policy in enforcing an award of exemplary damages.[183] Similarly, although the court will not enforce a domestic wagering contract, enforcement of a foreign judgment based on a wagering contract will not be refused on public policy grounds.

12.4.15   In *Israel Discount Bank of New York v Hadjipateras*[184] the plaintiff brought proceedings in New York against the defendant and his father as guarantors of obligations assumed by a third party. In the New York proceedings the defendant swore an affidavit stating that he had entered the guarantees as a result of undue influence exerted by his father. The New York court gave judgment for the plaintiff, who started enforcement proceedings in England. The defendant sought to defend the English proceedings on the ground that a judgment which is based on an agreement obtained by undue influence is contrary to public policy. Although permission to defend was refused, the Court of Appeal seemed to accept the proposition that a foreign judgment based on an agreement which contravenes public policy may be unenforceable on the ground of public policy.

12.4.16   The premises on which the decision of the Court of Appeal appears to have been based have been subjected to devastating criticism.[185] First, the traditional view is that the public policy defence relates to the substance of the foreign judgment, not to the underlying cause of action. There is little or no authority for the proposition that a foreign judgment based on an agreement which contravenes public policy is unenforceable on the ground of public policy. Accordingly, the proposition must be regarded as, at best, questionable. Secondly, even if the Court of Appeal is right in thinking that it is contrary to public policy to enforce a foreign judgment based on an agreement which contravenes public policy, the Court of Appeal's view that an agreement concluded under undue influence is unenforceable by reason of public policy cannot be supported.

12.4.17   It is contrary to public policy to recognise or enforce a judgment if the defendant's right to a fair trial under Article 6 of the European Convention on Human Rights (ECHR) had not been respected in the context of the proceedings leading to the judgment by the original court.[186] With regard to enforcement proceedings in England, it is irrelevant whether or not the country of origin is a party to the ECHR.[187] However, somewhat controversially, in *Government of the United States v Montgomery (No 2)*[188] the House of Lords held, in the context of an application to

---

[182] Eg, the argument that a foreign judgment, alleged to be procured by means of fraud, is unenforceable on grounds of public policy because the foreign judiciary is part of and not independent from the state which was involved in the fraud, did not succeed in the absence of an indication from the UK government that embarrassing issues which would affect diplomatic relations arose: *Korea National Insurance Corporation v Allianz Global Corporate & Specialty AG* [2008] 2 CLC 837.

[183] Lord Denning MR in *SA Consortium General Textiles v Sun and Sand Agencies Ltd* [1970] QB 279, 300.

[184] [1984] 1 WLR 137. JG Collier, [1984] *CLJ* 47.

[185] JG Collier, [1984] *CLJ* 47.

[186] See, eg, *Maronier v Larmer* [2003] QB 620 (a case decided under the Brussels Convention).

[187] *Pellegrini v Italy* (2001) 35 EHRR 44.

[188] [2004] 1 WLR 2241.

register a US confiscation order under the Criminal Justice Act 1988, that Article 6 of the ECHR was engaged only if the procedure of the original court involved a flagrant denial of justice. This conclusion has been the subject of cogent criticism[189] and, as the case is an example of the House of Lords 'getting human rights law wrong',[190] it is to be hoped that the issue will be reconsidered.

Res Judicata

12.4.18   However sophisticated the courts try to be in handling questions of jurisdiction, situations arise in which the same issues are litigated in different jurisdictions. Accordingly, there are cases in which the courts of different countries give inconsistent answers to the same questions. The problem of irreconcilable judgments may arise either where a foreign judgment relates to a matter which has already been decided in England or where there are two foreign judgments on the same issue.

12.4.19   Where an English judgment creates an estoppel, the court will not recognise or enforce a foreign judgment which conflicts with it.[191] More difficult is the problem posed by two irreconcilable foreign judgments. If one judgment is entitled to recognition or enforcement in England and the other is not the solution is obvious. What is the position, however, if both judgments are *prima facie* entitled to recognition or enforcement in England? In *Showlag v Mansour*[192] the Privy Council decided that, as a general rule, the court should give effect to whichever judgment was rendered first. However, Lord Keith added that 'it is to be kept in mind that there may be circumstances under which the party holding the earlier judgment may be estopped from relying upon it'.[193] Lord Keith observed:

If there are circumstances connected with the obtaining of the second judgment which make it unfair for the party founding on the first to seek to enforce it, then it may be proper to refuse to allow him to do so.[194]

Civil Jurisdiction and Judgments Act 1982, Section 32

12.4.20   Where parties to a contract agree to a particular dispute-resolution mechanism, be it arbitration or litigation, the general policy of English law is to hold the parties to the agreement. This policy is extended to cases involving the recognition and enforcement of foreign judgments.[195] Section 32 of the Civil Jurisdiction and Judgments Act 1982 provides:

---

[189] A Briggs, (2004) 75 *BYIL* 537; A Briggs, (2005) 121 *LQR* 185.
[190] JJ Fawcett, 'The Impact of Article 6(1) of the ECHR on Private International Law' (2007) 56 *ICLQ* 1, 23.
[191] *Vervaeke v Smith* [1983] 1 AC 145; *ED & F Man (Sugar) Ltd v Haryanto (No 2)* [1991] 1 Lloyd's Rep 429. PB Carter, (1991) 62 *BYIL* 461.
[192] [1995] 1 AC 431.
[193] [1995] 1 AC 431, 440–1.
[194] [1995] 1 AC 431, 441.
[195] The Hague Choice of Court Convention 2005 provides that a judgment given by the court of a contracting state which is designated in an exclusive choice of court agreement must be recognised and enforced in other contracting states (Art 8). Art 9 sets out a list of grounds on which recognition or enforcement may be refused. These grounds largely correspond with the current position under English law

(1) Subject to the following provisions in this section, a judgment given by a court of an overseas country in any proceedings shall not be recognised or enforced in the United Kingdom if—

    (a) the bringing of those proceedings in that court was contrary to an agreement under which the dispute in question was to be settled otherwise than by proceedings in the courts of that country; and

    (b) those proceedings were not brought in that court by, or with the agreement of, the person against whom the judgment was given; and

    (c) that person did not counterclaim in the proceedings or otherwise submit to the jurisdiction of that court.

(2) Subsection (1) does not apply where the agreement referred to in paragraph (a) of that subsection was illegal, void or unenforceable or was incapable of being performed for reasons not attributable to the fault of the party bringing the proceedings in which the judgment was given.

(3) In determining whether a judgment given by a court of an overseas country should be recognised or enforced in the United Kingdom, a court in the United Kingdom shall not be bound by any decision of the overseas court relating to any matters mentioned in subsection (1) or (2).

12.4.21   In the context of proceedings in which one of the parties seeks to rely on a foreign judgment, the question whether a contract includes 'an agreement under which the dispute in question was to be settled otherwise than by proceedings in the courts of that country' for the purposes of section 32(1)(a) is to be determined by the English court in accordance with English conflicts principles. Where a question arises whether, for the purposes of subsection (2), a dispute-resolution clause is 'illegal, void or unenforceable or … incapable of being performed' English private international law prevails over the law of the country of origin.

12.4.22   In *Tracomin SA v Sudan Oil Seeds (No 1)*[196] the parties entered a contract which, according to English law (the law governing the contract), contained an English arbitration clause. The plaintiff started proceedings in Switzerland with a view to recovering damages for breach of contract. The defendant contested the jurisdiction of the Swiss court on the basis of the arbitration clause, but took no further part in the proceedings. Having decided that the arbitration clause was of no effect, the Swiss court exercised jurisdiction and gave judgment in favour of the plaintiff. The plaintiff then sought to enforce this judgment in England. Enforcement of the Swiss judgment was refused on the basis that, for the purposes of section 32(1)(a), the arbitration clause was, according to its proper law, a valid agreement 'under which the dispute in question was to be settled otherwise than by proceedings in the [Swiss] courts'. By virtue of section 32(3) the fact that the Swiss court had reached a contrary conclusion on the effectiveness of the arbitration clause was to be ignored.

12.4.23   The availability of the defence contained in section 32 depends on the party against whom the judgment was given not having taken part in the original proceedings. A defendant who does anything which amounts to submission to the

with the only possible 'new' ground being Art 9(1)(a). This allows for refusal if 'the agreement was null and void under the law of the State of the chosen court, unless the chosen court has determined that the agreement is valid'. As of 1 December 2010, the Convention had been signed by the United States of America, the European Union (on behalf of all the Member States) and acceded to by Mexico. The Convention will only enter into force three months after two states have ratified or acceded to it: Article 31(1).

[196] [1983] 1 WLR 1026.

jurisdiction of the original court cannot rely on the dispute-resolution clause in the context of proceedings in England concerning the recognition or enforcement of the foreign judgment.[197] Furthermore, section 32 does not apply to judgments given by the courts of Scotland and Northern Ireland,[198] foreign judgments which are entitled to recognition or enforcement under the Brussels regime (ie, the Brussels I Regulation, the Brussels Convention and the Lugano Convention),[199] or judgments given in proceedings arising under certain international conventions which are entitled to recognition or enforcement under the Foreign Judgments (Reciprocal Enforcement) Act 1933.[200]

Multiple Damages[201]

12.4.24 The main purpose of the Protection of Trading Interests Act 1980 is to nullify the extraterritorial effect in the United Kingdom of US legislation which provides for the award of multiple damages—notably, the Clayton and Sherman Acts (which apply in anti-trust cases) and the Racketeer Influenced and Corrupt Organisations Act (known as RICO). According to the terms of section 5 of the 1980 Act there are three types of judgment which are not enforceable in the United Kingdom.

12.4.25 First, the court shall not enforce a foreign judgment for multiple damages,[202] which is defined as:

a judgment for an amount arrived at by doubling, trebling or otherwise multiplying a sum assessed as compensation for the loss or damage sustained by the person in whose favour the judgment is given.[203]

Where, for example, the foreign court assesses the loss at $x, but awards damages of $3x, the judgment is unenforceable in its entirety.[204] The position is less straightforward where the foreign judgment contains more than one element—such as compensatory damages and another sum which is determined by multiplication. In *Lewis v Eliades*[205] the claimant, having obtained a judgment from the New York courts under, *inter alia*, the RICO statute (which allows for the trebling of damages in certain circumstances), applied to enforce the judgment in England. By the time the case came before the Court of Appeal, the RICO element of the damages award had been trebled and the defendant argued that, because of the RICO element, section 5 of the 1980 Act rendered the entire judgment unenforceable. The Court of Appeal dismissed the appeal against the first instance decision. Although the 1980 Act barred enforcement of the RICO element of the judgment, the Court

---

[197] *Marc Rich & Co AG v Società Italiana Impianti PA (No 2)* [1992] 1 Lloyd's Rep 624.
[198] Civil Jurisdiction and Judgments Act 1982, s 50.
[199] Civil Jurisdiction and Judgments Act 1982, s 32(4)(a).
[200] Civil Jurisdiction and Judgments Act 1982, s 32(4)(b).
[201] D Lloyd Jones, 'Protection of Trading Interests Act 1980' [1981] *CLJ* 41; L Collins, 'Blocking and Clawback Statutes: The United Kingdom Approach' [1986] *JBL* 372 and 452.
[202] Protection of Trading Interests Act, s 5(1)(a).
[203] Protection of Trading Interests Act, s 5(3).
[204] *Lewis v Eliades* [2004] 1 WLR 692. E Kellman, (2004) 53 *ICLQ* 1025.
[205] [2004] 1 WLR 692. A Briggs, (2003) 74 *BYIL* 549.

of Appeal concluded that the part of the New York judgment which related to compensatory damages was a separable part which remained entitled to enforcement in England.[206]

12.4.26 Secondly, the court shall not enforce a foreign judgment which is based on a provision or rule of law specified or described in an order of the Secretary of State.[207] An order may be made in respect of any provision or rule of law which appears to the Secretary of State:

to be concerned with the prohibition or regulation of agreements, arrangements or practices designed to restrain, distort or restrict competition in the carrying on of business of any description or to be otherwise concerned with the promotion of such competition as aforesaid.[208]

12.4.27 Thirdly, the court shall not enforce a judgment on a claim for contribution in respect of damages awarded by a judgment falling within either of the other two categories. It should also be noted that section 6 of the 1980 Act provides a mechanism which enables a judgment debtor who has satisfied or partially satisfied a judgment which falls within the scope of section 5 to claw back any sums paid which are in excess of the amount attributable to compensation.

12.5 RECOGNITION AND ENFORCEMENT OF JUDGMENTS *IN REM*

12.5.1 Judgments *in rem* may concern either the legal status of persons or the possession or ownership of property. In the commercial context, it is the second category which is of prime importance. The significant feature of a judgment *in rem* is that, whereas a judgment *in personam* operates *inter partes*, a judgment *in rem* operates *erga omnes*. A judgment *in rem* does not only resolve the rights and duties of the parties to the litigation; it determines possession or ownership of the *res* and is conclusive as regards the whole world. So, a judgment purporting actually to transfer or dispose of property (which is a judgment *in rem*) must be distinguished from a judgment determining the contractual rights of parties to property (which, notwithstanding the fact that the underlying subject-matter of the proceedings is property, is a judgment *in personam*).[209]

12.5.2 The basic framework for the recognition and enforcement of judgments *in rem* is the same as that for the recognition or enforcement of judgments *in personam*: the original court must have been a court of competent jurisdiction; the judgment must be final and conclusive; recognition or enforcement may be refused if one of a number of defences is established. There are, however, differences which should be noted.

---

[206] See also *Lucasfilm Ltd v Ainsworth* [2009] FSR 103, 187 (at [231]) (A Briggs, (2008) 79 *BYIL* 537). This issue was not considered by the Court of Appeal in the subsequent appeal: [2010] FSR 270.

[207] Protection of Trading Interests Act 1980, s 5(1)(b).

[208] Protection of Trading Interests Act 1980, s 5(4). See Protection of Trading Interests (Australian Trade Practices) Order 1988, SI 1988/569. The effect of this Order is that a judgment based on s 81(1A) of the Australian Trade Practices Act 1974 is not enforceable in the United Kingdom.

[209] See Lord Mance in *Pattni v Ali* [2007] 2 AC 85, 99 (at [25]).

Jurisdiction of the Original Court

12.5.3 A foreign court which grants a judgment *in rem* in relation to movable or immovable property is to be regarded as a court of competent jurisdiction only if the property in question was located within the territorial jurisdiction of the country of origin at the time when the proceedings were commenced.[210] No other basis of jurisdiction will suffice.

Defences

12.5.4 The extent to which defences which are generally available in the context of proceedings involving foreign judgments *in personam* are also applicable to foreign judgments *in rem* is not free from doubt. If the foreign judgment was procured by fraud or is contrary to public policy it seems that recognition or enforcement will be refused. It has been suggested, however, that the degree of recognition to be accorded to a foreign judgment *in rem*—at least a foreign judgment dealing with movable property—falls to be determined not so much by the rules governing the recognition of foreign judgments, but by the rules governing the validity of assignments of property.[211] On this basis, subject to the defences of public policy and fraud, the recognition of a foreign judgment *in rem* would be governed by the law of the *situs*.

Enforcement

12.5.5 In practice, the recognition of foreign judgments *in rem* is likely to be of more significance than their enforcement.[212] Indeed, certain foreign judgments *in rem*—for example, a foreign judgment which determines title to foreign land—cannot be enforced in England. There are, however, circumstances in which a judgment creditor may wish to enforce a judgment *in rem* in England.[213] There can be no doubt that a judgment *in rem* may be enforced in England by means of proceedings *in personam*. In addition, in *The Despina GK* Sheen J held that a foreign judgment *in rem* may be enforced in England by proceedings *in rem*:

A judgment creditor who has obtained a final judgment against a shipowner by proceeding in rem in a foreign admiralty court can bring an action in rem in this court against that ship to enforce the decree of the foreign court if that is necessary to complete the execution of that judgment, provided that the ship is the property of the judgment debtor at the time when she is arrested.[214]

---

[210] *Castrique v Imrie* (1870) LR 4 HL 414. See, however, the decision of the Privy Council in *Cambridge Gas Transport Corporation v The Official Committee of Unsecured Creditors of Navigator Holdings plc* [2007] 1 AC 508 and the discussion in para 18.2.43. See also A Briggs, (2006) 77 *BYIL* 575; GS Teo, (2008) 20 *SAcLJ* 784; CH Tham, 'Insolvency Proceedings and Shareholdings: When is a Judgment not a Judgment?' [2007] *LMCLQ* 129.

[211] L Collins *et al*, *Dicey, Morris and Collins on The Conflict of Laws* (London, Sweet & Maxwell, 14th edn, 2006) para 14–102.

[212] *Castrique v Imrie* (1870) LR 4 HL 414.

[213] See, eg, *The City of Mecca* (1879) 5 PD 28, reversed by the Court of Appeal on the ground that the foreign judgment was in fact a judgment *in personam* (1881) 6 PD 106; *The Despina GK* [1983] QB 214.

[214] [1983] QB 214, 219.

12.6 RECOGNITION AND ENFORCEMENT UNDER STATUTORY REGIMES BASED ON THE COMMON LAW

12.6.1   Although the common law rules are still extremely important in practice, the recognition and enforcement of foreign judgments has to some extent been put on a statutory basis by Part II of the Administration of Justice Act 1920 and the Foreign Judgments (Reciprocal Enforcement) Act 1933. Part II of the 1920 Act provides for the enforcement of judgments given by the superior courts of most commonwealth countries. The 1933 Act provides for the recognition and enforcement of (1) judgments given by the courts of foreign countries outside the Commonwealth to which the United Kingdom has assumed obligations under bilateral treaties;[215] (2) foreign judgments given in proceedings under a number of international conventions;[216] and (3) judgments given by the courts of some commonwealth countries.[217] The regimes established by the 1920 Act and the 1933 Act exist side by side and are mutually exclusive.

12.6.2   The basic scheme of the legislation is to provide a mechanism for the registration of judgments given by the superior courts of foreign countries. A registered judgment is enforceable in England in the same way as a judgment of an English court. The conceptual structure of the legislation mirrors that of the common law and to a considerable extent the legislation is a codification of common law principles. Accordingly, the meaning of many of the provisions of the 1920 and 1933 Acts is to be gleaned from earlier case law. Nevertheless, it is not appropriate to attempt to ascertain the common law position by reasoning backwards from the statutory provisions.[218]

Enforcement under Part II of the Administration of Justice Act 1920

12.6.3   Section 9 of the Administration of Justice Act 1920 sets out the scheme for the registration of various foreign judgments and the defences to registration. From the date of registration, a registered judgment is 'of the same force and effect ... as if it had been a judgment originally obtained or entered up on the date of registration in the registering court'.[219] The 1920 Act is concerned only with enforcement, not with recognition. The 1920 Act does not supersede the common law; the fact that a judgment is registrable under the 1920 Act does not deprive the judgment creditor of the right to sue on the obligation created by the foreign judgment.[220] It is provided, however, that where proceedings are

---

[215] The Foreign Judgments (Reciprocal Enforcement) Act 1933 applies to judgments given by the superior courts of the following non-Commonwealth countries: Austria, Belgium, Germany, France, Israel, Italy, the Netherlands, Norway, Suriname. It should be noted, however, that judgments given by the courts of an EU Member State in civil and commercial matters are governed by Chapter III of the Brussels I Regulation; similarly, judgments given by the courts of Iceland, Norway and Switzerland fall within the scope of the Lugano Convention. See ch 13.

[216] See L Collins *et al*, *Dicey, Morris and Collins on The Conflict of Laws* (London, Sweet & Maxwell, 14th edn, 2006) ch 15.

[217] It was originally intended that the 1933 Act should supersede Part II of the 1920 Act entirely. However, as the law now stands the 1933 Act applies to the judgments of few Commonwealth countries: Australia, Bangladesh, Canada, Guernsey, India, Isle of Man, Jersey, Pakistan, Tonga.

[218] *Henry v Geoprosco International Ltd* [1976] QB 726.

[219] Administration of Justice Act 1920, s 9(3)(a).

[220] *Yukon Consolidated Gold Corporation Ltd v Clark* [1938] 2 KB 241.

brought at common law on a judgment which is registrable under the 1920 Act the claimant is not entitled to recover the costs of the proceedings 'unless the application to register the judgment … has previously been refused or unless the court otherwise orders'.[221]

12.6.4 Section 9(1) provides that where a judgment has been obtained in a superior court of a territory to which the Act applies the judgment creditor may apply to the High Court:

at any time within twelve months after the date of the judgment, or such longer period as may be allowed by the court, to have the judgment registered in the court, and on any such application the court may, if in all the circumstances of the case they think it is just and convenient that the judgment should be enforced in the United Kingdom … order the judgment to be registered accordingly.[222]

Section 9(1) applies only to judgments 'whereby any sum of money is made payable'[223] and confers a discretion on the High Court whether to order registration. The 1920 Act does not, however, indicate the basis on which the discretion of the court should be exercised.[224]

12.6.5 Section 9(2) lists the circumstances in which registration must be refused:

(a) the original court acted without jurisdiction; or

(b) the judgment debtor, being a person who was neither carrying on business[225] nor ordinarily resident within the jurisdiction of the original court, did not voluntarily appear or otherwise submit or agree to submit to the jurisdiction of that court; or

(c) the judgment debtor, being the defendant in the proceedings, was not duly served with the process of the original court and did not appear, notwithstanding that he was ordinarily resident or was carrying on business within the jurisdiction of that court[226] or agreed to submit to the jurisdiction of that court; or

(d) the judgment was obtained by fraud; or

(e) the judgment debtor satisfies the registering court either that an appeal is pending, or that he is entitled and intends to appeal, against the judgment; or

(f) the judgment was in respect of a cause of action which for reasons of public policy or for some other similar reason could not have been entertained by the registering court.

Many of these provisions are the same as, or roughly equivalent to, defences to enforcement at common law. The defence of fraud provided by paragraph (d) is the same as the defence at common law.[227] It is assumed that reference to lack of jurisdiction in paragraph (a) refers to lack of jurisdiction by the standards of English private international law, rather than under the law of the original court. This interpretation, however, renders paragraph (b) largely redundant. There is no defence based on natural justice as such; paragraph (c) is limited to cases where the defendant has not been duly served. Furthermore, the public policy defence in paragraph (f) is more limited

---

[221] Administration of Justice Act 1920, s 9(5).

[222] The relevant procedure for obtaining registration under this section is to be found in CPR Pt 74.

[223] Administration of Justice Act 1920, s 12(1).

[224] See *Svenska Petroleum Exploration AB v Government of the Republic of Lithuania (No 2)* [2007] QB 886 on whether s 1 of the State Immunity Act 1978 applies to an application to register a judgment under s 9 of the 1920 Act.

[225] See *Sfeir & Co v National Insurance Co of New Zealand* [1964] 1 Lloyd's Rep 330.

[226] See *Akande v Balfour Beatty Construction Ltd* [1998] ILPr 110.

[227] *Owens Bank Ltd v Bracco* [1992] 2 AC 443.

than the equivalent defence at common law as it refers to the cause of action, rather than the effect of the judgment. Paragraph (e) provides a basis for non-registration which is not a defence at common law; at common law a foreign judgment may be regarded as final and conclusive even though an appeal is pending.

12.6.6   The list of defences is incomplete—for example, the fact that the foreign judgment is incompatible with an English judgment is not expressly stated as a ground for refusing registration. However, in this type of case it is to be expected that the English court would exercise the discretion conferred by subsection (1) against registration. Presumably, an English court would, in the exercise of its discretion, refuse registration of a foreign judgment which was in the nature of a fine or other penalty. It should be added that the defences to enforcement provided by section 32 of the Civil Jurisdiction and Judgments Act 1982[228] and by the Protection of Trading Interests Act 1980[229] also apply to cases falling within the scope of the 1920 Act.

Recognition and Enforcement under the Foreign Judgments (Reciprocal Enforcement) Act 1933

12.6.7   Whereas the registration of foreign judgments under Part II of the Administration of Justice Act 1920 is discretionary, registration is mandatory in relation to foreign judgments which qualify under the Foreign Judgments (Reciprocal Enforcement) Act 1933. Furthermore, whereas the 1920 Act co-exists with the common law rules, the scheme provided by the 1933 Act, where applicable, supersedes the common law. Section 6 of the 1933 Act provides:

No proceedings for the recovery of a sum payable under a foreign judgment, being a judgment to which this Part of this Act applies, other than proceedings by way of registration of the judgment, shall be entertained by any court in the United Kingdom.

Enforcement: Conditions and Procedure

12.6.8   The 1933 Act applies to judgments given by the superior courts of foreign countries.[230] In order for a judgment to be enforced under the 1933 Act a number of conditions must be satisfied. First, the judgment must be final and conclusive between the parties.[231] A judgment is deemed to be final and conclusive even though the judgment may still be the subject of an appeal or even if an appeal is pending.[232] Secondly, the judgment must be a judgment for a sum of money, not being a sum payable in

---

[228] See paras 12.4.20–12.4.23.
[229] See paras 12.4.24–12.4.27.
[230] Certain types of judgments are, however, excluded: eg, a judgment given by a superior court on appeal from a court which is not a superior court and a judgment given by the superior court of a foreign judgment for the purposes of the enforcement of another judgment. See Foreign Judgments (Reciprocal Enforcement) Act 1933, s 1(2A). Cf the position in Hong Kong, where the equivalent legislation does not specifically exclude the enforcement of a judgment on a judgment: *Morgan Stanley & Co International Ltd v Pilot Lead Investments Ltd* [2006] 2 HKLRD 731.
[231] Foreign Judgments (Reciprocal Enforcement) Act 1933, s 1(2)(a).
[232] Foreign Judgments (Reciprocal Enforcement) Act 1933, s 1(3).

respect of taxes or other charges of a similar nature or in respect of a fine or other penalty.[233] Thirdly, the Act must have been extended to the foreign country in question by delegated legislation.[234]

12.6.9 Where a judgment satisfies these conditions the judgment creditor may apply for registration. A judgment creditor may apply to have the judgment registered in the High Court at any time within six years after the date of the foreign judgment, or, where there have been proceedings by way of appeal against the judgment, after the date of the last judgment given in those proceedings.[235] The procedure for registration is set out in Part 74 of the Civil Procedure Rules. Where a judgment is registered under the 1933 Act the judgment has the same force and effect as a judgment of the High Court: proceedings may be taken on the foreign judgment; the sum of money for which the judgment is registered carries interest; and the High Court has the same control over the execution of a registered judgment as in relation to a judgment of the High Court.[236] There are two bases on which registration is to be refused. First, if the foreign judgment has been wholly satisfied it may not be registered.[237] Where the foreign judgment has been partly satisfied, the judgment may be registered only to the extent of the balance remaining due at the date of the application for registration.[238] Secondly, registration is to be refused if the judgment cannot be enforced by execution in the country of origin.[239]

Resisting Enforcement

12.6.10 The defences to enforcement under the 1933 Act are contained in section 4, which lists the circumstances in which a registered judgment 'shall' or 'may' be set aside. Section 4 is drafted in a somewhat convoluted way.

IMPROPER REGISTRATION
12.6.11 Registration must be set aside if the judgment is not a judgment to which Part I of the 1933 Act applies or if the judgment was registered in contravention of the Act.[240] Furthermore, registration must be set aside if the rights under the judgment are not vested in the person by whom the application for registration was made.[241]

LACK OF JURISDICTION
12.6.12 If the original court did not have jurisdiction, registration must be set aside.[242] Lack of jurisdiction is extensively defined by section 4(2) and (3). Subsection (2)

---

[233] Foreign Judgments (Reciprocal Enforcement) Act 1933, s 1(2)(b).
[234] Foreign Judgments (Reciprocal Enforcement) Act 1933, s 1(2)(c).
[235] Foreign Judgments (Reciprocal Enforcement) Act 1933, s 2(1).
[236] Foreign Judgments (Reciprocal Enforcement) Act 1933, s 2(2).
[237] Foreign Judgments (Reciprocal Enforcement) Act 1933, s 2(1), proviso (a).
[238] Foreign Judgments (Reciprocal Enforcement) Act 1933, s 2(4).
[239] Foreign Judgments (Reciprocal Enforcement) Act 1933, s 2(1), proviso (b).
[240] Foreign Judgments (Reciprocal Enforcement) Act 1933, s 4(1)(a)(i).
[241] Foreign Judgments (Reciprocal Enforcement) Act 1933, s 4(1)(a)(vi).
[242] Foreign Judgments (Reciprocal Enforcement) Act 1933, s 4(1)(a)(ii).

lists certain circumstances in which the original court will be regarded as having had jurisdiction:

(a) in the case of an action in personam—

    (i) if the judgment debtor, being a defendant in the original court, submitted to the jurisdiction of that court by voluntarily appearing in the proceedings ...; or

    (ii) if the judgment debtor was plaintiff in, or counterclaimed in, the proceedings in the original court; or

    (iii) if the judgment debtor, being a defendant in the original court, had before the commencement of proceedings, agreed in respect of the subject-matter of the proceedings, to submit to the jurisdiction of that court or of the courts of the country of that court; or

    (iv) if the judgment debtor, being a defendant in the original court, was at the time when the proceedings were instituted resident in, or being a body corporate had its principal place of business in, the country of that court; or

    (v) if the judgment debtor, being a defendant in the original court, had an office or place of business in the country of that court and the proceedings in that court were in respect of a transaction effected through or at that office or place;

(b) in the case of a judgment given in an action of which the subject-matter was immovable property or in an action in rem of which the subject-matter was movable property, if the property in question was at the time of the proceedings in the original court situate in the country of that court;

(c) in the case of a judgment given in an action other than any such action as is mentioned in paragraph (a) or paragraph (b) of this subsection, if the jurisdiction of the original court is recognised by the law of the registering court.

To a significant extent this subsection reproduces the common law rules. The first three subparagraphs of paragraph (a) reflect the common law rules on submission. Subparagraphs (iv) and (v) define the type of connection between the judgment debtor and the original court which is regarded as sufficient to justify the original court's exercise of *in personam* jurisdiction. Whereas *Adams v Cape Industries Plc*[243] indicates that temporary presence is sufficient at common law, nothing less than residence will suffice under the 1933 Act. As regards corporations, the test is the presence of a place of business in the foreign country.

12.6.13 Subsection (2) is qualified by subsection (3) and by section 32 of the Civil Jurisdiction and Judgments Act 1982.[244] Subsection (3) provides that the original court is deemed not to have had jurisdiction if the subject-matter of the proceedings was immovable property not situated within the country of origin or if the judgment debtor, being a defendant in the original proceedings, was a person who under the rules of public international law was entitled to immunity in the country of origin and did not submit to the jurisdiction of that court. By virtue of section 32 of the 1982 Act recognition or enforcement of a foreign judgment shall be refused if the proceedings before the original court were contrary to an agreement under which the dispute in question was to be settled otherwise than by proceedings in the court of that country and the person against whom the judgment was given did not submit to the jurisdiction of the original court.[245]

---

[243] [1990] Ch 433. See paras 12.2.11–12.2.14.
[244] See paras 12.4.20–12.4.23.
[245] S 32 of the 1982 Act replaced s 4(3)(b) of the 1933 Act: Civil Jurisdiction and Judgments Act 1982, s 54 and sched 14.

DUE PROCESS, FRAUD AND PUBLIC POLICY

12.6.14 Section 4(1)(a)(iii) provides that registration shall be set aside if the registering court is satisfied:

that the judgment debtor, being the defendant in the proceedings in the original court, did not (notwithstanding that process may have been duly served on him in accordance with the law of the country of the original court) receive notice of those proceedings in sufficient time to enable him to defend the proceedings and did not appear.

This provision has certain aspects in common with the equivalent defence under the Brussels I Regulation.[246]

12.6.15 A foreign judgment which has been obtained by fraud shall not be recognised or enforced under the 1933 Act.[247] Similarly, registration of a foreign judgment shall be set aside if 'enforcement of the judgment would be contrary to public policy in the country of the registering court'.[248] It should be added that the defences to enforcement provided by section 5 of the Protection of Trading Interests Act 1980 also apply to cases falling within the scope of the 1933 Act.[249]

IRRECONCILABILITY

12.6.16 Section 4(1)(b) provides that registration of a judgment may be set aside if the registering court is satisfied that:

the matter in dispute in the proceedings in the original court had previously to the date of the judgment in the original court been the subject of a final and conclusive judgment by a court having jurisdiction in the matter.

The effect of this provision is that a foreign judgment which is *prima facie* entitled to registration under the 1933 Act may be denied enforcement if there is an earlier inconsistent judgment, whether an English judgment or the judgment of another foreign country which is entitled to recognition or enforcement in England.

WHEN AN APPEAL IS PENDING ABROAD

12.6.17 The fact that an appeal against the foreign judgment may be brought or has been commenced in the original country does not prevent enforcement under the 1933 Act. However, section 5(1) provides that, where the judgment debtor satisfies the court that he is entitled to appeal against the foreign judgment and intends to do so or that an appeal is pending, the court may set aside registration or adjourn the application to set aside registration for a suitable period during which time the foreign appeal can be heard. If registration is set aside under section 5(1) this does not preclude the judgment creditor from re-applying to register the judgment once the foreign appeal has been disposed of.[250]

---

[246] Art 34(2). See para 13.3.18.
[247] Foreign Judgments (Reciprocal Enforcement) Act 1933, s 4(1)(a)(iv). See paras 12.4.9–12.4.13.
[248] Foreign Judgments (Reciprocal Enforcement) Act 1933, s 4(1)(a)(v). See paras 12.4.14–12.4.17.
[249] See paras 12.4.24–12.4.27.
[250] Foreign Judgments (Reciprocal Enforcement) Act 1933, s 5(2).

Recognition

12.6.18 The 1933 Act provides for the recognition of judgments falling within the scope of the legislation without there being a need for the party in whose favour the judgment was granted to register the judgment.[251] Defences to enforcement are also defences to recognition. Although, as a general rule, a judgment which cannot be registered is not entitled to recognition, recognition shall not be refused on the basis that a sum of money is not payable under the judgment or the judgment has been wholly or partly satisfied or the judgment cannot be enforced by execution in the country of origin.[252] To qualify for recognition under the 1933 Act the foreign judgment must be a judgment on the merits.[253]

[251] Foreign Judgments (Reciprocal Enforcement) Act 1933, s 8(1).
[252] Foreign Judgments (Reciprocal Enforcement) Act 1933, s 8(1).
[253] *Black-Clawson International Ltd v Papierwerke Waldhof-Aschaffenburg AG* [1975] AC 591. For consideration of what is meant by the phrase 'on the merits', see paras 12.3.7–12.3.13.

13

RECOGNITION AND ENFORCEMENT OF JUDGMENTS UNDER THE BRUSSELS I REGULATION, JUDGMENTS AGAINST STATES AND EUROPEAN COMMUNITY JUDGMENTS

13.0.1 Among the statutory schemes for the recognition and enforcement of judgments, the most important is that to be found in the Brussels I Regulation.[1] The Brussels I Regulation contains a simplified procedure for the recognition and enforcement of judgments given by the courts of Member States (sections 13.1–13.4). The Brussels I Regulation also provides for the reciprocal enforcement of authentic instruments and court settlements (section 13.5). In order for a judgment to be entitled to recognition under Chapter III, there are five basic conditions which must be satisfied: first, the case must concern international recognition; secondly, the case must fall within the material scope of Article 1; thirdly, the judgment must have been granted by the court of a Member State; fourthly, the judgment must be a 'judgment' as defined by Article 32; and finally, the judgment must have been granted after the entry into force of the Regulation. To a significant extent, simplification as regards recognition and enforcement is made possible by the jurisdiction provisions, which assign jurisdiction in civil and commercial matters to the courts of Member States. Whereas, at common law, an important stage of the inquiry is whether the original court was a court of competent jurisdiction, in cases falling within the scope of the Brussels I Regulation the court addressed may not, as a general rule, review the basis on which the court of origin exercised jurisdiction. The grounds on which recognition or enforcement may be refused are limited. The Brussels I Regulation also contains detailed provisions which establish a mandatory, uniform procedure for the enforcement of judgments given by the courts of Member States. Since the material scope of the Regulation is limited to civil and commercial matters, the recognition and enforcement in England of judgments given by the courts of a Member State in matters which fall outside the scope of Article 1 has to be based on the common law or, where applicable, the Foreign Judgments (Reciprocal Enforcement) Act 1933. So, for example, the 1933 Act determines whether a judgment given by a French court in a social security matter is entitled to recognition or enforcement in England.

    13.0.2 Part II of the 1982 Act introduced a mechanism for the mutual recognition and enforcement of judgments given by the courts of the different parts of the United Kingdom (section 13.6). There are also statutory provisions dealing with the recognition and enforcement of foreign judgments given against the United Kingdom and other

---

[1] Whereas the Brussels I Regulation covers the reciprocal recognition and enforcement of judgments given by the courts of EU Member States, the almost identical Lugano Convention applies to the recognition and enforcement of judgments granted by the courts of Iceland, Norway and Switzerland.

states and with the recognition and enforcement of judgments of the institutions of the European Union (section 13.7).

13.0.3   The scheme for the recognition and enforcement of judgments established by the Brussels I Regulation is largely based on the theory of reciprocity or comity, rather than the notion of obligation. The courts of the United Kingdom are required to recognise and enforce the judgments of the courts of the other Member States, because the courts of the other Member States are required *mutatis mutandis* to recognise and enforce judgments given by the courts of the United Kingdom. Of course, this reciprocity is, to a significant extent, made possible because the Regulation lays down uniform jurisdiction rules which must be applied by the courts of all the Member States. However, because many of the jurisdictional safeguards are not extended to parties who are not domiciled in a Member State, there are circumstances in which the courts of one Member State are required to recognise or enforce a judgment given by the courts of another Member State notwithstanding the fact that the court of origin assumed jurisdiction on an exorbitant basis.[2]

13.1 BASIC CONDITIONS FOR RECOGNITION AND ENFORCEMENT UNDER THE BRUSSELS I REGULATION

The Scope of the Brussels I Regulation

13.1.1   In order for a judgment to be entitled to recognition or enforcement under the Brussels I Regulation the judgment must fall within its scope. This means, first, that the case must concern the recognition or enforcement of a judgment given in a Member State other than the state in which recognition or enforcement is sought. The Brussels I Regulation does not apply, for example, to the recognition or enforcement in England of judgments given by the courts of Scotland and Northern Ireland.[3] Secondly, the judgment must be in respect of a matter which is within the material scope of Article 1.[4] It should be noted that there may be situations in which the question whether proceedings fall within the scope of Article 1 arises both at the original stage and at the stage of recognition or enforcement. In this type of case, the decision of the court of origin does not bind the court of other Member States. The court addressed must determine for itself whether or not the proceedings are covered by Article 1.

What is a 'Judgment'?

The Basic Definition

13.1.2   The term 'judgment' is defined by Article 32 of the Brussels I Regulation as:

any judgment given by a court or tribunal of a Member State, whatever the judgment may be called, including a decree, order, decision or writ of execution, as well as the determination of costs or expenses by an officer of the court.

---

[2]   See paras 13.1.10–13.1.12.
[3]   See section 13.6.
[4]   See section 3.3. See also Case C–267/97 *Coursier v Fortis Bank* [1999] ECR I–2543.

Whereas under the common law only final judgments for a fixed sum of money are enforceable in England, there are no such restrictions under Chapter III.[5] Accordingly, provisional or interim measures, injunctions and orders for specific performance are, in principle, entitled to enforcement to the same extent as money judgments.[6] Having said that, to be entitled to recognition or enforcement under Chapter III, a provisional or protective measure must not go beyond the jurisdiction conferred by Article 31. This means that the court addressed is required to determine whether the order of the court of origin qualifies as a 'provisional measure' for the purposes of the Brussels I Regulation.[7] So, where a French court issues a judgment ordering interim payments, but the judgment neither contains a guarantee of repayment should the claim against the defendant fail nor relates to specific assets of the defendant located in France, the judgment does not fall within the scope of Article 31 of the Brussels I Regulation and is not entitled to recognition or enforcement under Chapter III.[8]

13.1.3   No distinction is drawn between judgments *in personam* and judgments *in rem*. However, recognition and enforcement are extended only to judicial decisions actually given by a court or tribunal of a Member State.[9] It is clear that in Article 32 'tribunal' does not include a tribunal appointed in accordance with an arbitration agreement in a commercial contract.[10] In order to be a 'judgment' for the purposes of the Brussels I Regulation the decision in question must emanate from a judicial body of a Member State deciding on its own authority on the issues between the parties.[11] In the absence of a specific decision of a judicial authority there is nothing to be recognised or enforced. So, a judicial decision which provisionally fixes the amount to which the liability of a shipowner will be limited is a judgment for the purposes of Article 32.[12] Whereas an order for costs is a 'judgment',[13] a bill of costs which is enforceable in the state of origin does not qualify as a 'judgment' if the bill is simply drawn up by one of the parties and its enforceability is not based on a decision of the court.[14] By the same token, a finding of a court as to costs is not without more a 'judgment', even if under the law of the state of origin the general principle is that the losing party is liable for the costs, since what is lacking is a decision of the court ordering one party or the other to pay specified costs.[15] Similarly, a court settlement is not entitled to recognition or enforcement as a 'judgment'—though Chapter IV contains special provisions dealing with the enforcement of authentic instruments and court settlements.[16] A court settlement

---

[5] See *Re Recognition of an Italian Judgment* [2002] ILPr 165 (Court of Appeal, Thessaloniki).

[6] Case 143/78 *de Cavel v de Cavel* [1979] ECR 1055; Case C–99/96 *Mietz v Intership Yachting Sneek BV* [1999] ECR I–2277; Case C–394/07 *Gambazzi v Daimler Chrysler Canada Inc* [2009] ILPr 637. See also *Landhurst Leasing plc v Marcq* [1998] ILPr 822; *Re Enforcement of a French Sequestration Order* [1979] ECC 321 (Federal Supreme Court, Germany); *Stolzenberg v Daimler Chrysler Canada Inc* [2005] ILPr 266 (Court of Cassation, France).

[7] See C–99/96 *Mietz v Intership Yachting Sneek BV* [1999] ECR I–2277, para 54. See also paras 10.3.6 and 10.4.12.

[8] *Comet Group Plc v Unika Computer SA* [2004] ILPr 10.

[9] Case C–414/92 *Solo Kleinmotoren GmbH v Boch* [1994] ECR I–2237, para 15.

[10] *CMA CGM SA v Hyundai MIPO Dockyard Co Ltd* [2009] 1 Lloyd's Rep 213.

[11] Case C–414/92 *Solo Kleinmotoren GmbH v Boch* [1994] ECR I–2237, para 17; Case C–39/02 *Maersk Olie & Gas A/S v Firma de Haan en de Boer* [2004] ECR I–9657, para 45.

[12] Case C–39/02 *Maersk Olie & Gas A/S v Firma de Haan en de Boer* [2004] ECR I–9657, para 47.

[13] *Re French Court Costs* [1992] ILPr 146 (Court of Appeal, Saarbrücken).

[14] *Re Enforcement of a Foreign Bill of Costs* [1981] ECC 551 (District Court, Maastricht).

[15] *Re French Court Costs* [1992] ILPr 146 (Court of Appeal, Saarbrücken).

[16] See section 13.5.

is not the same as a judgment by consent (where the defendant agrees to the judgment being entered by conceding the substantive issues raised by the claimant); such a judgment is entitled to recognition and enforcement under Chapter III in the same way as a default judgment.[17]

13.1.4   A judgment of a Member State court which has a bearing on territory which is not controlled by the Member State in question and in which the *acquis communautaire* is suspended is nevertheless entitled to recognition and enforcement under Chapter III of the Regulation. *Apostolides v Orams*[18] concerned judgments granted by the courts of the Republic of Cyprus; the judgments related *inter alia* to ownership of land situated in the territory commonly referred to as the Turkish Republic of Northern Cyprus (TRNC). When Cyprus joined the European Union, a protocol to the treaty of accession suspended the operation of the *acquis communautaire* in the TRNC. When the claimant applied for the recognition and enforcement of the Cypriot judgments in England, the defendants argued that the Brussels I Regulation did not apply as the protocol meant that the *acquis* (including the Regulation) was of no effect in connection with matters relating to the area controlled by the TRNC. Although the defendant's argument succeeded in the High Court,[19] notwithstanding its obvious weakness,[20] it was no surprise that, following the reference by the Court of Appeal, the Court of Justice decided that the suspension of the application of the *acquis communautaire* in the TRNC does not preclude the application of the Brussels I Regulation to judgments given by a Cypriot court sitting in the government-controlled area, but concerning land situated in the TRNC.[21]

Procedural Orders[22]

13.1.5   It has been held that 'interlocutory decisions which are not intended to govern the legal relationships of the parties, but to arrange the further conduct of the proceedings'[23] are not to be regarded as 'judgments' for the purposes of Chapter III. In *CFEM Façades SA v Bovis Construction Ltd*[24] the question was whether a French court order, which appointed experts to examine a building in London, to take evidence from witnesses and to draw conclusions as to the quality of the building, was entitled to recognition and enforcement in England. It was held that it was not:

[I]nterlocutory decisions in the course of civil and commercial litigation which do no more than regulate procedural matters and which neither govern the legal relationships of the parties

---

[17]   *Landhurst Leasing plc v Marcq* [1998] ILPr 822.
[18]   Case C–420/07 [2010] 1 All ER (Comm) 950. TC Hartley, 'Cyprus Land Rights: Conflict of Laws Meets International Politics' (2009) 58 *ICLQ* 1013.
[19]   [2007] 1 WLR 241.
[20]   See A Briggs, (2006) 77 *BYIL* 561.
[21]   Case C–420/07 [2010] 1 All ER (Comm) 950, 984–5 (para 39).
[22]   L Collins, 'Provisional Measures, the Conflict of Laws and the Brussels Convention' (1981) 1 *YBEL* 249.
[23]   Schlosser Report, [1979] OJ C59/127, para 187.
[24]   [1992] ILPr 561.

nor affect their proprietary rights are outside the scope of the recognition and enforcement provisions ... .[25]

Ex Parte Orders

13.1.6 Even as regards interlocutory orders which *prima facie* fall within the scope of Chapter III—by virtue of the fact that they are intended to govern the legal relationships of the parties—there are certain limits to their recognition and enforcement. Where protective or provisional measures are granted subsequent to an *inter partes* hearing—rather than on an application without notice—the court's order is entitled to recognition and enforcement under Chapter III. Conversely, a provisional measure which has been granted on the basis of an application without notice is not entitled to enforcement. In *Denilauler v Snc Couchet Frères* the Court of Justice ruled, in the context of a reference under the Brussels Convention, that:

judicial decisions authorising provisional or protective measures, which are delivered without the party against which they are directed having been summoned to appear and which are intended to be enforced without prior service, do not come within the system of recognition and enforcement provided for by Title III.[26]

For recognition or enforcement under Chapter III to be possible it is essential that before the judgment was delivered the defendant was given an opportunity to present arguments to the court; the crucial question is not whether an *inter partes* procedure actually took place, but whether such a procedure would have taken place had the defendant chosen to appear.[27] Accordingly, for the purposes of Article 32 of the Brussels I Regulation, a payment order made before the debtor has had the opportunity to be heard is not a 'judgment'.[28] Even if, after an *ex parte* order has been made, the defendant is given a reasonable opportunity under the law of the state of origin to apply to have the measure set aside, the order remains unenforceable in England.[29] Conversely, a freezing injunction is a 'judgment' if it was made *inter partes* or if the defendant had an opportunity to resist the making of the order.[30] Nevertheless, provisional or protective measures (such as freezing injunctions) will often not be entitled to recognition under the Brussels I Regulation; one of the key features of protective and provisional measures is the element of surprise, which can be achieved only by means of an application without notice.

13.1.7 The fact that a procedural or *ex parte* order is not entitled to international enforcement does not necessarily mean that the order is rendered ineffective; all it means is that the parties must look to the courts of the state of origin, rather than the

---

[25] Judge Goldblatt QC at [1992] ILPr 561, 577. See also *SA Trailigaz v Firma Krupp Industrietechnik GmbH* [1989] ECC 442 (Court of Appeal, Hamm).

[26] Case 125/79 [1980] ECR 1553, para 18. TC Hartley, (1981) 6 *EL Rev* 59; N March Hunnings, 'Enforceability of Ex Parte Orders in the EEC' [1981] *JBL* 243.

[27] Case C–39/02 *Maersk Olie & Gas A/S v Firma de Haan en de Boer* [2004] ECR I–9657, para 50.

[28] See *Re Enforcement of an Italian Judgment* [1993] ILPr 353 (Court of Appeal, Frankfurt am Main); *Re Enforcement of a French Interlocutory Order* [2001] ILPr 208 (Court of Appeal, Karlsruhe).

[29] *EMI Records Ltd v Modern Music Karl-Ulrich Walterbach GmbH* [1992] QB 115.

[30] *Normaco Ltd v Lundman* [1999] ILPr 381.

courts of other states, to control the implementation of the order. In a case in which speed and surprise are of the essence, a claimant who wishes to obtain provisional measures in more than one Member State has little choice but to make the necessary applications in all the jurisdictions in which such measures are required.

Penalties

13.1.8 At common law the English court will not enforce, either directly or indirectly, foreign judgments ordering the payment of taxes, fines or other penalties. It is apparent, however, that 'a judgment which orders a periodic payment by way of a penalty' is in principle entitled to enforcement under the Brussels I Regulation. However, a judgment of this type is not entitled to enforcement unless 'the amount of the payment has been finally determined by the courts of the Member State of origin'.[31] There is some uncertainty whether a judgment ordering a periodic payment by way of a penalty can be enforced under Chapter III when the payments accrue to the state, rather than to the judgment creditor.[32] It is to be expected that, as a general rule, a judgment of this type does not relate to civil and commercial matters and falls outside the scope of Article 1 altogether. However, if such a judgment is within the scope of Article 1, there is no reason why it should be excluded from the enforcement provisions contained in Chapter III.

Partial Enforcement

13.1.9 Article 48(1) of the Brussels I Regulation provides that:

Where a foreign judgment has been given in respect of several matters and the declaration of enforceability cannot be given for all of them, the court or competent authority shall give it for one or more of them.

It is further provided that an applicant may request partial enforcement of a judgment.[33] So, where a foreign order involves certain elements which fall within the scope of Article 1 and other elements which do not, the judgment creditor may apply for enforcement of only those elements which are covered by the Brussels I Regulation.

The Relationship between Chapter II and Chapter III

13.1.10 Chapter III (recognition and enforcement) is not directly linked to Chapter II (jurisdiction). The recognition and enforcement provisions in Chapter III are not limited to judgments which result from proceedings in which the court of origin exercised jurisdiction under the direct jurisdiction rules in Chapter II. Chapter III applies whether or not the parties are domiciled in a Member State and whatever their

---

[31] Brussels I Reg, Art 49. See, eg, *Medicale Equipex SA v Farmitalia Erba Srl* [1990] ILPr 192 (Court of Appeal, Versailles).
[32] Schlosser Report, [1979] OJ C59/132, para 213(bb).
[33] Brussels I Reg, Art 48(2).

nationality.[34] The key questions are whether the judgment falls both within Chapter I, which defines the material scope of the Brussels I Regulation, and within Chapter III.

13.1.11 Because the recognition and enforcement provisions do not depend on the court of origin having exercised jurisdiction under the direct jurisdiction provisions of Chapter II, the combination of Chapters I and III may have an oppressive effect on parties who are not domiciled in a Member State. If a French court assumes jurisdiction under Article 14 of the civil code against a defendant who is domiciled in, say, Japan and gives judgment against him, the judgment is *prima facie* entitled to recognition and enforcement in England under Chapter III. Similarly, if proceedings are brought in England against a New York company under CPR 6.36, the English judgment—if it concerns matters within the material scope of Chapter I—is enforceable in any of the Member States under Chapter III, even if the English court exercised jurisdiction on a basis which would not have been available had the defendant been domiciled in a Member State.

13.1.12 Put bluntly, the Brussels I Regulation endorses the application of double standards. As regards defendants domiciled in a Member State, recognition and enforcement under Chapter III is justified by the fact that the defendant has the benefit of the jurisdictional and procedural safeguards provided by Chapter II. The exorbitant bases of jurisdiction referred to by Article 3 and listed in Annex I cannot be invoked against a person who is domiciled in a Member State and Article 26 of the Brussels I Regulation must be applied in cases where a defendant who is domiciled in a Member State is sued in the courts of another Member State. However, as regards a defendant who is not domiciled in a Member State, the strict recognition and enforcement system of Chapter III is applicable, even though the defendant has none of the jurisdictional and procedural safeguards which are enjoyed by defendants domiciled in Member States. Perhaps not surprisingly, American commentators have been critical of this aspect of the Brussels regime,[35] which has rightly been regarded as overtly discriminating against outsiders:

Not only does it continue to authorise unreasonable jurisdictional assertions against outsiders; it enhances their effect by requiring unquestioning recognition of such judgments in all of the [Member States].[36]

13.2 THE PRINCIPLE OF AUTOMATIC RECOGNITION UNDER THE BRUSSELS I REGULATION

13.2.1 At common law a precondition for the recognition of a foreign judgment is that the original court had jurisdiction in the private international law sense.[37] The absence of internationally approved bases of jurisdiction—and the fact that

---

[34] Jenard Report, [1979] OJ C54/43.

[35] See, eg, KH Nadelmann, 'The Outer World and the Common Market Experts' Draft of a Convention on Recognition of Judgments' (1967–68) 5 *CML Rev* 409; AT von Mehren, 'Recognition and Enforcement of Sister-State Judgments: Reflections on General Theory and Current Practice in the European Economic Community and the United States' (1981) 81 *Col LR* 1044.

[36] PJ Borchers, 'Comparing Personal Jurisdiction in the United States and the European Community: Lessons for American Reform' (1992) 40 *Am J Comp L* 121, 132–3.

[37] See paras 12.2.2–12.2.24 and 12.3.2.

many countries readily assume jurisdiction over foreign defendants on exorbitant bases—justifies the common law rule that, when called upon to recognise a foreign judgment, the court is entitled to determine for itself whether the original court was a court of competent jurisdiction.

13.2.2   Chapter II, however, establishes common bases of jurisdiction—at least as regards defendants domiciled in Member States. This justifies the (almost) automatic recognition of judgments falling within the scope of Article 1. Article 33 of the Brussels I Regulation provides:

A judgment given in a Member State shall be recognised in the other Member States without any special procedure being required.

Although recognition is intended to be automatic, the process for recognition under Chapter III is not completely devoid of formalities. The party seeking recognition should normally produce a copy of the judgment.[38] Furthermore, the principle of automatic recognition is subject to the defences to recognition contained in other provisions.[39]

13.2.3   The apparent simplicity of Article 33, which provides merely that a judgment given in a Member State 'shall be recognised', masks a range of difficult questions. While it is reasonable to suppose that, depending on the circumstances, a judgment falling within the scope of Chapter III can give rise to either a cause of action estoppel or an issue estoppel, the conditions which have to be satisfied for a plea of estoppel *per rem judicatam* to succeed under Article 33 are unclear. In the context of enforcement proceedings, there is authority for the proposition that a foreign judgment which is entitled to recognition 'must in principle have the same effects in the State in which enforcement is sought as it does in the State in which judgment was given'.[40] Applying this approach to the recognition of judgments leads to the conclusion that the extent to which a judgment falling within Chapter III is entitled to recognition in England depends upon whether the judgment gives rise to an estoppel (whether in relation to the cause of action, an issue or a number of issues) according to the law of the state of origin.[41] The advantage of this approach is that a judgment falling within the scope of the Brussels I Regulation has the same legal effect in each Member State.

13.2.4   In a number of cases the Court of Appeal has adopted a different approach to the question of cause of action estoppel and issue estoppel. In *Berkeley Administration Inc v McClelland*[42] and *Berkeley Administration Inc v McClelland (No 2)*[43] the Court of Appeal had to consider the extent to which a French judgment was entitled to recognition. In the course of the Court of Appeal's judgments no consideration was given to the effect of the French judgment in France. Indeed, in each decision the Court of Appeal seems to have assumed that the extent to which a judgment

---

[38]   Brussels I Reg, Art 53(1).
[39]   Notably, Brussels I Reg, Arts 34 and 35.
[40]   Case 145/86 *Hoffmann v Krieg* [1988] ECR 645, para 11.
[41]   Further support for this approach is provided by the judgment of Saville LJ in *Boss Group Ltd v Boss France SA* [1997] 1 WLR 351, 359. See also *Re the Enforcement of a Foreign Courts Order* [1986] ECC 481 (Court of Appeal, Frankfurt am Main).
[42]   [1995] ILPr 201.
[43]   [1996] ILPr 772.

gives rise to an estoppel in England is to be regarded as a matter to be determined by English law rather than as a matter to be determined by reference to the law of the state of origin.[44] However, in relation to cause of action estoppel, it makes little difference whether regard is had to the law of the state of origin or the law of the forum as 'either the cause of action has been determined to exist or it has not'.[45]

13.3 DEFENCES TO RECOGNITION UNDER THE BRUSSELS I REGULATION

13.3.1 The Brussels I Regulation provides only a small number of potential defences to recognition.[46] This is consistent with the overall aim of the Regulation to facilitate the free flow of judgments between the Member States. Furthermore, the proper approach towards interpretation of the available defences should not be expanded further than is reasonably necessary to achieve their purpose.[47] However, once a defence has been established the court addressed has no discretion in the matter; the court must refuse recognition or enforcement as the case may be.[48]

No Review of the Merits

13.3.2 At common law, a litigant may not challenge a foreign judgment on the basis that a point of fact or law was wrongly decided by the original court.[49] The same principle is to be found in the Brussels I Regulation:

Under no circumstances may a foreign judgment be reviewed as to its substance.[50]

This means that the court addressed cannot review the accuracy of the findings of law or fact made by the court of origin.[51]

---

[44] See, eg, Hobhouse LJ in *Berkeley Administration Inc v McClelland* [1995] ILPr 201, 221 and Potter LJ in *Berkeley Administration Inc v McClelland (No 2)* [1996] ILPr 772, 796–7. See also *Papeteries de la Vesdre Raoul Collin Sprl v Velourspapiers und Tapeten Ditzel* [1984] ECC 547 (Commercial Court, Liège), in which a similar approach was adopted.

[45] P Barnett, 'The Prevention of Abusive Cross-Border Re-Litigation' (2002) 51 *ICLQ* 943, 955.

[46] See, in particular, Art 34 and 35. Where the original proceedings fall within the scope of one of a number of EC Regulations in the field of civil procedure, the process of enforcement is simplified and the judgment of the court of origin may be refused recognition or enforcement in another Member State on only one basis: that the judgment conflicts with an earlier judgment involving the same cause of action and the same parties; even this ground is available only if the irreconcilability was not, and could not have been, raised as an objection in the proceedings in the court of origin. See the European Enforcement Order Regulation, Art 21, Reg (EC) 805/2004, [2004] OJ L143/15; the European Order for Payment Procedure Regulation, Art 22, Reg (EC) 1896/2006 [2006] OJ L399/1; the European Small Claims Procedure Regulation, Art 22, Reg (EC) No 861/2007 [2007] OJ L199/1.

[47] See Rix LJ in *TSN Kunststoffrecycling GmbH v Jurgens* [2002] 1 WLR 2459, 2472 (at [49]).

[48] Case C–80/00 *Italian Leather SpA v WECO Polstermöbil GmbH & Co* [2002] ECR I–4995, paras 50–2.

[49] *Godard v Gray* (1870) LR 6 QB 139. This principle is subject to the defence of fraud. See paras 12.4.9–12.4.13.

[50] Art 36.

[51] See Case C–38/98 *Régie Nationale des Usines Renault SA v Maxicar SpA* [2000] ECR I–2973, para 29.

Limited Review of Jurisdiction

13.3.3 As a general principle, the court addressed is not entitled to examine the basis on which the court of origin exercised jurisdiction over the defendant. It is provided not only that the jurisdiction of the court of origin 'may not be reviewed,' but also that '[t]he test of public policy ... may not be applied to the rules relating to jurisdiction'.[52] Accordingly, the mere fact that the case was brought in a particular Member State cannot provide a ground for enforcement of the judgment being refused in another Member State.[53] Similarly, a judgment may not be refused recognition or enforcement on the basis that the court of origin, having misapplied Article 5(1)[54] or Article 27,[55] should not have assumed jurisdiction over the dispute. This principle is justified by the overall structure of the Brussels I Regulation:

The very strict rules of jurisdiction laid down in [Chapter II], and the safeguards granted ... to defendants who do not enter an appearance, make it possible to dispense with any review, by the court in which recognition or enforcement is sought, of the jurisdiction of the court in which the original judgment was given.[56]

13.3.4 Just as the rule which prevents review on questions of substance implies confidence in the courts of other Member States on questions of law and fact, the absence of a general jurisdictional defence at the stage of recognition or enforcement assumes the proper application of the jurisdiction provisions of Chapter II by the court of origin. Accordingly, if a defendant intends to challenge the jurisdiction of the court of origin he must do so before that court (and, in appropriate circumstances, the matter may be referred to the Court of Justice). A defendant who chooses not to take part in the proceedings in the state of origin cannot normally challenge the jurisdiction of the court of origin at the stage of recognition or enforcement and the fact that the court of origin assumed jurisdiction on an exorbitant basis or misapplied the provisions of Chapter II is irrelevant.[57]

13.3.5 There are, however, limited exceptions to the general principle that the assumption of jurisdiction by the court of origin may not be reviewed by the court addressed.[58] First, Article 35(1) provides that a judgment shall not be recognised

---

[52] Brussels I Reg, Art 35(3). See Case C–7/98 *Krombach v Bamberski* [2000] I–1935, para 31. The defence of public policy under the Brussels I Regulation is discussed at paras 13.3.9–13.3.17.

[53] See Gloster J in *Viking Line ABP v International Transport Workers' Federation* [2006] ILPr 50, 65 (at [79]).

[54] *Corapak (Société) v Jean Daujas (Société)* [2008] ILPr 211 (Court of Cassation, France).

[55] *Mikropolis-Informedica v Amstrad Plc* [2005] ILPr 356 (Supreme Court, Greece).

[56] Jenard Report, [1979] OJ C59/46.

[57] Case C–7/98 *Krombach v Bamberski* [2000] ECR I–1935, paras 32–3.

[58] In addition to the two exceptions discussed in the text, Art 35(1) of the Lugano Convention provides that recognition may also be refused in any case provided for by Art 64(3) or Art 67(4). Art 64(3) provides that recognition or enforcement may be refused if the ground of jurisdiction on which the judgment has been based differs from that resulting from the Lugano Convention and recognition or enforcement is sought against a party who is domiciled in a state bound by the Lugano Convention, unless the judgment may otherwise be recognised or enforced under any rule of law in the state addressed. This provision is relevant only in the context of the recognition or enforcement of a judgment granted by the court of a Member State in a non-EU country: Jenard-Möller Report, [1990] OJ C189/68, para 16(5). Art 67(1) provides that the Lugano Convention 'shall not affect any conventions by which the Contracting Parties and/or the States bound by this Convention are bound and which, in relation to particular matters, govern ... the recognition or enforcement of judgments'. Art 67(4) of the Lugano Convention provides that 'recognition

if it conflicts with the jurisdiction provisions in Section 3 (insurance), Section 4 (consumer contracts) and Section 6 (exclusive jurisdiction) of Chapter II of the Brussels I Regulation. However, Article 35(2) states that the court addressed 'shall be bound by the findings of fact on which the court of the Member State of origin based its jurisdiction'. The reason for this exception is not difficult to discern. As regards Article 22 of the Brussels I Regulation (the only provision of Section 6 of Chapter II), it is ultimately for the court of the Member State which has exclusive jurisdiction to determine its own jurisdiction. If the court of one Member State wrongly assumes jurisdiction when a court of another Member State has exclusive jurisdiction, it is right and proper that the court on which exclusive jurisdiction is conferred should refuse recognition or enforcement of the foreign judgment.[59] As regards judgments which conflict with the jurisdictional provisions relating to insurance matters (Section 3) and consumer contracts (Section 4), the exception to the general principle that there should be no review of jurisdiction by the court addressed is justified by the aim of the Brussels I Regulation to protect the weaker party.[60] Where, for example, a dispute arises in relation to a consumer contract concluded between an English consumer and an Italian supplier, Article 16(2) of the Brussels I Regulation provides that the consumer shall be sued in the country of his domicile.[61] If the supplier sues the consumer in Italy, it hardly seems reasonable to expect the consumer to appear in the Italian proceedings to contest the jurisdiction of the Italian court. The effect of Article 35(1) is that, should the Italian court erroneously assume jurisdiction over the consumer, the consumer is able to ignore the foreign proceedings and defend any subsequent enforcement proceedings in England on the basis that the exercise of jurisdiction by the court of origin was inconsistent with Section 4 of Chapter II. Given that the Brussels I Regulation also contains provisions which aim to protect employees,[62] it is surprising that it is not also provided that the courts of the state addressed may refuse to recognise or enforce a judgment which conflicts with the jurisdiction provisions relating to individual contracts of employment. The suggestion that employees do not require the same protection as consumers at the recognition or enforcement stage because 'any review of jurisdiction would affect only the applicant, who will generally be the worker'[63] is not wholly convincing.[64]

---

or enforcement may be refused if the State addressed is not bound by the convention on a particular matter and the person against whom recognition or enforcement is sought is domiciled in that State, or, if the State addressed is a Member State of the European Community and in respect of conventions which would have to be concluded by the European Community, in any of its Member States, unless the judgment may otherwise be recognised or enforced under any rule of law in the State addressed'. The ground for refusal under Art 67(4) confers a discretion on the court in which recognition or enforcement is sought. Even though Art 67(4) was included at the request of the EFTA countries, 'a judgment delivered in an EFTA Member State on the basis of a rule of jurisdiction provided for in a special convention might be refused recognition or enforcement ... in a Community Member State': Jenard-Möller Report, [1990] OJ C189/82, para 82.

[59] See *Prudential Assurance Co Ltd v Prudential Insurance Co of America* [2003] 1 WLR 2295.
[60] See *Re Jurisdiction in a Consumer Contract* [2002] ILPr 157 (Court of Appeal, Koblenz).
[61] This general rule must be read subject to the possibility of the parties (albeit in rather limited circumstances) agreeing to the exclusive jurisdiction of other courts. See paras 5.8.33–5.8.35.
[62] See section 5.8.
[63] European Commission, *Proposal*, COM (1999) 348 final, p 23.
[64] AAH van Hoek, (2001) 38 *CML Rev* 1011, 1025.

13.3.6   The defence which allows limited review of jurisdiction does not refer to the provisions which cover prorogation of jurisdiction—that is, Section 7 of Chapter II of the Brussels I Regulation. Recognition may not be refused on the basis that the court of origin wrongly assumed jurisdiction in breach of the terms of a jurisdiction agreement which, in the eyes of the court addressed, satisfies the requirements of Article 23 of the Brussels I Regulation. So, for example, a judgment given by a German court is entitled to recognition in England under Chapter III of the Brussels I Regulation even if the English court believes that the subject-matter of the dispute litigated in Germany falls within the scope of an English jurisdiction clause which is valid under Article 23. Although section 32 of the Civil Jurisdiction and Judgments Act 1982 provides a defence to recognition or enforcement of a foreign judgment which results from proceedings brought in breach of a dispute-resolution clause,[65] this provision does not apply to judgments which are entitled to recognition or enforcement under the Brussels I Regulation.[66]

13.3.7   There is a case for saying that the position should be different in a case where the court of a Member State exercises jurisdiction in defiance of an arbitration clause. However, it follows from the judgment of the Court of Justice in the *West Tankers* case[67] that where a court exercises jurisdiction and gives judgment on the merits of the dispute—notwithstanding the existence of an arbitration clause which, according to English conflicts principles, is valid under its proper law—the judgment does not fall outside the scope of the Regulation; the judgment's subject-matter is 'civil and commercial' in nature and it does not concern 'arbitration'.[68] As the judgment is within the scope of Article 1, recognition or enforcement cannot be refused on the basis that the bringing of the proceedings in the original court was 'contrary to an agreement under which the dispute in question was to be settled otherwise than by proceedings in the courts of that country'.[69]

13.3.8   Secondly, Article 35(1) of the Brussels I Regulation provides that a judgment shall not be recognised in a case provided for by Article 72.[70] This provision can only be understood against the background of some of its history. As already indicated, the Brussels I Regulation has the potential to operate harshly in relation to defendants not domiciled in Member States; as regards such defendants, claimants can rely on exorbitant bases of jurisdiction and the ensuing judgments are, in principle, entitled to recognition and enforcement in other Member States. Article 59 of the Brussels Convention permitted contracting states to enter into bilateral agreements with third states under the terms of which the courts of the contracting state would refuse to recognise or enforce judgments given by the courts of other contracting states in cases where the defendant was domiciled in the third state and the court of origin's jurisdiction was founded on one of the exorbitant bases of jurisdiction identified by Article 3. Although EU Member States can no longer enter such agreements—as, by virtue of the enactment of the Brussels I Regulation, the EU institutions have acquired this competence—it is intended that any

---

[65]   See paras 12.4.20–12.4.23.
[66]   Civil Jurisdiction and Judgments Act 1982, s 32(4).
[67]   Case C–185/07 *Allianz SpA (formerly Riunione Adriatica Di Sicurta SpA) v West Tankers Inc* [2009] 1 AC 1138.
[68]   See *DHL GBS (UK) Ltd v Fallimento Finmatica SPA* [2009] 1 Lloyd's Rep 430; *The Wadi Sudr* [2010] 1 Lloyd's Rep 193. See paras 3.3.28–3.3.32.
[69]   Civil Jurisdiction and Judgments Act 1982, s 32(1).
[70]   (Lugano Convention, Art 68.)

agreements concluded by Member States before the entry into force of the Brussels I Regulation should continue to operate. Accordingly, Article 72 provides that the Brussels I Regulation shall not effect agreements which Member States undertook pursuant to Article 59 of the Brussels Convention.

Public Policy

13.3.9   Article 34(1) of the Brussels I Regulation provides that a judgment given by the court of a Member State shall not be recognised 'if such recognition is manifestly contrary to public policy in the state in which recognition is sought'.

The Proper Approach to Public Policy

13.3.10   The public policy defence 'ought to operate only in exceptional cases'.[71] Furthermore, Article 35(3) expressly provides that public policy cannot be used as a basis for refusing to recognise a judgment in a situation where the court of origin misapplied the jurisdiction rules contained in Chapter II. The Court of Justice has confirmed that the public policy defence must be narrowly construed. In *Krombach v Bamberski*[72] the Court of Justice considered that recourse to the public policy defence can be envisaged only when recognition or enforcement of the foreign judgment 'would be at variance to an unacceptable degree with the legal order of the State in which enforcement is sought inasmuch as it infringes a fundamental principle'.[73] To justify the court addressed refusing to recognise or enforce the foreign judgment such infringement 'would have to constitute a manifest breach of a rule of law regarded as essential in the legal order of the State [addressed] or of a right recognised as being fundamental within that legal order'.[74] Where, for example, the defendant's right to a fair trial under Article 6 of the European Convention on Human Rights has not been respected in the state of origin, it is appropriate for the courts of the state addressed to refuse to recognise or enforce the judgment on grounds of public policy.[75] However, in *Gambazzi v Daimler Chrysler Canada Inc*[76] the Court of Justice pointed out that:

fundamental rights, such as respect for the rights of the defence, do not constitute unfet-tered prerogatives and may be subject to restrictions. ... [S]uch restrictions must in fact

---

[71]   Jenard Report, [1979] OJ C59/44. This view is supported by the Court of Justice in Case 145/86 *Hoffmann v Krieg* [1988] ECR 645. See also *Hupperichs v Dothu* [1990] ILPr 180 (Supreme Court, Netherlands).

[72]   Case C–7/98 [2000] ECR I–1935. AAH van Hoek, (2001) 38 *CML Rev* 1011.

[73]   Case C–7/98 [2000] ECR I–1935, para 37.

[74]   Case C–7/98 [2000] ECR I–1935, para 37. See also Case C–420/07 *Apostolides v Orams* [2010] 1 All ER (Comm) 950.

[75]   *Maronier v Larmer* [2003] QB 620 (A Briggs, (2002) 73 *BYIL* 468); *Citibank NA v Rafidian Bank* [2003] 2 All ER (Comm) 1054. See also *Pordea v Times Newspapers Ltd* [2000] ILPr 763 (Court of Cassation, France), in which enforcement of an English order for costs in a libel case was refused on the basis that the costs were set at a disproportionately high level, thereby infringing the judgment debtor's access to justice rights under Art 6 ECHR; *Stolzenberg v Daimler Chrysler Canada Inc* [2005] ILPr 266 (Court of Cassation, France). See also the discussion of JJ Fawcett, 'The Impact of Article 6(1) of the ECHR on Private International Law' (2007) 56 *ICLQ* 1.

[76]   Case C–394/07 [2009] ILPr 637.

correspond to the objectives of public interest pursued by the measure in question and must not constitute, with regard to the aim pursued, a manifest or disproportionate breach of the rights thus guaranteed.[77]

It follows that, as long as such restrictions are not manifestly disproportionate to the aim being pursued, namely the sound administration of justice, judgments which impose sanctions on defendants who fail to participate in civil proceedings or otherwise engage in delaying tactics are not necessarily contrary to public policy, notwithstanding the fact that the defendant's procedural rights are restricted.[78] In *Gambazzi* the claimant attempted to enforce an English judgment in Italy. Because the defendant had failed to comply with freezing and disclosure orders, the High Court barred him from taking any further part in the substantive proceedings and gave judgment for the claimant. According to the Court of Justice, given that the defendant's exclusion from participation in civil proceedings is the most serious restriction possible on the defendant's procedural rights, 'such a restriction must satisfy very exacting requirements if it is not to be regarded as a manifest and disproportionate infringement of those rights'.[79] It was for the court addressed to assess, in the light of all the specific circumstances of the proceedings, whether or not the sanction was disproportionate (and, therefore, whether recognition of the English orders was contrary to public policy).

13.3.11   In *Régie Nationale des Usines Renault SA v Maxicar SpA*[80] the Court of Justice ruled that public policy cannot be relied upon simply because the rule of law applied by the court of origin is different from the rule that would have been applied by the court addressed.[81] The position is not altered by the fact that the court addressed considers that the court of origin made an error relating to rules of EU law.[82] The questions referred to the Court of Justice arose out of the French plaintiff's application to enforce a French judgment in Italy. The French court had awarded damages for breach of the plaintiff's intellectual property rights by the defendant, an Italian company. Even if the French court, by upholding the plaintiff's intellectual property right in the circumstances of the case, was acting in breach of EU law (specifically, the rules relating to the free movement of goods and abuse of a dominant position), this did not justify enforcement of the French judgment being refused by the Italian court on the basis of public policy.[83]

13.3.12   This restrictive approach to questions of public policy is justified by the structure of the Brussels I Regulation.[84] Some of the areas in which public policy questions often arise are outside Article 1, which excludes proceedings concerning public law, social security and nearly all aspects of family law. Moreover, Chapter II tackles specific subject areas in which public policy may arise by means of direct jurisdiction rules. There are, for example, special jurisdiction rules dealing with consumer contracts, employment contracts and matters relating to insurance.

---

[77]   Case C–394/07 [2009] ILPr 637, 660 (para 29).

[78]   Case C–394/07 *Gambazzi v Daimler Chrysler Canada Inc* [2009] ILPr 637, 660 (paras 31–2).

[79]   Case C–394/07 [2009] ILPr 637, 660 (para 33).

[80]   Case C–38/98 ECR I–2973.

[81]   Case C–38/98 ECR I–2973, para 29.

[82]   Case C–38/98 ECR I–2973, para 32.

[83]   Case C–38/98 ECR I–2973, para 34.

[84]   M Forde, 'The "Ordre Public" Exception and Adjudicative Jurisdiction Conventions' (1980) 29 *ICLQ* 259, 271.

13.3.13 The exceptional nature of the public policy defence seems to have been largely accepted by national courts. For example, it has been said that, in order to be contrary to public policy, a judgment must violate principles of justice and reason which are considered fundamental to the forum's legal system in such a manner that recognition or enforcement of the judgment cannot be justified[85] and that, where a foreign judgment conflicts with the law of the forum, a refusal of its recognition or enforcement is justified only if the conflict is intolerable.[86] A judgment is not contrary to public policy simply because the court of origin awarded damages on a different basis from that applied by the court addressed[87] or because the court of origin upheld a contract which the court addressed would regard as having been procured by undue influence[88] or because the court of origin declared invalid an arbitration agreement which was regarded as valid by the court addressed.[89] As a general rule, one would expect an objection founded on public policy to be more likely to fail than to succeed.[90] Nevertheless, the French courts have held that recognition or enforcement of a foreign judgment which does not include the reasons of the court of origin would be contrary to public policy.[91]

Limits on Public Policy

13.3.14 The fact that specific grounds for refusing recognition are to be found in other paragraphs of Article 34 of the Brussels I Regulation means that the public policy defence should have no role to play where one of the more specific grounds for refusing recognition applies.[92] In *Hoffmann v Krieg*[93] the Court of Justice took the view that the public policy defence is precluded when the issue is whether a foreign judgment is compatible with a national judgment. In such a case 'the issue must be resolved on the basis of the specific provision ... which envisages cases in which the foreign judgment is irreconcilable with a judgment given in a dispute between the same parties in the state in which [recognition or] enforcement is sought'.[94] The same approach was adopted by the Court of Justice in *Hendrickman v Magenta Druck &*

---

[85] See *Hupperichs v Dothu* [1990] ILPr 180 (Supreme Court, Netherlands).
[86] See *Re a German Commercial Agent* [1980] ECC 207 (Federal Supreme Court, Germany); *Re Liability for Investment in Futures Options* [1999] ILPr 758 (Federal Supreme Court, Germany).
[87] See *Re a German Commercial Agent* [1980] ECC 207 (Federal Supreme Court, Germany); *Re a Shipowner's Liability* [1996] ILPr 497 (Court of Appeal, Hamburg).
[88] *Re Enforcement of a Guarantee* [2001] ILPr 425 (Federal Supreme Court, Germany).
[89] *The Wadi Sudr* [2010] 1 Lloyd's Rep 193.
[90] Judge Goldblatt QC in *CFEM Façades SA v Bovis Construction Ltd* [1992] ILPr 561, 571.
[91] *Dehbashi v Gerling Kozern* [1996] ILPr 104 (Court of Appeal, Poitiers); *Sàrl Polypetrol v Société Générale Routière* [1993] ILPr 107 (Court of Cassation, France); *Society of Lloyd's v X* [2009] ILPr 161 (Court of Cassation, France); G Cuniberti, 'The Recognition of Foreign Judgments Lacking Reasons in Europe: Access to Justice, Foreign Court Avoidance, and Efficiency' (2008) 57 *ICLQ* 25. Cf *Matériel Auxiliaire d'Informatique v Printed Forms Equipment Ltd* [2006] ILPr 803 (Court of Cassation, France). See also *Fortis Banque v Mancini* [2005] ILPr 731 (Court of Cassation, France) in which a rule of French insolvency procedure requiring all creditors to declare the debts due to them was regarded as being part of French public policy.
[92] Jenard Report, [1979] OJ C59/44.
[93] Case 145/86 [1988] ECR 645.
[94] Case 145/86 [1988] ECR 645, para 21.

Verlag GmbH,[95] a case where the defendant sought to resist the enforcement of a judgment either on the ground that he had not been duly served with the document instituting proceedings in sufficient time for him to arrange his defence or on the basis of public policy. In these circumstances the Court of Justice ruled that recourse to public policy 'is ... precluded when the issue must be resolved on the basis of a specific provision'.[96]

Public Policy and Fraud

13.3.15 At common law, fraud is a basis for refusing to recognise a foreign judgment even if the issue of fraud was raised in the original proceedings and rejected.[97] While fraud is not listed in the defences available under Article 35 of the Brussels I Regulation, it is clear that 'to obtain a judgment by fraud can in principle constitute an offence against the public policy of the state addressed'.[98] In what circumstances is it contrary to public policy to recognise a judgment which has been obtained by fraud?

13.3.16 In *Interdesco SA v Nullifire Ltd*[99] the plaintiff, a French paint manufacturer, entered an agreement with the defendant, an English company, under which the defendant was given exclusive distribution rights in the United Kingdom and Ireland in respect of the plaintiff's products. Before the agreement had expired, it was terminated by the defendant on the basis that, as the plaintiff's products failed to satisfy UK standards, they were unmarketable. The plaintiff brought proceedings in France for wrongful termination of the agreement. The French court, which relied on the results of tests conducted in France by the testing institution appointed by the parties in the distribution agreement, and attached little weight to contradictory English tests indicating that the paint was substandard, awarded damages to the plaintiff. When the plaintiff sought to enforce the judgment in England the defendant argued that as the judgment had been procured by fraud, enforcement would be contrary to English public policy.

13.3.17 The defence of public policy was rejected. Three important principles emerge from the judgment, which was subsequently approved by the Court of Appeal in *Société d'Informatique Service Réalisation Organisation v Ampersand Software BV*.[100] First, where the court of another Member State has ruled on precisely the matters that a defendant seeks to raise when challenging the judgment on the ground of fraud, the Brussels I Regulation precludes the court addressed from reviewing the conclusion of the foreign court.[101] Secondly, where a Member State judgment is challenged on the ground that the foreign court has been fraudulently deceived, the English court should first consider whether the defendant has a

---

[95] Case C–78/95 [1996] ECR I–4943.
[96] Case C–78/95 [1996] ECR I–4943, para 23.
[97] See paras 12.4.9–12.4.13.
[98] Schlosser Report, [1979] OJ C59/128, para 192(a).
[99] [1992] 1 Lloyd's Rep 180. See also *Turczynski v Wilde and Partners* [2003] ILPr 64 (Court of Cassation, France).
[100] [1994] ILPr 55.
[101] Phillips J at [1992] 1 Lloyd's Rep 180, 187.

remedy in the foreign jurisdiction in question. If so, it will normally be appropriate to leave the defendant to pursue his remedy in that jurisdiction.[102] Thirdly, it is not generally appropriate for the English court to deny recognition to a Member State judgment on the ground of public policy except in circumstances where it would permit a challenge to an English judgment.[103] It follows that, as a general rule, the public policy defence cannot be relied upon in cases of fraud unless, first, the party resisting recognition of the foreign judgment produces evidence which could not have been produced with reasonable diligence in the foreign proceedings and which, although not necessarily decisive, would probably have had an important influence on the result of the case and, secondly, there is no means of recourse under the law of the state of origin.

Safeguarding the Rights of the Defendant[104]

13.3.18   Although the aim of the Brussels I Regulation is to facilitate the mutual recognition and enforcement of foreign judgments between the Member States, Chapter III cannot be allowed to undermine in any way the defendant's right to a fair hearing.[105] Accordingly, one of the defences to recognition and enforcement is designed to ensure that the procedural rights of the defendant are effectively respected.[106] Article 34(2) provides that a judgment shall not be recognised:

> where it was given in default of appearance, if the defendant was not served with the document which instituted the proceedings or with an equivalent document in sufficient time and in a sufficient way to enable him to arrange for his defence, unless the defendant failed to commence proceedings to challenge the judgment when it was possible for him to do so.[107]

The Relationship between Article 26 and Article 34(2)

13.3.19   Article 26(2) provides that, where a defendant who is domiciled in one Member State is sued in another Member State, the court shall stay the proceedings unless it is shown that 'the defendant has been able to receive the document instituting the proceedings ... in sufficient time to enable him to arrange for his defence, or that all necessary steps have been taken to this end'. The ground for refusing recognition of a judgment under Article 34(2) overlaps to a considerable extent with Article 26(2). A question which arises is whether the person against whom the judgment is invoked

---

[102]   Phillips J at [1992] 1 Lloyd's Rep 180, 188.
[103]   Eg, the principle in *Henderson v Henderson* (1843) 3 Hare 100.
[104]   WA Kennett, 'Reviewing Service: Double Check or Double Fault?' (1992) 11 *CJQ* 115.
[105]   Case 49/84 *Debaecker v Bouwman* [1985] ECR 1779, para 10.
[106]   Case C–283/05 *ASML Netherlands BV v Semiconductor Industry Services GmbH (SEMIS)* [2006] ECR I–12041, para 20; Case C–420/07 *Apostolides v Orams* [2010] All ER (Comm) 950, 990 (para 75).
[107]   Under Art III of Protocol 1 to the Lugano Convention, Switzerland reserves the right to declare upon ratification that it will not apply the following part of the provision in Article 34(2): 'unless the defendant failed to commence proceedings to challenge the judgment when it was possible for him to do so'. If Switzerland makes such declaration, the other contracting parties shall apply the same reservation in respect of judgments rendered by the courts of Switzerland.

can rely on Article 34(2) when the court of origin has already decided, in the context of Article 26, that he was given sufficient time to prepare his defence: is the court addressed bound by the decision of the court of origin on this point? The purpose of Articles 26 and 34(2) is 'to ensure that the defendant's rights are effectively protected'.[108] According to the Court of Justice, in a case where a Dutch court decides that the defendant received the originating process in sufficient time and gives a default judgment in the claimant's favour, when the creditor applies to enforce the judgment in Germany, the German court is not bound by the decision of the Dutch court, but must examine for itself the question posed by Article 34(2), even though the same issue has been considered and decided by the Dutch court under Article 26(2).[109]

13.3.20   It should be noted that there is a very important distinction between the scope of Article 26 and the scope of Article 34(2). Whereas Article 26 applies to cases where proceedings are brought against a defendant who is domiciled in a Member State other than the state in which the original proceedings take place, Article 34(2) applies to all defendants regardless of their domicile. Accordingly, Article 34(2) is of particular importance in two sorts of case: first, where the original proceedings are brought against a defendant who is not domiciled in a Member State and, secondly, where the original proceedings are brought in the Member State in which the defendant is domiciled.[110]

One Defence or Two?

13.3.21   The effect of Article 34(2) is to give the defendant a double protection: first, the document must have been served; secondly, even where service has been effected, recognition can be refused if the court addressed considers that the document was not served in sufficient time or in such a way to enable the defendant to arrange for his defence. In *Klomps v Michel*[111] the Court of Justice confirmed that it is perfectly possible for a defendant to rely on the defence based on procedural fairness—because he had insufficient time to prepare for his defence—notwithstanding the fact that he was served with the document instituting the proceedings.

13.3.22   It would also seem that a defendant can, in principle, rely on Article 34(2)—even if he had sufficient time in which to prepare his defence—on the ground that he was not served with the document which instituted the proceedings.[112] It is difficult to imagine how such a case might arise in practice as a defendant will only have sufficient time in which to arrange for his defence if he has been informed in some way of the

---

[108] Case 228/81 *Pendy Plastic Products BV v Pluspunkt Handelsgesellschaft mbH* [1982] ECR 2723, para 13.

[109] *Ibid*. See also *Lafforgue v Sweet Factory International Ltd* [2005] ILPr 610 (Court of Cassation, France).

[110] Although this was implicit in the decision of the Court of Justice in Case 166/80 *Klomps v Michel* [1981] ECR 1593, it was expressly articulated in Case 49/84 *Debaecker v Bouwman* [1985] ECR 1779.

[111] Case 166/80 [1981] ECR 1593, para 15. TC Hartley, (1982) 7 *EL Rev* 419.

[112] This proposition follows from the reasoning of the Court of Justice in Case 305/88 *Isabelle Lancray SA v Peters und Sickert KG* [1990] ECR I–2725, notwithstanding that this case was decided under the different wording of Art 27(2) of the Brussels Convention.

proceedings that have been brought against him. However, it is possible to conceive of a situation in which there has been a failure of service, but the defendant learns about the impending proceedings from some other source. In such a case, the defendant ought to be able to rely on Article 34(2).[113]

'In Default of Appearance'

13.3.23   Although it has been suggested that the definition of 'appearance' should be a matter for the law of the state of origin,[114] the Court of Justice has accepted that the notion of 'appearance' is to be given a Europe-wide meaning. The fact that the proceedings are regarded as *inter partes* according to the law of the state of origin does not necessarily deprive the defendant of the defence provided by Article 34(2).[115]

13.3.24   In *Klomps v Michel* the Court of Justice held that if, after a judgment has been given, the defendant appears for the first time before the court of origin with a view to having the judgment set aside, the judgment is still to be regarded as having been given in default of appearance.[116] Furthermore, in *Hendrickman v Magenta Druck & Verlag GmbH* the Court of Justice ruled that a judgment is to be regarded as given in default of appearance in a case where 'proceedings are initiated against a person without his knowledge and a lawyer appears before the court first seised on his behalf but without his authority'.[117] Conversely, if the defendant appears to fight the case on the merits, reliance cannot be placed on Article 34(2). Similarly, where a civil claim is joined to criminal proceedings, if the defendant answers the criminal charge and is aware of the civil claim which is being made against him in the criminal proceedings, the plea to the criminal charge will be regarded as an appearance to the proceedings as a whole.[118]

13.3.25   The rationale for the defence in Article 34(2) is to ensure that the defendant has had the opportunity of defending himself.[119] It follows that the reason for the defendant's appearance is not relevant and that a defendant who, having been served with the document initiating the proceedings, appears solely to challenge the jurisdiction of the court cannot rely on Article 34(2).[120] The position would appear to be the same where the defendant appears to apply for proceedings to be adjourned.[121] It is unclear whether a judgment is given in default of appearance for the purposes of Article 34(2) in a case where the defendant lodges with the court of origin a formal document either challenging the court's jurisdiction or indicating an intention to defend the claim on the merits, but subsequently decides not to

---

[113] See *Tavoulareas v Tsavliris (No 2)* [2007] 1 WLR 1573.

[114] Advocate General Darmon in Case C172/91 *Sonntag v Waidmann* [1993] ECR I–1963, para 82.

[115] Case C–78/95 *Hendrickman v Magenta Druck & Verlag GmbH* [1996] ECR I–4943, para 18.

[116] Case 166/80 [1981] ECR 1593, paras 12–13.

[117] Case C–78/95 [1996] ECR I–4943, para 18. A Briggs, (1996) 16 *YBEL* 606; TC Hartley, (1997) 22 *EL Rev* 364. See also *Re Enforcement of a Guarantee* [2001] ILPr 425 (Federal Supreme Court, Germany).

[118] Case C–172/91 *Sonntag v Waidmann* [1993] ECR I–1963, para 41.

[119] Case C–172/91 *Sonntag v Waidmann* [1993] ECR I–1963, para 38; Case C–78/95 *Hendrickman v Magenta Druck & Verlag GmbH* [1996] ECR I–4943, para 15.

[120] Case C–39/02 *Maersk Olie & Gas A/S v Firma de Haan en de Boer* [2004] ECR I–9657, para 56.

[121] TC Hartley, *Civil Jurisdiction and Judgments* (London, Sweet & Maxwell, 1984) 90.

be present at any subsequent hearings.[122] The underlying purpose of Article 34(2) suggests that, in this type of case, the judgment should be regarded as not having been given in default of appearance.

13.3.26   There are situations where a broad view of 'appearance' may operate harshly. It is not obvious why, for example, a defendant who applies to the court of origin for more time for the preparation of his defence should be placed in a worse position than the defendant who chooses to ignore the proceedings entirely. The protection offered by Article 34(2) is significantly reduced if a defendant is deprived of the possibility of relying on the defence of insufficient time simply by making an application for an extension of time.

'Service in Sufficient Time and in Such a Way'

13.3.27   For the purposes of Article 34(2), what is important is that the defendant was given a proper opportunity of defending the proceedings brought against him. Whether the defendant was served in sufficient time and in such a way to enable him to arrange for his defence has to be considered from a substantive, as opposed to a technical, perspective. In *ASML Netherlands BV v Semiconductor Industry Services GmbH (SEMIS)* the Court of Justice ruled that Article 34(2) 'does not necessarily require the document which instituted the proceedings to be duly served, but does require that the rights of defence are effectively respected'.[123] So, the question is not whether the defendant was, as a matter of law, properly served prior to the proceedings; rather, the question is whether the defendant was, in a practical sense, able to mount a defence. In the earlier case of *Tavoulareas v Tsavliris (No 2)*[124] the Court of Appeal had held that the defendant must have been 'served' (in accordance with Article 30 of the Service Regulation[125]) and that it was not enough that 'the defendant was notified of the proceedings in a time and in a way that enabled him to defend if he wanted to'.[126] The Court of Appeal appears to have accepted that, where service has occurred but is defective in some way, the defendant cannot argue that there has been no service—this follows from the fact that Article 34(2) says 'served' rather than 'duly served'—but maintained that Article 34(2) must be available as a defence if proceedings in the court of origin have never been served at all (even if notice of the proceedings has come to the defendant's attention in some other way).

13.3.28   In considering whether or not the defendant has been served, it is important to identify the document instituting the proceedings. It is only this document which has to be served in sufficient time and in such a way as to enable the defendant to arrange for his defence. Whether or not other documents in the proceedings have been appropriately served is irrelevant.[127] For example, the fact that service of the

---

[122]   See *Tavoulareas v Tsavliris (No 2)* [2007] 1 WLR 1573.
[123]   Case C–283/05 [2006] ECR I–12041, para 20.
[124]   [2007] 1 WLR 1573.
[125]   Reg (EC) 1348/2000, [2008] OJ L160/37.
[126]   Longmore LJ at [2007] 1 WLR 1573, 1577 (at [6]).
[127]   *Société Biomécanique Intégrée v Fabrique Nationale de Herstal SA* [1993] ILPr 127 (Court of Cassation, France); *Gregori Sud-Est SA v Ziliani, t/a Cave Ferruccio Ziliani* [2001] ILPr (Court of

judgment was irregular does not provide a defence to recognition or enforcement under Article 34(2).[128] For the purposes of Article 34(2), the relevant document is:

the document or documents which must be ... served on the defendant in order to enable him to assert his rights before an enforceable judgment is given in the state of origin.[129]

13.3.29 In the context of the question whether the defendant has been given sufficient time, the period which should be considered is the time available to the defendant for the purposes of preventing the issue of a judgment in default which is enforceable against him.[130] It is the adequacy of the period leading up to the obtaining of the default judgment which must be considered; the fact that the defendant is given an opportunity to challenge a default judgment is irrelevant to the question whether sufficient time was given—though the availability of means of recourse against the judgment in the state of origin may have the effect of depriving the defendant of the defence under Article 34(2).[131] Where the foreign procedure allows the defendant 14 days in which to enter an appearance (failing which a default judgment may be entered), but, in the circumstances of the case, the default judgment is not actually made until five weeks after service of the originating process, the pertinent question is whether five weeks (not 14 days) is sufficient time for the defendant to arrange for his defence.[132]

13.3.30 In the simple situation where the defendant is personally served with the document instituting the proceedings it is obvious that time starts to run from the moment of service. More problematical is the situation where the defendant is not personally served and either he never becomes aware of the document or he only becomes aware of the document some time after service has been effected. This type of situation is most likely to arise in cases where the defendant is served by post—the originating process may go missing or be misdirected—or where some method of substituted service is used. The essential question in this situation is whether, given the way in which service was effected, the defendant was given sufficient time for the preparation of his defence.

13.3.31 Because Article 34(2), although derived from Article 27(2) of the Brussels Convention, is drafted in different terms, the case law of the Court of Justice under the Brussels Convention has to be treated with a degree of caution. For example, in *Debaecker v Bouwman*[133]—a case involving the enforcement of a Belgian judgment in the Netherlands—the question was whether the defendant could rely on Article 27(2) of the Brussels Convention in a case where proceedings were commenced by way of fictitious service in Belgium (because the plaintiff did not know the defendant's address), but the plaintiff, on later being informed by the defendant of a post-office box for correspondence, did nothing to inform the defendant of the proceedings.

Cassation, France); *Re Enforcement of a Judgment (Date Error in Translated Summons)* [2003] ILPr 523 (Federal Supreme Court, Germany).

[128] *Guittienne v Société Nationale de Crédit à l'Industrie* [1997] ILPr 522 (Court of Cassation, France).
[129] Case C–474/93 *Hengst Import BV v Campese* [1995] ECR I–2113, para 19. See also Case 166/80 *Klomps v Michel* [1981] ECR 1593, para 11.
[130] Case 166/80 *Klomps v Michel* [1981] ECR 1593, para 11.
[131] See para 13.3.34.
[132] *TSN Kunststoffrecycling GmbH v Jurgens* [2002] 1 WLR 2459. A Briggs, (2002) 73 *BYIL* 468.
[133] Case 49/84 [1985] ECR 1779. TC Hartley, (1987) 12 *EL Rev* 220.

In these circumstances, the Court of Justice ruled that the plaintiff's failure to inform the defendant at the postal address given by the defendant was 'in reality merely a factor which must be taken into account in order to establish whether service was effected in sufficient time'.[134] If the same facts were to arise under the Brussels I Regulation, the defendant should be able to rely on Article 34(2) on the basis that he was 'not served ... in such a way as to enable him to arrange for his defence'.

13.3.32   For the purposes of Article 34(2), there is no indication of the standard by which sufficiency of time is to be judged. It is reasonable to suppose that the standard cannot simply be that provided by the law of the state of origin, otherwise Article 34(2) would amount to no more than a verification by the court addressed that the court of origin correctly applied its own procedural law.[135] Nevertheless, it would hardly seem proper for an English court to refuse recognition of a foreign judgment simply on the ground that the time given to a defendant for the preparation of his defence under the law of the state of origin is less than the time given by English procedural law. Ultimately, the smooth operation of this aspect of Article 34(2) depends on the formulation of a supranational standard—or at least an appreciation that the courts cannot rely on purely national standards.

13.3.33   When applying Article 34(2), national courts are required to make a factual assessment in light of the surrounding circumstances.[136] Whether the time given in a particular situation and the method of service are sufficient will depend on all the circumstances of the case (including matters such as the kind of action involved, the parties to it, the need to obtain a legal adviser, and whether translations are required).[137] Accordingly, it is impossible to lay down fixed periods which are, or are not, sufficient. For example, although there are cases in which the German courts have taken the view that a period of 13 days[138] or even 20 days is insufficient for the preparation of a defence by a German defendant in an action in Belgium, there is also contrary German authority for the view that 12 days is sufficient time.[139] The Italian courts have also decided that periods of between 20 and 30 days are sufficient to enable the defendant to arrange his defence in another Member State.[140] In France it has been held that, where the hearing took place on 11 May, service of the originating process on 20 April did not give the defendant sufficient time to prepare his defence.[141]

'Waiving' the Defence

13.3.34   A defendant who was not served in sufficient time to arrange for his defence will cease to be able to rely on Article 34(2) if 'the defendant failed to commence

---

[134] Case 49/84 [1985] ECR 1779, para 27.

[135] See, eg, *Re Service Abroad of a Document* [1993] ILPr 289 (Court of Appeal, Koblenz).

[136] *Rosco BV v Sàrl Fraisgel* [1986] ECC 175 (Court of First Instance, Paris).

[137] Advocate General Reischl in Case 166/80 *Klomps v Michel* [1981] ECR 1593, 1621.

[138] *Re Time for Service of Belgian Default Proceedings* [1987] ECC 276 (Federal Supreme Court, Germany).

[139] *Re Recognition of a Default Judgment* [2005] ILPr 260 (Court of Appeal, Cologne).

[140] WA Kennett, 'Reviewing Service: Double Check or Double Fault?' (1992) 11 *CJQ* 115, 143.

[141] *Bettan v Simon* [1996] ILPr 55 (Court of Cassation, France).

proceedings to challenge the judgment when it was possible for him to do so'.[142] So, if a defendant fails to bring an appeal or to apply to have the judgment set aside by the court of origin, the judgment will be enforceable under the Brussels I Regulation, notwithstanding the procedural irregularity in the original proceedings.[143] However, the defence under Article 34(2) remains available if it was not possible for the defendant to challenge the judgment of the court of origin. Where, for example, the default judgment is not served on the defendant, the defendant is able to rely on Article 34(2) (assuming that the other conditions of that provision are satisfied); the defence under Article 34(2) is not lost simply because the defendant becomes aware of the existence of the judgment at the enforcement stage.[144] Conversely, if the debtor brings proceedings to challenge the default judgment in the country of origin (and that challenge fails), the defendant cannot rely on Article 34(2) at the enforcement stage as long as the proceedings challenging the judgment 'enabled him to argue that he had not been served with the document which instituted the proceedings ... in sufficient time and in such a way as to enable him to arrange for his defence'.[145] The effect of the proviso to Article 34(2)—and its 'very narrow interpretation'[146] by the Court of Justice—is to tilt the balance further in favour of judgment creditors. However, this is thought to be appropriate given that experience under the Brussels and Lugano Conventions showed that Article 27(2) provided judgment debtors with unmeritorious defences based on purely technical, rather than substantive, questions.[147] Furthermore, it is consistent with the general policy of the Brussels I Regulation; by not allowing defendants to raise at the recognition or enforcement stage matters which could have been raised before the court of origin, defendants are drawn into the proceedings in the court of origin, thereby simplifying the process of recognition and enforcement.

Irreconcilability

13.3.35 One of the aims of the Brussels I Regulation is to reduce the incidence of conflicting judgments. The most important mechanisms in this regard are Article 6 and the provisions dealing with concurrent proceedings.[148] It is, however, impossible entirely to prevent conflicting judgments—especially since the material scope of the

---

[142] This proviso was added to Art 34(2) to reverse the effect of Case C–123/91 *Minalmet GmbH v Brandeis Ltd* [1992] ECR I–5661 in which the Court of Justice had held that, in the context of the Brussels Convention, a defendant who had not been duly served could rely on Art 27(2) even though, after having become aware of the judgment in default, he neither applied to have the judgment set aside on the ground that service of the document instituting the proceedings was defective. See also *Re a Belgian Default Judgment* [1991] ILPr 483 (Court of Appeal, Cologne).

[143] See *Re Recognition of a Default Judgment* [2005] ILPr 260 (Court of Appeal, Cologne).

[144] Case C–283/05 *ASML Netherlands BV v Semiconductor Industry Services GmbH (SEMIS)* [2006] ECR I–12041.

[145] Case C–420/07 *Apostolides v Orams* [2010] 1 All ER (Comm) 950, 990 (para 80). See, however, the contrary view that had previously been taken by the German Federal Supreme Court in *Re the Enforcement of a Portuguese Judgment* [2005] ILPr 362.

[146] TC Hartley, 'Cyprus Land Rights: Conflict of Laws Meets International Politics' (2009) 58 *ICLQ* 1013.

[147] See, eg, Case 305/88 *Isabelle Lancray SA v Peters und Sickert KG* [1990] ECR I–2725.

[148] See sections 5.7 and 9.1.

Regulation is limited by Article 1. Accordingly, the grounds for refusing recognition or enforcement include cases involving conflicting judgments.

13.3.36 Article 34(3) of the Brussels I Regulation provides that a judgment given by the courts of a Member State shall be refused recognition if it conflicts with a judgment given in a dispute between the same parties in the state in which recognition is sought. Although for recognition or enforcement to be refused on this basis the proceedings leading to the irreconcilable judgments must have been between the same parties,[149] there is no requirement that the proceedings should have concerned the same cause of action. In order to ascertain whether the two judgments are irreconcilable for the purposes of this rule 'it should be examined whether they entail legal consequences that are mutually exclusive'.[150] This will not always be an easy task for a national court to undertake. It should also be noted that the application of this ground for refusing recognition or enforcement does not turn on which of the conflicting judgments was granted first. Where, in the context of English proceedings, recognition of a French judgment is resisted on the basis of Article 34(3) of the Brussels I Regulation there is no requirement that the English judgment should have been rendered before the French judgment.

13.3.37 The operation of this defence was considered by the Court of Justice in *Italian Leather SpA v WECO Polstermöbil GmbH & Co.*[151] The Italian plaintiff brought proceedings against the German defendant in Germany with a view to obtaining an interim injunction to restrain the defendant from marketing certain products in Germany. The German court dismissed the plaintiff's application on the basis that there was no ground justifying the grant of interim relief. Shortly before the German decision, the plaintiff also started proceedings in Italy, in the context of which the Italian court made an order prohibiting the defendant from using a particular brand name in various countries, including Germany. When the plaintiff sought to enforce the Italian order in Germany, the question arose whether enforcement was to be refused on the basis that it conflicted with the German decision. The Court of Justice confirmed, first, that the question was whether the two judgments entailed legal consequences which are mutually exclusive and, second, that it was irrelevant that the decisions in question concerned the granting of interim relief, rather than the substantive issues between the parties.[152] It went on to conclude that the two judgments were irreconcilable:

a foreign decision on interim measures ordering an obligor not to carry out certain acts is irreconcilable with a decision on interim measures refusing to grant such an order in a dispute between the same parties in the State where recognition is sought.[153]

13.3.38 The defence of irreconcilability is not limited to cases where the conflicting judgments both fall within the material scope of the Brussels I Regulation. Where a judgment creditor seeks to enforce a judgment under Chapter III, enforcement will be

---

[149] See the discussion of this issue in the context of *lis pendens* at paras 9.1.24–9.1.34.
[150] Case 145/86 *Hoffmann v Krieg* [1988] ECR 645, para 22.
[151] Case C–80/00 [2002] ECR I–4995. XE Kramer, (2003) 40 *CML Rev* 953.
[152] Case C–80/00 [2002] ECR I–4995, paras 40–1. See also *AGF Kosmos Assurances Générales v Surgil Trans Express* [2007] ILPr 363 (Court of Cassation, France).
[153] Case C–80/00 [2002] ECR I–4995, para 47.

refused under Article 34(3) if the judgment of another Member State is irreconcilable with a judgment of the court addressed in a matter falling outside the scope of Article 1. So, for example, a foreign judgment ordering a man to make maintenance payments to his wife (by virtue of his conjugal obligations to support her) is irreconcilable within the meaning of Article 34(3) with a divorce decree obtained in the state addressed, notwithstanding the fact that the divorce decree does not fall within the material scope of Article 1.[154]

13.3.39 Article 34(4) of the Brussels I Regulation provides that a judgment given by the courts of a Member State shall be refused recognition:

if the judgment is irreconcilable with an earlier judgment given in another Member State or in a third state involving the same cause of action and between the same parties, provided that the earlier judgment fulfils the conditions necessary for its recognition in the Member State addressed.

The solution provided by Article 34(4) is relatively straightforward. If, for example, A sues B in New York for breach of contract and obtains a judgment ordering B to pay damages and B subsequently obtains a declaration of non-liability from the Italian courts, the Italian judgment is not entitled to recognition in England under the Brussels I Regulation if the earlier New York judgment satisfies the conditions for recognition at common law. The result would be the same if the earlier judgment was given by the courts of another Member State and that judgment satisfied the conditions for recognition or enforcement under Chapter III of the Regulation. In the context of Article 34(4) the words 'cause of action' should be interpreted in the same way as under Article 27.[155]

Appeals in the State of Origin

13.3.40 Although a judgment against which an appeal is pending is enforceable under the Brussels I Regulation, there are obvious practical problems if, after a judgment granted by the courts of state A has been enforced in state B, an appeal against the judgment is upheld by the appellate courts of state A. Article 37 of the Brussels I Regulation provides:

A court of a Member State in which recognition is sought of a judgment given in another Member State may stay the proceedings if an ordinary appeal against the judgment has been lodged.

A court of a Member State in which recognition is sought of a judgment given in Ireland or the United Kingdom may stay the proceedings if enforcement is suspended in the state of origin, by reason of an appeal.

13.3.41 This provision is concerned with the situation where a party, in the course of litigation, wishes to plead a judgment which has been given in another Member State but which has not yet become unimpeachable. In order to remedy the inconvenience which would result if courts of the state of origin reversed the judgment, the court addressed is allowed 'to stay the proceedings upon the principal issue of which it is

---

[154] Case 145/86 *Hoffmann v Krieg* [1988] ECR 645. A Briggs, (1988) 8 *YBEL* 265; TC Hartley, (1991) 16 *EL Rev* 64.
[155] See paras 9.1.15–9.1.23.

seised, until the foreign judgment whose recognition is sought has become *res judicata* in the state in which it was given'.[156]

What is an 'Ordinary Appeal'?

13.3.42 While the idea behind Article 37 is apparent, there is a problem of interpretation surrounding the words 'ordinary appeal'. The Schlosser Report states that a 'clearly defined distinction between ordinary and extraordinary appeals is nowhere to be found'.[157] In *Industrial Diamond Supplies v Riva* the Court of Justice noted that:

although in some states the distinction between 'ordinary' and 'extraordinary' appeals is based on the law itself, in other legal systems the classification is made primarily or even purely in the works of learned authors while in a third group of states this distinction is completely unknown.[158]

Not surprisingly, therefore, the Court of Justice thought that the term 'ordinary appeal' has to be given an autonomous meaning.[159] The Court of Justice decided that a broad interpretation was appropriate; an ordinary appeal is 'any appeal which is such that it may result in the annulment or the amendment of the judgment which is the subject matter of the procedure for recognition or enforcement'.[160]

The Special Position of Appeals in Ireland and the United Kingdom

13.3.43 Although the decision of the Court of Justice in *Industrial Diamond Supplies v Riva* pre-dated the Convention whereby Ireland and the United Kingdom acceded to the Brussels Convention, it was decided that appeals against judgments given by the courts of Ireland and the United Kingdom required separate treatment. The Schlosser Report notes that there is no equivalent to the distinction between ordinary and extraordinary appeals in common law systems.[161] So, it is provided that, in cases involving the recognition of judgments given in Ireland or the United Kingdom, the court addressed may stay its proceedings in any case where an appeal in the state of origin has the effect of suspending enforcement of the judgment in that state.

The Exercise of Discretion

13.3.44 The court addressed may stay its proceedings on the application of either of the parties or of its own motion. However, no guidance is given on the criteria which the court should apply when deciding whether to exercise its discretion to grant a stay. The Court of Justice has indicated that the court addressed may, when considering an application for a stay in the context of the enforcement procedure, take into account only arguments

---

[156] Jenard Report, [1979] OJ C59/46–7.
[157] [1979] OJ C59/129, para 196(a). For a review of the approach adopted by the Member States, see Schlosser Report, [1979] OJ C59/12930, paras 196–202.
[158] Case 43/77 [1977] ECR 2175, para 22. TC Hartley, (1978) 3 *EL Rev* 160.
[159] Case 43/77 [1977] ECR 2175, para 27.
[160] Case 43/77 [1977] ECR 2175, para 42.
[161] [1979] OJ C59/128, para 195.

which the party against whom enforcement is authorised was unable to raise before the court of origin.[162] It would be appropriate for the same approach to be adopted in the context of cases where recognition, as opposed to enforcement, is at issue.

13.4 ENFORCEMENT OF JUDGMENTS UNDER THE BRUSSELS I REGULATION

Introduction

13.4.1   The basic idea underlying Chapter III is that enforcement should go hand in hand with recognition. Accordingly, enforcement can be refused only if there is a ground for refusing recognition.[163] Nevertheless, within Chapter III there are detailed rules governing the procedure for the enforcement of judgments granted by the courts of Member States in civil and commercial matters. Although as a general principle a judgment granted in one Member State should have the same effect in the state in which enforcement is sought as it does in the state of origin,[164] since the state in which enforcement is sought is obliged to lend its own remedies by way of execution,[165] the judgment may, in fact, be enforced rather differently from the way in which it would have been enforced in the state of origin.[166]

13.4.2   When the original Brussels Convention was being drafted the committee considered a number of possibilities: reference back to national laws, subject to certain rules of the Convention; ordinary contentious procedure; summary contentious procedure; or *ex parte* application. The committee decided to adopt a system based on an *ex parte* application.[167] One of the principles of the Brussels I Regulation is that the enforcement procedure is unified and simplified.[168] The basic procedure for enforcement of judgments under the Brussels I Regulation can be divided into four elements: (1) the application for enforcement; (2) the decision of the court whether or not to order enforcement; (3) appeals against enforcement; (4) appeals against non-enforcement.

Application for Enforcement

The Application

13.4.3   Article 38(1) of the Brussels I Regulation provides:

A judgment given in a Member State and enforceable in that State shall be enforced in another Member State when, on the application of any interested party, it has been declared enforceable there.

---

[162] Case C–183/90 *Van Dalfsen v Van Loon* [1991] ECR I–4743. See para 13.4.20.
[163] Jenard Report, [1979] OJ C95/47. See section 13.3.
[164] Case 145/86 *Hoffmann v Krieg* [1988] ECR 645, para 11.
[165] Case 148/84 *Deutsche Genossenschaftsbank v SA Brasserie du Pêcheur* [1985] ECR 1981.
[166] A Briggs, (1988) 8 *YBEL* 265, 266.
[167] Jenard Report, [1979] OJ C59/47.
[168] Almeida Cruz-Desantes Real-Jenard Report, [1990] OJ C189/38, para 4.

So far as English law is concerned, the procedure outlined in the Brussels I Regulation is supplemented by legislation[169] and Part 74 of the Civil Procedure Rules, which set out a registration scheme. Since the *exequatur* system for foreign judgments[170] does not exist in the law of the United Kingdom, it is provided that a judgment given in another Member State shall be enforced in England, Scotland or Northern Ireland where, on the application of any interested party,[171] it has been registered for enforcement in that part of the United Kingdom.[172] An application for registration in England, which is submitted to the High Court,[173] does not take the form of contentious proceedings; the application 'may be made without notice'.[174]

13.4.4 If the judgment is not enforceable in the state of origin, it cannot be enforced in other Member States under Chapter III.[175] In *Coursier v Fortis Bank*[176] the question was whether a French judgment for repayment of a loan (the first judgment) was enforceable in Luxembourg. Following the first judgment, there were further French proceedings, which became a court-supervised liquidation of the judgment debtor's business (the second judgment). The judgment debtor argued that the effect of the second judgment was to give him 'immunity from enforcement'—that is, the first judgment ceased to be enforceable against him in France, as a consequence of which it was no longer enforceable in Luxembourg under the Brussels Convention. The Court of Justice rejected the judgment debtor's argument. Having drawn attention to the distinction between enforceability and execution,[177] the Court of Justice decided that whether a judgment is 'enforceable':

refers solely to the enforceability, in formal terms, of foreign decisions and not to the circumstances in which such decisions may be executed in the State of origin.[178]

Although the first judgment could not be executed against the judgment debtor's assets in France, as the effect of the second judgment was not to extinguish the judgment creditor's rights, the first judgment remained 'enforceable'. This left the Court of Justice to consider the effect of the second judgment. This judgment was not entitled to recognition either under the Brussels Convention as it was excluded by Article 1(2) ('bankruptcy, proceedings relating to the winding-up of insolvent companies and other legal persons ...') or under the private international law of

---

[169] Civil Jurisdiction and Judgments Order 2001 (SI 2001/3929), sched 1.

[170] One of the questions raised by the Commission Green Paper is whether the *exequatur* procedure should be abolished, subject to the preservation of necessary safeguards: European Commission, Green Paper on the Review of Council Regulation (EC) No 44/2001 on jurisdiction and the recognition and enforcement of judgments in civil and commercial matters COM (2009) 175 final, pp 2–3.

[171] For consideration of some questions concerning whether a party is 'interested' for the purposes of Art 38, see *Re Haji-Ioannou (deceased)* [2009] ILPr 936.

[172] Art 38(2). See also Jenard-Möller Report, [1990] OJ C189/79, para 68.

[173] Art 39(1); Annex II.

[174] CPR 74.3(2).

[175] See *La Caisse Régionale de Crédit Agricole Nord de France v Ashdown* [2007] ILPr 348 (Tugendhat J), [2007] EWCA Civ 574. See also *Re Enforcement of an Italian Judgment* [1993] ILPr 353 (Court of Appeal, Frankfurt am Main).

[176] Case C–267/97 [1999] ECR I–2543. E Peel, (2001) 20 *YBEL* 352.

[177] See paras 13.4.28–13.4.29.

[178] Case C–267/97 [1999] ECR I–2543, para 29. See *Schmitz v Schmitz* [2006] ILPr 806 (Court of Cassation, France).

Luxembourg. Accordingly, there was no obstacle to the enforcement of the first judgment in Luxembourg.

13.4.5 A similar issue was raised in *Apostolides v Orams*,[179] in which the Court of Justice confirmed that whether a judgment is 'enforceable' in the state of origin for the purposes of Article 38(1) is a legal question, not a practical one. The defendants argued that a Cypriot judgment which related to land situated in the northern part of Cyprus, an area not under the control of the Republic of Cyprus, was not enforceable in England under the Brussels I Regulation on the basis that, in practical terms, the judgment could not be enforced in Cyprus. However, the Court of Justice held:

The fact that claimants might encounter difficulties in having judgments enforced in the northern area cannot deprive them of their enforceability and, therefore, does not prevent the courts of the Member State in which enforcement is sought from declaring such judgments enforceable. ... [T]he fact that a judgment given by the courts of a Member State concerning land situated in an area of that State over which its Government does not exercise effective control, cannot, as a practical matter, be enforced where the land is situated ... does not mean that such a judgment is unenforceable for the purposes of Article 38(1) of that regulation.[180]

Formalities

13.4.6 By way of general principle, Article 40(1) provides that the procedure for making the application 'shall be governed by the law of the Member State in which enforcement is sought'. The domestic law of the state in which enforcement is sought is relevant for determining matters such as:

the particulars which the application must contain, the number of copies which must be submitted to the court, the authority to which the application must be submitted, also, where necessary, the language in which it must be drawn up, and whether a lawyer should be instructed to appear.[181]

Indeed, the law of the state in which enforcement is sought governs the entire procedure for making the application.[182] However, the law of the state in which enforcement is sought must conform to the aims of the Brussels regime.[183]

13.4.7 A further requirement is imposed by Article 40(2), which provides that, as part of the application for an enforcement order, the applicant must 'give an address for service of process within the area of jurisdiction of the court applied to'.[184] The purpose of this requirement is twofold: first, it enables the applicant to be informed quickly of the court's decision on the application; secondly, it enables the defendant to institute an appeal.[185]

---

[179] Case C–420/07 [2010] 1 All ER (Comm) 950.
[180] Case C–420/07 [2010] 1 All ER (Comm) 950, 989 (paras 70–1).
[181] Jenard Report, [1979] OJ C59/49.
[182] Case 198/85 *Carron v Federal Republic of Germany* [1986] ECR 2437, para 10.
[183] Case 198/85 *Carron v Federal Republic of Germany* [1986] ECR 2437, para 14.
[184] Because furnishing an address for service is unknown in German law, Art 33(2) provides that, if the law of the state in which enforcement is sought does not provide for the furnishing of such an address, the applicant shall appoint a representative *ad litem*.
[185] Jenard Report, [1979] OJ C59/50.

13.4.8 Two points relating to the provision of the Brussels Convention which corresponds to Article 40 of the Regulation were considered by the Court of Justice in *Carron v Federal Republic of Germany*.[186] First, the Court of Justice ruled:

Where the law of the State in which enforcement is sought does not indicate the exact time at which an address for service is to be given, it must be held ... that it must be given sufficiently early to ensure that the proceedings are not improperly delayed and that the rights of the party against whom enforcement is sought are safeguarded. At the latest it must be given when the decision authorising enforcement is served.[187]

There is, however, no requirement that an address for service should be stated on the face of the enforcement order itself.[188] Secondly, the Court of Justice decided that, inasmuch as no sanction for non-compliance is provided, the sanction must be determined by the law of the state in which enforcement is sought.[189] An important qualification was, however, added to this principle. Any sanction imposed by the law of the state in which enforcement is sought 'may neither cast doubt on the validity of the enforcement order nor in any way prejudice the rights of the party against whom enforcement is sought'.[190]

13.4.9 Article 40(3) requires the applicant to attach to his application various documents including 'a copy of the judgment which satisfies the conditions necessary to establish its authenticity'[191] and it would seem from the terms of Chapter III that, if the person seeking an enforcement order is unable to produce a copy of the judgment or other appropriate documents, the court addressed is required to refuse to authorise enforcement. However, the Jenard Report suggests that the court should not refuse the application in this situation; instead 'the court may stay the proceedings and allow the applicant time to produce the documents'.[192] In *Van der Linden v Berufsgenossenschaft der Feinmechanik und Elektrotechnik*[193] the Court of Justice, having regard to the objectives of the Brussels Convention, adopted a flexible interpretation of the formal requirements. In this case, the Belgian court had ordered enforcement of a German judgment even though the plaintiff had not at that stage produced proof that the judgment had been served. The defendant appealed and, during the course of the appeal proceedings, the original judgment was re-served on the defendant in accordance with the requirements of Belgian law. The Court of Justice decided that the judgment was not rendered unenforceable by virtue of the fact that, at the time of the *ex parte* application for enforcement, the plaintiff did not provide proof that the judgment had been served.[194] If, however, the documents produced

---

[186] Case 198/85 [1986] ECR 2437.

[187] Case 198/85 [1986] ECR 2437, para 10. See *Office of Social Affairs and for Youth Karlsruhe v Ducatillon* [1991] ILPr 170 (Court of Cassation, France).

[188] *Rhatigan v Textiles y Confecciones Europeas SA* [1992] ILPr 40 (Supreme Court, Ireland).

[189] Case 198/85 [1986] ECR 2437, para 13.

[190] Case 198/85 [1986] ECR 2437, para 14.

[191] Art 53(1). However, it is not necessary for the judgment creditor to provide proof of due service of the document instituting the proceedings at the time of an application for a declaration of enforceability: *Re the Enforcement of an Austrian Judgment* [2005] ILPr 366 (Court of Appeal, Düsseldorf).

[192] [1979] OJ C59/50.

[193] Case C–275/94 [1996] ECR I–1393. A Briggs, (1996) 16 *YBEL* 601.

[194] Case C–275/94 [1996] ECR I–1393, para 19.

by the judgment creditor are not sufficient and the court cannot obtain sufficient information the application should be rejected.[195]

Security for Costs

13.4.10 One of the general principles of EU law is that Member States should not discriminate against citizens of other Member States on the basis of nationality. For this reason, the Court of Justice has ruled that a national procedural rule which requires a person from a Member State to give security for costs in a situation where no such security can be demanded from a national infringes EU law.[196] Article 50 provides that:

No security ... shall be required of any party who in one Member State applies for enforcement of a judgment given in another Member State on the ground that he is a foreign national or that he is not domiciled or resident in the State in which enforcement is sought.[197]

However, there is nothing to prevent the court requiring an applicant to give security in cases where, for some other reason, there is a good ground for doing so.[198]

The Decision

13.4.11 On completion of the formalities referred to in Article 40, '[t]he judgment shall be declared enforceable'.[199] The court's decision is based entirely on the *ex parte* application of the person seeking enforcement of the foreign judgment and '[t]he party against whom enforcement is sought shall not at this stage of the proceedings be entitled to make any submissions on the application'.[200] The insistence on the application for enforcement being by way of application without notice is to maintain the element of surprise which is necessary to ensure that the judgment debtor is not given an opportunity of withdrawing his assets from the jurisdiction.[201] At this stage of the process, the fact that the defendant may have a defence to enforcement is not a reason for the court refusing to make a declaration of enforceability. In England, the application is made to the High Court[202] and, once the decision to order enforcement has been made, the declaration of enforceability (which in England is referred to as the registration order) must be served on the party against whom enforcement is sought; if the judgment has not yet been served on the defendant, it should be served

---

[195] *Brähmer v Van Loon* [1986] ECC 178 (District Court, Breda).
[196] See Case C–43/95 *Data Delecta Aktiebolag v MSL Dynamics Ltd* [1996] ECR I–4661; Case C–323/95 *Hayes v Kronenberger GmbH* [1997] ECR I–1711; Case C–122/96 *Saldanha v Hiross Holding AG* [1997] ECR I–5325. See also Case C–398/92 *Mund & Fester v Hatrex International Transport* [1994] ECR I–467 (A Briggs, (1994) 14 *YBEL* 561).
[197] See Art 45; CPR 74.5(4).
[198] CPR 25.3.
[199] Art 41.
[200] Art 41. See *Re National Organisation Systems SA's Application* [2005] ILPr 728 (One Member First Instance Court, Athens).
[201] Jenard Report, [1979] OJ C59/50.
[202] Art 39, Annex II.

at this time along with the declaration of enforceability.[203] The registration order must inform the defendant of his right to appeal.[204]

Appeals against Enforcement

The First Appeal

13.4.12 Article 43(1) provides that the decision on the application for a declaration of enforceability may be appealed against by either party.[205] If a registration order is made by the High Court in relation to a judgment given in another Member State, the judgment debtor may appeal against this decision to the High Court.[206] It is provided that the appeal under Article 43(1) must be dealt with 'in accordance with the rules governing procedure in contradictory matters'.[207] The details of the procedure to be followed are to be found in Part 52 of the Civil Procedure Rules. Where an appeal is brought against the registration order, the appeal must be lodged within the period specified by Article 43. The general rule is that an appeal must be lodged within one month of the date of service of the declaration of enforceability; however, if the party against whom enforcement is authorised is domiciled in a Member State other than that in which the declaration of enforceability was given, the time for appealing is two months from the date of service of the order.[208] In *Société d'Informatique Service Réalisation Organisation v Ampersand Software BV* the Court of Justice indicated that the time limits for the lodging of an appeal must be strictly observed: 'No extension of time may be granted on account of distance.'[209]

13.4.13 However, in relation to a judgment debtor who is not domiciled in a Member State, the Jenard Report suggests that a certain amount of flexibility as regards time limits might be appropriate:

[I]f the party is domiciled outside the Community, the period within which an appeal may be lodged runs from the date when the decision is served or is deemed to have been served according to the law of the state in which the decision was given. In this case the period of one month may be extended on account of distance in accordance with the law of that state.[210]

English law provides that, where the person against whom enforcement is sought is not domiciled in a Member State, if an application is made within two months of

---

[203] Art 42.

[204] CPR 74.6(3)(c)(ii).

[205] Where C1 obtains a judgment against D in one Member State and a declaration of enforceability in another Member State, C2 (another of D's creditors) is not a 'party' for the purposes of Art 43 and cannot, therefore, lodge an appeal against the declaration of enforceability: Case C–167/08 *Draka NK Cables Ltd v Omnipol Ltd* [2009] ECR I–3477.

[206] Art 43(2), Annex III.

[207] Art 43(2).

[208] Art 43(5). In Case C–3/05 *Verdoliva v Van der Hoeven BV* [2006] ECR I–1597, the Court of Justice held that time started to run under the equivalent provision of the Brussels Convention from when the declaration of enforceability was duly served on the defendant; in the event of defective service, the mere fact that the defendant had notice of the declaration of enforceability was not sufficient to cause time to run.

[209] Case C–432/93 [1995] ECR I–2269, para 19. TC Hartley, (1996) 21 *EL Rev* 169.

[210] [1979] OJ C59/51.

service to extend time, the court may extend the period for filing an appellant's notice against the registration order.[211]

A Further Appeal on a Point of Law

13.4.14   Once the High Court has resolved the appeal against the registration order there is a further right of appeal, which—depending on the outcome of the first appeal—may be brought either by the judgment debtor or the judgment creditor. Under Article 44, a decision of the High Court on the first appeal (under Article 43), which is referred to as the 'judgment given on appeal', may be contested only by 'a single further appeal on a point of law' (the final appeal).[212] In the standard case, the final appeal will be heard by the Court of Appeal. However, in exceptional circumstances, the final appeal may be directed to the Supreme Court under the leap-frog procedure.

13.4.15   The scope of the final appeal provided for by Article 44 has been strictly limited by the Court of Justice. The final appeal relates only to the judgment given on appeal brought under Article 43—that is, the decision ruling on the merits of an appeal lodged against an enforcement order.[213] Article 44 does not permit an appeal either against interlocutory orders made by the court addressed in the context of the enforcement procedure[214] or against decisions taken by the court addressed under Article 46.[215] So, no appeal lies against a decision refusing to stay enforcement proceedings pending the outcome of an appeal in the state of origin.[216] Where, for example, the High Court refuses to grant a stay of enforcement under Article 46 (or grants a stay and subsequently lifts it), if the judgment debtor appeals to the Court of Appeal under Article 44 there can be no question of the Court of Appeal imposing a stay in the context of the 'single further appeal on a point of law'.[217] Even if the decision on the application under Article 46 is contained in the same judgment as the decision on the merits of the appeal against the enforcement order, there is no right of appeal under Article 44 against the decision taken under Article 46.[218] Moreover, it is only the judgment debtor (or judgment creditor) who can bring the final appeal under Article 44; no appeal can be brought by an interested third party.[219]

---

[211]   CPR 74.8(3).

[212]   Art 44, Annex IV.

[213]   Case C–183/90 *Van Dalfsen v Van Loon* [1991] ECR I–4743, para 21.

[214]   Case 258/83 *Calzaturificio Brennero sas v Wendel GmbH Schuhproduktion International* [1984] ECR 3971. TC Hartley, (1986) 11 *EL Rev* 95; K Lipstein, 'Enforcement of Judgments under the Jurisdiction and Judgments Convention: Safeguards' (1987) 36 *ICLQ* 873.

[215]   Case C–183/90 *Van Dalfsen v Van Loon* [1991] ECR I–4743.

[216]   See *Delloye v Lamberts* [1996] ILPr 504 (Court of Cassation, France).

[217]   Case C–432/93 *Société d'Informatique Service Réalisation Organisation v Ampersand Software BV* [1995] ECR I–2269, para 36. For differing views on this decision, see A Briggs, (1995) 15 *YBEL* 506 and JG Collier, [1996] *CLJ* 9.

[218]   Case C–183/90 *Van Dalfsen v Van Loon* [1991] ECR I–4743, paras 22–5.

[219]   Case C–172/91 *Sonntag v Waidmann* [1993] ECR I–1963, paras 34–5. See also *DSK Chornomorske Morske Paroplavstvo v Contship Containers Limited* [2004] ILPr 536 (Court of Cassation, Italy).

Grounds on which an Appeal may be Allowed

13.4.16   Article 45 provides:

(1) The court with which an appeal is lodged under Article 43 or Article 45 shall refuse or revoke a declaration of enforceability only on one of the grounds specified in Articles 34 and 35. It shall give its decision without delay.
(2) Under no circumstances may the foreign judgment be reviewed as to its substance.

Article 45(2) reiterates the rule contained in Article 36[220] and requires no further comment. The first paragraph is potentially misleading. Since there can be no enforcement of a judgment which is not entitled to recognition, it is entirely unexceptionable that Article 45(1) provides that the grounds in Articles 34 and 35 are an effective bar to enforcement of a foreign judgment under Chapter III. However, it would be wrong to think that these are the only grounds on which registration in England of judgments granted by the courts of other Member States may be refused. Two important points should be recalled. First, the judgment must be one which falls within the scope of Chapter III. This means that enforcement will be refused if the court addressed decides that the judgment is not within the material scope of Article 1,[221] whether or not the court of origin exercised jurisdiction over the defendant under the direct jurisdiction provisions contained in Chapter II. Similarly, enforcement will be refused if the order of the foreign court is not a 'judgment' within the meaning of Article 32.[222] Secondly, it is made clear in Article 38(1) that for a foreign judgment to be enforced under Chapter III it must be enforceable in the state of origin. So:

[i]f a judgment from which an appeal still lies or against which an appeal has been lodged in the state in which it was given cannot be provisionally enforced in that state, it cannot be enforced in the state in which enforcement is sought.[223]

Similarly, if the judgment has ceased to be enforceable in the country of origin, the judgment debtor's appeal should succeed.[224] Nevertheless, there is no general requirement that the judgment should be *res judicata* in order to be enforceable.[225] If, under the law of the state of origin, an appeal does not suspend the enforceability of the judgment, it is enforceable in the other Member States.

The Effect of an Appeal Pending before the Court of Origin

13.4.17   Where an appeal is brought under Article 43 or Article 44, Article 46(1) provides that the court addressed may stay the proceedings if an 'ordinary appeal'[226] has been lodged against the judgment in the state of origin or if the time for such an appeal has not

---

[220] See para 13.3.2.
[221] See section 3.3.
[222] See paras 13.1.2–13.1.9.
[223] Jenard Report, [1979] OJ C59/48.
[224] See the discussion of Advocate General La Pergola in Case C–267/97 *Coursier v Fortis Bank* [1999] ECR I–2543, paras 14–15.
[225] Case C–183/90 *Van Dalfsen v Van Loon* [1991] ECR I–4743, para 28.
[226] For the meaning of 'ordinary appeal' see para 13.3.42. As regards judgments given in Ireland and the United Kingdom Art 36(2) provides that an 'ordinary appeal' in this context means 'any form of appeal'.

yet expired. If an appeal has not yet been lodged the court addressed may specify the time within which such an appeal is to be lodged.[227] If, however, the time for the bringing of an appeal in the state of origin has expired, a stay cannot be granted under Article 46(1).[228] Where an appeal has been brought in the state of origin Article 46(3) permits the court addressed to make enforcement 'conditional on the provision of such security as it shall determine'. Article 46(3) does not, however, enable a court to order the applicant to provide security pending its own decision on the appeal against enforcement.[229]

13.4.18 In cases where an appeal has been lodged against the judgment in the state of origin—or the time for such an appeal has not yet expired—Article 46 gives the court addressed a broad range of options: the court may stay the proceedings (unconditionally or subject to terms); or authorise enforcement (with or without conditions); or, in appropriate cases, specify the time within which the defendant must lodge his appeal before the courts of the state of origin.[230] Any decision taken by the court addressed under Article 46 is final; there is no right of appeal under Article 44.[231]

13.4.19 The purpose of Article 46 is to enable the court addressed 'to stay the proceedings whenever reasonable doubt arises with regard to the fate of the decision in the state in which it was given'.[232] However, the effect of Article 46 is that 'the court before which recognition or enforcement is sought is not under a duty to stay the proceedings but merely has the power to do so'.[233] Since it provides an exception to the general principle that a judgment which is enforceable in the state of origin is entitled to enforcement in other Member States, Article 46 should be interpreted strictly.[234] In view of the fact that in no circumstances may the foreign judgment be reviewed on the merits,[235] the court addressed may not, when considering whether or not to grant a stay of enforcement proceedings under Article 46, take account of arguments which were raised before the court of origin,[236] or of the merits of the appeal brought by the judgment debtor in the state of origin.[237] Similarly, the scheme of Chapter III precludes the court addressed from considering arguments which could have been raised, but which were not raised before the court of origin.[238] The only arguments which the court may take into account for the purposes of Article 46 are 'arguments which the appellant was unable to raise before the court of the state where the judgment was given'.[239] The relevant factors are: the fact that the foreign judgment has been appealed against; the admissibility or

---

[227] Art 46(1).

[228] See *Noirhomme v Walklate* [1992] 1 Lloyd's Rep 427.

[229] Case 258/83 *Calzaturificio Brennero sas v Wendel GmbH Schuhproduktion International* [1984] ECR 3971.

[230] Jenard Report, [1979] OJ C59/52. P Kaye, 'Stay of Enforcement Proceedings under the European Judgments Convention: Factors Relevant to the Exercise of Discretion' [1991] *JBL* 261.

[231] Case C–183/90 *Van Dalfsen v Van Loon* [1991] ECR I–4743, para 25.

[232] Case 43/77 *Industrial Diamond Supplies v Riva* [1977] ECR 2175, para 33.

[233] Case 43/77 *Industrial Diamond Supplies v Riva* [1977] ECR 2175, para 32.

[234] Case C–183/90 *Van Dalfsen v Van Loon* [1991] ECR I–4743, para 30. A Briggs, (1991) 11 *YBEL* 530.

[235] Art 45(2).

[236] Case C–183/90 *Van Dalfsen v Van Loon* [1991] ECR I–4743, para 33.

[237] Case C–183/90 *Van Dalfsen v Van Loon* [1991] ECR I–4743, para 32.

[238] Case C–183/90 *Van Dalfsen v Van Loon* [1991] ECR I–4743, para 36.

[239] Case C–183/90 *Van Dalfsen v Van Loon* [1991] ECR I–4743, para 37.

inadmissibility of the appeal lodged before the court of origin; the nature of the injury which would be inflicted on the judgment debtor in the event of complete enforcement (and whether the injury would be irreversible); and whether protective measures would be sufficient from the judgment creditor's point of view if the enforcement proceedings were stayed.[240]

13.4.20 Article 46 does not allow judgment debtors to frustrate the enforcement process simply by bringing an appeal against the judgment in the state of origin. Since a judgment obtained in a Member State is *prima facie* enforceable, it would be wholly inappropriate for the court addressed to adopt a general practice of depriving a successful claimant of the fruits of the judgment by the imposition of a more or less automatic stay, merely on the ground that there is a pending appeal. Following the decision of the Court of Justice in *Van Dalfsen v Van Loon*[241] a stay of enforcement proceedings in cases where the judgment debtor has appealed in the state of origin should be a relatively rare occurrence. Nevertheless, the fact that the courts of the state of origin have refused to stay enforcement pending the judgment debtor's appeal does not mean that the courts of the state addressed should necessarily follow suit.[242] Article 46 requires the court addressed to strike a balance between the interests of the judgment creditor and those of the judgment debtor. By allowing unconditional enforcement, the court should not place the judgment debtor in a position such that he is unable to reverse the effects of enforcement. If the refusal of a stay would cause extreme hardship to the judgment debtor and the position of the judgment creditor can be protected by the grant of protective measures, it is not improper for the court to grant a stay of the enforcement proceedings pending the outcome of the appeal in the state of origin.[243]

Limitations on Enforcement

13.4.21 Since the application for enforcement is made by an application without notice, it would be unfair if, immediately on registration, the foreign judgment could be enforced by the judgment creditor without the judgment debtor being given the opportunity of being heard. Article 47(5), which deals with the period immediately following the determination of the application for enforcement, seeks to achieve a fair balance between the interests of the parties by providing that:

During the time specified for an appeal pursuant to Article 43(5) against the declaration of enforceability and until such an appeal has been determined, no measures of enforcement may be taken other than protective measures against the property of the party against whom enforcement is sought.

The protective measures which the applicant may obtain are those which are available under the law of the state in which enforcement is sought. It is important that during this initial period no irreversible measures of execution are taken against the judgment debtor.[244]

---

[240] Advocate General Van Gerven in Case C–183/90 *Van Dalfsen v Van Loon* [1991] ECR I–4743, para 19.

[241] Case C–183/90 [1991] ECR I–4743.

[242] *Société d'Informatique Service Réalisation Organisation v Ampersand Software BV* [1994] ILPr 55.

[243] *Petereit v Babcock International Holdings Ltd* [1990] 1 WLR 350.

[244] See the judgment of Moore-Bick J in *JH Rayner (Mincing Lane) Ltd v Republic of Brazil* [1999] 2 Lloyd's Rep 750.

13.4.22 Article 47(2) provides that the declaration of enforceability (which in the English context is the registration order) 'shall carry with it the power to proceed to any protective measures'. This means that the applicant may obtain protective measures *ex parte* before the defendant is informed of the court's decision to make a registration order in the applicant's favour. The Jenard Report stresses the importance of the availability of protective measures at the outset of the enforcement process; the applicant 'must be able to take quickly all measures necessary to prevent the judgment debtor from removing the assets on which execution is to be levied'.[245] In an appropriate case, the English court may make a worldwide freezing order under Article 47, even before the formalities required for registration have been completed.[246]

13.4.23 Article 47 is not a comprehensive code. For example, it does not give a list of the types of protective measures which may be taken, the kind and value of the property to which such measures may relate, the requirements for validity of the measures (such as whether the judgment creditor may carry out the measures himself or whether he is required to act through the medium of an officer of the court or other agent), the procedure for enforcing them and for verifying that they are in due form. Nevertheless, the power to grant protective measures is not a matter which is governed entirely by the procedural rules of the law of the state in which enforcement is sought.

13.4.24 Although the task of settling any matter which is not the subject of specific provisions in the Brussels I Regulation is left to the procedural law of the state addressed, the application of that law must not have the effect of contravening the principles laid down, whether expressly or by implication, by the Brussels regime.[247] In certain circumstances, the procedural law of the Member State in which enforcement is sought will have to yield to the requirements of the Brussels I Regulation. Whether a particular procedural rule is applicable depends on the content of the provision and its compatibility with the principles enshrined in Article 47.[248] For example, 'a judgment creditor on an application for protective measures cannot be required to prove or even make out a *prima facie* case on the merits, even if he might otherwise have to do so under national law'.[249]

13.4.25 Under English law equitable remedies, including injunctions, are discretionary. Moreover, the Civil Procedure Rules do not specify the circumstances in which protective measures under Article 47 should be granted. The Civil Procedure Rules state merely that the fact that there is an appeal against registration shall not 'prevent the court from making orders to preserve the property of the judgment debtor pending final determination of any issue relating to the enforcement of the judgment'.[250] Nevertheless, it would appear that the Brussels I Regulation has created a situation in which the court no longer has a discretion whether to allow

[245] [1979] OJ C59/52.
[246] *Banco Nacional de Commercio Exterior SNC v Empressa de Telecommunicaciones de Cuba SA* [2008] 1 WLR 1936.
[247] Case 119/84 *Capelloni v Pelkmans* [1985] ECR 3147, paras 20–1.
[248] Case 119/84 *Capelloni v Pelkmans* [1985] ECR 3147, para 21.
[249] Advocate General Slynn in Case 119/84 *Capelloni v Pelkmans* [1985] ECR 3147, 3150.
[250] CPR 74.9(3).

protective measures.[251] Where a judgment debtor appeals against a registration order, the logic of the scheme established by Chapter III is that the English court is obliged by Article 46 to grant a freezing injunction—up to the value of the judgment creditor's unsatisfied judgment—in respect of the defendant's assets. This was the solution adopted in Ireland in *Elwyn (Cottons) Ltd v Pearle Designs Ltd*[252] (albeit in a different domestic statutory framework). In this case the plaintiff, having obtained a judgment in England, applied both for its enforcement and for protective measures in the form of an order restraining the defendant from reducing its assets below a sum equivalent to the judgment debt. On an appeal against the decision refusing to grant the protective measures requested by the plaintiff Carroll J, having considered the Court of Justice's decision in *Capelloni v Pelkmans*, concluded that, since the measure applied for was one which the court had power to grant in respect of proceedings within its jurisdiction, the court was not entitled to refuse the order sought.[253] If the court determines the appeal brought by the judgment debtor pursuant to Article 43 in the applicant's favour—thereby confirming the registration order—Article 47 ceases to have any limiting effect and the applicant may proceed to execution.

Appeals Against a Refusal to Enforce

13.4.26   The procedure which allows a judgment debtor to appeal against a declaration of enforceability also permits a judgment creditor to appeal against a refusal to order enforcement.[254] As already noted, the appeal under Article 43(1) must be dealt with 'in accordance with the rules governing procedure in contradictory matters'.[255] This requirement has been strictly interpreted by the Court of Justice.[256] Even if the judgment creditor's application for enforcement under Article 38(1) is rejected on purely formal grounds (for example, because of the judgment creditor's failure to produce the documents required by Article 53) the appeal under Article 43 must be in the form of contentious proceedings, notwithstanding the fact that, by allowing the judgment debtor's participation, the enforcement proceedings are deprived of any element of surprise. If a judgment creditor's appeal under Article 43 is unsuccessful, there is the possibility of a single further appeal on a point of law under Article 44. As regards the first appeal, Article 43(4) provides that the judgment debtor is to be summoned to appear and, if he fails to do so, Article 26(2) and (4) shall apply even if the judgment debtor is not domiciled in a Member State.

---

[251] Jenard Report, [1979] OJ C59/52.
[252] [1990] ILPr 40. See G Hogan, 'The Judgments Convention and Mareva Injunctions in the United Kingdom and Ireland' (1989) 14 *EL Rev* 191, 200–04.
[253] [1990] ILPr 40, 42.
[254] Art 43(1).
[255] Art 43(2).
[256] Case 178/83 *Firma P v Firma K* [1984] ECR 3033. TC Hartley, (1985) 10 *EL Rev* 233.

The Relationship between National Law and Chapter III

The Exclusivity and Autonomy of the Brussels I Regulation

13.4.27 The procedure for enforcement set out in Chapter III is exclusive in the sense that judgments given in Member States which fall within the scope of Article 1 may be enforced only under Chapter III; a judgment creditor may not seek to rely on the common law.[257] The fact that the costs of enforcement under the Brussels I Regulation might be considerably higher than those under the common law does not entitle a judgment creditor to side-step the enforcement procedure laid down in Chapter III. Furthermore, in order to achieve the objective of simplifying enforcement procedures, Chapter III establishes 'an enforcement procedure which constitutes an autonomous and complete system, including the matter of appeals'.[258] The procedure established by Chapter III is comprehensive and may not be supplemented by the domestic law of the state in which enforcement is sought.

Enforcement and Execution

13.4.28 The Brussels I Regulation regulates the procedure for obtaining an order for enforcement but does not deal with execution itself, which continues to be governed by the domestic law of the court of the state in which execution is sought.[259] Consequently, a foreign judgment for which an enforcement order has been issued is executed in accordance with the procedural rules of the law of the country in which execution is sought, including its rules on legal remedies.[260]

13.4.29 The general principle that execution is left to the internal law of the state in which execution is sought is subject to an exception which was formulated in *Hoffmann v Krieg*.[261] The Court of Justice considered that the application, for the purposes of the execution of a judgment, of the procedural rules of the state in which enforcement is sought may not impair the effectiveness of the Brussels regime as regards enforcement orders.[262] Accordingly, as a general rule, a judgment debtor cannot rely on remedies available under the law of the state in which execution is sought when an appeal against execution of a foreign judgment for which an enforcement order has been issued is lodged 'by the same person who could have appealed against the enforcement order' and 'is based on an argument which could have been raised in such an appeal'.[263] A judgment debtor should not normally be allowed to use defences

---

[257] Case 42/76 *de Wolf v Harry Cox BV* [1976] ECR 1759.

[258] Case 148/84 *Deutsche Genossenschaftsbank v SA Brasserie du Pêcheur* [1985] ECR 1981, para 17.

[259] Case 148/84 *Deutsche Genossenschaftsbank v SA Brasserie du Pêcheur* [1985] ECR 1981, para 18; Case 119/84 *Capelloni v Pelkmans* [1985] ECR 3147, para 16.

[260] Case 145/86 *Hoffmann v Krieg* [1988] ECR 645, para 28. See *Noirhomme v Walklate* [1992] 1 Lloyd's Rep 427. See also *GN Preziosi di Gori & Nibi sdf v Swiss Gold Imports plc* [1997] ILPr 509 (Supreme Court, Sweden).

[261] Case 145/86 [1988] ECR 645.

[262] Case 145/86 [1988] ECR 645, para 29.

[263] Case 145/86 [1988] ECR 645, para 30.

to execution under the law of the state in which execution is sought as a way of avoiding the procedures and time-limits established by the Brussels I Regulation.[264]

13.5 AUTHENTIC INSTRUMENTS AND COURT SETTLEMENTS UNDER THE BRUSSELS I REGULATION

13.5.1   Chapter IV makes provision for the enforcement of authentic instruments and court settlements in the same way as judgments. The basic scheme for the enforcement of judgments (under Chapter III) is available (subject to some modifications) for the enforcement of authentic instruments and court settlements falling within the scope of the Brussels I Regulation.[265]

Authentic Instruments

13.5.2   The original Brussels Convention broke new ground in formulating rules for the enforcement of authentic instruments.[266] Although it appears that the cross-border enforcement of authentic instruments is relatively uncommon,[267] equivalent provisions were included in the Lugano Convention and in the Brussels I Regulation. An authentic instrument has a status which is different from an ordinary contract. To be regarded as authentic for the purposes of Chapter IV, an instrument must satisfy three conditions: first, the authenticity of the instrument should have been established by a public authority; secondly, this authenticity should relate to the content of the instrument and not only, for example, the signature; thirdly, the instrument has to be enforceable as such in the state of origin.[268] To fall within the enforcement regime an instrument must contain a statement of what has been agreed between the parties and must be made in the presence of an authorised person who is not himself concerned in the agreement. An order for costs which is drawn up by an authorised person, but for his own benefit, cannot be an authorised instrument for the purposes of Chapter IV.[269] Similarly, an acknowledgement of indebtedness, whose authenticity has not been established by a public authority or other authority empowered for that purpose, is not an authentic instrument notwithstanding that it is enforceable under the law of the state of origin.[270] There is no equivalent to an authentic instrument in English law.

---

[264] The position is different, however, if—as in *Hoffmann v Krieg* itself—the objection to execution raised by the judgment debtor is based on factors which are outside the material scope of the Brussels regime.

[265] See Civil Jurisdiction and Judgments (Authentic Instruments and Court Settlements) Order 1993, SI 1993/604; Civil Jurisdiction and Judgments (Authentic Instruments and Court Settlements) Order 2001, SI 2001/3928; CPR 74.11.

[266] Jenard Report, [1979] OJ C59/56.

[267] Jenard-Möller Report, [1990] OJ C189/80, para 72. But see Case 148/84 *Deutsche Genossenschaftsbank v SA Brasserie du Pêcheur* [1985] ECR 1981.

[268] Jenard-Möller Report, [1990] OJ C189/80, para 72.

[269] *Re Enforcement of a Foreign Bill of Costs* [1983] ECC 551 (District Court, Maastricht).

[270] Case C-260/97 *Unibank A/S v Christensen* [1999] ECR I-3715.

13.5.3   It is provided that the procedure for the enforcement of judgments is equally applicable to the enforcement of authentic instruments. Article 57(1) of the Brussels I Regulation states:

A document which has been formally drawn up or registered as an authentic instrument and is enforceable in one Member State shall, in another Member State, be declared enforceable there, on application made in accordance with the procedures provided for in Articles 38 et seq. The court with which an appeal is lodged under Article 43 or Article 44 shall refuse or revoke a declaration of enforceability only if enforcement of the instrument is manifestly contrary to public policy in the Member State addressed.

To be enforceable in other Member States the instrument must satisfy the conditions necessary to establish its authenticity in the state of origin.[271] The provisions of Section 3 of Chapter III apply as appropriate.[272]

Court Settlements

13.5.4   The regime that applies to authentic instruments also governs the recognition and enforcement of court settlements. Article 58 of the Brussels I Regulation provides:

A settlement which has been approved by a court in the course of proceedings and is enforceable in the Member State in which it was concluded shall be enforceable in the State addressed under the same conditions as authentic instruments.

This provision is included because under the laws of Germany and the Netherlands a settlement which has been approved by a court in the course of proceedings is enforceable without further formality.[273] Settlements occurring outside courts do not fall within Chapter IV; likewise, commercial bills and cheques are not covered.[274]

Grounds for Refusing Enforcement

13.5.5   The defences to recognition and enforcement relating to conflicting judgments under the Brussels I Regulation[275] do not apply by analogy to a case involving a conflict between, on the one hand, a judgment given by the courts of one Member State and, on the other, a court settlement obtained in another Member State.[276] It is provided that an authentic instrument or court settlement may be refused enforcement only if it is contrary to public policy in the state addressed. When considering whether to refuse enforcement of an authentic instrument on grounds of public policy, the court should have regard to the contents of the instrument as opposed to the circumstances surrounding the making of it.[277]

---

[271] Brussels I Reg, Art 57(3).
[272] Brussels I Reg, Art 57(4).
[273] Jenard Report, [1979] OJ C59/56.
[274] Jenard-Möller Report, [1990] OJ C189/80, para 72.
[275] Brussels I Reg, Art 34(3), (4). See paras 13.3.35–13.3.39.
[276] Case C–414/92 *Solo Kleinmotoren GmbH v Boch* [1994] ECR I–2237, para 19. A Briggs, (1994) 14 *YBEL* 568.
[277] *Guyot De Mischaegen v Generale Bankmij BV* [1990] ILPr 349 (District Court, Roermond).

13.5.6   It is not to be expected that, where a judgment has been granted in state A, a conflicting court settlement obtained in state B will be enforced in state A. In this type of case the courts of state A may decide that enforcement of the foreign court settlement is contrary to public policy. Similarly, where a court settlement is obtained in state A and a conflicting judgment is subsequently granted by the courts of state B, if the judgment creditor seeks to enforce the judgment in state A, enforcement of the judgment may be refused on the ground of public policy. Where necessary the public policy defence[278] can be applied to 'a case where the circumstances are quite out of the ordinary'.[279]

13.6 RECOGNITION AND ENFORCEMENT OF JUDGMENTS WITHIN THE UNITED KINGDOM

Introduction

13.6.1   Since the Judgments Extension Act 1868 there has been in existence a statutory regime designed to facilitate the reciprocal recognition and enforcement of judgments given within the United Kingdom. The Civil Jurisdiction and Judgments Act 1982 repealed all the earlier legislation and established a new regime, which is to be found in Part II of the Act: sections 18 and 19 (supplemented by schedules 6 and 7 to the 1982 Act) deal with enforcement and recognition respectively.

13.6.2   In the context of commercial matters the scope of sections 18 and 19 is very wide. The regime for the recognition and enforcement of judgments given by the courts of the constituent parts of the United Kingdom extends to 'any judgment or order (by whatever name called) given or made by a court of law in the United Kingdom',[280] as well as to 'any award or order made by a tribunal in any part of the United Kingdom which is enforceable in that part without an order of a court of law'[281] and to fines for contempt of court.[282] Section 18 also applies to arbitral awards.[283] There are, however, express exclusions from the scope of section 18, of which the most important are judgments given in the exercise of jurisdiction in relation to insolvency law, within the meaning of section 426 of the Insolvency Act 1986,[284] and provisional, including protective, measures (other than orders for the making of an interim payment).[285] Although the scope of section 19 is broadly the same as section 18,[286] there are a few additional minor exclusions.[287]

---

[278] Brussels I Reg, Art 34(1).
[279] Advocate General Gulmann in Case C–414/92 *Solo Kleinmotoren GmbH v Boch* [1994] ECR I–2237, para 32.
[280] Civil Jurisdiction and Judgments Act 1982, s 18(2)(a). Section 50 of the 1982 Act provides that a 'court of law' includes: (1) in Northern Ireland—the Court of Appeal, the High Court, and a county court; (2) in Scotland—the Court of Session and a sheriff court; and (3) the Supreme Court.
[281] Civil Jurisdiction and Judgments Act 1982, s 18(2)(d).
[282] Civil Jurisdiction and Judgments Act 1982, s 18(4)(b).
[283] The recognition and enforcement of arbitral awards under the 1982 Act is discussed at paras 24.5.1–24.5.3.
[284] Civil Jurisdiction and Judgments Act 1982, s 18(3)(ba).
[285] Civil Jurisdiction and Judgments Act 1982, s 18(5)(d).
[286] Civil Jurisdiction and Judgments Act 1982, s 19(2).
[287] Civil Jurisdiction and Judgments Act 1982, s 19(3).

Recognition

13.6.3   The recognition in England of judgments given by the courts of Scotland and Northern Ireland is dealt with by section 19(1), which provides:

A judgment to which this section applies given in one part of the United Kingdom shall not be refused recognition in another part of the United Kingdom solely on the ground that, in relation to that judgment, the court which gave it was not a court of competent jurisdiction according to the rules of private international law in force in that other part.

It is far from obvious what the effect of this provision is meant to be. Three points may, however, be noted. First, the mere fact that the original court did not have jurisdiction in the private international law sense is not a basis for refusing recognition. Secondly, recognition of a judgment given in Scotland or Northern Ireland cannot be refused on the basis of section 32 of the 1982 Act.[288] Thirdly, although section 19(1) makes no reference to the problem of irreconcilable judgments, the 1982 Act provides that enforcement may be refused if the judgment given in another part of the United Kingdom conflicts with an earlier judgment given by a court of the country addressed.[289] There is no reason why recognition of a judgment should not be refused on the same basis.

13.6.4   This still leaves a number of questions unanswered. The literal wording of section 19(1)—in particular, the use of the word 'solely'—suggests that a judgment given in Scotland or Northern Ireland may be refused recognition in England if the original court's lack of jurisdiction in the private international law sense is coupled with some other defence (such as fraud). From the point of view of policy, however, this interpretation makes little sense and should be rejected. An alternative view is that, since Part II of the 1982 Act makes no mention of the common law defences other than lack of jurisdiction in the international sense, a judgment given in Scotland or Northern Ireland may be refused recognition if the judgment was procured by fraud or if the original proceedings involved a breach of natural justice or if recognition of the judgment is contrary to English public policy.[290] The somewhat surprising consequence of this alternative view, however, is that a judgment given in Scotland and Northern Ireland would be more likely to be refused recognition than a judgment granted by the courts of another Member State.

13.6.5   Although the position cannot be regarded as anything other than uncertain, it seems likely that the traditional common law defences based on natural justice and fraud are not available in cases falling within Part II of the 1982 Act. Within the United Kingdom, it is not unreasonable that a party who alleges fraud or a breach of the principles of natural justice should pursue his remedies, if any, before the courts of the country of origin. However, it would be surprising if the English courts were unable to refuse recognition under Part II of the 1982 Act in a case where the judgment in question is contrary to English public policy.

---

[288] A judgment given in Scotland or Northern Ireland is not an 'overseas judgment': Civil Jurisdiction and Judgments Act 1982, s 50.

[289] Civil Jurisdiction and Judgments Act 1982, sched 6, para 10(b) and sched 7, para 9(b).

[290] A Layton and H Mercer, *European Civil Practice* (London, Sweet & Maxwell, 2nd edn, 2004) 1289.

Enforcement

Introduction

13.6.6   Although there are commentators who accept—either explicitly or implicitly—that the effect of Part II of the 1982 Act is to create situations in which a judgment which would be enforceable under section 18 may be refused recognition under section 19,[291] as a matter of general principle a judgment which is not entitled to recognition should not be enforced. Accordingly, a judgment given by the courts of Scotland or Northern Ireland should be refused enforcement in England not only in the circumstances expressly identified in section 18 (as supplemented by schedules 6 and 7), but to the extent that the judgment is not entitled to recognition. Section 18(1) provides:

In relation to any judgment to which this section applies—

(a) Schedule 6 shall have effect for the purpose of enabling any money provisions contained in the judgment to be enforced in a part of the United Kingdom other than the part in which the judgment was given; and
(b) Schedule 7 shall have effect for the purpose of enabling any non-money provisions so contained to be enforced.

13.6.7   The regime put in place by the 1982 Act is mandatory and exclusive. As regards those judgments falling within the scope of section 18, the only way in which the judgment of the courts of Scotland and Northern Ireland can be enforced is by registration under schedule 6 or 7.[292] Where a single judgment contains both money provisions and non-money provisions, the money provisions must be registered under schedule 6 and the non-money provisions under schedule 7.

Money Judgments: Schedule 6

13.6.8   The enforcement of a money judgment (which is defined as a 'provision for the payment of one or more sums of money'[293]) is effected by a system of registration. The basic scheme is for the person seeking enforcement to obtain a certificate from the court of the country of origin[294] and to register the certificate in the country where enforcement is sought. The certificate will state the sum or aggregate of sums payable under the judgment (including interest on the judgment debt).[295] There are various circumstances in which a certificate cannot be issued: first, if the time for bringing an appeal has not expired; or, secondly, if an appeal has been brought and has not been finally determined; or, thirdly, if enforcement of the judgment is stayed or suspended; or, fourthly, if the time for enforcement of the judgment has expired.[296]

   13.6.9   Once a certificate has been issued, any interested party may apply for registration in the High Court.[297] The reasonable costs of obtaining a certificate and

---

[291] See, eg, S Lane, 'Free Movement of Judgments within the EEC' (1986) 35 *ICLQ* 629, 633–4.
[292] Civil Jurisdiction and Judgments Act 1982, s 18(8). The regime is not, however, exclusive for arbitral awards within s 18(2)(e) of the Civil Jurisdiction and Judgments Act 1982.
[293] Civil Jurisdiction and Judgments Act 1982, sched 6, para 1.
[294] Civil Jurisdiction and Judgments Act 1982, sched 6, para 2.
[295] Civil Jurisdiction and Judgments Act 1982, sched 6, para 4.
[296] Civil Jurisdiction and Judgments Act 1982, sched 6, para 3.
[297] Civil Jurisdiction and Judgments Act 1982, sched 6, para 5. See CPR 74.15(2).

registering it are recoverable[298] and provision is made for the payment of interest on the judgment debt.[299] Once registered, the judgment is of the same force and effect as if the judgment had been given by the registering court.[300]

13.6.10   It is expressly provided that the court must set aside registration if registration is contrary to the provisions of schedule 6 and the court may set aside registration if it is satisfied that the matter in dispute in the proceedings in which the judgment was given had previously been the subject of a judgment by another court having jurisdiction in the matter.[301] The court may stay proceedings for enforcement if it is satisfied that any person against whom enforcement is sought is entitled and intends to apply to have the judgment quashed or set aside in the country of origin.[302]

Non-money Judgments: Schedule 7

13.6.11   Prior to the entry into force of the 1982 Act, it was not possible to enforce in England non-money judgments granted by the courts of Scotland and Northern Ireland. Since the Brussels regime makes provision for the recognition and enforcement of judgments irrespective of whether or not they are for a sum of money, it was appropriate to reform the internal law of the United Kingdom. Schedule 7 to the 1982 Act sets out the procedure for the enforcement of non-money judgments (which are defined as provisions 'for any relief or remedy not requiring payment of a sum of money').[303] The procedure is broadly similar to that provided by schedule 6.

13.6.12   The person seeking enforcement of a non-money judgment in England must obtain a certified copy of the judgment from the court of the country of origin.[304] The certified copy, which cannot be issued if certain conditions are satisfied,[305] must include both any money provisions and any provisions which relate to matters which fall outside the scope of section 18 of the 1982 Act.[306] The application must be made to the High Court and must be accompanied by the certified copy of the judgment and written evidence stating, *inter alia*, that the judgment is enforceable and that no appeal may be brought or is pending.[307] An application for registration of a non-money judgment may be made without notice.[308] Once registered in the High Court a non-money judgment has the same force and effect as if the judgment had been given by the English court.[309] The reasonable costs of obtaining a certified copy of the judgment and registering it are recoverable.[310]

---

[298] Civil Jurisdiction and Judgments Act 1982, sched 6, para 7.
[299] Civil Jurisdiction and Judgments Act 1982, sched 6, para 8.
[300] Civil Jurisdiction and Judgments Act 1982, sched 6, para 6.
[301] Civil Jurisdiction and Judgments Act 1982, sched 6, para 10.
[302] Civil Jurisdiction and Judgments Act 1982, sched 6, para 9.
[303] Civil Jurisdiction and Judgments Act 1982, sched 7, para 1.
[304] Civil Jurisdiction and Judgments Act 1982; sched 7, para 2.
[305] Civil Jurisdiction and Judgments Act 1982, sched 7, para 3. The substance of this paragraph is the same as para 3 of sched 6.
[306] Civil Jurisdiction and Judgments Act 1982, sched 7, para 4.
[307] Civil Jurisdiction and Judgments Act 1982, sched 7, para 5; CPR 74.18(3).
[308] CPR 74.18(2).
[309] Civil Jurisdiction and Judgments Act 1982, sched 7, para 6.
[310] Civil Jurisdiction and Judgments Act 1982, sched 7, para 7.

13.6.13   Registration must be refused if compliance with the judgment would involve a breach of English law[311] and registration must be set aside if registration is contrary to schedule 7.[312] The court may set aside registration if the subject-matter of the proceedings which led to the judgment in question had previously been the subject of a judgment by another court having jurisdiction in the matter.[313] The court may stay proceedings for enforcement if it is satisfied that any person against whom enforcement is sought is entitled and intends to apply to have the judgment quashed or set aside in the country of origin.[314]

13.7 JUDGMENTS AGAINST STATES AND EUROPEAN UNION JUDGMENTS

Recognition of Judgments Given against the United Kingdom

13.7.1   The regime for the recognition of judgments given against the United Kingdom is contained in the State Immunity Act 1978. Section 18 provides for the recognition of judgments given against the United Kingdom by the courts of other states which are also party to the European Convention on State Immunity of 1972. In order for such a judgment to be entitled to recognition in England it must be final and it must have been given in proceedings in which the United Kingdom was not entitled to immunity by virtue of provisions corresponding to those of sections 2–11 of the 1978 Act.[315]

13.7.2   There are, however, various defences to recognition. First, an English court may refuse to recognise a foreign judgment given against the United Kingdom if: (1) to accord recognition would be manifestly contrary to public policy; or (2) any party to the original proceedings did not have an adequate opportunity to present his case; or (3) the judgment was given in circumstances in which the provisions corresponding to section 12 of the 1978 Act[316] were not complied with and the United Kingdom neither entered an appearance nor applied to have the judgment set aside.[317] Secondly, an English court must refuse recognition if: proceedings between the same parties on the same issues are pending in the United Kingdom or in another state which is party to the 1972 Convention (as long as those proceedings were instituted first); or there is an earlier inconsistent judgment of the courts of the United Kingdom or of another state which is party to the 1972 Convention; or the foreign judgment concerns an interest of the United Kingdom in property and either an English court would not have regarded itself as having jurisdiction in such circumstances or an English court, applying English conflicts rules, would have arrived at a decision different from that of foreign court.[318]

---

[311] Civil Jurisdiction and Judgments Act 1982, sched 7, para 5(5).
[312] Civil Jurisdiction and Judgments Act 1982, sched 7, para 9.
[313] Civil Jurisdiction and Judgments Act 1982, sched 7, para 9.
[314] Civil Jurisdiction and Judgments Act 1982, sched 7, para 8.
[315] State Immunity Act 1978, s 18(1).
[316] See paras 2.3.58–2.3.63.
[317] State Immunity Act 1978, s 19(1).
[318] State Immunity Act 1978, s 19(2).

Recognition and Enforcement of Judgments Given against Other States

13.7.3 The 1978 Act does not deal with the question of foreign judgments given against foreign states. Section 31(1) of the Civil Jurisdiction and Judgments Act 1982 provides:

A judgment given by a court of an overseas country against a state other than the United Kingdom or the state to which that court belongs shall be recognised and enforced in the United Kingdom, if and only if—

(a) it would be so recognised and enforced if it had not been given against a State; and
(b) that court would have had jurisdiction in the matter if it had applied rules corresponding to those applicable to such matters in the United Kingdom in accordance with sections 2 to 11 of the State Immunity Act 1978.[319]

This provision does not apply to judgments which are given in proceedings under international conventions and which are entitled to recognition or enforcement under the Foreign Judgments (Reciprocal Enforcement) Act 1933.[320]

European Union Judgments

13.7.4 Secondary legislation provides the framework for the recognition and enforcement in the United Kingdom of judgments given by the Court of Justice of the European Union and decisions of other institutions which impose monetary obligations on parties other than states.[321] A judgment or decision to which the 1972 Order relates is registered in the High Court and takes effect in the same way as a decision of the High Court.[322]

---

[319] See *NML Capital Ltd v Republic of Argentina* [2009] QB 579. H Fox, 'Enforcement of judgments against foreign states: "… the kind of coherent law we ought to have?"' (2009) 125 *LQR* 544. For a discussion of the scope of State Immunity Act 1978, ss 2–11, see paras 2.3.11–2.3.38.
[320] Civil Jurisdiction and Judgments Act 1982, s 31(3).
[321] European Communities (Enforcement of Community Judgments) Order 1972, SI 1972/1590, as amended by European Communities (Enforcement of Community Judgments) (Amendment) Order 2003, SI 2003/3204.
[322] For the relevant procedure for enforcement, see CPR 74.19–26.

PART II

CHOICE OF LAW

14

CHOICE OF LAW IN CONTRACT

14.0.1 In the early 1990s the English choice of law rules relating to contractual obligations underwent a revolution. For most practical purposes the period of common law development came to a halt on 1 April 1991, when the Rome Convention on the Law Applicable to Contractual Obligations was brought into force by the Contracts (Applicable Law) Act 1990.[1] The Rome Convention was superseded by the Rome I Regulation on the law applicable to contractual obligations. The Regulation came into effect on, and applies to contracts concluded on or after, 17 December 2009 (section 14.1).[2]

14.0.2 General choice of law rules—the vast majority of which are to be found in the Rome I Regulation—can be divided into three groups. First, Articles 3 and 4 are the core provisions of the Regulation: Article 3 identifies the applicable law in cases where the parties have chosen the law to govern their contractual relations, whether or not expressly; Article 4 contains the provisions for ascertaining the applicable law in situations where the parties have not made a choice (section 14.2). Secondly, although the applicable law plays the predominant role in regulating the rights and obligations of the parties, there are circumstances in which the applicable law may yield to the mandatory rules of the forum (or of another country) or to public policy (section 14.3). Thirdly, not all aspects of a contract are necessarily governed by the same law. It is important to have regard to the way in which the various choice of law rules apply to specific aspects of a contract, such as material and formal validity, interpretation, performance and the quantification of contractual damages (section 14.4). Not all contracts are governed exclusively by these general rules. The Regulation includes specific choice of law rules for certain types of contract (section 14.5). The Regulation also has provisions covering issues such as assignment and subrogation (section 14.6).

14.0.3 While the Rome I Regulation is different from the Rome Convention in a number of significant respects, many of the Convention's provisions are transposed virtually unchanged to the Regulation. Thus, the body of English case law relating to

---

[1] See the 3rd edition of this work: J Hill, *International Commercial Disputes in English Courts* (Oxford, Hart Publishing, 3rd edn, 2005). See also AL Diamond, 'Conflict of Laws in the EEC' (1979) 22 *CLP* 155; TC Hartley, 'Beyond the Proper Law' (1979) 5 *EL Rev* 236; AJE Jaffey, 'The English Proper Law Doctrine and the EEC Convention' (1984) 33 *ICLQ* 531; O Lando, 'The EEC Convention on the Law Applicable to Contractual Obligations' (1987) 24 *CML Rev* 159; R Merkin, 'Contracts (Applicable Law) Act 1990' [1991] *JBL* 205; CGJ Morse, 'The EEC Convention on the Law Applicable to Contractual Obligations' (1982) 2 *YBEL* 107; PM North, 'The EEC Convention on the Law Applicable to Contractual Obligations' [1980] *JBL* 382; PR Williams, 'The EEC Convention on the Law Applicable to Contractual Obligations' (1986) 35 *ICLQ* 1; J Young, 'The Contracts (Applicable Law) Act 1990' [1991] *LMCLQ* 314.

[2] Reg (EC) 593/2008, [2008] OJ L177/6. See Art 24. A report shall be submitted by the Commission to the European Parliament, the Council and the European Economic and Social Committee on the application of the Regulation by 17 June 2013. The report may be accompanied by proposals to amend the Regulation. See Art 27(1).

the interpretation of the Convention[3] remains relevant for the interpretation of the Regulation for those provisions that remain unchanged. A drawback of an instrument in the form of a Regulation is that there is no official explanatory report accompanying it. However, an official report accompanied the Rome Convention, the Giuliano-Lagarde Report,[4] and this report remains good authority for the unchanged provisions in the Regulation; it is referred to below in relation to the Regulation where appropriate. There is also a large body of cases decided under the common law; some of these cases are used to illustrate the way in which the Regulation is intended to work, as many of the issues which arise under the Regulation are the same as (or similar to) issues considered by the courts in the context of the common law rules. However, two points should be stressed. First, in some respects the similarity between the common law rules and the provisions of the Regulation is more apparent than real. There are dangers in attempting to reason from the common law cases to a solution under the Regulation. Secondly, it must be remembered that precedents decided in the context of the common law have no direct authority when considering questions of interpretation which arise under the Regulation.

14.1 INTRODUCTION

The Common Law[5]

14.1.1 The development of choice of law rules in matters relating to contract has been described as 'one of the great achievements of the English judiciary'[6] in the late 19th and 20th centuries. The doctrine of the proper law of the contract reflects the doctrine of party autonomy, the underlying basis of English contract law itself. The influence of the common law rules in other jurisdictions has been considerable, the English private international law of contracts 'being recognised and followed in practically the whole world'.[7]

14.1.2 At common law parties are free to choose the law governing their contractual relationship. Furthermore, it would seem that the chosen law need not have any connection with the contract. In *Vita Food Products Inc v Unus Shipping Co Ltd*[8] the Privy Council upheld a choice of English law even though all the relevant factors

---

[3] The Court of Justice has handed down only one judgment so far on the interpretation of the Rome Convention: Case C–133/08 *ICF v Balkenende Oosthuizen BV* [2010] ILPr 37. The dearth of case law from the Court of Justice is partly due to the belated entry into force of the two Protocols on interpretation which conferred jurisdiction on the Court of Justice to interpret the Rome Convention; the Protocols were agreed in 1988 but were brought into force only in 2004 and 2005.

[4] [1980] OJ C282/1. This Report 'may be considered in ascertaining the meaning or effect of any provision' of the Convention: Contracts (Applicable Law) Act 1990, s 3(3)(a).

[5] For a detailed discussion of the common law rules, see PM North and JJ Fawcett, *Cheshire and North's Private International Law* (London, Butterworths, 11th edn, 1987) 447–503; L Collins *et al*, *Dicey and Morris on The Conflict of Laws* (London, Sweet & Maxwell, 11th edn, 1987) chs 32 and 33.

[6] FA Mann, 'The Proper Law of the Contract—an Obituary' (1991) 107 *LQR* 353. See also A Nussbaum, *Principles of Private International Law* (New York, OUP, 1943) 168.

[7] FA Mann, 'The Proper Law of the Contract—an Obituary' (1991) 107 *LQR* 353.

[8] [1939] AC 277.

were connected with Canada or the United States. Lord Wright expressed the view that:

> where there is an express statement by the parties of their intention to select the law of the contract, it is difficult to see what qualifications are possible, provided the intention expressed is bona fide and legal, and provided there is no reason for avoiding the choice on the ground of public policy.[9]

The precise scope of the proviso which purports to limit the parties' freedom of choice has never been properly determined. It has been suggested that 'too much has been made of Lord Wright's remark, which reads like a "throw-away" line'.[10] In any event, there is no reported case in which an English court has refused to uphold an express choice of law on the basis that it was *mala fide*, illegal or contrary to public policy.[11] Nevertheless, only a choice of the law of a *country* will be given effect.[12]

14.1.3 If the parties have not expressly chosen the governing law, the proper law of the contract is 'the system of law by reference to which the contract was made or that with which the transaction has its closest and most real connexion'.[13] This formulation distinguishes cases of implied choice ('the system of law by reference to which the contract was made') from cases in which the parties have made no choice (in which case the contract is governed by the objective proper law—that is, the law of the country 'with which the transaction has its closest and most real connection').[14]

14.1.4 The combined effect of the decision in *Vita Food Products Inc v Unus Shipping Co Ltd* and the *Bonython* formula is to produce a tripartite hierarchy of rules for determining the proper law of a contract. First, if the parties have made an express choice, the will of the parties is decisive (so long as the choice is *bona fide*, legal and not contrary to public policy). Secondly, if there is no express choice, the parties may have impliedly chosen the proper law. The court may imply a choice of law from the nature of the contract (such as use of a Lloyd's form[15]) or from an arbitration clause[16] or a jurisdiction agreement.[17] Thirdly, in the absence of express or implied choice, the objective proper law governs the contract. In the early stages of development the English courts used to approach cases where there was no choice from the point of view of presumptions, such as the place of contracting, the place of performance or the flag of the ship. However, these presumptions lost favour and the courts adopted an approach based on a wide-ranging inquiry into all the relevant factors.

---

[9] [1939] AC 277, 290.

[10] JG Collier, *The Conflict of Laws* (Cambridge, CUP, 1987) 147.

[11] See also *Peh Teck Quee v Bayerische Landesbank Girozentrale* [2001] 2 LRC 23 (Court of Appeal, Singapore). See, however, *Golden Acres Ltd v Queensland Estates Pty Ltd* [1969] Qd R 378 (Supreme Court, Queensland). DStL Kelly, 'International Contracts and Party Autonomy' (1970) 19 ICLQ 701.

[12] *Musawi v RE International (UK) Ltd* [2008] 1 Lloyd's Rep 326. A Briggs, (2007) 78 *BYIL* 624.

[13] Lord Simonds in *Bonython v Commonwealth of Australia* [1951] AC 201, 219.

[14] JHC Morris and GCC Cheshire, 'The Proper Law of a Contract in the Conflict of Laws' (1940) 56 *LQR* 320; FA Mann, 'The Proper Law of the Contract' (1950) 3 *ILQ* 60; JHC Morris, 'The Proper Law of the Contract: A Rejoinder' (1950) 3 *ILQ* 197; FA Mann, 'The Proper Law of the Contract: A Reply' (1950) 3 *ILQ* 597; EJ Cohn, 'The Objectivist Practice on the Proper Law of Contract' (1957) 6 *ICLQ* 373.

[15] *Amin Rasheed Shipping Corporation v Kuwait Insurance Co* [1984] AC 50.

[16] *James Miller and Partners Ltd v Whitworth Street Estates (Manchester) Ltd* [1970] AC 583; *Compagnie Tunisienne de Navigation SA v Compagnie d'Armement Maritime SA* [1971] AC 572.

[17] *The Komninos S* [1991] 1 Lloyd's Rep 370.

14.1.5 Although it was suggested by Lord Wilberforce that the second and third categories 'merge into each other'[18] the conceptual distinction between them is clear:

So long as the object of the court's inquiry is the intention of the parties, the language, termi-nology, form and terms of the contract will very often constitute a useful guide, bearing in mind that the search is for the system of law with which they intended (or assumed) would govern their contract. However, once that search has been abandoned, the determination of the parties' intention (or assumption) with any degree of realism being impossible, resort must perforce be had to a purely objective test (as distinct from one based upon an 'objectively' determined intention). Application of this purely objective test involves *geographical location* of the *trans-action*. It is then actual or contemplated factual activity, rather than inference from the form, etc, of the contract which is most relevant.[19]

The existence of a three-stage approach to determining the proper law of the contract was affirmed in *Zebrarise Ltd v De Nieffe*.[20]

14.1.6 There was strong opposition when the Rome Convention was being introduced into English law.[21] It was argued that the common law rules, 'grown by experience and developed by judicial wisdom', are innately superior to 'statutory tests drawn up by a committee of theorists speaking different languages and trained in different legal systems'.[22] Be that as it may, the common law rules are residual to the Convention and its successor, ie the Rome I Regulation.

The Rome I Regulation[23]

14.1.7 The proposal to modernise the Rome Convention stemmed from a Green Paper published by the European Commission in 2003.[24] Thereafter, the Commission put forward a proposal to transpose the Convention into a Regulation and modernise its provisions.[25] The Brussels I Regulation had already modernised the jurisdiction and recognition rules contained in the Brussels Convention and plans were already afoot for a proposed Rome II Regulation covering choice of law rules for non-contractual obligations.[26] It was therefore thought inappropriate for the Rome Convention to remain as the only Community instrument in treaty form[27] as all three instruments

---

[18] *Amin Rasheed Shipping Corporation v Kuwait Insurance Co* [1984] AC 50, 69.

[19] PB Carter, 'Contracts in English Private International Law' (1986) 57 *BYIL* 1, 21–2. (Emphasis in original.)

[20] [2005] 1 Lloyd's Rep 154, 161 (at [32]).

[21] See the 3rd edition of this work, 460–1; FA Mann, (1983) 32 *ICLQ* 265; PB Carter, 'Contracts in English Private International Law' (1986) 57 *BYIL* 1; FA Mann, 'The Proper Law of the Contract—an Obituary' (1991) 107 *LQR* 353.

[22] FA Mann, *The Times*, 14 December 1990.

[23] R Plender and M Wilderspin, *The European Private International Law of Obligations* (London, Thomson Reuters, 3rd edn, 2009) Pt 2; S Leible and F Ferrari (eds), *Rome I Regulation: The Law Applicable to Contractual Obligations in Europe* (Munich, Sellier, 2009).

[24] Green Paper on the conversion of the Rome Convention of 1980 on the law applicable to contractual obligations into a Community instrument and its modernisation, COM (2002) 654 final; hereafter 'Green Paper'.

[25] Proposal for a Regulation of the European Parliament and the Council on the law applicable to con-tractual obligations (Rome I) COM (2005) 650 final; hereafter 'Commission Proposal'.

[26] See ch 15.

[27] Not to mention that modernising the Rome Convention in treaty form would have been a time-consuming procedure as it would require negotiations between all intended signatories.

were intended to function as a unified set of private international law rules relating to contractual and non-contractual obligations in civil and commercial matters in the European Union.[28] There were also other advantages of transposing the Convention into a Regulation: it could be more easily amended; it would automatically apply to new Member States as part of the *acquis communautaire*; preliminary rulings to the Court of Justice would help ensure consistency of interpretation of the instrument; and it would be directly binding on national courts.[29]

14.1.8 Initial reaction in the United Kingdom to the proposed Regulation was not warm. The legal basis for the conversion of the Convention into a Regulation is what is now Article 81(c) of the Treaty on the Functioning of the European Union (TFEU), which allows measures aimed at ensuring the 'compatibility of the rules applicable in the Member States concerning the conflict of laws and of jurisdiction', particularly where the measures are 'necessary for the proper functioning of the internal market'. Yet the proposed Regulation was not intended to be confined to intra-EU fact situations. There was also disquiet over some of the proposed changes, particularly as reservations would no longer be possible for a Regulation.[30] Since the proposed Regulation fell within Title IV of the Treaty establishing the European Community and did not apply to the United Kingdom by virtue of the Protocol annexed to the Treaty unless the United Kingdom exercised its right to opt into the instrument, the UK government decided to opt out but continued to engage in the negotiations. It was perhaps inevitable that the decision to opt out would eventually be reversed given that the Brussels I Regulation and Rome II Regulation were part of English law and the United Kingdom risked being out of step with most of the rest of the European Union with its opt-out decision.[31] In 2008, the Ministry of Justice launched a consultation in which it recommended that the United Kingdom should opt in, as some changes had been made to the initial proposal; the outcome of the consultation process was the decision to seek permission to opt in to Rome I. Upon notification by the United Kingdom, the Commission approved of the United Kingdom's request to accept Rome I.[32]

The Scope of the Rome I Regulation

14.1.9 The Regulation is limited in both its material and its temporal scope. As regards contractual obligations not governed by the Regulation either the Rome Convention or the common law choice of law rules continue to apply.[33]

---

[28] Explanatory Memorandum, Commission Proposal, COM (2005) 650 final, p 2.

[29] European Parliament Report A6-0450/2007 (21.1.2007), p 42.

[30] In particular, there was concern over a provision giving the courts the discretion to apply the mandatory rules of the law of a country (not being the law applicable to the contract or the law of the forum) with which the situation has a close connection. See Commission Proposal, COM (2005) 650 final, Art 8(3). This provision was removed from the final text of the Regulation.

[31] The Regulation applies to all Member States apart from Denmark by virtue of its own Protocol on Title IV measures. Ireland, which could have opted out, chose to become a party to the Regulation right from the start. Note that in certain limited circumstances, Member States are allowed to conclude bilateral agreements with third countries relating to contractual (and non-contractual) obligations. See Reg (EC) 662/2009 establishing a procedure for the negotiation and conclusion of agreements between Member States and third countries on particular matters concerning the law applicable to contractual and non-contractual obligations, [2009] OJ L200/25.

[32] See Commission Decision, [2009] OJ L19/22.

[33] See para 14.1.22.

Material Scope

CHOICE OF LAW RELATING TO CONTRACTUAL OBLIGATIONS

14.1.10   Article 1 sets out the Regulation's material scope. The first paragraph, which determines the outer limits of the Regulation, provides:

This Regulation shall apply, in situations involving a conflict of laws, to contractual obligations in civil and commercial matters.

It shall not apply, in particular, to revenue, customs or administrative matters.

The phrase 'contractual obligation' is not defined in the Regulation. It is clear, though, that it has a European autonomous meaning as the counterpart phrase of 'non-contractual obligations' in the Rome II Regulation is expressly said to have a European autonomous meaning.[34] So, for the purpose of the Regulation, gifts and promises to give should be regarded as involving contractual obligations.[35] Conversely, a tortious or equitable duty of care which is imposed by law may arise from a voluntary assumption of responsibility, but is not consensual and therefore falls outside the Regulation as '[a] contractual obligation is by its very nature one which is voluntarily assumed by agreement'.[36] The phrase 'civil and commercial matters', which also determines the outer boundary of the Brussels I Regulation, also has a Europe-wide definition;[37] in particular, as the second sentence in the first paragraph explains, it does not include revenue, customs or administrative matters.

EXCEPTIONS

14.1.11   The material scope of the Regulation, as defined by the first paragraph of Article 1, is limited by the exceptions set out in the second and third paragraphs. These various exclusions to the Regulation are motivated by different reasons: as regards some of the excluded matters the choice of law rules in the Regulation would be inappropriate; some excluded matters are not regarded as being essentially contractual by some of the Member States; other specific matters were excluded because of legal developments in other contexts.

   14.1.12   Article 1(2)(a) excludes 'questions involving the status or legal capacity of natural persons'. This is, however, subject to the limited exception in Article 13.[38] Sub-paragraph (b) excludes 'obligations arising out of family relationships and relation-ships deemed by the law applicable to such relationships to have comparable effects, including maintenance obligations', while sub-paragraph (c) goes on to exclude all remaining questions of family law: obligations arising out of matrimonial property regimes, property regimes of relationships deemed by the law applicable to such rela-tionships to have comparable effects to marriage, and wills and succession. The net

---

[34]   Rome II Reg, Recital 11.
[35]   See, eg, *Re Bonacina* [1912] 2 Ch 394 (a case decided at common law).
[36]   Tuckey LJ in *Base Metal v Shamurin* [2005] 1 WLR 1157, 1167 (at [28]). A Dickinson, (2005) 121 *LQR* 374; TM Yeo, [2005] *LMCLQ* 144; A Briggs, (2004) 75 *BYIL* 572.
[37]   See, eg, Case 814/79 *Netherlands State v Rüffer* [1980] ECR 3807; Case C–172/91 *Sonntag v Waidmann* [1993] ECR I–1963. See, further, ch 4.
[38]   Contractual capacity is discussed further at paras 14.4.19–14.4.27.

effect of these two sub-paragraphs is that issues of parentage, marriage, affinity and collateral relatives fall outside the scope of the Regulation.[39] Recital 8 contains the rather puzzling sentence that the references to relationships which have comparable effects to family relationships and marriage 'should be interpreted in accordance with the law of the Member State in which the court is seised'.[40] If a civil partnership between two same-sex partners is registered in England and considered by English law to be comparable to marriage, but the court which is seised does not share the same view, which court's view prevails?

14.1.13   Choice of law questions concerning bills of exchange, cheques and promissory notes are excluded from the scope of the Regulation;[41] they are governed by the Bills of Exchange Act 1882. As regards negotiable instruments which are not bills of exchange, cheques or promissory notes, the rules laid down by the Regulation do not apply to those obligations which arise out of their negotiable character. The Regulation's rules do apply, however, to those obligations which do not arise out of their negotiable character. The effect of Article 1(2)(d) is that where a negotiable instrument is used as a method of payment (for example, in the context of a contract for the sale of goods), although the obligations arising out of the instrument fall outside the scope of the Regulation, the underlying contract does not. As regards a negotiable instrument which is not a bill of exchange, a cheque or a promissory note it is important to distinguish two different transactions: sale and negotiation. Whereas the sale of a negotiable instrument falls within the Regulation's scope,[42] its negotiation does not. Whether a document is characterised as a negotiable instrument is a matter for the law of the forum (including its conflicts rules).[43] Transactions which are related to negotiable instruments, but which are not themselves negotiable instruments (such as letters of credit) plainly fall within the scope of the Regulation.

14.1.14   It is provided that the Regulation does not apply to 'arbitration agreements and agreements on the choice of court'.[44] Many jurisdiction clauses are regulated by the Brussels I Regulation,[45] and the New York Convention of 1958 (which has been ratified by all the Member States) applies to arbitration agreements.[46] Jurisdiction clauses are excluded as choice of law issues, such as those relating to consent, will often not arise as the Brussels I Regulation requires jurisdiction agreements to be in writing.[47] As regards arbitration agreements, it was thought at the time the Rome Convention was drafted that 'any increase in the number of conventions in this area should be avoided'[48]—a position which the Regulation maintains. There are, however, cogent arguments in favour of the inclusion of dispute-resolution agreements within

---

[39] Recital 8.
[40] It is a reproduction of the Rome II Regulation, Recital 10.
[41] Art 1(2)(d).
[42] An identical provision is contained in the Rome Convention (Article 1(2)(c)) and it was interpreted in this manner: Giuliano-Lagarde Report, [1980] OJ C282/11. There is no reason to think that the position under the Regulation is different.
[43] Giuliano-Lagarde Report, [1980] OJ C282/11.
[44] Art 1(2)(e).
[45] Brussels I Reg, Art 23. See section 5.3.
[46] See section 22.2.
[47] See Giuliano-Lagarde Report, [1980] OJ C282/11.
[48] Giuliano-Lagarde Report, [1980] OJ C282/12.

the scope of the Regulation. First, although the Brussels I Regulation and the New York Convention deal with formal validity, it is doubtful that they also regulate all questions of material validity. Secondly, as a result of amendments it is no longer true that jurisdiction agreements in favour of the courts of a Member State have to be in writing.[49] Thirdly, an agreement in favour of the courts of a non-Member State is not governed by Article 23 of the Brussels I Regulation. The effect of the exclusion is that if choice of law questions arise in English proceedings in relation to an international contract which contains a jurisdiction or arbitration clause, the law governing the clause is to be determined by reference to the common law choice of law rules and the law governing the rest of the contract falls to be determined by the Regulation. It is likely in practice that, notwithstanding the fact that different choice of law regimes apply to different aspects of the same contract, the proper law of the clause will be the same as the law applicable to the contract as a whole. Nevertheless, the application of two different sets of choice of law rules might lead to the jurisdiction or arbitration agreement being governed by law of country X and the contract as a whole being governed by the law of country Y.

14.1.15   The Regulation does not apply to:

questions governed by the law of companies and other bodies corporate or unincorporate such as the creation, by registration or otherwise, legal capacity, internal organisation or winding-up of companies and other bodies corporate or unincorporated and the personal liability of officers and members as such for the obligations of the company or body.[50]

Acts which are necessary for the creation of a company or firm and for the regulation of its internal organisation and its winding up are all outside the scope of the Regulation. However, preliminary contracts whose sole purpose is to create obligations between interested parties with a view to forming a company or firm are regulated by the choice of law rules contained in the Regulation.[51] For example, where two persons enter a joint venture to stage a musical and the medium through which the joint venture is realised is a company established by the parties, the original joint venture agreement falls within the scope of the Regulation, although the liability of the organs of the company is a matter which is excluded.

14.1.16   The Regulation does not apply to 'the constitution of trusts and the relationship between settlors, trustees and beneficiaries'.[52] The Commission had proposed that the legal relationship between the principal and the third party in a contract concluded through an agent should be included, but this proposal fell by the wayside.[53] The Regulation therefore retains the same exclusion as the Convention and does not apply to 'the question whether an agent is able to bind a principal, or an organ to bind a company or body corporate or unincorporate, in relation to a third party'.[54] Nevertheless, to the extent that such relations are contractual, choice of law questions arising out of the relationship between, on the one hand, the principal and

---

[49] See section 5.3.
[50] Art 1(2)(f).
[51] Giuliano-Lagarde Report, [1980] OJ C282/12.
[52] Art 1(2)(h).
[53] Commission Proposal, COM (2005) 650 final, Art 7.
[54] Art 1(2)(g).

the agent and, on the other, between the agent and the third party are within the scope of the Regulation.

14.1.17   A proposed change which did make it to the final version of the Regulation is the exclusion of 'obligations arising out of dealings prior to the conclusion of a contract'.[55] For example, a claim may be made for money paid over in anticipation of a contract which ultimately does not come to fruition. Such a claim will be governed by the choice of law rules set out in the Rome II Regulation.[56]

14.1.18   Insurance contracts arising out of operations carried out by organisations other than undertakings which are referred to in Article 2 of Directive 2002/83/EC on life assurance[57] are also excluded.[58] Insurance contracts that fall within the Regulation's scope are governed by either the general choice of law rules set out in Articles 3 and 4, or the special choice of law rules set out in Article 7.

14.1.19   As a general principle, questions of procedure are for the law of the forum, regardless of the law which governs the substantive issues disputed by the parties. The Regulation adheres to this traditional analysis by excluding 'evidence and procedure'.[59] However, this exclusion is subject to Article 18, the first paragraph of which provides:

The law governing a contractual obligation under this Regulation shall apply to the extent that, in matters of contractual obligations, it contains rules which raise presumptions of law or determine the burden of proof.

The purpose of this rule is to include within the applicable law those rules—specific to contractual obligations—which are in reality rules of substance, even though phrased in terms of presumptions and the burden of proof. Article 18(2) provides that a contract may be proved in any manner permitted by the law of the forum or in any manner permitted by the law which renders the contract formally valid under Article 11.

Territorial Scope

UNIVERSAL APPLICATION
14.1.20   Article 2 provides:

Any law specified by this Regulation shall be applied whether or not it is the law of a Member State.

The Regulation is universal in scope in the sense that its rules could lead to the application of the law of a non-EU Member State. This rule leads to the welcome situation that the court needs to apply only one set of rules for both intra- and extra-EU cases.[60]

---

[55] Art 1(2)(i).
[56] See ch 15. This also follows the position adopted for the Brussels I Regulation, where the Court of Justice has held that pre-contractual liability is non-contractual and falls within Art 5(3) of the Regulation: Case C–334/00 *Fonderie Officine Meccaniche Tacconi SpA v Heinrich Wagner Sinto Maschinenfabrik GmbH* [2002] ECR I–7377.
[57] [2002] OJ L345/1, as amended by Dir 2008/19/EC, [2008] OJ L76/44.
[58] Art 1(2)(j).
[59] Art 1(3). See, however, Art 12(1)(c), discussed at paras 14.4.44–14.4.54.
[60] Although opponents of the Regulation pointed out that the inclusion of extra-EU situations within the Regulation's scope was irrelevant to the 'proper functioning of the internal market' (see Recital 6), the application of the Regulation regardless of the territorial connections of the dispute and the parties to it is justified.

'INTERNAL' CONFLICTS

14.1.21   As the United Kingdom is made up of three different legal systems—England, Scotland and Northern Ireland—choice of law questions may arise as between these different countries. Article 22(2) of the Regulation provides that a Member State which is made up of several territorial units, each with its own law of contract, is not required to apply the Regulation's rules to purely internal conflicts. Nevertheless, the UK government has chosen to extend the Regulation's rules to conflicts between the laws of different parts of the United Kingdom and conflicts between the laws of one or more parts of the United Kingdom and Gibraltar.[61] The application of one set of rules, rather than two, is always easier and there do not appear to be any reasons why different rules are warranted for intra-UK situations.[62]

Temporal Scope

14.1.22   Article 28 provides that the Regulation is to apply only to contracts concluded 'after' 17 December 2009. This has been clarified to mean contracts concluded 'as from' that date.[63] Other contracts will generally be governed by either the Rome Convention or the common law rules. The Rome Convention will apply to any contractual obligation entered into between 1 April 1991 and 16 December 2009, while the common law choice of law rules will continue to apply in relation to any contractual obligation entered into prior to 1 April 1991.

Exclusion of the Doctrine of *Renvoi*

14.1.23   The doctrine of *renvoi* has no role to play in the field of choice of law in contract. This was the position adopted by the English courts at common law[64] and the same rule is to be found in both the Rome Convention and the Rome I Regulation. Article 20 of the Regulation provides:

The application of the law of any country specified by this Regulation means the application of the rules of law in force in that country other than its rules of private international law, unless provided otherwise in this Regulation.

Where choice of law rules indicate that the law of Brazil is to be applied, the domestic rules of Brazilian law are exclusively relevant; Brazilian choice of law rules are irrelevant. So, Brazilian law would be the applicable law even if, through the application of Brazilian choice of law rules, a Brazilian court would regard Argentine law

---

[61] The Law Applicable to Contractual Obligations (England and Wales and Northern Ireland) Regs 2009, SI 2009/3064; The Law Applicable to Contractual Obligations (Scotland) Regs 2009, SSI 2009/410. A similar extension is made for insurance contracts falling within Art 7 of the Rome I Regulation by the Financial Services and Markets Act 2000 (Law Applicable to Contracts of Insurance) Regs 2009, SI 2009/3075.

[62] Ministry of Justice, *Rome I—Should the UK opt in?*, Consultation Paper CP05/08, 2 April 2008, 36 (para 91).

[63] Corrigendum to Reg (EC) 593/2008 on the law applicable to contractual obligations (Rome I), [2009] OJ L309/87.

[64] See Lord Diplock in *Amin Rasheed Shipping Corporation v Kuwait Insurance Co* [1984] AC 50, 61–2.

to be the applicable law. The Regulation, in limited circumstances, permits *renvoi*, for example in relation to certain insurance contracts.[65] Note must also be taken of Article 23, which provides that the Regulation shall not prejudice the application of provisions of EU law which lay down conflict of laws rules relating to contractual obligations.[66]

14.2 DETERMINING THE APPLICABLE LAW[67]

The Applicable Law in Cases of Choice

Introduction

THE PRINCIPLE OF PARTY AUTONOMY[68]

14.2.1   Article 3(1) embodies the 'cornerstone'[69] principle of party autonomy:

A contract shall be governed by the law chosen by the parties. The choice shall be made expressly or clearly demonstrated by the terms of the contract or the circumstances of the case.

There is nothing in the Regulation which says that there needs to be any connection between the chosen law and the contract or the parties. Even a choice made in bad faith (for example, with the express purpose of evading statutory provisions which would otherwise govern the contract) is valid. However, where the parties make an evasive choice, it is more than likely that the chosen law will be subject to the mandatory rules of the law which the parties have sought to evade.[70]

14.2.2   The parties' choice is limited to domestic systems of law.[71] The Commission initially proposed a radical change: that the parties be allowed to choose a non-state body of rules, such as the *UNIDROIT Principles of International Commercial Contracts* or the *Principles of European Contract Law*,[72] as the applicable law of the contract.[73] This suggestion did not survive the negotiations. Nevertheless, Recital 13 provides that parties are not precluded from incorporating by reference into their contract a non-state body of law or an international convention.[74] Recital 14 leaves open the possibility of the parties choosing an EU-wide instrument setting out rules of substantive

---

[65] See Art 7(3).

[66] See also Recital 40.

[67] See J Hill, 'Choice of Law in Contract under the Rome Convention: The Approach of the UK Courts' (2004) 53 *ICLQ* 325.

[68] See, generally, P Nygh, *Autonomy in International Contracts* (Oxford, Clarendon Press, 1999) and the discussion by J Harris, 'Contractual Freedom in the Conflict of Laws' (2000) 20 *OJLS* 247.

[69] Recital 11.

[70] See section 14.3.

[71] This has been held to be the same under the common law: *Musawi v RE International (UK) Ltd* [2008] 1 Lloyd's Rep 326. Cf the position where the parties have agreed to refer their dispute to arbitration: Arbitration Act 1996, s 46. See ch 23.

[72] But not the *lex mercatoria* as this 'is not precise enough': COM (2005) 650 final, p 5. Note, however, that strictly speaking, the *UNIDROIT Principles of International Commercial Contracts* (see the Preamble) and the *Principles of European Contract Law* (see Art 1:101) are codifications of part of the *lex mercatoria*.

[73] COM (2005) 650 final, proposed Art 3(2).

[74] See para 14.2.4.

contract law, such as the proposed common frame of reference for European contract law,[75] if that comes into existence.

CHOICE AND INCORPORATION

14.2.3   It is important to distinguish a choice of law from the incorporation of foreign legal provisions into a contract. Whether a particular contractual provision amounts to a choice of law or incorporation of specific provisions is a question of construction. Where, for example, parties choose French law to govern their contract as a whole, the chosen law determines the rights and obligations of the parties and it applies as 'a living and changing body of law'.[76] Accordingly, the parties take the risk that between the conclusion of the contract and its performance the chosen law will change in a way that alters their rights and obligations.[77] Incorporation operates in a different way. It is perfectly possible for a contract which is governed by the law of country X to incorporate rules of law from country Y. This is not, however, a case of the applicable law being split. Provisions of a foreign law which are incorporated into the text of the contract, whether by reference or verbatim, take effect as written terms which must be interpreted by the applicable law. So, for example, a contract which is governed by English law may provide that in case of breach the liability of the parties is to be governed by specific provisions of the French civil code. In this case, the incorporated provisions have to be construed as English contractual terms.[78] Moreover, the rights and obligations of the parties are fixed at the date of incorporation. Rules which are incorporated are not affected by any change in the law of which they form a part between the conclusion of the contract and its performance. Further, for there to be incorporation of rules from a body of law other than the applicable law, the rules to be incorporated must be clearly identified:

> The doctrine of incorporation can only sensibly operate where the parties have by the terms of their contract sufficiently identified specific 'black-letter' provisions of a foreign law or an international code or set of rules apt to be incorporated as terms of the relevant contract such as particular Articles of the French Civil Code or the Hague Rules.[79]

14.2.4   As mentioned above, Recital 14 allows the parties to incorporate a non-state body of law into the contract. The criterion of certainty applies *a fortiori*. The phrase 'the principles of the glorious Sharia' was held not to identify clearly the specific provisions of Sharia law which were intended to be incorporated especially where there was controversy and different schools of thought as to what was laid down by Sharia law.[80] In contrast, where there was a dispute between Orthodox Jews in *Halpern v*

---

[75] See Council of the European Union, Note from the General Secretariat to the Committee on Civil Law Matters (Contract Law), Consolidated version of the conclusion of the Council, 5784/09 (27 January 2009).

[76] M Wolff, 'The Choice of Law by the Parties in International Contracts' (1937) 49 *Jur Rev* 110, 124.

[77] *Re Chesterman's Trusts* [1923] 2 Ch 466.

[78] *GE Dobell & Co v Steamship Rossmore Co Ltd* [1895] 2 QB 408.

[79] Potter LJ in *Shamil Bank of Bahrain EC v Beximco Pharmaceuticals Ltd* [2004] 1 WLR 1784, 1799 (at [51]).

[80] *Shamil Bank of Bahrain EC v Beximco Pharmaceuticals Ltd* [2004] 1 WLR 1784, 1801 (at [55]).

Halpern, it was held that Jewish law could be incorporated into a contract provided there was common ground that it was a distinct body of law.[81]

14.2.5 Problems of construction may arise in a situation where a contract governed by English law expressly incorporates provisions of a foreign law or a non-state body of law. This is particularly likely when the incorporated provisions are provisions of foreign law that is identical to equivalent provisions of English law. If the English and foreign courts have interpreted identical statutory provisions differently, which interpretation is to prevail? In *The Stolt Sydness* Rix J posed the question in the following terms:

> Given that the incorporation of a foreign statute does not affect the choice of proper law ..., and given that the foreign statute is treated as so many terms incorporated wholesale into an English law contract, what if any is the relevance to that contract of the decisions upon the meaning of that foreign statute of the courts of the country of enactment?[82]

In answering this question Rix J confirmed that the general principle is that 'the question of construction must be answered as a matter of the proper law'.[83] This does not mean, however, that the decisions of foreign courts are necessarily irrelevant. Often the English courts may have to refer to foreign law in order to assist it in discovering the parties' presumed intentions. If, for example, the parties incorporate specific provisions of the French civil code into an English contract, the courts will turn to French law to elucidate the meaning of the incorporated provisions. Where, however, the incorporated provisions are the same as the equivalent English provisions the position is different:

> Where ... the English and the foreign law differ as to the meaning to be given to identical wording of an international rule enacted in both England and the foreign country, it is hard to think that there are any circumstances in which the foreign law's view could prevail over that of the proper law. But the ultimate question will still remain: What in accordance with the proper law, must be taken to be the presumed intention of the parties?[84]

THE EXISTENCE AND VALIDITY OF CHOICE

14.2.6 The Rome I Regulation does not lay down uniform requirements—either of form or substance—for the validity of a choice of law. In cases where it is alleged that the parties have made a choice of law (whether express or implied), that choice will be effective if it is valid by the applicable law. Accordingly, where parties contract on standard conditions which include both a jurisdiction clause and a choice of law clause, it is perfectly possible that the jurisdiction clause, if governed by the Brussels I Regulation, will be ineffective for failure to comply with the necessary formal requirements,[85] but that the choice of law clause will be valid according to its applicable law.[86]

---

[81] [2008] QB 195, 213 (at [33]). A Briggs, (2007) 78 *BYIL* 624.
[82] [1997] 1 Lloyd's Rep 273, 279.
[83] [1997] 1 Lloyd's Rep 273, 282.
[84] Rix J at [1997] 1 Lloyd's Rep 273, 282.
[85] Brussels I Reg, Art 23.
[86] See, eg, *Allpac Holding BV v Maier am Tor* [1982] ECC 200 (Court of Appeal, Amsterdam).

14.2.7   Questions of the existence and validity of a choice of law are governed by the general principles which apply to the existence and validity of any other contractual agreement. Article 3(5) provides that:

the existence and validity of the consent of the parties as to the choice of the applicable law shall be determined in accordance with the provisions of Articles 10, 11 and 13.

Article 10 applies to material validity, Article 11 to formal validity, and Article 13 to questions of capacity.[87]

Express Choice

14.2.8   Whether a contractual clause constitutes an express choice is a matter of construction. Most cases are entirely straightforward, since the parties simply agree that the contract is to be governed by the law of a particular country. If the court accepts that the contract has been concluded by reference to one of the parties' general conditions (which include a choice of law clause), the requirements of Article 3 are satisfied.[88] If, however, there was no clear consensus between the parties on the relevant term of the contract, the courts will conclude that the parties did not make an express choice of law. In *Iran Continental Shelf Oil Company v IRI International Corporation*[89] each party sought to rely on its own terms and conditions which contained inconsistent choice of law clauses and at no point did either party unequivocally accept the other party's terms. McCombe J, at first instance, held that in the circumstances of the case it could not be said that the parties had made an express choice of law[90] and, in the subsequent appeal, neither party sought to challenge this conclusion.[91] Similarly, where the draft contract prepared by one party contains a choice of law clause, but the other party deletes it before signing and returning the contract, the parties cannot be regarded as having made a choice of the governing law.[92] Furthermore, the parties' alleged choice of law may be unenforceable as a result of uncertainty.[93]

14.2.9   Problems may arise in cases where the parties seek to determine the applicable law indirectly. In *Compagnie Tunisienne de Navigation SA v Compagnie d'Armement Maritime SA*[94] the defendant, a French shipowner, and the plaintiff, a Tunisian company, entered into a contract for the shipment of oil between Tunisian ports. Clause 13 of the contract provided that the contract was to be governed by the 'the laws of the Flag of the Vessel carrying the goods'. The defendant owned four ships and through a subsidiary company controlled a fifth, all of which flew the French flag. Although the printed form which the parties used for the agreement was designed for a single voyage charterparty, it was envisaged that performance of

---

[87] See paras 14.4.3–14.4.27.
[88] See, eg, *Ferguson Shipbuilders Ltd v Voith Hydro GmbH & Co KG* 2000 SLT 229 (Court of Session, Scotland).
[89] [2002] CLC 372.
[90] [2002] CLC 372, 381 (at [34]).
[91] [2004] 2 CLC 696.
[92] *Samcrete Egypt Engineers and Contractors SAE v Land Rover Exports Ltd* [2002] CLC 533.
[93] See *Sonatrach Petroleum Corp v Ferrell International Ltd* [2002] 1 All ER (Comm) 627.
[94] [1971] AC 572.

the contract would require at least a dozen voyages. The printed form was therefore adapted to suit the contract in question. Ships of five different flags were used in the first six voyages. After the sixth voyage war broke out in the Middle East and the defendant ceased to perform the contract. The plaintiff contended that the contract was governed by English law and that the defendant was in breach. It was the defendant's argument that the contract was governed by French law, under which the contract was frustrated. One of the issues facing the House of Lords was the effect of clause 13.

14.2.10 The minority thought that clause 13 was meaningless and should be regarded 'as having failed in its purpose to determine the proper law of the contract'.[95] The majority, however, decided that, since the parties had envisaged that the shipowner would primarily use ships flying the French flag, clause 13 was operative as a choice of French law. Lord Diplock was motivated by a desire to give effect to what he understood to be the obvious intentions of the parties:

[I]n commerce business men frequently find it convenient to use printed forms of contract with which they are familiar to record their agreements about transactions for which the printed clauses are not literally apt, as they were drafted for use as contracts about transactions which have somewhat different characteristics. If the law is to give effect to their intentions ... the court must construe the words of the printed form not exclusively literally but, if necessary, analogistically. ... By clause 13 when used for a single voyage charter the parties clearly intended to choose the system of law with which the contract had its connection through the nationality of the carrying vessel. Had the parties contemplated that the contract would be performed exclusively by vessels owned or controlled by the French company there could be no question but that the parties intended to choose French law as the proper law of the contract. Is the court to treat the clause as meaningless simply because, notwithstanding that they did contemplate that vessels owned by the French company would be used primarily to perform the contract, they also contemplated that there might be exceptional occasions on which chartered vessels might be used? It does not seem to me that from the business point of view this could make any significant difference so far as choice of proper law was concerned.[96]

14.2.11 Although the *Compagnie Tunisienne* case was decided under the common law, the question of what constitutes a choice can arise under Article 3(1) of the Regulation. Whether a contractual term is an express choice of law is a question of construction to be determined in each case in the light of the relevant circumstances.

'Implied' Choice

14.2.12 It is extremely important to distinguish cases of implied choice, which fall within Article 3(1), from cases in which the parties have failed to make a choice, which are governed by Article 4. An implied choice must be 'clearly demonstrated by the terms of the contract or the circumstances of the case'.[97] Apart from Recital 12,[98] the Regulation does not offer further guidance as to how to identify an implied choice.

---

[95] Lord Reid at [1971] AC 572, 583.
[96] [1971] AC 572, 608–9.
[97] Art 3(1).
[98] See paras 14.2.16–14.2.20.

The Regulation appears to establish a higher threshold than that set out in the Rome Convention, which referred to a choice 'demonstrated with reasonable certainty'.[99] Nevertheless, the examples that were set out in the Giuliano-Lagarde Report (such as the use of standard forms, a jurisdiction clause or an arbitration agreement)—where it might be possible to discern a genuine choice, notwithstanding the fact that the choice is not express—are still relevant in the context of the Regulation, even though the Regulation imposes a higher burden of proof. Each of the factors referred to in the report may incline the court to conclude that the parties have made a real choice. However, none of the factors is in itself decisive; much depends on the surrounding circumstances. Notwithstanding the use of the word 'or' between 'the terms of the contract' and 'the circumstances of the case', the court is entitled to look at both the contractual terms and the surrounding circumstances.[100]

STANDARD FORMS

14.2.13   It is not uncommon for the courts to imply a choice of law from the parties' use of a particular standard form. A contract may be in 'a standard form which is known to be governed by a particular system of law even though there is no express statement to this effect, such as a Lloyd's policy of marine insurance'.[101] Where, for example, contracting parties agree to the application of the General German Forwarding Agents Conditions the court is entitled to conclude that the parties chose German law, against the background of which the General Conditions were drafted.[102] However, the fact that the parties have used a standard form in the English language does not necessarily imply a choice of English law. Some forms are in worldwide use and it would not be appropriate to imply a choice in all cases.[103] In *Amin Rasheed Shipping Corporation v Kuwait Insurance Co*[104] the plaintiff, a Liberian company resident in Dubai, owned a vessel which was insured with the defendant, a Kuwaiti insurance company. The policy, which was issued in Kuwait, was based on the Lloyd's SG form (as set out in schedule 1 to the Marine Insurance Act 1906) but did not contain a choice of law clause. When a dispute arose under the contract the plaintiff sought to bring proceedings in England under what is now CPR PD 6B para 3.1 (6)(c).[105] The first issue facing the court was whether the contract was by implication governed by English law.

14.2.14   The majority of the House of Lords thought that English law was the proper law of the contract by virtue of the choice of the parties. Having referred to a number of 'the more esoteric provisions of the policy of which the legal effect is

---

[99]   Rome Convention, Art 3(1).

[100]   See Aikens J in *Marubeni Hong Kong and South China Ltd v Mongolian Government* [2002] 2 All ER (Comm) 873, 885 (at [42]).

[101]   Giuliano-Lagarde Report, [1980] OJ C282/17. See also *Gard Marine & Energy Ltd v Tunicliffe* [2010] Lloyd's Rep IR 62.

[102]   See *Re a Fowarding Agent's Costs* [1993] ILPr 49 (Court of Appeal, Hamburg).

[103]   PA Stone, 'The proper law of a marine insurance policy' [1984] *LMCLQ* 438.

[104]   [1984] AC 50. JG Collier, [1983] *CLJ* 214. See also *Wasa International Insurance Co v Lexington Insurance Co* [2010] 1 AC 180, a case decided under the common law rules, where a contract of reinsurance concluded in English form which was brokered and issued in the English market was accepted to be impliedly governed by English law.

[105]   See paras 7.3.17 and 7.3.26–7.3.27.

undiscoverable except by reference to the Marine Insurance Act 1906', Lord Diplock ventured the opinion that:

Except by reference to the English statute and to judicial exegesis of the code that it enacts it is not possible to interpret the policy so as to determine what [the parties'] mutual rights and obligations are.[106]

On this basis it was concluded that the parties had impliedly chosen English law as the proper law of the contract. Lord Wilberforce, on the other hand, took the view that there was 'no basis for inferring, as between the parties to this contract, an intention that the contract should be governed either by English law or by the law of Kuwait'.[107] According to this analysis, the proper law was the system of law with which the contract had its closest and most real connection. Lord Wilberforce concluded, albeit '[w]ith no great confidence',[108] that the proper law of the contract was English. The approach of the majority was followed in *Gan Insurance Company Limited v Tai Ping Insurance Company Ltd.*[109] The Court of Appeal decided that a contract of reinsurance concluded between the claimant, a company which carried on reinsurance business on the London market, and the defendant, a Taiwanese insurance company, was governed by English law by virtue of Article 3, even though the parties had not made an express choice of law. Beldam LJ (with whom Brooke and Mummery LJJ agreed) considered that, in the absence of evidence of a common intention to choose any law other than English law, the fact that the contract was of a standard type and had been made in London between London underwriters and brokers was sufficient to indicate that the parties had intended English law to govern the contract. Although the circumstances were less clear-cut than in the *Amin Rashid* case, the conclusion that the parties had made an implied choice of English law is uncontroversial.[110]

14.2.15 In the *Amin Rashid* case, the outcome did not depend on whether the situation was regarded as involving an implied choice or an absence of choice; in either event the proper law was English. The fact that this will not always be the case is illustrated by the decision of the House of Lords in *James Miller and Partners Ltd v Whitworth Street Estates (Manchester) Ltd.*[111] This case concerned a contract—between an English company and a Scottish company—which was concluded on a Royal Institute of British Architects (RIBA) standard form (which included an arbitration clause). The subject-matter of the contract was the conversion of premises in Scotland into a bonded warehouse. A dispute arose, arbitration proceedings were commenced in Scotland and litigation ensued in which one of the questions facing the court was whether the contract was governed by English or Scots law. The argument in favour of English law was that the RIBA contract was in English form and that there was in common use at the time a Scottish form of contract drawn up by a different professional body. This argument persuaded two members of the House of Lords. Lord Hodson—with whom Viscount Dilhorne agreed—thought that the proper law

---

[106] [1984] AC 50, 64.
[107] [1984] AC 50, 69.
[108] [1984] AC 50, 71.
[109] [1999] ILPr 729.
[110] See also *Tiernan v The Magen Insurance Co Ltd* [2000] ILPr 517.
[111] [1970] AC 583.

was 'determined by the use of the English form, the selection of which shows the intention of the parties to be bound by English law'.[112] Lord Guest, who had 'no doubt that the parties never chose English law as the proper law of the contract or evinced any intention to be bound by this law',[113] thought that English law governed the contract as the objective proper law. The remaining two members of the House of Lords—Lord Reid and Lord Wilberforce—agreed with Lord Guest that the parties had not chosen English law, either expressly or impliedly, but concluded that Scots law was the law with which the contract had its closest and most real connection.[114]

PREVIOUS COURSE OF DEALING

14.2.16   In certain circumstances:

a previous course of dealing between the parties under contracts containing an express choice of law may leave the court in no doubt that the contract in question is to be governed by the law previously chosen where the choice of law clause has been omitted in circumstances which do not indicate a deliberate change of policy by the parties.[115]

However, the court should not be too ready to imply a choice of law on the basis of a previous course of dealing. The absence of a choice of law clause in a particular written contract may result from the fact that the parties were unable to reach an agreement. Even if the parties have contracted with each other previously, the absence of a choice of law may signify a change in policy by one of the parties. Furthermore, it cannot be implied from the fact that parties have repeatedly contracted for the sale of apples on a standard form which includes an express choice of law that the same parties intend that a contract for the sale of pears which does not include a choice of law should be governed by the same law.

DISPUTE-RESOLUTION CLAUSES

14.2.17   Recital 12 provides that party agreement on an exclusive jurisdiction clause in favour of one or more courts or tribunals of a Member State to determine disputes under the contract should be one of the factors to be taken into account when trying to determine if an implied choice has been made.[116] By necessity, this is restricted to exclusive dispute-resolution clauses as otherwise the applicable law may differ according to which court is seised. It is a question of interpretation, to be determined in accordance with the law governing the dispute-resolution agreement, whether the clause is exclusive or non-exclusive.[117] If the clause is one which falls within the scope of the Brussels I Regulation, it is presumed that the choice of court clause is exclusive.[118]

---

[112]   [1970] AC 583, 606.

[113]   [1970] AC 583, 607–8.

[114]   Viscount Dilhorne also indicated that, had the parties not impliedly chosen English law, the proper law would have been Scots law as the law of the country with which the transaction had its closest and most real connection: [1970] AC 583, 611.

[115]   Giuliano-Lagarde Report, [1980] OJ C282/17.

[116]   The Commission had proposed this to be part of Art 3(1) but, as a compromise, the proposal was implemented by a Recital.

[117]   *Evans Marshall & Co Ltd v Bertola SA* [1973] 1 WLR 349, 361–2.

[118]   Brussels I Reg, Art 23(1).

14.2.18 When the question under consideration is whether a dispute-resolution clause is to be treated as an implied choice of law, regard must be had to all the circumstances of the case. It will be a question of interpretation in all cases. In *The Komninos S*,[119] for example, the plaintiff was the owner of a cargo which was shipped on a vessel owned by the defendant. The bills of lading were in the English language and contained the following clause:

In case any controversies arise with respect to the construction of the foregoing terms the English text alone to be conclusive. All dispute[s] to be referred to British courts.

None of the parties to the dispute was English or connected with England. The contract was made in Greece between Greek shippers and Greek managers on behalf of the Cypriot owners of a Panamanian vessel to carry a cargo from Greece to Italy for freight payable in Greece in Greek currency. When the cargo was discharged in Italy it was discovered that it had been damaged during the voyage. The plaintiff commenced proceedings in England, alleging that the ship was unseaworthy and that the defendant had been negligent. The first issue was whether the bills of lading were governed by English law or Greek law. If Greek law applied, the plaintiff's claim was *prima facie* time-barred. The plaintiff, however, sought to rely on the jurisdiction clause as an implied choice of English law. At first instance, Leggatt J held that there had been no choice and that the bills of lading were governed by Greek law, being the law with which the transaction had its closest and most real connection; the very strong factual connections with Greece predominated over the equivocal reference to the British courts.[120] This decision was reversed on appeal. First, the Court of Appeal decided that the reference to British courts operated as a choice of English jurisdiction.[121] Secondly, in relation to the impact of the jurisdiction clause on the choice of law question, Bingham LJ (with whom Nourse and Lloyd LJJ agreed) thought that it was appropriate to 'infer that the parties intended their contracts to be governed by the law of the forum where disputes were to be tried unless there were strong indications that they did not intend or may not have intended this result'.[122] Even though the contract had its closest and most real connection with Greek law, there was no indication to displace the *prima facie* inference from the jurisdiction clause.

14.2.19 The English courts have adopted a similar approach to arbitration clauses.[123] At common law:

an arbitration clause is generally intended by the parties to operate as a choice of the proper law of the contract ... unless there are compelling indications to the contrary in the other terms of the contract or the surrounding circumstances of the transaction.[124]

---

[119] [1991] Lloyd's Rep 370.

[120] [1990] 1 Lloyd's Rep 541, 544.

[121] [1991] 1 Lloyd's Rep 370, 374.

[122] [1991] 1 Lloyd's Rep 370, 376.

[123] For a discussion of the position at common law, see DR Thomas, 'Arbitration agreements as a signpost of the proper law' [1984] *LMCLQ* 141.

[124] Lord Diplock in *Compagnie Tunisienne de Navigation SA v Compagnie d'Armement Maritime SA* [1971] AC 572, 609. See also *King v Brandywine Reinsurance Co (UK) Ltd* [2005] 1 Lloyd's Rep 655. A Briggs, (2005) 76 *BYIL* 660.

Although an agreement to refer disputes to arbitration in a particular country does not necessarily lead to the conclusion that the parties are to be regarded as having intended the law of that country to be the applicable law,[125] it would appear that, at common law, '[t]he mere fact that there are systems of law with which the transaction has a closer connection is not sufficient to rebut the implication'.[126]

14.2.20 It may be questioned whether the common law approach to dispute-resolution clauses should be adopted under the Regulation. The terms of Article 3(1) do not entitle the court to presume that a dispute-resolution clause is a choice of law unless there are strong indications to the contrary and Recital 12 indicates that the existence of an exclusive dispute resolution clause is merely one of the factors to be considered. The onus should be on the person seeking to rely on a dispute-resolution clause as an implied choice of law to 'clearly demonstrate' that a real choice was made by the parties. In principle, the court should require stronger evidence of the parties' intention in the context of Article 3(1) than was traditionally required under the common law.[127]

14.2.21 English courts accepted the idea that the traditional common law approach was equally applicable to cases falling under the Rome Convention notwithstanding the differences between the two regimes. In *Egon Oldendorff v Libera Corporation*[128] the plaintiff, a German company, sought permission to serve process on the defendant, a Japanese corporation, under what is now CPR PD 6B para 3.1(6)(c), alleging that the contract between the parties was 'by implication' governed by English law. The contract had no connections with England other than a clause providing for arbitration in England. Mance J gave permission for the defendant to be served out of the jurisdiction on the ground that there was a good arguable case that the contract was governed by English law. The defendant's suggestion that it was contemplated that the arbitration tribunal might apply a foreign law was dismissed as 'unconvincing'.[129] Subsequently, it was held that the contract was indeed governed by English law.[130] As regards the effect of the arbitration clause on the applicable law, Clarke J decided that, although the test under Article 3 is not the same as the common law test, it is very similar and that the factors considered at common law by the House of Lords in the *Compagnie Tunisienne* case are equally relevant to the correct application of the test under the Convention.[131] It was Clarke J's conclusion that 'if [the Convention] involves a change in emphasis from the approach by the common law it is a small one'.[132] The same approach has been followed in more recent cases[133] and should be continued under the Regulation. Although the

---

[125] See Lord Morris in *Compagnie Tunisienne de Navigation SA v Compagnie d'Armement Maritime SA* [1971] AC 572, 588.

[126] Lord Diplock in *Compagnie Tunisienne de Navigation SA v Compagnie d'Armement Maritime SA* [1971] AC 572, 609.

[127] CGJ Morse, 'The EEC Convention on the Law Applicable to Contractual Obligations' (1982) 2 *YBEL* 107, 117.

[128] [1995] 2 Lloyd's Rep 64.

[129] [1995] 2 Lloyd's Rep 64, 69.

[130] [1996] 1 Lloyd's Rep 380.

[131] [1996] 1 Lloyd's Rep 380, 389.

[132] [1996] 1 Lloyd's Rep 380, 390.

[133] See, eg, *Marubeni Hong Kong and South China Ltd v Mongolian Government* [2002] 2 All ER (Comm) 873. See also *The Hornbay* [2006] 2 Lloyd's Rep 44.

existence of a dispute-resolution clause is merely one of the factors to be taken into account, the fact that such a clause has been singled out in the Regulation suggests that, in the search of an implied choice of law, considerable weight should be given to an exclusive jurisdiction clause or an arbitration agreement. Practical advantages also accrue from this approach: the convenience of courts applying their own law in terms of time and costs hardly need to be stated.

REFERENCE TO PROVISIONS OF DOMESTIC LAW

14.2.22 The Giuliano-Lagarde Report on the Rome Convention suggests that:

references in a contract to specific Articles of the French Civil Code may leave the court in no doubt that the parties have deliberately chosen French law, although there is no expressly stated choice of law.[134]

A choice of law has to be distinguished from the incorporation of provisions of law into a contract.[135] Where provisions of law have been incorporated into a contract it does not follow that the contract as a whole is to be governed by that law. Much depends on the circumstances of the case. Where, for example, an Englishman and a Scotsman enter into a contract for the sale of goods, but agree that, in the event of breach, damages are to be determined by specific provisions of the French civil code, it would be wrong to assume that reference to the French civil code indicates an intention that French law should be the applicable law. Indeed, if anything, the reference to a provision of French law without a choice of French law suggests that the parties do not intend French law to be the applicable law. It must always be remembered that, for the purposes of Article 3(1), the choice must be 'clearly demonstrated'.

RELATED TRANSACTIONS

14.2.23 The Giuliano-Lagarde Report accepts the idea that a choice may be implied into a contract from 'an express choice of law in related transactions *between the same parties*'.[136] In *FR Lürssen Werft GmbH & Co KG v Halle*,[137] the parties had, in chronological order, entered into a construction contract for the building of a yacht, a commission agreement to cover the situation if the vessel was purchased by a client introduced by the builders and, lastly, a termination agreement which ended the construction contract. The first and third contracts contained express English choice of law clauses. The court held that a choice of English law for the commission agreement was clearly demonstrated from the circumstances for the purposes of the Rome Convention. At common law, however, the courts have gone considerably further—in the sense that the courts have taken the view that, where there is an express choice of law in a contract between A and B, it is possible to imply a choice into a related contract between B and C on the basis that the parties must have intended or assumed that the transactions would be governed by the same law. Where, for example, a charterparty is governed by English law the courts are prepared to imply that related bills

---

[134] [1980] OJ C282/17.
[135] See paras 14.2.3–14.2.5.
[136] [1980] OJ C282/17. (Emphasis added.)
[137] [2010] CP Rep 11.

of lading are also governed by English law, even though no specific intention can be gleaned from the terms of the bills of lading themselves.[138] Similarly, in cases involving a contract of guarantee, the court may imply that the law governing the primary obligation—by virtue of the parties' choice—should govern the contract of guarantee by implication.[139] By contrast, a letter of credit establishes an autonomous legal relationship and it cannot be assumed that the parties necessarily intended that the law governing the underlying contract should also govern the letter of credit.[140]

OTHER RELEVANT CIRCUMSTANCES

14.2.24   It is important to note that the various examples given by the Giuliano-Lagarde Report of circumstances or contractual terms from which a court may legitimately conclude that the parties have made a choice of law, albeit not an express one, are not exhaustive. This is illustrated by *American Motorists Insurance Co v Cellstar Corporation*[141] in which one of the issues facing the court was whether a contract of insurance between the claimant, an Illinois company authorised to conduct insurance business in Texas, and the first defendant, a company which—although incorporated in Delaware—had its principal place of business in Texas, was governed by the law of England or of Texas. The contract had been negotiated by the first defendant (on behalf of itself and its subsidiaries) from its base in Texas and the contract had been issued by the claimant in Texas.[142]

14.2.25   The Court of Appeal dismissed the defendant's appeal against David Steel J's decision that the contract was, by virtue of the parties' choice, governed by Texan law.[143] The factors which were regarded as particularly relevant by the judge were that the negotiation and issue of the policy in Texas was between a Texas broker and a Texas insurer and that one of the terms of the policy provided a time limit for suit of 12 months 'by the laws of the State in which such policy is issued'.[144] Mance LJ, with whom Mantell and Kennedy LJJ agreed, also considered that the terms of the contract were 'a strong indication of an understanding that the policy would be subject to the laws of the state in which it was issued'.[145] In addition, Mance LJ thought that the circumstances of the case—in particular, the fact that the contract was concluded by the first defendant on behalf of its whole corporate group from its place of business in Texas with insurers also based in Texas—was a relevant indicator of implied intent.[146]

---

[138]   *The Njegos* [1936] P 90; *The Freights Queen* [1977] 2 Lloyd's Rep 140.

[139]   *Broken Hill Pty Co Ltd v Xanakis* [1982] 2 Lloyd's Rep 304; *Mitsubishi Corporation v Alafouzos* [1988] 1 Lloyd's Rep 191. See also *Turkiye Is Bankasi AS v Bank of China* [1993] 1 Lloyd's Rep 132; *Wahda Bank v Arab Bank Plc* [1996] 1 Lloyd's Rep 470.

[140]   *Attock Cement Co Ltd v Romanian Bank for Foreign Trade* [1989] 1 WLR 1147.

[141]   [2003] ILPr 370. Compare *Evialis SA v SIAT* [2003] 2 Lloyd's Rep 377.

[142]   There was some uncertainty whether the case fell within the scope of the Rome Convention or whether it was excluded by Art 1(3) and governed by Insurance Companies Act 1982, sched 3A (subsequently replaced by the Financial Services and Markets Act 2000 (Law Applicable to Contracts of Insurance) Regs 2001, SI 2001/2635, as amended by SI 2001/3542.). However, the Court of Appeal considered that it did not need to decide which of the potentially applicable choice of law regimes governed the case as under both regimes contracting parties are permitted to make a choice of law and the test for determining whether or not such a choice has been made is the same.

[143]   [2002] 2 Lloyd's Rep 216.

[144]   See Mance LJ at [2003] ILPr 370, 391 (at [41]).

[145]   [2003] ILPr 370, 392 (at [41]).

[146]   [2003] ILPr 370, 392 (at [43]).

CONCLUDING REMARKS

14.2.26 The cases—those decided both at common law and under the Rome Convention—illustrate the problems which the English courts have experienced in attempting to draw a clear dividing line between an implied choice, on the one hand, and an absence of choice, on the other. This looks set to continue under the Rome I Regulation because there are no hard-and-fast rules on when a choice of law should be implied. In view of these difficulties the usefulness of the concept of an implied choice of law may be questioned:

Surely the only situation where it is clear what the parties' *actual* intentions are is where they have expressly provided for the governing law by a choice of law clause. The whole notion of inferring an *actual* intent is based, at best, upon making assumptions which may or may not be correct, and, at worst, upon a form of dishonesty. It would be better to apply a purely objective test in all cases where there is no express choice of law clause.[147]

Splitting the Applicable Law

14.2.27 While no contractual obligation can be governed simultaneously by the laws of more than one country, there is no obvious reason why all aspects of a contract should be governed by the same law. Splitting the applicable law can take a number of different forms: first, it is possible to apply different laws to different aspects of the same obligation (for example, formation and performance);[148] secondly, different terms of one contract may be governed by different laws (for example, an index-linking clause may be made subject to a different law from the rest of the contract[149]); thirdly, different groups of obligations may be governed by different laws (for example, a contract which is both a sale of goods and a distributorship agreement may be governed by the law of the manufacturer/seller as regards the sales aspects and by the law of the distributor/buyer as far as the distributorship aspects are concerned);[150] fourthly, the obligations of each party may be governed by a different law (for example, in a contract of sale the obligations of the seller may be governed by the law of one country and the obligations of the buyer by the law of another).[151]

14.2.28 The ideology of party autonomy inevitably leads to acceptance of the notion that parties to a contract may split the applicable law. The final sentence of Article 3(1) provides:

By their choice the parties can select the law applicable to the whole or to part only of the contract.

---

[147] PM North and JJ Fawcett, *Cheshire & North's Private International Law* (London, Butterworths, 11th edn, 1987) 461. (Emphasis in original.) This comment on the common law is equally applicable to the Regulation. See also JG Collier, [1983] All ER Ann Rev 86, 87.

[148] This is a true example of *dépéçage*.

[149] See Giuliano-Lagarde Report, [1980] OJ C282/17.

[150] O Lando, 'The EEC Convention on the Law Applicable to Contractual Obligations' (1987) 24 *CML Rev* 159, 168.

[151] For a general discussion, see C McLachlan, 'Splitting the Proper Law in Private International Law' (1990) 61 *BYIL* 311.

Accordingly, the parties may choose different laws for different parts or aspects of a single contract or may choose a law for part of a contract, leaving the remainder to be governed by the law resulting from the application of Article 4.

14.2.29   The extent to which Article 3(1) allows splitting of the applicable law is not entirely free from doubt. The Giuliano-Lagarde Report on the Rome Convention states that 'the choice must be logically consistent, ie it must relate to elements in the contract which can be governed by different laws without giving rise to contradictions'.[152] From a practical perspective, splitting the applicable law is most likely in cases involving a single contract which comprises in reality several contracts or parts which are separable and independent of each other from a legal and economic point of view. In this context, the application of different laws to different parts does not present significant problems. However, the report questions whether it would be appropriate to uphold a choice of law clause which purported to subject the obligations of each of the contracting parties to the laws of different countries.[153] As one commentator notes: 'The harmony between the obligations of the parties to a bilateral contract is disturbed if different laws are to be applied to the two obligations'.[154] Where the choices of the parties cannot be logically reconciled, Article 4 of the Regulation is applicable.[155]

Changing the Chosen Law[156]

14.2.30   The Regulation provides flexibility on when a choice of law can be made. Article 3(2) states:

The parties may at any time agree to subject the contract to a law other than that which previously governed it, whether as a result of an earlier choice made under this Article or of other provisions of this Regulation. Any change in the law to be applied that is made after the conclusion of the contract shall not prejudice its formal validity under Article 11 or adversely affect the rights of third parties.

By virtue of this provision the parties may, having included a choice of law clause in their contract, subsequently decide to change the applicable law by a new agreement. Alternatively, in a situation where the contract does not include a choice of law, the parties may agree on the applicable law at some later stage. Article 3(2) is a natural extension of the general principle of party autonomy. If parties are free to decide on the applicable law, there is no reason why they should not be able to change it.

14.2.31   The text of the Regulation is silent on this point. However, the Giuliano-Lagarde Report indicates that, as regards the way in which the choice of law can be changed, 'it is quite natural that this change should be subject to the same rules as the initial choice'[157]

---

[152] [1980] OJ C282/17.

[153] *Ibid.*

[154] O Lando, 'The EEC Convention on the Law Applicable to Contractual Obligations' (1987) 24 *CML Rev* 159, 169.

[155] Giuliano-Lagarde Report, [1980] OJ C282/17.

[156] For a discussion of post-contractual choice of law at common law, see A Briggs, 'The validity of "floating" choice of law and jurisdiction clauses' [1986] *LMCLQ* 508; A Beck, 'Floating choice of law clauses' [1987] *LMCLQ* 523; DG Pierce, 'Post-Formation Choice of Law in Contract' (1987) 50 *MLR* 176.

[157] [1980] OJ C282/18.

(ie, for the purposes of the Regulation, the choice of a new law may be either express or clearly demonstrated by the terms of the contract and/or the circumstances of the case). However, as the decision of the Court of Appeal in *The Aeolian*[158] illustrates, it will only be in rather unusual circumstances that the court will be able to imply the choice of a new law.

14.2.32   In *The Aeolian* the claimant supplied a turbo-charger to the defendant for installation into the engine of one of the defendant's vessels. This contract (contract A) was governed by Japanese law. The turbo-charger failed and, following an exchange of correspondence, the parties concluded a contract for spare parts. When the spare parts were delivered the defendant, having accepted some and rejected others, refused to pay for them. The claimant threatened to arrest the vessel to enforce its claim to the price and, in consideration of the claimant refraining from arresting the vessel, the defendant undertook to pay for the spares. This contractual undertaking (contract B) was expressly subject to English law and jurisdiction. When the claimant sought to enforce contract B, the defendant attempted to raise a counterclaim for damages under contract A. The defendant's argument was based on there being an implied term as to the quality and durability of the turbo-charger in contract A. Such a term could not have been implied into contract A if that contract was governed by Japanese law. Accordingly, it was an essential element of the defendant's argument that, by expressly choosing to subject contract B to English law and jurisdiction, the parties had demonstrated an intention to change the law applicable to contract A from Japanese law to English law (under which the term alleged by the defendant could be implied).

14.2.33   The defendant's argument only has to be stated for its intrinsic weakness to be apparent. Not surprisingly, neither the judge at first instance nor the Court of Appeal accepted that, by choosing the applicable law for contract B, the parties had indicated an intention to change the law governing contract A. As Potter LJ noted:

[Contract B] makes no reference whatsoever to [contract A]. If the parties had intended to change the proper law of [contract A], they could expressly so have provided; however, they did not. There is certainly no room in my view for the implication of such a term under the principles of English law applicable to the implication of contractual terms, whether on the basis of the business efficacy or 'officious bystander' test.[159]

Of course, one cannot attach too much weight to the negative inference which Potter LJ drew from the fact that the parties could have (but did not) expressly choose to change the law governing contract A. In any situation where it is argued that the parties made a choice of law, albeit not expressly, it can be said that the parties could have made an express choice. Taken to its logical conclusion, such a negative inference would limit Article 3 to cases of express choice only. Nevertheless, in the context of *The Aeolian*, it is difficult to see how, in the absence of an express agreement between the parties, there could have been a *common* intention to change the law applicable to contract A. As counsel for the claimant argued, there is no reason why the claimant would agree to forego the complete answer to the defendant's counterclaim which it enjoyed under Japanese law.

---

[158] [2001] 2 Lloyd's Rep 641. See also *Satyam Computer Services Ltd v Upaid Systems Ltd* [2008] 2 All ER (Comm) 465.
[159] [2001] 2 Lloyd's Rep 641, 645 (at [15]).

14.2.34 The problem revealed in *The Aeolian* is by no means the most difficult issue raised by Article 3(2). Having said that, it is almost certainly the case that some of the potential difficulties surrounding this provision are likely to remain more theoretical than practical. In particular, there is the question concerning which law governs the validity of the agreement varying the chosen law. Arguments can be advanced for three different possibilities. First, as a matter of principle, the original applicable law should govern the validity of the variation.[160] Secondly, it can be argued, on the basis of Article 10(1),[161] that the validity of the variation should be governed by the law which would apply if the variation were valid.[162] Thirdly, it has been argued that the terms of Article 3(2) itself treat the validity of the variation as a question to be determined by the law of the forum.[163] According to the second and third views, parties would be permitted to change the applicable law irrespective of whether the original governing law permits them to do so. Arguments of simplicity point in favour of the application of the law of the forum. Nevertheless, whichever solution is adopted, some problems are likely to remain. What, for example, is the solution to the problem posed by a contract which is void under the law which applies to it at its inception, but is valid according to the new applicable law after the variation? It should be noted that if a contract is formally valid at its inception a subsequent variation of the applicable law cannot have the effect of rendering the contract formally invalid, nor can a change in the applicable law adversely affect the rights of third parties.

14.2.35 Finally, the status of a floating choice of law clause under Article 3 should be considered. What is the effect of a clause which provides that a contract shall, at the option of one of the parties, be governed by the law of country X or the law of country Y? At common law such a clause, if governed by English law, is ineffective.[164] If, however, the event on which the selection of the proper law depends is not the unilateral choice of one party, but an external event, the clause is valid.[165] In view of the fact that the Regulation seeks to give full expression to the freedom of the parties, there is no obvious reason why a floating choice of law should be regarded as ineffective under Article 3. If the parties can agree to the applicable law at any time, a contractual agreement that one party may determine the applicable law at a future point would appear to fall within the scope of Article 3(2). Until such time as a final determination is made by the party authorised to make the choice, the contract is governed by the law designated by Article 4.

Mandatory Rules

14.2.36 Although there are no restrictions on the law which the parties may choose, some provisions of the chosen law may be overridden by mandatory rules of the laws of other countries or may be disapplied on grounds of public policy.[166]

---

[160] M Wolff, *Private International Law* (Oxford, Clarendon Press, 2nd edn, 1950) 426.
[161] See paras 14.4.5–14.4.9.
[162] CGJ Morse, 'The EEC Convention on the Law Applicable to Contractual Obligations' (1982) 2 *YBEL* 107, 121.
[163] AL Diamond, 'Conflict of Laws in the EEC' (1979) 22 *CLP* 155, 165.
[164] *Armar Shipping Co Ltd v Caisse Algérienne d'Assurance et de Réassurance* [1981] 1 WLR 207; *The Iran Vojdan* [1984] 2 Lloyd's Rep 380.
[165] *The Mariannina* [1983] 1 Lloyd's Rep 12.
[166] See section 14.3.

The Applicable Law in the Absence of Choice

Introductory Remarks

14.2.37   One of the biggest changes made by the Regulation is in Article 4, which sets out the choice of law rule in the absence of party choice.[167] The solution provided by the Rome Convention was that the general choice of law rule for this situation is that a contract is governed by the law of the country with which it is most closely connected,[168] with Article 4(2) providing the presumption that a contract is most closely connected with the country where the party who is to effect the characteristic performance of the contract ('the characteristic performer') is based.[169] The 'characteristic performance' of a contract is, generally, the performance for which payment is due.[170] However, according to Article 4(5), the presumption was to be disregarded if the characteristic performance cannot be determined or the contract is more closely connected with another country. The rather complicated structure set out in Article 4 of the Rome Convention caused problems; in particular, national courts interpreted the strength of the presumption (in Article 4(2)) and the availability of the escape clause (in Article 4(5)) in different ways. For example, the Dutch and Scottish courts have tended to rely on the presumption[171] while the English courts[172] have more freely invoked the escape clause to rebut the presumption. The correct approach to be adopted was clarified by the Court of Justice in *ICF v Balkenende Oosthuizen BV*.[173] The court held that there was no need to restrict recourse to the escape clause only to cases where the connecting criteria indicated in Article 4(2) to (4) do not have any genuine connecting value. Instead, the threshold was lower and it was legitimate to disregard the presumptions and invoke Article 4(5) where it is clear from the circumstances as a whole that the contract is more closely connected with a country other than that identified on the

---

[167] Art 4, however, does not apply to contracts of carriage (which are governed by Art 5), certain consumer contracts (Art 6), insurance contracts (Art 7) and individual employment contracts (Art 8).

[168] Rome Convention, Art 4(1).

[169] Depending on the circumstances, the characteristic performer's country may be that person's habitual residence, central administration, principal place of business or some other place of business through which the contract is to be performed. Art 4(2) of the Rome Convention was relevant for all contracts falling within the scope of Art 4 other than contracts relating to rights in immovable property (Art 4(3)) and contracts for the carriage of goods (Art 4(4)), for which there are separate presumptions.

[170] Giuliano-Lagarde Report, [1980] OJ C282/20.

[171] See, eg, *Caledonia Subsea Ltd v Micoperi Srl* 2001 SC 716 (OH); 2003 SC 70; *Société Nouvelle des Papeteries de l'Aa v Machinefabriek BOA*, 1992 Nederlands Jurisprudentie 750; noted and discussed by THD Struycken, 'Some Dutch judicial reflections on the Rome Convention, Art 4(5)' [1996] *LMCLQ* 18; *Baros AG v Embrica Maritim Hotelschiffe GmbH*, 17 October 2008 (Dutch Supreme Court).

[172] See, eg, *Bank of Baroda v Vysya Bank* [1994] 2 Lloyd's Rep 87; *Definitely Maybe (Touring) Ltd v Marek Lieberberg Konzertagentur GmbH* [2001] 1 WLR 1745 (R Fentiman, [2002] *CLJ* 50); *Samcrete Egypt Engineers and Contractors SAE v Land Rover Exports Ltd* [2002] CLC 533; *Kenburn Waste Management Ltd v Bergmann* [2002] CLC 644; *Marconi Communications v PT Pan Indonesia Bank* [2007] 2 Lloyd's Rep 72 (C Hare, [2005] *LMCLQ* 417); *Commercial Marine Piling Ltd v Pierse Contracting Ltd* [2009] ILPr 909. Cf *Ennstone Building Products Ltd v Stanger Ltd* [2002] 1 WLR 3059; *Iran Continental Shelf Oil Company v IRI International Corporation* [2004] 2 CLC 696; *Print Concept GmbH v GEW (EC) Ltd* [2002] CLC 352; *Ophthalmic Innovations International (UK) Ltd v Ophthalmic Innovations International Incorporated* [2005] ILPr 109; *Albon v Naza Motor Trading Sdn Bhd* [2007] 1 WLR 2489.

[173] Case C–133/08 [2010] ILPr 37.

basis of the presumption.[174] This interpretation generally accords with the English approach to Article 4(2) and (5).[175]

14.2.38   The *ICF* judgment came too late to save the version of Article 4 set out in the Convention and there is reason to be grateful for that fact. The balance between certainty and flexibility arguably tilted too far in favour of the latter in the scheme of the Convention. Article 4 of the Rome I Regulation seeks to avoid the problems associated with its predecessor. First, it does away with the use of presumptions altogether. Instead, Article 4(1) sets out fixed rules identifying the applicable law for eight categories of contracts. Secondly, Article 4(2) provides that the law of the country where the characteristic performer has his habitual residence governs the contract where the contract is either not covered by Article 4(1) or falls into more than one of the categories listed in Article 4(1).[176] Thirdly, Article 4(3) slightly refines the escape clause in favour of the law of closest connection. Fourthly, where the applicable law cannot be determined by reference to Article 4(1) or (2), Article 4(4) provides that the law of the country with which the contract is most closely connected applies.

The Fixed Rules

14.2.39   Article 4(1) provides rigid connecting factors for certain types of contracts. It sets out hard-and-fast choice of law rules which generally pinpoint the law of habitual residence of the characteristic performer of the contract. For example, a contract for the sale of goods is governed by the law of the country where the seller has his habitual residence[177] and a contract for the provision of services is governed by the law of the country where the service provider has his habitual residence.[178] In this respect, the effect of the new rigid rules does not significantly differ from the effect of Article 4(2) of the Rome Convention; the Convention's presumption has been crystallised into fixed rules. However, the Regulation does clear up the issue of what is the applicable law for certain contracts where courts have struggled to identify the characteristic performer under the Convention. A distribution agreement is a prime example: is the characteristic performer the distributor, because the distribution of the goods is, after all, the ultimate aim of the contract, or is it the supplier as, without him, there would be no goods to distribute? In *Print Concept GmbH v GEW (EC) Ltd*,[179] the Court of Appeal held that the supplier is the characteristic performer and that the supplier's law is applicable under Article 4(2)

---

[174]   Case C–133/08 [2010] ILPr 37, 67 (paras 61–4).

[175]   For the inter-relationship between Arts 4(2) and 4(5) of the Rome Convention, see J Hill, 'Choice of Law in Contract under the Rome Convention: The Approach of the UK Courts' (2004) 53 *ICLQ* 325; S Atrill, 'Choice of Law in Contract: The Missing Pieces of the Article 4 Jigsaw?' (2004) 53 *ICLQ* 549; WE O'Brian Jr, 'Choice of Law under the Rome Convention: The Dancer or the Dance' [2004] *LMCLQ* 375.

[176]   For the purposes of this rule, Art 19 lays down a special meaning for 'habitual residence'. See para 14.2.47.

[177]   Art 4(1)(a). 'Sale of goods' should be interpreted in the same way as for Art 5 of the Brussels I Regulation: Recital 17.

[178]   Art 4(1)(b). 'Provision of services' should be interpreted in the same way as for Art 5 of the Brussels I Regulation.

[179]   *Print Concept GmbH v GEW (EC) Ltd* [2002] CLC 352. See also *Ammann-Yanmar SA v Zwaans BVA* [2005] ECC 16 (Court of Cassation, France); cf *Elinga BV v British Wool International Ltd*, Nederlands International Privaatrecht 1998, No 288, noted R Plender and M Wilderspin, *The European Private International Law of Obligations* (London, Sweet & Maxwell, 3rd edn, 2009) 183.

of the Rome Convention. This conclusion, however, is reversed by Article 4(1)(f) of the Rome I Regulation, which provides that a distribution agreement shall be governed by the law of the country where the distributor has his habitual residence. Article 4(1)(e) in turn provides that a franchise contract shall be governed by the law of the country where the franchisee has his habitual residence. These rules reflect the desire to protect the distributor and franchisee who are regarded as the weaker parties.[180]

14.2.40 Parties to a contract for the sale of immovable property situated in country X are free to agree that the contract should be governed by the law of country Y. Such a choice is valid under Article 3(1). However, where the parties have not chosen the applicable law—either expressly or impliedly—Article 4(1)(c) provides that contracts relating to a right *in rem* in immovable property or to a tenancy of immovable property are governed by the law of the country where the property is situated.[181]

14.2.41 One of the major questions of interpretation surrounding Article 4(1)(c) concerns the phrase 'relating to a right *in rem* in immovable property'. It is clear that a contract for the construction or repair of immovable property is not within Article 4(1)(c); the subject-matter of such contracts is the construction or repair, rather than the property.[182] The central question is whether the scope of Article 4(1)(c) should be determined by the law of the forum, the law of the *situs* or by an independent definition. The problems concerning Article 4(1)(c) are similar to those which arise out of Article 22(1) of the Brussels I Regulation. That provision allocates exclusive jurisdiction to the courts of the Member State in which the property is situated where the proceedings 'have as their object rights *in rem* in immovable property, or tenancies of immovable property'. The Schlosser Report, which accompanied the 1978 Accession Convention, suggests that the question of whether proceedings concern a right *in rem* should be determined by the law of the *situs*.[183] This view was not, however, adopted by the Court of Justice which has formulated an autonomous definition;[184] the same approach will therefore be applicable under the Regulation.

14.2.42 Notwithstanding Article 4(1)(c), where the tenant is a natural person and both tenant and landlord habitually reside in the same country, tenancies of immovable property concluded for temporary private use for a period of no more than six consecutive months are governed by the law of the country of common habitual residence.[185] Article 4(1)(d) is the counterpart to the jurisdictional rule contained in Article 22(1) which provides a derogation from the general rule that courts of the *situs* have exclusive jurisdiction in matters concerning immovable property. Apart from ensuring coherence between the Rome I and Brussels I Regulations, the rule is sensible. If two Germans conclude a short-term holiday letting for a house in Italy, there are no compelling policy reasons which would warrant application of Italian law

---

[180] Commission Proposal, COM (2005) 650 final, p 6. However, in other instances the effect of Art 4 is to protect the stronger party; eg, in a contract of sale, the law of the seller will apply: Art 4(1)(a).

[181] In the Rome Convention, the equivalent rule is drafted in terms of a presumption in favour of the *lex situs* of the property: Art 4(3).

[182] [1980] OJ C282/21.

[183] [1979] OJ C59/121, para 168(c).

[184] Case C–115/88 *Reichert v Dresdner Bank* [1990] ECR I–27. See para 5.1.5.

[185] Art 4(1)(d).

unless the dispute concerns title to the holiday house. The net effect of Article 22(1) of the Brussels I Regulation and Article 4(1)(d) of the Rome I Regulation is that the German court will apply its own law to any dispute between the two German residents.[186] It is regrettable that the convenience of this result is impaired by the restrictive nature of Article 4(1)(d); for example, a contract between a German corporation who rents a short-term Italian holiday villa from another German (whether corporation or individual), or a contract between two Germans for the short-term rental of business premises in Italy, will be governed by Italian law under Article 4(1)(c).

14.2.43 Instead of subsuming a contract for the sale of goods by auction under a contract for the sale of goods, Article 4(1)(g) provides a special rule in favour of the law of the country where the auction takes place, if such a place can be determined.[187] This furnishes a clearer rule for the buyer than the law of the seller's habitual residence, and it is convenient from the auctioneer's point of view to have all contracts concluded at an auction governed by one single law.[188]

14.2.44 Article 4(1)(h) provides that:

a contract concluded within a multilateral system which brings together or facilitates the bringing together of multiple third-party buying and selling interests in financial instruments, as defined by Article 4(1), point (17) of Directive 2004/39/EC, in accordance with non-discretionary rules and governed by a single law, shall be governed by that law.

Stock exchanges and other multilateral trading systems[189] obviously handle complicated transactions and a high degree of legal certainty is required. This provision ensures that, when the parties have not specified a choice of law, a single law will govern such financial transactions. Multilateral systems such as stock exchanges are predicated on anonymous buyers and sellers, and participants would expect that common rules, namely the rules set out by the law under which the system is organised, would apply to all participants irrespective of nationality or habitual residence.[190] The reference to the EC Directive is merely to describe the financial instruments falling within the scope of this provision; the intention is not to limit the scope of this rule to an intra-EU context.

Law of Habitual Residence of the Characteristic Performer of the Contract

14.2.45 While the concept of the characteristic performer of the contract is indirectly utilised in Article 4(1), Article 4(2) overtly provides that:

Where the contract is not covered by paragraph 1 or where the elements of the contract would be covered by more than one of points (a) to (h) of paragraph 1, the contract shall be governed by the law of the country where the party required to effect the characteristic performance of the contract has his habitual residence.

---

[186] Cf Case C–241/83 *Rösler v Rottwinkel* [1985] ECR 99.

[187] Art 4(1)(g).

[188] Z Tang, 'Law Applicable in the Absence of Choice—The New Article 4 of the Rome I Regulation' (2008) 71 *MLR* 785, 790.

[189] Defined in Recital 18 as 'those in which trading is conducted, such as regulated markets and multilateral trading facilities as referred to in Article 4 of Directive 2004/39/EC of the European Parliament and of the Council of 21 April 2004 on markets in financial instruments, regardless of whether or not they rely on a central counterparty'.

[190] FJG Alferez, 'The Rome I Regulation: Exceptions to the Rule in Consumer Contracts and Financial Instruments' (2009) 5 *Journal of Private International Law* 85, 98.

Two conditions are laid down before Article 4(2) comes into play: the contract is not one of the eight types of contracts listed in Article 4(1)[191] or the contract falls into more than one of the eight categories. The overall effect of Article 4(1) and Article 4(2) is to ensure that in cases of doubt, the law of the characteristic performer's habitual residence will apply, assuming of course that the characteristic performer can be identified.[192] For example, the place of an auction which takes place electronically might be difficult to identify. Any resulting contract will not fall within Article 4(1)(g), and any debate over whether the contract falls within Article 4(1)(a) or Article 4(2) is unnecessary because both will lead to application of the law of the seller's habitual residence. Likewise, a contract to sell a ship that is built to the buyer's specifications could be considered to be a contract of sale falling within Article 4(1)(a), or a contract of services falling within Article 4(1)(b), or within both categories. Application of either Articles 4(1)(a) or (b), or 4(2) will lead to the same result, ie, application of the law of habitual residence of the builders.

CHARACTERISTIC PERFORMANCE

14.2.46   The concept of the 'characteristic performance' of the contract originated in Switzerland, rather than in any of the Member States. The use of this concept in an EU instrument has been justified in the following terms:

The submission of the contract, in the absence of a choice by the parties, to the law appropriate to the characteristic performance defines the connecting factor of the contract from the inside, and not from the outside by elements unrelated to the essence of the obligation such as the nationality of the contracting parties or the place where the contract was concluded. In addition it is possible to relate the concept of characteristic performance to an even more general idea, namely the idea that his [sic] performance refers to the function which the legal relationship involved fulfils in the economic and social life of any country. The concept of characteristic performance essentially links the contract to the social and economic environment of which it will form a part.[193]

In a contract consisting of a bundle of rights and obligations that could be classified in more than one of the eight types of contracts listed in Article 4(1), Recital 19 stipulates that the regard should be had to the 'centre of gravity' of the contract when identifying the characteristic performance of the contract.

14.2.47   Recital 19 tries to tie in the idea of the characteristic performance with the centre of gravity of the contract, but Article 4(2) does not necessarily lead to the application of the law of the centre of gravity of the contract. This is because it is not the place of characteristic performance which is important, but the territorial connections of the characteristic performer. Article 4(2) points to the law of the country with which the characteristic performer is connected rather than to the law of the country where the characteristic obligation is to be performed. For the same reason, Article 4(2) does not necessarily forge a link between the 'characteristic performance' and 'the social and economic environment' of which the contract forms a part.

---

[191] For a discussion of the applicable law in the absence of choice for intellectual property rights, see P Torremans, 'Licences and Assignments of Intellectual Property Rights under the Rome I Regulation' (2008) 4 *Journal of Private International Law* 397.

[192] If not, then the applicable law is determined in accordance with Art 4(4).

[193] Giuliano-Lagarde Report, [1980] OJ C282/20.

THE CONNECTING FACTOR

14.2.48   Article 19 of the Regulation helpfully defines 'habitual residence'. It is to be expected that in the commercial sphere most contracts—whether involving individuals or firms—will be entered into in the course of business of the characteristic performer. In such cases, the factor which localises the contract is either the principal place of business of the characteristic performer if that person is a natural person or, if the characteristic performance is to be effected by a company or other body, whether corporate or unincorporated, the place where that entity's central administration lies.[194] Where the contract is concluded in the course of the operations of a branch, agency or any other establishment the place where the branch, agency or any other establishment is located is treated as the place of habitual residence; the same applies if, under the contract, performance is the responsibility of that branch, agency or establishment.[195] In all cases, the relevant point in time in identifying the connecting factor is the time of the conclusion of the contract.[196]

14.2.49   It should be noted that the approach taken in the Regulation differs from that of the Brussels I Regulation where the defendant's domicile, a key jurisdictional ground, is capable of various locations.[197] Such an approach would have been inappropriate for choice of law purposes where, in the interests of legal certainty, it is necessary for only one law to be identified.[198]

14.2.50   The implications of Article 4(2) and Article 19 should be spelled out. While it is important to determine if the characteristic performer is acting in the course of business, it is irrelevant whether the party who is not the characteristic performer enters the contract in the course of his business. Where the characteristic performer is a natural person who is not acting in the course of his business activity, the contract is governed by the law of this person's habitual residence.[199] However, where the characteristic performer is a natural person who is acting in the course of his business activity, the applicable law is the law of this person's principal place of business.[200] Where the characteristic performer is a company or other corporate or unincorporated body, the contract is governed by the law of the country in which the central administration of the company or body is located.[201] This is the position in relation to Article 4(2) and Article 19(1). However, where the contract is concluded in the course of the operations of a branch, agency or any other establishment, or under the contract, performance is the responsibility of the subordinate entity, the law of the place where that entity is located is the applicable law. This is the result of Article 4(2) and Article 19(2).

14.2.51   Although the Regulation is more helpful than the Convention in terms of shedding light on the connecting factor in Article 4(2), some residual problems remain. Specifically, the Regulation does not attempt to define 'habitual residence' for cases where the characteristic performer is a natural person who is not acting in

---

[194] Art 19(1). This follows the definition set out in Rome II Reg, Art 23.
[195] Art 19(2).
[196] Art 19(3).
[197] Brussels I Reg, Arts 59 and 60.
[198] Recital 39.
[199] Assuming that the contract does not fall within one of the sub-paragraphs in Article 4(1).
[200] Art 4(2) and Art 19(1).
[201] Art 4(2) and Art 19(1).

the course of his business activity; nor are the concepts 'central administration' and 'principal place of business' defined. There is a significant body of English authority on what 'habitual residence' means in the context of domestic statutes in the field of family law[202] and Article 3 of the Hague Convention of the Civil Aspects of International Abduction (which is set out in schedule 1 to the Child Abduction and Custody Act 1985).[203] It is far better, though, for 'habitual residence' to be given an autonomous meaning.[204] On this point, the concept has been defined by the Court of Justice in other EU law contexts;[205] however, one must be wary of directly transposing these definitions to the Rome I Regulation. The Court of Justice has itself recognised that it is inappropriate for the definition of 'habitual residence', a term which is used in many areas of EU law, to be copied directly from one context to another.[206] The Court of Justice should develop an autonomous meaning that is specific to civil and commercial matters.[207] It is clear, though, that, contrary to English authorities,[208] a person can be habitually resident in only one country at a time for the purposes of the Regulation as only one law should be identified as the applicable law. Lastly, if a person cannot be regarded as habitually resident anywhere, Article 4(2) cannot be applied and one must move on to Article 4(4).

14.2.52 By the same token, 'central administration' and 'principal place of business' should also have autonomous meanings. These two concepts are used as connecting factors for the purposes of determining the domicile of a company or other legal person for the purposes of the Brussels I Regulation.[209] It seems sensible for the same definition to apply for the Rome I Regulation as well, notwithstanding that the concepts are used for the purposes of determining domicile for the Brussels I Regulation and habitual residence for the Rome I Regulation. The difference, however, is that, while it is not necessary for a company's 'central administration' or 'principal place of business' to be restricted to one place for the purpose of the Brussels I Regulation, only one location must be identified for choice of law purposes. Potential problems may therefore arise in certain cases, such as where the administration of a company is divided between different centres.

14.2.53 The problem is unlikely to be as acute when trying to identify a single principal place of business for a natural person acting in the course of his business activity as for a company because the company may have both an administrative

---

[202] See, eg, Matrimonial Causes Act 1973, Domicile and Matrimonial Proceedings Act 1974; Child Abduction and Custody Act 1985; Family Law Act 1986.

[203] See CMV Clarkson and J Hill, *The Conflict of Laws* (Oxford, OUP, 3rd edn, 2006) 43–50; EM Clive, 'The Concept of Habitual Residence' [1997] *Jur Rev* 136; EB Crawford, 'A Day is not Enough: Further Views on the Meaning of Habitual Residence' [2000] *Jur Rev* 89.

[204] See Case C–523/07 *Proceedings Brought by A* [2010] 2 WLR 527, 549 (para 34), where the Court of Justice states: 'According to settled case law, it follows from the need for uniform application of Community law and from the principle of equality that the terms of a provision of Community law which makes no express reference to the law of the Member States for the purpose of determining its meaning and scope must normally be given an autonomous and uniform interpretation throughout the European Community, having regard to the context of the provision and the objective pursued by the legislation in question'.

[205] See, eg, Case C–90/97 *Swaddling v Adjudication Officer* [1999] ECR I–1075; Case C–523/07 *Proceedings Brought by A* [2010] 2 WLR 527.

[206] Case C–523/07 *Proceedings Brought by A* [2010] 2WLR 527, 556 (para 36).

[207] The Rome II Regulation also contains the same concept.

[208] Eg, *Mark v Mark* [2006] 1 AC 98, 113 (at [37]).

[209] Brussels I Reg, Art 60. See paras 4.1.8–4.1.10.

centre (where important business decisions are taken) and a main business centre (where most business is transacted).[210] In the case of a natural person acting in the course of his business, it is highly likely that his principal place of business will, in most cases, coincide with his personal habitual residence.

14.2.54 The combination of Article 4(2) and Article 19(2) raises other issues. There are two limbs to Article 19(2): the place where the branch, agency or other establishment is located provides the connecting factor where (i) the contract is concluded in the course of the operations of that entity or (ii) performance is the responsibility of that entity. If a contract is made by the London branch of a New York bank with characteristic performance to be effected by the New York head office, should English or New York law govern the contract? On the one hand, the two-fold split in Article 19(2) may suggest that the provision seeks to ensure that the law of the place where the branch is located should govern whether or not it carries out the performance itself. This accords with a literal reading of the first limb of Article 19(2). On the other hand, the characteristic performer can be easily identified in the example given, that is, the New York head office. There appears to be no good reason to apply English law in this situation and New York law should be the applicable law. The latter analysis is perhaps the more intuitive one. However, this interpretation would render the first limb of Article 19(2) otiose as it would mean that the law of the place where the branch is located would never apply unless the contract is concluded in the course of its operations *and*[211] performance is to be carried out by that branch. Although it may seem intuitively unattractive, the first analysis must be the correct one so that the law of the place where the branch is located is the applicable law notwithstanding that its principal will be carrying out the characteristic performance of the contract.

14.2.55 The working of the second limb of Article 19(2) can be illustrated by reference to a case decided under the Rome Convention. In *Bank of Baroda v Vysya Bank Ltd*[212] the defendant, an Indian bank, issued a letter of credit in favour of an Irish buyer. Although the credit was confirmed by the plaintiff, another Indian bank, it was provided that the plaintiff's confirmation was to be effected through its London branch. Since the plaintiff was the characteristic performer in these circumstances, the relevant connecting factor was the plaintiff's London branch and the effect of Article 4(2) was to presume that the contract was governed by English law. Under the Regulation, application of Article 4(2) and the second limb of Article 19(2) leads to the same result. However, the second limb of Article 19(2) raises the question whether performance by the branch, agency or other establishment needs to be spelled out expressly in the contract itself, or whether it suffices that the parties envisaged that performance would be done by the branch, agency or other establishment in order for the law of habitual residence of the relevant entity to apply.[213] Given the change of terminology from 'under the terms of the contract' in Article 4(2) of the Rome

---

[210] See *The Polzeath* [1916] P 241; *The Rewia* [1991] 2 Lloyd's Rep 325.

[211] Whereas Art 19(2) uses the disjunctive 'or'.

[212] [1994] 2 Lloyd's Rep 87.

[213] Compare *Iran Continental Shelf Oil Company v IRI International Corporation* [2004] 2 CLC 696 with *Ennstone Building Products Ltd v Stanger Ltd* [2002] 1 WLR 3059.

Convention to the less stringent 'under the contract' in the Regulation, the latter interpretation is preferable.[214]

The Escape Clause

14.2.56 The Commission proposal did not contain any flexible exception in favour of the law of closest connection.[215] This was no doubt motivated by a desire to prevent the fixed rules being undermined. However, opinion was strongly in favour of retaining a flexible exception along the lines of Article 4(5) of the Rome Convention.[216] Thus, Article 4(3) of the Regulation states:

Where it is clear from all the circumstances of the case that the contract is manifestly more closely connected with a country other than that indicated in paragraphs 1 or 2, the law of that other country shall apply.

14.2.57 The word 'manifestly' is a new addition and is no doubt intended to avoid some of the problems generated by Article 4(5) of the Convention under which some national courts invoked the escape clause more readily than others.[217] The addition is an indication that the fixed rules should be disapplied only in exceptional circumstances. The change from presumptions to fixed rules in Article 4(1) of the Regulation, and the addition of the word 'manifestly', strongly suggest that national courts should be slow to find such exceptional circumstances. Nevertheless, such an exceptional circumstance may occur where there are related contracts, it being commercially desirable for the connected transactions to be governed by a single law rather than for different laws to govern the intertwined contracts.[218] The English authorities where the courts have disapplied the presumptions set out in Article 4 of the Rome Convention in favour of the law of closest connection are not necessarily good authority for Article 4 of the Regulation. Under the Convention, the English courts have tended to fall back on the escape clause where the characteristic performer's habitual residence is country A but country B is the place of performance,[219] at least where the characteristic performer's obligations are to be performed solely in country B.[220] However, while the place of performance is an important connecting factor, other factors must also be considered in deciding whether to fall back on Article 4(3). The practice of invoking the escape clause in the Convention simply on the basis that the place of

---

[214] Z Tang, 'Law Applicable in the Absence of Choice—The New Article 4 of the Rome I Regulation' (2008) 71 *MLR* 785, 796.

[215] COM (2005) 650 final, draft Art 4.

[216] See, eg, Opinion of the European Economic and Social Committee, [2006] OJ C318/56, para 3.2.4; Editorial comments, 'On the way to a Rome I Regulation' (2006) 43 *CML Rev* 913, 916–7; S Dutson, 'A Dangerous Proposal—The European Commission's Attempt to Amend the Law Applicable to Contractual Obligations' [2006] *JBL* 608, 613–14; S Dutson, 'A Misguided Proposal' (2006) 122 *LQR* 374, 374–6.

[217] See also the similar wording in the Rome II Reg, Art 4(3).

[218] See Recital 20. See also *Bank of Baroda v Vysya Bank* [1994] 2 Lloyd's Rep 87.

[219] See eg, *Definitely Maybe (Touring) Ltd v Marek Lieberberg Konzertagentur GmbH* [2001] 1 WLR 1745; *Kenburn Waste Management Ltd v Bergmann* [2002] CLC 644; *Marconi Communications International Ltd v PT Pan Indonesia Bank Ltd* [2007] 2 Lloyd's Rep 72.

[220] Cf *Ennstone Building Products Ltd v Stanger Ltd* [2002] 1 WLR 3059; *Iran Continental Shelf Oil Company v IRI International Corporation* [2004] 2 CLC 696.

performance differs from the habitual residence of the characteristic performer of the contract should not be continued under the Regulation.

The Law of Closest Connection

14.2.58 Lastly, Article 4(4) provides that:

Where the law applicable cannot be determined pursuant to paragraphs 1 or 2, the contract shall be governed by the law of the country with which it is most closely connected.

This provision is undoubtedly necessary. It would be impossible for Article 4(1) to set out fixed rules for each and every possible type of contract. The fall-back rule in Article 4(2) in favour of the law of habitual residence of the characteristic performer of the contract is also not fool-proof. There are certain types of contract in relation to which it is impossible to determine the characteristic performance, notably in cases where the parties undertake reciprocal obligations of a similar type.[221] For example, it will generally not be possible to identify the characteristic performance of a contract under the terms of which two or more enterprises agree to enter a joint venture. Similarly, Article 4(2) would not work in contracts of exchange. Recital 21 states that a factor to consider under Article 4(4) is whether the contract in question has a very close relationship with another contract or contracts. For example, where four contractual relationships arose in a case involving a complex web of contracts surrounding a letter of credit, it was held that it was undesirable for different contracts within the web of contracts created by a confirmed letter of credit to be governed by different laws.[222]

Conclusion on Article 4

14.2.59 The purpose of choice of law rules in contract is not merely to guide the courts in determining the applicable law in cases which are litigated before them. In cases where the parties have failed to make a choice of law, they may nevertheless legitimately expect their legal advisers to be able to identify the applicable law for them by reference to the relevant choice of law rules. It is also necessary for the choice of law rules to be highly foreseeable[223] so that the parties can decide whether or not to exercise their choice.[224] A test based purely on closest connection, as is adopted under the common law, is perfectly adequate for cases in which it is obvious that the contract is more closely connected with one country rather than another. However, in cases where the relevant connecting factors are more evenly divided between two or more different countries, a pure test of closest connection generates considerable uncertainty, since it may be very difficult to assess which factor or factors might be regarded by the court as crucial in tipping the balance one way or the other. The use of presumptions, as adopted under the Rome Convention, somewhat improved the situation, but created new problems.

---

[221] See *Apple Corps Limited v Apple Computer Inc* [2004] ILPr 597.
[222] *Bank of Baroda v Vysya Bank* [1994] 2 Lloyd's Rep 87.
[223] Recital 16.
[224] COM (2005) 650 final, p 5.

14.2.60   Article 4 contains some of the most radical changes from the Convention. There are merits to these changes. Whereas the choice of law rules at common law, and under the Rome Convention were balanced in favour of flexibility rather than certainty, the Regulation tilts the opposite way: certainty is key as illustrated by the provisions of Article 4(1), but flexibility and discretion are not abandoned altogether. The framework set out in Article 4, with its mixture of fixed rules and a discretionary escape clause, attempts to strike the appropriate balance between the competing policy objectives.

Scission

14.2.61   Article 3(1) provides for different laws to be applied to different parts of a single contract. A part of the contract may be governed by a different law from that governing the rest of the contract 'only where the object of that part is independent'.[225] For example, the contract cannot stipulate that the law of country A will govern X's right to be paid by Y but the law of country B will govern Y's obligation to pay.[226] The Giuliano-Lagarde Report on the Rome Convention indicates that courts should effect severance only 'by way of exception, for part of a contract which is independent and separable, in terms of the contract and not of the dispute' and should have recourse to severance 'as seldom as possible'.[227]

14.2.62   Scission of the contract may arise mainly in two different ways. First, the parties may choose different laws to govern different aspects of the contract. For example, they may choose English law to govern the issue of performance of the contract but German law to govern the consequences if the contract is found to be void. Secondly, different laws may apply to different parts of a contract as a consequence of the interaction of Articles 3 and 4. If the parties choose the applicable law in accordance with Article 3 in relation to only part of the contract, Article 4 determines the law which governs the remainder. In this situation the law which is identified under Article 4 may be different from the law chosen by the parties.

14.2.63   Where the parties have not chosen the applicable law at all, it is unlikely that different laws will apply to different parts of the contract.[228] For example, in a contract for the sale of machinery with the undertaking to provide after-sales advice, one could sever the aspect of sale from the aspect of service. The contract falls within more than one of the categories set out in Article 4(1), in which case, Article 4(2) dictates that the law of habitual residence of the characteristic performer, that is, the seller and service provider, is applicable.[229] Further, in contrast with Article 3, Article 4 does not refer to severance at all.[230]

---

[225] Case C–133/08 *ICF v Balkenende Oosthuizen BV* [2010] ILPr 37, 65 (para 48).

[226] See Case C–133/08 *ICF v Balkenende Oosthuizen BV* [2010] ILPr 37, 65 (para 47): 'the rules relating to the prescription of a right must fall under the same legal system as that applied to the corresponding obligation'.

[227] [1980] OJ C282/23.

[228] See, eg, Case C–133/08 *ICF v Balkenende Oosthuizen BV* [2010] ILPr 37.

[229] If it is construed as two separate contracts, one of sale and the other of service, the same law, ie the law of habitual residence of the seller/service provider, will again be applicable for both contracts.

[230] Cf Rome Convention, Art 4(1).

Mandatory Rules

14.2.64   In cases where the parties have failed to make a choice for the purposes of Article 3(1), specific rules which form part of the applicable law—as determined by the principles set out in Article 4—may be overridden by mandatory rules of the laws of other countries or may be disapplied on grounds of public policy.[231]

14.3 MANDATORY RULES AND PUBLIC POLICY

Introduction

14.3.1   The Regulation imposes no restrictions on the law which can be chosen by the parties to a contract. The choice of a law which is wholly unconnected with the transaction is perfectly valid. However, in certain circumstances specific rules which are part of the law chosen by the parties may yield to the mandatory rules of another law. Similarly, in cases where the parties have not made a choice of law and the applicable law is determined by Article 4, the applicable law may be overridden by the mandatory rules of another law.[232]

14.3.2   From a policy point of view almost all mandatory rules which have an impact on contractual relations fall into one of two categories.[233] First, many legal systems include rules which are intended to protect the weaker party. Classic examples of mandatory rules of this type include consumer legislation (such as legislation dealing with product liability, the right to cancel a contract, maximum interest rates, the right to be given certain information, the requirement that goods should be of a reasonable quality) and employment protection legislation (such as rules relating to hours of work, minimum wages, the freedom to strike, remedies for unfair dismissal and compensation for industrial injuries). Secondly, legal systems also include rules intended to promote the social and economic policies of the state.[234] Important examples of rules of this type include exchange control legislation, price control legislation, rules on cartels, monopolies and mergers and legislation relating to import and export controls. Although mandatory rules are most likely to be statutory in origin, it is perfectly possible for a common law rule to be mandatory for the purposes of the Regulation.[235]

14.3.3   The Regulation draws a distinction between two different types of mandatory rule. Article 3(3) defines the first category of mandatory rules as 'provisions ... which cannot be derogated from by agreement'. Article 9 defines a narrower category of rules[236]

---

[231]   See section 14.3.

[232]   There are also specific provisions dealing with consumer contracts and individual contracts of employment: see section 14.5.

[233]   TC Hartley, 'Beyond the Proper Law' (1979) 4 *EL Rev* 236, 238–9.

[234]   These rules fall within the category of 'overriding mandatory provisions' set out in Art 9 of the Regulation. They are also referred to in the literature as 'qualified mandatory rules' or 'conflicts mandatory rules' or 'internationally mandatory rules': see C Tillman, 'The Relationship between Party Autonomy and the Mandatory Rules in the Rome Convention' [2002] *JBL* 45, 49.

[235]   Cf Giuliano-Lagarde Report, [1980] OJ C282/27.

[236]   Recital 37 states that the concept of 'overriding mandatory provisions' should be distinguished from, and construed more restrictively than, the concept of 'provisions which cannot be derogated from by agreement'.

which not only are mandatory in the sense of Article 3(3)—in that they cannot be derogated from by agreement—but also must be applied 'irrespective of the law otherwise applicable to the contract under this Regulation'. The type of mandatory rules referred to in Article 9 are labelled 'overriding mandatory provisions' in the Regulation and are:

provisions the respect for which is regarded as crucial by a country for safeguarding its public interests, such as its political, social or economic organisation, to such an extent that they are applicable to any situation falling within their scope, irrespective of the law otherwise applicable to the contract under this Regulation.[237]

14.3.4   For ease of reference, the first category will be referred to as mandatory rules, while the second category will be referred to as overriding rules. Mandatory rules are provisions which the parties cannot by agreement exclude in a purely domestic contract which does not include among its terms a choice of law. There are numerous examples of rules of this type in English law. For example, it is an implied condition in a sale that the seller has a right to sell the goods; in the case of an agreement to sell it is an implied condition that the seller will have such a right at the time when the property is to pass.[238] These implied conditions cannot be excluded or restricted by reference to any contract term.[239] Similarly, in a lease of a dwelling-house for a term of less than seven years the landlord's implied covenant to keep the structure and exterior in repair[240] cannot be limited by the terms of the lease.[241] Overriding rules, however, are rules which are not only mandatory but which the parties cannot avoid by the selection of a foreign law, even though a foreign element is present.

14.3.5   Whether a particular rule of law is mandatory or overriding (or neither) is a question of construction, which can only be answered by reference to the law of which the particular rule forms a part. Although in certain circumstances it may be perfectly clear whether a rule is mandatory, in others the position will be obscure. English rules are particularly difficult to classify. The terminology and conceptual structure of the Regulation in relation to mandatory rules is alien to English law and it is unusual for English legislation to include any indication whether a particular rule of law is mandatory or overriding in nature.[242] The problems surrounding the classification of common law rules are even more pronounced.

---

[237] Art 9(1). This definition is culled from Joined Cases C–369/96 *Arblade* and C–376/96 *Leloup* [1998] ECR I–8453, para 30. See Commission Proposal, COM (2005) 650 final, p 8.
[238] Sale of Goods Act 1979, s 12(1).
[239] Unfair Contract Terms Act 1977, s 6(1)(a).
[240] Landlord and Tenant Act 1985, s 11(1)(a) and s. 13(1).
[241] Landlord and Tenant Act 1985, s 12(1).
[242] Eg, in *Chiron Corporation v Organon Teknika Ltd (No 2)* [1993] FSR 567 the Court of Appeal held that s 44(1) of the Patents Act 1977—which renders void various terms of 'a contract for the supply of a patented product or of a licence to work a patented invention, or of a contract relating to any such supply or licence'—applies to contracts which are governed by the law of a foreign country. See also *Lawson v Serco* [2006] 1 All ER 823 and *Crofts v Veta Ltd* [2006] 1 All ER 823, where the House of Lords had to decide on the territorial reach of s 94(1) of the Employment Rights Act 1996; and *Office of Fair Trading v Lloyds TSB Bank plc* [2008] 1 AC 316 where the House of Lords had to decide if s 75(1) of the Consumer Credit Act 1974 extended to a transaction made overseas pursuant to a UK credit card agreement. A Briggs, (2006) 77 *BYIL* 572.

The Application of Mandatory Rules

Mandatory Rules under Article 3(3)

14.3.6 Article 3(3), the purpose of which is to prevent the evasion of domestic rules which would in the normal course of events govern the parties' contractual obligations, provides:

Where all other elements relevant to the situation at the time of the choice are located in a country other than the country whose law has been chosen, the choice of the parties shall not prejudice the application of provisions of the law of that other country which cannot be derogated from by agreement.

This provision is concerned with the situation where parties have concluded an agreement which is to all intents and purposes a domestic contract, but have chosen the law of a foreign country to govern the contract.[243] In this type of case the choice of a foreign law does not prejudice the application of the mandatory rules of the law of the country with which all the relevant factors are connected. Article 3(3) does not, however, invalidate the choice of law. The choice is still operative as regards the contract as a whole. The effect of Article 3(3) is to supersede the chosen law only to the extent that mandatory rules of another legal system are applicable.

14.3.7 Although the basic purpose of Article 3(3) is to counteract an evasive choice of law in a domestic contract, the test applied by Article 3(3) is based on objective criteria, rather than the subjective intentions of the parties. For example, where the parties involved have significant territorial connections with more than one country, it cannot be said that the relevant elements are 'located in a country'.[244] Nevertheless, there is uncertainty surrounding the meaning of the word 'relevant'. To determine whether an element is 'relevant', the court cannot look solely to the foreign mandatory rules which are alleged to be applicable under Article 3(3). Article 3(3) refers to 'elements relevant to the situation', a concept which is even wider than 'elements relevant to the contract'.[245] The same phrase is used in the Rome Convention; however, the Giuliano-Lagarde Report sheds no light on what types of factors might be regarded as 'relevant to the situation' even though they are not relevant to the contract. What, for example, is the position where two German parties include a choice of English law in a contract for the sale of goods in Germany which are manufactured by the seller at a factory in France? The fact that the goods are made in France is not relevant to the contract, but is it 'relevant to the situation'? By referring to elements which are 'relevant to the situation', Article 3(3) appears to leave considerable latitude to the courts. It is suggested that a restrictive reading of what 'relevant to the situation' means would rob Article 3(3) of its basic aim to prevent evasion of the law. In the example given, the parties would likely have as their aim the avoidance of mandatory provisions of German law rather than rules of French law. The connection

---

[243] There is no common law rule corresponding to Art 3(3): *Tamil Nadu Electricity Board v ST-CMS Electric Co Private Ltd* [2008] 1 Lloyd's Rep 93, 104 (at [44]).
[244] *Caterpillar Financial Services Corporation v SNC Passion* [2004] 2 Lloyd's Rep 99.
[245] Cooke J in *Caterpillar Financial Services Corporation v SNC Passion* [2004] 2 Lloyd's Rep 99, 103 (at [17]–[18]).

with France is incidental and should be ignored so that Article 3(3) applies to this situation. Otherwise, the parties will succeed in evading the mandatory provisions of German law which would otherwise have applied to their contract.[246]

14.3.8 Another issue is whether Article 3(3) requires the application of the mandatory rules of the country with which all the factors relevant to the situation are connected or whether a discretion is conferred on the courts. As a matter of common sense, Article 3(3) should be interpreted in such a way that the forum gives effect to foreign mandatory rules only to the extent that they would be applied by the court of the country with which all the relevant elements are connected.[247]

Mandatory Rules of EU Law

14.3.9 The Regulation introduces a new category of mandatory rules not found in the Convention. Article 3(4) provides:

Where all other elements relevant to the situation at the time of the choice are located in one or more Member States, the parties' choice of applicable law other than that of a Member State shall not prejudice the application of provisions of Community law, where appropriate as implemented in the Member State of the forum, which cannot be derogated from by agreement.

The term 'Member State' in Article 3(4) includes Denmark as it means all the EU Member States, instead of the regular meaning of all Member States to which the Regulation applies.[248] The concern underlying Article 3(4) is to prevent parties from evading the operation of mandatory rules of EU law by the simple expedient of choosing the law of a non-EU Member State to govern the contract. The principle that EU law could be mandatory in nature was established in *Ingmar GB Ltd v Eaton Leonard Technologies Inc*.[249] The claimant, an English company, was employed by the defendant, a Californian company, as the defendant's exclusive agent in the United Kingdom and Ireland. The contract contained an express choice of Californian law. When the agency contract was terminated, the claimant started proceedings in England with a view to recovering payment of commission as provided by the Commercial Agents (Council Directive) Regulations.[250] The High Court rejected the claim on the basis that, because the contract was governed by Californian law, the Commercial Agents (Council Directive) Regulations were not relevant. However, on a reference from the Court of Appeal under what is now Article 267 TFEU, the Court of Justice ruled that the provisions dealing with compensation to which commercial agents are entitled after termination of the agency contract (which are designed to protect commercial agents who carry on their activity in a Member State) are overriding in nature.[251]

---

[246] See A Chong, 'The Public Policy and Mandatory Rules of Third Countries in International Contracts' (2006) 2 *Journal of Private International Law* 27, 51–3.

[247] CGJ Morse, 'The EEC Convention on the Law Applicable to Contractual Obligations' (1982) 2 *YBEL* 107, 123.

[248] Art 1(4).

[249] Case C–381/98 [2000] ECR I–9305. W-H Roth, (2002) 39 *CML Rev* 369; HLE Verhagen, 'The Tension between Party Autonomy and European Union Law' (2002) 51 *ICLQ* 135.

[250] SI 1993/3053, implementing Dir (EEC) 653/86 [1986] OJ L382/17.

[251] Case C–381/98 [2000] ECR I–9305, para 22.

The parties cannot evade their operation by the simple expedient of a choice of law clause; the purpose of the provisions requires that they be applied where the commercial agent carries on his activity in a Member State and regardless of the law governing the contract, even though the principal is established in a non-member country.[252] The facts of this case would neatly fall within the scope of Article 3(4). That said, the need for the inclusion of Article 3(4) in the Regulation is puzzling, as mandatory rules of EU law would constitute mandatory rules of national law and apply under Article 9(2) in any event.[253]

The Application of Overriding Rules

14.3.10 The application of overriding rules may arise both in cases where the parties have chosen a law and in cases where the applicable law is determined by Article 4.

Overriding Rules under Article 9(3)[254]

14.3.11 Article 9(3) provides:

Effect may be given to the overriding mandatory provisions of the law of the country where the obligations arising out of the contract have to be or have been performed, in so far as those overriding mandatory provisions render the performance of the contract unlawful. In considering whether to give effect to those provisions, regard shall be had to their nature and purpose and to the consequences of their application or non-application.

The initial version of Article 9(3) in the Commission Proposal[255] was a reiteration of Article 7(1) of the Rome Convention, which gave courts the discretion to apply the overriding rules of the law of a third country (not being the law of the forum or the applicable law of the contract) with which 'the situation has a close connection'. The United Kingdom, along with some other Member States,[256] had entered a reservation[257] against Article 7(1) of the Rome Convention[258] due to fears of uncertainty. The perceived uncertainty stemmed from two issues: first, the criterion of 'close connection' was thought to be too vague; secondly, it was left up to the court's discretion whether or not to apply the overriding rules of the third country. These concerns were raised afresh upon the appearance of a new version of Article 7(1) in the Commission Proposal as reservations would no longer be permitted in the context of a Regulation. Objections were raised especially in the City of London, and the concern over the

---

[252] Case C–381/98 [2001] ECR I–9305, para 26.

[253] Financial Markets Law Committee, *Legal Assessment of the conversion of the Rome Convention to a Community Instrument and the Provisions of the Proposed Rome I Regulations*, April 2006, p 11 (para 5.1).

[254] A Chong, 'The Public Policy and Mandatory Rules of Third Countries in International Contracts' (2006) 2 *Journal of Private International Law* 27; A Dickinson, 'Third Country Mandatory Rules Within the Law Applicable to Contractual Obligations: So Long, Farewell, Auf Wiedersehen, Adieu?' (2007) 3 *Journal of Private International Law* 51.

[255] COM (2005) 650 final, proposed Art 8(3).

[256] Germany, Ireland, Luxembourg, Portugal, Latvia and Slovenia had also entered a reservation against Art 7(1).

[257] Permitted by Rome Convention, Art 22(1)(a).

[258] Contracts (Applicable Law) Act 1990, s 2(2).

provision was the primary reason why the UK government decided to withdraw from the negotiations over the Rome I Regulation.[259]

14.3.12 Article 9(3) is a compromise solution that is narrower in scope than the original proposal. The discretion to apply the overriding rules of a third country is maintained, but the third country is identified as being solely the place of performance. Further, the overriding mandatory provisions of the place of performance may be given effect only in so far as those provisions render the performance of the contract unlawful.

14.3.13 A few points can be made about Article 9(3). First, the place of performance should be identified by the *lex fori* as it is a connecting factor:[260] 'the interpretation of a connecting factor is always a matter exclusively for English law as the *lex fori*. This is elementary, axiomatic, and could not be otherwise.'[261] Secondly, it was previously unclear whether the line of English cases[262] where the court had refused to enforce contracts governed by English law which involved performance that was illegal according to the place of performance survived the Rome Convention.[263] Article 9(3) lays this debate to rest for the purposes of the Regulation. It is clear that the facts of those common law cases fall within its scope; additionally, it will also cover contracts governed by a foreign law that are illegal according to the law of a different foreign place of performance. Thirdly, Article 9(3) covers both situations involving initial illegality (where the contract is illegal at its inception) and cases of subsequent illegality (where the contract is valid and legal at its inception, but is rendered illegal by a subsequent change in the law). This point is made because some of the cases under the common law on subsequent illegality, the most important one being *Ralli Bros v Compania Naviera Sota y Aznar*,[264] have seemingly hinged on the fact that English law was the governing law of the contract and English domestic contract law considered that illegality under the law of the place of performance frustrated the contract.[265] It will not be necessary under

---

[259] Ministry of Justice, *Rome I—Should the UK opt in?*, Consultation Paper CP05/08, 2 April 2008, p 32 (para 77).

[260] Cf O Lando and PA Nielsen, 'The Rome I Regulation' (2008) 45 *CML Rev* 1687, 1722.

[261] JG Collier, [1989] All ER Rev 61.

[262] Eg, *Foster v Driscoll* [1929] 1 KB 470; *Regazzoni v KC Sethia (1944) Ltd* [1958] AC 301.

[263] The debate centred on whether the cases involved the application of English public policy, or application of the mandatory rules of the place of performance. If it were the latter, the cases would not continue to apply under the Rome Convention given the United Kingdom's reservation on Art 7(1). If it were the former, it was argued that the cases would also not apply under the Convention as the public policy provision entails the negative disapplication of an objectionable foreign law, whereas the cases involved the positive application of a foreign rule. See JJ Fawcett and JM Carruthers, *Cheshire, North & Fawcett: Private International Law* (Oxford, OUP, 14th edn, 2008) 742; TC Hartley, 'Mandatory Rules in International Contracts: The Common Law Approach' (1997) 266 *Hag Rec* 341, 403; P Kaye, *The New Private International Law of Contract of the European Community* (Aldershot, Dartmouth Publishing, 1993) 347.

[264] [1920] 2 KB 287.

[265] JJ Fawcett and JM Carruthers, *Cheshire, North & Fawcett: Private International Law* (Oxford, OUP, 14th edn, 2008) 759–60; P Nygh, *Autonomy in International Contracts* (Oxford, Clarendon Press, 1999) 224; TC Hartley, 'Mandatory Rules in International Contracts: The Common Law Approach' (1997) 266 *Hag Rec* 341, 392; FA Mann, 'Proper Law and Illegality in Private International Law' (1937) 18 *BYIL* 97, 110–11; FA Mann, 'The Proper Law of Contracts Concluded by International Persons' (1959) 35 *BYIL* 34, 47.

Article 9(3) to consider whether the applicable law of the contract considers the contract frustrated before effect is given to the law of the place of performance.

14.3.14 The next issue is: when should the court exercise its discretion and give effect to the invalidating rules of the law of the place of performance? Article 9(3) asks courts to have regard to the 'nature and purpose and to the consequences of their application or non-application'. This owes something to American governmental interest analysis both in its phrasing and its substance. At common law there are many cases in which the courts have approved (*obiter*) a rule to the effect that a contract (whether lawful by its proper law or not) is, in general, invalid in so far as the performance of it is unlawful by the law of the country where the contract is to be performed.[266] For example, in *Libyan Arab Foreign Bank v Bankers Trust Co* Staughton J thought that there was no need to cite authority to support the proposition that performance of a contract is excused if 'it necessarily involves doing an act which is unlawful by the law of the place where the act has to be done'.[267] In view of the fact that Article 9(3) resurrects common law authorities that were thought to be redundant after the Rome Convention, it is likely that English courts at least would routinely exercise their discretion to apply the overriding mandatory provisions of the law of the place of performance. The doctrine of comity accords with this view. At common law, the contract must, either expressly or impliedly, require the performance of the act that is unlawful in the country of performance: 'It is not enough that an act of performance is unlawful by the law of the country in which it happens to be done'.[268] Whether the contract itself stipulates the performance of that illegal act will be a factor going towards the exercise of the court's discretion under Article 9(3).

Overriding Rules of the Forum under Article 9(2)[269]

14.3.15 Article 9(2) provides:

Nothing in this Regulation shall restrict the application of the overriding mandatory provisions of the law of the forum.

Whereas Article 3(3) is concerned with domestic rules which cannot be excluded by contractual agreement, Article 9 is directed at overriding rules—rules which not only are mandatory, in the sense that they cannot be derogated from by contract in the domestic context, but which must also be applied regardless of the applicable law. For example, in English law, the Unfair Contract Terms Act 1977 and the Carriage of Goods by Sea Act 1971 include examples of overriding rules.[270]

14.3.16 In a case where the parties choose the applicable law, both Article 3(3) and Article 9(2) may be relevant. Where, for example, a contract entirely connected with Germany contains a provision for disputes to be litigated in England according

---

[266] See L Collins *et al*, *Dicey and Morris on The Conflict of Laws* (London, Sweet & Maxwell, 11th edn, 1987) 1218 (Rule 184, Exception 1). This principle, which originated in the 1908 edition of the work, was approved by the Court of Appeal in *Ralli Brothers v Compania Naviera Sota y Aznar* [1920] 2 KB 287.

[267] [1989] QB 728, 743.

[268] Cooke J in *Tamil Nadu Electricity Board v ST-CMS Electric Co Private Ltd* [2008] 1 Lloyd's Rep 93, 104 (at [47]).

[269] S Knöfel, 'Mandatory Rules and Choice of Law: A Comparative Approach to Article 7(2) of the Rome Convention' [1999] *JBL* 239.

[270] Aspects of the Unfair Contract Terms Act 1977 are discussed in section 14.5.

to French law, three different laws are potentially relevant. First, French law is the applicable law by virtue of Article 3(1). Secondly, the effect of Article 3(3) is that French law is superseded by any mandatory rules of German law. Thirdly, Article 9(2) provides for the application of English overriding rules. If there is a conflict between the mandatory rules of German law and the overriding rules of the law of the forum, the latter prevail.

14.3.17 An example of an overriding mandatory provision of English law is Article VIII(2)(b) of the Bretton Woods Agreement,[271] which deals with exchange contracts.[272] Under English law, exchange contracts are contracts which involve the exchange of one currency for another, including such contracts which are disguised as something else.[273] Article VIII(2)(b) provides:

Exchange contracts which involve a currency of any member and which are contrary to the exchange control regulations of any member maintained or imposed consistently with this Agreement shall be unenforceable in the territories.

Article VIII(2)(b) is an overriding rule—in the sense that it is applicable regardless of the law governing the contract.[274] In cases where Article VIII(2)(b) is applicable, as a general rule, it is not open to the court to disregard the foreign exchange control legislation on grounds of public policy.[275] Where Article VIII(2)(b) arises, the court, having identified any monetary transaction—whether concealed or not—which constitutes a relevant exchange contract, must refuse to enforce the monetary transaction or any linked transaction or contract which, if enforced, would give effect to the monetary transaction.[276]

14.3.18 The operation of Article 9(2) can also be illustrated by considering the Unfair Contract Terms Act 1977. The primary purpose of the 1977 Act is to regulate clauses which limit or exclude contractual liability. Many of the controls contained in the Act are directed at consumer contracts. Nevertheless, some provisions apply to ordinary commercial contracts as well as to consumer contracts. The scope of the controls contained in the 1977 Act is defined by sections 26 and 27. The limits imposed by the Act do not apply to international supply contracts which are governed by English law.[277] Furthermore, sections 2–7 of the 1977 Act do not apply in cases where the applicable law is English law 'only by choice of the parties'.[278] Conversely, in certain circumstances the Act applies, notwithstanding the fact that the applicable law is the law of a country outside the United Kingdom. Section 27(2), which defines

---

[271] The Agreement was made part of English law by the Bretton Woods Agreements Order in Council 1946, SR & O 1946 No 36 (made under the Bretton Woods Agreements Act 1945).

[272] For discussion of the problems arising out of exchange control legislation, see section 16.4 of the 3rd edition of this work.

[273] *Wilson, Smithett & Cope Ltd v Terruzzi* [1976] QB 683; *United City Merchants (Investments) Ltd v Royal Bank of Canada* [1983] 1 AC 168. See JP Corbett, 'Exchange contracts and the international sale of goods' [1977] *LMCLQ* 310; J Crawford, (1976–7) 48 *BYIL* 337; K Lipstein, [1976] *CLJ* 203; JG Collier, [1983] *CLJ* 49; J Crawford, (1982) 53 *BYIL* 288; FA Mann, 'Documentary Credits and Bretton Woods' (1982) 98 *LQR* 526.

[274] *United City Merchants (Investments) Ltd v Royal Bank of Canada* [1983] 1 AC 168.

[275] C Proctor, *Mann on the Legal Aspect of Money* (Oxford, Clarendon Press, 6th edn, 2005) 376–8.

[276] Neill LJ in *Mansouri v Singh* [1986] 1 WLR 1393, 1403.

[277] Unfair Contract Terms Act 1977, s 26. See *Amiri Flight Authority v BAE Systems plc* [2004] 1 All ER (Comm) 385.

[278] Unfair Contract Terms Act 1977, s 27(1).

the extent to which the Act contains overriding rules for the purposes of Article 9(2) of the Regulation, provides:

This Act has effect notwithstanding any contract term which applies or purports to apply the law of some country outside the United Kingdom, where (either or both)—

(a) the term appears to the court ... to have been imposed wholly or mainly for the purpose of enabling the party imposing it to evade the operation of this Act; or

(b) in the making of the contract one of the parties dealt as consumer, and he was then habitually resident in the United Kingdom, and the essential steps necessary for the making of the contract were taken there, whether by him or by others on his behalf.

14.3.19 Where, for example, an English traveller buys a train ticket from a foreign railway operator for transportation between two foreign cities, a clause in the contract which excludes the railway operator's liability for death or personal injury will be void in England by virtue of Article 9(2) if the traveller takes all the essential steps necessary for the making of the contract in England, even though the contract contains an express choice of law in favour of the foreign law under which the contractual exclusion is valid.[279] The effect of section 27(2) is that the 1977 Act (which includes a provision which renders void any contract term which seeks to exclude or restrict liability for death or personal injury resulting from negligence)[280] is overriding in these circumstances.

14.3.20 The Unfair Contract Terms Act 1977 is unusual among English statutes in that it contains express provisions which determine its sphere of application in cases involving a foreign element. In the absence of such provisions, it is for the courts to determine whether or not a particular rule is to be regarded as overriding for the purposes of Article 9(2). Some of the cases decided at common law indicate that whether a statutory rule has overriding effect is ultimately a question of policy to be determined by reference to the purpose of the rule in question.[281]

14.3.21 *Boissevain v Weil*[282] concerned a contract under which a British subject borrowed foreign currency in Monaco during the Second World War. At that time statutory provisions laid down that British subjects were not allowed to borrow foreign currency in various foreign countries (including Monaco). The House of Lords held that, even if the contract were governed by the law of Monaco, the statutory provisions rendered the contract void. The wartime regulations were regarded as having overriding effect.

14.3.22 In the Scottish case of *English v Donnelly*[283] the defender, a Scottish resident, entered into a hire-purchase agreement in Scotland with the pursuer, an English company. The contract contained an express choice of English law. When the defender failed to pay in accordance with the terms of the agreement, the pursuer commenced proceedings in Scotland. The defender sought to rely on the Hire-Purchase and Small Debt (Scotland) Act 1932, which provided that a hire-purchase agreement was void if the hirer was not provided with a copy of the agreement within a specified period.

---

[279] This will be a contract of carriage falling within Art 5(2). See paras 14.5.1–14.5.3.

[280] Unfair Contract Terms Act 1977, s 2(1).

[281] See S Dutson, 'The Conflict of Laws and Statutes: The International Operation of Legislation Dealing With Matters of Civil Law in the United Kingdom and Australia' (1997) 60 *MLR* 668.

[282] [1950] AC 327.

[283] 1958 SC 494 (Sheriff Court, Hamilton).

The Scots court held that the statute applied to all hire-purchase contracts made in Scotland, regardless of whether Scots law was the law governing the contract. The substance of the court's decision was that the statutory provision relied upon by the defender was a rule having overriding effect.

Overriding Rules of the Applicable Law of the Contract

14.3.23 It should be pointed out that when the parties choose a law in accordance with Article 3, they choose that law in its entirety, that is, including its overriding mandatory rules. This is the same when the law is determined in the absence of choice; the applicable law is inclusive of its overriding mandatory rules. As such, there is no separate provision in the Regulation providing for the overriding rules of the law applicable to the contract.[284]

14.3.24 In *Re Helbert Wagg & Co Ltd*[285] the defendant, a German company, owed a sum of money payable in sterling to the plaintiff, an English company, under a contract governed by German law. After the conclusion of the contract Germany enacted exchange control legislation which had the effect of enabling the defendant to pay the sum owed in German currency to a government agency in Berlin. Under German law payment in this way discharged the obligation. When the plaintiff sought to recover the sum owing under the contract in England the claim was rejected. Upjohn J decided that the court must recognise the right of a foreign state to protect its economy by measures relating to foreign exchange control and by altering the value of its currency: 'Effect must be given to those measures where the law of the foreign state is the proper law of the contract'.[286]

Public Policy: Article 21

14.3.25 According to the traditional common law approach to cases involving contractual obligations, questions of public policy may generally be placed in one of two categories.[287] First, the doctrine of public policy may be invoked if the nature or content of the foreign rule is so unacceptably repugnant that it could never be applied in England. For example, a contract for the sale of slaves or a contract to bribe a public official would not be enforced in England. In *Kaufman v Gerson*[288] the plaintiff, a French resident, had threatened to institute criminal proceedings against the defendant's husband. The parties concluded an agreement in France according to the terms of which the defendant promised to pay the plaintiff a sum of money if he refrained from instituting the threatened criminal proceedings. When the defendant failed to pay the agreed sum, the plaintiff

---

[284] O Lando and PA Nielsen, 'The Rome I Regulation' (2008) 45 *CML Rev* 1687, 1719. Cf Max Planck Institute for Foreign Private and Private International Law, 'Comments on the European Commission's Green Paper on the conversion of the Rome Convention of 1980 on the law applicable to contractual obligations into a Community instrument and its modernization' (2004) *RabelsZ* 1, 75–6; Editorial comments, 'On the way to a Rome I Regulation' (2006) 43 *CML Rev* 913, 921.

[285] [1956] Ch 323.

[286] [1956] Ch 323, 351.

[287] See PB Carter, 'Rejection of Foreign Law: Some Private International Law Inhibitions' (1984) 55 *BYIL* 111, 123–5.

[288] [1904] 1 KB 591.

sought to enforce the agreement in England. The court rejected the plaintiff's claim on grounds of public policy, notwithstanding the fact that the agreement was valid by French law and had no meaningful connection with England. According to Romer LJ, the court will not enforce a contract which contravenes 'what by the law of this country is deemed an essential moral interest'.[289] It should be noted, however, that not every case involving duress raises questions of public policy.[290] Cases involving economic duress, for example, should not normally be seen as involving universal moral principles. Whether a contract is void or voidable for economic duress (or valid) is simply a matter for the applicable law and does not concern public policy.[291]

14.3.26   The second category of case is not so much focused on the content of a foreign rule, but on the undesirability of an English court being seen to act in a particular way:

The main thrust of public policy here is not to achieve the rejection of an intrinsically repugnant foreign rule, but rather to protect the public or national interest or image of the United Kingdom.[292]

In *Foster v Driscoll*[293] the Court of Appeal refused to enforce a contract for the introduction of alcohol into the United States of America during prohibition. In *Regazzoni v KC Sethia (1944) Ltd*[294] a contract designed to circumvent Indian export controls was refused enforcement by the House of Lords on grounds of public policy. These cases are an illustration of '[t]he overriding principle ... that an English court will decline to take action which would be liable to be significantly detrimental to the national or international interests of the United Kingdom'.[295] In cases of this type it is immaterial whether the applicable law is English law or the law of another country.[296]

14.3.27   As a general rule, international instruments in the field of private international law make some allowances for the fact that different countries apply different standards to certain fundamental questions. Article 21 provides:

The application of a provision of the law of any country specified by this Regulation may be refused only if such application is manifestly incompatible with the public policy (*ordre public*) of the forum.

Article 21 is different in its operation from Article 9(2). Whereas Article 9(2) is positive, in the sense that it provides that certain overriding rules of the forum displace the applicable law, the effect of Article 21 is negative; it involves the exclusion by the forum of a particular rule of the applicable law on the basis that it conflicts with the public policy of the forum. Nevertheless, in certain circumstances it may be difficult to determine whether an agreement is null and void because it violates the public

---

[289] [1904] 1 KB 591, 599–600.
[290] *Dimskal Shipping Co SA v International Transport Workers Federation (The Evia Luck) (No 2)* [1992] 2 AC 152.
[291] *Royal Boskalis Westminster NV v Mountain* [1999] QB 674.
[292] PB Carter, 'Rejection of Foreign Law: Some Private International Law Inhibitions' (1984) 55 *BYIL* 111, 124.
[293] [1929] 1 KB 470.
[294] [1958] AC 301.
[295] PB Carter, 'Rejection of Foreign Law: Some Private International Law Inhibitions' (1984) 55 *BYIL* 111, 125.
[296] See *Royal Boskalis Westminster NV v Mountain* [1999] QB 674.

policy of the forum (Article 21) or because an overriding rule of the forum makes it unenforceable (Article 9(2)). The result, however, is the same.[297]

14.3.28 Article 21 is intended to be very narrow in scope. The application of the foreign rule must be manifestly contrary to the public policy of the forum. Moreover, the fact that the content of a foreign rule is contrary to English public policy is not in itself a ground on which Article 21 may be invoked. The effect of Article 21 is that the court may refuse to apply a foreign rule of law only where the result of the application of the foreign rule of law is contrary to English public policy:

It may therefore happen that a foreign law, which might in the abstract be held to be contrary to the public policy of the forum, could nevertheless be applied, if the actual result of its being applied does not in itself offend the public policy of the forum.[298]

Cases such as *Foster v Driscoll* and *Regazzoni v KC Sethia (1944) Ltd* do not involve the disapplication of an objectionable rule of foreign law. They fall within the scope of Article 9(3), which deals with the application of the overriding mandatory provisions of the law of the place of performance.

14.4 PARTICULAR ASPECTS OF THE CONTRACT

Preliminary Remarks

14.4.1 The applicable law plays the most significant role in determining the rights and obligations of the parties to a contract. The applicable law is one of the systems of rules by which formal validity is tested[299] and the putative applicable law governs questions of material validity.[300] In addition, Article 12(1) provides a list of matters which are governed by the applicable law:

The law applicable to a contract by virtue of this Regulation shall govern in particular:

(a)   interpretation;
(b)   performance;
(c)   within the limits of the powers conferred on the court by its procedural law, the consequences of a total or partial breach of obligations, including the assessment of damages in so far as it is governed by rules of law;
(d)   the various ways of extinguishing obligations, and prescription and limitation of actions;
(e)   the consequences of nullity of the contract.

14.4.2 A number of general points should be made about this provision before examining the particular issues. First, the list in Article 12(1) is illustrative rather than exhaustive.[301] Secondly, there is an overlap in paragraph (e) with the Rome II

---

[297] O Lando, 'The EEC Convention on the Law Applicable to Contractual Obligations' (1987) 24 *CML Rev* 159, 208.

[298] Giuliano-Lagarde Report, [1980] OJ C282/38.

[299] Art 11.

[300] Art 10.

[301] Giuliano-Lagarde Report, [1980] OJ C282/32.

Regulation. Paragraph (e) deals with mainly unjust enrichment claims which fall within the scope of the Rome II Regulation.[302] Thirdly, there are some matters which are not governed by the applicable law at all or are not exclusively governed by the applicable law.

Consent and Material Validity: Article 10

Introduction

14.4.3 Under the common law, the formation of a contract is governed by the putative proper law—that is, the law which would be the proper law of the contract if the contract was validly concluded.[303] The rationale for the application of the putative proper law is that:

it is (or will be) the law governing validity, quite regardless of whether this is (or will be) because it represents the parties' choice or because it is the law of the country of closest and most real connection.[304]

According to this approach, a disputed choice of law clause is relevant for determining the law which will govern the validity of the clause itself and, if valid, the validity of the contract as a whole.

14.4.4 Article 10 adopts a similar principle in paragraph 1, but provides an exception in the second paragraph:

1. The existence and validity of a contract, or of any term of a contract, shall be determined by the law which would govern it under this Regulation if the contract or term were valid.
2. Nevertheless, a party, in order to establish that he did not consent, may rely upon the law of the country in which he has his habitual residence if it appears from the circumstances that it would not be reasonable to determine the effect of his conduct in accordance with the law specified in paragraph 1.

The Regulation draws a distinction between formal and material validity: Article 10 deals with material validity; Article 11 provides rules concerning formal validity. Article 10 'is intended to cover all aspects of formation of the contract other than general validity', including 'the existence and validity of the parties' consent as to

---

[302] The Rome Convention contained the same provision and the UK government had entered a reservation against it (Contracts (Applicable Law) Act 1990, s 2(2)) on the basis that the effects of nullity are classified under English law as concerning restitution rather than contract: 513 *HL Deb* cols 1258–9, 1271.

[303] *Marc Rich & Co AG v Società Italiana Impianti PA (No 2)* [1989] 1 Lloyd's Rep 548, 552. See also *The Parouth* [1982] 2 Lloyd's Rep 351.

[304] PB Carter, 'Contracts in English Private International Law' (1986) 57 *BYIL* 1, 26. Compare L Collins, 'Choice of Forum and the Exercise of Judicial Discretion—the Resolution of an Anglo-American Conflict' (1973) 22 *ICLQ* 332, 339–40. For further consideration of the position at common law, see DF Libling, 'Formation of International Contracts' (1979) 42 *MLR* 169; A Briggs, 'The Formation of international contracts' [1990] *LMCLQ* 192; KFK Low, 'Choice of Law in Formation of Contracts' (2004) 20 *J Cont L* 167; J Harris, 'Does Choice of Law Make Any Sense?' (2004) 57 *CLP* 305, 316–24; A Chong, 'Choice of Law for Void Contracts and Their Restitutionary Aftermath: The Putative Governing Law of the Contract' in P Giliker (ed), *Re-examining Contract and Unjust Enrichment* (Martinus Nijhoff, 2007) 155–81.

choice of the applicable law'.[305] The issues which fall within the scope of Article 10 include: whether the parties reached agreement; whether an agreement is unenforceable for want of consideration; whether a contract is void for mistake; whether a contract is void for illegality; whether a contract is voidable for duress, misrepresentation or undue influence.

The General Principle

14.4.5 Article 10(1) provides a simple—perhaps even simplistic—solution to potentially difficult questions. The general principle contained in Article 10(1) is that all questions of existence and validity (excluding questions of formal validity) are governed by the putative applicable law—that is, the law which would apply if the contract were valid. Where, for example, a seller refuses to deliver goods under an alleged contract of sale on the basis that the contract is void for mistake, the question whether the contract is void is to be determined by the putative applicable law as determined by Article 4(1)(a), which provides that the law of the seller's habitual residence governs.

14.4.6 The position is more complex in cases where the dispute over the existence of the contract also involves a dispute concerning the existence of a choice of law. Suppose that a buyer offers to buy specific goods from the seller on terms which include a choice of law clause in favour of the buyer's law; before the seller replies, the buyer purports to withdraw the offer; notwithstanding the purported revocation, the seller accepts the offer. Whereas under the buyer's law the revocation is effective, under the seller's law it is not. Is there a valid contract? There are two possible approaches to this question.

14.4.7 The first approach is to look at the contract as a whole. If the contract as a whole is valid it will include a choice of the buyer's law, according to which the revocation is effective. Accordingly, the contract is not valid according to its putative applicable law. This approach is questionable for two reasons. First, as a matter of logic, the choice of law clause is being used to determine the putative applicable law notwithstanding the fact that the choice of law is invalid. Secondly, Article 3(5) provides that the existence and validity of the consent of the parties as to the choice of the applicable law is to be determined according to the general principles which apply to other questions relating to the existence and validity of contractual terms. This entails treating the choice of law clause as severable from the contract itself.[306] So, whether a choice of law clause is materially valid is to be determined by the law which would govern it on the assumption that the clause is valid, before the issue of the contract's validity can be assessed.

14.4.8 The alternative approach to the question of the material validity of a contract which allegedly includes a choice of law clause is to approach the question in two stages. The first stage is to determine whether or not the choice of law clause is valid according to its putative law. The second stage involves a determination of

---

[305] Giuliano-Lagarde Report, [1980] OJ C282/28.
[306] See, generally, A Briggs, *Agreements on Jurisdiction and Choice of Law* (Oxford, OUP, 2008) ch 10.

the contract's validity. At the second stage the choice of law is relevant only if it is valid according to its putative applicable law. The application of this approach to the above example produces the following analysis. At the first stage, the combined effect of Article 3(5) and Article 10(1) is that the buyer's law, as the putative applicable law, governs the existence and validity of the term in question. However, as the revocation is effective under the buyer's law, the choice of law clause is invalid. Accordingly, the material validity of the contract as a whole has to be determined on the basis that the parties did not make a choice of law. In these circumstances, as a result of Article 10(1) and Article 4(1)(a), the putative applicable law will be the seller's law. Since the purported revocation of the buyer's offer is ineffective under the seller's law, the conclusion is that there is a valid contract, governed by the seller's law.

14.4.9   Opinion on the merits of Article 10(1) is divided. In terms of pure logic the approach adopted by Article 10(1) is questionable. On this basis it is thought by some to be 'wrong and misguided'.[307] Although Article 10(1) involves bootstraps reasoning, it is not obvious that any other solution would achieve uniformity across the contracting states. At least Article 10(1) 'cuts the knot by an arbitrary but convenient solution'.[308]

The Problem of Consent

14.4.10   Without the exception contained in paragraph 2, Article 10 could lead to potentially absurd and unjust results in cases where one of the parties claims that he did not consent. Suppose a French seller offers goods to an English buyer and expressly provides that the contract of sale is to be governed by Ruritanian law, according to which silence equals acceptance. The application of Article 10(1) to this situation leads to the conclusion that there is a binding contract, notwithstanding the fact that the buyer has done nothing positive to indicate his acceptance and that no contract comes into existence under the law of either the seller or the buyer. In this type of situation Article 10(2) allows the offeree to rely on the law of his habitual residence. If, according to the law of the offeree's habitual residence, silence does not constitute acceptance, the court may decide that no contract has been concluded.

14.4.11   A number of further points should be noted. First, Article 10(2) refers to 'conduct', and does not relate solely to silence. Secondly, Article 10(2) uses the term 'party' and therefore can be relied upon either by the offeror or the offeree. Thirdly, although Article 10(2) may invalidate an agreement which would be valid under its putative applicable law, it cannot have the effect of validating an agreement which would be invalid under its putative applicable law. Fourthly, Article 10(2) applies both to individuals and to companies, with the concept of 'habitual residence' to be determined in accordance with Article 19. Finally, Article 10(2) confers a discretion on the court, which must consider whether it is reasonable to allow the party in question to rely on the law of his habitual residence in order to establish his lack of consent. In *Egon Oldendorff v Libera Corporation*[309] the plaintiff, a German company, sought

---

[307] A Briggs, 'The formation of international contracts' [1990] *LMCLQ* 192, 193.
[308] AL Diamond, 'Conflict of Laws in the EEC' (1979) 22 *CLP* 155, 162.
[309] [1995] 2 Lloyd's Rep 64.

to enforce a charter agreement against the defendant, a Japanese corporation. The putative applicable law was English law, according to which the agreement was materially valid. However, the defendant sought to invoke the exception in what is now Article 10(2) and to rely on Japanese law, according to which, it was argued, consent was not established. Was it reasonable to determine the effect of the defendant's conduct in accordance with English law or was the defendant able to rely on Japanese law? The court decided that this question could not be answered from the viewpoint of the defendant's law or from the viewpoint of the putative applicable law; it can only be answered by the court before which it comes adopting 'a dispassionate, internationally minded approach'.[310] It was held that, in the circumstances, the application of English law to the question of the defendant's consent was not unreasonable in view of the fact that the disputed contract included an English arbitration clause from which a choice of English law could be implied. According to Mance J:

To ignore the arbitration clause would appear contrary to ordinary commercial expectations, when everything suggests that the defendants must actually have considered and accepted the clause (and even if they did not, ordinary commercial practice and common sense would suggest that they should have done), and when, moreover, the clause in question was precisely the sort of clause which would be expected in an international charter agreement.[311]

If the parties' contract contains an English arbitration clause and the transaction is an entirely conventional one, it is not unreasonable to determine the effect of the parties' conduct in accordance with English law.[312]

Formal Validity: Article 11

What are Questions of Form?

14.4.12 Although Article 11 does not define what is meant by formal validity, the Giuliano-Lagarde Report on the Rome Convention states that matters of form should be understood to include:

every external manifestation required on the part of a person expressing the will to be legally bound, and in the absence of which such expression of will would not be regarded as fully effective.[313]

The requirement under English law that a contract for the sale of land or an interest in land must be made in writing in order to be valid[314] is a classic example of a formal requirement.

---

[310] Mance J at [1995] 2 Lloyd's Rep 64, 70.
[311] [1995] 2 Lloyd's Rep 64, 71. See also *The Epsilon Rosa (No 2)* [2002] 2 Lloyd's Rep 701, in which David Steel J followed Mance J's approach. The appeal against David Steel J's decision was dismissed, but there was no consideration of the point on material validity by the Court of Appeal: *The Epsilon Rosa* [2003] 2 Lloyd's Rep 509.
[312] See David Steel J in *The Epsilon Rosa (No 2)* [2002] 2 Lloyd's Rep 701, 704 (at [12]).
[313] [1980] OJ C282/29.
[314] Law of Property (Miscellaneous Provisions) Act 1989, s 2.

14.4.13 More problematical are the requirements laid down by the Statute of Frauds 1677 in relation to contracts of guarantee. Section 4 of the Statute of Frauds provides that:

no action shall be brought ... whereby to charge the defendant upon any special promise to answer for the debt, default or miscarriages of another person ... unless the agreement upon which such action shall be brought or some memorandum or note thereof shall be in writing and signed by the party to be charged therewith or by some other person thereunto by him lawfully authorised.

In *Leroux v Brown*[315] it was held that section 4 was a procedural rule which rendered unenforceable a contract which was concluded in France and governed by French law. Although this decision has been widely criticised,[316] it has not been overruled.

14.4.14 The decision in *Leroux v Brown* is an example of the tendency of the English courts to characterise as procedural matters which continental courts would classify as questions of form. It is clear that the concepts employed in the Regulation cannot be approached from an entirely domestic point of view. Notwithstanding the decision in *Leroux v Brown* and the fact that matters of procedure are excluded from the scope of the Regulation,[317] section 4 of the Statute of Frauds should be regarded as laying down formal requirements for the purposes of Article 11.

Choice of Law Rules

14.4.15 The Regulation adopts a liberal attitude to questions of form. Accordingly, it should be very unusual for an international contract to be rendered formally invalid by the Regulation. The key provisions are set out in the first three paragraphs of Article 11, which draw a distinction between cases involving the conclusion of a contract by parties who are in the same country and cases where the parties are in different countries. The test for determining whether parties to a contract are in the same country or different countries would seem to be a purely factual one[318]; the habitual residence or place of business of the parties is not relevant. The Regulation does not indicate what is meant by the conclusion of a contract for the purposes of Article 11. If the terms of a contract are negotiated and agreed by telephone, but subsequently the parties sign a written agreement at a meeting in an airport departure lounge, is the contract concluded when the terms are orally agreed or when the written memorandum is signed?

14.4.16 Article 11(1) provides:

A contract concluded between persons who, or whose agents, are in the same country at the time of its conclusion is formally valid if it satisfies the formal requirements of the law which governs it in substance under this Regulation or of the law of the country where it is concluded.

---

[315] (1852) 12 CB 801.
[316] See, eg, JJ Fawcett and J Carruthers, *Cheshire, North and Fawcett: Private International Law* (Oxford, OUP, 14th edn, 2008) 76–7.
[317] Art 1(3).
[318] See Giuliano-Lagarde Report, [1980] OJ C282/30–1.

This rule is effectively the same as the Rome Convention and common law rules on formal validity.[319] The reference to the parties' agents should be construed liberally so as to include the situation where an organ of a company concludes a contract on the company's behalf. Paragraph 2, which deals with the situation where the parties are not in the same country at the time of the conclusion of the contract, provides:

A contract concluded between persons who, or whose agents, are in different countries at the time of its conclusion is formally valid if it satisfies the formal requirements of the law which governs it in substance under this Regulation, or of the law of either of the countries where either of the parties or their agent is present at the time of conclusion, or of the law of the country where either of the parties had his habitual residence at that time.[320]

This provision takes into account modern commercial life, where many contracts are not concluded face-to-face. Accordingly, if an English seller is in Spain when he enters a contract with a French buyer by e-mail according to the terms of which German law is the applicable law, the contract is formally valid if it satisfies the formal requirements of German, Spanish, English or French law.

14.4.17 Paragraph 3 deals with the formal validity of a unilateral act:

A unilateral act intended to have legal effect relating to an existing or contemplated contract is formally valid if it satisfies the formal requirements of the law which governs or would govern the contract in substance under this Regulation, or of the law of the country where the act was done, or of the law of the country where the person by whom it was done had his habitual residence at that time.

So, an offer will be valid if it satisfies the formal requirements of the putative applicable law, the law of the place where the offer is made or the law of the offeror's habitual residence.

14.4.18 Paragraph 5 deals with a contract which concerns a right *in rem* in immovable property or a tenancy of immovable property. Such a contract will have to fulfil the formal requirements of the law of the country where the property is situated if by that law:

(a) those requirements are imposed irrespective of the country where the contract is concluded and irrespective of the law governing the contract; and
(b) those requirements cannot be derogated from by agreement.

Capacity

14.4.19 As regards individuals, it is expressly provided by Article 1(2)(a) that, subject to Article 13, questions of contractual capacity do not fall within the scope of the Regulation. Accordingly, in those cases in which Article 13 does not apply, the common law conflicts rules continue to be relevant. In relation to corporations questions of capacity are entirely outside the Regulation's scope.[321]

---

[319] Giuliano-Lagarde Report, [1980] OJ C282/30.
[320] The option of a contract being formally valid under the law of either party's habitual residence is not available under the Rome Convention.
[321] Art 1(2)(f).

Individuals

GENERAL PRINCIPLES

14.4.20   The common law rules relating to contractual capacity are not entirely free from doubt. Many of the older cases are unsatisfactory[322] and there are few recent authorities which clarify the position. It has been suggested that a contract should be regarded as valid so far as capacity is concerned if each party has capacity either under the system of law with which the contract has its closest and most real connection or under the law of that party's domicile and residence.[323] Although the pedigree of this rule is not beyond question, it can be defended from the point of view of principle.

14.4.21   Since capacity is to some extent an extension of legal status, there is a natural connection between an individual's personal law and his contractual capacity. If an individual is regarded as having capacity—and not in need of protection—under the law of the country with which he is most closely connected (in this context, the country of his domicile and residence) there is no good reason why the contract should be invalidated on the basis of the individual's incapacity under any other law. So, if a 20-year old, domiciled and resident in England, buys goods abroad, the fact that the purchaser has capacity by English law should be sufficient to ensure that the contract is valid so far as capacity is concerned. Absence of capacity by the law of the place of contracting in these circumstances should not be relevant.

14.4.22   There are, however, strong arguments for not referring questions of capacity to an individual's personal law alone. If, for example, an English resident, aged 17, contracts to buy a motor-car from a foreign seller, the contract would not be valid if contractual capacity were regarded as being a matter solely for the personal law. On the assumption that the contract is more closely connected with the seller's law, should the seller be expected to take the risk that the buyer does not have capacity by his personal law? As a general rule an individual ought to be regarded as having the necessary capacity if he has capacity by the putative proper law.[324]

14.4.23   It is important to stress that the proper law in this context should mean the law with which the contract has its closest and most real connection and not the proper law chosen by the parties (whether expressly or impliedly). Some of the cases do not make this clear. In *Bodley Head Ltd v Flegon*[325] the Russian novelist, Alexander Solzhenitsyn, signed a power of attorney in Moscow authorising a Swiss lawyer to deal outside Russia with the former's literary works. The power of attorney, which was in the German language, contained the following jurisdiction and choice of law clause:

In regard to disputes arising out of this mandate, the donor of the power recognises the courts at the place of business of the attorney as competent, and Swiss law as applicable.

---

[322]   Eg, *Simonin v Mallac* (1860) 2 Sw & Tr 67, which seems to favour the law of the place of contracting.

[323]   L Collins *et al, Dicey, Morris and Collins on The Conflict of Laws* (London, Sweet & Maxwell, 14th edn, 2006) para 32R–216 (Rule 209).

[324]   See *Homestake Gold of Australia Ltd v Peninsula Gold Pty Ltd* (1996) 131 Fed LR 447 (Supreme Court, New South Wales).

[325]   [1972] 1 WLR 680.

The plaintiff acquired the right to produce an English language version of one of Solzhenitsyn's works in England. When the defendant proposed producing a rival English language version of the work, the plaintiff sought an injunction to restrain the defendant from producing this work on the basis that the copyright was vested in the plaintiff. To the extent that the plaintiff had rights in Solzhenitsyn's works they were derived from the power of attorney concluded between the author and the Swiss lawyer. It was the defendant's contention that the power of attorney was invalid on the basis that Solzhenitsyn did not have capacity under Russian law. Although it was held that the issue was one of material validity rather than capacity, Brightman J concluded that, even if the author had lacked capacity by Russian law, the contract would still have been valid on the ground that the author's capacity was to be tested by Swiss law, the proper law of the contract.[326]

14.4.24 To the extent that this decision accepts that, as regards capacity under the common law, the putative proper law of the contract should be determined by reference to the law which the parties expressly or impliedly chose, rather than by reference to the law of the country with which the contract has its closest and most real connection, it cannot be supported in principle. If, for the purpose of capacity rules, the proper law were to be determined subjectively rather than objectively, this would enable an individual who does not have capacity by his personal law to confer capacity on himself merely by the choice of a law under which no such incapacity exists—thereby nullifying the protective effect of the individual's personal law.

ARTICLE 13

14.4.25 Article 13 provides:

In a contract concluded between persons who are in the same country, a natural person who would have capacity under the law of that country may invoke his incapacity resulting from the law of another country, only if the other party to the contract was aware of this incapacity at the time of the conclusion of the contract or was not aware thereof as a result of negligence.

The purpose behind Article 13 is to protect a party who in good faith believed himself to be contracting with a person of full capacity and who, after the contract has been entered into, is confronted by the incapacity of the other contracting party.[327] Article 13 has no application to situations where the parties are in different countries when the contract is concluded. Where parties are in the same country, the effect of Article 13 will be generally to validate the contract where both parties have capacity under the law of the place of contracting. The burden of proof lies on the incapacitated party to show that the other party knew of his incapacity or should have known of it.[328] If the person raising the incapacity cannot satisfy the burden of proof, that person will be regarded as having the necessary capacity if he has capacity under the law of the place of contracting.

---

[326] [1972] 1 WLR 680, 689.
[327] Giuliano-Lagarde Report, [1980] OJ C282/34.
[328] *Ibid.*

14.4.26   So far as the English courts are concerned, it is unlikely that Article 13 will have much of a role to play. First, it seems that questions of contractual capacity occur infrequently in modern practice. Secondly, Article 13 is relevant only if there is a conflict of laws:

The law which, according to the private international law of the court hearing the case, governs the capacity of the person claiming to be under a disability must be different from the law of the country where the contract was concluded.[329]

As regards proceedings in England, Article 13 comes into the picture only if an individual has capacity under the law of the place of contracting but does not have capacity according to English conflicts rules. Since a person who concludes a contract abroad will usually be regarded as having capacity for the purposes of the common law rules if he has capacity under the law of the place of contracting—because the law of the place of contracting will frequently also be the objective proper law—Article 13 will rarely be relevant.

Corporations

14.4.27   The contractual capacity of a corporation is governed both by the law governing the constitution of the company and the law governing the transaction in question.[330] First, a corporation does not have capacity to enter transactions unless authorised to do so by its constitution; an *ultra vires* act is invalid. Secondly, if the company does not have capacity by the law governing the transaction, the transaction is invalid. For the purposes of this rule it would seem that, as regards contractual obligations, the governing law must be determined by reference to common law principles, rather than the provisions of the Regulation.

Performance

The Applicable Law

14.4.28   Article 12(1)(b) provides that 'performance' is to be governed by the applicable law. The Giuliano-Lagarde Report lists various matters which fall within the scope of sub-paragraph (b):

the diligence with which the obligation must be performed; conditions relating to the place and time of performance; the extent to which the obligation can be performed by a person other than the party liable; the conditions as to performance of the obligation both in general and in relation to certain categories of obligation (joint and several obligations, alternative obligations, divisible and indivisible obligations, pecuniary obligations); where performance consists of the payment of

---

[329]   *Ibid.*
[330]   L Collins *et al, Dicey, Morris and Collins on The Conflict of Laws* (London, Sweet & Maxwell, 14th edn, 2006) para 30R–020 (Rule 162). See *Merrill Lynch Capital Services Inc v Municipality of Piraeus* [1997] 6 Bank LR 241.

a sum of money, the conditions relating to the discharge of the debtor who made the payment, the appropriation of the payment, the receipt, etc.[331]

14.4.29 The approach of the Regulation reflects the position under the common law. For example, in *Jacobs, Marcus & Co v Crédit Lyonnais*[332] the defendant contracted to sell to the plaintiff goods which were to be shipped by a French company from Algeria to London. Before all the goods had been delivered, hostilities broke out in Algeria, as a consequence of which the defendant failed to perform the remainder of the contract. The plaintiff commenced proceedings for breach of contract in England. Notwithstanding the fact that English law governed the contract, the defendant sought to rely on the law of the place of performance, under which the defendant was not in breach, since the outbreak of hostilities would be treated as *force majeure*. Under English law, however, the defendant was liable in damages since the events in question did not have the effect of frustrating the contract. In the course of his judgment Bowen LJ said:

If a contract made in England by English subjects or residents, and upon which payment is to be made in England, has to be performed in part abroad, it might not be unreasonable to assume that the mode in which any part of it has to be performed abroad was intended to be in accordance with the law of the foreign country, and to construe the contract as incorporating silently to that extent all provisions of a foreign law which would regulate the method of performance, and which were not inconsistent with the English contract. But it cannot be gathered from such a contract as the present that the parties desired to go further and to discharge the defendants from performance whenever circumstances arose which would, according to the foreign law, excuse them.[333]

The issue of the liability of the defendant for failure to perform the contract is not concerned with the mode or manner of performance, but with the substance of the defendant's obligation, and is governed by the applicable law.[334]

Performance and Manner of Performance

14.4.30 Although performance is governed by the applicable law, when it comes to the manner of performance attention should be paid to the law of the place of performance. Article 12(2) provides:

In relation to the manner of performance and the steps to be taken in the event of defective performance, regard shall be had to the law of the country in which performance takes place.

A few questions arise regarding the relationship between Article 12(1)(b) and Article 12(2). First, what is meant by the 'manner of performance' of an obligation? According to the Giuliano-Lagarde Report, although this question has to be answered by reference to the law of the forum, the following matters should normally be regarded as concerned

---

[331] [1980] OJ C282/32–3.

[332] (1884) 12 QBD 589.

[333] (1884) 12 QBD 589, 604.

[334] See also *Catalyst Recycling Ltd v Nickelhütte Aue GmbH* [2009] Env LR 29, especially Collins LJ at 47 (at [57]). The contract was governed by English law, and performance, which required permission from the German authorities, took place in Germany. The mode of performance depended on German law, but the effect of any failure to obtain the permission was determined by English law.

with the manner of performance: the rules governing public holidays, the manner in which goods are to be examined, and the steps to be taken if they are refused.[335]

14.4.31 Secondly, as regards the significance which should be attached to the law of the place of performance the report gives the following guidance:

[T]he court may consider whether such law has any relevance to the manner in which the contract should be performed and has a discretion whether to apply it in whole or in part so as to do justice between the parties.[336]

14.4.32 Thirdly, how is the line to be drawn between 'performance' and 'manner of performance'? The division between the two concepts is somewhat elusive. For example, the Giuliano-Lagarde Report lists 'time of performance' as an issue going to the 'performance' of the contract while 'rules governing public holidays' is categorised under 'manner of performance'. It is possible, though, to construe a contract providing for the delivery of goods on a date which happens to be a public holiday in Utopia (under whose law performance is unlawful) but which is valid according to the applicable law of the contract, Ruritanian law, in two ways.[337] It could be seen as a contract for the delivery of goods on that specified date, so that the issue of non-delivery by the seller is seen as one pertaining to 'performance'. Alternatively, it could be construed as a contract for the delivery of goods, with the question of whether delivery can take place on a certain date being classified as involving the 'manner of performance'.

14.4.33 *East West Corporation v DKBS 1912*[338] concerned the application of Article 10(2) of the Rome Convention, which is identical to Article 12(2) of the Regulation. The defendant was under an obligation to deliver a cargo against presentation of an original bill of lading in Chile. Although the bill of lading was governed by English law, Thomas J accepted that:

To the extent that the law of Chile contained provisions specifying the manner in which cargo in Chile had to be delivered, … it must be correct to have regard to the law of Chile under art 10.[339]

So, even though the obligation under the bills of lading in English law contemplated the bills being surrendered to the carrier and kept by him, the effect of Article 10(2)—which allowed regard to be had to the law of Chile—was to enable that obligation to be discharged by the bills of lading being presented to the carrier and returned (because Chilean law requires that the original bills of lading have to be retained by a customs agent).[340]

14.4.34 In *East West Corporation*, the mode of discharge of the obligation under the law of Chile was consistent with English law, the law governing the contract.[341] Thomas J expressly left open the situation if Chilean law had been incompatible

---

[335] [1980] OJ C282/33.
[336] *Ibid.*
[337] A Chong, 'The Public Policy and Mandatory Rules of Third Countries in International Contracts' (2006) 2 *Journal of Private International Law* 27, 56.
[338] [2002] 2 Lloyd's Rep 182.
[339] [2002] 2 Lloyd's Rep 182, 205–6 (at [131]).
[340] See [2002] 2 Lloyd's Rep 182, 206 (at [131] and [134]).
[341] [2002] 2 Lloyd's Rep 182, 206 (at [134]).

with English law.[342] This raises a fourth question on the relationship between Article 12(1)(b) and Article 12(2), that is, whether regard shall be had to the law of the place of performance with respect to the manner of performance only to the extent that it is not incompatible with the law applicable to the contract. In the example given above concerning a Ruritanian contract to deliver goods to Utopia on a public holiday, on one interpretation non-delivery by the seller could be seen as falling under the issue of 'performance'. 'Performance' is governed by Ruritanian law, which means that the seller is liable for breach. On the other interpretation, the court has the discretion to have regard to Utopian law, so that if the seller delivers on the day after the public holiday, the seller will not be liable. Which is the correct interpretation? On the one hand, the imperative nature of the phrase 'shall govern' in Article 12(1)(b) compared with the phrase 'regard shall be had' in Article 12(2) suggests that the applicable law of the contract is dominant with respect to all aspects of performance and therefore the mode of performance would also need to comply with this law. On the other hand, this interpretation obviously robs Article 12(2) of any significance. It is suggested that compatibility between the applicable law of the contract and the law of the place of performance is not required before regard is had to the latter law with respect to the manner of performance. After all, the applicable law is concerned with the overall substance of performance, and not with the more minor details of performance.[343]

Discharging Foreign Currency Obligations

14.4.35   The significance of the distinction between performance (which is governed by the applicable law) and manner of performance (in relation to which regard may be had to the law of the place of performance) emerges in the situation where the discharge of a foreign currency obligation involves payment in a currency other than the money of account. If, for example, the applicable law provides that all debts must be discharged in the money of account, but the law of the place of performance insists that all debts be discharged in the local currency, the effect of Article 12(2) is to enable the court to treat the discharge of a debt in the local currency of the place of payment as good discharge. Although Article 12(2) allows the court to have regard to the law of the place of performance, Article 12(1) makes it clear that the applicable law governs questions relating to the substance of the obligation.[344] If, for example, a contract which is not governed by English law provides for payment of a sum of money in England, the court may have regard to English law but the application of English rules on the discharge of foreign currency obligations may not be allowed to alter the substance of the obligation.

14.4.36   Whether payment is to be effected in England or abroad, the exchange rate to be applied should be determined by the law applicable to the obligation, rather than

---

[342] [2002] 2 Lloyd's Rep 182, 206 (at [135]).

[343] A Chong, 'The Public Policy and Mandatory Rules of Third Countries in International Contracts' (2006) 2 *Journal of Private International Law* 27, 56.

[344] This analysis of the Rome I Regulation is consistent with the generally accepted position under the common law: *Report on Foreign Money Liabilities*, Law Com No 124 (1983) p 4 (para 2.2).

by the law of the place of payment.[345] Where the obligation is governed by English law, if the debtor chooses to discharge in England a foreign currency obligation in sterling, the rate of exchange is that at which 'units of the foreign legal tender can, on the day when the money is paid, be bought in London in a recognised and accessible market, irrespective of any official rate of exchange between that currency and sterling'.[346] If the debtor tenders the appropriate amount in the foreign currency[347] potential problems concerning exchange rates can be avoided.

Interpretation

14.4.37 The substantive obligations of the parties to a contract are governed by the applicable law. It follows that a court must interpret a contract by reference to its applicable law.[348] Article 12(1)(a) of the Regulation provides that 'interpretation' is governed by the applicable law. The position under the Regulation accords with the common law.[349] So, where a contract of sale states that the purchase price is to be paid in 'dollars', the canons of construction of the applicable law determine the money of account.[350]

Discharge

14.4.38 By virtue of Article 12(1)(d) the applicable law governs 'the various ways of extinguishing obligations, and prescription and limitation of actions'. At common law, the proper law of the contract governs the question whether a debtor is discharged by performance,[351] by bankruptcy,[352] by legislation,[353] by outbreak of war,[354] by a moratorium,[355] or by subsequent impossibility.[356] In this respect Article 12(1)(d) follows the common law.

14.4.39 Traditionally, the common law regarded English limitation periods as procedural rather than substantive. Accordingly, at common law a claim arising

---

[345] *Report on Foreign Money Liabilities*, Law Com No 124 (1983) p 4, n 15. Although the report discusses the common law, the position under the Rome I Regulation is the same. See also C Proctor, *Mann on the Legal Aspect of Money* (Oxford, Clarendon Press, 6th edn, 2005) 473.

[346] L Collins *et al, Dicey, Morris and Collins on The Conflict of Laws* (London, Sweet & Maxwell, 14th edn, 2006) para 36R–051 (Rule 240). See, eg, *George Veflings Rederi A/S v President of India* [1979] 1 WLR 59.

[347] See, eg, *Marrache v Ashton* [1943] AC 311.

[348] *OT Africa Line Ltd v Magic Sportswear Corp* [2005] 2 Lloyd's Rep 170, 177 (at [20]).

[349] *St Pierre v South American Stores (Gath and Chaves) Ltd* [1936] 1 KB 382.

[350] 'Money of account' is to be contrasted with 'money of payment'; the former determines the quantum of the debt while the latter is the instrument of payment. Eg, for an obligation expressed as '10,000 Swiss francs payable in pounds sterling', the money of account is Swiss francs and the money of payment is sterling. For further discussion of foreign currency obligations see ch 16 of the third edition of this work.

[351] *Jacobs, Marcus & Co v Crédit Lyonnais* (1884) 12 QBD 589.

[352] *Ellis v M'Henry* (1871) LR 6 CP 228.

[353] *Mount Albert Borough Council v Australasian Temperance and General Mutual Life Assurance Society Ltd* [1938] AC 224.

[354] *Re Anglo-Austrian Bank* [1920] 1 Ch 69.

[355] *Re Helbert Wagg & Co Ltd* [1956] Ch 323.

[356] *Jacobs, Marcus & Co v Crédit Lyonnais* (1884) 12 QBD 589.

under a contract which was time-barred under the applicable law could nevertheless be brought in England so long as the English limitation period had not expired. Since Article 12(1)(d) treats defences based on limitation as substantive rather than procedural, whether a claim is barred by lapse of time is governed by the applicable law rather than the law of the forum. It should be remembered, however, that by virtue of Article 21 of the Regulation the application of a rule of the governing law may be refused on grounds of public policy. Accordingly, notwithstanding Article 12(1)(d) there may be circumstances in which, relying on Article 21, an English court may refuse to apply a foreign limitation period.[357]

Nullity

14.4.40 Article 12(1)(e) states that the applicable law also governs 'the consequences of nullity of the contract'. The UK government entered a reservation against the identical provision in the Rome Convention[358] on the basis that under English law the consequences of nullity are regarded as forming part of the law of restitution, rather than the law of contract.[359] A reservation is not possible for the Regulation and, in any case, is not necessary. The effect of paragraph (e) is the same as the choice of law rule for unjust enrichment claims set out in the Rome II Regulation. This provides that where an obligation to restore a benefit arises out of a contract, the claim shall be governed by the law governing the contract.[360] At common law, the proper law of the unjust enrichment claim arising in connection with a contract will be the proper law of the contract.[361] For nearly all practical purposes Article 12(1)(e), the Rome II Regulation and the common law rules lead to the same results.[362]

Illegality[363]

14.4.41 At common law the English courts formulated a number of principles relating to problems of illegality. In considering questions involving illegality it is

---

[357] In cases not falling within the Regulation the common law was replaced by the Foreign Limitation Periods Act 1984, s 1 of which provides that the limitation rules of the applicable law are to be applied in litigation which takes place in England. S 2 provides for the possibility of the English court deciding to disapply a foreign limitation period on the ground of public policy. There is no reason to think that the results achieved by the application of Art 21 of the Rome I Regulation are any different from those reached through the operation of s 2. For a detailed discussion of the Act, see ch 17 of the 3rd edition of this work.

[358] Contracts (Applicable Law) Act 1990, s 2(2).

[359] 513 *HL Deb* cols 1258–9, 1271.

[360] Rome II Reg, Art 10(1).

[361] L Collins *et al, Dicey, Morris and Collins on The Conflict of Laws* (London, Sweet & Maxwell, 14th edn, 2006) para 34R–001 (Rule 230(2)(a)).

[362] For an exception (albeit arising out of a rather unlikely set of hypothetical facts), see PM North, 'The EEC Convention on the Law Applicable to Contractual Obligations (1980): Its History and Main Features' in PM North (ed), *Contract Conflicts* (Amsterdam, North-Holland Publishing Co, 1982) 17.

[363] FA Mann, 'Proper Law and Illegality in Private International Law' (1937) 18 *BYIL* 97.

important to distinguish cases involving initial illegality (where the contract is illegal
at its inception) from cases of subsequent illegality (where the contract is valid and
legal at its inception, but is rendered illegal by a subsequent change in the law). There
are various different laws which may potentially be relevant to questions of illegality:
the applicable law, the law of the place of performance and the law of the forum.

Initial Illegality

14.4.42   If a contract is void on grounds of illegality by the putative applicable law,
it is not enforceable in England.[364] In this situation it is irrelevant whether or not the
parties knew of the illegality at the time when the contract was concluded. It is not
contrary to English public policy to enforce a contract which is valid by its applicable law, but is contrary to the public policy of the law of the place of performance.[365] Nevertheless, the English courts have taken the view that where contracting
parties intend the doing, or the procuring of the doing by a third party, of an act in
a friendly foreign country which is illegal by its law the contract is contrary to public policy and cannot be enforced.[366] Where, however, the contract is illegal neither
under the applicable law nor under the law of the place of performance, the fact that
the contract is illegal under the law of another country is irrelevant,[367] unless the
contract in some way breaches English public policy or an overriding rule.

14.4.43   In *Foster v Driscoll*[368] a number of English residents entered an agreement
for the shipment of whisky across the Atlantic, the purpose of which was to smuggle
the whisky into the United States at a time when the import of alcohol into the United
States was illegal. The majority of the Court of Appeal refused to enforce the contract
on the ground of public policy. Sankey LJ thought that a contract should be held
invalid on account of illegality:

if the real object and intention of the parties necessitates them joining in an endeavour to
perform in a foreign and friendly country some act which is illegal by the law of such country
notwithstanding the fact that there may be, in a certain event, alternative modes or places of
performing which permits the contract to be performed legally.[369]

Although in *Foster v Driscoll* the applicable law was English law, it is generally
accepted that, since the decision depended on English public policy, the contract
would have been refused enforcement had the applicable law been the law of a foreign
country. Where only one party knows of the illegal design, public policy prevents
that party from enforcing the contract. This rule applies whether the applicable law is
English law or the law of another country.[370]

---

[364]   Art 10(1).
[365]   *Lemeda Trading Co Ltd v African Middle East Petroleum Co Ltd* [1988] QB 448. JG Collier, [1988] *CLJ* 169.
[366]   *De Wutz v Hendricks* (1824) 2 Bing 314; *Foster v Driscoll* [1929] 1 KB 470; *Regazzoni v KC
Sethia (1944) Ltd* [1958] AC 301 (FA Mann, 'Illegality and the Conflict of Laws' (1958) 21 *MLR* 130;
RY Jennings, [1958] *CLJ* 17).
[367]   *JSC Zestafoni G Nikoladze Ferroalloy Plant v Ronly Holdings Ltd* [2004] 2 Lloyd's Rep 335.
[368]   [1929] 1 KB 470. This case is subjected to exhaustive analysis by Lindsay J in *S v A Bank* [1997]
6 Bank LR 163. See also *Ispahani v Bank Melli Iran* [1998] Lloyd's Rep Banking 133.
[369]   [1929] 1 KB 470, 521–2.
[370]   *Royal Boskalis Westminster NV v Mountain* [1999] QB 674. See also *Mahonia Ltd v JP Morgan Chase
Bank* [2003] 2 Lloyd's Rep 911.

14.4.44 A case such as *Foster v Driscoll* could be decided in the same way under the Regulation by virtue of Article 9(3). Article 9(3) gives a discretion to the court to apply the overriding mandatory provisions of the law of the place of performance which render the performance of the contract unlawful. In *Foster v Driscoll* the applicable law was English law but the same discretion is available to the court under Article 9(3) even if the applicable law is not English law.

Subsequent Illegality

14.4.45 As regards subsequent illegality, four factual situations may arise. First, if after a contract is concluded it becomes illegal under the applicable law for one or more of the parties to perform their obligations, the contract is unenforceable in England to the extent that it is unenforceable under its applicable law. This follows from the rule that the discharge of contractual obligations is governed by the applicable law.[371] Secondly, it is a rule of English domestic law that a contract which becomes impossible to perform by the law of the place of performance is frustrated.[372] However, the fact that performance becomes illegal under the law of a foreign country amounts to frustration of the contract only if the contract requires performance in that country:

the fact that performance in that country was within the contemplation of both parties is not enough; such performance must be required by a term of the contract express or implied.[373]

So, in relation to a contract which is governed by English law, if performance becomes illegal under the law of the place of performance after the conclusion of the contract, the contracting party who under the terms of the contract is required to perform in that place is discharged.[374] Thirdly, following the conclusion of the contract, performance becomes illegal by the law of the place of performance, but by the foreign applicable law illegality by the law of the place of performance does not frustrate the contract. This situation again falls within the scope of Article 9(3) and the court may, in the exercise of its discretion, apply the law of the place of performance to render performance of the contract illegal. Fourthly, where a contract is illegal neither by its applicable law nor by the law of the place of performance, illegality by the law of a third country is irrelevant.[375]

Remedies

14.4.46 One of the fundamental distinctions in private international law is the distinction between substance and procedure. Whereas substantive questions are

---

[371] Art 12(1)(d).
[372] *Ralli Brothers v Compania Naviera Sota y Aznar* [1920] 2 KB 287. Whether the rule in *Ralli Bros* is also a conflicts rule which applies to contracts not governed by English law has yet to be definitively determined: *Peh Teck Quee v Bayerische Landesbank Girozentrale* [2001] 2 LRC 23 (Court of Appeal, Singapore).
[373] Millett LJ in *Bangladesh Export Import Co Ltd v Sucden Kerry SA* [1995] 2 Lloyd's Rep 1, 6.
[374] Art 12(1)(d).
[375] As in *Kleinwort, Sons & Co v Ungarische Baumwolle Industrie Aktiengesellschaft* [1939] 2 KB 678.

governed by the applicable law, questions of procedure are governed by the law of the forum. In accordance with this general principle it is provided that 'evidence and procedure' are excluded from the material scope of the Regulation.[376] It follows that, as regards proceedings in England, English law, as the law of the forum, determines the nature of the remedy for breach of contract regardless of the law governing the contract. For example, English law alone determines whether or not a claimant in English proceedings is entitled to an injunction or an order of specific performance rather than damages. Another example is the rule set out in *Miliangos v George Frank (Textiles) Ltd*,[377] where the House of Lords decided for the first time that judgments may be given in a foreign currency.[378] This is a procedural rule which must be applied by the court regardless of the law applicable to the obligation in question.

14.4.47 According to English principles of classification, rules relating to remoteness of damage and heads of damage are substantive. Similarly, whether the defendant can rely on a defence as a means of limiting his liability—such as contributory negligence or set-off—is a substantive matter governed by the applicable law.[379] By contrast, rules governing the quantification of damage are procedural.[380] So, at common law, whether the claimant is entitled to recover damages for inconvenience and distress is a matter for the proper law of the contract, but if this head of damage is available under the proper law, the level of compensation which is recoverable depends on the procedural law of the forum.

14.4.48 Although 'evidence and procedure' are excluded from the Regulation's scope, Article 12(1)(c) provides that the applicable law governs:

within the limits of the powers conferred on the court by its procedural law, the consequences of a total or partial breach of obligations, including the assessment of damages in so far as it is governed by rules of law.

The expression 'consequences of ... breach' refers to the consequences which the law or the contract attaches to the breach of a contractual obligation, whether it is the liability of the party who has committed the breach or a claim to terminate the contract for breach.[381] Any requirement for service of notice on the party to assume his liability also comes within the scope of this provision.[382]

14.4.49 As regards the assessment of damages, the solution adopted by the Regulation is different from the position at common law. To the extent that

---

[376] Art 1(3).

[377] [1976] AC 443. PB Carter, (1974–5) 47 *BYIL* 369; SL Isaacs, 'Foreign currency claims and the English courts' [1977] *LMCLQ* 356; DG Powles, 'Foreign currency judgments' [1979] *LMCLQ* 485. For an American view of the decision, see JD Becker, 'The Currency of Judgment' (1977) 25 *Am J Comp L* 152. See also S Stern, 'Judgments in Foreign Currencies: A Comparative Analysis' [1997] *JBL* 266; J Knott, 'A Quarter of a Century of Foreign Currency Judgments: The Wealth-time Continuum in Perspective' [2004] *LMCLQ* 325.

[378] For a discussion of the *Miliangos* rule and the background leading to it, see section 16.3 of the 3rd edition of this work.

[379] *Meridien Baio Bank GmbH v Bank of New York* [1997] 1 Lloyd's Rep 437.

[380] *D'Almeida Araujo Lda v Sir Frederick Becker & Co Ltd* [1953] 2 QB 329; *Harding v Wealands* [2007] 2 AC 1.

[381] Giuliano-Lagarde Report, [1980] OJ C282/33.

[382] *Ibid.*

quantification of damage is regulated by rules of law,[383] the applicable law governs. Although the principle is easy enough to state, its application is more problematical. For example, to what extent are rules relating to matters such as the time at which loss is to be assessed and whether the claimant is entitled to the loss value of damaged property or to the cost of repair to be treated as 'rules of law' for the purposes of Article 12(1)(c)?

14.4.50   It should be emphasised that the principle in Article 12(1)(c) is subject to the limits of the procedural law of the forum. It has been suggested that 'if the applicable law provides for the payment of damages by instalments and the procedural rules of the forum are not suited to the task of supervising such payments ... the judge of the forum could require a single lump sum payment instead'.[384]

Money of Account for Damages

14.4.51   The effect of Article 12(1)(c) is also that it is for the applicable law to determine the money of account in which damages are to be assessed. This does not, of course, mean that damages will necessarily be assessed in the currency of the country whose law governs the obligation. Where a contract is not governed by English law it is for the foreign applicable law to determine the currency in which damages are to be assessed.

14.4.52   Although in many cases concerning contracts governed by English law it is appropriate for the court to award damages in sterling, situations arise in which not only is it inappropriate to give judgment in sterling, but there is more than one eligible foreign currency. In this type of case the determination of the currency in which damages are to be awarded depends on 'general principles of the law of contract and on rules of conflict of laws'.[385]

THE PARTIES' AGREEMENT

14.4.53   As regards damages in contract, the first principle is that, in deciding the currency in which damages should be awarded, the court should start by looking at the contract:

If the proper law is English, the first step must be to see whether, expressly or by implication, the contract provides an answer to the currency question. This may lead to selection of the 'currency of the contract'. If from the terms of the contract it appears that the parties have accepted a currency as the currency of account and payment in respect of all transactions arising under the contract, then it would be proper to give judgment for damages in that currency. ... But there may be cases in which, although obligations under the contract are to be met in a specified currency, or currencies, the right conclusion may be that there is no intention shown that damages for breach of contract should be given in that currency or currencies.[386]

---

[383] The reference to 'rules of law' excludes situations where the assessment of damages is a question of fact to be determined by the court after taking into account the economic and social conditions in its country, or the amount is fixed by a jury: see Giuliano-Lagarde Report, [1980] OJ C282/33.

[384] R Plender and M Wilderspin, *The European Private International Law of Obligations* (London, Sweet & Maxwell, 3rd edn, 2009) 415–6.

[385] Lord Wilberforce in *Services Europe Atlantique Sud (SEAS) v Stockholms Rederiaktiebolag Svea* [1979] AC 685, 700.

[386] Lord Wilberforce at [1979] AC 685, 700.

14.4.54   The fact that a contract is denominated in a particular currency does not necessarily lead to the conclusion that damages for breach of contract should be paid in that currency. For example, in *Services Europe Atlantique Sud (SEAS) v Stockholms Rederiaktiebolag Svea*,[387] although the contract—which was governed by English law—was denominated in US dollars, this was not in itself sufficient to justify a conclusion that the parties had agreed that damages should be payable in that currency. If, however, the contract specifies a currency of payment, damages should normally be awarded in the agreed currency of payment. In *The Agenor*[388] a charterparty provided for demurrage at $6,000 per day, but provided that payments under the charterparty should be made in sterling. (The contract also included an agreed rate of exchange between US dollars and sterling.) In these circumstances, it was held that, although the agreed money of account was US dollars, damages should be awarded in sterling, the money of payment.

IF THERE IS NO AGREEMENT

14.4.55   In the absence of an agreement—regardless of whether the claim is for damages in contract or tort or for restitution of money—if English law is the applicable law, the claimant should be 'compensated for the expense or loss in the currency which most truly expresses his loss'.[389] The currency which most truly expresses the claimant's loss is not necessarily that in which it first arose. To determine the currency which most truly expresses the claimant's loss the court must ask:

what is the currency, payment in which will as nearly as possible compensate the [claimant] in accordance with the principle of restitution, and whether the parties must be taken reasonably to have had this in contemplation.[390]

QUALIFICATIONS

14.4.56   Two qualifications to the general principles formulated by the courts should be noted. First, the burden is on the claimant to prove that he conducts his operations in a particular currency and that the loss was felt in that currency. If the claimant is unable to prove this, damages will be expressed in the currency or currencies in which the loss immediately arose. In the case of delivery of damaged goods, for example, the ordinary measure of damages leads to the *prima facie* result that the currency of loss is the currency of the place of discharge.[391] Secondly, the House of Lords has not laid down a hard-and-fast rule that, in all cases where a claimant suffers a loss or damage in a foreign currency, the right currency to take for the purposes of the claim is the

---

[387] [1979] AC 685. R Bowles and C Whelan, 'Judgments in Foreign Currencies: Extension of the Miliangos Rule' (1979) 42 *MLR* 452. For a summary of the principles laid down by the House of Lords, see the judgment of Brandon J in *The Federal Huron* [1985] 3 All ER 378.

[388] [1985] 1 Lloyd's Rep 155.

[389] Lord Wilberforce in *Services Europe Atlantique Sud (SEAS) v Stockholms Rederiaktiebolag Svea* [1979] AC 685, 701.

[390] *Ibid.*

[391] Bingham J in *The Kefalonia Wind* [1986] 1 Lloyd's Rep 273, 291.

'claimant's currency'.[392] In the words of Gatehouse J in *Metaalhandel JA Magnus BV v Ardfields Transport Ltd*:

The fact that a foreign plaintiff will necessarily have his bank accounts in, keep his financial books in, and fund his purchases of other currencies from the currency of his own country cannot automatically result in an award of damages in our courts in that currency. It must depend on the particular circumstances of the case.[393]

The principle underlying the flexible approach is that the claimant should be properly compensated for his loss; a decision on the currency in which the loss was felt is equivalent to a finding as to the currency which most appropriately or justly reflects the recoverable loss.[394]

14.4.57   Where damages are assessed in a foreign currency under the foregoing principles the claimant has to stand the risk of any fluctuations in the value of that currency which take place after the date on which the cause of action accrues. The object of an award in damages is to put the claimant in the position he would have been in had the defendant performed his obligation, not to indemnify the claimant against the fall in the value of the currency in which he operates:

The proper approach is to identify, in accordance with established principle, the appropriate currency in which the award of damages is to be made, and to award an appropriate sum by way of damages in that currency, and also of interest in that currency to compensate for the delay between the date of breach and the date of judgment.[395]

14.5 PARTICULAR CONTRACTS

Contracts of Carriage

14.5.1   Article 5 covers contracts for the carriage of goods and contracts for the carriage of passengers. Contracts for the carriage of goods are covered by Article 5(1).[396] Parties are allowed to choose the applicable law in accordance with Article 3. If party autonomy has not been exercised, Article 5(1) provides that the applicable law shall be the law of the country of the carrier's habitual residence, provided that the place of receipt or the place of delivery or the habitual residence of the consignor is also situated in that country. However, if the law of the carrier's habitual residence does not coincide with at least one of the other three connecting factors mentioned, the applicable law shall be the law of the country where the place of delivery as agreed by the parties is situated. For example, where the carrier's habitual residence is in country X, the ports of loading and discharge are in country Y and the consignor's habitual residence is in country Z, the law of country Y shall apply.

---

[392] See Lord Wilberforce in *Services Europe Atlantique Sud (SEAS) v Stockholms Rederiaktiebolag Svea* [1979] AC 685, 698.
[393] [1988] 2 Lloyd's Rep 197, 205.
[394] Brandon J in *The Federal Huron* [1985] 3 All ER 378, 381.
[395] Lord Goff in *The Texaco Melbourne* [1994] 1 Lloyd's Rep 473, 476–7.
[396] This is an updated version of Rome Convention, Art 4(4).

14.5.2   Recital 22 provides that contracts for the carriage of goods include single-voyage charterparties and other contracts whose main purpose is the carriage of goods. This is a reproduction of the last sentence of Article 4(4) of the Rome Convention. The issue has arisen whether charterparties other than single-voyage charterparties fall within the scope of Article 4(4). The Court of Justice held that where a party undertakes not only to make a means of transport available to the charterer but also undertakes to carry the goods, such a contract is a contract of carriage within the meaning of Article 4(4) provided that its main purpose is the carriage of goods.[397] In construing the main purpose of the contract, the objective of the contractual relationship and the obligations of the characteristic performer of the contract must be taken into consideration.[398] It does not matter if the contract is classified as a charterparty under national law instead of a carriage of goods contract.[399]

14.5.3   Party autonomy is restricted for contracts for the carriage of passengers; parties are allowed to choose as the applicable law only the law of certain countries, namely, the law of the passenger's habitual residence; the law of the carrier's habitual residence; the law of the country where the carrier has his place of central administration; the law of the country of departure; or the law of the country of destination.[400] If the applicable law has not been so chosen, it shall be the law of the country where the passenger has his habitual residence, provided that either the place of departure or the place of destination is situated in that country. Article 5(2) goes on to provide that if these requirements are not met, the law of the country where the carrier has his habitual residence shall apply. The intention behind Article 5(2) is to provide increased consumer protection for contracts for the carriage of passengers.[401] Finally, Article 5(3) provides an escape clause in favour of the law of the more (or most) closely connected country other than that indicated in Article 5(1) or (2).

Certain Consumer Contracts

14.5.4   Article 6 of the Regulation includes a number of specific choice of law rules which apply only to consumer contracts.[402] The basic purpose of these rules is to ensure that the consumer is not deprived of consumer protection legislation. The Rome Convention also has a consumer contract provision[403] which was subject to heavy criticism, such as the lack of adequate protection for mobile consumers and its inability to cope with the development of e-commerce and modern distance selling techniques.[404] It also leads to a hybrid legal framework consisting of two applicable laws which in turn entail legal costs which were out of proportion with the small

---

[397] Case C–133/08 *ICF v Balkenende Oosthuizen BV* [2010] ILPr 37, 63 (paras 34–7).

[398] Case C–133/08 *ICF v Balkenende Oosthuizen BV* [2010] ILPr 37, 63 (para 34).

[399] Case C–133/08 *ICF v Balkenende Oosthuizen BV* [2010] ILPr 37, 63 (para 34).

[400] Art 5(2).

[401] Ministry of Justice, *Rome I—Should the UK opt in?*, Consultation Paper CP05/08, 2 April 2008, p 24 (para 57). The Rome Convention did not have a special choice of law rule for these contracts.

[402] For international consumer contracts, see generally J Hill, *Cross-Border Consumer Contracts* (Oxford, OUP, 2008).

[403] Rome Convention, Art 5.

[404] Green Paper, COM (2002) 654 final, 29. For a discussion of consumer e-commerce contracts and choice of law, see LE Gillies, 'Choice-of-Law Rules for Electronic Consumer Contracts: Replacement of

claims usually brought by consumers.[405] The opportunity to improve the consumer contracts provision for the Regulation was therefore seized upon and Article 6 is heavily revised from its predecessor.[406]

Scope of Article 6

14.5.5   If the parties have not chosen the applicable law, Article 6(1) provides that:

Without prejudice to Articles 5 and 7, a contract concluded by a natural person for a purpose which can be regarded as being outside his trade or profession (the consumer) with another person acting in the exercise of his trade or profession (the professional) shall be governed by the law of the country where the consumer has his habitual residence, provided that the professional:

(a)   pursues his commercial or professional activities in the country where the consumer has his habitual residence, or
(b)   by any means, directs such activities to that country or to several countries including that country,

and the contract falls within the scope of such activities.

This provision is modelled on Article 15(1)(c) of the Brussels I Regulation and the intention is for both provisions to be interpreted harmoniously.[407] Sub-paragraph (a) suggests that some physical presence in the country of the consumer's habitual residence is necessary.[408] Sub-paragraph (b) is wider in scope; it takes into account the 'targeted activity' criterion,[409] which seeks to accommodate distance selling techniques via the internet.[410] For example, interactive websites or websites inviting buyers to fax an order which are accessible in the country of the consumer's habitual residence would fall within the scope of Article 6(1).[411] Recital 24 emphasises that it is insufficient for sub-paragraphs (a) or (b) to be fulfilled; the contract must also be concluded within the framework of activities pursued or directed by the professional. This requirement means that if an electronics firm advertises its range of mobile phones in the consumer's habitual residence but not its range of laptops, a contract for the sale of a phone, but not a laptop, would fall within the scope of Article 6(1). Conversely, if the firm advertises generally in the consumer's habitual residence without highlighting specific goods but merely to increase brand recognition, both

the Rome Convention by the Rome I Regulation' (2007) 3 *Journal of Private International Law* 89; Z Tang, 'Parties' Choice of Law in E-Consumer Contracts' (2007) 3 *Journal of Private International Law* 113.

[405] Commission Proposal, COM (2005) 650 final, p 6; Editorial comments, 'On the way to a Rome I Regulation' (2006) 43 *CML Rev* 913, 917.

[406] The Commission is specifically to evaluate the application of Art 6 in its report due by 17 June 2013. See Art 27(1)(b).

[407] Recital 24.

[408] P Cachia, 'Consumer Contracts in European Private International Law: The Sphere of Operation of the Consumer Contract Rules in the Brussels I and Rome I Regulations' (2009) 34 *EL Rev* 476, 483.

[409] Art 6(1)(b). The concept of directed activity in the context of Art 15(1)(c) is the subject of references to the Court of Justice by the Austrian Supreme Court: Case C–585/08 *Pammer v Reederei Karl Schlüter GmbH & Co KG* [2009] OJ C44/40; Case C–144/09 *Hotel Alpenhof GesmbH v Heller* [2009] OJ 153/26.

[410] See Recital 24.

[411] Commission Proposal, COM (2005) 650 final, pp 6–7. See Recital 24.

contracts would be caught by Article 6(1).[412] This choice of law rule is obviously aimed at protection of the consumer, the weaker party, due to the consumer's familiarity with the law and language and the ease of obtaining legal advice on the law of his home country.[413]

14.5.6   Party autonomy was initially excluded in the Commission Proposal but was reinstated after objections.[414] It was argued that the exclusion of party auton-omy would require businesses to research the contract law of countries to which its goods and services were supplied to consumers and interfere with the operation of the internal market.[415] Article 6(2) therefore provides that parties may expressly or impliedly choose the law applicable to a contract which fulfils the requirements of Article 6(1). However, the choice of law cannot have the effect of depriving the consumer of the protection of the mandatory rules of the law of the country where he is habitually resident. Where the contract does not fulfil the requirements of Article 6(1), the law applicable to a contract between a consumer and a professional will be determined pursuant to the normal choice of law rules set out in Articles 3 and 4.[416]

14.5.7   Consumer contracts of carriage and insurance are subject to Article 5 and Article 7 respectively.[417] Article 6(4) sets out a list of other exclusions to which the special choice of law rules set out in Article 6(1) and (2) do not apply:

(a) a contract for the supply of services where the services are to be supplied to the consumer exclusively in a country other than that in which he has his habitual residence;
(b) a contract of carriage other than a contract relating to package travel within the meaning of Council Directive 90/314/EEC of 13 June 1990 on package travel, package holidays and package tours[418];
(c) a contract relating to a right *in rem* in immovable property or a tenancy of immovable prop-erty other than a contract relating to the right to use immovable properties on a timeshare basis within the meaning of Directive 94/47/EC;
(d) rights and obligations which constitute a financial instrument and rights and obligations constituting the terms and conditions governing the issuance or offer to the public and public take-over bids of transferable securities, and the subscription and redemption of units in collective investment undertakings in so far as these activities do not constitute provision of a financial service;
(e) a contract concluded within the type of system falling within the scope of Article 4(1)(h).

---

[412] See the approach taken under Art 13(1)(3) of the Brussels Convention by Advocate General Jacobs in Case C–464/01 *Gruber v Bay Wa AG* [2005] ECR I–439, paras 61–3.

[413] Opinion of the European Economic and Social Committee, [2006] OJ C318/59, para 3.3.1.

[414] Eg, Opinion of the European Economic and Social Committee, [2006] OJ C318/59, para 3.3.1; cf LE Gillies, 'Choice-of-Law Rules for Electronic Consumer Contracts: Replacement of the Rome Convention by the Rome I Regulation' (2007) 3 *Journal of Private International Law* 89, 97–9. Another change is that the special consumer contract rule in the Commission Proposal was limited to EU resident consumers; Art 6 of the Regulation is not limited in this way.

[415] Ministry of Justice, *Rome I—Should the UK opt in?*, Consultation Paper CP05/08, 2 April 2008, p 26 (para 61).

[416] Art 6(3).

[417] Recital 32 states that this is due to the particular nature of such contracts which require specific provi-sions to ensure an adequate level of protection of passengers and policy holders.

[418] [1990] OJ L158/59.

The first two exclusions are carried over from the Rome Convention. They lead to a number of arbitrary distinctions.[419] If an English resident concludes a contract for a room in a Parisian hotel and separately purchases an airline ticket to fly from London to Paris, the contract with the hotel is excluded by paragraph 4(a) because 'the services are to be supplied to the consumer exclusively in a country other than that in which he has his habitual residence' and the contract of carriage is excluded from the scope of Article 6 by paragraph 4(b). If, however, the same consumer purchases a package holiday, involving a flight from London to Paris and accommodation in a Parisian hotel, the contract falls within the scope of the consumer contract provisions. The third exclusion merely reflects the general policy that contracts relating to a proprietary right in immovable property should be governed by the *lex situs*.[420] The more noteworthy exclusions are those contained in sub-paragraphs (d) and (e)[421] which deal with situations where it is imperative that one single law governs,[422] that single law not being necessarily the law of the consumer's habitual residence.[423]

14.5.8 Sub-paragraph (d) deals with three items, that is, financial instruments,[424] public issues or offers and public takeover bids,[425] and the subscription and redemption of units in collective investment undertakings.[426] These fall generally into the area of the Markets in Financial Instruments Directive (MiFID),[427] which extensively harmonises this area of the financial sector. The exclusion carved out by sub-paragraph (d) is necessary to preserve the operation of the Directive, which is 'intended to foster a thriving internal market in investment services and to deliver savings to MiFID regulated firms, and thereby to their clients'.[428] Recital 29 gives an indication of the types of issues falling within the scope of the exclusion and which are intended to be governed by one single law: the allocation of securities or units, rights in the event of over-subscription, withdrawal rights and similar matters in the context of the offer as well as consent and material validity, formal validity, scope of the applicable law, and capacity of the parties to contract. It should be noted that Article 6 still applies to contracts

---

[419] See the Giuliano-Lagarde Report's attempt to justify the situation under the Rome Convention: [1980] OJ C282/24–5. Cf CGJ Morse, 'Consumer Contracts, Employment Contracts and the Rome Convention' (1992) 41 *ICLQ* 1, 4–6.

[420] See Art 4(1)(c).

[421] For a detailed examination of these two exclusions, see FJG Alferez, 'The Rome I Regulation: Exceptions to the Rule on Consumer Contracts and Financial Instruments' (2009) 5 *Journal of Private International Law* 85.

[422] Eg, financial instruments are a bundle of rights which must be governed by one law as each instrument must confer identical rights to the different holders. See FJG Alferez, 'The Rome I Regulation: Exceptions to the Rule on Consumer Contracts and Financial Instruments' (2009) 5 *Journal of Private International Law* 85, 90.

[423] Recital 28.

[424] As referred to in Article 4 of the Markets in Financial Instruments Directive, Dir 2004/39/EC on markets in financial instruments amending Dirs 85/611/EEC and 93/6/EEC and Dir 2000/12/EC repealing Dir 93/22/EEC, [2004] OJ L145/1. Article 4 of this Directive also provides the definition for 'transferable securities'. See Rome I Reg, Recital 30.

[425] See further Recital 29.

[426] See further Recital 29.

[427] Dir 2004/39/EC on markets in financial instruments amending Dirs 85/611/EEC, 93/6/EEC and 2000/12/EC and repealing Dir 93/22/EEC [2004] OJ L145/1. See Rome I Reg, Recital 30.

[428] Ministry of Justice, *Rome I—Should the UK opt in?*, Consultation Paper CP05/08, 2 April 2008, 27 (para 67).

for the purchase of financial instruments by a consumer as the exclusion refers only to the financial instrument itself.[429] By the same token, contracts for the provision of financial services such as the reception and transmission of orders in relation to one or more financial instruments, the underwriting of financial instruments, or the safekeeping and administration of financial instruments are also included within Article 6.[430]

14.5.9 Sub-paragraph (e) excludes contracts concluded in the context of multilateral systems such as stock markets. The usual course of things, though, is that individual investors will have to act through a broker or intermediary who will buy or sell shares in their names, albeit on behalf of the investors. Such contracts would not qualify as consumer contracts under Article 6 anyway[431]; sub-paragraph (e) functions to close any loopholes that may exist. However, a contract concerning the provision of financial services between the investor and broker, such as the reception and transmission of orders in relation to one or more financial instruments, the execution of order, or the provision of investment advice, will fall within the scope of Article 6.[432]

14.5.10 Lastly, it should be noted that contracts concluded in securities settlement systems,[433] which involve individual investors who may be consumers, do not fall within Article 6(1). These contracts are governed by the general choice of law rules set out in Articles 3 and 4, although this is without prejudice to the rules set out in Directive 98/26/EC of the European Parliament and of the Council on settlement finality in payment and securities settlement systems.[434]

The Application of Mandatory Rules in Cases where the Parties have Chosen a Law

14.5.11 Article 6(2) provides that a choice of law made by parties to a consumer contract within the scope of Article 3 shall not have the result of depriving the consumer of the protection afforded to him by the mandatory rules of the law of the country in which he has his habitual residence.[435] The purpose of Article 6(2) is to ensure that a choice of law cannot have the effect of avoiding the application of the mandatory rules which would have applied had the parties not made the choice. So, if an English consumer receives an advertising catalogue from a Californian seller inviting him to purchase the seller's goods, the consumer is able to rely on the Unfair Terms in Consumer Contracts Regulations 1999[436] and those provisions of the Unfair Contract

---

[429] Unless the contracts for the purchase of financial instruments are concluded in the context of a public offer or multilateral trading system: FJG Alferez, 'The Rome I Regulation: Exceptions to the Rule on Consumer Contracts and Financial Instruments' (2009) 5 *Journal of Private International Law* 85, 90–1.

[430] See Dir 2004/39/EC, Annex I, Sections A and B; referred to in Rome I Reg, Recital 26.

[431] FJG Alferez, 'The Rome I Regulation: Exceptions to the Rule on Consumer Contracts and Financial Instruments' (2009) 5 *Journal of Private International Law* 85, 101.

[432] See Recital 26.

[433] As defined by Dir 98/26/EC on settlement finality in payment and securities settlement systems, Art 2(a) [1998] OJ L166/45. The gist is that these systems comprise 'institutional arrangements for confirmation, clearance and settlement of securities' trade and safekeeping of securities': FJG Alferez, 'The Rome I Regulation: Exceptions to the Rule on Consumer Contracts and Financial Instruments' (2009) 5 *Journal of Private International Law* 85, 101. An example would be the CREST share settlement system in the United Kingdom.

[434] [1998] OJ L166/45. See Rome I Reg, Recital 31.

[435] See Recital 25.

[436] SI 1999/2083.

Terms Act 1977 which cannot be derogated from by contract, notwithstanding the fact that the contract is concluded on the seller's standard terms and conditions which include a Californian choice of law.

14.5.12 An interesting question arises if the applicable law under Article 3(1) is more generous to the consumer than the law of the place where the consumer is habitually resident. Can the consumer rely on the chosen law in these circumstances? The proper solution would appear to be that the applicable law should be applied where it provides a greater degree of protection than the law which would have applied in the absence of choice. Paragraph 2 talks in terms of the consumer being 'deprived' of the benefit of the mandatory rules of the law of the country where he is habitually resident. There can be no 'deprivation' if the standards of the chosen law are higher than those of the law of the country where the consumer is habitually resident. Article 6(2) does no more than lay down a minimum standard.[437] If the parties have chosen the law of a non-EU Member State to govern a contract in a case where all the elements relevant to the situation at the time of the choice are located in one or more Member States, the contract will be subject to provisions of EU law which cannot be derogated from by agreement.[438]

Overriding Rules

14.5.13 Consumer contracts which are governed by Article 6 are also subject to the general choice of law rules in the Regulation relating to mandatory rules. Accordingly, the applicable law may be modified by the overriding rules of the forum.[439] The Unfair Terms in Consumer Contracts Regulations 1999 implement rules which are common to all the EU Member States.[440] The Regulations, which provide that certain types of contractual term are not binding on consumers,[441] expressly state that, if the contract has a close connection with the territory of the Member States, the Regulations apply notwithstanding any contract term which applies or purports to apply the law of a non-Member State. Accordingly, for the purposes of the Rome I Regulation, the Regulations are overriding rules in cases where the contract has the specified connection with a Member State.

14.5.14 Section 27(2) of the Unfair Contract Terms Act 1977—which exists along-side the 1999 Regulations—indicates that the controls of the Act apply regardless of a choice of the law of a foreign country by the parties if either (a) the choice of law was imposed 'wholly or mainly for the purpose of enabling the party imposing it to evade the operation of this Act' or (b) 'one of the parties dealt as consumer, and he was then habitually resident in the United Kingdom, and the essential steps necessary for the making of the contract were taken there, whether by him or by others on his behalf'.[442]

---

[437] See CGJ Morse, 'Consumer Contracts, Employment Contracts and the Rome Convention' (1992) 41 *ICLQ* 1, 8–9.

[438] Art 3(4).

[439] Art 9(2). For consideration of the distinction between mandatory rules and overriding rules, see paras 14.3.3–14.3.4.

[440] Dir 93/13/EEC [1993] OJ L95/29.

[441] Reg 5(1).

[442] See FA Mann, 'Unfair Contract Terms Act 1977 and the Conflict of Laws' (1978) 27 *ICLQ* 661.

14.5.15 In the consumer context, section 27(2) of the 1977 Act has—to a significant extent—been superseded by the Rome I Regulation. If a contract falls within the scope of Article 6, the consumer receives the protection of the mandatory rules which form part of the law of the country where he is habitually resident, whether or not the contract includes a choice of law.[443] Furthermore, if a contract contains a choice of the law of a foreign country and all the factors relevant to the situation are connected with England, the mandatory rules of English law are applicable by virtue of Article 3(3) of the Regulation.[444]

14.5.16 However, even in the consumer context, section 27(2) of the 1977 Act may be relevant in two situations. First, if a contract includes a choice of the law of a foreign country, the court may, relying on Article 9(2), apply the Unfair Contract Terms Act 1977 if it appears that the purpose of the choice of law was to evade the operation of the Act, even though not all the factors relevant to the situation are connected with England.[445] Secondly, as regards those consumer contracts which do not fall within the scope of Article 6 of the Regulation (either because the subject-matter is excluded by paragraph 4 or because none of the qualifying conditions in paragraph 1 is satisfied) section 27(2)(b) directs that the controls of the Act are to apply, notwithstanding the fact that the contract contains a choice of foreign law, if a contracting party—who is habitually resident in the United Kingdom—dealt as consumer and the essential steps necessary for the making of the contract were taken in the United Kingdom. Lastly, it should be noted that effect may also be given to overriding rules of the law of the place of performance that render performance of the contract unlawful.[446]

Formal Validity

14.5.17 Article 11(4) provides that the formal validity of a consumer contract within the scope of Article 6 is governed by the law of the country in which the consumer has his habitual residence.

Insurance Contracts

14.5.18 The Regulation introduces a special choice of law rule covering insurance contracts.[447] Under previous legislation, the choice of law rules for insurance contracts were rather convoluted, consisting of overlapping regimes, with different rules applicable depending on where the risk is located or where the insurer is established.[448] Article 7 of the Regulation ameliorates the situation to a certain extent. The choice of

---

[443] Art 6(1) and (2).The applicable law in the absence of choice is the law of the consumer's habitual residence, which includes that law's mandatory provisions.

[444] For a discussion of Art 3(3) see paras 14.3.6–14.3.8.

[445] If all the factors relevant to the case are connected with England, English mandatory rules (which by definition include overriding rules) would apply by virtue of Art 3(3).

[446] Art 9(3).

[447] The Commission is specifically to study the law applicable to insurance contracts and the impact which the new provisions have had in its report due by 17 June 2013; see Art 27(1)(a).

[448] See, generally, F Seatzu, *Insurance in Private International Law: A European Perspective* (Oxford, Hart Publishing, 2003); L Collins *et al, Dicey, Morris and Collins on The Conflict of Laws* (London, Sweet & Maxwell, 14th edn, 2006) paras 33R–136–207.

law rules in Article 7 largely mirror the rules found in the EC Insurance Directives.[449] Article 7 covers insurance contracts covering a large risk, wherever situated, and all other insurance contracts covering risks situated inside the territory of Member States.[450] Insurance contracts covering non-large risks situated outside the territory of Member States and reinsurance contracts[451] are excluded from the scope of Article 7; they are governed by the general choice of law rules set out in Articles 3 and 4, with Article 6 being applicable to consumer insurance contracts. The phrase 'Member State' as used in Article 7 refers to all Member States and not just those to which the Regulation applies.[452]

'Large Risk' Insurance Contracts

14.5.19 A 'large risk' is defined by reference to Article 5(2)(d) of the First Council Directive 73/239/EEC on the co-ordination of laws, regulations and administrative provisions relating to the taking-up and pursuit of the business of direct insurance other than life insurance.[453] Examples include contracts covering damage to or loss of railway rolling stock, aircraft, goods in transit or baggage irrespective of the form of transport; liability arising out of the use of ships, vessels or boats on the sea, lakes, rivers or canals; and suretyship and credit insolvency where the risk relates to the policyholder's business. Generally, the choice of law rules for insurance contracts covering large risks follow the general choice of law framework set out in the Regulation. Party autonomy is respected, but where choice has not been exercised, the applicable law is the law of the country where the insurer has his habitual residence. However, where it is clear from all the circumstances of the case that the contract is manifestly more closely connected with another country, the law of that other country will govern the insurance contract.[454]

Non-large Risks Situated within the EU

14.5.20 Other rules are provided for insurance contracts covering non-large risks situated inside the territory of EU Member States. Article 7(3) allows for a more

---

[449] Dir 73/239 [1973] OJ 238/3, Dir 88/357/EEC [1988] OJ 172/1 and Dir 92/49/EEC [1992] OJ 228/1 (general/non-life insurance); Dir 2002/83/EC [2002] OJ L 345/1 (life assurance directive; repealing Dir 79/267/EEC [1979] OJ 63/1, Dir 90/619/EEC [1990] OJ 330/50, Dir 92/96/EEC [1992] OJ 360/1). The Insurance Directives were implemented into English law by the Financial Services and Markets Act 2000 (Law Applicable to Contracts of Insurance) Regs 2001, SI 2001/2635, as amended by SI 2001/3542. The Insurance Directives also bind EFTA Member States and Denmark.

[450] Art 7(1).

[451] See *Wasa International Insurance Co v Lexington Insurance Co* [2010] 1 AC 180. See also on choice of law and reinsurance generally, R Merkin, 'The Rome I Regulation and Reinsurance' (2009) 5 *Journal of Private International Law* 69.

[452] Art 1(4).

[453] [1973] OJ L228/3; as amended by Dir 88/357/EEC on the co-ordination of laws, regulations and administrative provisions relating to direct insurance other than life assurance and laying down provisions to facilitate the effective exercise of freedom to provide services and amending Dir 73/239/EEC [1988] OJ L172/1.

[454] Art 7(2).

restricted form of party autonomy. Choice is allowed but the parties may choose only between:

(a) the law of any Member State where the risk is situated at the time of conclusion of the contract;
(b) the law of the country where the policy holder has his habitual residence;
(c) in the case of life assurance, the law of the Member State of which the policy holder is a national;
(d) for insurance contracts covering risks limited to events occurring in one Member State other than the Member State where the risk is situated, the law of that Member State;
(e) where the policy holder of a contract falling under this paragraph pursues a commercial or industrial activity or a liberal profession and the insurance contract covers two or more risks which relate to those activities and are situated in different Member States, the law of any of the Member States concerned or the law of the country of the habitual residence of the policy holder.

However, where the relevant Member State in paragraphs (a), (b) or (e) allocates greater freedom of choice of the law to the parties, the parties 'may take advantage of that freedom'.[455] If the applicable law has not been chosen in accordance with the rules set out above, the applicable law is the law of the Member State in which the risk is situated at the time of conclusion of the contract. Article 7(6) contains further directions on how the country in which the risk is situated is to be identified.[456]

14.5.21 If the contract covers risks that are situated in more than one Member State, 'the contract shall be considered as constituting several contracts each relating to only one Member State'.[457] Severance is also the method employed in the event that the risks insured are situated within and without the EU. Recital 33 states that:

Where an insurance contract not covering a large risk covers more than one risk, at least one of which is situated in a Member State and at least one of which is situated in a third country, the special rules on insurance contracts in this Regulation should apply only to the risk or risks situated in the relevant Member State or Member States.

Therefore, where an insurance policy is taken out by a German corporation over its buildings in Germany and Korea, the law governing coverage over the German building is determined by Article 7 while the law applicable to coverage over the Korean building has to be ascertained in accordance with the general choice of law rules set out in Articles 3 and 4. While severance may be tenable where the risks can be divided in this manner, certain risks may be considered 'indivisible'.[458] It is unclear what rule should be applied in this situation unless it is possible to identify the risk as being situated predominantly in a particular country.[459]

---

[455] Art 7(3). This is a limited form of *renvoi*. For the position in the United Kingdom, see the Financial Services and Markets Act 2000 (Law Applicable to Contracts of Insurance) Regs 2009, SI 2009/3075, reg 4.

[456] Specifically, by referring to Dir 88/357/EEC, Art 2(d) (for general/non-life insurance) and Dir 2002/83/EC, Art 1(1) (for life insurance).

[457] Art 7(5).

[458] L Collins *et al, Dicey, Morris and Collins on The Conflict of Laws* (London, Sweet & Maxwell, 14th edn, 2006) para 33–146; L Merrett, 'Choice of Law in Insurance Contracts Under the Rome I Regulation' (2009) 5 *Journal of Private International Law* 49, 54–5.

[459] L Collins *et al, Dicey, Morris and Collins on The Conflict of Laws* (London, Sweet & Maxwell, 14th edn, 2006) para 33–146.

Mandatory Insurance Contracts

14.5.22   Article 7(4) sets out additional rules for insurance contracts covering risks for which a Member State imposes an obligation to take out insurance. The risks may be large risks or non-large risks. First, the obligation to take out insurance will not be fulfilled unless the contract complies with the specific provisions relating to that insurance as mandated by the law of the relevant Member State. Where there is a conflict between the law of the Member State in which the risk is situated and the law of the Member State imposing the obligation to take out insurance, the latter prevails. Secondly, a Member State may lay down that the insurance contract shall be governed by the law of the Member State that imposes the obligation to take out the insurance. Derogation in this manner from the choice of law rules laid out in Article 7(2) and (3) is thus permitted, although it should be pointed out that the derogation is on the Member States' and not the parties' part.

Consumer Insurance Contracts

14.5.23   Article 7 prevails over the consumer contract provisions set out in Article 6. This impacts on consumer contracts concerning a large risk, such as insurance taken out on a yacht. Although the policy holder may be a consumer, he will not benefit from the more protective rules of Article 6 and the law governing the insurance contract will be determined by Article 7(1). The same position applies for a consumer contract concerning a non-large risk where the risk is located within the EU. Consumers in these contracts will have to look for protection via application of Article 3(3) and (4) (if the parties have chosen the applicable law) and Article 9.[460] Conversely, consumers in contracts concerning a non-large risk situated outside the EU will benefit from the protective rules set out in Article 6.

Individual Employment Contracts

Introduction

14.5.24   Article 8 does not differ substantively from its predecessor, Article 6 of the Rome Convention, although there are differences of terminology and structure. As a starting point, party autonomy will be recognised, although some restriction by way of mandatory rules is imposed (Article 8(1)). If the parties have not chosen a law, the contract will be governed by the law of the country in which, or from which, the employee habitually carries out his work (Article 8(2)). Where the law cannot be identified pursuant to Article 8(2), the law of the place of business through which the employee was engaged will be applicable (Article 8(3)). Lastly, there is a flexible escape clause in favour of the law of the closer or closest connection (Article 8(4)).

---

[460]   See section 14.3.

What is an Individual Employment Contract?

14.5.25   There is little guidance on the scope of the special provisions concerning individual employment contracts contained in Article 8. However, Article 8 presumably 'covers the case of void contracts and also de facto employment relationships, in particular those characterised by failure to respect the contract imposed by law for the protection of employees'.[461] An autonomous meaning must be ascribed to the concept 'individual employment contract'. The Court of Justice has pronounced on the meaning of this concept for the purposes of Article 5(1) of the Brussels Convention. These cases have been interpreted by Field J in *WPP Holding Italy Srl v Benatti* to indicate that the objective criteria of an individual employment contract are: the provision of services by one party over a period of time for which remuneration is paid; control and direction over the provision of services by the counterparty; and the integration to some extent of the provider of the services within the organisational framework of the counterparty.[462] These however are 'not "hard edged" criteria which can be mechanistically applied'.[463] The drawback to adopting a European autonomous definition for employment contracts is that it 'could well have the result that a particular state's employment law would have to be applied to a particular contract even though that state would regard the contract as being, say, one of agency rather than one of employment'.[464]

Party Autonomy and the Application of Mandatory Rules

14.5.26   Article 8(1) provides:

An individual employment contract shall be governed by the law chosen by the parties in accordance with Article 3. Such a choice of law may not, however, have the result of depriving the employee of the protection afforded to him by provisions that cannot be derogated from by agreement under the law that, in the absence of choice, would have been applicable pursuant to paragraphs 2, 3 and 4 of this Article.

Article 8(1) is inspired by the same philosophy as Article 6(2)—an intention to protect the weaker party by ensuring that a choice of law does not prejudice the application of protective legislation which would apply in the absence of choice. If, for example, a French resident is employed by a German subsidiary of a New York corporation to work in different countries in the Middle East under a contract which is expressly governed by New York law, Article 8(1) requires the application of any relevant rules that cannot be derogated from by agreement of the law of the country which would have applied in the absence of choice (which would probably be German law by virtue of Article 8(3)) even though the contract is governed by New York law. The protective rules will consist of provisions relating to the contract of employment itself and 'provisions such as those concerning industrial safety and hygiene which are regarded in

---

[461]   Giuliano-Lagarde Report, [1980] OJ C282/25–6.
[462]   [2006] 2 Lloyd's Rep 610, 622 (at [69]).
[463]   Toulson LJ in *WPP Holding Italy Srl v Benatti* [2007] 1 WLR 2316, 2331 (at [47]).
[464]   CGJ Morse, 'Consumer Contracts, Employment Contracts and the Rome Convention' (1992) 41 *ICLQ* 1, 13.

certain Member States as being provisions of public law'.[465] English domestic contract rules on restrictive covenants in employment contracts do not qualify as mandatory for the purposes of Article 8(1).[466]

14.5.27 In deciding whether a mandatory rule should be applied by virtue of Article 8(1) it is important to have regard to the legal system of which the rule forms a part. The point has been made that it is often the case that employment protection legislation only applies if the relevant employment is in the enacting country, whatever law may be applicable to the contract of employment.[467] It would be absurd for a court in which a dispute is litigated to give effect to foreign legislation which according to its own terms is not applicable. If the applicable law gives the employee more extensive protection than the law which would be applicable in the absence of choice, the wording of the Regulation indicates that the employee obtains the benefit of the law which is more favourable.[468]

14.5.28 Any choice made has to be in accordance with Article 3. Therefore, Article 3(4) also applies to an employment contract. The mandatory provisions of EU law will be superimposed onto the contract where all the elements relevant to the situation at the time of choice are located within the European Union, but the parties choose the law of a non-EU Member State to govern the contract.

The Applicable Law in Cases where the Parties Have not Made a Choice of Law

THE COMMON LAW

14.5.29 The leading common law authority on the proper law of a contract of employment is the decision of the Court of Appeal in *Sayers v International Drilling Co NV*.[469] In this case the plaintiff, an English resident, entered into a contract of employment with the defendant, a Dutch company. The contract stated that, although the work was expected to be done in Nigeria, the defendant had the right to change the venue of work. Under the terms of the contract the plaintiff agreed that in the event of his suffering injury or disability at work he would accept the benefits payable under the 'voluntary death and disability compensation program' maintained by the defendant as his 'exclusive remedy in lieu of all other claims, rights, demands or actions, whether at common law or under the statutes of the United Kingdom'. The contract did not contain an express choice of law. The plaintiff was injured while working on one of the defendant's oilrigs situated off the Nigerian coast. In the plaintiff's action against the defendant in England a preliminary issue arose concerning

---

[465] Giuliano-Lagarde Report, [1980] OJ C282/25.

[466] *Duarte v Black & Decker Corp* [2008] 1 All ER (Comm) 401. However, the court held (*obiter*) that if the covenants are valid and enforceable under the applicable law of the contract containing the covenants but invalid and unenforceable under English law, the covenants may be struck down as being against English public policy where the employee was working in England at the time the covenants were entered into pursuant to a contract of employment governed by English law.

[467] CGJ Morse, 'The EEC Convention on the Law Applicable to Contractual Obligations' (1982) 2 *YBEL* 107, 139.

[468] WA Allwood, 'Characteristic Performance and Labour Disputes under the Brussels Convention: Pandora's Box' (1987) 7 *YBEL* 131, 154. See also Recital 23.

[469] [1971] 1 WLR 1176. R Smith, 'International Employment Contracts—Contracting Out' (1972) 21 *ICLQ* 164.

the law governing the contract. Whereas the exclusion of liability in the contract was valid under Dutch law, under English law it was void.[470] The majority of the Court of Appeal decided that the contract of employment was governed by Dutch law. Among the various factors considered by Salmon LJ one of the most important was the fact that the employer was based in the Netherlands:

[S]ince the Dutch employers were engaging people of various nationalities in different parts of the world to work abroad together it certainly gives the greatest business efficacy to such contracts to presume that the parties must have intended to adhere to the law of Holland, or, put in a different way, that that system of law has the closest and most real connection with the contract.[471]

ARTICLE 8(2)

14.5.30   As regards individual employment contracts concluded as from 17 December 2009 the choice of law rules contained in the Regulation apply. If the parties fail to make a choice of law, the applicable law is not determined by Article 4, but by Article 8(2), which provides:

To the extent that the law applicable to the individual employment contract has not been chosen by the parties, the contract shall be governed by the law of the country in which or, failing that, from which the employee habitually carries out his work in performance of the contract. The country where the work is habitually carried out shall not be deemed to have changed if he is temporarily employed in another country.

14.5.31   First, how is the test in Article 8(2) to be applied? In *Sayers v International Drilling Co NV* the plaintiff was employed to work on an oilrig in Nigerian territorial waters, but the contract provided that the defendant had the right to change the venue of work. Could it be said that the employee habitually worked in Nigeria? The problems surrounding the identification of the place where the employee habitually works have been considered by the Court of Justice in the context of the jurisdiction provisions relating to individual contracts of employment.[472] It is not unreasonable to assume that the approach adopted in the context of jurisdiction disputes may be relevant to the interpretation of the Rome I Regulation.[473] However, although Recital 7 exhorts that consistency should be maintained between the Brussels I, Rome I and Rome II Regulations, there are important differences which need to be noted. Whereas, in the context of a jurisdiction rule, it is not necessary for the relevant connecting factor to be constant, it is vital that the connecting factor which determines the applicable law is stable. Accordingly the place where 'the employee habitually carries out his work' may have to be given different interpretations in different contexts.

14.5.32   Note must be taken of 'temporary employment' situations which commonly crop up in relation to a group of companies where an employee employed by a company in country X will be sent to work in an affiliated company in country Y. Sometimes this is done without any revision of the original contract of employment. More commonly

---

[470] By virtue of s 1(3) of the Law Reform (Personal Injuries) Act 1948.
[471] [1971] 1 WLR 1176, 1184.
[472] See paras 5.8.40–5.8.42.
[473] See Recital 7.

though, new contracts will be concluded: one between the employee and the employer in country X containing the terms of re-employment of the employee upon finishing his work in country Y, and another between the employee and the employer in country Y which may be required for the purposes of obtaining a work permit in country Y.[474] It is unclear whether an employee in such a situation would be considered to have changed the place where he habitually works. Recital 36 clarifies that the phrase 'temporary employment' captures situations where the employee is expected to resume work in the country of origin after carrying out work abroad. In particular, '[t]he conclusion of a new contract of employment with the original employer or an employer belonging to the same group of companies as the original employer should not preclude the employee from being regarded as carrying out his work in another country temporarily'. The duration for which employment will be considered to be more than temporary is not specified and is left up to the courts.[475] It has been suggested that the court should look at the subjective will of the parties as to the nature of the new employment.[476] Therefore, in the example given above, the employee will be considered still habitually to work in country X provided that the duration of his employment in country Y is not so long as to indicate that the parties intend that the employee will not return to his original job.

14.5.33 The phrase 'in which, or failing that, from which' was used to ensure consistency with the Court of Justice's pronouncements on Article 18 of the Brussels I Regulation.[477] Article 8(2) seeks specifically to encompass aircraft personnel within its scope provided that the work is organised from a fixed base and the employee performs other work in that fixed place such as registration and safety checks.[478] Many aircraft personnel conclude contracts in the company headquarters in country A and are then transferred to a base in country B where they will receive instructions on their flying schedule and perform other tasks.[479] The law of country B will be applicable under Article 8(2) as it will be the country 'from which' the personnel habitually carries out his work in performance of the contract.

14.5.34 It is unclear whether contracts with more peripatetic employees, such as seagoing personnel, would be governed by Article 8(2). Although a fixed base may be identified, the proportion of time spent at, and work done in, the base would be so insignificant for many seagoing personnel that it would be difficult to describe seagoing

---

[474] Max Planck Institute for Foreign Private and Private International Law, 'Comments on the European Commission's Green Paper on the conversion of the Rome Convention of 1980 on the law applicable to contractual obligations into a Community instrument and its modernization' (2004) *RabelsZ* 1, 60.

[475] The difficulties of imposing an objective time limit are discussed by Max Planck Institute for Foreign Private and Private International Law, 'Comments on the European Commission's Green Paper on the conversion of the Rome Convention of 1980 on the law applicable to contractual obligations into a Community instrument and its modernization' (2004) *RabelsZ* 1, 61–2.

[476] Max Planck Institute for Foreign Private and Private International Law, 'Comments on the European Commission's Green Paper on the conversion of the Rome Convention of 1980 on the law applicable to contractual obligations into a Community instrument and its modernization' (2004) *RabelsZ* 1, 61.

[477] Commission Proposal, COM (2005) 650 final, p 7.

[478] Commission Proposal, COM (2005) 650 final, p 7. See *Crofts v Veta Ltd* [2006] 1 All ER 823, where the House of Lords held that s 94(1) of the Employment Rights Act 1996 applied to a pilot who was employed to work for a Hong Kong airline when the pilot was based at Heathrow and lived in the United Kingdom. A Briggs, (2006) 77 *BYIL* 572.

[479] Max Planck Institute for Foreign Private and Private International Law, 'Comments on the European Commission's Green Paper on the conversion of the Rome Convention of 1980 on the law applicable to contractual obligations into a Community instrument and its modernization' (2004) *RabelsZ* 1, 66.

personnel as habitually carrying out work in the country where the base is located. An alternative would be to identify the ship as the place where the sailor habitually carries out his work and apply the law of the country of the ship's flag. However, a ship obviously moves through waters belonging to different countries and sometimes a ship flies a flag of convenience with no other connection with the country of the flag.[480] It is suggested that maritime employment contracts, and other similar contracts, should instead be governed by Article 8(3).[481]

ARTICLE 8(3)

14.5.35   Article 8(3) provides that:

Where the law applicable cannot be determined pursuant to paragraph 2, the contract shall be governed by the law of the country where the place of business through which the employee was engaged is situated.

There are difficulties in interpreting the relationship between paragraphs 2 and 3. The problem of which provision covers contracts of employment for peripatetic employees, such as seagoing personnel, has been discussed above. Another problem concerns the interpretation of the phrase 'the place of business though which the employee was engaged' for the purposes of Article 8(3). In *Sayers v International Drilling Co NV* the plaintiff was recruited in England by an agent acting on behalf of a Dutch company. On these facts would Article 8(3) point to England, where the agent's place of business was located, or to the Netherlands, where the employer's place of business was located? It makes little sense to interpret 'the place of business though which the employee was engaged' as referring to the agent's place of business; it is the employer's place of business which constitutes the more significant connecting factor. Typically, the only connection between the contract and the agent's place of business (if any) is that the contract is concluded there.

ARTICLE 8(4)

14.5.36   Article 8(4) provides an escape clause:

Where it appears from the circumstances as a whole that the contract is more closely connected with a country other than that indicated in paragraphs 2 or 3, the law of that other country shall apply.

The relationship between paragraphs 2 and 3, on the one hand, and paragraph 4, on the other, is unclear. In what circumstances do the rules in paragraphs 2 and 3 yield to the test of closest connection?[482] In *Sayers v International Drilling Co NV* the majority of the Court of Appeal laid particular emphasis on the fact that the employer's administrative centre was located in the Netherlands. Would this be sufficient to justify the conclusion that the contract was most closely connected with

---

[480] Where the country of the flag has no connection with the ship, some countries apply the law of closest connection; others, the law of the place of business through which the sailor was engaged. See Max Planck Institute for Foreign Private and Private International Law, 'Comments on the European Commission's Green Paper on the conversion of the Rome Convention of 1980 on the law applicable to contractual obligations into a Community instrument and its modernization' (2004) *RabelsZ* 1, 63–4.

[481] Cf Max Planck Institute for Foreign Private and Private International Law, 'Comments on the European Commission's Green Paper on the conversion of the Rome Convention of 1980 on the law applicable to contractual obligations into a Community instrument and its modernization' (2004) *RabelsZ* 1, 65.

[482] These problems mirror those surrounding the relationship between the fixed rules in Art 4(1) and Art 4(3) of the Regulation. See paras 14.2.55–14.2.56.

the Netherlands, bearing in mind that the applicable law presumptively identified by sub-paragraph (a) or (b) is only displaced if the *contract* is more closely connected with another country?[483] There are no simple answers to many of the questions raised by Article 8[484]; they will have to be answered in due course by the Court of Justice.

Overriding Rules

14.5.37 Apart from the superimposition of the mandatory rules of the law applicable in the absence of choice when the parties have made a choice of law,[485] an individual employment contract is subject to other overriding rules. The underlying objective is not to deprive employees of protection afforded to them by giving effect to overriding rules when this is to the employees' benefit.[486]

14.5.38 Whether or not parties have chosen a law, Article 9(2) provides for the application of the overriding mandatory rules of the forum. Legislation in the United Kingdom rarely indicates whether particular provisions are or are not overriding. For example, section 1(3) of the Law Reform (Personal Injuries) Act 1948 simply provides:

Any provision contained in a contract of service or apprenticeship, or in an agreement collateral thereto (including a contract or agreement entered into before the commencement of this Act), shall be void in so far as it would have the effect of excluding or limiting any liability of the employer in respect of personal injuries caused to the person employed or apprenticed by the negligence of persons in common employment with him.

Although this provision is a mandatory rule—in the sense that it cannot be excluded by agreement in a domestic contract—the extent to which section 1(3) is to be regarded as a rule which is capable of overriding the law chosen by the parties in an international contract is not obvious from the terms of the legislation itself. As a general principle, legislation of this type is not regarded as having extraterritorial effect. So, on the one hand, where an employee is injured by the negligence of a fellow employee in England, the effect of section 1(3) of the 1948 Act is to override an exclusion clause in the contract of employment even if the clause is valid under the applicable law.[487] If, on the other hand, injuries result from negligence committed in a foreign country, it seems that section 1(3) is not to be regarded as an overriding rule for the purposes of Article 9(2).[488]

14.5.39 In addition, Recital 34 provides for the application of the overriding mandatory provisions of the country to which a worker is posted in accordance with Directive 96/71/EC of the European Parliament and of the Council concerning the posting of workers in the framework of the provision of services.[489] The Directive is of a more restricted scope than the Rome I Regulation as it is concerned only with intra-EU situations, that is, when an employee of an undertaking established in a Member State is posted to the

---

[483] See *Booth v Phillips* [2004] 1 WLR 3292.

[484] For English decisions on Art 6 of the Rome Convention, see *Base Metal Trading Ltd v Shamurin* [2002] CLC 322, [2004] ILPr 74; *Booth v Phillips* [2004] 1 WLR 3292.

[485] And the mandatory rules of EU law if the requirements of Art 3(4) are fulfilled.

[486] See Recital 35.

[487] This result follows from the analysis of the Court of Session in *Brodin v A/R Seljan* 1973 SLT 198.

[488] *Sayers v International Drilling Co NV* [1971] 1 WLR 1176.

[489] [1997] OJ L18/1. For consideration of the Directive, see P Davies, 'Posted Workers: Single Market or Protection of National Labour Law Systems?' (1997) 34 *CML Rev* 571; R Smith and C Villiers, 'Protecting Internationally Posted Workers' [1996] *Jur Rev* 167.

territory of another Member State for a limited period. It mandates the application of the overriding rules of the law of the latter state notwithstanding the law applicable to the employment contract. Examples of the rules targeted are minimum wage rules or health and safety regulations.[490] These overriding mandatory provisions would be applicable anyway by virtue of Article 23 of the Regulation but Recital 34 serves to clear up any doubt as to the applicability of the Directive in the context of employment contracts falling within the scope of the Rome I Regulation. Lastly, the overriding mandatory provisions of the law of the country where the employee will perform or has performed his obligations may apply if they affect the validity of the contract.[491]

14.6 MISCELLANEOUS PROVISIONS

Voluntary Assignment and Contractual Subrogation

14.6.1   Voluntary assignment and contractual subrogation of the creditor's rights are covered in the same provision as both serve the same economic purpose.[492] Article 14 provides:

1. The relationship between the assignor and assignee under a voluntary assignment or contractual subrogation of a claim against another person (the debtor) shall be governed by the law that applies to the contract between the assignor and assignee under this Regulation.
2. The law governing the assigned or subrogated claim shall determine its assignability, the relationship between the assignee and the debtor, the conditions under which the assignment or subrogation can be invoked against the debtor and whether the debtor's obligations have been discharged.

Article 14 basically covers triangular transactions involving an assignor (creditor), assignee and debtor. Paragraph 3 explains that outright transfers of claims, transfers of claims by way of security and pledges or other security rights over claims are included in Article 14.

14.6.2   Article 14(1) covers issues such as the date on which the assignee should pay the assignor or what are the assignee's rights against the assignor when the debtor defaults.[493] According to the Giuliano-Lagarde Report, the predecessor to Article 14(2), which has the same wording, covers issues such as:

the assignability of the debt, the relationship between the assignee and the debtor, the conditions under which the assignment can be invoked against the debtor and any question whether the debtor's obligations have been discharged.

---

[490] Dir 96/71/EC concerning the posting of workers in the framework of the provision of services, [1997] OJ L18/1, Art 3(1).

[491] Art 9(2).

[492] Commission Proposal, COM (2005) 650 final, p 8.

[493] M Bridge, 'The Proprietary Aspects of Assignment and Choice of Law' (2009) 125 *LQR* 671, 690. However, the liquidator of an insolvent assignor is not subject to the law governing the relationship between the assignor and assignee with respect to his obligations towards the assignee: *Cofacredit v Morris* [2007] 2 BCLC 99, 134–5 (at [109]). It was held that the law governing the assignee's rights against the liquidator depended on the nature of its claim, so that a restitutionary claim will be governed by the choice of law rule for restitution.

The words 'conditions under which the assignment can be invoked' cover the conditions of transferability of the assignment as well as the procedures required to give effect to the assignment in relation to the debtor.[494]

14.6.3 The way in which Article 14 functions can be illustrated by a simple example. A (debtor) owes a debt to B (creditor/assignor). The debt is governed by English law. B chooses to assign his claim against A for the debt to bank C (assignee) in return for the bank paying him the amount of the debt. The contract of assignment is governed by French law. Whether the debt is assignable depends on the law governing the debt, that is, English law (application of Article 14(2)). Under English law, the debt may be unassignable, for example, because the contract under which the debt arose has a valid anti-assignment clause. The assignment would then fail. If under English law, the debt can be assigned, a further question could arise, that is, has the debt been validly assigned? This depends on the law governing the relationship between the assignor and assignee, namely French law (application of Article 14(1)). The solution engendered by the framework of Article 14 is laudable in so far as the debtor's legitimate expectations are protected so that his rights and obligations remain unaffected by any assignment.

14.6.4 The above simple illustration, however, does not reveal the complexities inherent in assignments. Assignments involve contractual and proprietary aspects. After all, a person who is owed a debt also *owns* it. At common law, the line distinguishing between property and contractual issues in an assignment is not clear and the vagueness in domestic law impacts at the choice of law level. This raises an issue as to the scope of Article 14, namely, is it intended to cover only the contractual aspects of assignment, given that the Rome I Regulation only covers contractual obligations, or does it cover the proprietary aspects of assignment as well? For example, which law determines whether ownership of the debt has been validly transferred from the assignor to the assignee? Or, which law determines who has priority when the assignor assigns the same right to successive assignees? Member States have taken differing approaches under the Rome Convention. The Dutch Supreme Court has taken the view that the proprietary effects of an assignment not only as between assignor and assignee, but also against third parties other than the debtor[495] is governed by the applicable law of the contract between the assignor and the assignee (Article 14(1)), although it did not specifically address the question of priority among successive assignees.[496] The German Federal Supreme Court has held that claims of priority between successive assignments are determined in accordance with the law governing the right assigned (Article 14(2)).[497]

---

[494] Giuliano-Lagarde Report, [1980] OJ C282/34–5. See also *Salfinger v Niugini Mining (Australia) Pty Ltd (No 3)* [2007] FCQ 1532, at [113]: the assignability of causes of action in tort or equity is to be determined by the law under which the causes of action or rights were created.

[495] On the facts of that case, the debtor had already paid the amount due into a specific account; therefore the Supreme Court did not have to consider the proprietary effects of the assignment as against the debtor.

[496] *Bransma qq v Hansa* HR 16 May 1997, NJ 1998, 585. THD Struycken, [1998] *LMCLQ* 345; ME Koppenol-Laforce, [1998] *NILR* 129. Mance LJ, in his judgment in *Raiffeisen Zentralbank Österreich AC v Five Star Trading LLC*, found himself unable to follow the Dutch Supreme Court's reasoning in this case, although he preferred not to express any definite views on it, not having read a full translation of the judgment: [2001] 1 QB 825, 847 (at [52]).

[497] VIII ZR 158/89 (1990) RIW 670; discussed by Mance LJ in *Raiffeisen Zentralbank Österreich AC v Five Star Trading LLC* [2001] 1 QB 825, 846 (at [49]).

14.6.5 The leading case under English law is *Raiffeisen Zentralbank Österreich AC v Five Star Trading LLC*.[498] A policy of marine insurance over a ship, *Mount I*, was taken out with French insurers, with the policy being governed by English law. By a deed of assignment, the Dubai shipowners assigned their 'right, title and interest in and to the insurances' to an Austrian bank. This assignment was valid according to its governing law, English law,[499] but invalid according to French law because the assignment did not comply with French requirements on notice to be given to the insurers. When the *Mount I* collided with another ship, the *ICL Vikraman*, the owners of the *ICL Vikraman* and the owners of the cargo on board that ship sought to attach the insurance proceeds. The Austrian bank in turn sought various declarations, including a declaration that, from the date of the assignment, the owners of *Mount I* no longer had any right, title or interest in or to the insurances and that those rights and interests belonged to the bank. The cargo owners argued that the issue was a proprietary one, concerning the validity of the assignment against third parties. This issue was said to be governed by the *lex situs* of the attached debt, that is, French law, on the basis that France was the place where the debtor (the French insurers) resided.[500] Conversely, the bank argued that the issue was a contractual one involving the question whether the right to claim the debt from the insurers was validly assigned. This issue was said to be governed by Article 12(2) of the Rome Convention, which corresponds to Article 14(2) of the Rome I Regulation. This pointed towards English law. Mance LJ, with whom the other two members of the Court of Appeal agreed, held that the issue boiled down to a simple question: who was in the circumstances entitled to claim as against the debtor?[501] This was an issue which fell within the scope of Article 12(2). On the point that Article 12 was merely concerned with *contractual* issues on assignment, Mance LJ stated that: '[T]here is no hint in Article 12(2) of any intention to distinguish between contractual and proprietary aspects of assignment. The wording appears to embrace all aspects of assignment.'[502] Notwithstanding this finding, the judgment proceeded on the basis that the issue of what steps are required to be taken in relation to the debtor for the assignment to take effect as between the assignee and debtor was a contractual one and governed by Article 12(2).[503] This meant that English law applied, with the result

---

[498] [2001] QB 825. R Stevens and THD Struycken, (2002) 118 *LQR* 15; A Briggs, (2001) 72 *BYIL* 461–4.

[499] The contract of assignment also contained an English jurisdiction clause.

[500] A debt is situated where the debtor resides: *Kwok Chi Leung Karl v Commissioner of Estate Duty* [1988] 1 WLR 1035.

[501] [2001] QB 825, 842 (at [35]).

[502] [2001] QB 825, 845 (at [45]).

[503] [2001] QB 825, 845–6 (at [48]). It has been argued that the characterisation of the issue in *Raiffeisen* as contractual was incorrect, as there was no contractual nexus between the debtor and the assignee: JJ Fawcett and JM Carruthers, *Cheshire, North & Fawcett: Private International Law* (Oxford, OUP, 14th edn, 2008) 1237. The authors conclude, though, that application of the law governing the right to which the assignment relates is a sensible choice of law rule. Cf M Bridge, 'The Proprietary Aspects of Assignment and Choice of Law' (2009) 125 *LQR* 671, 688–9, who argues that the characterisation depends on the purpose of the notice requirement: ie, whether it was to indicate that only the assignee could give a good discharge (contractual) or whether it was to indicate that the assignor could no longer dispose of the debt (proprietary). See also E McKendrick, *Goode on Commercial Law* (London, Penguin, 4th edn, 2010) 1239–41; M Moshinsky, 'The Assignment of Debts in the Conflict of Laws' (1992) 108 *LQR* 591.

that the right or title to such claim and sums as against the insurers belonged to the Austrian bank.

14.6.6   *Raiffeisen* illustrates the thorny problem of characterisation. As Mance LJ remarked: '[The] opposing analyses both assume that the factual complex raises only one issue and, in their differing identification of that issue, emphasise different aspects of the facts.'[504] At the heart the issue may have been who had the right to claim against the debtor but this in turn involved the question of who owned the debt so that he had the right to make that claim. The case raised intertwined contractual and proprietary issues. The court arguably should have first considered the question of who owned the debt, and then, secondly, whether the owner could invoke the debt against the debtor.

14.6.7   It is clear now that the first question falls under Article 14(1) of the Regulation.[505] There was a change of terminology from Article 12(1) of the Rome Convention to Article 14(1) of the Regulation. The Rome Convention refers to the law applicable to the contract between the assignor and assignee as governing the 'mutual *obligations* of assignor and assignee'. The Rome I Regulation has replaced this phrase with simply the 'relationship between assignor and assignee'. Recital 38 explains that:

the term 'relationship' should make it clear that Article 14(1) also applies to the property aspects of an assignment, as between assignor and assignee, in legal orders where such aspects are treated separately from the aspects under the law of obligations.

This means that the validity of the transfer of the ownership in the right assigned as between assignor and assignee falls within the scope of Article 14(1) and is governed by the law applicable to the contract between assignor and assignee. For example, if the applicable law of the contract of assignment is English law, while the law under which the debt arises is Italian law, English law governs the issue of the validity of the transfer of ownership of the debt. However, if notice has not been given to the debtor in accordance with Italian law, the assignment cannot be invoked against the debtor.[506] So the assignee who has a valid title according to English law will have to seek recourse against the assignor in accordance with English law.

14.6.8   This still leaves the question of which law governs the issue of priority between successive assignments. It is clear that application of Article 14(1) to the issue of priorities is not tenable. For example, B might assign a right to C, with the contract of assignment governed by German law, and subsequently C assigns that same right to D with a contract governed by Spanish law. German law and Spanish law may hold that C and D respectively own the same right. The same problem arises when there is a chain of assignments of one right when the assignments are governed by different laws.

---

[504] [2001] QB 825, 838 (at [20]).

[505] See *Cofacredit v Morris* [2007] 2 BCLC 99, 136 (at [115]), where Warren J hints that a proprietary claim in respect of bank balances representing assigned debts should be governed by the law governing the relationship between the assignor and assignee.

[506] It is likely that the result in *Raiffeisen* would have been the same under the Regulation as both the contract of assignment and the debt were governed by English law.

Another choice of law rule is required. The Commission, in its Proposal, suggested a new provision:

The question whether the assignment or subrogation may be relied on against third parties shall be governed by the law of the country in which the assignor or the author of the subrogation has his habitual residence at the material time.[507]

14.6.9 This provision was based on the solution found in the United Nations Convention on the Assignment of Receivables in International Trade 2001.[508] However, objections were raised against the new provision, primarily because of a fear that it would increase legal complexity by adding a third law (other than those stipulated by Article 14(1) and (2)) to the matrix and that the debtor may not have adequate protection.[509] The provision was ultimately deleted from the final text of the Regulation. However, Article 27(2) stipulates that the Commission must submit 'a report on the question of the effectiveness of an assignment or subrogation of a claim against third parties and the priority of the assigned or subrogated claim over a right of another person' and suggest a solution if appropriate by 17 June 2010. It thus appears that proprietary aspects of an assignment vis-à-vis third parties are not included within the scope of either Article 14(1) or (2). Recourse must be had to the common law. Therein lies another problem as the cases on this are ambiguous and capable of being interpreted in favour of the *lex situs* of the right assigned or the law governing the assigned right.[510] Between the law of the assignor's habitual residence,[511] the *lex situs*[512] and the law governing the assigned right, it is suggested that the last option is preferable. The right itself is a constant common denominator among all the contracts of assignment[513] and all assignees should be aware of the law applicable to the right. Further, it would be advisable to restrict the number of laws applicable to assignments; if the choice of law rule were to favour the law of the assignor's habitual residence or the *lex situs* potentially three different laws could apply to the factual matrix. One drawback, though, is that in the case of bulk or global assignments or receivables financing there may be as many different laws

---

[507] COM (2005) 650 final, proposed Art 13(3).

[508] See Arts 22 and 30.

[509] Ministry of Justice, *Rome I—Should the UK opt in?*, Consultation Paper CP05/08, 2 April 2008, p 34 (para 85). The latter fear is said to be 'exaggerated' by M Bridge, 'The Proprietary Aspects of Assignment and Choice of Law' (2009) 125 *LQR* 671, 674, who points out that Article 14(2) would protect the debtor in so far as it identifies to the debtor the payee who will give him a good discharge. Supporters also argue that this option protects the interests of third parties such as creditors of the insolvent assignor and facilitates bulk assignments.

[510] See, eg, *Kelly v Selwyn* [1905] 2 Ch 117; *Le Feuvre v Sullivan* (1855) 10 Moo PC 1. The Ministry of Justice, *Rome I—Should the UK opt in?*, Consultation Paper CP05/08, 2 April 2008, p 34 (para 85) considers that the common law rule here is for 'the law of the original claim', ie the law governing the right assigned.

[511] For detailed criticisms against this choice of law option, see R Verhagen, 'Assignment in the Commission's "Rome I Proposal"' [2006] *LMCLQ* 270; L Steffens, 'The New Rule on the Assignment of Rights in Rome I—The Solution to All Our Proprietary Problems? Determination of the Conflict of Laws Rule in Respect of the Proprietary Aspects of Assignment' (2006) 14 *European Review of Private Law* 543, 564–76.

[512] This suffers from the fiction of attributing a *situs* to intangibles. See P Rogerson, 'The Situs of Debts in the Conflict of Laws—Illogical, Unnecessary and Misleading' [1990] *CLJ* 441.

[513] Whereas the habitual residence of the assignor could potentially change and also may not be apparent to the assignees at the time of conclusion of the contracts of assignments.

as there are rights assigned. One solution to this is to apply the law of the assignor's residence as an exception in this case.[514]

Legal Subrogation

14.6.10   Contractual subrogation is covered by Article 14 whereas legal subrogation falls within Article 15. This provision states:

Where a person (the creditor) has a contractual claim against another (the debtor) and a third person has a duty to satisfy the creditor, or has in fact satisfied the creditor in discharge of that duty, the law which governs the third person's duty to satisfy the creditor shall determine whether and to what extent the third person is entitled to exercise against the debtor the rights which the creditor had against the debtor under the law governing their relationship.[515]

Multiple Liability

14.6.11   Several debtors may be liable for the same claim against the same creditor. If one of the debtors pays off the claim in whole or in part, this debtor may be able to claim a contribution from the other debtors. Whether he may do so is governed by the law governing the debtor's obligations towards the creditor. The other debtors may raise defences that they had against the creditor against the debtor claiming a contribution to the extent that this is allowed by the law governing their obligations towards the debtor.[516]

Set-off

14.6.12   The Regulation contains a new provision on set-off. Article 17 provides that:

Where the right to set-off is not agreed by the parties, set-off shall be governed by the law applicable to the claim against which the right to set-off is asserted.

For example, A and B may have claims against each other but have not agreed on the right to set-off. A's claim against B is governed by German law while B's claim against A is governed by French law. If A wishes to set off his claim on B against B's claim on him, French law determines whether A has the right to insist on set-off.[517]

---

[514]   R Goode, *Commercial Law* (London, Penguin, 2nd edn, 1995) 1128; M Moshinsky, 'The Assignment of Debts in the Conflict of Laws' (1992) 108 *LQR* 591, 613 (although it should be pointed out that both Goode and Moshinsky prefer application of the *lex situs* in the first place). Cf L Steffens, 'The New Rule on the Assignment of Rights in Rome I—The Solution to All Our Proprietary Problems? Determination of the Conflict of Laws Rule in Respect of the Proprietary Aspects of Assignment' (2006) 14 *European Review of Private Law* 543, 560, who argues that the problem of multiple laws applying is overstated as more often than not the rights which an assignor has against each of his debtors will be governed by the same law.
[515]   This provision is similar to Rome II Reg, Art 19.
[516]   Art 16. For a critical analysis, see paras 15.1.104–15.1.106 on Rome II Reg, Art 20, which is similar to Art 16.
[517]   See U Magnus, 'Set-Off and the Rome I Proposal' (2006) 8 *Yearbook of Private International Law* 113.

15

CHOICE OF LAW: NON-CONTRACTUAL OBLIGATIONS

15.0.1 The choice of law regime for non-contractual obligations in the United Kingdom is quite convoluted. There are separate rules for, on the one hand, tortious obligations and, on the other, other non-contractual obligations (particularly, those relating to unjust enrichment). Furthermore, the area of non-contractual obligations has seen the common law rules (and domestic legislative rules) largely superseded by the European rules contained in Regulation (EC) 864/2007 ('the Rome II Regulation') (section 15.1). The Regulation sets out a comprehensive scheme for choice of law both for torts and for other non-contractual obligations.[1] The Regulation applies from 11 January 2009 and covers events giving rise to damage that occur after its entry into force on 20 August 2007. There is, however, one significant exception: defamation is still governed by the common law choice of law rules (section 15.2). Outside the field of defamation, the common law choice of law rules were replaced by Part III of the Private International Law (Miscellaneous Provisions) Act 1995 (section 15.3); Part III of the 1995 Act applies only to (i) torts which were committed before the entry into force of the Rome II Regulation and (ii) situations which are excluded from the scope of Rome II and do not involve defamation claims (which are still covered by the common law). For example, where a German claimant sues an English defendant in England for invasion of privacy, Part III of the 1995 Act is relevant because the subject-matter of the claim is excluded from the scope of Rome II. Notwithstanding the pre-eminence of the Rome II Regulation in the field of non-contractual obligations, the Regulation does not explicitly address the potential difficulties surrounding situations where the claimant seeks to advance his claim on more than one legal basis (such as contract and tort) or surrounding the potential interaction of contract choice of law rules and tort choice of law rules (section 15.4).

15.1 THE ROME II REGULATION[2]

Background of Events Leading to the Rome II Regulation

15.1.1 The initiative to harmonise the choice of law rules within the European Union was taken in the late 1960s. Four areas were identified: the law applicable to corporeal

---

[1] The common law choice of law rules in the field of unjust enrichment, restitution and equitable obligations are relevant only with regard to cases which pre-date the entry into force of the Rome II Regulation and cases which are excluded from the scope of Rome II. For consideration of the common law rules, see the 3rd edition of this work, section 15.5.

[2] A Dickinson, *The Rome II Regulation: The Law Applicable to Non-Contractual Obligations* (Oxford, OUP, 2008); R Plender and M Wilderspin, *The European Private International Law of Obligations* (London, Sweet & Maxwell, 3rd edn, 2009) Pt 3; (2007) 9 *Yearbook of Private International Law* 1–222 (various authors); TC Hartley, 'Choice of Law for Non-Contractual Liability: Selected Problems under the Rome II Regulation' (2008) 57 *ICLQ* 899; ThM de Boer, 'The Purpose of Uniform Choice of Law Rules: The Rome II Regulation' (2009) 56 *NILR* 295.

and incorporeal property; the law applicable to contractual and non-contractual obligations; the law applicable to the form of legal transactions and evidence; and general matters under the foregoing heads (such as *renvoi*, classification, application of foreign law, acquired rights, public policy, capacity and representation). It was later decided that efforts should be focused on the law applicable to contractual and non-contractual obligations and a preliminary draft convention covering both these areas was produced in 1972. Ultimately, though, the scope of the convention was narrowed to cover only contractual obligations and the Rome Convention of 1980 was the result.

15.1.2 In 2002, the European Commission took steps to revitalise the attempt to harmonise choice of law rules for non-contractual obligations by launching a public consultation. Further to the consultation, in July 2003 it published a Proposal for a Regulation of the European Parliament and the Council on the Law Applicable to Non-Contractual Obligations.[3] Given that the Brussels I Regulation sets out rules on jurisdiction and the recognition and enforcement of judgments in civil and commercial matters for both contractual and non-contractual obligations, and the Rome Convention (since modernised as the Rome I Regulation) covers choice of law for contractual obligations, the Rome II Regulation was said to be a 'natural extension' of the European Union's efforts to harmonise the private international law rules relating to contractual and non-contractual obligations in civil and commercial matters in the European Union.[4] All three instruments are supposed to constitute 'a coherent set of instruments covering the general field of private international law in matters of civil and commercial obligations'.[5]

15.1.3 The Rome II Regulation is a result of the co-decision procedure whereby the Council and Parliament act as co-legislators.[6] The legal basis for the Regulation is what is now Article 81 of the Treaty on the Functioning of the European Union (TFEU), which refers to the adoption of measures 'particularly when necessary for the proper functioning of the internal market'.[7] Reservations were expressed about the European Union's competence in this area given that the Rome II Regulation is not restricted to intra-EU disputes.[8] Views culled from industry, commerce, the media and legal practitioners also did not reveal a widespread belief that there was any practical need for an EU-wide measure.[9] Nevertheless, the UK government chose to

---

  [3] COM (2003) 427 final.

  [4] Commission of the European Communities, *Explanatory Memorandum attached to the Proposal for a Regulation of the European Parliament and the Council on the Law Applicable to Non-Contractual Obligations ('Rome II')*, COM (2003) 427 final, p 3 (hereafter *Explanatory Memorandum*).

  [5] COM (2003) 427 final, p 8. However, in certain limited circumstances, Member States are allowed to conclude bilateral agreements with third countries relating to non-contractual (and contractual) obligations. See Reg (EC) 662/2009 establishing a procedure for the negotiation and conclusion of agreements between Member States and third countries on particular matters concerning the law applicable to contractual and non-contractual obligations [2009] OJ L200/25.

  [6] Now Art 294 TFEU.

  [7] See, previously Art 61(c) and 65 TEC.

  [8] Art 3. See the House of Lords European Union Committee, *The Rome II Regulation, 8th Report, HL Paper 66* (London, HMSO, 2004) pp 18–24 (hereafter *8th Report*); Response of the Government of the UK, October 2002, Introduction, paras 2–5.

  [9] House of Lords European Union Committee, *8th Report*, pp 24–5.

opt into the Rome II Regulation.[10] The Regulation applies to all EU Member States apart from Denmark.[11]

General Overview of the Rome II Regulation

Material Scope

15.1.4   Article 1 sets out the Regulation's scope. It provides that the Regulation 'shall apply, in situations involving a conflict of laws, to non-contractual obligations in civil and commercial matters'.

15.1.5   The phrase 'non-contractual obligations' has a European autonomous meaning.[12] So too does the phrase 'civil and commercial matters'. This latter phrase also appears in the Brussels I Regulation and the Rome I Regulation and previous Court of Justice judgments on the interpretation of the phrase in relation to these other instruments and their predecessors apply equally in the context of the Rome II Regulation.

15.1.6   Article 1 states that the Regulation 'shall not apply' not only 'to revenue, customs or administrative matters' but also 'to the liability of the State for acts and omissions in the exercise of State authority (*acta iure imperii*)'.[13] The exclusion of revenue, customs or administrative matters is also found under the Brussels I Regulation and the Rome I Regulation and is based on the idea of the sovereignty of states.

15.1.7   The reference to *acta iure imperii* is a departure from the text of the Brussels I Regulation. However, this exclusion incorporates into the wording of Rome II aspects of the way in which the Court of Justice has interpreted 'civil and commercial matters' in the context of the Brussels regime. When considering the question whether actions involving public authorities are within the meaning of the phrase 'civil and commercial matters',[14] the Court of Justice has taken the view that the key question is whether the actions of the public authority were specific to its public authority powers.[15]

EXCEPTIONS

15.1.8   Article 1(2) sets out further exclusions from the scope of Rome II. These exclusions are to be interpreted strictly, as they are exceptions from the choice of law rules set out in the Regulation.[16]

15.1.9   Sub-paragraph (a) excludes non-contractual obligations arising out of family relationships or similar relationships whilst sub-paragraph (b) excludes non-contractual obligations arising out of matrimonial property regimes or similar

---

[10]   The Regulation falls under Title IV of the Treaty establishing the European Community and does not apply to the United Kingdom by virtue of the Protocol annexed to the Treaty unless the United Kingdom exercises its right to opt into the instrument. Ireland also chose to opt into the Regulation.

[11]   See Recital 40.

[12]   Recital 11.

[13]   The explicit exclusion of *acta iure imperii* does not appear in the Brussels I Regulation.

[14]   See, eg, Case 814/79 *Netherlands State v Rüffer* [1980] ECR 3807; Case C–172/91 *Sonntag v Waidmann* [1993] ECR I–1963.

[15]   See paras 3.3.5–3.3.9.

[16]   *Explanatory Memorandum*, COM (2003) 427 final, p 9.

property regimes, wills and succession. These exclusions concern matters with social repercussions which are more appropriately dealt with by separate instruments.[17]

15.1.10   Article 1(2)(c) is identical to Article 1(2)(d) of the Rome I Regulation. Both exclude obligations arising under bills of exchange, cheques and promissory notes. Section 72 of the Bills of Exchange Act 1882 sets out choice of law rules for bills of exchange, cheques and promissory notes for England. Several of the other Member States are signatories of other instruments which govern these matters.[18]

15.1.11   Non-contractual obligations arising under other negotiable instruments are also excluded by sub-paragraph (c) to the extent that they arise out of their negotiable character. For example, any non-contractual claim that may be pursued against a thief who has successfully cashed a cheque will still fall within Rome II. However, the non-contractual rights or liabilities of the drawer and payee of the cheque towards each other—which arise out of the cheque itself—are outside Rome II.

15.1.12   Company law matters pertaining to the creation, legal capacity, internal organisation or winding up of companies and other bodies corporate or unincorporate, the personal liability of officers and members for the obligations of the company and the personal liability of auditors to a company or its members are excluded.[19] Such questions are inextricably linked with the company statutes themselves and are more suitably regulated by the law governing the company.[20] However, an allegation that a company has been negligent in discharging its duties falls within the scope of Rome II.

15.1.13   Sub-paragraph (e) excludes 'non-contractual obligations arising out of relations between settlors, trustees and beneficiaries of a trust created voluntarily'. Clearly, the exclusion covers express trusts, which are governed by the Recognition of Trusts Act 1987.[21] The focus of the exclusion on 'a trust created voluntarily' logically means that trusts created involuntarily are within the scope of Rome II. Under English law, issues relating to involuntary trusts could include claims of 'constructive trusteeship' which arise upon breach of fiduciary duty (which, presumably, fall within Rome II) and the proprietary notion of resulting and constructive trusts, which appear to fall outside Rome II.[22] These issues are considered further below.[23]

15.1.14   Non-contractual obligations arising out of nuclear damage are also excluded.[24] Like many other EU Member States, the United Kingdom is a signatory to the Paris Convention of 29 July 1960 on Third Party Liability in the Field of

---

[17] See the European Economic and Social Committee, *Opinion of the EESC on the 'Proposal for a Regulation of the European Parliament and the Council on the law applicable to non-contractual obligations (Rome II)'*, para 4.2.

[18] Such as the Geneva Convention of 7 June 1930 for the Settlement of Certain Conflicts of Laws in Connection with Bills of Exchange and Promissory Notes and the Geneva Convention of 19 March 1931 for the Settlement of Certain Conflict of Laws in Connection with Cheques.

[19] Art 1(2)(d).

[20] A similar exclusion is found in Art 1(2)(e) of the Rome Convention and Art 1(2)(f) of the Rome I Regulation.

[21] The 1987 Act enacts the Hague Convention of 1 July 1985 on the Law Applicable to Trusts and on their Recognition into English law.

[22] Some resulting and constructive trusts are covered by the Hague Trusts Convention as s 1(2) of the Recognition of Trusts Act 1987 extends the ambit of the Convention to 'any other trusts of property arising under the law of any part of the United Kingdom or by virtue of a judicial decision whether in the United Kingdom or elsewhere'.

[23] See paras 15.1.86–15.1.94.

[24] Art 1(2)(f).

Nuclear Energy and the Vienna Convention of 21 May 1963 on Civil Liability for Nuclear Damage, and the rules contained in those instruments apply to this issue.

15.1.15   The last exception in sub-paragraph (g) relates to 'violations of privacy and rights relating to personality, including defamation'. The preliminary draft proposal contained a provision dealing with defamation.[25] However, ensuing hostility, particularly from the newspaper and broadcasting industries, eventually led to the provision being dropped and sub-paragraph (g) being inserted.[26]

15.1.16   Article 1(3) stipulates that the Regulation 'shall not apply to evidence and procedure, without prejudice to Articles 21 and 22'.[27] The effect of Article 1(3) is that the prevailing position under English law—that is, that matters of evidence and procedure are for the *lex fori*—still stands under the Regulation. It is possible, however, that Rome II has brought about a change in terms of the matters which ought to be classified as 'evidence and procedure' for the purposes of the choice of law rules.[28]

Territorial Scope

UNIVERSAL APPLICATION

15.1.17   Article 3 provides that:

Any law specified by this Regulation shall be applied whether or not it is the law of a Member State.

Although it has been pointed out that the applicability under the Regulation of the laws of third states as well as of EU Member States makes the link between the Regulation and the 'proper functioning of the internal market' tenuous,[29] it is preferable that the same choice of law rules apply to intra-EU disputes and disputes which are closely connected with a country which is not an EU Member State. A split regime comprising different choice of law rules which depended on the territorial connections of the case would unnecessarily complicate matters and could also be said to discriminate against non-EU systems of laws.[30] The approach taken in Article 3, therefore, has the merit of simplicity.

INTERNAL CONFLICTS

15.1.18   Each territorial unit of the United Kingdom is considered as a country for the purposes of identifying the applicable law under the Rome II Regulation.[31]

---

[25] Art 7 of the preliminary draft proposal for a Council Regulation on the law applicable to non-contractual obligations.

[26] Pursuant to the review clause in Art 30, a report on this area was made: 'Comparative Study on the Situation in the 27 Member States as regards the Law Applicable to Non-Contractual Obligations Arising out of Violations of Privacy and Rights Relating to Personality' JLS/2007/C4/028 Final Report (February 2009). The Report concluded that the current stalemate would best be resolved by the adoption of a Directive setting out an EU-wide minimum substantive threshold reconciling media rights and personality rights.

[27] On Arts 21 and 22, see paras 15.1.107–15.1.108.

[28] See para 15.1.101.

[29] O Remien, 'European Private International Law, the European Community and its Emerging Area of Freedom, Security and Justice' (2001) 38 *CML Rev* 53, 75–76; Response of the Government of the UK, Introduction, para 4; House of Lords European Union Committee, *8th Report*, pp 29–30. Cf J Basedow, 'The Communitarisation of The Conflict of Laws under the Treaty of Amsterdam' (2000) 37 *CML Rev* 687, 701.

[30] Opinion of the European Economic and Social Committee, [2004] OJ C241/3, para 4.6.

[31] Art 25(1).

The United Kingdom is not required to apply the Regulation's rules to a purely internal conflict.[32] However, it is not surprising that the UK government has chosen to do so. The Law Applicable to Non-Contractual Obligations (England and Wales and Northern Ireland) Regulations 2008 extends the Rome II Regulation's rules to cases involving conflicts between (a) the laws of different parts of the United Kingdom, or (b) between the laws of one or more parts of the United Kingdom and Gibraltar. [33]

Temporal Scope

15.1.19 Article 31 provides that the Regulation 'shall apply to events giving rise to damage which occur after its entry into force'. In the absence of any date specified for its entry into force, the Regulation entered into force on the 20th day follow-ing its publication in the Official Journal, that is, 20 August 2007.[34] Article 32 then stipulates that the Regulation shall apply from 11 January 2009.[35] This seems to mean that events giving rise to damage which occur on or after 20 August 2007 will be subject to the Rome II Regulation's rules if proceedings are commenced on or after 11 January 2009. If the event giving rise to damage occurred before 20 August 2007 (or if proceedings were commenced before 11 January 2009), then the situation is gov-erned by the common law rules or the rules set out in the Private International Law (Miscellaneous Provisions) Act 1995 (as the case may be).[36]

Exclusion of the Doctrine of Renvoi

15.1.20 The doctrine of *renvoi* has little or no application in the commercial sphere. It has no role to play in relation to contractual obligations either at common law or under the Rome I Regulation.[37] Article 24, which makes it clear that the doctrine also has no role to play in the field of non-contractual obligations, provides that:

The application of the law of any country specified by this Regulation means the application of the rules of law in force in that country other than its rules of private international law.

For example, if the law applicable to a tort under the Regulation is the law of country X, the English court should apply the tort law of country X. This is so regardless of whether a court of country X, if seised of the matter, would apply its own law or would, by virtue of the operation of its choice of law rules, apply the law of country Y.[38]

---

[32] Art 25(2).
[33] SI 2008/2986, reg 6. The Regulations also amend the Private International Law (Miscellaneous Provisions) Act 1995 and the Foreign Limitation Periods Act 1984 to make it clear that these Acts yield to Rome II in cases where Rome II applies. The corresponding Scottish legislation is the Law Applicable to Non-Contractual Obligations (Scotland) Regs 2008, SSI 2008/404.
[34] Art 297 TFEU.
[35] Apart from Art 29, which applies from 11 July 2008.
[36] Cf A Dickinson, *The Rome II Regulation: The Law Applicable to Non-Contractual Obligations* (Oxford, OUP, 2008) 285–90.
[37] See para 14.1.23.
[38] Cf *Neilson v Overseas Projects Corporation of Victoria Ltd* (2005) 221 ALR 213, where the High Court of Australia, by a six-to-one majority, unexpectedly accepted the availability of *renvoi* for international torts.

Choice of Law Rules for Tort

The Recognition of Party Autonomy

15.1.21 Party autonomy provides the primary choice of law rule under the Rome II Regulation. Party autonomy, of course, has long been recognised for contract choice of law[39] and although such recognition has been slower to come in the field of non-contractual obligations, is not totally unknown.[40] In *Trafigura Beheer BV v Kookmin Bank Co*,[41] proceedings characterised as tortious had been brought on the failure of Trafigura, the beneficiary of a letter of credit, to return all original copies of a bill of lading to Kookmin, the issuer of the letter of credit, which then deprived Kookmin of its security interest in the cargo. Application of section 11(2)(c) of the Private International Law (Miscellaneous Provisions) Act 1995[42] led to Singapore law—the law of the country where Trafigura surrendered the bills of lading to the carrier contrary to Kookmin's instructions and where Trafigura took and then put the second set of claused bills which were useless as security for the cargo into the banking chain—being the applicable law. However, the letter of credit which underpinned the parties' contractual relationship was governed by English law. The question then arose as to whether English law could displace Singaporean law under the exception in section 12[43] on the basis that, having regard to the various connecting factors, it was substantially more appropriate that English law should be the governing law. Aikens J held that parties' express or implied choice of law to govern their pre-existing contractual relationship is 'a factor connecting the tort … with another country' within the meaning of section 12 if that relationship gives rise to events constituting the alleged tort in question. It was noted that 'it is substantially more appropriate that the applicable law governing the contractual relationship between Trafigura and Kookmin for issues relating to tort should be the same as that governing their contractual relationship … it would seem bizarre for all those parties' contractual relations to be governed by one applicable law, yet hold that the law of another country is to determine non-contractual rights and obligations.'[44] The problem with this analysis is that section 12 calls for factors connecting the tort with a *country*, not a law.[45] The Court of Appeal in *Morin v Bonhams & Brooks*[46] found its way out of this problem by treating the law of a country as being 'after all a feature of the country'.[47] However, this statement was only *obiter* and Mance LJ ultimately preferred to leave

---

R Mortensen, (2006) 2 *Journal of Private International Law* 1; A Briggs, [2006] *LMCLQ* 1; A Dickinson, (2006) 122 *LQR* 183; E Schoeman, (2006) 25 *UQLJ* 203; M Davies, (2006) *Melb Univ L Rev* 244.

[39] Rome I Reg, Art 3(1); *Vita Food Products Inc v Unus Shipping Co Ltd* [1939] AC 277.

[40] For a hint that party choice may be given effect under the common law double actionability rule, see *The Rainbow Joy* [2005] 3 SLR 719 (Court of Appeal, Singapore). TM Yeo [2005] *Sing JLS* 448, 458–59.

[41] [2006] 2 Lloyd's Rep 455; A Briggs (2007) 123 *LQR* 18.

[42] See para 15.3.6.

[43] See paras 15.3.7–15.3.11.

[44] [2006] 2 Lloyd's Rep 455, 473 (at [118]).

[45] A Briggs, (2007) 123 *LQR* 18, 19.

[46] [2004] 1 Lloyd's Rep 702. S Houseman, [2004] *LMCLQ* 426.

[47] [2004] Lloyd's Rep 702, 709 (at [23]).

open the question of whether a parties' choice of law of a particular country is a factor which connects a tort with a country under section 12.

15.1.22 When compared to the position under the 1995 Act, Article 14(1) of the Regulation provides for a more unequivocal recognition of party autonomy.[48] It provides not just for a choice made after the event giving rise to the damage occurred,[49] but also gives effect to 'an agreement freely negotiated before the event giving rise to the damage occurred' provided that 'all the parties are pursuing a commercial activity'.[50]

15.1.23 The Commission's first draft allowed a choice made after, but not before, the occurrence of a dispute.[51] The concern then appeared to be that allowing a pre-dispute choice would undermine a weaker party.[52] Similar concerns have been echoed by others.[53] In addition, it was thought that an anterior choice would not be appropriate because parties at that point in time cannot properly contemplate a future tort occurring; details such as who will injure whom or the nature and severity of the injury are obviously unknown.[54]

15.1.24 However, these concerns can be allayed. Weaker parties are protected to a certain extent by the need for the parties to be in a commercial activity and to have 'freely negotiated'[55] a pre-dispute choice of law.[56] This means that an anterior choice will only be effective if the parties are already in a pre-existing commercial relationship. That relationship would in most cases be a contractual one where each party would have had the chance to negotiate at arm's length and determine on whose shoulders certain risks will fall. If the contract falls within the scope of

---

[48] Or under the conflicts legislation of most civil law countries for that matter. Art 128 of the Swiss Federal Statute of Private International Law of 1 January 1989 allows the parties to choose the *lex fori*. Party autonomy under Art 42 of the German EGBGB is not restricted to the *lex fori* but allows party choice only after the event giving rise to a non-contractual obligation has arisen.

[49] Art 14(1)(a).

[50] Art 14(1)(b). The Law Commission and Scottish Law Commission initially recommended that the parties should be allowed to agree on what law governs their mutual liability in tort or delict before or after the tort or delict occurred. See *Consultative Memorandum No 62, Private International Law: Choice of Law in Tort and Delict* (London, HMSO, 1984) p 265. However, this recommendation was not followed up in the final report (*Law Com No 193*, London, HMSO, 1990) nor the Private International Law (Miscellaneous Provisions) Act 1995. See J Carruthers and E Crawford, 'Variations on a Theme of Rome II. Reflections on Proposed Choice of Law Rules for Non-Contractual Obligations: Part I' (2005) 9 *Edin LR* 65, 83.

[51] COM (2003) 427 final, Draft Art 10(1).

[52] *Explanatory Memorandum*, COM (2003) 427 final, p 22.

[53] S Symeonides, 'Rome II and Tort Conflicts: A Missed Opportunity' (2008) 56 *Am J Comp Law* 173, 215–16; Hamburg Group for Private International Law, *Comments on the European Commission's Draft Proposal for a Council Regulation on the Law Applicable to Non-Contractual Obligations*, p 38.

[54] S Symeonides, 'Rome II and Tort Conflicts: A Missed Opportunity' (2008) 56 *Am J Comp Law* 173, 215.

[55] Whether this requirement excludes a choice of law clause in a standard form contract altogether is unclear. The requirement of free negotiation stemmed from the European Parliament's Report and was contemplated to exclude clauses in standard form contracts: A6-0211/2005, p 17. The Commission (after refining the Parliament's version for greater precision) thought that the clause would protect 'consumers and employees from ill-thought-out choices and exclude the possibility of such choices being *imposed* in standard contracts': COM (2006) 83 final, p 4 (emphasis added). The word 'imposed' suggests an element of compulsion and it is submitted that provided the parties had the opportunity to negotiate the terms in the standard form contract, the contract and choice of law clause is still freely negotiated even if the contract ultimately is entered into on those standard conditions.

[56] For a more sceptical view, see A Rushworth and A Scott, 'Rome II: Choice of law for non-contractual obligations' [2008] *LMCLQ* 274, 293.

the Rome I Regulation, any choice made by the parties will also be subject to the protective rules set out in the Regulation and help to ensure that the weaker party is not taken advantage of.

15.1.25   The practical reality is that most parties will not be able to reach agreement on a choice of law once a dispute has arisen thereby rendering a rule in favour of only an *ex ante* choice largely ineffectual.[57] Conversely, giving effect to party choice, whether made before or after the tort occurs, will mean that the same law will apply should parallel claims be made in both contract and tort. This will prevent irreconcilable judgments. It will also increase legal certainty and predictability. Parties will not need to litigate just to find out what law applies to their claim. All this means that the final version of Article 14(1) is to be supported.

15.1.26   Article 14(1) goes on to say that '[t]he choice shall be expressed or demonstrated with reasonable certainty by the circumstances of the case and shall not prejudice the rights of third parties'. There is some uncertainty as to what kind of wording is required for a clause to be construed to cover non-contractual obligations. In *Fiona Trust & Holding v Privalov*,[58] the House of Lords held that semantics had no place when determining the intentions of rational businessmen in international commercial contracts and that one should liberally construe what fell within the scope of an arbitration clause.[59] This reasoning should equally apply to choice of law clauses and one should not make 'fussy distinctions'[60] as to what is covered by phrases like 'arising out of', 'arising under', 'arising in connection with' or any of the other common terminology used for contractual choice of law clauses.[61] For example, a choice of law clause may be phrased in terms of the law of country X governing 'any dispute arising out of the contract'. If the issue is the supply of a defective product pursuant to the contract, one must be cognisant that the supply only took place because of the contract.[62] Taking a commonsense view, any tortious claim that may be pursued as a result of the defective product should be considered to fall within the scope of the choice of law clause. In addition, party intentions would usually be that a choice of law clause in their contract would govern any disputes that develop as a result of their contractual relationship; this would include any contractual or non-contractual claims.[63]

15.1.27   Lastly, party autonomy has no role to play in relation to unfair competition and acts restricting free competition[64] or the infringement of intellectual

---

[57] Memorandum by the City of London Law Society, *Written Evidence to the House of Lords European Union Committee, 8th Report*, para 8.1.

[58] [2007] 4 All ER 951. A Briggs, [2008] *LMCLQ* 1.

[59] See also *Empresa Exportadora de Azucar v Industria Azucarera Nacional SA, The Playa Larga* [1983] 2 Lloyd's Rep 171, 183; *Continental Bank NA v Aeokos Cia Naviera SA* [1994] 1 WLR 588, 592; *Caterpillar Financial Services Corporation v SNC Passion* [2004] 2 Lloyd's Rep 99, 103; *Leo Laboratories v Crompton BV* [2005] 2 IR 225, 239 (Supreme Court, Ireland).

[60] Lord Hope at [2007] 4 All ER 951, 961 (at [27]).

[61] Cf A Briggs, [2003] *LMCLQ* 389.

[62] See *Leo Laboratories v Crompton BV* [2005] 2 IR 225 (Supreme Court, Ireland), a case on the scope and effect of a jurisdiction clause.

[63] In *Roy v North American Leisure Group* (2004) 73 OR (3d) 561, 246 DLR (4th) 306, the Ontario Court of Appeal accepted without demur that a choice of law clause in a contract specifying that English law would govern any action arising out of the contract governed the tortious claim.

[64] Art 6(4).

property rights.[65] The public interests that arise for the former and the territorial scope of the latter make them inappropriate areas for the recognition of party autonomy.[66]

15.1.28 Article 14(2) is 'inspired' by Article 3(3) of the Rome Convention.[67] It deals with the situation where all elements relevant to the situation at the time when the event giving rise to the damage occurs are located in country X, but the parties have chosen the law of country Y to govern. In this situation, Article 14(2) provides that the choice of the law of country Y by the parties shall not prejudice the application of the provisions of the law of country X which cannot be derogated from by agreement. In other words, the choice of the law of country Y still stands but the domestic mandatory rules of the law of country X will supersede the chosen law to the extent that it conflicts with them.

15.1.29 It is unclear what the phrase 'all elements relevant to the situation' covers. If a tortious claim, agreed by the parties to be governed by Suburbian law, concerns the sale and use of a defective product in Ruritania between Ruritanian parties with consequent suffering of injury in Ruritania, the fact that the product was manufactured in Utopia must surely take the case outside Article 14(2). This is because the defective manufacture of the product is a significant element of the tortious claim. However, what if the manufacture, sale, use and damage suffered are localised within Ruritania but the person injured is a Utopian tourist? The residence of the parties is arguably not an element that is as relevant to the tortious claim as the place of manufacture of the defective product.

15.1.30 The explanation given by the European Commission is that Article 14(2) is intended to deal with 'a purely internal situation' that falls under the scope of Rome II because the parties have chosen another law to govern the claim.[68] Given this, it would appear that not only the choice of Suburbian law but also the Utopian residence of the claimant internationalises the claim. Therefore, Article 14(2) is not applicable to either of scenarios set out in the previous paragraph.[69] The scope of Article 14(2) thus appears to be extremely restricted. It is suggested that a more nuanced analysis of the applicability of Article 14(2) is preferable.

15.1.31 Article 14(3) provides that:

Where all elements relevant to the situation at the time when the event giving rise to the damage occurs are located in one or more of the Member States, the parties' choice of the law applicable other than that of a Member State shall not prejudice the application of provisions of Community law, where appropriate as implemented in the Member State of the forum, which cannot be derogated from by agreement.

The purpose underlying Article 14(3) is similar to that underlying Article 14(2); namely to avoid the parties from evading the application of mandatory rules of EU law through a choice of the law of a non-EU Member State. The uncertainty over

---

[65] Art 8(3).

[66] Hamburg Group for Private International Law, *Comments on the European Commission's Draft Proposal for a Council Regulation on the Law Applicable to Non-contractual Obligations*, p 38.

[67] *Explanatory Memorandum*, COM (2003) 427 final, p 22.

[68] *Explanatory Memorandum*, COM (2003) 427 final, p 22.

[69] Cf A Dickinson, 'Cross-Border Torts in EC Courts—A Response to the Proposed "Rome II" Regulation' [2002] *EBLR* 369, 379.

what the phrase 'all elements relevant to the situation' covers arises in relation to Article 14(3) just as it does in relation to Article 14(2).

General Choice of Law Rule for Torts/Delicts

15.1.32   In the absence of the exercise of party autonomy pursuant to Article 14, Chapter II of the Regulation sets out a general choice of law framework for torts/delicts.

15.1.33   Article 4(1) provides a choice of law rule in favour of the law of the place of the wrong (*lex loci deliciti commissi*). Although many jurisdictions adopt a form of *lex loci delicti* rule for torts, the *lex loci delicti* could be identified by means of different connecting factors such as the place where the event occurs,[70] the place where the damage arises[71] or the place where the indirect consequences are felt.[72] Article 4(1), however, is quite precise about which connecting factor is relevant; it provides that:

Unless otherwise provided for in this Regulation, the law applicable to a non-contractual obligation arising out of a tort/delict shall be the law of the country in which the damage occurs irrespective of the country in which the event giving rise to the damage occurred and irrespective of the country or countries in which the indirect consequences of that event occur.

15.1.34   Consider the case where X is given negligent advice by Y in Belgium. X acts on that advice by ordering his stockbroker to buy certain shares in the New York stock market. When the value of the shares plummets, X suffers the financial consequences in England, where he resides. The country in which the event giving rise to damage occurred is Belgium; the country in which the damage occurs is New York; and the country in which the indirect consequences are suffered is England. Article 4(1) points towards New York law and is thus specifically a *lex loci damni* rule.[73]

15.1.35   The law of the place of damage was chosen because it was thought to correspond in most cases to the law of the injured party's country of residence.[74] It also strikes a good balance between protecting the interests of the victim and the legitimate interests of the person causing the injury. On the one hand, Y, in the example above, may expect Belgian law to apply; however, the law of the place of the event is generally within the defendant's control and given that tort is concerned with the violation of the victim's rights and interests, it is unfair to place too much weight on Y's expectations.[75] On the other hand, X may expect that English law should apply as England is where he predominantly suffers financial loss. However, in some cases, the tortfeasor may not be able to foresee this when he commits the tortious

---

[70] Austrian Federal Statute of 15 June 1978 on Private International Law, § 48(1).

[71] Private International Law (Miscellaneous Provisions) Act 1995, s 11(2).

[72] *Oceanic Sun Line Special Shipping Company v Fay* (1998) 165 CLR 197 (where leave was given to serve out on the basis that damage was suffered partly in New South Wales when the plaintiff was injured on board a Greek ship in Greek waters but had to seek medical treatment in New South Wales).

[73] Recital 16.

[74] *Explanatory Memorandum*, COM (2003) 427 final, p 11.

[75] However, the rules of safety and conduct which were in force at the place and time of the event giving rise to liability are taken into account: Art 17.

act. Therefore, the law of the place of damage prioritises the protection of the victim, without unduly ignoring the legitimate expectations of the defendant.[76]

15.1.36   Nevertheless, there are a few issues to consider. The damage may be sustained in more than one country. In this situation, the laws of all the countries concerned will be applied on a distributive basis in accordance with the German law concept of *Mosaikbetrachtung*.[77] This means that if chemicals that seep into the Rhine from X's factory in Switzerland cause damage to crops grown by different farmers on the banks of the Rhine in Germany, France and the Netherlands, Article 4(1) provides that X's liability towards the farmer in Germany will be subjected to German law, his liability towards the French farmer victims will be governed by French law and Dutch law determines X's liability towards the Dutch farmer.[78] Insofar as this results in different laws applying to the same wrongful act, the position is not ideal, but the end result is not objectionable.[79] The result may be less palatable if a farmer owns a plot of land that spans both Austria and Germany which is affected by X's chemicals. The law applicable to the damage caused to the Austrian portion of the land will be subject to Austrian law and the law applicable to the damage caused to the German portion of the land will be subject to German law. It may be more convenient here for one law to govern the victim's claims through application of Article 4(3).[80]

15.1.37   Another concern that has been raised about Article 4(1) has to do with direct harm being caused to 'indirect' victims.[81] For example, the death of X which occurs due to the negligence of Y while he is on holiday in Ruritania will cause the bereavement of his spouse who resides in Utopia. On the one hand, 'damage' could be understood to refer to the damage caused to the wife—such as her grief and suffering—which she suffers in Utopia.[82] However, it may be argued that Y has no reason to foresee that the wife resides in Utopia. So, on the other hand, one could argue that the direct harm is the death of her husband which occurs in Ruritania.[83] Given the emphasis on balancing the interests of the victim and the tortfeasor,[84] the latter interpretation may be the more satisfactory one.[85]

15.1.38   It may also be difficult to identify where the damage occurs in economic loss cases. For example, a misrepresentation may be made in Ruritania which induces X to enter into a contract to buy a car in Utopia. X pays the purchase price for the car by transferring the money from his Suburbian bank account. Although X arguably is

---

[76] European Economic and Social Committee, *Opinion of the EESC on the 'Proposal for a Regulation of the European Parliament and the Council on the law applicable to non-contractual obligations (Rome II)'* [2004] OJ C241/3, para 5.1.

[77] *Explanatory Memorandum*, COM (2003) 427 final, p 11.

[78] If the wrong constitutes 'environmental damage' (rather than nuisance), Art 7(1) allows the victim to opt for the application of the law of the country in which the event giving rise to the damage occurred. See paras 15.1.63–15.1.65.

[79] Cf for jurisdiction in defamation claims: Case C–68/93 *Shevill v Presse Alliance SA* [1995] ECR I–415.

[80] See paras 15.1.42–15.1.46.

[81] A Briggs, *Written Evidence to the House of Lords European Union Committee, 8th Report*, para 7.

[82] *Booth v Phillips* [2004] 1 WLR 3292.

[83] See the opinion of Advocate General Darmon in Case C–220/88 *Dumez France SA v Hessische Landesbank* [1990] ECR I–49, para 52.

[84] *Explanatory Memorandum*, COM (2003) 427 final, pp 11–12.

[85] See also the position taken in relation to Art 5(3) of the Brussels I Regulation; see, especially, para 5.6.67.

hardest hit in Suburbia, the place of damage must be Utopia, where the car bought by X does not accord with its prior representation.[86]

15.1.39 Article 4(2) allows for the application of the law of the parties' common habitual residence at the time when the damage occurs.[87] Habitual residence is in turn defined in Article 23. For companies and other bodies, corporate or unincorporated, their habitual residence is the place of central administration. However, where the event giving rise to the damage occurs or arises in the course of the operation of a branch, agency or any other establishment, the location of that branch, agency or any other establishment shall be the place of habitual residence.[88] The habitual residence of a natural person acting in the course of his or her business is the place of his or her principal place of business.[89] There is no provision defining habitual residence for a natural person who is not acting in the course of his or her business; this must presumably be for national courts, applying their own laws, to decide[90] although there is a strong argument that the phrase should be given an autonomous meaning.[91]

15.1.40 The law of the parties' common habitual residence at the time when the damage occurs prevails over Article 4(1). The inclusion of this rule is partly practical—if the parties share a common habitual residence, it is likely that any litigation will take place in that same country and there are obvious advantages if the court can apply its own law—and partly based on the idea that parties who are habitually resident in the same country would have a reasonable expectation that the law of their common habitual residence would apply. However, it has been argued that it may sometimes be inappropriate to apply the law of the parties' common habitual residence. For example, if two Englishmen have a road traffic accident in Malta,[92] English law should not apply to determine whether the defendant is liable. Rather, Maltese law has an obvious and legitimate interest in having its standards of safety and conduct upheld. Therefore, Article 17 stipulates that:

In assessing the conduct of the person claimed to be liable, account shall be taken, as a matter of fact and in so far as is appropriate, of the rules of safety and conduct which were in force at the place and time of the event giving rise to the liability.

15.1.41 Article 17 should work both ways; that is, offer protection to both the victim and the person causing the injury.[93] In the example above, if the defendant is not liable under English law (the applicable law under Article 4(2)) but is liable under Maltese law, account must be taken of Maltese law. Similarly, account must be taken

---

[86] See *Morin v Bonham & Brooks Ltd* [2004] 1 Lloyd's Rep 702.

[87] This rule mirrors American cases such as *Babcock v Jackson* [1963] 2 Lloyd's Rep 286 (Court of Appeals, New York) where the law of the parties' common residence was applicable to torts occurring elsewhere. However, the American cases were based on the delicate process of weighing governmental interests whereas Art 4(2) is unconcerned with such deliberations and merely sets out an inflexible rule in favour of the law of the parties' common habitual residence.

[88] Art 23(1). This is to protect the legitimate expectations of the parties: *Explanatory Memorandum*, (2003) 427 final, p 27.

[89] Art 23(2).

[90] Cf Brussels I Reg, Art 59.

[91] See para 14.2.50.

[92] Facts of *Boys v Chaplin* [1971] AC 356.

[93] Cf S Symeonides, 'Rome II and Tort Conflicts: A Missed Opportunity' (2008) 56 *Am J Comp L* 173, 213–15.

of Maltese law in the converse situation where the defendant is liable under Maltese law but not under English law. However, it is unclear exactly what 'account shall be taken'[94] means. It cannot signify that the defendant's liability will ultimately hinge on whether he is liable under the law of the place of the event giving rise to damage since Article 17 is merely discretionary and is not a proper choice of law rule. How far and how much 'account shall be taken' of the rules of safety and conduct in the place of event giving rise to liability is something which regrettably has to be established over time. It might have been more suitable for clearer wording to have been employed.[95]

15.1.42   Article 4(3) contains another displacement rule. It provides that:

Where it is clear from all the circumstances of the case that the tort/delict is manifestly more closely connected with a country other than that indicated in paragraphs 1 or 2, the law of that other country shall apply. A manifestly closer connection with another country might be based in particular on a pre-existing relationship between the parties, such as a contract, that is closely connected with the tort/delict in question.

Given that tortious claims run the gamut from a simple traffic accident to the giving of negligent advice which causes financial loss, an inflexible choice of law rule runs the risk of causing injustice in individual cases. An escape clause such as Article 4(3) is a sensible addition to any tortious choice of law framework.

15.1.43   There are a few points to note about Article 4(3). First, it is to be invoked only in exceptional circumstances, where the tort is *manifestly* more closely connected with another country.[96] An example is given of when this might occur—where there is a pre-existing relationship between the parties that is closely connected with the tort in question. The court could then apply the law governing that relationship to the tort. If the parties have chosen French law to govern a contract between them which has no connections with France but most connections with Germany, does Article 4(3) point towards French law or German law?[97] This leads to the second point: Article 4(3) is phrased in terms of connections with a *country*, not a law. This suggests that German law is applicable under Article 4(3) as the relationship between the parties has most of its connections with Germany; there is no connection with France, merely a connection with its law. However, the law of a country has been said to be 'a feature of the country'.[98] The European Commission also seems to envisage that it is the law applicable to the pre-existing relationship which is all-important, not the objective law of closest connection to the pre-existing relationship.[99] This means that Article 4(3) points towards French law.

15.1.44   This is by no means an undesirable result. The same law will apply to contractual or non-contractual claims arising out of the parties' relationship or even

---

[94] The analogous phrasing used in Art 12(2) of the Rome I Regulation—ie 'regard shall be had' to the law of the place of performance in relation to the manner of performance—has been interpreted to cover the more 'minor' details rather than the substance of performance itself. See paras 14.4.30–14.4.34.

[95] A Dickinson, 'Cross-Border Torts in EC Courts—A Response to the Proposed "Rome II" Regulation' [2002] *EBLR* 369, 375. Maltese law could be applicable in its own right (ie, not by way of it being taken into account) under Art 4(3); see paras 15.1.42–15.1.46.

[96] *Explanatory Memorandum*, COM (2003) 427 final, p 12; cf the form of words used in the Rome Convention, Art 4(5).

[97] See Symeonides, 'Rome II and Tort Conflicts: A Missed Opportunity' (2008) 56 *Am J Comp L* 173, 203–4.

[98] *Morin v Bonhams & Brooks* [2004] 1 Lloyd's Rep 702, 709 (at [23]).

[99] COM (2003) 427 final, p 12.

contemplated relationship.[100] There are obvious advantages in terms of practicality and the avoidance of irreconcilable judgments. This interpretation also reinforces the importance of party autonomy within the scheme of Rome II; if courts have been unduly narrow in construing the scope of contractual choice of law clauses, Article 4(3) may prove to be the means by which party autonomy and expectations may be upheld.

15.1.45 Of course, it should be noted that the courts are not bound to apply the law governing a pre-existing relationship between the parties to a tortious claim; it is merely a factor that could be considered by the courts in order to decide whether the manifestly closer connection with another country exists, thereby displacing the applicable law under the general rules set out in Articles 4(1) and 4(2).

15.1.46 One drawback is that Article 4(3) espouses an 'all or nothing' approach.[101] If another country is manifestly more closely connected to the *tort as a whole*, then the law of that other country shall apply. There does not seem to be the possibility of isolating a particular issue and considering whether that issue has a manifestly closer connection with another country. For example, if two Englishmen have a road traffic accident in Malta, the issue of what heads of damages are available may appropriately be governed by English law as the law of the parties' common habitual residence; however, the issue of whether the defendant has acted negligently may more appropriately be governed by Maltese law, as Maltese law has a legitimate interest in regulating driving standards within its jurisdiction. As it is, since Article 4(3) stipulates that courts have to consider factors which relate to the tort and not the particular issue at stake, the more sophisticated issue-by-issue analysis does not seem possible.[102] Any attempt to give effect to Maltese driving standards must be through the operation of Article 17.

Special Choice of Law Rules

15.1.47 Articles 5 to 9 set out special choice of law rules for product liability, unfair competition and acts restricting free competition, environmental damage, infringement of intellectual property rights and industrial action.

PRODUCT LIABILITY

15.1.48 Article 5 deals with special choice of law rules for product liability[103] but its effectiveness may be somewhat limited. Priority is given to party choice pursuant to Article 14 and the law of the parties' common habitual residence

---

[100] COM (2003) 427 final, p 13.

[101] See S Symeonides, 'Rome II and Tort Conflicts: A Missed Opportunity' (2008) 56 *Am J Comp L* 173, 200–3; A Dickinson, 'Cross-Border Torts in EC Courts—A Response to the Proposed "Rome II" Regulation' [2002] *EBLR* 369, 375; R Morse, *Written Evidence to the House of Lords European Union Committee, 8th Report*, para 4.

[102] Cf Private International Law (Miscellaneous Provisions) Act 1995, s 12; *Boys v Chaplin* [1971] AC 356.

[103] Art 5 obviously does not cover cases such as a traffic accident where a pedestrian is injured by a car (a product) due to the driver's negligence; it only covers cases where the injury itself stems from a defect of the car and not the negligence of the driver. See J Kozyris, 'Rome II: Tort Conflicts on the Right Track! A Postscript to Symeon Symeonides' "Missed Opportunity"' (2008) 56 *Am J Comp L* 471, 487–8; A Rushworth and A Scott, 'Rome II: Choice of law for non-contractual obligations' [2008] *LMCLQ* 274, 283.

under Article 4(2) over the choice of law rules set out in Article 5. In addition, the Hague Convention on the Law Applicable to Products Liability takes precedence in those EU Member States which have ratified it.[104] There is also a substantial degree of harmonisation on product liability within the European Union due to Directive 85/374 on the approximation of the laws, regulations and administrative provisions of the Member States concerning liability for defective products.[105] However, Directive 85/374 covers only strict liability actions and certain types of damage. Consequently, the scope of Article 5 is broader than the scope of Directive 85/374.

15.1.49 The person claimed to be liable under Article 5 of Rome II could be the manufacturer of the finished product, the producer of a component or commodity or an intermediary or a retailer.[106] The definition of product and defective product for Article 5 is to be referred to Articles 2 and 6 of Directive 85/374. Article 2 defines 'product' to mean all movables including electricity, with the exception of primary agricultural products (products of the soil, of stock-farming and of fisheries, excluding products which have undergone initial processing) and game. Article 6 in turn defines a defective product as one which does not provide the safety which a person is entitled to expect, taking into account circumstances such as the presentation of the product, the use to which it could reasonably be expected that the product would be put and the time when the product was put into circulation.

15.1.50 In order of hierarchy, Article 5(1) sets out choice of law rules in favour of the law of the country in which the person sustaining the damage had his or her habitual residence when the damage occurred (Article 5(1)(a)),[107] the law of the country in which the product was acquired (Article 5(1)(b))[108] and the law of the country in which the damage occurred (Article 5(1)(c)). In all instances, it must be shown that the product was marketed in the relevant country. However, there is a proviso: if the defendant could not reasonably foresee the marketing of the product or a product of the same type in the relevant country, the law applicable shall be the law of the country in which the defendant is habitually resident.

15.1.51 The rationale for not relying on the general rule set out in Article 4(1) for product liability cases is that application of the *lex loci damni* could lead to fortuitous results. For example, drugs which are made by an English company and bought in France by an Italian tourist on a world-wide tour may cause injury when ingested by the tourist while in South Africa. The Italian tourist may not have a reasonable expectation that the law of South Africa will govern his claims against the English company as he bought the drugs in France and he himself brought them

---

[104] By virtue of Art 28. The United Kingdom has not signed up to this Hague Convention.

[105] [1985] OJ L210/29; as amended by Dir 199/34/EC [1999] OJ L141/20. The Product Liability Directive is implemented in the United Kingdom by the Consumer Protection Act 1987.

[106] *Explanatory Memorandum*, COM (2003) 427 final, p 15.

[107] This may be criticised for favouring residents in developed countries who may have higher standards of product safety compared to developing countries: S Symeonides, 'Rome II and Tort Conflicts: A Missed Opportunity' (2008) 56 *Am J Comp L* 173, 208–9.

[108] This is the choice of law rule preferred by J Kozyris, 'Rome II: Tort Conflicts on the Right Track! A Postscript to Symeon Symeonides' "Missed Opportunity"' (2008) 56 *Am J Comp L* 471, 491–2.

to South Africa.[109] Importantly, the English company would not be able to foresee in which country the tourist will ultimately take the drugs and suffer damage.[110] Foreseeability is an important factor so that a manufacturer is able to calculate the risks involved in production and distribution and take out adequate insurance accordingly.[111]

15.1.52   The emphasis in Article 5 is on making sure that the person claimed to be liable is able to foresee the applicable law by requiring that the product must have been marketed in the country concerned.[112] This also ensures that all competitors in a particular market are subject to the same safety standards.[113]

15.1.53   An issue that arises in relation to the proviso is its place within the framework of Article 5. In the example of the English drugs bought by the Italian tourist in France which causes injury in South Africa, let us assume that the product was marketed in Italy and France. Application of Article 5(1)(a) points towards Italian law; however, the English manufacturer is able to show that it could not reasonably foresee the marketing of the medication in Italy. Will the next step then be application of Article 5(1)(b), which leads towards French law (assuming that the English company is unable to show that it could not reasonably foresee the marketing of the medication in France), or can the defendant invoke the proviso which thereby leads to English law as the law of the defendant's habitual residence? If it is the latter,[114] then Article 5 seems to favour the defendant, unless American experience that it will be rare for the defendant to be able to rely on the proviso[115] holds true in Europe as well.

15.1.54   Article 5(2) sets out an escape clause that is substantively the same as Article 4(3). As a result, if there is a contractual relationship between the claimant and the defendant which pertains to the defective product, the applicable law of that contract should normally govern the claim.

UNFAIR COMPETITION AND ACTS RESTRICTING FREE COMPETITION

15.1.55   Unfair competition is not defined in Rome II. This was a particular concern for English lawyers given that English law does not have a general action for unfair competition,[116] unlike most other Member States. Some guidance can be gleaned from the Commission's *Explanatory Memorandum*, which explains that Article 6 covers acts

---

[109] T Graziano, 'The Law Applicable to Product Liability: The Present State of the Law in Europe and Current Proposals for Reform' (2005) 54 *ICLQ* 475, 481.

[110] T Graziano, 'The Law Applicable to Product Liability: The Present State of the Law in Europe and Current Proposals for Reform' (2005) 54 *ICLQ* 475, 477.

[111] Hamburg Group for Private International Law, *Comments on the European Commission's Draft Proposal for a Council Regulation on the Law Applicable to Non-contractual Obligations*, p 16.

[112] Similar emphasis is placed on the act of putting the defective product on the market in the jurisdictional context; see *Castree v ER Squibb* [1980] 1 WLR 1248; *Distillers v Thompson* [1971] AC 458.

[113] *Explanatory Memorandum*, COM (2003) 427 final, p 15.

[114] This is the assumption of S Symeonides, 'Rome II and Tort Conflicts: A Missed Opportunity' (2008) 56 *Am J Comp L* 173, 207.

[115] S Symeonides, 'Rome II and Tort Conflicts: A Missed Opportunity' (2008) 56 *Am J Comp L* 173, 207–8.

[116] Although there is protection against unfair competition by way of torts such as malicious falsehood and passing-off under English law.

such as misleading advertising, forced sales, disruption of deliveries by competitors, enticing away a competitor's staff, boycotts, and passing off.[117]

15.1.56   Article 6 has a tri-partite objective.[118] First, to ensure that all participants in a market will be subject to the same rules. Secondly, to protect competitors. Thirdly, to protect consumers and the public in general.[119] Given the wider societal interests at stake, parties are not able to choose the law applicable to torts falling within the scope of Article 6.[120]

15.1.57   Article 6(1) provides that:

The law applicable to a non-contractual obligation arising out of an act of unfair competition shall be the law of the country where the competitive relations or the collective interests of consumers are, or are likely to be, affected.

15.1.58   Application of the law of the market where the competitors' or consumers' interests are affected ensures that all market players have to abide by the same rules and protects the victims' normal expectation that the law governing their economic environment will apply.[121] Yet it also leads generally to the *lex loci damni* and raises the question of why it was necessary to formulate a special provision for unfair competition when it could have been adequately covered by Article 4.[122] Recital 21 attempts to provide a justification by saying that Article 6 is 'not an exception to the general rule in Article 4(1) but rather a clarification of it'.

15.1.59   Article 6(2) stipulates that where an act of unfair competition affects exclusively the interests of a specific competitor, the general rule under Article 4 shall apply. The *Explanatory Memorandum* gives as examples acts such as enticing away a competitor's staff, corruption, industrial espionage, disclosure of business secrets and inducing breach of contract.[123]

15.1.60   Article 6(3) deals with acts restricting free competition.[124] Article 6(3)(a) provides for application of the law of the country where the market is, or is likely to be, affected. It must be noted that, although Article 6(3)(a) refers to the law of a *country*, thereby indicating that the laws of a non-EU Member State could be applicable, Recital 23 refers to acts which are prohibited by what are now Articles 101 and 102 TFEU[125] or by the law of a Member State. This suggests that Article 6(3)(a) only leads to the application of the law of an EU Member State. However, the wording of

---

[117] *Explanatory Memorandum*, COM (2003) 427 final, p 16.

[118] *Explanatory Memorandum*, COM (2003) 427 final, p 16.

[119] This objective is derived from Dir 2005/29/EC concerning unfair business-to-consumer commercial practices in the internal market and amending Dir 84/450/EEC, Dirs 97/7/EC, 98/27/EC and 2002/65/EC and Reg (EC) 2006/2004 ('Unfair Commercial Practices Directive') [2005] OJ L149/22, implemented into English law by the Consumer Protection for Unfair Trading Regs 2008, SI 2008/1277. That claims falling within this third objective is a matter relating to tort, delict or quasi-delict is established by Case C–167/00 *Verein für Konsumenteninformation v Henkel* [2002] ECR I–8111, where the Court of Justice held that an action for an injunction brought by a consumer association to prevent a trader from using unfair terms in contracts with private individuals fell within Art 5(3) of the Brussels Convention.

[120] Art 6(4).

[121] *Explanatory Memorandum*, COM (2003) 427 final, p 16.

[122] House of Lords European Union Committee, *8th Report*, p 34.

[123] COM (2003) 427 final, p 16.

[124] ER Pineau, 'Conflict of Laws Comes to the Rescue of Competition Law' (2009) 5 *Journal of Private International Law* 311; J Fitchen, 'Choice of Law in International Claims Based on Restrictions of Competition: Article 6(3) of the Rome II Regulation' (2009) 5 *Journal of Private International Law* 337.

[125] These set out rules on competition within the common market.

Article 6(3)(a) is clear enough and recital 23 is probably only reiterating the 'effects principle'[127] upon which EU competition law is based.[126] Given that civil courts have been extremely reluctant to apply foreign competition law, the generous approach of Article 6(3)(a) could be thought a bit surprising.[128]

15.1.61 Where the market is affected in more than one country, the claimant has the option of choosing the *lex fori*. The first part of Article 6(3)(b) sets out that:

the person seeking compensation for damage who sues in the court of the domicile of the defendant, may instead choose to base his or her claim on the law of the court seised, provided that the market in that Member State is amongst those directly and substantially affected by the restriction of competition out of which the non-contractual obligation on which the claim is based arises ...

15.1.62 If the claimant pursues multiple claims, then the second part of Article 6(3)(b) provides that:

where the claimant sues, in accordance with the applicable rules on jurisdiction, more than one defendant in that court, he or she can only choose to base his or her claim on the law of that court if the restriction of competition on which the claim against each of these defendants relies directly and substantially affects also the market in the Member State of that court.

Article 6(3)(b) reflects the general consensus that only the direct substantial effects of an act of unfair competition are relevant as an unfair act may have repercussions in several markets.[129]

ENVIRONMENTAL DAMAGE

15.1.63 Article 7 provides that:

The law applicable to a non-contractual obligation arising out of environmental damage or damage sustained by persons or property as a result of such damage shall be the law determined pursuant to Article 4(1), unless the person seeking compensation for damage chooses to base his or her claim on the law of the country in which the event giving rise to the damage occurred.

By allowing the claimant to make a unilateral choice of law, the underlying policy of Article 7 is to try to provide the maximum level of legal protection for the environment possible. The person who sustains the damage can choose to base his claim on either the law of the country in which the damage is sustained or the law of the country in which the event giving rise to the damage occurred.[130] This echoes the European Court of Justice's interpretation of Article 5(3) of the Brussels Convention[131] and is in line with

---

[126] 'Effects principle' relates to 'the assertion by a state that its law applies (or may apply) to regulate conduct that has or is intended to have effect within its territory, even when the conduct itself takes place outside its territory': A Lowenfeld, *International Litigation and the Quest for Reasonableness* (Oxford, OUP, 1996) 29. See Case 48/69 *Imperial Chemical Industries v Commission* [1972] ECR 619; Case 89/85 *Re Wood Pulp Cartel; Ahlström Osakeyhtiö v Commission* [1988] ECR 5193. It is clear that the choice of law rules set out in Art 6 are a manifestation of the 'effects principle'.

[127] 'Editorial Comments: Sometimes it takes thirty years and even more ...' (2007) 44 *CML Rev* 1567, 1573 (n 18).

[128] 'Editorial Comments: Sometimes it takes thirty years and even more ...' (2007) 44 *CML Rev* 1567, 1572–3.

[129] *Explanatory Memorandum*, (2003) COM 427 final, p 16.

[130] The stage in proceedings at which the option must be exercised is left to the procedural rules of the forum: Recital 25.

[131] Case 21/76 *Handelskwekerij GJ Bier v Mines de Potasse d'Alsace SA* [1976] ECR 1735.

the 'polluter pays' principle.[132] The rationale behind offering the victim a choice is that he or she will presumably choose the law which increases the operator's liability. The hope is that this will induce operators to adopt measures which will minimise the risk that their actions will cause environmental damage; they will not be able to escape liability simply by setting up operations in countries with lower standards of environmental protection.[133] The choice of law approach adopted in Article 7 also deters potential polluters from choosing to establish operations near a border where wind directions or river flows may mean that the effects of any polluting activity are felt in a neighbouring country with lower standards of environmental protection.[134] Another reason for the exception to the *lex loci damni* rule is that it is reasonable for the operator to expect his actions to be assessed by application of the law of the place where he carries out his activities.[135]

15.1.64   There is no role for the law of common habitual residence or a flexible escape clause here. The exclusion of the former can be justified as the greater societal interests in cases of environmental damage diminish the importance of personal connecting factors. A role is, however, envisaged for Article 17 on rules of safety and conduct.[136] The example given in the Commission's *Explanatory Memorandum* is where toxic emissions in state A are legitimate according to the laws of state A, but illegal according to the laws of state B where the damage is sustained. Under Article 17, the court must take into account the fact that the polluter has complied with the laws of the country in which he is in business.[137] Reliance on Article 17 in environmental damage cases would seem to undermine the overarching general legislative policy to increase environmental standards within the European Union.[138]

15.1.65   Recital 24 states that '[e]nvironmental damage should be understood as meaning adverse change in a natural resource, such as water, land or air, impairment of a function performed by that resource for the benefit of another natural resource or the public, or impairment of the variability among living organisms'. Presumably, it is permissible to refer to Directive 2004/35/EC on environmental liability with regard to the prevention and remedying of environmental damage[139] to fill in any gaps. Clearly, nuisance should not fall under Article 7 given that the category of environmental damage is concerned with the negative impact on wider societal interests when a polluting activity is carried out.[140]

---

[132] Recital 25.
[133] *Explanatory Memorandum*, COM (2003) 427 final, p 19.
[134] *Explanatory Memorandum*, COM (2003) 427 final, pp 19–20.
[135] S Symeonides, 'Rome II and Tort Conflicts: A Missed Opportunity' (2008) 56 *Am J Comp L* 173, 210.
[136] See above, para 15.1.41.
[137] COM (2003) 427 final, p 20.
[138] See Dir 79/409/EEC on the conservation of wild birds [1979] OJ L103/1 (as amended); Dir 92/43/EEC on the conservation of natural habitats and of wild fauna and flora [1992] OJ L206/7 (as amended), and Dir 2004/35/EC on environmental liability with regard to the prevention and remedying of environmental damage [2004] OJ L143/56 (as amended). S Symeonides, 'Rome II and Tort Conflicts: A Missed Opportunity' (2008) 56 Am J Comp L 173 suggests that lower standards in state A should be rejected if damage in state B is foreseeable. However, this compromise solution still undermines the overall objective of Art 7 and is out of line with environmental protection policy, which tends to espouse strict liability.
[139] [2004] OJ L143/56.
[140] Note the reference to 'public' benefit in Recital 24. The original heading for this category was 'Violation of the environment', which has connotations of some extensive environmental damage rather than the infringement of private rights which gives rise to an action for nuisance.

INFRINGEMENT OF INTELLECTUAL PROPERTY RIGHTS

15.1.66   Intellectual property rights[141] include copyright, related rights, the *sui generis* right for the protection of databases and industrial property rights.[142] Article 8(1) provides that the law applicable to the infringement of such rights shall be the law of the country for which protection is claimed. Article 8(1) therefore sets out the traditionally accepted principle of the *lex loci protectionis*.[143] It means that, for example, the law applicable to the infringement of a patent registered in France is governed by French law and the law applicable to the infringement to a trademark registered in Germany will be German law. If a copyright is infringed in Ireland, the applicable law will be Irish law as the law of the country where the copyright was infringed.

15.1.67   Application of the *lex loci protectionis* is based on the principle of the territoriality of intellectual property rights.[144] The principle of territoriality means that an intellectual property right that is protected by the laws of a country is only protected within the territory of that country. For example, a trademark registered in the United Kingdom is only protected within UK borders so that there is no infringement when the trademark is used by an unauthorised person in France.[145] Building on this point, since intellectual property rights are granted by countries, the same object may be protected independently by different laws. For example, X may register the same trademark in England, Germany and France. The trademark is then independently protected by English, German and French laws. The principle of territoriality also explains why there is no scope for party autonomy in relation to the infringement of intellectual property rights.[146]

15.1.68   Given that intellectual property rights confer monopoly rights, there is the clear potential for overlap between infringement of intellectual property rights and unfair competition. Intellectual property rights are said to be 'restrictions on competition in furtherance of competition'.[147] However, the same law would probably be applicable no matter how a claim is classified. For example, passing off is classified as a species of unfair competition and governed by Article 6 whereas the infringement of copyright and industrial property rights such as patents and trademarks are considered to fall under Article 8. It is likely, though, that the law applicable to a claim based on the tort of passing off would be the same under Article 6 or Article 8. Passing off claims will usually involve application of Article 6(2), which points back towards the general *lex loci damni* rule. So if X alleges that the goodwill attached to his product has been damaged by Y's actions in selling in France a similar product which is advertised in a

---

[141]   See, in general, K Lipstein, 'Intellectual Property: Parallel Choice of Law Rules' [2005] *CLJ* 593; JJ Fawcett and P Torremans, *Intellectual Property and Private International Law* (Oxford, Clarendon Press, 1998).

[142]   Recital 26.

[143]   The principle of the *lex loci protectionis* forms the basis of the Berne Convention for the Protection of Literary and Artistic Works of 1886 and the Paris Convention for the Protection of Industrial Property of 1883.

[144]   See the Paris Convention for the Protection of Industrial Property of 20 March 1883; Convention of the Grant of European Patents of 5 October 1973.

[145]   This illustrates why it would have been inappropriate for infringement of intellectual property rights to be subjected to the general rule in Art 4(1).

[146]   Art 8(3).

[147]   JJ Fawcett and P Torremans, *Intellectual Property and Private International Law* (Oxford, Clarendon Press, 1998) 494.

manner which would have confused buyers into thinking it was X's product, French law would apply because the damage (to goodwill) occurs in France. If the claim had been dealt with under Article 8, the *lex loci protectionis* would also be French law as France is where X wants the goodwill attached to his product to be protected.

15.1.69 Article 8(2) provides that:

In the case of a non-contractual obligation arising from an infringement of a unitary Community intellectual property right, the law applicable shall, for any question that is not governed by the relevant Community instrument, be the law of the country in which the act of infringement was committed.

Article 8(2) covers infringements of rights such as the EU trade mark, EU designs and similar rights which may be created in future. There are a few EU instruments which set out a regime for EU intellectual property rights.[148] If there is no unitary EU solution to a particular matter in those instruments, then the applicable law shall be the law of the country in which the act of infringement was committed. Different laws may then apply to a case of multi-state infringement of the same EU intellectual property right.

INDUSTRIAL ACTION

15.1.70 Article 9 provides:

Without prejudice to Article 4(2), the law applicable to a non-contractual obligation in respect of the liability of a person in the capacity of a worker or an employer or the organisations representing their professional interests for damages caused by an industrial action, pending or carried out, shall be the law of the country where the action is to be, or has been, taken.

This provision was a result of the European Parliament's initiative. It is limited to the issue of liability of employers, workers and/or trade unions when there is industrial action such as strikes or lockouts. It is not intended to extend to relationships vis-à-vis third parties.[149] If the parties share a common habitual residence, the law of that common habitual residence applies under Article 4(2). This exception recognises that most of the national law provisions which regulate industrial action tend to be mandatory in nature[150] and ensures that those provisions will be given effect.[151]

Choice of Law Rules for Other Non-contractual Obligations

15.1.71 Chapter III of the Rome II Regulation sets out choice of law rules for unjust enrichment, *negotiorum gestio* and *culpa in contrahendo*. Party autonomy pursuant to Article 14 precedes the choice of law rules set out for these categories

---

[148] Eg, Reg (EC) 40/94 on the Community trade mark [1994] OJ L11/1 (as amended). See Reg (EC) 207/2009 (codified version) [2009] OJ L78/1.

[149] Communication from the Commission to the European Parliament pursuant to the second subparagraph of Art 251(2) of the EC Treaty concerning the common position of the Council on the adoption of a Regulation of the European Parliament and of the Council on the law applicable to non-contractual obligations ('Rome II') , COM (2006) 566 final, para 3.2.

[150] J Kozyris, 'Rome II: Tort Conflicts on the Right Track! A Postscript to Symeon Symeonides' "Missed Opportunity"' (2008) 56 *Am J Comp L* 471, 497.

[151] Under the Rome II Regulation, only the overriding mandatory rules of the forum are applicable.

of other non-contractual obligations. There is also another exception: Article 13 stipulates that Article 8 shall apply to non-contractual obligations arising from an infringement of an intellectual property right for the purposes of Chapter III. This is to ensure that only one law is applicable to the same dispute.[152] For example, a claim based on unjust enrichment arising from an infringement of an intellectual property right will be governed by Article 8 and not the choice of law rules set out in Chapter III.

Unjust Enrichment

15.1.72   The UK government and various academic commentators objected to the inclusion of an unjust enrichment choice of law rule in Rome II. It was thought premature to try to harmonise the choice of law rules for unjust enrichment given that this area is still developing and that, amongst the Member States, there was a lack of substantial uniformity between the domestic laws of unjust enrichment.[153]

15.1.73   Be that as it may, prior to Rome II, the choice of law rules for unjust enrichment in England were never terribly clear. The choice of law framework set out in *Dicey, Morris and Collins*[154] has always been prefaced with the word *semble*.[155] The advantage of Rome II setting out a harmonised choice of law rule for unjust enrichment is that there is much greater clarity as to what exactly the choice of law rules are.

15.1.74   There is, however, a problem of characterisation. Unjust enrichment belongs within the rubric of the more encompassing label of the law of restitution. However, in England the two labels are frequently used interchangeably. Although the analysis is not entirely free from controversy, it is generally accepted that, under English domestic law, restitution consists of three areas: unjust enrichment, restitution for wrongs and proprietary restitution.[156] Unjust enrichment, as a category within the law of restitution, more accurately means autonomous unjust enrichment[157] and it concerns situations where the defendant has been unjustly enriched at the expense of the claimant (for example, where money has been paid over pursuant to a mistake, leading to an action for money had and received). Restitution for wrongs covers the situation where a wrongdoer who has profited from a wrong is made to disgorge the benefits obtained to the claimant (for example, a trustee who makes a profit by exploiting his position as a trustee may be liable to hand over that profit to the beneficiary). Proprietary restitution deals with claims which are founded on the vindication of the claimant's property rights (for example, a claim that property is held on a resulting trust for the claimant).

15.1.75   Several factors complicate this picture. First, it will be noted from the examples above that the law of restitution is focused on depriving the defendant of a gain

---

[152] *Explanatory Memorandum*, COM (2003) 427 final, p 22.

[153] Lord Chancellor's Department, *Consultation Response: Preliminary draft proposal for a Council Regulation on the Law Applicable to Non-Contractual Obligations (Response of the Government of the United Kingdom)* para 20.

[154] L Collins *et al, Dicey, Morris and Collins on The Conflict of Laws* (London, Sweet & Maxwell, 14th edn, 2006).

[155] Rule 230 in the 14th edn, para 34R–001.

[156] See G Virgo, *The Principles of the Law of Restitution* (Oxford, OUP, 2nd edn, 2006).

[157] Or unjust enrichment by subtraction.

rather than compensating the claimant for a loss. It is this feature which marks restitution out from contract and tort. Simply put, the law of restitution is concerned with the law of remedies.[158] There are, of course, no choice of law rules for remedies as remedies are generally considered to be procedural in nature and governed by the *lex fori*.[159] Secondly, the unjust enrichment principle is thought by some not only to provide the basis for autonomous unjust enrichment claims, but also restitution for wrongs and proprietary restitution.[160] Others think that restitution for wrongs is based on the particular wrong itself, whereas proprietary restitution is based on the vindication of pre-existing property rights and neither have anything to do with the principle of unjust enrichment.[161] Thirdly, all this is based on the murky picture of the English domestic law of restitution. For conflict of laws purposes, an internationalist outlook must be adopted.[162] Recital 11 of Rome II recognises that 'the concept of a non-contractual obligation varies from one Member State to another. Therefore for the purposes of this Regulation non-contractual obligation should be understood as an autonomous concept.'

15.1.76   What can be concluded is this: the characterisation of restitution (and unjust enrichment) as being purely remedial for conflicts purposes can be dismissed quickly. Restitution is recognised[163] as forming an independent branch of the law which stands alongside contract[164] and tort and there are detailed, substantive rules governing its operation. More crucially, it is important to determine, for the purposes of Rome II and the conflict of laws in general, what scope is to be attributed to the unjust enrichment principle in order to be able to tell what claims fall within or outwith Article 10. Given the rather convoluted case law in this area, this objective might prove to be difficult to achieve.

15.1.77   It is clear that Article 10 covers autonomous unjust enrichment claims. The provisions of Article 10 will be dealt with first before the more problematic issue of whether its scope covers restitution for wrongs and claims for proprietary restitution is considered.

THE CHOICE OF LAW FRAMEWORK: ARTICLE 10

15.1.78   Article 10(1) provides that:

If a non-contractual obligation arising out of unjust enrichment, including payment of amounts wrongly received, concerns a relationship existing between the parties, such as one arising out of a contract or a tort/delict, that is closely connected with that unjust enrichment, it shall be governed by the law that governs that relationship.

This choice of law rule is similar to that adopted under English law.[165] There are many clear advantages to it. This rule leads to application of the law governing the

---

[158] G Virgo, *The Principles of the Law of Restitution* (Oxford, OUP, 2nd edn, 2006) 3.

[159] *Phrantzes v Argenti* [1960] 2 QB 19; *Harding v Wealands* [2007] 2 AC 1, 13 (at [24]).

[160] Eg A Burrows, *The Law of Restitution* (London, Butterworths, 2nd edn, 2002).

[161] Eg G Virgo, *The Principles of the Law of Restitution* (Oxford, OUP, 2nd edn, 2006).

[162] Eg, *Re Bonacina* [1912] 2 Ch 394.

[163] Albeit rather belatedly in England: *Lipkin Gorman v Karpnale Ltd* [1991] 2 AC 548.

[164] The United Kingdom made a reservation against Art 10(1)(e) of the Rome Convention on the grounds that 'the consequences of nullity of the contract' belonged within the law of restitution and not contract: Contracts (Applicable Law) Act 1990, s 2(2).

[165] *Fibrosa Spolka Akcyjna v Fairbairn Lawson Combe Barbour Ltd* [1943] AC 432; *Dimskal Shipping Co SA v International Transport Workers Federation (No 2)* [1992] 2 AC 152; *Arab Monetary Fund v Hashim*

relationship between the parties when the unjust enrichment happens *because of* that relationship and thus leads to the application of the law most closely connected to the claim. For example, where rights to a debt had been transferred from X to Y and the debtor continues to pay X, Y's claim against X to recover the payment should be governed by the law governing the contract between X and Y. This is because the right of Y to recover the payment from X 'arises only because of the contract: without it, there would be no such right'.[166] To give another example: if an insurance company has paid over money on a policy under the mistaken belief that the policy is still subsisting, the only reason why money is paid over is the policy. Therefore, the law applicable to the policy, being the law governing the relationship between the parties, is the most appropriate law and has the closest connection to any consequential unjust enrichment claim. Conversely, if trust money is paid over to a third party in breach of trust and the beneficiary pursues an unjust enrichment claim against that third party, the law governing the trustee–beneficiary relationship has no application under Article 10(1). This is because Article 10(1) refers to the law governing the relationship between the parties to the claim—that is, the beneficiary and the third party. This result is justified because a claim between the beneficiary and third party does not have its roots in the relationship between the trustee and beneficiary.

15.1.79   Relationships in this context must also be understood to cover intended relationships.[167] For example, if services are rendered pursuant to a void contract which contains a clause choosing German law, German law is the putative applicable law of the contract[168] and will govern the unjust enrichment claim.[169] If the relationship is a contractual one, the Rome I Regulation determines what is the applicable (or putative applicable) law of the contract. If the relationship stems from a tort or delict, the rules set out in the Rome II Regulation apply.

15.1.80   Apart from generally leading to the law of closest connection, the choice of law rule in Article 10 has other advantages. Application of the law governing the relationship protects parties' legitimate expectations as they would probably expect that that law should govern *all* matters arising from their relationship. Moreover, the same law would end up being applicable to matters arising from a unitary factual situation. For example, the putative applicable law of the contract may determine that the contract is void and then go on to govern the unjust enrichment claim arising in the aftermath of voidness. Application of the same law to both of these related issues is not only convenient, but also ensures logically consistent outcomes.

[1993] 1 Lloyd's Rep 543, reversed on other grounds [1996] 1 Lloyd's Rep 589 (CA). For criticisms of the strength of the authority of these cases, see J Bird, 'Choice of Law' in F Rose (ed), *Restitution and the Conflict of Laws* (Oxford, Mansfield Press, 1995) 120–1. But the reasons of principle supporting this choice of law rule are evident.

[166] *Cofacredit SA v Morris* [2007] 2 BCLC 99, 133 (at [104]).
[167] *Explanatory Memorandum*, COM (2003) 427 final, p 21.
[168] Rome I Reg, Art 10(1).
[169] However, if the contract is void because there was no meeting of minds to enter into the contract, such as where *non est factum* is pleaded, then there is no reason to give effect to any purported choice of law clause. See *CIMB Bank Sdn Bhd v Dresdner Kleinwort* [2008] 4 SLR 543, 555–65 (at [29]–[57]) (A Chong, (2009) 21 *SAcLJ* 545). See also J Harris, 'Does Choice of Law Make Any Sense?' (2004) 57 CLP 305, 324–8; A Chong, 'Choice of Law for Void Contracts and Their Restitutionary Aftermath: The Putative Governing Law of the Contract' in P Giliker (ed), *Re-examining Contract and Unjust Enrichment* (Leiden/Boston, Martinus Nijhoff, 2007) 170–81.

15.1.81   If the applicable law cannot be determined on the basis of Article 10(1), Article 10(2) favours the law of the common habitual residence of the parties when the event giving rise to unjust enrichment occurs. Article 10(2), therefore, only comes into play when the claim is not closely connected to a relationship existing between the parties. Reasons of convenience and practicality justify this choice of law rule;[170] the rule also accords with the parties' legitimate expectations.[171]

15.1.82   Article 10(3) provides that:

Where the law applicable cannot be determined on the basis of paragraphs 1 or 2, it shall be the law of the country in which the unjust enrichment took place.

This rule deals with the situation where the unjust enrichment does not concern a relationship between the parties and the parties do not share a common habitual residence at the time when the event giving rise to unjust enrichment occurs. Although the language of Article 10(3) is not as unambiguous as it could be, it is tolerably clear that the 'law of the country in which the unjust enrichment took place' should be understood to mean the law of the country in which the enrichment took place and not the law of the country in which the event giving rise to the enrichment occurred. This interpretation follows from the fact that Article 10(2) expressly refers to the 'event giving rise to unjust enrichment' and the same form of words is not reproduced in Article 10(3). In addition, European conflicts legislation which appears to have influenced the drafters of Rome II, such as the Swiss Federal Statute on Private International Law,[172] includes choice of law rules in favour of the law of the country where the enrichment occurred.[173]

15.1.83   The application of the law of the place of enrichment[174] has received judicial approval in England[175] although it is worth noting that support from many commentators has been lukewarm.[176] The main criticisms of this rule are that the applicable law may be difficult to identify and fortuitous. The oft-cited example is along the lines of: what if money is mistakenly credited into the defendant's bank account in country X but the defendant withdraws the money in country Y? Should the choice of law rule point towards the law of country X (law of the place of immediate

---

[170] See above, paras 15.1.39–15.1.40.

[171] *Explanatory Memorandum*, COM (2003) 427 final, p 21.

[172] *Explanatory Memorandum*, COM (2003) 427 final, p 22.

[173] Swiss Federal Statute on Private International Law, Art 128(2).

[174] In the form of Rule 230(2)(c): L Collins *et al*, *Dicey, Morris and Collins on The Conflict of Laws* (London, Sweet & Maxwell, 14th edn, 2006) para 34R–001.

[175] *Chase Manhattan Bank NA v Israel-British Bank* [1981] Ch 105; *Re Jogia* [1988] 1 WLR 484; *El Ajou v Dollar Land Holdings* [1993] 3 All ER 717, reversed on other grounds [1994] 2 All ER 685 (CA); *Kuwait Oil Tanker Co SAK v Al Bader*, Moore-Bick J, unreported, 16 November 1998, affirmed [2000] All ER (Comm) 271. In *Cofacredit v Morris* [2007] 2 BCLC 99, a claim against a liquidator of a company who had received payment of debts owed to the company where such debts had been assigned to another company (the liquidator not being part of the contract of assignment of debt) was governed by English law as the law of the place where payment was received from the debtor. Overseas: *Hong Kong and Shanghai Banking Corp Ltd v United Overseas Bank* [1992] 2 Sing LR 495. See however, the more cautious support given to the law of place of enrichment by Lawrence Collins J in *Barros Mattos Junior v MacDaniels Ltd* [2005] ILPr 630, 665 (at [117]); see also [2005] ILPr 630, 655–62 (at [86]–[105]).

[176] Eg A Burrows, *The Law of Restitution* (London, Butterworths, 2nd edn, 2002) 617–18; A Briggs, *The Conflict of Laws* (Oxford, OUP, 2nd edn, 2008) 213; G Panagopoulos, *Restitution in Private International Law* (Oxford, Hart Publishing, 2000) 133–40.

enrichment) or the law of country Y (law of the place of ultimate enrichment)?[177] If it is the latter, country Y could have little connection with the claim or the parties.

15.1.84 If one draws an analogy between Article 4(1) of the Rome II Regulation[178] and the interpretation of Article 5(3) of the Brussels I Regulation,[179] both of which emphasise the place where direct, rather than indirect damage occurs for tortious claims, the law of the place of immediate enrichment should be the key. The place of immediate enrichment will also tend to be less fortuitous. It is less easy to be manipulated by any of the parties compared to the law of the place of ultimate enrichment as the latter is solely in the hands of the defendant. Therefore, it is submitted that Article 10(3) refers to the law of the place of enrichment and that the place of enrichment should be interpreted to mean the place of *immediate* enrichment.[180]

15.1.85 Article 10(4) contains an escape clause:

Where it is clear from all the circumstances of the case that the non-contractual obligation arising out of unjust enrichment is manifestly more closely connected with a country other than that indicated in paragraphs 1, 2 and 3, the law of that other country shall apply.

In view of the fact that under English law at least, the exact scope of unjust enrichment claims remains uncertain, an escape clause will be a useful tool to enable the court to arrive at the most just solution in certain cases. However, it must be emphasised that the strong form of words used in Article 10(4)—which mirrors the wording of Article 4(3) in the context of tortious obligations—indicates that the escape clause should be invoked only in exceptional circumstances.

Restitution for Wrongs

15.1.86 It is clear that Article 10 will cover autonomous unjust enrichment claims. What is less clear is whether its scope extends to restitution for wrongs and proprietary restitution.

15.1.87 As mentioned above, restitution for wrongs raises serious characterisation problems. Some, but not all, are convinced that restitution for wrongs also has as its basis the reversal of unjust enrichment under English domestic law. For conflicts purposes, the cases in this area are confusing and it is hard to discern any consistent and strong line of authority.

15.1.88 There are a few possible approaches. The first approach is to focus on the equitable basis that underlies many restitution for wrongs claims. The reasoning here is that, since equity acts *in personam*, the *lex fori* should govern equitable claims.[181] However, the inappropriateness of this solution has been persuasively

---

[177] For a more elaborate example, see Hwang JC in *Hong Kong and Shanghai Banking Corp v United Overseas Bank* [1992] 2 SLR 495, 500–1.

[178] See paras 15.1.33–15.1.38.

[179] Case 220/88 *Dumez France and Tracoba v Hessische Landesbank* [1990] ECR 49; Case C–364/93 *Marinari v Lloyds Bank plc* [1995] ECR I–2719.

[180] See A Chong, 'Choice of Law for Unjust Enrichment/Restitution and the Rome II Regulation' (2008) 57 *ICLQ* 863, 886–7.

[181] *Attorney-General (UK) v Heinemann Publishers Australia Pty Ltd* (1987) 10 NSWLR 86, 151, 192; *United States Surgical Corporation v Hospital Products International Pty Ltd & Ors* [1982] 2 NSWLR 766,

demonstrated[182] and has been conclusively rejected by Christopher Clarke J in *OJSC Oil Company Yugraneft v Abramovich*.[183] It has been shown that the principle that the *lex fori* should govern equitable claims derived from an age when the jurisdictional rules insisted on there being a substantial connection between England and the defendant before the Court of Chancery would assume jurisdiction.[184] Even modern application of the *lex fori* rule has been modulated: in *Paramasivam v Flynn*, the Federal Court of Australia applied the *lex fori* to breach of a fiduciary relationship whilst noting that this approach may not be correct if the source of the fiduciary relationship is a contract or if the issue raised is the duty owed to a foreign corporation by its directors or officers.[185] The court also held that 'where the circumstances giving rise to the asserted duty or the impugned conduct (or some of it) occurred outside the jurisdiction, the attitude of the law of the place where the circumstances arose or the conduct was undertaken is likely to be an important aspect of the factual circumstances in which the court determines whether a fiduciary relationship existed and, if so, the scope and content of the duties to which it gave rise.'[186]

15.1.89   The second possible approach is to characterise wrongs, or at least certain wrongs, as being restitutionary in character and governed by the restitutionary choice of law rule. English courts have done so and have tended to classify the claim as restitutionary and to apply the law of the place of enrichment. For example, in *Douglas v Hello! Ltd (No. 6)*,[187] the Court of Appeal thought that a breach of confidence claim was restitutionary and governed by the law of the country where the enrichment occurred.[188] Cases involving breach of fiduciary duties have also been thought to be governed by the law of the place of enrichment.[189] In *Kuwait Oil Tanker SAK v Al Bader*, the law of the place of enrichment was applied to a claim for breach of fiduciary duty[190] This analysis has also been thought to apply to knowing receipt claims[191] and to the recovery of bribe money from dishonest fiduciaries.[192]

15.1.90   On the other hand, after engaging in an extensive review of the case law which has supported the application of the law of the place of enrichment, Lawrence Collins J concluded that the authorities were weak.[193] There have also been authorities for the application of other laws. In *Base Metal Trading Ltd v Shamurin*,[194] the

---

797–8; *National Commercial Bank v Wimborne* (1978) 5 BPR 11958 (NSW). Cf RW White, 'Equitable Obligations in Private International Law: The Choice of Law' (1986) 11 *Sydney LR* 92.

[182] RW White, 'Equitable Obligations in Private International Law: The Choice of Law' (1986) 11 *Sydney LR* 92; TM Yeo, *Choice of Law for Equitable Doctrines* (Oxford, OUP, 2004) 17–39.

[183] [2008] EWHC 2613 (Comm) at [171]–[185].

[184] This is now no longer the case, especially with the advent of the Brussels I Regulation.

[185] (1998) 160 ALR 203, 217. TM Yeo, (1999) 115 *LQR* 571.

[186] (1998) 160 ALR 203, 217.

[187] [2006] QB 125, 160 (R Bagshaw, (2005) 121 *LQR* 550), reversed in part on other grounds [2008] 1 AC 1.

[188] [2006] QB 125, 160.

[189] *Kuwait Oil Tanker SAK v Al Bader* [2000] 2 All ER (Comm) 271; *Trustor v Smallbone* [2000] EWCA Civ 150.

[190] The basis on which the court did so, though, is rather unclear; A Briggs, (2000) 71 *BYBIL* 435, 471–2.

[191] *El Ajou v Dollar Land Holdings* [1993] 3 All ER 717; *Trustor v Smallbone* [2000] EWCA Civ 150.

[192] *Thahir v Pertamina* [1994] 3 SLR 257.

[193] *Barros Mattos Junior v MacDaniels Ltd* [2005] ILPr 630, 665 (at [117]) (A Briggs, (2005) 76 *BYIL* 671). See also Christopher Clarke J in *OJSC Oil Company Yugraneft v Abramovich* [2008] EWHC 2613 (Comm) at [246]–[247].

[194] [2005] 1 WLR 1157.

Court of Appeal applied the law of place of incorporation of the company for the breach of an equitable duty of care owed by a company director. In *Arab Monetary Fund v Hashim*,[195] the court preferred to apply a flexible 'proper law of the restitution-ary obligation' approach to determine the applicable law in a claim for the recovery of bribe money. Dishonest assistance in a breach of trust has been held to be neither restitutionary[196] nor tortious in character,[197] whilst at the same time it has been acknowledged that it shares marked similarities with a tort.[198]

15.1.91 This leads, then, to consideration of a third, and preferable, approach, support for which can be derived from *OJSC Oil Company Yugraneft v Abramovich*.[199] It is obvious from the above that it is not possible to have a category called 'wrongs' and hope that a single choice of law rule will be able to encompass the various dif-ferent wrongs.[200] Instead, the particular wrong involved needs to be isolated and characterised. In doing so, one must not be distracted by the fact that the remedy may be restitutionary in nature, in the sense that the defendant is being stripped of a gain. What is important is that the cause of action is predicated upon the commission of a particular wrong by the defendant and that it is the cause of action, and not the remedy, that needs to be characterised.[201] It should also not matter if the particular wrong is equitable in nature as equitable claims should be treated in the same man-ner as legal claims.[202] It should then be possible to fit in the various wrongs into the existing main choice of law categories such as contract, tort, property and unjust enrichment.[203] For example, if the claim involves restitutionary damages for breach of contract, the claim should be characterised as being contractual and governed by the Rome I Regulation. If the claim involves a breach of fiduciary duties arising from a relationship between the parties, the claim is analogous to a contractual claim and the law governing that relationship should also govern the claim.[204] If a third party

---

[195] *Arab Monetary Fund v Hashim* [1993] 1 Lloyd's Rep 543, reversed on other grounds [1996] 1 Lloyd's Rep 589 (CA). See also *Baring Brothers v Cunninghame District Council* [1997] CLC 108 (Court of Session, Scotland).

[196] *Grupo Torras SA v Al-Sabah* [2001] Lloyd's Rep Bank 36.

[197] *Metall & Rohstoff v Donaldson Lufkin & Jenrette Inc* [1990] 1 QB 391, 474.

[198] *Arab Monetary Fund v Hashim (No 9)*, The Times, 11 October 1994. For three possible interpretations of Chadwick J's decision, see TM Yeo, *Choice of Law for Equitable Doctrines* (Oxford, OUP, 2004) 276–8. In the jurisdictional context, see *Dubai Aluminium v Salaam* [1999] 1 Lloyd's Rep 415, 467; cf *Metall & Rohstoff v Donaldson Lufkin & Jenrette Inc* [1990] 1 QB 391, 474.

[199] [2008] EWHC 2613 (Comm). A Briggs, (2008) 79 *BYIL* 543. See also *Rickshaw Investments Ltd v Nicolai Baron von Uexkull* [2007] 1 Sing LR 377 (TM Yeo, (2007) 9 *Yearbook of Private International Law* 459).

[200] Cf L Barnard, 'Choice of Law in Equitable Wrongs: A Comparative Analysis' [1992] *CLJ* 474, who argues for a 'proper law' approach for equitable wrongs.

[201] Remedies are generally procedural in nature and for the *lex fori*: *Phrantzes v Argenti* [1960] 2 QB 19.

[202] TM Yeo, *Choice of Law for Equitable Doctrines* (Oxford, OUP, 2004) chs 1 and 2.

[203] See generally TM Yeo, *Choice of Law for Equitable Doctrines* (Oxford, OUP, 2004). See also G Panagopoulos, *Restitution in Private International Law* (Oxford, Hart Publishing, 2000) 81–94; J Bird, 'Choice of Law' in F Rose (ed), *Restitution and the Conflict of Laws* (Oxford, Mansfield Press, 1995) 76; R Stevens, 'The Choice of Law Rules of Restitutionary Obligations' in F Rose (ed), *Restitution and the Conflict of Laws* (Oxford, Mansfield Press, 1995) 187–91; G Virgo, *Written Evidence to the House of Lords European Union Committee, 8th Report*, para 7.

[204] *Rickshaw Investments Ltd v Nicolai Baron von Uexkull* [2007] 1 Sing LR 377, 403–7 (at [74]–[83]). Cf In *Base Metal Trading v Shamurin*, the Court of Appeal held that the imposition of a tortious or equitable duty of care did not fall within the expression 'contractual obligations' in Art 1(1) of the Rome Convention. The analogy between fiduciary and contractual duties was also overlooked in *WPP Holdings Italy Srl v Benatti* [2007] 1 WLR 2316. The case involved allegations of breach of contractual and fiduciary duties.

wrongfully assists in a breach of trust, it has been held that the choice of law rule for tort should be applicable as there are enough similarities between dishonest assistance and tort to characterise the claim as being tortious.[205] This means that dishonest assistance claims should be governed by Article 4 of the Rome II Regulation. If a personal knowing receipt claim is pursued, then the claim should be characterised as being restitutionary and governed by Article 10.[206] This means that if there is a contractual relationship or other similar relationship between the parties (the parties not having a common habitual residence), the governing law of that relationship is the applicable law for the knowing receipt claim; otherwise, the law of the place of enrichment should be the applicable law.[207]

Proprietary Restitution

15.1.92 A related issue to consider is whether or not claims for proprietary restitution fall within the scope of Article 10. Remedial constructive trusts are accepted to arise from unjust enrichment. Such trusts are not currently part of the English domestic law of restitution,[208] but it has been argued by some that other proprietary restitution claims also have as their basis the unjust enrichment principle. [209]

15.1.93 Insofar as proprietary restitution claims are based on the vindication of property rights, the answer seems to be straightforward: the Rome II Regulation covers non-contractual *obligations*; not property matters. But the clumsy drafting of Article 1(2)(e) and the Court of Justice's jurisprudence on trusts complicate matters. Article 1(2)(e) excludes 'non-contractual obligations arising out of relations between settlors, trustees and beneficiaries of a trust created *voluntarily*'; it stands to reason that the exclusion does not cover non-contractual obligations arising out of a trust that has been created *involuntarily*. Drawing from English trusts law, examples of trusts that may arise involuntarily include a resulting trust which arises when a contribution towards the purchase price of property is not reflected in the documents of title[210] and a constructive trust which arises when property is transferred pursuant to a contract which subsequently fails.[211] In these situations, the beneficiary's

---

The Court of Appeal held that it had jurisdiction for the breach of contractual duties under Art 5(1) and jurisdiction for breach of fiduciary duties under Art 5(3) of the Brussels I Regulation.

[205] See Christopher Clarke J in *OJSC Oil Company Yugraneft v Abramovich* [2008] EWHC 2613 (Comm) especially at [221]–[223]. See also *Arab Monetary Fund v Hashim (No 9)*, The Times, 11 October 1994; *Dubai Aluminium v Salaam* [1999] 1 Lloyd's Rep 415, 467; *Grupo Torras SA v Al-Sabah* [2001] Lloyd's Rep Banking 36.

[206] See *El Ajou v Dollar Land Holdings* [1993] 3 All ER 717, 736. See also *Grupo Torras SA v Al-Sabah* [2001] Lloyd's Rep Banking 36 (at [122]).

[207] See Christopher Clarke J in *OJSC Oil Company Yugraneft v Abramovich* [2008] EWHC 2613 (Comm) at [247].

[208] *Westdeutsche Landesbank Girozentrale v Islington London Borough Council* [1996] AC 669; *Re Polly Peck (No 2)* [1998] 3 All ER 812.

[209] Cf *NABB Bros Ltd v Lloyd's Bank International (Guernsey) Ltd* [2005] ILPr 506, 524 (at [76]–[77]), where Lawrence Collins J expressed tentative support for the view that equitable proprietary claims, although not based on unjust enrichment, fell within the ambit of what is now CPR PD 6B, para 3.1(16), which allows service out of the jurisdiction where 'a claim is made for restitution where the defendant's alleged liability arises out of acts committed within the jurisdiction'.

[210] Eg, *Sekhon v Alissa* [1989] 2 FLR 94.

[211] Eg, *Westdeutsche Landesbank Girozentrale v Islington London Borough Council* [1996] AC 669.

claim is predicated upon his holding an equitable proprietary interest in the property. Whilst this would be considered a proprietary claim under English law, the Court of Justice has held that beneficiaries' rights under such trusts are not rights *in rem*.[212]

15.1.94 The better view, however, is that resulting and constructive trusts which have their basis in the assertion of equitable proprietary rights do not fall within the scope of Rome II. They are property matters and should be governed by the property choice of law rule.[213] It is likely that the wording of Article 1(2)(e) was to make clear that claims of 'constructive trusteeship' which may arise in response to unjust enrichment are not caught by the exclusion and fall within the Rome II Regulation.[214] 'Constructive trusteeships' are imposed on wrongdoers or fiduciaries who breach their duties; such constructive trusteeship concerns the defendants' *personal* liability to account for losses caused or profits obtained. Depending on the wrong involved, such claims could be characterised as being tortious or concerned with unjust enrichment and therefore properly fall within the scope of Rome II.

Negotiorum Gestio

15.1.95 *Negotiorum gestio* is a cause of action that is unknown under English law.[215] It concerns 'an act performed without due authority in connection with the affairs of another person'.[216] Although conflicts of law cases on *negotiorum gestio* are rare, it is right for Rome II to have a provision for such a category since *negotiorum gestio* is obviously a non-contractual obligation and falls within the Regulation's scope.[217]

15.1.96 The choice of law rules here are similar to those under Article 4 for torts. Under Article 11(1), the applicable law in this area will be the law governing the relationship between the parties if the non-contractual obligation concerns a relationship existing between the parties, such as one arising out of a contract or a tort/delict, that is closely connected with that non-contractual obligation. Where there is no relationship or the relationship is not closely connected with the *negotiorum gestio*, the law of the parties' common habitual residence will apply if they share a common habitual residence when the event giving rise to damage occurs.[218] Where it is not possible to determine the

---

[212] Case C–294/92 *Webb v Webb* [1994] ECR I–1717.

[213] A Chong, 'The Common Law Choice of Law Rules for Resulting and Constructive Trusts' (2005) 54 *ICLQ* 855; R Stevens, 'The Choice of Law Rules of Restitutionary Obligations' in F Rose (ed), *Restitution and the Conflict of Laws* (Oxford, Mansfield Press, 1995) 182–5, 216. Cf G Panagopoulos, *Restitution in Private International Law* (Oxford, Hart Publishing, 2000) 67.

[214] See D Wallis, *Report on the proposal for a regulation of the European Parliament and of the Council on the law applicable to non-contractual obligations ('Rome II')*, A6-0211/2005 (27.6.2005) p 15; European Commission, *Explanatory Memorandum attached to the Amended proposal for a European Parliament and Council Regulation on the Law Applicable to Non-Contractual Obligations ('Rome II')*, COM (2006) 83 final, p 4. See also A Chong, 'Choice of Law for Unjust Enrichment/Restitution and the Rome II Regulation' (2008) 57 *ICLQ* 863, 894.

[215] Cf D Sheehan, '*Negotiorum Gestio*: A Civilian Concept in the Common Law?' (2006) 55 *ICLQ* 253.

[216] Art 11(1).

[217] Hamburg Group for Private International Law, *Comments on the European Commission's Draft Proposal for a Council Regulation on the Law Applicable to Non-contractual Obligations*, pp 33–4.

[218] Art 11(2).

applicable law by either method above, then the claim shall be governed by the law of the country in which the unauthorised act was performed.[219] Article 11(4) then sets out an escape clause in favour of the law of the country of manifestly closer connection.

Culpa in Contrahendo

15.1.97   Article 12 was a belated addition to the text of the Regulation. *Culpa in contrahendo* has a European autonomous meaning and should not necessarily be interpreted by reference to domestic laws.[220] Recital 30 states that the concept should include the violation of the duty of disclosure and the breakdown of contractual negotiations. This means that the factual scenarios which arose in cases such as *Agnew v Längsförsäkringsbolagens*[221] and *Fonderie Officine Meccaniche Tacconi SpA v Heinrich Wagner Sinto Maschinenfabrik GmbH*[222] are within the scope of Article 12 although, for jurisdictional purposes, the *Agnew* case was held to involve 'a matter relating to a contract' and in *Tacconi* the situation concerned 'a matter relating to tort, delict or quasi-delict' for the purposes of the Brussels I Regulation.[223]

15.1.98   Article 12 does not cover the classic German *culpa in contrahendo* case where a prospective customer entered a carpet store and was injured when two rolls of carpet fell from a shelf.[224] This is because Recital 30 states that 'Article 12 covers only non-contractual obligations presenting a direct link with the dealings prior to the conclusion of a contract. This means that if, while a contract is being negotiated, a person suffers personal injury, Article 4 or other relevant provisions of this Regulation should apply.' Article 12, however, applies 'regardless of whether the contract was actually concluded or not'.[225]

15.1.99   If money has been paid in anticipation of a contract which never comes to fruition, it is unclear whether the claim will fall within Article 10 or Article 12. On the one hand, the claim will be based on unjust enrichment; on the other hand, the unjust enrichment covers pre-contractual dealings.[226] But if the circumstances are such that a putative applicable law can be identified,[227] the same law is applicable anyway—whether under Article 10(1) or Article 12(1). Article 12(1) stipulates that the law applicable shall be 'the law that applies to the contract or that would have been applicable to it had it been entered into'.

15.1.100   If the applicable law cannot be determined on the basis of Article 12(1), Article 12(2) sets out a list of familiar connecting factors. The applicable law shall then be the law of the country in which the damage occurs, irrespective of the country in which the event giving rise to the damage or countries in which the

---

[219] Art 11(3).
[220] Recital 30.
[221] [2001] 1 AC 223.
[222] Case C–344/00 [2002] ECR I–7377.
[223] See paras 5.6.18–5.6.20.
[224] 78 RGZ 239 (1911).
[225] Art 12(1).
[226] A Rushworth and A Scott, 'Rome II: Choice of law for non-contractual obligations' [2008] *LMCLQ* 274, 290.
[227] Using the Rome I Regulation rules.

indirect consequences occurred[228] or, if the parties have the same habitual residence at the time when the event giving rise to the damage occurs, it shall be the law of the parties' common habitual residence.[229] However, where it is clear from all the circumstances of the case that the non-contractual obligation is manifestly more closely connected with another country, then the applicable law shall be the law of that country.[230]

Other Provisions

Scope of the Applicable Law

15.1.101   Article 15 sets out a non-exhaustive list of matters that fall within the scope of the applicable law. The applicable law shall govern in particular:

(a) the basis and extent of liability, including the determination of persons who may be held liable for acts performed by them;

The 'basis of liability' covers questions such as whether the liability is strict or fault-based and, if the latter, the definition of fault; the causal link between the event giving rise to the damage and the damage and the persons potentially liable. The 'extent of liability' refers to limitations laid down by the law on liability. These would include the maximum extent of that liability, the contribution to be made by each of the persons liable for the damage and division of liability between joint perpetrators.[231]

(b) the grounds for exemption from liability, any limitation of liability and any division of liability;

Whereas Article 15(a) refers to intrinsic factors of liability, Article 15(b) refers to the extrinsic factors of liability. So a defendant's liability may be exempted or limited by the operation of *force majeure*, necessity, third-party fault, fault by the victim and rules which forbid actions between spouses or exclude liability in relation to certain categories of persons.[232] This means that whether the defence of contributory negligence can be raised (and, if so, whether the defence is partial or total) will be governed by the applicable law.[233]

(c) the existence, the nature and the assessment of damage or the remedy claimed;

The existence and nature of the damage or remedy and assessment of remedy is uncontroversial and will cover issues such as whether a claim will lie for particular heads of damage and whether the claimant is under a duty to mitigate his loss. The 'assessment of damage' is potentially more problematic. Nevertheless, it almost certainly means that quantification of damages is for the applicable law of the

---

[228] Art 12(2)(a).
[229] Art 12(2)(b).
[230] Art 12(2)(c).
[231] *Explanatory Memorandum*, COM (2003) 427 final, p 23.
[232] *Explanatory Memorandum*, COM (2003) 427 final, p 23.
[233] The defence of contributory negligence was accepted to be inextricably linked with the issue of causation such that the defence should be considered to be substantive in nature in *Dawson v Broughton* (CC (Manchester), 31 July 2007) (2007) 151 Sol J 1167.

non-contractual obligation.[234] If this is correct[235]—which in view of Recital 32 it must be[236]—it means that the established division under English law between heads of damage being substantive and governed by the *lex causae* and quantification of damages being procedural and governed by the *lex fori*[237] does not apply under the Rome II Regulation. This interpretation is advantageous in that, in a case where the foreign tort on which the claim is based is unknown under English law, the court would have difficulty in applying English law to quantify the loss. Some qualification to quantification being for the *lex causae* is introduced in Recital 33—although the text is vague and its effect is uncertain.[238]

> (d) *within the limits of powers conferred on the court by its procedural law, the measures which a court may take to prevent or terminate injury or damage or to ensure the provision of compensation;*

This provision covers, for example, the question whether the court may order payment of damages or grant an interlocutory injunction.[239]

> (e) *the question whether a right to claim damages or a remedy may be transferred, including by inheritance;*
> (f) *persons entitled to compensation for damage sustained personally;*

---

[234] Given that Art 12(1)(c) of the Rome I Regulation provides for assessment of damages to be for the applicable law of the contract it may be that the intention is for Art 15(c) to do the same. Note also that Art 12(1)(c) of the Rome I Regulation provides for the assessment of damages *in so far as it is governed by rules of law* to be governed by the *lex causae*. It is unclear if the omission of this restriction from the final text of the Rome II Regulation (it had appeared in earlier drafts) has any important bearing. Cf A Rushworth and A Scott, 'Rome II: Choice of law for non-contractual obligations' [2008] *LMCLQ* 274, 294.

[235] If this is the meaning, the phrase 'assessment of damages' would have been clearer. The European Parliament thought the same: an 's' was added to the word 'damage' in their amendment: *Report on the proposal for a regulation of the European Parliament and of the Council on the law applicable to non-contractual obligations*, A6-0211/2005, p 28.

[236] Recital 32 states that the forum may, on the basis of public policy, disapply 'a provision of the law designated by this Regulation which would have the effect of causing non-compensatory, exemplary or punitive damages of an excessive nature to be awarded'. This Recital only makes sense on the basis that quantification is determined by the *lex causae* rather than by the *lex fori*.

[237] *Boys v Chaplin* [1971] AC 356; *Roerig v Valiant Trawlers* [2002] 1 WLR 2304; *Harding v Wealands* [2007] 2 AC 1 (C Dougherty and L Wyles, (2007) 56 *ICLQ* 443; P Beaumont and S Tang, (2008) 12 *Edin LR* 131; P Rogerson, [2006] *CLJ* 515; H Seriki, (2007) 26 *CJQ* 28; A Scott, [2007] *LMCLQ* 44). See also M Illmer, 'Neutrality Matters—Some Thought About the Rome Regulations and the So-Called Dichotomy of Substance and Procedure in European Private International Law' (2009) 28 *CJQ* 237. In an intra-Australian tort case, the High Court of Australia held that all questions of the kinds of damage or amount of damages were substantive and governed by the *lex causae*: *Pfeiffer v Rogerson* (2000) 203 CLR 503, 543–4. Whether this applied to foreign torts was left open by the High Court of Australia in *Régie Nationale des Usines Renault SA v Zhang* (2002) 210 CLR 491, 520.

[238] Recital 33 states: 'According to the current national rules on compensation awarded to victims of road traffic accidents, when quantifying damages for personal injury in cases in which the accident takes place in a State other than that of the habitual residence of the victim, the court seised should take into account all the relevant actual circumstances of the specific victim, including in particular the actual losses and costs of after-care and medical attention.' It is doubtful that the Recital goes so far as to permit a court to use the escape clause in Art 4(3) to displace the applicable law on the basis that the law of manifestly closer connection is the law of habitual residence of the victim; the Recital does not set out a choice of law rule.

[239] *Explanatory Memorandum*, COM (2003) 427 final, p 24.

This provision refers particularly to whether an 'indirect' victim can be compensated following damage being suffered by the 'direct' victim[240]—such as a wife whose husband has been killed by the defendant's wrongful act.

(g) liability for the acts of another person;

This paragraph covers vicarious liability and also the liability of parents for their children and of principals for their agents.[241]

(h) the manner in which an obligation may be extinguished and rules of prescription and limitation, including rules relating to the commencement, interruption and suspension of a period of prescription or limitation.

It used to be thought that rules laying down limitation periods were procedural in nature (and, therefore, that the limitation period of the *lex fori* was applicable). Since the 1980s, however, English law has recognised that a rule which lays down the period in which a particular claim may be brought is substantive in nature and that the question whether a claim is time-barred is governed by the *lex causae*.[242] Unsurprisingly, the Rome II Regulation adopts the same approach as the Rome I Regulation and provides that questions of limitation are for the applicable law. So, subject to the possible disapplication of the relevant limitation period on grounds of public policy,[243] a tortious claim governed by the law of country X is time-barred if the limitation period under the law of country X has expired even though the claim is within the limitation period prescribed by the *lex fori*.

Direct Action against the Insurer of the Person Liable

15.1.102 Article 18 is a bit anomalous as it sets out a substantive rule, as opposed to a choice of law rule. It allows the claimant to bring his or her claim against the insurer of the person liable to provide compensation if the law applicable to the non-contractual obligation or the law applicable to the insurance contract so provides. The right of direct action had already been incorporated into English law pursuant to the Fourth Motor Directive.[244] However, Article 18 covers more than motor accident cases and there was concern that the pro-claimant stance of Article 18 did not strike a reasonable balance between the parties or offer predictability for the defendant.[245] Nevertheless, many forms of damage do not require compulsory insurance[246] and

---

[240] *Explanatory Memorandum*, COM (2003) 427 final, p 24.
[241] *Explanatory Memorandum*, COM (2003) 427 final, p 24.
[242] Foreign Limitation Periods Act 1984.
[243] See para 15.1.111.
[244] There has been a series of Directives on the approximation of the laws of the Member States relating to insurance against civil liability in respect of the use of motor vehicles; these Directives have been consolidated into a codified version: Dir 2009/103/EC relating to insurance against civil liability in respect of the use of motor vehicles, and the enforcement of the obligation to insure against such liability [2009] OJ L263/11. The Directives are implemented in the United Kingdom by Financial Services and Markets Act 2000 (Fourth Motor Insurance Directive) Regs 2002 (SI 2002/2706), Fourth Motor Insurance Directive Instrument 2002 (FSA 2002/74); Motor Vehicles (Compulsory Insurance) (Information Centre and Compensations Boards) Regs 2003 (SI 2003/37); Financial Services and Markets Act 2000 (Motor Insurance) Regs 2007 (SI 2007/2403). Note that direct actions against insurers are also provided for in limited circumstances under the Third Parties (Rights against Insurers) Act 1930.
[245] House of Lords European Union Committee, *8th Report*, pp 45–6.
[246] For example, product and environmental damage.

where insurance is taken out, it is likely that claims would be passed on to the insurers at an early stage anyway.[247] In short, the implications of Article 18 are probably not as pervasive as initially thought.

Subrogation

15.1.103   Article 19 sets out that:

Where a person (the creditor) has a non-contractual claim upon another (the debtor), and a third person has a duty to satisfy the creditor, or has in fact satisfied the creditor in discharge of that duty, the law which governs the third person's duty to satisfy the creditor shall determine whether, and the extent to which, the third person is entitled to exercise against the debtor the rights which the creditor had against the debtor under the law governing their relationship.

Article 19 is consistent with Article 15 of the Rome I Regulation. It applies in particular to insurance situations where the insurer may pay the tort victim because of the contract of insurance with the insured. The governing law of the contract of insurance will then determine whether, and to what extent the insurer may be subrogated to the rights which the tort victim had against the insured.

Multiple Liability

15.1.104   Article 20 deals with multiple liability and provides that:

If a creditor has a claim against several debtors who are liable for the same claim, and one of the debtors has already satisfied the claim in whole or in part, the question of that debtor's right to demand compensation from the other debtors shall be governed by the law applicable to that debtor's non-contractual obligation towards the creditor.

It could be argued that this rule is inappropriate as it means that a joint debtor may be faced with a claim for contribution under a different law from that which governs his liability towards the creditor. Also, where there is a pre-existing relationship between the joint tortfeasors, this solution may not be suitable. For example, if several directors of a company are jointly liable in tort for injury caused to the creditor and director A has satisfied the creditor's claim, the law governing the company and the directors' relationships with each other may be a more appropriate option to govern any contribution claim by director A against the other directors.[248]

15.1.105   However, Article 20 can be justified. The debtor who has already satisfied the creditor's claim is worse off compared to the other joint debtors as he is already out of pocket. Applying the law under which he had to satisfy the creditor's claim to determine whether he can seek contribution from other tortfeasors would be fairer to him.[249]

15.1.106   This provision also lays to rest, for the purposes of the Rome II Regulation at least, the previous debate as to whether claims for contribution are

---

[247] See Association of British Insurers, *Written Evidence to the House of Lords European Union Committee, 8th Report,* paras 2.9–2.14.

[248] Cf Hamburg Group for Private International Law, p 55.

[249] Hamburg Group for Private International Law, *Comments on the European Commission's Draft Proposal for a Council Regulation on the Law Applicable to Non-contractual Obligations,* p 54.

tortious or restitutionary.[250] If the debtor had to pay the creditor on the basis of a tortious claim, then the law applicable to the tort will govern the debtor's claim for contribution from the other tortfeasors. If the debtor had to pay the creditor on the basis of an unjust enrichment claim, then the law applicable to the unjust enrichment will govern the debtor's claim for contribution from the other tortfeasors.[251]

Formal Validity

15.1.107 Article 21 stipulates that:

A unilateral act intended to have legal effect and relating to a non-contractual obligation shall be formally valid if it satisfies the formal requirements of the law governing the non-contractual obligation in question or the law of the country in which the act is performed.

This provision is similar to Article 11 of the Rome I Regulation and sets out a generous approach towards formal validity. It is likely, though, that it will not be frequently invoked because, as the *Explanatory Memorandum* acknowledges, 'the concept of formal validity plays a minor role in the creation of non-contractual obligations'.[252]

Burden of Proof

15.1.108 Article 22, which is identical to Article 18 of the Rome I Regulation, provides that the applicable law under the Rome II Regulation's rules 'shall apply to the extent that, in matters of non-contractual obligations, it contains rules which raise presumptions of law or determine the burden of proof'.[253] Apart from this, the Rome II Regulation does not apply to evidence and procedure.[254]

Public Policy and Overriding Mandatory Rules

15.1.109 Articles 16 and 26 preserve the operation of the forum's overriding mandatory rules and public policy. Article 16 provides that:

Nothing in this Regulation shall restrict the application of the provisions of the law of the forum in a situation where they are mandatory irrespective of the law otherwise applicable to the non-contractual obligation.

---

[250] Restitutionary: *Sweedman v Transport Accident Commission* (2006) 224 ALR 625, 632. The Law Commission and Scottish Law Commission were also of the view that claims for contribution were restitutionary, not delictual in character: *Private International Law: Choice of Law in Tort and Delict—Law Com No 193* (London, HMSO, 1990) p 25.
  Tortious: *Hewden Tower Cranes v Wolffkran GmbH* [2007] 2 Lloyd's Rep 138, 143 (at [31]–[32]), where a claim for contribution under the Civil Liability (Contribution) Act 1978 was held to be a matter 'relating to tort, *delict or quasi-delict*' under Art 5(3) of the Brussels I Reg. (The 1978 Act has also been held to be applicable automatically (without the need to consider choice of law rules) if the claim fell with within its scope: *Arab Monetary Fund v Hashim (No 9)*, The Times, 11 October 1994.)
[251] See also Art 16 of the Rome I Regulation and, generally, K Takahashi, *Claims for Contribution and Reimbursement in an International Context* (Oxford, OUP, 2000) ch 3.
[252] COM (2003) 427 final, p 26.
[253] Cf the common law: *Re Fuld's Estate (No. 3)* [1968] P 675; *Re Cohn* [1945] Ch 5.
[254] Art 1(3).

The mandatory rules referred to in Article 16 are of the 'international' variety meaning that they are rules which apply regardless of the applicable law. This is in contrast with the mandatory rules referred to in Article 14(2), which cover 'domestic' mandatory rules that apply only when the *lex causae* is also that of the law containing those 'domestic' mandatory rules.

15.1.110   Article 26 maintains the forum's right to refuse to apply a provision of the law of any country specified by Rome II if 'such application is manifestly incompatible with the public policy (*ordre public*) of the forum'. An example where resort may be had to Article 26 is given in Recital 32, which refers to non-compensatory, exemplary or punitive damages of an excessive nature being awarded. While English public policy is obviously a matter for the English courts, the European Court of Justice has, in recent cases, held that it is competent to review the limits within which the court of a Member State relies on the public policy concept in the context of other European legislation.[255]

15.1.111   In the context of the Foreign Limitation Periods Act 1984, there are cases where the English court has held that it would be contrary to public policy to allow the claim to be barred by the limitation rule of the applicable law. In *Jones v Trollope Colls Cementation Overseas Ltd*,[256] for example, the plaintiff, who had been injured in a road accident in Pakistan, started proceedings in England against the driver's employer. Not long after the accident the plaintiff had been flown to Germany, where she spent seven months in hospital. Although the proceedings in England were commenced within the three-year limitation period, the claim was time barred under the law of Pakistan, where the limitation period was one year. The Court of Appeal held that the application of the one-year limitation period would cause undue hardship to the plaintiff and disapplied the foreign limitation period; of particular significance was the fact that before starting proceedings in England the plaintiff had been in correspondence with a representative of the defendant who had made statements suggesting that her claim would be settled by the defendant's insurers.[257] Notwithstanding the fact that public policy should be invoked only in exceptional circumstances, it is not unreasonable to think that this case would be decided in the same way under the Rome II Regulation.

15.1.112   The paradigm situation in which public policy might be invoked is where the claimant seeks to establish the defendant's liability under the foreign law applicable to the tort and the defendant argues that the application of the foreign rule which imposes liability on him is contrary to public policy. However, this is not the only situation in which the issue of public policy may arise. For example, the claimant may wish to avoid the application of a rule forming part of the law governing the tort which has the effect of excluding the defendant's liability. This was the situation which arose in *Kuwait Airways Corpn v Iraqi Airways Co (Nos 4 and 5)*.[258] One element of the case concerned six of the claimant's aircraft which

---

[255] Case C–7/98 *Krombach v Bamberski* [2000] ECR I–1935; Case C–38/98 *Régie Nationale des Usines Renault SA v Maxicar SpA* [2000] ECR I-2973; Case C–341/04 *Eurofood IFSC* [2006] ECR I–3813. For a discussion of the development of a common EU public policy, see HP Meidanis, 'Public Policy and Order Public in the Private International Law of the EU: Traditional Positions and Modern Trends' (2005) 31 *EL Rev* 95.

[256] *The Times, 26 January 1990.*

[257] See also, in the contractual context, *The Komninos S* [1991] 1 Lloyd's Rep 370.

[258] [2002] 2 AC 883. A Briggs, (2002) 73 *BYIL* 490; JM Carruthers and EB Crawford, (2003) 52 *ICLQ* 761; R O'Keefe, [2002] *CLJ* 499; E Peel, 'The Scope of Double Actionability and Public Policy' (2003) 119

had been confiscated by the Republic of Iraq at the start of the Gulf War in 1990 and then transferred to the defendant.[259] The claimant sued the defendant for the tort of conversion and applied for an order for the delivery up of the aircraft and consequential damages. The defendant argued that the claim must fail: although the Iraqi law of usurpation was substantially the same as the English tort of conversion, Iraqi legislation ('Resolution 369') had been passed conferring title to the aircraft on the defendant under the law of Iraq. Therefore, the claimant could not establish that the defendant's act was tortious under the law of the place where the alleged tort was said to have occurred. The majority of the House of Lords rejected the defendant's argument. Resolution 369 was a breach of public international law; the United Nations Security Council had condemned the invasion of Kuwait by Iraq and had authorised military action against Iraq with a view to restoring the legitimate government of Kuwait. In these circumstances, the House of Lords decided that recognition of Resolution 369 should be declined on the basis of public policy. Accordingly, the claimant was entitled to establish the defendant's liability by relying on the fact that, if Resolution 369 was ignored, the defendant's conduct was tortious under Iraqi law.

15.1.113   The situation considered in *Kuwait Airways Corpn v Iraqi Airways Co (Nos 4 and 5)* was truly exceptional. Not only was the factual background to the case 'highly unusual',[260] the use of public policy as a sword (by the claimant), rather than as a shield (by the defendant), is uncommon—to the point of being almost unique. Accordingly, the extent to which the case lays down principles which are likely to be of much significance in run-of-the-mill tort cases is somewhat limited. Furthermore, it would be wrong to conclude from the House of Lords' decision that it is appropriate for the English courts to refuse to apply all foreign rules which are in conflict with public international law. Lord Nicholls referred to Iraq's invasion of Kuwait and seizure of its assets as 'a gross violation of established rules of international law of fundamental importance'.[261] Similarly, Lord Steyn considered that it was appropriate to extend the public policy exception 'to flagrant breaches of public international law'.[262]

Relationship with Other Provisions of EU Law and Existing International Conventions

15.1.114   Article 27 provides that:

This Regulation shall not prejudice the application of provisions of Community law which, in relation to particular matters, lay down conflict-of-law rules relating to non-contractual obligations.

LQR 1. See also P Rogerson, '*Kuwait Airways Corp v Iraqi Airways Corp*: The Territoriality Principle in Private International Law—Vice or Virtue?' (2002) 55 *CLP* 265.

[259] The claimant also unsuccessfully claimed damages for the loss of four other aircraft which had been destroyed during the war.
[260] Lord Hope at [2000] 2 AC 883, 1108 (at [135]).
[261] [2000] 2 AC 883, 1081 (at [29]).
[262] [2002] 2 AC 883, 1102 (at [114]). See also Lord Hope at [2002] 2 AC 883, 1116 (at [168]).

Recital 35 states that Rome II shall not prejudice the application of other instruments laying down provisions designed to contribute to the proper functioning of the internal market in so far as they cannot be applied in conjunction with the law designated by the rules of this Regulation, such as the E-Commerce Directive.[263]

15.1.115 Article 28 enables Member States to continue to respect existing international conventions which have been adopted and which lay down conflict of laws rules relating to non-contractual obligations.[264] However, the Rome II Regulation shall, between Member States, take precedence over conventions concluded exclusively between two or more of them in so far as such conventions concern matters governed by Rome II.[265]

15.2 CHOICE OF LAW IN TORT: COMMON LAW RULES

Background to the English Choice of Law Rules

The Importance of the Place of the Wrong

15.2.1 As regards torts committed in England the traditional common law view is that English law alone applies.[266] Where, however, the tort is committed abroad, the courts have had regard to both English law, as the law of the forum, and the law of the place of the wrong. The determination of the place of the wrong presents no problems in cases where all the elements constituting the tort occur in the same country. If a claimant is injured in a road accident in France, France is clearly the place of the wrong. The position is less straightforward in a multiple locality case—where the defendant commits the wrongful act in one country, but the claimant suffers the harm in another. Is the place of the wrong where the defendant acted or where the claimant was harmed?

15.2.2 After a degree of uncertainty in some of the early cases[267] it came to be accepted that, in seeking to determine where a tort was committed, the court should look back over the series of events constituting the tort and ask the following question: 'Where in substance did this cause of action arise?'[268] Although such an open-textured test has an advantage in providing flexibility, it is arguably unpredictable. In practice, the cases show that the place where the claimant suffered the harm is generally regarded as being the place of the wrong. For example, in defamation cases, the wrong occurs where the defamatory material is published.[269] It would, however, be wrong to conclude

---

[263] Dir 2000/31/EC on certain legal aspects of information society services, in particular electronic commerce, in the Internal Market [2000] OJ L178/1.

[264] Art 28(1).

[265] Art 28(2).

[266] *Szalatnay-Stacho v Fink* [1947] KB 1; *Metall und Rohstoff AG v Donaldson Lufkin & Jenrette Inc* [1990] 1 QB 391; *Base Metal Trading Ltd v Shamurin* [2002] CLC 322; *Ennstone Building Products Ltd v Stanger Ltd* [2002] 1 WLR 3059 (J Perkins, [2003] *CLJ* 274).

[267] See, eg, *George Monro Ltd v American Cyanamid and Chemical Corporation* [1944] 1 KB 432; *Cordova Land Co Ltd v Victor Brothers Inc* [1966] 1 WLR 793.

[268] See Lord Pearson in *Distillers Co (Biochemicals) Ltd v Thompson* [1971] AC 458, 468.

[269] *Bata v Bata* [1948] WN 366; *Church of Scientology of California v Commissioner of Metropolitan Police* (1976) 120 Sol J 690.

that a tort is invariably to be regarded as having been committed where the harm is suffered. On the facts of the case, the place where the defendant committed the wrongful act may constitute the place where, in substance, the cause of action arose.[270]

Torts Committed Abroad

15.2.3 The foundation of the common law rules on choice of law in tort is to be found in two cases decided at the end of the 19th century. *The Halley*,[271] a case decided by the Privy Council, involved a collision between two ships in Belgian territorial waters. The collision resulted from the negligence of the pilot of the defendant's ship. Even though the events constituting the tort occurred abroad, the plaintiff's action was rejected on the basis that, under English law, the defendant was not vicariously liable for the pilot's negligence.

15.2.4 In *Phillips v Eyre*[272] the plaintiff brought an action in England for false imprisonment. The defendant was the Governor of Jamaica and the events which gave rise to the alleged tort had occurred in Jamaica. In the course of his judgment Willes J said:

As a general rule, in order to found a suit in England for a wrong alleged to have been committed abroad, two conditions must be fulfilled. First, the wrong must be of such a character that it would have been actionable if committed in England. ... Secondly, the act must not have been justifiable by the law of the place where it was done.[273]

15.2.5 The first limb of the rule in *Phillips v Eyre* was derived from *The Halley*. The precise verbal formulation of the second limb of the rule can be explained by the facts in *Phillips v Eyre*. Although, at common law, the defendant's action constituted a tort, the imprisonment of the plaintiff had taken place within the context of the defendant's efforts to put down a rebellion on the island of Jamaica and, subsequently, the local parliament had passed legislation which retrospectively legitimated the defendant's actions. So, although the defendant's action was tortious at the time of commission, his action was 'justifiable' in view of the subsequent legislation. In *Machado v Fontes*[274] it was held by the Court of Appeal that the second limb of the rule was satisfied in circumstances where the defendant's conduct abroad gave rise to criminal liability, but not to civil liability. The plaintiff alleged that he had been libelled by the defendant in Brazil. While the defendant's action was a tort under English law, libel under Brazilian law was a criminal offence but did not give rise to civil liability. The Court of Appeal took the view that the plaintiff was entitled to recover damages in England, since not only did the defendant's conduct amount to a tort in English law, it was not 'justifiable' under the law where the act took place. Accordingly, English law alone determined questions of the defendant's civil liability.

15.2.6 There are various ambiguities in *Phillips v Eyre*, one of which may be dealt with at this stage. From the terms of Willes J's judgment it is not clear that the

---

[270] See, eg, *Dimskal Shipping Co SA v International Transport Workers Federation (No 2)* [1989] 1 Lloyd's Rep 166, 177, reversed on other grounds: [1990] 1 Lloyd's Rep 319 (CA); [1992] 2 AC 152 (HL).
[271] (1868) LR 2 PC 193.
[272] (1870) LR 6 QB 1.
[273] (1870) LR 6 QB 1, 28–9.
[274] [1897] 2 QB 231.

double-limbed rule was intended as a choice of law rule at all. In subsequent cases it was argued (and by some judges accepted) that the *Phillips v Eyre* rule was either a jurisdiction rule or that the first part of the rule was a jurisdiction rule and the second part was a choice of law rule. This particular uncertainty was, however, resolved by *Boys v Chaplin*,[275] in which the House of Lords confirmed that the decision in *Phillips v Eyre* had laid down a double-barrelled choice of law rule.

The Modern Common Law Position

Boys v Chaplin: Outline

15.2.7   *Boys v Chaplin*[276] involved a road accident in Malta in which the plaintiff suffered injuries caused by the defendant's negligence. Both parties were members of the British forces serving in Malta. The plaintiff started proceedings in England with a view to recovering damages for negligence. Under Maltese law the defendant was liable for special damages, but damages for pain and suffering were not recoverable. Under English law the defendant was liable both for special damages (£53) and for damages for pain and suffering (£2,250). The key question was whether the plaintiff was entitled to recover damages for pain and suffering.

15.2.8   A majority of the House of Lords—comprising Lord Guest, Lord Hodson and Lord Wilberforce—advocated a reinterpretation of the rule in *Phillips v Eyre* and adopted the Scottish approach.[277] For the purposes of the second limb of the rule, 'justifiable' should not be equated with 'innocent'; rather, liability for a foreign tort cannot be established unless the defendant's conduct gives rise to civil liability (whether contractual or non-contractual) according to the law of the place of the wrong. The application of the reformulated rule in *Phillips v Eyre* to the facts of *Boys v Chaplin* would have prevented the plaintiff from recovering damages for pain and suffering because Maltese law, the law of the place of the wrong, did not impose liability for such losses. Lord Guest allowed recovery for pain and suffering on the basis that this was a procedural matter governed by the law of the forum. This reasoning, however, was rejected by a different majority (comprising Lord Hodson, Lord Wilberforce and Lord Pearson). Lord Hodson and Lord Wilberforce proposed that there should be an exception to the reformulated rule in *Phillips v Eyre* and Lord Pearson (who was part of the minority who favoured the retention of *Machado v Fontes*) also thought that in certain circumstances a qualification of the general rule might be appropriate.

---

[275] [1971] AC 356.

[276] [1971] AC 356. PB Carter, (1970) 44 *BYIL* 222; RH Graveson, 'Towards a Modern Applicable Law in Tort' (1969) 85 *LQR* 505; I Karsten, 'Chaplin v Boys: Another Analysis' (1970) 19 *ICLQ* 35; L Lazar, 'Phillips v Eyre Revisited' (1969) 32 *MLR* 638; H McGregor, 'The International Accident Problem' (1970) 33 *MLR* 1; PM North and PRH Webb, 'The Effect of Chaplin v Boys' (1970) 19 *ICLQ* 24; A Shapira, 'A Transatlantic Inspiration: The "Proper Law of the Tort" Doctrine' (1970) 33 *MLR* 27. See also JJ Fawcett, 'Policy Considerations in Tort Choice of Law' (1984) 47 *MLR* 650.

[277] See *MacKinnon v Iberia Shipping Co Ltd* 1955 SC 20 (Court of Session, Scotland); *McElroy v McAllister* 1949 SC 110 (Court of Session, Scotland).

15.2.9   The identification of the true *ratio decidendi* of *Boys v Chaplin* is not without its difficulties.[278] However, in *Church of Scientology of California v Commissioner of Metropolitan Police*[279] the Court of Appeal took the view that Lord Wilberforce's speech provides the most authoritative guidance on what was decided by the House of Lords and in *Armagas Ltd v Mundogas SA* Goff LJ thought that 'the applicable principle in respect of foreign torts is as stated by Lord Wilberforce in his speech in *Boys v Chaplin*'.[280] In subsequent cases the courts have accepted this view which allows them 'to go, and to go alone, to the speech of Lord Wilberforce'.[281]

Lord Wilberforce's Speech and its Application

THE GENERAL RULE: DOUBLE ACTIONABILITY

15.2.10   The major part of Lord Wilberforce's speech is a reappraisal of the rule in *Phillips v Eyre*. Lord Wilberforce was content to accept 'the orthodox judicial view that the first part of the rule is laying down, not a test of jurisdiction, but what we now call a rule of choice of law'.[282] As regards the first part of the rule, 'actionability as a tort under and in accordance with English law is required'.[283] As regards the second part of the rule Lord Wilberforce thought that:

a person should not be permitted to claim in England in respect of a matter for which civil liability does not exist, or is excluded, under the law of the place where the wrong was committed.[284]

Accordingly, the choice of law rule favoured by Lord Wilberforce, as a general rule, is a rule of double actionability which requires actionability as a tort according to English law, subject to the condition that civil liability in respect of the relevant claim exists as between the actual parties under the law of the foreign country where the act was done.[285] To succeed under the general rule the claimant must establish that, in the particular circumstances of the case, the defendant is actually liable under both English law and the law of the place of the wrong:

it is the relevant claim as between the actual parties that must be looked at, and not whether such a claim could in theory be actionable.[286]

15.2.11   In relation to the general rule, what significance should be attached to defences under the law of the place of the wrong? What, for example, is the solution in a case where the defence of contributory negligence operates as a complete defence under the law of the place of the wrong? Since defences are to be regarded as substantive, a complete defence under the law of the place of the wrong defeats the claim in

---

[278] A Briggs, 'What Did Boys v Chaplin Decide?' (1984) 12 *Anglo-Am LR* 237. See Hodgson J in *Coupland v Arabian Gulf Oil Co* [1983] 1 WLR 1136, 1145.

[279] (1976) 120 Sol J 690.

[280] [1986] AC 717, 740.

[281] Hodgson J in *Coupland v Arabian Gulf Oil Co* [1983] 1 WLR 1136, 1146. See also *Dimskal Shipping Co SA v International Transport Workers Federation (No 2)* [1992] 2 AC 152; *Johnson v Coventry Churchill International Ltd* [1992] 3 All ER 14; *Red Sea Insurance Co v Bouygues SA* [1995] 1 AC 190.

[282] [1971] AC 356, 385.

[283] [1971] AC 356, 387.

[284] [1971] AC 356, 389.

[285] [1971] AC 356, 389.

[286] Dunn LJ in *Armagas Ltd v Mundogas SA* [1986] AC 717, 753.

England. Similarly, if the limitation period under the law of the place of the wrong has expired, the claim will fail under the second limb of the double actionability rule.[287]

THE EXCEPTION

15.2.12   The general rule can cause injustice since the requirement of double actionability gives the claimant the worst of both worlds.[288] If, for example, there are two heads of damage (A and C) under the law of the forum and two heads of damage (B and C) under the law of the place of the wrong, the double actionability rule allows the claimant to recover only C, the lowest common denominator. *Boys v Chaplin* was a case of this type; according to the general rule propounded by Lord Wilberforce, the plaintiff was entitled only to special damages, since under Maltese law damages for pain and suffering were not recoverable. As Lord Wilberforce noted, the question whether there should be an exception to the general rule highlights two conflicting pressures: 'the first in favour of certainty and simplicity in the law, the second in favour of flexibility in the interest of individual justice'.[289] Both Lord Wilberforce and Lord Hodson thought that the requirements of justice may in certain circumstances outweigh the arguments in favour of certainty. In cases where the double actionability rule has the effect of limiting or excluding liability the possibility of applying an exception to the general rule should be considered.[290]

15.2.13   The exception to the general rule has been formulated in the following terms:

a particular issue between the parties … may be governed by the law of the country which, with respect to that issue, has the most significant relationship with the occurrence and the parties.[291]

Although this formulation 'has not received the seal of explicit judicial approval',[292] neither litigants nor members of the judiciary have sought to challenge its accuracy.[293] It is important to stress that the exception should not be invoked too readily:

The general rule must apply unless clear and satisfying grounds are shown why it should be departed from and what solution, derived from what other rule, should be preferred.[294]

The exception will not be applied unless, in the light of all the circumstances, justice requires that the exception should be applied in preference to the general rule.[295]

15.2.14   In *Boys v Chaplin* Lord Wilberforce thought that it was appropriate to apply the exception to the general rule: neither party had significant connections with Malta; there was no reason to think that the Maltese state had any interest in applying

---

[287] Foreign Limitation Periods Act 1984, s 1; *Arab Monetary Fund v Hashim* [1993] 1 Lloyd's Rep 543. The English court may disapply a foreign limitation rule on the basis of public policy: Foreign Limitation Periods Act 1984, s 2(2).

[288] For a graphic example, see *McElroy v McAllister* 1949 SC 110 (Court of Session, Scotland).

[289] [1971] AC 356, 389.

[290] [1971] AC 356, 389.

[291] L Collins *et al*, *Dicey, Morris and Collins on The Conflict of Laws* (London, Sweet & Maxwell, 14th edn, 2006) para 35R–123 (Rule 235(3)).

[292] Slade LJ in *Metall und Rohstoff AG v Donaldson Lufkin & Jenrette Inc* [1990] 1 QB 391, 440.

[293] See, eg, *Johnson v Coventry Churchill International Ltd* [1992] 3 All ER 14; *Red Sea Insurance Co v Bouygues SA* [1995] 1 AC 190.

[294] Lord Wilberforce in *Boys v Chaplin* [1971] AC 356, 391.

[295] Judge Kay QC in *Johnson v Coventry Churchill International Ltd* [1992] 3 All ER 14, 26.

the rule denying damages for pain and suffering to persons not resident in Malta or in denying the application of the English rule allowing recovery.[296] Accordingly, Lord Wilberforce was prepared to segregate the availability of damages for pain and suffering from other questions arising in the case and to apply English law to this particular issue.

15.2.15   The methodology proposed by Lord Wilberforce was applied in subsequent cases. In *Johnson v Coventry Churchill International Ltd*[297] the plaintiff, an English carpenter, was employed by the defendant, an English company, to work in Germany. While working on a construction site in Stuttgart the plaintiff fell and suffered personal injuries. The plaintiff commenced proceedings in England, alleging that the injuries were caused by the defendant's negligent failure to provide a safe system of work. Although under English law the defendant's default would have amounted to a tort had the events occurred in England, the defendant was not civilly liable under German law.[298] The judge approached the question whether the exception to the general rule should be applied in two stages: first, the judge thought that 'there is nothing in the policy underlying the foreign rule that was ever intended to have any application to the case of an English citizen working for an English employer'[299]; secondly, England was 'the country with the most significant relationship with the occurrence and the parties'.[300] The important connections were with England: the plaintiff was English; the defendant was an English company; the contract giving rise to the defendant's duty was made in England and was governed by English law; the intended duration of the plaintiff's period of employment in Germany was only 13 weeks; and the failure to act that led to the accident could be traced back to decisions made in England.

15.2.16   In *Boys v Chaplin* the effect of invoking the exception to the general rule was to justify the application of English law. Furthermore, Lord Wilberforce advocated the application of English law only to one specific issue which arose out of the litigation—namely, the recovery of damages for pain and suffering—rather than to the whole of the claim. Similarly, in *Johnson v Coventry Churchill International* resort to the exception led to the application of the law of the forum at the expense of the law of the place of the wrong. These decisions left two important questions concerning the scope of the exception unanswered. First, can the exception be invoked in favour of a law other than the law of the forum? Secondly, can the law applicable under the exception be applied to the whole of the claim? In *Red Sea Insurance Co Ltd v Bouygues SA*[301] the Privy Council gave a positive answer to both questions; where the situation has its most real and substantial connection with a country which is neither the forum nor the place of the wrong, the court may apply the law of that country by way of exception.

---

[296] [1971] AC 356, 392.

[297] [1992] 3 All ER 14. PB Carter, (1992) 63 *BYIL* 530; P Rogerson, [1992] *CLJ* 439.

[298] Germany has a system of social security payments for persons injured at work and s 636 of the German Social Security Act exempts the employer from liability except in cases where the employee's injury is the result of a wilful breach of duty.

[299] [1992] 3 All ER 14, 24.

[300] [1992] 3 All ER 14, 25.

[301] [1995] 1 AC 190. A Briggs, '*The Halley*: Holed, but Still Afloat?' (1995) 111 *LQR* 18; PB Carter, [1995] *CLJ* 38; A Dickinson, 'Further thoughts on foreign torts: *Boys v Chaplin* explained?' [1994] *LMCLQ* 463; P Rogerson, 'Choice of Law in Tort: A Missed Opportunity?' (1995) 44 *ICLQ* 650.

15.2.17   As noted already, the scope of the common law rules has been severely cut down by legislation. The only cases in which the common law rules apply—that is, the double actionability rule and the exception—are cases which involve defamation claims.[302] The statutory scheme introduced by Part III of the Private International Law (Miscellaneous Provisions) Act 1995 did not apply to 'defamation claims', which are defined as:

(a) any claim under the law of any part of the United Kingdom for libel or slander or for slander of title, slander of goods or other malicious falsehood and any claim under the law of Scotland for verbal injury; and
(b) any claim under the law of any other country corresponding to or otherwise in the nature of a claim mentioned in paragraph (a) above.

The Rome II Regulation, which largely replaced Part III of the 1995 Act, also excludes 'non-contractual obligations arising out of violations of privacy and rights relating to personality, including defamation' from its scope.[303]

15.2.18   The effect of these provisions is that defamation claims continue to be governed by the double actionability rule or, where appropriate, the exception to it. Accordingly, if the publisher of an English newspaper with a worldwide circulation is sued in England on the ground that it has published material which is defamatory according to the law of a foreign country, liability can be imposed only if the material is also defamatory according to English law. If, for example, the publisher has a defence under English law (such as justification or fair comment) no liability can be imposed under the double actionability rule even if the publisher has no defence under the law of the place of the alleged wrong.

15.3 CHOICE OF LAW UNDER PART III OF THE PRIVATE INTERNATIONAL LAW (MISCELLANEOUS PROVISIONS) ACT 1995

Introduction

Background to the 1995 Act

15.3.1   Over the years the rule in *Phillips v Eyre* was subjected to extensive criticism and, although the common law was not without its supporters,[304] in the 1980s it became widely recognised that the law was defective and in need of reform. The case for reform was based largely on the inappropriateness of the dominant role played by the law of the forum.

15.3.2   The essence of the reform effected by Part III of the Private International Law (Miscellaneous Provisions) Act 1995 was the abolition of the common law rules (both the double actionability rule and the proper law exception) and their replacement

---

[302] See R Morse, 'Rights Relating to Personality, Freedom of the Press and Private International Law: Some Common Law Comments' (2005) 58 *CLP* 133.

[303] Art 1(2)(g).

[304] For a spirited defence of the common law, see PB Carter, 'Choice of Law in Tort and Delict' (1991) 107 LQR 405.

with a general rule which, in substance, stipulates the law of the place of the wrong to be the applicable law (section 11) and an exception in cases where the law of a country other than the place of the wrong is more appropriate (section 12). Looked at in most general terms, the effect of the statutory provisions was to reverse the effect of *The Halley*[305] (according to which there can be no liability for a foreign tort if the defendant is not liable under the law of the forum).

The Scope of the Statutory Rules

15.3.3 Part III applies to torts (other than defamation) committed after the entry into force of the 1995 Act—that is, 1 May 1996[306]—and before the entry into force of the Rome II Regulation—20 August 2007.[307] Part III also applies to torts committed after the entry into force of Rome II if the tort is excluded from the scope of the Regulation, but is not in the nature of defamation. In terms of the 1995 Act's material scope, it applies to issues relating to tort.[308] It is for the English court to characterise issues according to the conceptual categories of English private international law and the fact that a foreign law might classify a situation as contractual rather than tortious does not prevent the case falling within the material scope of Part III the 1995 Act.[309] It would, however, make no sense if the scope of Part III did not also extend to wrongs under foreign laws which are broadly analogous to English torts. Any other approach would stifle the proper operation of the statutory rules and would be tantamount to restoring the double actionability rule by the back door. If, for example, a claimant brings proceedings in England alleging that the defendant committed the tort of seduction in Botswana, the case should be regarded as falling within the scope of Part III. Although seduction does not constitute a tort under English domestic law, for private international law purposes foreign wrongs which have no English counterpart should be classified by reference to their closest English analogue. Although there was an argument that the 1995 Act has no application in cases where the tort was committed in England,[310] the statutory rules are applicable regardless of where the tort is committed.[311]

The General Rule

15.3.4 Part III follows the common law in establishing a general rule, the operation of which is tempered by an exception. The general rule is set out in section 11, the exception in section 12. Section 11 draws a distinction between single locality

---

[305] (1868) LR 2 PC 193.

[306] SI 1996/995.

[307] Part III also applies to claims which are not defamation claims but which fall outside the scope of the Rome II Regulation.

[308] 'Tort' under the 1995 Act should be taken to include a claim for dishonest assistance: see Christopher Clarke J in *OJSC Oil Company Yugraneft v Abramovich* [2008] EWHC 2613 (Comm) at [223].

[309] See Mance LJ in *Morin v Bonhams & Brooks Ltd* [2004] 1 Lloyd's Rep 702, 707 (at [12]).

[310] See the 3rd edition of this work at paras 15.3.10–15.3.11.

[311] See s 9(6) and *Roerig v Valiant Trawlers Ltd* [2002] 2 WLR 2304.

cases, where the events constituting the tort occur in one country, and multiple locality cases, where the events constituting the tort are spread between two or more countries. There is no suggestion in the 1995 Act that, as regards tortious obligations, the parties may make a choice of law (as they can in relation to contractual obligations[312]). Where tortious obligations arise in a situation which is closely linked to a contract, the impact of a choice of law in the contract on the law governing the tortious obligations is unclear. In *Morin v Bonhams & Brooks Ltd*[313] it was held that a choice of law clause in a related contract was irrelevant for the purposes of determining the law applicable to tortious obligations under section 11; the question whether such a clause is to be regarded as a relevant factor under section 12 was left open.[314]

Single Locality Cases

15.3.5   The general rule in single locality cases is to be found in section 11(1), which provides:

The general rule is that the applicable law is the law of the country in which the events constituting the tort or delict in question occur.

It would be hard to imagine a simpler rule. Instead of the double actionability rule and its attendant problems, the general rule in straightforward cases is that the law of the place of the wrong is the applicable law.[315]

Multiple Locality Cases

15.3.6   The localisation of a tort in cases where the events constituting the tort do not all occur in one country presents certain conceptual difficulties. To some extent the 1995 Act sidesteps these difficulties by not seeking to stipulate the place of the tort. Instead, the 1995 Act identifies the applicable law directly. Section 11(2) provides:

Where elements of those events occur in different countries the applicable law under the general rule is to be taken as being—

(a) for a cause of action in respect of personal injury caused to an individual or death resulting from personal injury, the law of the country where the individual was when he sustained the injury;
(b) for a cause of action in respect of damage to property, the law of the country where the property was when it was damaged; and
(c) in any other case, the law of the country in which the most significant element or elements of those events occurred.

---

[312] Rome Convention, Art 3(1).
[313] [2004] 1 Lloyd's Rep 702. See also *Trafigura Beheer BV v Kookmin Bank Co* [2006] 2 Lloyd's Rep 455; *Middle Eastern Oil LLC v National Bank of Abu Dhabi* [2009] 1 Lloyd's Rep 251.
[314] See para 15.1.21.
[315] *Edmunds v Simmonds* [2001] 1 WLR 1003, *Roerig v Valiant Trawlers Ltd* [2002] 1 WLR 2304; *Bristow Helicopters Ltd v Sikorsky Aircraft Corporation* [2004] 2 Lloyd's Rep 150; *Glencore International AG v Metro Trading International Inc* [2001] 1 Lloyd's Rep 284.

In cases involving personal injury and property damage section 11(2) identifies the law of the place where the harm is inflicted as the applicable law. This provision is unlikely to generate much difficulty in practice. In cases involving economic loss the place of harm is less tangible than in cases involving personal injury or property damage; it may, in itself, be a connecting factor of limited significance. Accordingly, in cases not involving personal injury or property damage, the 1995 Act does not seek to identify the applicable law by reference to a single connecting factor. Instead, section 11(2)(c) stipulates that the applicable law is the law of the country 'in which the most significant element or elements of [the events constituting the tort] occurred'. This test gives the courts considerable room to manoeuvre and is sufficiently flexible that it 'might yield different answers in different cases even in relation to the same kind of tort'.[316]

The Exception

15.3.7   Just as the common law developed an exception to the double actionability rule to counteract the potential injustice to which the general rule could give rise, the 1995 Act provides in section 12 an exception to the general rule in section 11. Section 12(1) reads:

If it appears, in all the circumstances, from a comparison of—

(a) the significance of the factors which connect a tort ... with the country whose law would be the applicable law under the general rule; and
(b) the significance of any factors connecting the tort ... with another country,

that it is substantially more appropriate for the applicable law for determining the issues arising in the case, or any of those issues, to be the law of the other country, the general rule is displaced and the applicable law for determining those issues or that issue (as the case may be) is the law of that other country.

15.3.8   Section 12 requires a comparison to be made between the factors that connect the tort to the country whose law is the applicable law under section 11 (country X) and the factors which connect the tort with another country (country Y). Section 12 requires that it be 'substantially more appropriate' to apply the law of country Y rather than the law of country X. Accordingly, it is not appropriate to apply the exception in section 12 simply on the ground that the situation surrounding the tort was marginally more closely connected with a country other than the country whose law is the applicable law under section 11.

   15.3.9   Section 12(2) provides:

The factors that may be taken into account as connecting a tort or delict with a country for the purposes of this section include, in particular, factors relating to the parties, to any of the events which constitute the tort or delict in question or to any of the circumstances or consequences of those events.

---

[316] Moore-Bick J in *Protea Leasing Ltd v Royal Air Cambodge Co Ltd* [2002] EWHC 2731 (Comm) at [78].

This list of factors is not intended to be exhaustive and does not suggest what weight should be attached to any particular factor. Indeed, it is a statutory provision of very limited value. The listed factors suggest, however, that section 12 is firmly rooted within a traditional choice of law methodology; section 12(2) is not drafted in the language of interest analysis and does not overtly invite an analysis of the policies of the potentially conflicting rules.

15.3.10   The arguments in favour of the application of the exception are strongest in a case where the tort is committed in country Y and both the parties have strong territorial connections with country X (and no more than weak connections with country Y). So, where D commits an invasion of C's privacy in England and both C and D are habitually resident in Germany, the applicable law under Part III is likely to be German law (by virtue of section 12) rather than English law (by virtue of section 11).

15.3.11   It should be noted that whereas section 11 identifies a unitary law which is applicable to the tort as a whole, section 12 allows for different issues to be governed by different laws. The court may apply the law identified by the exception to 'the issues arising in the case, or any of those issues'.[317] As regards the exception, there is no requirement that it should be all or nothing. In this respect section 12 adopts the same approach as the common law.

The Scope of the Applicable Law: Substance and Procedure

15.3.12   It is a well-established principle of English private international law that, whereas questions of substance are governed by the applicable law, matters of procedure are governed by the law of the forum. Section 14(3)(b) of the 1995 Act provides that nothing in Part III 'affects any rules of evidence, pleading or practice or authorises questions of procedure to be determined otherwise than in accordance with the law of the forum'. The statutory regime of the 1995 Act is intended to leave the traditional dividing line between substance and procedure intact.

15.3.13   Following the decision of the House of Lords in *Boys v Chaplin*[318] it is established that whether or not the claimant is entitled to recover damages for a particular head of damage is a substantive matter to be governed by the applicable law.

15.3.14   By contrast the quantification of damages is a procedural matter. So, whereas whether the claimant is entitled to recover damages for the loss of an eye is a substantive question governed by the applicable law, the amount of compensation to which the claimant is entitled is a procedural matter for the law of the forum.[319] Similarly, whether in the assessment of damages deductions should be made for benefits received by the claimant is a procedural question.[320] In *Harding v Wealands*[321] the House of Lords held that New South Wales legislation laying down statutory maxima for certain types of injury were procedural in nature and were, therefore, irrelevant to

---

[317] Private International Law (Miscellaneous Provisions) Act 1995, s 12(1).
[318] [1971] AC 356.
[319] *Edmunds v Simmonds* [2001] 1 WLR 1003; *Hulse v Chambers* [2001] 1 WLR 2386. See JM Carruthers, 'Substance and Procedure in the Conflict of Laws: A Continuing Debate in Relation to Damages' (2004) 53 *ICLQ* 691.
[320] *Roerig v Valiant Trawlers Ltd* [2002] 1 WLR 2304.
[321] [2007] 2 AC 1. C Dougherty and L Wyles, (2007) 56 *ICLQ* 443; P Beaumont and S Tang, (2008) 12 *Edin LR* 13; P Rogerson, [2006] *CLJ* 515; H Seriki, (2007) 26 *CJQ* 28; A Scott, [2007] *LMCLQ* 44.

the quantification of the claimant's damages even though the defendant's liability was governed by the law of New South Wales.[322]

Public Policy and Overriding Rules

Public Policy

15.3.15 The choice of law regime introduced by sections 11 and 12 gives no weight to the law of the forum as such. Of course, if the tort is more closely connected with England than with the law of the place of the wrong, English law will normally be applicable under the exception in section 12. However, it is possible that the law applicable under sections 11 and 12 is significantly different from English principles governing tortious liability. For example, under the applicable law liability may be strict in circumstances where under English law liability is based on fault; contributory negligence under the applicable law may be a complete defence; the applicable law may include types of tort which have no direct counterpart in English law. It is provided that the court may refuse to apply a foreign rule of law if its application 'would conflict with principles of public policy'.[323] From the point of view of principle, the applicable law (whether under the general rule or the exception) should not be excluded on the ground of public policy simply on the basis that the applicable law is different from the law of the forum. The legislation also makes provision for the application of the overriding mandatory rules of the law of a country which is closely connected with the dispute.[324]

15.4 PARALLEL CLAIMS AND THE POTENTIAL INTERACTION OF CONTRACT AND TORT CHOICE OF LAW RULES

Parallel Claims

15.4.1 As a matter of English common law, a claimant is free to (i) formulate his claim in whichever choice of law category he wishes; and (ii) advance parallel claims in as many legal categories for which there is a choice of law rule on the basis of the breach of a single duty. The latter was confirmed in *Base Metal v Shamurin*,[325] where the claimant was allowed to advance alternative claims in tort and breach of equitable duty of care.[326] The former can be illustrated by *Matthews v Kuwait Bechtel*

---

[322] See also *Maher v Groupama Grand Est* [2010] 2 All ER 455; *Knight v Axa Assurances* [2009] Lloyd's Rep IR 667.

[323] S 14(3).

[324] S 14(4).

[325] [2005] 1 WLR 1157. TM Yeo, [1995] *LMCLQ* 144; A Dickinson, (2005) 121 *LQR* 374; A Briggs, (2004) 75 *BYIL* 572.

[326] Whether a claimant should have such freedom of choice has been questioned: A Briggs, 'Choice of choice of law?' [2003] *LMCLQ* 12. See also Tomlinson J in *Base Metal Trading Limited v Shamurin* [2004] ILPr 74, 101.

Corporation.[327] The plaintiff had been injured while working for the defendant in Kuwait. The contract of employment was governed by English law. As the defendant had no place of business in England, the plaintiff sought permission to serve the defendant out of the jurisdiction on the basis of what is now CPR PD 6B para 3.1(6)(c). The defendant argued that the claim was in tort and that, since the alleged tort had been committed abroad, the plaintiff was unable to invoke the English court's jurisdiction. The Court of Appeal concluded, however, that the acts alleged by the plaintiff gave rise to a claim for damages either in tort or for breach of contract. Accordingly, the plaintiff could choose to frame his claim in contract and take advantage of the rule which allows the English court to assume jurisdiction in a case involving a contract governed by English law.

15.4.2 This approach was confirmed in *Coupland v Arabian Gulf Oil Co*,[328] in which the plaintiff was injured while working for the defendant in Libya. Whereas the plaintiff in *Matthews v Kuwait Bechtel Corporation* framed his claim in contract, in *Coupland v Arabian Gulf Oil Co* the plaintiff commenced proceedings in England claiming damages in tort. The defendant argued that the plaintiff's claim was in contract rather than tort and that the contract of employment was governed by Libyan law, according to which the defendant was not liable for breach of contract. The Court of Appeal rejected the first limb of this argument:

The plaintiff can advance his claim, as he wishes, either in contract or in tort; and no doubt he will, acting on advice, advance the claim on the basis which is most advantageous to him.[329]

15.4.3 The position is somewhat different in cases in which jurisdiction is determined by Chapter II of the Brussels I Regulation. For the purposes of Article 5, the question whether proceedings concern 'matters relating to a contract' or 'matters relating to tort' is to be answered by reference to EU law, rather than to the law of the forum.[330] So, a court may not assume jurisdiction under Article 5(1) if the proceedings involve 'matters relating to tort' as defined by the Court of Justice. However, the classification of proceedings for jurisdictional purposes does not determine how the claim is to be regarded for choice of law purposes. An English court may, for example, exercise jurisdiction under Article 5(1) pursuant to an unjust enrichment claim arising out of a valid contract on the basis that it is a 'matter relating to a contract'[331] but apply Article 10 of the Rome II Regulation to determine the applicable law.

15.4.4 The advent of the harmonised European choice of law rules for contractual and non-contractual obligations raises a question as to whether parallel claims are permitted for a matter falling within the scope of the Rome I and Rome II Regulations. On the jurisdictional front, the Court of Justice has held that a claim must be either 'a matter relating to a contract' within Article 5(1) or 'a matter relating to tort' within Article 5(3) of the Brussels I Regulation; that is to say, the two categories

---

[327] [1959] 2 QB 57. GJ Webber, 'Servant Suing Master for Negligence in Contract' (1959) 22 *MLR* 521; JA Jolowicz, [1959] *CLJ* 163.

[328] [1983] 1 WLR 1136.

[329] Goff LJ at [1983] 1 WLR 1136, 1153.

[330] Case C–26/91 *Jakob Handte & Co GmbH v Société Traitements Mécano-chimiques des Surfaces* [1992] ECR I–3967; Case 189/87 *Kalfelis v Bankhaus Schröder, Münchmeyer, Hengst & Co* [1988] ECR 5565. See paras 5.6.65–6.7.

[331] See Lord Goff in *Kleinwort Benson Ltd v Glasgow City Council* [1999] 1 AC 153, 170–1.

are mutually exclusive.[332] It seems reasonably clear that the Rome I and Rome II Regulations are also intended to be *generally* mutually exclusive; one need only refer to their scopes, that is, contractual obligations and non-contractual obligations respectively. Nevertheless, some overlap appears to be inevitable. For example, both Article 12(1)(e) of the Rome I Regulation and Article 10 of the Rome II Regulation cover unjust enrichment claims arising out of a void contract. Furthermore, it is clear from the terms of the Rome II Regulation that there are circumstances in which a claimant may advance a tortious claim (which falls within the scope of Rome II) notwithstanding the fact that there exists a pre-existing contractual relationship between the parties; Article 4(3) provides that, in this type of case, the law of the place where the damage occurs (which would normally be the applicable law under Article 4(1)) may be displaced in favour of the law governing the contract on the basis that, where a contract is closely connected with the tort, the tort may be manifestly more closely connected with the country whose law governs the contract.

15.4.5 Even if both Regulations were intended to be mutually exclusive, it is suggested that this is not a bar to the advancement of alternative claims which do not all fall within the scope of one Regulation.[333] The analogy drawn with Articles 5(1) and 5(3) of the Brussels I Regulation is not a perfect one: it would be problematic if the Brussels I Regulation were to allocate jurisdiction to the courts of different countries depending upon whether the same claim was framed in contract or tort; however, as Tuckey LJ observed in *Base Metal Trading Ltd v Shamurin*, 'there is not the same problem with a court which has jurisdiction having to apply different laws'.[334] The same factual scenario can give rise to multiple causes of action. Mutual exclusivity is only relevant in the context of a *single* cause of action: that cause of action and issues arising from it can only fall within one of the Regulations. However, if one claim is framed on the basis of breach of a contractual obligation, and the other claim is phrased in terms of breach of a non-contractual obligation, the first claim would be governed by the Rome I Regulation, and the second by the Rome II Regulation. However unattractive it may be for the defendant to have to defend himself against multiple claims,[335] there is nothing in both Regulations to suggest that only one claim may proceed. Pending future clarification from the Court of Justice, it is suggested that it is up to national laws to determine whether concurrent claims are permitted. The question that then arises is whether the relevant national law should be the *lex fori* or the *lex causae*. It has been suggested that whether concurrent causes of action are allowed is to be answered by the respective *leges causae*.[336] So, for example, if the claimant pursues a claim based on breach of contract and a claim based on tort out of the same factual scenario (for example, an employee who is injured in the course

---

[332] Case 189/87 *Kalfelis v Bankhaus Schröder, Münchmeyer, Hengst & Co* [1988] ECR 5565.

[333] Cf JJ Fawcett and JM Carruthers, *Cheshire, North and Fawcett: Private International Law* (Oxford, OUP, 14th edn, 2008) 779–80; the authors suggest that, if there is concurrent liability in contract and tort, the tortious classification should prevail.

[334] [2005] 1 WLR 1157, 1169 (at [34]).

[335] A Briggs. 'Choice of Choice of Law?' [2003] *LMCLQ* 12, 15, uses a sporting analogy: 'The defendant has to defend his goal against an opponent who may be playing with as many as five footballs at once but who stands to win damages, interest and costs if he misses with four but scores with the fifth.'

[336] R Plender and M Wilderspin, *The European Private International Law of Obligations* (London, Sweet & Maxwell, 3rd edn, 2009) 73–4.

of his employment due to the negligence of his employers may base a claim either on the tort of negligence or on the breach of the employer's implied contractual duty to take care) application of the Rome I Regulation to the contractual claim may point towards French law while application of the Rome II Regulation to the tortious claim may point towards German law.[337] It will then be necessary to assess according to French and German laws whether parallel claims are allowed. The obvious problem with this approach is that parallel claims may be denied by French law but allowed by German law. There is no justifiable means by which one claim could be said to be dominant to the other and it is that particular *lex causae*'s rule on parallel claims that should prevail. The simple and more persuasive position is that the possibility of concurrent causes of action is purely a matter of procedure and thus left to the *lex fori*.[338] The Regulations do not impinge on the forum's right to determine this issue.[339] If this is correct, this would leave the position under English law untouched.

The Potential Interaction of Contract and Choice of Law Rules

15.4.6   A different problem that arises is where mixed issues of contract and tort arise in the course of determining a single claim. There are various situations in the conflict of laws where this might occur. The simplest situation is where a foreign contract is relied upon by the defendant as a defence to a tort which is alleged to have been committed in England. In *Galaxias Steamship Co Ltd v Panagos Christofis*[340] the defendants worked on a ship which was owned by the plaintiff. The parties were Greek and the contract of employment between the plaintiff and the defendants was governed by Greek law. When the ship was docked in England, the plaintiff paid off the defendants, having purported to terminate their contract of employment. The defendants failed to leave the ship and the plaintiff sued them for trespass. The defendants sought to rely on the contract of employment as a defence, alleging that they were still entitled under the contract to remain on board. For the plaintiff to establish the tort of trespass, it had to be shown that the defendants' presence was unlawful; if the contract gave the defendants the right to remain on board, no tort could be established. In this case, the rights of the parties under the contract had to be determined by reference to Greek law as the law governing the contract. Since under Greek law the plaintiff had validly discharged the defendants, the defendants' presence on the ship was unlawful and the plaintiff's claim in trespass succeeded.

---

[337] In practice, however, in this type of case, there will be a tendency for the law governing the contract also to govern the claim in tort on the basis that the tort is manifestly more closely connected with the country whose law governs the contract: see Art 4(3) of the Rome II Regulation.

[338] Cf A Briggs, 'Choice of Choice of Law?' [2003] *LMCLQ* 12, 20, who argues that the accumulation of causes of action should be seen as part of the process of characterisation and thus arises prior to the division of issues as substantive or procedural.

[339] Cf R Plender and M Wilderspin, *The European Private International Law of Obligations* (London, Sweet & Maxwell, 3rd edn, 2009) 72, who argue that although the initial question of concurrency of claims is for the procedural law of the forum, once a foreign law is pleaded, there is still a need to determine according to the foreign *lex causae* whether concurrency is allowed.

[340] (1948) 81 Ll L Rep 499. This case is discussed by PM North, 'Contract as a Tort Defence in the Conflict of Laws' (1977) 26 *ICLQ* 914, 915–16.

15.4.7 *Galaxias Steamship Co Ltd v Panagos Christofis* is a straightforward case because the contract issue and the tort issue can be segregated and different laws can be applied to each issue. More problematical are cases which involve the interrelationship between contract and tort rules. The most important and difficult questions surround the potential impact of a contractual exemption clause on a tort claim. These issues arise most frequently in the context of cases in which an employee suffers personal injury as a result of an accident at work.

The Position if the Claimant Advances the Claim in Contract

15.4.8 If the claimant chooses to advance his claim in contract, the matter is governed exclusively by contract choice of law rules. Where the contract is concluded on or after 17 December 2009, the applicable law is to be determined by the Rome I Regulation.[341] If the contract contains a clause which purports to limit or exclude the defendant's liability under the contract, the validity of such a clause is determined in accordance with the applicable law.[342] If a contractual term is invalid under the applicable law, the defendant is unable to rely on it. If, on the other hand, the contractual term is valid according to the applicable law, as a general rule, the claim in contract will be limited or defeated.

15.4.9 It must, however, be remembered that under the Rome I Regulation there are circumstances in which the applicable law is superseded or overridden by the mandatory rules of other legal systems.[343] In the context of individual contracts of employment, Article 8(1) of the Regulation provides that, where the contract contains a choice of law, that choice shall not deprive the employee of the benefit of the mandatory rules of the law which would have applied in the absence of choice. Furthermore, Article 9(2) of the Regulation provides that the applicable law yields to the overriding mandatory rules of the law of the forum and Article 9(3) provides for the same effect with respect to certain of the overriding mandatory rules of the law of the place of performance.[344] Accordingly, the fact that a contractual exclusion of liability is valid by the applicable law does not necessarily mean that a claim in contract will fail.

The Position if the Claimant Advances the Claim in Tort

PRELIMINARY REMARKS
15.4.10 If the claimant advances his claim in tort, the main practical issue to be considered is the effect of any term of the contract which purports to limit or exclude the defendant's liability. The decided cases in this area are not entirely consistent and the analysis of the courts has not always been convincing. The position at common law will be considered first before the approach to be taken under the Rome II Regulation is considered.

---

[341] See ch 14. For specific rules relating to contracts of employment, see paras 14.5.23–14.5.38.
[342] Rome I Reg, Art 10(1).
[343] See section 14.3.
[344] Under Art 9(3) overriding mandatory rules of the law of the place of performance may supersede the applicable law only in so far as they render performance of the contract unlawful.

THE SIMPLE ANALYSIS

15.4.11 According to the simple analysis, if a contractual defence is relevant to a claim which is framed in tort, the claim in tort and the contractual defence are treated independently. The effect of this approach is that a contractual defence which is valid according to the law applicable to the contract operates to limit or bar the claim in tort. This seems to be the view taken by the majority of the Court of Appeal in *Sayers v International Drilling Co NV*[345] and *Coupland v Arabian Gulf Oil Co*.[346] These cases are, however, not entirely satisfactory as authorities.

15.4.12 *Sayers v International Drilling Co NV* involved an appeal on a very narrow issue. Salmon LJ indicated that only one point was raised in the appeal: 'Was the judge right in coming to the conclusion that the proper law of the contract of employment was Dutch law?'[347] Neither Salmon LJ nor Stamp LJ, both of whom concluded that the law governing the contract was Dutch law, expressly addressed the problems posed by the potential interaction of contract and tort choice of law rules. Nevertheless, it is clear that the plaintiff's claim was in tort[348] and it is implicit in the judgments of Salmon and Stamp LJJ that if the exclusion of liability was valid according to the law governing the contract, the plaintiff's claim was bound to fail.

15.4.13 In *Coupland v Arabian Gulf Oil Co* it was argued by the defendant that the contract of employment, which was governed by Libyan law, had to be considered in the context of the plaintiff's claim in tort. Hodgson J rejected this argument on the basis that the defendant had failed to show that the contract contained any defence to the plaintiff's claim in tort.[349] When the matter came before the Court of Appeal, Robert Goff LJ indicated that:

the contract is only relevant to the claim in tort in so far as it does, on its true construction in accordance with the proper law of the contract, have the effect of excluding or restricting the tortious claim.[350]

However, this apparent endorsement of the view that the effect on a claim in tort of a contractual defence, valid under its applicable law, should be governed by the law applicable to the contract rather than the law applicable to the tort was *obiter*, since on the facts of the case there was no contractual defence available to the defendants.

THE DEVELOPED ANALYSIS

15.4.14 The simple analysis has been convincingly criticised. In cases involving contractual exclusion clauses there are two issues to consider.[351] The first question is whether the exemption clause is valid. This is a contractual issue to be determined by the

---

[345] [1971] 1 WLR 1176. PB Carter, (1971) 45 *BYIL* 404; R Smith, 'International Employment Contracts—Contracting Out' (1972) 21 *ICLQ* 164.

[346] [1983] 1 WLR 1136. PB Carter, (1983) 54 *BYIL* 301.

[347] [1971] 1 WLR 1176.

[348] Lord Denning MR stated that 'the claim by the plaintiff is a claim founded in tort': [1971] 1 WLR 1176, 1180. Salmon LJ described the plaintiff's action as an action 'for damages for negligence': [1971] 1 WLR 1176, 1182.

[349] [1983] 1 WLR 1136, 1151.

[350] [1983] 1 WLR 1136, 1153.

[351] See PM North, 'Reform, But Not Revolution: General Course on Private International Law' (1990) 220 *Hag Rec* 9, 230; CGJ Morse, 'Tort, Employment Contracts and the Conflict of Laws' (1984) 33 *ICLQ* 449, 459.

law applicable to the contract. If the clause is invalid under the law governing the contract there can be no question of its providing a defence to a claim in tort. If the clause is valid, however, the second issue arises, namely whether the contractual clause operates as a defence to the tort claim under the law governing the tort (rather than under the law governing the contract). If the contract provides a good defence to a tort claim under the law applicable to the tort, the claim will fail. There are a number of cases which either support or are consistent with this analysis, rather than the simple analysis.

FURTHER PRELIMINARY CHOICE OF LAW QUESTIONS

15.4.15 Although the validity of the contractual term on which the defendant seeks to rely as a defence to the claim in tort is to be considered under the law applicable to the contract, which choice of law rules are to be used to determine the law applicable to the contract: the conflicts rules of the forum or the conflicts rules of the law governing the tort? The purist view is that the conflicts rules of the law governing the tort are relevant,[352] since to know whether an exemption clause will be given effect to under the law governing the tort, it is important to know whether under that country's law (including its choice of law rules) the clause is valid.[353] The pragmatic view is that 'it must be for the *lex fori* to determine the validity of the contractual exemption clause according to its proper law'.[354] The pragmatic view is more convenient and simpler to apply.[355]

15.4.16 It has been suggested that where there is a pre-existing contractual relationship between the parties, the contract might be relevant for the purpose of determining the law applicable to the tort.[356] If this suggestion is accepted there will be a tendency for the law applicable to the tort to follow the law governing the contract. The decided cases point in different directions. On the one hand, in *Sayers v International Drilling Co NV*[357] Lord Denning MR thought that English law was the law applicable to the contract, but that Dutch law was the law of the country with which the parties and the acts done had the most significant connection.[358] On the other hand, in *Johnson v Coventry Churchill International Ltd*[359] the fact that the contract of employment between the parties was concluded in England and was governed by English law was one of the factors which the judge took into account in deciding that English law governed the claim in tort.

THE APPLICATION OF THE DEVELOPED ANALYSIS

15.4.17 The simple analysis yields simple solutions. According to the simple analysis, if the contractual term on which the defendant seeks to rely as a defence is valid under

---

[352] PM North, 'Contract as a Tort Defence in the Conflict of Laws' (1977) 26 *ICLQ* 914, 927.

[353] PM North, 'Reform, But Not Revolution: General Course on Private International Law' (1990) 220 *Hag Rec* 9, 231.

[354] L Collins, 'Interaction between Contract and Tort in the Conflict of Laws' (1967) 16 *ICLQ* 103, 115.

[355] PM North, 'Reform, But Not Revolution: General Course on Private International Law' (1990) 220 *Hag Rec* 9, 231.

[356] CGJ Morse, 'Tort, Employment Contracts and the Conflict of Laws' (1984) 33 *ICLQ* 449, 460.

[357] [1971] 1 WLR 1176.

[358] Two points should be noted: (1) the majority thought that Dutch law was the law applicable to the contract; (2) Lord Denning MR's interpretation of *Boys v Chaplin* [1971] AC 356 was highly unorthodox and in the light of subsequent cases must be regarded as wrong.

[359] [1992] 3 All ER 14.

the law applicable to the contract the claim is limited or defeated, as the case may be, both in tort and in contract. According to the developed analysis, however, when a contractual defence is raised in the context of a claim which is framed in tort, the basic issues which the court should consider are, first, the validity of the contractual term according to the law applicable to the contract and, secondly, the availability of a contractual term as a defence to a claim in tort under the law applicable to the tort. If the contractual term is valid by the law governing the contract and is available as a defence under the law applicable to the tort the claimant cannot recover in tort. If, however, under the law governing the tort the contractual defence is not available, there is no reason in principle why the claimant should not be able to recover in tort, notwithstanding the validity of the contractual term under the law governing the contract.

15.4.18 In *Brodin v A/R Seljan*[360] the pursuer's husband was a seaman who died as a consequence of injuries sustained in an accident on board a fishing vessel owned by the defender, a Norwegian company. The pursuer's husband was employed by the defender under a contract of employment which was governed by Norwegian law. The accident took place in Scottish waters. When the pursuer sued the defender in Scotland claiming damages for negligence the defender sought to rely on a term in the contract of employment which exempted the defender from liability for negligence. Under Scots law the contractual exclusion of liability was void by virtue of section 1(3) of the Law Reform (Personal Injuries) Act 1948. The court held that the defender was liable in tort on the basis that Scots law, the law governing the tort, prevailed over Norwegian law, the law governing the contract. Although *Brodin v A/R Seljan* did not involve a foreign tort—as Scotland was both the forum and the place of the wrong—the court's analysis is the appropriate one to adopt in cases involving foreign torts. Accordingly, the result should be the same in a case where the tort is committed abroad and under the law applicable to the tort the contractual term is not available as a defence.

15.4.19 Only if the contractual term is available as a defence to the tort under the law applicable to the tort should the claim be defeated. In *Canadian Pacific Railway Co v Parent*,[361] a case decided by the Privy Council on appeal from the Supreme Court of Canada, the plaintiff's husband was killed as a result of an accident on a train in Ontario. The accident was caused by the negligence of employees of the defendant, the railway owner. At the time of the accident the plaintiff's husband was travelling at a reduced fare and the contract between the plaintiff's husband and the defendant provided that, in relation to a person travelling at less than full fare, the defendant was not liable for that person's death or personal injury, whether caused by negligence or otherwise. The plaintiff started proceedings against the defendant in Quebec claiming damages for negligence. The plaintiff's claim failed since under the law of Ontario—the place where the accident occurred—the terms of the contract were effective to bar the plaintiff's claim in tort.

15.4.20 If the contractual term is invalid by the law governing the contract, the claimant can maintain a claim in contract. It is also reasonable to suppose that the

---

[360] 1973 SLT 198. JM Thompson, 'International Employment Contracts—The Scottish Approach' (1974) 23 *ICLQ* 458.
[361] [1917] AC 195.

claimant may succeed in tort in these circumstances. There is no obvious reason why the forum should give any effect to a contractual term which is invalid by its applicable law.

THE APPROACH UNDER THE ROME II REGULATION

15.4.21 It is doubtful that either the simple or developed analysis will be available for claims falling under the scope of the Rome II Regulation. Article 15(b) provides that the law applicable to the non-contractual obligation shall govern 'the grounds of exemption from liability, any limitation of liability and any division of liability'. The advancement of a contractual exemption clause as a defence to a tortious claim clearly falls within this provision. Whether the contractual exemption clause can be raised as a defence to a tort claim is to be determined by the applicable law of the tort. This accords with one part of the developed analysis advanced at common law. However, it appears that the validity of the contractual exemption clause is also to be determined by the law applicable to the tort, rather than the law governing the contract.[362] Although this does not follow the second part of the developed analysis, note should be taken of Article 4(3) of the Rome II Regulation.[363] This provides for the displacement of the law of the country in which the damage occurs or the law of common habitual residence of the parties in favour of the law of another country with which the tort is manifestly more closely connected. Crucially, Article 4(3) states that: 'A manifestly closer connection with another country might be based in particular on a pre-existing relationship between the parties, such as a contract, that is closely connected with the tort/delict in question.' It would appear, therefore, that Article 4(3) points towards the law applicable to the tort following the law governing the contract and that, in the context of a claim in tort, the law governing the contract should be applied to assess the validity of the contractual exemption clause. This leads to the result that the law applicable to the contract will determine (i) the validity of the contractual exemption clause; and (ii) whether a valid contractual exemption clause may be raised as a defence to the tortious claim.[364] It is difficult to read Article 4(3) and Article 15 as allowing the two issues to be split and governed by different applicable laws as under the developed analysis. Thus, it seems clear that under the Rome II Regulation, one law and one law only will determine whether a contractual exemption clause is valid and whether it may be raised as a defence to a non-contractual claim.

---

[362] The issue of the validity of such clauses is seemingly covered by Art 8 of the Hague Convention on the Law Applicable to Traffic Accidents 1971 which formed the basis for Art 15 of the Rome II Reg. See the *Explanatory Report* which accompanies the Convention (by EW Essén) 29. See JJ Fawcett and JM Carruthers, *Cheshire, North and Fawcett: Private International Law* (Oxford, OUP, 14th edn, 2008) 843.

[363] Note the *Explanatory Memorandum,* COM (2003) 427 final, pp 12–13.

[364] Cf JJ Fawcett and JM Carruthers, *Cheshire, North and Fawcett: Private International Law* (Oxford, OUP, 14th edn, 2008) 866–7.

16

PROOF OF FOREIGN LAW[1]

16.0.1   The fact that, in a case with a foreign element, English conflicts rules indicate that the applicable law is the law of a foreign country does not necessarily mean that the foreign law will be applied. As a general rule, foreign law is treated as a fact which must be pleaded and proved by the party seeking to rely on it (section 16.1). There are, however, certain situations where foreign law does not have to be proved (section 16.2). Where foreign law is disputed the court has to rely on expert evidence (section 16.3). Although foreign law is treated as a question of fact, appeals on questions of foreign law are regarded differently from appeals on other questions of fact (section 16.4).

16.1 FOREIGN LAW: A QUESTION OF FACT

16.1.1   There are many cases in which English choice of law rules point towards the law of a foreign country as the applicable law. Whereas the court has judicial notice of English law (which includes EU law[2] and public international law[3]), there is no similar principle as regards the laws of foreign countries. Foreign law is for evidential purposes treated in English courts as a question of fact, which must be pleaded and proved by appropriate evidence. It is for the party seeking to establish the foreign law to plead the relevant rules of law and prove them.[4] If the foreign law is not pleaded, or cannot be proved to the satisfaction of the court, English law is applied by default.[5] So, where a claimant sues a defendant in England in relation to a tort which was committed abroad, if neither party pleads the law of the country where the wrong was committed the defendant's liability is determined by English law. It is sometimes said that the court assumes that foreign law is the same as English law unless it is proved to be different.[6] However, this presumption is 'not applied inflexibly'[7] and is subject to a number of exceptions.[8] For example, the presumption has not been used when the

---

[1] R Fentiman, *Foreign Law in English Courts* (Oxford, OUP, 1998); R Fentiman, 'Laws, Foreign Laws and Facts' (2006) 59 *CLP* 391.

[2] European Communities Act 1972, s 3; as amended by European Union (Amendment) Act 1986, s 2 and European Union (Amendment) Act 2008, s 3(3), sched, part 1.

[3] *Trendtex Trading Corporation v Central Bank of Nigeria* [1977] QB 529.

[4] See, eg, the judgment of Mann LJ in *The Amazonia* [1990] 1 Lloyd's Rep 236, 247.

[5] *Dynamit AG v Rio Tinto Co* [1918] AC 260; *Guaranty Trust Co of New York v Hannay & Co* [1918] 2 KB 623; *Callwood v Callwood* [1960] AC 659 (PB Carter, (1960) 36 *BYIL* 408).

[6] See, eg, the judgment of Purchas LJ in *Bumper Development Corporation v Commissioner of Police of the Metropolis* [1991] 1 WLR 1362, 1368.

[7] Peter Gibson LJ in *Shaker v Al-Bedrawi* [2003] Ch 350, 371 (at [64]). See also *National Auto-Glass Supplies (Australia) Pty Ltd v Nielsen & Moller Autoglass (NSW) Pty Ltd (No 8)* [2007] FCA 1625 (at [41]) (Federal Court of Australia).

[8] See R Fentiman, 'Laws, Foreign Laws and Facts' (2006) 59 *CLP* 391, 408–14.

proper law of a contract was the law of Saudi Arabia but the parties had not proved the content of that law.[9] Reliance on the presumption was also refused where expert evidence had been produced but it did not cover the point of foreign law which was argued.[10] It has been suggested that the terminology of presumption should be abandoned.[11] It is better simply to say that, since English law is the only law of which the court has judicial notice, if the foreign law is not proved, the court has no choice but to apply English law.[12]

16.1.2   Although foreign law is treated as a fact, in those cases where a judge sits with a jury the foreign law has to be proved to the satisfaction of the judge, rather than the jury. Section 69(5) of the Supreme Court Act 1981 provides:

Where … it is necessary to ascertain the law of any other country which is applicable to the facts of the case, any question as to the effect of the evidence given with respect to that law shall, instead of being submitted to the jury, be decided by the judge alone.

16.1.3   The question arises whether, in a case involving the application of either the Rome I Regulation on the law applicable to contractual obligations[13] or the Rome II Regulation on the law applicable to non-contractual obligations[14] the English court might be required of its own motion to apply the law of a foreign country if the Regulation's choice of law rules provide for the application of a law other than English law. According to Article 2 of the Rome I Regulation and Article 3 of the Rome II Regulation, any law specified by the Regulation 'shall be applied'. It could be argued that, in certain circumstances, the court should apply rules of foreign law, even if not pleaded or proved by either of the parties. However, both Regulations exclude 'evidence and procedure' from their scope[15] and it seems clear that questions relating to the proof of foreign law concern 'evidence and procedure' and, therefore, fall outside the scope of the Regulations. Furthermore, in relation to the Rome I Regulation, Article 3(2) provides that the parties may agree to subject a contract to a law other than that which previously governed it (whether as a result of an earlier choice or as a result of other provisions of the Regulation which determine the applicable law in the absence of choice by the parties). Where in English proceedings the parties choose not to plead the applicable law, the parties' conduct may legitimately be interpreted as an implied agreement to subject the contract to English law.

16.2 CASES IN WHICH FOREIGN LAW DOES NOT HAVE TO BE PROVED

16.2.1   In certain rather limited circumstances a court may have judicial notice of a law other than English law. First, in some instances, the laws of Scotland and

---

[9] *Global Multimedia International Ltd v ARA Media Services* [2007] 1 All ER (Comm) 1160.
[10] *Tamil Nadu Electricity Board v ST-CMS Electric Co Private Ltd* [2008] 1 Lloyd's Rep 93, 113 (at [97]–[101]). A Mills, [2008] *CLJ* 25.
[11] See L Collins *et al*, *Dicey, Morris and Collins on The Conflict of Laws* (London, Sweet & Maxwell, 14th edn, 2006) para 9024. See also R Fentiman, 'Laws, Foreign Laws, and Facts' (2006) 59 *CLP* 391, who argues that the presumption no longer exists.
[12] *Global Multimedia International Ltd v ARA Media Services* [2007] 1 All ER (Comm) 1160, 1175–6 (at [38]).
[13] [2008] OJ L177/6.
[14] [2007] OJ L199/40.
[15] Rome I Reg, Art 1(3); Rome II Reg, Art 1(3).

Northern Ireland do not have to be proved. Generally speaking, for the purpose of English private international law, the laws of Scotland and Northern Ireland are treated in the same way as the laws of politically foreign countries, such as France and Germany. So, in a case involving a contract governed by Scots law, since an English judge does not have judicial notice of the applicable law, a party wishing to enforce his rights under the applicable law has to plead and prove the relevant Scottish rules. However, the Supreme Court, which has jurisdiction to hear appeals from England and Wales, Scotland and Northern Ireland, has judicial notice of the laws of all parts of the United Kingdom when hearing an appeal from the courts of one of the parts. It may also be presumed that the Supreme Court has judicial notice of the laws of those countries in relation to which it exercises appellate jurisdiction.

16.2.2 Secondly, there may be circumstances in which the court has judicial notice of a rule of foreign law as a notorious fact. For example, the English courts have taken judicial notice of the fact that roulette is not unlawful in Monte Carlo.[16] Thirdly, the parties may dispense with the aid of witnesses and request the court to decide a question of foreign law without proof. The court is not, however, obliged to accede to the parties' request. Except in cases where the substantive issue turns on the interpretation of a foreign statute, the court is reluctant to decide questions of foreign law without having had the benefit of expert evidence.[17] Finally, statute may expressly provide that the court shall have judicial notice of the laws of a foreign country.[18]

16.3 MODE OF PROOF

The Requirement of Evidence

16.3.1 Foreign law has to be proved to the satisfaction of the judge in the same manner as other facts. If the foreign law is admitted, no proof is necessary.[19] Where, however, the foreign law is disputed, evidence is required. It is not sufficient for the party pleading the foreign law simply to place before the court the relevant primary and secondary sources of law (statutes, decided cases and commentaries), leaving the judge to draw his own conclusions.[20] What is required is the evidence of qualified experts in the foreign law.[21] When it comes to questions of foreign law the judge 'has

---

[16] *Saxby v Fulton* [1909] 2 KB 208.

[17] L Collins *et al*, *Dicey, Morris and Collins on The Conflict of Laws* (London, Sweet & Maxwell, 14th edn, 2006) para 9–008, citing *Beatty v Beatty* [1924] 1 KB 807. For Australian discussion of the issue, see *Damberg v Damberg* (2001) 52 NSWLR 492 (Court of Appeal, New South Wales); *Tisand Pty Ltd v Owners of the Ship MV Cape Moron* (2005) 219 ALR 48 (Federal Court of Australia); *Neilson v Overseas Projects Corp of Victoria Ltd* (2005) 221 ALR 213 (High Court, Australia) (A Briggs, [2006] *LMCLQ* 1; E Schoeman, (2006) 25 *UQLJ* 203; M Keyes, (2007) 15 *Torts LJ* 1; SGA Pitel, (2006) 43 *Can Bus LJ* 171; M Davies, (2006) 30 *Melb U LR* 244; A Mills, [2006] *CLJ* 37; A Dickinson, (2006) 122 *LQR* 183).

[18] Eg, s 22(2) of the Maintenance Orders Act 1950 provides that in certain circumstances the court of one part of the United Kingdom shall have judicial notice of the laws of the other parts.

[19] *Prowse v European and American Steam Shipping Co* (1860) 13 Moo PC 484; *Moulis v Owen* [1907] 1 KB 746.

[20] See Atkin LJ in *Buerger v New York Life Assurance Co* (1927) 96 LJKB 930, 940.

[21] See Lord Wright in *Lazard Brothers & Co v Midland Bank Ltd* [1933] AC 289, 298.

not organs to know and to deal with the text of that law, and therefore requires the assistance of a lawyer who knows how to interpret it'.[22] The principle which requires the parties to prove the foreign law means that if an expert refers only to part of a foreign legal text the judge may not refer to other parts which have not been put in evidence and is not entitled to conduct his own researches into the foreign law.[23] If the evidence put before the court is not satisfactory the judge is not entitled 'to search for himself into the sources of knowledge from which witnesses have drawn, and produce for himself the fact which is required to be proved as part of the case before him'.[24] While the court may allow evidence to be given in written form, it is usual for experts to be required to give their evidence orally, with the consequence that they may be subjected to cross-examination.

Uncontradicted Evidence

16.3.2   Where the evidence of an expert is uncontradicted, the court will not generally reject it.[25] However, the court is not required to accept the uncontradicted evidence of an expert. The judge is free to scrutinise the witness and what he says as on any other question of fact and there are examples where expert evidence has been rejected on the basis that it was obviously wrong:

The witness, however expert in the foreign law, cannot prevent the court using its common sense; and the court can reject his evidence if he says something patently absurd, or something inconsistent with the rest of his evidence—including the correct translation, for instance, of a foreign statute which *ex hypothesi* has been proved and therefore is before the court.[26]

Conflicting Evidence

16.3.3   Where the evidence of the expert witnesses conflicts, the court is required to determine these differences in the same way as he must in the case of other conflicting evidence of fact.[27] Where the experts do not agree, 'the judge has the comparatively easy task of choosing between them'.[28] Of course, the court is 'not obliged to accept

---

[22] Lord Brougham in the *Sussex Peerage Case* (1844) 11 Cl & Fin 85, 115.
[23] *Bumper Development Corporation v Commissioner of Police of the Metropolis* [1991] 1 WLR 1362, 1371.
[24] Lord Chelmsford in *Duchess Di Sora v Phillips* (1863) 10 HL Cas 624, 640.
[25] *Buerger v New York Life Assurance Co* (1927) 96 LJKB 930; *Koechlin & Cie v Kestenbaum Brothers* [1927] 1 KB 616; *Re Banque des Marchands de Moscou (Koupetschesky)* [1958] Ch 182; *Sharif v Azad* [1967] 1 QB 605.
[26] Scott LJ in *A/S Tallinna Laevauhisus v Estonian State Steamship Line* (1947) 80 Ll L Rep 99, 108. It is clear that the circumstances in which uncontradicted evidence may be rejected are not limited to cases in which the evidence presented is 'patently absurd': Foskett J in *Harley v Smith* [2009] 1 Lloyd's Rep 359, 367 (at [47]) and 371 (at [74]).
[27] *Bumper Development Corporation v Commissioner of Police of the Metropolis* [1991] 1 WLR 1362, 1368; *Islamic Republic of Iran v Barakat Galleries Ltd* [2009] QB 22, 43 (at [47]).
[28] Roxburgh J in *Re Banque des Marchands de Moscou (Koupetschesky)* [1958] Ch 182, 195. See also *Catalyst Recycling Ltd v Nickelhütte Aue GmbH* [2009] Env LR 29, 44–6 (at [49]–[52]).

the evidence of any witness in its entirety';[29] the judge may accept the views of one expert on some points and those of another expert on others.[30] If the evidence of several expert witnesses conflicts concerning the effect of foreign sources, the court is entitled and, indeed, bound to look at those sources in order to decide between conflicting testimony.[31]

Who is an Expert?

16.3.4   There is no statutory definition of an expert; in order to be an expert a person does not have to be qualified to practise law in the relevant foreign jurisdiction. Section 4(1) of the Civil Evidence Act 1972 provides:

It is hereby declared that in civil proceedings a person who is suitably qualified to do so on account of his knowledge or experience is competent to give expert evidence as to the law of any country or territory outside the United Kingdom or of any part of the United Kingdom other than England and Wales, irrespective of whether he has acted or is entitled to act as a legal practitioner there.

This provision is thought to be declaratory of the pre-existing common law. While some of the older cases suggest that even a bank manager,[32] a former colonial governor,[33] or a diplomatic official[34] may be suitably qualified to give expert evidence on questions of foreign law with which they are familiar by virtue of their profession or calling, the modern practice is to use as expert witnesses legal practitioners and academic lawyers who have specialised in the foreign legal system.

Decisions on Points of Foreign Law in Subsequent Cases

16.3.5   At common law, a decision on a point of foreign law is not binding in subsequent cases. This is a logical consequence of the doctrine which states that in English proceedings foreign law is a question of fact. In *Lazard Brothers & Co v Midland Bank Ltd* Lord Wright indicated that the court may not take judicial cognisance of the law of a foreign country 'even though the foreign law has already been proved before it in another case'.[35] The common law rule is that the court must act upon the evidence before it in the actual case.

16.3.6   The strict common law position has, however, been modified by section 4(2) of the Civil Evidence Act 1972, which provides:

Where any question as to the law of any country or territory outside the United Kingdom, or any part of the United Kingdom other than England and Wales, with respect to any matter

---

[29] Stuart-Smith LJ in *Grupo Torras SA v Sheikh Fahad Mohammed al Sabah* [1995] ILPr 667, 684.

[30] As in *Dubai Bank Ltd v Galadari (No 5)* The Times, 26 June 1990; *Protea Leasing Ltd v Royal Air Cambodge Co Ltd* [2002] EWHC 2731 (Comm), The Times, 3 January 2003 at [81]–[103].

[31] *Bumper Development Corporation v Commissioner of Police of the Metropolis* [1991] 1 WLR 1362, 1369.

[32] *De Beéche v South American Stores (Gath and Chaves) Ltd* [1935] AC 148.

[33] *Cooper-King v Cooper-King* [1900] P 65.

[34] *In the Goods of Dost Aly Khan* (1880) 6 PD 6.

[35] [1933] AC 289, 297–98.

has been determined (whether before or after the passing of this Act) in any such proceedings as are mentioned in subsection (4) below, then in any civil proceedings (not being a court which can take judicial notice of the law of that country, territory or part with respect to that matter):

(a) any finding made or decision given on that question in the first-mentioned proceedings shall, if reported or recorded in citable form, be admissible in evidence for the purpose of proving the law of that country, territory or part with respect to that matter; and

(b) if that finding or decision, as so reported or recorded, is adduced for that purpose, the law of that country, territory or part with respect to that matter shall be taken to be in accordance with that finding or decision unless the contrary is proved:

Provided that paragraph (b) above shall not apply in the case of a finding or decision which conflicts with another finding or decision on the same question adduced by virtue of this subsection in the same proceedings.[36]

The proceedings, whether civil or criminal, to which subsection (2) applies are listed in subsection (4):

(a) proceedings at first instance in any of the following courts, namely the High Court, the Crown Court …;

(b) appeals arising out of any such proceedings as are mentioned in paragraph (a) above;

(c) proceedings in the Judicial Committee of the Privy Council on appeal (whether to Her Majesty in Council or to the Judicial Committee as such) from any decision of any court outside the United Kingdom.

16.3.7   The effect of these provisions is that, whereas normally it is for the party pleading the foreign law to prove it, once a particular question of foreign law has been decided by an English court, the English judgment is evidence of the foreign law unless it can be proved to be wrong. Section 4(2) does not, however, create a system of binding precedent in cases involving questions of foreign law, since the existence of an English decision on a point of foreign law raises no more than a presumption.[37]

16.4 APPEALS

16.4.1   As a general rule appellate courts are unwilling to overturn findings of fact made by courts of first instance. Where questions of foreign law are involved, appellate courts are more ready to interfere on the basis that a question of foreign law is 'a question of fact of a peculiar kind'.[38] The appellate court will examine the evidence of foreign law which was before the lower court and decide for itself whether that evidence justifies the conclusion to which the lower court came.[39] Where the issue of foreign law is essentially one of statutory interpretation, the Court of Appeal considers

---

[36] This provision is supplemented by CPR 33.7.

[37] See *Phoenix Marine Inc v China Ocean Shipping Co* [1999] CLC 478.

[38] Megaw LJ in *Dalmia Dairy Industries Ltd v National Bank of Pakistan* [1978] 2 Lloyd's Rep 223, 286.

[39] Cairns J in *Parkasho v Singh* [1968] P 233, 250. See *King v Brandywine Reinsurance Co* [2005] 1 Lloyd's Rep 655.

that it is entitled to form its own view on the issue of construction.[40] However, the appellate court should not forget that 'the trial judge had the undoubted initial advantage of having seen and heard the witnesses'.[41] Accordingly, the Court of Appeal 'should be extremely reluctant to substitute its own views where questions of credibility are concerned'.[42]

---

[40] *MCC Proceeds Inc v Bishopsgate Investment Trust plc* [1999] CLC 417.
[41] Megaw LJ in *Dalmia Dairy Industries Ltd v National Bank of Pakistan* [1978] 2 Lloyd's Rep 223, 286.
[42] Stuart-Smith LJ in *Grupo Torras SA v Sheikh Fahad Mohammed al Sabah* [1995] ILPr 667, 684.

PART III

INTERNATIONAL INSOLVENCY

17

EC REGULATION ON INSOLVENCY PROCEEDINGS

17.0.1 Council Regulation 1346/2000 on Insolvency Proceedings entered into force on 31 May 2002. The Regulation sets out harmonised rules on jurisdiction, choice of law and the recognition and enforcement of judgments in insolvency proceedings. The Regulation has its roots in a 1995 European Union Convention on Insolvency Proceedings which was opened for signature on 23 November 1995 for a period of six months.[1] It was signed by all Member States at that time except the United Kingdom;[2] as a result of the United Kingdom's failure to sign, the Convention lapsed.

17.0.2 The need for better regulation and co-ordination of international insolvencies, however, was undeniable. Without some sort of international framework and co-operation, debtors are at liberty to engage in forum shopping and transfer disputes and assets from one country to another.[3] Creditors may also pursue their own individual claims without regard to claims by other creditors or survivability of the debtor.

17.0.3 In 1999 Germany and Finland proposed reviving the 1995 Convention in the form of a Regulation.[4] This then led to the adoption of the Insolvency Regulation in 2000. The Regulation transposes the text of the 1995 Convention with some amendments, two of which are of substance,[5] and the rest of which take into account the different legal nature of the two instruments. Because the substantive text of the Regulation is mainly a reproduction of the 1995 Convention, the unofficial Explanatory Report which accompanied the Convention (the 'Virgos-Schmit Report')[6] is generally acknowledged to be a legitimate reference for interpretation

---

[1] Although the European Commission had started work on a harmonised international insolvency Convention in the 1960s. That project collapsed due to lack of sufficient consensus in 1985. See I Fletcher, *Insolvency in Private International Law* (Oxford, OUP, 2nd edn, 2005) 341–2, 346–52; Virgos-Schmit Report, para 3.

[2] The reluctance of the United Kingdom to become a signatory appears to stem not so much from doubts about the Convention itself, but rather unconnected political reasons. See I Fletcher, *Insolvency in Private International Law* (Oxford, OUP, 2nd edn, 2005) 344–6.

[3] The Council of Europe concluded the European Convention on Certain International Aspects of Bankruptcy in 1990 (the Istanbul Convention) but that Convention has yet to enter into force as only one (Cyprus) out of a minimum three Member States has ratified it. For a detailed look at the Istanbul Convention, see I Fletcher, *Insolvency in Private International Law* (Oxford, OUP, 2nd edn, 2005) ch 6.

[4] See Initiative of the Federal Republic of Germany and the Republic of Finland with a view to the adoption of a Council Regulation on insolvency proceedings, submitted to the Council on 26 May 1999: [1999] OJ C221/8.

[5] Namely, Arts 5 and 42.

[6] The Virgos-Schmit Report was never published in the Official Journal or formally approved by the Council. It can be found in Council Document 6500/1/96 (Annex); and is reproduced in I Fletcher, *Insolvency in Private International Law* (Oxford, OUP, 2nd edn, 2005) Appendix VII and G Moss, I Fletcher and S Isaacs (eds), *The EC Regulation on Insolvency Proceedings: A Commentary and Annotated Guide* (Oxford, OUP, 2002) Appendix 2.

of the Regulation.[7] This proposition is further bolstered by the fact that some of the Recitals to the Regulation are culled from the Virgos-Schmit Report.[8]

17.0.4   The legal bases for the Regulation are what are now Article 67(4) and Article 81 of the Treaty on the Functioning of the European Union (TFEU) (formerly Article 61(c) and Article 65 TEC). Although instruments adopted under these provisions do not apply to the United Kingdom and Ireland, the United Kingdom and Ireland exercised their prerogative to take part in the adoption and application of the Insolvency Regulation under the Protocol on the position of the United Kingdom and Ireland which was annexed to the EC Treaty.[9] Conversely, Denmark, in accordance with the Protocol on the position of Denmark, also annexed to the EC Treaty, did not participate in the adoption of the Insolvency Regulation and is therefore not bound by it or subject to its application.[10] Unless otherwise indicated, references to 'Member State' must therefore be understood to mean all EU Member States except Denmark.

17.0.5   The European Court of Justice has jurisdiction to interpret provisions of the Regulation under Article 267 TFEU. Only courts from whose decisions there is no further appeal or judicial remedy under national law can seek a preliminary ruling from the Court of Justice on the interpretation of the Regulation.

17.1 SCOPE OF THE INSOLVENCY REGULATION

General

17.1.1   Article 1(1) provides that:

This Regulation shall apply to collective insolvency proceedings which entail the partial or total divestment of a debtor and the appointment of a liquidator.

The key phrases in Article 1(1) are further defined in Article 2. Interestingly, though, 'insolvency' is nowhere defined in the Regulation. This concept is left to the national laws of Member States and to a shared understanding as to what the term means.[11] For example, German law relies on the balance sheet test, where the value of assets is less than the amount of liabilities, whilst French law applies the illiquidity test, which examines the ability to pay a mature debt. The test under UK law is a combination of the cashflow test, which asks whether the debtor is unable to pay debts as they fall due,

---

[7] I Fletcher, *Insolvency in Private International Law* (Oxford, OUP, 2nd edn, 2005) 356–7; L Collins *et al*, *Dicey, Morris and Collins on The Conflict of Laws* (London, Sweet & Maxwell, 14th edn, 2006) para 30–150. In *Re BRAC Rent-A-Car International Inc* [2003] 1 WLR 1421, 1427, Lloyd J thought that he 'ought to take some account of [the Virgos-Schmit Report's] contents'. The Report was also referred to in, *inter alia*, *Stojevic v Komercni Banka AS* [2007] BPIR 141; *Geveran Trading Co Ltd v Skjevesland* [2003] BCC 209, affirmed [2003] BCC 391; *Re The Salvage Association* [2004] 1 WLR 174, 180; *Syska and another v Vivendi Universal SA and others* [2009] 2 All ER (Comm) 891, 896–7 (at [20]–[21]); and the opinion of Advocate General Jacobs in Case C–341/04 *Eurofood IFSC Ltd* [2006] ECR I–3813.

[8] Eg, Recital 13 is extracted from para 75 of the Virgos-Schmit Report.

[9] Recital 32.

[10] Recital 33.

[11] M Balz, 'The European Union Convention on Insolvency Proceedings' (1996) 70 *Am Bank LJ* 485, 501. Balz was intimately involved with the drafting of the 1995 Convention.

and the balance sheet test.[12] As long as either test is satisfied, insolvency proceedings may be opened.

17.1.2 Four fundamental conditions can be identified in Article 1(1) in order for proceedings to fall within the scope of the Regulation. First, the proceedings must be based on the insolvency of the debtor; secondly, it has to be a 'collective insolvency proceeding'. This is opposed to an individual insolvency proceeding, which involves only one creditor. Annex A lists insolvency proceedings for each Member State which fall within the scope of the Regulation.[13] For the United Kingdom, five types of proceedings are listed: winding-up by or subject to the supervision of the court;[14] creditors' voluntary winding-up (with confirmation by the court); administration, *including appointments made by filing prescribed documents with the court*;[15] voluntary arrangements under insolvency legislation; and bankruptcy or sequestration.

17.1.3 Several observations may be made. Winding-up proceedings under English law also serve purposes other than in connection with the insolvency of a company.[16] Winding-up proceedings which are not based on the debtor's insolvency do not fall within the scope of the Regulation.[17] In addition, non-judicial proceedings, such as creditors' voluntary winding-up,[18] are covered by the Regulation; this is practical as a significant percentage of corporate insolvency cases are settled through a non-judicial route.[19] Creditors' voluntary winding-up does not usually require court involvement under English law, which was why a new procedure was introduced for judicial confirmation of such proceedings for the purposes of the Regulation.[20] It should also be observed that receiverships, which play an important role in UK insolvency laws, are excluded from the Regulation.[21] This can be explained as receiverships are more akin to enforcement remedies for one particular type of secured creditor rather than a 'true' collective insolvency proceeding.[22]

---

[12] Insolvency Act 1986, s 123.

[13] For amendments to Annexes A, B and C, see Reg (EC) 603/2005 [2005] OJ L100/1 and the Corrigendum [2007] OJ L49/36; Reg (EC) 694/2006 [2006] OJ L121/1; Reg (EC) 1791/2006 [2006] OJ L363/1; Reg (EC) 681/2007 [2007] OJ L159/1; Reg (EC) 788/2008 [2008] OJ L213/1. For further proposed amendments, see COM (2009) 564 final.

[14] Winding-up under the supervision of the court has been abolished in England and Wales, Scotland and Northern Ireland but still exists in Gibraltar, which is subject to the Regulation.

[15] The italicised words were added by Reg (EC) 603/2005, [2005] OJ L100/1, and came into effect on 21 April 2005.

[16] For example, a company may be wound up because the number of members falls below the required minimum or there has been a lengthy suspension of business.

[17] Virgos-Schmit Report, para 49(b).

[18] On the other hand, a members' voluntary winding-up will not be within the Regulation because that procedure is not based on the insolvency of the company. See Insolvency Act 1986, ss 89 and 90. However, a members' voluntary winding-up could be converted into a creditors' voluntary winding-up if the company becomes insolvent (Insolvency Act 1986, s 96). Once judicial confirmation is obtained, the Regulation will apply.

[19] Virgos-Schmit Report, para 52; I Fletcher, 'The European Union Convention on Insolvency Proceedings: An Overview and Comment, with US Interest in Mind' (1997) 23 *Brooklyn J Int Law* 25, 30.

[20] See Insolvency Rules 1986, rr 7.62 and 7.63 (inserted by Insolvency (Amendment) Rules 2002, SI 2002/1307, rr 9 and 12). See also Form 7.20.

[21] Such as administrative receiverships and receiverships available under Insolvency Act 1986, Part III and Law of Property Act 1925, s 101(1)(iii).

[22] I Fletcher, *Insolvency in Private International Law* (Oxford, OUP, 2nd edn, 2005) 360; (E McKendrick Goode on, *Commercial Law* (London, Penguin Books, 4th edn, 2010) 922.

17.1.4 The third fundamental criterion set out in Article 1(1) is that the proceedings must entail 'partial or total divestment' of a debtor. This means that the debtor's powers of administration and disposal over all or part of his assets must be transferred over to the liquidator or the liquidator has the right to control the debtor's exercise of such powers.[23] The Virgos-Schmit Report emphasises that partial divestment, whether of the debtor's assets or power of administration, is sufficient.[24]

17.1.5 Fourthly, as is clear from the point above, the proceedings must involve the appointment of a 'liquidator'. Article 2(b) defines a 'liquidator' as 'any person or body whose function is to administer or liquidate assets of which the debtor has been divested or to supervise the administration of his affairs'. That this is a broad concept of a 'liquidator' is borne out by Annex C, which lists persons and bodies who are considered to be liquidators for the purposes of the Regulation. For the United Kingdom, such persons are a liquidator, supervisor of a voluntary arrangement, administrator,[25] official receiver, trustee, provisional liquidator[26] and judicial factor.

17.1.6 A fifth, and very fundamental, criterion can be added to the four above. The Regulation only applies where the centre of the debtor's main interests is located in the European Union.[27] If the debtor's centre of main interests lies outside the European Union, then English private international law rules will govern. This restriction is necessary as the rules set out in the Regulation require a degree of inter-connected economic and legal frameworks. The concept of 'centre of main interests' is examined below.

17.1.7 Two further points can be noted. No distinctions are made between a natural person or a legal person, a trader or an individual debtor—the Regulation covers all.[28] Moreover, proceedings covered by the Regulation are not dependent on the realisation of the debtor's assets as the Regulation extends to both winding-up proceedings and proceedings which are aimed at reorganisation of the debtor.[29]

Exclusions

17.1.8 Article 1(2) excludes insolvency proceedings involving certain entities from the scope of the Regulation as insolvencies involving such entities are or are intended to be subject to specific EU Directives.[30] The exclusion encompasses insolvency proceedings concerning insurance undertakings,[31] credit institutions,[32] investment

---

[23] Virgos-Schmit Report, para 49(c).

[24] Para 49(c).

[25] An issue that has arisen is whether an administrator conducting an out-of-court administration would be recognised under the Regulation given the Regulation's emphasis on court-activated insolvency proceedings. See G McCormack, 'Jurisdictional Competition and Forum Shopping in Insolvency Proceedings' [2009] *CLJ* 169, 193–4.

[26] This was inserted by Reg (EC) 603/2005, [2005] OJ L100/1, and came into effect on 21 April 2005.

[27] See Recital 14.

[28] Recital 9.

[29] See Virgos-Schmit Report, para 51.

[30] Virgos-Schmit Report, para 54.

[31] Covered by Dir 2001/17/EC on the reorganisation and winding-up of insurance undertakings [2001] OJ L110/28; implemented in the United Kingdom by the Insurers (Reorganisation and Winding-Up) Regs 2004, SI 2004/353, as amended by SI 2004/546, SI 2007/851, SI 2007/108 and SI 2007/126.

[32] Covered by Dir 2001/24 on the reorganisation and winding-up of credit institutions [2001] OJ L125/1; implemented in the United Kingdom by the Credit Institutions (Reorganisation and Winding Up) Regs 2004, SI 2004/1045, as amended by SI 2007/830, SI 2007/108 and SI 2007/126.

undertakings which provide services involving the holding of funds or securities for third parties, or collective investment undertakings.

Insolvency-related Proceedings

17.1.9 An issue that was previously left unclear was whether insolvency-related proceedings were covered by the Regulation, as the Regulation does not contain specific jurisdictional rules geared towards such actions, nor are such actions listed in Annex A.[33] This issue was finally cleared up in *Seagon v Deko Marty Belgium NV*.[34] The Court of Justice held that an action to set aside a transaction by virtue of a debtor's insolvency falls within the scope of the Regulation.[35] The Court referred to Recital 6[36] and the second subparagraph of Article 25(1),[37] both of which refer to proceedings which are closely connected to insolvency proceedings.[38] Taking into account the intention of the legislature and the objective of improving the effectiveness and efficiency of insolvency proceedings,[39] the Court concluded that the action to set aside a transaction should be governed by the rules set out in the Regulation. Although the case concerned only one type of action, it is clear that other insolvency-related actions which are closely connected to insolvency proceedings[40] should be treated in a similar manner. However, actions which are not derived from insolvency proceedings (that is, actions which could have been pursued independently) are excluded from the Regulation.[41] In *German Graphics Graphische Maschinen GmbH v Schee*,[42] a Dutch company was the subject of main insolvency proceedings in the Netherlands. An action by the German company invoking a reservation of title clause in its favour in the contract between the two companies with respect to machines located in the Netherlands was held to be independent of the insolvency proceedings as it was not

---

[33] See A Dutta, 'Jurisdiction for insolvency-related proceedings caught between European legislation' [2008] *LMCLQ* 88. The Brussels I Report (B Hess, T Pfeiffer and P Schlosser, *Report on the Application of Regulation Brussels I in the Member States,* Study JLS/C4/2005/03, September 2007, pp 349–50) recommends that the delimitation between matters falling within the Brussels I Regulation and the Insolvency Regulation should be clarified and that it is made clear that even collective proceedings and proceedings related to insolvency proceedings which are not explicitly listed in Annex A of the Insolvency Regulation are dealt with by either instrument.

[34] Case C–399/07 [2009] 1 WLR 2168.

[35] Such an action was previously held to be outside the scope of the Brussels Convention: Case C–133/78 *Gourdain v Nadler* [1979] ECR 733.

[36] Recital 6 provides: 'In accordance with the principle of proportionality this Regulation should be confined to provisions governing jurisdiction for opening insolvency proceedings and judgments which are delivered directly on the basis of the insolvency proceedings and are *closely connected* with such proceedings' (emphasis added).

[37] This provision deals with the automatic recognition of decisions handed down by a court taking jurisdiction under the Regulation. Judgments that are closely linked with insolvency proceedings are also covered by the automatic recognition principle. See para 17.4.6.

[38] Case C–399/07 [2009] 1 WLR 2168, 2190 (paras 20 and 26).

[39] Case C–399/07 [2009] 1 WLR 2168, 2190 (paras 21 and 22).

[40] The Virgos-Schmit Report mentions examples such as actions on the personal liability of directors based upon insolvency law, actions relating to the admission or the ranking of a claim, disputes between the liquidator and the debtor on whether an asset belongs to the bankrupt's estate: para 196.

[41] Virgos-Schmit Report, para 196.

[42] Case C–292/08 [2010] ILPr 15.

based on the law of the insolvency proceedings and required neither the opening of such proceedings nor the appointment of a liquidator.[43]

Intra-UK Insolvencies

17.1.10   The Regulation does not apply to intra-UK insolvencies. Recital 15 makes the point that:

The rules of jurisdiction set out in this Regulation establish only international jurisdiction, that is to say, they designate the Member State the courts of which may open insolvency proceedings. Territorial jurisdiction within that Member State must be established by the national law of the Member State concerned.

17.2 JURISDICTION

Two Sets of Conflicting Doctrines

17.2.1   A problem that arises in international insolvencies is that the debtor may have assets in more than one jurisdiction. Two sets of conflicting doctrines are put forward to deal with this situation: universality versus territoriality and unity versus plurality.[44]

17.2.2   The first set of conflicting doctrines focuses on the assets of the debtor. The doctrine of universality supposes that insolvency proceedings opened in one country will apply to all the debtor's assets, wherever situated. The fallacy behind this doctrine, though, is that a state is usually reluctant to allow proceedings conducted in another state to determine the fate of assets located within its jurisdiction. The converse doctrine of territoriality espouses that insolvency proceedings can be opened in whichever jurisdiction the debtor has assets and that those proceedings only have effect within that particular jurisdiction.

17.2.3   The second set of conflicting doctrines largely follows the lines drawn between universalists and territorialists. Thus the doctrine of unity supports giving exclusive jurisdiction to the courts of one state whereas the doctrine of plurality accepts that there may be as many proceedings as countries in which the debtor has assets.

17.2.4   The lack of a uniform Europe-wide system of security rights and the differences in national insolvency laws of Member States as to which class of creditor should be given priority made a scheme based on the principles of universality and unity unviable.[45] Thus, the Regulation sets out what may be described as a

---

[43] Case C–292/08 [2010] ILPr 15, 22 (paras 31–2).

[44] For more details, see I Fletcher, *Insolvency in Private International Law* (Oxford, OUP, 2nd edn, 2005) 11–15.

[45] Virgos-Schmit Report, para 12. Cf Economic and Social Committee, Opinion of the Economic and Social Committee on the 'Initiative of the Federal Republic of Germany and the Republic of Finland with a view to the adoption of a Council Regulation on insolvency proceedings, submitted to the Council on 26 May 1999' (hereafter 'EESC Opinion') [2000] OJ C75/1, paras 3.4.1–3.4.5.

'mitigated or modified universality'[46] scheme. It gives jurisdiction to the courts of the Member State within the territory of which the centre of a debtor's main interests is situated.[47] Proceedings in this Member State are termed 'main proceedings' and they have universal scope—that is, they are intended to encompass all the debtor's assets within the European Union. However, the Regulation also allows courts of another Member State to open insolvency proceedings against the debtor if the debtor possesses an establishment within the territory of that Member State. These are territorial proceedings which are restricted to assets situated within the jurisdiction of the particular Member State.[48] If these territorial proceedings are opened after the main proceedings, they must be winding-up proceedings and are termed 'secondary proceedings'.[49] If the territorial proceedings are opened prior to the opening of the main proceedings, they are termed 'independent proceedings' as they are not subordinated to any main proceedings.[50] If main proceedings are subsequently opened, then 'independent proceedings' may be converted into 'secondary proceedings'.

Main Proceedings

17.2.5 Main proceedings are opened by the courts of the Member State within the territory in which the centre of the debtor's main interests is situated. The Regulation thus only applies if the debtor's centre of main interests is within the territory of a Member State.[51] Main proceedings could be either winding-up or reorganisation proceedings as set out in Annex A.

17.2.6 Only one set of main proceedings can be opened within the European Union.[52] The Virgos-Schmit Report concedes that there is no resolution where concurrent jurisdiction is claimed in accordance with Article 3(1), but anticipates that such cases 'must be an exception, given the necessarily uniform nature of the criteria of jurisdiction used'.[53] The Court of Justice emphasises the principle of 'mutual trust' to avoid parallel claims of jurisdictional competence.[54]

17.2.7 Article 3(1) allocates jurisdiction to the 'courts' of the Member State in which the debtor's centre of main interests is situated to open insolvency proceedings. 'Court' is further defined in Article 2(d) to mean 'the judicial body or any other competent body of a Member State empowered to open insolvency proceedings or to take decisions in the course of such proceedings'. This non-traditional definition of 'court' for the purposes of the Regulation appears broad enough to encompass members and

---

[46] C Paulus, 'Group Insolvencies—Some Thoughts About New Approaches' (2006/07) 42 *Texas Int LJ* 819, 821; M Balz, 'The European Union Convention on Insolvency Proceedings' (1996) 70 *Am Bank LJ* 485, 496.
[47] Art 3(1).
[48] Art 3(2).
[49] Art 3(3).
[50] Art 3(4).
[51] Recital 14.
[52] Virgos-Schmit Report, para 73.
[53] Para 79.
[54] Case C–341/04 *Eurofood IFSC* [2006] ECR I–3813, para 42.

creditors of a company who agree on a voluntary winding-up procedure based on the insolvency of the company.[55]

Centre of Main Interests

WHAT IS THE 'CENTRE OF MAIN INTERESTS'?

17.2.8 The concept of 'centre of main interests'[56] not only is important in identifying the court in which main proceedings can be opened, but also generally determines what law is applicable to the proceedings; the Regulation's main choice of law rule stipulates that the applicable law is the law of the state in which the main proceedings are opened.[57] Furthermore, once a judgment is handed down by the court of the debtor's centre of main interests, that judgment is entitled to automatic recognition and enforcement throughout the EU Member States. Given that the concept of centre of main interests is not only fundamental to the jurisdictional scheme but also has repercussions beyond that, it is surprising that only limited guidance is given in the Regulation as to what is meant by this crucial concept.

17.2.9 According to the Virgos-Schmit Report, the word 'interests' is intended to denote that not only commercial, industrial or professional activities are considered but also general economic activities which include the activities of private individuals such as consumers.[58] 'Main' denotes that the primary interest is paramount when the debtor carries on activities of different types in various jurisdictions.[59]

17.2.10 For companies, Article 3(1) provides: 'In the case of a company or legal person, the place of the registered office shall be presumed to be the centre of its main interests in the absence of proof to the contrary.' It is assumed that the place of the registered office will normally also correspond with the debtor's head office.[60]

17.2.11 There is no guidance for identifying the 'centre of main interests' for individuals in the Regulation itself, but the Virgos-Schmit Report states that the centre of main interests will generally be the place of professional domicile for professionals and the place of habitual residence for other natural persons.[61] In *Geveran Trading Co Ltd v Skjevesland*,[62] it was held that a natural person's centre of main interests ought to be the place where he can be contacted. Factors to be considered are where the debtor's home is located, where he conducts his business, where his emotional ties are and how much time he spends in different places. However, a debtor's indirect economic interests in companies should not be confused with his own interests: where a natural person spends considerable time in London as a shadow director of an English company and as the owner of another company, but whose settled,

---

[55] G Moss, T Smith *et al*, 'Commentary on Council Regulation 1346/2000 on Insolvency Proceedings' in G Moss, I Fletcher and S Isaacs (eds), *The EC Regulation on Insolvency Proceedings: A Commentary and Annotated Guide* (Oxford, OUP, 2002) 163; Virgos-Schmit Report, para 66.

[56] The concept is borrowed from Art 4 of the Istanbul Convention and it is by no means the only concept derived from the Istanbul Convention that influenced the shape of the Regulation.

[57] Art 4.

[58] Virgos-Schmit Report, para 75.

[59] Virgos-Schmit Report, para 75.

[60] Virgos-Schmit Report, para 75.

[61] Para 75.

[62] [2003] BCC 209, affirmed [2003] BCC 391.

permanent home is in Austria with his family, Austria is his centre of main interests.[63] Conversely, where a German doctor moved to England to work and spent more time in England in connection with his work than in Germany, where his wife continued to live, his centre of main interests was held to be in England.[64]

17.2.12   One principle underlying the concept of 'centre of main interests' is that expectations of third parties should be preserved. Thus Recital 13 states: 'The "centre of main interests" should correspond to the place where the debtor conducts the administration of his interests on a regular basis and is therefore ascertainable by third parties.' The third parties referred to here are primarily, although not only,[65] potential creditors.[66] Insolvency is a foreseeable risk and by emphasising the place where the debtor primarily conducts his business, potential creditors can pinpoint a discernible jurisdiction in which litigation may be pursued and the law by reference to which they are able to calculate the risks of conducting business with the debtor.[67]

WHEN ARE PROCEEDINGS OPENED?

17.2.13   The 'centre of main interests' is assessed at the time the proceedings are opened. This then leads to the question of when exactly proceedings are 'opened'. 'Time of the opening of proceedings' is defined in Article 2(f) as the 'time at which the judgment opening proceedings becomes effective, whether it is a final judgment or not'. In *Staubitz-Schreiber*,[68] the Court of Justice upheld the traditional principle of *perpetuatio fori*; it decided that where a debtor has lodged a request for the opening of insolvency proceedings in Germany but moved to Spain to live and work before the proceedings were opened, the German courts retained jurisdiction to open the main proceedings. The Court of Justice noted that to permit the transfer of jurisdiction from the court originally seised to another court would be contrary to the Regulation's aim to avoid incentives for the parties to transfer assets or judicial proceedings from one Member State to another.[69] From the point of view of the creditors, to permit such a transfer would oblige them to be in continual pursuit of the debtor wherever he chooses to establish himself.[70]

---

[63] *Stojevic v Komercni Banka AS* [2007] BPIR 141. Cf *Cross Construction Sussex Ltd v Tseliki* [2006] BPIR 888, 893 (at [13]), where Lewison J appeared to accept that the discharge by a director of a company of his duties as director can amount to the administration by the director of his own interests and thereby indicate the location of his own centre of main interests.

[64] *Official Receiver v Eichler* [2007] BPIR 1636.

[65] P Torremans, 'Coming to Terms with the COMI Concept in the European Insolvency Regulation' in P Omar (ed), *International Insolvency Law: Themes & Perspectives* (Aldershot Hampshire, Ashgate, 2008) 180, points out that the Regulation uses the term 'third parties' as a generic term, and specifically uses the term 'creditors' in some places.

[66] Virgos-Schmit Report, para 71; *Re Daisytek-ISA Ltd* [2003] BCC 562, 566; *Geveran Trading Co Ltd v Skjevesland* [2003] BCC 209, 223; *Stojevic v Komercni Banka AS* [2007] BPIR 141, 158, [33] (at). Cf C Paulus, 'Group Insolvencies—Some Thoughts About New Approaches' (2006/07) 42 *Texas Int LJ* 819, 824.

[67] Virgos-Schmit Report, para 75. See the Court of Justice's decision in Case C–341/04 *Eurofood IFSC* [2006] ECR I–3813, which emphasised the primacy of foreseeability by creditors.

[68] Case C–1/04 [2006] ECR I–701.

[69] Case C–1/04 [2006] ECR I–701, para 25 and see Recital 4.

[70] Case C–1/04 [2006] ECR I–701, para 26. The Court of Justice's apparent equation of the centre of main interests with the place where the debtor's centre of main interests was situated when creditors entered into a legal relationship with him (para 27) must be treated with caution as this results in a static centre of main interests.

17.2.14   Nevertheless, a debtor's centre of main interests may not be static.[71] On the assumption that the presumption in Article 3(1) is not rebutted, the problem that arises is that a debtor may strategically relocate his administrative centre to another state in anticipation of imminent insolvency proceedings being opened against him.[72] Given the emphasis on the need for third parties to be able to ascertain the debtor's centre of main interests, it is suggested that it would be unattractive in principle to give effect to a transfer of centre of main interests that is undertaken for tactical purposes.[73]

17.2.15   Insolvency proceedings may be judged to have been opened at quite an early stage of the process. In *Eurofood*,[74] the Court of Justice held that the appointment of a provisional liquidator by the Irish court meant that an insolvency proceeding under the Regulation had been opened in Ireland on the date of the court order, notwithstanding that the court did not adjudicate on whether the debtor was insolvent or whether its centre of main interests was in Ireland until a later date. The Court of Justice said that:

a 'decision to open insolvency proceedings' for the purposes of the Regulation must be regarded as including not only a decision which is formally described as an opening decision by the legislation of the Member State of the court that handed it down, but also a decision handed down following an application, based on the debtor's insolvency, seeking the opening of proceedings referred to in Annex A to the Regulation, where that decision involves the divestment of the debtor and the appointment of a liquidator referred to in Annex C to the Regulation.[75]

This extended concept of what constitutes a 'decision to open insolvency proceedings' for the purposes of the Regulation has been criticised;[76] the most important critique is that it incongruously requires neither the existence of insolvency nor the debtor's centre of main interests to be established for an order to be classified as having opened insolvency proceedings.

LOCATION OF THE 'CENTRE OF MAIN INTERESTS'

17.2.16   English law places a premium on the place of incorporation. However, under the Regulation, the place of incorporation is irrelevant. In *Enron Directo SA*,[77] the English court held that it had jurisdiction under Article 3(1) to make an

---

[71]   *Shierson v Vlieland-Boddy* [2005] 1 WLR 3966, 3985 (at [55]).

[72]   I Fletcher, *Insolvency in Private International Law* (Oxford, OUP, 2nd edn, 2005) 367–8.

[73]   In Case C–210/06 *Application brought by Cartesio Oktató és Szolgáltató bt (a limited partnership)* [2009] Ch 354, the Court of Justice ruled that a Member State's legislation providing that a company incorporated under its law may not transfer its seat to another Member State whilst retaining its status as a company governed by the law of the state of its incorporation was not against the principle of freedom of establishment enshrined in Art 54 TFEU. If the Court had reached the opposite conclusion (as urged by Advocate General Maduro in his opinion), tactical migrations of a company's centre of main interests would have been more easily facilitated.

[74]   Case C–341/04 [2006] ECR I–3813.

[75]   Case C–341/04 [2006] ECR I–3813, para 54.

[76]   See G Moss, 'When is a Proceeding Opened' (2008) 21 *Insolv Int* 33; J Garašić, 'What is Right and What is Wrong in the ECJ's Judgment on *Eurofood IFSC Ltd*' (2006) 8 *Yearbook of Private International Law* 87, 96–101. Other criticisms are that the decision undermines the utility of the third subparagraph of Art 25(1) which accords automatic recognition and enforcement upon preservation measures and favours Member States whose systems provide for provisional orders.

[77]   4 July 2002, High Court (ChD) (Lightman J). No judgment was given but the case is noted in I Fletcher, *Insolvency in Private International Law* (Oxford, OUP, 2nd edn, 2005) 381.

administration order in relation to a company which had been incorporated in Spain but which had its centre of main interests in England.

17.2.17 The fact that the company has been incorporated in a third state also does not matter so long as its centre of main interests is located in England. In *Re BRAC Rent-A-Car International Inc*,[78] the English court held that it had jurisdiction under Article 3(1) of the Regulation when a petition was made for an administration order in relation to a company which was incorporated and had its registered address in the United States but which conducted its operations almost entirely in the United Kingdom. To do otherwise would have provided an incentive for forum shopping and manipulation whereby a company may strategically be incorporated outside the European Union but has its business assets and operates within the European Union.[79]

17.2.18 Thus it is clear that so long as the debtor's centre of main interests is situated in the United Kingdom, the fact that it has been incorporated in another EU Member State or in a third state does not preclude the operation of the Regulation. As mentioned above, Denmark will be regarded as a third state for the purposes of the Regulation; accordingly, the English court has to apply its own private international rules to a debtor whose centre of main interests is located in Denmark.[80]

PROBLEMS WITH THE CONCEPT OF 'CENTRE OF MAIN INTERESTS': *EUROFOOD IFSC*[81]

17.2.19 The lack of a concrete definition of 'centre of main interests' raises at least a couple of questions, both of which were dealt with, amongst other issues, by the Court of Justice in *Eurofood IFSC*.[82] First, how strong is the presumption set out in Article 3(1) that the centre of main interests of a company correlates with the place of the company's registered office? In the particular context of the *Eurofood* case, a parent–subsidiary relationship was involved and the issue was whether the centre of main interests for the parent was the centre of main interests for the subsidiary. Secondly, what if more than one court identifies the centre of the debtor's main interests as being situated within its territory?

17.2.20 Eurofood was registered in Ireland and was a subsidiary of Parmalat SpA, a company incorporated in Italy. Both the Irish and the Italian courts claimed international jurisdiction on the basis that Eurofood's centre of main interests was within their respective territories. The Irish proceedings had been commenced first by the appointment of a provisional liquidator by the Irish High Court, though no finding of insolvency was made at that time. Next, the District Court of Parma decided that it had international jurisdiction under the Regulation. Thereafter, the Irish

---

[78] [2003] 1 WLR 1421.

[79] [2003] 1 WLR 1421, 1427.

[80] *Arena Corporation Ltd (In Provisional Liquidation) v Customs and Excise Commissioners* [2004] BPIR 375 (Lawrence Collins J); [2004] BPIR 415 (CA). The ingenious argument made there was that the term 'Member State' is not defined in the Regulation and Denmark is an EU Member State. At first instance, Lawrence Collins J rightly rejected this argument by pointing out that Denmark did not opt into the Regulation and that therefore the term 'Member State' for the purposes of the Regulation must be interpreted as excluding Denmark; otherwise 'Denmark would have all the benefit of the Council Regulation without any of its burden': [2004] BPIR 375, 385 (at [46]).

[81] Case C–341/04 [2006] ECR I–3813. G Moss, (2006) 19 *Insolv Intel* 97; J Armour, [2006] *CLJ* 505; J Garašić, (2006) 8 *Yearbook of Private International Law* 87.

[82] Case C–341/04 [2006] ECR I–3813.

High Court determined that the centre of Eurofood's main interests was in Ireland and that Eurofood was insolvent. Under Irish law, the insolvency proceedings were taken to have been opened in Ireland on the date when the provisional liquidator was appointed. On appeal by the Italian administrator, the Irish Supreme Court referred a number of questions to the Court of Justice.

17.2.21   Eurofood regularly conducted the administration of its interests in Ireland but Parmalat had the power to appoint Eurofood's directors and control its policy. The Court of Justice therefore had to consider how a parent–subsidiary relationship might affect where the subsidiary's centre of main interests lies. On this point, the Court of Justice held that 'reference to criteria that are both objective and ascertainable by third parties' was paramount when identifying the centre of main interests 'in order to ensure legal certainty and foreseeability'.[83] Therefore, the presumption that the centre of main interests is the place of registration 'can be rebutted only if factors which are both objective and ascertainable by third parties enable it to be established that an actual situation exists which is different from that which locating it at that registered office is deemed to reflect'.[84] The mere fact that the subsidiary's economic choices are or can be controlled by a parent company in another Member State was not enough to rebut the presumption.[85] An example given of when the presumption may be rebutted was the case of a 'letterbox' company which does not carry out any business in the territory of the Member State in which its registered office is located.[86]

17.2.22   It is unclear whether the last proposition still stands if the company or legal person carries out minimal activity in the Member State in which the registered office is located and the greater part of its activities take place in another Member State. It might be that one would need to differentiate between different types of activities. Given the Court of Justice's emphasis on ascertainability by third parties, it appears sensible to focus on evidence of economic rather than management activity to bolster the presumption. Emphasising management activity may assist forum shopping[87] as it would be easier to transfer management rather than economic activity from one Member State to another.[88]

17.2.23   The Regulation does not contain rules that are specifically tailored to groups of companies.[89] This leads to the problem that arose in *Eurofood*, that is, more than one court claiming international jurisdiction under the Regulation in an insolvency concerning a group of companies. On this problem, the Court of Justice emphasised the 'principle of mutual trust', which underpins the Regulation.[90] This principle means that once main insolvency proceedings have been opened in one Member State, the courts of other Member States must recognise that decision without being able to review the basis on which the first court assumed jurisdiction.[91]

---

[83] Case C–341/04 [2006] ECR I–3813, para 33.
[84] Case C–341/04 [2006] ECR I–3813, para 34.
[85] Case C–341/04 [2006] ECR I–3813, para 36.
[86] Case C–341/04 [2006] ECR I–3813, para 35.
[87] See paras 17.2.28–17.2.29.
[88] J Garašić, 'What is Right and What is Wrong in the ECJ's Judgment on *Eurofood IFSC Ltd*' (2006) 8 *Yearbook of Private International Law* 87, 93.
[89] See paras 17.2.25–17.2.27.
[90] See Recital 22.
[91] Case C–341/04 [2006] ECR I–3813, para 42.

Any challenge to the first court's jurisdiction must be made before that court itself.[92] This approach echoes the one taken with respect to the Brussels I Regulation.

CONCLUSION ON 'CENTRE OF MAIN INTERESTS'

17.2.24 The concept of centre of main interests lies at the heart of the Regulation. In *Eurofood IFSC*, the Court of Justice sought to clarify some of the uncertainties surrounding this concept. However, the inherent malleability of the concept inevitably means that there will always be some uncertainty over its application and some ambiguity over where a debtor's centre of main interests truly lies. This might be exploited in various ways. For example, there might be a race to open main insolvency proceedings in a favourable forum to pre-empt the opening of proceedings elsewhere. The extended concept of when proceedings have been opened as approved in *Eurofood* also raises problematic issues. In addition, there is no verdict yet on whether a tactical move of a debtor's centre of main interests prior to the opening of insolvency proceedings is valid. Furthermore, the concept raises serious problems in the context of group insolvencies where principle and pragmatism may collide. However, defenders of the concept could well argue that its adoption renders forum shopping more difficult. These last two issues are examined further below.

Group Insolvencies

17.2.25 An insolvent company which is part of a group of affiliated companies will frequently cause a 'domino effect' leading to the insolvencies of other group members. It has been alleged that group-related cases account for 99 out of 100 cases of cross-border insolvencies.[93] From this perspective, one of the biggest problems with the Regulation is that it offers no rule for insolvencies involving groups of affiliated companies.[94] The Regulation adheres to the principle of 'one company, one insolvency, one proceeding'.[95] Each company within an affiliated group is treated as a legal entity of its own.[96] Thus, there can be as many main proceedings as there are subsidiary companies in different Member States in an affiliated group of companies.

---

[92] Case C–341/04 [2006] ECR I–3813, para 43.

[93] C Paulus, 'A Vision of the European Insolvency Law' (2008) 17 *Norton J of Bankruptcy Law & Practice* 607, 610.

[94] Conceded in the Virgos-Schmit Report, para 76. Suggestions on how group insolvencies should be dealt with can be found in, eg: C Paulus, 'Group Insolvencies—Some Thoughts About New Approaches' (2006/07) 42 *Texas Int LJ* 819, 825–30; I Mevorach, 'The Road to a Suitable and Comprehensive Global Approach to Insolvencies Within Multinational Corporate Groups' (2006) 15 *Norton J of Bankruptcy Law and Practice* 455; I Mevorach, 'The "Home Country" of a Multinational Enterprise Group Facing Insolvency' (2008) 57 *ICLQ* 427. The UNCITRAL Model Law on Cross-Border Insolvency also does not have a separate rule dealing with group insolvencies although there are plans to come up with such a rule. For a brief general comparison between the UNCITRAL Model Law, the EC Insolvency Regulation, and English rules falling outside these two instruments, see section 19.7.

[95] C Paulus, 'Group Insolvencies—Some Thoughts About New Approaches' (2006/07) 42 *Texas Int LJ* 819, 820.

[96] See, eg, *Telia AB v Hilcourt (Docklands) Ltd* [2003] BCC 856, where the English court decided that the presence of a subsidiary in England did not amount to an 'establishment' of the parent company, which would have entitled the English court to open secondary proceedings against the parent company.

17.2.26 Having separate main proceedings for each subsidiary in a different Member State is 'wasteful, duplicative, expensive, and likely to impede a rescue, reconstruction, or beneficial realization of the business of the group'.[97] The English courts have tried to tackle this potential problem by taking what some might call an inventive approach in identifying where a subsidiary's centre of main interests lies. It has been held that the centre of main interests of French and German companies was located in England where the English holding company managed and co-ordinated the operations of the companies within the European sub-group.[98] Despite an initial uproar over what was perceived to be an overly imperialistic attitude by the English courts, other Member State courts have followed this 'head-office functions'[99] approach to reach the conclusion that the centres of main interests of affiliated companies are located within one Member State.[100] The advantage of centralising insolvency proceedings for groups within one jurisdiction is obvious: it allows the crafting of a coherent insolvency regime for the group of companies as a whole, which is especially crucial for a group which functions as an integrated economic unit; moreover, the liquidator or administrator does not have to worry about insolvency proceedings being opened in other jurisdictions which could jeopardise liquidation or rescue plans.[101] This advantage is clearly illustrated in *Re Collins & Aikman Europe SA*[102] where, subject to some minor exceptions, administrators in charge of the English main proceedings managed to avoid the opening of secondary proceedings by promising the local creditors that they would respect their financial positions under the relevant local laws as far as

---

[97] G Moss, 'Group Insolvency—Choice of Forum and Law: The European Experience Under the Influence of English Pragmatism' (2006/07) 32 *Brooklyn J Int Law* 1005, 1008.

[98] *Re Daisytek-ISA Ltd* [2003] BCC 562. See also *Crisscross Telecommunications Group*, Chancery Division, 20 May 2003, unreported; *Aim Underwriting Agencies (Ireland) Ltd* [2005] ILPr 254; *Re Parkside Flexibles SA* [2006] BCC 589; *Re Sendo Ltd* [2006] 1 BCLC 395; *Re Lennox Holdings Plc* [2009] BCC 155. Cf *Re Stanford International Bank Ltd (In Receivership)* [2009] BPIR 1157, 1174 (at [61]).

[99] This concept is referred to in the opinion of Advocate General Jacobs in Case C–341/04 *Eurofood IFSC* [2006] ECR I–3813, para 111: 'The focus must be on the head office functions rather than simply on the location of the head office because a head office can be just as nominal as a registered office if head office functions are not carried out there.' According to the Commercial Court of Nanterre, factors to be considered under the 'head office functions' approach include: the place of meetings of the board of directors, the law governing the main contracts, the location of the business relations with clients, the location where the commercial policy of the group is defined, the existence of a prior authorisation of the parent company to enter into certain financial arrangements, the location of creditors and the centralised management of the purchasing policy, of the staff, of the accounts and of the computing systems: *MPOTEC GmbH* [2006] BCC 681, 687.

[100] Eg, *Hettlage AG* Amtsgericht München [AG] 4 May 2004, ZIP 20/2004, 962 (FRG); *Parmalat Group* Municipal Court of Fejer/Szeeksfehervar (Hung.); *MTOPEC GmbH* [2006] BCC 681 (Commercial Court of Nanterre, 15 February 2006); *Eurotunnel Finance Ltd* (Paris Commercial Court, 2 August 2006). These cases are briefly described in G Moss, 'Group Insolvency—Choice of Forum and Law: The European Experience Under the Influence of English Pragmatism' (2006/07) 32 *Brooklyn J Int Law* 1005, 1012–13. See also *Re Energotech Sarl* [2007] BCC 123 (Court of First Instance, Lure).

[101] See *Re Nortel Networks SA and Others* [2009] ILPr 722, where English administration constituted the main insolvency proceedings of a number of companies in the Nortel group of companies. The court authorised the sending of appropriate letters of request to the judicial authorities of other states in which the parent company had subsidiaries for the joint administrators to be notified of any request to open secondary proceedings in those states and the opportunity to be heard on any such application; the joint administrators wished to avoid the opening of secondary insolvency proceedings which would have impeded the planned global restructuring of the Nortel group.

[102] [2006] BCC 606.

possible. The joint administration resulted in a significantly higher than expected sale price for the group business.

17.2.27   However, the pragmatic approach pioneered by English courts towards group insolvencies received a setback in the Court of Justice's decision in *Eurofood*.[103] The Court of Justice's insistence that where a subsidiary carries on business in the territory of the Member State in which its registered office is situated, this means, more often than not, that the presumption that the subsidiary's centre of main interests is located within that Member State (notwithstanding the abrogation of control of some of its activities to a parent company situated in another Member State) would stand. Given the higher threshold required to rebut the presumption under *Eurofood*, it is unclear whether, in the aftermath of the *Eurofood* case, Member State courts are still able to engage in resourceful interpretations of what 'centre of main interests' means in order to achieve a pragmatic result in cross-border group insolvencies. Indications are that the courts would probably not do so.[104] In *BenQ Holding BV*, Amsterdam and Munich courts strictly followed the decision in *Eurofood*.[105] The court in Amsterdam stated that the presumption set out in Article 3(1) can be rebutted 'only if no or hardly any activities are conducted in the country where the registered office is situated'.[106] Hopefully the Court of Justice will soon have an opportunity to clarify whether this decision reflects a misplaced deference to the *dictum* in *Eurofood*.

Forum Shopping

17.2.28   Some commentators question whether forum shopping should be considered to be such an evil in international insolvencies; it has been argued that it can be beneficial for both the debtor and its creditors.[107] Nevertheless, the Regulation aims to prevent forum shopping[108] and the Regulation's adoption of the centre of main interests concept by itself renders forum shopping more difficult. For example, it would seem to require considerable expense and effort for a company to shift its centre of main interests,[109] especially if economic rather than management activities provide the indicator of the centre of main interests. Although the Court of Justice has yet

---

[103]   Case C–341/04 [2006] ECR I–3813. Most of the cases which applied the 'head-office functions' concept were decided before *Eurofood IFSC*. In *Re Stanford International Bank Ltd (In Receivership)* [2009] BPIR 1157, 1174 (at [61]), Lewison J considered that he had been wrong to apply the 'head office functions' test in *Re Lennox Holdings Plc* [2009] BCC 155 as '[p]re-*Eurofood* decisions by English courts should no longer be followed' in determining the centre of main interests.

[104]   Whether they *may* do so is another issue.

[105]   J Sarra, 'Maidum's Challenge, Legal and Governance Issues in Dealing with Cross-Border Business Enterprise Group Insolvencies' (2008) 17 *Int Insolv Rev* 73, 112–14; C Paulus, 'The Aftermath of "Eurofood"—BenQ Holding BV and the Deficiencies of the ECJ Decision' (2007) 20 *Insolv Int* 85, 85–7.

[106]   [2008] BCC 489, 495. C Paulus, 'The Aftermath of "Eurofood"—BenQ Holding BV and the Deficiencies of the ECJ Decision' (2007) 20 *Insolv Int* 85, 86. See also *Re Stanford International Bank Ltd (In Receivership)* [2009] BPIR 1157.

[107]   W-G Ringe, 'Forum Shopping under the EU Insolvency Regulation' (2008) 9 *European Business Organisation Law Review* 579.

[108]   Recital 4; Case C–1/04 *Staubitz-Schreiber* [2006] ECR I–701, para 25.

[109]   J Pottow, 'The Myth (and Realities) of Forum Shopping in Transnational Insolvency' (2006/07) 32 *Brooklyn J Int Law* 785, 797–8. However, the implementation of Dir 2005/56/EC on cross-border mergers of limited liability companies [2005] OJ L310/1 (implemented in the United Kingdom by the Companies (Cross-Border Mergers) Regs 2007, SI 2007/2974) may make the transfer of a company's centre of main

to pronounce on the situation where a debtor has strategically moved his centre of main interests prior to the opening of insolvency proceedings, anything other than a legitimate shift which satisfies the criterion of ascertainability by third parties would be unlikely to suffice.[110]

17.2.29   It should be noted that jurisdictional competence under the Regulation does not depend on the presence of the debtor's assets within jurisdiction. This goes towards mitigating forum shopping. A debtor cannot escape insolvency proceedings being conducted in a particular Member State by moving highly liquid and mobile assets (such as money held in bank accounts by electronic transfer) from a less favourable jurisdiction to a more favourable one just prior to the opening of insolvency proceedings.[111]

Territorial Proceedings

17.2.30   If the debtor's centre of main interests is situated within the territory of a Member State, Article 3(2) allows proceedings to be opened in other Member States in which the debtor has an establishment. The effects of these proceedings are confined to assets of the debtor situated within the jurisdiction of the forum in which the proceedings under Article 3(2) take place.[112] These territorial insolvency proceedings can be divided into two types: 'secondary proceedings' and 'independent proceedings'.

17.2.31   Article 3(2) was one of the most debated provisions of the Convention from which the Regulation is derived.[113] The idea of basing the opening of insolvency proceedings on the presence of the debtor's assets within the jurisdiction was also mooted but in the end rejected in favour of basing jurisdiction solely on whether the debtor has a place of 'establishment' within the jurisdiction.[114]

17.2.32   'Establishment' refers to 'any place of operations where the debtor carries out a non-transitory economic activity with human means and goods'.[115] The phrase 'with human means' suggests that at least one other person apart from the debtor must

---

interests easier. See W-G Ringe, 'Forum Shopping under the EU Insolvency Regulation' (2008) 9 *European Business Organisation Law Review* 579, 592–3.

[110] See *Hans Brochier Holdings Ltd v Exner* [2007] BCC 127; *Re TXU Europe German Finance BV* [2005] BCC 90, para 19; *Re Ci4net.com Inc* [2005] BCC 277. Cf the successful transfer of the centre of main interests by the German companies Schefenacker and Deutsche Nickel to England to benefit from the more favourable English insolvency laws, described in W-G Ringe, 'Forum Shopping under the EU Insolvency Regulation' (2008) 9 *European Business Organisation Law Review* 579, 585–7.

[111] However, as J Pottow points out, whilst territorialism may affect those assets which have been moved out to a more favourable jurisdiction, universalism would affect *all* assets if the debtor's centre of main interests is successfully shifted: 'The Myth (and Realities) of Forum Shopping in Transnational Insolvency' (2006/07) 32 *Brooklyn J Int Law* 785, 813.

[112] The Virgos-Schmit Report, however, envisages that the secondary liquidator would have to act extraterritorially in certain circumstances; eg, to recover an asset moved outside the jurisdiction after the opening of the secondary proceedings or in fraud against the creditors of the secondary proceedings: para 224.

[113] Virgos-Schmit Report, para 70.

[114] The concern about allowing asset-based jurisdiction was that there would be a rapid increase in the number of small bankruptcies in the jurisdiction where the debtor had real estate, bank accounts or gold deposits: M Balz, 'The European Union Convention on Insolvency Proceedings' (1996) 70 *Am Bank LJ* 485, 505.

[115] Art 2(h).

be involved.[116] The Virgos-Schmit Report further explains that 'place of operations' means a place from where commercial, industrial or professional economic activities are exercised externally on the market.[117]

17.2.33   In *Shierson v Vlieland-Boddy*,[118] the Court of Appeal held that a debtor had an 'establishment' in England when a nominee company carried out the activity of letting and managing English property owned by the debtor in circumstances where the debtor was suspected to have some sort of involvement in the nominee company.[119] In addition, there needs to be a minimal level of organisation as a purely occasional place of operations cannot be classified as an 'establishment' and what is decisive is how the activity appears externally, rather than the subjective intention of the debtor.[120]

17.2.34   Despite the attempts of the Regulation and the Virgos-Schmit Report, the concept of 'establishment' is still rather elusive. The 'very open definition'[121] has been criticised,[122] but is most probably the result of the need to appease those who favoured also allowing asset-based proceedings. It has been argued that the present tense used in the relevant provisions indicates that the debtor's place of establishment must be currently operational in order for secondary proceedings to be opened[123] but this issue has yet to be addressed by the Court of Justice.

17.2.35   In addition to criticisms about the elusive nature of 'establishment', the scheme of allowing simultaneous insolvency proceedings in different Member States has raised concerns. One concern is that it could 'render the main proceedings meaningless in economic terms'.[124] Given that the EU countries form a single market, it has been argued that the principle of universality should prevail and that the Regulation should only allow a single insolvency proceeding.[125]

17.2.36   That said, there are several reasons in favour of the 'mitigated universality' scheme adopted by the Regulation. First, local creditors will be in the same legal position as in domestic proceedings even though the debtor's centre of main interests may be located in another Member State.[126] Thus, entitlement to dividends

---

[116] *Re Stojevic*, Vienna Higher Regional Council (Oberlandsgericht Wien), 17 November, 2004; G Moss, 'A Very Peculiar "Establishment"' (2006) 19 *Insolv Int* 20, 23. In *BenQ Holdings NV* Docket No 1503 IE 4371/06 Munich, 5 February, 2007, the Munich Court held that 'human means' does not just mean a company's own employees, but also includes persons engaged under business or agency agreements to act on the company's behalf with regard to third parties. See J Sarra, 'Maidum's Challenge, Legal and Governance Issues in Dealing with Cross-Border Business Enterprise Group Insolvencies' (2008) 17 *Int Insolv Rev* 73, 114.

[117] Para 71.

[118] [2005] 1 WLR 3966.

[119] This decision has been criticised; see G Moss, 'A Very Peculiar "Establishment"' (2006) 19 *Insolv Int* 20.

[120] Virgos-Schmit Report, para 71.

[121] As acknowledged by the Virgos-Schmit Report, para 70.

[122] Eg, CGJ Morse, 'Cross-Border Insolvency in the European Union' in J Zekoll and P Borchers (eds), *International Conflict of Laws for the Third Millennium: Essays in Honor of Friedrick K Juenger* (Ardsley NY, Transnational Publishers, 2001) 244.

[123] I Fletcher, 'A Culling of Sacred Cows—The Impact of the EC Insolvency Regulation on English Conflict of Laws' in JJ Fawcett, *Reform and Development of Private International Law: Essays in Honour of Sir Peter North* (Oxford, OUP, 2002) 178–80; I Fletcher, *Insolvency in Private International Law* (Oxford, OUP, 2nd edn, 2005) 377.

[124] EESC Opinion, para 3.4.4.

[125] EESC Opinion, para 3.4.2.

[126] Virgos-Schmit Report, para 32.

that can be satisfied out of local assets and priority are protected through territorial proceedings.[127] Local creditors will also not be liable for the additional costs that may be incurred from their claims having to be lodged in foreign proceedings.[128] All this serves to protect local interests. Secondly, territorial proceedings supplement the main proceedings. Thus, the liquidator in the main proceedings has the power[129] to request the opening of secondary proceedings where required for the efficient administration of the estate.[130] This may occur where 'the estate of the debtor is too complex to administer as a unit, where differences in the legal systems concerned are so great that difficulties may arise from the extension of effects deriving from the law of the State of the opening to the other States where the assets are located'.[131] The leeway to open concurrent proceedings reflects the Regulation's desire to maintain a balance between the twin principles of universality and unity, on the one hand, and local interests, on the other.

Secondary Proceedings

17.2.37 If territorial proceedings are opened after the main proceedings, they are called 'secondary proceedings'. Secondary proceedings must be winding-up proceedings.[132] This inflexible rule could jeopardise rescue and rehabilitation plans in the main proceedings.[133] At the same time, co-ordination between main proceedings and secondary rehabilitation proceedings could prove to be too complicated.[134]

17.2.38 'Winding-up proceedings' is defined in Article 2(c) as insolvency proceedings 'involving realising the assets of the debtor, including where the proceedings have been closed by a composition or other measure terminating the insolvency, or closed by reason of the insufficiency of the assets'. For the purposes of the United Kingdom, winding-up proceedings referred to in Article 2(c) are winding-up by or subject to the supervision of the court, winding-up through administration including appointments made by filing prescribed documents with the court,[135] creditors' voluntary winding-up (with confirmation by the court) and bankruptcy or sequestration.[136]

---

[127] I Fletcher, 'The European Union Convention on Insolvency Proceedings: An Overview and Comment, with US Interest in Mind' (1997/98) *Brooklyn J Int L* 25, 42–3.

[128] European Parliament, Report on the proposal for a Council regulation on insolvency proceedings, 23 February 2000, A5-39/2000, 14; M Balz, 'The European Union Convention on Insolvency Proceedings' (1996) 70 *Am Bank LJ* 485, 520.

[129] Art 29.

[130] Virgos-Schmit Report, para 33.

[131] Recital 19; Virgos-Schmit Report, para 33.

[132] Art 3(3).

[133] I Fletcher, 'The European Union Convention on Insolvency Proceedings: An Overview and Comment, with US Interest in Mind' (1997) 23 *Brooklyn J Int Law* 25, 42; G McCormack, 'Jurisdictional Competition and Forum Shopping in Insolvency Proceedings' [2009] *CLJ* 169, 195.

[134] Virgos-Schmit Report, para 221. It was also said to be difficult to conceive of an establishment dependent on a debtor proved to be insolvent at the centre of his main interests being separately the subject of reorganisation: Virgos-Schmit Report, para 221. The problems that would arise if secondary rehabilitation proceedings were allowed in tandem with main liquidation or main rehabilitation proceedings are set out in greater detail in M Balz, 'The European Union Convention on Insolvency Proceedings' (1996) 70 *Am Bank LJ* 485, 498–501.

[135] This was inserted by Reg (EC) 603/2005, [2005] OJ L100/1, and came into effect on 21 April 2005.

[136] Annex B.

CO-ORDINATION BETWEEN MAIN AND SECONDARY PROCEEDINGS

17.2.39 Secondary proceedings are subordinate to main proceedings. The liquidator in the main proceedings has the right to request the opening of secondary proceedings, as does any other person or authority empowered to request the opening of insolvency proceedings under the law of the Member State within the territory in which the opening of secondary proceedings is requested.[137]

17.2.40 Given that secondary proceedings must be winding-up proceedings, a concern is that the opening of secondary proceedings may jeopardise reorganisation plans in the main proceedings. Therefore, one important power in the hands of the liquidator in the main proceedings is that he can request that the court which opened the secondary proceedings temporarily stay such proceedings.[138] The main liquidator could thereby 'buy time' and negotiate a settlement with the creditors of the secondary proceedings which may then allow the removal of assets from the secondary forum to the main forum,[139] or a preservation of the assets with a view to a sale or with a view to a composition undertaken via main proceedings.[140]

17.2.41 The court in which secondary proceedings have been opened can reject the request for a stay only if it is manifestly of no interest to the creditors in the main proceedings.[141] If the stay is granted, some protection to creditors involved in the secondary proceedings is provided as the court can require the liquidator in the main proceedings to take any suitable measure to guarantee the interests of the creditors in the secondary proceedings and of individual classes of creditors.[142]

17.2.42 Similarly, to minimise any disruption that may be caused by secondary proceedings to the aim pursued by main proceedings, the liquidator in the main proceedings is empowered to suggest the closure of secondary proceedings without liquidation by a rescue plan, a composition or a comparable measure where this is allowed by the law applicable to the secondary proceedings.[143] Any measures agreed upon by creditors in the secondary proceedings need to be approved by the liquidator in the main proceedings in order to safeguard the rights of the general body of creditors; if his approval is not forthcoming, the measures may become final if the financial interests of the creditors in the main proceedings are not affected.[144] Measures agreed upon in the secondary proceedings can affect the debtor's assets which are located abroad only if the consent of all the creditors having an interest affected by the measure give their consent.[145] In the event of a stay of the process of liquidation in secondary proceedings, only a composition that is proposed by the liquidator in the main proceedings or the debtor with the former's consent may be put forward;[146] this

---

[137] Art 29.
[138] Art 33(1).
[139] M Balz, 'The European Union Convention on Insolvency Proceedings' (1996) 70 *Am Bank LJ* 485, 526.
[140] Virgos-Schmit Report, para 243.
[141] Art 33(1). Such stays may be ordered for up to three months and renewed for similar periods. Art 33(2) provides that the court shall terminate the stay upon request of either (i) the liquidator in the main proceedings; or (ii) a creditor or the liquidator in the secondary proceedings if the stay no longer appears justified.
[142] Art 33(1).
[143] Art 34(1).
[144] Art 34(1), second subparagraph.
[145] Art 34(2).
[146] Art 34(3).

is to safeguard the interests of creditors for whose benefit the stay was granted in the first place.[147]

17.2.43   A creditor may lodge his claim in the main proceedings or in any secondary proceedings;[148] this means that local proceedings are not solely for local creditors. Creditors who lodge claims in more than one proceeding cannot recover twice over.[149] To ensure that all creditors are treated fairly, a creditor who has obtained a dividend on his claim in an insolvency proceeding can only share in distributions made in other proceedings where creditors of the same ranking or category have obtained an equivalent dividend in those other proceedings.[150]

17.2.44   To facilitate the exercise of creditors' rights and to allow liquidators to reinforce their influence in other proceedings,[151] liquidators shall lodge in other proceedings claims which have already been lodged in the proceedings for which they were appointed when the interests of creditors in the latter proceedings are served.[152] This is, however, subject to the right of creditors generally to withdraw their claims where the law applicable to the proceedings in which the claim is presented so allows; creditors may wish to exercise this right if they run the risk of incurring additional costs.[153]

17.2.45   In order to ensure efficiency and the proper functioning of the internal market,[154] liquidators in the main and secondary proceedings are duty bound to co-operate with each other and communicate information which may be relevant to the other proceedings.[155] Such information may include information about the assets, actions planned or under way in order to recover assets, ranking of creditors and proposed compositions.[156] In the event that some assets remain after the secondary proceedings have been wrapped up, those assets shall be transferred to the liquidator in the main proceedings.[157] The imposition of the duties of co-operation and the communication of information is an attempt to deal with the problem of co-ordinating different proceedings in different jurisdictions. That said, the Regulation does not provide for the imposition of sanctions if the duties of co-operation and the communication of information are not fulfilled. However, the *lex concursus* should step in and the problem is mitigated if the *lex concursus* of the Member State under which the particular liquidator who has not fulfilled these duties has been appointed provides for sanctions to be imposed.[158]

---

[147] Virgos-Schmit Report, para 251.
[148] Art 32(1).
[149] Art 20(1). See further paras 17.5.1–17.5.2
[150] Art 20(2).
[151] Virgos-Schmit Report, para 236.
[152] Art 32(2).
[153] Virgos-Schmit Report, para 239.
[154] Recital 2.
[155] Art 31(1) and (2). The duty of co-operation set out in Art 31 may be framed in terms of co-operation between the insolvency officeholders, but has been held to extend to courts too; see *Re Nortel Networks SA and Others* [2009] ILPr 722, 725 (at [11]) (citing the Vienna Higher Regional Court in *Re Stojevic* (9 Nov 2004, 28 R 225/04w).
[156] For further examples, see Virgos-Schmit Report, para 230.
[157] Art 35.
[158] G Moss, T Smith *et al*, 'Commentary on Council Regulation 1346/2000 on Insolvency Proceedings' in G Moss, I Fletcher and S Isaacs (eds), *The EC Regulation on Insolvency Proceedings: A Commentary and Annotated Guide* (Oxford, OUP, 2002) 219.

17.2.46 Lastly, it should be noted that a temporary administrator that has been appointed by the court of the Member State in which main proceedings have been opened shall be empowered to request any preservation measures necessary to secure any of the debtor's assets situated in another Member State.[159] This is to ensure that, between the date on which the request to open proceedings and the date on which the judgment opening the proceedings is made, assets of the debtor are not moved around to the detriment of the creditors.[160]

Independent Territorial Proceedings

17.2.47 Territorial proceedings may be opened prior to, or even without, main proceedings being conducted in the Member State in which the debtor has his centre of main interests. These proceedings are termed 'independent territorial proceedings'. Article 3(4) sets out that independent territorial proceedings can be opened only where main insolvency proceedings cannot be opened because of the conditions laid down by the law of the Member State within the territory of which the centre of the debtor's main interests is situated or where there is a request for the opening of territorial proceedings by a creditor who has his domicile, habitual residence or registered office in the Member State within the territory of which the establishment is situated, or whose claim arises from the operation of that establishment.

17.2.48 Independent territorial proceedings need not, like secondary proceedings, be winding-up proceedings but must be proceedings that are listed in Annex A.[161] However, if main proceedings are subsequently opened in another Member State, it is unclear whether independent proceedings will necessarily be converted into secondary proceedings.[162] Recital 17 envisages that this will be so but the Virgos-Schmit Report does not maintain a consistent line on this.[163] The provisions of the Regulation merely provide that, where main proceedings are subsequently opened, Articles 31 to 35, which cover secondary proceedings, shall apply to independent territorial proceedings in so far as the progress of those proceedings so permits[164] and that the liquidator in the main proceedings could request for the conversion of independent proceedings into winding-up proceedings if this is in the interests of the creditors in the main proceedings.[165] However, no provision in the Regulation dictates that such a conversion must necessarily occur—although it is clear that independent territorial proceedings will become subordinate to the main proceedings once the latter are opened.

17.2.49 If independent territorial proceedings are opened in more than one Member State without any main proceedings, the same rules which serve to coordinate secondary proceedings should apply by analogy to coordinate the parallel independent territorial proceedings.[166]

---

[159] Art 38.
[160] Virgos-Schmit Report, para 262.
[161] And if they are not proceedings which are listed in Annex A, they will be outside the Regulation.
[162] And thereby converted into winding-up proceedings if the independent territorial proceedings were rehabilitation proceedings in the first place.
[163] Eg, compare paras 31, 37, 84 and 259 with paras 86 and 254.
[164] Art 36.
[165] Art 37.
[166] Virgos-Schmit Report, para 39.

17.3 CHOICE OF LAW

General Rule

17.3.1   The general principle is that the law of the state of the opening of proceedings, that is, the *lex concursus*, governs the conditions for the opening of insolvency proceedings, their conduct and closure.[167] This is the position for both main proceedings and territorial proceedings.[168] Reference to the *lex concursus* is to be taken as reference to the domestic law of the *lex concursus*.[169] In other words, *renvoi* is excluded. Although the Regulation does not explicitly set this out, there is no policy reason why the complexities of *renvoi* should be assumed to be part of the scheme of the Regulation.[170]

17.3.2   Article 4(2) sets out a non-exhaustive list of issues which are governed by the *lex concursus*. That law determines in particular:

(a) against which debtors insolvency proceedings may be brought on account of their capacity;

(b) the assets which form part of the estate and the treatment of assets acquired by or devolving on the debtor after the opening of the insolvency proceedings;

(c) the respective powers of the debtor and the liquidator;

(d) the conditions under which set-offs may be invoked;

(e) the effects of insolvency proceedings on current contracts to which the debtor is party;

(f) the effects of insolvency proceedings on proceedings brought by individual creditors, with the exception of lawsuits pending;

(g) the claims which are to be lodged against the debtor's estate and the treatment of claims arising after the opening of insolvency proceedings;

(h) the rules governing the lodging, verification and admission of claims;

(i) the rules governing the distribution of proceeds from the realization of assets, the ranking of claims and the rights of creditors who have obtained partial satisfaction after the opening of insolvency proceedings by virtue of a right in rem or through a set-off;

(j) the conditions for and the effects of closure of insolvency proceedings, in particular by composition;

(k) creditors' rights after the closure of insolvency proceedings;

(l) who is to bear the costs and expenses incurred in the insolvency proceedings;

(m) the rules relating to the voidness, voidability or unenforceability of legal acts detrimental to all the creditors.

17.3.3   This list is generally self-explanatory. One thing should be pointed out, however. Although a debtor's obligations may be governed by the applicable law of the contract if those obligations arose under that contract, Article 4(2)(m) provides that it is the *lex concursus* and not the applicable law of the contract which determines the discharge of that obligation. This overturns the general principle in contractual conflict of laws rules that a contract's applicable law determines the invalidity or unenforceability of contractual obligations. Article 4(2)(m) also makes clear that the cumulative application of the applicable law of the contract and the *lex concursus* to

---

[167] Art 4(2).
[168] See Art 28, which reiterates the choice of law rule for the *lex concursus* for secondary proceedings.
[169] Virgos-Schmit Report, para 87.
[170] I Fletcher, *Insolvency in Private International Law* (Oxford, OUP, 2nd edn, 2005) 397–8.

the issue of discharge, which is supported by some national laws, is not adopted by the Regulation.[171]

17.3.4 However, Article 13 states that Article 4(2)(m) shall be inapplicable where the person who benefited from an act detrimental to all the creditors provides proof that the said act is subject to the law of a Member State other than that of the state of the opening of proceedings, and that law does not allow any means of challenging that act in the relevant case. The aim of providing this defence against the effects of application of the *lex concursus* is to uphold the legitimate expectations of creditors and third parties.[172] According to the Virgos-Schmit Report, this defence can only be raised with regard to acts done prior to the opening of insolvency proceedings.[173]

Exceptions

17.3.5 A number of derogations have been made to the general rule that the *lex concursus* governs issues arising in insolvency proceedings. These are set out in Articles 5 to 15.

Rights in Rem

17.3.6 Article 5(1) states that:

The opening of insolvency proceedings shall not affect the rights in rem of creditors or third parties in respect of tangible or intangible, movable or immovable assets—both specific assets and collections of indefinite assets as a whole which change from time to time—belonging to the debtor which are situated within the territory of another Member State at the time of the opening of proceedings.

Rights *in rem* play an important role in the granting of credit as holders are protected against the risk of insolvency of the debtor and any intervention of third party rights.[174] The policy underlying Article 5 is therefore to protect the trade in the Member State in which the asset is situated and to preserve legal certainty.[175]

17.3.7 'Rights *in rem*' is not defined in the Regulation; but Article 5(2) provides a list of examples of rights which qualify as rights *in rem*, such as a lien, mortgage and beneficial rights to assets. Characterisation of a right *in rem* should be done by the relevant national laws, usually the *lex situs*.[176] The Virgos-Schmit Report goes on to caution that an unreasonably wide interpretation of the national concept of a right *in rem* will render harmonisation meaningless[177] but accepts that a 'floating charge'

---

[171] M Balz, 'The European Union Convention on Insolvency Proceedings' (1996) 70 *Am Bank LJ* 485, 508; I Fletcher, 'The European Union Convention on Insolvency Proceedings: Choice-of-Law Provisions' (1998) 33 *Texas Int LJ* 119, 128.

[172] Virgos-Schmit Report, para 138.

[173] Para 138.

[174] See Recital 25; Virgos-Schmit Report, para 97.

[175] Virgos-Schmit Report, para 97.

[176] Virgos-Schmit Report, para 100. Cf Brussels I Reg, Art 22(1), discussed in section 5.2.

[177] Virgos-Schmit Report, para 102.

recognised under English law can be characterised as a right *in rem* for the purposes of the Regulation.[178]

17.3.8   Article 5 applies only to rights *in rem* which were created prior to the opening of proceedings, and those rights must be over assets located within another Member State. If the asset is located in a third state, Article 5 is inapplicable and the *lex concursus* will determine the effect to be given to the right *in rem*. The *lex concursus* may also continue to be applicable where the *situs* of a movable asset at the time of creation is where the proceedings are eventually opened and this is different from the *situs* of the asset at the time of the opening of proceedings.[179] Courts of the *situs* may circumvent any tactical relocation of the moveable by referring to Article 5(4), which preserves the application of the *lex concursus* for actions for voidness, voidability or unenforceability as referred to in Article 4(2)(m).

17.3.9   Article 2(g) defines what is meant by 'the Member State in which assets are situated' for tangible property (the Member State within the territory of which the property is located), registrable property (the Member State under the authority of which the public register is kept) and 'claims' by the debtor against a third party (the Member State within the territory of which the third party required to meet them has the centre of his main interests as determined in Article 3(1)). The last of these localising rules has created some uncertainty as to whether the common law rule[180] that, where the debtor is resident in more than one country, a debt is situated at the place where the debt is stipulated to be payable[181] is applicable under the Regulation.[182]

17.3.10   The last point to note is that Article 5 only preserves rights *in rem* over assets located in other Member States; those assets are still subject to the universal effects of main proceedings conducted in the centre of the debtor's main interests. Therefore, a creditor who has satisfied the value of his claim against an asset must relinquish the surplus value of the asset to the debtor's estate.[183] Furthermore, the liquidator in the main proceedings can request for secondary proceedings to be opened where the asset is located if the debtor has an establishment in that Member State.[184]

Set-off

17.3.11   The treatment of set-off varies sharply amongst Member States. English law embraces the concept, whilst civil law systems are generally far less sympathetic.[185] Although Article 4(2)(d) provides that the *lex concursus* determines the conditions under which set-offs may be invoked, this is subject to Article 6(1), which provides: 'The opening of insolvency proceedings shall not affect the right of creditors to

---

[178] Virgos-Schmit Report, para 104.

[179] I Fletcher, 'The European Union Convention on Insolvency Proceedings: Choice-of-Law Provisions' (1998) 33 *Texas Int LJ* 119, 129.

[180] *Kwok Chi Leung Karl v Commissioner of Estate Duty* [1988] 1 WLR 1035 (PC).

[181] If the debtor is resident in one country, the debt will be situated in that country; the debtor's place of residence will generally coincide with the debtor's centre of main interests.

[182] See PStJ Smart, 'Rights In Rem, Article 5 and the EC Insolvency Regulation: An English Perspective' (2006) 15 *Int Insolv Rev* 17, 28–9.

[183] Virgos-Schmit Report, para 99.

[184] Art 29. This may be helpful if the *lex situs* (applicable law of the secondary proceedings) will subject secured creditors to certain restrictions which may help the main liquidator in his administration or rescue efforts.

[185] See I Fletcher, 'The European Union Convention on Insolvency Proceedings: Choice-of-Law Provisions' (1998) 33 *Texas Int LJ* 119, 131.

demand the set-off of their claims against the claims of the debtor, where such a set-off is permitted by the law applicable to the insolvent debtor's claim.'[186] It ought to be noted that Article 6(1) does not require that the law governing the insolvent debtor's claim be the law of a Member State. [187] Thus, where D, the debtor against whom insolvency proceedings have been opened in England, has a claim against C, a creditor, that is governed by Japanese law, C is entitled to demand the set-off of D's claim against him vis-à-vis his claim against D, if this is permitted by Japanese law. English law, the *lex concursus*, will be ousted on this issue.[188] However, Article 6(2) preserves the application of the *lex concursus* in relation to actions for voidness, voidability or unenforceability as referred to in Article 4(2)(m).

Reservation of Title

17.3.12 Reservation of title is treated in a similar manner to rights *in rem* under Article 5. Article 7(1) excludes the operation of the *lex concursus* where insolvency proceedings have been opened against the buyer and the seller retains title to an asset via a reservation of title clause. The seller's rights are not affected. The asset must be situated within the territory of a Member State other than the state of opening of proceedings at the time of opening of proceedings; any subsequent relocation of the asset does not affect the operation of the rule. Article 7(2) deals with the converse scenario where insolvency proceedings have been opened against the seller after delivery of the asset. The buyer is still entitled to pay up and acquire title so long as the assets are situated in a Member State other than the state of the opening of proceedings at the time of the opening of proceedings.[189]

17.3.13 It seems to be assumed that the seller's and buyer's rights in the two situations dealt with in Articles 7(1) and 7(2) respectively are subject to the *lex situs*, although this is not expressly spelled out in the provisions themselves.[190] There may be a role for the applicable law of the contract, though, whether through some sort of consideration by the *lex situs* of the effects of the applicable law of the contract,[191] or perhaps through a two-stage process whereby the *lex situs* decides whether reservation of title clauses are permissible; and if they are, the applicable law of the contract then assesses whether the specific clause is valid.

17.3.14 Article 7 is still subject to actions for voidness, voidability or unenforceability as referred to in Article 4(2)(m).[192]

---

[186] The mutual claims must have arisen prior to the opening of insolvency proceedings: Virgos-Schmit Report, para 110.

[187] Either the Rome I or Rome II Regulation should determine the law applicable to the insolvent debtor's claim against the creditor, depending on the nature of the claim. Both Regulations are universal in scope—in the sense that their application can lead to the law of a non-Member State being the applicable law.

[188] Of course, there is no need for recourse to Art 6 if English law itself allowed the set-off.

[189] Art 7(2) is not a choice of law rule but is a uniform substantive rule: Virgos-Schmit Report, para 112.

[190] L Collins *et al*, *Dicey, Morris and Collins on The Conflict of Laws* (London, Sweet & Maxwell, 14th edn, 2006) para 30–243; I Fletcher, *Insolvency in Private International Law* (Oxford, OUP, 2nd edn, 2005) 413.

[191] I Fletcher, 'Choice of Law Rules' in G Moss, I Fletcher and S Isaacs (eds), *The EC Regulation on Insolvency Proceedings: A Commentary and Annotated Guide* (Oxford, OUP, 2002) 58–9.

[192] Art 7(3).

Contracts Relating to Immovable Property

17.3.15   As mentioned above, the general rule is that the *lex concursus* will determine the effects of the insolvency proceedings on current contracts to which the debtor is party.[193] This may enable the liquidator to decide whether the best course is the fulfilment or termination of executory contracts.

17.3.16   Article 8, however, stipulates that the *lex situs* alone shall govern the effects of insolvency proceedings on a contract conferring the right to acquire or make use of immovable property, such as a contract for the sale, rental or lease of immovable property. Significantly, there is no derogation, as for the previous provisions, in favour of the *lex concursus* in relation to avoidance actions. This follows the general conflicts approach in relation to immovable property and underlines the importance of protecting party expectations and state interests in which the immovable property is located.

Payment Systems and Financial Markets

17.3.17   Payment systems and financial markets concern large-scale transactions which require special rules to ensure their smooth operation.[194] Article 9(1) subjects the effects of insolvency proceedings on the rights and obligations of the parties to a system or market solely to the law of the Member State applicable to that system or market. Article 9(2) bolsters the point by providing that the avoidance rules of the law applicable to the relevant payment system or financial market is applicable, instead of the Regulation's usual reference to the avoidance rules of the *lex concursus*. There is an exception when a right *in rem* of a creditor or third party is involved; this situation is governed by Article 5 and hence the *lex situs* of the asset.[195]

17.3.18   The objective of the rule set out in Article 9 is to preserve confidence in the mechanisms for regulating and settling transactions made in the context of payment systems and financial markets; it would be disastrous if different laws were to apply to mechanisms such as closing out contracts, netting operations or the realisation of securities located in a Member State. Multiple transactions operating within the same framework should also be subject to the same law.[196]

Contracts of Employment

17.3.19   Article 10 provides that the effects of insolvency proceedings on employment contracts and relationships shall be governed solely by the law of the Member State applicable to the contract of employment. The applicable law of the contract of employment would be determined in accordance with the Rome I Regulation.[197]

17.3.20   No role is allocated to the *lex concursus* insofar as the issues raised relate strictly to 'the effects of insolvency proceedings on employment contracts and

---

[193] Art 4(2)(e).
[194] Virgos-Schmit Report, para 120.
[195] Art 9(1).
[196] M Balz, 'The European Union Convention on Insolvency Proceedings' (1996) 70 *Am Bank LJ* 485, 513.
[197] See ch 14.

relationships'. For example, whether contracts of employment will be continued or terminated in the event of insolvency of the employer falls to be determined by the applicable law of the contract of employment.[198] However, the *lex concursus* will be applicable to issues that do not fall within the scope of Article 10, such as whether an employee claim arising out of his employment will be designated as a preferential debt, the amount protected and the priority of the claim.[199]

Effects of Rights Subject to Registration and Protection of Third-party Purchasers

17.3.21   Article 11 states that: 'The effects of insolvency proceedings on the rights of the debtor in immovable property, a ship or an aircraft subject to registration in a public register shall be determined by the law of the Member State under the authority of which the register is kept.'

17.3.22   The Virgos-Schmit Report points out that the word 'solely' is omitted in Article 11 thereby indicating that this exception is more limited than the exceptions contained in Articles 8, 9 and 10. Some sort of role is, therefore, envisaged for the *lex concursus*; 'a sort of cumulative application' of both the *lex concursus* and the law of the Member State under the authority of which the register is kept is said to be 'necessary'.[200] It is unclear exactly how the two laws should interact with each other—although presumably the law of the Member State under the authority of which the register is kept, being the law which is stipulated in the Article itself, would play the dominant role. The Virgos-Schmit Report states that:

the law of the [Member] State of registration will … determine the modifications which, required by the law of the State of the opening, may be prompted by the insolvency proceedings and affect the rights of the debtor over immovable property, ships and aircraft subject to registration, the requisite entries in the register and the consequences thereof. In consequence, the law of the [Member] State of registration decides which effects of the insolvency proceedings are admissible and affect the rights of the debtor subject to registration in that State.[201]

17.3.23   In close connection with Article 11 is Article 14, which deals with the rights of third-party purchasers of an immovable asset, ship or aircraft subject to registration in a public register,[202] or securities whose existence presupposes registration in a register laid down by law. Where the debtor has disposed of such assets for consideration[203] after the opening of insolvency proceedings, Article 14 subjects the validity of the debtor's acts to the law of the state[204] within the territory of which the immovable asset is situated or under the authority of which the register is kept. This protects the purchasers of such assets where the opening of proceedings or

---

[198]   Virgos-Schmit Report, para 125.

[199]   Virgos-Schmit Report, para 128.

[200]   Virgos-Schmit Report, para 130.

[201]   Para 130.

[202]   According to the Virgos-Schmit Report, para 69, 'public register' refers to a register for public access an entry in which binds third parties and need not necessarily be a register kept by a public authority.

[203]   Gratuitous beneficiaries cannot avail themselves of Art 14.

[204]   Note that Art 14 does not refer to the law of a Member State; thus the law of a third country could be applicable.

restrictions on the debtor have not yet been entered into the specific register. It also upholds the integrity of, and public confidence in, property registers.

Community Patents and Trade Marks

17.3.24 Article 12 provides that a Community patent,[205] a Community trade mark or any other similar right established by EU law may only be included in main proceedings opened where the debtor has his centre of main interests in a Member State. This provision replaces the rules found in other European instruments, which generally provide that EU intellectual property rights can only be included in the state in which insolvency proceedings are first opened, irrespective of whether they are main or territorial proceedings.[206] Where the debtor's centre of main interests is situated outside the European Union, the rules contained in the other instruments will prevail.

Effects of Insolvency Proceedings on Lawsuits Pending

17.3.25 While the effects of insolvency on individual enforcement actions[207] are governed by the *lex concursus*,[208] the Regulation supplies a special rule to deal with the effects of insolvency on lawsuits pending in relation to an asset or a right of which the debtor has been divested. This shall be governed 'solely by the law of the Member State in which that lawsuit is pending'. The procedural law of this state shall decide whether the pending lawsuits are to be suspended, how they are to be continued and whether any procedural modifications need to be made to take account of the fact that the debtor has lost or had his powers of disposal and administration restricted and a liquidator has stepped into his place.[209] It should be pointed out that Article 15 does not have general application to pending lawsuits and only applies to pending lawsuits 'concerning an asset or a right of which the debtor has been divested'.[210]

17.3.26 In *Syska v Vivendi Universal SA*,[211] the claimant, a Polish company, was declared to be insolvent in Poland. Prior to the opening of insolvency proceedings, the defendant had advanced breach of contract claims against the claimant in London pursuant to an arbitration agreement governed by English law. However, Polish law had an unusual provision which stipulated that (i) any arbitration clause concluded by the bankrupt shall lose its legal effect as at the date the insolvency is declared and (ii) any pending arbitration proceedings shall be discontinued. It was therefore argued that the pending arbitration on the breach of contract claims depended on the continuing validity

---

[205] Although proposals for a Community patent have been on the table for many years, agreement on legislation to bring the Community patent into existence has not yet been attained.

[206] Eg, Art 25 of Reg (EC) 2100/94 on Community plant variety rights [1994] OJ L227/1. However, Art 21(1) of Reg (EC) 207/2009 on the Community trade mark [2009] OJ L78/1 coheres with Art 12. It repealed the rule in favour of the state in which proceedings are first opened that was contained in Reg (EC) 40/94 on the Community trade mark [1994] OJ L11/1.

[207] Eg, distress, execution, attachment and sequestration.

[208] Art 4(2)(f).

[209] *Re Flightlease Ireland Ltd* [2005] IEHC 274, para 6.3 (High Court, Ireland); Virgos-Schmit Report, para 142.

[210] *Re Flightlease Ireland Ltd* [2005] IEHC 274, para 6.3.

[211] [2009] 2 All ER (Comm) 891. See also *Mazur Media Ltd v Mazur Media GmbH* [2004] 1 WLR 2966, 2979–84 (at [53]–[71]).

of the agreement to arbitrate. The effects of the insolvency proceedings on the arbitration agreement was to be governed by the *lex concursus* under Article 4(2)(e) as the agreement was a 'current contract' and the effect of Polish law was that the agreement was unenforceable. In the course of its judgment, the Court of Appeal considered the relationship between the general rule in Article 4 that the *lex concursus* governs choice of law issues and the exception to the general rule in relation to lawsuits pending in Article 15. Longmore LJ observed:

It is self-evidently the law of [the state of opening of insolvency proceedings] which must determine matters such as the amount of the debtor's estate which is available to satisfy creditors and the priority of competing claims on that estate. Likewise it is not difficult to see why pending lawsuits should be excluded from the general application of the *lex concursus*; a lawsuit (including a reference to arbitration) becomes necessary when there is a need to determine the existence or validity of a particular claim which (if valid) will then be permitted to participate in the insolvency proceedings. Until the validity of that particular claim is ascertained, it has no status in or relevance to the insolvency proceedings at all.[212]

His Lordship emphasised that the rationale behind the choice of law rules in the Regulation was to protect legitimate expectations and the certainty of transactions.[213] If no claim had been initiated before the opening of insolvency proceedings, the *lex concursus* should determine how any subsequent litigation or arbitration should proceed. However, the situation was different if litigation or arbitration had commenced prior to the insolvency proceedings. In this scenario, the natural expectation of businesses would be that it should be the law of the state in which the litigation or arbitration is pending that should determine whether the proceedings should continue or come to a halt.[214] It was held that if the argument on Article 4(2)(e) was accepted, Article 15 would hardly ever apply in practice because the *lex concursus* will invariably prevail.[215] The phrase 'lawsuit pending' in Article 15 included pending references to arbitration and therefore English law should be applied to determine whether the arbitration should continue or be discontinued.

17.4 RECOGNITION AND ENFORCEMENT

General

17.4.1   Article 16(1) provides that:

Any judgment opening insolvency proceedings handed down by a court of a Member State which has jurisdiction pursuant to Article 3 shall be recognized in all the other Member States from the time that it becomes effective in the State of the opening of proceedings.

This rule shall also apply where, on account of his capacity, insolvency proceedings cannot be brought against the debtor in other Member States.

---

[212] [2009] 2 All ER (Comm) 891, 895 (at [16]).
[213] [2009] 2 All ER (Comm) 891, 895–6 (at [17]). See Recital 24.
[214] [2009] 2 All ER (Comm) 891, 895 (at [16]).
[215] [2009] 2 All ER (Comm) 891, 896, (at [19]).

Article 16 sets out one of the cornerstone principles of the Regulation, namely, the mandatory automatic recognition of a judgment opening insolvency proceedings. The proceedings must be of a type listed in the Annexes to the Regulation but the judgment need not be a final judgment[216] so long as it is effective in the state of the opening of proceedings.[217] Although the wording of Article 16 encompasses both main and territorial proceedings, it will be of greater applicability for main proceedings which are of universal effect since the effects of territorial proceedings are limited to assets within the state of opening of the territorial proceedings.

17.4.2   The second paragraph of Article 16(1) deals with situations where the law of the recognising state does not permit insolvency proceedings to be brought against a debtor because he is, for example, a non-trader. The insolvency proceedings opened will still have to be recognised notwithstanding that the debtor may not have been subject to insolvency proceedings in the recognising state. The Virgos-Schmit Report states that the recognising state cannot invoke the public policy exception to oppose recognition in these circumstances.[218]

17.4.3   Article 16 is further bolstered by Article 17. Article 17(1) provides that a judgment opening main proceedings shall, with no further formalities, produce the same effects in any other Member State as under the *lex concursus* unless the Regulation provides otherwise and as long as no territorial proceedings are opened in that other Member State.[219] Therefore, assets and creditors located in Member States other than the state in which main proceedings are opened will be bound by the effects of the main proceedings. However, the opening of territorial proceedings in the recognising Member State will limit the recognition of main proceedings as it will be the law of the Member State in which territorial proceedings are opened which will determine the protection of local interests and the effects of proceedings on local assets.[220] So, main proceedings opened in Germany cannot affect the application of English law with respect to assets located in England in English territorial proceedings.

17.4.4   Article 17(2) sets out that the effects of territorial proceedings may not be challenged in other Member States. Thus, the liquidator in territorial proceedings may demand the return of assets which were transferred without authority out of the jurisdiction after the opening of proceedings.[221]

17.4.5   The effects of territorial proceedings are limited to local assets. If territorial proceedings result in some limitation of creditors' rights, such as authorising the debtor to postpone payment or a discharge of debt, the effects will only operate as against the debtor's estate which is located within the jurisdiction in which the territorial proceedings were opened. However, creditors may voluntarily agree to the

---

[216] Art 2(f).
[217] So a judgment that is stayed in the state of the opening of proceedings would not qualify.
[218] Para 148.
[219] The model of recognition adopted is called the 'extension model' whereby proceedings opened in another Member State are not equated with national proceedings, but instead the effects of those proceedings (as determined by the *lex concursus*) will be the same in the opening and recognising states. See Virgos-Schmit Report, para 153.
[220] Subject to the co-ordination and subordination rules to which territorial proceedings are subject. See above, paras 17.2.39–17.2.46.
[221] Virgos-Schmit Report, para 156.

limitation of their rights with respect to assets of the debtor which are located in other Member States.[222] This explains the second sentence of Article 17(2), which provides: 'Any restriction of the creditors' rights, in particular a stay or discharge, shall produce effects vis-à-vis assets situated within the territory of another Member State only in the case of those creditors who have given their consent.' For example, if English territorial proceedings result in an order of discharge of debt, the creditors involved in those proceedings may not further pursue their claim with respect to assets located in England, but there is nothing to stop them pursuing satisfaction against assets located outside England via other proceedings, unless they have agreed not to do so.

17.4.6 Article 25(1) extends the automatic recognition principle to judgments concerning the course[223] and closure of insolvency proceedings, and compositions approved by the court, in addition to judgments which are closely linked with the insolvency proceedings[224] and judgments relating to preservation measures taken after the request for the opening of insolvency proceedings.[225] Such judgments are stipulated to be enforced in accordance with Articles 31 to 51,[226] with the exception of Article 34(2), of the Brussels Convention.[227] Article 34(2) refers to the grounds upon which a judgment can be refused recognition under the Brussels Convention. It is clear that this now needs to be read as a reference to the equivalent (but differently numbered) provisions of the Brussels I Regulation.[228]

17.4.7 The omission of the grounds for non-recognition contained in the Brussels regime is filled in by Article 26 of the Insolvency Regulation which contains the traditional public policy exception. Article 26 enables any Member State to invoke its public policy, 'in particular its fundamental principles or the constitutional rights and liberties of the individual' to refuse to recognise insolvency proceedings opened in another Member State or to enforce a judgment handed down in such proceedings. Article 25(3) also allows the refusal of recognition and enforcement if the judgment might result in a limitation of personal freedom or postal secrecy.

17.4.8 The Court of Justice in *Eurofood* emphasised that the principle of mutual trust underpins the recognition provisions in the Regulation.[229] So the public policy exception can be exercised only in exceptional circumstances and must not be given

---

[222] This limitation has to be accepted personally and not by a majority vote: Virgos-Schmit Report, para 157.

[223] Eg, a decision by the court in which main proceedings have been opened that assets located in another Member State should be seized will have to be given effect in that other Member State under Art 25.

[224] Such actions must be closely linked with insolvency proceedings in the sense that they are based on insolvency law and could not have been undertaken without the commencement of insolvency proceedings. Eg, actions to set aside acts detrimental to the general body of creditors, actions on the personal liability of directors based on insolvency law, actions relating to the admission or the ranking of a claim, and disputes between the liquidator and the debtor on whether an asset belongs to the bankrupt's estate. See Virgos-Schmit Report, para 196. See Case C–399/07 *Seagon v Deko Marty Belgium NV* [2009] 1 WLR 2168; cf Case C–292/08 *German Graphics Graphische Maschinen GmbH v Schee* [2010] ILPr 15.

[225] Measures adopted both before and after the opening of insolvency proceedings, provided that they were adopted after the request for the opening of proceedings, are covered by Art 25.

[226] Therefore, the simplified exequatur system adopted in the Brussels I Regulation is also used for the enforcement of judgments under the Insolvency Regulation.

[227] This corresponds with Arts 38–58, with the exception of Art 45(1) of the Brussels I Regulation.

[228] See Art 68(2) of the Brussels I Reg.

[229] Case C–341/04 [2006] ECR I–3813, paras 39–42. See also Recital 22.

an unreasonably wide interpretation by national laws.[230] In particular, the recognising court may not question whether the court of the state of opening of proceedings took jurisdiction correctly under the Regulation, nor review the substance of the judgment.[231] The recognising court can only verify that the judgment is from a court of a Member State which has exercised jurisdiction on the basis of Article 3.[232] However, the fundamental right to be heard is a general principle of EU law and a creditor who has been denied a fair legal process will have grounds to argue for refusal of recognition under Article 26.[233]

17.4.9   The effect of Article 25(2) is that judgments other than those referred to in Article 25(1) shall be governed by the recognition and enforcement provisions of the Brussels I Regulation, provided that that Regulation is applicable. In considering whether a judgment should be recognised in accordance with Article 25(2), the court needs to determine first whether the judgment at issue is within the material scope of the Brussels I Regulation.[234]

Powers of the Liquidator

17.4.10   To facilitate the automatic recognition principle, Article 18 provides considerable powers to the liquidator.[235] The liquidator in the main proceedings may exercise all the powers conferred on him by the *lex concursus* in another Member State as long as no other insolvency proceedings have been opened there nor any preservation measure to the contrary has been taken there further to a request for the opening of insolvency proceedings in that state. The main liquidator has the power to remove the debtor's assets from the territory of the Member State in which they are situated, subject to Articles 5 and 7.[236] Similarly, the liquidator in territorial proceedings has the power to claim in other Member States movable property that was removed from the territory of the state of the opening of proceedings to that of other Member State after the opening of the insolvency proceedings.[237] However, the liquidator needs to comply with the law of the Member State within the territory of which he intends to take action.[238] The exercise of coercive powers in another Member State and the right to rule on legal proceedings or disputes are expressly excluded from the powers of

---

[230]   Virgos-Schmit Report, para 205. There is no European autonomous concept of public policy.

[231]   Any such challenges must be mounted before the court which took jurisdiction or handed down the judgment.

[232]   See Virgos-Schmit Report, para 202.

[233]   See Case 341/04 *Eurofood IFSC* [2006] ECR I–3813, paras 65–8. In *Eurofood*, it was alleged that the Italian administrator had not given the Irish provisional liquidator adequate notice of the Italian hearing. This was the basis of the Court of Justice's pronouncement on Art 26. However, as has been pointed out, given the Court of Justice's emphasis on basic procedural fairness, the Italian court should equally have been entitled to refuse recognition to the Irish order appointing the Irish provisional liquidator which had been made without notice. See G Moss, 'When is a Proceeding Opened?' (2008) 21 *Insolv Int* 33, 37.

[234]   Case C–292/08 *German Graphics Graphische Maschinen GmbH v Schee* [2010] ILPr 15, 21 (paras 19–20).

[235]   The ease and promptness in which the liquidator can go about his duties is facilitated by Art 19, which stipulates that the liquidator's appointment need only be evidenced by a certified copy of the original decision appointing him or by any other certificate issued by the relevant court.

[236]   Art 18(1).

[237]   Art 18(2).

[238]   Art 18(3).

liquidators. Instead, liquidators must petition the authorities of the Member State in which action is required to be taken for help.

17.5 MISCELLANEOUS

The 'Hotchpot' Rule

17.5.1 Article 20 encapsulates what is referred to under English law as the 'hotchpot' rule, which is aimed at the equal treatment of creditors and the principle of collective satisfaction of all creditors.[239] Thus, Article 20(1) provides that a creditor who, after the opening of main proceedings, has obtained by any means a total or partial satisfaction of his claim on the assets belonging to the debtor situated within the territory of another Member State, is required to return what he has obtained to the liquidator, subject to the rights *in rem* or reservation of title of third parties and creditors over those assets. Further, Article 20(2) stipulates that a creditor who has obtained satisfaction on his claim in an insolvency proceeding is only allowed to share in distributions made in other parallel proceedings where creditors of the same ranking or category have, in those other proceedings, obtained equivalent satisfaction.

17.5.2 An issue that arises is whether dividends obtained in insolvency proceedings opened in a non-Member State will also be factored in under Article 20.[240] Article 20(1) refers to assets situated within the territory of another Member State. Hence, a creditor who has obtained satisfaction on assets situated in a non-Member State will not be required to return his dividends to the liquidator in the main proceedings. In contrast, Article 20(2) does not refer to proceedings in a Member State so a creditor who has obtained satisfaction in Indian proceedings must wait until creditors in English proceedings have obtained an equivalent dividend before he is allowed a share of the English distribution. However, this interpretation is at odds with the Virgos-Schmit Report, which seems to envisage that Article 20(2) also only applies in relation to parallel insolvency proceedings which have been opened in Member States.[241]

Publication of Insolvency Proceedings

17.5.3 The Regulation itself does not make publication of the notice of the judgment opening insolvency proceedings mandatory,[242] although it would be advisable

---

[239] It was also inspired by the United States Bankruptcy Code: M Balz, 'The European Union Convention on Insolvency Proceedings' (1996) 70 *Am Bank LJ* 485, 517.

[240] CGJ Morse, 'Cross-Border Insolvency in the European Union' in J Zekoll and P Borchers (eds), *International Conflict of Laws for the Third Millennium: Essays in Honor of Friedrick K Juenger* (Ardsley NY, Transnational Publishers, 2001), 258–9.

[241] Para 174.

[242] See Art 21(1). Publication is only mandatory if the Member State within the territory of which the debtor has an establishment requires publication: Art 21(2). The situation is similar with respect to registration in a public register; see Art 22.

for the liquidator to pursue publication in at least the Member States in which the debtor has assets or a place of establishment. If the notice has not been published, a third party who has effected payment to the debtor subject to insolvency proceedings instead of to the liquidator shall be presumed to have been unaware of the proceedings and will be deemed to have discharged the debt. If the notice has been published, the third party who has effected payment to the debtor instead of to the liquidator shall be presumed to have been aware of the opening of proceedings and must therefore honour the debt towards the liquidator.[243]

Provision of Information for Creditors and Lodgement of their Claims

17.5.4   The Regulation sets out provisions to ensure equal access to insolvency proceedings by all creditors, even those who are not EU nationals.[244] Article 39 allows any creditor who has his habitual residence, domicile or registered office in a Member State other than the state of the opening of proceedings the right to lodge claims in the insolvency proceedings in writing. Significantly, it also allows the tax authorities and social security authorities of Member States that same right, thus abrogating the general rule on the unenforceability of foreign revenue laws.[245]

17.5.5   The court of the Member State which opens proceedings or the liquidator appointed by that court has a duty immediately to inform known creditors who have their habitual residences, domiciles or registered offices in the other Member States upon the opening of the insolvency proceedings.[246] The immediate imposition of this duty upon the opening of proceedings serves to reduce any disadvantages that may be suffered by foreign creditors due to a delay in receiving information. The information, which should include in particular information on time limits, penalties laid down in regard to those time limits, the body or authority empowered to accept the lodging of claims, will have to be given by individual notice.[247] In turn, a creditor needs to send copies of supporting documents indicating the nature and details of the claim.[248]

---

[243] Art 24(2).

[244] The Regulation thereby does more than is required under EU law which generally enshrines the principle of non-discrimination only between citizens of different EU states.

[245] *Government of India v Taylor* [1955] AC 491.

[246] Art 40(1).

[247] Art 40(2). The information shall be provided in the official language or one of the official languages of the state of the opening of proceedings: Art 42(1). However, the invitation to lodge claims and of the time limits to be observed must be given in all the official languages of the institutions of the European Union.

[248] Art 41. The claim may be lodged in the official language or one of the official languages of his habitual residence, domicile or registered office in a Member State, although a translation into the official language or one of the official languages of the state of the opening of proceedings may be required: Art 42(2).

18

INTERNATIONAL INSOLVENCIES FALLING OUTSIDE THE EC INSOLVENCY REGULATION

18.0.1 It must first be remembered that the EC Insolvency Regulation has had a significant impact on the operation of English rules on international insolvency. If the debtor has his centre of main interests in an EU Member State,[1] then the Insolvency Regulation applies. This means that if the debtor's centre of main interests is in England, the English courts may open main insolvency proceedings on the basis of Article 3(1). If the debtor's centre of main interests is in another EU Member State but the debtor has a place of establishment in England, the English court has jurisdiction to open territorial insolvency proceedings under Article 3(2). Therefore, the contents of this chapter must be understood mainly to cover situations falling outside the scope of the EC Insolvency Regulation. That said, some of the rules discussed here will still be relevant in cases falling within the Regulation. When the court assumes jurisdiction under Article 3 of the Regulation, Article 4 dictates that English law will be applicable and, thus, the court will have to consult English rules on, for example, set-off, priority and the discharge of debts. The contents of this chapter should, however, be read subject to the prior discussion of the Regulation in Chapter 17. Another regime which has recently been made part of English law, the UNCITRAL Model Law on Cross-Border Insolvency,[2] deals mainly with easing cross-border co-operation and the recognition of foreign officeholders and proceedings. Because it does not contain any direct jurisdictional[3] or choice of law rules and its provisions on co-operation exist alongside existing English rules, it does not substantially affect the rules that are discussed in this chapter. The UNCITRAL Model Law is examined in detail in Chapter 19.

18.0.2 Whilst personal and corporate insolvencies share certain similarities, such as rules on proof, priority and the avoidance of certain transactions, the two regimes fundamentally differ in that the former involves the discharge of the bankrupt from his liabilities, so that he can start with a clean slate, whereas the latter almost invariably[4] results in the dissolution of the company.[5] Some of the rules for the two regimes are therefore the same, and the precedents from one area are equally authoritative for the other. Nevertheless, the inherent differences between the two regimes require

---

[1] For the purposes of this chapter, the phrase 'EU Member State', when used in connection with the EC Insolvency Regulation, does not include Denmark.

[2] Implemented in Great Britain by the Cross-Border Insolvency Regs 2006, SI 2006/1030.

[3] Apart from a provision dealing with the allocation of jurisdiction between the courts of England and Scotland; see Art 4.

[4] There is a possibility that the company may emerge from the procedure intact, eg where a successful Company Voluntary Arrangement (CVA) under Part I of the Insolvency Act 1986 takes place.

[5] R Goode, *Principles of Corporate Insolvency Law* (London, Sweet & Maxwell, 3rd edn, 2005) 25.

separate treatment of the two areas, although it will be pointed out where they overlap. It should also be noted that, while English law adopts different terminology for personal and corporate insolvencies, using 'bankruptcy' for the former and 'winding up' or 'liquidation' for the latter,[6] not all legal systems adopt different nomenclature for the two.[7] The discussion which follows adopts the English terminology.

18.1 PERSONAL INSOLVENCY/BANKRUPTCY

Jurisdiction

18.1.1   According to section 265(1) of the Insolvency Act 1986, an English court has jurisdiction to open insolvency proceedings against an individual debtor who:

(a) is domiciled in England and Wales,
(b) is personally present in England and Wales on the day on which the petition is presented, or
(c) at any time in the period of 3 years ending with that day—

   (i) has been ordinarily resident, or has had a place of residence, in England and Wales, or
   (ii) has carried on business in England and Wales.

18.1.2   The bases of jurisdiction set out in section 265(1) are alternative. To reiterate the point made above, section 265 is subject to the conditions set out in Article 3 of the EC Insolvency Regulation,[8] and thus will be relevant only where the debtor's centre of main interests is located outside the European Union.

Bases of Jurisdiction

DOMICILE[9]
18.1.3   'Domicile' in the context of section 265(1)(a) should be understood to refer to the common law concept of domicile.[10] The connotation of the word 'domicile' is that it should point towards a person's 'permanent home'.[11] Every person is ascribed one, and only one, domicile. In a state which comprises more than one country or law district, such as the United Kingdom, a person is domiciled in one of the constituent countries and not the United Kingdom as a whole.[12] There are three ways in which a person's domicile might be identified: by reference to the person's origin, choice,

---

   [6] Of course, there are other modes of insolvency proceedings for companies.
   [7] Eg, the concept of 'bankruptcy' applies to both individuals and corporations under the US insolvency regime.
   [8] S 265(3).
   [9] For a detailed look at the common law concept of domicile, see L Collins *et al*, *Dicey, Morris and Collins on The Conflict of Laws* (London, Sweet & Maxwell, 14th edn, 2006) ch 6 (hereafter '*Dicey, Morris and Collins*'); JJ Fawcett and JM Carruthers, *Cheshire, North & Fawcett: Private International Law* (Oxford, OUP, 14th edn, 2008) ch 9.
   [10] A special definition of 'domicile' is adopted for the purposes of the Brussels I Regulation; see paras 4.1.1–4.1.7.
   [11] Lord Cranworth in *Whicker v Hume* (1858) 10 HLC 124, 160.
   [12] Except for certain tax purposes; see, eg, Inheritance Tax Act 1984, s 267.

or, in cases where a person is dependent on another, to that other person's domicile. The last covers mainly children or mentally incapable people and would have little utility in the field of international insolvency. The domicile of origin depends on the father's domicile at the time of birth,[13] unless the child is illegitimate or is born after the father's death, in which case it depends on the mother's domicile at the time of birth.[14] The enduring nature[15] of the domicile of origin has led to particularly archaic results whereby persons who may not have set foot in their domicile of origin for a substantial number of years have still been held to be domiciled in that place.[16] A domicile of choice may displace the domicile of origin, although the domicile of origin will be revived when the domicile of choice is abandoned, unless the evidence shows the acquisition of a new domicile of choice.[17] A domicile of choice is acquired when a person resides in a place with the intention of continuing to do so permanently or indefinitely. There are two criteria involved: the objective criterion of residence and the subjective criterion of intention. Residence is usually easily established; it depends on quality rather than quantity.[18] Intention is more difficult; the intention needs to be *bona fide*,[19] and difficult issues arise if the intention to reside permanently is dependent on a contingency which may or may not happen.[20] Given the imperfect and outdated[21] principles on the common law concept of 'domicile' and the fact that the concept has been developed mainly in family and tax matters, some degree of caution may be advisable when the court is seeking to assume bankruptcy jurisdiction over an individual debtor on the basis of section 265(1)(a). The traditional principles were, however, applied without any modifications in a bankruptcy context in *Barlow Clowes International Ltd v Henwood*.[22] A debtor with an English domicile of origin, who later acquired a Manx domicile of choice, failed in a challenge to the English court's bankruptcy jurisdiction against him when the evidence showed that he had abandoned his domicile of choice in the Isle of Man but had not acquired a new domicile of choice elsewhere. His domicile of origin was held to have revived in these circumstances.

PRESENCE

18.1.4 In order to found jurisdiction on the basis of presence, the debtor must be personally present in England on the day on which the bankruptcy petition is

---

[13] *Re Duleep Singh* (1890) 6 TLR 385; Lord Westbury in *Udny v Udny* (1869) LR 1 Sc & Div 441, 457.

[14] Lord Westbury in *Udny v Udny* (1869) LR 1 Sc & Div 441, 457.

[15] See Lord MacNaghten in *Winans v A-G* [1904] AC 287, 290: 'its character is more enduring, its hold stronger, and less easily shaken off.'

[16] See, eg, *Winans v A-G* [1904] AC 287; *Ramsay v Liverpool Royal Infirmary* [1930] AC 588.

[17] *Udny v Udny* (1869) LR 1 Sc & Div 441; *Barlow Clowes International Ltd v Henwood* [2008] BPIR 778.

[18] *Ramsay v Liverpool Royal Infirmary* [1930] AC 588; *Barlow Clowes International Ltd v Henwood* [2008] BPIR 778.

[19] See Baroness Hale in *Mark v Mark* [2006] 1 AC 98, 116 (at [47]).

[20] See, eg, *Re Fuld's Estate (No 3)* [1968] P 675; *IRC v Bullock* [1976] 1 WLR 1178; *Cramer v Cramer* [1987] 1 FLR 116.

[21] This area was studied by the English and Scottish Law Commissions (*The Law of Domicile* (Law Com No 168, 1987)) which made several proposals but its recommendations were rejected for England and Wales (*Thirtieth Annual Report 1995* (Law Com No 239, 1996) 10 (n 24)).

[22] [2008] BPIR 778. A Briggs, (2008) 79 *BYIL* 549.

presented. Whereas establishing the debtor's personal presence is crucial to validate the exercise of jurisdiction when the bankruptcy petition is presented by a creditor, it is unclear if the debtor's presence needs to be established where the bankruptcy petition is filed by an agent or representative of the debtor.[23] Temporary presence suffices, although the court has a discretion to decline jurisdiction if this would result in injustice.[24]

ORDINARY RESIDENCE OR PLACE OF RESIDENCE

18.1.5 The English court can assume jurisdiction if the debtor has been ordinarily resident or has had a place of residence in England at any time in the period of three years ending with the date on which the petition is presented. Thus a debtor who was ordinarily resident in England in the three-year period but who emigrated to another country at the date on which the petition is presented would still fall within section 265(1)(c)(i). 'Ordinary residence' has not been precisely defined, but it is generally thought to be nearly synonymous with the more widely used concept of 'habitual residence'.[25] There needs to be some degree of continuity in terms of physical presence in England, with an allowance for temporary absences.[26] Residence must be voluntarily adopted and there must be a degree of settled purpose.[27] The courts have resisted linking the concept to a particular duration of stay in England.[28]

18.1.6 'Place of residence' is the modern manifestation of the phrase 'dwelling-house' which was used in previous legislation.[29] Case law on the older phrase shows a generous interpretation of what suffices to permit the English courts to assume jurisdiction. A lease or licence over an abode has been thought to be sufficient.[30] It is probable that the same approach remains under the new terminology adopted by the Insolvency Act 1986; that is, ownership of the place of residence is not required under section 265(1)(c)(i).[31]

CARRYING ON A BUSINESS

18.1.7 A debtor will also be subject to the English court's jurisdiction if he has carried on a business in England at any time in the period of three years ending with the day on which the bankruptcy petition is presented.[32] 'Business' is stated to include 'a trade or profession'.[33] It is well established that 'trading does not cease when, as the expression is, "the shutters are put up," but continues until the sums due are collected

---

[23] I Fletcher, *Insolvency in Private International Law* (Oxford, OUP, 2nd edn, 2005) 43–4 (hereafter 'Fletcher'). It should be noted that the English bankruptcy regime covers both voluntary and involuntary proceedings.

[24] For further discussion, see paras 18.1.11–18.1.12.

[25] *Barnet London Borough Council v Shah* [1983] 2 AC 309. Cf *Nessa v Chief Education Officer* [1999] 1 WLR 1937, 1941. See also *Stojevic v Komercni Banka AS* [2007] BPIR 141; *Cross Construction Sussex Ltd v Tseliki* [2006] BPIR 888; *Geveran Trading Co Ltd v Skjevesland* [2003] BCC 209, affirmed [2003] BCC 391.

[26] *Barnet London Borough Council v Shah* [1983] 2 AC 309, 341–2; *Levene v IRC* [1928] AC 217, 225.

[27] *Barnet London Borough Council v Shah* [1983] 2 AC 309, 344.

[28] Eg, *Levene v IRC* [1928] 1 AC 217, 225, 232.

[29] Eg, Bankruptcy Act 1914, s 4(1)(d) (repealed).

[30] *Re Hecquard* (1889) 24 QBD 71; *Re Brauch* [1978] Ch 316, 334. Cf *Re Norris* (1888) 4 TLR 452.

[31] See Fletcher, 48.

[32] Insolvency Act 1986, s 265(1)(c)(i).

[33] Insolvency Act 1986, s 436.

and all debts paid'.[34] This is on the ground that a debtor continues to trade until all the obligations imposed upon the debtor pursuant to the trade have been performed.[35] It has been confirmed that the same meaning is to be ascribed to the words 'carried on business' for the purposes of section 265(1)(c)(ii).[36]

18.1.8   Section 265(2) further explains that 'carrying on business' includes:

(a) the carrying on of business by a firm or partnership of which the individual is a member, and

(b) the carrying on of business by an agent or manager for the individual or for such a firm or partnership.

This means that a debtor who does not visit England within the relevant time-frame may still come within the court's bankruptcy jurisdiction if he is involved with a firm or partnership which carries on business in England at some point within that time-frame.

Presentation of a Bankruptcy Petition

18.1.9   The English bankruptcy regime covers voluntary and involuntary proceedings. A bankruptcy petition may be presented by the debtor himself, by a creditor or jointly by more than one creditor, or by the supervisor of, or any person (other than the debtor) who is for the time being bound by, a voluntary arrangement proposed by the debtor and approved under Part VIII of the 1986 Act.[37] The last, being an extension of an arrangement to which the debtor is a party, should not raise any particular jurisdictional complaints on the part of the debtor.[38] Other persons who may present a petition are a temporary administrator (within the meaning of Article 38 of the EC Insolvency Regulation) and a liquidator (within the meaning of Article 2(b) of the Regulation in respect of proceedings commenced under Article 3(1) of the Regulation); these additions were made to adapt English law to the EC Insolvency Regulation.

18.1.10   Where the petition is filed by the creditor or creditors, a copy of the petition is required to be served on the debtor.[39] If the debtor is out of the jurisdiction, the court may give leave to serve the petition on the debtor in such a manner as it thinks fit.[40] Substituted service is likely to be ordered if the court is satisfied that the debtor is keeping out of the way to avoid service.[41]

Discretion to Decline Jurisdiction or Stay Proceedings

18.1.11   Early case law shows that English courts were reluctant to decline jurisdiction or stay English proceedings in a bankruptcy case; this may, however, be explained

---

[34] *Theophile v Solicitor-General* [1950] 1 AC 186, 201. See also, eg, *Re Dagnall* [1896] 2 QB 407; *Re Reynolds* [1915] 2 KB 186; *Re Allen* [1915] 1 KB 285; *Re Bird* [1962] 1 WLR 686.

[35] *Re Dagnall* [1896] 2 QB 407, 410–1.

[36] *Re a Debtor (No 784 of 1991)* [1992] Ch 554.

[37] Insolvency Act 1986, s 264.

[38] *Dicey, Morris and Collins*, para 31–004; Fletcher, 35.

[39] Insolvency Rules 1986 (SI 1986/1925), r 6.14.

[40] Insolvency Rules 1986 (SI 1986/1925), r 12.12; CPR 6.36–6.43 and PD 6B.

[41] See *Re Urquhart* (1890) 24 QBD 723. Cf *Re A Judgment Debtor (No 1539 of 1936)* [1937] Ch 137; *Re A Debtor (No 419 of 1939)* [1939] 3 All ER 429.

by the fact that previous bankruptcy legislation generally did not expressly give the courts any discretion[42] and that the doctrine of *forum non conveniens* had yet to be fully developed. However, section 266(3) of the Insolvency Act 1986 states that:

The court has a general power, if it appears to it appropriate to do so on the grounds that there has been a contravention of the rules or for any other reason, to dismiss a bankruptcy petition or to stay proceedings on such a petition, and, where it stays proceedings on a petition, it may do so on such terms and conditions as it thinks fit.

18.1.12   That said, there is little authority on which factors may be relevant when consideration is being given to whether this discretion should be exercised in favour of granting a stay or dismissal. Courts have, under previous bankruptcy legislation, given weight to factors such as the lack of assets in England and the existence of a foreign bankruptcy adjudication against the debtor.[43] However, the debtor has a heavy burden to discharge when seeking to show that any bankruptcy proceedings would be in vain because he has no assets: in a case decided under section 266(3), it was said that: 'the burden on him is to prove that he is too poor to be made bankrupt.'[44] In addition, it should be noted that the existence of a foreign bankruptcy adjudication against the debtor is not a bar against the English court assuming jurisdiction;[45] it is merely a factor to be considered in determining the exercise of discretion against taking jurisdiction or staying proceedings. Other factors that may be considered include: whether the debtor had been given a legitimate expectation that proceedings would not be pursued,[46] whether the English proceedings amount to an abuse of legal process,[47] and the location of the creditors (that is, the general body of creditors as well as creditors petitioning the English court).[48] The aim is to seek to determine, looking at the overall justice of the case, whether the English court should assume jurisdiction. It is likely, though, that, given the specific nature of insolvency proceedings, a wholesale exportation of the test of *forum non conveniens*, which was developed and is applied in other commercial contexts, will not work for section 266(3); nevertheless, some of the factors considered under the *forum non conveniens* doctrine may be relevant in certain insolvency cases.[49]

---

[42]   Although an inherent discretion remained: James LJ in *Re McCulloch* (1880) 14 ChD 716, 723. This discretion was, however, rarely exercised.

[43]   *Re Robinson* (1883) 22 ChD 816; *Re Behrends* (1865) 12 LT 149.

[44]   Rimer J in *Her Majesty's Revenue and Customs v Crossman (Junior)* [2008] 1 All ER 483, 498 (at [42]). See also *Re Thulin* [1995] 1 WLR 165.

[45]   *Re McCulloch* (1880) 14 ChD 716; *Re Robinson* (1883) 22 ChD 816; *Re Artola Hermanos* (1890) 24 QBD 640; *Re a Debtor (No 199 of 1922)* [1922] 2 Ch 470; *Re a Debtor (No 737 of 1928)* [1929] 1 Ch 362; *Re Thulin* [1995] 1 WLR 165.

[46]   *Her Majesty's Revenue and Customs v Crossman (Junior)* [2008] 1 All ER 483.

[47]   Eg, where the creditor is seeking to harass the debtor or where the debtor frequently files petitions to take advantage of the short time period in which one could be discharged from bankruptcy under English law (see Insolvency Act 1986, s 279). See also *Re Betts* [1901] 2 KB 39.

[48]   See PStJ Smart, 'Forum Non Conveniens in Bankruptcy Proceedings' [1989] *JBL* 126.

[49]   See PStJ Smart, 'Forum Non Conveniens in Bankruptcy Proceedings' [1989] *JBL* 126; Fletcher, 58–9, 64–5. For a consideration of the application of the doctrine of *forum non conveniens* to the winding-up of foreign companies, see K Dawson, 'The Doctrine of Forum Non Conveniens and the Winding Up of Insolvent Foreign Companies' [2005] *JBL* 28. For a consideration of how the modern principles governing anti-suit injunctions which have been developed in international commercial cases could be adapted for use in the insolvency context, see LC Ho, 'Anti-Suit Injunctions in Cross-Border Insolvency: A Restatement'

Choice of Law

18.1.13 Generally, if England is the forum for the bankruptcy proceedings, English law, being the *lex concursus,* will be applicable to all matters, both procedural and substantive, relating to the bankruptcy. This means that English rules on issues such as proof, what are the assets comprising the estate and their distribution, set-off,[50] priorities,[51] and the hotchpot rule,[52] will be applicable. That said, incidental recourse to foreign law may be necessary in order to determine, for example, the validity of a debt governed by French law or a secured right alleged to have been created under Singaporean law. Once the validity of the right asserted has been established under the foreign applicable law,[53] English law governs other aspects of the claim, such as the order in which that right would rank as against other claims.

18.1.14 The court has the power, by virtue of sections 339 (for individuals) and 238 (for companies), to set aside a transaction which is made at an undervalue.[54] Such transactions defraud the general body of creditors by improperly removing property from the debtor's estate.[55] The provisions give the court the discretion to set aside transactions entered into 'with any person at an undervalue'.[56] The issue considered in *Re Paramount Airways Ltd*[57] was whether the court's power extended to transactions which were entered into by the debtor with a Jersey company which did not carry on business in England. The Court of Appeal held that the expression 'any person' bears its literal and natural meaning. The potential width of the court's power is, however, tempered by two safeguards: first, that the defendant needs to have a sufficient connection with England for it to be just for the order to be made notwithstanding the foreign element;[58] secondly, when the court is

---

(2003) 52 *ICLQ* 697; I Fletcher, *The Law of Insolvency* (London, Sweet & Maxwell, 4th edn, 2009) 969–72. See also *Barclays Bank plc v Homan* [1993] BCLC 680.

[50] *Meyer v Dresser* (1864) 16 CB (NS) 646. In *Re Bank of Credit and Commerce International SA (No 10)* [1997] Ch 213, the High Court held that English rules of set-off (Insolvency Rules 1986, SI 1986/1925, r 4.90) were applicable notwithstanding that the English insolvency proceedings were ancillary to principal proceedings in Luxembourg. Cf *Re HIH Casualty & General Insurance Ltd* [2008] 1 WLR 852, where the House of Lords remitted English assets to Australia where principal insolvency proceedings were taking place for the assets to be distributed in accordance with Australian rules. Where there are no English insolvency proceedings, the English court will apply the set-off rule of the law of the place where the bankruptcy proceedings are taking place: *Macfarlane v Norris* (1862) 2 B&S 783, 121 ER 1263.

[51] Lord Cairns in *Thurburn v Steward* (1869–1871) LR 3 PC 478, 513; *Ex parte Melbourn* (1870–71) LR 6 Ch App 64.

[52] *Banco de Portugal v Waddell* (1879–1880) 5 App Cas 161.

[53] The foreign applicable law having been identified using English choice of law rules.

[54] See LC Ho, 'Conflict of Laws in Insolvency Transaction Avoidance' (2008) 20 *SAcLJ* 343. See also UNCITRAL Model Law on Cross-Border Insolvency, Art 23 (as implemented in Great Britain by the Cross-Border Insolvency Regs 2006).

[55] See also Insolvency Act 1986, ss 423–5.

[56] Insolvency Act 1986, s 339(1) and s 238(2).

[57] [1993] Ch 223. See also *Jyske Bank (Gibraltar) Ltd v Spjeldnaes* [1999] 2 BCLC 101 (English court exercised its discretion to set aside a transaction involving a contract between Irish companies to purchase land in Ireland); *The WD Fairway (No 3)* [2009] 2 Lloyd's Rep 420 (Insolvency Act 1986, s 423 was applied to a situation where there was no formal insolvency).

[58] In considering whether there is a sufficient connection, 'the court will look at all the circumstances, including the residence and place of business of the defendant, his connection with the insolvent, the nature and purpose of the transaction being impugned, the nature and locality of the property involved, the circumstances in which the defendant became involved in the transaction or received a benefit from it

considering whether to give permission to serve out on the defendant abroad, it will take into account the strength or weakness of the claimant's claim in the proceedings.[59] The 1986 Act contains equivalent provisions giving the court similar discretion to set aside a preference (that is, where the debtor does anything or suffers anything to be done which puts a creditor into a better position in the event of the debtor's insolvency than he would have been in otherwise).[60] It should be noted that Nicholls V-C in *Re Paramount Airways Ltd* mentioned that one of the factors relevant to the exercise of the discretion under section 238 is 'whether under any relevant foreign law the defendant acquired an unimpeachable title free from any claims even if the insolvent had been adjudged bankrupt or wound up locally';[61] thus some recourse to foreign law may be required in application of the avoidance provisions of the Act.

18.1.15 Application of foreign law may also be entailed under the provisions of the Insolvency Act 1986 which deal with cross-border judicial co-operation with certain designated countries. In dealing with such a request for assistance, the English court is, according to section 426(5):

to apply, in relation to any matters specified in the request, the insolvency law which is applicable by either court in relation to comparable matters falling within its jurisdiction.

In exercising its discretion under this subsection, a court shall have regard in particular to the rules of private international law.[62]

The effect of the last paragraph is somewhat obscure.[63] However, the provision has enabled English courts to apply foreign insolvency law when assisting foreign proceedings.[64] However, in *Re HIH Casualty and General Insurance Ltd*,[65] in which the court was faced with a request for the remittal of assets to Australia, Lord Hoffman made the point that, although section 426(5) may authorise the court to apply a foreign law of distribution, namely, the law of the requesting court, this is not what a court directing remittal of assets is doing:

[The English court] is exercising its power under English law to direct the liquidator to remit the assets and leave their distribution to the courts and liquidators in Australia. It is they who apply Australian law, not the English ancillary liquidator.[66]

---

or acquired the property in question, whether the defendant acted in good faith, and whether under any relevant foreign law the defendant acquired an unimpeachable title free from any claims even if the insolvent had been adjudged bankrupt or wound up locally. The importance to be attached to these factors will vary from case to case': Nicholls V-C in *Re Paramount Airways Ltd* [1993] Ch 223, 240.

[59] It should be noted that CPR 6.36 is not applicable here; Insolvency Rules 1986, r 12.12 is.
[60] See Insolvency Act 1986, s 340 (individuals) and s 239 (companies).
[61] [1993] Ch 223, 240.
[62] Insolvency Act 1986, s 426(5).
[63] A Briggs, (2008) 79 *BYIL* 501, 505 argues that it covers the common law principle of private international law that English proceedings may be treated as ancillary to principal proceedings taking place elsewhere and that the court's approach could differ according to how the proceedings are characterised.
[64] See, eg, *England v Smith* [2001] 1 Ch 419.
[65] [2008] 1 WLR 852.
[66] [2008] 1 WLR 852, 861 (at [26]). Cf A Briggs, (2008) 79 *BYIL* 501, 503–4.

Effects of an English Bankruptcy Order

The Universalist Effects of an English Bankruptcy Order

18.1.16 A bankruptcy order made by an English court results in the immediate vesting of the bankrupt's estate in the trustee.[67] No conveyance, assignment or transfer is necessary to effect this.[68] The bankrupt's estate is defined as including all of the bankrupt's property at the commencement of the bankruptcy.[69] 'Property' in turn:

includes money, goods, things in action, land and every description of property wherever situated and also obligations and every description of interest, whether present or future or vested or contingent, arising out of, or incidental to, property.[70]

This means that, ostensibly, title to property located within a foreign jurisdiction will pass according to English law. This is obviously contrary to orthodox conflicts principle whereby title to property (immovables and tangible movables) is generally determined by the *lex situs*. However, the English court has recognised that a judgment *in rem* that is delivered by the courts of the *situs*, even if delivered after the start of English insolvency proceedings, will exclude the relevant property from the debtor's estate.[71] Thus, a secured creditor will not be prevented from enforcing its security abroad after the commencement of English proceedings.[72] There is also some authority that the English doctrine of 'relation back',[73] whereby dispositions of the debtor's property made after the commencement of the insolvency proceedings are void unless the court otherwise orders, does not apply with respect to property located abroad.[74]

18.1.17 The Act stipulates that nothing in it is to be construed as restricting the capacity of the trustee to exercise his powers outside England.[75] Provisions in the Act mandate co-operation between courts in the different parts of the United Kingdom;[76] this will assist in perfecting the title of a trustee in English insolvency proceedings over property located in Scotland and Northern Ireland.[77] Outside the United Kingdom, however, it remains up to the foreign court to decide what effect, if any, it should give to the universalist implications of an English bankruptcy order; some countries are more receptive to co-operation than others.[78] If the

---

[67] Insolvency Act 1986, s 306(1).

[68] Insolvency Act 1986, s 306(2).

[69] Insolvency Act 1986, s 283.

[70] Insolvency Act 1986, s 436.

[71] *Minna Craig Steamship Co v Chartered Mercantile Bank* [1897] 1 QB 460.

[72] *Moor v Anglo Italian Bank* [1980] 10 ChD 681.

[73] See Insolvency Act 1986, s 284 (individuals), s 127 (companies). The doctrine used to be more expansive; see Bankruptcy Act 1914, s 37.

[74] *Galbraith v Grimshaw* [1910] AC 508, 513; *Re Paramount Airways Ltd* [1993] Ch 223, 238.

[75] Insolvency Act 1986, s 314(8).

[76] Insolvency Act 1986, s 426.

[77] Albeit s 426(2) diplomatically stipulates that a court in any part of the United Kingdom is not required, in relation to property situated within its jurisdiction, to enforce any order made by a court in any other part of the United Kingdom.

[78] Mainly due to historical ties with the United Kingdom; see Fletcher, 79–83.

foreign court does not recognise the English order, indirect means of enforcement will have to be relied on. For example, an alternative route towards transferring title to property abroad to the trustee would be for the English court to exert jurisdiction *in personam* against the bankrupt (assuming that it enjoys such jurisdiction) by ordering the bankrupt to transfer title to the trustee in bankruptcy. The Act facilitates this route by obliging the bankrupt to co-operate with the official receiver and trustee in bankruptcy in terms of delivering possession of his estate, assisting in the protection of property which cannot be delivered, and giving information as may be required by the trustee to carry out his duties.[79]

18.1.18 The above regime is, however, subject to the EC Insolvency Regulation for cases falling within that Regulation.[80] If the court takes jurisdiction on the basis of the existence of a place of establishment within England and opens territorial proceedings (whether secondary or independent), the effects of its order are restricted to assets which are situated in England. If the court has jurisdiction to open main proceedings, then the universalist aspirations of an English order are maintained.

Discharge in English Insolvency Proceedings[81]

18.1.19 Generally, if the English court is asked to recognise an order of discharge under a foreign bankruptcy, a debt is regarded as discharged only if it is discharged in accordance with the law applicable to the contract or debt.[82] However, a double standard is adopted: an order of discharge made in an English bankruptcy is universally valid regardless of whether it is valid by the law applicable to the contract or debt.[83] A discharge issued under a Scottish[84] or Northern Ireland[85] bankruptcy has the same effect. Two points can be noted:[86] first, it goes against the general principle that matters relating to an obligation, such as the discharge of the obligation, is to be governed by the applicable law of the obligation;[87] secondly, the creditor who had no knowledge of the English proceedings will be faced with a valid defence if he tries to sue for the debt before an English court.[88] In view of the rather old authorities on which the principle of universal discharge depends, a reformed approach which takes into account the applicable law of the obligation and the demands of international comity would be preferable.[89]

---

[79] See Insolvency Act 1986, ss 291, 312 and 333.

[80] See Insolvency Act 1986, s 436A.

[81] This paragraph applies to both personal and corporate insolvencies.

[82] *Wight v Eckhardt Marine GmbH* [2004] 1 AC 147; *AWB (Geneva) SA v North America Steamships Ltd* [2007] 2 Lloyd's Rep 315. See generally, PStJ Smart, *Cross-Border Insolvency* (London, Butterworths, 2nd edn, 1998) ch 9 (hereafter 'Smart').

[83] Insolvency Act 1986, s 281(1); exceptions are listed in ss 281(2)–(6).

[84] Bankruptcy (Scotland) Act 1985, s 55(1); exceptions are listed in s 55(2).

[85] *Simpson v Mirabita* (1869) LR 4 QB 257.

[86] Fletcher, 108–9.

[87] See Rome I Regulation, Art 12(d).

[88] *Simpson v Mirabita* (1869) LR 4 QB 257.

[89] See Fletcher, 109.

Position of Creditors in English Insolvency Proceedings[90]

18.1.20 No distinction is made between foreign and local creditors or whether debts are governed by foreign law or English law; all claimants are entitled to prove in English insolvency proceedings. However, English insolvency rules will be applicable; for example, a creditor would be ranked in accordance with English priority rules notwithstanding that he would have been ranked differently according to the law governing the debt or the law of his home country. The *pari passu* principle, whereby the debtor's estate will be distributed rateably amongst creditors,[91] is the bedrock of English insolvency law. This principle will generally apply,[92] although the position may be different if the English proceedings are ancillary to principal proceedings taking place elsewhere.[93] If, in proceedings abroad, a creditor has obtained partial or total satisfaction of the debt owed, he will be required to bring into the common fund what he has obtained abroad before he is entitled to dividends under English insolvency proceedings in accordance with the 'hotchpot' rule. This rule provides that a creditor who has proved in foreign proceedings and obtained a dividend can only participate in the English insolvency proceedings to the extent that he brings into hotchpot his foreign dividends.[94] Two points should be noted. First, the 'hotchpot' rule does not cover property that has been acquired before the commencement of English insolvency proceedings,[95] or a secured interest that is realised before or after the commencement of English insolvency proceedings.[96] As Lord Steyn remarked: 'the hotchpot requirement applies only to assets that, under English law, are regarded as forming part of the estate in liquidation.'[97] Secondly, the operation of 'hotchpot' is dependent on the creditor taking part in English proceedings; if the creditor refuses to do so, he can be compelled to refund the value of the property to the debtor's estate only if the English court is able to exercise jurisdiction over him. However, the older authorities upon which this principle is based concerned cases where the creditor was resident in England and was aware of the existence of or the imminence of English proceedings;[98] it is unclear whether this remedy would be available in other contexts.[99]

---

[90] This paragraph applies to both personal and corporate insolvencies.

[91] Albeit in reality rateable distribution is rarely achieved: Report of the Review Committee on Insolvency Law and Practice (commonly known as the Cork Report), Cmnd 8558, 1982, para 1396. For a criticism of the view that the *pari passu* principle forms a fundamental part of insolvency law, see RJ Mokal, 'Priority as Pathology: The *Pari Passu* Myth' [2001] *CLJ* 581.

[92] *Selkrig v Davies* (1814) 2 Rose 291, 318; *Banco de Portugal v Waddell* (1880) 5 App Cas 161; *Re Douglas, ex p Wilson* (1872) LR 7 Ch App 490.

[93] *Re HIH Casualty and General Insurance Ltd* [2008] 1 WLR 852, where the English *pari passu* scheme was disapplied in favour of the Australian scheme and English assets were remitted to Australia to be distributed in accordance with Australian rules; the English proceedings in that case were ancillary to the Australian proceedings. See also CH Tham, 'Ancillary liquidations and *pari passu* distribution in a winding-up by the court' [2009] *LMCLQ* 113.

[94] *Cleaver v Delta American Insurance Co* [2001] 2 AC 328 (PC).

[95] See *Cleaver v Delta America Reinsurance Co* [2001] 2 AC 328, 339 (at [20]); and for a review of the hotchpot authorities, 338–41 (at [18]–[29]).

[96] *Re Somes, ex p De Lemos* (1896) 3 Mans 131; *Callender Sykes & Co v Lagos Colonial Secretary* [1891] AC 460. See Insolvency Rules 1986, r 4.88 (liquidation of companies).

[97] *Cleaver v Delta America Reinsurance Co* [2001] 2 AC 328, 340 (at [26]) (PC).

[98] *Sill v Worswick* (1791) 1 H Bl 665, 693; *Hunter v Potts* (1791) 4 TR 182, 193–4; *Phillips v Hunter* (1795) 2 H Bl 402, 404–5.

[99] See Fletcher, 107; *Dicey, Morris and Collins*, para 31–042; PM North and JJ Fawcett, *Cheshire and North's Private International Law* (London, Butterworths, 12th edn, 1992) 908–11.

Recognition

Recognition of Intra-UK Insolvencies[100]

18.1.21   Section 426(1) of the Insolvency Act 1986, which covers both personal and corporate insolvency, provides that:

An order made by a court in any part of the United Kingdom in the exercise of jurisdiction in relation to insolvency law shall be enforced in any other part of the United Kingdom as if it were made by a court exercising the corresponding jurisdiction in that other part.

Thus, a bankruptcy order made by the courts in Scotland or Northern Ireland will be accorded automatic recognition[101] by English courts. Importantly, a discharge granted by the Scottish or Northern Irish courts would be a valid discharge in England irrespective of whether it is similarly valid under the law applicable to the contract or debt.[102]

18.1.22   By the same token, the trustee in bankruptcy or assignee in the Scottish or Northern Ireland proceedings gains title to the property of the debtor, wherever situated.[103] With respect to property located in England, section 426(2) provides that a court in any part of the United Kingdom is not required to enforce, in relation to property situated in that part, any order made by a court in any other part of the United Kingdom. Nevertheless, the provisions requiring co-operation between the courts of the different parts of the United Kingdom will more likely than not persuade English courts to exercise their discretion to assist in perfecting the title of the Scottish and Northern Irish trustees or assignees over property in England.[104] In particular, the Secretary of State, with the concurrence of the Lord Chancellor, may make such an order securing the title of the trustee or assignee.[105]

Recognition of Foreign Bankruptcies

18.1.23   The first thing that should be noted is that the normal English conflicts rules on recognition and enforcement are not applicable in an insolvency context. Lord Hoffman has observed that, whilst judgments *in rem* and judgments *in personam* are judicial determinations of the existence of rights, the purpose of bankruptcy proceedings on the other hand is not to determine or establish the existence of rights but to provide a mechanism for collective execution against the property of the debtor by creditors whose rights are admitted or established.[106] Although the proposition that

---

    [100]   See also the Cross-Border Insolvency Regs 2006, reg 7.
    [101]   Albeit the word used in s 426(1) is 'enforcement', but recognition is a necessary precursor to enforcement.
    [102]   Bankruptcy (Scotland) Act 1985, s 55(1); exceptions are listed in s 55(2); *Simpson v Mirabita* (1869) LR 4 QB 257 (Northern Ireland).
    [103]   Bankruptcy (Scotland) Act 1985, s 31(1) and (8); Insolvency (Northern Ireland) Order 1989, Art 279.
    [104]   Insolvency Act 1986, s 426(4)–(6).
    [105]   Insolvency Act 1986, s 426(3).
    [106]   *Cambridge Gas Transport Corp v Official Committee of Unsecured Creditors of Navigator Holdings Plc* [2007] 1 AC 508, 516 (at [13]–[14]). See also Lord Hoffman's remarks in *Wight v Eckhardt Marine GmbH* [2004] 1 AC 147, 155 (at [26]).

bankruptcy proceedings do not involve the adjudication of rights might be thought by some to be dubious,[107] it is clearly established that different rules on recognition and enforcement apply for foreign insolvency orders. It has been said:

[A decree of insolvency] is not the mere settlement by a foreign tribunal of a dispute between two litigants; it affects the rights of third parties who were never before the foreign court; and not only does it affect such rights, but it regulates in the future the dealings between the insolvent and all other persons. It is, in fact, a species of arrest or execution upon the property of the insolvent, followed by a distribution of it among his various creditors; it restricts the ordinary legal remedies of those creditors, and it imposes upon the insolvent disabilities which tend in the direction of an impairment of his status. To enforce such a decree absolutely and entirely in this country, as if it were a foreign judgment, is, therefore, out of the question.[108]

BASES OF RECOGNITION

18.1.24 It is well established that an English court may recognise and enforce foreign bankruptcy proceedings.[109] Outside the context of intra-UK insolvencies and insolvencies falling within the scope of the EC Insolvency Regulation, the foreign court must have assumed bankruptcy jurisdiction on a basis that is recognised by the English court.[110] The Insolvency Act 1986 is silent on what the relevant bases may be; recourse must be had to the admittedly unclear[111] common law. According to case law, the English court will recognise that a foreign court has exercised bankruptcy jurisdiction validly if the debtor either was domiciled in that foreign country at the time the bankruptcy petition is presented,[112] or submitted to the jurisdiction of the foreign court.[113]

18.1.25 The concept of domicile used here is the one developed by the common law.[114] The debtor's domicile was adjudged to be an appropriate base on which to gauge the validity of a bankruptcy order by a foreign court because bankruptcy impacts on a debtor's personal status and capacity[115] and the operation of the (now outdated) maxim *mobilia sequuntur personam*.[116] Indeed, it used to be thought that domicile was the sole basis upon which the jurisdictional competence of a foreign court in bankruptcy proceedings should be recognised.[117]

---

[107] A Briggs, (2006) 77 *BYIL* 578; CH Tham, [2007] *LMCLQ* 129.

[108] Innes JP in *ex p Stegmann* 1902 TS 40, 47. See also Lord Hoffman in *Wight v Eckhardt Marine GmbH* [2004] 1 AC 147, 155 (at [26]).

[109] *Solomons v Ross* (1764) 1 H Bl 131n. KH Nadelman, (1946) 9 *MLR* 154.

[110] The UNCITRAL Model Law on Cross-Border Insolvency (as implemented in Great Britain by the Cross-Border Insolvency Regs 2006) also contains rules on recognition of foreign insolvency proceedings and the consequences of such recognition; see ch 19.

[111] *Dicey, Morris and Collins* describe the question as being 'vexed and controversial': para 31–064.

[112] *Re Blithman* (1866) LR 2 Eq 23.

[113] *Re Davidson's Settlement* (1872–73) LR 15 Eq 383; *Bergerem v Marsh* (1921) 6 B & CR 195.

[114] See above, para 18.1.3.

[115] Fletcher, 112.

[116] 'Movables follow the person.' The maxim is outdated as it is now established that the *lex situs* governs the transfer of movable property.

[117] See *Re Artola Hermanos* (1890) 24 QBD 640.

18.1.26 It is, however, well established that submission is accepted as a second basis of recognition. Submission includes various forms of participation in the foreign bankruptcy proceedings; the debtor may present the bankruptcy petition himself,[118] appear personally or have a legal representative in the proceedings,[119] or appeal against an adjudication.[120] Conversely, an appearance that is made solely to contest the foreign court's jurisdiction should not count as submission.[121]

18.1.27 As a result of this jurisdictional approach, a fraudulent bankrupt who runs up debts when carrying on business in, say, China, would have his English assets protected in the event of Chinese bankruptcy proceedings if he is neither domiciled in China nor submits to the Chinese courts. To address the apparent injustice of this type of situation, it has been suggested that recognition of foreign bankruptcy judgments should also be founded on two other jurisdictional bases: where the debtor carries on business in the foreign jurisdiction[122] or the debtor is resident there.[123] A further two potential bases, namely the presence of assets within the foreign jurisdiction[124] and comity,[125] are less likely to constitute sufficient grounds for recognition.

18.1.28 Lastly, it should be pointed out that even though one of the bases of jurisdiction is present, the English court may refuse to give effect to the foreign bankruptcy proceedings on the usual grounds on which recognition of a foreign judgment may be refused,[126] namely: that it would be contrary to English public policy,[127] the foreign judgment was procured by fraud,[128] the foreign proceedings were in breach of natural justice,[129] or where it would involve the enforcement of a foreign penal[130] or revenue law.[131]

CONSEQUENCES OF RECOGNITION

18.1.29 There are two consequences which merit discussion. The first deals with the assignment of property to the foreign administrator or trustee and the second concerns the discharge of debts. First, if the foreign court has bankruptcy jurisdiction

---

[118] *Re Davidson's Settlement Trusts* (1873) LR 15 Eq 383.

[119] *Re Anderson* [1911] 1 KB 896; *Re Craig* (1916) 86 LJ Ch 62.

[120] *Bergerem v Marsh* (1921) 6 B&CR 195.

[121] Smart, 147.

[122] PStJ Smart, 'Carrying on Business as a Basis of Recognition of Foreign Bankruptcies in English Private International Law' (1989) 9 *OJLS* 557; Smart, 148–53. There is some Scottish authority for this base of jurisdiction: *Obers v Paton's Trustees* (1897) 24 R 719; *Home's Trustee v Home's Trustees* 1926 SLT 214.

[123] Smart, 157–9; *Dicey, Morris and Collins*, para 31–065.

[124] *Re Artola Hermanos* (1890) 24 QBD 640, 649.

[125] *Felixstowe Dock and Railway Co v United States Lines Inc* [1989] QB 360, 373–6. That said, the concept of comity featured strongly in the House of Lords' decision in *Re HIH Casualty & General Insurance* [2008] 1 WLR 852, in relation to the decision to remit assets to Australia pursuant to a request for assistance from the Australian court.

[126] See, in general, Smart, ch 7.

[127] Goulding J in *Re A Debtor, ex p Viscount of the Royal Court of Jersey* [1981] Ch 384, 402.

[128] *Re Henry Hooman* (1859) 1 LT 46.

[129] *Bergerem v Marsh* (1921) 6 B&CR 195. Cf *Re Behrends* (1865) 12 LT 149.

[130] *Schemmer v Property Resources Ltd* [1975] Ch 273.

[131] *Government of India v Taylor* [1955] AC 491. Cf EC Insolvency Regulation, Art 39 and UNCITRAL Model Law on Cross-Border Insolvency, Art 13(3) (as implemented in Great Britain by the Cross-Border Insolvency Regs 2006).

over the debtor according to English private international law, an extra-territorial assignment of the debtor's property to the assignee in accordance with the foreign law will be effective as an assignment of movable property located in England.[132] The vesting of title takes place automatically, and will oust an English execution which takes effect after the foreign bankruptcy assignment. However, the title of the foreign trustee is subject to any charge or encumbrance that may be imposed on the property under English law.[133]

18.1.30 This principle does not extend to immovables located in England;[134] no automatic assignment of title to English land to the foreign trustee takes place upon the making of a foreign bankruptcy order. That said, the English court has the discretion to appoint a receiver of the rents and profits of the immovables.[135] If the foreign court is from a 'relevant country or territory',[136] section 426(4) of the 1986 Act, which deals with judicial co-operation in cross-border insolvencies, may be prayed in aid to achieve this.

18.1.31 The above is subject to the EC Insolvency Regulation, which provides that the *lex concursus* of the main proceedings will determine the assets which form part of the debtor's estate.[137]

18.1.32 Secondly, in contrast with a discharge granted in UK bankruptcy proceedings, a discharge granted in foreign proceedings will only be recognised in England if it is a valid discharge under the law applicable to the contract.[138] In other words, the debt must be governed by the law of the country in which the proceedings take place, assuming that that court applies, as is the usual course of things, the *lex concursus* generally to insolvency matters. For example, a discharge of a debt governed by Malaysian law that is granted in Chinese bankruptcy proceedings will be valid only if the discharge is valid under Malaysian law, notwithstanding the fact that the Chinese court may have bankruptcy jurisdiction in English eyes.

18.1.33 The effect of this approach is that a debtor's assets may be recognised as having passed to his foreign trustee in bankruptcy, but his liability is not at the same time recognised as being discharged.[139] Thus, 'the debtor has lost his assets but not his liability'.[140] One suggestion that has been made to ameliorate this anomaly is that the foreign discharge is also to be recognised in England if it is recognised to be effective by the courts of the country of the law governing the contract.[141]

---

[132] This includes after-acquired property of the debtor: eg, *Re a Debtor, Ex p Viscount of the Royal Court of Jersey* [1981] Ch 384.

[133] *Galbraith v Grimshaw* [1910] AC 508. Cf *Al Sabah v Grupo Torras SA* [2005] 2 AC 333, 352–4 (at [39]–[45]).

[134] *Cockerell v Dickens* (1840) 3 Moo PC 98; *Waite v Bingley* (1882) 21 ChD 674, 682.

[135] *Re Levy's Trusts* (1885) 30 ChD 119, 123–5; *Re Kooperman* (1928) 13 B&CR 49; *Re Osborn* (1931–32) 15 B&CR 189.

[136] Insolvency Act 1986, s 426(11).

[137] Art 4(2)(b).

[138] *Burrows v Jemino* (1726) 2 Str 733; *Potter v Brown* (1804) 5 East 124; *Gardiner v Houghton* (1862) 2 B&S 743; *Bartley v Hodges* (1861) 1 CBNS 375; *Wight v Eckhardt Marine GmbH* [2004] 1 AC 147 (PStJ Smart, [2004] *CLJ* 39).

[139] *Smith v Buchanan* (1800) 1 East 6; *Gibbs v Société Industrielle des Métaux* (1890) 25 QBD 399.

[140] PM North and JJ Fawcett, *Cheshire and North's Private International Law* (London, Butterworths, 12th edn, 1992) 918.

[141] Smart, 261; *Dicey, Morris and Collins*, para 31–097.

18.1.34 This is, however, subject to Article 4(2)(j) of the EC Insolvency Regulation, which provides that the *lex concursus* of the main proceedings will determine the conditions for, and effects of, closure of insolvency proceedings; thus, a discharge which is effective according to the *lex concursus* will be treated as effective in England notwithstanding that it is not so according to the law applicable to the contract.

Concurrent Proceedings

18.1.35 The situation may arise where concurrent insolvency proceedings take place in more than one jurisdiction. It should be noted that the existence of foreign insolvency proceedings does not bar the English court from opening its own proceedings.[142] There are two potential scenarios: where England provides the forum for one of several insolvency proceedings; and where the proceedings are all taking place in foreign jurisdictions. The general rule for both situations is that the English court will give effect to the proceedings which were opened earliest in time,[143] provided, of course, that any foreign court that is earliest in time has jurisdiction in accordance with English private international law. There appears to be some leeway for creative judicial approaches; in *Re P MacFadyen & Co*,[144] the court authorised an agreement between English and Indian trustees to pool all the debtor's assets and distribute them rateably among English and Indian creditors, recognising that it was a common-sense arrangement that benefited all the parties.

18.1.36 A problem that may arise is tied in with the rule that discharge of a debt is recognised only if it is in accordance with the law applicable to the debt. A creditor is allowed to enter proof in more than one set of proceedings, provided that he brings into hotchpot any dividends obtained abroad if he also wishes to enter a claim in England. However, due to costs or other reasons, a creditor may choose to enter proof in only one set of proceedings. If, for example, the creditor chooses to enter a claim in English, but not Ruritanian, proceedings which are opened at around the same time, he may be faced with a problem if the Ruritanian court discharges the debt in accordance with its applicable law much more quickly than the English court. That discharge would then be recognised in England and the creditor would have no claim in the English proceedings.[145] The same problem occurs where the creditor enters claims in both English and Ruritanian proceedings and the debt is more quickly discharged under Ruritanian law.[146]

18.2 CORPORATE INSOLVENCY

18.2.1 At common law, the law of the place of incorporation determines the most important questions relating to a corporation. The place of incorporation provides

---

[142] *Re McCulloch* (1880) 14 ChD 716; *Re Robinson* (1883) 22 ChD 816; *Re Artola Hermanos* (1890) 24 QBD 640; *Re a Debtor (No 199 of 1922)* [1922] 2 Ch 470; *Re a Debtor (No 737 of 1928)* [1929] 1 Ch 362; *Re Thulin* [1995] 1 WLR 165.
[143] *Re Anderson* [1911] 1 KB 896; *Re Temple* [1947] Ch 345.
[144] [1908] 1 KB 675.
[145] PStJ Smart and CD Booth, 'Cross-border insolvency and the discharge of debts' (2004) 20 *Insolv Law & Practice* 147, 148.
[146] *Ibid.*

the domicile of the company,[147] and the law of the place of incorporation governs all matters concerning the constitution of a corporation such as its formation, existence and dissolution.[148] The emphasis on the place of incorporation reflects the fact that a corporation needs to be created, and it can only be created in accordance with a system of law. Registration under a country's relevant laws will give legal personality to a corporation.

18.2.2 In cases of corporate insolvency, several avenues may be pursued. By way of background, under English law, a range of procedures are possible: the company may be wound up (liquidated) and such winding-up can be either voluntary or compulsory;[149] the company may be put into administration[150] or administrative receivership;[151] statutory compromises, composition and arrangements with creditors may be agreed upon;[152] or a reorganisation may be attempted.[153] Not all of these may have equivalents under foreign laws.

18.2.3 The questions that arise pursuant to personal insolvencies arise in relation to corporate insolvencies too, namely: when will an English court assume jurisdiction over an insolvent corporation; what is the applicable law; what are the effects of an English order; and when will a foreign order be recognised? Nevertheless, there are significant differences between the corporate insolvency and personal insolvency regimes, although it will be pointed out where the earlier discussion of personal insolvency is equally applicable in the corporate context. In addition, it should be remembered that the following discussion covers situations falling outside the EC Insolvency Regulation and that it should be read subject to that Regulation's rules.

Jurisdiction

Jurisdiction to Make a Winding-up Order

COMPANIES REGISTERED IN ENGLAND

18.2.4 This area is covered by Part IV of the Insolvency Act 1986. Rather unsurprisingly, English courts have jurisdiction to wind up companies which are registered in

---

[147] *Gasque v Commissioners of Inland Revenue* [1940] 2 KB 80; *National Trust Co Ltd v Ebro Irrigation & Power Co Ltd* [1954] 3 DLR 326 (Ont).

[148] See, eg, *Bateman v Service* (1881) 6 App Cas 386, 389; *National Bank of Greece and Athens SA v Metliss* [1958] AC 509; *Carl Zeiss Stiftung v Rayner & Keller (No 2)* [1967] 1 AC 853, 972; *Grupo Torras SA v Al-Sabah* [1996] 1 Lloyd's Rep 7; *Base Metal v Shamurin* [2005] 1 WLR 1157; *Speed Investments Ltd v Formula One Holdings Ltd* [2005] 1 WLR 1936.

[149] A voluntary winding-up usually results from the members of the company passing a resolution to put the company into winding-up and the process is primarily in the control of the creditors. A compulsory winding-up is a winding-up made by order of the court upon presentation of a petition by the directors or one or more of the creditors and other persons listed in Insolvency Act 1986, s 124.

[150] Introduced as a result of proposals made in the Cork Report (Cmnd 8558, 1982), ch 9. The objective of an administration procedure is to rehabilitate the company, or achieve a better result for creditors as a whole than would have been possible if the company had gone into liquidation straight away. See Part II of the Insolvency Act 1986, as amended by the Enterprise Act 2002.

[151] Administrative receiverships have been partially abolished; see Insolvency Act 1986, s 72A.

[152] Companies Act 2006, Pt 26.

[153] For more details, see R Goode, *Principles of Corporate Insolvency Law* (London, Sweet & Maxwell, 3rd edn, 2005) 18–29.

England.[154] This jurisdiction exists notwithstanding the fact that there is little connection with England apart from England being the place of registration; the company's directors and shareholders may not be English and the company may conduct most of its business outside England.

18.2.5   Section 147 of the 1986 Act gives the court a discretion to stay proceedings, whether temporarily or permanently, on such terms and conditions as it thinks fit.[155] With the advent of the EC Insolvency Regulation, however, the English courts' jurisdiction with respect to winding up insolvent[156] English companies is subject to the Regulation;[157] thus, if the company has its centre of main interests in an EU Member State, English courts may open main insolvency proceedings against an English company only if its centre of main interests is located in England, or territorial proceedings if the company has its centre of main interests in another Member State and a place of establishment in England. In the latter situation, the English proceedings are limited territorially to assets of the debtor within England. If the English company has its centre of main interests in another EU Member State so that the Regulation applies, but does not have a place of establishment in England, the English court has no jurisdiction to wind it up.[158] If the English company has its centre of main interests outside the European Union, the court will have jurisdiction to wind it up whether or not it has a place of establishment in England.

COMPANIES THAT ARE NOT REGISTERED IN ENGLAND (FOREIGN COMPANIES)

18.2.6   This area is covered by Part V of the Insolvency Act 1986. Unregistered companies can be wound up by an English court as provided for by section 221.[159] Although foreign companies are rather surprisingly not expressly referred to by that provision, companies which have been incorporated abroad have long been held to fall within the Act's definition of 'unregistered companies'.[160] If the company has its centre of main interests in England, the English courts have jurisdiction to open main insolvency proceedings under the EC Insolvency Regulation; if the company has its centre of main interests in another Member State but has a place of establishment in England, the English courts have jurisdiction to open territorial proceedings under the Regulation.

18.2.7   Outside the Regulation, the English court will have jurisdiction to wind up an unregistered company which has its centre of main interests outside an EU Member State. The following discussion is based on the assumption that the Regulation is inapplicable.

---

[154] Insolvency Act 1986, s 117.

[155] See *Re Harrods (Buenos Aires) Ltd* [1992] Ch 72 on the exercise of judicial discretion against assuming jurisdiction to wind up a *solvent* company incorporated in England but with its place of business and central management based in Argentina.

[156] The winding-up of solvent companies is unaffected by the EC Insolvency Regulation; however, that topic is outside the scope of this chapter.

[157] Insolvency Act 1986, s 117(7).

[158] The corollary to this is that, under the EC Insolvency Regulation, the English court has jurisdiction to wind up a foreign company which has its centre of main interests in England.

[159] See Insolvency Act 1986, s 221. The winding up of solvent companies is outside the scope of this chapter.

[160] See Insolvency Act 1986, s 220(1). International organisations set up by treaties do not fall within s 220(1): *JH Rayner (Mincing Lane) Ltd v Department of Trade and Industry* [1990] 2 AC 418, 482.

18.2.8   Under section 221(5) of the Insolvency Act 1986, an unregistered company may be wound up[161] in three circumstances:

(a) if the company is dissolved, or has ceased to carry on business, or is carrying on business only for the purpose of winding up its affairs;
(b) if the company is unable to pay its debts;
(c) if the court is of opinion that it is just and equitable that the company should be wound up.

This section appears to give English courts an exorbitant jurisdiction since no tie with England is required before assumption of jurisdiction to wind up the foreign company. However, English courts have been circumspect and insisted on some sort of nexus with England before it will assume jurisdiction under section 221(5). Earlier case law had placed importance on the existence of assets in England.[162] However, there may be other reasons why an English winding-up order is requested other than the realisation of assets to creditors; for example, it may be required to trigger other legislation.[163] The reality is also that a simple 'presence of assets' test can be easily manipulated by transferring the assets out of the jurisdiction. It is now accepted that the presence of assets in England is not a condition of the English courts' jurisdictional competence to wind up a foreign company.[164]

18.2.9   Knox J in *Re Real Estate Development Co* articulated three core requirements that need to be satisfied before jurisdiction is exercised over a foreign company:

(1) There must be a sufficient connection with England and Wales, but that does not mean that assets must be situate within the jurisdiction.
(2) There must be a reasonable possibility, if a winding up order is made, of benefit accruing to those applying for the winding-up order.
(3) One or more persons interested in the distribution of the assets must be persons over whom the court could exercise jurisdiction.[165]

There is some uncertainty as to whether the principles go towards the issue of whether the court has jurisdiction to wind up a foreign company or whether the court should exercise its discretion to do so.[166] Given that the terms of the Insolvency Act 1986, albeit not expressly,[167] give statutory jurisdiction to the courts to wind up a foreign

---

[161] No voluntary winding-up of a foreign company is possible, except in accordance with the EC Insolvency Regulation; see Insolvency Act 1986, s 221(4). In contrast, both court-ordered winding-up and voluntary winding-up (creditors' voluntary winding-up) are permissible under the Insolvency Act 1986 for English registered companies.

[162] Eg, *Re Matheson Brothers Ltd* (1884) 27 Ch D 225; *Banque des Marchands de Moscou v Kindersley* [1951] Ch 112, 126; *Re Azoff-Don Commercial Bank* [1954] 1 Ch 315.

[163] Eg, *Re Compania Merabello San Nicholas* [1973] Ch 75. See K Dawson, 'The Doctrine of Forum Non Conveniens and the Winding Up of Insolvent Foreign Companies' [2005] *JBL* 28, 31–2.

[164] *Re Eloc Electro-Optieck BV* [1982] Ch 43; *Re A Company (No 000359 of 1987)* [1988] Ch 210; *Banco Nacional de Cuba v Cosmos Trading Corp* [2000] 1 BCLC 813; *Stocznia Gdanska SA v Latreefers Inc (No 2)* [2001] 2 BCLC 116.

[165] Knox J in *Re Real Estate Development Co* [1991] BCLC 210, 217. These requirements were approved by the Court of Appeal in later cases such as *Banco Nacional de Cuba v Cosmos Trading Corp* [2000] 1 BCLC 813; *Stocznia Gdanska SA v Latreefers Inc (No 2)* [2001] 2 BCLC 116. The requirements have also been applied to the approval of a scheme of arrangement under the Companies Act 1985, s 425 (now see Companies Act 2006, Pt 26): *Re Drax Holdings Ltd* [2004] 1 WLR 1049.

[166] See *Re Paramount Airways Ltd* [1993] Ch 223, 240; *Stocznia Gdanska SA v Latreefers Inc (No 2)* [2001] 2 BCLC 116, 140 (at [30]); *Re Drax Holdings Ltd* [2004] 1 WLR 1049, 1054 (at [23]).

[167] Save in the context of s 225, on which, see para 18.2.14.

company, the likelier inference is that the core requirements set out by Knox J go towards the issue of discretion.[168] In any event, little will turn on either interpretation in the winding-up context as:

The English court will not wind up a foreign company where it has no legitimate interest to do so, for that would be to exercise an exorbitant jurisdiction contrary to international comity, and for that purpose it does not matter whether the preconditions are couched in terms of the existence of jurisdiction or the exercise of jurisdiction.[169]

18.2.10   However, it may make a difference when the court is asked to approve a scheme of arrangement under what is now Part 26 of the Companies Act 2006 as the second and third requirements are formulated in the context of winding-up. In *Re Drax Holdings Ltd*,[170] the issue was whether Knox J's core requirements had to be fulfilled in the context of a scheme of arrangement (under section 425 of the Companies Act 1985) which referred to companies 'liable to be wound up'[171] under the Insolvency Act 1986. If Knox J's requirements relate to the existence of jurisdiction, the requirements would need to be fulfilled even for schemes of arrangement. Sensibly, Lawrence Collins J preferred to interpret the requirements as referring to the discretion of the court as, given that schemes of arrangement arise in many non-insolvency-related contexts, the alternative interpretation would lead to 'very odd and artificial consequences'.[172]

18.2.11   In the normal course of things, the presence of assets in England would constitute a good reason for making a winding-up order. However, if the asset is so small or of such a character that the link with England is tenuous it would not persuade the court to assume jurisdiction.[173] In all cases, clear evidence of a sufficient connection with England needs to be demonstrated; for example, the company may carry on business in England,[174] or a relevant agreement may be governed by English law and be negotiated, executed and require performance in England,[175] or the company may be a member of a group of companies that comprises mainly English companies whose directors are English residents.[176] In relation to the second requirement, the fact that a similar benefit might be achieved by other means might be a reason for the court to decline to exercise its winding-up jurisdiction, but this must depend on all the circumstances; in particular, it is not necessary that a winding-up be a remedy of last resort.[177] Thus, the availability of an easier UNCITRAL procedure to a foreign liquidator was outweighed where the foreign liquidator was neither fluent in the

---

[168]   *Re OJSC Ank Yugraneft* [2009] 1 BCLC 298, 306.
[169]   Lawrence Collins J in *Re Drax Holdings Ltd* [2004] 1 WLR 1049, 1054 (at [24]).
[170]   [2004] 1 WLR 1049.
[171]   Companies Act 1985, s 425(6)(a). See now Companies Act 2006, s 895(2).
[172]   [2004] 1 WLR 1049, 1054 (at [27]). On jurisdiction to approve schemes of arrangements, see further *Re DAP Holdings NV* [2006] BCC 48; *Re The Home Insurance Co* [2006] 2 BCLC 476; *Re Sovereign Marine & General Insurance Co* [2007] 1 BCLC 228.
[173]   Eg, *Re Real Estate Development Co* [1991] BCLC 210.
[174]   Knox J in *Re Real Estate Development Co* [1991] BCLC 210, 217; *Re A Company (No 003102 of 1991)* [1991] BCLC 539; *Re Eloc Electro-Optieck BV* [1982] Ch 43; *Atlantic & General Investment Trust Ltd v Richbell Information Services Inc* [2000] 2 BCLC 778.
[175]   *Re A Company (No 000359 of 1987)* [1988] Ch 210.
[176]   *Atlantic & General Investment Trust Ltd v Richbell Information Services Inc* [2000] 2 BCLC 778.
[177]   *Re OJSC Ank Yugraneft* [2009] 1 BCLC 298, 315.

English language nor familiar with English court procedure. Commencing winding-up proceedings would lead to a licensed insolvency practitioner who was familiar with the intricacies of English litigation presiding over a complex liquidation and account-able to the English court; the creditors would also be protected in the event of the for-eign liquidator being unable to continue in office.[178] A fourth principle is sometimes added to Knox J's requirements: that there is no other more appropriate jurisdiction in which to wind up the company[179]; this ties in with the argument that the doctrine of *forum non conveniens* should have a role to play in this area.[180] The fact that the causes of action are situated in England and there is no prospect of proceedings abroad has been held to be a relevant factor under this fourth requirement.[181]

18.2.12   Although English courts are prepared to wind up a company incorpo-rated abroad, some heed is taken of the place of incorporation; in *Banco Nacional de Cuba v Cosmos Trading Corp*[182] it was held that, if the company continues trading in the country where it is incorporated, it is 'thoroughly undesirable'[183] for the English court to assume jurisdiction to wind up the company, although in this case there was limited connection with England in the first place.

18.2.13   There are two conceptual puzzles underlying section 221(5)(a), which, it will be recalled, permits the court to wind up a foreign company which is dissolved. First, if the company has already been dissolved abroad, what is there left for the English court to wind up? English courts have ingeniously held that the dissolved company is revived, thereby enabling it to be wound up and then dissolved again by the court.[184] The second puzzle is related to the first: when a company is dissolved, its property and rights are deemed to be *bona vacantia* under English law,[185] thereby rendering otiose any winding-up order. To get around this, the Crown's title to the English assets is treated as being defeated upon the making of a winding-up order under section 221(5)(a) so that title revests in the revived company.

FOREIGN COMPANIES WHICH HAVE BEEN DISSOLVED UNDER
THE LAW OF THE PLACE OF INCORPORATION

18.2.14   Section 225(1) of the Insolvency Act 1986 states that:

Where a company incorporated outside Great Britain which has been carrying on business in Great Britain ceases to carry on business in Great Britain, it may be wound up as an unregistered company under this Act, notwithstanding that it has been dissolved or otherwise

---

[178] *Re OJSC Ank Yugraneft* [2009] 1 BCLC 298, 315. However, Clarke J ultimately dismissed the winding-up petition on grounds that the petitioners had failed to disclose material facts to the court.

[179] *Re A Company (No 000359 of 1987)* [1988] Ch 210, 226–7; *Re A Company (No 003102 of 1991)* [1991] BCLC 539, 541.

[180] See K Dawson, 'The Doctrine of Forum Non Conveniens and the Winding Up of Insolvent Foreign Companies' [2005] *JBL* 28.

[181] *Re Compania Merabello San Nicholas* [1973] Ch 75; *Re Allobrogia Steamship Corp* [1978] 3 All ER 423.

[182] [2000] 1 BCLC 813.

[183] Scott V-C at [2000] 1 BCLC 813, 819.

[184] *Russian and English Bank and Florance Montefiore Guedalla v Baring Bros & Co Ltd* [1936] AC 405.

[185] See Companies Act 2006, s 1012. See also *Re Higginson and Dean* [1899] 1 QB 325; *Re Wells, Swinburne-Hanham v Howard* [1933] 1 Ch 29; *Re Banque Industrielle de Moscou* [1952] Ch 919; *Re Azoff-Don Commercial Bank* [1954] Ch 315.

ceased to exist as a company under or by virtue of the laws of the country under which it was incorporated.

The enactment of the predecessor of this subsection is generally thought to be 'merely for the removal of doubt'[186] over whether the English courts had jurisdiction to wind up Russian companies dissolved by Soviet decrees after the 1917 revolution.[187] It was decided by Bennett J that what is now section 225 did not apply with retrospective effect to companies which had been dissolved before the provision came into force in 1928;[188] this is now considered to be erroneous, since this would defeat the very objective of the provision's enactment.[189] Section 225 is largely redundant as the jurisdiction it espouses is covered by the broader jurisdiction set out in section 221(5)(a)[190] and there appears to be no reported case in which section 225(1) has been utilised.[191]

COMPANIES REGISTERED IN OTHER PARTS OF THE UNITED KINGDOM
18.2.15   The general rule is that within the United Kingdom, only the courts of the place where the company is incorporated have jurisdiction to wind up that company. Therefore Scottish, not English, courts have the jurisdiction to wind up Scottish-registered companies.[192] However, an unregistered company which has a principal place of business in both England and Scotland is considered to be registered in both countries[193] and English courts will therefore have jurisdiction to wind it up under section 221.

18.2.16   The situation is a bit more complicated for Northern Irish companies. First, it is clear that a company incorporated in Northern Ireland which has been carrying on business in Great Britain but has ceased to do so may be wound up in England pursuant to section 225. However, outside the rather limited scope of section 225, it is uncertain whether the English court can claim jurisdiction to wind up a Northern Irish company. In *Re A Company (No 007946 of 1993)*,[194] the question facing the court was whether section 221, which is contained in Part V of the 1986 Act, which deals with the winding up of unregistered companies, could be used as a basis for such jurisdiction. To answer this question, one had to consider section 441(2), which provides that nothing in the Insolvency Act 1986 extends to Northern Ireland or applies to or in relation to companies registered or incorporated in Northern Ireland apart from certain identified provisions[195] (which are irrelevant for the current discussion) and 'any provision expressly relating to companies incorporated elsewhere than in Great Britain'. The issue was therefore whether section 220, which defines what is an 'unregistered company' for the purposes of Part V, could be said

---

[186] Megarry J in *Re Compania Merabello San Nicholas SA* [1973] Ch 75, 86.
[187] See also M Mann, (1952) 15 *MLR* 479; M Mann, (1955) 4 *ICLQ* 226.
[188] *Re Russian and English Bank* [1932] 1 Ch 663.
[189] See Lord Blanesburgh in *Russian and English Bank and Florance Montefiore Guedalla v Baring Bros & Co Ltd* [1936] AC 405, 415–6. See also Lord Atkin at [1936] AC 405, 424–5.
[190] See, eg, *IRC v Highland Engineering Ltd* 1975 SLT 203.
[191] *Dicey, Morris and Collins*, para 30–054.
[192] Insolvency Act 1986, s 120.
[193] Insolvency Act 1986, s 221(3).
[194] [1994] Ch 198.
[195] Set out in Insolvency Act 1986, s 441(1).

to 'expressly relate to companies incorporated elsewhere than in Great Britain'.[196]
On the face of it, section 220 did not do so, as section 220(1) merely states that:

(1) For the purposes of this Part, the expression 'unregistered company' includes ..., any association and any company, with the following exceptions—

   (a) ...
   (b) a company registered in any part of the United Kingdom under the Joint Stock
       Companies Acts or under the legislation (past or present) relating to companies in
       Great Britain.

18.2.17   However, Morritt J held that:

it is quite possible, as a matter of ordinary English usage, to have an express relation without
an express reference. For example, a provision which referred expressly to citrus fruits would
be a provision expressly relating to oranges and lemons even though they were not expressly
mentioned in the provision. Thus, in my judgment, the fact that section 220 of the Insolvency
Act 1986 does not refer expressly to companies incorporated elsewhere in Great Britain is by
no means conclusive.[197]

It was held that section 220 was 'a provision expressly relating to companies incorporated elsewhere than in Great Britain notwithstanding that there is no express
reference to such a company'.[198] Upon consideration of other provisions, Morritt J
ultimately held that the court had jurisdiction to wind up the Northern Irish company
as an unregistered company pursuant to section 221.[199]

18.2.18   It has been pointed out that Morritt J's judgment is based on a distortion
of the historical lineage of the particular provisions and a misunderstanding of them.
For example, Morritt J relied on section 221(2), which provides:[200]

If an unregistered company has a principal place of business situated in Northern Ireland; it
shall not be wound up under this Part [V] unless it has a principal place of business situated in
England and Wales or Scotland, or in both England and Wales and Scotland.

He considered that section 221(2) was evidence of the draftsman's intention that a
company incorporated in Northern Ireland could be wound up in England as an
unregistered company because 'a company with a principal place of business in
Northern Ireland would most commonly be a company incorporated there'.[201] This,
however, is argued to be misconceived, because section 221(2) originates from the
Companies Act 1862 where, at that time, Ireland was part of the United Kingdom
and it was clear that courts of one part of the United Kingdom could not wind up

---

[196] S 225 obviously fulfilled this criterion.
[197] [1994] Ch 198, 203.
[198] [1994] Ch 198, 203.
[199] Provided the company had a principal place of business in England and Wales (see Insolvency Act
1986, s 221(2)); the company did not suggest that it did not have such a place of business.
[200] Morritt J also referred to s 225, noting at [1994] Ch 198, 204 that: 'It would be most surprising if
a company incorporated in Northern Ireland might be wound up in England if it had ceased to carry on
business in England and had been dissolved in Northern Ireland, but not otherwise.' This, however, mis-
interprets s 225, which does not require a company to be dissolved in the place of incorporation before
the provision can be invoked but provides that the provision can be invoked even if the company has been
dissolved.
[201] [1994] Ch 198, 203.

companies incorporated under the Companies Act in another part.[202] Some commentators, therefore, persuasively argue that the correct position is that an English court only has jurisdiction to wind up a Northern Irish company under section 225, and not under section 220.[203]

Jurisdiction to Make Administration Orders

18.2.19 English courts obviously have jurisdiction to make an administration order in respect of a company registered in England.[204] It is less clear whether there is a similar jurisdiction with respect to foreign companies. It has been assumed in some cases that the court does not have jurisdiction to make an administration order in respect of a foreign company.[205] However, in *Re International Bulk Commodities Ltd*,[206] it was held that receivers appointed over the property of an unregistered company were administrative receivers[207] within Part III of the Insolvency Act 1986 and not merely contractual receivers appointed out of court with powers limited to those conferred by the terms of the debenture. The authoritativeness of this case is unclear and it was not followed in relation to a receiver of an unregistered English company.[208] Further, Mummery J in *Re International Bulk Commodities Ltd* noted that the two remedies of administrative receiver and administrators are different in nature, albeit similar in purpose, and therefore it does not necessarily follow that any confinement of the court's power to appoint an administrator over foreign companies[209] would be the same for an administrative receiver.[210] Although it would be convenient if an English court could put a foreign company into administration,[211] the legislative history of the relevant provisions and enactment of subsequent legislation suggests that the Insolvency Act 1986 does not give the court the power to make an administrative order over foreign companies.[212]

---

[202] Smart, 116–7.

[203] Smart, 113–20 (note the additional arguments he makes); *Dicey, Morris and Collins*, para 30–070.

[204] Insolvency Act 1986, Pt II, sched B1, paras 10–13, as amended by the Enterprise Act 2002. Under the 2002 Act, an administrator can also be appointed by the holder of a qualifying floating charge or by the company or its directors.

[205] *Felixstowe Dock and Rly Co v US Lines Inc* [1989] QB 360, 376; *Re Dallhold Estates (UK) Pty Ltd* [1992] BCLC 621, 623.

[206] [1993] Ch 77.

[207] A receiver is someone appointed to collect and receive the company's property by or on behalf of debenture holders under a debenture secured by a floating charge. Under English law, there are administrative receiverships which cover the whole or substantially the whole of the company's assets, and receiverships that are confined to a particular asset or assets (which includes receiverships under the Law of Property Act 1925). Only the former is considered to be an insolvency regime. See R Goode, *Principles of Corporate Insolvency Law* (London, Sweet & Maxwell, 3rd edition, 2005) 22–4. The entitlement to appoint an administrative receiver has been partially abolished; see Insolvency Act 1986, s 72A.

[208] *Re Devon and Somerset Farmers Ltd* [1994] Ch 57.

[209] Mummery J declined to decide whether the assumption that the court has no power to make an administration order in relation to a foreign company is right or wrong: [1993] Ch 77, 88.

[210] [1993] Ch 77, 88.

[211] Eg, if an attempt is being made to rescue a group of companies, all bar one of which are English companies. See Smart, 132–3.

[212] See Smart, 130–6. Cf G Moss, 'Administration Orders for Foreign Companies' (1993) 6 *Insolv Int* 19.

Choice of Law

18.2.20   As with bankruptcies, English law will apply to both substantive and pro-cedural questions.[213] English law remains applicable even if the English liquidation proceedings are ancillary to foreign liquidation proceedings.[214] Referring to a line of authorities where courts had disclaimed the power to disapply English law notwith-standing that the English proceedings were merely ancillary, Scott V-C in *Re BCCI SA (No 10)*[215] held that the court had no inherent common law discretion to disapply the statutory scheme of set-off contained in rule 4.90 of the Insolvency Rules 1986. So, this rule was held to be applicable in the situation where English liquidators had requested directions on whether assets should be remitted to Luxembourg where the principal liquidation was being conducted, and where the English rule would have been ignored by the Luxembourg court; moreover, if the court did have discretion to disapply English law, it should not be exercised in this situation. Scott V-C was not prepared to remit the assets unless provision was made to ensure that the distribution was in accordance with English rules. It should be noted that, whilst Lord Hoffman in *Re HIH Casualty & General Insurance Ltd*[216] thought that the decision was correct because of the close connection of the underlying transactions with England,[217] the various members of the House of Lords[218] did not agree that the court's jurisdiction to remit assets abroad was restricted to situations where the foreign court had similar distribution rules to England.[219]

18.2.21   Some reference to foreign law may be necessary, such as to determine whether a debt is valid according to its governing law. Recourse to the law of the place of incorporation may be necessary to determine issues such as the validity of the appointment of officers and directors of the company,[220] whether a shareholder has to make payment as a contributory, or the identity of persons entitled to surplus assets.[221]

Effects of an English Winding-up Order

18.2.22   The discussion on issues such as the discharge of debts, the position of creditors and the operation of the hotchpot rule, which was examined in relation to the effects of an English bankruptcy order,[222] applies in the same manner to corporate

---

[213] For more details, see paras 18.1.13–18.1.14.

[214] *Re English, Scottish and Australian Chartered Bank* [1893] 3 Ch 385, 394; *Re Sudair International Airways Ltd* [1951] Ch 165, 172–3; *Re Bank of Credit and Commerce International SA (No 10)* [1997] Ch 213; *Re OJSC Ank Yugraneft* [2009] 1 BCLC 298, 315 (at [62]).

[215] [1997] Ch 213.

[216] [2008] 1 WLR 852.

[217] The mutual debts which were set off against each other were governed by English law.

[218] Albeit on different grounds; see paras 18.3.9–18.3.14.

[219] [2008] 1 WLR 852, 860 (at [24]). See also Lord Hoffman's remarks at [2008] 1 WLR 852, 860–1 (at [26]–[27]) on whether the application of s 426(5), in the particular context of that case, involved the application of Australian insolvency law (Australia being the state requesting assistance) or English law.

[220] *Banco de Bilbao v Sancha* [1938] 2 KB 176.

[221] *Re Banque des Marchands de Moscou* [1958] Ch 182.

[222] See paras 18.1.16–18.1.20.

insolvencies. Instances where the effects of a winding up order may differ from the effects of a bankruptcy order are considered below.

The Universalist Effects of an English Winding-up Order

18.2.23   Like an English bankruptcy order, a winding-up order purports to cover all the company's assets[223] and creditors, wherever situated. The difference is that the Insolvency Act 1986 does not provide for the automatic vesting of the company's property in the liquidator. However, the 1986 Act does enable the court to make an order vesting all or part of the company's property in the liquidator upon application,[224] and also provides that the liquidator or provisional liquidator (as the case may be) shall take into his custody or under his control the company's property.[225] Under the common law, it is well established that the insolvent company's property is impressed with a trust upon the making of a winding-up order,[226] although the trust that arises in this situation is acknowledged to be a 'legal construct',[227] being one which strips the company of its beneficial interest in the property[228] but which does not correspondingly hand that beneficial interest to the creditors.[229] In any event, whether under the 1986 Act or through operation of the common law, the company can be deprived of the management and use of its assets. The liquidator steps in and the legislation spells out the liquidator's functions, powers and duties and determines when he may be removed.[230]

18.2.24   As has been noted previously, the encompassing definition of property provided by section 436 covers property situated abroad. But the liquidator's ability to take control of property located outside England depends on the *lex situs* and whether the foreign court recognises the authority of the liquidator.

18.2.25   It should also be noted that in cases where the court regards the English proceedings as ancillary to main proceedings commenced in the place of incorporation, the court is prepared to depart from universalism and confine the English liquidator to collecting assets located in England.[231]

Dissolution of the Company

18.2.26   The ultimate effect of winding-up is that the company is dissolved. However, the company's debts are not discharged as in the case of a bankruptcy:

---

[223]   For the definition of 'property', see Insolvency Act 1986, s 436.

[224]   Insolvency Act 1986, s 145.

[225]   Insolvency Act 1986, s 144(1).

[226]   *Re Oriental Inland Steam Co* (1874) LR 9 Ch App 557; *New Zealand Loan and Mercantile Agency Co Ltd v Morrison* [1898] AC 349; *Ayerst v C&K (Construction) Ltd* [1976] AC 167; *Re Bank of Credit and Commerce International SA (No 10)* [1997] Ch 213.

[227]   Burnton LJ in *Bloom v Harms Offshore AHT 'Taurus' GmbH & Co KG* [2010] 2 WLR 349, 358 (at [24]).

[228]   Cf *Federal Commissioner of Taxation v Linter Textiles Australia Ltd* (2005) 220 CLR 592 (High Court, Australia); *International Transportation Service Inc v The Owners and/or Demise Charterers of the Ship or Vessel 'Convenience Container'* [2006] 2 Lloyd's Rep 556 (High Court, Hong Kong).

[229]   Millett LJ in *Mitchell v Carter* [1997] 1 BCLC 673, 684.

[230]   Insolvency Act 1986, ss 143–6, 160, 163–174.

[231]   See para 18.2.50.

[The debts] are discharged by the winding-up only to the extent that they are paid out of dividends. But when the process of distribution is complete, there are no further assets against which they can be enforced. There is no equivalent of the discharge of a personal bankrupt which extinguishes his debts. When the company is dissolved, there is no longer an entity which the creditor can sue.[232]

As a result, a creditor who has not obtained full satisfaction of his claim has no practical recourse. However, if an asset is discovered, the company can be restored for the process of distribution to resume.[233] If a composition or scheme of arrangement has been concluded, a discharge of debt can be agreed upon by the company and its creditors.

    18.2.27 There is little difficulty in accepting that an English winding-up order legitimately dissolves an English incorporated company. However, the notion that an order made by the English court applying English law will also similarly dissolve a foreign company sits rather uncomfortably with the notion that, as regards fundamental aspects of a company, including its dissolution, overriding importance should be attached to the law of the place of incorporation.[234] It might be that a definitive dissolution may need to be sought in the country of incorporation.

Automatic Stays and Executions

18.2.28 Section 130(2) of the 1986 Act provides that when a winding-up order has been made or a provisional liquidator has been appointed, no other proceedings may be brought against the company except by leave of the court and subject to such terms as the court may impose. This means that, as a general rule, any other proceedings against the company are subject to an automatic stay. However, it is important to note that this automatic stay is imposed only on proceedings in courts within the United Kingdom and does not extend beyond. This means that when an English winding-up order has been made, an automatic stay will be imposed on proceedings brought against the company in Scotland but not proceedings brought against the company in Melbourne.[235] Section 130(2) also has no effect on English proceedings against a company where that company is subject to insolvency proceedings abroad.[236] The automatic stay may be waived; a secured creditor will be granted leave pursuant to section 130(2) to enforce his security.[237] In cases falling outside section 130(2), the court can still rely on its inherent jurisdiction[238] to stay English proceedings, although exceptionally strong grounds must be shown for the court to exercise this power.[239]

---

[232] Lord Hoffman in *Wight v Eckhardt GmbH* [2004] 1 AC 147, 156 (at [27]) (PC).

[233] Lord Hoffman in *Wight v Eckhardt GmbH* [2004] 1 AC 147, 156 (at [27]). See Companies Act 2006, ss 1024–34 on how a company may be restored after dissolution has taken place. On how the discovered assets may be distributed, see Fletcher, 198–200.

[234] See, further, Fletcher, 196–8.

[235] *Re Vocalion (Foreign) Ltd* [1932] 2 Ch 196.

[236] *Mazur Media Ltd v Mazur Media GmbH* [2004] 1 WLR 2966.

[237] *Moor v Anglo-Italian Bank* (1879) 10 ChD 681; *Re Wanzer Ltd* [1891] 1 Ch 305; *Re West Cumberland Iron and Steel Co* [1893] 1 Ch 713; *Minna Craig Steamship Co v Chartered Mercantile Bank of India, London and China* [1897] 1 QB 460. Cf *Re International Pulp and Paper Co* (1876) 3 ChD 594.

[238] Reinforced by the Supreme Court Act 1981, s 49(3).

[239] *Mazur Media Ltd v Mazur Media GmbH* [2004] 1 WLR 2966.

18.2.29   In addition, any benefit gained from an execution or attachment that is only completed after the commencement of winding-up proceedings cannot be retained.[240] This, again, does not apply to executions and attachments that have been obtained in a foreign court.[241]

18.2.30   The 1986 Act also provides that:

Where a company registered in England and Wales is being wound up by the court, any attachment, sequestration, distress or execution put in force against the estate or effects of the company after the commencement of the winding-up is void.[242]

Although the reference is to 'a company registered in England and Wales', this provision has been held also to apply to a foreign company, on the basis that section 221(1) makes it clear that all the provisions of the Act about winding-up apply to an unregistered company as well.[243]

18.2.31   Despite the territorial limitations of some of the Act's provisions, a creditor who is within the court's *in personam* jurisdiction can still be restrained, in accordance with the court's inherent jurisdiction, from commencing foreign proceedings[244] against the company to ensure that he does not obtain more than his fair share of dividends; this does not depend on whether the creditor has proved in the English proceedings.[245] The discretion to issue an anti-suit injunction against a creditor also applies to bankruptcy cases.

18.2.32   One of the objectives of stays and injunctions in this context is the prevention of a creditor getting more than his fair share of dividends. It should be noted that the operation of the hotchpot rule, which operates for liquidations in the same manner as was discussed previously for bankruptcies, also militates against this risk.

18.2.33   Lastly, it should be noted that the 1986 Act contains an equivalent to section 130(2) for companies under administration. Paragraph 43(6) of Schedule B1 provides:

No legal process (including legal proceedings, execution, distress and diligence) may be instituted or continued against the company or property of the company except—

(a) with the consent of the administrator, or
(b) with the permission of the court.

This provision, like section 130(2), has no extra-territorial effect.[246] The court nevertheless still has an inherent power to prevent creditors from seeking to put themselves in a better position to other creditors by pursuing foreign proceedings against assets abroad:

If the court has a jurisdiction to protect the assets of a company that is being wound up by the Court from foreign attachments and executions, ... it has a similar jurisdiction in the case of a company in administration.[247]

---

[240] Insolvency Act 1986, s 183.
[241] *Mitchell v Carter* [1997] 1 BCLC 673.
[242] Insolvency Act 1986, s 128(1).
[243] *Re Lineas Navieras Bolivianas SAM (The Bolivia)* [1995] BCC 666, 669F. PStJ Smart, [1996] *LMCLQ* 168.
[244] There is a difference between this and restraining a creditor from proving in a foreign insolvency; the latter is unobjectionable as the creditor is merely seeking to share in the insolvent's assets rather than gaining a priority over other creditors. See Smart, 294–5.
[245] *Re Central Sugar Factories of Brazil (Flack's Case)* [1894] 1 Ch 369.
[246] Burnton LJ in *Bloom v Harms Offshore AHT 'Taurus' GmbH & Co KG* stated that he 'found it difficult' to decide otherwise, although in the end he held that it was unnecessary to arrive at a conclusion on the facts of the case: [2010] 2 WLR 349, 357–8 (at [21]–[22]).
[247] Burnton LJ in *Bloom v Harms Offshore AHT 'Taurus' GmbH & Co KG* [2010] WLR 349, 358 (at [24]).

18.2.34 In *Bloom v Harms Offshore AHT 'Taurus' GmbH & Co KG*,[248] creditors had 'set a trap' for administrators by obtaining attachment orders against assets of the company in New York, not informing the New York court that the company was subject to an English administration order. When the administrators paid over money into a New York bank account in ignorance of the attachment orders, the money was attached. The Court of Appeal held that it had jurisdiction to prevent the creditors from taking advantage of a foreign attachment and that, given the creditors' improper and oppressive conduct, the facts of the case merited the exercise of that jurisdiction.

18.2.35 Thus the court has the power to take whatever steps are open to it within the limits of its jurisdiction to enable the liquidator or the administrator to carry out his duties, although the exercise of that jurisdiction would always depend on the facts of each case.

Recognition

Recognition of Intra-UK Insolvency Proceedings

18.2.36 Liquidations conducted by courts in other parts of the United Kingdom are accorded automatic recognition under section 426(1), which stipulates that an order made by a court in any part of the United Kingdom in the exercise of jurisdiction in relation to insolvency law shall be enforced in other parts of the United Kingdom as if it were made by the recognising court. Therefore, a liquidator appointed in Scotland will be recognised by the English court. Strictly speaking, if the Scottish liquidator seeks to recover assets in England, he is not seeking enforcement of a Scottish court order but rather seeking recognition of his authority to act under Scottish law.[249] Pedantry, however, should not obscure the effect and intention of the provision that, in this situation,[250] the English court should accede to the liquidator's request.[251]

18.2.37 In relation to receivers appointed elsewhere in Great Britain, section 72(1) of the Insolvency Act 1986 provides:

A receiver appointed under the law of either part of Great Britain in respect of the whole or any part of any property or undertaking of a company and in consequence of the company having created a charge which, as created, was a floating charge may exercise his powers in the other part of Great Britain so far as their exercise is not inconsistent with the law applicable there.

The same is applicable for receivers appointed under the law of Northern Ireland.[252]

Recognition of Foreign Liquidations[253]

18.2.38 In keeping with the importance that is attached to the place of incorporation for companies, a liquidation that is conducted by the country where the company

---

[248] [2010] 2 WLR 349.
[249] Smart, 214.
[250] See paras 18.1.21–18.1.22.
[251] Subject to s 426(2); see para 18.1.22.
[252] The powers of Northern Irish receivers are still covered by the Administration of Justice Act 1977, s 7; this provision originally covered receivers appointed under the law of any part of the United Kingdom but is now superseded by the Insolvency Act 1986, s 72, in relation to English and Scottish receivers.
[253] The UNCITRAL Model Law on Cross-Border Insolvency also contains rules on recognition of foreign insolvency proceedings and the consequences of such recognition; see ch 19.

is incorporated will be accorded recognition by the English courts.[254] The authority of the liquidator or equivalent office holder appointed by the courts of the country of incorporation will be recognised by the court and assistance will be granted to enable him to carry out his duties efficiently.

18.2.39 Outside this context, it is somewhat unclear on what basis foreign liquidations will be recognised, although it is at least established that recognition is not based on the same grounds on which the English court itself assumes jurisdiction to wind up a foreign company.[255] If the foreign liquidation concerns a company which is not incorporated in the country where the liquidation proceedings take place, there is a good case for saying that the English court should likewise recognise the liquidation if the courts of the place of incorporation do so.[256] Further, it has been suggested that, if the company carries on business in a particular country, an order made by the courts of that country will also be recognised.[257] It might also be postulated that, if an English company is the subject of the foreign liquidation, English courts may be less ready to recognise the legitimacy of the foreign court's jurisdiction unless it can be shown that the company has substantial ties with that jurisdiction.[258] If there are concurrent proceedings taking place in England and in the foreign jurisdiction with respect to an English company, the foreign proceedings could be treated as being ancillary to the English winding-up;[259] conversely, if the other proceedings involve a winding-up of a company incorporated in that jurisdiction, the English proceedings are likely to be treated as ancillary.[260] If the concurrent proceedings are taking place in the place of incorporation and a third state, the English courts will be likely to deem the proceedings being conducted in the place of incorporation as being the main proceedings and any other proceedings merely ancillary.[261]

18.2.40 Once it is established that the foreign liquidation is recognised, a liquidator appointed in those proceedings will be entitled to seek assistance from the English courts. The assistance extends to helping the liquidator gain control of property of the company in England, whether by vesting title to the property in the liquidator, or appointing him as receiver with the power to receive rents and profits. The helpful approach adopted by the court overcomes the practical difficulty that a foreign liquidation does not automatically vest the property of the company in the liquidator.[262] As has been said: 'recognition carries with it the active assistance of the court.'[263]

---

[254] *Baden, Belvaux and Lecuit v Société Générale pour Favoriser le Développement du Commerce et de l'Industrie en France SA* [1983] BCLC 325.

[255] *Re Trepca Mines Ltd* [1960] 1 WLR 1273, 1281; *Société Co-opérative Sidmetal v Titan International Ltd* [1966] 1 QB 828, 838–41; *Schemmer v Property Resources Ltd* [1975] Ch 273, 287. Cf *Re Dulles' Settlement (No 2)* [1951] Ch 842, 851 (albeit not in the context of insolvency).

[256] Smart, 167. See *Felixstowe Dock and Rly Co v United States Lines Inc* [1989] QB 360.

[257] Smart, 168–175. See *Queensland Mercantile Agency Co Ltd v Australasian Investment Co Ltd* (1888) 15 R 935; *North Australian Territory Co Ltd v Goldsbrough, Mort and Co Ltd* (1889) 61 LT 716; *Barclays Bank v Homan* [1993] BCLC 680.

[258] Fletcher, 202–3.

[259] See *North Australian Territory Co Ltd v Goldsbrough, Mort and Co Ltd* (1889) 61 LT 716.

[260] See paras 18.2.48–18.2.50.

[261] Fletcher, 203.

[262] *Cambridge Gas Transport Corp v Navigator Holdings plc Creditors' Committee* [2007] 1 AC 508, 517–8 (at [20]) PC.

[263] Innes CJ in *Re African Farms Ltd* [1906] TS 373, 377; cited with approval in *Cambridge Gas Transport Corp v Navigator Holdings plc Creditors' Committee* [2007] 1 AC 508, 518 (at [20]).

By recognising the foreign liquidator or other foreign office holder, the need for parallel proceedings with its consequent costs to be opened in England is avoided, and the creditors would be entitled to the same remedies to which they would have been entitled if the equivalent proceedings had taken place in England.[264]

18.2.41 It should be noted that the principle that debts are only considered to be discharged if they are discharged by the law applicable to the debt applies here as in the case of bankruptcies. [265]

Recognition of Foreign Reorganisations or Administrations

18.2.42 It may be that, instead of liquidation, the company which is facing financial trouble will undergo a scheme of reorganisation undertaken with a view to rehabilitate its fortunes. The insolvency laws of many countries, including England, provide for such procedures.[266] If an English court is asked to recognise a foreign reorganisation scheme, it remains unclear what prerequisites are necessary.[267] On the one hand, in *Felixstowe Dock and Railway Co v US Lines Inc*,[268] Hirst J refused to authorise the release of frozen English assets, which had been injuncted[269] by the plaintiffs, for transfer to the United States to be administered in accordance with Chapter 11 proceedings. Notwithstanding acknowledgment of the principle of comity, the fact that the remittal would have prejudiced the plaintiffs, as they would not have derived any benefit from the remittal, held greater sway.

18.2.43 On the other hand, the fact of a reorganisation scheme conducted under the auspices of a foreign jurisdiction indicates that the company has submitted to the foreign court and submission may furnish a compelling reason for recognition.[270] Thus, in *Barclays Bank v Homan*,[271] administration of the company was commenced first in the United States, then in England. Hoffman J declined to issue an injunction prohibiting the administrators from proceeding in the US court. This was upheld by the Court of Appeal. Ultimately, a harmonised disposal of the company's assets was achieved due to the high level of co-operation between the English and US courts.[272] In a case involving a complicated corporate structure, however, a party affected by reorganisation plans denied having submitted to the proceedings in which the plans were approved. In *Cambridge Gas Transport Corp v Official Committee of Unsecured*

---

[264] See Lord Hoffman in *Cambridge Gas Transport Corp v Navigator Holdings plc Creditors' Committee* [2007] 1 AC 508, 518 (at [22]).

[265] See paras 18.1.32–18.1.34.

[266] Eg, the Administration procedure set out in Insolvency Act 1986, Pt II, as amended by the Enterprise Act 2002; Chapter 11 Bankruptcy under the United States Bankruptcy Code.

[267] Foreign administration falls within the scope of the UNCITRAL Model Law on Cross-Border Insolvency (as implemented in Great Britain by the Cross-Border Insolvency Regs 2006). See para 19.2.3.

[268] [1989] QB 360. See also *Jefferies International Ltd v Landsbanki Islands HF* [2009] EWHC 894 (Comm).

[269] By means of a *Mareva* injunction, now called a freezing injunction.

[270] Smart, 178.

[271] [1993] BCLC 680.

[272] The administrators in the English proceedings were recognised as the corporate governance of the company in the US proceedings whilst the person appointed as examiner in the US proceedings was recognised by the English court as having the authority to assist the administrators to formulate a scheme of rearrangement.

Creditors of Navigator Holdings Plc,[273] Navigator Holdings, a Manx company, had petitioned for Chapter 11 relief in New York. Navigator was in turn held through a web of companies incorporated in other offshore jurisdictions, the most important ones being Cambridge Gas (a Cayman company which owned at least 70 per cent of the issued share capital of Navigator) and Vela Energy Holdings Ltd (a Bahamian company which owned all the issued share capital in Cambridge). Under the scheme of arrangement approved by the New York court, title to the Navigator shares vested automatically in the creditors' committee as interim shareholders. The vesting required the assistance of the Manx court and the creditors petitioned the High Court of the Isle of Man for an order vesting title to the Navigator shares in their representative. The issue facing the Privy Council on appeal was whether the New York order was a judgment *in rem*, in which case it could not extra-territorially affect shares in a Manx company, or a judgment *in personam*, in which case the sticking point was that Cambridge had not submitted to the jurisdiction of the New York court.[274] Lord Hoffman held that bankruptcy proceedings were neither judgments *in rem* nor *in personam*, and that the Manx court could properly assist the New York proceedings by vesting title to the Navigator shares in the creditors' committee, noting that Cambridge, as a shareholder, was bound by the transactions into which Navigator had entered.[275] Thus, it appears that a shareholder is bound by decrees handed down by a foreign court where the company in which it holds shares submits to (or is present in) the jurisdiction of a foreign court, notwithstanding the fact that the shareholder is not personally amenable to that court's jurisdiction. Insofar as a shareholder must be taken to have acceded to the constitution of the company and, therefore, be bound by the company's actions, this reduces what appears, at first glance, to be the rather shocking effect of the case: that an English court will sanction a foreign order which seeks to confiscate property located outside that foreign jurisdiction[276] belonging to someone also outside that foreign court's jurisdiction.

18.2.44 It may be suggested that if the reorganisation or administration scheme is pursued in the place of incorporation, the English court should recognise it.[277] Similarly, if the reorganisation proceedings take place in the country where the company's central management and administration lie, or where it has its principal place of business, recognition should also be accorded.[278] The sensible benchmark seems to be whether the company has a sufficient connection with the reorganisation forum so that creditors would calculate the risks involved in transacting with the company by

---

[273] [2007] 1 AC 508. A Briggs, (2006) 77 *BYIL* 578; CH Tham, [2007] *LMCLQ* 129; GS Teo, (2008) 20 *SAcLJ* 784.

[274] Cambridge argued that it had never submitted to the jurisdiction of the New York court although its parent company, Vela Energy Holdings Ltd, had participated in the Chapter 11 proceedings. This argument was accepted at first instance and upheld by the Staff of Government Division; there was no further appeal on this point, although Lord Hoffman described it as a 'surprising' finding: [2007] 1 AC 508, 515 (at [10]). See also *Rubin v Eurofinance* [2010] 1 All ER (Comm) 81.

[275] [2007] 1 AC 508, 519 (at [26]).

[276] Shares in a Manx company must be located in the Isle of Man. The general rule is that shares are located where the share register is kept, or, if the transfer of the shares does not depend on registration, where the company is incorporated: see *Dicey, Morris and Collins*, para 22–044.

[277] See *Re Phoenix Kapitaldienst GmbH* [2008] BPIR 1082.

[278] See *Re Phoenix Kapitaldienst GmbH* [2008] BPIR 1082.

reference to that forum and its laws.[279] The gloss added to this by the *Cambridge Gas* case is that, in the specific context of a foreign reorganisation scheme which seeks to divest a shareholder of his rights, the foreign court need only have jurisdiction[280] over the company, not the shareholder.

Recognition of Foreign Receivers

18.2.45 A receiver[281] is a person who is appointed to collect or protect the company's property. A receiver also frequently acts as a manager who carries on the business with a view to restoring profitability, or more usually, with a view to a sale of the business for the benefit of the secured creditors. [282] A distinction needs to be drawn between a receiver appointed out of court and a court-appointed receiver. The former is appointed by a creditor pursuant to rights which he holds; under English domestic law, this creditor is typically a debenture holder exercising his rights under the terms of a debenture. There is no direct authority on the status of foreign out-of-court receivers but it is suggested by commentators that the appointment of a foreign receiver will be recognised in England if the powers he seeks to exercise are authorised by the law of the place of incorporation.[283]

18.2.46 For foreign receivers appointed by a court, a 'sufficient connection' needs to be shown between the company and the jurisdiction in which the foreign receiver was appointed to justify recognition of the extra-territorial effects of the foreign court's order.[284] As to what constitutes a 'sufficient connection', it is clear that the place of incorporation is an appropriate connecting factor;[285] the relevance of other factors remains unclear. *Schemmer v Property Resources*[286] concerned an American receiver seeking to have himself appointed receiver of English assets of a company incorporated in the Bahamas. Goulding J held that submission by the company's subsidiaries to the US court did not suffice. The lack of evidence that the courts of the Bahamas would recognise the American decree as affecting English assets, that

---

[279] See Fletcher, 222.

[280] According to English rules.

[281] Under English law, there are administrative receiverships which cover the whole or substantially the whole of the company's assets, and receiverships that are confined to a particular asset or assets. Only the former is considered as an insolvency regime. See R Goode, *Principles of Corporate Insolvency Law* (London, Sweet & Maxwell, 3rd edn, 2005) 22–4. Administrative receiverships have been partially abolished by the Insolvency Act 1986, s 72A. Administrative receiverships do not fall within the scope of the UNCITRAL Model Law on Cross-Border Insolvency (as implemented in Great Britain by the Cross-Border Insolvency Regulations 2006). See para 19.2.3.

[282] For a detailed examination of the role of an administrative receiver in the context of corporate insolvency under English law, see R Goode, *Principles of Corporate Insolvency Law* (London, Sweet & Maxwell, 3rd edn, 2005) ch 9.

[283] See *Dicey, Morris and Collins*, para 30–124 (Rule 167(2)); Fletcher, 218. See further L Collins, 'Floating Charges, Receivers and Managers and the Conflict of Laws' in *Essays in International Litigation and the Conflict of Laws* (Oxford, Clarendon Press, 1994) 433. See also *CA Kennedy & Co Ltd v Stibbe-Monk Ltd* (1976) 74 DLR (3d) 87; *Cretanor Maritime Co Ltd v Irish Marine Management Ltd* [1978] 1 WLR 966, 975.

[284] *Schemmer v Property Resources Ltd* [1975] Ch 273, 287. See also *Re Stanford International Bank Ltd (In Receivership)* [2009] BPIR 1157, 1186–87 (at [101]–[107]).

[285] *Macaulay v Guaranty Trust Co of New York* (1927) 44 TLR 99.

[286] [1975] Ch 273.

the company had ever conducted business in the United States or that the seat of its central management and control was located there also did not persuade him that a 'sufficient connection' was present. Although his judgment was phrased in negative terms, it might be postulated that submission by the company (not its subsidiaries) and recognition by the courts in the place of incorporation would be likely to lead the English courts to recognise a foreign receiver. Goulding J was more equivocal about the relevance of a company conducting business or having its central management in the foreign jurisdiction, stating that he expressed 'no view, one way or the other, on the materiality of those two circumstances'.[287] The principles of comity and reciprocity, that is that English courts should recognise a jurisdiction which they themselves claim,[288] would also seem to be irrelevant here.[289]

18.2.47 The court could assist a recognised foreign receiver by appointing an English provisional liquidator whose function is to assist the foreign receiver by recovering and administering local assets; those assets may subsequently be transmitted to the foreign jurisdiction to be administered globally and the English winding-up will be dismissed.[290]

Concurrent Liquidations

18.2.48 Having more than one set of liquidation proceedings ongoing in different countries results in increased costs and disorder. Two or more liquidators may take action to recover the same debt and it may be unclear which court or liquidator can grant a discharge.[291] Nevertheless, English proceedings may be advisable, even though proceedings have been commenced elsewhere, if this would lead to a more efficient method of distributing the company's assets. A foreign liquidator may also want to bring English winding-up proceedings in order to take advantage of provisions that are only available to an English liquidator—such as the automatic stay of proceedings against the company or its property under section 130(2) of the Insolvency Act 1986.

18.2.49 The concept of ancillary liquidation[292] was developed by the courts;[293] it has no clear statutory basis.[294] An ancillary liquidation may come about through a

---

[287] An alternative ground for denying the US receiver's request was that it would involve enforcing a foreign penal law.

[288] See *Travers v Holley* [1953] P 246 (case on recognition of a foreign divorce decree). The principle of comity has been rejected in the context of company insolvency in cases such as *Re Trepca Mines Ltd* [1960] 1 WLR 1273; *Felixstowe Dock and Rly Co v United States Lines Inc* [1989] QB 360.

[289] *Schemmer v Property Resources Ltd* [1975] Ch 273, 287.

[290] See *Re Daewoo Motor Company Ltd (No 366 of 2001)* (unreported, 18 Jan 2001, ChD, Lightman J) and *Re Daewoo Motor Co Ltd* [2006] BPIR 415.

[291] C Grierson, 'Issues in Concurrent Insolvency Jurisdiction: English Perspectives' in JS Ziegel (ed), *Current Developments in International and Comparative Corporate Insolvency Law* (Oxford, Clarendon Press, 1994) 577, 585.

[292] For a detailed discussion, see Smart, ch 14; S Frisby, 'Cross-border Insolvency and Vulnerable Transaction' in J Amour and H Bennett (eds), *Vulnerable Transactions in Corporate Insolvency* (Oxford, Hart Publishing, 2003) 447–51.

[293] *Re Matheson Brothers Ltd* (1884) 27 ChD 225; *Re Commercial Bank of South Australia* (1886) 33 ChD 174; *Re English, Scottish and Australian Chartered Bank* [1893] 3 Ch 385.

[294] Smart, 362.

request for assistance by a court designated as a 'relevant country or territory' under section 426(4) of the Insolvency Act 1986. In general:

One knows that where there is a liquidation of one concern the general principle is—ascertain what is the domicil of the company in liquidation; let the Court of the country of domicil act as the principal Court to govern the liquidation; and let the other Courts act as ancillary, as far as they can, to the principal liquidation.[295]

Where liquidation proceedings have been commenced in the place of incorporation and the foreign liquidator and a large proportion of the creditors and contributories actively invite the English court to exercise its discretion to conduct an ancillary winding-up, the court would be inclined to do so.[296]

18.2.50 If the court directs that the English winding-up is to be ancillary to the principal winding-up in the place of incorporation, the English liquidator will generally be restricted to settling a list of the creditors who sent in proofs and collecting English assets. The implication, without which the concept of an ancillary liquidation is meaningless, is that at some stage in the process the court will authorise the English liquidators to transmit the assets they have collected to the principal liquidators.[297] The universalist effects of an English winding-up are therefore abrogated in this instance and the ultimate aim is the distribution of all the company's assets in a single set of proceedings.[298] It should be noted, though, that characterising the English proceedings as ancillary does not mean that the English court acts as an agent for the courts conducting the principal liquidation;[299] thus, the court still applies English law in conducting the English proceedings.[300] Principles of comity and co-operation underlie the willingness of the court to order that the English winding up be ancillary in nature.[301]

18.3 JUDICIAL CO-OPERATION

18.3.1 The preceding sections show how international insolvency will often give rise to convoluted scenarios that, out of commercial necessity, require some form of cross-border judicial assistance. Assets and creditors may be located out of the jurisdiction of the court conducting insolvency proceedings and the insolvency of a multinational corporation inevitably requires the close judicial co-operation of different jurisdictions. English courts have shown themselves ready to proffer assistance in cross-border insolvencies. Deeming English proceedings to be ancillary to proceedings taking place

---

[295] Vaughan Williams J in *Re English, Scottish and Australian Chartered Bank* [1893] 3 Ch 385, 394.
[296] *Re OJSC Ank Yugraneft* [2009] 1 BCLC 298, 315.
[297] *Re BCCI SA (No 10)* [1997] Ch 213, 247. See also *Re SwissAir Schweizerische Luftverkehr-Aktiengesellschaft* [2009] BPIR 1505. It should be noted that the court may order English assets to be remitted to a liquidation that is taking place in a jurisdiction other than the place of incorporation if this would promote equality between creditors worldwide: see *Re Alfred Shaw & Co Ltd* (1897) 8 QLJ 93.
[298] See *Re HIH Casualty & General Insurance Ltd* [2008] 1 WLR 852, 857 (at [10]).
[299] See North J in *Re Queensland Mercantile Agency Co Ltd* (1888) 58 LT 878, 879.
[300] *Re English, Scottish and Australian Chartered Bank* [1893] 3 Ch 385, 394; *Re BCCI SA (No 10)* [1997] Ch 213.
[301] See, eg, *Re HIH Casualty and General Insurance Ltd* [2008] 1 WLR 852.

elsewhere is one example. Nevertheless, the court will refuse assistance if there is a risk of prejudging English proceedings or appearing to do so; where a company and its subsidiaries were subject to parallel proceedings under the insolvency laws of England and the United States, the court refused an application for the two courts to communicate with each other via a telephone conference call on controversial matters which were in dispute between the parties and which might later come before the court for decision; assistance was limited to informing the US court on the issues that would involve questions of English insolvency law and procedure.[302]

18.3.2 There are several bases on which assistance could be granted: the UNCITRAL Model Law on Cross-Border Insolvency,[303] the common law and the Insolvency Act 1986. The UNCITRAL Model Law is considered in detail in Chapter 19; this section considers the common law and the 1986 Act.[304] Of the two, the latter is more restricted, being confined to certain countries and providing only for court-to-court assistance.[305] The common law, in contrast, has entertained requests for assistance from foreign liquidators or other office holders appointed abroad, with no restriction on the jurisdictions from which the court would accede to a request for assistance, save for the usual caveat that the assistance must not be against English public policy.[306] So, for example, the liquidator could request that title to property in England be vested in his name, or that he be appointed as receiver of immovables with the power to receive rents and profits. It has been doubted, though, whether assistance at common law could consist of applying provisions of foreign insolvency law which form no part of English domestic insolvency law.[307]

18.3.3 The statutory scheme is set out in section 426 of the Insolvency Act 1986.[308] Section 426(4) provides that:

The courts having jurisdiction in relation to insolvency law in any part of the United Kingdom shall assist the courts having the corresponding jurisdiction in any other part of the United Kingdom or any relevant country or territory.

According to section 426(11), 'any relevant country' or territory means:

(a) any of the Channel Islands or the Isle of Man; or
(b) any country or territory designated for the purposes of this section by the Secretary of State by order made by statutory instrument.

18.3.4 As noted above, section 426 envisages the court providing assistance pursuant to a request from a foreign court identified under section 426(11). So far, the list

---

[302] *Re T&N Ltd* [2005] BCC 982.

[303] Implemented in Great Britain by the Cross-Border Insolvency Regs 2006.

[304] For a brief comparison between the UNCITRAL Model Law, the EC Insolvency Regulation, and English rules falling outside these two instruments, see section 19.7.

[305] So the foreign liquidator must first approach the relevant foreign court and ask it to issue a letter of request to the English court.

[306] Albeit public policy is not the only reason against giving assistance; see *Hughes v Hannover Rückversicherungs-Aktiengesellschaft* [1997] 1 BCLC 497, 518 (in the context of assistance requested under Insolvency Act 1986, s 426(4).

[307] Lord Hoffman in *Cambridge Gas Transport Corp v Official Committee of Unsecured Creditors of Navigator Holdings Plc* [2007] 1 AC 508, 518 (at [22]). See also Lord Hoffman's remarks in *Re HIH Casualty & General Insurance Ltd* [2008] 1 WLR 852, 860–1 (at [26]–[27]).

[308] The effect of s 426 on intra-UK assistance is considered at paras 18.1.21–18.1.22.

of designated countries under section 426(11)(b) numbers twenty, of which most are members of the Commonwealth.[309]

18.3.5 Although the word 'shall' is used in section 426(4), assistance is not mandatory; it remains up to the court, in its discretion, whether assistance could 'properly be granted'.[310] At the same time, it has been said that assistance ought to be granted 'unless there is some compelling reason why that should [not] be done'.[311] In relation to the nature of assistance, section 426(5) states that:

For the purposes of subsection (4) a request made to a court in any part of the United Kingdom by a court in any other part of the United Kingdom or in a relevant country or territory is authority for the court to which the request is made to apply, in relation to any matters specified in the request, the insolvency law which is applicable by either court in relation to comparable matters falling within its jurisdiction.

In exercising its discretion under this subsection, a court shall have regard in particular to the rules of private international law.

The proviso[312] can most sensibly be read as being directed towards the requested court and not the requesting court; that is, the requested court should have regard to its private international law rules when exercising its discretion whether to apply its own law or the law of the requesting court to the matters specified in the request.[313] So, for example, the English court would decline to grant the requested assistance if to do so would be against the private international rule of non-enforcement of foreign penal, revenue and public laws.

18.3.6 It has been held that English courts can look to three sources of law when dealing with a request for assistance: (a) its own general jurisdiction and powers and either (b) the insolvency law of England and Wales (as defined in section 426(10)) or (c) so much of the law of the relevant country as corresponds to that comprised in (b).[314] In deciding which law to apply, the court should take into account factors such as the connections of the parties with England and with the foreign country.[315]

18.3.7 The measures that are available under section 426(4) are, therefore, not limited to measures that are available under English insolvency law or even measures that are available under English law generally. So, for example, the court could assist

---

[309] Currently, the countries are: Anguilla, Australia, the Bahamas, Bermuda, Botswana, Brunei Darussalam, Canada, Cayman Islands, Falkland Islands, Gibraltar, Hong Kong, Republic of Ireland, Malaysia, Montserrat, New Zealand, St Helena, South Africa, Turks and Caicos Islands, Tuvalu and the Virgin Islands. See Co-operation of Insolvency Courts (Designation of Relevant Countries and Territories) Orders: SI 1986/2123; SI 1996/253; and SI 1998/2766.

[310] *Hughes v Hannover Rückversicherungs-Aktiengesellschaft* [1997] 1 BCLC 497, 518. See also *Re Dallhold Estates (UK) Pty Ltd* [1992] BCLC 621; *Re BCCI SA (No 9)* [1994] 3 All ER 764 (reversed in part, but not on this point, [1994] 1 WLR 708 (CA)); *Re Focus Insurance Co Ltd* [1997] 1 BCLC 219; *Re Television Trade Rentals Ltd* [2002] BCC 807.

[311] Chadwick J in *Re Dallhold Estates (UK) Pty Ltd* [1992] BCLC 621, 627. See also Rattee J in *Re BCCI SA (No 9)* [1994] 3 All ER 764, 785. Both dicta were quoted by Morritt LJ in *Hughes v Hannover Rückversicherungs-Aktiengesellschaft* [1997] 1 BCLC 497, 513–4.

[312] Criticised by Lawrence Collins J as being an 'obscure and ill-thought out provision' in *Re Television Trade Rentals Ltd* [2002] BCC 807, 812 (at [17]).

[313] See Rattee J in *Re BCCI SA (No 9)* [1994] 3 All ER 764, 782. Cf the contrary view expressed by Chadwick J in *Re Dallhold Estates (UK) Pty Ltd* [1992] BCLC 621, 625.

[314] *Hughes v Hannover Rückversicherungs-Aktiengesellschaft* [1997] 1 BCLC 497, 517.

[315] *Re Television Trade Rentals Ltd* [2002] BCC 807, 812 (at [17]).

a foreign court by granting a freezing injunction[316] or an anti-suit injunction.[317] In *Re Dallhold Estates (UK) Pty Ltd*,[318] the Federal Court of Australia requested assistance in the form of an administration order. Even though it was likely[319] that the English court would have no jurisdiction to make such an order with respect to a company incorporated overseas, Chadwick J held that:

It appears to me clear that the purpose of s 426(5) of the Insolvency Act 1986 is to give to the requested court a jurisdiction that it might not otherwise have under domestic insolvency law in order that it can give the assistance to the requesting court which, by subs (4), it is directed to give.[320]

18.3.8   In a similar vein, the Court of Appeal in *England v Smith*[321] chose to apply Australian law and ordered that an officer of a company be examined in accordance with the principles and practice of the Supreme Court of South Australia (the requesting court) notwithstanding that such examination may have been refused on the basis of oppression if a comparable application had been made by the liquidator of a company being wound up in England.[322] Section 426 has also been used to apply to foreign companies provisions in the Insolvency Act 1986 relating to remedies against fraudulent company directors and officers and the setting aside of transactions at an undervalue where there was no counterpart in the foreign legislation.[323] Thus, it can be seen that section 426 operates to extend the jurisdiction of the English court: giving it a jurisdiction it may not otherwise have, and extending the choice of law available to the court by enabling it to apply a foreign law when it ordinarily may not do so.[324]

Re HIH Casualty and General Insurance Ltd[325]

18.3.9   One of the cases which explores the extent to which the court will assist another in the spirit of comity and judicial co-operation—and is worth exploring in detail—is *Re HIH Casualty and General Insurance Ltd.*[326]

    18.3.10   Four Australian insurance companies which were part of the HIH Group were the subject of insolvency proceedings in New South Wales. The companies had

---

[316] See *Fourie v Le Roux* [2007] 1 WLR 320 (although the order was discharged on the facts of the case because of procedural deficiencies).

[317] See *Hughes v Hannover Rückversicherungs-Aktiengesellschaft* [1997] 1 BCLC 497 (although the court did not exercise its discretion to make the order as there had been a change in circumstances which removed the reasons for which the letter of request was made).

[318] [1992] BCLC 621.

[319] See para 18.2.19.

[320] [1992] BCLC 621, 625.

[321] [2001] Ch 419. See also *Re Duke Group Ltd* [2001] BCC 144. Cf *Re JN Taylor Finance Pty Ltd* [1999] 2 BCLC 256.

[322] Australian law, however, had specific protections in place to prevent oppression in the conduct of the examination.

[323] *Re BCCI SA (No 9)* [1994] 3 All ER 764, reversed in part, but not on this point, [1994] 1 WLR 708 (CA).

[324] See Lord Hoffman in *Re HIH Casualty and General Insurance Ltd* [2008] 1 WLR 852, 861 (at [28]).

[325] [2008] 1 WLR 852. PStJ Smart, (2008) 124 *LQR* 554; J Townsend, (2008) 71 *MLR* 811; GS Teo, (2008) 20 *SAcLJ* 784; P Rogerson, [2008] *CLJ* 476; MS Wee, [2009] *LMCLQ* 18; A Briggs, (2008) 79 *BYIL* 501; G Moss, (2008) 21 *Insolv Intel* 145.

[326] [2008] 1 WLR 852.

assets, mainly reinsurance claims on policies taken out in London, in England and pro-visional liquidators had been appointed in England to safeguard those assets. The New South Wales court, upon the request of the Australian liquidators, wrote to the English High Court, requesting that the English provisional liquidators remit the English assets (after payment of their expenses) to Australia for distribution via the Australian proceed-ings. The problem was that, whereas English law adopted a statutory scheme of *pari passu* distribution, Australian law gave priority to the insurance creditors. The issues for the English court were: first, whether the English court had the power to make the order of remittal to Australia where the outcome for creditors would be different compared with the situation if English law had been applied, and secondly, if there was such a power, whether that power should be exercised. Although all members of the House of Lords reached the same conclusion—that English courts had the power and that the assets should be remitted to Australia—two different lines of reasoning were adopted.

18.3.11   On the one hand, Lord Hoffman, with whom Lord Walker agreed, held that the courts had inherent jurisdiction at common law to direct the remittal of English assets, notwithstanding the different schemes of distribution in the foreign state and England. In support of this conclusion, Lord Hoffman relied on the prin-ciple of (modified) universalism which:

has been the golden thread running through English cross-border insolvency since the 18th century. That principle requires that English courts should, so far as is consistent with justice and UK public policy, co-operate with the courts in the country of the principal liquidation to ensure that all the company's assets are distributed to its creditors under a single system of distribution.[327]

Lord Hoffman did not conceive that any principle of justice would be offended if the assets were remitted to Australia, all the more so given that English law had, since the appointment of the provisional liquidators, adopted a scheme of distribution that also gives priority to insurance creditors.[328] Furthermore, policy holders and other creditors of an Australian insurance company would expect that their rights would be determined by Australian law in the event of insolvency.[329]

18.3.12   On the other hand, Lord Scott based his decision solely on the power given by section 426 and the fact that Australia is designated as a 'relevant country or territory' for the purposes of that section. This fact also confirmed that the Australian insolvency scheme was acceptable by English law standards so that the grant of the remittal order was not against English public policy.[330] Lord Scott did not accept that the courts had an inherent common law power to render assistance to the New South Wales court in a situation where the Australian distribution rules were not identical to English distribution rules.[331] Lord Neuberger adopted the same reasoning as Lord

---

[327] [2008] 1 WLR 852, 861–2 (at [30]).

[328] Insurers (Reorganisation and Winding Up) Regs 2004 (SI 2004/353), reg 21(2), which implements Dir 2001/17/EC on the reorganisation and winding-up of insurance undertakings [2001] OJ L110/28. The Regulations were inapplicable to the case because they were not in force when the provisional liquidators were appointed.

[329] [2008] 1 WLR 852, 862 (at [33]).

[330] [2008] 1 WLR 852, 872 (at [62]).

[331] [2008] 1 WLR 852, 870–872 (at [59]–[61]). See also *Re SwissAir Schweizerische Luftverkehr-Aktiengesellschaft* [2009] BPIR 1505.

Scott. The fifth member of the House, Lord Phillips, declined to decide whether or
not there was a common law discretion to accede to the request of the Australian
liquidators, preferring to base his decision on the ground (which all members of the
House of Lords accepted) that there was such a power.[332] Lord Phillips thought that
this power should be used to accede to the request of the Australian court on the facts
of the case in accordance with international comity and the principle of universalism
elucidated by Lord Hoffman.

18.3.13   Several points may be made. First, the fact that foreign insolvency law is
different from English insolvency law is not a bar to the court exercising its discretion to come to the aid of a foreign court.[333] Secondly, for a majority of the House
of Lords,[334] the principle of universalism, or modified universalism, underlined the
court's power to direct remittal of English assets abroad. The majority's embrace of
universalism is suggested to be the preferable route. To insist, as the minority did, on
foreign priority rules being substantially similar to English rules before the English
court should remit assets to that foreign jurisdiction if section 426 were inapplicable,[335]
is unattractive.[336] It will be highly unlikely for foreign insolvency rules to be identical
to English insolvency rules. Priority rules, in particular, reflect legislative choices on
who should be accorded preferential treatment and how the risks of insolvency should
be allocated. All that should be is required is to ascertain that the operation of the
foreign rules is not against English public policy.[337] The minority's stance goes against
the spirit of comity and judicial co-operation that is required to facilitate a solution to
a cross-border insolvency. Even Lord Scott had to concede that: 'It is, of course, desirable as a general proposition that there should be one universally applicable scheme of
distribution of the assets of an insolvent company.'[338] Lord Hoffman's more generous
interpretation of the court's common law powers is more in tandem with cross-border
insolvency initiatives like the EC Insolvency Regulation and the UNCITRAL Model
Law. The principle of universalism should be an important factor whenever courts are
deciding whether to co-operate with foreign insolvency proceedings, whether under
section 426 or under their common law power.

18.3.14   Thirdly, Lord Hoffman recognised that the court's power to remit assets
to a foreign jurisdiction is exercised when the foreign jurisdiction is a more appropriate jurisdiction than England for the purpose of dealing with the questions arising

---

[332] According to Lord Phillips, all members of the House agreed that s 426 gave the court jurisdiction to
remit the assets to Australia. See, however, the remarks at [2008] 1 WLR 852, 861 (at [28]), which suggest
that Lord Hoffman thought that s 426 was inapplicable on the facts of the case.

[333] Cf *Re BCCI SA (No 10)* [1997] Ch 213.

[334] Lord Phillips also based his decision on international comity and the principle of universalism: [2008]
1 WLR 852, 864 (at [43]). This means that three members of the House of Lords (Lords Hoffman, Walker
and Phillips) supported universalism.

[335] Lord Scott at [2008] 1 WLR 852, 871–2 (at [61]–[62]); Lord Neuberger at [2008] 1 WLR 852, 875–876
(at [76]).

[336] Lord Hoffman commented that it would make 'no sense': [2008] 1 WLR 852, 859 (at [21]).

[337] Public policy is highlighted in the judgments: Lord Hoffman [2008] 1 WLR 852, 862–3 (at [31]–[32],
[34]), Lord Scott at [2008] 1 WLR 852, 872 (at [62]) and Lord Neuberger at [2008] 1 WLR 852, 876 (at
[80]).

[338] [2008] 1 WLR 852, 871 (at [61]).

in the winding-up proceedings.[339] This contains a hint that the doctrine of *forum non conveniens*, or a similar doctrine modified to suit international insolvency cases, should possibly play a role in deciding whether assets would be better distributed through proceedings in a foreign jurisdiction. The questions asked in a *forum non conveniens* enquiry would seem to fit international insolvency scenarios whereby an English court is trying to decide whether another court is the more appropriate one to deal with particular issues.[340]

[339] [2008] 1 WLR 852, 861 (at [28]).
[340] See GS Teo, (2008) 20 *SAcLJ* 784, 792, 797–8. See also K Dawson, 'The Doctrine of Forum Non Conveniens and the Winding Up of Insolvent Foreign Companies' [2005] *JBL* 28.

THE CROSS-BORDER INSOLVENCY REGULATIONS 2006

19.1 INTRODUCTION

19.1.1 The Cross-Border Insolvency Regulations 2006[1] came into force on 4 April 2006. The 2006 Regulations are the UK enactment of the United Nations Commission on International Trade Law Model Law on Cross-Border Insolvency (commonly known as the UNCITRAL Model Law on Cross-Border Insolvency) which was adopted by UNCITRAL on 30 May 1997.[2] The 2006 Regulations were made pursuant to section 14 of the Insolvency Act 2000, which allows the Secretary of State, with the agreement of the Lord Chancellor insofar as they extend to England and Wales and of the Scottish Ministers insofar as they extend to Scotland, to make any provision which he considers necessary or expedient for the purpose of giving effect to the UNCITRAL Model Law. The Regulations apply to Great Britain; Regulation 2(1) provides that the UNCITRAL Model Law shall have force of law in Great Britain in the form set out in schedule 1 to the Regulations. The Model Law was extended to Northern Ireland in 2007.[3]

19.1.2 According to the UNCITRAL website, the countries which have enacted the Model Law as of 1 December 2009 are: Australia (2008), British Virgin Islands; overseas territory of the United Kingdom of Great Britain and Northern Ireland (2003), Colombia (2006), Eritrea (1998), Great Britain (2006), Japan (2000), Mauritius (2009), Mexico (2000), Montenegro (2002), New Zealand (2006), Poland (2003), Republic of Korea (2006), Romania (2003), Serbia (2004), Slovenia (2007), South Africa (2000), and the United States of America (2005). However, in contrast with an international convention, enacting states do not need to notify the United Nations or other states that may have also enacted it.[4]

19.1.3 As far as England is concerned, one of the major drawbacks of the EC Insolvency Regulation and section 426 of the Insolvency Act 1986 is that these instruments do not cover its major trading partners such as Japan and the United States of America. Enacting the Model Law is one means of filling that gap by providing for

---

[1] SI 2006/1030. See generally, LC Ho (ed), *Cross-Border Insolvency: A Commentary on the UNCITRAL Model Law* (London, Globe Business Publishing, 2nd edn, 2009).

[2] Official Records of the General Assembly, Fifty-second Session, Supplement No 17, Annex I (pp 68–78).

[3] The Cross-Border Insolvency Regs (Northern Ireland) 2007 (SRNI 2007/115), in force from 12 April 2007. There are some differences between the Northern Ireland enactment and the 2006 Regs; see I Fletcher, *The Law of Insolvency* (London, Sweet & Maxwell, 4th edn, 2009) 1056–8.

[4] *Guide to Enactment of the UNCITRAL Model Law*, Document A/CN.9/442 (hereafter '*Guide to Enactment*') para 11.

a more structured mechanism for cross-border co-operation.[5] It was also considered that the move to enact the Model Law might serve as an encouragement to implementation by other countries, thereby eventually leading to a situation where British insolvency officeholders might enjoy the same benefits as their counterparts abroad.[6] In keeping with this sentiment, the 2006 Regulations do not impose a condition of reciprocity; some other states, when implementing the Model Law, have done so with the result that its courts will not recognise a foreign officeholder or co-operate with a foreign court in accordance with the Model Law unless that foreign state itself has implemented the Model Law.[7]

19.1.4 Enacting states have considerable freedom to modify or leave out some of the Model Law's provisions. Some modifications were made in the UK version as enacted in schedule 1 to the 2006 Regulations; however, the British government tried to follow UNCITRAL's exhortation[8] to make as few changes as possible in incorporating the Model Law so as to ensure consistency, certainty, and harmonisation with other countries enacting it.[9] Note should also be taken of Article 8, which provides that: 'In the interpretation of this Law, regard is to be had to its international origin and to the need to promote uniformity in its application and the observance of good faith'.[10] Furthermore, the UNCITRAL Secretariat produced a *Guide to Enactment* primarily to assist states in enacting the Model Law; regulation 2(2) states that, without prejudice to any of the courts as to matters which may be considered apart from this provision, the *Guide*, along with the UNCITRAL Model Law itself (in its original form) and any documents of UNCITRAL and its working group relating to the preparation of the Model Law can be considered by courts in ascertaining the meaning or effect of any provision of the Model Law. Thus, although there is a risk of substantial deviation amongst the different countries enacting the Model Law, countries committed to ensuring harmonisation across the board have the means by which to go about doing it.

19.1.5 The Model Law, as enacted in schedule 1 to the 2006 Regulations, is divided into five parts: Chapter I sets out the general provisions; Chapter II deals with the access of foreign representatives and creditors to courts in Great Britain; Chapter III comprises provisions pertaining to the recognition of foreign proceedings and relief; Chapter IV concerns co-operation with foreign courts and foreign representatives; and Chapter V deals with concurrent proceedings.[11] The structure of this chapter follows that of the Model Law. Those who are familiar with the EC

---

[5] The other is through application of common law rules.

[6] Department of Trade and Industry, *Explanatory Memorandum to the Cross-Border Insolvency Regulations 2006* (SI 2006/1030) para 7.2 (hereafter '*Explanatory Memorandum*').

[7] Eg, Mexico and South Africa: see P Wood, *Principles of International Insolvency Law* (London, Sweet & Maxwell, 2nd edn, 2007) 949.

[8] *Guide to Enactment*, para 12.

[9] *Explanatory Memorandum*, para 7.18.

[10] The hope is that the information system CLOUT ('Case Law on UNCITRAL Texts'), where abstracts of judicial decisions that interpret conventions and model laws emanating from the Commission are published, will facilitate a harmonised interpretation of the Model Law. See *Guide to Enactment*, para 92. See also *Rubin v Eurofinance SA* [2010] 1 All ER (Comm) 81.

[11] Sched 2 deals with procedural matters in England and Wales; sched 3 with procedural matters in Scotland; sched 4 with the delivery of notices to the registrar of companies; and sched 5 sets out the forms that are to be used in connection with proceedings under the Regulations.

Insolvency Regulation will be struck by the similarities between the Model Law and the EC Regulation[12]; for example, the Model Law divides up proceedings into 'main' and 'non-main' proceedings analogously with the Regulation's division of 'main' and 'territorial' proceedings. However, whereas the Regulation sought to set out a comprehensive framework for international insolvencies in terms of covering jurisdiction, choice of law, and recognition and enforcement, the Model Law's aims are more modest, being mainly confined to recognition and co-operation.[13] References to the Model Law below are to the version that is found in schedule 1 to the 2006 Regulations, unless stated otherwise.

19.2 GENERAL

Scope

19.2.1 Article 1(1) provides that the Model Law applies where:

(a) assistance is sought in Great Britain by a foreign court or a foreign representative in connection with a foreign proceeding; or
(b) assistance is sought in a foreign State in connection with a proceeding under British insolvency law; or
(c) a foreign proceeding and a proceeding under British insolvency law in respect of the same debtor are taking place concurrently; or
(d) creditors or other interested persons in a foreign State have an interest in requesting the commencement of, or participating in, a proceedings under British insolvency law.

The phrase 'British insolvency law' is, in relation to England and Wales, defined as:

provision extending to England and Wales and made by or under the Insolvency Act 1986 (with the exception of Part 3 of that Act) or by or under that Act as extended or applied by or under any other enactment (excluding these Regulations).[14]

Regulation 3(1) provides that the above definition and Part 3 of the Insolvency Act 1986 shall apply with such modifications as the context requires for the purpose of giving effect to the provisions of the Regulations.[15] It should also be noted that Article 2(q) states that 'references to the law of Great Britain include a reference to the law of either part of Great Britain (including its rules of private international law)'.

19.2.2 Article 1(2) sets out a list of exceptions to which the Model Law does not apply, such as water companies, railway companies, energy companies and building

---

[12] For a brief comparison between the UNCITRAL Model Law, the EC Insolvency Regulation, and English rules falling outside these two instruments, see section 19.7.
[13] There are no choice of law rules. The version of the Model Law enacted in Great Britain has a jurisdictional rule dealing with the allocation of jurisdiction between English and Scottish courts (Art 4); apart from this, the Model Law can at most be described as containing only rules of indirect jurisdiction in the sense that the recognition of a foreign proceeding (and the relief that follows) and degree of co-operation to be accorded to a foreign representative depends on the basis on which the foreign court assumed jurisdiction. See I Fletcher, *The Law of Insolvency* (London, Sweet & Maxwell, 4th edn, 2009) 1034.
[14] Art 2(a)(i).
[15] However, see Reg 3(2).

societies.[16] These are subject to their own insolvency regimes. Credit institutions and insurance companies are subject to extensive EU legislation and are also excluded from the Model Law for the time being; they may be included in the future once the interaction between the Model Law and the relevant EU legislation is worked out.[17]

19.2.3   Administrative receiverships and foreign equivalents are excluded from the scope of the Regulations[18] as the Model Law is designed to cover collective judicial or administrative proceedings, as illustrated by the definition in Article 2(i) of a 'foreign proceeding':

a collective judicial or administrative proceeding in a foreign State, including an interim proceeding, pursuant to a law relating to insolvency in which proceeding the assets and affairs of the debtor are subject to control or supervision by a foreign court, for the purpose of reorganisation or liquidation.[19]

Administrative receiverships are not collective procedures; actions by individual creditors such as execution, attachment and garnishment are also excluded for the same reason. It is clear, though, that an English administration under Part II of the Insolvency Act 1986 and the foreign equivalent would fall within the scope of the Model Law; it is thought that other collective procedures such as creditors' voluntary winding-up[20] and voluntary arrangements between debtors and creditors[21] should also fall within the Model Law although this is not as clear, as the role played by the court in these procedures is less obvious.[22] There is also some concern over whether the phrase 'pursuant to a law relating to insolvency' excludes foreign proceedings which are based on legislation which is not explicitly concerned with insolvency law.[23] However, the word 'relating' should indicate to the court that it should not take a narrow view of what counts as a 'foreign proceeding' and that it should include within that definition proceedings which may be imported from other parts of the law but which clearly form part of the insolvency process under the law of that foreign state.

19.2.4   Lastly, it should be noted that nothing in the Model Law prevents the court from refusing to take an action which is 'manifestly' contrary to the public policy of Great Britain.[24] The word 'manifestly' denotes that the public policy exception should

---

[16]   See also Arts 1(4)–(6) for further restrictions on the operation of the Model Law.

[17]   See *Explanatory Memorandum*, para 7.20.

[18]   An administrative receiver is expressly excluded from persons identified as being a 'British insolvency officeholder' in Art 2(b). See also *Re Stanford International Bank Ltd (In Receivership)* [2009] BPIR 1157.

[19]   The meaning of the word 'debtor' is that ascribed to it by the foreign court in the insolvency proceedings, so that it does not matter if the debtor has no legal personality according to English law: *Rubin v Eurofinance SA* [2010] 1 All ER (Comm) 81. See also *Re Bud-bank Leasings SP ZO O*, 29 June 2009 (Mr Registrar Baister).

[20]   Eg, Insolvency Act 1986, Pt IV, Chs IV and V.

[21]   Eg, Companies Act 2006, s 895.

[22]   See P Wood, *Principles of International Insolvency Law* (London, Sweet & Maxwell, 2nd edn, 2007) 954; L Collins *et al, Dicey, Morris and Collins on The Conflict of Laws, 2nd supplement to the 14th edn* (London, Sweet & Maxwell, 2008) S30-362; I Fletcher, *The Law of Insolvency* (London, Sweet & Maxwell, 4th edn, 2009) 1035.

[23]   I Fletcher, *Insolvency in Private International Law, Supplement to the Second Edition* (Oxford, OUP, 2007) 92.

[24]   Art 6.

be invoked only under exceptional circumstances involving matters of fundamental importance to the forum.[25]

Allocation of Jurisdiction between Courts in Great Britain

19.2.5 Article 4(1) provides that, as regards England and Wales, the functions referred to in the Model Law relating to recognition of foreign proceedings and co-operation with foreign courts shall be performed by the High Court and assigned to the Chancery Division.[26] As to which court has jurisdiction, Article 4(2) states that:

Subject to paragraph 1 of this article, the court in either part of Great Britain shall have jurisdiction in relation to the functions referred to in that paragraph if—

(a) the debtor has—
  (i) a place of business; or
  (ii) in the case of an individual, a place of residence; or
  (iii) assets, situated in that part of Great Britain; or
(b) the court in that part of Great Britain considers for any other reason that it is the appropriate forum to consider the question or provide the assistance requested.

19.2.6 Paragraph (b) might be thought to confer a wide discretion on the court, but Article 4(3) furnishes guidance on how that discretion should be exercised: it states that, when considering whether it is the appropriate forum to hear an application, the court shall take into account the location of any court in which a proceeding under British insolvency law is taking place in relation to the debtor and the likely location of any future proceedings under British insolvency law in relation to the debtor.

Co-operation between Courts in Great Britain

19.2.7 Regulation 7 dictates that an order made by a court in either part of Great Britain in the exercise of jurisdiction in relation to the subject matter of the Regulations shall be enforced in the other part of Great Britain as if it were made by a court exercising the corresponding jurisdiction in that other part.[27] However, this does not require a court in either part of Great Britain to enforce, in relation to property situated in that part, any order made by a court in the other part of Great Britain.[28] Nevertheless, the courts having jurisdiction in relation to the subject matter of the Regulations in either part of Great Britain are obliged to assist the courts having the corresponding jurisdiction in the other part of Great Britain.[29]

---

[25] *Guide to Enactment*, para 89. It is assumed that the public policy of Great Britain comprises the public policies of England and Scotland. Cf L Collins *et al*, *Dicey, Morris and Collins on The Conflict of Laws, 2nd supplement to the 14th edn* (London, Sweet & Maxwell, 2008) S30-369.

[26] The Court of Session will assume that role for Scotland.

[27] Reg 7(1). See *Gerrard, Petitioner* 2009 SLT 659.

[28] Reg 7(2).

[29] Reg 7(3).

Inter-relationship between the Model Law and other International Instruments

19.2.8 In the *Explanatory Memorandum* to the 2006 Regulations,[30] it was noted that there is a significant overlap between the Model Law and the EC Insolvency Regulation.[31] However, the EC Insolvency Regulation does not deal with matters extending beyond Member States of the European Union; thus, the Model Law was thought to provide a complementary regime that would deal with cases of international insolvency and cross-border co-operation with countries outside the European Union.[32]

19.2.9 Article 3 of the Model Law states that if there is a conflict between the Model Law and the United Kingdom's obligations under the EC Insolvency Regulation, the requirements of the latter shall prevail. For example, if a foreign main proceeding in Japan has been recognised under the Model Law and subsequently main proceedings are opened in Germany pursuant to the EC Insolvency Regulation, the English court can review and either terminate or modify the recognition of,[33] or relief[34] accorded to, the Japanese proceeding under the Model Law.[35] The Model Law also does not preclude the court from having recourse to other sources of law such as the principles relating to the recognition of foreign insolvency proceedings and cross-border assistance developed at common law and under section 426 of the Insolvency Act 1986[36] (which sets out a statutory scheme for judicial co-operation in cross-border insolvencies).[37] Regulation 3(2) states that in the case of any conflict between any provision of British insolvency law or of Part 3 of the Insolvency Act 1986 and the provisions of the 2006 Regulations, the latter shall prevail. Thus, the hierarchical order is, from the 'strongest' to the 'weakest' instrument: the EC Insolvency Regulation, the 2006 Regulations, and British insolvency law as defined in Article 2 of the UNCITRAL Model Law.

British Insolvency Officeholder Acting Abroad

19.2.10 In relation to England, a 'British insolvency officeholder' means[38]:

(i) the official receiver within the meaning of section 399 of the Insolvency Act 1986 when acting as liquidator, provisional liquidator, trustee, interim receiver or nominee or supervisor of a voluntary arrangement;

(ii) a person acting as an insolvency practitioner within the meaning of section 388 of that Act[39] but shall not include a person acting as an administrative receiver.

---

[30] Department of Trade and Industry, *Explanatory Memorandum to the Cross-Border Insolvency Regulations 2006* (SI 2006/1030).

[31] See also section 19.7.

[32] Para 7.4.

[33] Art 17(4).

[34] Arts 20(6) and 22(3).

[35] Insolvency Service, *Implementation of UNCITRAL Model Law on Cross-Border Insolvency in Great Britain: Summary of Responses and Government Reply* (March, 2006) p 15 (para 55).

[36] Although s 426 could have been amended to adapt it to the Model Law (see Insolvency Act 2000, s 14(2)(c)), the UK government decided that it would be better for all existing procedures to be maintained so as to afford the widest array of choice to applicants. See Insolvency Service, *Implementation of UNCITRAL Model Law on Cross-Border Insolvency in Great Britain: Summary of Responses and Government Reply* (March 2006) p 5 (para 7).

[37] See Art 7.

[38] Art 2(b).

[39] Amended by Insolvency Act 2000, s 4.

A British insolvency officeholder is authorised to act in a foreign state on behalf of British insolvency proceedings, but this is only to the extent that it is permitted by the applicable foreign law.[40] It is not necessary for that particular foreign state to have enacted legislation based on the Model Law.[41]

19.3 ACCESS OF FOREIGN REPRESENTATIVES AND CREDITORS TO ENGLISH COURTS

19.3.1 'Foreign representative' is defined as:

a person or body, including one appointed on an interim basis, authorised in a foreign proceeding to administer the reorganisation or the liquidation of the debtor's assets or affairs or to act as a representative of the foreign proceeding.

A hallmark of the Model Law is the provision of expedited and direct access for the foreign representative administering a foreign insolvency to the courts of the enacting state.[42] A foreign representative can apply to commence a proceeding under British insolvency law if the conditions for commencing such a proceeding are met[43]; prior recognition of the foreign proceeding is not necessary as, in certain circumstances, it is imperative to act urgently to preserve the debtor's assets.[44] The foreign representative is also entitled to participate in a proceeding regarding the debtor under British insolvency law; recognition of the foreign proceeding is a prerequisite in this situation.[45] This provision serves to give the foreign representative standing to make such petitions, requests or submissions as may be required for the realisation and distribution of the debtor's assets or co-operation with the foreign proceeding. Exactly what petitions or requests may be made by the foreign representative is left up to British insolvency law.[46]

19.3.2   However, the sole fact that a foreign representative has made an application to the court is not grounds for the court to take jurisdiction over the foreign representative, assets and affairs of the debtor for any purpose other than that stipulated in the application.[47] That said, the court is not prevented from exercising jurisdiction on other grounds, such as a tort committed by the foreign representative.[48]

19.3.3   The Model Law also enshrines the principle of non-discrimination of foreign creditors. Foreign creditors are to be treated equally with local creditors; thus, according to Article 13(1) they have the same rights regarding the commencement of and participation in British insolvency proceedings. There is, however, an exception in Article 13(2):

Paragraph 1 of this article does not affect the ranking of claims in a proceeding under British insolvency law, except that the claim of a foreign creditor shall not be given a lower priority

---

[40] Art 5.
[41] *Guide to Enactment*, para 85.
[42] Art 9.
[43] Art 11.
[44] *Guide to Enactment*, para 99.
[45] Art 12.
[46] *Guide to Enactment*, paras 100–1.
[47] Art 10.
[48] *Guide to Enactment*, para 95.

than that of general unsecured claims solely because the holder of such a claim is a foreign creditor.

The *Guide to Enactment* explains that, whilst the Model Law allows for foreign creditors to be assigned a special ranking if that is provided for by the law of the enacting state, the safety net is that the foreign creditors cannot be ranked lower than general unsecured claims.[49]

19.3.4   Article 13(3) is worthy of note as it provides that the claim may not be challenged solely on the ground that it is a claim by a foreign tax or social security authority.[50] This provision overrides the general common law rule that foreign tax and revenue laws cannot be enforced through the English courts. However, it does not destroy the parallel common law rule of non-enforcement of foreign penal laws as Article 13(3) goes on to provide that such a claim may still be challenged (a) on the ground that it is in whole or in part a penalty, or (b) on any other ground that a claim might be rejected in a proceeding under British insolvency law. Thus, a foreign tax law which is also penal in character will not be enforced in proceedings to which the Model Law applies.

19.3.5   Article 14 sets out the requirements by which notification of English proceedings to foreign creditors is to be undertaken. Notification needs to be made individually but, if this would entail excessive cost or not be feasible, the provision allows other forms of notification if the court thinks this would be more appropriate.[51] If the local creditors are to be notified by advertisement only, it would be permissible to notify foreign creditors by advertisement in the appropriate foreign newspapers.[52] However the notification is given, it shall: indicate a reasonable time period for filing claims[53] and specify the place for their filing; indicate whether secured creditors need to file their secured claims; and contain any other information required pursuant to the law of Great Britain and the orders of the court.[54]

19.4 RECOGNITION OF A FOREIGN PROCEEDING

19.4.1   The definition of 'foreign proceeding' as set out in Art 2(i) is considered above.[55] Foreign proceedings are divided into 'main' and 'non-main' proceedings.[56] The distinction between the two is important as it has repercussions for the type of relief available upon recognition; relief for non-main proceedings is discretionary in nature whilst some of the relief open to main proceedings is mandatory in character. If the proceeding does not fall within either definition, the Model Law is not applicable; assistance may be available under either the common law or section 426 of the Insolvency Act 1986.

---

[49] Para 104.
[50] See, to similar effect, EC Insolvency Regulation, Art 39.
[51] Art 14(2)(a).
[52] Art 14(2)(b).
[53] What would be a 'reasonable' time period is not set out.
[54] Art 14(3).
[55] See para 19.2.3.
[56] See Art 17(2).

19.4.2 A 'foreign main proceeding' is one taking place in the state where the debtor has the centre of its main interests[57]; whilst the concept of 'centre of main interests' is not defined, it is presumed that, in the absence of proof to the contrary, the debtor's registered office, or habitual residence in the case of an individual, is the centre of the debtor's main interests.[58] A 'foreign non-main proceeding' is a foreign proceeding, other than a foreign main proceeding, taking place in a state where the debtor has an establishment.[59] 'Establishment' in turn means any place of operations where the debtor carries out a non-transitory economic activity with human means and assets or services.[60] There is an obvious similarity between the Model Law and the EC Insolvency Regulation in terms of the framework and terminology used.[61] The inspiration which the former evidently took from the latter should serve as an encouragement to courts implementing the Model Law to consider the authorities on the EC Insolvency Regulation when trying to construe identical or markedly similar concepts to those found in the Regulation. Although it may be that EU courts which are bound by the EC Insolvency Regulation will naturally gravitate towards a familiar interpretation of similar concepts, it is more debatable whether the same approach will be (or should be) taken by courts of non-EU Member States. Although there is some advantage in terms of uniformity of interpretation,[62] a court referring to the Regulation for some guidance on the Model Law must always take into consideration the different nature and background of the two instruments and the fact that key concepts in the Regulation are still evolving. Nevertheless, in *Re Stanford International Bank Ltd (In Receivership)* it was suggested that 'the framers of the Model Law envisaged that the interpretation of [centre of main interests] in the EC Regulation ... would be equally applicable to [centre of main interests] in the Model Law'.[63] The judge embarked on a lengthy analysis of case law concerning the concept of centre of main interests in relation to the Regulation in order to interpret the same concept under the 2006 Regulations.[64]

19.4.3 Article 15 states that a foreign representative may apply to the court for recognition of the proceedings in which he has been appointed and sets out details of the documentation that is required. The court shall recognise a foreign proceeding if it fulfils the definition of 'foreign proceeding' in Article 2(i); the foreign

---

[57] Art 2(g).

[58] Art 16(3). The concept of the centre of main interests is also central to the EC Insolvency Regulation; Art 3(1) of the Regulation furnishes the same presumption with respect to a company. See paras 17.2.5–17.2.18.

[59] Art 2(h).

[60] Art 2(e). The definition of 'establishment' in the UK enactment is slightly different from that provided in the original text of the Model law; it is clear, though, that both versions were inspired by the definition in Art 2(h) of the Regulation.

[61] The EC Insolvency Regulation divides up proceedings into 'main' proceedings, which take place where the debtor has its centre of main interests, and 'territorial' proceedings (which could be either independent or secondary proceedings) which may be opened where the debtor has a place of establishment.

[62] Although the degree of uniformity may still be admittedly rather small as enacting states may modify the Model Law when implementing it.

[63] Lewison J at [2009] BPIR 1157, 1169–70 (at [45]–[46]).

[64] However, Lewison J did not see the need to decide whether he was strictly bound to follow the interpretation of centre of main interests under the EC Insolvency Regulation as counsel for the parties agreed that he should follow the same interpretation for the purposes of the 2006 Regs: [2009] BPIR 1157, 1173 (at [60]).

representative applying for recognition is a person or body within the meaning of Art 2(j); the application is accompanied by the documents required under Article 15(2) which go towards establishing the existence of the foreign proceeding and of the appointment of the foreign representative; and the application has been submitted to the appropriate court. A statement identifying all foreign proceedings, proceedings under British insolvency law and section 426 requests[65] in respect of the debtor that are known to the foreign representation must accompany the application for recognition.[66] The court is required to decide upon the application at the earliest possible time.[67] To expedite the process, the court is entitled to presume that the documents required under Article 15(2) that accompany the application are authentic, whether or not they have been legalised.[68] If recognition is given and it is later shown that the grounds for granting recognition were fully or partially lacking or have fully or partially ceased to exist, the court may modify or terminate recognition, either altogether or for a limited time, and on such terms and conditions as the court thinks fit. This may be done on the application of the foreign representative or a person affected by recognition or of its own motion.[69]

Relief Available upon the Application for Recognition of a Foreign Proceeding

19.4.4   Article 19 provides for relief to be granted from the time of filing an application for recognition until the application is decided upon, where such relief is urgently required to protect the assets of the debtor or the interests of the creditors. The court, upon request by the foreign representative, may grant provisional relief including: (a) staying execution against the debtor's assets; (b) entrusting the administration or realisation of all or part of the debtor's assets located in Great Britain to the foreign representative or another person designated by the court in order to protect and preserve the value of assets which are perishable, susceptible to devaluation or otherwise in jeopardy; and (c) any relief mentioned in Article 21(c), (d) or (g).[70] The court may extend the relief granted,[71] for example, to avoid a gap between the relief granted before recognition and after recognition,[72] but in the normal course of events relief granted under Article 19 terminates when the application for recognition is decided upon.[73] The court may, of course, deny relief, as relief under Article 19 is discretionary; in particular, the court may refuse to grant relief in relation to a foreign non-main proceeding if it would interfere with the administration of a foreign main proceeding.[74]

---

[65] Defined as 'a request for assistance in accordance with section 426 of the Insolvency Act 1986 made to a court in any part of the United Kingdom': Art 2(l).
[66] Art 15(3).
[67] Art 17(3).
[68] Art 16(2). See also Art 16(1).
[69] Art 17(4).
[70] See para 19.4.8.
[71] Art 21(f).
[72] *Guide to Enactment*, para 139.
[73] Art 19(2).
[74] Art 19(3).

Effects of Recognition of a Foreign Main Proceeding

19.4.5   Upon the recognition of a foreign main proceeding, there will be an automatic stay of any individual actions or individual proceedings, concerning the debtor's assets, rights, obligations, or liabilities and execution against the debtor's assets.[75] Further, the right to transfer, encumber or otherwise dispose of any assets of the debtor is suspended.[76] That said, the stay and suspension does not affect certain rights—in particular, the right to take any steps to enforce security[77] over the debtor's property, to repossess goods in the debtor's possession under a hire-purchase agreement, the right exercisable under or by virtue of or in connection with the provisions referred to in Article 1(4) and to set-off.[78] In order to escape the automatic moratorium, these rights must have been exercisable if the debtor had been adjudged bankrupt or had been made the subject of a winding-up order under the Insolvency Act 1986. In addition, there is a right to commence individual actions or proceedings necessary to preserve a claim against the debtor.[79] This is to deal with any limitation issues; once the claim is preserved, the automatic stay will apply.[80] The right to commence or continue any criminal proceedings or any action or proceedings by a person or body having regulatory, supervisory, or investigative functions of a public nature that is brought in the exercise of those functions, is also preserved.[81]

19.4.6   The stay or suspension may be modified or terminated by the court pursuant to Article 20(6). In relation to this it should be noted that foreign interim proceedings are also designated as foreign proceedings and, therefore, the effects set out above also apply to foreign interim proceedings. However, it may be that the foreign interim proceeding subsequently ceases to have a sufficient basis for an automatic stay to be imposed against actions against the debtor and his assets; in this situation, the court could then lift the automatic stay.[82] The court could also use its powers under Article 20(6) to terminate or modify the automatic stay against arbitral proceedings especially if it would be hard to enforce the automatic stay if the arbitration does not take place in England.[83]

19.4.7   The recognition of a foreign main proceeding is not a bar to the English court commencing a proceeding under English insolvency law.[84]

Relief Available upon the Recognition of a Foreign Proceeding

19.4.8   Whereas the provisions of Article 20 are mandatory in nature and cover only foreign main proceedings, Article 21 deals with discretionary relief that is available upon

---

[75] Art 20(1).

[76] The stay and suspension is to be of the same scope and effect as if the debtor had been subjected to proceedings under the Insolvency Act 1986 and subject to the same powers of the court and the same prohibitions, limitations, exceptions and conditions as would apply under the law of Great Britain: Art 20(2).

[77] 'Security' and 'secured creditor' are defined in Arts 2(n) and (m) respectively.

[78] Art 20(3).

[79] Art 20(4)(a).

[80] *Guide to Enactment*, para 151.

[81] Art 20(4)(b).

[82] *Guide to Enactment*, para 144.

[83] See *Guide to Enactment*, para 145.

[84] Art 20(5).

the recognition of both foreign main and non-main proceedings. Where necessary to protect the assets of the debtor or the interests of the creditors, the court may, at the request of the foreign representative, grant relief including: (a) staying against the commencement or continuation of individual actions or individual proceedings concerning the debtor's assets, rights, obligations or liabilities, to the extent they have not been stayed under Article 20(1)(a); (b) staying execution against the debtor's assets to the extent it has not been stayed under Article 20(1)(b); (c) suspending the right to transfer, encumber or otherwise dispose of any assets of the debtor to the extent this right has not been suspended under Article 20(1)(c); (d) providing for the examination of witnesses, the taking of evidence or the delivery of information concerning the debtor's assets, affairs, rights, obligations or liabilities; (e) entrusting the administration or realisation of all or part of the debtor's assets located in Great Britain to the foreign representative or another person designated by the court; (f) extending relief under Article 19(1); (g) granting any additional relief that may be available to a British insolvency officeholder under the law of Great Britain, including any relief provided under paragraph 43 of schedule B1 to the Insolvency Act 1986. The list set out in Article 21(1) covers the common types of relief that may arise in insolvency proceedings but is non-exhaustive.

19.4.9   Article 21(2)[85] empowers the court to entrust the foreign representative with the distribution of all or part of the debtor's assets located in Great Britain; however, the court must first be satisfied that the interests of creditors in Great Britain are adequately protected. In granting relief generally under Article 21 to a representative of a foreign non-main proceeding, the court must be satisfied that the relief relates to assets that, under the law of Great Britain, should be administered in the foreign non-main proceeding or concerns information required in that proceeding.[86] This is to ensure that the relief granted by the court does not confer unnecessarily wide powers on the foreign representative of a non-main proceeding which might interfere with the administration of another insolvency proceeding, in particular the main proceeding.[87]

19.4.10   It should be pointed out that the Model Law is silent on what sanctions will be imposed if a stay is violated; this is left to English law.

Protection of Creditors and Other Interested Persons

19.4.11   Article 22 seeks to achieve a balance between the relief that may be granted to the foreign representative and the interests of persons who may be affected by the granting of the relief, [88] such as creditors. Therefore, when granting or denying discretionary relief under Articles 19 or 21, or modifying or terminating relief under Articles 22(3) or 20(6), the court must be satisfied that the interests of all creditors and other interested persons (including if appropriate, the debtor), are adequately protected.[89] The relief granted under

---

[85] See *Re SwissAir Schweizerische Luftverkehr-Aktiengesellschaft* [2009] BPIR 1505.
[86] Art 21(3).
[87] *Guide to Enactment*, para 158.
[88] *Guide to Enactment*, para 161.
[89] Art 22(1). See *Warner v Verfides* [2009] BPIR 153.

Article 19 or Article 21 may be subject to conditions which the court considers appropriate,[90] and the court may also modify or terminate such relief of its own motion, or upon the request of the foreign representative or a person affected by the relief.[91]

19.4.12 It should also be noted that, on making an order pursuant to an Article 23 application (which is considered below[92]), the court may give such directions regarding the distribution of any proceeds of the claim by the foreign representative as it thinks fit; the purpose of such directions is to ensure that the interests of creditors in Great Britain are adequately protected.[93]

Avoidance

19.4.13 Article 23 deals with actions to avoid acts that are detrimental to creditors. According to Article 23(1), upon recognition of a foreign proceeding, the foreign representative will have standing to make an application to the court for an order under, or in connection with, certain sections of the Insolvency Act 1986 dealing with the setting aside of transactions at an undervalue,[94] preferences,[95] extortionate credit transactions,[96] certain floating charges transactions,[97] transactions defrauding creditors,[98] and the recovery of excessive pension contributions.[99] Where such an application (called an 'Article 23 application') is made, the provisions referred to in Article 23(1) and other specified sections,[100] shall apply whether or not the debtor has been adjudged bankrupt or is being wound up or is in administration (as the case may be) under British insolvency law and with the modifications set out in Article 23(3). These modifications concern the identification of the 'relevant time' for the avoidance provisions, the 'relevant time' involving the 'date of the opening of the relevant foreign proceeding'. According to Article 23(4), the date of opening of the foreign proceeding shall be determined in accordance with the law of the state in which the foreign proceeding is taking place, including any rule of law by virtue of which the foreign proceeding is deemed to have opened at an earlier time. This means that any rule of the foreign state involving the doctrine of 'relation back' will be relevant.[101]

19.4.14 Even if an Article 23 application is made, a British insolvency officeholder is still allowed to make any application under or in connection with any of the provisions referred to in Article 23(1).[102] Further, Article 23(1) does not apply to

---

[90] Art 22(2).
[91] Art 22(3).
[92] See paras 19.4.13–19.4.16.
[93] Art 23(7).
[94] Insolvency Act 1986, ss 238 and 339.
[95] Insolvency Act 1986, ss 239 and 340.
[96] Insolvency Act 1986, ss 244 and 343.
[97] Insolvency Act 1986, s 245.
[98] Insolvency Act 1986, s 423.
[99] Insolvency Act 1986, s 342A.
[100] Namely, Insolvency Act 1986, ss 240, 241, 341, 342, 342B to F, 424 and 425.
[101] Cf the unsettled situation under the EC Insolvency Regulation, see the opinion of Advocate General Jacobs in Case C–341/04 *Re Eurofood IFSC Ltd* [2006] ECR I–3813, paras 89–95. The Court of Justice refrained from dealing with this issue (see para 59).
[102] Art 23(8).

transactions which were entered into before the date on which the 2006 Regulations entered into force, that is, 4 April 2006.[103] Any challenge to transactions entered into before that date must be made by opening an English insolvency proceeding and for the officeholder to avoid the transactions using the English insolvency rules, a course of action which is preserved by Articles 20(5) and 23(8).[104]

19.4.15 To ensure that the foreign representative of a recognised foreign non-main proceeding does not obtain wider powers than necessary, Article 23(5) stipulates that the court must be satisfied that the Article 23 application in relation to a foreign non-main proceeding concerns assets that, under the law of Great Britain, should be administered in the foreign non-main proceeding.

19.4.16 To co-ordinate concurrent proceedings taking place in England and abroad, Article 23(6) provides that in this situation, the foreign representative shall not make an Article 23 application except with the permission of the High Court.

19.4.17 The final provision in Chapter III is Article 24, which stipulates that upon the recognition of a foreign proceeding, the foreign representative may intervene in any proceedings in Great Britain in which the debtor is a party, provided that the requirements of the law of Great Britain are met. The intervention may be in individual court actions or other proceedings (including extrajudicial proceedings) which are instituted by the debtor against a third party, or instituted by a third party against the debtor.[105]

19.5 CO-OPERATION WITH FOREIGN COURTS AND FOREIGN REPRESENTATIVES

19.5.1 Chapter IV of the Model Law sets out a framework for co-operation in international insolvency cases and is in many ways the heart of the Model Law. Speed and timing are essential in international insolvencies and, therefore, the framework set out eases co-operation by obviating the need to comply with time-consuming formalities.[106]

19.5.2 Article 25 provides that:

the court may co-operate to the maximum extent possible with foreign courts or foreign representatives, either directly or through a British insolvency officeholder.

Of particular note is the word 'may', which replaces the mandatory 'shall' in the original text of the Model Law. It was considered to be preferable to give the courts some discretion as to whether to co-operate, though it was anticipated that the court would refuse to co-operate only where it has good reasons for doing so.[107] To facilitate

---

[103] Art 23(9).

[104] See Insolvency Service, *Implementation of UNCITRAL Model Law on Cross-Border Insolvency in Great Britain: Summary of Responses and Government Reply* (March, 2006) p 33 (para 142); I Fletcher, *The Law of Insolvency* (London, Sweet & Maxwell, 4th edn, 2009) 1053.

[105] *Guide to Enactment*, para 169.

[106] See P Wood, *Principles of International Insolvency Law* (London, Sweet & Maxwell, 2nd edn, 2007) 966.

[107] Insolvency Service, *Implementation of UNCITRAL Model Law on Cross-Border Insolvency in Great Britain: Summary of Responses and Government Reply* (March 2006) p 34 (para 149).

co-operation, the court is entitled to communicate directly with, or to request information or assistance directly from, foreign courts or foreign representatives.[108]

19.5.3 Article 26 deals with the position of a British insolvency officeholder when co-operating with a foreign court or foreign representative. Article 26(1) provides that:

a British insolvency officeholder shall to the extent consistent with his other duties under the law of Great Britain, in the exercise of his functions and subject to the supervision of the court, co-operate to the maximum extent possible with foreign courts or foreign representatives.

The mandatory nature of the British insolvency officeholder's duty to co-operate is in contrast with the discretion that is given to the courts. The phrase 'subject to the supervision of the court' does not indicate any change in the pre-existing English rules regarding the supervisory functions of the court over the insolvency officeholder and the *Guide to Enactment* stresses that there is no suggestion that *ad hoc* authorisation would be needed for each communication between the insolvency officeholder and a foreign body.[109]

19.5.4 It should be noted that co-operation within Articles 25 and 26 does not require a previous formal decision to recognise the foreign proceeding,[110] thus expediting the process further.

19.5.5 Finally, Article 27 sets out examples of the forms which the co-operation can take, namely: (a) appointment of a person to act at the direction of the court; (b) communication of information by any means considered appropriate by the court; (c) co-ordination of the administration and supervision of the debtor's assets and affairs; (d) approval or implementation by courts of any agreement concerning the co-ordination of proceedings; (e) co-ordination of concurrent proceedings regarding the same debtor. This list is not exhaustive. However, the co-operation requested should not cause the English court to disregard its own rules of private international law. Where adversarial proceedings against third parties were brought pursuant to Chapter 11 bankruptcy proceedings in the United States, the *in personam* judgment against the third parties was not entitled to be enforced in England because the third parties had not submitted to the US bankruptcy court.[111]

19.6 CONCURRENT PROCEEDINGS

19.6.1 The fact that a foreign main proceeding has been recognised does not prevent the commencement of a British proceeding. However, Article 28 provides that the effects of a British proceeding in this situation shall be restricted to the debtor's assets that are located in Great Britain and, to the extent necessary to implement co-operation and co-ordination under Articles 25, 26 and 27, to other assets of the debtor that, under the law of Great Britain, should be administered in that proceeding. The original version of

---

[108] Art 25(2).
[109] Para 180.
[110] *Guide to Enactment*, para 177.
[111] *Rubin v Eurofinance SA* [2010] 1 All ER (Comm) 81.

Article 28 in the Model Law provided for local proceedings to be commenced only if the debtor has assets in the enacting state; however, the presence of assets[112] is not required under English insolvency rules in cases falling outside the EC Insolvency Regulation. This omission in the British enactment means, therefore, that in England, the English rules on jurisdiction for insolvency in cases falling outside the EC Insolvency Regulation will apply for cases falling within the Model Law.[113]

19.6.2   Article 29 deals with the situation where proceedings have been commenced concurrently under British insolvency law and abroad. It provides that the court may still seek co-operation and co-ordination under Articles 25, 26 and 27; the fact that an English proceeding has commenced does not prevent or terminate the recognition of the foreign proceeding and the provision of relief in favour of the foreign proceeding.[114] However, if the English proceeding is taking place when the application for recognition of the foreign proceeding is filed, any relief granted under Article 19 or 21 must be consistent with the English proceeding and, if the foreign proceeding is recognised as a foreign main proceeding, Article 20 is inapplicable.[115] This last rule is logically necessary as Article 20 imposes a mandatory stay upon recognition of a foreign main proceeding. If the English proceeding is commenced after the filing of the application for recognition of the foreign proceeding, three effects are spelled out in Article 29(b): (i) any relief under Article 19 or 21 shall be reviewed by the court and shall be modified or terminated if inconsistent with the English proceeding; (ii) if the foreign proceeding is a foreign main proceeding, the stay and suspension referred to in Article 20(1) shall be modified or terminated pursuant to Article 20(6), if inconsistent with the English proceeding; and (iii) any proceedings brought by the foreign representative pursuant to Article 23(1) before the English proceeding shall be reviewed by the court and the court may give such directions as it thinks fit regarding the continuation of those proceedings. Thus, it is clear that the provisions of Article 29 give primacy to the local proceeding over the foreign proceeding. Finally, Article 29(c) safeguards against the granting of excessive powers to a foreign representative of a non-main proceeding by providing that in granting, extending or modifying relief granted to such a person, the court must be satisfied that the relief relates to assets that, under English law, should be administered in the foreign non-main proceeding or concerns information required in that proceeding.

19.6.3   Article 30 deals with the situation where the court is asked to recognise more than one foreign proceeding. The court may seek co-operation and co-ordination under Articles 25, 26 and 27. The following shall also apply:

(a) any relief granted under Article 19 or 21 to a representative of a foreign non-main proceeding after recognition of a foreign main proceeding must be consistent with the foreign main proceeding;

(b) if a foreign main proceeding is recognised after the filing of an application for recognition of a foreign non-main proceeding, any relief in effect under Article 19 or 21 shall be reviewed by the court and shall be modified or terminated if inconsistent with the foreign main proceeding; and

---

[112] Note that the presence of assets alone is also not sufficient to grant international recognition under the Model Law to proceedings commenced on the basis of this ground.
[113] See paras 18.2.4–18.2.19.
[114] *Guide to Enactment*, para 189.
[115] Art 29(a).

(c) if, after the recognition of a foreign non-main proceeding, another foreign non-main proceeding is recognised, the court shall grant, modify or terminate relief for the purpose of facilitating coordination of the proceedings.[116]

19.6.4 Primacy is given to the foreign main proceeding; however, no priority is stipulated where there are two or more foreign non-main proceedings. Article 30 is not dependent on there being an insolvency proceeding pending in England. However, if there is a proceeding in England, in addition to two or more foreign proceedings, both Articles 29 and 30 will be applicable.[117]

19.6.5 Article 31 sets out a rebuttable presumption that:

In the absence of evidence to the contrary, recognition of a foreign main proceeding is, for the purpose of commencing a proceeding under British insolvency law, proof that the debtor is unable to pay its debts or, in relation to Scotland, is apparently insolvent within the meaning given to those expressions under British insolvency law.

This presumption means that it is not necessary to establish insolvency under English law which might be time-consuming; however, note that the presumption does not operate in relation to recognition of a foreign non-main proceeding.

19.6.6 Article 32 preserves the operation of the English 'hotchpot' rule which seeks to treat all creditors within the same class equally. It provides that:

Without prejudice to secured claims or rights in rem, a creditor who has received part payment in respect of its claim in a proceeding pursuant to a law relating to insolvency in a foreign State may not receive a payment for the same claim in a proceeding under British insolvency law regarding the same debtor, so long as the payment to the other creditors of the same class is proportionately less than the payment the creditor has already received.

This provision does not affect the ranking of claims in accordance with English law.

19.7 CONCLUSION AND OVERVIEW

19.7.1 As the economic crisis in 2008 demonstrated, globalisation has increased the significance of international insolvencies. There is obviously a need for cross-border co-operation and co-ordination between different jurisdictions. The EC Insolvency Regulation, English rules such as section 426 of the Insolvency Act and the common law's inherent jurisdiction to assist foreign insolvency proceedings, and the Model Law, are all attempts to cater for the phenomenon of international insolvencies.[118] A significant drawback of all these regimes is that none have rules catering specifically for group insolvencies.[119]

19.7.2 The value of judicial co-operation operating outside international instruments must not be underestimated. Section 426 of the Insolvency Act 1986 is a boon

---

[116] Art 30.

[117] *Guide to Enactment*, para 192.

[118] Other international initiatives are described in I Fletcher, *Insolvency in Private International Law* (Oxford, OUP, 2nd edn, 2005) ch 5; and B Wessels, *Cross-Border Insolvency Law: International Instruments and Commentary* (Alphen aan den Rijn, Kluwer, 2007).

[119] There are plans to incorporate such rules in the UNCITRAL Model Law.

that is unfortunately limited to only a certain number of countries, but the common law's inherent jurisdiction which enables the English court to provide assistance to foreign courts has proved to be malleable to the exigencies of the situation.[120] However, judicial co-operation has been said to be more easily achieved between common law jurisdictions as: 'The common law judicial mindset means that co-operation with judges in other states appears natural.'[121] There is therefore a need for a more structured mechanism for achieving global cross-border co-operation.

19.7.3   This brings us to the UNCITRAL Model Law. The Preamble to the Model Law states that the purpose of the Law is to promote: co-operation between courts and other competent authorities of the various states; greater legal certainty for trade and investment; the fair and efficient administration of cross-border insolvencies that protects the interests of all the creditors and other interested parties, including the debtor; protection and maximisation of the value of the debtor's assets; and facilitation of the rescue of financially troubled businesses. The hope is that the Model Law will be a modern, harmonised and fair framework for dealing with cross-border insolvencies in enacting states.[122] The Model Law has strengths, such as getting rid of many time-consuming formalities which may obstruct liquidators from taking control of the debtor's assets expeditiously and simplifying the procedure for recognition of foreign proceedings; however, the utopian ideals set out in its Preamble cannot be said to have been fully achieved. The Model Law suffers a disadvantage from being merely a Model Law. Enacting states are free to modify the provisions and only enact those which it thinks suitable, thereby undermining the objective of harmonising previously divergent laws. Yet the form of a Model Law and the flexibility inherent in its status as a Model Law was perhaps necessary to persuade countries reluctant to give up their autonomy in international insolvency situations to incorporate it as part of their law. This leads to the next point. The biggest problem for the Model Law is convincing states from myriad backgrounds and which may not have significant ties with each other to subscribe fully to the spirit of internationalism and co-operation and to relinquish part of their autonomy in this area; this task is all the harder given that insolvencies involve public policy, social security and economic issues.[123] That the Model Law had to be fairly restricted in its scope is a testament to the difficulty of the task.

19.7.4   Given that the element of trust between states is vital for any cross-border insolvency instrument to work, it is not surprising that the EC Insolvency Regulation is the more successful of the two instruments. The closer economic and social ties between the EU Member States have enabled the Regulation to be fairly comprehensive in scope, with harmonised jurisdiction, choice of law and recognition rules. Uniform implementation is also greatly enhanced by the fact that the Court of Justice

---

[120] Some prefer the flexibility of informal judicial co-operation rather than rigid rules such as those set out in the UNCITRAL Model Law. See J Ziegel, 'Canada–United States Cross-Border Insolvency Relations and the UNCITRAL Model Law' (2006–07) 32 *Brooklyn J Int Law* 1041, 1061–3.

[121] JJ Spigelman, 'Cross-border Insolvency: Co-operation or Conflict?' (2009) 83 *ALJ* 44.

[122] *Guide to Enactment*, para 1.

[123] P Torremans, *Cross Border Insolvencies in EU, English and Belgian Law* (The Hague, Kluwer, 2002) 224.

is authorised to rule on the interpretation of the Regulation; this is in contrast with the lack of an over-arching judicial body for the Model Law.[124]

19.7.5   While it may be that regional-based initiatives have more hope of success, the fact of the matter is that insolvencies cannot be arranged so as to have all their effects contained within one region. A debtor's assets and his creditors can be located worldwide. There is a need for a global instrument. Whatever its flaws, the Model Law should at least be applauded as an attempt to cater for such a need. It lays a foundation which can hopefully be built upon.

[124] Art 8 is inadequate to fill in this gap.

PART IV

ARBITRATION

ARBITRATION: INTRODUCTION

20.1 WHAT IS ARBITRATION LAW?

20.1.1 There are various general characteristics of arbitration which distinguish it from litigation. Perhaps the most fundamental aspect of the arbitral process is that it is built on the foundation of the agreement of the parties. Whereas the jurisdiction of the courts is derived directly from the law, the jurisdiction of an arbitrator is derived from the arbitration agreement itself. Unlike litigation, which is public, arbitration is essentially a private mechanism for the resolution of disputes.[1] This, indeed, is one of its attractions.[2] Furthermore, arbitration provides a dispute-resolution mechanism which has a greater appearance of neutrality than international litigation—which is often conducted in a forum which is the home forum of one of the parties and foreign to the other:

In a dispute between an Israeli seller and an Egyptian buyer, a Swiss arbitrator can usually be characterised as more neutral than an Israeli or an Egyptian. A Spanish buyer and a North African seller accept arbitration in Geneva as comparatively more neutral than litigation before national courts in Algiers or Madrid.[3]

Although it is sometimes asserted that the essence of arbitration is to enable parties to a dispute to obtain a speedy and cheap decision without having recourse to the courts,[4] in the international context commercial arbitration is rarely cheap and can be a very lengthy process. Nevertheless, in arbitration it is easier to tailor the procedure to the specific dispute—thereby avoiding unnecessary delay and expense.[5]

20.1.2 There are various ways in which arbitration resembles litigation. From a procedural point of view there is a common principle to both litigation and arbitration: it is fundamental that the parties should have a right to a fair hearing. In addition,

---

[1] On confidentiality in arbitration, see *Redfern and Hunter on International Commercial Arbitration* (London, Sweet & Maxwell, 5th edn, 2009) 136–45. See also *Dolling-Baker v Merrett* [1990] 1 WLR 1205; *Hassneh Insurance Company of Israel v Mew* [1993] 2 Lloyd's Rep 243; *Ali Shipping Corpn v Shipyard Trogir* [1999] 1 WLR 314; *Associated Electric Gas Insurance Services Ltd v European Reinsurance Co of Zurich* [2003] 1 WLR 1041; S Males, 'Confidence in arbitration' [1998] *LMCLQ* 245; H Smit, 'Breach of Confidentiality as a Ground for Avoidance of the Arbitration Agreement' (2000) 11 *Am Rev Int'l Arb* 567.

[2] See M Kerr, 'International Arbitration v Litigation' [1980] *JBL* 164; Departmental Advisory Committee, *Report on the Arbitration Bill* (1996) p 8 (para 12).

[3] WW Park, 'Neutrality, Predictability and Economic Co-operation' (1995) 12(4) *J Int Arb* 99, 103.

[4] Eg, see the opinion of Advocate General Reischl in Case 102/81 *Nordsee Deutsche Hochseefischerei GmbH v Reederei Mond Hochseefischerei AG & Co KG* [1982] ECR 1095, 1122.

[5] M Saville, 'An Answer to Some Criticisms of the Arbitration Act 1996' [1997] *ADRLJ* 155, 157. See also CR Drahozal, 'Of Rabbits and Rhinoceri: A Survey of Empirical Research on International Commercial Arbitration' (2003) 20(1) *J Int Arb* 23; RA Pepper, 'Why Arbitrate?: Ontario's Recent Experience with Commercial Arbitration' (1998) 36 *Osgoode Hall LJ* 807.

an award is not a negotiated settlement; it is a decision which is reached by the application of rules of law. In this respect arbitration is clearly distinguishable from mediation and conciliation. Nevertheless, it has been observed that the role of an arbitrator in the private sector is significantly different from that of a judge in the public sector.[6]

20.1.3 The focus of arbitration law is the relationship between the courts and the arbitral process. In the final analysis, the effectiveness of arbitration as a dispute-resolution mechanism depends on the coercive powers which the state entrusts to its courts. In the absence of voluntary compliance by the parties, it is the exercise of the coercive powers of the state which determines whether the acts of arbitrators are effective or ineffective.[7] The fundamental question is not whether the court should play a role in the arbitral process but what the limits of that role should be. Arbitration law defines the nature and extent of the court's powers in relation to the arbitral process.

20.2 VARIOUS TYPES OF ARBITRATION

Domestic and International

20.2.1 Arbitration, like litigation, may be entirely domestic or it may involve a foreign element. Where all the elements relevant to an arbitration are connected with England, English law governs the validity of the agreement, the procedure to be followed, the availability of interlocutory orders, the form of the award, the grounds on which the award may be challenged and the enforcement of the award. However, many arbitrations which take place in England have connections with other countries.

20.2.2 There are three types of international arbitration which may arise from contractual obligations: first, arbitration between states (or other international persons); secondly, arbitration between parties subject respectively to the jurisdiction of different states; and, thirdly, arbitration between states and private persons of foreign nationality or residence.[8] Only an arbitration within the first of these categories is truly international—in the sense that it is divorced from any municipal law and is submitted to public international law. The second and third categories are international only in the sense that they are connected with more than one country. They are, however, normally governed not by public international law, but by municipal law.[9]

20.2.3 Under the laws of some countries the same legal rules apply to all arbitrations. However, other legal systems seek to distinguish domestic from international (or non-domestic) arbitrations with a view to relaxing the degree of control exercised by the courts in international cases. Traditionally, English law distinguished between

---

[6] M Kerr, 'Concord and Conflict in International Arbitration' (1997) 13 *Arb Int* 121, 124–5.

[7] M Kerr, 'Arbitration and the Courts: the UNCITRAL Model Law' (1985) 34 *ICLQ* 1.

[8] FA Mann, 'State Contracts and International Arbitration' (1967) 42 *BYIL* 1.

[9] Although, as a general rule, an arbitration between a state and a private individual or corporation is subject to municipal law, arbitration under the auspices of the International Centre for the Resolution of Investment Disputes (ICSID) is wholly independent from municipal arbitration law—except regarding questions of enforcement See paras 24.5.8–24.5.10.

domestic and non-domestic arbitrations in three contexts. First, whereas the grant of a stay of proceedings brought in breach of an arbitration agreement was mandatory in non-domestic cases,[10] it was discretionary in domestic cases.[11] Secondly, it was easier to exclude the right to appeal to the courts on points of law under the Arbitration Act 1979 in non-domestic cases than in domestic ones.[12] Thirdly, the Consumer Arbitration Agreements Act 1988 rendered certain consumer arbitration agreements unenforceable in domestic cases,[13] but not in non-domestic cases.[14]

20.2.4 In 1996 the distinction between domestic and non-domestic cases came under attack from two directions. Within the context of a complete overhaul of English arbitration law,[15] the Departmental Advisory Committee suggested that consideration should be given to the abolition of the distinction. The basis of this proposal was that the rules which apply in non-domestic cases 'fit much more happily with the concept of party autonomy than our domestic rules, which were framed at a time when attitudes to arbitration were very different and the courts were anxious to avoid what they described as usurpation of their process'.[16] More significantly, in *Phillip Alexander Securities and Futures Ltd v Bamberger*[17] it was held—in the context of the Consumer Arbitration Agreements Act 1988—that the distinction between domestic and non-domestic cases was not compatible with EC law in that it discriminated against nationals of other EC Member States.[18]

20.2.5 Although it would have been possible to comply with EC law by extending the scope of the domestic rules to cases involving nationals of other EC states as well as to domestic cases involving UK nationals, this solution was very unattractive from the policy point of view and it would have involved a breach of the international obligations assumed by the United Kingdom on ratification of the New York Convention of 1958.[19] Therefore, to comply with the requirements of both EC law and international law, the only practical solution was to remove the special provisions for domestic arbitrations and to apply the same regime to all arbitrations. Following the entry into force of the Arbitration Act 1996, so far as English law is concerned, the same legal regime applies both to domestic cases and to cases with a foreign element.

Ad Hoc and **Institutional**

20.2.6 The words '*ad hoc*' in relation to international arbitration signify a situation where the parties conclude an agreement which provides a framework for the

---

[10] Arbitration Act 1975, s 1.
[11] Arbitration Act 1950, s 4.
[12] Arbitration Act 1979, s 3(6).
[13] Consumer Arbitration Agreements Act 1988, s 1.
[14] Consumer Arbitration Agreements Act 1988, s 2(a).
[15] See paras 20.3.11–20.3.13.
[16] *Report on the Arbitration Bill* (1996), p 66 (para 320).
[17] [1997] ILPr 73 (Waller J); [1997] ILPr 104 (CA). See also *Zellner v Phillip Alexander Securities and Futures Ltd* [1997] ILPr 730.
[18] The Court of Appeal relied on a number of cases decided by the Court of Justice: Cases 262/82 and 26/83 *Luisi and Carbone v Ministero del Tesoro* [1984] ECR 377; Case 186/87 *Cowan v Trésor Public* [1989] ECR 195; Case C–45/93 *Commission v Spain* [1994] ECR I–911; Case C–384/93 *Alpine Investments BV* [1995] ECR I–1141.
[19] See J Hill, 'Some Private International Law Aspects of the Arbitration Act 1996' (1997) 46 *ICLQ* 274, 276–80.

resolution of their disputes by arbitration without any assistance from an arbitration institution.[20] A clause providing for *ad hoc* arbitration may set out in detail the procedures to be followed at all the various stages. It is not uncommon, however, for the parties to incorporate a set of arbitration rules—such as the UNCITRAL Arbitration Rules—into the arbitration agreement. The model arbitration clause suggested by the UNCITRAL Arbitration Rules is in the following form:

Any dispute, controversy or claim arising out of or relating to this contract, or the breach, termination or invalidity thereof, shall be settled by arbitration in accordance with the UNCITRAL Arbitration Rules as at present in force.

The effect of this clause is to import into the arbitration agreement all the procedural elements contained in the rules. If the parties choose *ad hoc* arbitration but decide not to use a set of arbitration rules there is a greater danger that it will be necessary to have resort to the court to supplement the arbitration agreement.

20.2.7 Institutional arbitration refers to an arbitration which is carried out under the auspices of an institution which administers the progress of the arbitration. Some of the more important of the numerous arbitration institutions which are to be found throughout the world are the International Chamber of Commerce (ICC),[21] the London Court of International Arbitration (LCIA)[22] and the International Centre for Dispute Resolution (ICDR), which is a division of the American Arbitration Association (AAA). Generally, an institutional arbitration is conducted according to the rules of the institution in question. So, where parties adopt the standard arbitration clause suggested by the ICC, the parties agree to an arbitration administered by the ICC and governed by the ICC Rules of Arbitration.

20.2.8 One of the reasons for favouring institutional arbitration, rather than *ad hoc* proceedings, is the assistance provided by the institution to avoid delay and obstruction of the process.[23] The institution has a number of functions: first, it assists in the constitution of the tribunal if the parties do not specify in their agreement how the tribunal is to be appointed; secondly, it provides a mechanism for the challenge and replacement of arbitrators; and, thirdly, it provides the necessary back-up during the arbitration proceedings (such as the communication of documents). Furthermore, the fact that an award is obtained under the auspices of a well-known institution adds international respectability to the award and reduces the chances of the losing party defaulting or resisting enforcement. There are, however, certain drawbacks to institutional arbitration. It can be very expensive since the institution requires payment for its services; these costs are in addition to the

---

[20] Somewhat confusingly '*ad hoc*' is sometimes also used to describe an agreement to submit an existing dispute to arbitration (ie, a submission agreement). See *LG Caltex Gas Co Ltd v China National Petroleum Corpn* [2001] 1 WLR 1892 (W Godwin, [2002] *LMCLQ* 292).

[21] The ICC Rules were most recently revised in 1998: see WL Craig, WW Park and J Paulsson, *Annotated Guide to the 1998 ICC Arbitration Rules with Commentary* (Dobbs Ferry NY, Oceana Publications, 1998); MA Calvo, 'The New ICC Rules of Arbitration' (1997) 14(4) *J Int Arb* 41; EA Schwartz, 'The ICC Adopts New Arbitration Rules' [1997] *ADRLJ* 281.

[22] See M Kerr, 'The London Court of International Arbitration 1892–1992' (1992) 8 *Arb Int* 317; SN Lebedev, 'The LCIA Rules for International Commercial Arbitration' (1992) 8 *Arb Int* 321.

[23] MS Donahey, 'Defending the Arbitration against Sabotage' (1996) 13(1) *J Int Arb* 93, 94.

general costs of an arbitration, which include the arbitrator's fees and expenses, costs of hiring rooms, travelling costs, legal fees etc.

Specialised Arbitrations

20.2.9 Arbitration in trade and commodity fields has developed along its own lines. There are many trade associations which have their own arbitration rules—such as the Federation of Oils, Seeds and Fats Association (FOSFA) and the Grain and Food Trade Association (GAFTA). Standard contracts entered into by members of these associations normally incorporate the association's rules. Trade and commodity arbitrations are often of the 'look and sniff'[24] variety. Many commodity disputes concern questions such as whether goods which have been sold by sample conform to the sample. In this type of case the main task of the arbitrator is to resolve factual rather than legal questions.

20.3 TRENDS IN INTERNATIONAL COMMERCIAL ARBITRATION

Encouragement

20.3.1 The general trends in the second half of the 20th century were to encourage and facilitate international commercial arbitration and to make it more effective. First, the scope of the court's supervisory role over the arbitration process was reduced. Secondly, the enforcement of arbitration agreements and awards was made much easier by the New York Convention of 1958 (which was first implemented in England by the Arbitration Act 1975). If a successful claimant is not confident of being able to enforce an award abroad, arbitration in the international context remains a relatively unattractive prospect. In the absence of effective enforcement mechanisms an award is unlikely to be 'the end of the dispute-resolution process, or even the beginning of the end, but only the end of the beginning'.[25] As soon as enforcement abroad becomes readily available, arbitration becomes a more realistic alternative to the resolution of international disputes by litigation. Furthermore, the integrity of the arbitral process is protected if courts are required to uphold the agreement of the parties to refer their disputes to arbitration.

Harmonisation

20.3.2 Arbitration law is rooted in national legal systems which enjoy different cultures and traditions. Even in those cases where arbitration involves parties from different countries, the arbitral process is nevertheless regulated by national legal systems,

---

[24] Donaldson J in *Faure, Fairclough Ltd v Premier Oil and Cake Mills Ltd* [1968] 1 Lloyd's Rep 237, 238.
[25] PL Bruner and MT McCormick, 'Enforcement of Foreign Arbitral Awards: The US View of International Arbitration's "Final Frontier"' [1994] *ICLR* 128.

both as regards the conduct of the arbitration and the enforcement of the award. The second half of the 20th century saw developments—achieved largely through the work of international organisations—aimed at bringing national arbitration laws closer together.

The Geneva Protocol 1923 and the Geneva Convention 1927

20.3.3 Many legal systems have traditionally been suspicious of and hostile to arbitration. In the 1920s the international community took the first steps towards promoting international arbitration. These developments were accomplished with the backing of the League of Nations. The Geneva Protocol of 1923 was designed to promote the enforcement of arbitration clauses—which at that time were pro-hibited by many national laws—by imposing an obligation on national courts to refer to arbitration disputes in respect of which an arbitration agreement had been concluded. The Geneva Convention of 1927 sought to facilitate the enforcement of foreign awards. These conventions were no more than a limited success; they fell a long way short of guaranteeing the international enforcement of arbitral agree-ments and awards.

The New York Convention 1958

20.3.4 The New York Convention of 1958[26] is by far the most important develop-ment in international commercial arbitration during the last hundred years. Well over 100 states—including all the EU Member States and the Lugano contracting states—have acceded to the 1958 Convention. It should be noted, however, that not all the states which have signed the Convention have effectively implemented it.[27] The Convention, which is a significant improvement on the earlier international instruments in the field of arbitration, is designed to achieve two things: first, to ensure the respect of arbitration agreements by requiring national courts to decline jurisdiction over the merits of a dispute where the parties have agreed to arbitra-tion;[28] secondly, to provide a simple mechanism for the enforcement of foreign arbitral awards.[29]

UNCITRAL Arbitration Rules[30]

20.3.5 The institution of arbitration has traditionally been seen by the develop-ing world as one of the tools employed by former colonial governments and west-ern corporations to secure advantages over their contracting partners. States and

---

[26] See AJ van den Berg, *The New York Arbitration Convention of 1958* (Deventer, Kluwer, 1981). See also S Pisar, 'The United Nations Convention on Foreign Arbitral Awards' [1959] *JBL* 219.

[27] See M Kerr, 'Concord and Conflict in International Arbitration' (1997) 13 *Arb Int* 121, 130–1.

[28] See section 21.2.

[29] See section 24.2.

[30] JP Dietz, 'Introduction: Development of the UNCITRAL Arbitration Rules' (1979) 27 *Am J Comp L* 449; P Sanders, 'Procedures and Practices under the UNCITRAL Rules' (1979) 27 *Am J Comp L* 453.

corporations in developing countries have, therefore, tended to regard arbitration with a degree of mistrust:

African countries rightfully feel threatened by the overwhelming power of certain multinational corporations whose financial resources far surpass their own and whose tentacles extend into many different countries. Whether such fears are well grounded or not, they obviously still produce feelings of insecurity and dependence and a deep suspicion of a hidden agenda essentially for the benefit of big business. Without sufficient information on how the arbitral process benefits them immediately, African lawyers and their governments are understandably unwilling to get too involved in a process which they perceive as largely benefiting the trading entities of the west.[31]

20.3.6   To some extent the image of arbitration was given a boost in the developing world by the UNCITRAL Arbitration Rules, which were unanimously approved by the General Assembly of the United Nations in 1976. The rules have been successful in promoting arbitration in parts of the world which were traditionally hostile to arbitration as a mechanism for resolving commercial disputes. The fact that the UNCITRAL Arbitration Rules have the seal of approval from the United Nations gives them an international respectability not enjoyed by the institutional rules of all arbitration institutions.

20.3.7   Although the rules were originally designed for use in *ad hoc* arbitrations, their influence on institutional arbitration has been considerable. The arbitration rules of some arbitration institutions are very closely modelled on the UNCITRAL Arbitration Rules. Furthermore, some arbitration institutions are willing to administer arbitrations conducted under the UNCITRAL Arbitration Rules.

The UNCITRAL Model Law

20.3.8   The New York Convention of 1958 provides a framework for the enforcement of arbitration agreements and awards; it does not regulate in a general way the relationship between the arbitral process and national courts. So, the court's powers to grant interim relief or to set aside an award are derived entirely from municipal law.

20.3.9   International commercial arbitration is hindered by differences in national arbitration laws. For example, the setting aside of an award in the country where the arbitration was conducted is a ground on which enforcement of the award may be refused under the New York Convention.[32] Accordingly, an award which would be regarded as acceptable by most legal systems is nevertheless vulnerable to the idiosyncrasies of the municipal law of the country where the award is made.

20.3.10   There were various ways in which the international community might have sought to deal with the problems posed by the lack of uniformity in the field of arbitration law. The most ambitious solution would have been for the United Nations to draft a uniform law. However, this option was regarded as impractical on the basis that, even if international agreement could be reached on a text, a convention which gave no flexibility would be unlikely to receive very many ratifications. The alternative approach, which was the one adopted by UNCITRAL, was to encourage

---

[31] SL Sempasa, 'Obstacles to International Commercial Arbitration in African Countries' (1992) 41 *ICLQ* 387, 393.

[32] Art V(1)(e); Arbitration Act 1996, s 103(2)(f).

harmonisation in the field of arbitration by the adoption of a 'model' law. In 1985 a resolution of the General Assembly of the United Nations was passed recommending the UNCITRAL Model Law on Arbitration. In general terms, the aim of the Model Law is 'to facilitate international commercial arbitration and to ensure its proper functioning and recognition'.[33] More specifically, there are three main policy objectives in the Model Law: first, to allow the parties freedom to choose the procedure for the resolution of the dispute; secondly, to ensure fairness in arbitration proceedings; and, thirdly, to provide a legal framework which ensures that an arbitration can be completed notwithstanding disagreement by the parties. Countries which decide to adopt the Model Law are free to adapt it to suit their own requirements. The Model Law is, however, drafted in such a way that it can be adopted in its entirety without amendment. A number of countries have enacted the Model Law, either without change or with minor modifications.[34] Although the Model Law has not been embraced wholesale by any of the major arbitration centres, the Model Law set the agenda for the reform of arbitration law even in those countries which prefer to follow their own traditions.

The Evolution of English law

20.3.11   English arbitration law used to be a complex combination of 'incoherent and fragmentary'[35] statutes (in particular, the Arbitration Acts of 1950, 1975 and 1979) and case law. Given the unsatisfactory form of English arbitration law, the Departmental Advisory Committee on Arbitration Law was given the task of considering how English arbitration law should be reformed and whether the UNCITRAL Model Law should be implemented in England. In 1989 the Departmental Advisory Committee concluded that the Model Law should not be adopted in England.[36] The Model Law was rejected primarily on the basis that England already had an extremely sophisticated and highly developed body of arbitration law, based on statute, case law, writings and usages. However, the committee did recommend that English arbitration law should be amended in certain respects and that its form should be altered. In particular, English law 'should be set out in a logical order, and expressed in language which is sufficiently clear and free from technicalities to be readily comprehensible to the layman' and '[c]onsideration should be given to ensuring that any such new statute should, so far as possible, have the same structure and language as the Model Law, so as to enhance its accessibility to those who are familiar with the Model Law'.[37]

---

[33] MS Donahey, 'Defending the Arbitration against Sabotage' (1996) 13(1) *J Int Arb* 93.

[34] P Sanders, 'Unity and Diversity in the Adoption of the Model Law' (1995) 11 *Arb Int* 1: P Sanders, 'UNCITRAL's Model Law on International and Commercial Arbitration: Present Situation and Future' (2005) 21 *Arb Int* 443.

[35] M Mustill, 'Transnational Arbitration in English Law' [1984] *CLP* 133, 136.

[36] For a discussion of the Committee's report, see C Reymond, 'The Report of the Mustill Committee: A Foreign View' (1990) 106 *LQR* 431. The Model Law was adopted in Scotland: Law Reform (Miscellaneous Provisions) (Scotland) Act 1990, s 66 and sched 7. For an analysis of the Model Law and its impact in Scotland, see F Davidson, *International Commercial Arbitration: Scotland and the UNCITRAL Model Law* (Edinburgh, W Green, 1991) and 'International commercial arbitration in Scotland' [1992] *LMCLQ* 376.

[37] Departmental Advisory Committee on Arbitration Law, *A Report on the UNCITRAL Model Law on International Commercial Arbitration* (1989) p 34 (para 108(7)).

20.3.12 Following the recommendations of the committee, the task of promoting a new Arbitration Act was commenced by a private group of arbitration practitioners, acting in consultation with the Department of Trade and Industry and the chairman of the Departmental Advisory Committee. The project was later adopted by the Department of Trade and Industry so that the reform proposals could proceed as a government measure. Throughout the process the proposals were the subject of extensive consultation. Early attempts at consolidating the existing legislation were the subject of considerable criticism—largely on the basis that what was needed was comprehensive reform rather than mere consolidation[38]—and the final version of the Bill was much more ambitious in its aim. Whereas the aim of the draft Bill circulated in 1994 was, according to the long title, '[t]o consolidate, with amendments, the Arbitration Act 1950, Arbitration Act 1975, Arbitration Act 1979 and related enactments', the 1995 draft envisaged an Act 'to restate and improve the law relating to arbitration pursuant to an arbitration agreement'. In 1996, after 'a gestation period which [was] elephantine in its proportions',[39] comprehensive reforming legislation was enacted.

20.3.13 The Arbitration Act 1996 repealed Part I of the 1950 Act and the Acts of 1975 and 1979. While it does not purport to provide an exhaustive code on the subject of arbitration,[40] it does provide a comprehensive statement of the principles on which the law is based. Although in 1989 the Departmental Advisory Report had rejected the Model Law, the wisdom of that decision had been questioned.[41] As the reform project advanced the influence of the Model Law appears to have increased; in particular, the Model Law became 'a yardstick by which to judge the quality of ... existing arbitration legislation and to improve it'.[42] There can be no doubt that the Model Law had an impact on the 1996 Act from the point of view of structure, style and content.[43] Notwithstanding the fact that English law retains a number of distinctive features,[44] the 1996 Act brought English law more into line with modern international practice.[45] Although the 1996 Act attracted some criticism,[46] in general it was received with enthusiasm.[47] Few would dispute that the 1996 Act significantly improved the state of English arbitration law and further enhanced London's standing as a centre for international commercial arbitration.[48] While many of the provisions of the 1996

---

[38] See, eg, B Davenport, 'Problems of Arbitration Law Reform' (1994) 110 *LQR* 372; AH Hermann, 'The Draft English Bill: Pulling the Wrong Punches' (1994) 10 *Arb Int* 185.

[39] J Steyn, 'England's Response to the UNCITRAL Model Law of Arbitration' (1994) 10 *Arb Int* 1.

[40] Departmental Advisory Committee, *Report on the Arbitration Bill* (1996) p 8 (para 9).

[41] See, eg, J Uff and D Keating, 'Should England Reconsider the UNCITRAL Model Law or Not?' (1994) 10 *Arb Int* 179.

[42] J Steyn, 'England's Response to the UNCITRAL Model Law of Arbitration' (1994) 10 *Arb Int* 1. See M Saville, 'The Arbitration Act 1996' [1997] *LMCLQ* 502, 504–6.

[43] Departmental Advisory Committee, *Report on the Arbitration Bill* (1996) p 6 (para 4).

[44] See AS Reid, 'The UNCITRAL Model Law on International Commercial Arbitration and the English Arbitration Act 1996: Are the Two Systems Poles Apart?' (2004) 21(3) *J Int Arb* 227.

[45] See R Briner, 'Domestic Arbitration: Practice in Continental Europe and its Lessons for Arbitration in England' (1997) 13 *Arb Int* 155.

[46] See, eg, Anon, 'British Gelatin: Is It Consolidated, or Are You Petrified?' [1997] *ADRLJ* 169; IND Wallace, 'First Impressions of the 1996 Arbitration Act' [1997] *ICLR* 71.

[47] R Aird, 'Cross Border Aspects of Arbitration' (1996) 17 *Bus LR* 95; F Davidson, 'The New Arbitration Act—A Model Law?' [1997] *JBL* 101.

[48] GL Benton and RJ Rogers, 'The Arbitration of International Technology Disputes under the English Arbitration Act 1996' (1997) 13 *Arb Int* 361, 372–3.

Act are based on repealed legislation, almost no provision of the previous statutes has been restated in its original words. Accordingly, it is not always easy to determine where 'restatement ends and improvement begins'.[49] Some guidance may be found in the *travaux préparatoires* of the Departmental Advisory Committee.[50]

20.4 OUTLINE OF ENGLISH ARBITRATION LAW

20.4.1   The Arbitration Act 1996 provides the cornerstone of English arbitration law.[51] The ideology of the legislation is set out in the general principles contained in section 1, which overarch the whole of Part I of the Act:

(a) the object of arbitration is to obtain the fair resolution of disputes by an impartial tribunal without unnecessary delay or expense;
(b) the parties should be free to agree how their disputes are resolved, subject only to such safeguards as are necessary in the public interest;
(c) in matters governed by this Part the court should not intervene except as provided by this Part.

This section is important in the sense that it makes a decisive break with the past. Traditionally, English courts adopted an interventionist approach to arbitration, though the courts' powers of intervention were curtailed to some extent by the 1979 Act. By contrast, the 1996 Act starts from the principle of party autonomy and limits the role of the courts to giving effect to the parties' wishes and protecting the public interest. The modern view is that the role of the court is 'to support rather than to displace the arbitral process'.[52] Accordingly, although the 1996 Act confers extensive powers on the court, these powers are exercised more sparingly than was the case under the law which pre-dated the entry into force of the 1996 Act.[53] If the 1996 Act does not confer a power on the court to make a particular order, the court has no power to do so.[54]

The Foundations of Arbitration: the Arbitration Agreement

20.4.2   Arbitration is a consensual process based on an arbitration agreement. Such agreements may take the form of a submission agreement entered into after the dispute has arisen or an arbitration clause which refers to arbitration disputes which may arise in the future out of a particular legal relationship. A variation of the standard arbitration agreement is the *Scott v Avery*[55] clause, which may take the form of either a contractual term which provides that a reference to arbitration and the making of

---

[49] R Lord and S Salzedo, *Guide to the Arbitration Act 1996* (London, Cavendish, 1996) p x.
[50] In particular, *Report on the Arbitration Bill* (1996).
[51] The 1996 Act applies to arbitrations commenced on or after 31 January 1997.
[52] Departmental Advisory Committee, *Report on the Arbitration Bill* (1996) p 11 (para 22).
[53] See, eg, *Kalmneft JSC v Glencore International AG* [2002] 1 All ER 76.
[54] *ASM Shipping Ltd of India v TTMI Ltd of England (No 2)* [2007] 2 Lloyd's Rep 155.
[55] (1856) 5 HL Cas 811.

an award shall be a condition precedent to the commencement of any litigation, or a provision to the effect that the defendant's only contractual obligation is to pay such sum as the arbitrator shall award.[56] Under English law submission agreements and arbitration clauses (including *Scott v Avery* clauses) are equally valid. Although English law does not impose formal requirements which have to be satisfied for a valid arbitration agreement, in practice an oral agreement is difficult to enforce and the provisions of the Arbitration Act 1996 apply only if the arbitration agreement is in writing.[57]

The Doctrine of Separability

20.4.3 A submission agreement—under which the parties agree to refer a particular dispute to arbitration—is obviously a discrete contract. Similarly, an arbitration clause in a contract constitutes a self-contained contract, collateral or ancillary to the principal contract of which it forms a part.[58] This is the doctrine of separability (or severability).[59]

20.4.4 Since many contractual claims are referred to arbitration following the termination of the contract it would, in practical terms, seriously detract from the usefulness of arbitration as a method of dispute resolution if an arbitration clause applied only to pre-termination disputes. In a series of cases starting with the decision of the House of Lords in *Heyman v Darwins Ltd*[60] and culminating in the decision of the Court of Appeal in *Harbour Assurance Co (UK) Ltd v Kansa General International Insurance Co Ltd*,[61] the common law gradually adopted the doctrine of separability. This doctrine was placed on a statutory basis by the Arbitration Act 1996, section 7 of which provides:

Unless otherwise agreed by the parties, an arbitration agreement which formed or was intended to form part of another agreement (whether or not in writing) shall not be regarded as invalid, non-existent or ineffective because that other agreement is invalid, or did not come into existence or has become ineffective, and it shall for that purpose be treated as a distinct agreement.

Subject to the parties' contrary agreement, the principle of separability applies where English law is the law applicable to the arbitration agreement, even if the seat of arbitration is in a country other than England (or has not been designated or determined).[62] An arbitration agreement 'must be treated as a "distinct agreement" and can be void or voidable only on grounds which relate directly to the arbitration

---

[56] DR Thomas, 'Scott v Avery agreements' [1991] *LMCLQ* 508.

[57] Arbitration Act 1996, s 5(1).

[58] Arbitration Act 1996, s 7. For a consideration of the position at common law, see Lord Diplock in *Bremer Vulkan Schiffbau und Maschinenfabrik v South India Shipping Corporation Ltd* [1981] AC 909.

[59] For consideration of the doctrine of separability and its relationship with the conceptually distinct, but not unrelated, doctrine known as *Kompetenz-Kompetenz* (or *compétence-compétence*), see WW Park, 'The Arbitrability Dicta in *First Options v Kaplan*: What Sort of Kompetenz-Kompetenz Has Crossed the Atlantic?' (1996) 12 *Arb Int* 137.

[60] [1942] AC 356.

[61] [1993] QB 701. P Gross, 'Separability Comes of Age in England: *Harbour v Kansa* and Clause 3 of the Draft Bill' (1995) 11 *Arb Int* 85. See also A Rogers and R Launders, 'Separability—the Indestructible Arbitration Clause' (1994) 10 *Arb Int* 77.

[62] Arbitration Act 1996, s 2(5).

agreement'[63] (rather than to the contract as a whole). Accordingly, an appropriately drafted arbitration clause is effective to confer jurisdiction on the arbitrator not only in relation to contractual disputes which arise following the termination of a valid contract (whether by repudiation, frustration, rescission or supervening illegality),[64] but also in relation to disputes surrounding the initial existence or validity of the contract. There are cases where an arbitration clause is binding even though the underlying contract has not come into existence.[65] It should be noted, however, that there are limits to the doctrine of separability. An arbitrator does not have jurisdiction in cases where the ground on which the arbitration agreement is either invalid or non-existent is the same as the ground on which the contract as a whole is invalid or non-existent. For example, notwithstanding the doctrine of separability, an arbitration clause cannot survive in a case where it is successfully argued that the alleged contract containing the arbitration clause is a forgery. In such a case, the arbitration clause never comes into existence, because there was no consensus between the parties on the alleged agreement. The result is the same in cases where the alleged arbitration agreement never came into existence because of *non est factum*, threat, mistake about the identity of the other party or signature by someone lacking authority to agree on behalf of the party alleged to be bound.[66]

Validity and Scope of the Arbitration Agreement

20.4.5 The arbitrator's jurisdiction is derived from the arbitration agreement. If the arbitration agreement is for any reason invalid, or if the dispute falls outside the scope of the arbitration agreement, the arbitrator has no jurisdiction.[67] The validity and scope of an arbitration clause are to be determined by its proper law.[68] The proper law of the arbitration agreement governs whether the parties consented to the arbitration clause and determines the meaning to be given to various words and phrases which are commonly found in arbitration clauses (for example, 'disputes', 'differences', 'arising out of', 'in relation to', 'with regard to').

The Powers of the Tribunal[69]

General Powers of the Tribunal

20.4.6 The approach of the 1996 Act is to place primary responsibility for the conduct of an arbitration on the parties and the tribunal, rather than on the court. The obligations of the tribunal are to 'act fairly and impartially between the parties'

---

[63] Lord Hoffman in *Fiona Trust & Holding Corporation v Privalov* [2007] 4 All ER 951, 959 (at [17]). See also *El Nasharty v J Sainsbury plc* [2008] 1 Lloyd's Rep 360.
[64] *DDT Trucks of North America v DDT Holdings Ltd* [2007] 2 Lloyd's Rep 213.
[65] See *UR Power GMBH v Kuok Oils and Grains Pte Ltd* [2009] 2 Lloyd's Rep 495.
[66] MS McNeill and B Juratowitch, (2008) 24 *Arb Int* 475, 487.
[67] See, eg, *Metal Distributors (UK) Ltd v ZCCM Investment Holdings plc* [2005] 2 Lloyd's Rep 37.
[68] See section 21.1.
[69] M Hunter, 'The Procedural Powers of Arbitrators under the English 1996 Act' (1997) 13 *Arb Int* 345.

and to 'adopt procedures suitable to the circumstances of the particular case'.[70] Although there had been indications that, at common law, the arbitrator was the master of his own procedure,[71] the 'conventional wisdom'[72] was that arbitrators were required to adopt an adversarial model of procedure and were bound by the same rules of evidence as the courts.[73] The 1996 Act replaces the conventional wisdom with the principle that it is 'for the tribunal to decide all procedural and evidential matters, subject to the right of the parties to agree any matter'.[74] If the parties adopt particular rules of evidence (such as the International Bar Association Rules of Evidence)[75] the arbitrator is bound to apply those rules. In the absence of agreement by the parties, the tribunal has considerable room for manoeuvre. For example, an arbitrator may, in an appropriate case, choose to conduct an arbitration along inquisitorial rather than adversarial lines and may choose not to apply strict rules of evidence. Indeed, it has generally come to be accepted that arbitral tribunals 'should not accept the historical role of the common law judge as a more-or-less passive referee who merely holds the balance between opposing counsel'.[76] However, the arbitrator does not have the power to order the consolidation of related arbitral proceedings unless the parties have agreed to confer such a power on the tribunal.[77]

20.4.7 In the absence of contrary agreement by the parties, the arbitral tribunal may appoint experts or legal advisers to assist it[78]; it may order a claimant to provide security for the costs of the arbitration,[79] give directions in relation to property which is the subject of the proceedings,[80] direct that a witness be examined on oath[81] or give directions for the preservation of evidence in the parties' custody or control.[82]

---

[70] Arbitration Act 1996, s 33. See *The Magdalena Oldendorff* [2008] 1 Lloyd's Rep 7.

[71] See Goff J in *Carlisle Place Investments Ltd v Wimpey Construction (UK) Ltd* (1980) 15 BLR 109.

[72] A Marriott, 'Tell It To The Judge … But Only If You Feel You Must' (1996) 12 *Arb Int* 1, 15.

[73] *Halsbury's Laws*, Vol 2, 'Arbitration', para 672; MJ Mustill and SC Boyd, *Commercial Arbitration* (London, Butterworths, 2nd edn, 1989) 352. See also *Town & City Properties (Development) Ltd v Wiltshier Southern Ltd and Gilbert Powell* (1988) 44 BLR 114.

[74] Arbitration Act 1996, s 34(1). For consideration of the pros and cons of the arbitral tribunal's discretion to determine procedural questions, see WW Park, 'Arbitration's Protean Nature: The Value of Rules and the Risks of Discretion' (2003) 19 *Arb Int* 279.

[75] See H Bagner, 'Need for Rules of Evidence in International Arbitration' (1997) 25 *Int Bus Lawyer* 175.

[76] M Kerr, 'Concord and Conflict in International Arbitration' (1997) 13 *Arb Int* 121, 126.

[77] Arbitration Act 1996, s 35.

[78] Arbitration Act 1996, s 37.

[79] Arbitration Act 1996, s 38(3). Prior to the entry into force of the 1996 Act, the court had the power to order the claimant to provide security for costs under s 12(6)(a) of the 1950 Act. For consideration of the circumstances in which the court would order such security, see *SA Coppée Lavalin NV v Ken-Ren Chemicals and Fertilizers Ltd* [1995] 1 AC 38. In the words of the Departmental Advisory Committee, 'the proposition that the court should involve itself in such matters as deciding whether a claimant in an arbitration should provide security for costs has received universal condemnation in international arbitration' and the actual decision of the majority of the House of Lords in the *Ken-Ren* case 'was greeted with dismay by those in the international arbitration community who have at heart the desire to promote our country as a world centre of arbitration': *Report on the Arbitration Bill* (1996) p 44 (para 193). On the question of the court's power to order security for costs in the context of proceedings relating to the enforcement of an award under the Arbitration Act 1996, see *Gater Assets Ltd v NAK Naftogaz Ukrainiy* [2007] 2 Lloyd's Rep 588.

[80] Arbitration Act 1996, s 38(4). See *Emmott v Michael Wilson & Partners (No 2)* [2009] 1 Lloyd's Rep 233.

[81] Arbitration Act 1996, s 38(5).

[82] Arbitration Act 1996, s 38(6).

The Problem of Delay

20.4.8   The whole process of arbitration is potentially vulnerable to delay.[83] There are broadly speaking two kinds of problem. First, a claimant may, having commenced an arbitration, fail to prosecute the claim with appropriate vigour. If a claimant allows an arbitration to fall asleep, the question arises whether the claimant should be permitted to revive the arbitration at a subsequent point—maybe years after the commencement of the procedure. At common law, the English courts failed to deal very effectively with the problem of delay on the part of the claimant. Although, in the context of litigation, the court may dismiss a claim for want of prosecution in cases where the claimant is guilty of excessive delay, it was held that, at common law, the court does not have similar powers in relation to arbitration proceedings.[84] Furthermore, the courts decided that an arbitrator has no inherent power to dismiss arbitration proceedings for want of prosecution.

20.4.9   Since the common law proved singularly incapable of dealing with stale arbitrations, Parliament intervened to deal with the practical problems of delay on the part of the claimant, first, by section 5(2) of the 1979 Act and, secondly, following the recommendations of the Mustill Committee,[85] by section 13A of the 1950 Act. Both these provisions were repealed by the 1996 Act which confers a power on the arbitrator to dismiss a claim in the event of delay on the part of the claimant. Section 41, which is based on section 13A of the 1950 Act,[86] provides that, in the absence of contrary agreement by the parties, the tribunal may make an award dismissing the claim:

If the tribunal is satisfied that there has been inordinate and inexcusable delay on the part of the claimant in pursuing his claim and that the delay (a) gives rise, or is likely to give rise, to a substantial risk that it is not possible to have a fair resolution of the issues in that claim, or (b) has caused, or is likely to cause, serious prejudice to the respondent.

Unless there are very special circumstances, the arbitrator should not normally consider dismissing a claim for delay before the limitation period has expired.[87] It is also provided that, if the claimant fails to comply with the orders or directions of the tribunal, the tribunal may, in appropriate cases, dismiss the claim.[88]

20.4.10   Secondly, a respondent may seek to disrupt an arbitration by employing delaying tactics.[89] Under the 1996 Act the tribunal enjoys a range of powers to deal

---

[83] AI Okekeifere, 'The UNCITRAL Model Law and the Problem of Delay in International Commercial Arbitration' (1997) 14(1) *J Int Arb* 125.

[84] *Bremer Vulkan Schiffbau und Maschinenfabrik v South India Shipping Corporation Ltd* [1981] AC 909; *Paal Wilson & Co A/S v Partenreederei Hannah Blumenthal* [1983] 1 AC 854; *Food Corporation of India v Antclizo Shipping Corporation* [1988] 1 WLR 603. For an account of the development of the common law in this area, see P Owsia, 'Consensual Abandonment of Contract: Innovatory Developments under English Law in the Eighties Concerning Arbitration References' (1991) 8(4) *J Int Arb* 55.

[85] Departmental Advisory Committee on Arbitration Law, *A Report on the UNCITRAL Model Law on International Commercial Arbitration* (1989). DR Thomas, 'Arbitral Delay and the Recommendations of the Departmental Advisory Committee' [1990] *JBL* 110.

[86] Aspects of s 13A were considered by the House of Lords in *L'Office Cherifien des Phosphates v Yamahita-Shinnihon Steamship Co Ltd* [1994] 1 AC 486. JL Draeger, 'Arbitrators' power to strike out for want of prosecution' [1994] *LMCLQ* 198.

[87] *James Lazenby & Co v McNicholas Construction Co Ltd* [1995] 1 WLR 615.

[88] Arbitration Act 1996, s 41(5) and (6). See *TAG Wealth Management v West* [2008] 2 Lloyd's Rep 699.

[89] C Harris, 'Abuse of the Arbitration Process—Delaying Tactics and Disruptions' (1992) 9(2) *J Int Arb* 87. See also R Briner, 'Interim Awards' (1997) 25 *Int Bus Lawyer* 153; MS Donahey, 'Defending the

with problems posed by a failure by the respondent to co-operate in the conduct of the arbitration. If a party fails to attend oral hearings or to present written submissions, the tribunal may continue with the reference without that party and may make a default award.[90]

The Powers of the Court

20.4.11   In relation to disputes which the parties have agreed to refer to arbitration, the court serves two functions. On the one hand, the court provides assistance and support and, on the other, it supervises and controls. The control exercised by the court over the arbitral process is the price to be paid for the court's support. The state cannot reasonably be expected to allow a court of law to exercise its coercive powers to compel enforcement of an award unless it is satisfied that the arbitral procedure and the resulting award meet certain minimum standards. If, for example, the arbitral procedure has not complied with the basic requirements of due process, the state is justified in refusing to allow its sovereign powers to be used to obtain enforcement of the award.[91]

Assistance and Support

ENFORCING THE AGREEMENT TO ARBITRATE
20.4.12   Where proceedings are brought in England in breach of the terms of an arbitration agreement the proceedings must be stayed if certain conditions are satisfied.[92] In this way, the court forces the claimant to pursue the agreed method of dispute resolution.

THE CONSTITUTION OF THE ARBITRAL TRIBUNAL
20.4.13   Often the arbitration agreement sets out, either directly or indirectly, the mechanism for the appointment of the arbitrator or arbitrators. For example, an *ad hoc* arbitration clause may provide for a sole arbitrator to be appointed by agreement of the parties; alternatively, the agreement may make provision for a tribunal of two,[93] or more commonly, a tribunal of three with each party appointing one arbitrator and these two arbitrators appointing the third (to act either as chairman or as umpire).[94] A well-drafted clause also nominates an appointing authority (such as the President of the LCIA) so that the tribunal can be established in cases of a failure to appoint or disagreement. If the parties agree to institutional arbitration the rules of the institution provide a comprehensive scheme which ensures that the tribunal will be properly constituted. However, in cases where the arbitration agreement does not include a watertight set of provisions for the proper constitution of the tribunal, the court may be called upon to appoint an arbitrator.[95]

Arbitration against Sabotage' (1996) 13(1) *J Int Arb* 93; WW Park, 'Arbitration's Discontents: Of Elephants and Pornography' (2001) 17 *Arb Int* 263.

[90] Arbitration Act 1996, s 41(4).
[91] WL Craig, 'Uses and Abuses of Appeal from Awards' (1988) 4 *Arb Int* 174, 182.
[92] See section 21.2.
[93] See, eg, *Fletamentos Maritimos SA v Effjohn International BV* [1995] 1 Lloyd's Rep 311.
[94] See Arbitration Act 1996, s 16.
[95] See, in particular, Arbitration Act 1996, s 18; *The Villa* [1998] 1 Lloyd's Rep 195.

EXTENDING TIME LIMITS

20.4.14 A civil claim may be barred by lapse of time under the Limitation Act 1980. The statutory period of limitation applies to arbitrations in the same way as to court proceedings.[96] In the absence of agreement by the parties, arbitral proceedings are regarded as commencing either when one party serves on the other a notice in writing[97] requiring the submission of a matter to the arbitrator designated in the arbitration agreement or, if the arbitral tribunal has yet to be appointed, when one party puts in motion the process for its appointment.[98]

20.4.15 Many arbitration clauses stipulate time limits which are much shorter than the statutory limitation period, which in most cases is six years.[99] Such clauses normally provide that a claim which is not brought within the stipulated time—for example, 14 days or three months—is barred or extinguished. Similarly, an arbitration agreement may impose a time limit for the making of the award. If the time limit for making a claim (or for the making of the award) is allowed to elapse, the arbitrator ceases to have jurisdiction over the matter.

20.4.16 The 1996 Act contains various provisions for the extension of time limits. First, in certain circumstances, where the arbitration agreement provides that a claim is barred or the claimant's right extinguished if arbitral proceedings are not commenced within a specified period, the court may extend the time for commencing the proceedings. The court's power to extend time limits is restricted by section 12(3)[100] to cases where the court is satisfied:

(a) that the circumstances are such as were outside the reasonable contemplation of the parties when they agreed the provision in question, and that it would be just to extend the time, or

(b) that the conduct of one party makes it unjust to hold the other party to the strict terms of the provision in question.

This section replaces section 27 of the 1950 Act according to which the court was permitted to extend time limits in cases of 'undue hardship'.[101] Under the 1996 Act the court's power arises not only in cases where the arbitration clause imposes an absolute time limit, but also in cases where the agreement confers a discretion on the arbitrator to extend the contractual period in which a claim must be brought.[102] However,

---

[96] Arbitration Act 1996, s 13.

[97] See *Allianz Versicherungs AG v Fortuna Co Inc* [1999] 1 WLR 2117. A document sent by e-mail to a party's e-mail address is properly served: *Bernuth Lines Ltd v High Seas Shipping Ltd* [2006] 1 CLC 403.

[98] Arbitration Act 1996, s 14. See *Seabridge Shipping AB v AC Orssleff's Eftf's A/S* [1999] 2 Lloyd's Rep 685; *Taylor Woodrow Construction v RMD Kwikform Ltd* [2008] 2 Lloyd's Rep 345; *The Voc Gallant* [2009] 1 Lloyd's Rep 418.

[99] Limitation Act 1980, s 5. See, eg, *The Casco* [2005] 1 Lloyd's Rep 565.

[100] For the court's interpretation, see *Vosnoc Ltd v Transglobal Projects Ltd* [1998] 1 WLR 101; *Cathiship SA v Allanasons Ltd* [1998] 3 All ER 714; *Grimaldi Compagnia di Navegazione SpA v Sekhihyo Lines Ltd* [1999] 1 WLR 708; *Harbour and General Works Ltd v Environment Agency* [2000] 1 WLR 950; *Thyssen Inc v Calypso Shipping Corp SA* [2001] CLC 805.

[101] For discussion of the 1950 Act, see DR Thomas, 'Power of court to extend time for commencing arbitration proceedings' [1981] *LMCLQ* 529. The leading cases were: *The Aspen Trader* [1981] 1 Lloyd's Rep 273; *The Jocelyne* [1984] 2 Lloyd's Rep 569; *Comdel Commodities Ltd v Siporex Trade SA (No 2)* [1991] 1 AC 148.

[102] In this respect the 1996 Act follows the court's interpretation of s 27 of the 1950 Act: *Comdel Commodities Ltd v Siporex Trade SA (No 2)* [1991] 1 AC 148.

it is expressly provided that the court's power to extend a time limit under section 12 does not arise unless the claimant has exhausted any arbitral process for obtaining an extension of time.[103]

20.4.17 Secondly, section 50 provides that, unless otherwise agreed by the parties, the court may, on the application by the tribunal or one of the parties, extend any time limit for the making of an award. The court may exercise the power to extend such a time limit if any available arbitral process for obtaining an extension of time has been exhausted and if the court is satisfied that refusing to grant the extension of time would cause 'substantial injustice'.[104] Thirdly, the 1996 Act provides for the court to extend the period of time in which a party may challenge an award.[105]

THE CONDUCT OF PROCEEDINGS

20.4.18 The court has various powers in relation to the conduct of proceedings. Specific powers in relation to arbitral proceedings are contained in sections 42–45 of the 1996 Act. First, unless the parties have excluded the court's power by agreement, the court may make an order requiring a party to comply with a peremptory order made by the tribunal.[106] Secondly, a party to arbitral proceedings may use the same court procedures as are available in relation to legal proceedings to secure the attendance of witnesses before the arbitral tribunal.[107] Although this power may not be excluded by agreement, a party may make use of court procedures only if he obtains the consent of the tribunal or the other party and if the witness is in the United Kingdom.[108]

20.4.19 Thirdly, section 44(2) lists various powers which the court may exercise unless they have been excluded by agreement of the parties.[109] These powers are the same as the powers the court enjoys in legal proceedings in relation to the following matters:

(a) the taking of the evidence of witnesses;
(b) the preservation of evidence;
(c) making orders relating to property which is the subject of the proceedings or as to which any question arises in the proceedings—

(i) for the inspection, photographing, preservation, custody or detention of the property, or
(ii) ordering that samples to be taken from, or any observation be made of or experiment conducted upon, the property;

and for that purpose authorising any person to enter any premises in the possession or control of a party to the arbitration;

---

[103] Arbitration Act 1996, s 12(2).
[104] Arbitration Act 1996, s 50(2) and (3).
[105] Arbitration Act ss 79 and 80(5). See *Kalmneft v Glencore International AG* [2002] 1 Lloyd's Rep 128; *The Joanna V* [2003] 2 Lloyd's Rep 617; *Gold Coast Ltd v Naval Gijon SA* [2006] 2 Lloyd's Rep 400.
[106] Arbitration Act 1996, s 42(1).
[107] Arbitration Act 1996, s 43(1). See *BNP Paribas v Deloitte Touche LLP* [2004] 1 Lloyd's Rep 233.
[108] Arbitration Act 1996, s 43(2) and (3).
[109] For consideration of this provision, see *Tsakos Shipping and Trading SA v Orizon Tanker Co Ltd* [1998] CLC 2003; *Commerce and Industry Insurance Co of Canada v Certain Underwriters at Lloyd's of London* [2002] 1 WLR 1323; *Hiscox Underwriting Ltd v Dickson Manchester & Co Ltd* [2004] 1 All ER (Comm) 753.

(d)   the sale of any goods the subject of the proceedings;
(e)   the granting of an interim injunction or the appointment of a receiver.[110]

It is also provided that, '[i]f the case is one of urgency, the court may, on the application of a party or proposed party to the arbitral proceedings, make such orders as it
thinks necessary for the purpose of preserving evidence or assets'.[111]

20.4.20   One of the most important aspects of the court's support of the arbitral
process is the power to grant provisional measures under section 44(2)(e). However, it
is not the intention that powers should be taken out of the hands of the arbitrator and
exercised by the court. Accordingly, the court's powers under section 44 are limited
by the principle that the court shall act only if or to the extent that the tribunal 'has
no power or is unable for the time being to act effectively'.[112] Where the parties have
adopted institutional arbitration rules, those rules invariably confer on the arbitrator various powers, including the power to order provisional measures. For example,
Article 26(1) of the UNCITRAL Arbitration Rules provides:

At the request of either party, the arbitral tribunal may take any interim measures it deems necessary in respect of the subject-matter of the dispute, including measures for the conservation
of the goods forming the subject-matter in dispute, such as ordering their deposit with a third
person or the sale of perishable goods.

Although the parties are under a general duty to 'do all things necessary for the proper
and expeditious conduct of the arbitral proceedings'[113] and, more specifically, are required
'to comply without delay ... with any order or directions of the tribunal',[114] the tribunal's
lack of formal coercive powers prevents it from granting some of the most potent interim
measures.[115] For instance, since an arbitral tribunal may not direct orders to third parties,
it cannot effectively make an order freezing a bank account. Moreover, if the assistance
of the court is required as a result of the failure by one of the parties to comply with the
arbitrator's order, the element of surprise is lost. Accordingly, there are many situations
where an application to the court for interim measures is either the only available course
of action or is the most effective one to pursue.[116]

20.4.21   Fourthly, it is provided by section 45 of the 1996 Act that, subject to the
parties' contrary agreement, a party to an arbitration may—during the course of the
arbitral proceedings—refer a question of law for determination by the court. Such
an application must be made either with the permission of the tribunal or with the
agreement of the other parties to the arbitration. Section 45 of the 1996 Act is derived
from section 2 of the 1979 Act, which was of very limited significance and was little
used in practice. It would appear that section 45 of the 1996 Act is not proving to be
any more popular.[117]

---

[110]   Arbitration Act 1996, s 44(2). S 44 does not give the court the power to grant pre-action disclosure:
EDO Corporation v Ultra Electronics Ltd [2009] 2 Lloyd's Rep 349.
[111]   Arbitration Act 1996, s 44(3). See *Cetelem SA v Roust Holdings Ltd* [2005] 1 WLR 3555 (H Main,
'Court Ordered Interim Relief: Developments in English Arbitration Law' (2005) 22(6) *J Int Arb* 505);
National Insurance and Guarantee Corporation Ltd v M Young Legal Services Ltd [2005] 2 Lloyd's Rep 46.
[112]   Arbitration Act 1996, s 44(5).
[113]   Arbitration Act 1996, s 40(1).
[114]   Arbitration Act 1996, s 40(2)(a).
[115]   See *Pacific Maritime (Asia) Ltd v Holystone Overseas Ltd* [2008] 1 Lloyd's Rep 371.
[116]   See, eg, *Hiscox Underwriting Ltd v Dickson Manchester & Co Ltd* [2004] 1 All ER (Comm) 753.
[117]   See, eg, *Dredging and Construction Co Ltd v Delta Civil Engineering Co Ltd (No 2)* (2000) 72 Con
LR 99.

ENFORCEMENT OF THE AWARD

20.4.22   The overwhelming majority of awards are complied with by the losing party voluntarily. Where, however, the losing party fails to honour an award, the successful party will have to apply to the court for enforcement. The court's powers in relation to English awards are to be found in section 66 of the 1996 Act. As regards foreign awards, the position is regulated by common law and statute (most notably, Part III of the 1996 Act).[118]

Supervision and Control

20.4.23   The supervisory role of the court is based on a number of statutory powers contained in the 1996 Act. Some of the bases of intervention under the previous legislation have been abolished. Moreover, the grounds on which the court is entitled to intervene have been carefully circumscribed. The function of control is exercised by removing an arbitrator, by exercising control over costs and fees, by ruling on the scope of the arbitrator's jurisdiction, by setting aside the award or by reviewing the award on procedural or substantive grounds.[119]

THE REMOVAL OF AN ARBITRATOR

20.4.24   There are two relevant provisions of the 1996 Act relating to the revocation of an arbitrator. First, section 18 provides that, in the event of a failure in the procedure for the appointment of the arbitral tribunal, the court may, in the absence of the parties' agreement to the contrary, revoke any appointment which has already been made. Secondly, and more importantly, section 24 sets out certain grounds on which an arbitrator may be removed by the court.[120] An arbitrator may be removed if the court is satisfied:

(a) that circumstances exist that give rise to justifiable doubts as to his impartiality;
(b) that he does not possess the qualifications required by the arbitration agreement;
(c) that he is physically or mentally incapable of conducting the proceedings or there are justifiable doubts as to his capacity to do so;
(d) that he has refused or failed—

  (i) properly to conduct the proceedings, or
  (ii) to use all reasonable dispatch in conducting the proceedings or making the award,

and that substantial injustice has been or will be caused to the applicant.

20.4.25   It should be noted that the court's power is residual. Where the parties have agreed on institutional arbitration and, according to the institutional rules, the

---

[118] See ch 24.

[119] If a party to arbitral proceedings takes part, or continues to take part, in proceedings without making an objection (for example, that the proceedings have been improperly conducted or there has been a failure to comply with the 1996 Act) that objection cannot normally be raised later: Arbitration Act 1996, s 73. See, eg, *ASM Shipping Ltd of India v TTMI Ltd of England* [2006] 1 Lloyd's Rep 575; *The Ythan* [2006] 1 Lloyd's Rep 457.

[120] See *Laker Airways Inc v FLS Aerospace Ltd* [1999] 2 Lloyd's Rep 45; *Rustal Trading Ltd v Gill & Duffus SA* [2000] 1 Lloyd's Rep 14; *ASM Shipping Ltd of India v TTMI Ltd of England* [2006] 2 Lloyd's Rep 375 (permission to appeal refused: [2007] 1 Lloyd's Rep 136); *Norbrook Laboratories Ltd v Tank* [2006] 2 Lloyd's Rep 485; *ASM Shipping Ltd v Harris* [2008] 1 Lloyd's Rep 61; *Sumukan Ltd v Commonwealth Secretariat (No 2)* [2007] 1 Lloyd's Rep 370.

institution has the power to remove an arbitrator, the court's power under section 24 arises only if the court is satisfied that 'the applicant has first exhausted any available recourse to that institution'.[121]

COSTS AND FEES

20.4.26   The legislation gives the court a degree of control over the costs of an arbitration and the arbitrator's fees. There are two aspects of the provisions relating to costs and fees. First, all parties are jointly and severally liable for the arbitrators' fees; however, such liability is limited to 'such reasonable fees and expenses (if any) as are appropriate in the circumstances'.[122] The reasonableness of the arbitrator's fees is ultimately in the hands of the court; a party may apply to the court for the arbitrators' fees to be adjusted.[123] If the fees have already been paid, the court may order their repayment to the extent that they exceed what is reasonable.[124]

20.4.27   Secondly, as in litigation, 'when one party is successful, that party should normally recover at least a proportion of his costs'.[125] Although costs are within the discretion of the arbitrator,[126] the 1996 Act provides that, in the absence of special factors, '[u]nless the parties otherwise agree, the tribunal shall award costs on the general principle that costs should follow the event'.[127] Any decision of the tribunal as regards the recovery of costs is reviewable in the same way as any other award.[128]

DETERMINATION OF THE ARBITRATOR'S JURISDICTION

20.4.28   Although the 1996 Act provides that the arbitrator may rule on his own jurisdiction,[129] the court will generally have the final say.[130] A challenge to the tribunal's jurisdiction must be made as early as possible—normally, not later than when the party making the challenge takes his first step in the proceedings.[131] If, however, a question relating to the scope of the arbitrator's jurisdiction arises for the first time during the course of the proceedings, a challenge may be made at that stage.

20.4.29   When a jurisdictional challenge is made, there are various routes whereby the matter can be brought before the court.[132] First, the tribunal may rule on its own jurisdiction either as a preliminary point or in the final award, which also deals with the merits of the dispute. Regardless of when the tribunal rules on jurisdictional questions, the award is reviewable by the court[133]—unless the award is made under a separate agreement that the tribunal should rule on its jurisdiction.[134] Secondly,

---

[121] Arbitration Act 1996, s 24(2).
[122] Arbitration Act 1996, s 28(1).
[123] Arbitration Act 1996, s 28(2); *Hussman (Europe) Ltd v Al Ameen Development & Trade Co* [2000] 2 Lloyd's Rep 83. See also Arbitration Act 1996, s 64.
[124] Arbitration Act 1996, s 28(3).
[125] Departmental Advisory Committee, *Report on the Arbitration Bill* (1996) p 30 (para 121).
[126] Arbitration Act 1996, s 61(1).
[127] Arbitration Act 1996, s 61(2).
[128] See, eg, *Gbangbola v Smith & Sherriff Ltd* [1998] 3 All ER 730.
[129] Arbitration Act 1996, s 30(1).
[130] See *Vee Networks Ltd v Econet Wireless International Ltd* [2005] 1 Lloyd's Rep 192.
[131] Arbitration Act 1996, s 31(1).
[132] See Departmental Advisory Committee, *Report on the Arbitration Bill* (1996) pp 33–5 (paras 140–9).
[133] Arbitration Act 1996, s 67(1)(a).
[134] See *LG Caltex Gas Co Ltd v China National Petroleum Corpn* [2001] 1 WLR 1892, 1905 (at [50]).

an application may be made to the court under section 32 of the 1996 Act for the substantive jurisdiction of the tribunal to be determined before any award is made. The court may not consider an application under section 32 unless the application is made with the written agreement of all the parties or unless it is made with the permission of the tribunal.[135] The rationale for the mechanism provided by section 32 is that, in a case where one party refuses to take part in an arbitration on the basis of an objection to the arbitrator's jurisdiction, 'it might very well be cheaper and quicker for the party wishing to arbitrate to go directly to the court to seek a favourable ruling on jurisdiction rather than seeking an award from the tribunal'.[136] Thirdly, section 72 of the 1996 Act provides that a person alleged to be a party to arbitral proceedings, but who takes no part in those proceedings, may apply to the court for the determination of whether or not there is a valid arbitration agreement.[137]

RECOURSE AGAINST THE AWARD[138]

20.4.30 In an ideal world, the decisions of arbitral tribunals would be reached swiftly and economically and they would be clear and legally accurate. In practice, however, there is a tension between two conflicting goals—the finality of an award and its legality. The goal of finality would be promoted by reducing the circumstances in which an arbitral award can be challenged in the courts. The goal of legality would be advanced by allowing a party to appeal to the courts on any question of substance or procedure. No modern legal system adopts either extreme position: 'The real problem is, as it has always been, to strike a realistic balance between meddling and indifference.'[139] How the balance between finality and legality should be struck is controversial.

20.4.31 The general trend in English law has been to reduce the avenues by which an arbitral award can be challenged in the courts. It is well established that the tribunal is the final arbiter on questions of fact.[140] Although, traditionally, parties to an English arbitration had a right to appeal to the courts on points of law, this right has been severely curtailed by legislation. Such a right is not found at all in many other legal systems.

20.4.32 Most legal systems accept that, even if the tribunal has the final word on questions of law and fact, this does not mean that arbitral awards should be entirely excluded from the scrutiny of the courts. One of the supervisory functions of the courts is to ensure that the arbitral process operates according to principles of natural justice. So far as English law is concerned, whereas the right to appeal on a point of law may be excluded by the agreement of the parties, the general supervisory jurisdiction of the court may not.[141]

---

[135] See *ABB Lummus Global Ltd v Keppel Fels Ltd* [1999] 2 Lloyd's Rep 24; *Film Finance Inc v Royal Bank of Scotland* [2007] 1 Lloyd's Rep 382.

[136] Departmental Advisory Committee, *Report on the Arbitration Bill* (1996) p 33 (para 141).

[137] See *Law Debenture Trust Corporation plc v Elektrim Finance BV* [2005] 2 Lloyd's Rep 755.

[138] See O Chukwumerije, 'Judicial Supervision of Commercial Arbitration: the English Arbitration Act of 1996' (1999) 15 *Arb Int* 171.

[139] MJ Mustill and SC Boyd, *Commercial Arbitration* (London, Butterworths, 2nd edn, 1989) 453, n 10.

[140] See, eg, *Demco Investments & Commercial SA v SE Banken Forsakring Holding AB* [2005] 2 Lloyd's Rep 650.

[141] Arbitration Act 1996, s 4(1), sched 1. For consideration of potential problems if either the courts of the seat do not have powers of supervision or such powers may be excluded by agreement of the parties, see AA Asouzu, 'A Threat to Arbitral Integrity' (1995) 12(4) *J Int Arb* 145.

20.4.33 The 1996 Act provides that an award may be challenged on two general bases: lack of jurisdiction and serious irregularity. The current legislation swept away the rather complex (and potentially confusing) legislation and case law relating to misconduct. Section 67(1) provides that a party to arbitral proceedings may apply to the court:

(a) challenging any award of the arbitral tribunal as to its substantive jurisdiction; or
(b) for an order declaring an award made by the tribunal on the merits to be of no effect, in whole or in part, because the tribunal did not have substantive jurisdiction.

In cases where an award is challenged on the basis that the tribunal did not have substantive jurisdiction, the court may, depending on the circumstances, confirm the award, vary it or set it aside (either in whole or in part). If an award is set aside, it is a nullity; it is as if the award had never been made. If only part of the award is set aside, only that part is a nullity; the rest remains valid.

20.4.34   Section 68 sets out a mechanism whereby an award may be challenged on the basis of serious irregularity.[142] Serious irregularity is defined by section 68(2) as:

(a) failure by the tribunal to comply with section 33 (general duty of tribunal);[143]
(b) the tribunal exceeding its powers (otherwise than by exceeding its substantive jurisdiction: see section 67);
(c) failure by the tribunal to conduct the proceedings in accordance with the procedure agreed by the parties;
(d) failure by the tribunal to deal with all the issues which were put to it;[144]
(e) any arbitral or other institution or person vested by the parties with powers in relation to the proceedings or the award exceeding its powers;
(f) uncertainty or ambiguity as to the effect of the award;
(g) the award being obtained by fraud or the award or the way in which it was procured being contrary to public policy;[145]
(h) failure to comply with the requirements as to the form of the award; or
(i) any irregularity in the conduct of the proceedings or in the award which is admitted by the tribunal or by any arbitral or other institution or person vested by the parties with powers in relation to the proceedings or the award.

20.4.35 If, in the court's opinion, an irregularity of one of the kinds listed in section 68(2) 'has caused or will cause substantial injustice to the applicant' the court is presented with a number of options (under section 68(3)). The court may remit the award to the tribunal (in whole or in part) for reconsideration or set aside the award (in whole or in part) or declare the award to be of no effect (in whole or in part).[146] Remission, which is a less draconian remedy than setting aside, may be appropriate

---

[142] See *Egmatra AG v Marco Trading Corporation* [1999] 1 Lloyd's Rep 862; *Hussman (Europe) Ltd v Al Ameen Development & Trade Co* [2000] 2 Lloyd's Rep 83; *Lesotho Highlands Development Authority v Impregilo SpA* [2006] 1 AC 221.

[143] See, eg, *Margulead Ltd v Exide Technologies* [2005] 1 Lloyd's Rep 324; *OAO Northern Shipping Co v Remolcadores de Marin SL* [2007] 2 Lloyd's Rep 302.

[144] See, eg, *World Trade Corporation v Czarnikow Sugar Ltd* [2005] 1 Lloyd's Rep 422; *Fidelity Management SA v Myriad International Holdings BV* [2005] 2 Lloyd's Rep 508; *Van der Giessen-de-Nord Shipbuilding Division BV v Imtech Marine & Offshore BV* [2009] 1 Lloyd's Rep 273.

[145] See, eg, *Thyssen Canada Ltd v Mariana Maritime SA* [2005] 1 Lloyd's Rep 640; *R v V* [2009] 1 Lloyd's Rep 97.

[146] See, eg, *F Ltd v M Ltd* [2009] 1 Lloyd's Rep 537.

in a case where the parties have referred a number of issues to the arbitrator, but the award does not determine all of them. If only part of an award is remitted, the arbitrator may reconsider only the part of the award which has been remitted.

20.4.36   The court's power to intervene in cases of lack of jurisdiction or serious irregularity cannot be used as an excuse for backdoor tampering with the merits of an arbitral award; the court will not look sympathetically on an attempt to dress up as an irregularity what is in reality a question of law.[147] The purpose of the power to remit or set aside for lack of jurisdiction or serious irregularity is to guarantee the fundamental integrity of the arbitral process.[148] In the words of the Departmental Advisory Committee:

The test of 'substantial justice' is intended to be applied by way of support for the arbitral process, not by way of interference with that process. Thus, it is only in those cases where it can be said that what has happened is so far removed from what could reasonably have been expected of the arbitral process that we would expect the court to take action.[149]

Accordingly, the power to remit 'cannot be used merely to enable the arbitrator to correct errors of judgment, whether on fact or law, or to have second thoughts, even if they would be better thoughts'.[150] The only way in which errors of law can be corrected is by an appeal under section 69 of the 1996 Act; an error of law involves the erroneous exercise of an available power, but does not involve an excess of power under section 68 of the 1996 Act and, therefore, does not entitle the court to remit or set aside the award for lack of jurisdiction or serious irregularity.[151]

APPEALS ON A POINT OF LAW

20.4.37   Although appeals in arbitration are rare, they are not unknown. Parties may, for example, expressly agree to a two-tier procedure which provides for an appeal on the merits against the decision of the arbitral tribunal. More importantly, some institutional arbitration rules, such as those of the Grain and Feed Trade Association (GAFTA), provide for an internal appeal procedure. However, this form of procedure is not common outside the sphere of commodities arbitration.

20.4.38   Whereas most legal systems provide for judicial review of the arbitral process in order to prevent 'improper conduct, breaches of the principle of natural justice, or decisions which clearly transcend any standard of objective reasonableness',[152] English law is unusual in also providing a mechanism for the parties to appeal from the decision of the arbitrator to the court on a point of law. The justification of the approach adopted by English law is the principle of legality; if awards were not subject to the supervision of the court on points of law 'the result might be that in time codes of law would come to be administered in various trades differing substantially from the English mercantile law'.[153]

---

[147]   *Protech Projects Construction (Pty) Ltd v Al-Kharafi & Sons* [2005] 2 Lloyd's Rep 779.
[148]   See, eg, *Bank Mellat v GAA Development and Construction Co* [1988] 2 Lloyd's Rep 44.
[149]   *Report on the Arbitration Bill* (1996) p 58 (para 280).
[150]   Lord Donaldson MR in *King v Thomas McKenna Ltd* [1991] 2 QB 480, 492.
[151]   *Lesotho Highlands Development Authority v Impreglio SpA* [2006] 1 AC 221.
[152]   M Kerr, 'Arbitration and the Courts: The UNCITRAL Model Law' (1985) 34 *ICLQ* 1, 15.
[153]   Atkin LJ in *Czarnikow v Roth, Schmidt & Co* [1922] 2 KB 478, 491.

20.4.39   In the international context it is necessary for the law to strike a balance between control by the courts of the seat of arbitration and the independence of the arbitral process. It can be presumed that parties who choose to refer their disputes to arbitration are aware of the strengths and weaknesses of the process and are prepared to take the risk that the arbitrator will make mistakes of law—just as they take the risk of errors of fact.

20.4.40   Before the entry into force of 1979 Act a party to an arbitration who wished to appeal on a point of law could require the arbitrator to state a case for the opinion of the High Court—so long as the dispute involved a genuine question of law. In the post-war years 'those who wished to delay the evil day when they had to meet their commitments came to realise that the special case procedure could be manipulated to produce very considerable delay'.[154] The existence of an appeal procedure which was open to abuse did little to encourage the international business community to regard England as an appropriate place for international commercial arbitration. Indeed, the very existence of a right of appeal to the court on a point of law—which is not found in continental legal systems—undermines the finality of the arbitrator's decision. The 1979 Act radically altered the position; the old forms of appeal were abolished[155] and a new limited right of appeal was introduced.[156]

20.4.41   Although the law was further amended by the repeal of the 1979 Act and its replacement with section 69 of the 1996 Act, the current provisions are largely based on the earlier legislation and its interpretation by the courts. The operation of section 69 depends on a number of principles. First, there can be no right of appeal if no point of law is involved. Where, for example, the parties adopt an equity clause, according to which the dispute is to be resolved by reference to the principle of fairness, 'the parties are in effect excluding any right to appeal to the court (there being no "point of law" to appeal)'.[157] Similarly, if the dispute is determined by reference to the law of a country other than England, there can be no right of appeal;[158] so far as English law is concerned questions of foreign law are treated as questions of fact, rather than as questions of law.[159] So, permission to appeal against an arbitral award will be refused in a case where the parties' contract is subject to the laws of England 'except to the extent it may conflict with Islamic Shari'a which shall prevail' and the parties' dispute relates exclusively to the reach of Shari'a law;[160] where Swiss law governs the contract out of which the dispute referred to arbitration arises;[161] where the challenge relates to the arbitral tribunal's decision on a point of Greek law;[162] and where Indian law is the law governing the contract, even if the relevant rules of Indian law are the same as English law.[163] Secondly, where a point of law is involved, there is a right to appeal to the court unless that right is excluded

---

[154] J Donaldson, 'Commercial Arbitration—1979 and After' [1983] *CLP* 1, 3.

[155] Arbitration Act 1979, s 1(1).

[156] J Donaldson, 'Commercial Arbitration—1979 and After' [1983] *CLP* 1; EA Marshall, 'The Arbitration Act 1979' [1979] *JBL* 241; DR Thomas, 'An appraisal of the Arbitration Act 1979' [1981] *LMCLQ* 199.

[157] Departmental Advisory Committee, *Report on the Arbitration Bill* (1996) p 49 (para 223).

[158] See the definition of 'question of law' in Arbitration Act 1996, s 82(1).

[159] See ch 16.

[160] *Sanghi Polyesters Ltd (India) v International Investor (KCFC) (Kuwait)* [2000] 1 Lloyd's Rep 480.

[161] *Egmatra AG v Marco Trading Corporation* [1999] 1 Lloyd's Rep 862.

[162] *Athletic Union of Constantinople v National Basketball Association* [2002] 1 Lloyd's Rep 305.

[163] *Reliance Industries Ltd v Enron Oil and Gas India Ltd* [2002] 1 All ER (Comm) 59.

by the parties' agreement. Thirdly, where the right of appeal exists (because it has not been excluded by the parties' agreement) an appeal is normally possible only if the court grants permission and such permission will be given in limited circumstances. It is for this reason that the courts must be careful to ensure that applications which are, in substance, appeals on points of law are not dressed up as challenges under either section 67 (lack of jurisdiction) or section 68 (serious irregularity), for which the permission of the court is not required.[164]

20.4.42 Section 69(1) provides:

Unless otherwise agreed by the parties, a party to arbitral proceedings may (upon notice to the other parties and to the tribunal) appeal to the court on a question of law arising out of an award made in the proceedings.

An appeal under this subsection can be brought only with either the agreement of all the other parties or with the permission of the court.[165] Under the 1979 Act there was a significant body of case law dealing with the question of when the court would grant permission. In *The Nema*[166] and *The Antaios*[167] the House of Lords laid down strict guidelines which had to be satisfied before permission would be granted. On the basis of the House of Lords' interpretation of the 1979 Act there was always a presumption in favour of finality and, where there was nothing to rebut it, an application for permission was unceremoniously refused.[168] Under the 1979 Act cases could be placed on a spectrum ranging from, at one end, a case concerning the construction of a one-off contract in which the arbitrator possibly made an error of law and, at the other, a case concerning the interpretation of a widely used standard-form contract on a point on which there were conflicting judicial decisions. In the first case permission would invariably be refused; in the second, permission would be given almost as a matter of course. Between the two extremes it was often difficult to predict whether, in particular circumstances, permission would be granted.

20.4.43 The 1996 Act attempts to codify the guidelines laid down by the House of Lords in section 69(3), which provides:

Leave to appeal shall be given only if the court is satisfied—

(a) that the determination of the question will substantially affect the rights of one or more of the parties,
(b) that the question is one which the tribunal was asked to determine,
(c) that, on the basis of the findings of fact in the award—
  (i) the decision of the tribunal on the question is obviously wrong, or
  (ii) the question is one of public importance and the decision of the tribunal is at least open to doubt, and
(d) that, despite the agreement of the parties to resolve the matter by arbitration, it is just and proper in all the circumstances for the court to determine the question.

---

[164] See, eg, *The Petro Ranger* [2001] 2 Lloyd's Rep 348, 351; *Lesotho Highlands Development Authority v Impreglio SpA* [2006] 1 AC 221, 233–4 (at [25]).
[165] Arbitration Act 1996, s 69(2).
[166] *Pioneer Shipping Ltd v BTP Tioxide Ltd* [1982] AC 724. C Lewis, 'Leave to appeal under the Arbitration Act 1979' [1982] *LMCLQ* 271.
[167] *Antaios Compania Naviera SA v Salen Rederierna AB* [1985] AC 191. DR Thomas, 'The Antaios: The Nema Guidelines Reconsidered' [1985] *JBL* 200.
[168] Lord Donaldson MR in *Ipswich BC v Fisons Plc* [1990] Ch 709, 724.

Not surprisingly, the case law decided under the 1979 Act[169] continues to be of relevance to cases falling within section 69 of the 1996 Act.[170] Under section 69(7) the court may confirm the award, vary the award, remit the award to the tribunal (in whole or in part) for reconsideration,[171] or set aside the award (in whole or in part).

20.4.44 Section 69(1) of the 1996 Act provides that the right to appeal exists unless excluded by the parties. Under the 1979 Act the effectiveness of an agreement excluding the right to appeal depended on a number of factors: whether the agreement was domestic or not; whether the subject-matter of the dispute fell within the so-called special categories (which comprised insurance, commodities and admiralty matters); and whether the agreement was concluded before or after the commencement of the arbitration. These distinctions have not been adopted by the 1996 Act,[172] which treats all arbitration agreements equally.

20.4.45 The mechanism whereby the parties may exclude the right of appeal is an agreement in writing.[173] In order to exclude the right to appeal there is no requirement that the agreement should adopt any particular form of words. The arbitration rules of the major arbitral institutions are drafted in a way which effects an exclusion of the parties' right of appeal. So, for example, Article 28.6 of the ICC Rules of Arbitration provides:

Every Award shall be binding on the parties. By submitting the dispute to arbitration under these Rules, the parties undertake to carry out any Award without delay and shall be deemed to have waived their right to any form of recourse insofar as such waiver can validly be made.

An agreement to refer disputes to arbitration under the ICC Rules of Arbitration is interpreted as excluding the jurisdiction of the court on points of law.[174] An agreement to refer disputes under the LCIA Arbitration Rules has the same effect.[175] The position as regards an *ad hoc* arbitration conducted under the UNCITRAL Arbitration Rules is less clear. Where parties decide to refer disputes to arbitration in England under the UNCITRAL Arbitration Rules and wish to exclude the right of appeal it is sensible to include a specific provision in the contract. An agreement excluding the right to appeal might be in the following form:

The award of the arbitrators shall be final and binding on the parties and shall not be subject to appeal under section 69 of the Arbitration Act 1996.

---

[169] For an exhaustive analysis of the 1979 Act, see DR Thomas, *The Law and Practice relating to Appeals from Awards: A Thematic Analysis of the Arbitration Act 1979* (London, LLP, 1994).

[170] For the courts' approach to Arbitration Act 1996, s 69(3), see, eg, *CMA CGMSA v Beteiligungs-KG MS 'Northern Pioneer' Schiffahrtsgesellschaft mbH & Co* [2003] 1 WLR 1015; *The Agios Dimitrios* [2005] 1 Lloyd's Rep 23.

[171] See *The Johnny K* [2006] 1 Lloyd's Rep 666.

[172] The decision to abolish the so-called special categories was taken after the Departmental Advisory Committee's consultation exercise in 1993. See 'The "Special Categories" under the English Arbitration Act 1979—Memorandum from the Departmental Advisory Committee' (1993) 9 *Arb Int* 405.

[173] Arbitration Act 1996, s 5.

[174] *Arab African Energy Corporation Ltd v Olieprodukten Nederland BV* [1983] 2 Lloyd's Rep 419; *Marine Contractors Ltd v Shell Petroleum Development Co of Nigeria Ltd* [1984] 2 Lloyd's Rep 77; *Sanghi Polyesters Ltd (India) v International Investor (KCFC) (Kuwait)* [2000] 1 Lloyd's Rep 480; *Sumukan Ltd v Commonwealth Secretariat* [2007] 3 All ER 342.

[175] *Royal & Sun Alliance Insurance plc v BAE Systems (Operations) Ltd* [2008] 1 Lloyd's Rep 712.

Where, according to its proper interpretation, a contract includes a provision excluding the right to appeal on a point of law under section 69, the parties' rights to a fair trial under Article 6 of the European Convention on Human Rights are not infringed.[176]

---

[176] *Sumukan Ltd v Commonwealth Secretariat* [2007] 3 All ER 342.

21

THE AGREEMENT TO ARBITRATE

21.0.1   In relation to the arbitration agreement there are two main questions to be considered. First, which law governs the arbitration agreement (section 21.1)? Secondly, to what extent does an arbitration agreement have an effect on the substantive jurisdiction of the court (section 21.2)? Where, for example, the parties agree to refer disputes to arbitration, what should the court do if one of the parties commences proceedings in England with regard to the merits of the dispute?

21.1 THE LAW GOVERNING THE ARBITRATION AGREEMENT

21.1.1   Under the doctrine of separability the agreement to arbitrate is separate from the contract of which it forms a part.[1] While it is to be expected that the proper law of the arbitration agreement will normally be the same as the law applicable to the contract as a whole, it is possible for the arbitration agreement to be governed by the law of country X, but for the substantive obligations of the parties under the contract to be governed by the law of country Y.[2] Arbitration agreements are excluded from the material scope of the Rome I Regulation[3] and the Arbitration Act 1996 does not address the question of which law governs such agreements. So, the proper law of an arbitration agreement is determined by the common law choice of law rules formulated by the English courts.[4]

21.1.2   If an arbitration agreement expressly includes a choice of law, the agreement is governed by the chosen law.[5] For the purposes of this principle, the chosen law must be the law of a country. Where, for example, contracting parties agree that their substantive dispute is to be decided by reference to a non-national system of law (such as Shari'a law), the arbitration agreement is not governed by the chosen 'law'; in such circumstances the arbitration agreement is governed by the law of the seat of arbitration—that is, the place where the arbitration is, from a legal point of view, centred[6]—on the basis that the law of the seat is the system of law with which the

---

[1] Arbitration Act 1996, s 7.

[2] *James Miller and Partners Ltd v Whitworth Estates (Manchester) Ltd* [1970] AC 583; *Black Clawson International Ltd v Papierwerke Waldhof-Aschaffenburg AG* [1981] 2 Lloyd's Rep 446; *Tamil Nadu Electricity Board v ST-CMS Electric Company Private Ltd* [2008] 1 Lloyd's Rep 93.

[3] Art 1(2)(e).

[4] See DR Thomas, 'Proper law of arbitration agreements' [1984] *LMCLQ* 304; A Arzandeh & J Hill, 'Ascertaining the proper law of an arbitration clause under English law' (2009) 5 *Journal of Private International Law* 425.

[5] *Naviera Amazonica Peruana SA v Compania Internacional de Seguros del Peru* [1988] 1 Lloyd's Rep 116. See also *Tamil Nadu Electricity Board v ST-CMS Electric Company Private Ltd* [2008] 1 Lloyd's Rep 93.

[6] For consideration of the meaning and significance of the 'seat of arbitration', see paras 22.1.4–22.1.9.

arbitration agreement has its most real and substantial connection.[7] In the days before acceptance in English law of the doctrine of separability, it was acknowledged that, if a contract contained an express choice of law clause, the chosen law governed both the underlying contract and the agreement to arbitrate.[8] Even following the adoption of the doctrine of separability in England, there are several cases which support the view that, if the underlying contract contains an express choice of law, the arbitration clause will be governed by the law chosen to govern the underlying contract, since an arbitration clause (as distinct from a submission agreement) is part of the substance of the underlying contract.[9] This approach appears, however, to have been rejected by the Court of Appeal. In *C v D*,[10] a case where the parties agreed to arbitration in London, but chose New York law as the law governing the contract, the Court of Appeal concluded that the agreement to arbitrate was governed by English law, rather than by New York law. According to the analysis of Longmore LJ, in a case where the law chosen to govern the contract is not the law of the seat of arbitration and there is no express choice of the law applicable to the arbitration clause itself, the court's task is to determine whether the law with which the agreement to arbitrate has its closest and most real connection is the law of the underlying contract or the law of the seat of arbitration.[11] This approach leads to the conclusion that, where parties to a contract governed by the law of country X agree that disputes arising under the contract should be referred to arbitration in country Y, the agreement to arbitrate will normally be the law of country Y:

The reason is that an agreement to arbitrate will normally have a closer and more real connection with the place where the parties have chosen to arbitrate than with the place of the law of the underlying contract in cases where the parties have deliberately chosen to arbitrate in one place disputes which have arisen under a contract governed by the law of another place.[12]

21.1.3 If a contract which contains an arbitration clause does not include an express choice of law, the law governing the contract (including the arbitration clause) will normally be implied from the parties' choice of the seat of arbitration.[13] Even if the law governing the contract is not implied from the choice of the seat, the arbitration clause is governed by the law of the seat.[14] In a situation where the parties neither make an express choice of law nor designate the seat of arbitration, the agreement is normally governed by the law which governs the contract as a whole (which is the law

---

[7] See *Musawi v RE International (UK) Ltd* [2008] 1 Lloyd's Rep 326, 338.

[8] See Longmore LJ in *C v D* [2008] 1 Lloyd's Rep 239, 246 (at [23]).

[9] See Potter J in *Sumitomo Heavy Industries Ltd v Oil and Natural Gas Commission* [1994] 1 Lloyd's Rep 45, 57. See also *The Amazonia* [1990] 1 Lloyd's Rep 236; *Sonatrach Petroleum Corp v Ferrell International Ltd* [2002] 1 All ER (Comm) 627; *Peterson Farms Inc v C&M Farming Ltd* [2004] 1 Lloyd's Rep 603.

[10] [2008] 1 Lloyd's 239. See also the judgment of Toulson J in *XL Insurance Ltd v Owens Corning* [2000] 2 Lloyd's Rep 500.

[11] [2008] 1 Lloyd's 239, 246 (at [22]).

[12] Longmore LJ in *C v D* [2008] 1 Lloyd's 239, 247 (at [26]).

[13] *Compagnie Tunisienne de Navigation SA v Compagnie d'Armement Maritime SA* [1971] AC 572; *Egon Oldendorff v Libera Corporation* [1996] 1 Lloyd's Rep 380; *Sonatrach Petroleum Corp v Ferrell International Ltd* [2002] 1 All ER (Comm) 627.

[14] *Hamlyn & Co v Talisker Distillery* [1894] AC 202; *Deutsche Schachtbau- und Tiefbohrgesellschaft mbH v Shell International Petroleum Co Ltd* [1990] 1 AC 295; *XL Insurance Ltd v Owens Corning* [2000] 2 Lloyd's Rep 500.

of the country with which it most closely connected);[15] the law governing the contract as a whole must also govern the arbitration clause if the contract contains an express choice of law, but no designation of the seat.

21.1.4 It seems that, in certain circumstances, the operation of the principles of English private international law may lead to an arbitration agreement being governed by international law, rather than the law of a particular country. In *Republic of Ecuador v Occidental Exploration and Production Co*[16] the Court of Appeal suggested, without deciding the issue one way or the other, that, where an arbitration agreement is closely connected to an international treaty between states, it may make sense for the agreement to arbitrate to be subject to international law. This solution may be appropriate in the context of a case involving a bilateral investment treaty between state X and state Y which, *inter alia*, makes provision for disputes between state X and investors who are nationals or companies of state Y to be referred to arbitration.[17]

21.1.5 The proper law governs the validity and effect of the arbitration agreement,[18] the consequences which flow from its breach and the remedies which are available. The proper law also governs questions relating to the jurisdiction of the arbitrator and the scope of the arbitration agreement.[19] An arbitration agreement must be interpreted according to the canons of construction of its proper law.[20] The proper law determines whether the agreement has been brought to an end whether by repudiation, frustration or voluntary termination.[21] Equally, the proper law covers such questions as whether the agreement is void, voidable or illegal.[22] However, the scope of the arbitrator's jurisdiction may also be limited by the procedural rules governing the arbitration. In *Econet Satellite Services Ltd v Vee Networks Ltd*[23] a dispute arising from a contract governed by English law was referred to arbitration under the UNCITRAL Arbitration Rules. When the defendant sought to raise a set-off under a different contract between the parties the arbitral tribunal ruled that it had no jurisdiction to determine the set-off. This conclusion was based on Article 19(3) of the UNCITRAL Rules, which provides that a defendant 'may make a counter-claim arising out of the same contract or rely on a claim arising out of the same contract for the purpose of a set-off'. The defendant argued that, because the contract (including the arbitration clause) was governed by English law, the arbitral tribunal's jurisdiction extended to a set-off which the defendant was entitled to raise as a matter of English law even though it did not arise out of the same contract. Although Field J recognised that there was a certain tension between Article 19(3) and the English

---

[15] *The Star Texas* [1993] 2 Lloyd's Rep 445.

[16] [2006] 2 WLR 70. R O'Keefe, (2005) 76 *BYIL* 585.

[17] See Mance LJ at [2006] 2 WLR 70, 92–4 (at [33]–[34]). To the extent that the judgment of Hobhouse J in *Dallal v Bank Mellatt* [1986] QB 441 might be read as insisting that the law governing an arbitration agreement must be the law of a municipal legal system, the Court of Appeal did not agree with it.

[18] See, eg, *The Amazonia* [1990] 1 Lloyd's Rep 236.

[19] *Nova (Jersey) Knit Ltd v Kammgarn Spinnerei* [1977] 1 WLR 713; *Grupo Torras SA v Sheikh Fahad Mohammed al Sabah* [1995] 1 Lloyd's Rep 374; *Peterson Farms Inc v C&M Farming Ltd* [2004] 1 Lloyd's Rep 603. See DR Thomas, 'Proper law of arbitration agreements' [1984] *LMCLQ* 304, 309.

[20] *AB Bofors-Uva CAV Ltd v AB Skandia Transport* [1982] 1 Lloyd's Rep 410. See also *Mangistaumunaigaz Oil Production Association v United World Trade Inc* [1995] 1 Lloyd's Rep 617.

[21] *Black-Clawson International Ltd v Papierwerke Waldhof-Aschaffenburg AG* [1981] 2 Lloyd's Rep 446.

[22] *Dalmia Dairy Industries Ltd v National Bank of Pakistan* [1978] 2 Lloyd's Rep 223.

[23] [2006] 2 Lloyd's Rep 423.

choice of law clause, he held that the arbitral tribunal's view as to its jurisdiction was correct: in this type of case; the governing law of the contract cannot prevail over the conflicting procedural rules which regulate the arbitration and have the effect of limiting the matters which the arbitral tribunal is entitled to decide.

21.1.6 Where the existence of the contract containing an arbitration clause or the arbitration agreement itself is contested on the basis of some factor which makes the arbitration agreement void *ab initio*, there is, strictly speaking, no proper law, only a putative proper law—that is, the law which would govern if there were a valid agreement. In these circumstances the putative proper law is determined subjectively, full weight being given to the (disputed) arbitration clause itself.[24] Even if one of the parties denies having agreed to a clause providing for disputes to be referred to arbitration in England, the existence and validity of the arbitration agreement are governed by English law as the putative proper law. While the logic of the analysis adopted by the English courts may be questionable, the principle seems to be firmly established.[25]

21.2 ENFORCEMENT OF THE AGREEMENT TO ARBITRATE

Introduction

21.2.1 If a court accepts jurisdiction over the substance of a dispute which the parties agreed to refer to arbitration, the institution of arbitration is undermined. There can be no objection to the court exercising its jurisdiction if the parties to an arbitration agreement subsequently choose to litigate their dispute. Where one party to an arbitration agreement starts court proceedings the defendant may choose to waive the arbitration clause and to fight the claim on the merits. However, since the undertaking to arbitrate involves both an immediate irrevocable obligation to refer a dispute to arbitration and an obligation to settle the dispute by means of arbitration in preference and prior to any other type of legal proceedings,[26] in cases where court proceedings are commenced in breach of the terms of an arbitration agreement the defendant should be able to rely on the agreement and ask the court to decline jurisdiction. Whereas judges used to view arbitration agreements as tending to oust the jurisdiction of the courts, it is now appreciated that a less interventionist approach is appropriate: 'there is no good reason why the courts should strive to take matters out of the hands of the tribunal into which the parties have by agreement undertaken to place them.'[27]

21.2.2 One of the aims of the New York Convention on the Recognition and Enforcement of Foreign Arbitral Awards was to ensure the respect of arbitration

---

[24] *The Parouth* [1982] 2 Lloyd's Rep 351; *Marc Rich & Co AG v Società Italiana Impianti PA* [1989] 1 Lloyd's Rep 548.

[25] For different approaches to this question, see A Briggs, 'The formation of international contracts' [1990] *LMCLQ* 192; R Plender and M Wilderspin, *The European Contracts Convention* (London, Sweet & Maxwell, 2nd edn, 2001) 70–2; A Chong, 'Choice of Law for Void Contracts and Their Restitutionary Aftermath: The Putative Governing Law of the Contract' in P Giliker (ed), *Re-examining Contract and Unjust Enrichment* (Leiden, Martinus Nijhoff, 2007) 155–70.

[26] H Fox, 'States and the Undertaking to Arbitrate' (1988) 37 *ICLQ* 1.

[27] Saville J in *Hayter v Nelson* [1990] 2 Lloyd's Rep 265, 269.

agreements and to prevent a party who had entered an arbitration agreement from being able to opt for litigation instead. Although the Convention has been implemented in the United Kingdom, it should be noted that there are some differences between the Convention and the implementing legislation. To the extent that the Act and the Convention diverge the provisions of the Act prevail.

21.2.3 Section 9 of the 1996 Act provides:

(1) A party to an arbitration agreement against whom legal proceedings are brought (whether by way of claim or counterclaim) in respect of a matter which under the agreement is to be referred to arbitration may (upon notice to the other parties to the proceedings) apply to the court in which the proceedings have been brought to stay the proceedings so far as they concern that matter.

(2) An application may be made notwithstanding that the matter is to be referred to arbitration only after the exhaustion of other dispute resolution procedures.

(3) An application may not be made by a person before taking the appropriate procedural step (if any) to acknowledge the legal proceedings against him or after he has taken any step in those proceedings to answer the substantive claim.

(4) On an application under this section the court shall grant a stay unless satisfied that the arbitration agreement is null and void, inoperative, or incapable of being performed.

(5) If the court refuses to stay the legal proceedings, any provision that an award is a condition precedent to the bringing of legal proceedings in respect of any matter is of no effect in relation to those proceedings.

The territorial scope of section 9 is clear; it is a provision of universal application. Section 2(2), which follows the position adopted at common law,[28] expressly provides that section 9 applies 'even if the seat of arbitration is outside England and Wales ... or no seat has been designated or determined'. The duty to stay proceedings arises not only regardless of the territorial connections of the parties, but regardless of whether the parties agreed to refer disputes to arbitration in England, Scotland, France or any other place in the world.[29] Attempts to challenge section 9 on the basis that it conflicts with the right to fair trial under Article 6 of the European Convention on Human Rights have not been successful.[30]

Conditions for the Grant of a Stay under Section 9

21.2.4 The court does not have the power to impose arbitration when both parties are content to have the dispute adjudicated by the court. There can be no question of the court staying legal proceedings of its own motion on the basis that the dispute between the parties ought to be referred to arbitration. Furthermore, the only person who may apply for a stay is the person against whom legal proceedings are being brought.[31] In a case involving a claim by X against Y (which falls outside

---

[28] See Staughton LJ in *Channel Tunnel Group Ltd v Balfour Beatty Construction Ltd* [1992] QB 656, 671.

[29] Arbitration Act 1996, s 2(2).

[30] See *Stretford v Football Association Ltd* [2007] 2 Lloyd's Rep 31.

[31] In the paragraphs which follow, the person against whom proceedings are being brought is referred to as the defendant.

the scope of the parties' arbitration agreement) and a counterclaim by Y against X (which falls within the scope of the agreement), it is possible for X to obtain a stay of the counterclaim on the basis that it is a matter which ought to be referred to arbitration. It is irrelevant that X initiated the legal proceedings.[32] Section 9 cannot apply if the parties to the court proceedings are not the parties[33] to the arbitration agreement.[34]

21.2.5 Before a stay can be granted under section 9 a number of conditions must be satisfied: first, there must be an arbitration agreement between the parties; secondly, the arbitration agreement must be within the scope of the legislation; thirdly, there must be a dispute falling within the scope of the arbitration agreement; fourthly, the defendant must apply for a stay at the appropriate time; fifthly, the arbitration agreement must not be null and void, inoperative or incapable of being performed. If these statutory conditions are satisfied, a stay is mandatory, however inconvenient this may be.[35] The court cannot refuse a stay on the basis that the effect of staying the proceedings will be that related proceedings will end up being decided by different tribunals.[36]

An Arbitration Agreement between the Parties

21.2.6 If, in the context of legal proceedings in England, the defendant applies for a stay under section 9 of the 1996 Act, the court will consider the grant of a stay only if there is an arbitration agreement between the parties. If there is an unresolved issue of fact as to whether an arbitration agreement was ever concluded between the parties (for example, where the defendant in English proceedings applies for a stay on the basis of an arbitration agreement and the claimant argues that the alleged arbitration agreement is a forgery) and the issue cannot be resolved by the English court on the written evidence, the threshold requirements of section 9 are not satisfied; in this situation the court does not have jurisdiction under section 9 to grant a stay[37] and the court's choice is between, on the one hand, giving directions for the trial of that issue by the court and, on the other, granting a stay under its inherent jurisdiction so that the issue can be resolved in the arbitration.[38] The court will not

---

[32] *The New Vanguard* [1995] 1 Lloyd's Rep 191.

[33] Or persons claiming through or under a party: Arbitration Act 1996, s 82(2).

[34] *City of London v Sancheti* [2009] 1 Lloyd's Rep 117.

[35] For consideration of some of the technicalities concerning appeals against the decision to grant (or refuse) a stay under s 9, see *Inco Europe Ltd v First Choice Distribution* [2000] 1 WLR 586; *Henry Boot Construction (UK) Ltd v Malmaison Hotel (Manchester) Ltd* [2000] 2 Lloyd's Rep 625. For consideration of the Australian legislation which equates to s 9 of the 1996 Act, see R Garnett, 'The Current Status of International Arbitration Agreements in Australia' (1999) 15 J *Cont Law* 29.

[36] *Wealands v CLC Contractors Ltd* [1999] 2 Lloyd's Rep 739. See also *John Kaldor Fabricmaker Pty Ltd v Mitchell Cotts Freight (Australia) Pty Ltd* (1989) 90 ALR 244 (Commercial Division, New South Wales).

[37] *Albon v Naza Motor Trading Sdn Bhd (No 3)* [2007] 2 All ER 1075. N Pengelley, 'Necessity for the Court to Find that there *is* an Arbitration Agreement Before Determining that it is Null and Void' (2008) 24 *Arb Int* 171.

[38] See Lightman J in *Albon v Naza Motor Trading Sdn Bhd (No 3)* [2007] 2 All ER 1075, 1081 (at [13]).

normally refer the matter to the arbitral tribunal unless it is 'virtually certain'[39] that there is a concluded arbitration agreement between the parties.

21.2.7 What constitutes an arbitration agreement? This question is answered—at least in part—by section 6, which provides:

(1) In this Part an 'arbitration agreement' means an agreement to submit present or future disputes (whether contractual or not).
(2) The reference in an agreement in a written form of arbitration clause or to a document containing an arbitration clause constitutes an arbitration agreement if the reference is such as to make that clause part of the agreement.

Whether an agreement satisfies the definition in subsection (1) is a question of construction. It has been held, for example, that an agreement that one party, but not the other, may insist on arbitration is an arbitration agreement.[40] Conversely, an agreement, governed by the law of Abu Dhabi, which could not compel both parties to enter into arbitration, is not an arbitration agreement for the purposes of section 9.[41] Subsection (2) raises the question of incorporation, though does not seek to provide a definitive answer to it. The paradigm problem concerns whether, in the context of a dispute arising out of a bill of lading, an arbitration clause in the charterparty has been incorporated into the bill of lading.[42] If one party to the bill of lading starts legal proceedings, the other party's entitlement to a stay under section 9 depends on establishing that the arbitration clause has been effectively incorporated. The Departmental Advisory Committee, having noted that there is 'some conflicting authority on the question as to what is required for the effective incorporation of an arbitration clause by reference', expressed the view that it is 'really a matter for the court to decide'.[43] On the one hand, there is a view that, in the absence of special circumstances, the strict approach which emerges from the charterparty/bill of lading cases[44]—that general words of incorporation are not sufficient to effect incorporation of an arbitration clause—should be extended to other situations.[45] On the other hand, there is authority supporting the view that standard terms, including arbitration clauses, can be incorporated by the use of general words; exceptionally and for reasons of commercial certainty, a stricter rule (which requires there to be an express reference to the arbitration clause which is alleged to be incorporated) is applicable in two-contract cases (ie, where one of the parties to the contract which refers to another

---

[39] Waller LJ in *Al-Naimi v Islamic Press Agency Ltd* [2000] 1 Lloyd's Rep 522, 525.
[40] *Pittalis v Sherefettin* [1986] QB 868; *NB Three Shipping Ltd v Harebell Shipping Ltd* [2005] 1 Lloyd's Rep 509. Where, on its proper construction, a dispute-resolution clause allows X to choose between arbitration and litigation, but obliges Y to refer disputes to arbitration, the court will not stay proceedings brought by X against Y: *Law Debenture Trust Corporation plc v Elektrim Finance BV* [2005] 2 Lloyd's Rep 755.
[41] *Abu Dhabi Investment Co v H Clarkson & Co Ltd* [2006] 2 Lloyd's Rep 381.
[42] P Todd, 'Incorporation of Arbitration Clauses into Bills of Lading' [1997] *JBL* 331. For a discussion of divergent international practice, see J Trappe, 'The arbitration clause in a bill of lading' [1999] *LMCLQ* 337. Similar questions arise in disputes arising out of construction contracts: P Sheridan, 'The Consensus Challenged: Incorporation of Arbitration Agreements by Reference into Construction Contracts' [1996] *ADRLJ* 274.
[43] *Report on the Arbitration Bill* (1996) p 16 (para 42).
[44] See, eg, *The Epsilon Rosa* [2003] 2 Lloyd's Rep 509.
[45] *Trygg Hansa Insurance Co Ltd v Equitas Ltd* [1998] 2 Lloyd's Rep 439 (in which the question was whether an arbitration clause in an insurance contract had been incorporated into a reinsurance contract).

contract containing an arbitration clause is not a party to that other contract). In the words of Langley J in *The Athena (No 2)*:

English law accepts incorporation of standard terms by the use of general words and ... particularly so when the terms are readily available and the question arises in the context of established dealers in a well known market. The principle ... does not distinguish between a term in an arbitration clause and one which addresses other issues. In contrast and for the very reason that it concerns other parties a 'stricter rule' is applied in charter party/bills of lading cases. The reason given is that the other party may have no knowledge nor ready means of knowledge of the relevant terms. Further as the authorities illustrate, the terms of an arbitration clause may require adjustment if they are to be made to apply to the parties to a different contract.[46]

21.2.8   Where a litigant is not an original party to the contract which includes an arbitration agreement, a question may arise as to whether that person is bound by the arbitration clause. The legislation provides that a party to an arbitration agreement includes 'any person claiming under or through a party to the agreement'.[47] Accordingly, an assignee is entitled to a stay under section 9 to the same extent as the original contracting party.[48] However, a mere legal or commercial connection between the claimant and another person who is bound by the arbitration agreement (for example, between a parent company and a wholly-owned subsidiary) is not enough.[49]

An Arbitration Agreement within the Scope of Section 9

21.2.9   Section 9 does not apply to all arbitration agreements. To fall within the scope of section 9 two conditions must be satisfied: the subject-matter of the dispute must be arbitrable; and the arbitration agreement must satisfy the formal requirements set out in section 5.

CAPABLE OF SETTLEMENT BY ARBITRATION
21.2.10   Under the 1975 Act it was a condition that the dispute was one which is 'capable of settlement by arbitration'.[50] Although the structure of the 1996 Act is different from the legislation which it replaced, a stay will not be granted unless the dispute is arbitrable. Section 81(1) provides:

Nothing in this Part shall be construed as excluding the operation of any rule of law consistent with the provisions of this Part, in particular, any rule of law as to—

(a) matters which are not capable of settlement by arbitration ...

This section is of limited assistance. What is the position where one of the parties starts proceedings in England in relation to a matter which is not arbitrable under English law but is arbitrable under the law of the seat agreed by the parties? There

---

[46] [2007] 1 Lloyd's Rep 280, 289 at [65]. See also *The Federal Bulker* [1989] 1 Lloyd's Rep 103.
[47] Arbitration Act 1996, s 82(2).
[48] *The League* [1984] 2 Lloyd's Rep 259.
[49] *City of London v Sancheti* [2009] 1 Lloyd's Rep 117, overruling (in part) *Roussel-Uclaf v GD Searle & Co Ltd* [1978] 1 Lloyd's Rep 225.
[50] Arbitration Act 1975, s 7(1).

is nothing in the legislation to indicate the system of law by reference to which the question of arbitrability is to be tested and there is no English authority directly on this point. There are various possibilities: first, the law of the seat of arbitration; secondly, the proper law of the arbitration agreement (as determined by the conflicts rules of the forum); thirdly, the law of the forum in which the litigation has been brought.

21.2.11 There is little agreement among the commentators. One view is that, as a matter of principle, arbitrability should not be decided by the law of the seat and that Article II(1) of the New York Convention, which the 1996 Act seeks to implement in England, expressly provides that the law which governs the arbitration agreement should determine the question of arbitrability.[51] Another view is that, although the proper law of the arbitration agreement determines the validity of an arbitration agreement, questions of arbitrability are fundamentally tied up with the compulsory jurisdiction of the courts (rather than the validity of the arbitration agreement) and should, therefore, be regulated by the *lex fori*.[52] According to this view, the English court is entitled to refuse a stay under section 9 of the 1996 Act if the dispute is not arbitrable under English law, even if, under the law of the seat chosen by the parties or under the law governing the arbitration agreement, there is no such restriction. A third view, which has much to commend it, is that arbitrability under section 9 of the 1996 Act should be referred to the law of the seat of arbitration.[53]

21.2.12 Under English law there are very few restrictions on the types of dispute which are arbitrable.[54] It has been suggested that 'any dispute or claim concerning legal rights which can be the subject of an enforceable award, is capable of being settled by arbitration'.[55] For example, it has been accepted that competition claims under what are now Articles 101 and 102 TFEU are arbitrable.[56] There are, however, certain practical limitations on the matters which can be the subject of a binding award. Arbitrators do not enjoy the coercive powers of the state and have no authority over persons who are not parties to the arbitration agreement. So, for example, an arbitrator may not make an award *in rem* in a shipping dispute nor make an award winding up a company.[57] While intellectual property disputes are generally arbitrable—to the extent that they involve the rights and obligations of the parties *inter se*—it seems that an arbitrator is not entitled to rule on the validity of a registered intellectual property right.[58] Although questions of EU law in general are arbitrable,[59] any matter which

---

[51] B Hanotiau, 'What Law Governs the Issue of Arbitrability?' (1996) 12 *Arb Int* 391, 393–5.

[52] H Arfazadeh, 'Arbitrability under the New York Convention: the *Lex Fori* Revisited' (2001) 17 *Arb Int* 73, 80–3; AJ van den Berg, *The New York Arbitration Convention of 1958* (Deventer, Kluwer, 1981) 152.

[53] See M Danov, 'The law governing arbitrability under the Arbitration Act 1996' [2008] *LMCLQ* 536, 537–41.

[54] For a comparative perspective, see A Kirry, 'Arbitrability: Current Trends in Europe' (1996) 12 *Arb Int* 373.

[55] MJ Mustill and SC Boyd, *Commercial Arbitration* (London, Butterworths, 2nd edn, 1989) 149.

[56] *Et Plus SA v Welter* [2006] 1 Lloyd's Rep 251, 264 (at [51]).

[57] *Exeter City AFC Ltd v Football Conference Ltd* [2004] EWHC 831 (Comm) (s 9 of the 1996 Act does not apply to a petition brought under s 459 of the Companies Act 1985).

[58] P Nützi, 'Intellectual Property Arbitration' [1997] 4 *EIPR* 192.

[59] See, eg, *Bulk Oil (Zug) Ltd v Sun International Ltd* [1984] 1 WLR 147.

would give rise to administrative measures or penalties under EU law is not capable of being resolved by arbitration in England.[60]

FORMAL REQUIREMENTS

21.2.13   An arbitration agreement does not fall within the scope of the provisions of the 1996 Act unless it is 'an agreement in writing'.[61] What constitutes an agreement in writing for the purposes of the 1996 Act is defined by section 5:

(2) There is an agreement in writing—
    (a) if the agreement is made in writing (whether or not it is signed by the parties),
    (b) if the agreement is made by exchange of communications in writing, or
    (c) if the agreement is evidenced in writing.
(3) Where parties agree otherwise than in writing by reference to terms which are in writing, they make an agreement in writing.
(4) An agreement is evidenced in writing if an agreement made otherwise than in writing is recorded by one of the parties, or by a third party, with the authority of the parties to the agreement.
(5) An exchange of written submissions in arbitral or legal proceedings in which the existence of an agreement otherwise than in writing is alleged by one party against another party and not denied by the other party in his response constitutes as between those parties an agreement in writing to the effect alleged.
(6) References in this Part to anything being written or in writing include its being recorded by any means.

It can be seen that section 5 provides a broad definition of 'writing'.[62] In particular, an agreement in writing does not have to be signed by the parties[63] and such an agreement may be entered into by an authorised agent.[64] Furthermore, an oral agreement which refers to written terms is regarded as made in 'writing' for the purposes of the Act. This rule is designed to deal with common situations—such as salvage operations—where parties habitually contract orally by reference to standard terms which include an arbitration clause. It also covers situations where an agreement is concluded by conduct. The Departmental Advisory Committee gives the following example:

[P]arty A may agree to buy from party B a quantity of goods on certain terms and conditions (which include an arbitration clause) which are set out in writing and sent to party B, with a request that he sign and return the order form. If, which is by no means uncommon, party B fails to sign the order form, or send any document in response to the order, but manufactures and delivers the goods in accordance with the contract to party A, who pays for them in

---

[60]   See JH Dalhuisen, 'The Arbitrability of Competition Law' (1995) 11 *Arb Int* 151. See also J Bridgman, 'The Arbitrability of Competition Law Disputes' [2008] *EBLR* 147; D de Groot, 'Arbitration and the Modernisation of EC Competition Law' [2008] *EBLR* 175.
[61]   Arbitration Act 1996, s 5(1).
[62]   See T Landau, 'The Effect of the New English Arbitration Act on Institutional Arbitration' (1996) 13(4) *J Int Arb* 113, 121–3.
[63]   Arbitration Act 1996, s 5(2)(a), confirming the position adopted by the courts under the previous legislation: *The St Raphael* [1985] 1 Lloyd's Rep 403.
[64]   See, eg, *The Altair* [2008] 2 Lloyd's Rep 90, in which it was held that, through the operation of the Salvage Convention 1989 (which has the force of law in England), an arbitration clause in a contract for salvage services concluded by the master of a vessel on behalf of the cargo owners was binding on the cargo owners.

accordance with the contract, this could constitute an agreement *'otherwise than in writing by reference to terms which are in writing ...'*, and could therefore include an effective arbitration agreement.[65]

21.2.14   The broad definition of 'writing' adopted by the 1996 Act confirms the decision of the Court of Appeal in *Zambia Steel and Building Supplies Ltd v James Clark & Eaton Ltd*,[66] a case decided under the 1975 Act, to the effect that the oral acceptance of a written proposal to arbitrate qualified as an agreement in writing within the meaning of the Act.[67] The defendant, an English company, provided the plaintiff, a Zambian company, with a written price quotation for goods 'made on our terms of business'. The defendant's standard terms—which were set out on the back of the price quotation—included an arbitration clause which provided for arbitration in England. The plaintiff ordered goods from the defendant and orally assented to the defendant's terms. When the plaintiff, claiming that the goods were damaged on delivery, started proceedings in England, the defendants sought a stay on the basis of the arbitration clause. O'Conner LJ decided that 'if it is established that a document with an arbitration clause in writing forms part of a contract between the parties, the assent by one party orally to the contract is sufficient'.[68] Ralph Gibson LJ took a similar view:

If the term containing the agreement to submit is incorporated in a document and it is proved that the party is bound by an agreement which includes the terms of that document, then no further proof of the agreement to submit ... is required.[69]

21.2.15   The Act also follows the UNCITRAL Model Law[70] by providing that an exchange of written submissions which refer to an arbitration agreement is an agreement in writing.[71] It should be noted, however, that there is a not insignificant difference between the Model Law and the 1996 Act on this point:

it is not enough [under the 1996 Act] for one party to allege in a written submission that there is an arbitration agreement, in circumstances where the other party does not respond at all. If this were enough, an unfair obligation would be placed on any party ... to take the active step of serving a written submission in order to deny this allegation. Therefore, in order to satisfy [the 1996 Act] there must be a failure to deny an allegation by a party who has submitted a response submission.[72]

21.2.16   Although the 1975 Act followed the wording of the New York Convention by referring to 'an agreement contained in an exchange of letters or telegrams',[73] the courts did not interpret the formal requirements too literally. In *Arab African Energy*

---

[65] *Report on the Arbitration Bill* (1996) p 15 (para 36).
[66] [1986] 2 Lloyd's Rep 225. For conflicting views on this decision, see FA Mann, 'An "Agreement in Writing" to Arbitrate' (1987) 3 *Arb Int* 171; A Samuel, 'The Effect of the Place of Arbitration on the Enforcement of the Agreement to Arbitrate' (1992) 8 *Arb Int* 257.
[67] See also *Abdullah M Fahem & Co v Mareb Yemen Insurance Co* [1997] 2 Lloyd's Rep 738.
[68] [1986] 2 Lloyd's Rep 225, 229.
[69] [1986] 2 Lloyd's Rep 225, 235.
[70] Art 7(2).
[71] Arbitration Act 1996, s 5(2)(a).
[72] Departmental Advisory Committee, *Report on the Arbitration Bill* (1996) p 15 (para 38).
[73] Arbitration Act 1975, s 7(1).

Corporation Ltd v Olieprodukten Nederland BV[74] it was held that an exchange of telexes containing the words 'English law-arbitration, if any, London according ICC Rules' satisfied the formal requirements imposed by the Act. The 1996 Act confirms the liberal approach adopted under the 1975 Act by providing that 'in writing' means 'recorded by any means'.[75] So, an exchange of facsimile or e-mail messages would satisfy section 5 of the 1996 Act. However, since section 5 is, to some extent, based on Article 7(2) of the UNCITRAL Model Law, which refers to 'other means of tele-communication which provide a record of the agreement', the formal requirements of section 5 would not be satisfied in a case where the alleged agreement had been recorded as speech, rather than as text.[76] Finally, it has been held that an arbitration agreement does not cease to be an agreement in writing simply because, in the process of its interpretation by the court, the words of the clause are 'manipulated or adapted'.[77]

21.2.17   In its definition of 'writing' the 1996 Act goes considerably further than the New York Convention (which the 1996 Act implements). Under the Convention the obligation to grant a stay arises in relation to an 'agreement in writing' which, according to the English text of Article II(2), 'shall include an arbitral clause in a contract or an arbitration agreement, signed by the parties or contained in an exchange of letters or telegrams'. There are three types of arbitration agreement which clearly fall within the scope of both the Convention and the 1996 Act: first, an arbitral clause in a contract which is signed by the parties; secondly, a submission agreement which is signed by the parties; thirdly, an arbitration agreement contained in an exchange of letters or telegrams.

21.2.18   Some have doubted whether the English legislation is consistent with the Convention. The purpose of Article II(2) of the Convention was to exclude 'an arbitration agreement which is proposed in writing and accepted orally or tacitly'.[78] Although an agreement in this form may satisfy the 1996 Act, it constitutes neither an agreement contained in a contract signed by the parties nor an exchange of letters or telegrams. It has been argued that Article II(2) is intended as a uniform rule which lays down both a minimum and a maximum requirement. According to this approach, 'a court may not require more, but also may not accept less than is provided by Article II(2) for the form of the arbitration agreement'.[79]

21.2.19   However, the Departmental Advisory Committee considered that the 1996 Act is consonant with Article II(2) of the English text of the Convention:

The non-exhaustive definition in the English text ('shall include') may differ in this respect from the French and Spanish texts, but the English text is equally authentic under Article XVI of the New York Convention itself, and also accords with the Russian authentic text.[80]

---

[74] [1983] 2 Lloyd's Rep 419.
[75] Arbitration Act 1996, s 5(6).
[76] See Departmental Advisory Committee, *Report on the Arbitration Bill* (1996) p 14 (para 33).
[77] Saville LJ in *The Nerano* [1996] 1 Lloyd's Rep 1, 5.
[78] AJ van den Berg, *The New York Arbitration Convention of 1958* (Deventer, Kluwer, 1981) 196. See, however, the flexible interpretation by the courts of some other European countries: V van Houtte, 'Consent to Arbitration through Agreement to Printed Contracts: The Continental Experience' (2000) 16 *Arb Int* 1.
[79] AJ van den Berg, *The New York Arbitration Convention of 1958* (Deventer, Kluwer, 1981) 179.
[80] *Report on the Arbitration Bill* (1996) p 14 (para 34).

In addition, from a policy point of view, the English approach is not hard to defend. It is inherently unfair if a party, having orally accepted a written contract which includes an arbitration clause, can disregard the arbitration clause but rely on the other terms of the contract. Some commentators think that both the Convention and the Model Law 'fail to provide a satisfactory solution to problems that arise in practice'[81] and that the 1996 Act adopts a more realistic solution.[82]

A Dispute within the Scope of the Agreement

21.2.20 For the defendant to be entitled to a stay, the legal proceedings must involve 'a matter which under the agreement is to be referred to arbitration'.[83] Since standard agreements refer disputes and/or differences to arbitration, the defendant is not entitled to a stay unless there is a dispute[84] between the parties which falls within the scope of the arbitration clause. The fact that the defendant does not have a plausible defence to the claim does not mean that there is no dispute—otherwise arbitrators would have jurisdiction to decide cases only where there is a *bona fide* defence.[85] Regardless of whether there is a plausible defence to the claim, there is a dispute between the parties whenever one party puts forward a claim and the other party disputes the claim, rejects it, ignores it or prevaricates.[86] In effect, if one party advances a claim the only circumstance in which there is no dispute between the parties is if the other party admits the claim unreservedly—though even in this situation there is an argument for saying that the claimant would be entitled to an award if the respondent subsequently refused to satisfy the claim.[87] Furthermore, if the parties' agreement provides that, whenever there are sums owing by one party to the other under the contract, there is deemed to be a 'dispute', whether or not the debtor acknowledges that the sums are owing, the court should treat such a deemed dispute as a 'dispute' for the purposes of section 9 of the 1996 Act and, assuming that the other conditions are satisfied, grant a stay.[88]

21.2.21 Although an application for a stay under section 9 will arise in cases where the claimant commences litigation on the substance of the dispute between the parties, similar issues may arise in the context of procedural applications. For example, an application to the court for an extension of time for the commencement of an arbitration under section 12 of the 1996 Act may raise substantive issues which the respondent is not willing to have resolved by the court. In such circumstances, the

---

[81] See, eg, *Smal v Goldroyce* [1994] 2 HKC 526 (High Court, Hong Kong).
[82] N Kaplan, 'Is the Need for Writing as Expressed in the New York Convention and the Model Law Out of Step with Commercial Practice?' (1996) 12 *Arb Int* 27, 29.
[83] Arbitration Act 1996, s 9(1).
[84] For the purposes of the legislation it is provided that 'dispute' includes 'any difference': Arbitration Act 1996, s 82(1).
[85] M Saville, 'An Answer to Some Criticisms of the Arbitration Act 1996' [1997] *ADRLJ* 155, 156.
[86] P Sheridan, 'Stay of Proceedings: the New Law in Construction Matters' [1997] *ADRLJ* 208, 212. See *Wealands v CLC Contractors Ltd* [1999] 2 Lloyd's Rep 739.
[87] See Clarke J in *Halki Shipping Corporation v Sopex Oils Ltd* [1997] 1 WLR 1268, 1277.
[88] This proposition follows logically from the Court of Appeal's analysis in *Glencore Grain Ltd v Agros Trading Ltd* [1999] 2 Lloyd's Rep 410; discussed by A Berg, 'Arbitration: legal set-off and enforcing admitted claims' [2000] *LMCLQ* 153.

right course for the court to take is to stay the proceedings and to allow the arbitral tribunal to determine the substantive issues.[89] Where a claimant brings legal proceedings in relation to a dispute which the parties did not agree to refer to arbitration, and the defendant raises as a cross-claim a matter which does fall within the parties' arbitration clause, the claimant is entitled to a mandatory stay under section 9 in relation to the matter raised in the cross-claim.[90]

21.2.22   In principle, whether the subject-matter of the dispute falls within the scope of the parties' arbitration clause is a question of construction which should be determined by the canons of construction of the proper law of the agreement. In the past there have been cases in which the English courts have held that, according to its proper construction, an arbitration clause does not adequately cover all potential disputes between the parties.[91] In recent years, however, there has been a tendency by the courts to assume that the parties intended to agree to 'one-stop' adjudication for the resolution of their disputes.[92] In *Fiona Trust & Holding Corporation v Privalov*[93] the House of Lords was even more emphatic: 'the construction of an arbitration clause should start from the assumption that the parties, as rational businessmen, are likely to have intended any dispute arising out of the relationship into which they have entered or purported to enter to be decided by the same tribunal. The clause should be construed in accordance with this presumption unless the language makes it clear that certain questions are intended to be excluded from the arbitrator's jurisdiction.'[94] Consequently, a potentially ambiguous arbitration clause will be construed broadly, rather than narrowly[95] and the previous case law in which the courts have attempted to determine the precise meaning of terms such as 'arising out of', 'regarding' or 'concerning' has been swept away.[96]

The Timing of the Application

21.2.23   Where one of the parties commences court proceedings, a defendant who wishes to force the claimant to refer the dispute to arbitration must first take the

---

[89] See *Grimaldi Compagnia di Navegazione SpA v Sekhihyo Lines Ltd* [1999] 1 WLR 708.

[90] *The New Vanguard* [1995] 1 Lloyd's Rep 191. See also *Prekons Insaat Sanayi AS v Rowlands Castle Contracting Group Ltd* [2007] 1 Lloyd's Rep 98.

[91] See, eg, *May & Hassell Ltd v Vsesojuznoje Objedinenije "Exportles"* (1940) 66 Ll L Rep 103; *Fillite (Runcorn) Ltd v Aqua-Lift (a firm)* (1989) 45 BLR 27.

[92] See, eg, *Harbour Assurance Co (UK) Ltd v Kansa General International Insurance Co Ltd* [1993] QB 701; *Capital Trust Investments Ltd v Radio Design TJ AB* [2002] 2 All ER 159; *ET Plus SA v Welter* [2006] 1 Lloyd's Rep 251.

[93] [2007] 4 All ER 951. A Briggs, 'Construction of an Arbitration Agreement: Deconstruction of an Arbitration Agreement' [2008] *LMCLQ* 1; A Briggs, (2007) 78 *BYIL* 588; S Gee, (2008) 24 *Arb Int* 467; A Samuel, (2008) 24 *Arb Int* 489; C Style & M Knowles, (2008) 24 *Arb Int* 499. For discussion of the decision of the Court of Appeal ([2007] 1 All ER (Comm) 891), see A Berg, 'Arbitration under a Contract Alleged Not to Exist' (2007) 123 *LQR* 352; TD Grant, 'International Arbitration and English Courts' (2007) 56 *ICLQ* 871; G McMeel, 'Arbitration Agreements: Construction and Distinctiveness—A New Dawn?' [2007] *LMCLQ* 292; N Pengelley, 'Separability Revisited: Arbitration Clauses and Bribery' (2007) 24(5) *J Int Arb* 445. See also P Shine, 'Establishing Jurisdiction in Commercial Disputes: Arbitral Autonomy and the Principle of Kompetenz-Kompetenz' [2008] *JBL* 202.

[94] Lord Hoffman at [2007] 4 All ER 951, 958 (at [13]).

[95] See, eg, *Emmott v Michael Wilson & Partners Ltd (No 2)* [2009] 1 Lloyd's Rep 233.

[96] See Lord Hoffman at [2007] 4 All ER 951, 958 (at [12]).

appropriate step to acknowledge the legal proceedings. An application for a stay under section 9 cannot be brought before that point. However, if the defendant takes any step in the legal proceedings to answer the substantive claim, he will be treated as having waived the arbitration clause and he will be deprived of the right to a stay.

21.2.24 Section 1 of the 1975 Act provided that an application for a stay had to be made 'before delivering any pleadings or taking any other steps in the proceedings'. In the context of this provision it was held, for example, that a defendant who fails in an application for a declaration that an alleged arbitration agreement does not exist[97] or who negotiates with the claimant an extension of time for service of the defence[98] is not regarded as having taken a step in the proceedings. There is no reason to think that these decisions do not remain relevant in the context of applications under section 9 of the 1996 Act. However, some decisions under the 1975 Act may be of limited significance. Whereas a defendant would lose the right to a stay under the 1975 Act by taking any step in the proceedings, under the 1996 Act a defendant is not deprived of the right unless he takes a step 'to answer the substantive claim'; the fact that the defendant took a step in the proceedings is not conclusive that he took a step to answer the substantive claim. The fundamental question is whether or not the defendant did some act which involves an acceptance of the court's substantive jurisdiction and which is inconsistent with an application for a stay or which demonstrates an election to abandon the right to a stay in favour of allowing the litigation to proceed. For example, a party does not lose the right to a stay under section 9 by applying for summary judgment, if he makes it clear that this application is only advanced in the event of the application for a stay being unsuccessful,[99] or by applying for a default judgment to be set aside unconditionally and for permission to defend, while clearly stating in his written evidence that he intends to seek a stay.[100]

Null and Void, Inoperative or Incapable of being Performed

21.2.25 If the arbitration agreement is 'null and void, inoperative or incapable of being performed' the defendant has no right to a stay.[101] On this point, the 1996 Act follows the precise wording of the Convention.

NULL AND VOID
21.2.26 The words 'null and void' denote an arbitration agreement which is affected by some invalidity. The 1996 Act does not indicate the law by which the validity or invalidity of the clause is to be tested. The various possibilities include the law of the seat, the law of the forum and the (putative) proper law of the arbitration agreement. In principle, whether an arbitration agreement is null and void should be governed by its proper law; if, under the applicable law, there is no binding arbitration agreement between the parties, a stay should not be granted under

---

[97] *Metal Scrap Trade Corporation v Kate Shipping Co Ltd* [1990] 1 WLR 115.
[98] *The Nerano* [1996] 1 Lloyd's Rep 1.
[99] *Capital Trust Investments Ltd v Radio Design TJ AB* [2002] 2 All ER 159.
[100] *Patel v Patel* [2000] QB 551.
[101] Arbitration Act 1996, s 9(4).

section 9.[102] According to this view there is an obvious relationship between the doctrine of separability[103] and the rule that a stay will be refused if the arbitration agreement is null and void.

21.2.27   Where the arbitration agreement is governed by English law a stay will be refused if there was no consensus between the parties either on the arbitration agreement itself or on the main contract of which the arbitration clause forms a part or where the arbitration agreement itself is void. The fact that the contract of which the arbitration clause forms a part is void *ab initio* (whether for illegality or some other reason) is not, however, a basis for refusing a stay, since a suitably drafted arbitration clause is capable of surviving the initial invalidity of the contract.[104] The 1996 Act leans in favour of the grant of a stay. In a case where the validity of an arbitration clause is questioned, the burden is on the party seeking to resist the stay to establish that the clause is null and void.[105] Where a claimant seeks to resist a stay on the basis that the arbitration agreement is null and void, if the court is unable to determine the issue on the basis of the evidence before it, a decision has to be made between ordering a trial of the issue or granting a stay (and leaving the jurisdictional question to be decided, in the first instance, by the arbitrator). If a trial of the issue would extend widely over the substantive dispute between the parties (rather than being confined to a reasonably circumscribed area of investigation) the appropriate tribunal to resolve the jurisdictional issues is more likely to be the arbitral tribunal than the English court; if the English court is unable to resolve to its satisfaction the issues arising under section 9(4), it 'should stand back and allow the arbitrator to proceed to determine his own jurisdiction'[106] (particularly in a case where the arbitration agreement is governed by a foreign law and the seat of arbitration is outside England).

21.2.28   Although, as a general principle, the validity of an arbitration clause is to be determined exclusively by its proper law, the court will not give effect to an arbitration agreement which conflicts with mandatory rules of English law—regardless of the agreement's validity under its proper law. *AB Bofors-Uva CAV Ltd v AB Skandia Transport*[107] concerned an arbitration agreement which was governed by Swedish law and provided for arbitration in Sweden. When the plaintiff started litigation in England the defendant sought to rely on the arbitration clause and applied for a stay. The court refused to grant a stay on the ground that the arbitration clause was invalid. It was held that the clause infringed the Convention on the International Carriage of Goods by Road (CMR Convention)—which is incorporated into English law by the Carriage of Goods by Road Act 1965—because it did not expressly provide that the arbitrators should apply the CMR Convention.

---

[102] *Abu Dhabi Investment Co v H Clarkson & Co Ltd* [2006] 2 Lloyd's Rep 381.
[103] See paras 20.4.3–20.4.4.
[104] *Harbour Assurance Co (UK) Ltd v Kansa General International Insurance Co Ltd* [1993] QB 701.
[105] See Colman J in *A v B* [2007] 1 Lloyd's Rep 237, 261 (at [137]). For the position under the 1975 Act, see *Overseas Union Insurance Ltd v AA Mutual International Insurance Co Ltd* [1988] 2 Lloyd's Rep 63.
[106] Colman J in *A v B* [2007] 1 Lloyd's Rep 237, 261 (at [139]).
[107] [1982] 1 Lloyd's Rep 410. For the very limited application of the Unfair Terms in Consumer Contracts Regs 1999 (SI 1999/2083) in the commercial context, see *Heifer International Inc v Christiansen* [2008] 2 All ER (Comm) 831.

INOPERATIVE OR INCAPABLE OF BEING PERFORMED

21.2.29 In principle, the question whether an arbitration agreement has become inoperative or incapable of being performed should also be governed by the proper law of the arbitration agreement. However, it has been noted that in practice the English court is likely to determine these matters for itself, uninfluenced by foreign law.[108] An arbitration clause will be regarded as inoperative in cases where a valid arbitration agreement is subsequently terminated (for example, by a subsequent agreement by the parties). A stay will also be refused where, on the application of traditional contractual principles, the parties' arbitration clause has been repudiated by one of them and the repudiation has been unequivocally accepted by the other. In *Downing v Al Tameer Establishment*[109] the claimant alleged that the parties had concluded a contract which included an arbitration clause. When a dispute arose, the claimant invited the defendant to agree to the appointment of arbitrators under the arbitration clause, but the defendant responded by denying that any contract was concluded between them. The claimant then started legal proceedings and the defendant applied for a stay under section 9 of the 1996 Act. The Court of Appeal decided that the defendant's denial of the alleged contract containing the arbitration clause was a repudiatory breach which had been unequivocally accepted by the commencement of proceedings by the claimant. Accordingly, a stay under section 9 was refused. It would be wrong, however, to conclude that the commencement of legal proceedings following a repudiatory breach of the arbitration clause will always deprive the defendant of the right to a stay under section 9:

> The question whether or not the issue and service of proceedings is an unequivocal acceptance of the repudiation will depend upon the previous communications of the parties and whether or not, on an objective construction of the state of play when the proceedings are commenced, the fact of the issue and service of the [claim form] amounts to an unequivocal communication to the defendant that his earlier repudiatory conduct has been accepted.[110]

21.2.30 Only rarely will an arbitration clause be regarded as incapable of being performed. Indeed, there appears to be no reported case in which an English court has refused a stay on this basis. It is clear that the financial position of the parties is not a relevant factor in the decision whether a stay should be granted. In *The Rena K*[111] the plaintiff resisted the application for a stay on the basis that if an award was made against him he would not be able to honour it. Brandon J thought that this consideration was wholly irrelevant:

> [T]he words 'incapable of being performed' should be construed as referring only to the question of whether an arbitration agreement is capable of being performed up to the stage when it results in an award; and should not be construed as extending to the question whether, once an award has been made, the party against whom it is made will be capable of satisfying it.[112]

---

[108] L Collins *et al*, *Dicey, Morris and Collins on The Conflict of Laws* (London, Sweet & Maxwell, 14th edn, 2006) para 16–077.
[109] [2002] 2 All ER (Comm) 545.
[110] Potter LJ at [2002] 2 All ER (Comm) 545, 555 (at [35]).
[111] [1979] QB 377.
[112] [1979] QB 377, 393.

The refusal of a stay is not justified by the fact that the claimant in the litigation is unable to afford the deposit for the costs of arbitration.[113] Furthermore, the fact that if a stay is granted the claim will necessarily be dismissed (for example, because the agreed time limits have not been complied with) does not render the arbitration agreement incapable of being performed.[114]

21.2.31   Nevertheless, an arbitration agreement is incapable of being performed if the arbitration cannot be set in motion. Accordingly, an application for a stay under section 9 might be refused in a case where the arbitrator refuses to act and the court with jurisdiction over the arbitration is unable to replace him or where the mechanism for constituting the arbitral tribunal breaks down completely and the relevant court is unable to rectify the situation (or refuses to do so).

No Other Conditions

21.2.32   The 1975 Act provided that the court's duty to stay the proceedings did not arise if 'there is not in fact any dispute between the parties with regard to the matter agreed to be referred'.[115] This requirement could be exploited, in certain circumstances, by a claimant who wished to avoid the impact of an arbitration agreement. The paradigm case arose where, notwithstanding the fact that parties had agreed to arbitration, the claimant applied for summary judgment under what is now Part 24 of the Civil Procedure Rules.[116] When the defendant relied on the arbitration clause and applied for a stay, the claimant would resist the application on the basis that, as the defendant had no defence to the claim, there was no dispute between the parties within the meaning of section 1 of the 1975 Act. The traditional approach of the courts to this situation was to treat the refusal of a stay and an order for summary judgment as two sides of the same coin. This approach had the result that, if the claimant could satisfy the court that the defendant had no defence, the court would refuse a stay and exercise jurisdiction in relation to a matter which the parties had agreed to refer to arbitration.

21.2.33   There were various arguments against the position under the 1975 Act. First, as the rule under the 1975 Act—that the court would refuse a stay if there was not in fact any dispute between the parties—had no counterpart in the text of the Convention which the 1975 Act purported to implement it was doubtful whether the addition of this further condition to those set out in the Convention was permissible under international law.[117] Secondly, from the point of view of principle, if parties agree to refer a dispute to arbitration it is for the arbitrator, not the court, to decide whether there is a defence to the claim. Thirdly, theoretical problems surrounding the relationship between the court's jurisdiction to give summary judgment and section 1

---

[113] *Paczy v Haendler and Nattermann GmbH* [1981] 1 Lloyd's Rep 302.

[114] *The Merak* [1965] P 223.

[115] This phrase has an interesting history: it was inserted into the Arbitration Clauses (Protocol) Act 1924 by s 8 of the Arbitration (Foreign Awards) Act 1930; when the arbitration legislation was consolidated the phrase appeared in s 4(2) of the Arbitration Act 1950; s 4(2) of the 1950 Act was in turn repealed by the 1975 Act, but the phrase was included in the text of s 1(1) of the 1975 Act.

[116] Formerly RSC Ord 14.

[117] C Reymond, 'The Channel Tunnel Case and the Law of International Arbitration' (1993) 109 *LQR* 337, 340.

of the 1975 Act were exposed in a number of cases, in particular *Hayter v Nelson*.[118] If the court has jurisdiction in a case where the defendant has no defence to the claim (because there is no dispute), it should follow logically that the arbitrator has no jurisdiction in such a case (as, under a standard arbitration clause, the arbitrator's jurisdiction extends only to disputes).

21.2.34 The Departmental Advisory Committee decided that the additional words, which do not appear in the New York Convention, were 'confusing and unnecessary'.[119] Accordingly, section 9 of the 1996 Act does not reproduce the additional words which were contained in section 1 of the 1975 Act. Following the entry into force of the 1996 Act a claimant is unable to circumvent an arbitration agreement by seeking summary judgment. If the claimant applies for summary judgment (on the basis that the defendant has no defence to the claim) and the defendant seeks a stay under section 9, the duty of the court is to grant a stay—assuming that the various conditions of section 9 are satisfied. In *Halki Shipping Corporation v Sopex Oils Ltd*[120] a majority of the Court of Appeal decided that the grant of a stay is mandatory if there is a dispute between the parties and that, for the purposes of section 9, a dispute exists in a case where the claimant advances a claim which the defendant does not admit.[121] Whereas some cases have treated a dispute as a situation where the defendant has not made an unequivocal admission of liability and quantum,[122] others have gone further and held that there is also a dispute between the parties in a case where the defendant admits liability, but refuses to pay.[123]

21.2.35 In cases where there is no plausible defence to the claim, the claimant may consider that proceedings under Part 24 of the Civil Procedure Rules are a more attractive option than arbitration. Since it seems that it often takes longer to resolve a simple dispute by arbitration proceedings than by legal proceedings under Part 24, there is always the danger that, if the matter is referred to arbitration, the respondent will be able to delay the moment of payment.[124] Nevertheless, the parties have to accept that having agreed to arbitration, they must take the rough with the smooth. As Lord Mustill observed:

The parties choose arbitration for better or for worse. They relish the better features, of which there are many. When things take a turn for the worse there are limits beyond which they cannot be allowed, consistently with their arbitration agreement, to run to the courts for help.[125]

21.2.36 Finally, section 9(2) makes it clear that the grant of a stay is not dependent on the parties being in a position to proceed immediately to arbitration. If, for example, the parties have agreed to a two-stage process (such as where in a construction contract the parties agree to refer disputes, first to a panel of experts, and then

---

[118] [1990] 2 Lloyd's Rep 265. See also M Saville, 'The Origin of the New Arbitration Act 1996: Reconciling Speed with Justice in the Decision-Making Process' (1997) 13 *Arb Int* 237, 244.

[119] *Report on the Arbitration Bill* (1996) p 19 (para 15).

[120] [1998] 1 WLR 728. M Whiteley, 'Stays and summary judgment under the Arbitration Act 1996' [1998] *LMCLQ* 164. For a robust criticism of the decision, see IND Wallace, 'Arbitration: Another Nail in the Coffin' [1998] *ICLR* 371.

[121] See Swinton Thomas LJ at [1998] 1 WLR 728, 761.

[122] *Tri-MG Intra Asia Airlines v Norse Air Charter* [2009] 1 Lloyd's Rep 258 (High Court, Singapore).

[123] *Exfin Shipping Ltd v Tolani Shipping Co Ltd* [2006] 2 Lloyd's Rep 388.

[124] See J Rawlings, 'A Mandatory Stay' (1997) 13 *Arb Int* 421.

[125] *SA Coppée Lavalin NV v Ken-Ren Chemicals and Fertilizers Ltd* [1995] 1 AC 38, 65.

to an arbitral tribunal if necessary) the court must grant a stay under the 1996 Act even if, when the litigation is started, the first stage of the agreed dispute-resolution mechanism has yet to be commenced.[126] Section 9(2) was included—probably unnecessarily—to address the concerns expressed by Lord Mustill in *Channel Tunnel Group Ltd v Balfour Beatty Construction Ltd.*[127]

The Effect of a Stay under Section 9

21.2.37   If the conditions for the grant of a stay are satisfied the court has no discretion; a stay must be granted. When a stay is granted under section 9 the court has no general power to impose conditions.[128] However, the grant of a stay does not fetter in any way the power of the court to order protective measures.[129] The court may, for example, grant an injunction (assuming that the court has the necessary jurisdiction) under section 44 of the 1996 Act.[130] Similarly, where the court stays proceedings *in rem* under section 9 the court may, in appropriate circumstances, refuse to order the release of a ship which has been properly arrested, or make release conditional on the provision of equivalent security.[131]

Inherent Jurisdiction

21.2.38   Prior to the entry into force of the 1996 Act, it had been held that even if the conditions for the grant of a stay under the 1975 Act were not satisfied, in exceptional circumstances the court had an inherent power to stay proceedings brought before it in breach of an arbitration agreement (or some other form of dispute-resolution agreement).[132]

21.2.39   The role to be played by this inherent jurisdiction is relatively limited following the entry into force of the 1996 Act. Nevertheless, there are still cases where the court's inherent jurisdiction may be relevant.[133] Although a stay will be granted under section 9 of the 1996 Act if the court is satisfied that there is an arbitration clause and the subject-matter of the proceedings falls within that clause, the court may, under its inherent jurisdiction, grant a stay in cases where it cannot be sure that the conditions for a stay under section 9 are satisfied, but considers that, in terms of case management,

---

[126] For a discussion of problems which can arise in cases where the parties agree to an arbitration clause which requires the parties to attempt to reach an amicable settlement (or pursue some other dispute-resolution process) before referring their dispute to arbitration, see T Varady, 'The Courtesy Trap' (1997) 14(4) *J Int Arb* 5.

[127] [1993] AC 334, 354. For further discussion, see J Hill, 'Some Private International Law Aspects of the Arbitration Act 1996' (1997) 46 *ICLQ* 274, 281–2.

[128] *The Rena K* [1979] QB 377.

[129] *Channel Tunnel Group Ltd v Balfour Beatty Construction Ltd* [1993] AC 334.

[130] See paras 10.3.18–10.3.21 and paras 20.4.19–20.4.20.

[131] Arbitration Act 1996, s 11 (replacing Civil Jurisdiction and Judgments Act 1982, s 26). See para 10.2.4.

[132] *Channel Tunnel Group Ltd v Balfour Beatty Construction Ltd* [1993] AC 334. See also *Roussel-Uclaf v GD Searle & Co Ltd* [1978] 1 Lloyd's Rep 225; *Etri Fans Ltd v NMB (UK) Ltd* [1987] 1 WLR 1110.

[133] See *A v B* [2007] 1 Lloyd's Rep 237.

it makes more sense for the arbitral tribunal to consider the whole matter first.[134] In addition, it is provided that the Act should not be construed as excluding the operation of any rule of law, which is not inconsistent with the Act, in relation to, *inter alia*, 'the effect of an oral arbitration agreement'.[135] Where, for example, the parties conclude an arbitration agreement which does not satisfy the formal requirements of section 5 there would appear to be no obstacle to the court granting a stay of any legal proceedings brought in breach of the terms of the agreement under its inherent jurisdiction. Similarly, the court may in the exercise of its inherent jurisdiction stay proceedings which are brought in breach of an agreement to refer disputes to an alternative dispute-resolution mechanism other than arbitration.[136] The power of the court to stay proceedings under its inherent jurisdiction, which is discretionary rather than mandatory, should be exercised only in an exceptional case.[137]

[134] *Al-Naimi v Islamic Press Agency Ltd* [2000] 1 Lloyd's Rep 522; compare *T & N Ltd v Royal & Sun Alliance plc* [2002] CLC 1342.
[135] Arbitration Act 1996, s 81(1)(b).
[136] See, eg, *Cott UK Ltd v FE Barton Ltd* [1997] 3 All ER 540; *Cable & Wireless plc v IBM United Kingdom Ltd* [2002] 2 All ER (Comm) 1041 (J Lee, [2003] *LMCLQ* 164; K Mackie, 'The Future for ADR Clauses After *Cable & Wireless v IBM*' (2003) 19 *Arb Int* 345).
[137] *Albon v Naza Motor Trading Sdn Bhd (No 3)* [2007] 2 All ER 1075.

22

THE LAW GOVERNING THE CONDUCT OF AN ARBITRATION AND THE SCOPE OF THE COURT'S POWERS

22.1 INTRODUCTION

Preliminary Remarks

22.1.1 Arbitration is a dispute-resolution mechanism which is regulated by rules. Just as the process of litigation is regulated by procedural rules, so there are procedural rules which regulate an arbitration. The rules governing the procedural aspects of an arbitration are often referred to as the curial law.[1] There are two different aspects to consider. One element of the curial law relates to the internal aspect of the procedure.[2] How is the arbitrator to conduct the arbitration? What are the relevant rules of evidence? What are the arbitrator's powers? The second element of the curial law governs the external aspect of the procedure by determining the procedures under which the court exercises powers of supervision and support and the circumstances in which the court is able to intervene:

The law governing the arbitration comprises the rules governing interim measures (eg, court orders for the preservation or storage of goods), the rules empowering the exercise by the court of supportive measures to assist an arbitration which has run into difficulties (eg, filling a vacancy in the composition of the tribunal if there is no other mechanism) and rules providing for the exercise by the court of its supervisory jurisdiction over arbitrations (eg, removing an arbitrator for misconduct).[3]

The 'Delocalisation' Theory

22.1.2 Arbitration depends for its existence on the agreement of the parties; if there is no arbitration agreement there can be no arbitration. In the 20th century much attention was directed by commentators towards establishing the independence of the arbitral process from national courts. By emphasising the principle of party autonomy and the contractual foundation of arbitration, certain commentators suggested that, at least at the international level, arbitration may be liberated from the control

---

[1] See G Petrochilos, *Procedural Law in International Arbitration* (Oxford, OUP, 2004); DR Thomas, 'The curial law of arbitration proceedings' [1984] *LMCLQ* 491.
[2] FA Mann, 'State Contracts and International Arbitration' (1967) 42 *BYIL* 1, 6.
[3] Steyn J in *Paul Smith Ltd v H & S International Holding Inc* [1991] 2 Lloyd's Rep 127, 130.

of municipal law. The theory has been propounded that, in international cases, an arbitration agreement creates an exclusive and self-sufficient legal regime, as a result of which the arbitral process is to be regarded as being detached from the system of municipal law of the country where the arbitration is conducted. As a result of this theory, international arbitration is described as 'delocalised' (or 'denationalised' or 'anational').[4] The theory is largely based on a practical consideration which flows from the fact that the municipal laws of some countries are outmoded and overzealous in their desire to control the arbitral process. If international arbitration can be 'delocalised', it may be possible to escape the peculiarities of the law of the seat of arbitration. There are, of course, strong arguments against the theory of 'delocalisation'. For example, it has been shown that the theory is 'riddled with inconsistencies'.[5] Furthermore, the viability of arbitration as a mechanism for resolving international commercial disputes depends upon confidence that the system operates fairly. This confidence is fostered by the fact that the municipal legal systems which give binding force to arbitration can also be relied upon to guarantee its integrity.[6]

22.1.3 The theory of 'delocalisation' has made little headway in England[7] and it has been doubted 'whether in its purest sense the doctrine ... commands widespread support'.[8] Recognition that the agreement of the parties provides the foundation of the arbitral process cannot hide the fact that a state's jurisdiction over its territory provides a justification for the supervision of the arbitral process and the enforcement of awards by the courts.[9] The traditional view is that—except in truly international cases, where both parties are states or other international persons—all arbitrations are subject to a municipal system of law:

Although, where international aspects of some kind arise, it is not uncommon and, on the whole, harmless to speak, somewhat colloquially, of international arbitration, the phrase is a misnomer. In the legal sense no international commercial arbitration exists. Just as, notwithstanding its notoriously misleading name, every system of private international law is a system of national law, every arbitration is a national arbitration, that is to say, subject to a specific system of national law.[10]

This view was adopted by the English courts, which rejected 'the concept of arbitral procedures floating in the transnational firmament, unconnected with any municipal

---

[4] See J Paulsson, 'Arbitration Unbound: Award Detached from the Law of its Country of Origin' (1981) 30 *ICLQ* 358; WW Park, 'The *Lex Loci Arbitri* and International Commercial Arbitration' (1983) 32 *ICLQ* 21; J Paulsson, 'Delocalisation of International Commercial Arbitration: When and Why it Matters' (1983) 32 *ICLQ* 53; T Rensmann, 'Anational Arbitral Awards' (1998) 15(2) *J Int Arb* 37; P Read, 'Delocalization of International Commercial Arbitration: Its Relevance in the New Millennium' (1999) 10 *Am Rev Int'l Arb* 177.

[5] R Goode, 'The Role of the *Lex Loci Arbitri* in International Commercial Arbitration' (2001) 17 *Arb Int* 19, 28.

[6] WW Park, 'National Law and Commercial Justice: Safeguarding Procedural Integrity in International Arbitration' (1989) 63 *Tulane LR* 647, 658.

[7] See MJ Mustill, 'Transnational Arbitration in English Law' [1984] *CLP* 133.

[8] Lord Mustill in *SA Coppée Lavalin NV v Ken-Ren Chemicals and Fertilizers Ltd* [1995] 1 AC 38, 52.

[9] H Fox, 'States and the Undertaking to Arbitrate' (1988) 37 *ICLQ* 1.

[10] FA Mann, 'Lex Facit Arbitrum' in P Sanders (ed), *International Arbitration: Liber Amicorum for Martin Domke* (The Hague, Martinus Nijhoff, 1967) 159. See also, H Smit, 'A-National Arbitration' (1989) 63 *Tulane LR* 629.

system of law'.[11] The 1996 Act also has the same starting point—for it is premised on the notion that arbitration must rely for its existence in the legal order upon some law which renders the process valid and effective.

The Importance of the Seat of Arbitration

22.1.4 Where an arbitration is conducted in England, which rules apply to the internal and external procedural aspects of the arbitration? It does not follow from the mere fact that an arbitration is being conducted in England that all aspects of the procedure will be governed by English law. Where an arbitration is being conducted abroad, the question arises whether the English court may exercise the powers set out in the 1996 Act. Where, for example, two English companies enter a contract which provides for disputes to be referred to arbitration in Geneva, does it follow from the fact that the parties are amenable to English jurisdiction that the court has the power to set aside any resulting Swiss award under sections 67 and 68 of the 1996 Act?

22.1.5 With regard to the procedural aspects of an arbitration, central to the operation of the 1996 Act is the determination of the 'seat of arbitration'. On procedural matters, primacy is given to the law of the seat. The seat is the place where, from a legal point of view, the arbitration is centred; it is usually 'the place where the arbitration is actually conducted: but this is not necessarily so, particularly if different parts of the proceedings are held in different countries'.[12] It is for the parties to determine the seat of arbitration by their agreement.[13] In principle, whether or not the parties have designated the seat (either expressly or impliedly) is a matter to be determined by reference to the proper law of the arbitration agreement.[14] A well-drafted arbitration clause normally includes an express reference to the intended seat. Where, for example, an arbitration clause refers disputes to arbitration in accordance with the ICC Arbitration Rules and provides that the venue of the arbitration shall be London, the parties make a choice of London as the juridical seat of the arbitration for the purposes of section 3 of the 1996 Act.[15] Alternatively, a clause may give one of the parties a choice as to the seat of arbitration; a clause may provide, for example, that disputes are 'referred to arbitration in Beijing or London at defendant's option'.[16] Although it is easy enough for parties expressly to designate the seat, problems of interpretation may arise if the drafting of the arbitration agreement is not

---

[11] Kerr LJ in *Bank Mellat v Helliniki Techniki SA* [1984] QB 291, 301. See also *Amin Rasheed Shipping Corporation v Kuwait Insurance Co* [1984] AC 50 (FA Mann, 'England Rejects "Delocalised" Contracts and Arbitration' (1984) 33 *ICLQ* 193); *Naviera Amazonica Peruana SA v Compania Internacional de Seguros del Peru* [1988] 1 Lloyd's Rep 116; *Arab National Bank v El-Abdali* [2005] 1 Lloyd's Rep 541.

[12] Departmental Advisory Committee, *Report on the Arbitration Bill* (1996) p 12 (para 26). See, eg, *The Bay Hotel v Cavalier Construction Co Ltd* [2001] UKPC 34 (discussed by K Dharmandara, 'The Unconscious Choice: Reflections on Determining the *Lex Arbitri*' (2002) 19(2) *J Int Arb* 151; P Mitchell, 'Party Autonomy and Implied Choice in International Commercial Arbitration' (2003) 14 *Am Rev Int Arb* 571).

[13] Arbitration Act 1996, s 3(a).

[14] See Potter J in *Sumitomo Heavy Industries Ltd v Oil and Natural Gas Commission* [1994] 1 Lloyd's Rep 45, 58.

[15] See Cooke J in *Shashoua v Sharma* [2009] 2 Lloyd's Rep 376, 380 (at [27]).

[16] *The Star Texas* [1993] 2 Lloyd's Rep 445. PB Carter, (1993) 64 *BYIL* 475; MN Howard, 'Floating choice of law clauses' [1995] *LMCLQ* 1.

as clear as it might be. For example, in *Braes of Doune Wind Farm (Scotland) Ltd v Alfred McAlpine Business Services Ltd*[17] the parties' agreement was, on the face of it, inconsistent. Although clause 20.2(c) stated that 'the seat of the arbitration shall be Glasgow, Scotland', it was also provided that 'the Parties agree that the courts of England and Wales have exclusive jurisdiction to settle any dispute arising out of or in connection with the Contract'. The arbitration clause also expressly referred to English law and the Arbitration Act 1996; there was no mention at all of Scots law. As, from a legal point of view, an arbitration cannot have two seats, the judge had to decide whether the seat was in Scotland or in England. Stressing that section 3 of the Arbitration Act 1996 is focused on the 'juridical seat' of the arbitration, as opposed to its physical location, Akenhead J held that, properly understood, the parties, by agreeing that the English court had supervisory jurisdiction over the arbitration, had agreed that England was the 'juridical seat' of the arbitration for the purposes of section 3, notwithstanding the wording of clause 20.2(c), and that the express reference to Glasgow was simply to indicate that any hearings in the context of the arbitration would take place in Scotland. So, even though hearings would be held in Scotland, Part I of the 1996 Act would govern the arbitration procedure.

22.1.6   In the absence of express designation by the parties, the seat may be implied from the curial law.[18] Where, in the context of an arbitration agreement governed by English law, the parties choose English law as the curial law without expressly designating the seat, it is implied that England is intended to be the seat.[19] Similarly, an arbitration clause which provides that '[d]isputes shall be settled in accordance with Singapore law' is an implied choice of Singapore as the seat of arbitration.[20] Since party autonomy is given free rein in relation to the determination of the seat, the parties are free to change the seat designated by the arbitration agreement after the dispute has arisen.[21]

22.1.7   It is relatively unusual for the parties to fail to designate the seat, whether expressly or impliedly. In such a case the seat may be fixed by the arbitral institution (if the parties have agreed to institutional arbitration) or by the tribunal.[22] Failing any such designation, the seat has to be determined 'having regard to the parties' agreement and all the relevant circumstances'.[23] Once the seat has been determined in this way, it cannot be changed other than by an express choice by the parties or by the arbitral institution (if any) or by the tribunal.[24] In *Dubai Islamic Bank PJSC v Paymentech Merchant Services Inc*[25] the claimant applied for the setting aside of an award made under the VISA International Operating Regulations which include a

---

[17] [2008] 1 Lloyd's Rep 608.

[18] See, eg, *Arab National Bank v El-Abdali* [2005] 1 Lloyd's Rep 541.

[19] *Naviera Amazonica Peruana SA v Compania Internacional de Seguros del Peru* [1988] 1 Lloyd's Rep 116. M Hunter, [1988] *LMCLQ* 23; FA Mann, '*Lex Arbitri* and *Locus Arbitri*' (1988) 104 *LQR* 348; EA Marshall, [1988] *JBL* 405.

[20] *ABB Lummus Global Ltd v Keppel Fels Ltd* [1999] 2 Lloyd's Rep 24.

[21] *ABB Lummus Global Ltd v Keppel Fels Ltd* [1999] 2 Lloyd's Rep 24.

[22] Arbitration Act 1996, s 3(b)(c).

[23] Arbitration Act 1996, s 3.

[24] See Aikens J in *Dubai Islamic Bank PJSC v Paymentech Merchant Services Inc* [2001] 1 Lloyd's Rep 65, 73 (at [48]).

[25] [2001] 1 Lloyd's Rep 65. G Petrochilos, 'On the juridical character of the seat in the Arbitration Act 1996' [2002] *LMCLQ* 66.

mechanism for the resolution of disputes between members of the VISA system. The court's jurisdiction to entertain the claimant's application depended upon England being the seat of arbitration. Aikens J rejected the claimant's argument that because the award in question had been made by the VISA board of directors at an international board meeting in London, the award was made in England.

22.1.8 Central to Aikens J's analysis was the observation that the various powers which a court may exercise in relation to an arbitration within its jurisdiction are relevant at different stages of the process—from the very inception of the arbitration (when the court may be called upon to appoint an arbitrator) to after the award has been made (when, as in *Dubai Islamic Bank PJSC v Paymentech Merchant Services Inc*, one of the parties seeks to have the award set aside). As Aikens J made clear, it goes without saying that, in the standard case, the seat of arbitration will remain constant throughout the duration of the arbitration (even if different elements of the arbitration procedure and proceedings take place in different countries).[26] Accordingly, in cases where the seat has neither been chosen by the parties nor designated by the tribunal or arbitral institution, the court's task under section 3 of the 1996 Act is to determine the seat having regard only to circumstances prior to the commencement of the arbitration, rather than to the whole history of the arbitration leading up to the award.[27] On the facts of the case, there could be little doubt that England was not the seat of arbitration: the parties were based in Dubai and Texas and VISA was based in California; although the VISA Regulations did not contain any choice of law provisions, VISA had its headquarters in California and the regulations seemed to envisage that VISA's Californian offices would provide administrative support for VISA arbitrations; the dispute between the parties arose out of a transaction in Florida; and the fact that the board of directors reached its decision at a board meeting in London was fortuitous, as the board meets periodically in several cities around the world. In these circumstances, Aikens J thought that the seat of arbitration was probably California.

22.1.9 Although the law of the seat is of fundamental importance, it must be remembered that one of the starting points of the 1996 Act is the principle of party autonomy. As a general rule, parties are free to determine how their disputes are to be resolved. Accordingly, in principle, parties to an arbitration agreement may select procedural rules to govern the arbitration which are different from (and may conflict with) the rules which form part of the law of the seat. One of the central issues which the law has to resolve is the extent to which the law of the seat prevails over the parties' agreement and the extent to which the law of the seat yields to the parties' wishes.

22.2 THE SCOPE OF THE STATUTORY PROVISIONS: GENERAL PRINCIPLES

22.2.1 In the field of arbitration there is a tension between the principle of party autonomy (according to which parties are free to determine the procedure whereby their disputes are to be resolved) and the principle of territoriality (according to which

---

[26] *PT Garuda Indonesia v Birgen Air* [2002] 5 LRC 560 (Court of Appeal, Singapore).
[27] Aikens J at [2001] 1 Lloyd's Rep 65, 73 (at [48]).

the state exercises control over disputes resolved within its borders). The starting point for a set of rules for determining the scope of arbitration rules must be either an autonomy criterion (the rules apply because they have been chosen by the parties) or a territorial criterion (the rules apply because the seat of the arbitration is in a particular country). Article 1(2) of the UNCITRAL Model Law uses a 'territorial criterion'[28] and the 1996 Act adopts the same starting point. Section 2(1) provides that the various provisions of Part I 'apply where the seat of the arbitration is in England and Wales'. So, if parties agree to arbitration in England the arbitration is governed by the 1996 Act as regards both the internal and external procedural aspects by virtue of the simple fact that the seat of arbitration is in England.

22.2.2 It should be stressed, however, that the territorial criterion is the starting point, not the whole story. The 1996 Act would be seriously defective if the parties' control over procedural aspects of an arbitration were limited to the choice of the seat of arbitration or if the power of the courts to intervene in an arbitration were limited to cases where the seat of arbitration is England. The principle of party autonomy is given expression by a number of features of the 1996 Act which counter-balance the general principle in section 2(1). Furthermore, the principle of territoriality is subject to exceptions.

22.2.3 As arbitration is a consensual process, the parties should, in general, be able to decide for themselves how their dispute is to be resolved. There is nothing in principle objectionable in allowing the parties to exclude the law of the seat—whether by an *ad hoc* agreement or by the adoption of institutional arbitration rules or by choosing the law of another country. Nevertheless, the principle of party autonomy must be subordinate to the public interest of the country in which the seat of arbitration is located. Since the law of the seat has a legitimate interest in ensuring that the arbitral process meets certain basic standards of justice and fairness, parties to an arbitration cannot be entitled to exclude procedural rules which are mandatory according to the law of the seat. In addition, as the courts of one country may make a positive contribution to proceedings being conducted in other countries, it is legitimate for the court to exercise certain types of power to support foreign arbitral proceedings.

22.2.4 The general principle set out in section 2(1) is modified by a number of other rules. First, subsections (2)–(5) provide that some sections of the 1996 Act apply even if the seat of arbitration is outside England and Wales or if the seat of arbitration has not been determined or designated. Secondly, the sections of Part I of the 1996 Act are divided into two groups: mandatory provisions (which are listed in schedule 1) and non-mandatory provisions. In general, the mandatory provisions are designed 'to support and assist the arbitral process and the stated objective of arbitration';[29] the non-mandatory provisions exist as 'fall-back' rules,[30] which apply if the parties do not provide for the particular matter in question. As regards the mandatory provisions, if the seat of arbitration is in England,

---

[28] See HM Holzmann and JE Neuhaus, *A Guide to the UNCITRAL Model Law of International Commercial Arbitration: Legislative History and Commentary* (Deventer, Kluwer, 1989) 35–6. See also *PT Garuda Indonesia v Birgen Air* [2002] 5 LRC 560 (Court of Appeal, Singapore).

[29] Departmental Advisory Committee, *Report on the Arbitration Bill* (1996) p 13 (para 19).

[30] Departmental Advisory Committee, *Report on the Arbitration Bill* (1996) p 13 (para 28).

they cannot be excluded by the parties' agreement.[31] The non-mandatory provisions, however, may be departed from by the parties. Most of the non-mandatory provisions take one of two forms: either they state that 'the parties are free to agree' a particular issue (and that, failing such agreement, the statutory rules apply) or they provide that a particular rule shall apply 'unless otherwise agreed by the parties'.[32] The non-mandatory provisions can be excluded by the parties' agreement (in writing)[33] either expressly or impliedly (for example, by the adoption of a set of institutional arbitration rules, such as the ICC Rules of Arbitration, or by a choice of the law of another country as the curial law). Whether the terms of the parties' agreement are sufficient to effect such an exclusion is a question of interpretation. In *Re Q's Estate*[34] the arbitration clause provided that any dispute deriving from or in connection with the parties' agreement was to be submitted 'to the exclusive jurisdiction of arbitration in London'. When the claimant applied for a freezing injunction from the English court, the defendant argued that the court's power under section 44(2)(e) of the 1996 Act was excluded by the parties' agreement through the use of the phrase 'exclusive jurisdiction' in the arbitration clause. Rix J rejected this argument and decided that, to exclude the court's power, something more explicit was required:

the word 'exclusive' in the present clause is merely intended to underline the general rule, which is that substantive proceedings must be by way of arbitration, rather than to introduce the exceptional situation where the parties are barred from ancillary proceedings in Court ... It seems to me that if the parties wanted to exclude the right to resort to the Court under s 44 for assistance in ancillary matters, they could have done so by more specific wording.[35]

22.3 THE SCOPE OF THE STATUTORY PROVISIONS: CASES WHERE THE SEAT OF ARBITRATION IS IN ENGLAND

Introduction

22.3.1   In the standard case where the parties agree to arbitration in England and the parties either choose English law as the curial law or make no choice, the position

---

[31] Arbitration Act 1996, s 4(1) and sched 1. The following mandatory provisions are listed in sched 1: ss 9–11 (stay of legal proceedings); s 12 (power of court to extend agreed time limits); s 13 (application of Limitation Acts); s 24 (power of court to remove arbitrator); s 26(1) (effect of death of arbitrator); s 29 (immunity of arbitrator); s 31 (objection to substantive jurisdiction of arbitrators); s 32 (determination of preliminary point of jurisdiction); s 33 (general duty of tribunal); s 37(2) (items to be treated as expenses of arbitrators); s 40 (general duty of parties); s 43 (securing the attendance of witnesses); s 56 (power to withhold award in case of non-payment); s 60 (effectiveness of agreement for payment of costs in any event); s 66 (enforcement of award); ss 67 and 68 (challenging the award: substantive jurisdiction and serious irregularity) and ss 70 and 71 (supplementary provisions; effect of order of court) so far as relating to ss 67 and 68; s 72 (saving for rights of person who takes no part in proceedings); s 73 (loss of right to object); s 74 (immunity of arbitral institutions, &c); s 75 (charge to secure payment of solicitors' costs).

[32] The following provisions either apply 'unless the parties otherwise agree' (or 'unless otherwise agreed by the parties' or 'subject to the right of the parties to agree') or state that 'the parties are free to agree' a particular matter: ss 7–8, 14–18, 20–3, 25, 26(2), 27, 30, 34–6, 37(1), 38–9, 41–2, 44–5, 47–8, 57–8, 61–5, 69, 76–9.

[33] Arbitration Act 1996, s 5.

[34] [1999] 1 Lloyd's Rep 931.

[35] [1999] 1 Lloyd's Rep 931, 938.

under the 1996 Act is straightforward enough; section 2(1) states that the provisions of Part I are applicable. Of course, the provisions of the 1996 Act which are not listed in schedule 1, not being mandatory, can be excluded by the parties. In this type of case whether or not the situation involves a foreign element is, in a formal sense, largely irrelevant in terms of the conduct of the arbitration and the powers of the court.

Internal Aspects of the Procedure

22.3.2   The bulk of the provisions of the 1996 Act which relate to internal aspects of the procedure are not mandatory. Accordingly, the parties are largely free to determine how the arbitration is to be conducted. First, the arbitration agreement, which is the foundation of the arbitrator's authority, may expressly determine many aspects of the arbitral process (such as the procedure to be adopted). Secondly, the parties may expressly incorporate into the arbitration agreement a set of arbitration rules—whether institutional or *ad hoc*—which play a major role in shaping the way in which the arbitration is conducted.[36] Section 4(3) of the 1996 Act provides:

The parties may make such arrangements by agreeing to the application of institutional rules or providing any other means by which a matter may be decided.

22.3.3   For example, Articles 15–30 of the UNCITRAL Arbitration Rules indicate the general shape which the proceedings should take. Article 15(1) provides:

Subject to these Rules, the arbitral tribunal may conduct the arbitration in such manner as it considers appropriate, provided that the parties are treated with equality and that at any stage of the proceedings each party is given full opportunity of presenting his case.

The other relevant rules govern the following matters: Article 16 (place of arbitration); Article 17 (language); Articles 18–20 (statement of claim and statement of defence); Article 21 (pleas as to the jurisdiction of the arbitral tribunal); Article 22 (further written statements); Article 23 (periods of time); Article 24 and 25 (evidence and hearings); Article 26 (interim measures of protection); Article 27 (experts); Article 28 (default); Article 29 (closure of hearings); Article 30 (waiver of rules). These rules tend to be very general. For example, Article 23, which deals with time limits, merely states:

The periods of time fixed by the arbitral tribunal for the communication of written statements (including the statement of claim and statement of defence) should not exceed forty-five days. However, the arbitral tribunal may extend the time-limits if it concludes that an extension is justified.

22.3.4   Arbitration rules such as the ICC Rules of Arbitration are 'designed to cover every aspect of arbitrations conducted under their terms, from the inception of the arbitration to the issue of a final award'.[37] Nevertheless, the details of the procedure (such as the extent to which there is to be disclosure of documents, the relative importance of written submissions and oral hearings) have to be worked out by the

---

[36] See, eg, *Paul Smith Ltd v H & S International Holding Inc* [1991] 2 Lloyd's Rep 127.
[37] Kerr LJ in *Bank Mellat v Helliniki Techniki SA* [1984] QB 291, 304.

arbitrator in each individual case. Although an arbitral tribunal has considerable discretion in determining the procedure to be employed, it must normally respect the express wishes of the parties.

22.3.5 Instead of adopting institutional rules, the parties may choose the law of a foreign country. English law gives the contracting parties freedom to determine the rules governing the internal conduct of an arbitration; whether that procedure is provided by an *ad hoc* arbitration clause, by a set of rules (such as the UNCITRAL Arbitration Rules) or by the procedural law of a sovereign state, makes no difference in principle. Section 4(5) of the 1996 Act provides:

The choice of a law other than the law of England and Wales ... as the applicable law in respect of a matter provided for by a non-mandatory provision of this Part is equivalent to an agreement making provision about that matter.

For this purpose an applicable law determined in accordance with the parties' agreement, or which is objectively determined in the absence of any express or implied choice, shall be treated as chosen by the parties.

So, in relation to an English arbitration, the choice of a foreign curial law operates as a contractual incorporation in the same manner as the adoption of the rules of an arbitral institution.[38] Where, for example, parties agree to arbitration in England in accordance with German procedural law, all the non-mandatory provisions of the 1996 Act are displaced by the relevant provisions of German law.

22.3.6 To the extent that the rules governing the internal conduct of the arbitration are not agreed by the parties, the law of the seat applies. For example, if the seat of arbitration is England, a party to arbitral proceedings may be represented in the proceedings by a lawyer or other person chosen by him (unless the parties have agreed to the contrary).[39] Furthermore, as regards English arbitrations, if there is a conflict between the procedural rules chosen by the parties and a mandatory provision of the 1996 Act, the statutory rule must prevail. The parties' freedom to determine the arbitral procedure 'exists only if and to such extent as it is granted by the law of the arbitration tribunal's seat'.[40] For example, the parties to an English arbitration cannot by agreement exclude their joint and several liability to pay the arbitrators for their reasonable fees and expenses.[41]

External Aspects of the Procedure

22.3.7 With regard to the external aspects of the procedure of an English arbitration, the provisions of the 1996 Act are likely to play the predominant role for three reasons. First, the parties' agreement will often not seek to regulate external aspects of the procedure. In the absence of express agreement by the parties, the provisions of the 1996 Act apply in full. Secondly, although '[t]here is ... no reason in theory

---

[38] For the position at common law, see *Union of India v McDonnell Douglas Inc* [1993] 2 Lloyd's Rep 48; DR Thomas, 'The curial law of arbitration proceedings' [1984] *LMCLQ* 491, 497–8.
[39] Arbitration Act 1996, s 36.
[40] FA Mann, 'English Procedural Law and Foreign Arbitrations' (1970) 19 *ICLQ* 693, 695.
[41] Arbitration Act 1996, s 28(1).

which precludes parties to agree that an arbitration shall be held at a place or in a country X but subject to the procedural laws of Y',[42] such agreements are rare. From a practical point of view 'there is no useful reason to agree to arbitrate in one country under the arbitration law of another country'.[43] The potential problems of an arbitration in country X being subject to the curial law of country Y can easily be avoided, since there is no requirement that hearings should be conducted at the legal seat of arbitration.[44] This is spelt out in many institutional rules; Article 16(2) of the LCIA Rules, for example, provides that '[t]he Arbitral Tribunal may hold hearings, meetings and deliberations at any convenient geographical place in its discretion'. If the most convenient geographical location for the hearings is country X, but the parties want the arbitration to be governed by the law of country Y, instead of fixing the seat in country X and choosing the law of country Y as the curial law, the parties should choose country Y as the seat and conduct the hearings in country X.[45] Thirdly, a number of the provisions of the 1996 Act which confer powers of supervision on the court are mandatory. To the extent that the provisions of the Act are mandatory they prevail over any contrary agreement of the parties. So, for example, the parties cannot exclude the power of the court to set aside an arbitral award on the basis of serious irregularity[46] or the power of the court to remove an arbitrator on various grounds (such as physical or mental incapacity or lack of appropriate qualifications).[47]

22.3.8   Nevertheless, it is relevant to note that many of the powers conferred on the court by the 1996 Act—even those conferred by provisions listed in schedule 1 which cannot be excluded by the parties' agreement—are discretionary. There is no provision in the 1996 Act which specifically seeks to direct how the court's discretion should be exercised. The only guidance given by the 1996 Act is to be found in the general principles set out in section 1, which stipulates in paragraph (b) that the provisions of Part I must be construed in accordance with the principle that 'the parties should be free to agree how their disputes are resolved, subject only to such safeguards as are necessary in the public interest'.

22.3.9   In a case where parties, none of whom is connected with England, choose England as the seat of arbitration, guidance on how the court should exercise its discretion may be found in the observations of Lord Mustill in *SA Coppée Lavalin NV v Ken-Ren Chemicals and Fertilizers Ltd*.[48] This case concerned an application for

---

[42] Kerr LJ in *Naviera Amazonica Peruana SA v Compania Internacional de Seguros del Peru* [1988] 1 Lloyd's Rep 116, 120.

[43] AJ van den Berg, 'Non-Domestic Arbitral Awards under the 1958 New York Convention' (1986) 2 *Arb Int* 191, 201.

[44] Kerr LJ in *Naviera Amazonica Peruana SA v Compania Internacional de Seguros del Peru* [1988] 1 Lloyd's Rep 116, 120–1.

[45] See *PT Garuda Indonesia v Birgen Air* [2002] 5 LRC 560 (Court of Appeal, Singapore) (seat in Indonesia; hearings in Singapore).

[46] Arbitration Act 1996, s 68.

[47] Arbitration Act 1996, s 24.

[48] [1995] 1 AC 38. This case has been extensively discussed: NH Andrews, [1994] *CLJ* 470; J Beechey, 'International Arbitrations and the Award of Security for Costs in England' [1994] *ADRLJ* 242; D Branson, 'The Ken-Ren Case: It is an Ado Where More Aid is Less Help' (1994) 10 *Arb Int* 313; B Davenport, 'The Ken-Ren Case: Much Ado About Nothing Very Much' (1994) 10 *Arb Int* 303; J Hill, 'Security for costs in

an order for security for costs under section 12(6)(a) of the 1950 Act[49] in the context of an ICC arbitration between foreign companies. Lord Mustill placed particular emphasis on two points.[50] First, regard should be paid to the degree of connection that the parties or the arbitration have with England and its legal system. The court should generally be less willing to intervene in cases where the parties have little connection with England than in cases where both parties have strong connections with England. Secondly, the court should 'recognise and give effect to any agreement between the parties, express or tacit, as to the way in which the arbitration should be conducted'.[51] This second point is an important one. Under the 1996 Act the non-mandatory provisions may be excluded by the parties' agreement. So, for example, the parties, having decided to refer their dispute to arbitration in England, can agree that the court's power to grant interim injunctions (under section 44 of the 1996 Act) should be excluded. For the purposes of the 1996 Act 'agreement' means an agreement in writing (or evidenced in writing) in accordance with the formal requirements laid down in section 5. Therefore, only an express, written agreement can *exclude* the powers conferred by the 1996 Act. However, the implication of Lord Mustill's speech in the *Coppée Lavalin* case is that, even where the parties have not excluded the court's powers by written agreement, the court should, as a matter of discretion, only exercise its powers if to do so would not be inconsistent with the type of dispute-resolution process to which the parties impliedly committed themselves. In a case where the parties have chosen a foreign curial law, although that choice cannot exclude the court's supervisory powers, to the extent that the court's powers of supervision are discretionary the parties' choice is a factor which should be considered; the court may decide not to exercise its powers, notwithstanding the fact that the seat of arbitration is in England.[52]

22.4 SCOPE OF THE STATUTORY PROVISIONS: CASES WHERE THE SEAT IS ABROAD OR NO SEAT HAS BEEN DESIGNATED OR DETERMINED

22.4.1 Where the seat of arbitration is in another country and the parties do not choose English law as the curial law, the provisions of the 1996 Act are, in general, irrelevant; section 2(1) states that the provisions of Part I apply if the seat of arbitration is in England. Does this mean that the English court has no role to play in relation to foreign arbitrations? In *Channel Tunnel Group Ltd v Balfour Beatty Construction Ltd*[53] the House of Lords held that the powers conferred by section 12(6) of the 1950 Act were exercisable only in relation to an English arbitration. Lord

---

ICC arbitration' [1995] *LMCLQ* 19; C Reymond, 'Security for Costs in International Arbitration' (1994) 110 *LQR* 501.

[49] Under the 1996 Act the court does not have the power to make orders for security for costs. However, unless the parties agree to the contrary, the tribunal may order a claimant to provide security for the costs of the arbitration: Arbitration Act 1996, s 38(3).

[50] Although Lord Mustill was in the minority in deciding that the court should not make an order for security for costs, there was unanimous support for the approach which was advocated.

[51] Lord Mustill at [1995] 1 AC 38, 51.

[52] Saville J in *Union of India v McDonnell Douglas Inc* [1993] 2 Lloyd's Rep 48, 51.

[53] [1993] AC 334.

Mustill thought that there was 'no reason why Parliament should have had the least concern to regulate the conduct of an arbitration carried on abroad pursuant to a foreign arbitral law'.[54]

22.4.2 The 1996 Act approaches the court's powers to intervene in a foreign arbitration differently. First, section 2(2) provides that certain sections apply even if the seat of arbitration is outside England or no seat has been designated or determined. Under this provision the sections relating to the staying of proceedings are of universal application;[55] the same is true of the provisions relating to a court's power to order the enforcement of an award in the same manner as a judgment.[56]

22.4.3 Secondly, section 2(3) provides that the powers conferred by section 43 (securing the attendance of witnesses) and section 44 (court powers exercisable in support of arbitral proceedings) apply even if the seat of arbitration is outside England or no seat has been designated or determined. The power conferred by section 43 applies where the arbitral proceedings are being conducted in England. The court could, for example, make an order under section 43 in a situation where the parties have chosen France as the seat, but have decided to hold the hearings in England. The power is limited, however, to cases where the witness is in the United Kingdom. Section 44 allows the court to exercise, with regard to an arbitration, various powers which it enjoys in the context of litigation. The matters in relation to which the powers can be exercised include the taking of evidence of witnesses,[57] the preservation of evidence and property, the sale of goods and the granting of interim injunctions or the appointment of a receiver.[58]

22.4.4 The idea which underlies section 2(3) is the distinction between powers of supervision and powers of support. The process of arbitration is subject to certain limitations, in particular the fact that the arbitrator is not invested with many of the coercive powers which are enjoyed by the courts.[59] While it would be wholly inappropriate to confer on the English court the power to supervise a foreign arbitration being conducted in accordance with a foreign law, there is nothing in principle improper about the courts of one country assisting an arbitration being conducted in another jurisdiction. The practical value of assistance rendered by the courts of one country to the resolution of a dispute in another country is well recognised in the context of international litigation[60] and the 1996 Act enables the English court to exercise similar powers in support of foreign arbitral proceedings.

22.4.5 Of course, the possibility that the English court may make procedural orders in relation to a foreign arbitration involves certain risks. There is a danger that the English court and the courts of the country in which the seat is located might come into conflict

---

[54] [1993] AC 334, 359. It was held that, under s 37(1) of the Supreme Court Act 1981, the court could grant the injunction sought by the plaintiffs, but that, in the exercise of its discretion, it should not do so.

[55] Arbitration Act 1996, ss 9–11.

[56] Arbitration Act 1996, s 66. Nothing in s 66 affects the recognition or enforcement of an award under other statutory provisions, in particular under Part III of the Act: s 66(4). See ch 24.

[57] See, eg, *Commerce and Industry Insurance Co of Canada v Certain Underwriters at Lloyd's of London* [2002] 1 WLR 1323 (in which Moore-Bick J exercised his discretion against ordering witnesses to provide evidence for use in a New York arbitration).

[58] Arbitration Act 1996, s 44(2). See para 20.4.19.

[59] See *Pacific Maritime (Asia) Ltd v Holystone Overseas Ltd* [2008] 1 Lloyd's Rep 371.

[60] See paras 10.3.6–10.3.17.

by issuing inconsistent orders in relation to the same matters. It is, therefore, important that the English court should exercise caution when invited to come to the assistance of a foreign arbitration; special circumstances need to be shown to justify the English court's intervention.[61] Indeed, the 1996 Act encourages such caution by providing that the court may refuse to exercise any power if the fact that the seat of arbitration is outside England and Wales makes it inappropriate to exercise that power.[62] The court should also be guided by Lord Mustill's observation in the *Channel Tunnel* case that, where the seat of arbitration is located in a foreign country, the court of that country is 'the natural court for the source of interim relief'.[63] In a case where the arbitration is abroad and the parties have no connections with England, the English court will not normally be an appropriate forum for an application for an injunction in aid of such arbitration.[64] If, in a case involving an arbitration being conducted abroad, an application for interim relief is made in England it is for the claimant to show why the English court, rather than the relevant foreign forum, should grant relief. If, for example, a particular form of relief is not available under the law of the seat, this is a factor which the English court has to weigh in the balance. It does not follow, however, that the absence of a remedy in the foreign forum would, in itself, justify the intervention of the English court. Where the form of relief sought by the claimant under section 44 is a freezing injunction extending to assets of the defendant located outside the jurisdiction, the court will only be prepared to exercise its discretion to support a foreign arbitration if the defendant or the dispute has a sufficiently strong link to England or where there is some other factor of sufficient strength to justify the making of an order in the absence of such a link; the presence of substantial assets in England might in appropriate circumstances demonstrate a relevant link.[65]

22.4.6 Thirdly, section 2(4) states that the court may exercise a power conferred by any provision in Part I not mentioned in subsection (2) or (3) for the purpose of supporting the arbitral process where no seat of arbitration has been designated or determined and the connection with England makes it appropriate to do so.

22.4.7 It should be noted that section 1(c) provides that in matters governed by Part I 'the court should not intervene except as provided by [Part I]'. It follows that the courts should not follow the approach adopted by the House of Lords in the *Channel Tunnel* case—where it was held that, although relief could not be given under the Arbitration Acts, the court did have the power to grant an injunction under the general power conferred by section 37(1) of the Supreme Court Act 1981. It is intended that the 1996 Act should be all-embracing; if the court cannot exercise (or chooses not to exercise) the powers conferred by the 1996 Act that should be the end of the matter.

22.4.8 It is possible that parties to a foreign arbitration might choose English law as the curial law. At common law, the proper approach to this type of case was not free from doubt.[66] Under the 1996 Act the role of the English court in relation to foreign

---

[61] *Weissfisch v Julius* [2006] 1 Lloyd's Rep 716.
[62] Arbitration Act 1996, s 2(3).
[63] [1993] AC 334, 368.
[64] *Econet Wireless Ltd v Vee Networks Ltd (No 2)* [2006] 2 Lloyd's Rep 428.
[65] *Mobil Cerro Negro Ltd v Petroleos de Venezuela SA* [2008] 1 Lloyd's Rep 684.
[66] See *James Miller and Partners Ltd v Whitworth Street Estates (Manchester) Ltd* [1970] AC 583; *Naviera Amazonica Peruana SA v Compania Internacional de Seguros del Peru* [1988] 1 Lloyd's Rep 116; *Channel Tunnel Group Ltd v Balfour Beatty Construction Ltd* [1992] QB 656.

arbitrations is determined by section 2, which does not allow for the application of the provisions of Part I on the basis of an express choice of English law as the curial law. Although subsections (2)–(4) provide that some sections are applicable in cases where the seat is abroad or where the seat has not been designated or determined, according to the general rule in section 2(1), the powers conferred by Part I cannot be exercised unless the seat of arbitration is in England. With regard to a foreign arbitration, there can, for example, be no question of the English court being able to exercise its power to replace an arbitrator (under section 24) or to set aside an award for serious irregularity (under section 68). Even if the parties have expressly chosen English law as the curial law, these are matters which are to be dealt with by the appropriate foreign courts. Where, for example, the parties agree to arbitration in Scotland, the parties may not have recourse to the appeals procedure laid down by the English legislation,[67] even if the law governing the merits of the dispute is English law.

22.4.9 By adopting as its starting point a territorial criterion, rather than an autonomy criterion, the 1996 Act appears to render an express choice of English law as the curial law wholly irrelevant. It should be recalled, however, that the powers which may be exercised under sections 43 and 44 are discretionary and that section 2(3) requires the court to consider the appropriateness or inappropriateness of exercising its powers in cases where England is not the seat of arbitration. One of the factors which the court is entitled to take into account is the express wishes of the parties. It is not unreasonable to suppose that the court may be more willing to exercise the powers conferred by section 44 if the parties have chosen English law as the curial law.

22.4.10 Although the scope of the court's powers under the 1996 Act is determined primarily by the seat of arbitration, section 2(5) provides that section 7 (separability of arbitration agreement) and section 8 (death of a party) apply where English law is the law applicable to the arbitration agreement—regardless of the seat of arbitration. Section 2(5) is the one provision which determines the scope of statutory provisions by reference to the proper law of the arbitration agreement. It should be noted, however, that sections 7 and 8 are not mandatory and may be excluded by the parties' agreement.

22.5 JURISDICTION IN PROCEEDINGS ANCILLARY TO AN ARBITRATION

22.5.1 Once it is established that the court is able to exercise the powers conferred by the 1996 Act, there remains the question of how proceedings under the 1996 Act are to be commenced and how process is to be served on the respondent. For applications under the 1996 Act, the relevant procedural rules are to be found in Part 62 of the Civil Procedure Rules, which replaced RSC Order 73. For the purposes the Civil Procedure Rules an 'arbitration claim' is defined as:

(a) any application to the court under the 1996 Act;
(b) a claim to determine—

---

[67] Arbitration Act 1996, s 69.

(i) whether there is a valid arbitration agreement;
(ii) whether an arbitration tribunal is properly constituted; or
(iii) what matters have been submitted to arbitration in accordance with an arbitration agreement;

(c) a claim to declare that an award made by an arbitral tribunal is not binding on a party; and
(d) any other application affecting—

(i) arbitration proceedings (whether started or not); or
(ii) an arbitration agreement.[68]

Certain types of proceeding are not within this definition of 'arbitration claim', in particular claims to enforce arbitral awards.[69] It should also be noted that where proceedings are commenced abroad in breach of an arbitration clause, the court does not have jurisdiction under Part 62 to grant an anti-suit injunction to restrain the foreign proceedings; an application for an anti-suit injunction is not 'an application under the 1996 Act' within the meaning of the Civil Procedure Rules.[70]

22.5.2 An arbitration claim normally has to be commenced in the High Court[71] and must comply with the requirements laid down by Part 62 of the Civil Procedure Rules. The general rule is that the claim form should be served on the respondent personally within the jurisdiction.[72] If the claim from cannot be served in England (either on the respondent personally or on his agent) the applicant may seek the court's permission to serve the claim form out of the jurisdiction. The Civil Procedure Rules list three types of application which may be served abroad and the conditions which must be satisfied (if any).[73]

22.5.3 First, with regard to an application challenging an arbitral award or appealing to the court on a question of law arising from an award, permission to serve out may be given only if the award was made in England.[74] An award is treated as made in England only if the seat of arbitration was in England.[75] Secondly, if the application is for an order under section 44 of the 1996 Act (for example, an application for interim relief in support of a foreign arbitration), no special requirements have to be satisfied.[76] Thirdly, where the claimant seeks some other remedy or requires a question to be decided by the court affecting an arbitration (whether started or not), an arbitration agreement or an arbitration award, the court may give permission either if the seat of arbitration is (or will be) in England or if the conditions in section 2(4) are

---

[68] CPR 62.2(1).

[69] For procedural aspects of enforcement (other than enforcement by means of a common law action on the award), see CPR 62.17–62.21.

[70] See *Sokana Industries Inc v Freyre Co Inc* [1994] 2 Lloyd's Rep 57. The reasoning of this decision—which is based on the pre-1996 legislation—applies equally to cases falling under the 1996 Act.

[71] See High Court and County Courts (Allocation of Arbitration Proceedings) Order 1996 (SI 1996/3215); High Court and County Courts (Allocation of Arbitration Proceedings) (Amendment) Order 1999 (SI 1999/1010); Civil Procedure (Modification of Enactments) Order 2002 (SI 2002/439).

[72] See section 7.1.

[73] CPR 62.5.

[74] CPR 62.5(1)(a).

[75] Arbitration Act 1996, s 53.

[76] CPR 62.5(1)(b).

satisfied[77]—that is to say, notwithstanding the fact that the seat of arbitration has not been designated or determined, there is a connection with England.

22.5.4   A question arises whether the court may authorise service of an arbitration claim form on a person who is not a party to the arbitration agreement out of which the dispute arises. Where, for example, a dispute between A and B is referred to arbitration in England, the court may, by virtue of section 44(2)(a) of the 1996 Act, make orders relating to 'the taking of the evidence of witnesses'. If one of the witnesses, C, is not present within the jurisdiction, may the court give permission for service out of the jurisdiction of an arbitration claim form? The problem posed by third parties who cannot be served within the jurisdiction was considered by Clarke J in *The Cienvik*[78] in the context of the old Rules of the Supreme Court. The rationale for allowing service of arbitration proceedings abroad is that:

the parties to an arbitration agreement have consented to the determination of their disputes by arbitration in England. It makes sense for the rules to permit service out of the jurisdiction of applications by one party against the other relating to the arbitrations between them. There is, however, no similar rational basis for saying that the English court should have power to allow service out of the jurisdiction of proceedings relating to an arbitration to which the proposed defendant is not a party.[79]

Clarke J concluded that the provision of the Rules of the Supreme Court which enabled the court to give permission for service out of the jurisdiction 'is properly to be regarded as being concerned only with applications by and against parties to an arbitration which relate to the arbitration to which they are parties'.[80] If it were intended that the court should be able to allow service abroad on non-parties out of the jurisdiction, there would be an express provision to that effect.[81] The decision of Clarke J in *The Cienvik*[82] was considered in *Vale do Rio Doce Navegaçao SA v Shanghai Bao Steel Ocean Shipping Co Ltd*.[83] Thomas J followed Clarke J's reasoning and concluded that permission to serve an arbitration claim form out of the jurisdiction can be given only where the application is between the parties to the arbitration agreement (or persons alleged to be parties) or between the parties to an arbitration pursuant to such an agreement.[84]

22.5.5   Although Part 62 does not deal expressly with the issue, whether permission is given must be a matter for the court's discretion, which will normally only be given if the court is satisfied that England is the proper place in which to bring the claim.[85] On the basis of the cases decided under the old Rules of the Supreme Court,[86] it would seem that the relevant criteria for determining whether England is the proper

---

[77]   CPR 62.5(1)(c).
[78]   [1996] 2 Lloyd's Rep 395.
[79]   Clarke J at [1996] 2 Lloyd's Rep 395, 405. See also *Tate & Lyle Industries Ltd v Cia Usina Bulhoes* [1997] 1 Lloyd's Rep 355.
[80]   [1996] 2 Lloyd's Rep 395, 405.
[81]   As under CPR 6.36, PD 6B para 3.1(3) and (4).
[82]   [1996] 2 Lloyd's Rep 395.
[83]   [2000] 2 Lloyd's Rep 1.
[84]   [2000] 2 Lloyd's Rep 1, 8.
[85]   See CPR 6.37(3).
[86]   See *Marc Rich & Co AG v Società Italiana Impianti PA* [1989] 1 Lloyd's Rep 548, 553; *Sokana Industries Inc v Freyre & Co Inc* [1994] 2 Lloyd's Rep 57, 64.

place in which to bring the claim are those laid down in the context of what is now CPR 6.36.[87] There are three limbs to the test: first, there must be a serious issue to be tried; secondly, there must be a good arguable case that the proceedings fall within the rule relied upon; thirdly, England must be the *forum conveniens*.[88] It is reasonable that the first two limbs of the test should be applied in the same way, regardless of whether the application for permission to serve out is brought under CPR 6.36 or under Part 62. So, if the applicant seeks permission to serve out of the jurisdiction in a case where the respondent disputes that the seat is or will be in England, the applicant must satisfy the court—under the second limb of the test—that there is a good arguable case that England is (or will be) the seat of arbitration.[89]

22.5.6 However, as regards the third limb of the test, the decision of the Court of Appeal in *The John C Helmsing*[90]—a case concerning an application for the appointment of an arbitrator by the court—indicates that special considerations must be taken into account when the applicant seeks permission under Part 62. It would not be appropriate for the court simply to apply the *forum conveniens* test as laid down in *Spiliada Maritime Corporation v Cansulex Ltd*.[91] Because cases come within the scope of Part 62 only if the parties agreed to refer their dispute to arbitration such cases are more akin to cases involving jurisdiction clauses—in which the court's inclination is to hold the parties to their agreement[92]—than standard CPR 6.36 cases. In cases falling within Part 62:

the [claimant] has ex hypothesi bound himself to refer differences to arbitration and cannot therefore pursue his substantive claim against the defendant in legal proceedings abroad. He may also be bound to pursue the arbitration reference here ... If, therefore, the court exercises discretion so as to prevent the [claimant] achieving a properly constituted arbitration tribunal, it may leave him with no means of pursuing his claim anywhere, this being a notable distinction with the position under [CPR 6.36].[93]

22.5.7 Although Part 62 provides specifically for the service of arbitration claim forms out of the jurisdiction in cases where the application cannot be served on the respondent in England, it would seem that certain legal proceedings arising out of an arbitration also fall within the more general rules concerning service out of the jurisdiction contained in CPR 6.36 (as supplemented by CPR PD 6B, para 3.1). Where, for example, a party to an arbitration agreement which was concluded in England seeks a declaration that the agreement has been discharged by consent, the claim falls within CPR PD 6B, para 3.1(6)(a), one of the grounds on which permission to serve out may be granted under CPR 6.36. When a situation appears to fall within the scope of both Part 62 and CPR PD 6B, para 3.1, permission to serve out should be sought under Part 62, which is 'very much more specific and therefore more apt'.[94] Where proceedings which are ancillary to arbitration do not involve an arbitration claim—and therefore

---

[87] See section 7.3.
[88] *Seaconsar Far East Ltd v Bank Markazi Jomhouri Islami Iran* [1994] 1 AC 438.
[89] Potter J in *Sumitomo Heavy Industries Ltd v Oil and Natural Gas Commission* [1994] 1 Lloyd's Rep 45, 55.
[90] [1990] 2 Lloyd's Rep 290.
[91] [1987] AC 460.
[92] See paras 7.3.44–7.3.46 and section 9.3.
[93] Bingham LJ in *The John C Helmsing* [1990] 2 Lloyd's Rep 290, 293.
[94] Bingham LJ in *The John C Helmsing* [1990] 2 Lloyd's Rep 290, 293.

fall outside Part 62—if the defendant cannot be served in England, the claimant may seek to rely on CPR 6.36. Where a claimant wishes to enforce an English arbitration clause by means of an anti-suit injunction restraining the defendant from pursuing litigation abroad the claim falls within the scope of CPR PD 6B, para 3.1(6)(c).[95]

---

[95] *Schiffahrtsgesellschaft Detlev von Appen GmbH v Voest Alpine Intertrading GmbH* [1997] 2 Lloyd's Rep 279.

THE LAW APPLICABLE TO THE MERITS OF A DISPUTE REFERRED TO ARBITRATION

23.1 INTRODUCTION

Types of Choice of Law Clause[1]

23.1.1 In situations where the contracting parties include a choice of law clause in their agreement, but do not agree to arbitration, the clause normally involves the choice of the law of a particular country. The parties may choose the law of a country with which one of the parties has a particular connection or the law of a third country. Clauses in arbitration agreements which seek to determine the body of rules to govern the substantive rights and obligations of the parties may be much more complex. Parties to an arbitration agreement may decide to refer to one or more of the following: (1) the law of a particular country; (2) public international law; (3) the rules of law common to two or more countries[2] or common to the law of a country and public international law; (4) international trade law (also referred to as 'transnational law', 'the international law of contracts' or the *lex mercatoria*); or (5) equity and good conscience (arbitration *ex aequo et bono* or *amiable composition*).

Legal Background

23.1.2 A judge in England is required to apply the law of the forum; this includes not only domestic law, but, where relevant, the rules of English private international law. Where the parties have chosen the applicable law, the court will respect that choice—subject to the possible application of mandatory rules of a law (or laws) not chosen by the parties; where the parties have failed to make a choice, the court will, as a general rule, apply the law of the country with which the contract is most closely connected.[3] Arbitrators are in a position which is analogous to that of a judge, in the sense that they are required to decide the dispute which has been referred to them in a judicial manner. However, their position is different since the immediate source

---

[1] See *Redfern and Hunter on International Commercial Arbitration* (London, Sweet & Maxwell, 5th edn, 2009) 193–229; P Lalive, 'Contracts between a State or a State Agency and a Foreign Company' (1964) 13 *ICLQ* 987, 992; K-H Böckstiegel, 'States in the International Arbitral Process' (1986) 2 *Arb Int* 22, 28–9.

[2] See M Rubino-Sammartano, 'The Channel Tunnel and the *Tronc Commun* Doctrine' (1993) 10(3) *J Int Arb* 59; P Raoul-Duval, 'English and French Law: the Search for Common Principles' (1997) 25 *Int Bus Lawyer* 181.

[3] For a discussion of choice of law in contract, see ch 14.

of their jurisdiction is the agreement of the parties. It does not logically follow from the fact that an arbitrator has a role which is analogous to that of a judge that the arbitrator is bound by the choice of law rules which must be applied by a court in legal proceedings. The basic principle is that the law of the seat's choice of law rules determine the law which the arbitrator must apply.[4] The laws of some continental countries have provided for many years that, in the absence of a choice of law by the parties, an arbitrator is free to apply such choice of law rules (or such substantive rules of law) as he considers appropriate.[5] Furthermore, in many countries, the law expressly provides that the parties may authorise an arbitrator to act *ex aequo et bono* or as *amiable compositeur*.[6]

23.1.3   Traditionally, the position in England was different. Prior to the Arbitration Act 1996 there was no specific legislation dealing with the law to be applied by an arbitrator to the merits of the dispute. At common law, the traditional view was that stated by Scrutton LJ in *Czarnikow v Roth, Schmidt & Co* in the following terms: 'Arbitrators, unless expressly otherwise authorised, have to apply the laws of England.'[7] Accordingly, the traditional view was that where England was the seat of arbitration, an arbitrator should apply English conflicts rules to determine the applicable law:

Just as the judge has to apply the private international law of the forum, so the arbitrator has to apply the private international law of the arbitration tribunal's seat ... Any other solution would involve the conclusion that it is open to the arbitrator to disregard the law.[8]

Although the traditional view was never properly tested in the courts, there were indications in some of the cases that the courts were becoming increasingly prepared to adopt a less strict approach to arbitration agreements which incorporated equity clauses or which authorised the arbitrator to determine the dispute by reference to the *lex mercatoria*.

23.2 THE POSITION UNDER THE 1996 ACT

Section 46 of the 1996 Act

23.2.1   When English law was restated and overhauled by the Arbitration Act 1996, it was decided that the traditional view should be jettisoned and that a more flexible

---

[4] *Norske Atlas Insurance Co Ltd v London General Insurance Co Ltd* (1927) 28 Ll L Rep 104; *Union Nationale des Coopératives Agricoles de Céréales v Robert Catterall & Co Ltd* [1959] 2 QB 44.
[5] See, eg, Art 1496 of the French new code of civil procedure and Art 1054(2) of the Dutch code of civil procedure.
[6] See, eg, Art 1497 of the French new code of civil procedure; Art 1054(3) of the Dutch code of civil procedure; Art 187(2) of the Swiss Private International Law Act.
[7] [1922] 2 KB 478, 488.
[8] FA Mann, 'Lex Facit Arbitrum' in P Sanders (ed), *International Arbitration: Liber Amicorum for Martin Domke* (The Hague, Martinus Nijhoff, 1967) 167. See also DR Thomas, 'Commercial Arbitration—Justice According to Law' (1983) 2 *CJQ* 166; AJE Jaffey, 'Arbitration of Commercial Contracts: the Law to be Applied by the Arbitrators' in DL Perrott and I Pogany (eds), *Current Problems in International Business Law* (Aldershot, Avebury, 1988) 129–51.

approach along the lines of the UNCITRAL Model Law should be adopted. Section 46 of the 1996 Act provides:

(1) The arbitral tribunal shall decide the dispute—

    (a) in accordance with the law chosen by the parties as applicable to the substance of the dispute, or

    (b) if the parties so agree, in accordance with such other considerations as are agreed by them or determined by the tribunal.

(2) For this purpose the choice of the laws of a country shall be understood to refer to the substantive laws of that country and not its conflict of laws rules.

(3) If or to the extent that there is no such choice or agreement, the tribunal shall apply the law determined by the conflict of laws rules which it considers applicable.

The Exclusion of Section 46

23.2.2 Section 46 yields to the contrary intention of the parties; it is a non-mandatory provision which can be excluded by the parties' agreement. Where the parties have agreed to institutional arbitration or to arbitration in accordance with a set of arbitration rules such as the UNCITRAL Arbitration Rules, the arbitration rules are effectively incorporated into the parties' agreement. Accordingly, the applicable choice of law provisions are those set out in the arbitration rules (rather than the provisions of section 46).

23.2.3 In substance, some arbitration rules are similar to section 46 of the 1996 Act. For example, Article 33(1) of the UNCITRAL Arbitration Rules provides that, in the absence of choice by the parties, the tribunal shall 'apply the law determined by the conflict of laws rules which it considers applicable'. In *Deutsche Schachtbau- und Tiefbohrgesellschaft mbH v Shell International Petroleum Co Ltd*,[9] which was concerned with an ICC arbitration conducted in Switzerland, Donaldson MR considered the effect of the relevant choice of law provision of the ICC Rules of Arbitration which, like the UNCITRAL Arbitration Rules, then provided that, in the absence of a choice of the applicable law by the parties, the arbitrator 'shall apply the law designated as the proper law by the rules of conflict which he deems appropriate'.[10]

23.2.4 The arbitrators, in reliance on this provision, took the view that the rights and obligations of the parties were to be governed by 'internationally accepted principles of law governing contractual relations'. In the context of proceedings in England to enforce the award, Donaldson MR said:

By choosing to arbitrate under the rules of the ICC ... the parties have left [the] proper law to be decided by the arbitrators and have not in terms confined the choice to national systems of law. I can see no basis for concluding that the arbitrators' choice of proper law—a common denominator of principles underlying the laws of the various nations governing contractual relations—is outwith the scope of the choice which the parties left to the arbitrators.[11]

---

[9] [1990] 1 AC 295 (CA).

[10] Art 13. The choice of law provision in the current ICC Rules of Arbitration (Art 17) is substantially different from Art 13 of the earlier rules.

[11] [1990] 1 AC 295, 316.

However, the conclusion of Donaldson MR may be questioned. The better view is that, where the relevant choice of law provision requires the arbitral tribunal to apply the law determined by the conflict of laws rules which it considers applicable, the tribunal should follow the traditional conflicts methodology with a view to identifying the law of a particular country as the applicable law.[12]

23.2.5 Some institutional rules adopt a more direct approach to the determination of the applicable law and dispense with the need for choice of law rules. For example, Article 17(3) of the 1998 ICC Rules of Arbitration provides that, in the absence of agreement by the parties, the arbitral tribunal shall 'apply the rules of law which it determines to be appropriate'; similarly, Article 22(3) of the 1998 LCIA Rules states that, if the parties have not made a choice, the arbitral tribunal shall 'apply the law(s) or rules of law which it considers appropriate'. Under these institutional rules, the tribunal may, but is not required to, adopt traditional conflicts methodology. Since the tribunal is entitled to select the applicable rules of law directly, rather than through the application of choice of law rules, the tribunal may conclude that the *lex mercatoria* or some other set of non-national rules furnishes the applicable rules of law.

23.2.6 Most institutional arbitration rules also accept the possibility that, if authorised by the parties to do so, the tribunal may decide the dispute by reference to extra-legal criteria. Article 33(2) of the UNCITRAL Arbitration Rules, for example, provides:

The arbitral tribunal shall decide as *amiable compositeur* or *ex aequo et bono* only if the parties have expressly authorised the arbitral tribunal to do so and if the law applicable to the arbitral procedure permits such arbitration.[13]

The Three Circumstances Envisaged by Section 46

Choice of Law

23.2.7 If the parties have not effectively excluded the operation of section 46—by the adoption of a set of arbitration rules which contains choice of law provisions— the starting point for the choice of law process under section 46(1)(a) is the expressed wishes of the parties. If the parties agree that their rights and obligations are to be governed by the law of country X that choice is effective and should be respected by the arbitrator. Failure by the arbitrators to apply the law chosen by the parties exposes the resulting award to the possibility of challenge by one of the parties.[14] Reported arbitral awards show that arbitrators invariably apply the law selected by the parties.[15] It seems that, while some do so without referring to any choice of law rules, others justify upholding the parties' choice by reference to the choice of law rules of the law of the seat.[16] The fact that the parties have made a

---

[12] Departmental Advisory Committee, *Report on the Arbitration Bill* (1996) p 50 (para 225); compare E Gaillard, 'Transnational Law: A Legal System or a Method of Decision Making?' (2001) 17 *Arb Int* 59, 65–71.

[13] See also, Art 22.4 of the LCIA Rules; Art 17.3 of the ICC Rules of Arbitration.

[14] *Peterson Farms Inc v C&M Farming Ltd* [2004] 1 Lloyd's Rep 603.

[15] JDM Lew, 'Determination of Applicable Substantive Law' (1997) 25 *Int Bus Lawyer* 157, 158.

[16] O Lando, 'The Law Applicable to the Merits of the Dispute' (1986) 2 *Arb Int* 104, 107.

choice of law does not, however, impose an obligation on the arbitral tribunal to take active steps to discover the content of the foreign law. Where England is the seat of arbitration, but the parties have chosen the law of another country to govern the merits of the dispute, section 46(1)(a) does not impose a mandatory requirement on the tribunal to obtain general advice and guidance on the chosen law:

If there is no suggestion by the parties that there is an issue under the applicable system of law which is different from the law of England and Wales, or the tribunal does not itself raise a specific issue, then the tribunal is free to decide the matter on the basis of the presumption that the applicable system of law is the same as the law of England and Wales.[17]

23.2.8   A question arises whether for the purposes of section 46(1)(a) a choice of law has to be express, or whether an implied choice will suffice. At common law, in cases where the parties have failed to make an express choice of law, an arbitration clause is generally regarded as an implied choice of the law of the seat of arbitration. So, if parties agree to arbitration in England, the presumption at common law would generally be that the parties intend the merits of the dispute to be governed by English law.[18] Whether an implied choice suffices for the purposes of section 46(1)(a) is unlikely to be of practical interest. In a case where the parties agree to arbitration in England, it makes no real difference whether the arbitrator concludes that English law is the law applicable to the merits of the dispute by virtue of a choice under section 46(1)(a) or, on the assumption that the parties failed to make a choice, by virtue of the application of the principle *qui indicem forum elegit ius* under section 46(3).

23.2.9   A contract concluded by two states (or other international persons) is normally governed by public international law rather than by the municipal law of any country. Furthermore, a contract between a state and a national corporation may include a clause to the effect that the contract should be governed by public international law. In these situations, the tribunal should respect the parties' choice of public international law as the law applicable to the merits of the dispute. The only question is whether public international law is a 'law' for the purposes of section 46(1)(a) or should be regarded as 'other considerations' within the scope of section 46(1)(b). The better view is that public international law should be regarded as 'law' within section 46(1)(a).[19] In practical terms, however, it makes no difference within which paragraph an express choice of public international law falls.

Choice of Other Considerations

23.2.10   Although English law has traditionally been hostile to arbitration according to extra-legal criteria—as opposed to arbitration according to law—section 46(1)(b) allows the parties to authorise the arbitral tribunal to determine the substance of

---

[17] Thomas J in *Hussman (Europe) Ltd v Al Ameen Development & Trade Co* [2000] 2 Lloyd's Rep 83, 94.

[18] *Hamlyn & Co v Talisker Distillery* [1894] AC 202; *Compagnie Tunisienne de Navigation SA v Compagnie d'Armement Maritime SA* [1971] AC 572; *Egon Oldendorff v Libera Corporation* [1995] 2 Lloyd's Rep 64. See DR Thomas, 'Arbitration agreements as a signpost of the proper law' [1984] *LMCLQ* 141.

[19] F Davidson, 'The New Arbitration Act—A Model Law?' [1997] *JBL* 101, 121.

the dispute by reference to 'such other considerations' as they choose to specify. An arbitration agreement may include an equity clause or may adopt the *lex mercatoria* as the applicable law;[20] by the same token, parties to an arbitration agreement may agree that the merits of the dispute are to be decided by reference to a system of law which is not the law of a country, such as Jewish law[21] or Sharia law.[22] This change of policy is to be welcomed. Parties to a contract are generally free to decide whether to enforce their legal rights. A and B may settle a dispute by agreement and, so long as mandatory rules of law are not infringed, such an agreement is not regarded as posing a threat to the legal order. Arbitration *extra legem* is no more of a threat. Within the limits laid down by mandatory rules and general principles of natural justice, 'nothing of any particular consequence turns on the question whether or not the award is in tune with contemporary commercial law'.[23] From the point of view of the applicable law, an arbitral award is, in terms of policy, more like a settlement in litigation than a judicial determination of the parties' rights. Although, as a general principle, commercial arbitrators should act in accordance with legal principles, it is equally supportable that arbitrators should have the power to decide *extra legem* when that is the express wish of the contracting parties.[24]

EQUITY AND GOOD CONSCIENCE: *AMIABLE COMPOSITION* AND ARBITRATION *EX AEQUO ET BONO*[25]

23.2.11 Although strictly speaking the French and Latin expressions are not really synonyms, the terms *amiable composition* and arbitration *ex aequo et bono* are generally used interchangeably. In each case an arbitrator may, to some extent, dispense with rules of law. An *amiable compositeur* is not, however, a mediator or conciliator; he may not, for example, modify the terms of the contract.[26] The importance of the distinction between arbitrators who decide according to rules of law and those who decide as *amiables compositeurs* can be exaggerated; under both systems arbitrators are bound by relevant mandatory procedural and substantive rules and by public policy. It has been said that 'the difference between the two systems is certainly not as great as many ... are inclined to think'.[27]

---

[20] S 46(1)(b) does not apply to arbitration agreements concluded before 31 January 1997: SI 1996/3146, Arbitration Act 1996 (Commencement No 1) Order 1996, sched 2, para 4. Accordingly, the effect of an equity clause (or a clause expressly adopting the *lex mercatoria*) concluded prior to 31 January 1997 is governed by the old law (with all its uncertainties). See section 17.3 of the first edition of this work.

[21] *Halpern v Halpern (Nos 1 & 2)* [2008] QB 195.

[22] *Musawi v RE International (UK) Ltd* [2008] 1 Lloyd's Rep 326.

[23] DR Thomas, 'Commercial Arbitration—Justice According to Law?' (1983) 2 *CJQ* 166, 181–2.

[24] C Schmitthoff, 'Arbitration: The Supervisory Jurisdiction of the Courts' [1967] *JBL* 318; R Goode, 'The Adaptation of English Law to International Commercial Arbitration' (1992) 8 *Arb Int* 1.

[25] M Rubino-Sammartano, '*Amiable Compositeur* (Joint Mandate to Settle) and *Ex Bono et Aequo* (Discretional Authority to Mitigate Strict Law)' (1992) 9(1) *J Int Arb* 5.

[26] WW Park, 'National Law and Commercial Justice: Safeguarding Procedural Integrity in International Arbitration' (1989) 63 *Tulane LR* 647, 648 n 1.

[27] P Sanders, 'Trends in the Field of International Commercial Arbitration' (1975) 145 *Hag Rec* 205, 238.

LEX MERCATORIA[28]

23.2.12   Although the parties to an international contract may expressly choose the law of a particular country to govern their agreement, there are contexts in which a choice of this type may not seem appropriate. For example, in investment contracts between a state and a foreign corporation, if the contract is governed by the law of the host state, the foreign corporation runs the risk of the host state changing the law in a way which benefits the state and is detrimental to the other contracting party. In this situation, the corporation needs a choice of law clause which avoids the tangles of nationalisation and unilateral action by the host state.[29] The host state is, however, equally unlikely to be willing to submit to the law of a foreign country. Even in a contract between two private persons neither party may wish to submit to the law of the other or to the law of a country with which neither party is closely connected. In these situations the parties may choose to submit to the *lex mercatoria*, the new law merchant, by using one of a number of different formulas—such as general principles of law, principles of law recognised by civilised nations or principles of law applied by international tribunals.[30] While the meaning of such formulas may not always be self-evident, it is clear that by adopting one of them the parties are seeking to avoid the idiosyncrasies of the laws of particular countries.

23.2.13   The *lex mercatoria* is said to be made up of public international law, principles derived from uniform laws, general principles recognised by commercial nations, rules of international organisations, customs and usages, clauses in standard-form contracts and reported awards.[31] The subject of the *lex mercatoria* provokes strong feelings. Some argue that it is the panacea for the problems posed by transnational commercial transactions; others, for whom the *lex mercatoria* is like the emperor's new clothes, regard the whole notion with a high degree of scepticism.

23.2.14   Notwithstanding the claims made by proponents of the theory, it has been suggested that even if the methodological problems surrounding the identification or creation of rules which go to make up the *lex mercatoria* are put to one side, the *lex mercatoria* is far from being a self-sufficient system of rules. One critic of the new law merchant writing in the 1980s, having listed 20 rules and principles which are said to constitute the *lex mercatoria* in its then present form, suggested that '[t]his list, incomplete as it may be, seems a rather modest haul for twenty-five years of international arbitration'.[32] Others go further: 'It is not even possible to supply more than a meagre inventory, loaded with vagueness and charged with logical and analytical legal error.'[33] Similarly, it has been said that

---

[28] For a discussion by one of the leading proponents of the *lex mercatoria* see B Goldman, 'The Applicable Law: General Principles of Law—The *Lex Mercatoria*' in JDM Lew (ed), *Contemporary Problems in International Arbitration* (Dordrecht, Kluwer, 1987) 113 *ff*. See also T Carbonneau (ed), *Lex Mercatoria and Arbitration: A Discussion of the New Law Merchant* (Dobbs Ferry NY, Transnational Juris Publications, 1990).

[29] K Highet, 'The Enigma of the *Lex Mercatoria*' (1989) 63 *Tulane LR* 613, 628.

[30] GR Delaume, 'Comparative Analysis as a Basis of Law in State Contracts: the Myth of the *Lex Mercatoria*' (1989) 63 *Tulane LR* 574, 583. See also the examples given by DW Rivkin, 'Enforceability of Arbitral Awards based on *Lex Mercatoria*' (1993) 9 *Arb Int* 67, 68–72.

[31] O Lando, 'The *Lex Mercatoria* in International Commercial Arbitration' (1985) 34 *ICLQ* 745, 748–51. See also A Goldstajn, 'The New Law Merchant' [1961] *JBL* 12.

[32] MJ Mustill, 'The New *Lex Mercatoria*: The First Twenty-Five Years' (1988) 4 *Arb Int* 86, 114.

[33] K Highet, 'The Enigma of the *Lex Mercatoria*' (1989) 63 *Tulane LR* 613, 623.

the *lex mercatoria* 'does not constitute an ascertainable, certain, enforceable, autonomous body of law which international merchants can rely on'.[34] Some of these perceived problems have, however, been addressed by the emergence of non-national 'codes' of contract law (such as the UNIDROIT Principles of International Commercial Contracts and the Lando Commission's Principles on European Contract Law),[35] which can be chosen by contracting parties as an alternative to the laws of a particular country or which can be used by arbitrators as a source of rules in cases where the parties have chosen the *lex mercatoria*. Whereas, in its traditional formulation, the *lex mercatoria* leaves the arbitral tribunal with a considerable margin of appreciation in determining its content, the adoption of a non-national code, either by the parties or by the arbitrators, gives the tribunal much less scope for rule creation.

23.2.15   Whatever may be the arguments for or against the theory, the *lex mercatoria* seems to fulfil a need—in the sense that some members of the international business community indicate, by choosing the *lex mercatoria*, a desire not to submit transnational legal disputes to national laws. Furthermore, there have been arbitral awards based on the *lex mercatoria* and it seems that, as a general rule, national courts are prepared to enforce such awards.[36] Finally, it is important that the issue of the *lex mercatoria* should be kept in proportion. The majority of international commercial agreements which provide for the resolution of disputes by arbitration contain choice of law clauses which select the law of a particular country. In practice, the appeal of the *lex mercatoria* has been limited largely to economic development agreements between states and foreign investors. Even in this limited field, 'departures from conflicts methodology are not as widespread as the abundant literature on point might suggest'.[37]

Absence of Choice

23.2.16   In the absence of choice by the parties it may legitimately be presumed that, since the parties must have envisaged that their contract would be governed by

---

[34] VLD Wilkinson, 'The New *Lex Mercatoria*: Reality or Academic Fantasy?' (1995) 12(2) *J Int Arb* 103, 115. Compare M Brunetti, 'The *Lex Mercatoria* in Practice: The Experience of the Iran-United States Claims Tribunal' (2002) 18 *Arb Int* 355; A Fall, 'Defence and Illustration of *Lex Mercatoria* in Maritime Arbitration' (1998) 15(1) *J Int Arb* 83.

[35] See KP Berger, *The Creeping Codification of the Lex Mercatoria* (The Hague, Kluwer, 1999). See also MJ Bonnell, *An International Restatement of Contract Law: The UNIDROIT Principles of International Commercial Contracts* (Irvington-on-Hudson NY, Transnational Publishers, 2nd edn, 1997); KP Berger, 'International Arbitral Practice and the UNIDROIT Principles of International Commercial Contracts' (1998) 46 *Am J Comp L* 129; LY Fortier, 'The New, New *Lex Mercatoria* or, Back to the Future' (2001) 17 *Arb Int* 121; AC Sinclair, 'Using the UNIDROIT Principles of International Commercial Contracts in International Commercial Arbitration' (2003) 6(3) *Int ALR* 65; H van Houtte, 'The UNIDROIT Principles of International Commercial Contracts' (1995) 11 *Arb Int* 373. It is also possible to access a version of the *lex mercatoria* via the Internet: KP Berger, '*Lex Mercatoria* Online: the CENTRAL Transnational Law Database at www.tldb.de' (2002) 18 *Arb Int* 83.

[36] See P Freeman, '*Lex Mercatoria*: Its Emergence and Acceptance as a Legal Basis for the Resolution of International Disputes' [1997] *ADRLJ* 289, 293–8. See also W Kühn, 'Choice of Substantive Law in the Practice of International Arbitration' (1997) 25 *Int Bus Lawyer* 148.

[37] GR Delaume, 'Comparative Analysis as a Basis of Law in State Contracts: the Myth of the *Lex Mercatoria*' (1989) 63 *Tulane LR* 575, 578.

some law, they must have intended the arbitrator to determine the applicable law.[38] For dealing with cases where the parties have failed to make a choice, there are two policy options. The first is for the law to give the arbitrator complete discretion on the choice of the applicable rules. For example, under Dutch law, if the parties to an arbitration agreement fail to make a choice of law 'the arbitral tribunal shall make its award in accordance with the rules of law which it considers appropriate'.[39] The alternative approach is to require the arbitral tribunal to select the applicable law by reference to the choice of law rules which it considers applicable. Although the first view has its supporters,[40] it is the second option which is adopted by section 46(3). The effect of section 46(3) is that, in the absence of choice by the parties, the arbitrator's task is to apply whichever choice of law rules he considers applicable, with a view to ascertaining the law applicable to the merits of the dispute. The tribunal is not obliged to apply the principles which the English court would apply, though it is of course free to do so if it thinks that English choice of law rules are applicable.

23.2.17   What is the scope of the arbitrator's discretion under section 46(3)? For example, would the approach taken by the arbitrator in the *Sapphire* arbitration[41] be legitimate? This arbitration concerned a dispute arising under a contract between a Canadian oil company and the National Iranian Oil Company. The arbitrator, having taken the view that he was not bound to conform to the conflicts rules of the seat of arbitration, decided as follows:

It is quite clear … that the parties intended to exclude the application of Iranian law. But they have not chosen another positive legal system and this omission is on all the evidence deliberate. All the connecting factors … point to the fact that the parties therefore intended to submit the interpretation and performance of their contract to principles of law generally recognised by civilised nations … The arbitrator will therefore apply these principles, in taking account, when necessary, of the decisions taken by international tribunals.[42]

23.2.18   Unless the parties have authorised him to do so under section 46(1)(b), the arbitrator is not entitled to decide the dispute by reference to standards of equity or fairness. An arbitral tribunal may not act as *amiable compositeur* or decide the dispute *ex aequo et bono* unless expressly authorised by the parties to do so. The position with regard to the *lex mercatoria* should be equally straightforward. Section 46(3) is based on Article 28(2) of the UNCITRAL Model Law. According to the drafters of the Model Law, in a case falling within Article 28(2), the tribunal is bound to apply the law of a specified legal system. In such a case the tribunal is not entitled to select 'rules of law', which is a more open-textured term covering, for example, 'the rules embodied in a convention or similar text elaborated on the international level, even if not yet

---

[38] AJE Jaffey, 'Arbitration of Commercial Contracts: the Law to be Applied by the Arbitrators' in DL Perrott and I Pogany (eds), *Current Problems in International Business Law* (Aldershot, Avebury, 1988) 136.

[39] Art 1054(2) of the code of civil procedure.

[40] See, eg, M Blessing, 'Choice of Substantive Law in International Arbitration' (1997) 14(2) *J Int Arb* 39.

[41] Part of the award is reproduced as an appendix to P Lalive, 'Contracts Between a State or a State Agency and a Foreign Company' (1964) 13 *ICLQ* 987, 1011–21.

[42] (1964) 13 *ICLQ* 987, 1015. See also the discussion of similar cases by AFM Maniruzzaman, 'State Contracts and Arbitral Choice-of-Law Process and Techniques' (1998) 15(3) *J Int Arb* 65.

in force'.[43] Since the intention of the drafters of the 1996 Act was to follow the Model Law, it seems reasonable to conclude that, in the absence of choice by the parties, the tribunal is bound to apply the choice of law rules which it considers appropriate with a view to identifying the law of a particular country as the applicable law. This is the view of the Departmental Advisory Committee:

In such circumstances the tribunal must decide what conflicts of law rules are applicable, and use those rules in order to determine the applicable law. It cannot simply make up rules for this purpose.[44]

23.2.19 Against this view is the decision of the Court of Appeal in *Deutsche Schachtbau- und Tiefbohrgesellschaft mbH v Shell International Petroleum Co Ltd*,[45] a case involving an ICC arbitration, in which the view was expressed that an arbitrator could adopt 'internationally accepted principles of law governing contractual rela- tions' as the applicable law on the basis that it was 'the law designated as the proper law by the rules of conflict which he deems appropriate' for the purposes of the applicable arbitration rules. Not too much significance should be attached to this decision. Not only did the case involve the interpretation of the ICC Rules (rather than section 46(3) of the 1996 Act), but also the decision did not find favour with leading commentators on ICC arbitration.[46] It may be questioned whether the *Deutsche Schachtbau* case should be regarded as even of persuasive authority in cases involving the interpreta- tion of section 46(3).

23.2.20 While it is easy enough to say what the arbitral tribunal should not do under section 46(3), it is more difficult to say exactly what it should do. Reported arbitral awards indicate a number of possible approaches.[47] Of course, the arbitrator may adopt the conflicts rules of the law of the country where the seat of arbitration is located. In an English arbitration, the tribunal might apply the choice of law regime to be found in the Rome I Regulation.[48] However, the tribunal may consider that, in the circumstances of the case, the conflicts rules of the law of the seat are not appro- priate. One possibility is for the arbitrator to apply a cumulative approach, which involves consideration of the conflict of laws rules of all the countries connected with the dispute. If these rules all lead to the same applicable law, the tribunal will inevi- tably apply that law; if the relevant conflict of laws rules point to different laws, the tribunal might adopt 'the law which emerges most frequently as the applicable law'.[49] Alternatively, the arbitrator might apply general principles of private international law (rather than any national set of conflicts rules). It would seem that section 46(3) gives unfettered discretion to the arbitral tribunal, so long as the tribunal operates

---

[43] HM Holzmann and JE Neuhaus, *A Guide to the UNCITRAL Model Law of International Commercial Arbitration: Legislative History and Commentary* (Deventer, Kluwer, 1989) 768.

[44] *Report on the Arbitration Bill* (1996) p 50 (para 225). See also SR Shackleton, 'The Applicable Law in International Arbitration under the New English Arbitration Act 1996' (1997) 13 *Arb Int* 375.

[45] [1990] 1 AC 295.

[46] WL Craig, WW Park and J Paulsson, *International Chamber of Commerce Arbitration* (Dobbs Ferry NY, Oceana Publications, 2nd edn, 1990) 300.

[47] See AFM Maniruzzaman, 'Conflict of Laws Issues in International Commercial Arbitration: Practice and Trends' (1993) 9 *Arb Int* 371, 384–95; O Chukwumerije, 'Applicable Substantive Law in International Commercial Arbitration' (1994) 22 *Anglo-Am LR* 265, 294–303.

[48] Reg (EC) 593/2008, [2008] OJ L177/6.

[49] JDM Lew, 'Determination of Applicable Substantive Law' (1997) 25 *Int Bus Lawyer* 157, 159.

within some system of choice of law rules.[50] In practice, in the absence of choice by the parties, the likelihood is that the arbitrator will decide the merits of the case by reference to the law of the country with which the contract in question is most closely connected.

Cases where the Arbitrator Misapplies Section 46

23.2.21   Under the terms of the Model Law there is no real sanction if the arbitral tribunal fails to apply the choice of law principles set out in Article 28.[51] The relevant provisions of the 1996 Act dealing with recourse against the award are significantly different from the equivalent provisions of the Model Law. Not only does the 1996 Act make provision for a party to appeal to the court on a point of law,[52] an award may be remitted or set aside for serious irregularity, which includes 'the tribunal exceeding its powers'[53] and 'the award ... being contrary to public policy'.[54]

23.2.22   When considering the remedies which are potentially available in cases where the arbitrator misapplies section 46, it is important to know whether the right to appeal on a point of law has been excluded by the parties. As a general principle, when an arbitrator makes an error of law, there exists a right of appeal to the court.[55] Although traditionally English arbitration law placed legality above the finality of arbitration proceedings, the court's supervisory jurisdiction on points of law is severely limited by the 1996 Act. The right to appeal on a point of law may be simply excluded by the parties' agreement.[56]

Where the Right to Appeal Has not Been Excluded

23.2.23   Where the parties have not excluded the right to appeal, if the arbitrator fails to apply section 46 properly, there is a right of appeal to the court with permission under section 69. If the court gives permission and finds that the arbitrator made a mistake as to the applicable law, the court may vary or set aside the award or remit it to the arbitrator for reconsideration.[57] For example, in a case where the parties have not chosen the applicable law, if the arbitrator decides that the *lex mercatoria*

---

[50] For situations in which arbitrators are given discretion as to which choice of law rules to apply, a three-stage procedure has been proposed by B Wortmann, 'Choice of Law by Arbitrators: The Applicable Conflict of Laws System' (1998) 14 *Arb Int* 97: (1) applying the cumulative approach, if all the relevant choice of law rules identify the same law, that law should be applied; (2) if the cumulative approach does not produce unanimity, the choice of law rules of the seat of arbitration should be applied—so long as the seat has been chosen by the parties; (3) if the cumulative approach does not produce unanimity and the parties have not chosen the seat of arbitration, the tribunal should apply general principles of private international law.

[51] Art 34 (recourse against the award) limits the grounds on which an award may be set aside to the grounds on which enforcement of an award may be refused under Art V of the New York Convention.

[52] Arbitration Act 1996, s 69.

[53] Arbitration Act 1996, s 68(2)(b).

[54] Arbitration Act 1996, s 68(2)(g).

[55] Arbitration Act 1996, s 69.

[56] Arbitration Act 1996, s 69(1).

[57] Arbitration Act 1996, s 69(7).

furnishes the applicable law, this constitutes an error of law which may be corrected by the court under the 1996 Act. If, however, the parties have expressly authorised the arbitrator to determine the dispute by standards other than a national system of law (for example, by agreeing to arbitration *ex aequo et bono*) the court cannot intervene, notwithstanding the fact that the right of appeal has not been excluded, since there is no question of law which the court can review.

Where the Right to Appeal Has Been Excluded

23.2.24 Where the parties have excluded the right to appeal on points of law under section 69, one must distinguish cases in which the arbitrator makes an error of law from situations in which there is serious irregularity (for example, as a result of the arbitrator wholly disregarding the agreement of the parties). This is because, although the right to appeal on a point of law may be simply excluded by the parties' agreement, the court's setting aside jurisdiction under section 68 cannot.[58] In cases where the right to appeal under section 69 has been excluded, it may be difficult to draw the dividing line between mere errors of law (which are not reviewable) and serious irregularities (which may be dealt with under section 68).

23.2.25 The court's power under section 68 to set aside an award for serious irregularity may not be exercised where the only defect alleged is merely an error of law in a reasoned award. A simple mistake by an arbitrator in his assessment of the parties' substantive rights and obligations under a contract cannot amount to a serious irregularity, regardless of whether the parties' substantive rights are governed by English or foreign law.[59] The only way to challenge an error of English law is to seek permission to appeal under section 69. Accordingly, in those cases where the parties have excluded the right of appeal to the court on a point of law, there is no mechanism whereby simple errors of law can be corrected. In this situation, English law adopts the position that the finality of the award should prevail over its legality.

23.2.26 What is the position, however, if the arbitrator wholly disregards the terms of the arbitration agreement (for example, where the arbitrator decides *ex aequo et bono* notwithstanding the fact that the parties have agreed that the merits of the dispute should be governed by the law of a particular country or applies French law even though the parties' contract includes an express choice of English law)? There is case for saying that, in this type of case, the arbitrator's failure to act in accordance with the parties' agreement amounts to a serious irregularity.[60] According to this view, where an arbitrator fails to carry out the parties' mandate, for example, by ignoring or rejecting the relevant rules of law, a party who suffers substantial injustice as a result should be able to challenge the award under section 68(2)(b) on the basis that the arbitrator exceeded his powers[61] and that, in appropriate cases, the award should

---

[58] Arbitration Act 1996, s 4 (1) and sched 1.
[59] Steyn J in *Bank Mellat v GAA Development and Construction Ltd* [1988] 2 Lloyd's Rep 44, 52.
[60] AJE Jaffey, 'Arbitration of Commercial Contracts: the Law to be Applied by the Arbitrators' in DL Perrott and I Pogany (eds), *Current Problems in International Business Law* (Aldershot, Avebury, 1988) 138.
[61] F Davidson, 'The New Arbitration Act—A Model Law?' [1997] *JBL* 101, 122.

be set aside by the court.[62] However, in *Lesotho Highlands Development Authority v Impreglio SpA*[63] the House of Lords held that arbitrators had not exceeded their powers when, having decided that the determination of the currency for the payment of damages was a question of procedure rather than substance, they awarded damages to be paid in currencies other than those provided by the contract under its applicable law. The analysis of the House of Lords in this case suggests that a refusal by the arbitral tribunal to apply the law chosen by the parties to govern the contract would not constitute an excess of jurisdiction or power.[64]

The Impact of Mandatory Rules

23.2.27 Mandatory rules comprise rules of law that cannot be derogated from by contract, including rules which a legal system regards as being of such importance that they must be applied irrespective of the applicable law. Mandatory rules include competition laws, exchange control legislation, environmental protection laws, laws implementing trade sanctions and laws designed to protect the weaker party in consumer and employment contracts.

23.2.28 It is widely acknowledged that whatever methodology is employed for determining the applicable law, an arbitrator is required to have regard to mandatory rules—even if the parties have chosen the *lex mercatoria* or have authorised the arbitrator to decide the dispute *extra legem*. For example, arbitrators must be bound by EU law—at least if the seat of arbitration is situated in a Member State[65]—and it has generally been accepted that the decision of the Court of Justice in *Eco Swiss China Time Ltd v Benetton International NV*[66] means that arbitrators are obliged to apply mandatory provisions of EU law even if the relevant issue is not raised by the parties to the dispute.[67] Failure by the arbitrator to have regard to relevant mandatory rules may result in the award either being set aside by the court with supervisory jurisdiction over the arbitration or being unenforceable in other countries on the ground of public policy.[68] It goes without saying that the mandatory rules of the law applicable to the merits of the dispute must be applied. If, for example, a

[62] See the discussion by WW Park, 'National Law and Commercial Justice: Safeguarding Procedural Integrity in International Arbitration' (1989) 63 *Tulane LR* 647, 675.

[63] [2006] 1 AC 221. See also the discussion of WW Park, 'The Nature of Arbitral Authority: A Comment on *Lesotho Highlands*' (2005) 21 *Arb Int* 483.

[64] A Samuel, '*Lesotho Highlands*: "Denaturing" an Arbitration Statute and an Express Choice of Law does not Involve the Arbitrator Exceeding his Powers' (2006) 23(3) *J Int Arb* 259, 261.

[65] H van Houtte, 'The Application by Arbitrators of Articles 81 & 82 and Their Relationship with the European Commission' [2008] *EBLR* 63. There is no reason to suppose that EU competition law, for example, would form part of the public policy of a non-Member State.

[66] Case C–126/97 [1999] ECR I–3055. TD de Groot, 'The Impact of the *Benetton* Decision on International Commercial Arbitration' (2003) 20(4) *J Int Arb* 365; C Liebscher, 'European Public Policy After *Eco Swiss*' (1999) 10 *Am Rev Int'l Arb* 81; P Pinsolle, 'Private Enforcement of European Community Competition Rules by Arbitrators' (2004) 7 *Int ALR* 14; RB von Mehren, 'The *Eco-Swiss* Case and International Arbitration' (2003) 19 *Arb Int* 465.

[67] See, eg, G Blanke, 'The Role of EC Competition Law in International Arbitration: A Plaidoyer' [2005] *EBLR* 169.

[68] See P Mayer, 'Mandatory Rules of Law in International Arbitration' (1986) 2 *Arb Int* 274; D Hochstrasser, 'Choice of Law and "Foreign" Mandatory Rules' (1994) 11(1) *J Int Arb* 57. See also H Arfazadeh, 'In the

contract governed by French law infringes economic sanctions imposed by French law, the arbitrator should declare the contract to be null and void.[69]

23.2.29   If the parties agree that the tribunal should decide the dispute in accordance with principles of fairness or by reference to the *lex mercatoria*, the tribunal is given, in effect, a broad discretion to apply the rules and principles which it considers appropriate. In such a case the tribunal might decide that a party who has failed to keep his side of the bargain should be excused performance if performance is illegal under the law of country where performance was to be effected or that an agreement which violates 'good morals' (where, for example, one party agrees, in return for payment, to bribe public officials on behalf of the other) should be unenforceable.

23.2.30   In a case where the parties fail to make a choice of law (or other considerations), the tribunal may conclude—by reference to the choice of law rules which it considers appropriate—that, notwithstanding the fact that the law of country X is *prima facie* the applicable law, certain mandatory rules of the law of country Y or of the law of the country in which the seat of arbitration is located should prevail over the law of country X. In reaching such a conclusion the tribunal could, for example, rely on Article 9(3) of the Rome I Regulation[70] as a 'conflict of laws rule ... which it considers applicable'. Whether mandatory rules of the law of the seat should prevail over the law applicable to the merits of the dispute should depend on the circumstances. Although it is reasonable for an arbitrator to apply the mandatory rules of the law of the seat in those cases where the arbitrator can be seen simply as a substitute for the local courts, in international situations the arbitrator takes the place of all the courts which might have had jurisdiction to determine the dispute in the absence of the arbitration agreement. It is perfectly possible that, had the parties not agreed to arbitration, the dispute could not have been litigated in the country chosen as the seat of arbitration. Logically, it would follow that, except in cases where the dispute has a close connection with the seat of arbitration, an arbitrator should not be regarded as under a legal obligation to apply the mandatory rules of the law of the seat, but should be limited only by international public policy. In practice, however, the arbitrator ignores mandatory rules of the law of the seat at his peril.

23.2.31   Although section 46 of the 1996 Act does not address the situation where there is a conflict between the law applicable to the merits of the dispute and mandatory rules of English law, this does not necessarily mean that the arbitral tribunal is free to have regard only to the law chosen by the parties in such circumstances.[71] Account must also be taken of other statutory provisions concerning public policy which have some bearing on the matter, albeit somewhat obliquely. The 1996 Act provides that permission to enforce an award in England shall not be given to the extent that its enforcement would be contrary to public policy[72] and that an award may be

---

Shadow of the Unruly Horse: International Arbitration and the Public Policy Exception' (2002) 13 *Am Rev Int'l Arb* 43.

[69]   H van Houtte, 'Trade Sanctions and Arbitration' (1997) 25 *Int Bus Lawyer* 166.

[70]   See para 14.3.11–14.3.15.

[71]   See M Blessing, 'Mandatory Rules of Law *versus* Party Autonomy in International Arbitration' (1997) 14(4) *J Int Arb* 23.

[72]   Arbitration Act 1996, s 66(3)(b). This provision is concerned only with cases where England is the seat of arbitration; it does not apply to the enforcement of foreign awards, which fall within Part III of the 1996 Act.

set aside on the basis that the award (or the way in which it was procured) is contrary to public policy.[73] Accordingly, as regards an arbitration conducted in England, if the arbitrator fails to have regard to a mandatory rule of English law which in the court's eyes ought to have been applied, the award is likely to be refused enforcement in England or set aside by the English court. If an award is set aside by the courts of the seat the award will generally cease to be enforceable in other countries under the New York Convention.[74]

23.2.32 Similar problems may arise in cases where the law chosen by the parties conflicts with the mandatory rules of the law of a country which is not the seat of arbitration but with which the contract is closely connected. As regards the applicability of mandatory rules which form part neither of the law chosen by the parties nor of the law of the seat, academic opinion is divided. One view is that 'the overriding principle of international arbitration should be to follow the parties' choice of law even if such law is in conflict with mandatory rules of another country connected with the contract'.[75] The opposing approach is that, as a general rule, an arbitrator 'must consider any strong principle of public policy of a country closely connected with the contract'.[76]

23.2.33 From a practical perspective, it must always be borne in mind that one of the grounds on which an award may be refused enforcement under the New York Convention is that it offends the public policy of the country in which enforcement is being sought.[77] As one commentator has noted:

The award is the *raison d'être* of every arbitration; if the award is unenforceable the whole arbitration proceeding will have been a waste of time and money. If the arbitrator's award is not enforceable because it violates the public policy of the place of performance, the arbitrator will have failed in the responsibility vested in him.[78]

Given that arbitrators are under a general duty to render an enforceable award,[79] an arbitral tribunal should have regard to the public policy of the country (or countries) where enforcement is likely to be sought. Failure to do so will normally have the result that the award will be rendered unenforceable.

---

[73] Arbitration Act 1996, s 68(2)(g).

[74] Art V(1)(e).

[75] W Kühn, 'Choice of Substantive Law in the Practice of International Arbitration' (1997) 25 *Int Bus Lawyer* 148, 150.

[76] O Lando, 'The *Lex Mercatoria* in International Commercial Arbitration' (1985) 34 *ICLQ* 747, 766–7.

[77] Art V(2).

[78] JDM Lew, *Applicable Law in International Commercial Arbitration* (Dobbs Ferry NY, Oceana Publications, 1978) 537.

[79] GJ Horvath, 'The Duty of the Tribunal to Render an Enforceable Award' (2001) 18(2) *J Int Arb* 135.

RECOGNITION AND ENFORCEMENT OF ARBITRATION AWARDS

24.1 PRELIMINARY ISSUES

The Relationship between Enforcement and Setting Aside

24.1.1   If the arbitrator decides in favour of the claimant, the respondent may seek to challenge the award in two different ways. First, the respondent may take the initiative and apply to the courts of the country of origin to have the award set aside. Secondly, the respondent may wait and let the claimant take the initiative; if the claimant seeks to enforce the award the respondent may challenge the award in the context of the enforcement proceedings. It is clear that a person against whom an award has been made is not bound to make a challenge in the country of origin in order to be able to resist recognition or enforcement in another country.[1] If the claimant seeks to enforce the award in a country other than the country of origin the rules governing the enforcement of foreign awards apply.

24.1.2   If an award has been set aside in the country of origin, an attempt by the successful party to enforce the award in another country will normally fail.[2] Whereas setting aside operates *erga omnes*, the result reached by the courts in enforcement proceedings is strictly territorial. So, where the court of country Y refuses to enforce an award made in country X (for example, on the ground that the respondent was not given proper notice of the arbitration proceedings), the decision of the court of country Y does not preclude enforcement of the award in country Z. However, by virtue of the doctrine of estoppel *per rem judicatam*, a foreign judgment refusing to enforce an award may give rise to one or more issue estoppels if the relevant conditions are satisfied.[3]

The Enforcement of Domestic Awards

24.1.3   An award is unlike a judgment in the sense that it is not self-executing. If the debtor fails to comply voluntarily with the award, the creditor who wishes to enforce the award has to invoke the jurisdiction of the court. Where the award is made in England, the creditor may seek enforcement in one of two ways. First, the creditor may bring a claim on the award based on the debtor's breach of the implied obligation to comply with the terms of the award.[4] If the award is upheld, the court essentially translates the award

---

[1] *Svenska Petroleum Exploration AB v Government of the Republic of Lithuania (No 2)* [2007] QB 886; *Dallah Real Estate and Tourism Holding Co v Pakistan Ministry of Religious Affairs* [2010] 2 WLR 805.
[2] New York Convention, Art V(1)(e); Arbitration Act 1996, s 103(2)(f).
[3] *The Good Challenger* [2004] 1 Lloyd's Rep 67. See section 12.3.
[4] Arbitration Act 1996, s 66(4).

into a judgment for the amount awarded by the arbitrator. Secondly, the creditor may make an application to the court under section 66 of the 1996 Act, which provides:

(1) An award made by the tribunal pursuant to an arbitration agreement may, by leave of the court, be enforced in the same manner as a judgment or order of the court to the same effect.

(2) Where leave is so given, judgment may be entered in terms of the award.

An application for permission to enforce an award in the same manner as a judgment may be made without notice.[5] If the court gives permission to enforce, the award may be enforced in the same manner as a judgment. The order giving permission to enforce the award must be served on the debtor either in England or out of the jurisdiction; if necessary, the order may be served out of the jurisdiction without permission.[6]

24.1.4   Although permission to enforce an award is not automatic, unless there is real ground for doubting the validity of the award, permission to enforce under section 66 should be given.[7] Nevertheless, it should be stressed that section 66 'does not require the court to order enforcement, but only gives it a discretion to do so'.[8] That discretion is fettered in a negative way in a number of respects—that is to say, there are certain cases where enforcement shall not be ordered. It is provided that permission to enforce the award shall not be given if 'the tribunal lacked substantive jurisdiction'.[9] In addition, permission to enforce should be refused if it conflicts with 'public policy'[10] or if the subject-matter of the award was 'not capable of settlement by arbitration'.[11] These are not the only circumstances in which enforcement under section 66 will be refused as 'there is no closed list of cases where leave to enforce an award may be refused'.[12] The court may refuse permission to enforce where the case raises a question of law which cannot be disposed of without trial. If the court refuses permission to enforce under section 66, the creditor's only means of enforcement is by a claim on the award. In order to save time and expense, where permission to enforce is refused, the court may—in the exercise of its general powers of management—direct a separate trial of the contentious issue.[13]

The Enforcement of Foreign Arbitration Awards

24.1.5   International commercial arbitration could not function effectively without an adequate mechanism for the enforcement of awards in countries other than the country where the award was made:

The effectiveness of international arbitration depends ultimately on the question whether the award can be enforced against the losing party. That is not to say that most arbitrations lead

---

[5] CPR 62.18(1).
[6] CPR 62.18(8).
[7] *Middlemiss & Gould v Hartlepool Corporation* [1972] 1 WLR 1643.
[8] Departmental Advisory Committee, *Report on the Arbitration Bill* (1996) p 78 (para 374).
[9] Arbitration Act 1996, s 66(3).
[10] Arbitration Act 1996, s 81(1)(c).
[11] Arbitration Act 1996, s 81(1)(a).
[12] Departmental Advisory Committee, *Report on the Arbitration Bill* (1996) p 78 (para 374).
[13] CPR 3.1(2)(i).

to enforcement proceedings before the courts of some state. Quite the contrary, awards are complied with voluntarily in a large number of cases. But this large degree of voluntary compliance is, for a significant part, probably due to the fact that effective international enforcement measures are generally available to the winning party.[14]

In this regard the New York Convention of 1958, implemented in England by Part III of the 1996 Act (which replaced equivalent provisions of the 1975 Act), is of prime importance. As a result of the Convention 'the odds have been turned against the award-debtor and ... significant progress has been made to ensure the effectiveness of international awards'.[15] Furthermore, the success of the New York Convention has produced a situation where, on the international plane, it is generally easier to enforce arbitration awards than judgments.

24.1.6 Part III of the 1996 Act is not the only legal regime for the enforcement of foreign awards. Under English law a foreign award may be enforced at common law or may be entitled to enforcement under other statutory provisions. To a considerable extent the other legal regimes for enforcement are preserved by the 1996 Act. A foreign award may be enforced in England under one (or more) of the following regimes: (1) the 1996 Act; (2) the common law; (3) Part II of the 1950 Act (which implements the Geneva Protocol of 1923 and the Geneva Convention of 1927); (4) Part II of the Civil Jurisdiction and Judgments Act 1982 (as regards awards made in another part of the United Kingdom); (5) Part I of the Foreign Judgments (Reciprocal Enforcement) Act 1933; (6) Part II of the Administration of Justice Act 1920; and (7) the Arbitration (International Investment Disputes) Act 1966 (which implements the Washington Convention of 1965). The relationship between these various regimes is rather complex: some of them are mutually exclusive; in certain circumstances a creditor can choose which set of rules to rely upon.

24.1.7 To be entitled to recognition or enforcement in England under any of the schemes, the decision must qualify as an 'arbitration award'. This means that the decision must be one which determines the rights and obligations of the parties to the dispute. Accordingly, an interlocutory order made by an arbitral tribunal is not to be regarded as an award.[16] In addition, the decision must emanate from a tribunal on which jurisdiction has been conferred by the agreement of the parties. So, where a testator's Trusteeship Council, which was not a party to the dispute in question, referred to the Shari'a Council in London a dispute between parties entitled under the will, the decision of the Shari'a council could not be treated as an arbitral award.[17]

---

[14] AJ van den Berg, 'Recent Enforcement Problems under the New York and ICSID Conventions' (1989) 5 *Arb Int* 2. It is reckoned that more than 90 per cent of ICC awards are complied without enforcement measures being required: P-Y Gunter, 'Enforcement of Arbitral Awards, Injunctions and Orders' [1999] *ADRLJ* 265, 268.

[15] GR Delaume, 'Reflections on the Effectiveness of International Awards' (1995) 12(1) *J Int Arb* 5.

[16] *Re Resort Condominiums International Inc* [1995] 1 Qd 406 (Supreme Court, Queensland). For criticism of this decision, see T Kojovic, 'Court Enforcement of Arbitral Decisions on Provisional Relief: How Final is Provisional?' (2001) 18(5) *J Int Arb* 511.

[17] *Al Midani v Al Midani* [1999] 1 Lloyd's Rep. 923.

24.2 RECOGNITION AND ENFORCEMENT OF FOREIGN AWARDS UNDER PART III OF THE ARBITRATION ACT 1996[18]

24.2.1 To be entitled to recognition or enforcement under Part III of the 1996 Act an award must be a 'New York Convention award' and the person seeking to rely on the award must produce various documents. Even if these conditions are satisfied, recognition or enforcement may be refused if the party against whom the award is invoked can establish a ground for refusing recognition or enforcement.

24.2.2 Section 101(1) of the 1996 Act provides that, as a general principle, '[a] New York Convention award shall be recognised as binding on the persons as between whom it was made, and may accordingly be relied on by those persons by way of defence, set-off or otherwise in any legal proceedings in England and Wales or Northern Ireland'. So, not only may a successful claimant seek to enforce a New York Convention award in England under the 1996 Act, but a successful respondent may rely on a New York Convention award as a defence to subsequent legal proceedings in England on the same cause of action. In order for an award to be regarded as creating either a cause of action estoppel or issue estoppel, the decision of the arbitral tribunal must be final and conclusive under the law of the seat of arbitration.[19] Although the New York Convention does not explicitly authorise partial enforcement, the view in England is that enforcement of a New York Convention does not have to be an 'all or nothing' issue: there is 'no objection in principle to enforcement of part of an award provided the part to be enforced can be ascertained from the face of the award and judgment can be given in the same terms as the award'.[20]

The Scope of Part III of the 1996 Act

The Arbitration Agreement

24.2.3 The 1996 Act applies to the recognition and enforcement of awards made 'in pursuance of an arbitration agreement'.[21] For the purposes of this provision an arbitration agreement is 'an agreement in writing' as defined by section 5 of the 1996 Act.[22] An award which is based on an arbitration agreement which does not satisfy the formal requirements of section 5 is not entitled to recognition or enforcement under Part III of the 1996 Act.[23]

---

[18] See JDM Lew, 'The Arbitration Act 1975' (1975) 24 *ICLQ* 870; DR Thomas, 'International commercial arbitration agreements and the enforcement of foreign arbitral awards—a commentary on the Arbitration Act 1975' [1981] *LMCLQ* 17, 30–9. The leading work on the New York Convention is AJ van den Berg, *The New York Arbitration Convention of 1958* (Deventer, Kluwer, 1981).

[19] *Svenska Petroleum Exploration AB v Government of the Republic of Lithuania* [2005] 1 Lloyd's Rep 515; *Svenska Petroleum Exploration AB v Government of the Republic of Lithuania (No 2)* [2006] 1 All ER (Comm) 731, affirmed [2007] QB 886.

[20] Tuckey LJ in *Nigerian National Petroleum Corporation v IPCO (Nigeria) Ltd (No 2)* [2009] 1 Lloyd's Rep 89, 93 [at [14]]).

[21] Arbitration Act 1996, s 100(1).

[22] Arbitration Act 1996, s 100(2). See paras 21.2.13–21.2.19.

[23] In these circumstances the award might be entitled to recognition or enforcement at common law. See section 24.3.

Territorial Scope

INTRODUCTION

24.2.4 The Convention provides that it shall apply both to the recognition and enforcement of 'arbitral awards made in the territory of a state other than the state where the recognition and enforcement of such awards are sought' (foreign awards) and to 'arbitral awards not considered as domestic awards in the state where their recognition and enforcement are sought' (non-domestic awards).[24] The second category is intended to confer on the courts of country X a discretion to include within the Convention's scope an award which is made in country X under the procedural law of country Y.[25]

24.2.5 From a practical perspective it is only the recognition and enforcement of foreign awards under the Convention which is of importance; the reference to non-domestic awards in the Convention is almost a dead letter.[26] Part III of the 1996 Act provides for the enforcement of awards 'made ... in the territory of a State, other than the United Kingdom, which is party to the New York Convention'.[27] More than 140 states are bound by the Convention, including all, or nearly all, significant trading nations. Since most major arbitration centres are located in states which have ratified the Convention the vast majority of foreign awards are New York Convention awards for the purposes of the 1996 Act. For an award to fall within the scope of Part III there is no requirement that the arbitration should be international; an award made in Lagos in an arbitration involving two Nigerian corporations is a New York Convention award.[28]

24.2.6 The 1996 Act does not provide for the enforcement of non-domestic awards (that is, awards made in England under the curial law of a foreign country); permission to enforce such awards may be given under section 66 of the 1996 Act. Also, Part III of the 1996 Act does not apply to the enforcement in England of awards made in Scotland or Northern Ireland.

WHERE IS AN AWARD MADE?

24.2.7 Normally, the award is signed or deemed to have been signed by the arbitrator at the seat of arbitration. For example, Article 16(4) of the UNCITRAL Arbitration Rules provides that the award 'shall be made at the place of arbitration'; Article 25(3) of the ICC Rules of Arbitration states that the award 'shall be deemed to be made at the place of the arbitration'.

24.2.8 What is the position if the arbitration is conducted in country X, but the award is signed in country Y? The view adopted by academic commentators is that

---

[24] Art I(1).

[25] AJ van den Berg, *The New York Arbitration Convention of 1958* (Deventer, Kluwer, 1981) 22–8; AJ van den Berg, 'Non-Domestic Arbitral Awards under the 1958 New York Convention' (1986) 2 *Arb Int* 191, 200–01. See also M Pryles, 'Foreign Awards and the New York Convention' (1993) 9 *Arb Int* 259.

[26] AJ van den Berg, *The New York Arbitration Convention of 1958* (Deventer, Kluwer, 1981) 28. See, however, *Bergesen v Jospeh Muller Corp*, 710 F 2d 928 (2d Cir, 1983); *Jain v de Méré*, 51 F3d 686 (7th cir, 1995); *Yusuf Ahmed Alghanim & Sons v Toys 'R' Us Inc*, 126 F3d 15 (2d cir, 1997).

[27] Arbitration Act 1996, s 100(1).

[28] *IPCO (Nigeria) Ltd v Nigerian National Petroleum Corporation* [2005] 2 Lloyd's Rep 326, 329. See also the view of AJ van den Berg, *The New York Arbitration Convention of 1958* (Deventer, Kluwer, 1981) 17.

an award is made in the country where the arbitration took place. This view, which is based on the notion that '[t]he rendering of the award forms part of the arbitral procedure',[29] was, however, rejected by the House of Lords in *Hiscox v Outhwaite*.[30] In this case, although the arbitration had been conducted in England, with hearings having taken place in London, the arbitrator signed and dated the award in Paris. The plaintiff applied to the English court for leave to appeal against the award on a point of law and for the award to be remitted to the arbitrator for further consideration. The defendant, however, sought to enforce the award in England, arguing that the award was 'made' in France and that the award was entitled to enforcement in England as a New York Convention award.

24.2.9   The House of Lords accepted the defendant's argument that the award was 'made' in France—on the basis that the award was perfected in France, because that was where it was signed[31]—and was a New York Convention award.[32] This conclusion was described as 'truly startling'[33] and it is hardly surprising that the decision was vigorously criticised.[34] While the view that an award is made at the seat of arbitration attributes a somewhat strained meaning to the word 'made', the interpretation favoured by the House of Lords ran the risk of giving rise to bizarre results.[35]

24.2.10   Fortunately, the drafters of the 1996 Act took the opportunity to rectify the potential anomalies generated by the decision in *Hiscox v Outhwaite*. First, unless otherwise agreed by the parties, 'where the seat of arbitration is in England and Wales … any award in the proceedings shall be treated as made there, regardless of where it was signed, despatched or delivered to any of the parties'.[36] So, under the 1996 Act, on facts such as those which occurred in *Hiscox v Outhwaite*, the award is not a New York Convention award within the scope of Part III. Secondly, it is provided that, to determine whether an award is a New York Convention award for the purposes of Part III, 'an award shall be treated as made at the seat of the arbitration, regardless of where it was signed, despatched or delivered to any of the parties'.[37] So, if the seat of arbitration is in France (which is a New York Convention state), but the arbitrator signs the award in another country (which is not), the award is to be regarded as 'made' in France and is therefore entitled to recognition and enforcement according to the rules set out in Part III of the 1996 Act.

---

[29] P Sanders, 'Trends in the Field of International Commercial Arbitration' (1975) 145 *Hag Rec* 205, 274. See also FA Mann, 'Where is an Award "Made"?' (1985) 1 *Arb Int* 107, 108; AJ van den Berg, *The New York Arbitration Convention of 1958* (Deventer, Kluwer, 1981) 294–5.

[30] [1991] AC 334.

[31] See Lord Oliver at [1992] 1 AC 562, 594.

[32] It was also held that the court retained its supervisory jurisdiction over English arbitrations, even if the award happens to be made in a foreign country. Accordingly, enforcement of the award was suspended pending the outcome of the plaintiff's applications.

[33] DR Thomas, 'Reflections on Recent Judicial Development of the Concept of a Convention Award' (1992) 11 *CJQ* 352, 358.

[34] F Davidson, 'Where Is An Arbitral Award Made?—Hiscox v Outhwaite' (1992) 41 *ICLQ* 637; C Reymond, 'Where Is An Arbitral Award Made?' (1992) 108 *LQR* 1; FA Mann, 'Foreign Awards' (1992) 108 *LQR* 6.

[35] See M Broberg, 'The Interpretation of Section 5(2)(b) of the English Arbitration Act 1975' (1994) 11(3) *J Int Arb* 119.

[36] Arbitration Act 1996, s 53.

[37] Arbitration Act 1996, s 100(2)(b).

TEMPORAL SCOPE

24.2.11   The relevant time for deciding whether an award was made in the territory of a state which is a party to the New York Convention is the time when enforcement proceedings are commenced in England. *Minister of Public Works of the Government of the State of Kuwait v Sir Frederick Snow and Partners*[38] concerned an application to enforce an award made in Kuwait. It was held that the award was entitled to enforcement in England under the legislation which implemented the Convention. It was sufficient that, although Kuwait was not a party to the Convention at the time the award was made, it had become a party by the time enforcement of the award was sought in England.

Conditions for Obtaining Recognition or Enforcement

The Relevant Documents

24.2.12   Section 102 of the 1996 Act provides:

(1) A party seeking the recognition or enforcement of a New York Convention award must produce—

    (a) the duly authenticated original award or a duly certified copy of it, and
    (b) the original arbitration agreement or a duly certified copy of it.

(2) If the award or agreement is in a foreign language, the party must also produce a translation of it certified by an official or sworn translator or by a diplomatic or consular agent.

Once the party seeking recognition or enforcement has produced the documents required by section 102, the award is *prima facie* entitled to recognition or enforcement. In terms of section 102(1)(b), all that is required is:

apparently valid documentation, containing an arbitration clause, by reference to which the arbitrators have accepted that the parties had agreed on arbitration or in which the arbitrators have accepted that an agreement to arbitrate was recorded with the parties' authority.[39]

Similarly, the party seeking to rely on an award must produce an award of the arbitrators, a condition which would not be satisfied by the production of a forgery; but, the party invoking the award does not have to prove its validity and, in terms of section 102(1)(a), it is irrelevant that the award may subsequently be shown to be invalid.[40] Once the party seeking recognition or enforcement satisfies section 102, the onus shifts to the party against whom the award is invoked to establish that there is a good reason for refusing recognition or enforcement; if that party wishes to challenge the award on the basis that the arbitration agreement or the award is invalid, such challenge can be pursued only within the framework of section 103.[41]

---

[38] [1984] AC 426. J Crawford, (1984) 55 *BYIL* 336.
[39] Mance LJ in *Dardana Ltd v Yukos Oil Co* [2002] 2 Lloyd's Rep 326, 332 (at [12]).
[40] Mance LJ in *Dardana Ltd v Yukos Oil Co* [2002] 2 Lloyd's Rep 326, 331 (at [10]).
[41] *Ibid.*

PROCEDURAL STEPS

24.2.13 Section 101(2) provides that a New York Convention award 'may, by leave of the court, be enforced in the same manner as a judgment or order of the court to the same effect'. The summary procedure for obtaining permission to enforce is commenced by the creditor making an application for permission to enforce the award; the application may be made without notice.[42] If the application is made without notice the court may nevertheless direct that the application be served on other parties.[43] If the application cannot be served on the defendant within the jurisdiction, the court may give permission to serve the application out of the jurisdiction.[44] If permission to enforce is given without notice, the order giving permission to enforce must be served on the debtor either in England or out of the jurisdiction; service out of the jurisdiction does not require the court's permission.[45] The award may not be enforced until after the expiration of the period during which the debtor may apply to have the order set aside or, if the debtor makes an application during that period, until after the application has been finally disposed of.[46]

24.2.14 There may be difficulties in obtaining enforcement in England by this summary procedure in the international context. In *Dalmia Cement Ltd v National Bank of Pakistan*[47] Kerr J held that awards which in their operative parts directed payment 'in India' could not be summarily enforced because the court could not give judgment in such terms. By contrast, in *Bank Mellat v GAA Development and Construction Co*[48] a statement in the reasons (rather than in the operative parts of the award) that the respondent should 'pay the awarded sum in Switzerland' did not prevent summary enforcement of the award in England.

24.2.15 The creditor may choose to seek enforcement by a claim on the award, rather than by the summary procedure. Where the creditor seeks enforcement by way of a claim on the award, the proceedings are commenced by service of a claim form. If the debtor is not otherwise amenable to the jurisdiction of the court, the creditor has to obtain permission of the court to serve the claim form out of the jurisdiction. One of the grounds on which service out may be given under CPR 6.36 is provided by CPR PD 6B, para 3.1(10) of which refers to a situation where 'a claim is made to enforce any … arbitral award'. The presence of the defendant's assets is not sufficient to give the court jurisdiction in enforcement proceedings. Neither, however, is the presence of assets within the jurisdiction a precondition for permission to be given.[49] As regards the question of *forum conveniens*, when the issue is whether a foreign award should be enforced in England 'there cannot be any forum in which that can be debated other than the English court'.[50]

---

[42] CPR 62.18(1).
[43] CPR 62.18(2).
[44] CPR 62.18(4).
[45] CPR 62.18(7)–(8).
[46] CPR 62.18(9).
[47] [1979] QB 9.
[48] [1988] 2 Lloyd's Rep 44.
[49] Steyn J in *Rosseel NV v Oriental Commercial & Shipping Co (UK) Ltd* [1991] 2 Lloyd's Rep 625, 629.
[50] Waller J in *Arab Business Consortium International Finance and Investment Co v Banque Franco-Tunisienne* [1996] 1 Lloyd's Rep 485, 492.

Grounds for Refusing Recognition or Enforcement

The Statutory Framework

24.2.16 The eight grounds on which the recognition or enforcement of a New York Convention award may be refused are set out in subsections (2)–(4) of section 103.[51] Subsection (2)—which is supplemented by subsection (4)—lists six grounds on which recognition or enforcement may be refused: (1) the party against whom the award is invoked lacked capacity; (2) the arbitration agreement on which the award was based was invalid; (3) the arbitration proceedings did not comply with principles of natural justice; (4) the arbitrator lacked jurisdiction; (5) there was a failure to comply with the applicable procedural rules; (6) the award is not binding or has been set aside in the country of origin. In addition, subsection (3) provides two further grounds on which enforcement may be refused: (7) the award is contrary to public policy; (8) the subject-matter of the dispute was not arbitrable.

24.2.17 The grounds for refusal listed in subsection (2) must be proved by 'the person against whom the award is invoked'. By contrast, the two defences enumerated in subsection (3) may be raised by the court of its own motion. In practice, however, if the grounds for refusal in subsection (3) are invoked it is invariably by the party seeking to resist recognition or enforcement.

24.2.18 It would seem from the English text of the Convention—which is substantially reproduced in the 1996 Act—that even if the party against whom the award is invoked establishes one of the grounds for refusal of enforcement, the court still has a discretion not to allow the defence and to grant enforcement of the award.[52] There is, however, no indication in either the Convention or the 1996 Act of how such discretion might be exercised. The English courts have taken a restrictive approach to the question of discretion. To the extent that discretion is conferred on the court addressed, it is not an 'open discretion';[53] the discretion is a narrow one.[54] As Rix LJ made clear in *Dallah Real Estate and Tourism Holding Co v Pakistan Ministry of Religious Affairs*, 'the strong inference' from the framework of the New York Convention is that 'a proven defence is a defence'.[55] This means that, in a case where a defence is established, the court will not normally consider enforcing an award except on the basis of some 'recognisable legal principle'.[56]

24.2.19 There are two types of case where the courts seem to have accepted that an award may be enforced notwithstanding the fact that the respondent can establish

[51] The relationship between s 103 of the 1996 Act and the equivalent provisions of the New York Convention of 1958 is as follows: Art V(1)(a) = s 103(2)(a) and (b); Art V(1)(b) = s 103(2)(c); Art V(1)(c) = s 103(2)(d) and s 103(4); Art V(1)(d) = s 103(2)(e); Art V(1)(e) = s 103(2)(f); Art V(2) = s 103(3); Art VI = s 103(5).

[52] AJ van den Berg, *The New York Arbitration Convention of 1958* (Deventer, Kluwer, 1981) 267; J Paulsson, 'May or Must under the New York Convention: An Exercise in Syntax and Linguistics' (1998) 14 *Arb Int* 227.

[53] Mance LJ in *Dardana Ltd v Yukos Oil Co* [2002] 2 Lloyd's Rep 326, 330 (at [8]). See also *Kanoria v Guinness* [2006] 1 Lloyd's Rep 701.

[54] See, eg, Rix LJ in *Dallah Real Estate and Tourism Holding Co v Pakistan Ministry of Religious Affairs* [2010] 2 WLR 805, 837 (at [88]).

[55] [2010] 2 WLR 805, 837 (at [89]).

[56] Mance LJ in *Dardana Ltd v Yukos Oil Co* [2002] 2 Lloyd's Rep 326, 333 (at [18]).

one of the relevant grounds in section 103 of the 1996 Act. First, in *Dardana Ltd v Yukos Oil Co* Mance LJ accepted that a respondent's right to rely upon a defence may be lost by another agreement or estoppel.[57] This dictum follows the opinion of the leading commentator on the New York Convention who suggested it would be appropriate to order enforcement 'where the respondent can be deemed to be estopped from invoking the ground for refusal'.[58] Secondly, the court is prepared to exercise its discretion in favour of enforcing the award in a case where the defect which brings one of the grounds for refusal into play is trivial or merely technical (rather than substantial).[59] Conversely, if there is something unsound in 'the fundamental structural integrity of the arbitration proceedings' it is unlikely that the court will exercise discretion in favour of enforcing the award.[60] The fact that the party seeking to resist recognition or enforcement of the award could have applied to the courts of the seat of arbitration to have the award set aside (but failed to do so) does not prevent that party from challenging recognition or enforcement of the award in England on any of the grounds set out in section 103(2) of the 1996 Act.[61] In principle, the fact that the party resisting enforcement has not applied to have the award set aside in proceedings at the seat of arbitration is not something that the court ought to take into account when deciding how to exercise its discretion.[62]

24.2.20 As regards cases falling within the scope of the 1996 Act, the grounds set out in section 103 are exhaustive.[63] Section 103(1) provides that recognition or enforcement of a New York Convention award 'shall not be refused except in the cases' set out in the legislation. If none of the grounds for refusal under the 1996 Act is established, recognition or enforcement cannot be refused for a reason outside the legislation.[64] However, if the person against whom the award is invoked has brought proceedings in the country of origin with a view to having the award set aside the court may, in certain circumstances, adjourn the decision on the recognition or enforcement of the award under section 103(5).[65]

Lack of Capacity: Section 103(2)(a)

24.2.21 Section 103(2)(a) provides that recognition or enforcement of an award may be refused if 'a party to the arbitration agreement was (under the law applicable to him) under some incapacity'. The precursor of Article V(1)(a) (on which section 103(2)(a) is based) was Article 2(1)(b) of the Geneva Convention of 1927, which provides that enforcement of an award shall be refused if the person against whom enforcement is sought 'being under a legal incapacity … was not properly represented'. Although it has been suggested that it would be reasonable for Article V(1)(a)

---

[57] Mance LJ in *Dardana Ltd v Yukos Oil Co* [2002] 2 Lloyd's Rep 326, 330 (at [8]).
[58] AJ van den Berg, *The New York Arbitration Convention of 1958* (Deventer, Kluwer, 1981) 267.
[59] *China Agribusiness Development Corporation v Balli Trading* [1998] 2 Lloyd's Rep 76.
[60] May LJ in *Kanoria v Guinness* [2006] 1 Lloyd's Rep 701, 706 (at [30]).
[61] *Svenska Petroleum Exploration AB v Government of the Republic of Lithuania (No 2)* [2006] QB 886, 921.
[62] *Paklito Investment Ltd v Köckner East Asia Ltd* [1993] 2 HKLR 39 (High Court, Hong Kong).
[63] AJ van den Berg, *The New York Arbitration Convention of 1958* (Deventer, Kluwer, 1981) 265.
[64] *Rosseel NV v Oriental Commercial & Shipping Co (UK) Ltd* [1991] 2 Lloyd's Rep 625.
[65] See paras 24.2.56–24.2.61.

of the Convention to be interpreted in the same sense,[66] this suggestion fails to take into account the fact that Article V(1)(a) is aimed not at the improper representation of a party in the arbitral proceedings (which must be very unusual), but at the invalidity of the arbitration agreement on the basis of the incapacity of one of the parties (which is more likely).

24.2.22   Article V(1)(a) and section 103(2)(a) state simply that, where the incapacity of one of the parties to the arbitration agreement is raised, the relevant law is 'the law applicable to' the party in question. In the absence of any indication in the Convention to the contrary, it is assumed that the applicable law in this context is to be determined by reference to the conflicts rules of the country in which the proceedings are brought. While English law in this area is not free from doubt, it is generally accepted that an individual is regarded as having contractual capacity if he has capacity either under the law of the country where he is domiciled and resident, or under the law of the country with which the contract has its closest and most real connection.[67] As regards corporations, capacity is to be judged by reference to the law under which the company in question is incorporated.[68] Where one of the parties is a state or a state entity the law of that state determines whether that party has the necessary capacity.

Invalidity of the Arbitration Agreement: Section 103(2)(b)

24.2.23   If the arbitration agreement is invalid, any resulting award may be denied recognition or enforcement.[69] The types of question which can arise under section 103(2)(b) obviously include issues that relate to the formal or essential validity of an arbitration agreement. However, this paragraph is broader than its language might suggest. It has been held, for example, that the question whether an alleged party to an arbitration agreement is bound by the agreement is within the scope of the phrase 'the arbitration agreement was not valid'.[70]

24.2.24   Section 103(2)(b) contains two principles: first, recognition or enforcement of an award may be refused if 'the arbitration agreement was not valid under the law to which the parties subjected it'; secondly, where the parties gave no indication of which law should govern the arbitration agreement, recognition or enforcement of an award may be refused if the arbitration agreement was not valid 'under the law of the country where the award was made'. The second principle is premised on the notion that, where the parties have failed to choose the applicable law, an arbitration agreement is governed by the law of the seat of arbitration.[71]

---

[66] P Contini, 'The United Nations Convention on the Recognition and Enforcement of Foreign Arbitral Awards' (1959) 8 *Am J Comp L* 283, 301.

[67] See paras 14.4.19–14.4.26.

[68] See para 14.4.27.

[69] See, eg, *Dalmia Dairy Industries Ltd v National Bank of Pakistan* [1978] 2 Lloyd's Rep 223 (a case decided at common law).

[70] *Dardana Ltd v Yukos Oil Co* [2002] 2 Lloyd's Rep 326; *Dallah Real Estate and Tourism Holding Co v Pakistan Ministry of Religious Affairs* [2010] 2 WLR 805.

[71] S Pisar, 'The United Nations Convention on Foreign Arbitral Awards' [1959] *JBL* 219, 221. See section 21.1.

24.2.25 A question arises whether the first principle applies not only in cases where the parties have expressly chosen a law to govern the arbitration agreement itself but also in cases where the parties have chosen the law to govern the contract of which the arbitration agreement is a part. According to the leading commentator on the New York Convention, the first principle applies only where the parties have expressly selected the law applicable to the arbitration agreement.[72] The second principle in section 103(2)(b), which applies in other cases (including those where the parties' contract includes a choice of law clause, but does not explicitly choose the law to govern the arbitration agreement), makes sense only if the 'the law of the country where the award was made' is understood to mean the law of the seat of arbitration.[73] For the purposes of Part III of the 1996 Act, an award is treated as made at the seat of arbitration.[74] Given that the law of the seat is relevant because it is the proper law of the arbitration agreement, 'the law of the country where the award was made' signifies the substantive law of that country, rather than the substantive law of the country designated by the seat's choice of law rules.[75] Although the courts may recognise or enforce an award even if the arbitration agreement is invalid, they will only do so in exceptional circumstances, for example, where the right to rely upon section 103(2)(b) has been lost through estoppel.[76] It is difficult to imagine circumstances in which it would be appropriate for the court to exercise its discretion in favour of enforcing an award in a case where the party resisting enforcement can satisfy the court that he is not a party to the relevant arbitration agreement.[77]

Procedural Unfairness: Section 103(2)(c)

24.2.26 Section 103(2)(c) provides the party against whom an award is invoked with a defence to recognition or enforcement in cases where the arbitration was conducted in a manner which is not consistent with principles of natural justice. The due process defence contained in section 103(2)(c) has three alternative elements: recognition or enforcement of an award may be refused if the person against whom the award is invoked can prove, first, that 'he was not given proper notice of the appointment of the arbitrator', or secondly, that 'he was not given proper notice of … the arbitration proceedings', or thirdly, that he was 'otherwise unable to present his case'.

24.2.27 Section 103(2)(c) enables the courts of the country addressed to provide a check on the procedural requirements of the curial law. The fact that the procedural rules of the law of the seat of arbitration were complied with is not sufficient to deprive the party against whom the award is invoked of the possibility of resisting recognition or enforcement of the award under section 103(2)(c). To a large extent,

---

[72] AJ van den Berg, *The New York Arbitration Convention of 1958* (Deventer, Kluwer, 1981) 293.

[73] P Sanders, 'Trends in the Field of International Commercial Arbitration' (1975) 145 *Hag Rec* 205, 275.

[74] Arbitration Act 1996, s 100(2)(b).

[75] *Dallah Real Estate and Tourism Holding Co v Pakistan Ministry of Religious Affairs* [2008] 2 Lloyd's Rep 535 (J Grierson and M Taok, 'Comment on *Dallah v Pakistan*' (2009) 26(3) *J Int Arb* 467), affirmed without discussion of this point [2010] 2 WLR 805.

[76] See Mance LJ in *Dardana Ltd v Yukos Oil Co* [2002] 2 Lloyd's Rep 326, 330 (at [8]).

[77] See Moore-Bick LJ in *Dallah Real Estate and Tourism Holding Co v Pakistan Ministry of Religious Affairs* [2010] 2 WLR 805, 826 (at [61]).

the defence under section 103(2)(c) involves questions of fact.[78] It is for the court addressed to determine—according to its own standards of fairness—whether the party resisting recognition or enforcement was given proper notice of the appointment of the arbitrator and the proceedings and whether the party resisting recognition or enforcement was able to present his case. In order to be able to establish that it was unable to present its case within the meaning of section 103(2)(c), the party against whom the award is invoked must be able to establish that he was prevented from presenting his case as a result of matters beyond his control; where the alleged procedural defect is a consequence of a failure to take advantage of the opportunity given to him, he cannot rely on section 103(2)(c).[79]

24.2.28   Where parties agree to arbitrate under institutional arbitration rules the arbitrator generally has a broad discretion over the internal conduct of the arbitration. Article 14.2 of the LCIA Arbitration Rules, for example, provides:

Unless otherwise agreed by the parties ... the Arbitral Tribunal shall have the widest discretion to discharge its duties allowed under such law(s) or rules of law as the Arbitral Tribunal may determine to be applicable.

Except in a most unusual case, the mere fact that the arbitrator adopts one procedural model rather than another does not justify the court in refusing recognition or enforcement under section 103(2)(c). So, for example, where the arbitrator declines to hear oral evidence this cannot, without more, entitle the court to refuse recognition or enforcement on the ground that one of the parties was given insufficient opportunity to present his case.[80] A person seeking to resist the recognition or enforcement of a foreign award may, however, rely on section 103(2)(c) in cases where the tribunal failed to treat the parties equally;[81] the arbitral tribunal must act in a judicial manner[82] and comply with the principle of *audi alteram partem*.[83] So, if the outcome of the arbitration was affected by pressure brought to bear on the arbitrator by a third party, or if the award was based on evidence which was not made available to one of the parties to enable him to comment upon it, the defence in section 103(2)(c) should be available.[84] In a situation where serious illness prevents the respondent from attending the arbitration proceedings and the award is based on allegations of which the respondent was not informed and which he had no opportunity to refute, recognition or enforcement of the award will be refused.[85] The defence in section 103(2)(c) should also be available in cases where the procedural model adopted by the arbitrator unfairly prejudices one party, for example, if the arbitrator conducts a documents-only arbitration in a situation where the evidence of one of the parties consists almost entirely of oral testimony.

---

[78] See, eg, *Irvani v Irvani* [2000] 1 Lloyd's Rep 412.
[79] *Minmetals Germany GmbH v Ferco Steel Ltd* [1999] CLC 647, 657–8.
[80] *Dalmia Dairy Industries Ltd v National Bank of Pakistan* [1978] 2 Lloyd's Rep 223.
[81] *Re Enoch and Zeretsky, Bock & Co's Arbitration* [1910] 1 KB 327 (a case decided at common law).
[82] This would follow from the decision of the Court of Appeal in *Adams v Cape Industries Plc* [1990] Ch 433.
[83] *Minmetals Germany GmbH v Ferco Steel Ltd* [1999] CLC 647.
[84] *Irvani v Irvani* [2000] 1 Lloyd's Rep 412.
[85] *Kanoria v Guinness* [2006] 1 Lloyd's Rep 701.

24.2.29   Finally, it should be recalled that the 1996 Act does not require the court to refuse recognition or enforcement simply because the party against whom the award is invoked establishes one of the grounds in section 103(2). Where the party resisting recognition or enforcement satisfies the court that there was a breach of the principles of natural justice, it may nevertheless be legitimate for the court to uphold the award if it is obvious that the decision of the arbitrator would have been the same even if the irregularity had not occurred.[86] Nevertheless, in the words of May LJ in *Kanoria v Guinness*: 'If the structural integrity [of the arbitration proceedings] is fundamentally unsound, the court is unlikely to make a discretionary decision in favour of enforcing the award.'[87]

Excess of Jurisdiction: Section 103(2)(d) and Section 103(4)

24.2.30   The arbitrator's jurisdiction is determined by the terms of the arbitration agreement. If the arbitrator exceeds his jurisdiction, the award is a nullity and may be set aside by the court with supervisory jurisdiction over the arbitration. However, even if the courts of the seat have not vacated the award for lack of jurisdiction, section 103(2)(d) provides that recognition or enforcement of a New York Convention award may be refused if 'the award deals with a difference not contemplated by or not falling within the terms of the submission to arbitration, or contains decisions on matters beyond the scope of the submission to arbitration'. Whether the arbitrator had the necessary jurisdiction over the dispute dealt with in the award is essentially a question of construction of the arbitration agreement. Accordingly, the scope of the defence is to be determined by reference to the proper law of that agreement. Whether the arbitral tribunal's decision was within its jurisdiction turns solely on the scope of the submission (in terms of the substantive issues raised); for the purposes of section 103(2)(d), the procedure adopted by the tribunal is irrelevant.[88] Where it is possible to distinguish those matters in relation to which the arbitrator did have jurisdiction from those in relation to which he did not, the court may recognise or enforce the award to the extent that it deals with matters falling within the arbitrator's jurisdiction.[89]

24.2.31   The operation of the defence in section 103(2)(d) can be illustrated by *Kianta Osekeyhtio v Britain and Overseas Trading Co Ltd*,[90] a case decided under Part II of the 1950 Act. A Finnish timber merchant contracted to sell a quantity of pit props to an English buyer. The contract, which was governed by Finnish law, included an arbitration clause making provision for the reference of disputes to arbitrators in Finland. When the buyer refused to take delivery of part of the last shipment, the parties entered a compromise agreement, which did not include the arbitration clause. When a dispute arose under the compromise agreement the seller commenced arbitration proceedings in Finland. An award was made in the seller's favour, the buyer having taken no part in the proceedings. The seller then sought to enforce the award

---

[86] AJ van den Berg, *The New York Arbitration Convention of 1958* (Deventer, Kluwer, 1981) 301–02.
[87] [2006] 1 Lloyd's Rep 701, 706 (at [30]).
[88] See Colman J in *Minmetals Germany GmbH v Ferco Steel Ltd* [1999] CLC 647, 656.
[89] Arbitration Act 1996, s 103(4).
[90] [1954] 1 Lloyd's Rep 247.

in England and the question facing the court was whether the arbitration clause in the original contract of sale conferred jurisdiction on the arbitrators in relation to a dispute under the compromise agreement. The Court of Appeal held that, since under Finnish law (which was not different from English law in any material respect) the arbitration clause in the original agreement did not confer jurisdiction on the arbitrators to decide a dispute arising under the compromise agreement, enforcement of the award in England should be refused.

Failure to Comply with the Relevant Procedural Rules: Section 103(2)(e)

24.2.32 Section 103(2)(e) contains two rules: first, recognition or enforcement of an award may be refused if 'the composition of the arbitral authority or the arbitral procedure was not in accordance with the agreement of the parties'; secondly, failing an agreement on these matters, recognition or enforcement of an award may be refused if the composition of the arbitral authority or the arbitral procedure was not in accordance with 'the law of the country where the arbitration took place'. The second of these rules does not give rise to significant problems of interpretation. In the absence of agreement by the parties, procedural matters such as the mechanism for the appointment of the tribunal or the rules regulating the internal conduct of the arbitration are governed by the law of the seat. Failure by the arbitrator to comply with the applicable procedural rules is likely to be a ground for setting aside the award by the court with supervisory jurisdiction over the arbitration as well as providing a basis for refusing recognition or enforcement. However, it is increasingly recognised in international commercial arbitration that a party, who knows (or should have known) that the relevant procedural rules have not been complied with but continues with the arbitration without raising the procedural irregularity with the arbitral tribunal, should be regarded as having waived that procedural irregularity.[91] By the same token, a party who is regarded as having waived a procedural irregularity in the context of the arbitration proceedings should not normally be able to raise that irregularity as a defence to recognition or enforcement under section 102(3)(e).[92]

24.2.33 As regards the operation of the first rule, two situations should be distinguished. First, if there is no conflict between the procedure chosen by the parties and the procedural rules of the law of the seat, it is obvious that the arbitrator should comply with the terms of the parties' agreement, since failure to do so provides a basis for recognition or enforcement of the award being refused. Nevertheless, if the failure to follow the agreed procedure was not significantly prejudicial to the party seeking to resist the award, the court will exercise its discretion in favour of upholding the award.[93] Secondly, if the parties agree on a procedure which is at variance with mandatory procedural rules of the law of the seat, the arbitrator would appear to

---

[91] The relevant rule of English law is to be found in Arbitration Act 1996, s 73; see *Athletic Union of Constantinople v National Basketball Association* [2002] 1 Lloyd's Rep 305. The arbitration rules of many arbitral institutions contain a similar provision: see, eg, Art 33 of the ICC Rules of Arbitration; Art 30 of the UNCITRAL Arbitration Rules.

[92] *Minmetals Germany GmbH v Ferco Steel Ltd* [1999] CLC 647, 659.

[93] *China Agribusiness Development Corporation v Balli Trading* [1998] 2 Lloyd's Rep 76; *Tongyuan (USA) International Trading Group v Uni-Clan Ltd* (2001, unreported).

be placed in an insoluble dilemma. If, on the one hand, the procedure agreed by the parties is followed, the award is liable to be set aside by the court with supervisory jurisdiction over the arbitration—as a consequence of which the ground for refusing recognition or enforcement under Article V(1)(e) of the Convention[94] becomes available. If, on the other hand, the arbitrator ignores the agreement of the parties and complies with the mandatory rules of the law of the seat, recognition or enforcement of the award may be refused under Article V(1)(d) of the Convention.[95]

    24.2.34 As a matter of policy, if the arbitrator departs from the procedure chosen by the parties in order to comply with mandatory rules of the law of the seat, the award should not be denied recognition or enforcement.[96] The discretion conferred by section 103(2) on the court addressed should be exercised in favour of upholding the award in a situation where the arbitrator complies with the mandatory rules of the law of the seat rather than the agreement of the parties. This approach is supported, to some extent, by the Convention's *travaux préparatoires*. The Italian representative on the working party expressed the view that the text of Article V(1)(d) 'should not be interpreted to mean that parties could agree to disregard all national laws and determine some special procedure applicable to their case alone'.[97]

Invalid Award: Section 103(2)(f)

NOT BINDING

24.2.35 The Geneva Convention of 1927—the forerunner of the New York Convention—provides that a foreign award is not enforceable unless it has 'become final in the country in which it was made'.[98] Because the burden is placed on the party seeking to rely on an award to show that the award is 'final', in practice, enforcement of a foreign award under the Geneva Convention depends on the party seeking to rely on the award obtaining a so-called double *exequatur,* that is, an order for enforcement from the courts of the country of origin and an order for enforcement from the court of the country addressed.

    24.2.36 Under the first part of section 103(2)(f) an award may be refused recognition or enforcement if it 'has not yet become binding on the parties'. By using the term 'binding' rather than 'final' the drafters of the Convention intended to avoid the complications generated by the Geneva Convention. So, for the purposes of section 103(2)(f) in order for an award to be 'binding' it does not have to be final in the absolute sense; an award is 'binding' if it has obligatory force between the parties under the curial law and it is no longer open to a genuine appeal on the merits to a second arbitral instance or to a court. Only if there is still the possibility of a genuine appeal in full should an award be regarded as not 'binding'.[99]

---

[94] The corresponding provision of the 1996 Act is s 103(2)(f).
[95] The corresponding provision of the 1996 Act is s 103(2)(e).
[96] AJ van den Berg, 'Recent Enforcement Problems under the New York and ICSID Conventions' (1989) 5 *Arb Int* 2, 9–10. Compare R Nazzini, 'The Law Applicable to the Arbitral Award' (2002) 5(6) *Int ALR* 179.
[97] Cited by P Contini, 'The United Nations Convention on the Recognition and Enforcement of Foreign Arbitral Awards' (1959) 8 *Am J Comp L* 283, 301.
[98] Art I(d); Arbitration Act 1950, s 37(1)(d).
[99] AJ van den Berg, *The New York Arbitration Convention of 1958* (Deventer, Kluwer, 1981) 345.

24.2.37   According to this interpretation, where an arbitration is conducted under the GAFTA arbitration rules, which provide that any party dissatisfied with an arbitration award has a right to appeal to a board of appeal, the award only becomes 'binding' for the purposes of the 1996 Act if either an appeal has been heard or the time limit for bringing an appeal has expired. On the other hand, the possibility of an appeal on a point of law under section 69 of the 1996 Act is not sufficient to deprive an English award of its 'binding' nature for the purposes of the Convention.[100] *A fortiori*, an award is not to be regarded as not 'binding' simply because there is the possibility of proceedings for setting aside the award in the country of origin.[101]

SET ASIDE OR SUSPENDED

24.2.38   The second limb of the defence in section 103(2)(f) provides that recognition or enforcement may be refused if the award 'has been set aside or suspended by a competent authority of the country in which, or under the law of which, it was made'. On the basis of this provision, where an award is made under an arbitration agreement providing for arbitration in France, if the French court sets aside the award, the award may be refused enforcement in England. As it is clear that, for the purposes of this provision, the drafters of the Convention intended that 'the country in which … [the award] was made' should signify the country in which the seat of arbitration was located,[102] the English legislation provides that an award is treated as made at the seat of arbitration, regardless of where it is signed.[103] Although the court has discretion whether to enforce a foreign award in cases where one of the defences in section 103(2) is established, the English court should normally respect a decision of the court of origin and should refuse to recognise or enforce an award which has been set aside in the country of origin. It is to be expected that, if the party against whom an award is invoked is able to make out the defence in section 103(2)(f), the court will normally refuse to recognise or enforce the award.[104] Notwithstanding instances in which the courts of some other countries have enforced awards which have been set aside in the country of origin,[105] in the absence of exceptional circumstances (such as where

---

[100]   *Ibid.*

[101]   *AB Götaverken v General National Maritime Transport Co* (1981) 6 *YB Comm Arb* 237 (Supreme Court, Sweden).

[102]   P Sanders, 'Trends in the Field of International Commercial Arbitration' (1975) 145 *Hag Rec* 205, 274.

[103]   Arbitration Act 1996, s 102(b).

[104]   In *Tongyuan (USA) International Trading Group v Uni-Clan Ltd* (2001, unreported) Moore-Bick J accepted the idea that, in the event of the arbitration proceedings being a nullity, the court ought not to enforce the award.

[105]   See HG Gharavi, *The International Effectiveness of the Annulment of an Arbitral Award* (The Hague, Kluwer, 2002). For discussion of the French and US cases, see DH Freyer, 'United States Recognition and Enforcement of Annulled Foreign Arbitral Awards' (2000) 17(2) *J Int Arb* 1; E Gaillard, '*Baker Marine* and *Spier* Strike a Blow to the Enforceability in the United States of Awards Set Aside at the Seat' (2000) 3(2) *Int ALR* 37; P Lastenouse, 'Why Setting Aside an Arbitral Award is not Enough to Remove it from the International Scene' (1999) 16(2) *J Int Arb* 25; G Petrochilos, 'Enforcing Awards Annulled in their State of Origin under the New York Convention' (1999) 48 *ICLQ* 856; MD Slater, 'On Annulled Arbitral Awards and the Death of *Chromalloy*' (2009) 25 Arb Int 271; P Wahl, 'Enforcement of Foreign Arbitral Awards Set Aside in their Country of Origin' (1999) 16(4) *J Int Arb* 131; T Webster, 'Evolving Principles in Enforcing Awards Subject to Annulment Proceedings' (2006) 23(3) *J Int Arb* 201; C Koch, 'The Enforcement of Awards Annulled in their Place of Origin' (2009) 26(2) *J Int Arb* 267. For the position in Austria and Germany, see GJ Horvath, 'What Weight Should be Given to the Annulment of an Award under the

the award was improperly set aside by the court of origin[106] or where the judgment setting aside the award conflicts with the public policy of the country addressed), the arguments against the recognition or enforcement of awards which have been annulled by the courts of the seat are normally overwhelming.[107] It is worth noting, however, that in *Dallah Real Estate and Tourism Holding Co v Pakistan Ministry of Religious Affairs* the Court of Appeal somewhat elliptically suggested that the court's discretion to permit enforcement, notwithstanding that the award has been set aside in the country of origin, 'may be somewhat broader than has previously been recognised'.[108]

24.2.39   In some legal systems an application to set aside an award suspends the award by operation of law; in others the court of the country of origin may, on an application to set aside, make an order suspending the award.[109] If a party seeks to enforce a foreign award in England, and the person against whom the award is invoked applies to have the award set aside in the country of origin, may the English court order enforcement, notwithstanding the fact that the award is suspended in the country of origin? According to a leading commentator, recognition or enforcement may be refused only if the party resisting recognition or enforcement proves that suspension of the award has been ordered by the court in the country of origin[110] and this view has been followed by the English courts.[111] According to this view, the automatic suspension of the award by operation of law in the country of origin is not sufficient.

24.2.40   As a final point it should be noted that section 103(2)(f) is intended also to deal with the rare situations where the parties, by express agreement, sever the link between the curial law and the seat of arbitration. In a case where parties agree to refer disputes to arbitration in country X under the curial law of country Y, recognition or enforcement of the award may be refused in England if the award is set aside in country X or in country Y.

Non-arbitrability

24.2.41   Section 103(3) provides that recognition or enforcement of an award 'may also be refused if the award is in respect of a matter which is not capable of settlement by arbitration'. The 1996 Act does not state the law by reference to which the arbitrability of the dispute is to be referred. The provision of the Convention on which section 103(3) is based indicates that recognition or enforcement may be refused

---

Lex Arbitri?' (2009) 26(2) *J Int Arb* 249. See also CR Drahozal, 'Enforcing Vacated International Arbitration Awards: An Economic Approach' (2002) 11 *Am Rev Int'l Arb* 451.

[106] See Rix LJ in *Dallah Real Estate and Tourism Holding Co v Pakistan Ministry of Religious Affairs* [2010] 2 WLR 805, 838 (at [90]).

[107] R Goode, 'The Role of the *Lex Loci Arbitri* in International Commercial Arbitration' (2001) 17 *Arb Int* 19, 29–38.

[108] Moore-Bick LJ at [2010] 2 WLR 805, 826 (at [59]).

[109] Where an application is made to set aside an English award the court has inherent jurisdiction to suspend the award pending the outcome of the setting aside proceedings in England (thereby providing a defence against the award's enforcement under Art V(1)(e)—the equivalent of s 103(2)(f) of the 1996 Act—in other New York Convention states): *Apis AS v Fantazia Kereskedelmi KFT* [2001] 1 All ER (Comm) 348.

[110] AJ van den Berg, *The New York Arbitration Convention of 1958* (Deventer, Kluwer, 1981) 352.

[111] *IPCO (Nigeria) Ltd v Nigerian National Petroleum Corporation* [2005] 2 Lloyd's Rep 326, 328.

if the subject-matter of the dispute is not capable of settlement by arbitration under the law of the country addressed.[112] Under English law, however, there are very few restrictions as to the type of dispute which may be referred to arbitration,[113] and there is no reported case in which enforcement of a New York Convention award in England has been resisted on this basis. It has been argued[114] that the English court may, in reliance on section 103(3) of the 1996 Act, refuse to enforce an award in a case where the dispute was not arbitrable under the law of the seat of arbitration. [115]

24.2.42   Two further points should be noted: first, if the dispute is not arbitrable under the proper law of the arbitration agreement, the arbitration agreement may be regarded as invalid[116]—in which case recognition or enforcement of the award could be refused under section 103(2)(b); secondly, if the dispute is not arbitrable under the law of the seat the award is likely to be set aside—as a consequence of which recognition or enforcement may be refused under section 103(2)(f).

Public Policy

24.2.43   Section 103(3) also provides that the court may refuse to recognise or enforce an award 'if it would be contrary to public policy' to do so; in this context, the public policy referred to is the public policy of England (as the country in which recognition or enforcement is sought). Since EU law is part of national law, for the purposes of section 103(3) of the 1996 Act, public policy includes EU public policy as well as English public policy. In *Eco Swiss China Time Ltd v Benetton International NV*,[117] in the context of a dispute arising out of a licensing agreement, a Dutch arbitral tribunal ordered the respondent to pay damages to the claimant. The respondent brought proceedings in the Dutch courts contending that the licensing contract was a nullity under Article 81 EC and that the award should be set aside on the ground that it was contrary to public policy. During the arbitration proceedings the argument that the licensing contract might be contrary to EC law had not been raised. Following a reference under Article 234 EC, the Court of Justice ruled that:

a national court to which application is made for annulment of an arbitration award must grant that application if it considers that the award in question is in fact contrary to Article 81 EC (ex Article 85), where its domestic rules of procedure require it to grant an application for annulment founded on failure to observe national rules of public policy.[118]

---

[112]   Art V(2).

[113]   See paras 20.2.10–20.2.12.

[114]   See M Danov, 'The law governing arbitrability under the Arbitration Act 1996' [2008] *LMCLQ* 536, 542–4.

[115]   According to this argument, enforcement in England of a Belgian award relating to a dispute arising from a distributorship agreement may be refused on the basis that the dispute is not arbitrable under Belgian law. See *Audi-NSU Auto Union AG v Adelin Petit et Cie SA* [1980] ECC 235 (Court of Cassation, Belgium).

[116]   See para 21.2.11.

[117]   Case C–126/97 [1999] ECR I–3055. TD de Groot, 'The Impact of the *Benetton* Decision on International Commercial Arbitration' (2003) 20(4) *J Int Arb* 365; C Liebscher, 'European Public Policy After *Eco Swiss*' (1999) 10 *Am Rev Int'l Arb* 81; P Pinsolle, 'Private Enforcement of European Community Competition Rules by Arbitrators' (2004) 7 *Int ALR* 14; RB von Mehren, 'The *Eco-Swiss* Case and International Arbitration' (2003) 19 *Arb Int* 465.

[118]   Case C–126/97 [1999] ECR I–3055, para 39.

The Court of Justice also indicated that the provisions of Article 81 EC should be regarded as a matter of public policy within the meaning of the New York Convention.[119] So, where an arbitrator upholds and enforces a contract which is in breach of the terms of EU competition law, the award should be refused enforcement.[120]

24.2.44   Nevertheless, the scope of public policy should be narrowly circumscribed: 'The reference to public policy in section 103(3) was not intended to furnish an open-ended escape route for refusing enforcement of New York Convention awards.'[121] The mere fact that the court would have decided the dispute differently from the arbitral tribunal is not enough to justify the invocation of public policy; recognition or enforcement should not be refused on the ground of public policy unless recognition or enforcement 'would violate the forum state's most basic notions of morality and justice'.[122] In *Deutsche Schachtbau- und Tiefbohrgesellschaft mbH v Shell International Petroleum Co Ltd* Donaldson MR thought that an award should not be refused enforcement on the ground of public policy unless:

there is some element of illegality or that the enforcement would be clearly contrary to the public good or, possibly, that enforcement would be wholly offensive to the ordinary reasonable and fully informed members of the public on whose behalf the powers of the state are exercised.[123]

The mere fact that the arbitral tribunal reached a different conclusion from that which the court would have reached is not a ground for refusing to recognise or enforce the award on grounds of public policy.[124]

AWARDS BASED ON THE *LEX MERCATORIA* OR ARBITRATION *EXTRA LEGEM*

24.2.45   It is not contrary to public policy to enforce a foreign award in cases where the arbitrator decided the merits of the dispute on the basis of 'some system of "law" which is not that of England or any other state or is a serious modification of

---

[119]   Case C–126/97 [1999] ECR I–3055, para 38.

[120]   See the decision of the German Bundesfinanzhof (Decision of 27 February 1969, (1969) 22 NJW 978–80; cited by G Bebr, 'Arbitration Tribunals and Article 177 of the EEC Treaty' (1985) 22 *CML Rev* 489, 498 n 16) in which the court refused to allow the enforcement of an award on the ground that the award settled a dispute in a way which was contrary to what is now Art 101 TFEU. For conflicting views on the significance of the decision of the Paris court of appeal in *Thalès Air Defence BV v GIR Euromissile*, see D Bensaude, '*Thalès Air Defence BV v GIR Euromissile*: Defining the Limits of Scrutiny of Awards Based on Alleged Violations of European Competition Law' (2005) 22(3) *J Int Arb* 239; G Blanke, 'Defining the Limits of Scrutiny of Awards Based on Alleged Violations of European Competition Law: A *Réplique* to Denis Bensaude's "*Thalès Air Defence BV v GIR Euromissile*"' (2006) 23(3) *J Int Arb* 239; T Thomasi, 'The Paris court of appeal looks at a request for the annulment of an award for breach of EC competition law: a first application in France of the principles laid down by the ECJ in *Eco Swiss*' (2005) 8(2) Int ALR 55. See also the more recent decision of the Court of Cassation in *Société SNF SAS v Société Cytec industries BV*: www.courdecassation.fr/jurisprudence_2/premiere_chambre_civile_568/arrets_569/br_arret_11652.html.

[121]   Gross J in *IPCO (Nigeria) Ltd v Nigerian National Petroleum Corporation* [2005] 2 Lloyd's Rep 326, 329 (at [13]).

[122]   *Parsons & Whittemore Overseas Co Inc v Société Générale de l'Industrie du Papier* 508 F 2d 969 (2d Cir, 1974). See also *Amaltal Corporation Ltd v Maruha (NZ) Corporation Ltd* [2003] 2 NZLR 92 (High Court, New Zealand); *Broström Tankers AB v Factorias Vulcano SA* [2004] 2 IR 191 (High Court, Ireland).

[123]   [1990] 1 AC 295, 316.

[124]   See, eg, *Amaltal Corporation Ltd v Maruha (NZ) Corporation Ltd* [2004] 2 NZLR 614 (Court of Appeal, New Zealand), a case in which the arbitral tribunal enforced a contractual penalty clause which the court would not have upheld.

such a law'.[125] Recognition or enforcement of an award made under an arbitration agreement in which the parties agree that the 'applicable law' to govern the dispute is 'some set of principles not law or a law other than the law of a particular country'[126] (such as Sharia law or Jewish law) is entitled to enforcement under the 1996 Act. In *Norske Atlas Insurance Co Ltd v London General Insurance Co Ltd* the court ordered enforcement in England of a Norwegian award, notwithstanding the fact that the parties had expressly provided that the arbitrators 'must not necessarily judge according to the strict law but as a general rule ought chiefly to consider the principles of practical business'.[127] If the parties to the agreement intended to create legally enforceable rights and obligations and if the resulting agreement is sufficiently certain to constitute a legally enforceable contract, the award is *prima facie* enforceable.[128] The mere fact that the arbitrator decided the dispute according to 'internationally accepted principles of law governing contractual relations' does not render the award unenforceable on grounds of public policy.[129]

ILLEGALITY AND COMITY

24.2.46 *Dalmia Dairy Industries Ltd v National Bank of Pakistan*[130]—a case decided at common law—involved two awards made following arbitrations conducted in Geneva under the ICC Rules of Arbitration. The awards directed the defendant to make certain payments in India. The defendant raised two points of public policy: first, it was argued that enforcement of the award would be contrary to public policy on the basis that in order to comply with the award the defendant, a bank registered in Pakistan, would have to perform acts which were unlawful under the law of Pakistan, namely the transfer of foreign exchange from Pakistan to India; secondly, the defendant argued that it was contrary to public policy to enforce an award between persons who are nationals of foreign states at war with each other.

24.2.47 On the second point, the Court of Appeal rejected the defendant's argument:

[I]t would [not] be harmful to this country's international relations with friendly countries if it were to allow the machinery of its courts to be used to enforce a judgment, or an arbitral award, in favour of a national of one foreign state, friendly to the United Kingdom, against the national of another foreign state, also friendly to the United Kingdom, where the two foreign states are enemies of one another.[131]

There is, however, an implicit acceptance of the idea that, if enforcement of an award would involve a breach of comity, the defence of public policy may be invoked.

---

[125] Donaldson MR in *Deutsche Schachtbau- und Tiefbohrgesellschaft mbH v Shell International Petroleum Co Ltd* [1990] 1 AC 295, 315.
[126] See Waller LJ in *Halpern v Halpern (Nos 1 & 2)* [2008] QB 195, 214 (at [37]).
[127] MacKinnon J at (1927) 28 Ll L Rep 104, 107.
[128] Donaldson MR in *Deutsche Schachtbau- und Tiefbohrgesellschaft mbH v Shell International Petroleum Co Ltd* [1990] 1 AC 295, 316.
[129] *Deutsche Schachtbau- und Tiefbohrgesellschaft mbH v Shell International Petroleum Co Ltd* [1990] 1 AC 295. See also DW Rivkin, 'Enforceability of Arbitral Awards Based on *Lex Mercatoria*' (1993) 9 *Arb Int* 67.
[130] [1978] 2 Lloyd's Rep 223.
[131] [1978] 2 Lloyd's Rep 223, 300.

24.2.48 The first point was rejected on the authority of *Kleinwort, Sons & Co v Ungarische Baumwolle Industrie Aktiengesellschaft*.[132] On the facts of the case, the act to be done by the defendant, both under the contract and under the awards, was to make a payment in India, not in Pakistan, and by Indian law the payment was lawful.[133] However, what emerges from this decision is an implicit acceptance that, had the award been in terms such that the debtor was required to perform an obligation which was illegal by the law of the place of performance, the court would have refused to enforce the award on the basis of public policy. This is the significance of the observation by Donaldson MR in the *Deutsche Schachtbau* case to the effect that the public policy defence may succeed if 'there is some element of illegality'.[134]

24.2.49 The extent to which the recognition or enforcement of awards should be refused on public policy grounds in cases involving illegality was considered further by the courts in a series of cases decided in the 1990s. In general terms, if the allegation that the underlying contract was illegal was raised before the arbitral tribunal and rejected by it, there is no reason for the award not to be recognised or enforced in England.[135] In *Westacre Investments Ltd v Jugoimport-SPDR Holding Co Ltd*[136] the plaintiff sought to enforce an arbitral award made by ICC arbitrators in Switzerland. The defendant argued that enforcement of the award should be refused on grounds of public policy; it was the defendant's contention that the underlying contract between the parties—a consultancy agreement under the terms of which the plaintiff undertook to exercise personal influence in Kuwait with a view to certain contracts for the supply of military equipment being awarded to the defendant—was, in reality, a contract whose purpose was the bribery of Kuwaiti officials and was illegal under the law of Kuwait. This issue had been raised in the arbitral proceedings in Geneva, but the arbitral tribunal had upheld the contract and made an award ordering the defendant to pay various sums due under the contract to the claimant. Furthermore, the bribery issue had been raised and rejected in setting aside proceedings brought by the defendant in the Swiss courts. When the defendant sought to raise the illegality issue in the English enforcement proceedings, the questions facing the court were whether the alleged illegality of the underlying contract could be re-opened and whether enforcement of the award should be refused on grounds of public policy. A majority of the Court of Appeal held that, given that the bribery allegation had been made, entertained and rejected by the arbitral tribunal, in the absence of fresh evidence which had not been available to the defendant at the time of the hearing before the tribunal, there was no justification either for allowing the illegality point to be re-opened in the English enforcement proceedings or for refusing to enforce the award.[137]

24.2.50 In *Soleimany v Soleimany*[138] a dispute between two Iranian Jews (father and son) had been referred to arbitration in England before the Beth Din under

---

[132] [1939] 2 KB 678.

[133] Kerr J at [1978] 2 Lloyd's Rep 223, 267.

[134] [1990] 1 AC 295, 316.

[135] *Soinco SACI v Novokuznetsk Aluminium Plant* [1998] 2 Lloyd's Rep 337.

[136] [2000] 1 QB 288. N Enonchong, 'The enforcement of foreign arbitral awards based on illegal contracts' [2000] *LMCLQ* 495.

[137] See the judgment of Mantell LJ at [2000] 1 QB 288, 316–17. See also *R v V* [2009] 1 Lloyd's Rep 97 (a case involving an application to set aside an English award on the ground of public policy under Arbitration Act 1996, s 68(2)(g)).

[138] [1999] QB 785. J Harris and F Meisel, 'Public policy and the enforcement of international arbitration awards: controlling the unruly horse' [1998] *LMCLQ* 568.

Jewish law. Although the arbitrator found that he was dealing with an illicit enterprise under which it was the parties' common intention that carpets would be smuggled illegally out of Iran for re-sale in the United Kingdom and elsewhere, he upheld the contract (which was not illegal under Jewish law) and made an award ordering the defendant to pay various sums to the plaintiff. When the plaintiff sought to enforce the award, the defendant argued that enforcement should be refused on grounds of public policy. The Court of Appeal refused to enforce the award:

An English court will not enforce … a contract governed by the law of a foreign and friendly state, or which requires performance in such a country, if performance is illegal by the law of that country … This rule applies as much to the enforcement of an arbitration award as to the direct enforcement of a contract in legal proceedings.[139]

24.2.51   Both the *Westacre* and *Soleimany* cases were considered by Timothy Walker J in *Omnium de Traitement et de Valorisation SA v Hillmarton Ltd*,[140] another case involving an award made by ICC arbitrators in Switzerland. The dispute between the parties arose out of a consultancy contract under the terms of which H undertook to approach public servants and members of the government in Algeria with a view to a public works contract being awarded to OTV, which undertook to pay commission to H if it was awarded the contract. Although it was awarded the contract OTV paid only half the agreed fees. In the award, the arbitrators acknowledged that the parties' contract 'wittingly' breached an Algerian statute which prohibits the intervention of middlemen in public works contracts. Nevertheless, the award ordered OTV to pay the other half of the agreed fees. When H sought to enforce the award in England, OTV argued that, on the authority of the *Soleimany* case, enforcement of the award should be refused on grounds of public policy as the underlying contract between the parties was unlawful under the law of the place of performance (Algerian law). Timothy Walker J, however, ordered enforcement of the award; in his view, the important point was that, although the contract was illegal under Algerian law, the arbitrators had found that there was no element of corruption or illicit practice. Accordingly, the case was to be regarded as being more akin to *Westacre Investments Ltd v Jugoimport-SPDR Holding Co Ltd,* in which the arbitral tribunal had rejected the defendant's bribery allegations.

24.2.52   Although it might be conceded that the illegality under Algerian law in *Omnium de Traitement et de Valorisation SA v Hillmarton Ltd* was less serious than the illegality under Iranian law in the *Soleimany* case, it is difficult to reconcile Timothy Walker J's decision with the Court of Appeal's analysis in *Soleimany v Soleimany*. The basis of the *Soleimany* decision is that the English courts will not enforce—either directly or indirectly—contracts whose performance is illegal at the place of performance. As Waller LJ noted:

Where public policy is involved, the interposition of an arbitration award does not isolate the successful party's claim from the illegality which gave rise to it.[141]

It is clear from Timothy Walker J's judgment[142] that, had the underlying contract between H and OTV come before the English courts, its enforcement would have

---

[139] Waller LJ at [1999] QB 785, 803–04.
[140] [1999] 2 Lloyd's Rep 222. J Hill, 'Illegality under the law of the place of performance and the enforcement of arbitration awards' [2000] *LMCLQ* 311.
[141] [1999] QB 785, 800.
[142] [1999] 2 Lloyd's Rep 222, 224.

been refused on the authority of *Regazzoni v KC Sethia (1944) Ltd.*[143] In such circumstances, enforcement of the award in *Omnium de Traitement et de Valorisation SA v Hillmarton Ltd* should have been refused under section 103(3) of the 1996 Act.

SUBSTANTIAL JUSTICE

24.2.53 In parallel with the defence under section 103(2)(c) (which allows a court to refuse recognition or enforcement on the grounds of procedural irregularity), the defence of public policy extends to cases where the award was arrived at by means which were contrary to the requirements of substantial justice contained in English law as explained in *Adams v Cape Industries plc*[144] by the Court of Appeal.[145] However, in such cases, the court is often being invited to sit in judgment on the courts of the seat, which have supervisory jurisdiction over the arbitration and whose role it is to provide remedies in cases of procedural mishap. Accordingly, the policy of upholding the requirements of substantial justice has to balanced against 'the policy of sustaining the finality of international awards' and 'the policy of sustaining the finality of the determination of properly referred procedural issues by the courts of the supervisory jurisdiction'.[146] There may be some exceptional cases in which the supervisory powers of the courts of the seat are so limited that substantial injustice cannot be corrected by those courts; in such cases, recognition or enforcement of the award may be refused under section 103(3). However, where the party against whom an award is invoked seeks to rely on the defence of public policy, the English court should not normally become involved in a re-investigation of alleged procedural defects which were considered by the courts of the seat.

FRAUD

24.2.54 In a case where an award is procured by fraud (or by conduct which is tantamount to fraud), recognition or enforcement of the award would be contrary to public policy. If, for example, a claimant obtains an award in his favour by deliberately suppressing the existence of a document which is detrimental to his claim, the award is obtained by fraud and its recognition or enforcement would be contrary to public policy.[147] The party seeking to resist recognition or enforcement must be able to point to 'some form of reprehensible or unconscionable conduct' by the successful party which 'contributed in a substantial way' to the award being obtained in that party's favour.[148] The type of conduct which would bring public policy into the picture is 'conduct which we would feel comfortable in describing as fraud, conduct dishonestly intended to mislead'.[149]

---

[143] [1958] AC 301. See para 14.3.26.
[144] [1990] Ch 433. See paras 12.4.4–12.4.8.
[145] *Minmetals Germany GmbH v Ferco Steel Ltd* [1999] CLC 647, 659.
[146] Colman J in *Minmetals Germany GmbH v Ferco Steel Ltd* [1999] CLC 647, 661.
[147] *Profilati Italia Srl v PaineWebber Inc* [2001] 1 Lloyd's Rep 715.
[148] Tomlinson J in *Gater Assets Ltd v Nak Naftogaz Ukrainiy (No 2)* [2008] 1 Lloyd's Rep 479, 497 (at [40]).
[149] Tomlinson J in *Gater Assets Ltd v Nak Naftogaz Ukrainiy (No 2)* [2008] 1 Lloyd's Rep 479, 497 (at [41]).

No Review of the Merits

24.2.55 In cases falling within the scope of the 1996 Act the list of grounds for refusing recognition or enforcement is exhaustive.[150] Accordingly, as a general rule, there can be no review of a New York Convention award on the merits by the court addressed, even if the arbitrator has manifestly erred on questions of fact or law.

Discretion to Adjourn the Decision on Recognition or Enforcement

24.2.56 Section 103(2)(f) enables the court to refuse recognition or enforcement if the award has been set aside in the country of origin. Section 103(5) deals with the situation where proceedings to have the award set aside have been commenced in the country of origin, but before those proceedings are resolved an application is made to enforce the award (or have it recognised) in England. Section 103(5), which confers a discretion on the English court, provides:

Where an application for the setting aside or suspension of the award has been made to such a competent authority as is mentioned in subsection (2)(f), the court before which the award is sought to be relied upon may, if it thinks fit, adjourn the decision on the recognition or enforcement of the award.

It may also on the application of the party claiming recognition or enforcement of the award order the other party to give suitable security.

The rationale of section 103(5) is clear. If, after an award has been made in country X, the creditor applies for enforcement in country Y and the debtor applies to have the award set aside in country X, it would be unfortunate if the courts of country Y ordered enforcement, only for the courts of country X to set aside the award. The court's power to grant a stay does not arise unless an application has been made as contemplated by section 103(2)(f).[151] If such an application has been made, the court has the power to consider of its own motion whether a stay should be granted, even if neither of the parties applies for the decision on the recognition or enforcement of the award to be adjourned.[152]

24.2.57 There is some disagreement about the correct approach which should be adopted to the exercise of the discretion under section 103(5). At one extreme it has been suggested that recognition or enforcement should invariably be postponed when an application for setting aside the award has been made, particularly when security for the award is provided by the respondent in the context of the proceedings in which recognition or enforcement is claimed.[153] This suggestion cannot, however,

---

[150] *Rosseel NV v Oriental Commercial & Shipping Co (UK) Ltd* [1991] 2 Lloyd's Rep 625.

[151] See Waller J in *Arab Business Consortium International Finance and Investment Co v Banque Franco-Tunisienne* [1996] 1 Lloyd's Rep 485, 492; Mance LJ in *Dardana Ltd v Yukos Oil Co* [2002] 2 Lloyd's Rep 326, 335 (at [27]).

[152] See Waller J in *Arab Business Consortium International Finance and Investment Co v Banque Franco-Tunisienne* [1996] 1 Lloyd's Rep 485, 492; Mance LJ in *Dardana Ltd v Yukos Oil Co* [2002] 2 Lloyd's Rep 326, 334 (at [23]).

[153] VS Deshpande, 'Enforcement of Foreign Awards in India, UK and USA' (1987) 4(1) *J Int Arb* 41, 53.

be supported; if the courts invariably stay enforcement proceedings, they present the unsuccessful respondent with a simple means of frustrating the claimant's legitimate interests by slowing down the enforcement process. Experience shows that the chances of the respondent being successful in his application to have the award set aside in the country of origin are likely to be small. Since the delay caused by the stay will prejudice the claimant by depriving him of the spoils of victory, as a general rule, a stay should be refused. A stay is only appropriate if the respondent offers 'some summary proof that the award is tainted by a defect which is likely to cause its setting aside in the country of origin'.[154]

24.2.58 The court of the country addressed has a discretion whether the party seeking to resist the award should have to provide security (for example, in the form of a bank guarantee) to secure the amount of the award and accruing interest. The view has been expressed that 'it is difficult to think of any circumstances in which security would not be warranted'.[155] This view has not, however, commended itself to the Court of Appeal:

If, for example, the challenge to the validity of an award is manifestly well-founded, it would be quite wrong to order security until that is demonstrated in a foreign court.[156]

24.2.59 In *Soleh Boneh International Ltd v Government of the Republic of Uganda* the Court of Appeal decided that there are two important factors which should be considered in the context of an application to adjourn enforcement proceedings:

The first is the strength of the argument that the award is invalid, as perceived on a brief consideration of the court which is asked to enforce the award while proceedings to set it aside are pending elsewhere. If the award is manifestly invalid, there should be an adjournment and no order for security; if it is manifestly valid, there should either be an order for immediate enforcement, or else an order for substantial security. In between there will be various degrees of plausibility in the argument for invalidity and the judge must be guided by his preliminary conclusion on the point. The second point is that the court must consider the ease or difficulty of enforcement of the award, and whether it will be rendered more difficult, for example, by movement of assets or by improvident trading, if enforcement is delayed.[157]

On the basis of this approach, where the court considers that the losing party has little prospect of persuading the courts of the seat of arbitration to set aside the award, it would not be inappropriate to adjourn enforcement but to order security of a sum representing 80 per cent of the claim (plus interests and costs).[158] Where part of the sum awarded by the arbitral tribunal is indisputably due, the English court may order immediate enforcement of this sum—notwithstanding the setting aside proceedings in the country of origin—and, as regard the remainder, order such security as is appropriate in all the circumstances.[159]

---

[154] AJ van den Berg, *The New York Arbitration Convention of 1958* (Deventer, Kluwer, 1981) 353–4.

[155] WM Tupman, 'Staying Enforcement of Arbitral Awards under the New York Convention' (1987) 3 *Arb Int* 209, 223.

[156] Staughton LJ in *Soleh Boneh International Ltd v Government of the Republic of Uganda* [1993] 2 Lloyd's Rep 208, 212.

[157] Staughton LJ at [1993] 2 Lloyd's Rep 208, 212.

[158] See Colman J in *Minmetals Germany GmbH v Ferco Steel Ltd* [1999] CLC 647, 654.

[159] See *IPCO (Nigeria) Ltd v Nigerian National Petroleum Corporation* [2005] 2 Lloyd's Rep 326; *Nigerian National Petroleum Corporation v IPCO (Nigeria) Ltd (No 2)* [2009] 1 Lloyd's Rep 89.

24.2.60 Exceptionally, the claimant may, having commenced enforcement proceedings in England, apply for a stay of those proceedings pending the outcome of a challenge to the award brought before the courts of the seat of arbitration. In such a case, the court has discretion to order security—though there can be no question of making the provision of security a condition of adjournment, otherwise the respondent could be unfairly deprived of the opportunity of having its application under section 103(2)(f) determined on its merits.[160] Unless the claimant produces some evidence that there is a danger that, during the adjournment, the respondent will act in such a way that enforcement of the award will be rendered more difficult, there is no obvious reason why the court should exercise its discretion in favour of ordering security.

24.2.61 Although the court has no inherent jurisdiction to postpone enforcement of an award for reasons other than those contemplated by section 103(5),[161] it has been held that the court enjoys a wider discretion once the claimant has converted an award into an English judgment by obtaining permission to enforce the award under the summary procedure. In *Far Eastern Shipping Co v AKP Sovcomflot*,[162] after the plaintiff had obtained leave to enforce a New York Convention award in the same manner as a judgment, the defendant applied for a stay of enforcement. The plaintiff contested the court's jurisdiction to grant the stay. Potter J decided that the court did have the necessary jurisdiction:

[H]aving elected to convert an award into an English judgment, the plaintiff ought in principle to be subject to the same procedural rules and conditions as generally apply to the enforcement of such judgments.[163]

It should be added, however, that Potter J recognised that the court will rarely, if ever, regard it as appropriate to make an order staying enforcement in respect of a New York Convention award[164] and, on the facts of the case, a stay was refused.

24.3 RECOGNITION AND ENFORCEMENT OF FOREIGN AWARDS AT COMMON LAW

The Relationship between the Arbitration Act 1996 and the Common Law

24.3.1 A foreign award which is not entitled to recognition or enforcement under the 1996 Act (for example, because the party against whom the award is invoked successfully raises one of the grounds for refusal under Part III of the 1996 Act) may nevertheless be entitled to recognition or enforcement in England under the common law. It was the aim of the New York Convention to facilitate the international recognition and enforcement of awards, not to abrogate national regimes for the recognition and enforcement of awards which are less stringent than the Convention regime.

---

[160] *Dardana Ltd v Yukos Oil Co* [2002] 2 Lloyd's Rep 326, 335 and 342 (at [29] and [53]).
[161] See Waller J in *Arab Business Consortium International Finance and Investment Co v Banque Franco-Tunisienne* [1996] 1 Lloyd's Rep 485, 492.
[162] [1995] 1 Lloyd's Rep 521.
[163] [1995] 1 Lloyd's Rep 521, 523–4.
[164] [1995] 1 Lloyd's Rep 521, 524.

Accordingly, Article VII(1) of the Convention (the 'more favourable right' clause) provides that the provisions of the Convention shall not 'deprive any interested party of any right he may have to avail himself of an arbitral award in the manner and to the extent allowed by the law or the treaties of the country where such award is sought to be relied upon'. This provision is implemented by section 104, which states that nothing in the 1996 Act 'affects any right to rely upon or enforce a New York Convention award at common law'. Of course, an award which is made in a country which is not a party to the Convention cannot be enforced under the Convention; it may, however, be enforceable at common law.

Methods of Enforcement

24.3.2 A foreign award which is entitled to enforcement at common law may be enforced in the same manner as a domestic award. The party seeking to rely on the award is not restricted to bringing a claim on the award; a foreign award may be enforced by obtaining permission to enforce under section 66 of the 1996 Act.[165] Nevertheless, two limitations on the scope of section 66 should be noted in this context. First, section 66 is not available where, according to the terms of the award which the claimant is seeking to enforce, the defendant is obliged to make payment in a foreign country.[166] Secondly, it is to be expected that the more frequently used method of enforcing a foreign award at common law is by means of a claim on the award. Indeed, even where summary enforcement under section 66 is in principle available, the court may refuse to give permission to enforce:

In many, and perhaps most, cases of non-convention awards there may well be circumstances which would lead the court to the conclusion that the summary method of enforcement … is not an appropriate remedy if this is challenged.[167]

Conditions for Recognition or Enforcement at Common Law

24.3.3 A New York Convention award is presumed to be entitled to recognition or enforcement, the burden being placed on the party seeking to resist the award to establish a ground of refusal. At common law, however, there are conditions which must be satisfied by the person seeking to rely on the award before recognition or enforcement of a foreign award can be considered.

24.3.4 In order for a foreign award to be entitled to recognition or enforcement in England at common law, the person claiming recognition or enforcement must prove, first, 'that there was a submission', secondly, 'that the arbitration was conducted in pursuance of the submission' and, thirdly, 'that the award is a valid award, made pursuant to the provisions of the submission, and valid according to the *lex fori* of the place where the arbitration was carried out and where the award was

---

[165] See the judgment of Kerr J in *Dalmia Cement Ltd v National Bank of Pakistan* [1975] QB 9, 20–3.
[166] *Dalmia Ltd Cement v National Bank of Pakistan* [1975] QB 9. JG Collier, [1975] *CLJ* 44.
[167] Kerr J in *Dalmia Cement Ltd v National Bank of Pakistan* [1975] QB 9, 23.

made'.[168] In addition, the award must be final and conclusive according to the law governing the arbitration proceedings.[169] The requirement that the award should be in accordance with an agreement to arbitrate which is valid by its proper law does not seem to give rise to problems in practice; the requirements that the award should be valid and final according to the law governing the arbitration proceedings may be illustrated by examples.

24.3.5 If the award is invalid under the law governing the arbitration proceedings, it cannot be enforced in England at common law. In *Bankers and Shippers Insurance Co of New York v Liverpool Marine and General Insurance Co Ltd*[170] the parties entered a contract which included an agreement providing for arbitration in New York. A dispute arose and the claimant appointed an arbitrator. On the respondent's failure to appoint, the claimant, relying on the terms of the arbitration agreement, appointed a second arbitrator. The arbitral tribunal made an award in the claimant's favour. When the claimant sought enforcement in England the respondent resisted on the basis that the award was invalid under the curial law. It was established that, under the law of New York, where the respondent failed to appoint an arbitrator, the arbitration could proceed only if allowed to do so by an order of the court; failure to obtain an order of the court rendered the award invalid. Accordingly, the House of Lords refused to enforce the award in England.

24.3.6 As with the validity of an award, the finality of an award is, in principle, a question to be determined by the law governing the arbitration proceedings. There is, however, an important qualification. Although it is for the law governing the arbitration proceedings to determine the effects of the award, whether the award is final is a question of classification which is determined by English law. Although the question whether the award is final in the country of origin depends on the law of that country, the law of the country of origin is directed to showing whether it is final as that word is understood in English law.[171]

24.3.7 The requirement of finality must not be confused with enforceability. The importance of this distinction is illustrated by *Union Nationale des Coopératives Agricoles de Céréales v Robert Catterall & Co Ltd*,[172] a case concerning proceedings for the enforcement of a Danish award. It was established that there was no time limit under Danish law for raising objections to the validity of an award and that execution of a Danish award in Denmark depended on a judgment having been obtained from the court based on the award. When enforcement proceedings were commenced in England, the plaintiff had not obtained a judgment on the award in Denmark. Even though the award was not enforceable in Denmark, the Court of Appeal concluded that the award was final and entitled to enforcement in England. As a general

---

[168] *Norske Atlas Insurance Company Ltd v London General Insurance Co Ltd* (1927) 28 Ll L Rep 104, 106–07.

[169] *Dalmia Dairy Industries Ltd v National Bank of Pakistan* [1978] 2 Lloyd's Rep 223.

[170] (1926) 24 Ll L Rep 85.

[171] Lord Evershed MR in *Union Nationale des Coopératives Agricoles de Céréales v Robert Catterall & Co Ltd* [1959] 2 QB 44, 53. Although this decision was made in the context of Part II of the Arbitration Act 1950, the principle is equally applicable in cases governed by the common law.

[172] [1959] 2 QB 44.

principle, an award is 'valid, final and binding unless and until it is set aside by any procedure available for this purpose'.[173]

Defences at Common Law

24.3.8   Even if the person seeking to rely on a foreign award shows that the award is valid and final, the party against whom the award is invoked may nevertheless resist recognition or enforcement by establishing a valid defence. The authorities concerning defences to the enforcement of foreign awards at common law are few and far between. The relevant principles are, however, reasonably clear.

Matters which Are not Defences

24.3.9   First, although there is no authority directly on the point, it is universally accepted that the court cannot refuse to enforce a foreign award on the ground that the arbitral tribunal made an error of law or fact. In this respect foreign awards are to be treated in the same way as foreign judgments—in relation to which there can be no review of the merits by the court addressed.[174] Secondly, an allegation of serious irregularity, which may found a claim for setting aside an award before the courts of the country of origin, is no defence to the enforcement of a foreign award at common law.[175] Thirdly, it was once thought, on the basis of *Merrifield, Ziegler & Co v Liverpool Cotton Association*,[176] that the court would not enforce a foreign award unless it was actually enforceable in the country of origin. If correct, this rule would lead to the result that in most cases the plaintiff would have to obtain a judgment on the award in the country of origin before seeking enforcement in England. However, in *Union Nationale des Coopératives Agricoles de Céréales v Robert Catterall & Co Ltd*[177] it was established that enforcement depends on the validity and finality of the foreign award, rather than its enforceability. In subsequent cases the rule in *Union Nationale des Coopératives Agricoles de Céréales v Robert Catterall & Co Ltd* has been regarded as laying down the relevant principle.[178]

Valid Defences

EXCESS OF JURISDICTION
24.3.10   Recognition or enforcement of a foreign award will be refused if the arbitral tribunal had no jurisdiction to make the award. The defence of excess of jurisdiction at common law corresponds to section 103(2)(d) of the 1996 Act.[179] The jurisdiction of

---

[173] Kerr J in *Dalmia Dairy Industries Ltd v National Bank of Pakistan* [1978] 2 Lloyd's Rep 223, 247.

[174] *Godard v Gray* (1870) LR 6 QB 139.

[175] See *Dalmia Dairy Industries Ltd v National Bank of Pakistan* [1978] 2 Lloyd's Rep 223.

[176] (1911) 105 LT 97.

[177] [1959] 2 QB 44 (a case decided under Part II of the 1950 Act).

[178] See, eg, Kerr J in *Dalmia Dairy Industries Ltd v National Bank of Pakistan* [1978] 2 Lloyd's Rep 223, 249–50.

[179] See paras 24.2.30–24.2.31.

the arbitrator is to be determined by reference to the arbitration agreement, construed in accordance with its proper law.[180] For the purposes of section 103(2)(d) of the 1996 Act if the party seeking to rely on a New York Convention award produces the documents required by section 102, the burden is on the party against whom the award is invoked to show that the arbitrator did not have the necessary jurisdiction. At common law (and under Part II of the 1950 Act) the position is as follows: it is for the party who is setting up the award to prove that the arbitrator acted within the terms of the authority which was given to him; but, if the party who is setting up the award produces a document which appears to be regular and in circumstances in which the tribunal had jurisdiction, the onus passes to the other party to prove that the award is defective in that it has dealt with matters beyond the scope of the arbitration agreement.[181]

BREACH OF THE PRINCIPLES OF NATURAL JUSTICE

24.3.11 The natural justice defence at common law broadly corresponds with the ground for refusing enforcement to a New York Convention award provided by section 103(2)(c) of the 1996 Act.[182] In *Dalmia Dairy Industries Ltd v National Bank of Pakistan*[183] the issue of natural justice was raised in relation to arbitrations conducted under the ICC Rules of Arbitration. The arbitrator had followed the usual practice in ICC arbitration and, in his discretion, declined to hear any oral evidence. The defendant's contention that this involved a breach of the principles of natural justice—thereby rendering the awards unenforceable—was rejected.

PUBLIC POLICY AND FRAUD

24.3.12 The courts may refuse to enforce a foreign award where to do so would be contrary to public policy.[184] It may also be assumed that, at common law, the person against whom an award is invoked may seek to resist the enforcement of a foreign award on the ground that the award was procured by fraud. Although there is no clear authority on this point, the only reference to the issue being a *dictum* in a decision of the Privy Council,[185] it is reasonable to suppose that, if a foreign judgment may be refused enforcement on the basis of fraud, the same should be true in relation to a foreign award. However, if an analogy is to be drawn between foreign judgments and foreign awards, there are limitations on the availability of the defence of fraud. Where, for example, a party has sought to challenge an award on the basis of fraud in the country of origin, it should not be possible to raise the defence in the context enforcement proceedings in England, if the courts of the country of origin decide that the allegation of fraud is not made out.[186]

---

[180] *Kianta Osekeyhtio v Britain and Overseas Trading Co Ltd* [1954] 1 Lloyd's Rep 247; *Dalmia Dairy Industries Ltd v National Bank of Pakistan* [1978] 2 Lloyd's Rep 223.

[181] *Kianta Osekeyhtio v Britain and Overseas Trading Co Ltd* [1954] 1 Lloyd's Rep 247, 250–1.

[182] See paras 24.2.26–24.2.29.

[183] [1978] 2 Lloyd's Rep 223.

[184] The defence of public policy is considered in the context of recognition and enforcement under the Arbitration Act 1996. For a discussion of the relevant English case law, both at common law and under the legislation implementing the New York Convention, see paras 24.2.43–25.2.52.

[185] Viscount Cave in *Oppenheim & Co v Mahomed Haneef* [1922] 1 AC 482, 487.

[186] This proposition is consistent with the decision of the Court of Appeal in *House of Spring Gardens Ltd v Waite* [1991] QB 241 (discussed at para 12.4.10).

24.4 RECOGNITION AND ENFORCEMENT OF FOREIGN AWARDS UNDER PART II OF THE ARBITRATION ACT 1950

The Relationship between Part II of the 1950 Act and Other Regimes

24.4.1 The first international attempts to facilitate the mutual recognition and enforcement of awards date from the 1920s. The Arbitration (Foreign Awards) Act 1930 was passed to give effect to the Geneva Convention on the Execution of Foreign Arbitral Awards of 1927. The 1930 Act was re-enacted in Part II of the 1950 Act. The recognition and enforcement of awards under this statutory scheme is unnecessarily complex.

24.4.2 The 1996 Act leaves Part II of the 1950 Act in place, but very significantly cuts down its scope. Part II of the 1950 Act plays only a residual role since an award which is a New York Convention award within the scope of the 1996 Act is not entitled to recognition or enforcement under Part II of the 1950 Act; to this extent the earlier enactment is superseded by the 1996 Act. Part II of the 1950 Act is relevant to 'foreign awards' (as defined by section 35 of the 1950 Act) which are not New York Convention awards within the scope of Part III of the 1996 Act.[187] In view of the number of states which have ratified the New York Convention, Part II of the 1950 Act is almost entirely of historical interest. Part II of the 1950 Act, where applicable, is not exclusive; a creditor may seek enforcement at common law, rather than under the statutory scheme.[188]

Conditions for Recognition and Enforcement

24.4.3 In order for an award to be entitled to recognition and enforcement in England under Part II of the 1950 Act it must be a 'foreign award' within the meaning of section 35(1) of the 1950 Act (but not a New York Convention award within the scope of the 1996 Act). An award is a 'foreign award' if three conditions are satisfied: first, the award must have been made in a state to which the 1927 Convention has been declared to apply, but which has not ratified the 1958 Convention;[189] secondly, the award must have been made under an arbitration agreement which is not governed by English law and to which the Geneva Protocol on Arbitration Clauses of 1923 is applicable;[190] thirdly, the arbitration agreement under which the award was made must be between parties who are subject to the jurisdiction of different states which have been declared to be parties to the 1927 Convention.[191]

---

[187] Arbitration Act 1996, s 99.
[188] Arbitration Act 1950, s 40.
[189] Arbitration Act 1950, s 35(1)(c); Arbitration Act 1996, s 99. There are only a handful of states, none of them important arbitration centres, which satisfy this condition. For a list of the countries to which Part II of the 1950 Act has been declared to apply by Order in Council see MJ Mustill and SC Boyd, *Commercial Arbitration* (London, Butterworths, 2nd edn, 1989) 670–71.
[190] Arbitration Act 1950, s 35(1)(a).
[191] Arbitration Act 1950, s 35(1)(b).

24.4.4 A 'foreign award' must satisfy the criteria laid down by section 37(1), which provides:

In order that a foreign award may be enforceable under this Part of this Act it must have—

(a) been made in pursuance of an agreement for arbitration which was valid under the law by which it was governed;
(b) been made by the tribunal provided for in the agreement or constituted in manner agreed upon by the parties;
(c) been made in conformity with the law governing the arbitration procedure;
(d) become final in the country where it was made;
(e) been in respect of a matter which may lawfully be referred to arbitration under the law of England;

and the enforcement thereof must not be contrary to the public policy or the law of England.

24.4.5 The party seeking to enforce a 'foreign award' must produce the documents specified by section 38(1) (or where appropriate a certified translation):[192]

(a) the original award or a copy thereof duly authenticated in manner required by the law of the country in which it was made; and
(b) evidence proving that the award has become final; and
(c) such evidence as may be necessary to prove that the award is a foreign award and that the conditions mentioned in paragraphs (a), (b) and (c) of subsection (1) of the last foregoing section are satisfied.

Subject to the defences listed in section 37(2), an award which satisfies all these conditions may be enforced by a claim on the award or by an application under section 66 of the 1996 Act.[193]

Defences to Enforcement

24.4.6 The defences to enforcement under Part II of the 1950 Act are listed in section 37(2), which provides:

Subject to the provisions of this subsection, a foreign award shall not be enforceable under this Part of this Act if the court dealing with the case is satisfied that—

(a) the award has been annulled in the country in which it was made; or
(b) the party against whom it is sought to enforce the award was not given notice of the arbitration proceedings in sufficient time to enable him to present his case, or was under some legal incapacity and was not properly represented; or
(c) the award does not deal with all the questions referred or contains decisions on matters beyond the scope of the agreement for arbitration:

Provided that, if the award does not deal with all the questions referred, the court may, if it thinks fit, either postpone the enforcement of the award or order its enforcement subject to the giving of such security by the person seeking to enforce it as the court may think fit.

---

[192] Arbitration Act 1950, s 38(2).
[193] Arbitration Act 1950, s 36(1).

24.5 OTHER REGIMES FOR THE RECOGNITION AND ENFORCEMENT OF FOREIGN ARBITRAL AWARDS

Part II of the Civil Jurisdiction and Judgments Act 1982

24.5.1 Part II of the Civil Jurisdiction and Judgments Act 1982 provides a simple mechanism for the recognition and enforcement of judgments given by the courts of one part of the United Kingdom in other parts of the United Kingdom.[194] By virtue of the definition of 'judgment' for the purposes of Part II of the 1982 Act the same regime applies to awards. Section 18(2) of the Civil Jurisdiction and Judgments Act 1982 provides:

In this section 'judgment' means any of the following (references to the giving of a judgment being construed accordingly)—

...

(e) an arbitration award which has become enforceable in the part of the United Kingdom in which it was given in the same manner as a judgment given by a court of law in that part.

An award made in Scotland or Northern Ireland for a sum of money may be enforced in England under schedule 6 to the 1982 Act and non-money awards may be enforced under schedule 7. In order to enforce an award made in Scotland or Northern Ireland under Part II of the 1982 Act the party seeking to set up the award must obtain a certificate from the court which gave the judgment or made the order by virtue of which the award has become enforceable in the country of origin.[195] When a certificate has been issued it can then be registered in England.[196] The effect of registration is that the award has the same force as if the English court had given permission to enforce under section 66 of the 1996 Act.[197]

24.5.2 Sections 18 and 19 of the 1982 Act provide that the court may not refuse to recognise or enforce a judgment given by the courts of Scotland or Northern Ireland solely on the ground that the court of origin did not have jurisdiction under English private international law rules. The position is different as regards awards made in Scotland or Northern Ireland. It is provided in this context that if the court of origin did not have jurisdiction to make the judgment or order by virtue of which the award has become enforceable the award may be refused enforcement in England.[198] This ground for refusing recognition and enforcement is in addition to other defences which may be available.

24.5.3 In relation to awards the regime provided by Part II of the 1982 Act is not exclusive in those cases falling within its scope. The party seeking to set up the award may seek to enforce the award by a claim on the award or by an application for permission to enforce under section 66 of the 1996 Act.[199]

---

[194] See section 13.6.
[195] Civil Jurisdiction and Judgments Act 1982, sched 6, para 2(2)(e); sched 7, para 2(2)(e).
[196] Civil Jurisdiction and Judgments Act 1982, sched 6, para 5; sched 7, para 5.
[197] Civil Jurisdiction and Judgments Act 1982, sched 6, para 6; sched 7, para 6.
[198] Civil Jurisdiction and Judgments Act 1982, s 19(3)(b).
[199] Civil Jurisdiction and Judgments Act 1982, s 18(8).

Part II of the Administration of Justice Act 1920

24.5.4 Certain judgments may be registered under Part II of the Administration of Justice Act 1920, in consequence of which they become enforceable in England as if they were judgments of the High Court.[200] For the purposes of Part II of the 1920 Act, 'judgment' is defined as extending to awards which have become enforceable in the same manner as a judgment given by a court.[201]

Part I of the Foreign Judgments (Reciprocal Enforcement) Act 1933

24.5.5 A similar regime to that existing under Part II of the Administration of Justice Act 1920 was established under the Foreign Judgments (Reciprocal Enforcement) Act 1933. Indeed, the original intention was that the 1933 Act should supersede the earlier legislation. The basic condition for enforcement under the 1933 Act is the same as that which must be satisfied under Part II of the 1920 Act; in pursuance of the law in force in the place where it was made the award must have become enforceable in the same manner as a judgment given by a court in that place. In practice, this means that the award must have been accorded judicial recognition in the foreign country by some process analogous to that created by section 66 of the 1996 Act. The grounds for setting aside registration under section 4(1) of the 1933 Act apply to awards just as they do to foreign judgments.

24.5.6 An arbitration award made in a country other than the United Kingdom which is a party to the Geneva Convention in the International Carriage of Goods by Road (which is implemented by the Carriage of Goods by Road Act 1965) is enforceable under the 1933 Act if two conditions are satisfied: first, the award is enforceable in the country where the award was made and, secondly, the arbitration agreement provided that the arbitrator should apply the CMR Convention. When deciding whether the second condition is satisfied it is not sufficient that the substantive rights and obligations of the parties are governed by a national law which has incorporated the CMR Convention; the arbitration agreement must expressly provide that the tribunal shall apply the CMR Convention.[202]

24.5.7 A judgment falling within the scope of the 1933 Act may not be enforced except under the statutory provisions; a judgment creditor cannot rely on the common law.[203] The Act is not exclusive, however, as regards awards falling within its scope.[204]

Arbitration (International Investment Disputes) Act 1966

24.5.8 The Arbitration (International Investment Disputes) Act 1966 was passed to give effect to the United Kingdom's treaty obligations under the Washington Convention of 1965 for the settlement of investment disputes between states and

---

[200] See paras 12.6.3–12.6.6.
[201] Administration of Justice Act 1920, s 12(1).
[202] *AB Bofors-Uva CAV Ltd v AB Skandia Transport* [1982] 1 Lloyd's Rep 410.
[203] Foreign Judgments (Reciprocal Enforcement) Act 1933, s 6.
[204] Foreign Judgments (Reciprocal Enforcement) Act 1933, s 10A.

nationals of other states. The 1965 Convention set up the International Centre for Settlement of Investment Disputes (ICSID). The purpose of the Washington Convention was to promote private investment in developing countries by providing a mechanism for the settlement of disputes between states and foreign investors.[205]

24.5.9   ICSID helps to promote dispute resolution by arbitration or conciliation, depending on the choice of the parties. Although the jurisdiction of the centre is dependent on the consent of the parties (effected by means of a suitable clause in the principal contract or a submission agreement after the dispute has arisen), there are additional conditions which have to be satisfied if arbitration under ICSID is to take place: the dispute must be between a contracting state and a national of another contracting state; and the difference between the parties must be a legal dispute arising out of investment.[206]

24.5.10   Compared with other arbitration institutions relatively few awards have been rendered under the auspices of ICSID.[207] An ICSID award may be registered in the High Court.[208] Once registered, such an award has the same effect as a judgment of the High Court.[209] There are no grounds on which enforcement of an award which has been registered can be refused; enforcement may not be refused even on grounds of public policy. However, either party to a dispute arbitrated under ICSID may seek annulment of an award under the internal appeal procedure set out in the ICSID Convention, which provides that requests for annulment shall be heard by an *ad hoc* committee appointed by the President of the World Bank.[210] Furthermore, although there have been few successful judicial challenges to the enforcement of ICSID awards, experience has shown that there are various tactics that losing parties may employ in national courts in attempts to delay or to avoid having to comply with an ICSID award.[211] For example, in *AIG Capital Partners Inc v Republic of Kazakhstan*[212] the defendant successfully argued that the assets in England against which the claimant, having obtained an ICSID award in its favour, sought to obtain execution were immune from enforcement under the State Immunity Act 1978.

Recognition of Awards Made by the Iran–US Claims Tribunal

24.5.11   The Iran–US Claims Tribunal was established pursuant to the Algiers Declaration of 1981. The purpose of the tribunal was to settle claims between, on

---

[205] See, generally, PF Sutherland, 'The World Bank Convention on the Settlement of Investment Disputes' (1979) 28 *ICLQ* 367.

[206] See CF Amerasinghe, 'Jurisdiction *Ratione Personae* under the Convention on the Settlement of Investment Disputes Between States and Nationals of Other States' (1974–75) 47 *BYIL* 227.

[207] '[T]here have been only 180 ICSID arbitrations in the entire fifty-year history of ICSID': E Baldwin, M Kantor and M Nolan, 'Limits to Enforcement of ICSID Awards' (2006) 23(1) *J Int Arb* 1. See also WM Tupman, 'Case Studies in the Jurisdiction of the International Centre for Settlement of Investment Disputes' (1986) 35 *ICLQ* 813.

[208] Arbitration (International Investment Disputes) Act 1966, s 1; CPR 62.21.

[209] Arbitration (International Investment Disputes) Act 1966, s 2(1).

[210] See WL Craig, 'Uses and Abuses of Appeal from Awards' (1988) 4 *Arb Int* 174, 209–14.

[211] See E Baldwin, M Kantor and M Nolan, 'Limits to Enforcement of ICSID Awards' (2006) 23(1) *J Int Arb* 1.

[212] [2006] 1 WLR 1420.

the one hand, US nationals and corporations and, on the other, Iran and Iranian state corporations. The tribunal was established in The Hague and the procedure adopted by the tribunal was that laid down in the UNCITRAL Arbitration Rules. Awards were satisfied out of a specially established fund and were binding on the parties.

24.5.12   In *Dallal v Bank Mellat*[213] the plaintiff, whose claim had been rejected by the tribunal, started proceedings in England on the same cause of action. The defendant sought to raise the tribunal's award as a defence and the question arose whether the award was entitled to recognition in England so as to bar the plaintiff's claim. Hobhouse J held that the award was not entitled to recognition under the common law or the legislation implementing the New York Convention, since it was established that the 'arbitration agreement'—on which the jurisdiction of the tribunal was based—was void under its proper law (which was regarded as being Dutch law). Nevertheless, it was held that the award was entitled to recognition. This result was arrived at by treating the award as arising out of a statutory arbitration established under public international law; the competence of the tribunal was derived from international law and that competence was recognised in England. Although the reasoning adopted by Hobhouse J may be less than entirely convincing, it is highly desirable that awards of the tribunal should be entitled to recognition in England.

24.6 AWARDS, JUDGMENTS AND THE CAUSE OF ACTION

24.6.1   There are three different questions concerning the relationship between judgments, awards and the cause of action. First, what is the solution in a case where there is a conflict between a foreign judgment and an award? Secondly, does a foreign award, which has been the subject of a foreign judgment on the award, remain enforceable in England as an award? Thirdly, does a foreign award extinguish the cause of action?

Conflicting Judgments and Awards

24.6.2   Just as problems can arise in cases where conflicting judgments are granted by the courts of different countries, similar problems arise in cases involving conflicting judgments and awards. What is the position where an award made in one country conflicts with a judgment granted in another country? In considering this question it is important to distinguish judgments granted under the Brussels I Regulation from other judgments.

Cases Involving Judgments of Non-Member States

24.6.3   Section 32 of the Civil Jurisdiction and Judgments Act 1982 provides that a foreign judgment shall be refused recognition and enforcement if the bringing of the

---

[213] [1986] 1 QB 441. J Crawford, (1986) 57 *BYIL* 410; A Shindler, 'Arbitration Still Bound' (1986) 102 *LQR* 500; PF Kunzlik, [1986] *CLJ* 377.

foreign proceedings was 'contrary to an agreement under which the dispute in question was to be settled otherwise than by proceedings in the courts of that country'.[214] So, where there is a conflict between a foreign award which is entitled to enforcement in England and a foreign judgment given in defiance of the arbitration agreement, the foreign judgment is not entitled to recognition or enforcement and does not call into question the enforceability of the award. Even if the foreign court is recognised as having had jurisdiction (for example, because the defendant was resident in the country in question when the proceedings were commenced), a foreign judgment will not be recognised or enforced in England if it conflicts with an earlier arbitral award (which is entitled to recognition or enforcement in England).[215]

Cases Involving Judgments of Member States

24.6.4 There is some doubt whether the result is the same where a judgment is granted by a court of a Member State. For example, can a Belgian award be enforced in England under the 1996 Act in a situation where, notwithstanding the parties' agreement to refer the dispute to arbitration in Belgium, a Spanish court either renders a judgment declaring the arbitration agreement to be null and void or, in disregard of the arbitration agreement, renders a conflicting judgment on the merits? In these circumstances, the first issue is whether the Spanish judgment concerns 'arbitration' for the purposes of Article 1 of the Brussels I Regulation. If the judgment falls outside the scope of the Regulation and the English court does not share the view of the Spanish courts that the arbitration agreement is invalid, recognition of the judgment may be refused under section 32 of the 1982 Act and the award is enforceable under the 1996 Act. However, following the decision of the Court of Justice in the *West Tankers* case,[216] it is clear that, if the underlying substance of the dispute between the parties (such as a dispute arising out of a commercial contract) concerns 'civil and commercial matters', a judgment which, in the context of such a dispute, rules on the validity or effect of an arbitration clause falls within the scope of the Regulation.[217] If, for example, a Spanish court renders a judgment in which it decides that an alleged arbitration clause is not incorporated into the contract between the parties, that judgment does not concern 'arbitration' and falls within the scope of the Brussels I Regulation.[218] If, in this type of case, the parties' dispute is referred to arbitration in Belgium and the tribunal renders an award, both the award and the judgment are *prima facie* entitled to recognition (under the 1996 Act and the Brussels I Regulation respectively). There are several possible solutions to this problem, three of which merit consideration.

24.6.5 First, there is an argument that the Spanish judgment, even though it is within the Regulation's material scope, is not entitled to recognition or enforcement

---

[214] See paras 12.4.20–12.4.23.
[215] *The Joanna V* [2003] 2 Lloyd's Rep 617.
[216] Case C–185/07 *Allianz SpA (formerly Riunione Adriatica Di Sicurta SpA) v West Tankers Inc* [2009] 1 AC 1138.
[217] See, eg, *DHL GBS (UK) Ltd v Fallimento Finmatica SPA* [2009] 1 Lloyd's Rep 430.
[218] *The Wadi Sudr* [2010] 1 Lloyd's Rep 193.

under the Regulation in the context of English proceedings which themselves fall outside the scope of the Regulation. This was the analysis adopted by Gloster J in *The Wadi Sudr*[219] and, although it may be superficially appealing, this aspect of the decision was rejected by the Court of Appeal.[220] Gloster J sought to rely on authorities decided in the context of jurisdiction disputes in which it has been held that Articles 27 and 28 of the Regulation do not apply unless the proceedings brought in the court second seised fall within the material scope of the Regulation.[221] However, reliance on such authorities in relation to the recognition or enforcement of foreign judgments under the Regulation is wholly misplaced. The Regulation provides that a judgment of a Member State court, whose subject-matter is within the scope of the Regulation, is entitled to recognition and, where appropriate, enforcement in other Member States. The idea that such recognition applies only in the context of legal proceedings which are themselves within the scope of the Regulation makes no sense; a foreign judgment either has effect within a particular legal order or it does not.

24.6.6 Secondly, it could be argued that, in such circumstances, recognition or enforcement of the Spanish judgment should be refused on the basis of public policy and that the Belgian award should take priority. Notwithstanding the attractions of this solution (which was suggested by Waller J in *Phillip Alexander Securities & Futures Ltd v Bamberger*[222] and supported at first instance in *The Wadi Sudr*[223]) its adoption is problematic as Article 35(3) of the Brussels I Regulation expressly provides that the test of public policy 'may not be applied to the rules relating to jurisdiction'. In *The Wadi Sudr*, the Court of Appeal recognised that public policy cannot be used as a means for refusing to recognise a Spanish judgment which fails to uphold the validity and effectiveness of an arbitration clause which, from the perspective of English private international law, is valid and binding on the parties.[224] As the Court of Justice made clear in *Krombach v Bamberski*,[225] the judgment of the courts of another Member State is not contrary to public policy simply because the court of origin has reached a decision which the court addressed thinks is wrong.[226]

24.6.7 Thirdly, Article 71(1) of the Brussels I Regulation[227] provides that it 'shall not affect any conventions to which the Member States are parties and which in relation to particular matters, govern jurisdiction'. There is no doubt that the New York Convention, as well as providing for the recognition and enforcement of arbitral awards, regulates jurisdiction (as Article II requires the courts of states which are parties to the New York Convention not to exercise jurisdiction in relation to disputes which the parties agreed to refer to arbitration). Accordingly, it can be argued that to recognise or enforce the Spanish judgment under the Brussels I Regulation (thereby denying recognition or enforcement to the Belgian award under the New York

---

[219] [2009] 1 Lloyd's Rep 666.
[220] See Waller LJ at [2010] 1 Lloyd's Rep 193, 205 at [59].
[221] *Through Transport Mutual Insurance Association (Eurasia) Ltd v New India Assurance Co Ltd* [2005] 1 Lloyd's Rep 67.
[222] [1997] ILPr 73, 94–102.
[223] [2009] 1 Lloyd's Rep 666.
[224] [2010] 1 Lloyd's Rep 193.
[225] Case C–7/98 [2000] ECR I–1935, paras 36–8.
[226] See Moore-Bick LJ at [2010] 1 Lloyd's Rep 193, 216 at [130].
[227] (Lugano Convention, Art 67.)

Convention) would be contrary to Article 71 as it would affect a convention 'to which the Member States are parties and which in relation to particular matters, govern[s] jurisdiction'. An argument along similar lines was put forward in *The Wadi Sudr* and, although it held some attraction for the judge at first instance, the Court of Appeal rejected it.[228]

The Effect of a Foreign Judgment on the Award

24.6.8 Enforcement under Part II of the Civil Jurisdiction and Judgments Act 1982 or Part II of the Administration of Justice Act 1920 or the Foreign Judgments (Reciprocal Enforcement) Act 1933 is dependent on the award having become enforceable under the law of the seat. However, none of these statutory regimes provide an exclusive code for the enforcement of foreign awards falling within its scope. Accordingly, in principle, an award which is enforceable under one of these regimes, as a judgment, may, in appropriate circumstances, be enforceable at common law or as a New York Convention award under the 1996 Act. For a foreign award to be entitled to enforcement in England either at common law or under the 1996 Act there is no requirement that the award should be enforceable by the law governing the arbitration proceedings.[229] Under the 1996 Act the requirement is simply that the award should be 'binding'.[230]

24.6.9 In those cases where a foreign award has become enforceable abroad it is important to distinguish two different situations: first, the award may have become enforceable by a summary procedure (for example, by deposit of the award with the court); secondly, the award may have been converted into a judgment by a procedure analogous to a claim on the award at common law. In the first category of case, if the appropriate conditions are satisfied, there can be no doubt that the award remains enforceable as such in England. Indeed, it has been argued that, for the purposes of the recognition and enforcement of judgments, an execution order should not be regarded as a judgment.[231] Accordingly, where the order of the foreign court is in a form similar to an English order giving permission to enforce the award (under section 66 of the 1996 Act), it is the award, rather than the foreign judgment, which is enforceable.

24.6.10 In the second category, however, the question is whether the foreign judgment and/or the foreign award is entitled to enforcement in England. There is clear authority for the proposition that, in cases where there has been a foreign judgment on a foreign award, the judgment is entitled to enforcement in England according to general principles.[232] Furthermore, as a result of the abolition of the non-merger rule in relation to foreign judgments,[233] it is possible that, provided that the judgment

---

[228] See Waller LJ at [2010] 1 Lloyd's Rep 193, 206 at [69] and Moore-Bick LJ [2010] 1 Lloyd's Rep 193, 216 at [127].

[229] *Union Nationale des Coopératives Agricoles des Céréales v Robert Catterall & Co Ltd* [1959] 2 QB 44.

[230] See paras 24.2.35–24.2.37.

[231] DT Hascher, 'Recognition and Enforcement of Arbitration Awards and the Brussels Convention' (1996) 12 *Arb Int* 233, 238.

[232] *East India Trading Co Inc v Carmel Exporters and Importers Ltd* [1952] 2 QB 439.

[233] Civil Jurisdiction and Judgments Act 1982, s 34.

satisfies the relevant conditions, it is the judgment alone, and not the award, which is entitled to enforcement.[234]

24.6.11 However, as a matter of principle, the merger of the award with the judgment in the country of origin should not be regarded as having extraterritorial effect and the award should remain enforceable in these circumstances:

The fact that leave for enforcement has the effect of absorbing the award in the country of origin is a technical aspect for the purposes of enforcement within that country. The award can therefore be deemed to remain a cause of action for enforcement in other countries.[235]

In *Marc Rich & Co AG v Società Italiana Impianti PA* Advocate General Darmon went further and suggested that:

the 'merger' of the award must be regarded as limited to the territory of the court which delivered the judgment and *only* the award must be taken into account for the purpose of recognition and enforcement in other States.[236]

24.6.12 As a matter of policy, there is no reason why an award should cease to be enforceable as such when foreign proceedings have converted the award into a judgment.[237] Assuming that the award and the judgment satisfy the relevant conditions for enforcement, the creditor should be able to choose the route which best serves his interests. Such an approach is consistent with Article VII of the New York Convention (the 'more favourable right' clause).[238]

The Effect of a Foreign Arbitral Award on the Cause of Action

24.6.13 Under the common law rules which applied before the entry into force of the Civil Jurisdiction and Judgments Act 1982 a foreign judgment was not effective to extinguish the original cause of action. As a result a plaintiff who had obtained a judgment abroad was not prevented from suing on the original cause of action in England. The doctrine of non-merger was laid to rest by section 34 of the 1982 Act.[239]

24.6.14 Since section 34 refers only to foreign judgments, the question arises whether the doctrine of non-merger applies to foreign awards. There is no judicial authority on this point, but common sense suggests that the original cause of action should be regarded as merging with the award:

there is no reason of policy or principle why the obsolete and anomalous rule of non-merger in relation to foreign judgments should be extended to foreign awards. Indeed the consensual and contractual character of arbitration means that parties to an arbitration agreement impliedly

---

[234] L Collins *et al*, *Dicey, Morris and Collins on The Conflict of Laws* (London, Sweet & Maxwell, 14th edn, 2006) para 16–106.

[235] AJ van den Berg, *The New York Arbitration Convention of 1958* (Deventer, Kluwer, 1981) 347.

[236] Case C–190/89 [1991] ECR I–3855, para 69.

[237] RM Mosk and RD Nelson, 'The Effects of Confirming and Vacating an International Arbitration Award on Enforcement in Foreign Jurisdictions' (2001) 18(4) *J Int Arb* 463, 471.

[238] DT Hascher, 'Recognition and Enforcement of Arbitral Awards and the Brussels Convention' (1996) 12 *Arb Int* 233, 246.

[239] See para 12.3.4.

promise to perform a valid award, and it should follow that they also promise not to take any action inconsistent with their submission to arbitration. Bringing proceedings on the original cause of action would be wholly inconsistent with the obligation under the submission and the subsequent award.[240]

---

[240] L Collins *et al*, *Dicey, Morris and Collins on The Conflict of Laws* (London, Sweet & Maxwell, 14th edn, 2006) para 16–104. See also MJ Mustill and SC Boyd, *Commercial Arbitration* (London, Butterworths, 2nd edn, 1989) 415.

INDEX